THE BEST LAWYERS IN AMERICA

THE BEST LAWYERS IN AMERICA

STEVEN NAIFEH

AND

GREGORY WHITE SMITH

Harvard Law School 1977

———

LUCIENNE POTTERFIELD STEC

Senior Editor

———

1991–1992

WOODWARD / WHITE

Aiken, South Carolina

PLEASE NOTE

Woodward/White has used its best efforts in assembling material for inclusion in *The Best Lawyers in America* but does not warrant that the information contained in the book is complete or accurate, and does not assume, and hereby disclaims, any liability to any person for any loss or damage caused by errors or omissions in *The Best Lawyers in America* whether such errors or omissions result from negligence, accident, or any other cause.

Copyright © 1991 by Woodward/White, Inc.
129 First Avenue, SW, Aiken, SC 29801

Designed by JOEL AVIROM

Library of Congress Cataloging-in-Publication Data

Naifeh, Steven W., 1952–
   The best lawyers in America : 1991–1992 / Steven Naifeh and Gregory White Smith.
      p.   cm.
   ISBN 0-913391-04-2 : $95.00
      1. Lawyers—United States—Directories.   2. Lawyers—Specialties and specialists—United States—Directories.   I. Smith, Gregory White.   II. Title.
KF190.N23   1991
340'.025'73—dc20   91-11810
                                                                                            CIP

PRINTED IN THE UNITED STATES OF AMERICA

We would like to acknowledge our debt to the thousands of attorneys who gave of their time and expertise in the process of compiling these lists.

CONTENTS

INTRODUCTION

We are proud to present *The Best Lawyers in America, 1991-1992*. As those who are familiar with previous editions will see immediately, the new Fourth Edition has been thoroughly revised. The new edition is larger than ever, due primarily to the addition of five new categories: First Amendment Law, Health Care Law, Immigration Law, Intellectual Property Law, and Public Utility Law. Most of the individual lists, in fact, have grown only modestly in size, if at all, and some have even shrunk.

In addition, we have listed subspecialties for many lawyers. (While most of these have been provided by the listed lawyers themselves, others have been provided by nominating and voting lawyers and, therefore, may or may not reflect the listed lawyer's preferred view of his or her expertise.) We have also indicated by means of an asterisk (*) following a lawyer's name that the attorney has informed us that he or she has litigated at least one case to conclusion within the past two years. (N.B. The absence of such an asterisk does *not* necessarily indicate that an attorney has *not* litigated a case to conclusion in the past two years.)

Most importantly, every one of the existing lists has been completely revised on the basis of a new, nationwide survey even more rigorous and comprehensive than those we conducted for previous editions. The quality of the lists continues to be the backbone of this book, and, more than ever before, we have bent every effort to ensure that these lists are reliable, accurate, and current.

COMPILING THE FOURTH EDITION

We began with the lists from the third edition of *The Best Lawyers in America* as a starting point only. (A detailed description of the methodology used in the first three editions is included in the introductions to the earlier volumes.) For the first time, we began the polling process by sending a "ballot" to every one of the 10,048 lawyers listed in the 1989-1990 edition, asking them to (1) vote on the other listed lawyers in their area in their category, (2) nominate attorneys not previously listed, and (3) nominate attorneys in the five new categories.

As a result of the ballot process, we received 5,751 nominations. We then evaluated this list through a vast telephone survey of lawyers in every relevant legal community. Of the original nominations, only 2,211 were included in this edition, 1,036 of those in the five new categories. As in the past, we did not attempt to articulate the criteria for judging professional excellence either in the ballot or in the survey; we left that to the individual attorney. We did, however, routinely couch our inquiry in the following terms: "If you had a close friend or a relative who needed a real estate lawyer (for example), and you couldn't handle the case yourself—for reasons of conflict of interests or time—to whom would you refer them?" All comments, we promised, would remain confidential.

We continued to call lawyers on the lists, registering positive and negative votes, until a consensus emerged. Many names received unanimous praise. Others earned mixed assessments. In the latter instance, final decisions were made on a case-by-case basis after additional calls.

In revising the lists, of course, we again faced the most difficult problem: when to delete a name that was listed in the previous edition. *The Best Lawyers in America* is designed to be a current reference work—a picture of the legal profession at a given moment—not a monument to reputations. As a result, we have deleted the names of hundreds of lawyers as part of the revision process. Some, of course, died; others retired or moved into government service. Still others had curtailed their activity to the point where it was no longer appropriate to include them on what is essentially a referral list. A few simply did not receive the necessary number of affirmative votes to be included on the list.

In this fourth edition, we have also continued to make a concerted effort to correct for methodological biases. While the book still tends somewhat to favor older, established lawyers over young but equally capable lawyers (reputations, after all, take time to build), the revised lists include a higher percentage of lawyers under forty than previous lists, especially in relatively new fields such as Environmental Law and Health Care Law, as well as a higher percentage of female attorneys. We have also continued our effort to include more lawyers from relatively small firms and more lawyers from outside the large commercial centers in each state.

In regard to the problem of how to rank a lawyer who wields considerable political influence in his or her community but is no longer involved in the everyday minutiae of legal work—a problem especially acute in fields like Corporate Law, Real Estate Law, Labor Law, and Entertainment Law, where a lawyer's ability to make deals is at least as important as his precise command of the law—we have chosen once again to leave the determination of invidual cases in the hands of those who cast the votes. As a result, we believe that, for the most part, these lists represent an appropriate mix of successful power-brokers and "lawyers' lawyers."

Even with all these efforts, the current lists continue to represent largely subjective judgments—if not ours, then those of the lawyers we surveyed—and, like any subjective assessments, they are vulnerable to criticism. In the interest of honesty and by way of disclaimer, we should note as we have in previous editions that the lists may tend to reward visibility or popularity over sheer ability. Lawyers who write articles or give lectures are more likely to come to the attention of their colleagues than lawyers who work quietly outside the public eye. This is especially true in fields such as Tax or Trusts and Estates in which lawyers often have little reason to contact one another professionally. In addition, lawyers with agreeable personalities are more likely to be nominated than lawyers who may offend their fellow lawyers while satisfying their clients.

We remain confident, however, that these lists continue to represent the most useful guide to the best lawyers in the United States ever compiled.

THE EDITORS

Steven Naifeh and Gregory White Smith are both Harvard-trained attorneys. Mr. Naifeh worked briefly for the New York firm of Milbank, Tweed, Hadley & McCloy; Mr. Smith for the San Francisco firm of Morrison & Foerster. Between them, they have written twelve nonfiction books including four national bestsellers. Mr. Smith has also written a thirteen-part television series on the American Constitution with Archibald Cox.

Please direct all comments or inquiries to Woodward/White, Inc., 129 First Avenue, Aiken, SC 29801. Telephone: 803-648-0300.

METHOD OF ORGANIZATION

Within each state, lawyers are listed alphabetically: by category, city, and last name, in that order.

THE BEST LAWYERS
IN AMERICA

ALABAMA

BANKRUPTCY LAW

David B. Anderson · Cabaniss, Johnston, Gardner, Dumas & O'Neal · 1700 AmSouth Sonat Tower · 1900 Fifth Avenue North · P.O. Box 830612 · Birmingham, AL 35203 · 205-252-8800

Charles L. Denaburg · Najjar Denaburg · 2125 Morris Avenue · Birmingham, AL 35203 · 205-250-8400

Alan D. Levine · Levine & Schilling · 433 Frank Nelson Building · Birmingham, AL 35203 · 205-328-0460

Robert B. Rubin · Sirote & Permutt · 2222 Arlington Avenue, South · P.O. Box 55727 · Birmingham, AL 35255-5727 · 205-933-7111

Jerry W. Schoel* · Schoel, Ogle, Benton, Gentle and Centeno · 600 Financial Center · 505 North 20th Street · P.O. Box 1865 · Birmingham, AL 35201-1865 · 205-521-7000

John P. Whittington · Bradley, Arant, Rose & White · 1400 Park Place Tower · Birmingham, AL 35203 · 205-521-8000

George W. Finkbohner, Jr. · (Business Reorganization, Creditors' Rights, Bankruptcy Litigation) · Finkbohner, Lawler & Olen · Landmark Square Building · 169 Dauphin Street · P.O. Box 3085 · Mobile, AL 36652 · 205-438-5871

Irvin Grodsky · Grodsky & Mitchell · 1510 First National Building · P.O. Box 3123 · Mobile, AL 36652 · 205-433-3657

Donald J. Stewart · Cabaniss, Johnston, Gardner, Dumas & O'Neal · 63 South Royal Street, Suite 700 · P.O. Box 2906 · Mobile, AL 36652 · 205-433-6961

Charles N. Parnell III · (Business Reorganization, Creditors' Rights, Debtors' Rights, Bankruptcy Litigation) · Parnell, Crum & Anderson · 641 South Lawrence Street · P.O. Box 2189 · Montgomery, AL 36102-2189 · 205-832-4200

BUSINESS LITIGATION

Michael L. Edwards* · Balch & Bingham · 1710 Sixth Avenue North · P.O. Box 306 · Birmingham, AL 35201 · 205-251-8100

Edgar M. Elliott III* · Rives & Peterson · 1700 Financial Center · 505 North 20th Street · Birmingham, AL 35203-2607 · 205-328-8141

Samuel H. Franklin · Lightfoot, Franklin, White & Lucas · 300 Financial Center 505 Twentieth Street North · Birmingham, AL 35203-2706 · 205-581-0700

James W. Gewin · Bradley, Arant, Rose & White · 1400 Park Place Tower · Birmingham, AL 35203 · 205-521-8000

William C. Knight, Jr.* · Burr & Forman · SouthTrust Tower, Suite 3000 · 420 Twentieth Street North · Birmingham, AL 35203-3284 · 205-251-3000

Warren B. Lightfoot* · (also Appellate) · Lightfoot, Franklin, White & Lucas · 300 Financial Center · 505 Twentieth Street North · Birmingham, AL 35203-2706 205-581-0700

Crawford S. McGivaren, Jr. · Cabaniss, Johnston, Gardner, Dumas & O'Neal · 1700 AmSouth Sonat Tower · 1900 Fifth Avenue North · P.O. Box 830612 · Birmingham, AL 35203 · 205-252-8800

Hobart A. McWhorter, Jr. · Bradley, Arant, Rose & White · 1400 Park Place Tower · Birmingham, AL 35203 · 205-521-8000

John H. Morrow · Bradley, Arant, Rose & White · 1400 Park Place Tower · Birmingham, AL 35203 · 205-521-8000

J. Vernon Patrick, Jr. · Patrick & Lacy · 1201 Financial Center · Birmingham, AL 35203 · 205-323-5665

J. Michael Rediker · Ritchie & Rediker · 312 North 23rd Street · Birmingham, AL 35203 · 205-251-1288

Charles E. Sharp · Sadler, Sullivan, Sharp & Stutts · SouthTrust Tower, Suite 2500 · 420 North 20th Street · Birmingham, AL 35203 · 205-326-4166

Henry E. Simpson · Lange, Simpson, Robinson & Somerville · 1700 First Alabama Bank Building · 417 North 20th Street · Birmingham, AL 35203 · 205-250-5000

L. Vastine Stabler, Jr. · Cabaniss, Johnston, Gardner, Dumas & O'Neal · 1700 AmSouth Sonat Tower · 1900 Fifth Avenue North · P.O. Box 830612 · Birmingham, AL 35203 · 205-252-8800

Louis E. Braswell* · (Banking, Commercial) · Hand, Arendall, Bedsole, Greaves & Johnston · 3000 First National Bank Building · P.O. Box 123 · Mobile, AL 36601 · 205-432-5511

James J. Duffy, Jr.* · Inge, Twitty & Duffy · First Alabama Bank Building · 56 St. Joseph Street · P.O. Box 1109 · Mobile, AL 36633 · 205-433-3200

William H. Hardie, Jr.* · Johnstone, Adams, Bailey, Gordon and Harris · Royal St. Francis Building · 104 St. Francis Street · P.O. Box 1988 · Mobile, AL 36633 · 205-432-7682

Broox G. Holmes* · Armbrecht, Jackson, DeMouy, Crowe, Holmes & Reeves · 1300 AmSouth Center · P.O. Box 290 · Mobile, AL 36601 · 205-432-6751

John N. Leach, Jr. · Coale, Helmsing, Lyons, Sims & Leach · The Laclede Building · 150 Government Street · P.O. Box 2767 · Mobile, AL 36652 · 205-432-5521

Champ Lyons, Jr. · (Appellate) · Coale, Helmsing, Lyons, Sims & Leach · The Laclede Building · 150 Government Street · P.O. Box 2767 · Mobile, AL 36652 · 205-432-5521

Robert C. Black · Hill, Hill, Carter, Franco, Cole & Black · Hill Building, Second Floor · P.O. Box 116 · Montgomery, AL 36101-0116 · 205-834-7600

Charles M. Crook · Balch & Bingham · The Winter Building · Two Dexter Avenue, Court Square · P.O. Box 78 · Montgomery, AL 36101 · 205-834-6500

Richard H. Gill · Copeland, Franco, Screws & Gill · 444 South Perry Street · P.O. Box 347 · Montgomery, AL 36101-0347 · 205-834-1180

Robert A. Huffaker* · (Appellate, Commercial) · Rushton, Stakely, Johnston & Garrett · 184 Commerce Street · P.O. Box 270 · Montgomery, AL 36195 · 205-834-8480

Oakley Melton, Jr.* · (also Appellate) · Melton, Espy & Williams · 540 South Perry Street · P.O. Box 5130 · Montgomery, AL 36103-5130 · 205-263-6621

M. Roland Nachman, Jr.* · (Antitrust, Appellate, Banking, RICO) · Balch & Bingham · The Winter Building · Two Dexter Avenue, Court Square · P.O. Box 78 · Montgomery, AL 36101 · 205-834-6500

Robert D. Segall* · Copeland, Franco, Screws & Gill · 444 South Perry Street · P.O. Box 347 · Montgomery, AL 36101-0347 · 205-834-1180

Maury D. Smith* · Balch & Bingham · The Winter Building · Two Dexter Avenue, Court Square · P.O. Box 78 · Montgomery, AL 36101 · 205-834-6500

Thomas W. Thagard, Jr.* · (Antitrust, Commercial, RICO, Securities) · Balch & Bingham · The Winter Building · Two Dexter Avenue, Court Square · P.O. Box 78 · Montgomery, AL 36101 · 205-834-6500

John V. Denson · Samford, Denson, Horsley, Pettey, Martin & Barrett · 709 Avenue A · P.O. Box 2345 · Opelika, AL 36803-2345 · 205-745-3504

William F. Horsley · Samford, Denson, Horsley, Pettey, Martin & Barrett · 709 Avenue A · P.O. Box 2345 · Opelika, AL 36803-2345 · 205-745-3504

Sam M. Phelps · Phelps, Owens, Jenkins, Gibson & Fowler · 1201 Greensboro Avenue · Tuscaloosa, AL 35401 · 205-345-5100

CORPORATE LAW

John P. Adams · Bradley, Arant, Rose & White · 1400 Park Place Tower · Birmingham, AL 35203 · 205-521-8000

Louis H. Anders, Jr. · (Mergers & Acquisitions) · Burr & Forman · SouthTrust Tower, Suite 3000 · 420 Twentieth Street North · Birmingham, AL 35203-3284 · 205-251-3000

John Bingham · Balch & Bingham · 1710 Sixth Avenue North · P.O. Box 306 · Birmingham, AL 35201 · 205-251-8100

Thomas Neely Carruthers, Jr. · Bradley, Arant, Rose & White · 1400 Park Place Tower · Birmingham, AL 35203 · 205-521-8000

Richard J. Cohn · Sirote & Permutt · 2222 Arlington Avenue, South · P.O. Box 55727 · Birmingham, AL 35255-5727 · 205-933-7111

Fournier J. Gale III · Maynard, Cooper, Frierson & Gale · 2400 AmSouth/Harbert Plaza · 1901 Sixth Avenue North · Birmingham, AL 35203-2602 · 205-254-1000

John E. Grenier · Lange, Simpson, Robinson & Somerville · 1700 First Alabama Bank Building · 417 North 20th Street · Birmingham, AL 35203 · 205-250-5000

William Lyle Hinds, Jr. · Bradley, Arant, Rose & White · 1400 Park Place Tower · Birmingham, AL 35203 · 205-521-8000

Harold B. Kushner · Berkowitz, Lefkovits, Isom & Kushner · 1100 Financial Center · Birmingham, AL 35203 · 205-328-0480

Arnold K. Lefkovits · Berkowitz, Lefkovits, Isom & Kushner · 1100 Financial Center · Birmingham, AL 35203 · 205-328-0480

Daniel H. Markstein III · Maynard, Cooper, Frierson & Gale · 2400 AmSouth/Harbert Plaza · 1901 Sixth Avenue North · Birmingham, AL 35203-2602 · 205-254-1000

George F. Maynard · Maynard, Cooper, Frierson & Gale · 2400 AmSouth/Harbert Plaza · 1901 Sixth Avenue North · Birmingham, AL 35203-2602 · 205-254-1000

J. Fred Powell · Burr & Forman · SouthTrust Tower, Suite 3000 · 420 Twentieth Street North · Birmingham, AL 35203-3284 · 205-251-3000

J. Michael Rediker · Ritchie & Rediker · 312 North 23rd Street · Birmingham, AL 35203 · 205-251-1288

Joseph G. Stewart · Burr & Forman · SouthTrust Tower, Suite 3000 · 420 Twentieth Street North · Birmingham, AL 35203-3284 · 205-251-3000

Robert C. Walthall · Bradley, Arant, Rose & White · 1400 Park Place Tower · Birmingham, AL 35203 · 205-521-8000

Charles Larimore Whitaker · (Mergers & Acquisitions, Securities) · Bradley, Arant, Rose & White · 1400 Park Place Tower · Birmingham, AL 35203 · 205-521-8000

John A. Caddell · Harris, Caddell & Shanks · 214 Johnston, SE · P.O. Box 1727
Decatur, AL 35602 · 205-340-8045

Marshall J. DeMouy · Armbrecht, Jackson, DeMouy, Crowe, Holmes & Reeves
1300 AmSouth Center · P.O. Box 290 · Mobile, AL 36601 · 205-432-6751

J. Manson Murray · Vickers, Riis, Murray and Curran · Merchants National Bank
Building, Eighth Floor · P.O. Box 990 · Mobile, AL 36601 · 205-432-9772

E. B. Peebles III · (Banking, Corporate Finance, Insurance) · Armbrecht, Jackson,
DeMouy, Crowe, Holmes & Reeves · 1300 AmSouth Center · P.O. Box 290 ·
Mobile, AL 36601 · 205-432-6751

CRIMINAL DEFENSE

Albert C. Bowen, Jr.* · (Federal Court, State Court) · Beddow, Erben & Bowen
2019 Building, Second Floor · 2019 Third Avenue North, Second Floor · Birmingham, AL 35203 · 205-322-7651

William N. Clark* · Redden, Mills & Clark · 940 First Alabama Bank Building ·
Birmingham, AL 35203 · 205-322-0457

William M. Dawson, Jr. · Dawson, Ramsey & Wiley · 490 Park Place Tower ·
2001 Park Place North · Birmingham, AL 35203 · 205-323-6171

Arthur Parker · Frank Nelson Building, Suite 500 · Birmingham, AL 35203 ·
205-324-9517

L. Drew Redden · Redden, Mills & Clark · 940 First Alabama Bank Building ·
Birmingham, AL 35203 · 205-322-0457

Lawrence B. Sheffield, Jr. · Sheffield, Sheffield, Sheffield & Lentine · 730 Frank
Nelson Building · Birmingham, AL 35203 · 205-328-1365

Thomas M. Haas · Haas & Knight · 255 St. Francis Street · Mobile, AL 36602 ·
205-432-0457

Barry Hess · Hess, Atchison & Horne · 301 St. Joseph Street · P.O. Box 1706 ·
Mobile, AL 36633 · 205-432-4546

William A. Kimbrough, Jr.* · (Federal Court, State Court) · Turner, Onderdonk,
Kimbrough & Howell · 1359 Dauphin Street · P.O. Box 2821 · Mobile, AL 36652
205-432-2855

M. A. Marsal · Seale, Marsal & Seale · 200 Church Street · P.O. Box 1746 ·
Mobile, AL 36652 · 205-432-6685

Dennis N. Balske* · (Violent Crimes, Non-Violent Crimes, Federal Court, State Court) · Balske & Van Almen · 644 South Perry Street · P.O. Box 2104 · Montgomery, AL 36102-2104 · 205-263-4700

George L. Beck, Jr. · 22 Scott Street · P.O. Box 5019 · Montgomery, AL 36103 205-832-4878

David B. Byrne, Jr. · Robison & Belser · 210 Commerce Street, Second Floor · P.O. Drawer 1470 · Montgomery, AL 36102 · 205-834-7000

FAMILY LAW

Stephen R. Arnold · Durward and Arnold · City Federal Building, Suite 803 · 2026 Second Avenue North · Birmingham, AL 35203 · 205-324-6654

Robert C. Barnett* · Barnett, Noble, Hanes, O'Neal & Cotton · City Federal Building, Suite 1600 · 2026 Second Avenue North · Birmingham, AL 35203 · 205-322-0471

Gerard J. Durward · Durward and Arnold · City Federal Building, Suite 803 · 2026 Second Avenue North · Birmingham, AL 35203 · 205-324-6654

James M. Fullan, Jr. · Fullan & Fullan · Frank Nelson Building, Suite 610 · 205 North 20th Street · Birmingham, AL 35203 · 205-251-8596

L. Drew Redden · Redden, Mills & Clark · 940 First Alabama Bank Building · Birmingham, AL 35203 · 205-322-0457

Herndon Inge, Jr. · Inge, McMillan, Adams, Coley & Ledyard · SouthTrust Bank Building, 12th Floor · 61 St. Joseph Street · P.O. Box 2345 · Mobile, AL 36602-2345 · 205-433-6506

Albert J. Seale · Seale, Marsal & Seale · 350 Church Street · P.O. Box 1746 · Mobile, AL 36633 · 205-432-6685

David B. Byrne, Jr. · Robison & Belser · 210 Commerce Street, Second Floor · P.O. Drawer 1470 · Montgomery, AL 36102 · 205-834-7000

John L. Capell III · Capell, Howard, Knabe & Cobbs · 57 Adams Avenue · P.O. Box 2069 · Montgomery, AL 36102-2069 · 205-241-8000

Oakley Melton, Jr.* · Melton, Espy & Williams · 540 South Perry Street · P.O. Box 5130 · Montgomery, AL 36103-5130 · 205-263-6621

Maury D. Smith* · Balch & Bingham · The Winter Building · Two Dexter Avenue, Court Square · P.O. Box 78 · Montgomery, AL 36101 · 205-834-6500

FIRST AMENDMENT LAW

James C. Barton, Sr. · Johnston, Barton, Proctor, Swedlaw & Naff · 1100 Park Place Tower · 2001 Park Place · Birmingham, AL 35203 · 205-322-0616

Gilbert E. Johnston, Jr. · Johnston, Barton, Proctor, Swedlaw & Naff · 1100 Park Place Tower · 2001 Park Place · Birmingham, AL 35203 · 205-322-0616

Warren B. Lightfoot* · Lightfoot, Franklin, White & Lucas · 300 Financial Center · 505 Twentieth Street North · Birmingham, AL 35203-2706 · 205-581-0700

James E. Simpson · Lange, Simpson, Robinson & Somerville · 1700 First Alabama Bank Building · 417 North 20th Street · Birmingham, AL 35203 · 205-250-5000

Ferris S. Ritchie, Jr. · Ritchie & Ritchie · 1910 Twenty-Eighth Avenue South · P.O. Drawer 590069 · Homewood, AL 35259-0069 · 205-868-6800

M. Roland Nachman · Balch & Bingham · The Winter Building · Two Dexter Avenue, Court Square · P.O. Box 78 · Montgomery, AL 36101 · 205-834-6500

HEALTH CARE LAW

Sydney L. Lavender · Johnston, Barton, Proctor, Swedlaw & Naff · 1100 Park Place Tower · 2001 Park Place · Birmingham, AL 35203 · 205-322-0616

John T. Mooresmith · 100 Brookwood Place, Suite 202 · P.O. Box 20238 · Birmingham, AL 35216 · 205-871-3437

Wade B. Perry · Johnstone, Adams, Bailey, Gordon and Harris · Royal St. Francis Building · 104 St. Francis Street · P.O. Box 1988 · Mobile, AL 36633 · 205-432-7682

E. Watson Smith · Johnstone, Adams, Bailey, Gordon and Harris · Royal St. Francis Building · 104 St. Francis Street · P.O. Box 1988 · Mobile, AL 36633 · 205-432-7682

INTELLECTUAL PROPERTY LAW

Thad G. Long · Bradley, Arant, Rose & White · 1400 Park Place Tower · Birmingham, AL 35203 · 205-521-8000

Robert J. Veal · (Drafting Claims) · Jennings, Carter, Thompson & Veal · 2001 Park Place North, Suite 525 · Birmingham, AL 35203 · 205-324-1524

LABOR AND EMPLOYMENT LAW

James Patrick Alexander · (Management) · Bradley, Arant, Rose & White · 1400 Park Place Tower · Birmingham, AL 35203 · 205-521-8000

James U. Blacksher · (Individuals) · 300 North 21st Street · Birmingham, AL 35203 · 205-322-1100

Harold A. Bowron, Jr.* · (Management) · Balch & Bingham · 1710 Sixth Avenue North · P.O. Box 306 · Birmingham, AL 35201 · 205-251-8100

Stephen E. Brown* · (Management) · Maynard, Cooper, Frierson & Gale · 2400 AmSouth/Harbert Plaza · 1901 Sixth Avenue North · Birmingham, AL 35203-2602 205-254-1000

John James Coleman, Jr. · (Management) · Bradley, Arant, Rose & White · 1400 Park Place Tower · Birmingham, AL 35203 · 205-521-8000

Jerome A. Cooper · (Labor) · Cooper, Mitch, Crawford, Kuykendall & Whatley 409 North 21st Street, Suite 201 · Birmingham, AL 35203 · 205-328-9576

John C. Falkenberry* · (Labor, Individuals, Civil Rights) · Title Building, Fifth Floor · 300 Twenty-First Street North · Birmingham, AL 35203 · 205-322-1100

Sydney F. Frazier, Jr. · (Management) · Cabaniss, Johnston, Gardner, Dumas & O'Neal · 1700 AmSouth Sonat Tower · 1900 Fifth Avenue North · P.O. Box 830612 · Birmingham, AL 35203 · 205-252-8800

William F. Gardner · (Management) · Cabaniss, Johnston, Gardner, Dumas & O'Neal · 1700 AmSouth Sonat Tower · 1900 Fifth Avenue North · P.O. Box 830612 · Birmingham, AL 35203 · 205-252-8800

Harry L. Hopkins* · (Management) · Lange, Simpson, Robinson & Somerville · 1700 First Alabama Bank Building · 417 North 20th Street · Birmingham, AL 35203 · 205-250-5000

J. Fredric Ingram · (Management) · Burr & Forman · SouthTrust Tower, Suite 3000 · 420 Twentieth Street North · Birmingham, AL 35203-3284 · 205-251-3000

Peyton Lacy, Jr. · (Management) · Lange, Simpson, Robinson & Somerville · 1700 First Alabama Bank Building · 417 North 20th Street · Birmingham, AL 35203 · 205-250-5000

George C. Longshore* · (Labor) · City Federal Building, Suite 2104 · 2030 Second Avenue North · Birmingham, AL 35203 · 205-323-8504

Charles A. Powell III · (Management) · Powell, Tally & Frederick · 2100 First Avenue North, Suite 700 · Birmingham, AL 35203 · 205-324-4996

C. V. Stelzenmuller* · (Management) · Burr & Forman · SouthTrust Tower, Suite 3000 · 420 Twentieth Street North · Birmingham, AL 35203-3284 · 205-251-3000

Joe R. Whatley, Jr.* · (Labor, Individuals) · Cooper, Mitch, Crawford, Kuykendall & Whatley · 409 North 21st Street, Suite 201 · Birmingham, AL 35203 · 205-328-9576

Robert L. Wiggins, Jr.* · (Individuals) · Gordon, Silberman, Wiggins & Childs · 1400 SouthTrust Tower · Birmingham, AL 35203-3204 · 205-328-0640

Willis C. Darby, Jr. · (Management) · 200 St. Anthony Street · P.O. Box 2565 · Mobile, AL 36652 · 205-432-2635

J. Cecil Gardner* · (Labor) · Gardner, Middlebrooks & Fleming · Southtrust Bank Building, 16th Floor · P.O. Drawer 3103 · Mobile, AL 36652 · 205-433-8100

Brock B. Gordon · (Management) · Johnstone, Adams, Bailey, Gordon and Harris Royal St. Francis Building · 104 St. Francis Street · P.O. Box 1988 · Mobile, AL 36633 · 205-432-7682

Frank McRight* · (Management) · McRight, Jackson, Myrick & Moore · 1100 First Alabama Bank Building · P.O. Box 2846 · Mobile, AL 36652 · 205-432-3444

Paul D. Myrick · (Management) · McRight, Jackson, Myrick & Moore · 1100 First Alabama Bank Building · P.O. Box 2846 · Mobile, AL 36652 · 205-432-3444

Gregory B. Stein · (Individuals) · Stein & Brewster · Van Antwerp Building, Suite 405 · 103 Dauphin Street · Mobile, AL 36633-1051 · 205-433-2002

William C. Tidwell III* · (Management) · Hand, Arendall, Bedsole, Greaves & Johnston · 3000 First National Bank Building · P.O. Box 123 · Mobile, AL 36601 205-432-5511

Bruce J. Downey III* · (Management, Individuals) · Capell, Howard, Knabe & Cobbs · 57 Adams Avenue · P.O. Box 2069 · Montgomery, AL 36102-2069 · 205-241-8000

MARITIME LAW

Joseph M. Allen, Jr. · Johnstone, Adams, Bailey, Gordon and Harris · Royal Saint Francis Building · 104 St. Francis Street · P.O. Box 1988 · Mobile, AL 36633 · 205-432-7682

Douglas L. Brown · Armbrecht, Jackson, DeMouy, Crowe, Holmes & Reeves · 1300 AmSouth Center · P.O. Box 290 · Mobile, AL 36601 · 205-432-6751

Alexander F. Lankford III · Hand, Arendall, Bedsole, Greaves & Johnston · 3000 First National Bank Building · P.O. Box 123 · Mobile, AL 36601 · 205-432-5511

Abram L. Philips, Jr.* · (Charter Parties, Personal Injury, Cargo, Collision, Immigration) · Reams, Philips, Killion, Brooks, Schell, Gaston & Hudson · The Pillans Building · 3662 Dauphin Street · P.O. Box 8158 · Mobile, AL 36608 · 205-344-4721

A. Clay Rankin · Hand, Arendall, Bedsole, Greaves & Johnston · 3000 First National Bank Building · P.O. Box 123 · Mobile, AL 36601 · 205-432-5511

W. Boyd Reeves* · (Personal Injury, Workmen's Comp LHWCA) · Armbrecht, Jackson, DeMouy, Crowe, Holmes & Reeves · 1300 AmSouth Center · P.O. Box 290 · Mobile, AL 36601 · 205-432-6751

G. Hamp Uzzelle III* · Hand, Arendall, Bedsole, Greaves & Johnston · First National Bank Building, Suite 3000 · P.O. Box 123 · Mobile, AL 36601 · 205-432-5511

NATURAL RESOURCES AND ENVIRONMENTAL LAW

Fournier J. Gale III · Maynard, Cooper, Frierson & Gale · 2400 AmSouth/Harbert Plaza · 1901 Sixth Avenue North · Birmingham, AL 35203-2602 · 205-254-1000

William H. Satterfield · Balch & Bingham · 1710 Sixth Avenue North · P.O. Box 306 · Birmingham, AL 35203 · 205-251-8100

Macbeth Wagnon, Jr. · Bradley, Arant, Rose & White · 1400 Park Place Tower Birmingham, AL 35203 · 205-521-8000

Conrad P. Armbrecht II · Armbrecht, Jackson, DeMouy, Crowe, Holmes & Reeves · 1300 AmSouth Center · P.O. Box 290 · Mobile, AL 36601 · 205-432-6751

Norton W. Brooker, Jr.* · (Oil & Gas, Timber, Litigation, Energy) · Lyons, Pipes & Cook · Two North Royal Street · P.O. Drawer 2727 · Mobile, AL 36652-2727 · 205-432-4481

Rae M. Crowe · Armbrecht, Jackson, DeMouy, Crowe, Holmes & Reeves · 1300 AmSouth Center · P.O. Box 290 · Mobile, AL 36601 · 205-432-6751

Donald F. Pierce* · Hand, Arendall, Bedsole, Greaves & Johnston · 3000 First National Bank Building · P.O. Box 123 · Mobile, AL 36601 · 205-432-5511

PERSONAL INJURY LITIGATION

Frank J. Tipler, Jr.* · (Plaintiffs, Products Liability, Automobile Collision, Airplane Collision) · Tipler & Tipler · Tipler Building · 218 South Threenotch Street P.O. Box 1397 · Andalusia, AL 36420 · 205-222-4148

Bibb Allen* · (Defendants) · Rives & Peterson · 1700 Financial Center · 505 North 20th Street · Birmingham, AL 35203-2607 · 205-328-8141

M. Clay Alspaugh · Hogan, Smith, Alspaugh, Samples & Pratt · 2323 Second Avenue North · Birmingham, AL 35203 · 205-324-5635

Leon David Ashford · Hare, Wynn, Newell and Newton · City Federal Building, Seventh Floor · 2026 Second Avenue North · Birmingham, AL 35203 · 205-328-5330

Harold A. Bowron, Jr.* · (Defendants, Airplane Collision) · Balch & Bingham · 1710 Sixth Avenue North · P.O. Box 306 · Birmingham, AL 35201 · 205-251-8100

Frank O. Burge, Jr. · (Plaintiffs) · Burge & Wettermark · 2300 South Trust Tower 420 North 20th Street · Birmingham, AL 35203 · 205-251-9729

Thomas W. Christian* · (Defendants, Medical Malpractice, Products Liability) · Rives & Peterson · 1700 Financial Center · 505 North 20th Street · Birmingham, AL 35203-2607 · 205-328-8141

Edward O. Conerly · McDaniel, Hall, Conerly & Lusk · Financial Center, Suite 1400 · 505 North 20th Street · Birmingham, AL 35203 · 205-251-8143

Edgar M. Elliot III · (Defendants) · Rives & Peterson · 1700 Financial Center · 505 North 20th Street · Birmingham, AL 35203-2607 · 205-328-8141

Clifford Emond, Jr. · (Plaintiffs) · Emond & Vines · 1900 Daniel Building · P.O. Box 10008 · Birmingham, AL 35202-0008 · 205-324-4000

Samuel H. Franklin · (Defendants) · Lightfoot, Franklin, White & Lucas · 300 Financial Center · 505 Twentieth Street North · Birmingham, AL 35203-2706 · 205-581-0700

James W. Gewin · (Defendants) · Bradley, Arant, Rose & White · 1400 Park Place Tower · Birmingham, AL 35203 · 205-521-8000

Stephen D. Heninger* · (Plaintiffs, Medical Malpractice, Products Liability, Automobile Collision) · Heninger, Burdge & Vargo · Historic O'Neill Building · 2021 Third Avenue North, Suite 300 · Birmingham, AL 35203 · 205-322-5153

Warren B. Lightfoot* · (Defendants) · Lightfoot, Franklin, White & Lucas · 300 Financial Center · 505 Twentieth Street North · Birmingham, AL 35203-2706 · 205-581-0700

David H. Marsh · (Plaintiffs) · Pittman, Hooks, Marsh, Dutton & Hollis · Park Place Tower, Suite 800 · 2001 Park Place North · Birmingham, AL 35203 · 205-322-8880

Eugene D. Martenson* · (Defendants, Medical Malpractice, Products Liability, Professional Malpractice) · Huie, Fernambucq and Stewart · First Alabama Bank Building, Suite 825 · Birmingham, AL 35203 · 205-251-1193

William J. McDaniel* · (Defendants, Medical Malpractice, Products Liability, Professional Malpractice, Automobile Collision) · McDaniel, Hall, Conerly & Lusk · Financial Center, Suite 1400 · 505 North 20th Street · Birmingham, AL 35203 · 205-251-8143

Crawford S. McGivaren, Jr. · Cabaniss, Johnston, Gardner, Dumas & O'Neal · 1700 AmSouth Sonat Tower · 1900 Fifth Avenue North · P.O. Box 830612 · Birmingham, AL 35203 · 205-252-8800

Hobart A. McWhorter, Jr. · (Defendants) · Bradley, Arant, Rose & White · 1400 Park Place Tower · Birmingham, AL 35203 · 205-521-8000

John H. Morrow · (Defendants) · Bradley, Arant, Rose & White · 1400 Park Place Tower · Birmingham, AL 35203 · 205-521-8000

Neal C. Newell · (Plaintiffs) · Hare, Wynn, Newell and Newton · 2026 Second Avenue North, Suite 700 · Birmingham, AL 35203 · 205-328-5330

Alex W. Newton · (Plaintiffs) · Hare, Wynn, Newell and Newton · 2026 Second Avenue North, Suite 700 · Birmingham, AL 35203 · 205-328-5330

W. Lee Pittman* · (Plaintiffs) · Pittman, Hooks, Marsh; Dutton & Hollis · Park Place Tower, Suite 800 · 2001 Park Place North · Birmingham, AL 35203 · 205-322-8880

James R. PrattII · Hogan, Smith, Alspaugh, Samples & Pratt · 2323 Second Avenue North · Birmingham, AL 35203 · 205-324-5635

L. Drew Redden · Redden, Mills & Clark · 940 First Alabama Bank Building · Birmingham, AL 35203 · 205-322-0457

Charles E. Sharp · Sadler, Sullivan, Sharp & Stutts · SouthTrust Tower, Suite 2500 · 420 North 20th Street · Birmingham, AL 35203 · 205-326-4166

James E. Simpson · (Defendants, Products Liability) · Lange, Simpson, Robinson & Somerville · 1700 First Alabama Bank Building · 417 North 20th Street · Birmingham, AL 35203 · 205-250-5000

Clarence M. Small, Jr. · (Defendants) · Rives & Peterson · 1700 Financial Center 505 North 20th Street · Birmingham, AL 35203-2607 · 205-328-8141

William W. Smith · Hogan, Smith, Alspaugh, Samples & Pratt · 2323 Second Avenue North · Birmingham, AL 35203 · 205-324-5635

W. Stancil Starnes · (Defendants) · Starnes & Atchison · 100 Brookwood Place, Seventh Floor · Birmingham, AL 35209 · 205-868-6000

Lanny S. Vines · (Plaintiffs) · Emond & Vines · 1900 Daniel Building · P.O. Box 10008 · Birmingham, AL 35202-0008 · 205-324-4000

Robert O. Cox* · (Defendants) · Poellnitz, Cox & Jones · First National Bank Building · P.O. Box 876 · Florence, AL 35631 · 205-764-0821

James E. Davis, Jr. · (Defendants) · Lanier, Ford, Shaver & Payne · 200 West Court Square, Suite 5000 · Huntsville, AL 35801 · 205-535-1101

W. Stanley Rodgers · (Defendants) · Lanier, Ford, Shaver & Payne · 200 West Court Square, Suite 5000 · Huntsville, AL 35801 · 205-535-1101

Richard Bounds* · (Plaintiffs) · Cunningham, Bounds, Yance, Crowder & Brown 1601 Dauphin Street · P.O. Box 66705 · Mobile, AL 36600 · 205-471-6191

Robert T. Cunningham, Jr. · (Plaintiffs) · Cunningham, Bounds, Yance, Crowder & Brown · 1601 Dauphin Street · P.O. Box 66705 · Mobile, AL 36600 · 205-471-6191

James J. Duffy, Jr.* · (Defendants, Medical Malpractice, Products Liability, Professional Malpractice, Automobile Collision) · Inge, Twitty & Duffy · First Alabama Bank Building · 56 St. Joseph Street · P.O. Box 1109 · Mobile, AL 36633 205-433-3200

Broox G. Holmes* · (Defendants) · Armbrecht, Jackson, DeMouy, Crowe, Holmes & Reeves · 1300 AmSouth Center · P.O. Box 290 · Mobile, AL 36601 · 205-432-6751

Fred W. Killion, Jr. · Reams, Philips, Killion, Brooks, Schell, Gaston & Hudson The Pillans Building · 3662 Dauphin Street · P.O. Box 8158 · Mobile, AL 36608 205-344-4721

John N. Leach, Jr. · (Defendants) · Coale, Helmsing, Lyons, Sims & Leach · The Laclede Building · 150 Government Street · P.O. Box 2767 · Mobile, AL 36652 · 205-432-5521

Jerry A. McDowell · (Defendants) · Hand, Arendall, Bedsole, Greaves & Johnston · 3000 First National Bank Building · P.O. Box 123 · Mobile, AL 36601 205-432-5511

W. Boyd Reeves* · (Defendants, Medical Malpractice, Products Liability, Professional Malpractice) · Armbrecht, Jackson, DeMouy, Crowe, Holmes & Reeves 1300 AmSouth Center · P.O. Box 290 · Mobile, AL 36601 · 205-432-6751

Jere L. Beasley · Beasley, Wilson, Allen, Mendelsohn & Jemison · 207 Montgomery Street · P.O. Box 4160 · Montgomery, AL 36103 · 205-269-2343

Robert C. Black · (Defendants) · Hill, Hill, Carter, Franco, Cole & Black · Hill Building, Second Floor · P.O. Box 116 · Montgomery, AL 36101-0116 · 205-834-7600

Sterling G. Culpepper, Jr. · Balch & Bingham · The Winter Building · Two Dexter Avenue, Court Square · P.O. Box 78 · Montgomery, AL 36101 · 205-834-6500

Richard B. Garrett · (Defendants) · Rushton, Stakely, Johnston & Garrett · 184 Commerce Street · P.O. Box 270 · Montgomery, AL 36195 · 205-834-8480

Richard H. Gill* · (Commercial, Securities) · Copeland, Franco, Screws & Gill · 444 South Perry Street · P.O. Box 347 · Montgomery, AL 36101-0347 · 205-834-1180

Richard M. Jordan · Richard M. Jordan and Randy Myers · 302 Alabama Street Montgomery, AL 36104 · 205-265-4561

Thomas H. Keene · (Defendants, Medical Malpractice) · Rushton, Stakely, Johnston & Garrett · 184 Commerce Street · P.O. Box 270 · Montgomery, AL 36195 · 205-834-8480

Oakley Melton, Jr.* · (Defendants) · Melton, Espy & Williams · 540 South Perry Street · P.O. Box 5130 · Montgomery, AL 36103-5130 · 205-263-6621

Robert D. Segall* · Copeland, Franco, Screws & Gill · 444 South Perry Street · P.O. Box 347 · Montgomery, AL 36101-0347 · 205-834-1180

Maury D. Smith* · Balch & Bingham · The Winter Building · Two Dexter Avenue, Court Square · P.O. Box 78 · Montgomery, AL 36101 · 205-834-6500

Charles A. Stakely* · (Defendants, Medical Malpractice, Products Liability, Professional Malpractice, Appellate) · Rushton, Stakely, Johnston & Garrett · 184 Commerce Street · P.O. Box 270 · Montgomery, AL 36195 · 205-834-8480

Ralph D. Gaines, Jr. · (Defendants) · Gaines, Gaines & Gaines · 127 East North Street · P.O. Box 275 · Talladega, AL 35160 · 205-362-2386

Sam M. Phelps · (Defendants) · Phelps, Owens, Jenkins, Gibson & Fowler · 1201 Greensboro Avenue · Tuscaloosa, AL 35401 · 205-345-5100

PUBLIC UTILITY LAW

S. Eason Balch, Sr. · (Electric) · Balch & Bingham · 1710 Sixth Avenue North · P.O. Box 306 · Birmingham, AL 35201 · 205-251-8100

Robert A. Buettner · Balch & Bingham · 1710 Sixth Avenue North · P.O. Box 306 Birmingham, AL 35203 · 205-251-8100

REAL ESTATE LAW

Charles A. J. Beavers, Jr. · Bradley, Arant, Rose & White · 1400 Park Place Tower · Birmingham, AL 35203 · 205-521-8000

H. Hampton Boles · Balch & Bingham · 1710 Sixth Avenue North · P.O. Box 306 Birmingham, AL 35201 · 205-251-8100

Douglas P. Corretti · Corretti & Newsom · 1804 Seventh Avenue North · Birmingham, AL 35203 · 205-251-1164

J. Robert Fleenor · Bradley, Arant, Rose & White · 1400 Park Place Tower · Birmingham, AL 35203 · 205-521-8000

Frank C. Galloway, Jr. · Cabaniss, Johnston, Gardner, Dumas & O'Neal · 1700 AmSouth Sonat Tower · 1900 Fifth Avenue North · P.O. Box 830612 · Birmingham, AL 35203-0612 · 205-252-8800

Chervis Isom · Berkowitz, Lefkovits, Isom & Kushner · 1100 Financial Center · Birmingham, AL 35203 · 205-328-0480

Randolph H. Lanier · Balch & Bingham · 1710 Sixth Avenue North · P.O. Box 306 · Birmingham, AL 35201 · 205-251-8100

Jerome K. Lanning · Johnston, Barton, Proctor, Swedlaw & Naff · 1100 Park Place Tower · 2001 Park Place · Birmingham, AL 35203 · 205-322-0616

George F. Maynard · Maynard, Cooper, Frierson & Gale · 2400 AmSouth/ Harbert Plaza · 1901 Sixth Avenue North · Birmingham, AL 35203-2602 · 205-254-1000

James L. Permutt · Sirote & Permutt · 2222 Arlington Avenue, South · P.O. Box 55727 · Birmingham, AL 35255-5727 · 205-933-7111

J. Fred Powell · Burr & Forman · SouthTrust Tower, Suite 3000 · 420 Twentieth Street North · Birmingham, AL 35203-3284 · 205-251-3000

Harold Williams · Balch & Bingham · 1710 Sixth Avenue North · P.O. Box 306 Birmingham, AL 35201 · 205-251-8100

Stova F. McFadden · McFadden, Lyon, Willoughby & Rouse · 718 Downtowner Boulevard · Mobile, AL 36609 · 205-342-9172

Harold D. Parkman · (Commercial Transactions) · Hand, Arendall, Bedsole, Greaves & Johnston · 3000 First National Bank Building · P.O. Box 123 · Mobile, AL 36601 · 205-432-5511

Herman B. Franco · Copeland, Franco, Screws & Gill · 444 South Perry Street · P.O. Box 347 · Montgomery, AL 36101-0347 · 205-834-1180

Ralph A. Franco · (Estate Planning, Estate Administration) · Hill, Hill, Carter, Franco, Cole & Black · Hill Building, Second Floor · P.O. Box 116 · Montgomery, AL 36101-0116 · 205-834-7600

William Inge Hill, Jr. · Hill, Hill, Carter, Franco, Cole & Black · Hill Building, Second Floor · P.O. Box 116 · Montgomery, AL 36101-0116 · 205-834-7600

Rufus M. King · Capell, Howard, Knabe & Cobbs · 57 Adams Avenue · P.O. Box 2069 · Montgomery, AL 36102-2069 · 205-241-8000

William K. Martin · Capell, Howard, Knabe & Cobbs · 57 Adams Avenue · P.O. Box 2069 · Montgomery, AL 36102-2069 · 205-241-8000

TAX AND EMPLOYEE BENEFITS LAW

Louis H. Anders, Jr. · (Corporate & Partnership Transactions) · Burr & Forman SouthTrust Tower, Suite 3000 · 420 Twentieth Street North · Birmingham, AL 35203-3284 · 205-251-3000

Harold I. Apolinsky · Sirote & Permutt · 2222 Arlington Avenue, South · P.O. Box 55727 · Birmingham, AL 35255-5727 · 205-933-7111

Joseph W. Blackburn · Sirote & Permutt · 2222 Arlington Avenue, South · P.O. Box 55727 · Birmingham, AL 35255-5727 · 205-930-5154

Joseph S. Bluestein · (Employee Benefits) · Sirote & Permutt · 2222 Arlington Avenue, South · P.O. Box 55727 · Birmingham, AL 35255-5727 · 205-933-7111

Thomas Neely Carruthers, Jr. · Bradley, Arant, Rose & White · 1400 Park Place Tower · Birmingham, AL 35203 · 205-521-8000

John H. Cooper · Sirote & Permutt · 2222 Arlington Avenue, South · P.O. Box 55727 · Birmingham, AL 35255-5727 · 205-930-5108

Roy J. Crawford · Cabaniss, Johnston, Gardner, Dumas & O'Neal · 1700 AmSouth Sonat Tower · 1900 Fifth Avenue North · P.O. Box 830612 · Birmingham, AL 35203 · 205-252-8800

C. Fred Daniels · (Employee Benefits) · Dominick, Fletcher, Yeilding, Wood & Lloyd · 2121 Highland Avenue · Birmingham, AL 35205 · 205-939-0033

David S. Dunkle · (Employee Benefits) · Cabaniss, Johnston, Gardner, Dumas & O'Neal · 1700 AmSouth Sonat Tower · 1900 Fifth Avenue North · P.O. Box 830612 · Birmingham, AL 35283-0612 · 205-252-8800

Meade Frierson II · Maynard, Cooper, Frierson & Gale · 2400 AmSouth/Harbert Plaza · 1901 Sixth Avenue North · Birmingham, AL 35203-2602 · 205-254-1000

William Lyle Hinds, Jr. · Bradley, Arant, Rose & White · 1400 Park Place Tower Birmingham, AL 35203 · 205-521-8000

Robert G. Johnson · (Employee Benefits) · Bradley, Arant, Rose & White · 1400 Park Place Tower · Birmingham, AL 35203 · 205-521-8000

Harold B. Kushner · Berkowitz, Lefkovits, Isom & Kushner · 1100 Financial Center · Birmingham, AL 35203 · 205-328-0480

Arnold K. Lefkovits · Berkowitz, Lefkovits, Isom & Kushner · 1100 Financial Center · Birmingham, AL 35203 · 205-328-0480

J. William Lewis · Asbestos Litigation · 1027 Twenty-Second Street South, Suite 102 · Birmingham, AL 35203 · 205-328-9200

Edward M. Selfe · Bradley, Arant, Rose & White · 1400 Park Place Tower · Birmingham, AL 35203 · 205-521-8000

Robert C. Walthall · Bradley, Arant, Rose & White · 1400 Park Place Tower · Birmingham, AL 35203 · 205-521-8000

A. Brand Walton, Jr. · (Employee Benefits) · Burr & Forman · SouthTrust Tower, Suite 3000 · 420 Twentieth Street North · Birmingham, AL 35203-3284 · 205-251-3000

J. Gilmer Blackburn · Blackburn, Maloney & Schuppert · 201 Second Avenue · P.O. Box 1469 · Decatur, AL 35602 · 205-353-7826

Norman W. Harris, Jr. · Harris, Caddell & Shanks · 214 Johnston Street, SE · P.O. Box 2688 · Decatur, AL 35602-2688 · 205-340-8048

G. Porter Brock, Jr. · Hand, Arendall, Bedsole, Greaves & Johnston · 3000 First National Bank Building · P.O. Box 123 · Mobile, AL 36601 · 205-432-5511

Stephen G. Crawford · (Employee Benefits) · Hand, Arendall, Bedsole, Greaves & Johnston · 3000 First National Bank Building · P.O. Box 123 · Mobile, AL 36601 · 205-432-5511

Thomas F. Garth · (Corporate & Partnership Transactions, Employee Benefits) · Lyons, Pipes & Cook · Two North Royal Street · Drawer 2727 · Mobile, AL 36652-2727 · 205-432-4481

William B. Harvey · (Employee Benefits) · Armbrecht, Jackson, DeMouy, Crowe, Holmes & Reeves · 1300 AmSouth Center · P.O. Box 290 · Mobile, AL 36601 · 205-432-6751

Frederick G. Helmsing · Coale, Helmsing, Lyons & Sims · The Laclede Building, Suite 2000 · 150 Government Street · P.O. Box 2767 · Mobile, AL 36652 · 205-432-5521

J. Jeptha Hill · Hill and Hill · P.O. Box 16226 · Mobile, AL 36616-0226 · 205-478-6031

J. Thomas Hines, Jr. · Hand, Arendall, Bedsole, Greaves & Johnston · 3000 First National Bank Building · P.O. Box 123 · Mobile, AL 36601 · 205-432-5511

Vivian G. Johnston, Jr. · Hand, Arendall, Bedsole, Greaves & Johnston · 3000 First National Bank Building · P.O. Box 123 · Mobile, AL 36601 · 205-432-5511

F. M. Keeling · Armbrecht, Jackson, DeMouy, Crowe, Holmes & Reeves · 1300 AmSouth Center · P.O. Box 290 · Mobile, AL 36601 · 205-432-6751

Gregory L. Leatherbury, Jr. · (Tax, Employee Benefits) · Hand, Arendall, Bedsole, Greaves & Johnston · 3000 First National Bank Building · P.O. Box 123 · Mobile, AL 36601 · 205-432-5511

E. Watson Smith · (Tax, Employee Benefits) · Johnstone, Adams, Bailey, Gordon and Harris · Royal St. Francis Building · 104 St. Francis Street · P.O. Box 1988 · Mobile, AL 36633 · 205-432-7682

Henry B. Hardegree · Rushton, Stakely, Johnston & Garrett · 184 Commerce Street · P.O. Box 270 · Montgomery, AL 36195 · 205-834-8480

Gerald W. Hartley · Hill, Hill, Carter, Franco, Cole & Black · Hill Building, Second Floor · P.O. Box 116 · Montgomery, AL 36101-0116 · 205-834-7600

Henry H. Hutchinson · (Corporate & Partnership Transactions) · Capell, Howard, Knabe & Cobbs · 57 Adams Avenue · P.O. Box 2069 · Montgomery, AL 36102-2069 · 205-241-8000

D. Kyle Johnson · (Employee Benefits) · Capell, Howard, Knabe & Cobbs · 57 Adams Avenue · P.O. Box 2069 · Montgomery, AL 36102-2069 · 205-241-8000

Thomas G. Mancuso · (Corporate & Partnership Transactions) · Rushton, Stakely, Johnston & Garrett · 184 Commerce Street · P.O. Box 270 · Montgomery, AL 36195 · 205-834-8480

Alan E. Rothfeder · Kaufman, Rothfeder & Blitz · One Court Square · P.O. Drawer 4540 · Montgomery, AL 36103-4540 · 205-834-1111

James M. Scott · Capell, Howard, Knabe & Cobbs · 57 Adams Avenue · P.O. Box 2069 · Montgomery, AL 36102-2069 · 205-241-8000

Robert D. Thorington · Johnson & Thorington · 504 South Perry Street · P.O. Drawer 1748 · Montgomery, AL 36102-1748 · 205-834-6222

TRUSTS AND ESTATES

Harold I. Apolinsky · Sirote & Permutt · 2222 Arlington Avenue, South · P.O. Box 55727 · Birmingham, AL 35255-5727 · 205-933-7111

E. T. Brown, Jr. · Cabaniss, Johnston, Gardner, Dumas & O'Neal · 1700 AmSouth Sonat Tower · 1900 Fifth Avenue North · P.O. Box 830612 · Birmingham, AL 35203 · 205-252-8800

William Lyle Hinds, Jr. · Bradley, Arant, Rose & White · 1400 Park Place Tower Birmingham, AL 35203 · 205-521-8000

Kirby Sevier · Maynard, Cooper, Frierson & Gale · 2400 AmSouth/Harbert Plaza 1901 Sixth Avenue North · Birmingham, AL 35203-2602 · 205-254-1000

Judith F. Todd · Sirote & Permutt · 2222 Arlington Avenue, South · P.O. Box 55727 · Birmingham, AL 35255-5727 · 205-930-5249

Leonard Wertheimer III · One Independence Plaza, Suite 510 · Birmingham, AL 35209 · 205-870-9587

Paul O. Woodall · Burr & Forman · SouthTrust Tower, Suite 3000 · 420 Twentieth Street North · Birmingham, AL 35203-3284 · 205-251-3000

John N. Wrinkle · Bradley, Arant, Rose & White · 1400 Park Place Tower · Birmingham, AL 35203 · 205-521-8000

G. Porter Brock, Jr. · Hand, Arendall, Bedsole, Greaves & Johnston · 3000 First National Bank Building · P.O. Box 123 · Mobile, AL 36601 · 205-432-5511

Robert M. Galloway · Collins, Galloway & Smith · 3263 Cottage Hill Road · P.O. Box 16629 · Mobile, AL 36616-0629 · 205-476-4493

J. Jeptha Hill · (Estate Planning) · Hill and Hill · 3103 Airport Boulevard, Suite 630 · P.O. Box 16226 · Mobile, AL 36616 · 205-478-6031

Lyman F. Holland, Jr. · Hand, Arendall, Bedsole, Greaves & Johnston · 3000 First National Bank Building · P.O. Box 123 · Mobile, AL 36601 · 205-432-5511

Vivian G. Johnston, Jr. · Hand, Arendall, Bedsole, Greaves & Johnston · 3000 First National Bank Building · P.O. Box 123, Drawer C · Mobile, AL 36601 · 205-432-5511

F. M. Keeling · Armbrecht, Jackson, DeMouy, Crowe, Holmes & Reeves · 1300 AmSouth Center · P.O. Box 290 · Mobile, AL 36601 · 205-432-6751

Gregory L. Leatherbury, Jr. · Hand, Arendall, Bedsole, Greaves & Johnston · 3000 First National Bank Building · P.O. Box 123 · Mobile, AL 36601 · 205-432-5511

Henry B. Hardegree · Rushton, Stakely, Johnston & Garrett · 184 Commerce Street · P.O. Box 270 · Montgomery, AL 36195 · 205-834-8480

Gerald W. Hartley · Hill, Hill, Carter, Franco, Cole & Black · Hill Building, Second Floor · P.O. Box 116 · Montgomery, AL 36101-0116 · 205-834-7600

L. Lister Hill · (Estate Planning, Estate Administration, Charitable Trusts) · Capell, Howard, Knabe & Cobbs · 57 Adams Avenue · P.O. Box 2069 · Montgomery, AL 36102-2069 · 205-241-8000

ALASKA

BANKRUPTCY LAW

David H. Bundy · Guess & Rudd · 510 L Street, Seventh Floor · Anchorage, AK 99501 · 907-276-5121

Cabot Christianson · Law Office of Cabot Christianson · 911 West Eighth Avenue · Anchorage, AK 99501 · 907-258-6016

David W. Oesting · Davis Wright Tremaine · 550 West Seventh Avenue, Suite 1450 · Anchorage, AK 99501 · 907-276-4488

James D. DeWitt* · Guess & Rudd · Key Bank Building, Suite 500 · 100 Cushman Street · P.O. Box 2750 · Fairbanks, AK 99707 · 907-452-8986

BUSINESS LITIGATION

William M. Bankston · (Securities) · Bankston & McCullom · 1800 Enserch Center · 550 West Seventh Avenue, Suite 1800 · Anchorage, AK 99501 · 907-276-1711

John M. Conway · Atkinson, Conway & Gagnon · 420 L Street, Suite 500 · Anchorage, AK 99501-1989 · 907-276-1700

Jeffrey M. Feldman · Gilmore & Feldman · 310 K Street, Suite 308 · Anchorage, AK 99501 · 907-279-4506

Charles P. Flynn · Burr, Pease & Kurtz · 810 N Street · Anchorage, AK 99501-3293 · 907-276-6100

Bruce E. Gagnon* · (Commercial, Securities) · Atkinson, Conway & Gagnon · 420 L Street, Suite 500 · Anchorage, AK 99501-1989 · 907-276-1700

Julian L. Mason III* · Ashburn and Mason · 1130 West Sixth Avenue, Suite 100 · Anchorage, AK 99501 · 907-276-4331

Winston S. Burbank · Call, Barrett & Burbank · 711 Gaffney Road · Fairbanks, AK 99701 · 907-452-2211

Lloyd I. Hoppner · Hoppner & Paskvan · 714 Fourth Avenue, Suite 301 · P. O. Box 73888 · Fairbanks, AK 99707 · 907-452-1205

William B. Rozell · Faulkner, Banfield, Doogan & Holmes · 302 Gold Street · Juneau, AK 99801 · 907-586-2210

CORPORATE LAW

William M. Bankston · (Securities Regulation) · Bankston & McCullom · 1800 Enserch Center · 550 West Seventh Avenue, Suite 1800 · Anchorage, AK 99501 907-276-1711

Ralph E. Duerre · Burr, Pease & Kurtz · 810 N Street · Anchorage, AK 99501-3293 · 907-276-6100

Bruce E. Gagnon* · (Mergers & Acquisitions) · Atkinson, Conway & Gagnon · 420 L Street, Suite 500 · Anchorage, AK 99501-1989 · 907-276-1700

Andrew E. Hoge · Hoge and Lekisch · 437 E Street, Suite 500 · Anchorage, AK 99501 · 907-276-1726

L. S. Kurtz, Jr. · Burr, Pease & Kurtz · 810 N Street · Anchorage, AK 99501-3293 907-276-6100

Julian L. Mason III* · (Administrative) · Ashburn and Mason · 1130 West Sixth Avenue, Suite 100 · Anchorage, AK 99501 · 907-276-4331

Stanley H. Reitman · Delaney, Wiles, Hayes, Reitman & Brubaker · 1007 West Third Avenue, Suite 400 · Anchorage, AK 99501 · 907-279-3581

Winston S. Burbank · Call, Barrett & Burbank · 711 Gaffney Road · Fairbanks, AK 99701 · 907-452-2211

CRIMINAL DEFENSE

William P. Bryson* · (Violent Crimes, Non-Violent Crimes, Federal Court, State Court) · 810 West Second Avenue · Anchorage, AK 99501 · 907-276-8611

Jeffrey M. Feldman · Gilmore & Feldman · 310 K Street, Suite 308 · Anchorage, AK 99501 · 907-279-4506

James D. Gilmore* · Gilmore & Feldman · 310 K Street, Suite 308 · Anchorage, AK 99501 · 907-279-4506

James H. McComas · 330 L Street · Anchorage, AK 99501 · 907-258-7807

Phillip Paul Weidner* · (Trial & Appellate) · Phillip Paul Weidner and Associates 330 L Street, Suite 200 · Anchorage, AK 99501 · 907-277-7000

Dick L. Madson · 712 Eighth Avenue · Fairbanks, AK 99701 · 907-452-4215

FAMILY LAW

Douglas B. Baily* · (Divorce, Divorce Litigation) · Baily & Mason · 1130 West Sixth Avenue, Suite 100 · Anchorage, AK 99501 · 907-276-4331

Ken Brittain · Brittain, Mersereau & Pentlarge · 1400 West Benson Boulevard, Suite 550 · Anchorage, AK 99503-3690 · 907-276-1919

Joe M. Huddleston · Hughes, Thorsness, Gantz, Powell & Brundin · 509 West Third Avenue · Anchorage, AK 99501-2273 · 907-274-7522

Timothy M. Lynch · Lynch, Crosby & Sisson · The Enserch Building, Suite 1100 550 West Seventh Avenue · Anchorage, AK 99501 · 907-276-3222

FIRST AMENDMENT LAW

Robert H. Wagstaff · Wagstaff, Pope and Clocksin · 912 West Sixth Avenue · Anchorage, AK 99501 · 907-277-8611

LABOR AND EMPLOYMENT LAW

Fred B. Arvidson · (Management) · Perkins Coie · 1029 West Third Avenue, Suite 300 · Anchorage, AK 99501 · 907-279-8561

Charles A. Dunnagan · (Labor) · Jermain, Dunnagan & Owens · 3000 A Street, Suite 300 · Anchorage, AK 99503 · 907-563-8844

Charles P. Flynn · (Management) · Burr, Pease & Kurtz · 810 N Street · Anchorage, AK 99501-3293 · 907-276-6100

Parry E. Grover · (Management) · Davis Wright Tremaine · 550 West Seventh Avenue, Suite 1450 · Anchorage, AK 99501 · 907-276-4488

William K. Jermain · (Labor) · Jermain, Dunnagan & Owens · 3000 A Street, Suite 300 · Anchorage, AK 99503 · 907-563-8844

Thomas R. Lucas · (Management) · Hughes, Thorsness, Gantz, Powell & Brundin · 509 West Third Avenue · Anchorage, AK 99501-2273 · 907-274-7522

Thomas P. Owens, Jr.* · (Management) · Owens & Turner · 1500 West 33rd Avenue, Suite 200 · Anchorage, AK 99503-3639 · 907-276-3963

William B. Schendel · (Individuals) · Schendel & Callahan · National Bank Building · 613 Cushman Street · P.O. Box 2137 · Fairbanks, AK 99707 · 907-456-1136

NATURAL RESOURCES AND ENVIRONMENTAL LAW

Thomas E. Meacham · (Oil & Gas, Mining, Water, Alaska Native & Public Land Law) · Burr, Pease & Kurtz · 810 N Street · Anchorage, AK 99501-3293 · 907-276-6100

William B. Rozell · Faulkner, Banfield, Doogan & Holmes · 302 Gold Street · Juneau, AK 99801 · 907-586-2210

PERSONAL INJURY LITIGATION

Douglas B. Baily · (Plaintiffs, Medical Malpractice, Products Liability, Airplane Collision, Appellate) · Baily & Mason · 1130 West Sixth Avenue, Suite 100 · Anchorage, AK 99501 · 907-276-4331

Jeffrey M. Feldman · Gilmore & Feldman · 310 K Street, Suite 308 · Anchorage, AK 99501 · 907-279-4506

Bruce E. Gagnon* · (Professional Malpractice) · Atkinson, Conway & Gagnon · 420 L Street, Suite 500 · Anchorage, AK 99501-1989 · 907-276-1700

George N. Hayes · (Defendants) · Delaney, Wiles, Hayes, Reitman & Brubaker 1007 West Third Avenue, Suite 400 · Anchorage, AK 99501 · 907-279-3581

Roger F. Holmes · (Defendants) · Biss & Holmes · 705 Christensen Drive · Anchorage, AK 99501 · 907-277-8564

L. Ames Luce · (Plaintiffs) · The Law Offices of Luce & Hensley · 1015 West Seventh Avenue · Anchorage, AK 99501 · 907-276-1191

Theodore M. Pease, Jr.* · (Defendants, Medical Malpractice, Products Liability) Burr, Pease & Kurtz · 810 N Street · Anchorage, AK 99501-3293 · 907-276-6100

Eric T. Sanders* · (Plaintiffs, Medical Malpractice, Products Liability, Airplane Collision) · Young, Sanders & Feldman · 500 L Street, Suite 400 · Anchorage, AK 99501 · 907-272-3538

Robert H. Wagstaff · Wagstaff, Pope and Clocksin · 912 West Sixth Avenue · Anchorage, AK 99501 · 907-277-8611

Joseph L. Young* · (Plaintiffs) · Young & Sanders · 500 L Street, Suite 400 · Anchorage, AK 99501 · 907-272-3538

Lloyd I. Hoppner · Hoppner & Paskvan · 714 Fourth Avenue, Suite 301 · P.O. Box 73888 · Fairbanks, AK 99707 · 907-452-1205

O. Nelson Parrish · (Plaintiffs) · Parrish Law Office · 536 Fourth Avenue · Fairbanks, AK 99701 · 907-456-4070

William B. Rozell · Faulkner, Banfield, Doogan & Holmes · 302 Gold Street · Juneau, AK 99801 · 907-586-2210

Burton C. Biss · (Defendants) · Biss & Holmes · Star Route, Box 5111 · Wasilla, AK 99687 · 907-376-5318

PUBLIC UTILITY LAW

Andrew E. Hoge · Hoge and Lekisch · 437 E Street, Suite 500 · Anchorage, AK 99501 · 907-276-1726

Richard R. Huffman · Kemppel, Huffman & Ginder · 255 East Fireweed Lane, Suite 200 · Anchorage, AK 99503 · 907-277-1604

Mary K. Hughes · Hughes, Thorsness, Gantz, Powell & Brundin · 509 West Third Avenue · Anchorage, AK 99501-2273 · 907-274-7522

Roger R. Kemppel · Kemppel, Huffman & Ginder · 255 East Fireweed Lane, Suite 200 · Anchorage, AK 99503 · 907-277-1604

Julian L. Mason III · Ashburn and Mason · 1130 West Sixth Avenue, Suite 100 Anchorage, AK 99501 · 907-276-4331

REAL ESTATE LAW

William M. Bankston · Bankston & McCullom · 1800 Enserch Center · 550 West Seventh Avenue, Suite 1800 · Anchorage, AK 99501 · 907-276-1711

Peter C. Ginder · Kemppel, Huffman & Ginder · 255 East Fireweed Lane, Suite 200 · Anchorage, AK 99503 · 907-277-1604

Andrew E. Hoge · Hoge and Lekisch · 437 E Street, Suite 500 · Anchorage, AK 99501 · 907-276-1726

Peter A. Lekisch · Hoge and Lekisch · 437 E Street, Suite 500 · Anchorage, AK 99501 · 907-276-1726

Stanley H. Reitman · Delaney, Wiles, Hayes, Reitman & Brubaker · 1007 West Third Avenue, Suite 400 · Anchorage, AK 99501 · 907-279-3581

TAX AND EMPLOYEE BENEFITS LAW

Robert C. Brink · 1525 East Tudor Road · Anchorage, AK 99507 · 907-563-2114

Ralph E. Duerre · Burr, Pease & Kurtz · 810 N Street · Anchorage, AK 99501-3293 · 907-276-6100

Stanley H. Reitman · Delaney, Wiles, Hayes, Reitman & Brubaker · 1007 West Third Avenue, Suite 400 · Anchorage, AK 99501 · 907-279-3581

David G. Shaftel · (Corporate & Partnership Transactions, Tax Disputes) · Law Office of David G. Shaftel · First National Bank Building, Suite 700 · 425 G Street Anchorage, AK 99501 · 907-276-6015

TRUSTS AND ESTATES

Robert C. Brink · (Estate Planning) · 1525 East Tudor Road · Anchorage, AK 99507 · 907-563-2114

Trigg T. Davis · Davis & Goerig · 405 West 36th Avenue, Suite 200 · Anchorage, AK 99503 · 907-561-4420

Peter C. Ginder · Kemppel, Huffman & Ginder · 255 East Fireweed Lane, Suite 200 · Anchorage, AK 99503 · 907-277-1604

George E. Goerig, Jr. · Davis & Goerig · 405 West 36th Avenue, Suite 200 · Anchorage, AK 99503 · 907-561-4420

Robert L. Manley · (Estate Planning, Estate Administration, Estate Taxation) · Hughes, Thorsness, Gantz, Powell & Brundin · 509 West Third Avenue · Anchorage, AK 99501-2273 · 907-274-7522

David G. Shaftel · (Estate Planning, Estate Administration) · Law Office of David G. Shaftel · First National Bank Building, Suite 700 · 425 G Street · Anchorage, AK 99501 · 907-276-6015

ARIZONA

BANKRUPTCY LAW

Edward E. Davis · (Business Reorganization, Creditors' Rights, Debtors' Rights, Bankruptcy Litigation) · Davis & Lowe · Security Building, Suite 722 · 234 North Central Avenue · Phoenix, AZ 85004 · 602-253-2882

John J. Dawson · Streich, Lang, Weeks & Cardon · 2100 First Interstate Bank Plaza · P.O. Box 471 · Phoenix, AZ 85001 · 602-229-5200

Donald L. Gaffney · Snell & Wilmer · 3100 Valley Bank Center · Phoenix, AZ 85073-3100 · 602-257-7211

James M. Marlar* · 302 North First Avenue, Suite 450 · Phoenix, AZ 85003 · 602-254-4147

Peter J. Rathwell* · (Creditors' Rights, Bankruptcy Litigation) · Snell & Wilmer 3100 Valley Bank Center · Phoenix, AZ 85073-3100 · 602-257-7211

Gerald K. Smith · Lewis and Roca · Two Renaissance Square · 40 North Central Avenue · Phoenix, AZ 85004-4429 · 602-262-5311

Susan G. Boswell · Streich, Lang, Weeks & Cardon · 33 North Stone Avenue, Suite 1500 · Tucson, AZ 85701-1413 · 602-628-1419

Michael McGrath · (Business Reorganization, Debtors' Rights, Bankruptcy Litigation) · Mesch, Clark & Rothschild · 259 North Meyer Avenue · Tucson, AZ 85701-1090 · 602-624-8886

Lowell E. Rothschild · (Business Reorganization, Debtors' Rights, Bankruptcy Litigation) · Mesch, Clark & Rothschild · 259 North Meyer Avenue · Tucson, AZ 85701-1090 · 602-624-8886

Ralph E. Seefeldt · Seefeldt, Sparks & Neal · 110 South Church, Suite 3350 · Tucson, AZ 85701 · 602-623-8330

Clague A. Van Slyke · Snell & Wilmer · Citibank Tower, 15th Floor · One South Church Avenue · P.O. Box 871 · Tucson, AZ 85701 · 602-882-1237

BUSINESS LITIGATION

Robert E. B. Allen · Brown & Bain · Phoenix Plaza, Suite 2000 · 2901 North Central Avenue · P.O. Box 400 · Phoenix, AZ 85001-0400 · 602-351-8000

Peter D. Baird* · Lewis and Roca · Two Renaissance Square · 40 North Central Avenue · Phoenix, AZ 85004-4429 · 602-262-5311

John J. Bouma* · (Antitrust, Banking, Securities) · Snell & Wilmer · 3100 Valley Bank Center · Phoenix, AZ 85073-3100 · 602-257-7211

Jack E. Brown* · (Antitrust, Appellate, International) · Brown & Bain · Phoenix Plaza, Suite 2000 · 2901 North Central Avenue · P.O. Box 400 · Phoenix, AZ 85001-0400 · 602-351-8000

George Read Carlock · Ryley, Carlock & Applewhite · Security Bank Building, 26th Floor · 101 North First Avenue · Phoenix, AZ 85003 · 602-258-7701

Harry J. Cavanagh · O'Connor, Cavanagh, Anderson, Westover, Killingsworth & Beshears · One East Camelback Road, Suite 1100 · Phoenix, AZ 85012-1656 · 602-263-2400

Walter Cheifetz* · Cheifetz, Pierce, Cochran, Kozak & Mathew · 4041 East Thomas Road, Suite 210 · Phoenix, AZ 85018 · 602-381-0400

Daniel Cracchiolo* · Burch & Cracchiolo · 702 East Osborn Road · P.O. Box 16882 · Phoenix, AZ 85011 · 602-274-7611

Donald F. Daughton* · (Commercial) · Bryan, Cave, McPheeters & McRoberts 2800 North Central Avenue, 21st Floor · Phoenix, AZ 85004-1019 · 602-230-7000

Dan M. Durrant · Streich, Lang, Weeks & Cardon · 2100 First Interstate Bank Plaza · P.O. Box 471 · Phoenix, AZ 85001 · 602-229-5200

Jay Dushoff · Dushoff & McCall · 345 East Palm Lane, Suite 100 · Phoenix, AZ 85004 · 602-254-3800

Paul F. Eckstein* · (Antitrust, Appellate, First Amendment, Intellectual Property) · Brown & Bain · Phoenix Plaza, Suite 2000 · 2901 North Central Avenue · P.O. Box 400 · Phoenix, AZ 85001-0400 · 602-351-8000

John P. Frank · (Appellate) · Lewis and Roca · Renaissance Two · 40 North Central Avenue · Phoenix, AZ 85004-4429 · 602-262-5311

Susan M. Freeman · (Appellate) · Lewis and Roca · Two Renaissance Square · 40 North Central Avenue · Phoenix, AZ 85004-4429 · 602-262-5756

Philip T. Goldstein* · Goldstein, Kingsley & Myres · Professional Arts Building 1110 East McDowell Road · Phoenix, AZ 85006-2678 · 602-254-5581

Lawrence A. Hammond · Meyer, Hendricks, Victor, Osborn & Maledon · The Phoenix Plaza, Suite 2100 · 2929 North Central Avenue · P.O. Box 33449 · Phoenix, AZ 85067-3449 · 602-263-8700

Mark I. Harrison · Harrison, Harper, Christian & Dichter · 340 East Palm Lane, Suite 150 · Phoenix, AZ 85004 · 602-257-5800

William S. Hawgood II · (Appellate) · Streich, Lang, Weeks & Cardon · 2100 First Interstate Bank Plaza · P.O. Box 471 · Phoenix, AZ 85001 · 602-229-5200

Ed Hendricks* · (Commercial, Securities) · Meyer, Hendricks, Victor, Osborn & Maledon · The Phoenix Plaza, Suite 2100 · 2929 North Central Avenue · P.O. Box 33449 · Phoenix, AZ 85067-3449 · 602-640-9324

Michael J. LaVelle* · Allen, Kimerer & LaVelle · 2715 North Third Street · Phoenix, AZ 85004-1190 · 602-279-5900

John E. Lundin · Gallagher & Kennedy · 2600 North Central Avenue · Phoenix, AZ 85004-3020 · 602-530-8588

William J. Maledon* · Meyer, Hendricks, Victor, Osborn & Maledon · The Phoenix Plaza, Suite 2100 · 2929 North Central Avenue · P.O. Box 33449 · Phoenix, AZ 85067-3449 · 602-640-9000

Daniel McAuliffe · Snell & Wilmer · 3100 Valley Bank Center · Phoenix, AZ 85073-3100 · 602-257-7211

Newman R. Porter · Lewis and Roca · Renaissance Two · 40 North Central Avenue · Phoenix, AZ 85004-4429 · 602-262-5786

James Powers* · (Appellate, Commercial) · Fennemore Craig · Renaissance Building, Suite 2200 · Two North Central Avenue · Phoenix, AZ 85004-2390 · 602-257-8700

Richard A. Segal* · (Antitrust, Banking) · Gust, Rosenfeld & Henderson · 3300 Valley Bank Center · 201 North Central Avenue · Phoenix, AZ 85073-3300 · 602-257-7422

Kenneth J. Sherk* · Fennemore Craig · Renaissance Building, Suite 2200 · Two North Central Avenue · Phoenix, AZ 85004-2390 · 602-257-5383

Gerald K. Smith · Lewis and Roca · Two Renaissance Square · 40 North Central Avenue · Phoenix, AZ 85004-4429 · 602-262-5311

Paul G. Ulrich* · (Appellate) · 3030 North Central Avenue, Suite 1000 · Phoenix, AZ 85012 · 602-248-9465

Neil Vincent Wake* · (Administrative, Appellate, Commercial, Indian Affairs) · Law Offices of Neil Vincent Wake · The Brookstone, Suite 275 · 340 East Palm Lane · Phoenix, AZ 85004 · 602-271-4244

Phillip Weeks · Mariscal, Weeks, McIntyre & Friedlander · 201 West Coolidge Street · Phoenix, AZ 85013 · 602-285-5000

Thomas Chandler · Chandler, Tullar, Udall & Redhair · 1700 Arizona Bank Plaza 33 North Stone Avenue · P.O. Box 3069 · Tucson, AZ 85702 · 602-623-4353

David J. Leonard* · (Antitrust, Banking, Commercial, RICO) · Leonard, Felker, Altfeld, Nix & Krigbaum · 155 West Council Street · P.O. Box 191 · Tucson, AZ 85702-0191 · 602-622-7733

Robert O. Lesher · Lesher & Borodkin · 3773 East Broadway · Tucson, AZ 85716 602-795-4800

Gerald Maltz* · Miller, Pitt & McAnally · 111 South Church Avenue · Tucson, AZ 85701-1680 · 602-792-3836

Michael J. Meehan · (also Appellate) · Molloy, Jones & Donahue · 33 North Stone Avenue, Suite 2200 · P.O. Box 2268 · Tucson, AZ 85702 · 602-622-3531

John F. Molloy · Molloy, Jones & Donahue · 33 North Stone Avenue, Suite 2200 P.O. Box 2268 · Tucson, AZ 85702 · 602-622-3531

William H. Tinney* · Snell & Wilmer · Citibank Tower, 15th Floor · One South Church Avenue · P.O. Box 871 · Tucson, AZ 85701-1612 · 602-882-1236

CORPORATE LAW

Timothy W. Barton* · Jennings, Strouss and Salmon · One Renaissance Square Tower, Suite 1600 · Two North Central Avenue · Phoenix, AZ 85004-2393 · 602-262-5911

Marriner Cardon · 101 North Seventh Street, Suite 138 · Phoenix, AZ 85034 · 602-257-1483

George Read Carlock · Ryley, Carlock & Applewhite · Security Bank Building, 26th Floor · 101 North First Avenue · Phoenix, AZ 85003 · 602-258-7701

Jon S. Cohen · Snell & Wilmer · 3100 Valley Bank Center · Phoenix, AZ 85073-3100 · 602-257-7211

Stephen W. Craig · Brown & Bain · Phoenix Plaza, Suite 2000 · 2901 North Central Avenue · P.O. Box 400 · Phoenix, AZ 85001-0400 · 602-351-8000

Thomas J. Lang · Streich, Lang, Weeks & Cardon · 2100 First Interstate Bank Plaza · P.O. Box 471 · Phoenix, AZ 85001 · 602-229-5200

Paul R. Madden · Lewis and Roca · Renaissance Two · 40 North Central Avenue Phoenix, AZ 85004 · 602-262-5311

Paul J. Meyer · Meyer, Hendricks, Victor, Osborn & Maledon · The Phoenix Plaza, Suite 2100 · 2929 North Central Avenue · P.O. Box 33449 · Phoenix, AZ 85067-3449 · 602-640-9000

P. Robert Moya · (Corporate Finance, Leveraged Buyouts, Mergers & Acquisitions, Securities) · Gaston & Snow · 4722 North 24th Street, Suite 400 · Phoenix, AZ 85016 · 602-468-3600

Frederick H. Rosenfeld · Gust, Rosenfeld & Henderson · 3300 Valley Bank Center · 201 North Central Avenue · Phoenix, AZ 85073-3300 · 602-257-7422

Seymour Sacks · Sacks, Tierney, Kasen & Kerrick · Citibank Tower, 20th Floor 3300 North Central Avenue · Phoenix, AZ 85012-2576 · 602-279-4900

Morton M. Scult · Scult, Lazarus & French · One Arizona Center, 11th Floor · 400 East Van Buren · Phoenix, AZ 85004 · 602-266-4747

Charles L. Strouss, Jr. · Jennings, Strouss and Salmon · One Renaissance Square Tower, Suite 1600 · Two North Central Avenue · Phoenix, AZ 85004-2393 · 602-262-5911

David Victor · Meyer, Hendricks, Victor, Osborn & Maledon · The Phoenix Plaza, Suite 2100 · 2929 North Central Avenue · P.O. Box 33449 · Phoenix, AZ 85067-3449 · 602-640-9000

Larry R. Adamson · Fish, Duffield, Miller, Young, Adamson & Alfred · 177 North Church Avenue, Suite 711 · Tucson, AZ 85701 · 602-792-1181

Thomas Chandler · Chandler, Tullar, Udall & Redhair · 1700 Arizona Bank Plaza 33 North Stone Avenue · P.O. Box 3069 · Tucson, AZ 85702 · 602-623-4353

Richard Duffield · Fish, Duffield, Miller, Young, Adamson & Alfred · 177 North Church Avenue, Suite 711 · Tucson, AZ 85701 · 602-792-1181

Eugene C. Gieseler · Snell & Wilmer · Citibank Tower, 15th Floor · One South Church Avenue · P.O. Box 871 · Tucson, AZ 85701 · 602-882-1237

Lawrence M. Hecker · Hecker & Phillips · 405 West Franklin Street · Tucson, AZ 85701 · 602-798-3803

Russell E. Jones · Molloy, Jones & Donahue · 33 North Stone Avenue, Suite 2200 P.O. Box 2268 · Tucson, AZ 85702 · 602-622-3531

Gordon G. Waterfall · Waterfall, Economidis, Caldwell, Hanshaw & Villamana · Williams Centre, Eighth Floor · 5210 East Williams Circle · Tucson, AZ 85711 · 602-790-5828

CRIMINAL DEFENSE

Michael E. Benchoff · 3100 Valley Bank Center · 201 North Central Avenue · Phoenix, AZ 85073 · 602-257-7267

Larry L. Debus · Debus & Kazan · 335 East Palm Lane · Phoenix, AZ 85004 · 602-257-8900

Jordan Green* · Lewis and Roca · Two Renaissance Tower, Suite 1900 · 40 North Central Avenue · Phoenix, AZ 85004-4429 · 602-262-5311

Tom Karas* · 101 North First Avenue, Suite 2470 · Phoenix, AZ 85003 · 602-271-0115

Michael D. Kimerer* · (Non-Violent Crimes, Federal Court, State Court, Environmental Crimes) · Allen, Kimerer & LaVelle · 2715 North Third Street · P.O. Box 2800 · Phoenix, AZ 85004-1190 · 602-279-5900

Thomas A. Thinnes · 1005 North Second Street · Phoenix, AZ 85004 · 602-257-8408

Robert J. Hirsh · Hirsh & Sherick · Transamerica Building, Suite 877 · 177 North Church Avenue · Tucson, AZ 85701 · 602-884-9630

Michael L. Piccarreta · Davis & Piccarreta · 2730 East Broadway, Suite 250 · Tucson, AZ 85716 · 602-881-4500

FAMILY LAW

Philip C. Gerard* · O'Connor, Cavanagh, Anderson, Westover, Killingsworth & Beshears · One East Camelback Road, Suite 1100 · Phoenix, AZ 85012-1656 · 602-263-2400

Jolyon Grant* · O'Connor, Cavanagh, Anderson, Westover, Killingsworth & Beshears · One East Camelback Road, Suite 1100 · Phoenix, AZ 85012-1656 · 602-263-2400

Robert A. Jensen* · 805 North Second Street · Phoenix, AZ 85004 · 602-254-5557

Brian E. Kelley* · (Child Custody, Divorce, Domestic Torts) · O'Connor, Cavanagh, Anderson, Westover, Killingsworth & Beshears · One East Camelback Road, Suite 1100 · Phoenix, AZ 85012-1656 · 602-263-2400

Sheldon M. Mitchell* · (Child Custody, Divorce, Business Valuation) · Mitchell & Schwartz · 3238 North 16th Street · Phoenix, AZ 85016 · 602-265-1234

Phillip Weeks · Mariscal, Weeks, McIntyre & Friedlander · 201 West Coolidge Street · Phoenix, AZ 85013 · 602-285-5000

Peter Economidis · Waterfall, Economidis, Caldwell, Hanshaw & Villamana · Williams Centre, Eighth Floor · 5210 East Williams Circle · Tucson, AZ 85711 · 602-790-5828

Leonard Karp · Karp, Stolkin & Weiss · 33 North Stone Avenue, Suite 1800 · Tucson, AZ 85701 · 602-882-9705

James L. Stroud* · (Divorce, Marital Settlement Agreements, Equitable Division, Community Property) · Stompoly & Stroud · 1600 Citibank Tower · One South Church Avenue · P.O. Box 3017 · Tucson, AZ 85702-3017 · 602-798-5220

FIRST AMENDMENT LAW

Paul F. Eckstein* · Brown & Bain · Phoenix Plaza, Suite 2000 · 2901 North Central Avenue · P.O. Box 400 · Phoenix, AZ 85001-0400 · 602-351-8000

James F. Henderson · Gust, Rosenfeld & Henderson · 3300 Valley Bank Center 201 North Central Avenue · Phoenix, AZ 85073-3300 · 602-257-7403

Michael J. Meehan* · Molloy, Jones & Donahue · 33 North Stone Avenue, Suite 2200 · P.O. Box 2268 · Tucson, AZ 85702 · 602-622-3531

HEALTH CARE LAW

Richard B. Burnham · (Reimbursement) · Gammage & Burnham · Two North Central Avenue, 18th Floor · Phoenix, AZ 85004-2205 · 602-256-4489

Barry D. Halpern · Snell & Wilmer · 3100 Valley Bank Center · Phoenix, AZ 85073-3100 · 602-257-7211

Roger W. Kaufman · Lewis and Roca · Two Renaissance Square · 40 North Central Avenue · Phoenix, AZ 85004-4429 · 602-262-5729

Jay S. Ruffner · (Medicare Fraud & Abuse, Tax Exempt Entities) · Lewis and Roca · Two Renaissance Square · 40 North Central Avenue · Phoenix, AZ 85004-4429 · 602-262-5729

Beth J. Schermer · Lewis and Roca · Two Renaissance Square · 40 North Central Avenue · Phoenix, AZ 85004-4429 · 602-262-5311

Tracy P. Nuckolls · Dickerman & Nuckolls · 2195 East River Road, Suite 101 · Tucson, AZ 85718 · 602-299-2828

IMMIGRATION LAW

Roxana C. Bacon · Bryan, Cave, McPheeters & McRoberts · 2800 North Central Avenue, 21st Floor · Phoenix, AZ 85004-1019 · 602-230-7000

Nancy Jo Merritt · Bryan, Cave, McPheeters & McRoberts · 2800 North Central Avenue, 21st Floor · Phoenix, AZ 85004-1019 · 602-230-7000

Roger C. Wolf · Law Offices of Roger C. Wolf · 290 North Meyer Avenue · Tucson, AZ 85701 · 602-882-9633

LABOR AND EMPLOYMENT LAW

Gerald Barrett · (Labor) · Ward, Keenan & Barrett · 2020 North Central Avenue, Suite 1020 · Phoenix, AZ 85004 · 602-252-5606

Robert J. Deeny · (Management) · Snell & Wilmer · 3100 Valley Bank Center · Phoenix, AZ 85073-3100 · 602-257-7211

N. Douglas Grimwood · Twitty, Sievwright & Mills · 2702 North Third Street, Suite 4007 · Phoenix, AZ 85004-1142 · 602-248-9424

Daniel F. Gruender · (Management) · Shimmel, Hill, Bishop & Gruender · 3700 North 24th Street, Suite 200 · Phoenix, AZ 85016 · 602-224-9500

Marty Harper · (Management) · Lewis and Roca · Renaissance Two · 40 North Central Avenue · Phoenix, AZ 85004-4429 · 602-262-5311

William R. Hayden · (Management) · Snell & Wilmer · 3100 Valley Bank Center Phoenix, AZ 85073-3100 · 602-257-7211

James P. Hendricks · (Management) · Kaplan, Jacobowitz, Byrnes, Rosier & Hendricks · The Merabank Tower, Suite 1500 · 3003 North Central Avenue · Phoenix, AZ 85012 · 602-264-3134

Lawrence A. Katz · (Management) · Streich, Lang, Weeks & Cardon · 2100 First Interstate Bank Plaza · P.O. Box 471 · Phoenix, AZ 85001 · 602-229-5200

Michael J. Keenan · (Labor) · Ward, Keenan & Barrett · 2020 North Central Avenue, Suite 1020 · Phoenix, AZ 85004 · 602-252-5606

Stanley Lubin* · (Labor, Individuals) · Law Office of Stanley Lubin · 2700 North Central Avenue, Suite 975 · Phoenix, AZ 85004 · 602-285-4411

Jon E. Pettibone · (Management) · Lewis and Roca · Renaissance Two · 40 North Central Avenue · Phoenix, AZ 85004 · 602-262-5311

Tod F. Schleier* · (Individuals) · Schleier & Engle · 3030 North Third Street, Suite 1000 · Phoenix, AZ 85012 · 602-277-0157

Ralph B. Sievwright* · (Management) · Twitty, Sievwright & Mills · 2702 North Third Street, Suite 4007 · Phoenix, AZ 85004-1142 · 602-248-9424

Naida B. Axford* · (Individuals) · Hocker & Axford · 1700 East Elliot Road, Suite 501 · Tempe, AZ 85284-1630 · 602-897-0990

Max C. Richards · (Management, Individuals) · Richards & Pennington · 4750 North Oracle Road, Suite 316 · Tucson, AZ 85705 · 602-293-5525

John A. Robertson · (Management) · Snell & Wilmer · Citibank Tower, 15th Floor · One South Church Avenue · P.O. Box 871 · Tucson, AZ 85701 · 602-882-1237

Armand Salese* · (Individuals) · Salese & McCarthy · 130 West Cushing Street Tucson, AZ 85701 · 602-623-0341

Ronald J. Stolkin · (Individuals) · Karp, Stolkin & Weiss · 33 North Stone Avenue, Suite 1800 · Tucson, AZ 85701 · 602-882-9705

NATURAL RESOURCES AND ENVIRONMENTAL LAW

James G. Derouin · (Solid Waste, Hazardous Waste, Superfund Liability, Soil & Groundwater Contamination) · Meyer, Hendricks, Victor, Osborn & Maledon · The Phoenix Plaza, Suite 2100 · 2929 North Central Avenue · P.O. Box 33449 · Phoenix, AZ 85067-3449 · 602-640-9000

Fred E. Ferguson, Jr. · (Mining) · Lewis and Roca · Renaissance Two · 40 North Central Avenue · Phoenix, AZ 85004-3099 · 602-262-5308

Jerry L. Haggard · (Mining) · Apker, Apker, Haggard & Kurtz · 2111 East Highland Avenue, Suite 230 · P.O. Box 10280 · Phoenix, AZ 85064-0280 · 602-381-0085

James W. Johnson · Fennemore Craig · Renaissance Building, Suite 2200 · Two North Central Avenue · Phoenix, AZ 85004-2390 · 602-257-8700

David P. Kimball III · Kimball & Curry · 2600 North Central Avenue, Suite 1600 Phoenix, AZ 85004 · 602-222-5921

Elizabeth Ann Rieke · (Water) · Jennings, Strouss and Salmon · One Renaissance Square Tower, Suite 1600 · Two North Central Avenue · Phoenix, AZ 85004-2393 602-262-5880

James D. Vieregg · Meyer, Hendricks, Victor, Osborn & Maledon · 2929 North Central, 21st Floor · P.O. Box 33449 · Phoenix, AZ 85067 · 602-640-9356

John C. Lacy · (Mining) · DeConcini McDonald Brammer Yetwin & Lacy · 2525 East Broadway, Suite 200 · Tucson, AZ 85716 · 602-322-5000

PERSONAL INJURY LITIGATION

Daniel J. Stoops* · Mangum, Wall, Stoops & Warden · 222 East Birch Avenue · P.O. Box 10 · Flagstaff, AZ 86002 · 602-774-6664

Michael A. Beale · (Defendants) · Jennings, Strouss and Salmon · One Renaissance Square Tower, Suite 1600 · Two North Central Avenue · Phoenix, AZ 85004-2393 · 602-262-5911

Charles M. Brewer · (Plaintiffs) · 5500 North 24th Street · P.O. Box 10720 · Phoenix, AZ 85016 · 602-381-8787

James R. Broening · (Medical Malpractice) · Broening, Oberg & Woods · 1122 East Jefferson Street · Phoenix, AZ 85034 · 602-271-7700

Harry J. Cavanagh · (Defendants) · O'Connor, Cavanagh, Anderson, Westover, Killingsworth & Beshears · One East Camelback Road, Suite 1100 · Phoenix, AZ 85012-1656 · 602-263-2400

Walter Cheifetz* · Cheifetz, Pierce, Cochran, Kozak & Mathew · 4041 East Thomas Road, Suite 210 · Phoenix, AZ 85018 · 602-381-0400

Daniel Cracchiolo* · Burch & Cracchiolo · 702 East Osborn Road · Phoenix, AZ 85011 · 602-274-7611

Philip T. Goldstein* · Goldstein, Kingsley & Myres · 1110 East McDowell Road Phoenix, AZ 85006 · 602-254-5581

Arthur P. Greenfield · (Defendants) · Snell & Wilmer · 3100 Valley Bank Center Phoenix, AZ 85073-3100 · 602-257-7211

William R. Jones, Jr. · Jones, Skelton & Hochuli · 2702 North Third Street, Suite 3000 · Phoenix, AZ 85004 · 602-263-1700

James J. Leonard, Jr. · (Plaintiffs) · Leonard & Clancy · Luhrs Tower, Sixth Floor · 45 West Jefferson Street · Phoenix, AZ 85003 · 602-258-5749

Frank A. Parks · (Defendants) · Teilborg, Sanders & Parks · 3030 North Third Street, Suite 1300 · Phoenix, AZ 85012 · 602-230-5600

Warren E. Platt · (Defendants) · Snell & Wilmer · 3100 Valley Bank Center · Phoenix, AZ 85073-3100 · 602-257-7211

Philip A. Robbins · Robbins & Green · 1800 Citibank Tower · 3300 North Central Avenue · Phoenix, AZ 85012-9826 · 602-248-7999

Charles D. Roush · Roush, McCracken & Guerrero · 650 North Third Avenue · Phoenix, AZ 85003 · 602-253-3554

Richard A. Segal* · (Defendants, Professional Malpractice) · Gust, Rosenfeld & Henderson · 3300 Valley Bank Center · 201 North Central Avenue · Phoenix, AZ 85073-3300 · 602-257-7422

Richard T. Treon · (Plaintiffs) · Treon, Strick, Lucia & Aguirre · 2700 North Central Avenue, Suite 1400 · Phoenix, AZ 85004 · 602-285-4400

John H. Westover · O'Connor, Cavanagh, Anderson, Westover, Killingsworth & Beshears · One East Camelback Road, Suite 1100 · 3003 North Central Avenue · Phoenix, AZ 85012-1656 · 602-263-2400

Elliot G. Wolfe* · (Plaintiffs, Products Liability, Airplane Collision, Interstate Truck Collisions) · Langerman, Begam, Lewis and Marks · 1400 Arizona Title Building · 111 West Monroe Street · Phoenix, AZ 85003-1787 · 602-254-6071

Michael R. Murphy · Toci, Murphy, Lutey & Beck · Elks Building, Third Floor 117 East Gurley Street · P.O. Box 591 · Prescott, AZ 86302-0591 · 602-445-6860

Philip E. Toci* · Toci, Murphy, Lutey & Beck · Elks Building, Third Floor · 117 East Gurley Street · P.O. Box 591 · Prescott, AZ 86302-0591 · 602-445-6860

David Bury C. · (Defendants) · Bury, Moeller, Humphrey & O'Meara · 2606 East Tenth Street · Tucson, AZ 85716 · 602-795-8852

Leonard Everett · (Defendants) · Transamerica Building, Suite 608 · 177 North Church Avenue · Tucson, AZ 85701 · 602-623-1857

Dale Haralson · (Plaintiffs) · Haralson, Kinerk & Morey · 82 South Stone Avenue Tucson, AZ 85701 · 602-792-4330

Robert Q. Hoyt* · (Plaintiffs, Medical Malpractice, Products Liability, Automobile Collision, Airplane Collision) · 3501 North Campbell Avenue, Suite 101 · Tucson, AZ 85719 · 602-327-6801

William Kimble · (Defendants) · Kimble, Gothreau & Nelson · 5285 East Williams Circle, Suite 3500 · Tucson, AZ 85711 · 602-748-2440

Robert O. Lesher* · (Defendants) · Lesher & Borodkin · 3773 East Broadway · Tucson, AZ 85716 · 602-795-4800

Jack Redhair · (Defendants) · Chandler, Tullar, Udall & Redhair · 1700 Arizona Bank Plaza · 33 North Stone Avenue · P.O. Box 3069 · Tucson, AZ 85702 · 602-623-4353

Tom Slutes* · (Defendants) · Slutes, Sakrison, Even, Grant & Pelander · 1100 Security Pacific Bank Plaza · 33 North Stone Avenue · Tucson, AZ 85701-1489 · 602-624-6691

D. B. Udall · (Defendants) · Chandler, Tullar, Udall & Redhair · 1700 Arizona Bank Plaza · 33 North Stone Avenue · P.O. Box 3069 · Tucson, AZ 85702 · 602-623-4353

Thomas A. Zlaket · (Plaintiffs) · Zlaket & Zlaket · 2701 East Speedway, Suite 200 Tucson, AZ 85716 · 602-327-8777

PUBLIC UTILITY LAW

Steven M. Wheeler · Snell & Wilmer · 3100 Valley Bank Center · Phoenix, AZ 85073-3100 · 602-257-7211

REAL ESTATE LAW

Burton M. Apker* · Apker, Apker, Haggard & Kurtz · 2111 East Highland Avenue, Suite 230 · P.O. Box 10280 · Phoenix, AZ 85064-0280 · 602-381-0085

Marcia J. Busching · (Commercial Transactions) · Sacks, Tierney, Kasen & Kerrick · Citibank Tower, 20th Floor · 3300 North Central Avenue · Phoenix, AZ 85012-2576 · 602-279-4900

Marriner Cardon · 101 North Seventh Street, Suite 138 · Phoenix, AZ 85034 · 602-257-1483

Jay Dushoff · Dushoff & McCall · 345 East Palm Lane, Suite 100 · Phoenix, AZ 85004 · 602-254-3800

Grady Gammage, Jr. · Gammage & Burnham · Two North Central Avenue, 18th Floor · Phoenix, AZ 85004-2205 · 602-256-4489

James R. Huntwork · (Commercial Transactions, Industrial Transactions) · Jennings, Strouss and Salmon · One Renaissance Square Tower, Suite 1600 · Two North Central Avenue · Phoenix, AZ 85004-2393 · 602-262-5911

Robert V. Kerrick* · (Zoning, Land Use, Eminent Domain) · Sacks, Tierney, Kasen & Kerrick · CitiBank Tower, 20th Floor · 3300 North Central Avenue · Phoenix, AZ 85012-2576 · 602-279-4900

Thomas J. Lang · Streich, Lang, Weeks & Cardon · 2100 First Interstate Bank Plaza · P.O. Box 471 · Phoenix, AZ 85001 · 602-229-5200

Lyman A. Manser · Lewis and Roca · Renaissance Two · 40 North Central Avenue · Phoenix, AZ 85004-4429 · 602-262-5311

Bruce B. May · Streich, Lang, Weeks & Cardon · 2100 First Interstate Bank Plaza P.O. Box 471 · Phoenix, AZ 85003-1897 · 602-229-5200

Jay D. Wiley · Snell & Wilmer · 3100 Valley Bank Center · Phoenix, AZ 85073-3100 · 602-257-7211

Gerald B. Hirsch* · 111 South Church Avenue · Tucson, AZ 85701 · 602-624-9983

James F. Morrow · Streich Lang · 1500 Security Pacific Plaza · 33 North Stone Avenue · Tucson, AZ 85701-1413 · 602-628-1419

S. L. Schorr · Lewis and Roca · 5210 East Williams Circle, Suite 600 · Tucson, AZ 85711-4495 · 602-747-9901

Harold C. Warnock · Lesher & Borodkin · 3773 East Broadway · Tucson, AZ 85716 · 602-795-4800

John B. Wilkie · (Title Problems) · 6375 East Tanque Verde, Suite 140 · Tucson, AZ 85715 · 602-296-8550

Paul E. Wolf · Miller, Pitt & McNally · 111 South Church Avenue · Tucson, AZ 85701-1680 · 602-792-3836

TAX AND EMPLOYEE BENEFITS LAW

Marvin D. Brody · (Employee Benefits) · 4722 North 24th Street, Court Two, Suite 350 · Phoenix, AZ 85016 · 602-956-5050

John R. Christian · Jennings, Strouss and Salmon · One Renaissance Square Tower, Suite 1600 · Two North Central Avenue · Phoenix, AZ 85004-2393 · 602-262-5911

Robert D. Collins · 3010 East Camelback Road, Suite 100 · Phoenix, AZ 85016 602-954-0281

Anthony V. Ehmann · Ehmann & Hiller · 4722 North 24th Street, Court Two, Suite 350 · Phoenix, AZ 85016 · 602-956-5050

David R. Frazer · Frazer Ryan Goldberg Keyt & Lawless · 5353 North 16th Street, Suite 405 · Phoenix, AZ 85016-3224 · 602-277-2010

David L. Haga, Jr. · Mohr, Hackett, Pederson, Blakley, Randolph & Haga · 3807 North Seventh Street · Phoenix, AZ 85014 · 602-277-7600

Neil H. Hiller · (Employee Benefits) · Ehmann & Hiller · 4722 North 24th Street, Court Two, Suite 350 · Phoenix, AZ 85016 · 602-956-5050

William H. Isaacson · 3550 North Central Avenue, Suite 1701 · Phoenix, AZ 85012 · 602-264-2636

Leslie T. Jones, Jr. · Gallgher & Kennedy · 2600 North Central Avenue, 19th Floor · Phoenix, AZ 85004-3020 · 602-530-8303

Neal Kurn · Fennemore Craig · Renaissance Building, Suite 2200 · Two North Central Avenue · Phoenix, AZ 85004-2390 · 602-257-8700

Stephen E. Lee · Brown & Bain · Phoenix Plaza, Suite 2000 · 2901 North Central Avenue · P.O. Box 400 · Phoenix, AZ 85001-0400 · 602-351-8000

David E. Manch · (Employee Benefits) · Lewis and Roca · Renaissance Two · 40 North Central Avenue · Phoenix, AZ 85004-4429 · 602-262-5311

Joseph I. McCabe · McCabe, O'Donnell, Folk, Wright & Merritt · 300 East Osborn, Suite 2000 · Phoenix, AZ 85012 · 602-264-0800

Alfred J. Olsen · (Corporate & Partnership Transactions) · Olsen-Smith · 3300 Virginia Financial Plaza · 301 East Virginia Avenue · Phoenix, AZ 85004 · 602-254-1040

Michael E. Pietzsch · (Employee Benefits) · Pietzsch & Williams · 2930 East Camelback Road, Suite 155 · Phoenix, AZ 85016 · 602-955-3866

Leslie A. Plattner · (Employee Benefits) · Plattner, Schneidman & Schneider · 3010 East Camelback Road · Phoenix, AZ 85016 · 602-957-1872

James Powers* · (Tax Disputes) · Fennemore Craig · Renaissance Building, Suite 2200 · Two North Central Avenue · Phoenix, AZ 85004-2390 · 602-257-8700

Jay S. Ruffner · (Corporate & Partnership Transactions) · Lewis and Roca · Two Renaissance Square · 40 North Central Avenue · Phoenix, AZ 85004-4429 · 602-262-5729

Stephen E. Silver* · (Tax Disputes, Tax Litigation/Criminal & Civil) · Burch & Cracchiolo · 702 East Osborn Road · P.O. Box 16882 · Phoenix, AZ 85011 · 602-274-7611

Howard N. Singer · Meyer, Hendricks, Victor, Osborn & Maledon · The Phoenix Plaza, Suite 2100 · 2929 North Central Avenue · P.O. Box 33449 · Phoenix, AZ 85067-3449 · 602-640-9351

David E. Weiss, Jr. · Streich, Lang, Weeks & Cardon · 2100 First Interstate Bank Plaza · P.O. Box 471 · Phoenix, AZ 85001 · 602-229-5200

John C. Wesley · Gust, Rosenfeld & Henderson · 3300 Valley Bank Center · 201 North Central Avenue · Phoenix, AZ 85073-3300 · 602-257-7422

Stephen S. Case · Case & Bennett · 6740 East Camelback Road, Suite 100 · Scottsdale, AZ 85251 · 602-990-1133

Steven L. Bosse · (Employee Benefits) · Gabroy, Rollman & Bosse · 1840 East River Road, Suite 100 · Tucson, AZ 85718 · 602-577-1300

Bryan E. Daum · (Employee Benefits) · Snell & Wilmer · Citibank Tower, 15th Floor · One South Church Avenue · P.O. Box 871 · Tucson, AZ 85701 · 602-882-1237

John L. Donahue, Jr. · Molloy, Jones & Donahue · 33 North Stone Avenue, Suite 2200 · P.O. Box 2268 · Tucson, AZ 85702 · 602-622-3531

Eugene C. Gieseler · (Tax, Employee Benefits) · Snell & Wilmer · Citibank Tower, 15th Floor · One South Church Avenue · P.O. Box 871 · Tucson, AZ 85701 · 602-882-1237

Roger S. Levitan · Molloy, Jones & Donahue · 33 North Stone Avenue, Suite 2200 · P.O. Box 2268 · Tucson, AZ 85702 · 602-622-3531

Terry Marvin · (Employee Benefits) · Dickerman & Nuckolls · 2195 East River Road, Suite 101 · P.O. Box 41570 · Tucson, AZ 85717 · 602-299-2828

Douglas J. Newman · (Employee Benefits) · O'Connell & Newman · 1840 East River Road, Suite 100 · Tucson, AZ 85718 · 602-577-8880

Daniel H. O'Connell · O'Connell & Newman · 1840 East River Road, Suite 100 Tucson, AZ 85718 · 602-577-8880

Steven W. Phillips · Hecker & Phillips · 405 West Franklin Street · Tucson, AZ 85701 · 602-798-3803

Gordon G. Waterfall · (Tax, Employee Benefits) · Waterfall, Economidis, Caldwell, Hanshaw & Villamana · Williams Centre, Eighth Floor · 5210 East Williams Circle · Tucson, AZ 85711 · 602-790-5828

TRUSTS AND ESTATES

John R. Christian · Jennings, Strouss and Salmon · One Renaissance Square Tower, Suite 1600 · Two North Central Avenue · Phoenix, AZ 85004-2393 · 602-262-5911

Louis F. Comus, Jr. · Fennemore Craig · Renaissance Building, Suite 2200 · Two North Central Avenue · Phoenix, AZ 85004-2390 · 602-257-8700

Richard H. Elliott · Carson Messinger Elliott Laughlin & Ragan · 1900 Citibank Tower · 3300 North Central Avenue · P.O. Box 33907 · Phoenix, AZ 85067 · 602-264-2261

David R. Frazer · Frazer Ryan Goldberg Keyt & Lawless · 5353 North 16th Street, Suite 405 · Phoenix, AZ 85016-3224 · 602-277-2010

William H. Isaacson · 3550 North Central Avenue, Suite 1701 · Phoenix, AZ 85012 · 602-264-2636

Neal Kurn · Fennemore Craig · Renaissance Building, Suite 2200 · Two North Central Avenue · Phoenix, AZ 85004-2390 · 602-257-8700

Richard L. Lassen · (Estate Planning, Estate Administration) · Jennings, Strouss and Salmon · One Renaissance Square Tower, Suite 1600 · Two North Central Avenue · Phoenix, AZ 85004-2393 · 602-262-5911

Alfred J. Olsen · (Estate Planning, Estate Administration, Charitable Trusts) · Olsen-Smith · 3300 Virginia Financial Plaza · 301 East Virginia Avenue · Phoenix, AZ 85004 · 602-254-1040

Richard H. Whitney · Gust, Rosenfeld & Henderson · 3300 Valley Bank Center 201 North Central Avenue · Phoenix, AZ 85073-3300 · 602-257-7422

Stephen S. Case · Case & Bennett · 6740 East Camelback Road, Suite 100 · Scottsdale, AZ 85251 · 602-990-1133

Robert J. Rosepink · 7373 Scottsdale Road, Suite C126 · Scottsdale, AZ 85253 · 602-443-1280

Robert H. Norris · Norris & Adams · 10331 Coggins Drive · Sun City, AZ 85351 602-933-8274

Larry R. Adamson · Fish, Duffield, Miller, Young, Adamson & Alfred · 177 North Church Avenue, Suite 711 · Tucson, AZ 85701 · 602-792-1181

John L. Donahue, Jr. · Molloy, Jones & Donahue · 33 North Stone Avenue, Suite 2200 · P.O. Box 2268 · Tucson, AZ 85702 · 602-622-3531

Gregory V. Gardarian · Freund & Gardarian · 434 South Williams Boulevard, Suite 210 · Tucson, AZ 85711 · 602-745-2233

G. Eugene Isaak · Miller, Pitt & McAnally · 111 South Church Avenue · Tucson, AZ 85701-1680 · 602-792-3836

Clark W. Munger · Munger and Munger · 6131 East Grant Road · Tucson, AZ 85712 · 602-721-1900

Daniel H. O'Connell · O'Connell & Newman · 1840 East River Road, Suite 100 Tucson, AZ 85718 · 602-577-8880

William R. Poston · (Estate Planning) · 3444 North Country Club, Suite 202 · Tucson, AZ 85716 · 602-577-8880

Paul D. Slosser · (Estate Planning, Estate Administration, Charitable Trusts) · Molloy, Jones & Donahue · 33 North Stone Avenue, Suite 2200 · P.O. Box 2268 Tucson, AZ 85702 · 602-622-3531

Gordon G. Waterfall · Waterfall, Economidis, Caldwell, Hanshaw & Villamana · Williams Centre, Eighth Floor · 5210 East Williams Circle · Tucson, AZ 85711 · 602-790-5828

ARKANSAS

BUSINESS LITIGATION

Robert C. Compton* · (Commercial) · Compton, Prewett, Thomas & Hickey · 423 North Washington Avenue · P.O. Drawer 1917 · El Dorado, AR 71731 · 501-862-3478

Robert L. Jones, Jr. · Jones, Gilbreath, Jackson & Moll · 401 North Seventh Street · P.O. Box 2023 · Fort Smith, AR 72902 · 501-782-7203

Hillary Rodham Clinton* · Rose Law Firm · 120 East Fourth Street · Little Rock, AR 72201-2893 · 501-375-9131

Webster L. Hubbell · Rose Law Firm · 120 East Fourth Street · Little Rock, AR 72201-2893 · 501-375-9131

Alston Jennings, Sr.* · Wright, Lindsey & Jennings · 2200 Worthen Bank Building · 200 West Capitol Avenue · Little Rock, AR 72201-3699 · 501-371-0808

J. Thomas Ray · Shults, Ray & Kurrus · Worthen Bank Building, Suite 1600 · 200 West Capitol Avenue · Little Rock, AR 72201-3637 · 501-375-2301

William H. Sutton* · Friday, Eldredge & Clark · 2000 First Commercial Building 400 West Capitol Avenue · Little Rock, AR 72201-3493 · 501-376-2011

Michael G. Thompson · Friday, Eldredge & Clark · 2000 First Commercial Building · 400 West Capitol Avenue · Little Rock, AR 72201-3493 · 501-376-2011

William R. Wilson, Jr.* · Wilson, Engstrom, Corum & Dudley · 809 West Third Street · P.O. Box 71 · Little Rock, AR 72203 · 501-375-6453

Stephen A. Matthews · Bridges, Young, Matthews, Holmes & Drake · 315 East Eighth Avenue · P.O. Box 7808 · Pine Bluff, AR 71611 · 501-534-5532

James Blair · P.O. Drawer E · Springdale, AR 72764 · 501-756-4000

CORPORATE LAW

Philip S. Anderson · Williams & Anderson · 2200 Stephens Building · 111 Center Street · Little Rock, AR 72201 · 501-372-0800

Paul B. Benham III · (Corporate Finance, Mergers & Acquisitions, Securities) · Friday, Eldredge & Clark · 2000 First Commercial Building · 400 West Capitol Avenue · Little Rock, AR 72201-3493 · 501-376-2011

Herschel H. Friday* · Friday, Eldredge & Clark · 2000 First Commercial Building · 400 West Capitol Avenue · Little Rock, AR 72201-3493 · 501-376-2011

H. Maurice Mitchell · (Banking, Corporate Finance, Financial Institutions) · Mitchell, Williams, Selig & Tucker · 1000 Savers Federal Building · 320 West Capitol Avenue · Little Rock, AR 72201-3525 · 501-688-8800

John S. Selig · (Securities) · Mitchell, Williams, Selig & Tucker · 1000 Savers Federal Building · 320 West Capitol Avenue · Little Rock, AR 72201-3525 · 501-688-8800

Robert Shults · Shults, Ray & Kurrus · 1600 Worthen Bank Building · Little Rock, AR 72201 · 501-375-2301

Louis L. Ramsay, Jr. · (Banking, Financial Institutions) · Ramsay, Bridgforth, Harrelson and Starling · Simmons First National Building, 11th Floor · P.O. Drawer 8509 · Pine Bluff, AR 71611-8509 · 501-535-9000

CRIMINAL DEFENSE

Bobby R. McDaniel* · McDaniel & Wells · 400 South Main Street · Jonesboro, AR 72401 · 501-932-5950

William C. McArthur · McArthur Law Firm · 300 Spring Building, Suite 612 · Little Rock, AR 72201 · 501-376-6173

Richard N. Moore, Jr.* · Dodds, Kidd, Ryan & Moore · 313 West Second Street Little Rock, AR 72201 · 501-375-9901

Samuel A. Perroni · Perroni, Rauls, Looney & Barnes · 10810 Executive Center Drive, Suite 215 · Little Rock, AR 72211 · 501-227-8999

William R. Wilson, Jr.* · Wilson, Engstrom, Corum & Dudley · 809 West Third Street · P.O. Box 71 · Little Rock, AR 72203 · 501-375-6453

Damon Young · Young, Patton & Folsom · 4122 Texas Boulevard · P.O. Box 1897 Texarkana, AR 75504 · 501-774-3206

FAMILY LAW

Philip E. Dixon · Dover & Dixon · 425 West Capitol, Suite 3700 · Little Rock, AR 72201 · 501-375-9151

Stephen C. Engstrom · Wilson, Engstrom, Corum & Dudley · 809 West Third Street · P.O. Box 71 · Little Rock, AR 72203 · 501-375-6453

Dale Price · Howell, Price, Trice, Basham & Hope · 211 Spring Street · Little Rock, AR 72201 · 501-372-4144

William R. Wilson, Jr.* · Wilson, Engstrom, Corum & Dudley · 809 West Third Street · P.O. Box 71 · Little Rock, AR 72203 · 501-375-6453

FIRST AMENDMENT LAW

Phillip Carroll · Rose Law Firm · 120 East Fourth Street · Little Rock, AR 72201-2893 · 501-375-9131

Philip E. Kaplan · Kaplan, Brewer & Maxey · 415 Main Street · Little Rock, AR 72201 · 501- 372-0400

John T. Lavey · Lavey & Bernett · 904 West Second Street · P.O. Box 2657 · Little Rock, AR 72203 · 501-376-2269

William R. Wilson, Jr.* · Wilson, Engstrom, Corum & Dudley · 809 West Third Street · P.O. Box 71 · Little Rock, AR 72203 · 501-375-6453

HEALTH CARE LAW

Donald T. Jack, Jr. · Jack, Lyon & Jones · 3400 TCBY Tower Building · 425 West Capitol Avenue · Little Rock, AR 72201 · 501-375-1122

George D. Jernigan, Jr. · (Nursing Homes) · Smith & Jernigan · P.O. Box 3238 Little Rock, AR 72203 · 501-374-2215

Walter A. Paulson II · Friday, Eldredge & Clark · 2000 First Commercial Building 400 West Capitol Avenue · Little Rock, AR 72201-3493 · 501-376-2011

Harold H. Simpson · Simpson & Graham · Ozark Building, Suite 300 · 10201 West Markham Street · P.O. Box 5420 · Little Rock, AR 72215 · 501-221-7100

Jack A. McNulty · Bridges, Young, Matthews, Holmes & Drake · 315 East Eighth Avenue · P.O. Box 7808 · Pine Bluff, AR 71611 · 501-534-5532

INTELLECTUAL PROPERTY LAW

Robert R. Keegan · Law Office of Robert Keegan · 130 North College Avenue, Suite G · Fayetteville, AR 72701 · 501-521-4412

Steven D. Carver · Carver Law Offices · 2024 Arkansas Valley Drive, Suite 800 Little Rock, AR 72212 · 501-224-1500

LABOR AND EMPLOYMENT LAW

Tim Boe · (Management) · Rose Law Firm · 120 East Fourth Street · Little Rock, AR 72201-2893 · 501-375-9131

John L. Burnett* · (Labor, Individuals) · Lavey, Harmon and Burnett · 904 West Second Street · Little Rock, AR 72201 · 501-376-2269

Perlesta A. Hollingsworth · (Individuals) · 415 Main Street · Little Rock, AR 72201 · 501-374-3420

Philip E. Kaplan · (Management) · Kaplan, Brewer & Maxey · 415 Main Street Little Rock, AR 72201 · 501-372-0400

John T. Lavey* · (Labor, Individuals) · Lavey & Bernett · 904 West Second Street P.O. Box 2657 · Little Rock, AR 72203 · 501-376-2269

Philip K. Lyon* · (Management) · Jack, Lyon & Jones · 3400 TCBY Tower Building · 425 West Capitol Avenue · Little Rock, AR 72201 · 501-375-1122

James W. Moore* · (Management) · Friday, Eldredge & Clark · 2000 First Commercial Building · 400 West Capitol Avenue · Little Rock, AR 72201-3493 · 501-376-2011

Richard Quiggle* · (Individuals, Employment Discrimination) · 904 West Second Street · P.O. Box 2651 · Little Rock, AR 72203-2651 · 501-375-2963

John W. Walker · (Individuals) · 1723 Broadway · Little Rock, AR 72206 · 501-374-3758

Jay Thomas Youngdahl* · (Labor) · Youngdahl, Trother, McGowan & Farris · 103 West Capitol, Suite 1205 · P.O. Box 164808 · Little Rock, AR 72216 · 501-376-6355

James A. Gilker · (Management) · Gilker and Jones · Route 2 · P.O. Box 81 · Mountainburg, AR 72946 · 501-783-3109

PERSONAL INJURY LITIGATION

Otis H. Turner · (Defendants) · McMillan, Turner & McCorkle · 929 Main Street P.O. Box 607 · Arkadelphia, AR 71923 · 501-246-2468

H. David Blair* · (Plaintiffs, Medical Malpractice, Products Liability, Automobile Collision) · Blair & Stroud · First South Building, Suite 201 · 500 East Main · P.O. Box 2135 · Batesville, AR 72503 · 501-793-8350

Ted Boswell* · Boswell, Tucker & Brewster · Bryant Center · Bryant, AR 72022-0789 · 501-847-3031

Robert C. Compton* · (Plaintiffs, Defendants, Products Liability, Automobile Collision) · Compton, Prewett, Thomas & Hickey · 423 North Washington Avenue · P.O. Drawer 1917 · El Dorado, AR 71731 · 501-862-3478

Dennis L. Shackleford* · (Defendants) · Shackleford, Shackleford & Phillips · 100 East Church Street · P.O. Box 1854 · El Dorado, AR 71731 · 501-862-5523

P. H. Hardin · (Defendants) · Hardin, Jesson, Dawson & Terry · 1601 Rogers Avenue · P.O. Drawer 968 · Fort Smith, AR 72902-0968 · 501-783-6186

Robert L. Jones, Jr. · (Defendants) · Jones, Gilbreath, Jones, Jackson & Moll · 401 North Seventh Street · P.O. Box 2023 · Fort Smith, AR 72902 · 501-782-7203

Winslow Drummond* · (Plaintiffs, Medical Malpractice, Products Liability, Professional Malpractice) · McMath Law Firm · 711 West Third Street · P. O. Box 1470 · Little Rock, AR 72201 · 501-376-3021

Timothy O. Dudley · (Plaintiffs) · Wilson, Engstrom, Corum & Dudley · 809 West Third Street · P.O. Box 71 · Little Rock, AR 72203 · 501-375-6453

Sam Laser* · (Defendants, Products Liability, Professional Malpractice, Automobile Collision, Appellate) · Laser, Sharp, Mayes, Wilson, Bufford & Watts · 101 South Spring Street, Suite 300 · Little Rock, AR 72201-2488 · 501-376-2981

James M. Moody · (Defendants) · Wright, Lindsey & Jennings · 2200 Worthen Bank Building · 200 West Capitol Avenue · Little Rock, AR 72201-3699 · 501-371-0808

Laura Hensley Smith · (Defendants, Medical Malpractice) · Friday, Eldredge & Clark · 2000 First Commercial Building · 400 West Capitol Avenue · Little Rock, AR 72201-3493 · 501-370-1537

William H. Sutton* · (Defendants) · Friday, Eldredge & Clark · 2000 First Commercial Building · 400 West Capitol Avenue · Little Rock, AR 72201-3493 · 501-376-2011

William R. Wilson, Jr.* · Wilson, Engstrom, Corum & Dudley · 809 West Third Street · P.O. Box 71 · Little Rock, AR 72203 · 501-375-6453

Stephen A. Matthews · (Defendants) · Bridges, Young, Matthews, Holmes & Drake · 315 East Eighth Avenue · P.O. Box 7808 · Pine Bluff, AR 71611 · 501-534-5532

Nicholas H. Patton · (Plaintiffs) · Young, Patton & Folsom · 4122 Texas Boulevard · P.O. Box 1897 · Texarkana, AR 75504 · 501-774-3206

PUBLIC UTILITY LAW

Kent Foster · Mitchell, Williams, Selig & Tucker · 1000 Savers Federal Building 320 West Capitol Avenue · Little Rock, AR 72201-3525 · 501-688-8800

Herschel H. Friday* · Friday, Eldredge & Clark · 2000 First Commercial Building · 400 West Capitol Avenue · Little Rock, AR 72201-3493 · 501-376-2011

REAL ESTATE LAW

W. Christopher Barrier · (Zoning, Land Use, Commercial Transactions) · Mitchell, Williams, Selig & Tucker · 1000 Savers Federal Building · 320 West Capitol Avenue · Little Rock, AR 72201-3525 · 501-688-8800

George E. Campbell · Rose Law Firm · 120 East Fourth Street · Little Rock, AR 72201-2893 · 501-375-9131

Beresford L. Church, Jr. · 11101 Anderson Drive, Suite 307 · Little Rock, AR 72212 · 501-228-9952

Darrell D. Dover · Dover & Dixon · 425 West Capitol Avenue, Suite 3700 · Little Rock, AR 72201 · 501-375-9151

Edward L. Wright, Jr. · Wright, Lindsey & Jennings · 2200 Worthen Bank Building · 200 West Capitol Avenue · Little Rock, AR 72201-3699 · 501-371-0808

TAX AND EMPLOYEE BENEFITS LAW

Randall W. Ishmael · 603 Southwest Drive · P.O. Box 4096 · Jonesboro, AR 72403 · 501-972-1400

E. Chas. Eichenbaum · Eichenbaum, Scott, Miller, Liles & Heister · Union National Bank Building, Suite 1400 · 124 West Capitol Avenue · Little Rock, AR 72201 · 501-376-4531

Byron M. Eiseman, Jr. · (Corporate & Partnership Transactions, State Tax, Tax Disputes) · Friday, Eldredge & Clark · 2000 First Commercial Building · 400 West Capitol Avenue · Little Rock, AR 72201-3493 · 501-376-2011

Gregory B. Graham · (Corporate & Partnership Transactions, Employee Benefits) · Simpson & Graham · Ozark Building, Suite 300 · 10201 West Markham Street · P.O. Box 5420 · Little Rock, AR 72215 · 501-221-7100

Joseph B. Hurst, Jr. · (Employee Benefits) · Friday, Eldredge & Clark · 2000 First Commercial Building · 400 West Capitol Avenue · Little Rock, AR 72201-3493 · 501-376-2011

W. Wilson Jones · Rose Law Firm · 120 East Fourth Street · Little Rock, AR 72201-2893 · 501-375-9131

Lewis H. Mathis · Friday, Eldredge & Clark · 2000 First Commercial Building · 400 West Capitol Avenue · Little Rock, AR 72201-3493 · 501-376-2011

A. Wyckliff Nisbet, Jr. · (Employee Benefits) · Friday, Eldredge & Clark · 2000 First Commercial Building · 400 West Capitol Avenue · Little Rock, AR 72201-3493 · 501-376-2011

Thomas L. Overbey · (Tax, Employee Benefits) · Overbey Law Firm · 425 North University Avenue · Little Rock, AR 72205-3108 · 501-664-8105

Craig H. Westbrook · (Employee Benefits) · Mitchell, Williams, Selig & Tucker 1000 Savers Federal Building · 320 West Capitol Avenue · Little Rock, AR 72201-3525 · 501-688-8800

Richard A. Williams · Mitchell, Williams, Selig & Tucker · 1000 Savers Federal Building · 320 West Capitol Avenue · Little Rock, AR 72201-3525 · 501-688-8800

Ted N. Drake · Bridges, Young, Matthews, Holmes & Drake · 315 East Eighth Avenue · P.O. Box 7808 · Pine Bluff, AR 71611 · 501-534-5532

Robert H. Holmes · Bridges, Young, Matthews, Holmes & Drake · 315 East Eighth Avenue · P.O. Box 7808 · Pine Bluff, AR 71601 · 501-534-5532

TRUSTS AND ESTATES

Randall W. Ishmael · 603 Southwest Drive · P.O. Box 4096 · Jonesboro, AR 72403 · 501-972-1400

E. Chas. Eichenbaum · Eichenbaum, Scott, Miller, Liles & Heister · Union National Bank Building, Suite 1400 · 124 West Capitol Avenue · Little Rock, AR 72201 · 501-376-4531

Byron M. Eiseman, Jr. · (Estate Planning, Estate Administration, Charitable Trusts) · Friday, Eldredge & Clark · 2000 First Commercial Building · 400 West Capitol Avenue · Little Rock, AR 72201-3493 · 501-376-2011

James E. Harris · Friday, Eldredge & Clark · 2000 First Commercial Building · 400 West Capitol Avenue · Little Rock, AR 72201-3493 · 501-376-2011

Richard F. Hatfield · First Federal Plaza, Suite 502 · 401 West Capitol · Little Rock, AR 72201 · 501-374-9010

William D. Haught · Wright, Lindsey & Jennings · 2200 Worthen Bank Building 200 West Capitol Avenue · Little Rock, AR 72201-3699 · 501-371-0808

W. Wilson Jones · Rose Law Firm · 120 East Fourth Street · Little Rock, AR 72201-2893 · 501-375-9131

Thomas L. Overbey · Overbey Law Firm · 425 North University Avenue · Little Rock, AR 72205-3108 · 501-664-8105

Leonard L. Scott · Eichenbaum, Scott, Miller, Liles & Heister · Union National Bank Building, Suite 1400 · 124 West Capitol Avenue · Little Rock, AR 72201 · 501-376-4531

Richard A. Williams · Mitchell, Williams, Selig & Tucker · 1000 Savers Federal Building · 320 West Capitol Avenue · Little Rock, AR 72201-3525 · 501-688-8800

Ted N. Drake · Bridges, Young, Matthews, Holmes & Drake · 315 East Eighth Avenue · P.O. Box 7808 · Pine Bluff, AR 71611 · 501-534-5532

Robert H. Holmes · Bridges, Young, Matthews, Holmes & Drake · 315 East Eighth Avenue · P.O. Box 7808 · Pine Bluff, AR 71601 · 501-534-5532

James Lee Moore · Bridges, Young, Matthews, Holmes & Drake · 315 East Eighth Avenue · P.O. Box 7808 · Pine Bluff, AR 71611 · 501-534-5532

CALIFORNIA

BANKRUPTCY LAW

Lynn Anderson Koller · Koller & MacConaghy · 2354 Powell Street · Emeryville, CA 94608 · 415-652-5512

Stephen R. Brown · Luce, Forward, Hamilton & Scripps · Regents Square II · 4250 Executive Square, Suite 700 · La Jolla, CA 92037 · 619-455-6611

Merrill R. Francis · Sheppard, Mullin, Richter & Hampton · 333 South Hope Street, 48th Floor · Los Angeles, CA 90071 · 213-620-1780

Herman L. Glatt · Stutman, Treister & Glatt · 3699 Wilshire Boulevard, Suite 900 Los Angeles, CA 90010-2739 · 213-251-5100

Robert A. Greenfield · Stutman, Treister & Glatt · 3699 Wilshire Boulevard, Suite 900 · Los Angeles, CA 90010-2739 · 213-251-5100

Kenneth N. Klee* · (Business Reorganization, Creditors' Rights, Bankruptcy Litigation) · Stutman, Treister & Glatt · 3699 Wilshire Boulevard, Suite 900 · Los Angeles, CA 90010-2739 · 213-251-5100

Richard B. Levin · Stutman, Treister & Glatt · 3699 Wilshire Boulevard, Suite 900 · Los Angeles, CA 90010-2739 · 213-251-5100

Michael S. Lurey · (Business Reorganization, Creditors' Rights) · Latham & Watkins · 633 West Fifth Street, Suite 4000 · Los Angeles, CA 90071-2007 · 213-485-1234

Robert L. Morrison · Pillsbury Madison & Sutro · Citicorp Plaza, Suite 1200 · 725 South Figueroa Street · Los Angeles, CA 90017-2513 · 213-488-7100

Richard M. Neiter · Stutman, Treister & Glatt · 3699 Wilshire Boulevard, Suite 900 · Los Angeles, CA 90010-2739 · 213-251-5100

Prentice L. O'Leary · Sheppard, Mullin, Richter & Hampton · 333 South Hope Street, 48th Floor · Los Angeles, CA 90071 · 213-620-1780

Joel R. Ohlgren* · (Business Reorganization, Creditors' Rights, Bankruptcy Litigation, Out of Court Workouts) · Sheppard, Mullin, Richter & Hampton · 333 South Hope Street, 48th Floor · Los Angeles, CA 90071 · 213-620-1780

Ronald S. Orr* · (Business Reorganization, Creditors' Rights, Debtors' Rights, Bankruptcy Litigation) · Gibson, Dunn & Crutcher · 333 South Grand Avenue · Los Angeles, CA 90071 · 213-229-7000

Lawrence Peitzman · Morrison & Foerster · 333 South Grand Avenue, Suite 3800 Los Angeles, CA 90071-3168 · 213-626-3800

Richard T. Peters · Sidley & Austin · 2049 Century Park East, 35th Floor · Los Angeles, CA 90067 · 213-553-8100

Arnold M. Quittner · Gendel, Raskoff, Shapiro & Quittner · 1801 Century Park East, Sixth Floor · Los Angeles, CA 90067 · 213-277-5400

Bernard Shapiro · Gendel, Raskoff, Shapiro & Quittner · 1801 Century Park East, Sixth Floor · Los Angeles, CA 90067 · 213-277-5400

Bennett L. Silverman · Gibson, Dunn & Crutcher · 333 South Grand Avenue · Los Angeles, CA 90071 · 213-229-7000

Bruce H. Spector · Stutman, Treister & Glatt · 3699 Wilshire Boulevard, Suite 900 · Los Angeles, CA 90010-2739 · 213-251-5100

Irving Sulmeyer · (Business Reorganization, Creditors' Rights, Debtors' Rights, Bankruptcy Litigation) · Sulmeyer, Kupetz, Baumann & Rothman · 300 South Grand Avenue, 14th Floor · Los Angeles, CA 90071-3124 · 213-626-2311

George M. Treister · Stutman, Treister & Glatt · 3699 Wilshire Boulevard, Suite 900 · Los Angeles, CA 90010-2739 · 213-251-5100

J. Ronald Trost · Sidley & Austin · 2049 Century Park East, 35th Floor · Los Angeles, CA 90067 · 213-553-8100

Robert J. White · (Business Reorganization, Creditors' Rights, Bankruptcy Litigation) · O'Melveny & Myers · 400 South Hope Street · Los Angeles, CA 90071-2899 · 213-669-6000

Irving J. Kornfield* · (Creditors' Rights, Debtors' Rights, Bankruptcy Litigation) Kornfield, Paul & Bupp · Lake Merritt Plaza · 1999 Harrison Street, Suite 800 · Oakland, CA 94612 · 415-763-1000

Robert L. Ward · Law Office of Robert L. Ward · 610 Sixteenth Street, Suite 423 Oakland, CA 94612 · 415-834-6400

Steven H. Felderstein · (Business Reorganization, Creditors' Rights, Debtors' Rights, Workouts) · Diepenbrock, Wulff, Plant & Hannegan · 300 Capitol Mall, Suite 1700 · P.O. Box 3034 · Sacramento, CA 95812-3034 · 916-444-3910

Robert Ames · Gray, Cary, Ames & Frye · 1700 First Interstate Plaza · 401 B Street · San Diego, CA 92101-4219 · 619-699-2700

Michael T. Andrew · Luce, Forward, Hamilton & Scripps · The Bank of California Plaza, Suite 1700 · 100 West A Street · San Diego, CA 92101 · 619-236-1414

Theodore W. Graham · Brobeck, Phleger & Harrison · 550 West C Street, Suite 1300 · San Diego, CA 92101-8049 · 619-234-1966

Ralph M. Pray III · Gray, Cary, Ames & Frye · 1700 First Interstate Plaza · 401 B Street · San Diego, CA 92101-4219 · 619-699-2700

Victor A. Vilaplana · Sheppard, Mullin, Richter & Hampton · 501 West Broadway, 19th Floor · San Diego, CA 92101 · 619-338-6500

Michael H. Ahrens · Bronson, Bronson & McKinnon · 505 Montgomery Street, 11th Floor · San Francisco, CA 94111 · 415-986-4200

Peter J. Benvenutti · Heller, Ehrman, White & McAuliffe · 333 Bush Street · San Francisco, CA 94104-2878 · 415-772-6000

Penn Ayers Butler* · (Business Reorganization, Debtors' Rights, Bankruptcy Litigation) · Murphy, Weir & Butler · 101 California Street, 39th Floor · San Francisco, CA 94111 · 415-398-4700

Lawrence Goldberg · (Business Reorganization, Bankruptcy Litigation) · Goldberg, Stinnett & McDonald · 44 Montgomery Street, Suite 2900 · San Francisco, CA 94104 · 415-362-5045

John T. Hansen · (Business Reorganization, Debtors' Rights, Bankruptcy Litigation) · Thelen, Marrin, Johnson & Bridges · Two Embarcadero Center, Suite 2200 San Francisco, CA 94111 · 415-392-6320

Frederick D. Holden, Jr. · (Business Reorganization, Creditors' Rights, Debtors' Rights, Bankruptcy Litigation) · Brobeck, Phleger & Harrison · Spear Street Tower · One Market Plaza · San Francisco, CA 94105 · 415-442-0900

Thomas C. Holman · Pettit & Martin · 101 California Street, 35th Floor · San Francisco, CA 94111 · 415-434-4000

Robert E. Izmirian · Buchalter, Nemer, Fields & Younger · 101 California Street, Suite 2050 · San Francisco, CA 94111-5879 · 415-397-0277

William Kelly · Graham & James · One Maritime Plaza, Suite 300 · San Francisco, CA 94111 · 415-954-0200

James L. Lopes · (Business Reorganization, Creditors' Rights, Debtors' Rights, Bankruptcy Litigation) · Howard, Rice, Nemerovski, Canady, Robertson & Falk Three Embarcadero Center, Seventh Floor · San Francisco, CA 94111 · 415-434-1600

Dennis Montali · Pillsbury Madison & Sutro · 225 Bush Street · P.O. Box 7880 San Francisco, CA 94120-7880 · 415-983-1000

Patrick A. Murphy · (Business Reorganization, Creditors' Rights, Debtors' Rights, Bankruptcy Litigation) · Murphy, Weir & Butler · 101 California Street, 39th Floor · San Francisco, CA 94111 · 415-398-4700

Harvey S. Schochet · Steefel, Levitt & Weiss · One Embarcadero Center, 29th Floor · San Francisco, CA 94111 · 415-788-0900

Margaret Sheneman · Murphy, Weir & Butler · 101 California Street, 39th Floor San Francisco, CA 94111 · 415-398-4700

Philip S. Warden · Pillsbury Madison & Sutro · 225 Bush Street · P.O. Box 7880 San Francisco, CA 94120 · 415-983-1000

Kenneth J. Campeau · Campeau & Thomas · 55 South Market Street, Suite 1040 San Jose, CA 95113 · 408-295-9555

Harvey W. Hoffman · Bronson, Bronson & McKinnon · 100 B Street, Suite 400 Santa Rosa, CA 95401 · 707-527-8110

BUSINESS LITIGATION

Stephen A. Kroft · Rosenfeld, Meyer & Susman · First Interstate Bank Building, Fourth Floor · 9601 Wilshire Boulevard · Beverly Hills, CA 90210 · 213-858-7700

Joseph W. Cotchett* · Cotchett, Illston & Pitre · 840 Malcolm Road, Suite 200 Burlingame, CA 94010 · 415-697-6000

Susan Y. Illston · Cotchett, Illston & Pitre · 840 Malcolm Road, Suite 200 · Burlingame, CA 94010 · 415-697-6000

Robert E. Currie · Latham & Watkins · 650 Town Center Drive, 20th Floor · Costa Mesa, CA 92626 · 714-540-1235

Ellis J. Horvitz · (Appellate) · Horvitz & Levy · 15760 Ventura Boulevard, 18th Floor · Encino, CA 91436 · 818-995-0800

Joseph A. Ball · Carlsmith Ball · 301 East Ocean Boulevard, Suite 700 · Long Beach, CA 90802 · 213-435-5631

Samuel A. Keesal, Jr. · Keesal, Young & Logan · 310 Golden Shore · P.O. Box 1730 · Long Beach, CA 90801-1730 · 213-436-9051

Orville A. Armstrong · Baker & McKenzie · 725 South Figueroa Street, 36th Floor · Los Angeles, CA 90017 · 213-629-3000

Alfred E. Augustini · Augustini & Wheeler · 523 West Sixth Street, Suite 330 · Los Angeles, CA 90014 · 213-629-8888

Leo J. Biegenzahn · Pillsbury Madison & Sutro · Citicorp Plaza, Suite 1200 · 725 South Figueroa Street · Los Angeles, CA 90017-2513 · 213-488-7100

Maxwell M. Blecher* · (Antitrust) · Blecher & Collins · 611 West Sixth Street, 28th Floor · Los Angeles, CA 90017 · 213-622-4222

Richard H. Borow · Irell & Manella · 1800 Avenue of the Stars, Suite 900 · Los Angeles, CA 90067-4276 · 213-277-1010

Brad D. Brian · Munger, Tolles & Olson · 355 South Grand Avenue, 35th Floor · Los Angeles, CA 90071-1560 · 213-683-9100

William B. Campbell · Paul, Hastings, Janofsky & Walker · 555 South Flower Street, 23rd Floor · Los Angeles, CA 90071 · 213-683-6000

Robert E. Cooper · Gibson, Dunn & Crutcher · 333 South Grand Avenue · Los Angeles, CA 90071 · 213-229-7000

Richard P. Crane, Jr. · Girardi, Keese and Crane · 1126 Wilshire Boulevard · Los Angeles, CA 90017 · 213-489-5330

Peter Brown Dolan · Dolan & Forester · 333 South Grand Avenue · Los Angeles, CA 90071-3168 · 213-621-9513

Dean C. Dunlavey · Gibson, Dunn & Crutcher · 333 South Grand Avenue · Los Angeles, CA 90071 · 213-229-7000

Daniel Fogel · Fogel, Feldman, Ostrov, Ringer & Klevens · 5900 Wilshire Boulevard, 26th Floor · Los Angeles, CA 90036-5185 · 213-937-6250

Howard I. Friedman · Loeb and Loeb · 1000 Wilshire Boulevard, Suite 1800 · Los Angeles, CA 90017 · 213-688-3400

Max L. Gillam · Latham & Watkins · 633 West Fifth Street, Suite 4000 · Los Angeles, CA 90071-2007 · 213-891-8292

Marshall B. Grossman · Alschuler, Grossman & Pines · 1880 Century Park East, 12th Floor · Los Angeles, CA 90067 · 213-277-1226

Alan N. Halkett* · Latham & Watkins · 633 West Fifth Street, Suite 4000 · Los Angeles, CA 90071-2007 · 213-891-8286

C. Stephen Howard* · Milbank, Tweed, Hadley & McCloy · 601 South Figueroa Street, 30th Floor · Los Angeles, CA 90071 · 213-892-4000

Seth M. Hufstedler · Hufstedler, Kaus & Ettinger · 355 South Grand Avenue, 45th Floor · Los Angeles, CA 90071-3107 · 213-617-7070

Craig B. Jorgensen* · (RICO, Securities, Broker Dealer) · Kindel & Anderson · 555 South Flower Street, 29th Floor · Los Angeles, CA 90071-2498 · 213-680-2222

Stuart L. Kadison · Sidley & Austin · 2049 Century Park East, 35th Floor · Los Angeles, CA 90067 · 213-553-8100

Dennis E. Kinnaird · Munger, Tolles & Olson · 355 South Grand Avenue, 35th Floor · Los Angeles, CA 90071-1560 · 213-683-9100

Patrick Lynch · O'Melveny & Myers · 400 South Hope Street · Los Angeles, CA 90071-2899 · 213-669-6000

Ronald L. Olson · Munger, Tolles & Olson · 355 South Grand Avenue, 35th Floor · Los Angeles, CA 90071-1560 · 213-683-9100

Thomas P. Phillips · Rodi, Pollock, Pettker, Galbraith & Phillips · 801 South Grand Avenue, Suite 400 · Los Angeles, CA 90017 · 213-895-4900

John J. Quinn* · Quinn, Kully & Morrow · 520 South Grand Avenue, Eighth Floor · Los Angeles, CA 90071 · 213-622-0300

Frank Rothman · Skadden, Arps, Slate, Meagher & Flom · 300 South Grand Avenue, 34th Floor · Los Angeles, CA 90071 · 213-687-5000

Donald C. Smaltz · Morgan, Lewis & Bockius · 801 South Grand Avenue, 20th Floor · Los Angeles, CA 90017-3189 · 213-612-2500

Peter R. Taft · Munger, Tolles & Olson · 355 South Grand Avenue, 35th Floor · Los Angeles, CA 90071-1560 · 213-683-9100

Henry C. Thumann · O'Melveny & Myers · 400 South Hope Street · Los Angeles, CA 90071-2899 · 213-669-6000

William W. Vaughn · O'Melveny & Myers · 400 South Hope Street · Los Angeles, CA 90071-2899 · 213-669-6000

Charles S. Vogel* · Sidley & Austin · 2049 Century Park East, 35th Floor · Los Angeles, CA 90067 · 213-553-8100

Melvyn H. Wald · Munger, Tolles & Olson · 355 South Grand Avenue, 35th Floor Los Angeles, CA 90071-1560 · 213-683-9100

Robert S. Warren · Gibson, Dunn & Crutcher · 333 South Grand Avenue · Los Angeles, CA 90071 · 213-229-7000

Robert L. Winslow · Irell & Manella · 1800 Avenue of the Stars, Suite 900 · Los Angeles, CA 90067-4276 · 213-277-1010

Edwin A. Heafey, Jr.* · (Banking, Commercial, Finance, RICO, Securities) · Crosby, Heafey, Roach & May · 1999 Harrison Street · Oakland, CA 94612 · 415-763-2000

Raoul D. Kennedy · Crosby, Heafey, Roach & May · 1999 Harrison Street · Oakland, CA 94612 · 415-763-2000

Edmund L. Regalia* · (Appellate, Banking, Commercial, Finance) · Miller, Starr & Regalia · Ordway Building, 16th Floor · One Kaiser Plaza · Oakland, CA 94612 415-465-3800

Bruce G. Vanyo · Wilson, Sonsini, Goodrich & Rosati · Two Palo Alto Square · Palo Alto, CA 94306 · 415-493-9300

Eugene J. Majeski · Ropers, Majeski, Kohn, Bentley, Wagner & Kane · 1001 Marshall Street · Redwood City, CA 94063 · 415-364-8200

Don C. Brown · (Commercial) · Thompson & Colegate · 3610 Fourteenth Street P.O. Box 1299 · Riverside, CA 92502 · 714-682-5550

Enos C. Reid · Reid & Hellyer · 3880 Lemon Street, Fifth Floor · P.O. Box 1300 Riverside, CA 92502-3834 · 714-682-1771

James D. Ward* · Thompson & Colegate · 3610 Fourteenth Street · P.O. Box 1299 · Riverside, CA 92502 · 714-682-5550

Joseph S. Genshlea* · (Banking, Commercial, Finance, Securities) · Weintraub Genshlea & Sproul · 2535 Capitol Oaks Drive · P.O. Box 13530 · Sacramento, CA 95853-4530 · 916-648-9400

Frederick P. Crowell · Gray, Cary, Ames & Frye · 1700 First Interstate Plaza · 401 B Street · San Diego, CA 92101-4219 · 619-699-2700

Oscar F. Irwin · Hillyer & Irwin · 550 West C Street, Suite 1600 · San Diego, CA 92101 · 619-234-6121

William S. Lerach · (Securities) · Milberg Weiss Bershad Specthrie & Lerach · 2000 Coast Savings Tower · 225 Broadway · San Diego, CA 92101-5050 · 619-231-1058

Gerald L. McMahon* · Seltzer Caplan Wilkins & McMahon · 3003-3043 Fourth Avenue · P.O. Box X 33999 · San Diego, CA 92103 · 619-295-3003

David E. Monahan* · Gray, Cary, Ames & Frye · 1700 First Interstate Plaza · 401 B Street · San Diego, CA 92101-4219 · 619-699-2700

Robert G. Steiner · Luce, Forward, Hamilton & Scripps · 110 West A Street, Suite 1700 · San Diego, CA 92101 · 619-236-1414

William Alsup* · Morrison & Foerster · 345 California Street · San Francisco, CA 94104-2675 · 415-677-7206

David M. Balabanian* · (Antitrust, Commercial, Securities) · McCutchen, Doyle, Brown & Enersen · Three Embarcadero Center · San Francisco, CA 94111 · 415-393-2000

Stephen V. Bomse · Heller, Ehrman, White & McAuliffe · 333 Bush Street · San Francisco, CA 94104-2878 · 415-772-6000

William A. Brockett, Jr. · Keker & Brockett · 710 Samson Street · San Francisco, CA 94111 · 415-391-5400

James J. Brosnahan · Morrison & Foerster · 345 California Street, 35th Floor · San Francisco, CA 94104-2675 · 415-677-7000

Josef D. Cooper · The Law Offices of Josef D. Cooper · 100 The Embarcadero, Penthouse · San Francisco, CA 94105 · 415-788-3030

E. Judge Elderkin · Brobeck, Phleger & Harrison · Spear Street Tower · One Market Plaza · San Francisco, CA 94105 · 415-442-0900

Jerome B. Falk, Jr.* · (also Appellate) · Howard, Rice, Nemerovski, Canady, Robertson & Falk · Three Embarcadero Center, Seventh Floor · San Francisco, CA 94111 · 415-434-1600

Frederick P. Furth · Furth, Fahrner, Bluemle & Mason · Furth Building, Suite 1000 · 201 Sansome Street · San Francisco, CA 94104 · 415-433-2070

Melvin R. Goldman · Morrison & Foerster · 345 California Street, 34th Floor · San Francisco, CA 94104-2675 · 415-677-7000

James L. Hunt* · (Antitrust, Commercial) · McCutchen, Doyle, Brown & Enersen · Three Embarcadero Center · San Francisco, CA 94111 · 415-393-2000

John W. Keker · Keker & Brockett · 710 Samson Street · San Francisco, CA 94111 415-391-5400

Raoul D. Kennedy* · Crosby, Heafey, Roach & May · 333 Bush Street, Suite 2580 · San Francisco, CA 94111 · 415-543-8700

Moses Lasky · Lasky, Haas, Cohler & Munter · 505 Sansome Street, 12th Floor San Francisco, CA 94111-3183 · 415-788-2700

Richard J. Lucas* · Orrick, Herrington & Sutcliffe · Old Federal Reserve Building · 400 Sansome Street · San Francisco, CA 94111 · 415-773-5400

John S. Martel* · Farella, Braun & Martel · Russ Building, Suite 3000 · 235 Montgomery Street · San Francisco, CA 94104 · 415-954-4400

Charles O. Morgan, Jr. · 450 Sansome Street, Suite 1310 · San Francisco, CA 94111-3382 · 415-392-2037

James N. Penrod* · (Defendants) · Hassard, Bonnington, Rogers & Huber · Five Fremont Center, Suite 3400 · 50 Fremont Street · San Francisco, CA 94105 · 415-543-6444

M. Laurence Popofsky* · Heller, Ehrman, White & McAuliffe · 333 Bush Street · San Francisco, CA 94104-2878 · 415-772-6000

Robert D. Raven · Morrison & Foerster · 345 California Street, 35th Floor · San Francisco, CA 94104-2675 · 415-677-7000

Paul A. Renne* · (Securities, Professional Liability/Accountants) · Cooley, Godward, Castro, Huddleson & Tatum · One Maritime Plaza, 20th Floor · San Francisco, CA 94111 · 415-981-5252

Denis T. Rice* · (Securities) · Howard, Rice, Nemerovski, Canady, Robertson & Falk · Three Embarcadero Center, Seventh Floor · San Francisco, CA 94111 · 415-434-1600

Joseph W. Rogers, Jr. · Rogers, Joseph, O'Donnell & Quinn · 311 California Street, 10th Floor · San Francisco, CA 94104 · 415-956-2828

J. Thomas Rosch · McCutchen, Doyle, Brown & Enersen · Three Embarcadero Center, Suite 1800 · San Francisco, CA 94111 · 415-393-2000

Arthur J. Shartsis · Shartsis, Friese & Ginsburg · One Maritime Plaza, 18th Floor · San Francisco, CA 94111 · 415-421-6500

Michael Traynor* · Cooley Godward Castro Huddleson & Tatum · One Maritime Plaza,Suite 2000 · San Francisco, CA 94111-3580 · 415-981-5252

James P. Kleinberg · McCutchen, Doyle, Brown & Enersen · 55 South Market Street, Suite 1500 · San Jose, CA 95113 · 408-947-8400

Allen J. Ruby · Morgan, Ruby, Schofield, Franich & Fredkin · 99 Almaden Boulevard, Suite 1000 · San Jose, CA 95113 · 408-288-8288

A. Barry Cappello* · Cappello & Foley · 831 State Street · Santa Barbara, CA 93101-3227 · 805-564-2444

CORPORATE LAW

John C. McCarthy* · (Insurance) · 401 Harvard Avenue · Claremont, CA 91711 · 714-621-4984

Robert L. Adler · Munger, Tolles & Olson · 355 South Grand Avenue, 35th Floor · Los Angeles, CA 90071-1560 · 213-683-9100

Robert H. Baker · Jones, Day, Reavis & Pogue · 355 South Grand Avenue, Suite 3000 · Los Angeles, CA 90071 · 213-625-3939

Alan J. Barton · (Corporate Finance, Leveraged Buyouts, Mergers & Acquisitions, Securities) · Paul, Hastings, Janofsky & Walker · 555 South Flower Street, 23rd Floor · Los Angeles, CA 90071 · 213-683-6140

Ronald S. Beard · Gibson, Dunn & Crutcher · 333 South Grand Avenue · Los Angeles, CA 90071 · 213-229-7000

Barton Beek · O'Melveny & Myers · 400 South Hope Street · Los Angeles, CA 90071-2899 · 213-669-6000

Richard L. Bernacchi · (International, Mergers & Acquisitions, Computer) · Irell & Manella · 1800 Avenue of the Stars, Suite 900 · Los Angeles, CA 90067-4276 · 213-277-1010

Andrew E. Bogen · Gibson, Dunn & Crutcher · 333 South Grand Avenue · Los Angeles, CA 90071 · 213-229-7000

David M. Bosko · Sheppard, Mullin, Richter & Hampton · 333 South Hope Street, 48th Floor · Los Angeles, CA 90071 · 213-620-1780

Neal H. Brockmeyer · Kindel & Anderson · 555 South Flower Street, 29th Floor Los Angeles, CA 90071 · 213-680-2222

Robert E. Carlson · Paul, Hastings, Janofsky & Walker · 555 South Flower Street, 23rd Floor · Los Angeles, CA 90071 · 213-683-6000

Richard Carver · Latham & Watkins · 633 West Fifth Street, Suite 4000 · Los Angeles, CA 90071 · 213-485-1234

Louis M. Castruccio · Irell & Manella · 1800 Avenue of the Stars, Suite 900 · Los Angeles, CA 90067-4276 · 213-277-1010

R. Bradbury Clark · O'Melveny & Myers · 400 South Hope Street · Los Angeles, CA 90071-2899 · 213-669-6000

Michael J. Connell · Paul, Hastings & Janofsky · 555 South Flower Street, 23rd Floor · Los Angeles, CA 90071 · 213-683-6000

John J. Cost · Irell & Manella · 333 South Hope Street, Suite 3300 · Los Angeles, CA 90071 · 213-620-1555

James E. Cross · O'Melveny & Myers · 400 South Hope Street · Los Angeles, CA 90071-2899 · 213-669-6000

Robert E. Denham · (Corporate Finance, Mergers & Acquisitions) · Munger, Tolles & Olson · 355 South Grand Avenue, 35th Floor · Los Angeles, CA 90071-1560 · 213-683-9100

Thomas W. Dobson · Latham & Watkins · 633 West Fifth Street, Suite 4000 · Los Angeles, CA 90071-2007 · 213-891-8292

Stanley F. Farrar · Sullivan & Cromwell · 444 South Flower Street, Suite 1200 · Los Angeles, CA 90071 · 213-955-8000

William C. Farrer · Hill, Farrer & Burrill · Union Bank Square, 35th Floor · 445 South Figueroa Street · Los Angeles, CA 90071 · 213-620-0460

Ronald L. Fein · (Corporate Finance, Financial Institutions, Mergers & Acquisitions, Securities) · Wyman Bautzer Kuchel & Silbert · Two Century Plaza, 14th Floor · 2049 Century Park East · Los Angeles, CA 90067 · 213-556-8000

Robert T. Gelber · (Financial Institutions, International, Mergers & Acquisitions) Gibson, Dunn & Crutcher · 2029 Century Park East, Suite 4200 · Los Angeles, CA 90067 · 213-552-8500

William D. Gould · (Mergers & Acquisitions, Securities, Workouts) · Troy & Gould · 1801 Century Park East, 16th Floor · Los Angeles, CA 90067 · 213-553-4441

Gilbert E. T. Haakh · Baker & McKenzie · 725 South Figueroa Street, 36th Floor Los Angeles, CA 90017 · 213-629-3000

Guido R. Henry, Jr. · (Corporate Finance, Mergers & Acquisitions, Securities, Securities Regulation) · Milbank, Tweed, Hadley & McCoy · 601 South Figueroa Street, 30th Floor · Los Angeles, CA 90071 · 213-892-4000

Grover R. Heyler · Latham & Watkins · 633 West Fifth Street, Suite 4000 · Los Angeles, CA 90071-2007 · 213-891-8292

John D. Hussey · Sheppard, Mullin, Richter & Hampton · 333 South Hope Street, 48th Floor · Los Angeles, CA 90071 · 213-620-1780

Edmund M. Kaufman · Irell & Manella · 1800 Avenue of the Stars, Suite 900 · Los Angeles, CA 90067-4276 · 213-277-1010

C. Douglas Kranwinkle · O'Melveny & Myers · 400 South Hope Street · Los Angeles, CA 90071-2899 · 213-669-6000

Henry Lesser · (Corporate Finance, Leveraged Buyouts, Mergers & Acquisitions, Securities Regulation) · Fried, Frank, Harris, Shriver & Jacobson · Citicorp Plaza, Suite 3890 · 725 South Figueroa · Los Angeles, CA 90017-5438 · 213-689-0010

Ronald M. Loeb · (Corporate Finance, Leveraged Buyouts, Mergers & Acquisitions, Securities Regulation) · Irell & Manella · 1800 Avenue of the Stars, Suite 900 · Los Angeles, CA 90067-4276 · 213-277-1010

Francis D. Logan · (Banking) · Milbank, Tweed, Hadley & McCloy · 515 South Figueroa Street · Los Angeles, CA. 90071 · 213-892-4000

Simon M. Lorne · Munger, Tolles & Olson · 355 South Grand Avenue, 35th Floor Los Angeles, CA 90071-1560 · 213-683-9100

Joseph D. Mandel · Tuttle & Taylor · 355 South Grand Avenue, 40th Floor · Los Angeles, CA 90071-3101 · 213-683-0600

Harold Marsh, Jr. · 10920 Wilshire Boulevard, Suite 1000 · Los Angeles, CA 90024 · 213-208-1424

John P. McLoughlin · Latham & Watkins · 633 West Fifth Street, Suite 4000 · Los Angeles, CA 90071-2007 · 213-891-8292

Donn B. Miller · O'Melveny & Myers · 400 South Hope Street · Los Angeles, CA 90071-2899 · 213-669-6000

Gavin Miller · Heller, Ehrman, White & McAuliffe · 601 South Figueroa Street, 40th Floor · Los Angeles, CA 90071-5704 · 213-689-0200

Robert K. Montgomery · Gibson, Dunn & Crutcher · 333 South Grand Avenue Los Angeles, CA 90071 · 213-229-7000

Gary Olson · Latham & Watkins · 633 West Fifth Street, Suite 4000 · Los Angeles, CA 90071-2007 · 213-891-8292

Gerald L. Parsky · Gibson, Dunn & Crutcher · 33 South Grand Avenue · Los Angeles, CA 90071 · 213-229-7000

John H. Roney · O'Melveny & Myers · 400 South Hope Street · Los Angeles, CA 90071-2899 · 213-669-6000

Joseph Ryan · O'Melveny & Myers · 400 South Hope Street · Los Angeles, CA 90071-2899 · 213-669-6000

Reade H. Ryan, Jr. · (Banking, Corporate Finance, International Banking, Leveraged Buyouts) · Shearman & Sterling · 725 South Figueroa Street, 21st Floor Los Angeles, CA 90017-5421 · 213-239-0300

Myrl R. Scott · Sheppard, Mullin, Richter & Hampton · 333 South Hope Street, 48th Floor · Los Angeles, CA 90071 · 213-620-1780

Charles V. Thornton · Paul, Hastings, Janofsky & Walker · 555 South Flower Street, 23rd Floor · Los Angeles, CA 90071 · 213-683-6000

Paul D. Tosetti · (Mergers & Acquisitions) · Latham & Watkins · 633 West Fifth Street, Suite 4000 · Los Angeles, CA 90071-2007 · 213-485-1234

Joseph F. Troy · (Corporate Finance, Mergers & Acquisitions, Securities) · Troy & Gould · 1801 Century Park East, 16th Floor · Los Angeles, CA 90067 · 213-553-4441

Thomas Unterman · (Corporate Finance, Financial Institutions, Mergers & Acquisitions, Securities Regulation) · Morrison & Foerster · 333 South Grand Avenue, Suite 3800 · Los Angeles, CA 90071-3168 · 213-621-9683

George A. Vandeman · (Mergers & Acquisitions) · Latham & Watkins · 633 West Fifth Street, Suite 4000 · Los Angeles, CA 90071-2007 · 213-485-1234

Thomas B. Pitcher · Gibson, Dunn & Crutcher · 800 Newport Center Drive · Newport Beach, CA 92660 · 714-759-3800

Henry P. Massey, Jr. · Wilson, Sonsini, Goodrich & Rosati · Two Palo Alto Square · Palo Alto, CA 94306 · 415-493-9300

William D. Sherman · (Corporate Finance, Leveraged Buyouts, Mergers & Acquisitions, Securities, Securities Regulation) · Morrison & Foerster · 630 Hansen Way · Palo Alto, CA 94304 · 415-354-1500

Lawrence W. Sonsini · Wilson, Sonsini, Goodrich & Rosati · Two Palo Alto Square · Palo Alto, CA 94306 · 415-493-9300

Joseph S. Genshlea · Weintraub Genshlea & Sproul · 2535 Capitol Oaks Drive · P.O. Box 13530 · Sacramento, CA 95851-0208 · 916-648-9400

Malcolm S. Weintraub · (Administrative) · Weintraub Genshlea & Sproul · 2535 Capitol Oaks Drive · P.O. Box 13530 · Sacramento, CA 95853-4530 · 916-648-9400

John W. Brooks · (International, Mergers & Acquisitions) · Luce, Forward, Hamilton & Scripps · The Bank of California Plaza, Suite 1700 · 110 West A Street San Diego, CA 92101 · 619-236-1414

Robert G. Copeland · Gray, Cary, Ames & Frye · 1700 First Interstate Plaza · 401 B Street · San Diego, CA 92101-4219 · 619-699-2743

William N. Jenkins · Musick, Peeler & Garrett · 1900 Coast Savings Tower · 225 Broadway · San Diego, CA 92101 · 619-231-2500

Kenneth M. Poovey · Latham & Watkins · 701 B Street, Suite 2100 · San Diego, CA 92101-8197 · 619-236-1234

John C. Stiska · 1020 Prospect, Suite 210 · San Diego, CA 92101 · 619-459-3841

Cameron Baker · (Insurance, International, Mergers & Acquisitions) · Pettit & Martin · 101 California Street, 35th Floor · San Francisco, CA 94111 · 415-434-4000

Roland E. Brandel · Morrison & Foerster · 345 California Street, 33rd Floor · San Francisco, CA 94104-2675 · 415-677-7000

Alexander D. Calhoun · Graham & James · Alcoa Building · One Maritime Plaza, Suite 300 · San Francisco, CA 94111 · 415-954-0200

Maryellen B. Cattani · Morrison & Foerster · 345 California Street, 32nd Floor · San Francisco, CA 94104-2675 · 415-677-7675

James F. Crafts, Jr. · Orrick, Herrington & Sutcliffe · Old Federal Reserve Building · 400 Sansome Street · San Francisco, CA 94111 · 415-392-1122

Bartley C. Deamer · McCutchen, Doyle, Brown & Enersen · Three Embarcadero Center, Suite 1800 · San Francisco, CA 94111 · 415-393-2000

Frank E. Farella · Farella, Braun & Martel · Russ Building, 30th Floor · 235 Montgomery Street · San Francisco, CA 94104 · 415-954-4400

Margaret G. Gill · (Corporate Finance, Mergers & Acquisitions, Securities, Securities Regulation) · Pillsbury Madison & Sutro · 235 Montgomery Street · P.O. Box 7880 · San Francisco, CA 94120 · 415-983-1528

Leslie P. Jay · Orrick, Herrington & Sutcliffe · Old Federal Reserve Building · 400 Sansome Street · San Francisco, CA 94111 · 415-392-1122

Christopher L. Kaufman · Latham & Watkins · 505 Montgomery Street · San Francisco, CA 94104 · 415-395-8030

John W. Larson · Brobeck, Phleger & Harrison · Spear Street Tower · One Market Plaza · San Francisco, CA 94105 · 415-442-0900

Thomas A. Lee, Jr. · Morrison & Foerster · 345 California Street, 32nd Floor · San Francisco, CA 94104-2675 · 415-677-7000

Bruce Alan Mann · Morrison & Foerster · 345 California Street, 33rd Floor · San Francisco, CA 94104-2675 · 415-677-7000

Loyd W. McCormick* · McCutchen, Doyle, Brown & Enersen · Three Embarcadero Center · San Francisco, CA 94111 · 415-393-2000

David E. Nelson · Morrison & Foerster · 345 California Street, 32nd Floor · San Francisco, CA 94104-2675 · 415-677-7000

Denis T. Rice* · (Financial Institutions, Securities, Securities Regulation) · Howard, Rice, Nemerovski, Canady, Robertson & Falk · Three Embarcadero Center, Seventh Floor · San Francisco, CA 94111 · 415-434-1600

Marshall L. Small · Morrison & Foerster · 345 California Street · San Francisco, CA 94104-2675 · 415-677-7161

Charles R. Collins · Gibson, Dunn & Crutcher · One Almaden Boulevard, Suite 1000 · San Jose, CA 95113 · 408-998-2000

Jay L. Margulies · Pettit & Martin · 333 West Santa Clara · San Jose, CA 95113 408-295-3210

CRIMINAL DEFENSE

Anthony P. Brooklier · Marks & Brooklier · 8383 Wilshire Boulevard , Suite 7500 Beverly Hills, CA 90211 · 213-273-7166

Bruce I. Hochman · Hochman, Salkin and De Roy · West Tower, Seventh Floor 9100 Wilshire Boulevard · Beverly Hills, CA 90212 · 213-273-1181

Cristina C. Arguedas* · Cooper, Arguedas & Cassman · 5900 Hollis Street, Suite N Emeryville, CA 94608 · 415-654-2000

Penelope M. Cooper · Cooper, Arguedas & Cassman · 5900 Hollis Street, Suite N Emeryville, CA 94608 · 415-654-2000

Jules F. Bonjour, Jr.* · Bonjour, Gough, Thorman & Cohen · 24301 Southland Drive, Suite 312 · Hayward, CA 94545-1578 · 415-785-8400

Philip A. Schnayerson · Garcia & Schnayerson · 225 West Winton Avenue, Suite 208 · Hayward, CA 94544 · 415-782-7580

Leslie H. Abramson · 4929 Wilshire Boulevard, Suite 940 · Los Angeles, CA 90010 · 213-933-9002

Harland W. Braun · 2049 Century Park East, Suite 1800 · Los Angeles, CA 90067 213-277-4777

Douglas Dalton · Dalton & Godfrey · 4525 Wilshire Boulevard, Third Floor · Los Angeles, CA 90010-3886 · 213-933-4945

Max L. Gillam · Latham & Watkins · 633 West Fifth Street, Suite 4000 · Los Angeles, CA 90071-2007 · 213-891-8292

Stanley I. Greenberg · 11845 West Olympic Boulevard, Suite 1000 · Los Angeles, CA 90064 · 213-473-3333

Jan Lawrence Handzlik · Kirkland & Ellis · 300 South Grand Avenue, 30th Floor Los Angeles, CA 90071 · 213-680-8400

Mark O. Heaney* · (Federal Court) · Law Offices of Barry Tarlow · 9119 Sunset Boulevard · Los Angeles, CA 90069 · 213-278-2111

Thomas E. Holliday* · Gibson, Dunn & Crutcher · 2029 Century Park East · Los Angeles, CA 90067 · 213-552-8500

Richard H. Kirschner · AVCO Center, Fourth Floor · 10850 Wilshire Boulevard Los Angeles, CA 90024 · 213-474-6555

Joel Levine · 811 West Seventh Street, 11th Floor · Los Angeles, CA 90017 · 213-622-2635

Michael J. Lightfoot · (also Appellate) · Talcott, Lightfoot, Vandevelde, Woehrle & Sadowsky · 655 South Hope Street, 13th Floor · Los Angeles, CA 90017 · 213-622-4750

Vincent J. Marella* · (Federal Court, Environmental Crimes, White Collar Defense) · Bird, Marella, Boxer, Wolpert & Matz · 10960 Wilshire Boulevard, 24th Floor · Los Angeles, CA 90024 · 213-312-0300

Edward M. Medvene* · (Violent Crimes, Non-Violent Crimes, Federal Court) · Mitchell, Silberberg & Knupp · 11377 West Olympic Boulevard · Los Angeles, CA 90064-1683 · 213-312-2000

Alvin S. Michaelson · Michaelson & Levine · 1901 Avenue of the Stars, Suite 1708 · Los Angeles, CA 90067 · 213-278-4984

Stephen D. Miller · Miller & O'Connell · Biltmore Court, Seventh Floor · 520 South Grand Avenue · Los Angeles, CA 90071 · 213-627-1900

Donald M. Re · Law Offices of Donald M. Re · Wilshire Boulevard, Suite 1000 Los Angeles, CA 90024 · 213-208-0401

Robert M. Talcott · Talcott, Lightfoot, Vandevelde, Woehrle & Sadowsky · 655 South Hope Street, 13th Floor · Los Angeles, CA 90017 · 213-622-4750

Barry Tarlow* · (Violent Crimes, White-Collar Crimes, Federal Court, State Court) · Law Offices of Barry Tarlow · 9119 Sunset Boulevard · Los Angeles, CA 90069 · 213-278-2111

John D. Vandevelde · Talcott, Lightfoot, Vandevelde, Woehrle & Sadowsky · Roosevelt Building, Suite 430 · 727 West Seventh Street · Los Angeles, CA 90017 213-622-4750

Howard L. Weitzman · Wyman Bautzer Kuchel & Silbert · Two Century Plaza, 14th Floor · 2049 Century Park East · Los Angeles, CA 90067 · 213-556-8000

Dennis Roberts* · (Federal Court, State Court) · 370 Grand Avenue · Oakland, CA 94610 · 415-465-6363

George W. Porter, Jr. · Covington & Crowe · 1131 West Sixth Street · P.O. Box 1515 · Ontario, CA 91762 · 714-983-9393

Gary C. Scherotter* · Heritage Square · 901 Tahquitz Way, Suite C-203 · P.O. Box 2224 · Palm Springs, CA 92262 · 619-320-7111

Thomas J. Nolan* · Nolan & Armstrong · 600 University Avenue · Palo Alto, CA 94301 · 415-326-2980

Virginia M. Blumenthal · Blumenthal & Lomazow · The Riverside Barrister Building · 3993 Market Street · Riverside, CA 92501 · 714-682-5110

Steven L. Harmon* · Bridges and Harmon · Mission Square Plaza, Suite 240 · 3750 University Avenue · Riverside, CA 92501 · 714-682-2760

Gerald D. Polis · 3750 University Avenue, Suite 630 · Riverside, CA 92501 · 714-684-0131

Clyde M. Blackmon* · Blackmon & Drozd · 660 J Street, Suite 260 · Sacramento, CA 95814 · 916-441-0824

Michael Rothschild · Rothschild, Yim & Zappettini · 1303 H Street · Sacramento, CA 95814 · 916-446-4505

Michael S. Sands* · 800 Ninth Street, Third Floor · Sacramento, CA 95814 · 916-444-9845

Thomas S. Worthington* · (Violent Crimes, Non-Violent Crimes, Child Abuse) Civic Center Building, Suite 101 · 21 West Alisal Street · Salinas, CA 93901 · 408-758-1688

Juanita R. Brooks* · (Federal Court, White Collar Crimes) · 550 West C Street, Suite 1750 · San Diego, CA 92101 · 619-232-8118

John J. Cleary* · Cleary & Sevilla · 1010 Second Avenue, Suite 1601 · San Diego, CA 92101-4906 · 619-232-2222

Charles L. Goldberg · Goldberg, Frant & Hall · 2870 Fourth Avenue, Suite 100 San Diego, CA 92103 · 619-232-6671

Peter J. Hughes* · (Federal Court, State Court) · 1010 Second Avenue, Suite 1917 · San Diego, CA 92101 · 619-234-6695

Eugene G. Iredale · 625 Broadway · San Diego, CA 92101 · 619-233-1525

Michael Pancer · 625 Broadway, Suite 1140 · San Diego, CA 92101 · 619-236-1826

Elisabeth Semel · Semel & Feldman · 225 Broadway, Suite 810 · San Diego, CA 92101 · 619-236-9384

Charles M. Sevilla · Cleary & Sevilla · 1010 Second Avenue, Suite 1601 · San Diego, CA 92101-4906 · 619-232-2222

Milton J. Silverman* · (Plaintiffs) · The Quartermass-Wilde House · 2404 Broadway · San Diego, CA 92102 · 619-231-6611

William A. Brockett, Jr. · Keker & Brockett · 710 Samson Street · San Francisco, CA 94111 · 415-391-5400

James J. Brosnahan · Morrison & Foerster · 345 California Street, 35th Floor · San Francisco, CA 94104-2675 · 415-677-7000

Gilbert Eisenberg* · Filippelli & Eisenberg · 632 Commercial Street · San Francisco, CA 94111 · 415-433-3476

Patrick S. Hallinan · Hallinan, Poplack & Levine · 345 Franklin Street · San Francisco, CA 94102 · 415-861-1151

Susan B. Jordan* · (Violent Crimes, Non-Violent Crimes, Federal Court, State Court, Environmental Crimes) · 170 Columbus Street · San Francisco, CA 94133 707-462-2151

John W. Keker · Keker & Brockett · 710 Samson Street · San Francisco, CA 94111 415-391-5400

James Larson* · 632 Commercial Street, Third Floor · San Francisco, CA 94111 415-781-1800

Ephraim Margolin* · (Violent Crimes, Non-Violent Crimes, Federal Court, State Court) · Union Square · 240 Stockton Street, Suite 300 · San Francisco, CA 94108 415-421-4347

William L. Osterhoudt* · Law Offices of William L. Osterhoudt · 423 Washington Street, Third Floor · San Francisco, CA 94111 · 415-981-2122

Douglas R. Schmidt · Winslow & Schmidt · 3223 Webster Street · San Francisco, CA 94123 · 415-441-5943

M. Gerald Schwartzbach · (Violent Crimes, Non-Violent Crimes, Federal Court, State Court) · Law Offices of M. Gerald Schwartzbach · 901 Market Street, Suite 230 · San Francisco, CA 94103 · 415-777-3828

J. Tony Serra · Serra, Perelson, Anton, Lichter, Daar & Bustamante · 473 Jackson Street · San Francisco, CA 94111 · 415-986-5591

Marcus S. Topel* · (White-Collar Crimes, Federal Court, State Court, Complex Murder Cases) · Topel & Goodman · 832 Sansome Street, Fourth Floor · San Francisco, CA 94111 · 415-421-6140

George G. Walker · Law Offices of George G. Walker · 633 Battery, Suite 635 · San Francisco, CA 94111 · 415-421-6911

Doron Weinberg* · Law Offices of Doron Weinberg · 523 Octavia Street · San Francisco, CA 94102 · 415-431-3472

Guyton N. Jinkerson* · (Violent Crimes, White Collar Crimes, Federal Court, State Court) · 152 North Third Street, fourth Floor · San Jose, CA 95115 · 408-293-0463

Steven R. Manchester · Manchester & Williams · 100 Park Center Plaza, Suite 525 · San Jose, CA 95113 · 408-287-6193

Allen J. Ruby · Morgan, Ruby, Teter, Schofield, Franich & Fredkin · 99 Almaden Boulevard, Suite 1000 · San Jose, CA 95113 · 408-288-8288

Frank R. Ubhaus · Berliner, Cohen & Biagini · 10 Almaden Boulevard, 11th Floor San Jose, CA 95113 · 408-286-5800

John L. Williams* · Manchester & Williams · 100 Park Center Plaza, Suite 525 · San Jose, CA 95113 · 408-287-6193

Keith C. Monroe · 1428 North Broadway · Santa Ana, CA 92706 · 714-835-3883

James D. Riddet · Aronson & Riddet · 2677 North Main Street, Suite 100 · Santa Ana, CA 92701 · 714-835-8600

Marshall M. Schulman · Schulman & McMillan · 401 Civic Center Drive West, Suite 707 · Santa Ana, CA 92701 · 714-542-3989

Allan H. Stokke* · (Violent Crimes, Non-Violent Crimes, State Court) · 888 West Santa Ana Boulevard, Suite 200 · Santa Ana, CA 92701-4561 · 714-543-7704

James A. Stotler · 2372 Southeast Bristol Street, Suite A · Santa Ana, CA 92707 714-756-8080

John M. Sink · 114 State Street, Suite 211 · Santa Barbara, CA 93101 · 805-963-4266

Bradley Wm. Brunon* · 2400 Broadway, Suite 500 · Santa Monica, CA 90404 · 213-453-2393

Gerald Chaleff* · (Violent Crimes, Non-Violent Crimes, State Court, Environmental Crimes) · Chaleff, English & Catalano · Garden Suite · 1337 Ocean Avenue · Santa Monica, CA 90401 · 213-458-1691

Richard G. Hirsch* · Nasatir & Hirsch · 2115 Main Street · Santa Monica, CA 90405 · 213-399-3259

Michael D. Nasatir* · Nasatir & Hirsch · Main Street Law Building · 2115 Main Street · Santa Monica, CA 90405 · 213-399-3259

Brian O'Neill* · O'Neill & Lysaght · 100 Wilshire Boulevard, Suite 700 · Santa Monica, CA 90401-1142 · 213-451-5700

Victor Sherman · 2115 Main Street · Santa Monica, CA 90405 · 213-399-3259

Susan B. Jordan* · (Violent Crimes, Non-Violent Crimes, Federal Court, State Court, Environmental Crimes) · 514 South School Street · Ukiah, CA 95482 · 707-462-2151

ENTERTAINMENT LAW

Jay L. Cooper · (Film, Musical, Literary, Television) · Cooper, Epstein & Hurewitz · Maple Plaza · 345 North Maple Drive, Suite 300 · Beverly Hills, CA 90210-3863 · 213-278-1111

Jeffrey L. Nagin · Rosenfeld, Meyer & Susman · First Interstate Bank Building, Fourth Floor · 9601 Wilshire Boulevard · Beverly Hills, CA 90210 · 213-858-7700

Allen E. Susman · Rosenfeld, Meyer & Susman · First Interstate Bank Building, Fourth Floor · 9601 Wilshire Boulevard · Beverly Hills, CA 90210 · 213-858-7700

Eric Weissmann · (Film) · Weissmann, Wolff, Bergman, Coleman & Silverman · 9665 Wilshire Boulevard, Suite 900 · P.O. Box 5592 · Beverly Hills, CA 90209-5592 · 213-858-7888

Jacob A. Bloom · Bloom, Dekom and Hergott · 9255 Sunset Boulevard, 10th Floor · Los Angeles, CA 90069 · 213-278-8622

John G. Branca · Ziffren, Brittenham & Branca · 2121 Avenue of the Stars, 32nd Floor · Los Angeles, CA 90067 · 213-552-3388

Harry M. Brittenham · Ziffren, Brittenham & Branca · 2121 Avenue of the Stars, 32nd Floor · Los Angeles, CA 90067 · 213-552-3388

Peter J. Dekom · Bloom, Dekom & Hergott · 9255 Sunset, Suite 1011 · Los Angeles, CA 90069 · 213-859-6885

Donald S. Engel · Engel & Engel · 9200 Sunset Boulevard, Suite 505 · Los Angeles, CA 90069 · 213-550-7178

Bertram Fields* · Greenberg, Glusker, Fields, Claman & Machtinger · 1900 Building, 20th Floor · 1900 Avenue of the Stars · Los Angeles, CA 90067-4599 · 213-553-3610

John T. Frankenheimer · Loeb and Loeb · 10100 Santa Monica Boulevard, Suite 2200 · Los Angeles, CA 90067 · 213-282-2000

Barry L. Hirsh · Armstron & Hirsch · 1888 Century Park East, 18th Floor · Los Angeles, CA 90067 · 213-553-0305

David Nochimson · Ziffren, Brittenham & Branca · 2121 Avenue of the Stars, 32nd Floor · Los Angeles, CA 90067 · 213-552-3388

Donald S. Passman · Gang, Tyre, Ramer & Brown · 6400 Sunset Building · Los Angeles, CA 90028-7392 · 213-463-4863

Donald V. Petroni · O'Melveny & Myers · 1999 Avenue of the Stars, Suite 700 Los Angeles, CA 90067 · 213-553-6700

L. Lee Phillips · Manatt, Phelps & Phillips · Trident Center, East Tower · 11355 Olympic Boulevard · Los Angeles, CA 90064 · 213-312-4000

Bruce M. Ramer · Gang, Tyre, Ramer & Brown · 6400 Sunset Building · Los Angeles, CA 90028-7392 · 213-463-4863

Charles D. Silverberg · Silverberg, Katz, Thompson, Braun & Klein · One Century Plaza, Suite 1900 · 11766 Wilshire Boulevard, Suite 700 · Los Angeles, CA 90025 · 213-445-5800

Payson Wolff · (Musical) · Gang, Tyre, Ramer & Brown · 6400 Sunset Building Los Angeles, CA 90028-7392 · 213-463-4863

Kenneth Ziffren · Ziffren, Brittenham & Branca · 2121 Avenue of the Stars, 32nd Floor · Los Angeles, CA 90067 · 213-552-3388

John E. Mason, Jr. · Mason & Gilbert · Wilshire Palisades Building, Penthouse 1299 Ocean Avenue · Santa Monica, CA 90401 · 213-393-5345

Owen J. Sloane · 100 Wilshire Boulevard, Suite 2000 · Santa Monica, CA 90401 213-393-5345

FAMILY LAW

Harry M. Fain · Law Offices of Harry M. Fain · 121 South Beverly Drive · Beverly Hills, CA 90212 · 213-275-5132

Daniel J. Jaffe* · Jaffe & Clemens · 433 North Camden Drive, Suite 1000 · Beverly Hills, CA 90210 · 213-550-7477

David Keene Leavitt · (Adoption) · 9454 Wilshire Boulevard, Suite 200 · Beverly Hills, CA 90212 · 213-273-3151

Richard C. Berra · (Marital Settlement Agreements, Mediation & Special Master) Carr, McClellan, Ingersoll, Thompson & Horn · Security Pacific Building · 216 Park Road · P.O. Box 513 · Burlingame, CA 94011-0513 · 415-342-9600

Madeleine Simborg · Diamond, Bennington & Simborg · 300 Tamal Plaza, Suite 280 · Corte Madera, CA 94925 · 415-924-8870

S. Michael Love · McDougal, Love, Eckis, Grindle & O'Connor · 460 North Magnolia Street · P.O. Drawer 1466 · El Cajon, CA 92022-1466 · 619-440-4444

Ruth Miller · (Child Custody, Divorce, Marital Settlement Agreements, Mediation) · Davidson & Miller · 563 Pilgrim Drive, Suite D · Foster City, CA 94404 · 415-574-1215

Stephen A. Kalemkarian · 371 East Bullard Avenue, Suite 115 · Fresno, CA 93710 · 209-435-2525

William T. Richert · Lang, Richert & Patch · 2307 North Fine Avenue · Fresno, CA 93727 · 209-252-3600

Jerome L. Goldberg* · Goldberg and Andrus · 333 South Grand Avenue, Suite 1880 · Los Angeles, CA 90071 · 213-680-2616

Paul Gutman* · 1801 Century Park East, Suite 2211 · Los Angeles, CA 90067-2324 · 213-556-8999

A. David Kagon · Goldman & Kagon · 1801 Century Park East, Suite 2222 · Los Angeles, CA 90067 · 213-552-1707

Gerald E. Lichtig · Lichtig, Ellis and Meyberg · 11111 Santa Monica Boulevard, Suite 930 · Los Angeles, CA 90025 · 213-473-8899

Ira H. Lurvey* · (Child Custody, Marital Settlement Agreements, Community Property Division, Complex Assets) · Lurvey & Shapiro · 2121 Avenue of the Stars, Suite 1550 · Los Angeles, CA 90067 · 213-203-0711

S. David Rosenson · Wasser, Rosenson & Carter · One Century Plaza, Suite 1200 2029 Century Park East · Los Angeles, CA 90067 · 213-277-7117

Joseph Taback · 2029 Century Park East, Suite 2860 · Los Angeles, CA 90067 · 213-557-1200

Sorrell Trope · Trope & Trope · 12121 Wilshire Boulevard, Suite 801 · Los Angeles, CA 90025 · 213-879-2726

Dennis M. Wasser* · Wasser, Rosenson & Carter · One Century Plaza, Suite 1200 2029 Century Park East · Los Angeles, CA 90067 · 213-277-7117

O. A. John Goth* · (Divorce, Marital Settlement Agreements, Private Adjudication) · Goth & Silvestri · Menlo Suite 300 · 1010 El Camino Real · Menlo Park, CA 94025 · 415-322-2828

Dennis A. Cornell* · 728 West 19th Street · Merced, CA 95340 · 209-725-0804

Ronald A. Wagner · Hardin, Cook, Loper, Engel & Bergez · 1999 Harrison Street, 18th Floor · Oakland, CA 94612 · 415-444-3131

Michael E. Wald · Wald, Freedman, Chapman & Bendes · 1999 Harrison Street, Suite 1900 · Oakland, CA 94612 · 415-444-0560

William S. Love · Thoits, Love, Hershberger & McLean · 525 University Avenue Palo Alto, CA 94301 · 415-327-4200

George H. Norton · Lakin Spears · 285 Hamilton Avenue · P.O. Box 240 · Palo Alto, CA 94301 · 415-328-7000

Lee A. Lopez* · (Divorce, Marital Settlement Agreements, Equitable Division) · Simpson, Maire & Lopez · P.O. Drawer 4607 · Redding, CA 96099 · 916-243-1265

Francis A. Watson, Jr. · Watson, Hoffe & Barbieri · 3700 Barrett Avenue · Richmond, CA 94805 · 415-237-3700

Michael H. Clepper · 4192 Brockton Avenue, Suite 203 · Riverside, CA 92501 · 714-684-5530

Anthony S. Dick* · (Divorce, Marital Settlement Agreements, Equitable Division, Support) · Dick, Wasserman & Wagner · 797 University Avenue · Sacramento, CA 95825 · 916-920-9504

Robert J. O'Hair · Woodruff, O'Hair & Posner · 641 Fulton Avenue, Suite 200 · Sacramento, CA 95825 · 916-488-9334

Stephen James Wagner* · (Divorce, Marital Settlement Agreements, Property Valuation & Division) · Dick, Wasserman & Wagner · 797 University Avenue · Sacramento, CA 95825 · 916-920-9504

David L. Wasserman · Dick, Wasserman & Wagner · 797 University Avenue · Sacramento, CA 95825 · 916-920-9504

D. Thomas Woodruff* · (Divorce, Marital Settlement Agreements, Litigation) · Woodruff, O'Hair & Posner · 641 Fulton Avenue, Suite 200 · Sacramento, CA 95825 · 916-488-9334

Gerald L. Barry, Jr. · Barry & Pike · 520 West Ash Street, Suite 200 · San Diego, CA 92101 · 619-238-1234

Edward B. Huntington · (Taxation) · Huntington & Haviland · 1551 Fourth Avenue, Suite 700 · San Diego, CA 92101-3155 · 619-233-9500

John W. Lightner · Lightner, Castro, Schaefer & Schatz · 3104 Fourth Avenue · San Diego, CA 92103-5884 · 619-291-4500

Gary E. Pike · Barry & Pike · 520 West Ash Street, Suite 200 · San Diego, CA 92101 · 619-238-1234

Bonnie Nelson Reading* · Seltzer Caplan Wilkins & McMahon · 3003-3043 Fourth Avenue · P.O. Box X 33999 · San Diego, CA 92103 · 619-295-3003

Nordin F. Blacker* · (Adoption, Child Custody, Divorce, Marital Settlement Agreements) · Little Fox Building · 535 Pacific Avenue, First Floor · San Francisco, CA 94133 · 415-397-3222

C. Rick Chamberlin · Richmond & Chamberlin · 595 Market Street, Suite 2860 San Francisco, CA 94105 · 415-543-2990

Christopher Emley · (Child Custody) · Law Offices of Christopher Emley · 530 Bush Street, Suite 500 · San Francisco, CA 94108-3623 · 415-433-6166

Max Gutierrez, Jr. · Brobeck, Phleger & Harrison · Spear Street Tower · One Market Plaza · San Francisco, CA 94105 · 415-442-0900

Pamela E. Pierson* · (Child Custody) · Pierson & Toben · 685 Market Street, Suite 770 · San Francisco, CA 94105 · 415-495-4499

Diana Richmond* · (Child Custody, Divorce, Marital Settlement Agreements, Prenuptial Agreements, Mediation & Private Judging) · Richmond & Chamberlin 595 Market Street, Suite 2860 · San Francisco, CA 94105 · 415-543-2990

Merrill E. Steinberg · Leland, Parachini, Steinberg, Flinn, Matzger & Melnick · 333 Market Street, 27th Floor · San Francisco, CA 94105 · 415-957-1800

Lawrence H. Stotter · Stotter & Coats · 1772 Vallejo Street · San Francisco, CA 94123 · 415-928-5050

Lowell H. Sucherman* · Sucherman & Collins · 88 Kearny Street, Suite 1750 · San Francisco, CA 94108 · 415-956-5554

William L. Dok* · Dok, Levy & Perrin · 1550 The Alameda, Suite 300 · San Jose, CA 95126 · 408-287-7790

Philip L. Hammer* · (Child Custody, Divorce, Marital Settlement Agreements, Complex Property Issues) · Hammer & Jacobs · 1960 The Alameda, Suite 140 · San Jose, CA 95126 · 408-243-8200

Hugh T. Thomson · 2060 The Alameda · San Jose, CA 95126 · 408-247-2301

Harry A. Hanson, Jr.* · Hanson & Norris · 777 Mariners Island Boulevard, Suite 575 · San Mateo, CA 94404-1562 · 415-571-0600

Verna A. Adams* · Adams & Dornan · 633 Fifth Avenue · San Rafael, CA 94901-3214 · 415-454-8980

Richard F. Barry · 1000 Fourth Street, Suite 350 · P.O. Box 151257 · San Rafael, CA 94915-1257 · 415-453-0360

Cecilia D. Lannon · 2022 Fourth Street · San Rafael, CA 94901 · 415-457-0770

John P. McCall* · Riede & McCall · Courthouse Square, Suite 500 · 1000 Fourth Street · San Rafael, CA 94901 · 415-454-9880

James K. Batchelor* · (Child Custody, Divorce, Marital Settlement Agreements, Prenuptial Agreements) · 829 North Parton Street, Suite 1A · Santa Ana, CA 92701 714-542-2333

David L. Price · 600 West Santa Ana Boulevard, Suite 900 · Santa Ana, CA 92701 714-953-6831

Gertrude D. Chern · Chern, Brenneman & Garcia · 625 East Chapel · Santa Maria, CA 93454 · 805-922-4553

James A. Hennenhoefer · 316 South Melrose Drive, Suite 200 · Vista, CA 92083 619-941-2260

Steven D. Hallert · Hallert & Hallert · 710 South Broadway, Suite 312 · Walnut Creek, CA 94596 · 415-933-4033

FIRST AMENDMENT LAW

Rex S. Heinke · Gibson, Dunn & Crutcher · 333 South Grand Avenue · Los Angeles, CA 90071 · 213-229-7000

Robert S. Warren · Gibson, Dunn & Crutcher · 333 South Grand Avenue · Los Angeles, CA 90071 · 213-229-7326

John E. Carne · Crosby, Heafey, Roach & May · 1999 Harrison Street · Oakland, CA 94612 · 415-763-2000

Judith R. Epstein · (Defendants) · Crosby, Heafey, Roach & May · 1999 Harrison Street · Oakland, CA 94612 · 415-763-2000

James D. Ward* · Thompson & Colegate · 3610 Fourteenth Street · P.O. Box 1299 · Riverside, CA 92502 · 714-682-5550

Charity Kenyon · Diepenbrock, Wulff, Plant & Hannegan · 300 Capitol Mall, Suite 1700 · P.O. Box 3034 · Sacramento, CA 95812-3034 · 916-444-3910

Marilyn L. Huff · Gray, Cary, Ames & Frye · 1700 First Interstate Plaza · 401 B Street · San Diego, CA 92101-4219 · 619-699-2700

James J. Brosnahan · Morrison & Foerster · 345 California Street · San Francisco, CA 94104-2675 · 415-677-7000

Edward P. Davis, Jr. · Pillsbury Madison & Sutro · 225 Bush Street · P.O. Box 7880 · San Francisco, CA 94120 · 415-983-1000

Neil L. Shapiro · Brobeck, Phleger & Harrison · Spear Street Tower · One Market Plaza · San Francisco, CA 94105 · 415-442-0900

HEALTH CARE LAW

Robert J. Gerst · (Nursing Homes) · Weissburg & Aronson · 2049 Century Park East, Suite 3200 · Los Angeles, CA 90067 · 213-277-2223

Robert D. Girard · Jones, Day, Reavis & Pogue · 355 South Grand Avenue, Suite 3000 · Los Angeles, CA 90071 · 213-625-3939

Mark A. Kadzielski · (Medical Staff Issues) · Weissburg & Aronson · 2049 Century Park East, Suite 3200 · Los Angeles, CA 90067 · 213-277-2223

J. Robert Liset · Music, Peeler & Garrett · One Wilshire Boulevard, Suite 2000 Los Angeles, CA 90017 · 213-629-7683

James E. Ludlam · Music, Peeler & Garrett · One Wilshire Boulevard, Suite 2000 Los Angeles, CA 90017 · 213-629-7683

Douglas M. Mancino · McDermitt Will & Emery · 2029 Century Park East, 38th Floor · Los Angeles, CA 90067 · 213-277-4110

Ross E. Stromberg · Jones, Day, Reavis & Pogue · 355 South Grand Avenue, Suite 3000 · Los Angeles, CA 90071 · 213-625-3939

Carl Weissburg · Weissburg & Aronson · 2049 Century Park East, Suite 3200 · Los Angeles, CA 90067 · 213-277-2223

Gary F. Loveridge · McDonough, Holland & Allen · 555 Capitol Mall, Suite 950 · Sacramento, CA 95814 · 916-444-3900

T. Knox Bell · Gray, Cary, Ames & Frye · 1700 First Interstate Plaza · 401 B Street · San Diego, CA 92101-4219 · 619-699-2700

Thomas C. Geiser · (Managed Care) · Brobeck, Phleger & Harrison · Spear Street Tower · One Market Plaza · San Francisco, CA 94105 · 415-442-0900

Daniel B. Higgins · McCutchen, Doyle, Brown & Enersen · Three Embarcadero Center · San Francisco, CA 94111 · 415-393-2000

Carl H. Hitchner · Weissburg & Aronson · 555 Montgomery Street · San Francisco, CA 94014 · 415-434-4484

IMMIGRATION LAW

Angelo A. Paparelli · (Business Visa) · Bryan, Cave, McPheeters & McRoberts · 18881 Von Karman · Irvine, CA 92715-1500 · 714-757-8100

Ronald H. Bonaparte · Law Offices of Ronald H. Bonaparte · 11911 San Vicente Boulevard, Suite 355 · Los Angeles, CA 90049 · 213-471-3481

Josie Gonzalez · (Business Immigration, Employer Sanctions) · Gonzalez & Harris · 1805 North Vine Street · Los Angeles, CA 90028 · 213-469-8848

Peter N. Larrabee · Gray, Cary, Ames & Frye · 1700 First Interstate Plaza · 401 B Street · San Diego, CA 92101-4219 · 619-699-2700

Robert A. Mautino · Baxley & Mautino · 444 West C Street, Suite 320 · San Diego, CA 92101 · 619-235-9176

Gerald L. McVey · Law Offices Gerald L. McVey · 655 Montgomery Street, Suite 1150 · San Francisco, CA 94111 · 415-397-8291

Donald L. Ungar · Simmons, Ungar, Helbush, DiCostanzo & Steinberg · 517 Washington Street · San Francisco, CA 94111 · 415-421-0860

Frank D. Winston · Law Offices of Frank D. Winston · 101 California Street, 30th Floor · San Francisco, CA 94111-5833 · 415-434-7744

Polly A. Webber · 100 Park Center Plaza, Suite 530 · San Jose, CA 95113 · 408-947-7741

Charles M. Miller · The Miller Law Offices · 12441 Ventura Boulevard · Studio City, CA 91604 · 818-508-9005

INTELLECTUAL PROPERTY LAW

Kate H. Murashige · (Bio-Tech Patents) · Irell & Manella · 1800 Avenue of the Stars, Suite 900 · Los Angeles, CA 90067-4276 · 213-277-1010

Laurence H. Pretty · (Litigation) · Pretty, Schroeder, Brueggemann & Clark · 444 South Flower Street, Suite 2000 · Los Angeles, CA 90071 · 213-622-7700

Thomas E. Ciotti · (Bio-Tech Patents) · Irell & Manella · 545 Middlefield Road, Suite 200 · Menlo Park, CA 94025 · 415-327-7250

Ronald S. Laurie · (Computer Law) · Irell & Manella · 545 Middlefield Road, Suite 200 · Menlo Park, CA 94025 · 415-327-7250

G. Gervaise Davis · (Computer) · Schroeder, Davis & Orliss · 215 West Franklin Street, Fourth Floor · Monterey, CA 93940 · 408-649-1122

Lois W. Abraham · (High Tech Litigation) · Brown & Bain · 600 Hansen Way, Suite 100 · Palo Alto, CA 94306 · 415-856-9411

Neil Boorstyn · (Copyright) · McCutchen, Doyle, Brown & Enersen · Three Embarcadero Center · San Francisco, CA 94111 · 415-393-2000

Paul Goldstein · (Copyright) · Morrison & Foerster · 345 California Street · San Francisco, CA 94104-2675 · 415-723-0313

Carl A. Limbach · (Patent Litigation) · Limbach, Limbach & Sutton · 2001 Ferry Building · San Francisco, CA 94111 · 415-433-4150

J. Thomas McCarthy · (Trademark) · Limbach, Limbach & Sutton · 2001 Ferry Building · San Francisco, CA 94111 · 415-433-4150

Lynn H. Pasahow · (High Tech Litigation) · McCutchen, Doyle, Brown & Enersen · Three Embarcadero Center · San Francisco, CA 94111 · 415-393-2000

Neil A. Smith · (Trademark) · Limbach, Limbach & Sutton · 2001 Ferry Building San Francisco, CA 94111 · 415-433-4150

LABOR AND EMPLOYMENT LAW

A. Thomas Hunt* · (Employment Class Action) · The Wilshire San Vicente Plaza 8383 Wilshire Boulevard, Suite 7450 · Beverly Hills, CA 90211 · 213-653-4713

Leo Geffner · (Labor) · Taylor, Roth, Bush & Geffner · 3500 West Olive Avenue, Suite 1100 · Burbank, CA 91505 · 818-955-6400

Jay D. Roth · (Labor) · Taylor, Roth, Bush & Geffner · 3500 West Olive Avenue, Suite 1100 · Burbank, CA 91505 · 818-955-6400

John C. McCarthy* · (Individuals) · 401 Harvard Avenue · Claremont, CA 91711 714-621-4984

Howard C. Hay · (Management) · Paul, Hastings, Janofsky & Walker · 695 Town Center Drive, 17th Floor · Costa Mesa, CA 92626 · 714-668-6200

David C. Larsen · (Management) · Rutan & Tucker · Central Bank Tower, Suite 1400 · 611 Anton Boulevard · P.O. Box 1950 · Costa Mesa, CA 92628-1950 · 714-641-5100

Laurence P. Corbett · (Management) · Corbett & Kane · Watergate Tower III, Suite 1450 · 2000 Powell Street · Emeryville, CA 94608 · 415-547-2434

Joseph Posner · (Individuals) · 16311 Ventura Boulevard, Suite 555 · Encino, CA 91436 · 818-990-1340

James N. Adler · (Management) · Irell & Manella · 1800 Avenue of the Stars, Suite 900 · Los Angeles, CA 90067-4276 · 213-277-1010

Gloria R. Allred · (Individuals) · Allred, Maroko, Goldberg & Ribakoff · 6380 Wilshire Boulevard, Suite 1404 · Los Angeles, CA 90048 · 213-653-6530

Kenneth W. Anderson · (Management) · Gibson, Dunn & Crutcher · 333 South Grand Avenue · Los Angeles, CA 90071 · 213-229-7000

Paul W. Cane, Jr. · (Management) · Paul, Hastings, Janofsky & Walker · 555 South Flower Street, 23rd Floor · Los Angeles, CA 90071 · 213-683-6000

Willard Z. Carr, Jr. · (Management) · Gibson, Dunn & Crutcher · 333 South Grand Avenue · Los Angeles, CA 90071 · 213-229-7000

David A. Cathcart* · (Management) · Gibson, Dunn & Crutcher · 333 South Grand Avenue · Los Angeles, CA 90071 · 213-229-7000

Walter Cochran-Bond* · (Management) · Proskauer Rose Goetz & Mendelsohn 2121 Avenue of the Stars, Suite 2700 · Los Angeles, CA 90067-5010 · 213-557-2900

Richard J. Davis, Jr. · (Labor) · Pappy & Davis · 3424 Wilshire Boulevard, Suite 1100 · Los Angeles, CA 90010 · 213-385-3071

Robert M. Dohrmann · (Labor) · Schwartz, Steinsapir, Dohrmann & Sommers · 3580 Wilshire Boulevard, Suite 1820 · Los Angeles, CA 90010 · 213-487-5700

William J. Emanuel · (Management) · Morgan, Lewis & Bockius · 801 South Grand Avenue, 20th Floor · Los Angeles, CA 90017-3189 · 213-612-2500

Alan V. Friedman · (Management) · Munger, Tolles & Olson · 355 South Grand Avenue, 35th Floor · Los Angeles, CA 90071-1560 · 213-683-9100

Nathan Goldberg · (Individuals) · Allred, Maroko, Goldberg & Ribakoff · 6380 Wilshire Boulevard, Suite 1404 · Los Angeles, CA 90048 · 213-653-6530

Paul Grossman* · (Management) · Paul, Hastings, Janofsky & Walker · 555 South Flower Street, 23rd Floor · Los Angeles, CA 90071 · 213-683-6000

Joseph E. Herman · (Management) · Seyfarth, Shaw, Fairweather & Geraldson 2029 Century Park East, Suite 3300 · Los Angeles, CA 90067 · 213-277-7200

Gordon E. Krischer · (Management) · O'Melveny & Myers · 400 South Hope Street, Suite 1060 · Los Angeles, CA 90071-2899 · 213-669-6000

Michael Maroko · (Individuals) · Allred, Maroko, Goldberg & Ribakoff · 6380 Wilshire Boulevard, Suite 1404 · Los Angeles, CA 90048 · 213-653-6530

Anthony T. Oliver, Jr. · (Management) · Parker, Milliken, Clark, O'Hara & Samuelian · Security Pacific Plaza, 27th Floor · 333 South Hope Street · Los Angeles, CA 90071 · 213-683-6500

George A. Pappy · (Labor) · Pappy & Davis · 3424 Wilshire Boulevard, Suite 1100 Los Angeles, CA 90010 · 213-385-3071

Andrew C. Peterson* · (Management) · Paul, Hastings, Janofsky & Walker · 555 South Flower Street, 23rd Floor · Los Angeles, CA 90071 · 213-683-6000

Julius Reich · (Labor) · Reich, Adell & Crost · 501 Shatto Place, Suite 100 · Los Angeles, CA 90020 · 213-386-3860

Glenn Rothner · (Labor) · Reich, Adell & Crost · 501 Shatto Place, Suite 100 · Los Angeles, CA 90020 · 213-386-3860

Richard D. Sommers · (Labor) · Schwartz, Steinsapir, Dohrmann & Sommers · 3580 Wilshire Boulevard, Suite 1820 · Los Angeles, CA 90010 · 213-487-5700

Laurence D. Steinsapir · (Labor) · Schwartz, Steinsapir, Dohrmann & Sommers 3580 Wilshire Boulevard, Suite 1820 · Los Angeles, CA 90010 · 213-487-5700

William Stewart Waldo · (Management) · Paul, Hastings, Janofsky & Walker · 555 South Flower Street, 23rd Floor · Los Angeles, CA 90071 · 213-683-6000

John S. Welch · (Management) · Latham & Watkins · 633 West Fifth Street, Suite 4000 · Los Angeles, CA 90071-2007 · 213-891-8292

Kenneth E. Ristau, Jr. · (Management) · Gibson, Dunn & Crutcher · 800 Newport Center Drive, Suite 700 · P.O. Box 2490 · Newport Beach, CA 92660 · 714-759-3800

Richard C. White · (Management) · O'Melveny & Myers · Union Bank Building, Suite 1700 · 610 Newport Center Drive · Newport Beach, CA 92660-6429 · 714-760-9600

Timothy J. Murphy* · (Management) · Crosby, Heafey, Roach & May · 1999 Harrison Street · Oakland, CA 94612 · 415-763-2000

Guy T. Saperstein* · (Individuals) · Saperstein, Seligman, Mayeda & Larkin · 1300 Clay Street, 11th Floor · Oakland, CA 94612 · 415-763-9800

Brad S. Seligman* · (Class Action, Privacy) · Saperstein, Seligman, Mayeda & Larkin · 1300 Clay Street, 11th Floor · Oakland, CA 94612 · 415-763-9800

Paul E. Crost · (Labor) · Reich, Adell & Crost · 1918 West Chapman Avenue, Suite 205 · Orange, CA 92668-2654 · 714-978-6451

Raymond L. Wheeler* · (Management) · Morrison & Foerster · 630 Hansen Way · Palo Alto, CA 94304-1014 · 415-354-1156

Robert W. Bell, Jr. · (Management) · Gray, Cary, Ames & Frye · 1700 First Interstate Plaza · 401 B Street · San Diego, CA 92101-4219 · 619-699-2700

John D. Collins · (Management) · Sheppard, Mullin, Richter & Hampton · 501 West Broadway, Suite 1900 · San Diego, CA 92101 · 619-338-6500

Brian D. Monaghan · (Individuals) · Monaghan & Strauss · 1450 Front Street · San Diego, CA 92101 · 619-231-0059

Josiah L. Neeper · (Management) · Gray, Cary, Ames & Frye · 1700 First Interstate Plaza · 401 B Street · San Diego, CA 92101-4219 · 619-699-2700

Douglas F. Olins · (Labor) · Olins, Foerster & Siegel · 2214 Second Avenue · San Diego, CA 92101 · 619-238-1601

Richard A. Paul · (Management) · Gray, Cary, Ames & Frye · 1700 First Interstate Plaza · 401 B Street · San Diego, CA 92101-4219 · 619-699-2700

Richard D. Prochazka · (Labor) · Prochazka, McGrath & Cortez · 5333 Mission Center Road, Suite 220 · San Diego, CA 92108 · 619-296-7677

James K. Smith · (Management) · Gray, Cary, Ames & Frye · 1700 First Interstate Plaza · 401 B Street · San Diego, CA 92101-4219 · 619-699-2700

Fern M. Steiner · (Labor) · Georgiou & Tosdal · 600 B Street, Suite 1515 · San Diego, CA 92101-4506 · 619-239-7200

Thomas L. Tosdal* · (Labor) · Georgiou & Tosdal · 600 B Street, Suite 1515 · San Diego, CA 92101-4506 · 619-239-7200

John L. Anderson · (Labor) · Neyhart, Anderson, Nussbaum, Reilly & Freitas · 568 Howard Street · P.O. Box 7426 · San Francisco, CA 94120 · 415-495-4949

Douglas H. Barton · (Management) · Hanson, Bridget, Marcus, Vlahos & Rudy 333 Market Street, 23rd Floor · San Francisco, CA 94105 · 415-777-3200

Duane B. Beeson · (Labor) · Beeson, Tayer & Silbert · 100 Bush Street, Suite 1500 · San Francisco, CA 94104 · 415-986-4060

Marsha S. Berzon · (Labor, Appellate) · Altshuler, Berzon, Nussbaum, Berzon & Rubin · 177 Post Street, Suite 300 · San Francisco, CA 94108 · 415-421-7151

William H. Carder · Leonard, Zuckerman, Ross, Chin & Remar · 1188 Franklin Street · San Francisco, CA 94109-6839 · 415-771-6400

Gilmore F. Diekmann, Jr. · (Management) · Bronson, Bronson & McKinnon · 505 Montgomery Street, 11th Floor · San Francisco, CA 94111 · 415-986-4200

Alan B. Exelrod* · (Individuals) · 660 Market Street, Suite 300 · San Francisco, CA 94104-5014 · 415-392-2800

Wesley J. Fastiff · (Management) · Littler, Mendelson, Fastiff & Tichy · 650 California Street, 20th Floor · San Francisco, CA 94108 · 415-433-1940

Barry S. Jellison · (Labor) · Davis, Cowell & Bowe · 100 Van Ness Street, 20th Floor · San Francisco, CA 94102 · 415-626-1880

Robert M. Lieber · (Management) · Littler, Mendelson, Fastiff & Tichy · 650 California Street, 20th Floor · San Francisco, CA 94108 · 415-433-1940

John A. McGuinn · (Individuals) · McGuinn, Hillsman & Palefsky · 535 Pacific Avenue · San Francisco, CA 94133 · 415-421-9292

Stanley H. Neyhart · (Labor) · Neyhart, Anderson, Nussbaum, Reilly & Freitas 568 Howard Street · P.O. Box 7426 · San Francisco, CA 94120 · 415-495-4949

Peter D. Nussbaum · (Labor) · Allshuler, Berzon, Nussbaum, Berzon & Rubin · 177 Post Street, Suite 300 · P.O. Box 7426 · San Francisco, CA 94128 · 415-421-7151

Cliff Palefsky · (Individuals) · McGuinn, Hillsman & Palefsky · 535 Pacific Avenue · San Francisco, CA 94133 · 415-421-9292

James C. Paras · (Management) · Morrison & Foerster · 345 California Street · San Francisco, CA 94104-2675 · 415-677-7000

Mark S. Rudy · (Individuals) · Law Offices of Rudy & Zieff · 530 Bush Street, Suite 500 · San Francisco, CA 94108 · 415-433-6166

Jonathan H. Sakol · (Management) · McCutchen, Doyle, Brown & Enersen · Three Embarcadero Center · San Francisco, CA 94111 · 415-393-2000

Victor Schachter · Schachter, Kristoff, Ross, Sprague & Curiale · 505 Montgomery Street, 14th Floor · San Francisco, CA 94111 · 415-391-3333

Kenneth N. Silbert · Beeson, Tayer, Silbert, Bodine & Livingston · 100 Bush Street, Suite 1500 · San Francisco, CA 94104-3982 · 415-986-4060

Donald S. Tayer · (Labor) · Beeson, Tayer, Silbert, Bodine & Livingston · 100 Bush Street, Suite 1500 · San Francisco, CA 94104 · 415-986-4060

Victor J. Van Bourg · (Labor) · Van Bourg, Weinberg, Roger & Rosenfeld · 875 Battery Street · San Francisco, CA 94111 · 415-864-4000

Charles E. Voltz · (Management) · Pillsbury Madison & Sutro · 225 Bush Street P.O. Box 7880 · San Francisco, CA 94120-7880 · 415-983-1000

Stewart Weinberg · (Labor) · Van Bourg, Weinberg, Roger & Rosenfeld · 875 Battery Street · San Francisco, CA 94111 · 415-864-4000

M. Kirby C. Wilcox · (Management) · Morrison & Foerster · 345 California Street, 35th Floor · San Francisco, CA 94104-2675 · 415-677-7000

Nancy L. Abell* · (Management) · Paul, Hastings, Janofsky & Walker · 1299 Ocean Avenue, Fifth Floor · Santa Monica, CA 90401 · 213-451-1200

Robert F. Walker · (Management) · Paul, Hastings, Janofsky & Walker · 1299 Ocean Avenue, Suite 313 · Santa Monica, CA 90401 · 213-319-3300

MARITIME LAW

Lawrence D. Bradley, Jr.* · Pillsbury Madison & Sutro · Citicorp Plaza, Suite 1200 · 725 South Figueroa Street · Los Angeles, CA 90017-2513 · 213-488-7100

Robert E. Coppola · Baker, Hostetler, McCutchen & Black · 600 Wilshire Boulevard, Suite 1200 · Los Angeles, CA 90017 · 213-624-2400

Gordon K. Wright · Pillsbury Madison & Sutro · Citicorp Plaza, Suite 1200 · 725 South Figueroa Street · Los Angeles, CA 90017-2513 · 213-488-7100

William L. Banning · Pillsbury Madison & Sutro · 101 West Broadway, 18th Floor San Diego, CA 92101 · 619-544-3167

John Allen Flynn* · (Charter Parties, Personal Injury, Collision & Limitation of Liability) · Graham & James · Alcoa Building · One Maritime Plaza, Suite 300 · San Francisco, CA 94111 · 415-954-0200

D. Thomas McCune · (Charter Parties) · Lillick & Charles · Two Embarcadero Center, 26th Floor · San Francisco, CA 94111-3996 · 415-984-8200

Norman B. Richards · McCutchen, Doyle, Brown & Enersen · Three Embarcadero Center, Suite 1800 · San Francisco, CA 94111 · 415-393-2000

Graydon S. Staring · Lillick & Charles · Two Embarcadero Center, 26th Floor · San Francisco, CA 94111-3996 · 415-984-8200

NATURAL RESOURCES AND ENVIRONMENTAL LAW

Bryant C. Danner · Latham & Watkins · 633 West Fifth Street, Suite 4000 · Los Angeles, CA 90071-2007 · 213-891-8292

Richard J. Denny · Baker, Hostetler, McCutchen & Black · 600 Wilshire Boulevard, Suite 1200 · Los Angeles, CA 90017 · 213-624-2400

Betty-Jane Kirwan · Latham & Watkins · 633 West Fifth Street, Suite 4000 · Los Angeles, CA 90071-2007 · 213-891-8292

Joel S. Moskowitz* · Gibson, Dunn & Crutcher · 333 South Grand Avenue · Los Angeles, CA 90071 · 213-229-7000

M. William Tilden · (Mining) · Gresham, Varner, Savage, Nolan & Tilden · 600 North Arrowhead Avenue, Suite 300 · San Bernardino, CA 92401 · 714-884-2171

David R. Andrews · McCutchen, Doyle, Brown & Enersen · Three Embarcadero Center · San Francisco, CA 94111 · 415-393-2000

Michael R. Barr · Pillsbury Madison & Sutro · 225 Bush Street · P.O. Box 7880 San Francisco, CA 94120 · 415-983-1000

James A. Bruen · Landels, Ripley & Diamond · 350 Stuart Street · San Francisco, CA 94105-1250 · 415-788-5000

Michelle B. Corash · (Environmental) · Morrison & Foerster, 32nd Floor · 345 California Street · San Francisco, CA 94104-2675 · 415-677-7206

Barry P. Goode · McCutchen, Doyle, Brown & Enersen · Three Embarcadero Center · San Francisco, CA 94111 · 415-393-2000

Ronald C. Hausmann · Tuttle & Taylor · 33 New Montgomery Tower, 19th Floor · 33 New Montgomery Street · San Francisco, CA 94105-9781 · 415-957-4303

Robert C. Thompson · Graham & James · One Maritime Plaza, Suite 300 · San Francisco, CA 94111 · 415-954-0200

PERSONAL INJURY LITIGATION

Joseph W. Cotchett* · (Plaintiffs) · Cotchett & Illston · 840 Malcolm Road, Suite 200 · Burlingame, CA 94010 · 415-697-6000

Herbert Hafif · (Plaintiffs) · 269 West Bonita Avenue · Claremont, CA 91711 · 714-624-1671

William M. Shernoff · (Plaintiffs) · Shernoff, Bidart & Darras · 600 South Indian Hill · Claremont, CA 91711 · 714-621-4935

Marrs A. Craddick* · (Defendants, Medical Malpractice) · Craddick, Candland & Conti · 915 San Ramon Valley Boulevard, Suite 260 · P.O. Box 810 · Danville, CA 94526-0810 · 415-838-1100

Robert Roden · (Plaintiffs) · Roden, Ahler and Thompson · 225 East Third Avenue · Escondido, CA 92025 · 619-745-1484

James J. Pagliuso* · (Plaintiffs) · 801 North Brand Boulevard, Suite 320 · Glendale, CA 91203 · 818-244-2253

Thomas T. Anderson · (Plaintiffs) · Anderson & Associates · 45-926 Oasis Street Indio, CA 92201 · 619-347-3364

Joseph E. Thielen* · (Plaintiffs, Medical Malpractice, Products Liability, Professional Malpractice) · Thielen and Burke · 3233 East Broadway · Long Beach, CA 90803 · 213-439-0991

Ried Bridges* · (Defendants, Medical Malpractice, Professional Malpractice) · Bonne, Jones, Bridges, Mueller & O'Keefe · Wilshire Serrano Building · 3699 Wilshire Boulevard, 10th Floor · Los Angeles, CA 90010-2719 · 213-480-1900

Daniel C. Cathcart* · (Plaintiffs) · Magana, Cathcart, McCarthy & Pierry · Gateway West Building, Suite 810 · 1801 Avenue of the Stars · Los Angeles, CA 90067 213-553-6630

Larry R. Feldman · (Plaintiffs, Products Liability, Professional Malpractice, Airplane Collision) · Fogel, Feldman, Ostrov, Ringer & Klevens · 5900 Wilshire Boulevard, 26th Floor · Los Angeles, CA 90036-5185 · 213-937-6250

Thomas V. Girardi · (Plaintiffs) · Girardi, Keese and Crane · 1126 Wilshire Boulevard · Los Angeles, CA 90017 · 213-489-5330

David M. Harney* · (Plaintiffs) · Law Offices of David M. Harney · 201 North Figueroa Street, Suite 1300 · Los Angeles, CA 90012-2636 · 213-482-0881

George R. Hillsinger · (Defendants) · Hillsinger and Costanzo · 3055 Wilshire Boulevard, Seventh Floor · Los Angeles, CA 90010 · 213-388-9441

Raoul D. Magana · (Plaintiffs) · Magana, Cathcart, McCarthy & Pierry · Gateway West Building, Suite 810 · 1801 Avenue of the Stars · Los Angeles, CA 90067 · 213-553-6630

James J. McCarthy · (Plaintiffs) · Magana, Cathcart, McCarthy & Pierry · Gateway West Building, Suite 810 · 1801 Avenue of the Stars · Los Angeles, CA 90067 213-553-6630

Wm. Marshall Morgan · (Defendants) · Morgan, Wenzel & McNicholas · TWA Tower, Suite 800 · 1545 Wilshire Boulevard · Los Angeles, CA 90017 · 213-483-1961

Kenneth N. Mueller · (Defendants) · Bonne, Jones, Bridges, Mueller & O'Keefe 3699 Wilshire Boulevard, 10th Floor · Los Angeles, CA 90010-2719 · 213-480-1900

David J. O'Keefe · (Defendants, Medical Malpractice, Products Liability, Professional Malpractice) · Bonne, Jones, Bridges, Mueller & O'Keefe · Wilshire Serrano Building · 3699 Wilshire Boulevard, 10th Floor · Los Angeles, CA 90010-2719 · 213-480-1900

Timothy L. Walker* · (Defendants) · Shield & Smith · 1055 Wilshire Boulevard, 19th Floor · Los Angeles, CA 90017-1902 · 213-482-3010

G. Dana Hobart* · (Plaintiffs) · 4676 Admiralty Way, Suite 801 · Marina Del Rey, CA 90292 · 213-306-0063

Lewis L. Fenton* · (Defendants, Medical Malpractice, Products Liability) · Hoge, Fenton, Jones & Appel · 2801 Monterey-Salinas Highway · P.O. Box 791 Monterey, CA 93942-0791 · 408-373-1241

Larry Grassini* · (Plaintiffs, Products Liability, Professional Malpractice, Automobile Collision) · Hurley, Grassini and Wrinkle · 11313 Weddington Street · P.O. Box 590 · North Hollywood, CA 91603-0590 · 213-877-5422

Edwin A. Heafey, Jr.* · (Defendants, Medical Malpractice, Products Liability, Professional Malpractice) · Crosby, Heafey, Roach & May · 1999 Harrison Street Oakland, CA 94612 · 415-763-2000

Raoul D. Kennedy* · (Defendants) · Crosby, Heafey, Roach & May · 1999 Harrison Street · Oakland, CA 94612 · 415-763-2000

Gerald P. Martin · Martin, Ryan & Andrada · Ordway Building, Suite 2275 · One Kaiser Plaza · Oakland, CA 94612 · 415-763-6510

Ronald G. Sproat* · (Defendants, Medical Malpractice, Professional Malpractice, Automobile Collision) · Rankin, Sproat & Pollack · 1800 Harrison Street, Suite 1616 · P.O. Box 28765 · Oakland, CA 94604 · 415-465-3922

John J. Collins* · (Defendants) · Collins, Collins, Muir & Traver · 265 North Euclid, Suite 300 · P.O. Box 93490 · Pasadena, CA 91109-3490 · 818-793-1163

Ned Good* · (Plaintiffs, Products Liability, Automobile Collision, Airplane Collision) · Law Offices of Ned Good · 70 South Lake Avenue, Suite 600 · Pasadena, CA 91101 · 818-440-0000

George E. Moore · (Plaintiffs) · Oliver, Sloan, Moore, Vargas, McMillian, Jacobs & Picl · 350 West Colorado Boulevard, Suite 400 · Pasadena, CA 91105 · 818-440-1111

John M. Bentley · (Defendants) · Ropers, Majeski, Kohn, Bentley, Wagner & Kane · 1001 Marshall Street · Redwood City, CA 94063 · 415-364-8200

Eugene J. Majeski · (Defendants) · Ropers, Majeski, Kohn, Bentley, Wagner & Kane · 1001 Marshall Street · Redwood City, CA 94063 · 415-364-8200

Don C. Brown · (Defendants, Medical Malpractice, Products Liability) · Thompson & Colegate · 3610 Fourteenth Street · P.O. Box 1299 · Riverside, CA 92502 714-682-5550

Theodore D. Bolling, Jr.* · (Defendants) · Bolling, Walter & Gawthrop · 7919 Folsom Boulevard, Suite 300 · P.O. Box 255200 · Sacramento, CA 95865-5200 · 916-386-0777

Edward Freidberg* · (Plaintiffs, Professional Malpractice) · Freidberg Law Corporation · 77 Cadillac Drive, Suite 240 · Sacramento, CA 95825 · 916-929-9060

Morton L. Friedman* · (Plaintiffs) · Friedman, Collard & Poswall · 7750 College Town Drive, Suite 300 · Sacramento, CA 95826 · 916-381-9011

Russell G. Porter · (Defendants) · Porter, Scott, Weiberg & Delehant · 350 University Avenue, Suite 200 · Sacramento, CA 95865 · 916-929-1481

John M. Poswall* · (Products Liability, Professional Malpractice, Automobile Collision) · Friedman, Collard & Poswall · 7750 College Town Drive, Suite 300 · Sacramento, CA 95826-2386 · 916-381-9011

Leo H. Schuering, Jr.* · (Defendants) · Schuering Zimmerman Scully & Nolen 7919 Folsom Boulevard, Suite 100 · Sacramento, CA 95826 · 916-383-4427

Florentino Garza* · (Plaintiffs) · Law Offices of Florentino Garza · Vanir Tower, Suite 809 · 290 North D Street · P.O. Box 1601 · San Bernardino, CA 92402-1601 714-888-1733

Bruce D. MacLachlan · (Defendants) · MacLachlan, Burford & Arias · 150 West Fifth Street, Suite 103 · San Bernardino, CA 92401 · 714-885-4491

William G. Bailey* · (Defendants) · McInnis, Fitzgerald, Rees, Sharkey & McIntyre · 1230 Columbia Street, Suite 800 · San Diego, CA 92101 · 619-236-1711

Vincent J. Bartolotta, Jr.* · (Plaintiffs) · Thorsnes Bartolotta McGuire & Padilla Fifth Avenue Financial Center, 11th Floor · 2550 Fifth Avenue · San Diego, CA 92103 · 619-236-9363

Douglas M. Butz · (Defendants) · Butz, Lucas, Dunn & Enright · 101 West Broadway, 17th Floor · San Diego, CA 92101 · 619-233-4777

Edward D. Chapin* · (Defendants) · Chapin, Brewer & Winet · 1010 Second Avenue, Suite 1100 · San Diego, CA 92101 · 619-232-4261

Gordon S. Churchill · (Plaintiffs) · Churchill, Kaplan & Roberts · 101 West Broadway, Suite 1980 · San Diego, CA 92101 · 619-233-7241

Patrick R. Frega · (Plaintiffs) · Frega & Tiffany · 4370 LaJolla Village Drive, Suite 960 · San Diego, CA 92122 · 619-235-4044

Harvey R. Levine* · (Plaintiffs, Medical Malpractice, Products Liability, Insurance, Bad Faith Litigation) · Levine, Steinberg & DePasquale · 1200 Third Avenue, Suite 1400 · San Diego, CA 92101 · 619-231-9449

Patrick A. McCormick, Jr. · (Defendants) · Law Offices of Patrick A. McCormick, Jr. · Cabot Cabot & Forbes Building, Suite 700 · 550 West C Street · San Diego, CA 92101 · 619-231-8802

John F. "Mickey" McGuire* · (Plaintiffs, Construction Defect, Bad Faith Litigation) · Thorsnes Bartolotta McGuire & Padilla · Fifth Avenue Financial Center, 11th Floor · 2550 Fifth Avenue · San Diego, CA 92103 · 619-236-9363

James A. McIntyre · (Defendants) · McInnis, Fitzgerald, Rees, Sharkey & McIntyre · 1230 Columbia Street, Suite 800 · San Diego, CA 92101 · 619-236-1711

Brian D. Monaghan · (Plaintiffs) · Monaghan & Strauss · 1450 Front Street · San Diego, CA 92101 · 619-231-0059

Michael I. Neil · (Defendants) · Neil, Dymott, Perkins, Brown & Frank · 1010 Second Avenue, Suite 1712 · San Diego, CA 92101 · 619-238-1712

T. Michael Reed · (Plaintiffs) · Casey, Gerry, Casey, Westbrook, Reed & Hughes 110 Laurel Street · San Diego, CA 92101-1486 · 619-238-1811

Douglas R. Reynolds · (Defendants) · Lewis, Damato, Brisbois & Bisgaard · 550 West C Street, Suite 800 · San Diego, CA 92101 · 619-233-1006

Thomas E. Sharkey · (Defendants) · McInnis, Fitzgerald, Rees, Sharkey & McIntyre · 1230 Columbia Street, Suite 800 · San Diego, CA 92101 · 619-236-1711

John R. Wingert* · (Defendants) · Wingert, Grebing & Brubaker · Bank of America Plaza, Suite 1750 · 450 B Street · San Diego, CA 92101-8090 · 619-232-8151

Albert R. Abramson* · (Plaintiffs, Products Liability, Automobile Collision, Airplane Collision) · Abramson & Smith · 44 Montgomery Street, Suite 4211 · San Francisco, CA 94104 · 415-421-7995

Nelson C. Barry · (Defendants) · Bishop, Barry, Howe, Haney & Ryder · Merchants Exchange Building, 11th Floor · 465 California Street · San Francisco, CA 94104 · 415-421-8550

Ralph W. Bastian, Jr.* · (Plaintiffs) · Walkup, Shelby, Bastian, Melodia, Kelly, Echeverria & Link · The Hartford Building, 30th Floor · 650 California Street · San Francisco, CA 94108 · 415-981-7210

David B. Baum* · (Plaintiffs) · Townhouse Two · Boston Ship Plaza · San Francisco, CA 94111 · 415-956-5544

Salvatore Bossio · (Defendants) · Hassard, Bonnington, Rogers & Huber · 50 Fremont Street, Suite 3400 · San Francisco, CA 94105 · 415-543-6444

James S. Bostwick* · (Plaintiffs, Products Liability, Professional Malpractice, Automobile Collision) · Bostwick & Tehin · One Lombard, Third Floor · Lombard & Battery at The Embarcadero · San Francisco, CA 94111-1186 · 415-421-5500

Robert E. Dryden* · (Defendants, Products Liability) · Dryden, Margoles, Schimaneck, Hartman & Kelly · One California Street, Suite 3100 · San Francisco, CA 94111 · 415-362-6715

Edwin W. Green · (Defendants) · Bronson, Bronson & McKinnon · 505 Montgomery Street, 11th Floor · San Francisco, CA 94111 · 415-986-4200

Daniel J. Kelly* · (Plaintiffs, Medical Malpractice) · Walkup, Shelby, Bastian, Melodia, Kelly, Echeverria & Link · The Hartford Building, 30th Floor · 650 California Street · San Francisco, CA 94108 · 415-981-7210

Raoul D. Kennedy · (Defendants) · Crosby, Heafey, Roach & May · 333 Bush Street, Suite 2580 · San Francisco, CA 94104 · 415-543-8700

Edward J. McFetridge · (Defendants) · St. Clair, Zappettini, McFetridge & Griffin · Telesis Tower, Suite 1400 · One Montgomery Street · San Francisco, CA 94104 · 415-421-2462

Paul V. Melodia · (Plaintiffs) · Walkup, Shelby, Bastian, Melodia, Kelly, Echeverria & Link · The Hartford Building, 30th Floor · 650 California Street · San Francisco, CA 94108 · 415-981-7210

Charles O. Morgan, Jr. · 450 Sansome Street, Suite 1310 · San Francisco, CA 94111-3382 · 415-392-2037

James N. Penrod* · (Defendants) · Hassard, Bonnington, Rogers & Huber · Five Fremont Center, Suite 3400 · 50 Fremont Street · San Francisco, CA 94105 · 415-543-6444

Joseph W. Rogers, Jr. · (Defendants) · Rogers, Joseph, O'Donnell & Quinn · 311 California Street, 10th Floor · San Francisco, CA 94104 · 415-956-2828

Ronald H. Rouda · (Plaintiffs) · Rouda, Feder & Tietjen · 465 California Street, Suite 210 · San Francisco, CA 94104 · 415-398-5398

Gerald C. Sterns* · (Plaintiffs, Products Liability, Aviation Liability) · Law Offices of Gerald C. Sterns · 280 Utah Street · San Francisco, CA 94103 · 415-626-1000

Edward A. Hinshaw · (Defendants) · 152 North Third Street, Suite 300 · San Jose, CA 95115 · 408-293-5959

Archie S. Robinson* · (Defendants) · Robinson & Wood · 227 North First Street, Suite 300 · San Jose, CA 95113 · 408-298-7120

Norman W. Saucedo* · (Plaintiffs) · Ruocco & Saucedo · Riverpark Towers, Suite 600 · 333 West San Carlos Street · San Jose, CA 95110 · 408-289-1417

Wylie A. Aitken · (Plaintiffs) · Law Offices of Wylie A. Aitken · 600 West Santa Ana Boulevard, Penthouse Suite · Santa Ana, CA 92701 · 714-834-1424

Arthur N. Hews, Jr. · (Plaintiffs) · Hews, Munoz & Swift · 315 West Third Street Santa Ana, CA 92701 · 714-541-4331

H. Gilbert Jones · (Defendants) · Bonne, Jones, Bridges, Mueller & O'Keefe · 801 Civic Center Drive West, Suite 400 · Santa Ana, CA 92702-2018 · 714-835-1157

Robert C. Baker · (Defendants) · Baker, Silberberg & Keener · 2850 Ocean Park Boulevard, Suite 300 · Santa Monica, CA 90405 · 213-399-0900

Bruce A. Broillet* · (Plaintiffs, Products Liability, Professional Malpractice, Automobile Collision) · Greene, Broillet, Taylor & Wheeler · 100 Wilshire Boulevard, 21st Floor · Santa Monica, CA 90401 · 213-576-1200

Browne Greene · (Plaintiffs) · Greene, Broillet, Taylor & Wheeler · 100 Wilshire Boulevard, 21st Floor · Santa Monica, CA 90401 · 213-576-1200

Charles B. O'Reilly · 511 Wilshire Boulevard · Santa Monica, CA 90401 · 213-395-6660

Marshall Silberberg · (Defendants) · Baker, Silberberg & Keener · 2850 Ocean Park Boulevard, Suite 300 · Santa Monica, CA 90405 · 213-399-0900

Robert L. Anderson · (Defendants) · Anderson, Galloway & Lucchese · 1676 North California Boulevard, Suite 500 · Walnut Creek, CA 94596 · 415-943-6383

G. Patrick Galloway · (Defense, Medical Malpractice) · Anderson, Galloway & Lucchese · 1676 North California Boulevard, Suite 500 · Walnut Creek, CA 94596 · 415-943-6383

Thomas G. Stolpman · (Plaintiffs) · Silver, McWilliams, Stolpman, Mandel, Katzman, Krissman & Elber · 1121 North Avalon Boulevard · Wilmington, CA 90748 · 213-775-7300

PUBLIC UTILITY LAW

Earl Nicholas (Nick) Selby · 420 Florence Street, Suite 200 · Palo Alto, CA 94301 415-323-0990

Philip A. Stohr · Downey, Brand, Seymour & Rohwer · 555 Capitol Mall, 10th Floor · Sacramento, CA 95814 · 916-441-0131

Jerry R. Bloom · Morrison & Foerster, 28th Floor · 345 California Street · San Francisco, CA 94104-2675 · 415-677-7206

William H. Booth · Jackson, Tufts, Cole & Black · 650 California Street, 33rd Floor · San Francisco, CA 94108 · 415-433-1950

Gordon E. Davis · Brobeck, Phleger & Harrison · Spear Street Tower · One Market Plaza · San Francisco, CA 94105 · 415-442-0900

Thomas J. MacBride, Jr. · Armour, Goodin, Schlotz & MacBride · 505 Sansome Street, Ninth Floor · San Francisco, CA 94111 · 415-392-7900

David J. Marchant · Graham & James · Alcoa Building · One Maritime Plaza, Suite 300 · San Francisco, CA 94111 · 415-954-0200

Martin A. Mattes · Graham & James · Alcoa Building · One Maritime Plaza, Suite 300 · San Francisco, CA 94111 · 415-954-0200

David M. Wilson · Dinkelspiel, Donovan & Reder · One Embarcadero Center, Suite 2701 · San Francisco, CA 94111 · 415-788-1100

REAL ESTATE LAW

M. Rogue Hemley · Latham & Watkins · 650 Town Center Drive, 20th Floor · Costa Mesa, CA 92626 · 714-540-1235

John C. Gamble · Allen, Matkins, Leck, Gamble & Mallory · 18400 Von Karman, 4th Floor · Irvine, CA 92715-1597 · 714-553-1313

Frederick L. Allen · Allen, Matkins, Leck, Gamble & Mallory · 515 South Figueroa Street, Eighth Floor · Los Angeles, CA 90071-3398 · 213-622-5555

Dennis B. Arnold · Gibson, Dunn & Crutcher · 333 South Grand Avenue · Los Angeles, CA 90071 · 213-229-7000

Stephen Claman · Greenberg, Glusker, Fields, Claman & Machtinger · 1900 Avenue of the Stars, Suite 2000 · Los Angeles, CA 90067 · 213-553-3610

Robert M. Eller · Cadwalader, Wickersham & Taft · 660 South Figueroa Street Los Angeles, CA 90017 · 213-955-4610

Frank E. Feder · Loeb and Loeb · 10100 Santa Monica Boulevard, Suite 2200 · Los Angeles, CA 90067 · 213-282-2000

Louis A. Huskins · Irell & Manella · 1800 Avenue of the Stars, Suite 900 · Los Angeles, CA 90067-4276 · 213-277-1010

Russell L. Johnson · Gibson, Dunn & Crutcher · 333 South Grand Avenue · Los Angeles, CA 90071 · 213-229-7000

Alvin S. Kaufer* · (Land Use, Litigation) · Nossaman, Guthner, Knox & Elliott Union Bank Square, 31st Floor · 445 South Figueroa Street · Los Angeles, CA 90071-1672 · 213-612-7800

Mark L. Lamken · Richards, Watson & Gershon · Security Pacific Plaza, 38th Floor · 333 South Hope Street · Los Angeles, CA 90071 · 213-626-8484

David V. Lee · Latham & Watkins · 633 West Fifth Street, Suite 4000 · Los Angeles, CA 90071-2007 · 213-485-1234

Marvin Leon · Mitchell, Silverberg & Knupp · 11377 West Olympic Boulevard · Los Angeles, CA 90064 · 213-312-2000

Richard C. Mallory · Allen, Matkins, Leck, Gamble & Mallory · 515 South Figueroa Street, Eighth Floor · Los Angeles, CA 90071-3398 · 213-622-5555

Michael L. Matkins · Allen, Matkins, Leck, Gamble & Mallory · 515 South Figueroa Street, Eighth Floor · Los Angeles, CA 90071-3398 · 213-622-5555

Michael E. Meyer · (Commercial Transactions, Industrial Transactions) · Pillsbury Madison & Sutro · Citicorp Plaza, Suite 1200 · 725 South Figueroa Street · Los Angeles, CA 90017-2513 · 213-488-7100

O'Malley M. Miller · Allen, Matkins, Leck, Gamble & Mallory · 515 South Figueroa Street, Eighth Floor · Los Angeles, CA 90071-3398 · 213-622-5555

Phillip R. Nicholson · Cox, Castle & Nicholson · Two Century Plaza, 28th Floor 2049 Century Park East · Los Angeles, CA 90067 · 213-277-4222

Leo J. Pircher · Pircher, Nichols & Meeks · Century City North Building · 10100 Santa Monica Boulevard · Los Angeles, CA 90067 · 213-201-8900

Laurence G. Preble · O'Melveny & Myers · 400 South Hope Street · Los Angeles, CA 90071-2899 · 213-669-6000

Floyd Sayer · Floyd Sayer & Associates · 10960 Wilshire Boulevard · Los Angeles, CA 90024 · 213-477-6001

Ronald I. Silverman · Cox, Castle & Nicholson · Two Century Plaza, 28th Floor 2049 Century Park East · Los Angeles, CA 90067 · 213-284-2269

H. Randall Stoke · Latham & Watkins · 633 West Fifth Street, Suite 4000 · Los Angeles, CA 90071-2007 · 213-891-8292

Herbert J. Strickstein · (Condominiums) · Two Century Plaza, 12th Floor · 2049 Century Park East · Los Angeles, CA 90067 · 213-553-4888

Charles V. Thornton III · Paul, Hastings, Janofsky & Walker · 555 South Flower Street, 23rd Floor · Los Angeles, CA 90071 · 213-683-6000

David H. Vena · (Land Use, Commercial Transactions) · Latham & Watkins · 633 West Fifth Street, Suite 4000 · Los Angeles, CA 90071-2007 · 213-891-8292

Richard S. Volpert · Skadden, Arps, Slate, Meagher & Flom · 300 South Grand Avenue, 34th Floor · Los Angeles, CA 90071 · 213-687-5000

Paul R. Walker · Paul, Hastings, Janofsky & Walker · 555 South Flower Street, 23rd Floor · Los Angeles, CA 90071 · 213-683-6000

Alan Wayte · Dewey Ballantine · 333 South Hope Street, 30th Floor · Los Angeles, CA 90071 · 213-626-3399

John W. Whitaker · (Land Use, Commercial Transactions, Industrial Transactions) · Pillsbury Madison & Sutro · Citicorp Plaza, Suite 1200 · 725 South Figueroa Street · Los Angeles, CA 90017-2513 · 213-488-7100

Lowell C. Martindale, Jr. · O'Melveny & Myers · Union Bank Building, Suite 1700 · 610 Newport Center Drive · Newport Beach, CA 92660-6429 · 714-760-9600

John R. Simon · Sheppard, Mullin, Richter & Hampton · 4695 MacArthur Court, Seventh Floor · Newport Beach, CA 92660 · 714-752-6400

Ralph C. Wintrode · Gibson, Dunn & Crutcher · 800 Newport Center Drive, Suite 700 · P.O. Box 2490 · Newport Beach, CA 92660 · 714-759-3800

Michael A. Dean · Wendel, Rosen, Black, Dean & Levitan · Clorox Building, Suite 2000 · Oakland City Center · P.O. Box 2047 · Oakland, CA 94604-2047 · 415-834-6600

Harry D. Miller · Miller, Starr & Regalia · Ordway Building, 16th Floor · One Kaiser Plaza · Oakland, CA 94612 · 415-465-3800

Marvin B. Starr · Miller, Starr & Regalia · Ordway Building, 16th Floor · One Kaiser Plaza · Oakland, CA 94612 · 415-465-3800

Sharon D. Roseme · McDonough, Holland & Allen · 2260 Douglas Boulevard, Suite 200 · Roseville, CA 95661 · 916-773-2711

John V. Diepenbrock · (Land Use, Eminent Domain, Commercial Transactions, Industrial Transactions) · Diepenbrock, Wulff, Plant & Hannegan · 300 Capitol Mall, Suite 1700 · P.O. Box 3034 · Sacramento, CA 95812-3034 · 916-444-3910

David J. Spottiswood · McDonough, Holland & Allen · 555 Capitol Mall, Suite 950 · Sacramento, CA 95814 · 916-444-3900

Thomas C. Ackerman, Jr. · Gray, Cary, Ames & Frye · 1700 First Interstate Plaza 401 B Street · San Diego, CA 92101-4219 · 619-699-2700

Robert Caplan · Seltzer Caplan Wilkins & McMahon · 3003 Fourth Avenue · P.O. Box X 33999 · San Diego, CA 92163 · 619-295-3003

Louis E. Goebel · Goebel & Shensa · 1202 Kettner Boulevard, Suite 6000 · San Diego, CA 92101 · 619-239-2611

E. Ludlow Keeney, Jr.* · Mitchell, Keeney, Barry & Pike · 520 West Ash Street, Suite 200 · Columbia at Ash · San Diego, CA 92101 · 619-238-1234

Alex C. McDonald · McDonald, Hecht & Solberg · 1100 Financial Square · 600 B Street · San Diego, CA 92101 · 619-239-3444

Paul I. Meyer · Latham & Watkins · 701 B Street, Suite 2100 · San Diego, CA 92101-8197 · 619-236-1234

Christopher B. Neils · Sheppard, Mullin, Richter & Hampton · 501 West Broadway, Suite 1900 · San Diego, CA 92101 · 619-338-6500

Alan R. Perry · Musick, Peeler & Garrett · 1900 Central Savings Tower · 225 Broadway · San Diego, CA 92101 · 619-231-2500

Paul A. Peterson · Peterson & Price · 530 B Street, Suite 2300 · San Diego, CA 92101 · 619-234-0361

Stephen K. Cassidy · Cassidy & Verges · 20 California Street, Suite 500 · San Francisco, CA 94111 · 415-788-2020

William K. Coblentz · Coblentz, Cahen, McCabe & Breyer · 222 Kearny Street, Seventh Floor · San Francisco, CA 94108 · 415-391-4800

Stephen A. Cowan · O'Melveny & Myers · One Embarcadero West, Suite 2600 · San Francisco, CA 94111 · 415-984-8700

Philip E. Diamond · Landels, Ripley & Diamond · 350 Stuart Street · San Francisco, CA 94105-1250 · 415-788-5000

Pamela S. Duffy · Coblentz, Cahen, McCabe & Breyer · 222 Kearny Street, Seventh Floor · San Francisco, CA 94108 · 415-391-4800

Howard N. Ellman · Ellman, Burke, Hoffman & Johnson · One Ecker Building, Suite 200 · San Francisco, CA 94105 · 415-777-2727

Stephen R. Finn · Brobeck, Phleger & Harrison · Spear Street Tower · One Market Plaza · San Francisco, CA 94105 · 415-442-0900

Robert C. Herr · (Zoning, Land Use, Commercial Transactions, Commercial & Residential Development) · Pillsbury Madison & Sutro · 225 Bush Street · P.O. Box 7880 · San Francisco, CA 94120 · 415-983-1000

Bruce W. Hyman · Landels, Ripley & Diamond · 350 Stuart Street · San Francisco, CA 94105-1250 · 415-788-5000

Reverdy Johnson · Pettit & Martin · 101 California Street, 35th Floor · San Francisco, CA 94111 · 415-434-4000

Robert E. Merritt · McCutchen, Doyle, Brown & Enersen · Three Embarcadero Center · San Francisco, CA 94111 · 415-393-2000

Noel W. Nellis · (Commercial Transactions, Industrial Transactions, Real Estate Financing) · Morrison & Foerster · 345 California Street · San Francisco, CA 94104-2675 · 415-677-7111

Susan Jane Passovoy · Coblentz, Cahen, McCabe & Breyer · 222 Kearny Street, Seventh Floor · San Francisco, CA 94108 · 415-391-4800

Edward R. Steefel · Steefel, Levitt & Weiss · One Embarcadero Center, 29th Floor · San Francisco, CA 94111 · 415-788-0900

Robert A. Thompson · Pettit & Martin · 101 California Street, 35th Floor · San Francisco, CA 94111 · 415-434-4000

David M. Van Atta · Graham & James · Alcoa Building · One Maritime Plaza, Suite 300 · San Francisco, CA 94111 · 415-954-0200

Sanford A. Berliner · Berliner, Cohen & Biagini · 10 Almaden Boulevard, 11th Floor · San Jose, CA 95113 · 408-286-5800

David W. Mitchell · McCutchen, Doyle, Brown & Enersen · Market Post Tower, Suite 1500 · 55 South Market Street · San Jose, CA 95113 · 408-947-8400

Harris W. Seed · Seed, Mackall, Nida & Cole · 1006 Santa Barbara Street · P.O. Box 2578 · Santa Barbara, CA 93120 · 805-963-0669

TAX AND EMPLOYEE BENEFITS LAW

Bruce I. Hochman · Hochman, Salkin and DeRoy · West Tower, Seventh Floor 9100 Wilshire Boulevard · Beverly Hills, CA 90212 · 213-273-1181

Melvin S. Spears · Ervin, Cohen & Jessup · 9401 Wilshire Boulevard, Ninth Floor Beverly Hills, CA 90212-2974 · 213-273-6333

C. David Anderson · (Corporate & Partnership Transactions, State Tax, Employee Benefits, Tax Disputes) · Tuttle & Taylor · 355 South Grand Avenue, 40th Floor · Los Angeles, CA 90071-3101 · 213-683-0600

Norman B. Barker · Gibson, Dunn & Crutcher · 333 South Grand Avenue · Los Angeles, CA 90071 · 213-229-7000

S. David Blinn · (Employee Benefits) · Gibson, Dunn & Crutcher · 333 South Grand Avenue · Los Angeles, CA 90071 · 213-229-7000

Thomas G. Bost · Latham & Watkins · 633 West Fifth Street, Suite 4000 · Los Angeles, CA 90071-2007 · 213-485-1234

Richard S. Brawerman · Gibson, Hoffman & Pancione · 1901 Avenue of the Stars, Suite 1100 · Los Angeles, CA 90067 · 213-556-4660

James F. Childs, Jr. · Jones, Day, Reavis & Pogue · 355 South Grand Avenue, Suite 3000 · Los Angeles, CA 90071 · 213-624-3939

John R. Cohan · Irell & Manella · 1800 Avenue of the Stars, Suite 900 · Los Angeles, CA 90067-4276 · 213-277-1010

Terence F. Cuff · Loeb and Loeb · 1000 Wilshire Boulevard, Suite 1800 · Los Angeles, CA 90017 · 213-688-3400

Robert A. DeWitt · Paul, Hastings, Janofsky & Walker · 555 South Flower Street, 23rd Floor · Los Angeles, CA 90071 · 213-683-6000

David E. Gordon · (Employee Benefits) · O'Melveny & Myers · 400 South Hope Street · Los Angeles, CA 90071-2899 · 213-669-6000

Nancy L. Iredale · Paul, Hastings, Janofsky & Walker · 555 South Flower Street, 23rd Floor · Los Angeles, CA 90071 · 213-683-6000

Lawrence E. Irell · Irell & Manella · 1800 Avenue of the Stars, Suite 900 · Los Angeles, CA 90067-4276 · 213-277-1010

Philip D. Irwin · O'Melveny & Myers · 400 South Hope Street · Los Angeles, CA 90071-2899 · 213-669-6000

Robert K. Johnson · (Employee Benefits) · Munger, Tolles & Olson · 355 South Grand Avenue, 35th Floor · Los Angeles, CA 90071-1560 · 213-683-9100

James H. Kindel, Jr. · Kindel & Anderson · 555 South Flower Street, 26th Floor · Los Angeles, CA 90071 · 213-680-2222

Robert C. Kopple · Mitchel, Silberberg & Knupp · 11377 West Olympic Boulevard · Los Angeles, CA 90064 · 213-312-2000

Dudley M. Lang · Hufstedler, Kaus & Ettinger · 355 South Grade Avenue, 45th Floor · Los Angeles, CA 90071-3107 · 213-617-7070

Arthur Manella · Irell & Manella · 1800 Avenue of the Stars, Suite 900 · Los Angeles, CA 90067-4276 · 213-277-1010

James M. Murphy · Gibson, Dunn & Crutcher · 333 South Grand Avenue · Los Angeles, CA 90071 · 213-229-7000

William R. Nicholas · Latham & Watkins · 633 West Fifth Street, Suite 4000 · Los Angeles, CA 90071-2007 · 213-891-8292

Frederick A. Richman · O'Melveny & Myers · 400 South Hope Street · Los Angeles, CA 90071-2899 · 213-669-6000

Ronald S. Rizzo · (Employee Benefits) · Jones, Day, Reavis & Pogue · 355 South Grand Avenue, Suite 3000 · Los Angeles, CA 90071 · 213-625-3939

Donald R. Spuehler · (Employee Benefits) · O'Melveny & Myers · 400 South Hope Street · Los Angeles, CA 90071-2899 · 213-669-6000

Lawrence M. Stone · Irell & Manella · 1800 Avenue of the Stars, Suite 900 · Los Angeles, CA 90067-4276 · 213-277-1010

Clyde E. Tritt · O'Melveny & Myers · 400 South Hope Street · Los Angeles, CA 90071 · 213-669-6000

John S. Warren · Loeb and Loeb · 1000 Wilshire Boulevard, Suite 1800 · Los Angeles, CA 90017 · 213-688-3400

William P. Wasserman · Loeb and Loeb · 1000 Wilshire Boulevard, Suite 1800 · Los Angeles, CA 90017 · 213-688-3400

John S. Welch · (Employee Benefits) · Latham & Watkins · 633 West Fifth Street, Suite 4000 · Los Angeles, CA 90071-2007 · 213-891-8292

Robert L. Whitmire · Kindel & Anderson · 555 South Flower Street, 27th Floor · Los Angeles, CA 90071 · 213-680-2222

Robert M. Winokur · Crosby, Heafey, Roach & May · 1999 Harrison Street · Oakland, CA 94612 · 415-763-2000

James P. Fuller · Fenwick & West · Two Palo Alto Square, Eighth Floor · Palo Alto, CA 94306 · 415-494-0600

John R. Bonn · Sheppard, Mullin, Richter & Hampton · 501 West Broadway, Suite 1900 · San Diego, CA 92101 · 619-338-6500

Lawrence S. Branton · (Employee Benefits) · Branton & Wilson · 701 B Street, Suite 1255 · San Diego, CA 92101 · 619-236-1891

Robert K. Butterfield · Procopio, Cory, Hargreaves & Savitch · 530 B Street, Suite 1900 · San Diego, CA 92101 · 619-238-1900

George L. Damoose · Procopio, Cory, Hargreaves & Savitch · 530 B Street, Suite 1900 · San Diego, CA 92101 · 619-238-1900

Richard L. Kintz · (Corporate & Partnership Transactions) · Brobeck, Phleger & Harrison · 550 West C Street, Suite 1300 · P.O. Box 128047 · San Diego, CA 92101-8049 · 619-234-1966

Daniel N. Riesenberg · (Employee Benefits) · Luce, Forward, Hamilton & Scripps · The Bank of California Plaza, Suite 1700 · 110 West A Street · San Diego, CA 92101 · 619-236-1414

Luther J. Avery · Bancroft, Avery & McAlister · 601 Montgomery Street, Suite 900 · San Francisco, CA 94111 · 415-788-8855

Jeffry A. Bernstein · Coblentz, Cahen, McCabe & Breyer · 222 Kearny Street, Seventh Floor · San Francisco, CA 94108 · 415-391-4800

Robert A. Blum · (Employee Benefits) · Orrick, Herrington & Sutcliffe · Old Federal Reserve Building · 400 Sansome Street · San Francisco, CA 94111 · 415-392-1122

Edward D. Burmeister, Jr. · Baker & McKenzie · Two Embarcadero Center, Suite 2400 · San Francisco, CA 94111 · 415-576-3000

James M. Canty · Pillsbury Madison & Sutro · 225 Bush Street · P.O. Box 7880 San Francisco, CA 94120-7880 · 415-983-1000

Roy E. Crawford · (State Tax, Tax Disputes) · Brobeck, Phleger & Harrison · Spear Street Tower · One Market Plaza · San Francisco, CA 94105 · 415-442-0900

Richard M. Eigner · Pillsbury Madison & Sutro · 225 Bush Street · P.O. Box 7880 San Francisco, CA 94120-7880 · 415-983-1000

Nicholas S. Freud · (International Tax) · Kaplan Russin & Vecchi · 580 California Street, 16th Floor · San Francisco, CA 94104 · 415-421-1100

Joanne M. Garvey · Heller, Ehrman, White & McAuliffe · 333 Bush Street · San Francisco, CA 94104-2878 · 415-772-6000

Richard L. Greene · Greene, Radovsky, Maloney & Share · Spear Street Tower, Suite 4200 · One Market Plaza · San Francisco, CA 94105 · 415-543-1400

William T. Hutton · (Exempt Organizations) · Howard, Rice, Nemerovski, Canady, Robertson & Falk · Three Embarcadero Center, Seventh Floor · San Francisco, CA 94111 · 415-434-1600

Thomas F. Kostic · (Corporate & Partnership Transactions, Tax Disputes) · Pettit & Martin · 101 California Street, 35th Floor · San Francisco, CA 94111 · 415-434-4000

Alvin T. Levitt · Steefel, Levitt & Weiss · One Embarcadero Center, 29th Floor San Francisco, CA 94111 · 415-788-0900

Robert C. Livsey · Brobeck, Phleger & Harrison · Spear Street Tower · One Market Plaza · San Francisco, CA 94105 · 415-442-0900

John B. Lowry · McCutchen, Doyle, Brown & Enersen · Three Embarcadero Center · San Francisco, CA 94111 · 415-393-2000

Stephen J. Martin · Pillsbury Madison & Sutro · 225 Bush Street · P.O. Box 7880 San Francisco, CA 94120-7880 · 415-983-1000

T. Neal McNamara · (Employee Benefits) · Pillsbury Madison & Sutro · 225 Bush Street · P.O. Box 7880 · San Francisco, CA 94120 · 415-983-1551

James E. Merritt · (Tax Disputes, Tax Accounting & Transfer Prices) · Morrison & Foerster · 345 California Street · San Francisco, CA 94104-2675 · 415-677-7000

Stuart J. Offer · Morrison & Foerster · 345 California Street, 27th Floor · San Francisco, CA 94104-2675 · 415-677-7000

Jerry H. Robinson · (Corporate & Partnership Transactions, Tax Disputes) · Heller, Ehrman, White & McAuliffe · 333 Bush Street · San Francisco, CA 94104-2878 · 415-772-6132

Paul J. Sax* · (Corporate & Partnership Transactions, State Tax, Tax Disputes, Corporate Finance) · Orrick, Herrington & Sutcliffe · Old Federal Reserve Building · 400 Sansome Street · San Francisco, CA 94111 · 415-773-5949

Lawrence B. Silver · Greene, Radosky, Maloney & Share · Spear Street Tower, Suite 4200 · One Market Plaza · San Francisco, CA 94104 · 415-543-1400

Myron G. Sugarman · Cooley Godward Castro Huddleson & Tatum · One Maritime Plaza, 20th Floor · San Francisco, CA 94111-3580 · 415-981-5252

Prentiss Willson, Jr. · (Corporate & Partnership Transactions, State Tax, Tax Disputes) · Morrison & Foerster · 345 California Street · San Francisco, CA 94104-2675 · 415-677-7000

Cameron W. Wolfe, Jr.* · (Employee Benefits) · Orrick, Herrington & Sutcliffe Old Federal Reserve Building · 400 Sansome Street · San Francisco, CA 94111 · 415-392-1122

Owen G. Fiore · Law Offices of Owen G. Fiore · 101 Park Center Plaza, 13th Floor · San Jose, CA 95113 · 408-257-8545

John F. Hopkins · Hopkins & Carley · 150 Almaden Boulevard, 15th Floor · San Jose, CA 95113 · 408-286-9800

Charles M. Walker · Paul, Hastings, Janofsky & Walker · 1299 Ocean Avenue, Fifth Floor · Santa Monica, CA 90401 · 213-451-1200

TRUSTS AND ESTATES

Edward V. Brennan · Gray, Cary, Ames & Frye · 1200 Prospect Street, Suite 575 La Jolla, CA 92037 · 619-699-3498

Theodore J. Cranston · Gray, Cary, Ames & Frye · 1200 Prospect Street, Suite 575 · La Jolla, CA 92037 · 619-454-9101

Robert J. Durham, Jr. · Luce, Forward, Hamilton & Scripps · Regents Square II 4250 Executive Square, Suite 700 · La Jolla, CA 92037 · 619-455-6611

William E. Ferguson · Ferguson, Newburn & Weston · 7777 Fay Avenue, Suite 260 · P.O. Box 1107 · La Jolla, CA 92038 · 619-454-4233

Jonathan G. Blattmachr · Milbank, Tweed, Hadley & McCloy · 515 South Figueroa Street, 16th Floor · Los Angeles, CA 90071 · 213-892-4000

Theodore E. Calleton · Kindel & Anderson · 555 South Flower Street, 26th Floor Los Angeles, CA 90071 · 213-680-2222

John R. Cohan · Irell & Manella · 1800 Avenue of the Stars, Suite 900 · Los Angeles, CA 90067-4276 · 213-277-1010

Charles A. Collier, Jr. · Irell & Manella · 1800 Avenue of the Stars, Suite 900 · Los Angeles, CA 90067-4276 · 213-277-1010

Edmond R. Davis* · (Estate Planning, Estate Administration, Charitable Trusts, Estate & Trust Litigation) · Brobeck, Phleger & Harrison · 444 South Flower Street, Suite 4300 · Los Angeles, CA 90017 · 213-489-4060

Paul N. Frimmer · Irell & Manella · 1800 Avenue of the Stars, Suite 900 · Los Angeles, CA 90067-4276 · 213-277-1010

Jon J. Gallo · (Estate Planning, Estate Administration, Charitable Trusts) · Greenberg, Glusker, Fields, Claman & Machtinger · 1900 Avenue of the Stars, Suite 2000 · Los Angeles, CA 90067 · 213-553-3610

Andrew S. Garb · Loeb and Loeb · 000 Wilshire Boulevard, Suite 1800 · Los Angeles, CA 90017 · 213-688-3400

Joseph G. Gorman, Jr. · Sheppard, Mullin, Richter & Hampton · 333 South Hope Street, 48th Floor · Los Angeles, CA 90071 · 213-620-1780

Ronald E. Gother · Gibson, Dunn & Crutcher · 333 South Grand Avenue · Los Angeles, CA 90071 · 213-229-7000

Geraldine S. Hemmerling · Armstrong & Hirsch · 1888 Century Park East, 18th Floor · Los Angeles, CA 90067 · 213-553-0305

William E. Johnston · Johnson, Wohlwend, Johnston & Olivar · Gateway East, Suite 435 · 1800 Avenue of the Stars · Los Angeles, CA 90067 · 213-552-0175

Solomon M. Kamm · O'Melveny & Myers · 400 South Hope Street · Los Angeles, CA 90071-2899 · 213-669-6000

Edward A. Landry · Musick, Peeler & Garrett · One Wilshire Boulevard, Suite 2000 · Los Angeles, CA 90017 · 213-629-7600

Fred L. Leydorf · (Estate Planning, Estate Administration, Charitable Trusts) · Hufstedler, Kaus & Ettinger · 355 South Grand Avenue, 45th Floor · Los Angeles, CA 90071-3107 · 213-617-7070

Arne S. Lindgren · Latham & Watkins · 633 West Fifth Street, Suite 4000 · Los Angeles, CA 90071-2007 · 213-891-8292

Roy D. Miller · Gibson, Dunn & Crutcher · 333 South Grand Avenue · Los Angeles, CA 90071 · 213-229-7000

Wesley L. Nutten III · Sheppard, Mullin, Richter & Hampton · 333 South Hope Street, 48th Floor · Los Angeles, CA 90071 · 213-620-1780

John D. Pettker · Rodi, Pollock, Pettker, Galbraith & Phillips · 801 South Grand Avenue, Suite 400 · Los Angeles, CA 90017 · 213-895-4900

Matthew S. Rae, Jr. · Darling, Hall & Rae · 550 South Flower Street · Los Angeles, CA 90017 · 213-683-5337

Byron O. Smith* · (Estate Planning, Estate Administration, Probate Litigation) · Adams, Duque & Hazeltine · Pacific Mutual Building, 10th Floor · 523 West Sixth Street · Los Angeles, CA 90014 · 213-620-1240

George E. Stephens, Jr.* · Paul, Hastings, Janofsky & Walker · 555 South Flower Street, 23rd Floor · Los Angeles, CA 90071 · 213-683-6000

Stuart P. Tobisman · O'Melveny & Myers · 400 South Hope Street · Los Angeles, CA 90071-2899 · 213-669-6000

David D. Watts · (Estate Planning, Estate Administration, Charitable Trusts) · O'Melveny & Myers · 400 South Hope Street · Los Angeles, CA 90071-2899 · 213-669-6000

Harold Weinstock · (Estate Planning, Estate Administration) · Weinstock, Manion, Reisman & Shore · 1888 Century Park East, Suite 800 · Los Angeles, CA 90067-1712 · 213-553-8844

Joseph L. Wyatt, Jr.* · (Estate Planning, Charitable Trusts, Trust Litigation) · Hufstedler, Kaus & Ettinger · 355 South Grand Avenue, 45th Floor · Los Angeles, CA 90071-3107 · 213-617-7070

Francis J. Collin, Jr. · Dickenson, Peatman & Fogarty · 809 Coombs Street · Napa, CA 94559-2977 · 707-252-7122

John L. McDonnell, Jr. · Fitzgerald, Abbott & Beardsley · 1221 Broadway, 21st Floor · Oakland, CA 94612 · 415-451-3300

William E. Beamer · Gray, Cary, Ames & Frye · 1700 First Interstate Plaza · 401 B Street · San Diego, CA 92101-4219 · 619-699-2700

Stephen L. Newnham · Haskins, Nugent, Newnham & Kane · 1010 Second Avenue, Suite 2200 · San Diego, CA 921013944 · 619-236-1323

George E. Olmstead · Glenn, Wright, Jacobs & Schell · 2320 Fifth Avenue, Suite 300 · San Diego, CA 92101 · 619-239-1211

Margaret Anne Payne · Higgs, Fletcher & Mack · 2000 First National Bank Building · 40l West A Street · San Diego, CA 92101-7908 · 619-236-1551

D. Keith Bilter · Thelen, Marrin, Johnson & Bridges · Two Embarcadero Center, Suite 2200 · San Francisco, CA 94111 · 415-392-6320

Alan D. Bonapart · Bancroft, Avery & McAlister · 601 Montgomery Street, Suite 900 · San Francisco, CA 94111 · 415-788-8855

Raymond G. Ellis · Orrick, Herrington & Sutcliffe · Old Federal Reserve Building · 400 Sansome Street · San Francisco, CA 94111 · 415-392-1122

K. Bruce Friedman · Friedman & Olive · 425 California Street, Suite 2220 · San Francisco, CA 94104 · 415-434-1363

Max Gutierrez, Jr. · Brobeck, Phleger & Harrison · Spear Street Tower · One Market Plaza · San Francisco, CA 94105 · 415-442-0900

William L. Hoisington · Orrick, Herrington & Sutcliffe · Old Federal Reserve Building · 400 Sansome Street · San Francisco, CA 94111 · 415-773-555

Philip Hudner · Pillsbury Madison & Sutro · 225 Bush Street · P.O. Box 7880 · San Francisco, CA 94120 · 415-983-1000

Richard S. Kinyon · Morrison & Foerster · 345 California Street · San Francisco, CA 94104-2675 · 415-677-7000

Thomas B. McGuire · Heller, Ehrman, White & McAuliffe · 333 Bush Street · San Francisco, CA 94104-2878 · 415-772-6000

Robert A. Mills · McCutchen, Doyle, Brown & Enersen · Three Embarcadero Center · San Francisco, CA 94111 · 415-393-2000

Michael A. Roosevelt · Heller, Ehrman, White & McAuliffe · 333 Bush Street · San Francisco, CA 94104-2878 · 415-772-6000

Philip F. Spalding · Cooley, Godward, Castro, Huddleson & Tatum · One Maritime Plaza, 20th Floor · San Francisco, CA 94111-3580 · 415-981-5252

Charles G. Stephenson · (Estate Planning, Estate Administration, Charitable Trusts) · Jackson, Tufts, Cole & Black · 650 California Street, 33rd Floor · San Francisco, CA 94108 · 415-433-1950

Myron G. Sugarman · Cooley, Godward, Castro, Huddleson & Tatum · One Maritime Plaza, 20th Floor · San Francisco, CA 94111-3580 · 415-981-5252

Edward M. Alvarez · Ferrari, Alvarez, Olsen & Ottoboni · 333 West Santa Clara Street, Suite 700 · San Jose, CA 95113 · 408-280-0535

Charles W. Willey · Willey & Beckerman · 812 Presidio Avenue · Santa Barbara, CA 93101 · 805-965-4588

Edwin C. Anderson · Anderson, Zeigler, Bisharoon & Gray · 50 Old Courthouse Square · Santa Rosa, CA 95404 · 707-545-4910

COLORADO

BANKRUPTCY LAW

Ronald M. Martin* · Holland & Hart · Holly Sugar Building, Palmer Center, Suite 1300 · P.O. Box 2340 · Colorado Springs, CO 80901 · 719-475-7730

Craig A. Christensen · Lindquist, Vennum & Christensen · 600 Seventeenth Street South, Suite 2125 · Denver, CO 80202 · 303-573-5900

Carl A. Eklund · Faegre & Benson · 370 Seventeenth Street, Suite 2500 · Denver, CO 80202-4004 · 303-592-5900

Glen E. Keller, Jr. · Davis, Graham & Stubbs · 370 Seventeenth Street, Suite 4700 · P.O. Box 185 · Denver, CO 80201-0185 · 303-892-9400

Stephen E. Snyder · Holme Roberts & Owen · 1700 Lincoln Street, Suite 4100 · Denver, CO 80203 · 303-861-7000

Harry M. Sterling · Gelt, Fleishman & Sterling · 303 East 17th Avenue, Suite 1110 · Denver, CO 80203 · 303-861-1000

BUSINESS LITIGATION

Charles F. Brega · Brega & Winter · 1700 Lincoln Street, Suite 2222 · P.O. Box 5560 T.A. · Denver, CO 80203 · 303-866-9402

Peter Breitenstein · Fairfield and Woods · 1700 Lincoln Street, Suite 2400 · Denver, CO 80203 · 303-830-2400

Charles L. Casteel · Davis, Graham & Stubbs · 370 Seventeenth Street, Suite 4700 · P.O. Box 185 · Denver, CO 80201-0185 · 303-892-9400

Jeffrey A. Chase · Holme Roberts & Owen · 1700 Lincoln Street, Suite 4100 · Denver, CO 80203 · 303-861-7000

H. Thomas Coghill · Coghill & Goodspeed · 1675 Broadway, Suite 2800 · Denver, CO 80202 · 303-592-4400

Frederic K. Conover* · (Commercial, Energy, Telecommunications) · Faegre & Benson · Republic Plaza, Suite 2500 · 370 Seventeenth Street · Denver, CO 80202-4004 · 303-592-5900

Miles C. Cortez, Jr. · Cortez & Friedman · Dominion Plaza South, Suite 2800 South · 600 Seventeenth Street · Denver, CO 80202-5428 · 303-628-9400

William R. Fishman · 303 East 17th Avenue, Suite 800 · Denver, CO 80203 · 303-863-0060

Walter W. Garnsey, Jr.* · (Appellate, Commercial) · Kelly/Haglund/Garnsey & Kahn · 300 Blake Street Building · 1441 Eighteenth Street · Denver, CO 80202-1296 · 303-296-9412

Robert F. Hill · (Antitrust) · Hill & Robbins · 100 Blake Street Building · 1441 Eighteenth Street · Denver, CO 80202 · 303-296-8100

Daniel S. Hoffman · Holme Roberts & Owen · 1700 Lincoln Street, Suite 4100 Denver, CO 80203 · 303-861-7000

Edwin S Kahn* · (Appellate, Commercial, Securities) · Kelly/Haglund/Garnsey & Kahn · 300 Blake Street Building · 1441 Eighteenth Street · Denver, CO 80202-1296 · 303-296-9412

Alex Stephen Keller* · (Administrative, Appellate, Commercial) · Keller, Dunievitz & Johnson · 2480 Prudential Tower · 1050 Seventeenth Street · Denver, CO 80265 · 303-571-5302

James M. Lyons · Rothgerber, Appel, Powers & Johnson · One Taber Center, Suite 3000 · 1200 Seventeenth Street · Denver, CO 80202 · 303-628-9546

William C. McClearn · Holland & Hart · 555 Seventeenth Street, Suite 2900 · P.O. Box 8749 · Denver, CO 80201-8749 · 303-295-8000

Joseph E. Meyer III* · Pendleton & Sabian · 303 East 17th Avenue, Suite 1000 Denver, CO 80203 · 303-839-1204

Jane Michaels · Holland & Hart · 555 Seventeenth Street, Suite 2900 · P.O. Box 8749 · Denver, CO 80201-8749 · 303-295-8000

William E. Murane* · (Banking, Securities, Environmental) · Holland & Hart · 555 Seventeenth Street, Suite 2900 · P.O. Box 8749 · Denver, CO 80201-8749 · 303-295-8000

David G. Palmer* · (Antitrust, Banking, Securities) · Gibson, Dunn & Crutcher 1801 California Street, Suite 4200 · Denver, CO 80202 · 303-298-7200

Kenneth L. Starr* · Holmes & Starr · Colorado State Bank Building, 26th Floor 1600 Broadway · Denver, CO 80202-4926 · 303-860-1500

Roger P. Thomasch* · (Commercial, Finance, Securities, Director & Officer Liability) · Ballard, Spahr, Andrews & Ingersoll · 1225 Seventeenth Street, Suite 2300 · Denver, CO 80202 · 303-292-2400

Tucker K. Trautman* · Ireland, Stapleton, Pryor & Pascoe · 1675 Broadway, Suite 2600 · P.O. Box 1410 · Denver, CO 80201 · 303-623-2700

Michael A. Williams* · Sherman & Howard · 3000 First Interstate Tower North 633 Seventeenth Street · Denver, CO 80202 · 303-297-2900

CORPORATE LAW

Robert J. Ahrenholz · Kutak, Rock & Campbell · 2400 ARCO Tower · 707 Seventeenth Street · Denver, CO 80202-3424 · 303-297-2400

H. Gregory Austin · Holland & Hart · 555 Seventeenth Street, Suite 2900 · P.O. Box 8749 · Denver, CO 80201-8749 · 303-295-8000

George W. Bermant · Gibson, Dunn & Crutcher · 1801 California Street, Suite 4200 · Denver, CO 80202 · 303-298-7200

Harold S. Bloomenthal · Holme Roberts & Owen · 1700 Lincoln Street, Suite 4100 · Denver, CO 80203 · 303-861-7000

James T. Bunch · Davis, Graham & Stubbs · 370 Seventeenth Street, Suite 4700 P.O. Box 185 · Denver, CO 80201-0185 · 303-892-9400

David Butler · (Banking, Mergers & Acquisitions, Securities) · Holland & Hart · 555 Seventeenth Street, Suite 2900 · P.O. Box 8749 · Denver, CO 80201-8749 · 303-295-8000

Garth C. Grissom · (Corporate Finance, Mergers & Acquisitions, Securities, Securities Regulation) · Sherman & Howard · 3000 First Interstate Tower North 633 Seventeenth Street · Denver, CO 80202 · 303-297-2900

Cannon Y. Harvey · Holme Roberts & Owen · 1700 Lincoln Street, Suite 4100 · Denver, CO 80203 · 303-861-7000

Hardin Holmes · (International Finance, Mergers & Acquisitions, Securities, Securities Regulation) · Holmes & Starr · Colorado State Bank Building, 26th Floor · 1600 Broadway · Denver, CO 80202-4926 · 303-860-1500

Dennis M. Jackson · Holland & Hart · 555 Seventeenth Street, Suite 2900 · P.O. Box 8749 · Denver, CO 80201-8749 · 303-295-8000

David R. Johnson · Sherman & Howard · 3000 First Interstate Tower North · 633 Seventeenth Street · Denver, CO 80202 · 303-297-2900

John P. Kanouff · (Corporate Finance, Securities, Securities Regulation) · Hopper, Kanouff, Smith, Peryam and Terry · Union Square Building, Suite 200 · 1610 Wynkoop Street · Denver, CO 80202 · 303-892-6003

Francis P. King · Lentz, Evans and King · Lincoln Center Building, Suite 2900 1660 Lincoln Street · Denver, CO 80264 · 303-861-4154

Cathy S. Krendl · Krendl & Krendl · 303 East 17th Avenue, Suite 900 · Denver, CO 80203 · 303-830-9100

Mark R. Levy · (Corporate Finance, Financial Institutions, Mergers & Acquisitions, Securities) · Holland & Hart · 555 Seventeenth Street, Suite 2900 · P.O. Box 8749 · Denver, CO 80201-8749 · 303-295-8000

John G. Lewis · (Corporate Finance, Mergers & Acquisitions, Securities) · Ireland, Stapleton, Pryor & Pascoe · 1675 Broadway, Suite 2600 · P.O. Box 1410 · Denver, CO 80201 · 303-623-2700

Ernest W. Lohf · Lohf, Shaiman & Ross · 900 Cherry Tower · 950 South Cherry Street · P.O. Box 24188 · Denver, CO 80222 · 303-753-9000

John W. Low · Sherman & Howard · 3000 First Interstate Tower North · 633 Seventeenth Street · Denver, CO 80202 · 303-297-2900

Joseph W. Morrisey, Jr. · Holme Roberts & Owen · 1700 Lincoln Street, Suite 4100 · Denver, CO 80203 · 303-861-7000

John E. Moye · Moye, Giles, O'Keefe, Vermeire & Gorrell · 1225 Seventeenth Street, 29th Floor · Denver, CO 80202 · 303-292-2900

James C. Owen, Jr. · Holme Roberts & Owen · 1700 Lincoln Street, Suite 4100 Denver, CO 80203 · 303-861-7000

William D. Scheid · Scheid and Horleck · 707 Seventeenth Street, Suite 2800 · Denver, CO 80202-3428 · 303-292-4100

Richard G. Wohlgenant · Holme Roberts & Owen · 1700 Lincoln Street, Suite 4100 · Denver, CO 80203 · 303-861-7000

Lester R. Woodward · Davis, Graham & Stubbs · 370 Seventeenth Street, Suite 4700 · P.O. Box 185 · Denver, CO 80201-0185 · 303-892-9400

Robert S. Zinn · Davis, Graham & Stubbs · 370 Seventeenth Street, Suite 4700 P.O. Box 185 · Denver, CO 80201-0185 · 303-892-9400

CRIMINAL DEFENSE

Daniel C. Hale* · (Non-Violent Crimes, Federal Court, State Court, Environmental Crimes) · Miller, Hale and Harrison · 2305 Broadway · Boulder, CO 80304-4132 · 303-449-2830

Robert Bruce Miller · Miller, Hale and Harrison · 2305 Broadway · Boulder, CO 80302 · 303-449-2830

Theodore A. Borrillo* · (State Court) · 5353 West Dartmouth Avenue, Suite 510 Denver, CO 80227 · 303-985-8888

Charles F. Brega · Brega & Winter · 1700 Lincoln Street, Suite 2222 · P.O. Box 5560 T.A. · Denver, CO 80203 · 303-866-9402

Leonard M. Chesler · Law Offices of Leonard M. Chesler · 1343 Delaware Street Denver, CO 80204 · 303-893-8933

Lee D. Foreman · Haddon, Morgan & Foreman · 150 East 10th Avenue · Denver, CO 80203 · 303-831-7364

Walter L. Gerash · Gerash, Robinson & Miranda · 1439 Court Place · Denver, CO 80202 · 303-825-5400

Harold A. Haddon · Haddon, Morgan & Foreman · 1034 Logan Street · Denver, CO 80203 · 303-831-7364

Robert T. McAllister · Martin, McAllister & Murphy · The Chancery, Suite 1600 1120 Lincoln Street · Denver, CO 80203 · 303-830-0566

Grady Bryan Morgan · Haddon, Morgan & Foreman · 150 East Tenth Avenue · Denver, CO 80203 · 303-831-7364

Larry S. Pozner* · (Federal Court, State Court, Environmental Crimes) · Pozner Hutt & Kaplan · 1890 Gaylord Street · Denver, CO 80206 · 303-333-1890

Joseph Saint-Veltri* · 1570 Emerson Street · Denver, CO 80218 · 303-832-6777

Daniel J. Sears · 430 East Seventh Avenue, Suite 200 · Denver, CO 80203 · 303-860-8100

Daniel T. Smith* · 430 East Seventh Avenue, Suite 200 · Denver, CO 80203 · 303-860-8100

Craig L. Truman · 1444 Wazee Street, Suite 205 · Denver, CO 80202 · 303-595-8008

FAMILY LAW

Richard V. Lohman* · Susemihl, Lohman, Kent, Carlson & McDermott · 660 Southpointe Court, Suite 210 · Colorado Springs, CO 80906 · 719-579-6500

James T. Bayer* · (Child Custody, Divorce, Marital Settlement Agreements, Equitable Division) · Bayer, Carey & McGee · 1660 Downing Street · Denver, CO 80218 · 303-830-8911

Michael F. DiManna · DiManna & Jackson · 1741 High Street · Denver, CO 80218 · 303-320-4848

William L. Hunnicutt* · (Child Custody, Divorce, Marital Settlement Agreements, Equitable Division) · Sherman & Howard · 3000 First Interstate Tower North · 633 Seventeenth Street · Denver, CO 80202 · 303-297-2900

Terrance R. Kelly · Kelly/Haglund/Garnsey & Kahn · 300 Blake Street Building 1441 Eighteenth Street · Denver, CO 80202-1296 · 303-296-9412

Lawrence Litvak* · (Divorce, Marital Settlement Agreements, Equitable Division) · 430 East Seventh Avenue · Denver, CO 80203-3605 · 303-837-0757

Jerry N. Snyder* · (Divorce, Marital Settlement Agreements, Equitable Division) 1355 South Colorado Boulevard, Suite 600 · Denver, CO 80222 · 303-691-0788

Robert T. Hinds · Robert Hinds & Associates · 1709 West Littleton Boulevard · Littleton, CO 80120 · 303-795-1078

FIRST AMENDMENT LAW

Jeffrey A. Chase · Holme Roberts & Owen · 1700 Lincoln Street, Suite 4100 · Denver, CO 80203 · 303-861-7000

Edwin S. Kahn* · (Appellate, Commercial, Securities) · Kelly/Haglund/Garnsey & Kahn · 300 Blake Street Building · 1441 Eighteenth Street · Denver, CO 80202-1296 · 303-296-9412

Thomas B. Kelley · Cooper & Kelley · 1660 Wynkoop Street, Suite 900 · Denver, CO 80202 · 303-825-2700

Bruce D. Pringle · Baker & Hostetler · 303 East 17th Avenue, Suite 1100 · Denver, CO 80203 · 303-861-0600

Arthur M. Schwartz · 600 Seventeenth Street, Suite 2250-S · Denver, CO 80202 303-893-2500

HEALTH CARE LAW

Henry C. Cleveland · Yu, Stromberg, Huotari & Cleveland · Cherry Creek National Bank Building, Suite 700 · 3033 East First Avenue · Denver, CO 80206 · 303-388-9311

Paul C. Daw · Sherman & Howard · 3000 First Interstate Tower North · 633 Seventeenth Street · Denver, CO 80202 · 303-297-2900

George D. Dikeou · Faegre & Benson · Republic Plaza, Suite 2500 · 370 Seventeenth Street · Denver, CO 80202-4004 · 303-592-5900

Joseph C. Jaudon, Jr.* · Long & Jaudon · The Bailey Mansion · 1600 Ogden Street · Denver, CO 80218-1414 · 303-832-1122

IMMIGRATION LAW

Philip M. Alterman · Carter & Alterman · 621 Seventeenth Street, Suite 1555 · Denver, CO 80293 · 303-294-0707

John S. Castellano · (Business Related) · Holland & Hart · 555 Seventeenth Street, Suite 2900 · P.O. Box 8749 · Denver, CO 80201-8749 · 303-295-8000

Nancy B. Elkind · Stern & Elkind · 1763 Franklin Street · Denver, CO 80218 · 303-861-8580

Dan Kowalski · 621 Seventeenth Street, Suite 1555 · Denver, CO 80293 · 303-298-0005

Kenneth H. Stern · Stern & Elkind · 1763 Franklin Street · Denver, CO 80218 303-861-8580

Ann Allott · Law Office Ann Allott · 2305 East Arapahoe Road, Suite 260 · Littleton, CO 80122 · 303-797-8055

INTELLECTUAL PROPERTY LAW

Michael D. McIntosh · Sheridan, Ross & McIntosh · One United Bank Center, 35th Floor · 1700 Lincoln Street · Denver, CO 80203 · 303-863-9700

LABOR AND EMPLOYMENT LAW

Craig M. Cornish · (Individuals) · Cornish and Dellolio · 431 North Cascade Avenue, Suite One · Colorado Springs, CO 80903 · 719-475-1204

Walter C. Brauer III · (Labor) · Brauer, Buescher, Valentine, Goldhammer & Kelman · 1563 Gaylord Street · Denver, CO 80206 · 303-333-7751

Thomas B. Buescher · (Labor) · Brauer, Buescher, Valentine, Goldhammer & Kelman · 1563 Gaylord Street · Denver, CO 80206 · 303-333-7751

E. Lee Dale · (Management) · Sherman & Howard · 3000 First Interstate Tower North · 633 Seventeenth Street · Denver, CO 80202 · 303-297-2900

Gregory A. Eurich* · (Management) · Holland & Hart · 555 Seventeenth Street, Suite 2900 · P.O. Box 8749 · Denver, CO 80201-8749 · 303-295-8000

Lynn D. Feiger · (Individuals) · Feiger, Collison & Killmer · 1800 Grant Street, Suite 800 · Denver, CO 80203 · 303-830-8833

Joseph M. Goldhammer · (Labor) · Brauer, Buescher, Valentine, Goldhammer & Kelman · 1563 Gaylord Street · Denver, CO 80206 · 303-333-7751

James E. Hautzinger* · (Management) · Sherman & Howard · 3000 First Interstate Tower North · 633 Seventeenth Street · Denver, CO 80202 · 303-297-2900

John M. Husband* · (Management) · Holland & Hart · 555 Seventeenth Street, Suite 2900 · P.O. Box 8749 · Denver, CO 80201-8749 · 303-295-8000

Sander N. Karp* · (Individuals, Age Discrimination) · 1100 Stout Street, Suite 470 · Denver, CO 80204-2064 · 303-825-3995

Donald P. MacDonald* · (Labor) · Hornbein MacDonald Fattor & Hobbs · 1900 Colorado State Bank Building · 1600 Broadway · Denver, CO 80202-4969 · 303-861-7070

John W. McKendree · (Labor) · Creswell Mansion · 1244 Grant Street · Denver, CO 80203 · 303-861-8906

Robert R. Miller* · (Management) · Stettner, Miller and Cohn · Lawrence Street Center, Suite 1000 · 1380 Lawrence Street · Denver, CO 80204-2058 · 303-534-0273

Robert L. Morris · (Management) · Morris & Lower · Denver Technological Center, Suite 630 · 7800 East Union Avenue · Denver, CO 80237-2753 · 303-779-4664

Charles W. Newcom* · (Management) · Sherman & Howard · 3000 First Interstate Tower North · 633 Seventeenth Street · Denver, CO 80202 · 303-297-2900

Theodore A. Olsen · (Management) · Sherman & Howard · 3000 First Interstate Tower North · 633 Seventeenth Street · Denver, CO 80202 · 303-297-2900

Bruce W. Sattler · (Management) · Faegre & Benson · Republic Plaza, Suite 2500 370 Seventeenth Street, Suite 2500 · Denver, CO 80202-4004 · 303-592-5678

William F. Schoeberlein · (Management) · Sherman & Howard · 3000 First Interstate Tower North · 633 Seventeenth Street · Denver, CO 80202 · 303-297-2900

Kenneth R. Stettner · (Management) · Stettner, Miller and Cohn · Lawrence Street Center, Suite 1000 · 1380 Lawrence Street · Denver, CO 80204-2058 · 303-534-0273

Warren L. Tomlinson · (Management) · Holland & Hart · 555 Seventeenth Street, Suite 2900 · P.O. Box 8749 · Denver, CO 80201-8749 · 303-295-8000

Robert G. Good · (Management) · Good & Good · 5105 DTC Parkway, Suite 202 Englewood, CO 80111 · 303-773-9889

Earl K. Madsen · (Management) · Bradley, Campbell & Carney · 1717 Washington Avenue · Golden, CO 80401-1994 · 303-278-3300

Kathryn E. Miller · (Management, Individuals) · Miller & Leher · 1901 West Littleton Boulevard · Littleton, CO 80120 · 303-798-2525

Robert Truhlar · (Individuals) · Truhlar & Truhlar · 1901 West Littleton Boulevard · Littleton, CO 80120 · 303-794-2404

NATURAL RESOURCES AND ENVIRONMENTAL LAW

Stephen D. Alfers · (Mining) · Davis, Graham & Stubbs · 370 Seventeenth Street, Suite 4700 · P.O. Box 185 · Denver, CO 80201-0185 · 303-892-9400

Howard Lawrence Boigon · (Oil & Gas) · Davis, Graham & Stubbs · 370 Seventeenth Street, Suite 4700 · P.O. Box 185 · Denver, CO 80201-0185 · 303-892-9400

John U. Carlson · (Water) · Carlson, Hammond & Paddock · 1700 Lincoln Street, Suite 3900 · Denver, CO 80203 · 303-861-9000

Robert T. Connery · Holland & Hart · 555 Seventeenth Street, Suite 2900 · P.O. Box 8749 · Denver, CO 80201-8749 · 303-295-8000

Frank Erisman · Holme Roberts & Owen · 1700 Lincoln Street, Suite 4100 · Denver, CO 80203 · 303-861-7000

Alan J. Gilbert · (Mining, Water, Air, Hazardous Waste) · Sherman & Howard · 3000 First Interstate Tower North · 633 Seventeenth Street · Denver, CO 80202 303-297-2900

Paul D. Holleman · (Oil & Gas) · Holme, Roberts & Owen · 1700 Lincoln Street, Suite 4100 · Denver, CO 80203 · 303-861-7000

Julia Hook · (Oil & Gas, Coal, Mining, Indian) · Holland & Hart · 555 Seventeenth Street, Suite 2900 · P.O. Box 8749 · Denver, CO 80201-8749 · 303-295-8000

Kenneth D. Hubbard · (Mining, Oil & Gas, Coal, Mining) · Holland & Hart · 555 Seventeenth Street, Suite 2900 · P.O. Box 8749 · Denver, CO 80201-8749-8749 · 303-295-8000

Henry W. Ipsen · Holme Roberts & Owen · 1700 Lincoln Street, Suite 4100 · Denver, CO 80203 · 303-861-7000

James M. King · Sherman & Howard · 3000 First Interstate Tower North · 633 Seventeenth Street · Denver, CO 80202 · 303-297-2900

Rodney D. Knutson · (Oil & Gas, Mining) · Knutson, Brightwell & Reeves · 1200 Hudson's Bay Centre · 1600 Stout Street · Denver, CO 80202-3133 · 303-825-6000

Laura Lindley · (Oil & Gas) · Poulson, Odell & Peterson · 1775 Sherman Street, Suite 1400 · Denver, CO 80203 · 303-861-4400

William R. Marsh* · (Mining, Natural Resource Litigation) · Sherman & Howard 3000 First Interstate Tower North · 633 Seventeenth Street · Denver, CO 80202 303-297-2900

Harold G. Morris, Jr. · (Mining; Oil & Gas) · Lindquist, Vennum & Christensen 600 Seventeenth Street South, Suite 2125 · Denver, CO 80202 · 303-297-2900

Davis O. O'Connor · (Oil & Gas, Coal, Mining) · Holland & Hart · 555 Seventeenth Street, Suite 2900 · P.O. Box 8749 · Denver, CO 80201-8749 · 303-295-8000

William G. Odell · (Oil & Gas) · Poulson, Odell & Peterson · 1775 Sherman Street, Suite 1400 · Denver, CO 80203 · 303-861-4400

Randy L. Parcel · (Mining) · Parcel, Mauro, Hultin & Spaanstra · 1801 California Street, Suite 3600 · Denver, CO 80202 · 303-292-6400

Paul D. Phillips · (Air, Hazardous Waste) · Holland & Hart · 555 Seventeenth Street, Suite 2900 · P.O. Box 8749 · Denver, CO 80201-8749 · 303-295-8000

James M. Piccone · (Oil & Gas) · Davis, Graham & Stubbs · 370 Seventeenth Street, Suite 4700 · P.O. Box 185 · Denver, CO 80201-0185 · 303-892-9400

George E. Reeves · Knutson, Brightwell & Reeves · 1200 Hudson's Bay Centre 1600 Stout Street · Denver, CO 80202-3133 · 303-825-4877

Paul J. Schlauch · (Mining) · Sherman & Howard · 3000 First Interstate Tower North · 633 Seventeenth Street · Denver, CO 80202 · 303-297-2900

Don H. Sherwood* · (Mining) · Sherman & Howard · First Interstate Tower North · 633 Seventeenth Street · Denver, CO 80202 · 303-297-2900

Elizabeth H. Temkin · Davis, Graham & Stubbs · 370 Seventeenth Street, Suite 4700 · P.O. Box 185 · Denver, CO 80201-0185 · 303-892-9400

John F. Welborn · (Oil & Gas) · Welborn, Dufford, Brown & Tooley · 1700 Broadway, Suite 1700 · Denver, CO 80290-1701 · 303-861-8013

J. Kemper Will · Law Offices of J. Kemper Will · 5251 DTC Parkway · Englewood, CO 80111 · 303-796-2626

PERSONAL INJURY LITIGATION

John A. Purvis* · Buchanan, Gray, Purvis & Schuetze · The Exeter Building, Suite 501 · 1050 Walnut Street · Boulder, CO 80302 · 303-442-3366

Robert A. Schuetze · Buchanan, Gray, Purvis & Schuetze · The Exeter Building, Suite 501 · 1050 Walnut Street · Boulder, CO 80302 · 303-442-3366

William A. Trine · (Plaintiffs) · Williams, Trine, Greenstein and Griffith · 1435 Arapahoe Avenue · Boulder, CO 80302-6390 · 303-442-0173

Douglas E. Bragg* · (Plaintiffs) · Bragg, Baker & Cederberg · Dominion Plaza, North Tower, Suite 1700N · 600 Seventeenth Street · Denver, CO 80202 · 303-571-4030

Charles F. Brega · (Plaintiffs) · Brega & Winter · 1700 Lincoln, Suite 2222 · Denver, CO 80203 · 303-866-9400

John L. Breit* · (Professional Malpractice, Airplane Collision) · Breit, Best, Richman and Bosch · Writer Square, Suite 960 · 1512 Larimer Street · Denver, CO 80202 · 303-573-7777

Arthur H. Downey* · (Defendants, Medical Malpractice, Products Liability, Appellate) · Downey & Douglas · 312 Cherry Tower · 950 South Cherry Street · Denver, CO 80222 · 303-759-1350

Walter L. Gerash · (Plaintiffs) · Gerash, Robinson, Miller & Miranda · 1439 Court Place · Denver, CO 80202 · 303-825-5400

Daniel S. Hoffman · Holme Roberts & Owen · 1700 Lincoln Street, Suite 4100 · Denver, CO 80203 · 303-861-7000

Joseph C. Jaudon, Jr.* · (Defendants, Medical Malpractice, Products Liability/ Medical & Drug, Professional Malpractice, Complex Litigation) · Long & Jaudon · The Bailey Mansion · 1600 Ogden Street · Denver, CO 80218-1414 · 303-832-1122

William L. Keating · (Plaintiffs) · Fogel, Keating & Wagner · 1199 Bannock Street · Denver, CO 80204 · 303-534-0401

Alex Stephen Keller* · (Plaintiffs) · Keller, Dunievitz, Johnson & Wahlberg · 2480 Prudential Tower · 1050 Seventeenth Street · Denver, CO 80265 · 303-571-5302

Richard W. Laugesen · (Insurance) · Anderson, Campbell and Laugesen · 3464 South Willow Street · Denver, CO 80231 · 303-696-0894

Gerald P. McDermott* · (Plaintiffs) · McDermott, Hansen, Anderson & Reilly · 1890 Gaylord Street · Denver, CO 80206-1211 · 303-399-6037

Neil Hillyard* · (Plaintiffs, Medical Malpractice, Products Liability, Automobile Collision) · Branney, Hillyard and Kudla · First Interstate Center, 10th Floor · 3333 South Bannock Street · Englewood, CO 80110 · 303-761-5600

Irving G. Johnson · (Defendants) · Pryor, Carney and Johnson · 6200 South Syracuse Way, Suite 400 · P.O. Box 6559 · Englewood, CO 80155-6559 · 303-771-6200

Peter W. Pryor* · (Plaintiffs, Medical Malpractice, Professional Malpractice) · Pryor, Carney and Johnson · 6200 South Syracuse Way, Suite 400 · P.O. Box 6559 Englewood, CO 80155-6559 · 303-771-6200

PUBLIC UTILITY LAW

Steve Denman · Sherman & Howard · 3000 First Interstate Tower North · 633 Seventeenth Street · Denver, CO 80202 · 303-297-2900

Robert M. Pomeroy · Holland & Hart · 4601 DTC Boulevard, Suite 1050 · Denver, CO 80237 · 303-295-8000

Tucker K. Trautman* · Ireland, Stapleton, Pryor & Pascoe · 1675 Broadway, Suite 2600 · P.O. Box 1410 · Denver, CO 80201 · 303-623-2700

REAL ESTATE LAW

Joel C. Davis · Dietze, Davis and Porter · 2060 Broadway, Suite 400 · P.O. Box 1530 · Boulder, CO 80306 · 303-447-1375

Peter C. Dietze · Dietze, Davis and Porter · 2060 Broadway, Suite 400 · P.O. Box 1530 · Boulder, CO 80306 · 303-447-1375

Charles D. Calvin · Davis, Graham & Stubbs · 370 Seventeenth Street, Suite 4700 · P.O. Box 185 · Denver, CO 80201-0185 · 303-892-9400

Charlton H. Carpenter · Fairfield and Woods · One United Bank Center · 1700 Lincoln Street, Suite 2400 · Denver, CO 80203-4524 · 303-830-2400

Willis V. Carpenter · (Commercial Transactions) · Carpenter & Klatskin · 1500 Denver Club Building · 518 Seventeenth Street · Denver, CO 80202 · 303-534-6315

James E. Culhane · Davis, Graham & Stubbs · 370 Seventeenth Street, Suite 4700 · P.O. Box 185 · Denver, CO 80201-0185 · 303-892-9400

James L. Cunningham · Sherman & Howard · 3000 First Interstate Tower North 633 Seventeenth Street · Denver, CO 80202 · 303-297-2900

James E. Hegarty · Holland & Hart · 555 Seventeenth Street, Suite 2900 · P.O. Box 8749 · Denver, CO 80201-8749 · 303-295-8000

George M. Hopfenbeck, Jr. · Davis, Graham & Stubbs · 370 Seventeenth Street, Suite 4700 · P.O. Box 185 · Denver, CO 80201-0185 · 303-892-9400

Paul A. Jacobs · Holme Roberts & Owen · 1700 Lincoln Street, Suite 4100 · Denver, CO 80203 · 303-861-7000

Bruce B. Johnson · (Commercial Transactions, Industrial Transactions, Foreclosures) · Otten, Johnson, Robinson, Neff and Ragonetti · 1600 Colorado National Building · 950 Seventeenth Street · Denver, CO 80202 · 303-825-8400

John S. Kellogg · 4704 Harlan Street, Suite 300 · Denver, CO 80212 · 303-458-7117

Charles E. Rhyne · Gorsuch, Kirgis, Campbell, Walker and Grover · 1401 Seventeenth Street, Suite 1100 · P.O. Box 17180 · Denver, CO 80217-0180 · 303-534-1200

Frank L. Robinson · Otten, Johnson, Robinson, Neff and Ragonetti · 1600 Colorado National Building · 950 Seventeenth Street · Denver, CO 80202 · 303-825-8400

W. Dean Salter · Holme Roberts & Owen · 1700 Lincoln Street, Suite 4100 · Denver, CO 80203 · 303-861-7000

Richard G. Wohlgenant · Holme Roberts & Owen · 1700 Lincoln Street, Suite 4100 · Denver, CO 80203 · 303-861-7000

TAX AND EMPLOYEE BENEFITS LAW

Michael J. Abramovitz · Abramovitz, Merriam & Shaw · 1625 Broadway, Suite 770 · Denver, CO 80202 · 303-592-5404

Cynthia C. Benson · (Employee Benefits) · Sherman & Howard · 3000 First Interstate Tower North · 633 Seventeenth Street · Denver, CO 80202 · 303-297-2900

James E. Bye · Holme Roberts & Owen · 1700 Lincoln Street, Suite 4100 · Denver, CO 80203 · 303-861-7000

Douglas M. Cain · Sherman & Howard · 3000 First Interstate Tower North · 633 Seventeenth Street · Denver, CO 80202 · 303-297-2900

John DeBruyn · DeBruyn and Atlass · 2100 East 14th Avenue · Denver, CO 80206 · 303-377-0707

Stanley L. Drexler · Drexler & Wald · One Tabor Center, Suite 2350 · 1200 Seventeenth Street · Denver, CO 80202 · 303-825-3531

Bruce L. Evans · (Employee Benefits) · Lentz, Evans and King · Lincoln Center Building, Suite 2900 · 1660 Lincoln Street · Denver, CO 80264 · 303-861-4154

Theodore Z. Gelt · Gelt, Fleishman & Sterling · 303 East 19th Avenue, Suite 1110 · Denver, CO 80203 · 303-861-1000

Peter C. Guthery · Wade Ash Woods Hill & Guthery · 360 South Monroe Street, Suite 400 · Denver, CO 80209 · 303-322-8943

Samuel P. Guyton · Holland & Hart · 555 Seventeenth Street, Suite 2900 · P.O. Box 8749 · Denver, CO 80201-8749 · 303-295-8000

Marcia Chadwick Holt · (Employee Benefits) · Davis, Graham & Stubbs · 370 Seventeenth Street, Suite 4700 · P.O. Box 185 · Denver, CO 80201-0185 · 303-892-9400

Francis P. King · Lentz, Evans and King · Lincoln Center Building, Suite 2900 1660 Lincoln Street · Denver, CO 80264 · 303-861-4154

Hover T. Lentz · Lentz, Evans and King · Lincoln Center Building, Suite 2900 1660 Lincoln Street · Denver, CO 80264 · 303-861-4154

Claude M. Maer, Jr. · 288 Clayton Street, Suite 304 · Denver, CO 80206 · 303-377-3500

Bruce R. Muir · (Employee Benefits) · Lentz, Evans and King · Lincoln Center Building, Suite 2900 · 1660 Lincoln Street · Denver, CO 80264 · 303-861-4154

Donald J. O'Connor · Davis, Graham & Stubbs · 370 Seventeenth Street, Suite 4700 · P.O. Box 185 · Denver, CO 80201-0185 · 303-892-9400

Robert S. Rich · (Corporate & Partnership Transactions, Tax Disputes, International Tax) · Davis, Graham & Stubbs · 370 Seventeenth Street, Suite 4700 · P.O. Box 185 · Denver, CO 80201-0185 · 303-892-9400

R. Michael Sanchez · (Employee Benefits) · Sherman & Howard · 3000 First Interstate Tower North · 633 Seventeenth Street · Denver, CO 80202 · 303-297-2900

Joseph H. Thibodeau · Joseph H. Thibodeau PC · 155 South Madison Street, Suite 209 · Denver, CO 80209 · 303-320-1250

Robert J. Welter · Holme Roberts & Owen · 1700 Lincoln Street, Suite 4100 · Denver, CO 80203 · 303-861-7000

TRUSTS AND ESTATES

Christopher Brauchli · Brauchli—Snyder · Continental Building, Suite 400 · 1401 Walnut Street · Boulder, CO 80302 · 303-443-1118

William K. Brown · (Estate Planning, Estate Administration, Charitable Trusts) Holland & Hart · Holly Sugar Building, Palmer Center, Suite 1300 · P.O. Box 2340 · Colorado Springs, CO 80901 · 719-475-7730

Clifton B. Kruse, Jr. · (Estate Planning, Estate Administration) · Kruse & Lynch 1050 Holly Sugar Building · Chase Stone Center · Colorado Springs, CO 80903 · 719-473-9911

Walter B. Ash · Wade Ash Woods Hill & Guthery · 360 South Monroe Street, Suite 400 · Denver, CO 80209 · 303-322-8943

Theodore B. Atlass* · DeBruyn and Atlass · 2100 East 14th Avenue · Denver, CO 80206 · 303-377-0707

Donald H. Burkhardt · 1350 Seventeenth Street, Suite 360 · Denver, CO 80202 303-623-2112

William P. Cantwell · Sherman & Howard · 3000 First Interstate Tower North · 633 Seventeenth Street · Denver, CO 80202 · 303-297-2900

Jay H. Chapman · Chapman, Klein & Associates · 1355 South Colorado Boulevard, Suite 600 · Denver, CO 80222 · 303-759-4004

Kenneth G. Christianssen · (Estate Planning, Estate Administration, Estate, Gift & Fiduciary Income Tax) · Gorsuch, Kirgis, Campbell, Walker and Grover · 1401 Seventeenth Street, Suite 1100 · P.O. Box 17180 · Denver, CO 80217-0180 · 303-534-1200

Judson W. Detrick · Holme Roberts & Owen · 1700 Lincoln Street, Suite 4100 Denver, CO 80203 · 303-861-7000

J. Michael Farley · Holland & Hart · 555 Seventeenth Street, Suite 2900 · P.O. Box 8749 · Denver, CO 80201-8749 · 303-295-8000

Constance L. Hauver · Sherman & Howard · 3000 First Interstate Tower North 633 Seventeenth Street · Denver, CO 80202 · 303-297-2900

Joseph G. Hodges, Jr. · Law Offices of Joseph G. Hodges · 3300 East First Avenue, Suite 600 · Denver, CO 80206 · 303-377-0070

Marcia Chadwick Holt · Davis, Graham & Stubbs · 70 Seventeenth Street, Suite 4700 · P.O. Box 185 · Denver, CO 80201-0185 · 303-892-9400

William S. Huff · Holme Roberts & Owen · 1700 Lincoln Street, Suite 4100 · Denver, CO 80203 · 303-861-7000

Hover T. Lentz · Lentz, Evans and King · Lincoln Center Building, Suite 2900 1660 Lincoln Street · Denver, CO 80264 · 303-861-4154

William C. McGehee · Gorsuch, Kirgis, Campbell, Walker and Grover · 1401 Seventeenth Street, Suite 1100 · P.O. Box 17180 · Denver, CO 80210-0180 · 303-534-1200

Victor Quinn · Cockrell, Quinn & Creighton · Two United Bank Center, Suite 1516 · 1700 Broadway · Denver, CO 80290 · 303-860-7140

L. William Schmidt, Jr. · (Estate Planning) · One Tabor Center · 1220 Seventeenth Street, Suite 1000 · Denver, CO 80202-3357 · 303-629-4806

C. Jean Stewart · Holme Roberts & Owen · 1700 Lincoln Street, Suite 4100 · Denver, CO 80203 · 303-861-7000

Raymond L. Sutton, Jr. · Baker & Hostetler · 303 East 17th Avenue, Suite 1100 Denver, CO 80203 · 303-861-0600

James R. Wade · Wade Ash Woods Hill & Guthery · 360 South Monroe Street, Suite 400 · Denver, CO 80209 · 303-322-8943

Lucius E. Woods · Wade Ash Woods Hill & Guthery · 360 South Monroe Street, Suite 400 · Denver, CO 80209 · 303-322-8943

Joseph E. Doussard · Doussard Hodel & Markman · 143 Union Boulevard, Suite 660 · Lakewood, CO 80228 · 303-986-1523

David B. Shaw · Shaw & Quigg · 300 Thatcher Building · 501 North Main Street P.O. Box 5003 · Pueblo, CO 81002-5003 · 719-543-8596

CONNECTICUT

BANKRUPTCY LAW

Richard D. Zeisler · (Business Reorganization, Creditors' Rights, Debtors' Rights, Bankruptcy Litigation) · Zeisler & Zeisler · 558 Clinton Avenue · P.O. Box 3186 · Bridgeport, CT 06605-0186 · 203-368-4234

Richard F. Casher · Hebb & Gitlin · One State Street · Hartford, CT 06103-3178 203-549-0333

Richard A. Gitlin · Hebb & Gitlin · One State Street · Hartford, CT 06103-3178 203-549-0333

Martin W. Hoffman · 410 Asylum Street · Hartford, CT 06103 · 203-525-4287

Harold S. Horwich · Hebb & Gitlin · One State Street · Hartford, CT 06103-3178 203-549-0333

John B. Nolan · Day, Berry & Howard · CityPlace · 185 Asylum Street · Hartford, CT 06103-3499 · 203-275-0289

Michael J. Reilly · Hebb & Gitlin · One State Street · Hartford, CT 06103-3178 203-549-0333

Donald Lee Rome · Robinson & Cole · One Commercial Plaza · Hartford, CT 06103-3597 · 203-275-8200

Robert U. Sattin · Reid and Riege · One State Street · Hartford, CT 06103-3185 203-278-1150

Howard L. Siegel · Hoberman & Pollack · One State Street · Hartford, CT 06103 203-549-1000

Andrew M. DiPietro, Jr. · DiPietro, Kantrovitz & Brownstein · 64 Grove Street P.O. Drawer 1406 · New Haven, CT 06505 · 203-789-0070

John H. Krick · Sachs, Berman, Rashba & Shure · One Church Street, Seventh Floor · P.O. Box 1960 · New Haven, CT 06509 · 203-787-9514

BUSINESS LITIGATION

L. Douglas Shrader* · Zeldes, Needle & Cooper · 1000 Lafayette Boulevard · P.O. Box 1740 · Bridgeport, CT 06601-1740 · 203-333-9441

Jacob D. Zeldes · Zeldes, Needle & Cooper · 1000 Lafayette Boulevard · P.O. Box 1740 · Bridgeport, CT 06601-1740 · 203-333-9441

Ralph G. Elliot · Tyler, Cooper & Alcorn · City Place, 35th Floor · 185 Asylum Street · Hartford, CT 06103-3488 · 203-522-1216

Thomas J. Groark, Jr. · Day, Berry & Howard · CityPlace · 185 Asylum Street · Hartford, CT 06103-3499 · 203-275-0100

Edward F. Hennessey* · Robinson & Cole · One Commercial Plaza · Hartford, CT 06103-3597 · 203-275-8200

Wesley W. Horton · (Appellate) · Moller, Horton & Fineberg · 90 Gillett Street Hartford, CT 06105 · 203-522-8338

James A. Wade* · Robinson & Cole · One Commercial Plaza · Hartford, CT 06103-3597 · 203-275-8200

Albert Zakarian · Day, Berry & Howard · CityPlace · 185 Asylum Street · Hartford, CT 06103-3499 · 203-275-0100

J. Daniel Sagarin · Hurwitz & Sagarin · 147 North Broad Street · Milford, CT 06460-0112 · 203-877-6071

William J. Doyle* · Wiggin & Dana · One Century Tower · New Haven, CT 06508-1832 · 203-498-4400

Anthony M. Fitzgerald* · Carmody & Torrance · 59 Elm Street · P.O. Box 1990 New Haven, CT 06509 · 203-777-5501

William F. Gallagher* · (Appellate) · Gallagher, Gallagher & Calistro · 1377 Boulevard · P.O. Box 1925 · New Haven, CT 06509 · 203-624-4165

Ira B. Grudberg · Jacobs, Grudberg, Belt & Dow · 350 Orange Street · P.O. Box 606 · New Haven, CT 06503 · 203-772-3100

William R. Murphy* · Tyler, Cooper & Alcorn · 205 Church Street · P.O. Box 1936 · New Haven, CT 06509-1910 · 203-789-0700

Shaun S. Sullivan · Wiggin & Dana · One Century Tower · P.O. Box 1832 · New Haven, CT 06508-1832 · 203-498-4315

James R. Fogarty · Epstein & Fogarty · 733 Summer Street · Stamford, CT 06901 203-327-3400

Emanuel Margolis · Wofsey, Rosen, Kweskin & Kuriansky · 600 Summer Street Stamford, CT 06901 · 203-327-2300

John S. McGeeney* · Paul, Hastings, Janofsky & Walker · 1055 Washington Boulevard, Ninth Floor · Stamford, CT 06901 · 203-961-7403

Francis J. McNamara, Jr. · Cummings & Lockwood · 10 Stamford Forum · P.O. Box 120 · Stamford, CT 06904 · 203-327-1700

James F. Stapleton · (Marital Settlement Agreements) · Day, Berry & Howard · One Canterbury Green · Stamford, CT 06901 · 203-977-7300

Fredric H. Weisberg · (Banking, Commercial, RICO, Securities) · Cummings & Lockwood · 10 Stamford Forum · P.O. Box 120 · Stamford, CT 06904 · 203-327-1700

Lawrence W. Kanaga III · 830 Post Road East · P.O. Box 336 · Westport, CT 06881-0336 · 203-221-0696

CORPORATE LAW

David R. Chipman · (Corporate Finance, International, Leveraged Buyouts, Mergers & Acquisitions) · Gager & Henry · Danbury Executive Tower · 30 Main Street · Danbury, CT 06810 · 203-743-6363

Jennifer N. Boyd · Whitman & Ransom · Two Greenwich Plaza · P.O. Box 2250 Greenwich, CT 06836 · 203-869-3800

Morris W. Banks · Sorokin Sorokin Gross Hyde & Williams · One Corporate Center · Hartford, CT 06103-3291 · 203-525-6645

William Barnett · (Leveraged Buyouts) · Hoberman & Pollack · One State Street Hartford, CT 06103 · 203-549-1000

C. Duane Blinn · Day, Berry & Howard · CityPlace · 185 Asylum Street · Hartford, CT 06103-3499 · 203-275-0100

William H. Cuddy · Day, Berry & Howard · CityPlace · 185 Asylum Street · Hartford, CT 06103-3499 · 203-275-0100

Stanford N. Goldman, Jr. · Schatz & Schatz, Ribicoff & Kotkin · One Financial Plaza · 90 State House Square · Hartford, CT 06103-3902 · 203-522-3234

Timothy L. Largay · Murtha, Cullina, Richter and Pinney · CityPlace · P.O. Box 230197 · Hartford, CT 06123-0197 · 203-240-6000

James I. Lotstein · (Banking, Corporate Finance, Mergers & Acquisitions, Securities) · Cummings & Lockwood · CityPlace I · 185 Asylum Street · Hartford, CT 06103 · 203-275-6700

John S. Murtha · Murtha, Cullina, Richter and Pinney · CityPlace · P.O. Box 230197 · Hartford, CT 06123-0197 · 203-240-6000

Geoffrey W. Nelson · Murtha, Cullina, Richter and Pinney · CityPlace · P.O. Box 3197 · Hartford, CT 06103-0197 · 203-240-6000

Willard F. Pinney, Jr. · Murtha, Cullina, Richter and Pinney · CityPlace · P.O. Box 230197 · Hartford, CT 06123-0197 · 203-240-6000

Sanford L. Rosenberg · Sorokin Sorokin Gross Hyde & Williams · One Corporate Center · Hartford, CT 06103-3291 · 203-525-6645

Thomas L. Smith · Robinson & Cole · One Commercial Plaza · Hartford, CT 06103-3597 · 203-275-8200

Alan R. Spier · Robinson & Cole · One Commercial Plaza · Hartford, CT 06103-3597 · 203-275-8200

Michael Sudarsky · Murtha, Cullina, Richter and Pinney · CityPlace · P.O. Box 230197 · Hartford, CT 06123-0197 · 203-240-6000

Milton P. DeVane · Tyler, Cooper & Alcorn · 205 Church Street · P.O. Box 1936 New Haven, CT 06509 · 203-789-0700

Irving S. Schloss · Tyler, Cooper & Alcorn · 205 Church Street · P.O. Box 1936 New Haven, CT 06509 · 203-789-0700

Samuel S. Cross · Kelley, Drye & Warren · Six Stamford Forum · Stamford, CT 06901 · 203-324-1400

Harold B. Finn III · Finn Dixon & Herling · One Landmark Square, Suite 600 · Stamford, CT 06901 · 203-964-8000

F. Lee Griffith, III · Day, Berry & Howard · One Canterbury Green · Stamford, CT 06901 · 203-977-7300

Richard McGrath · (Corporate Finance, Mergers & Acquisitions, Securities, Securities Regulation) · Cummings & Lockwood · 10 Stamford Forum · P.O. Box 120 · Stamford, CT 06904 · 203-327-1700

Michael L. Widland · Schatz & Schatz, Ribicoff & Kotkin · One Landmark Square, 17th Floor · Stamford, CT 06901-2676 · 203-964-0027

David W. Collins · Carmody & Torrance · 50 Leavenworth Street · P.O. Box 1110 Waterbury, CT 06721 · 203-573-1200

Curtis V. Titus · Gager & Henry · One Exchange Place · P.O. Box 2480 · Waterbury, CT 06722 · 203-597-5100

David R. Levett · Levett, Rockwood & Sanders · 33 Riverside Avenue · P.O. Box 5116 · Westport, CT 06880 · 203-222-0885

CRIMINAL DEFENSE

John Robert Gulash · Gulash & Fleischmann · 135 Elm Street · P.O. Box 9118 Bridgeport, CT 06601 · 203-367-7440

Jacob D. Zeldes · Zeldes, Needle & Cooper · 1000 Lafayette Boulevard · P.O. Box 1740 · Bridgeport, CT 06601-1740 · 203-333-9441

Richard R. Brown · Brown, Paindiris & Zarella · 750 Main Street, Fourth Floor Hartford, CT 06103 · 203-522-3343

F. Mac Buckley* · (Non-Violent Crimes, Federal Court, State Court, Environmental Crimes) · 83 Oak Street · Hartford, CT 06106 · 203-293-1161

Hubert J. Santos · Santos, Peck & Smith · 51 Russ Street · Hartford, CT 06106 203-249-6548

James A. Wade* · Robinson & Cole · One Commercial Plaza · Hartford, CT 06103-3597 · 203-275-8200

J. Daniel Sagarin* · Hurwitz & Sagarin · 147 North Broad Street · P.O. Box 112 Milford, CT 06460-0112 · 203-877-6071

Ira B. Grudberg · Jacobs, Grudberg, Belt & Dow · 350 Orange Street · P.O. Box 606 · New Haven, CT 06503 · 203-772-3100

Hugh F. Keefe* · (Violent Crimes, Non-Violent Crimes, Federal Court, State Court) · Lynch, Traub, Keefe and Errante · 52 Trumbull Street · P.O. Box 1612 New Haven, CT 06506 · 203-787-0275

David S. Golub* · Silver, Golub & Teitell · 184 Atlantic Street · P.O. Box 389 · Stamford, CT 06904 · 203-325-4491

FAMILY LAW

Alfred R. Belinkie* · Belinkie & Blawie · 1087 Broad Street · Bridgeport, CT 06604-4379 · 203-368-4201

Michael A. Meyers* · Meyers, Breiner & Neufeld · 1000 Lafayette Boulevard · Bridgeport, CT 06604 · 203-333-9410

Dianne M. Andersen · Andersen & Ferlazzo · 72 North Street · Danbury, CT 06810 · 203-744-2260

Lloyd Cutsumpas* · Cutsumpas, Collins, Hannafin, Garamella, Jaber & Tuozzolo · 148 Deer Hill Avenue · P.O. Box 440 · Danbury, CT 06813 · 203-744-2150

Gaetano Ferro* · (Child Custody, Divorce, Marital Settlement Agreements, Equitable Division) · P.O. Box 175 · Greens Farms, CT 06436 · 203-254-3870

Donald J. Cantor · Hyman, Cantor, Seichter & Klau · 60 Washington Street · Hartford, CT 06106 · 203-549-6523

Bruce Louden · Louden & Forzani · 43 Woodland Street · Hartford, CT 06105 203-246-7200

C. Ian McLachlan* · Cummings & Lockwood · Cityplace I · Hartford, CT 06103 203-275-6700

Gerald A. Roisman* · (Child Custody, Divorce, Marital Settlement Agreements, Equitable Division) · Roisman & McClure · 31 Grand Street · Hartford, CT 06106-4692 · 203-549-6700

Morton E. Marvin* · Law Offices of Morton E. Marvin · 51 Locust Avenue · New Canaan, CT 06840 · 203-966-9655

Jeroll R. Silverberg* · P.O. Box 1026 · New Canaan, CT 06840 · 203-966-9547

Gary I. Cohen · Cohen & Rubin · 59 Elm Street · P.O. Box 1800 · New Haven, CT 06507-1800 · 203-782-9440

James R. Greenfield · Greenfield & Murphy · 234 Church Street · P.O. Box 1103 New Haven, CT 06504-1103 · 203-787-6711

Jean L. Welty · Law Office of Jean L. Welty · 385 Orange Street · P.O. Box 1662 New Haven, CT 06507 · 203-782-1616

Thomas A. Bishop* · (Child Custody, Divorce, Marital Settlement Agreements, Equitable Division) · Susman, Shapiro, Wool, Brennan & Gray · Mariner Square, Suite 240 · Eugene O'Neill Drive · P.O. Box 1591 · New London, CT 06320 · 203-442-4416

Francis J. Foley III* · Foley Horvitz & Gravalec · The Thayer Building · Sixteen Franklin Square · Norwich, CT 06360 · 203-889-5529

Robert A. Epstein · Epstein & Fogarty · 733 Summer Street · Stamford, CT 06901 · 203-327-3400

Samuel V. Schoonmaker III · Cummings & Lockwood · 10 Stamford Forum · P.O. Box 120 · Stamford, CT 06904 · 203-327-1700

Arthur E. Balbirer* · Berkowitz & Balbirer · 253 Post Road West · P.O. Box 808 Westport, CT 06881 · 203-226-1001

FIRST AMENDMENT LAW

Ralph G. Elliot · Tyler, Cooper & Alcorn · City Place, 35th Floor · Hartford, CT 06103-3488 · 203-522-1216

Mark R. Kravitz · Wiggin & Dana · One Century Tower · New Haven, CT 06508-1832 · 203-498-4400

Alan Neigher · Byelas & Neigher · 1804 Post Road East · Westport, CT 06880 · 203-259-0599

HEALTH CARE LAW

Raymond S. Andrews, Jr. · Robinson & Cole · One Commercial Plaza · Hartford, CT 06103-3597 · 203-275-8200

Stephen E. Ronai · Murtha, Cullina, Richter and Pinney · CityPlace · P.O. Box 3197 · Hartford, CT 06103-0197 · 203-240-6000

Melinda A. Agsten · Wiggin & Dana · One Century Tower · New Haven, CT 06508-1832 · 203-498-4400

J. Michael Eisner · Wiggin & Dana · One Century Tower · New Haven, CT 06508-1832 · 203-498-4400

David R. Levett · Levett, Rockwood & Sanders · 33 Riverside Avenue · P.O. Box 5116 · Westport, CT 06880 · 203-226-8025

LABOR AND EMPLOYMENT LAW

E. Terry Durant · (Management) · Durant, Sabanosh, Nichols & Houston · 1000 LaFayette Boulevard · P.O. Box 860 · Bridgeport, CT 06601-0860 · 203-366-3438

George N. Nichols · (Management) · Durant, Sabanosh, Nichols & Houston · 1000 LaFayette Boulevard · P.O. Box 860 · Bridgeport, CT 06601-0860 · 203-366-3438

Gregg D. Adler · (Individuals) · Gould, Livingston, Adler & Pulda · 606 Farmington Avenue · Hartford, CT 06105 · 203-233-9821

Brian Clemow · (Management) · Shipman & Goodwin · 799 Main Street · Hartford, CT 06103-2377 · 203-549-4770

Thomas M. Cloherty · (Management) · Murtha, Cullina, Richter and Pinney · CityPlace · P.O. Box 230197 · Hartford, CT 06123-0197 · 203-240-6000

William M. Cullina · (Management) · Murtha, Cullina, Richter and Pinney · CityPlace · P.O. Box 3197 · Hartford, CT 06103-0197 · 203-240-6000

Burton Kainen* · (Management) · Siegel, O'Connor, Schiff, Zangari & Kainen · 370 Asylum Street · Hartford, CT 06103 · 203-727-8900

Susan K. Krell · (Management) · Wiggin & Dana · One City Place · Hartford, CT 06103-3403 · 203-297-3700

Richard D. O'Connor · (Management) · Siegel, O'Connor, Schiff, Zangari & Kainen · 370 Asylum Street · Hartford, CT 06103 · 203-727-8900

Paul W. Orth* · (Individuals) · Shipman & Goodwin · 799 Main Street · Hartford, CT 06103-2377 · 203-549-4770

Emanuel N. Psarakis · (Management) · Robinson & Cole · One Commercial Plaza Hartford, CT 06103-3597 · 203-275-8200

Jay S. Siegel · (Management) · Siegel, O'Connor, Schiff, Zangari & Kainen · 370 Asylum Street · Hartford, CT 06103 · 203-727-8900

Felix J. Springer · (Management) · Day, Berry & Howard · CityPlace · 185 Asylum Street · Hartford, CT 06103-3499 · 203-275-0100

Albert Zakarian · (Management) · Day, Berry & Howard · CityPlace · 185 Asylum Street · Hartford, CT 06103-3499 · 203-275-0100

Janet Bond Arterton · (Individuals) · Garrison, Silbert & Arterton · 405 Orange Street · New Haven, CT 06511 · 203-777-4425

Joseph D. Garrison* · (Individuals) · Garrison, Silbert & Arterton · 405 Orange Street · New Haven, CT 06511 · 203-777-4425

David N. Rosen* · (Individuals, Class Actions) · Rosen & Dolan · 400 Orange Street · New Haven, CT 06511 · 203-787-3513

David M. Cohen · (Individuals) · Wofsey, Rosen, Kweskin & Kuriansky · 600 Summer Street · Stamford, CT 06901 · 203-327-2300

David S. Golub* · (Individuals) · Silver, Golub & Teitell · 184 Atlantic Street · P.O. Box 389 · Stamford, CT 06904 · 203-325-4491

William S. Zeman · (Labor) · Zeman & Ellis · 18 North Main Street · West Hartford, CT 06107 · 203-521-4430

Norman Zolot* · (Labor, Workers' Compensation) · 264 Amity Road · P.O. Box 3541 · Woodbridge, CT 06525 · 203-397-5346

NATURAL RESOURCES AND ENVIRONMENTAL LAW

Paul Jacobi · Miller & Jacobi · 300 Bic Drive · Milford, CT 06460 · 203-874-7110

PERSONAL INJURY LITIGATION

Robert B. Adelman* · (Plaintiffs, Medical Malpractice, Products Liability, Automobile Collision) · Cohen and Wolf · 1115 Broad Street · P.O. Box 1821 · Bridgeport, CT 06601 · 203-368-0211

Arnold Bai* · (Defendants, Medical Malpractice, Products Liability, Professional Malpractice, Airplane Collision) · Bai, Pollock and Dunnigan · The Connecticut Bank & Trust Tower · 10 Middle Street · Bridgeport, CT 06604 · 203-366-7991

Richard A. Bieder* · (Plaintiffs) · Koskoff, Koskoff & Bieder · 350 Fairfield Avenue · Bridgeport, CT 06604 · 203-336-4421

Robert J. Cooney* · (Defendants, Medical Malpractice, Products Liability, Professional Malpractice) · Williams, Cooney & Sheehy · One Lafayette Circle · Bridgeport, CT 06604 · 203-331-0888

Michael P. Koskoff · (Plaintiffs) · Koskoff, Koskoff & Bieder · 350 Fairfield Avenue · Bridgeport, CT 06604 · 203-336-4421

T. Paul Tremont* · (Plaintiffs) · Tremont & Sheldon · 64 Lyon Terrace · Bridgeport, CT 06604 · 203-335-5145

Ronald D. Williams · (Defendants, Medical Malpractice, Products Liability, Automobile Collision) · Williams, Cooney & Sheehy · One Lafayette Circle · Bridgeport, CT 06604 · 203-331-0888

James D. Bartolini · (Plaintiffs) · RisCassi and Davis · 131 Oak Street · P.O. Box 6550 · Hartford, CT 06106 · 203-522-1196

William R. Davis · (Plaintiffs) · RisCassi and Davis · 131 Oak Street · P.O. Box 6550 · Hartford, CT 06106 · 203-522-1196

John R. FitzGerald · (Defendants) · Howard, Kohn, Sprague & FitzGerald · 237 Buckingham Street · Hartford, CT 06106 · 203-525-3101

Edward F. Hennessey* · Robinson & Cole · One Commercial Plaza · Hartford, CT 06103-3597 · 203-275-8200

Joseph G. Lynch* · (Defendants) · Halloran & Sage · One Goodwin Square · 225 Asylum Street · Hartford, CT 06103 · 203-522-6103

F. Timothy McNamara* · 102 Oak Street · Hartford, CT 06106 · 203-249-8458

Francis H. Morrison · (Defendants) · Day, Berry & Howard · CityPlace · 185 Asylum Street · Hartford, CT 06103-3499 · 203-275-0231

Hubert J. Santos · (Plaintiffs) · Buckley & Santos · 51 Russ Street · Hartford, CT 06106 · 203-249-6548

John F. Scully · (Defendants) · Cooney, Scully and Dowling · Hartford Square North · 110 Columbus Boulevard · Hartford, CT 06106 · 203-527-1141

Joseph F. Skelley, Jr.* · (Defendants) · Skelley, Vinkels and Rottner · 12 Charter Oak Place · P.O. Box 14890 · Hartford, CT 06114-0890 · 203-246-6891

William J. Doyle* · (Defendants) · Wiggin & Dana · One Century Tower · New Haven, CT 06508-1832 · 203-498-4400

Anthony M. Fitzgerald* · Carmody & Torrance · 59 Elm Street · P.O. Box 1990 New Haven, CT 06509 · 203-777-5501

William F. Gallagher* · (Plaintiffs, Medical Malpractice, Products Liability, Appellate) · Gallagher, Gallagher & Calistro · 1377 Boulevard · P.O. Box 1925 · New Haven, CT 06509 · 203-624-4165

Ira B. Grudberg · (Plaintiffs) · Jacobs, Grudberg, Belt & Dow · 350 Orange Street P.O. Box 606 · New Haven, CT 06503 · 203-772-3100

Howard A. Jacobs* · (Plaintiffs) · Jacobs, Grudberg, Belt & Dow · 350 Orange Street · P.O. Box 606 · New Haven, CT 06503 · 203-772-3100

Stanley A. Jacobs · (Plaintiffs) · Jacobs & Jacobs · 555 Long Wharf Drive, Suite 13A · New Haven, CT 06511 · 203-777-2300

David W. Skolnick · (Plaintiffs) · Winnick, Skolnick, Rubin & Block · 110 Whitney Avenue · P.O. Box 1755 · New Haven, CT 06510 · 203-772-4400

Shaun S. Sullivan · (Defendants) · Wiggin & Dana · One Century Tower · P.O. Box 1832 · New Haven, CT 06508-1832 · 203-498-4315

Stephen I. Traub* · (Plaintiffs, Medical Malpractice, Professional Malpractice, Airplane Collision) · Lynch, Traub, Keefe and Errante · 52 Trumbull Street · P.O. Box 1612 · New Haven, CT 06506 · 203-787-0275

Dale Patrick Faulkner · Faulkner & Boyce · 216 Broad Street · P.O. Box 66 · New London, CT 06320 · 203-442-9900

Jeffrey B. Sienkiewicz · (Defendants) · Sienkiewićz, McKenna & Sienkiewicz · Nine South Main Street · P.O. Box 786 · New Milford, CT 06776 · 203-354-1583

Allyn L. Brown, Jr. · (Defendants) · Brown, Jacobson, Tillinghast, Lahan & King Uncas-Merchants National Bank Building · 22 Courthouse Square · Norwich, CT 06360 · 203-889-3321

Wayne G. Tillinghast · (Defendants) · Brown, Jacobson, Tillinghast, Lahan & King · Uncas-Merchants National Bank Building · 22 Courthouse Square · Norwich, CT 06360 · 203-889-3321

Richard A. Silver · (Plaintiffs) · Silver, Golub &Teitell · 184 Atlantic Street · P.O. Box 389 · Stamford, CT 06904 · 203-325-4491

Garrett M. Moore · Carmody & Torrance · 50 Leavenworth Street · P.O. Box 1110 · Waterbury, CT 06721 · 203-573-1200

Augustus R. Southworth II · (Defendants, Medical Malpractice) · Gager & Henry · One Exchange Place · P.O. Box 2480 · Waterbury, CT 06722-2480 · 203-597-5100

REAL ESTATE LAW

David O. Jackson · (Zoning, Land Use, Commercial Transactions, Industrial Transactions) · Pullman, Comley, Bradley & Reeves · 850 Main Street · P.O. Box 7006 · Bridgeport, CT 06601-7006 · 203-330-2000

Austin K. Wolf · (Zoning, Land Use, Commercial Transactions, Industrial Transactions) · Cohen and Wolf · 1115 Broad Street · P.O. Box 1821 · Bridgeport, CT 06601 · 203-368-0211

Robert J. Birnbaum · Cohn and Birnbaum · One Union Place, 14th Floor · 100 Pearl Street · Hartford, CT 06103-4500 · 203-549-7230

Gurdon H. Buck · (Zoning, Land Use, Condominiums, Land Development) · Robinson & Cole · One Commercial Plaza · Hartford, CT 06103-3597 · 203-275-8200

Barry Feldman · Murtha, Cullina, Richter and Pinney · CityPlace · P.O. Box 3197 · Hartford, CT 06103-0197 · 203-240-6000

John C. Glezen · Day, Berry & Howard · CityPlace · Hartford, CT 06103-3499 203-275-0100

J. Roger Hanlon · Day, Berry & Howard · CityPlace · 185 Asylum Street · Hartford, CT 06103-3499 · 203-275-0100

Harold F. Keith · Keith & Aparo · 100 Constitution Plaza · Hartford, CT 06103 203-728-0646

H. David Leventhal · Leventhal, Krasow & Roos · One Financial Plaza · 100 Pearl Street · Hartford, CT 06103 · 203-549-4100

Michael R. Levin · Levin & D'Agostino · One State Street · Hartford, CT 06103 203-527-0400

Dwight H. Merriam · (Zoning) · Robinson & Cole · One Commercial Plaza · Hartford, CT 06103-3597 · 203-275-8200

Mark Oland · Schatz & Schatz, Ribicoff & Kotkin · One Financial Plaza · 90 State House Square · Hartford, CT 06103-3902 · 203-522-3234

I. Milton Widem* · (Zoning, Land Use, Eminent Domain, Tax Appeals & Foreclosure) · Schatz & Schatz, Ribicoff & Kotkin · One Financial Plaza · 90 State House Square · Hartford, CT 06103-3902 · 203-522-3234

Michael Susman · (Zoning, Land Use, Eminent Domain, Commercial Transaction, Industrial Transactions, Real Estate Taxation) · Susman, Duffy & Segaloff 234 Church Street · P.O. Box 1684 · New Haven, CT 06507 · 203-624-9830

Jerome Berkman · Day, Berry & Howard · One Canterbury Green · Stamford, CT 06901 · 203-977-7300

Ronald King · King & King · 550 Summer Street · Stamford, CT 06901 · 203-327-1345

Thomas P. Skidd, Jr. · Cummings & Lockwood · 10 Stamford Forum · P.O. Box 120 · Stamford, CT 06904 · 203-327-1700

Richard Berkowitz · Berkowitz & Balbirer · 253 Post Road West · P.O. Box 808 Westport, CT 06881 · 203-226-1001

TAX AND EMPLOYEE BENEFITS LAW

Herbert H. Moorin · (Employee Benefits) · Pullman, Comley, Bradley & Reeves 850 Main Street · P.O. Box 7006. · Bridgeport, CT 06601-7006 · 203-334-0112

J. Danford Anthony, Jr. · (Corporate & Partnership Transactions, State Tax, Tax Disputes) · Day, Berry & Howard · CityPlace · Hartford, CT 06103-3499 · 203-275-0136

Frank S. Berall · (State Tax, Tax Disputes, Estate/Gift/Individual/Fiduciary Income Taxation) · Copp, Berall, Wellette, Carta & Sluis · 60 Washington Street · Hartford, CT 06106 · 203-249-5261

Michael L. Coyle · Reid and Riege · One State Street · Hartford, CT 06103-3185 203-278-1150

Ira H. Goldman · (Employee Benefits) · Shipman & Goodwin · 799 Main Street Hartford, CT 06103-2377 · 203-549-4770

John J. Jacobson · (Employee Benefits) · Reid and Riege · One State Street · Hartford, CT 06103-3185 · 203-278-1150

William R. Judy · (Tax, Employee Benefits) · Reid and Riege · One State Street Hartford, CT 06103-3185 · 203-278-1150

Alex Lloyd · Shipman & Goodwin · One American Row · Hartford, CT 06103-2819 · 203-549-4770

James B. Lyon · Murtha, Cullina, Richter and Pinney · CityPlace · P.O. Box 230197 · Hartford, CT 06123-0197 · 203-240-6000

Charles B. Milliken · (Corporate & Partnership Transactions, State Tax, Employee Benefits) · Shipman & Goodwin · 799 Main Street · Hartford, CT 06103-2377 · 203-549-4770

John T. Del Negro · (Corporate & Partnership Transactions, State Tax, Tax Disputes) · Murtha, Cullina, Richter and Pinney · CityPlace · P.O. Box 3197 · Hartford, CT 06103-0197 · 203-240-6000

Raymond J. Payne · (Employee Benefits, Tax Disputes) · Reid and Riege · One State Street · Hartford, CT 06103-3185 · 203-278-1150

Thomas Z. Reicher · (Employee Benefits) · Day, Berry & Howard · CityPlace · Hartford, CT 06103-3499 · 203-275-0100

Donald P. Richter · Murtha, Cullina, Richter and Pinney · CityPlace · P.O. Box 230197 · Hartford, CT 06123-0197 · 203-240-6000

John O. Tannenbaum · Robinson & Cole · One Commercial Plaza · Hartford, CT 06103-3597 · 203-275-8200

Richard W. Tomeo · Robinson & Cole · One Commercial Plaza · Hartford, CT 06103-3597 · 203-275-8200

Kenneth E. Werner · Day, Berry & Howard · CityPlace · Hartford, CT 06103-3499 · 203-275-0100

Barrie K. Wetstone · (Employee Benefits) · Sorokin Sorokin Gross Hyde & Williams · One Corporate Center · Hartford, CT 06103-3291 · 203-525-6645

Paul L. Behling · (Tax, Employee Benefits) · Wiggin & Dana · One Century Tower · New Haven, CT 06508-1832 · 203-498-4400

Stanley N. Bergman · Bergman, Horowitz & Reynolds · 157 Church Street · P.O. Box 426 · New Haven, CT 06502 · 203-789-1320

Newton D. Brenner · Brenner, Saltzman, Wallman & Goldman · 271 Whitney Avenue · P.O. Box 1746 · New Haven, CT 06507 · 203-772-2600

David L. Reynolds · (Employee Benefits) · Bergman, Horowitz & Reynolds · 157 Church Street · P.O. Box 426 · New Haven, CT 06502 · 203-789-1320

W. Parker Seeley, Jr. · (Corporate & Partnership Transactions, State Tax, Debt Restructurings) · Garcia, Seeley & Associates · 44 Trumbull Street · New Haven, CT 06510 · 203-773-3824

Nathan M. Silverstein · (Tax Disputes) · Silverstein & Osach · 234 Church Street, Suite 903 · P.O. Box 1727 · New Haven, CT 06507-1727 · 203-865-0121

John F. Strother · (Employee Benefits) · Cummings & Lockwood · 10 Stamford Forum · P.O. Box 120 · Stamford, CT 06904 · 203-327-1700

George G. Vest · Cummings & Lockwood · 10 Stamford Forum · P.O. Box 120 Stamford, CT 06904 · 203-327-1700

Richard A. Hoppe · (Tax, Employee Benefits) · Gager & Henry · One Exchange Place · P.O. Box 2480 · Waterbury, CT 06722-2480 · 203-597-5100

TRUSTS AND ESTATES

Peter Wilkinson · Marsh, Day & Calhoun · 955 Main Street · Bridgeport, CT 06604 · 203-368-4221

Robert T. Gilhuly · Cummings & Lockwood · Two Greenwich Plaza · P.O. Box 2505 · Greenwich, CT 06836 · 203-863-6506

R. Regner Arvidson · Robinson & Cole · One Commercial Plaza · Hartford, CT 06103-3597 · 203-275-8200

Frank S. Berall · (Estate Planning, Estate Administration, Charitable Trusts) · Copp, Berall, Wellette, Carta & Sluis · 60 Washington Street · Hartford, CT 06106 203-249-5261

James T. Betts · Shipman & Goodwin · One American Row · Hartford, CT 06103-2819 · 203-549-4770

Paul L. Bourdeau · Cummings & Lockwood · CityPlace I · 185 Asylum Street · Hartford, CT 06103 · 203-275-6700

Clifford S. Burdge, Jr. · Reid and Riege · One State Street · Hartford, CT 06103-3185 · 203-278-1150

John M. Donahue · Robinson & Cole · One Commercial Plaza · Hartford, CT 06103-3597 · 203-275-8200

John W. Hincks · Robinson & Cole · One Commercial Plaza · Hartford, CT 06103-3597 · 203-275-8200

Arthur B. Locke · Murtha, Cullina, Richter and Pinney · CityPlace · P.O. Box 230197 · Hartford, CT 06123-0197 · 203-240-6000

Warren S. Randall · Halloran & Sage · One Goodwin Square · 225 Asylum Street Hartford, CT 06103 · 203-522-6103

Martin Wolman · Day, Berry & Howard · CityPlace · 185 Asylum Street · Hartford, CT 06103-3499 · 203-275-0100

Stuyvesant K. Bearns · Shipman & Goodwin · Porter Street · P.O. Box 1809 · Lakeville, CT 06039 · 203-435-2539

Jeffrey L. Crown · 99 West Main Street · New Britain, CT 06051 · 203-229-6600

Charles C. Kingsley · Wiggin & Dana · One Century Tower · New Haven, CT 06508-1832 · 203-498-4400

James W. Venman · Pullman, Comley, Bradley & Reeves · 200 Pequot Avenue Southport, CT 06490 · 203-254-5000

Ronald O. Dederick · (Estate Planning, Estate Administration, Charitable Trusts) · Day, Berry & Howard · One Canterbury Green · Stamford, CT 06901 · 203-977-7300

Gayle Brian Wilhelm · (Estate Planning, Estate Administration, Estate & Trust Litigation) · Cummings & Lockwood · 10 Stamford Forum · P.O. Box 120 · Stamford, CT 06904 · 203-327-1700

DELAWARE

BANKRUPTCY LAW

Patrick Scanlon · Barros, McNamara & Scanlon · State & Loockerman Streets · P.O. Box 1298 · Dover, DE 19903-1298 · 302-734-8400

William L. Witham, Jr.* · (Business Reorganization, Creditors' Rights, Debtors' Rights, Bankruptcy Litigation) · Prickett, Jones, Elliott, Kristol & Schnee · 26 The Green · Dover, DE 19901 · 302-888-6500

Eric M. Doroshow · Doroshow, Pasquale & Linarducci · 1202 Kirkwood Highway Wilmington, DE 19805 · 302-998-0100

Richard G. Elliott, Jr. · Richards, Layton & Finger · One Rodney Square · P.O. Box 551 · Wilmington, DE 19899 · 302-658-6541

Eduard F. von Wettberg III · Morris, James, Hitchens & Williams · 222 Delaware Avenue · P.O. Box 2306 · Wilmington, DE 19899-2306 · 302-888-6800

Peter J. Walsh · Bayard, Handelman & Murdoch · 902 Market Street · P.O. Box 25130 · Wilmington, DE 19899 · 302-655-5000

BUSINESS LITIGATION

R. Franklin Balotti* · (Securities, Stocholders' Suits) · Richards, Layton & Finger One Rodney Square · P.O. Box 551 · Wilmington, DE 19899 · 302-658-6541

Victor F. Battaglia · Biggs and Battaglia · 1206 Mellon Bank Center · 10th and Market Streets · P.O. Box 1489 · Wilmington, DE 19899-1489 · 302-655-9677

Edmund N. Carpenter II* · Richards, Layton & Finger · One Rodney Square · P.O. Box 551 · Wilmington, DE 19899 · 302-658-6541

Arthur G. Connolly, Jr. · Connolly, Bove, Lodge & Hutz · 1220 Market Street P.O. Box 2207 · Wilmington, DE 19899-2207 · 302-658-9141

Charles S. Crompton, Jr. · Potter Anderson & Corroon · 350 Delaware Trust Building · 902 Market Street · P.O. Box 951 · Wilmington, DE 19899-0951 · 302-658-6771

Andrew B. Kirkpatrick, Jr. · Morris, Nichols, Arsht & Tunnell · 1201 North Market Street · P.O. Box 1347 · Wilmington, DE 19899-1347 · 302-658-9200

Irving Morris* · (Securities) · Morris, Rosenthal, Monhait & Gross · First Federal Plaza, Suite 214 · P.O. Box 1070 · Wilmington, DE 19899-1070 · 302-656-4433

Robert K. Payson · Potter Anderson & Corroon · 350 Delaware Trust Building · 902 Market Street · P.O. Box 951 · Wilmington, DE 19899-0951 · 302-658-6771

Charles F. Richards, Jr.* · Richards, Layton & Finger · One Rodney Square · P.O. Box 551 · Wilmington, DE 19899 · 302-658-6541

Steven J. Rothschild · Skadden, Arps, Slate, Meagher & Flom · One Rodney Square · P.O. Box 636 · Wilmington, DE 19899 · 302-651-3000

A. Gilchrist Sparks III* · (Securities) · Morris, Nichols, Arsht & Tunnell · 1201 North Market Street · P.O. Box 1347 · Wilmington, DE 19899-1347 · 302-658-9200

Bruce M. Stargatt · Young, Conaway, Stargatt & Taylor · Rodney Square North, 11th Floor · P.O. Box 391 · Wilmington, DE 19899-0391 · 302-571-6600

E. Norman Veasey · Richards, Layton & Finger · One Rodney Square · P.O. Box 551 · Wilmington, DE 19899 · 302-658-6541

Rodman Ward, Jr.* · Skadden, Arps, Slate, Meagher & Flom · One Rodney Square · P.O. Box 636 · Wilmington, DE 19899 · 302-651-3000

CORPORATE LAW

R. Franklin Balotti* · (Mergers & Acquisitions) · Richards, Layton & Finger · One Rodney Square · P.O. Box 551 · Wilmington, DE 19899 · 302-658-6541

Lewis S. Black, Jr. · Morris, Nichols, Arsht & Tunnell · 1201 North Market Street P.O. Box 1347 · Wilmington, DE 19899-1347 · 302-658-9200

Charles S. Crompton, Jr. · Potter Anderson & Corroon · 350 Delaware Trust Building · 902 Market Street · P.O. Box 951 · Wilmington, DE 19899-0951 · 302-658-6771

Robert K. Payson · Potter Anderson & Corroon · 350 Delaware Trust Building · 902 Market Street · P.O. Box 951 · Wilmington, DE 19899-0951 · 302-658-6771

Charles F. Richards, Jr.* · Richards, Layton & Finger · One Rodney Square · P.O. Box 551 · Wilmington, DE 19899 · 302-658-6541

A. Gilchrist Sparks III* · (Mergers & Acquisitions) · Morris, Nichols, Arsht & Tunnell · 1201 North Market Street · P.O. Box 1347 · Wilmington, DE 19899-1347 · 302-658-9200

Bruce M. Stargatt · Young, Conaway, Stargatt & Taylor · Rodney Square North, 11th Floor · P.O. Box 391 · Wilmington, DE 19899-0391 · 302-571-6600

E. Norman Veasey · Richards, Layton & Finger · One Rodney Square · P.O. Box 551 · Wilmington, DE 19899 · 302-658-6541

CRIMINAL DEFENSE

Sidney Balick* · 604 Mellon Bank Center · 10th and Market Streets · Wilmington, DE 19801 · 302-658-4265

Victor F. Battaglia · Biggs and Battaglia · 1206 Mellon Bank Center · 10th and Market Streets · P.O. Box 1489 · Wilmington, DE 19899-1489 · 302-655-9677

Joseph A. Hurley* · (Violent Crimes, Non-Violent Crimes, Federal Court, State Court) · 1215 King Street · Wilmington, DE 19801 · 302-658-8980

Eugene J. Maurer, Jr. · 1201-A King Street · Wilmington, DE 19801 · 302-652-7900

Carl Schnee · Prickett, Jones, Elliott, Kristol & Schnee · 1310 King Street · P.O. Box 1328 · Wilmington, DE 19899-1328 · 302-888-6500

FAMILY LAW

Gerald Z. Berkowitz* · (Child Custody, Divorce, Marital Settlement Agreements, Equitable Division) · Berkowitz, Greenstein, Schagrin & Coonin · 1218 Market Street · P.O. Box 1632 · Wilmington, DE 19899 · 302-652-3155

Bertram S. Halberstadt* · (Equitable Division, Domestic Relations Taxation) · Wier & Halberstadt · 1300 North Market Street, Suite 701 · Wilmington, DE 19801 · 302-654-0399

Michael K. Newell · Bayard, Handelman & Murdoch · 902 Market Street · P.O. Box 25130 · Wilmington, DE 19899 · 302-655-5000

H. Alfred Tarrant, Jr. · Cooch and Taylor · 824 Market Street Mall · P.O. Box 1680 · Wilmington, DE 19899 · 302-652-3641

FIRST AMENDMENT LAW

Richard G. Elliott · Richards, Layton & Finger · One Rodney Square · P.O. Box 551 · Wilmington, DE 19899 · 302-658-6541

Steven J. Rothschild · Skadden, Arps, Slate, Meagher & Flom · One Rodney Square · P.O. Box 636 · Wilmington, DE 19899 · 302-651-3030

HEALTH CARE LAW

Walter P. McEvilly, Jr. · Prickett, Jones, Elliott, Kristol & Schnee · 1310 King Street · P.O. Box 1328 · Wilmington, DE 19899-1328 · 302-888-6500

Peter J. Shanley · Saul, Ewing, Remick & Saul · 222 Delaware Avenue · P.O. Box 1266 · Wilmington, DE 19899 · 302-654-1413

INTELLECTUAL PROPERTY LAW

Douglas E. Whitney · Morris, Nichols, Arsht & Tunnell · 1201 North Market Street · P.O. Box 1347 · Wilmington, DE 19899-1347 · 302-658-9200

LABOR AND EMPLOYMENT LAW

Sheldon N. Sandler · (Management) · Young, Conaway, Stargatt & Taylor · Rodney Square North, 11th Floor · P.O. Box 391 · Wilmington, DE 19899-0391 302-571-6600

Robert F. Stewart, Jr. · (Management) · Duane, Morris & Heckscher · 1201 Market Street, Suite 1500 · P.O. Box 195 · Wilmington, DE 19899 · 302-571-5550

NATURAL RESOURCES AND ENVIRONMENTAL LAW

F. Michael Parkowski · Parkowski, Noble & Guerke · 116 West Water Street · P.O. Box 598 · Dover, DE 19903 · 302-678-3262

Thomas D. Whittington, Jr. · Whittington & Aulgur · Coffee Run Professional Centre · Lancaster Pike & Loveville Road · Hockessin, DE 19707 · 302-239-6100

Henry N. Herndon, Jr. · Morris, James, Hitchens & Williams · 222 Delaware Avenue · P.O. Box 2306 · Wilmington, DE 19899-2306 · 302-888-6800

Stephen E. Herrmann · Richards, Layton & Finger · One Rodney Square · P.O. Box 551 · Wilmington, DE 19899 · 302-658-6541

PERSONAL INJURY LITIGATION

Harold Schmittinger* · (Plaintiffs) · Schmittinger & Rodriguez · 414 South State Street · P.O. Box 497 · Dover, DE 19903-0497 · 302-674-0140

Sidney Balick* · (Plaintiffs) · Sidney Balick & Associates · 604 Mellon Bank Center · 10th and Market Streets · Wilmington, DE 19801 · 302-658-4265

Victor F. Battaglia · (Defendants) · Biggs and Battaglia · 1206 Mellon Bank Center · 10th and Market Streets · P.O. Box 1489 · Wilmington, DE 19899-1489 302-655-9677

Ben T. Castle · (Plaintiffs) · Young, Conaway, Stargatt & Taylor · Rodney Square North, 11th Floor · P.O. Box 391 · Wilmington, DE 19899-0391 · 302-571-6600

Mason E. Turner, Jr. · (Defendants) · Prickett, Jones, Elliott, Kristol & Schnee 1310 King Street · P.O. Box 1328 · Wilmington, DE 19899-1328 · 302-888-6500

F. Alton Tybout* · Tybout, Redfearn & Pell · Bank of Delaware Building, Suite 1110 · 300 Delaware Avenue · P.O. Box 2092 · Wilmington, DE 19801 · 302-658-6901

Bernard A. van Ogtrop* · (Plaintiffs, Automobile Collision) · Cooch and Taylor Marine Midland Plaza, Suite 1000 · 824 Market Street Mall · P.O. Box 1680 · Wilmington, DE 19899-1680 · 302-652-3641

REAL ESTATE LAW

Richard P. Beck · (Zoning, Land Use, Commercial Transactions, Industrial Transactions) · Morris, James, Hitchens & Williams · 222 Delaware Avenue · P.O. Box 2306 · Wilmington, DE 19899-2306 · 302-888-6800

Donald Nelson Isken · Morris, Nichols, Arsht & Tunnell · 1201 North Market Street · P.O. Box 1347 · Wilmington, DE 19899-1347 · 302-658-9200

Daniel L. Klein · Richards, Layton & Finger · One Rodney Square · P.O. Box 551 Wilmington, DE 19899 · 302-658-6541

Daniel M. Kristol · Prickett, Jones, Elliott, Kristol & Schnee · 1310 King Street P.O. Box 1328 · Wilmington, DE 19899-1328 · 302-888-6500

Richard H. May · Young, Conaway, Stargatt & Taylor · Rodney Square North, 11th Floor · P.O. Box 391 · Wilmington, DE 19899-0391 · 302-571-6600

Donald C. Taylor · Cooch and Taylor · 824 Market Street Mall · P.O. Box 1680 Wilmington, DE 19899 · 302-652-3641

Robert L. Thomas · Young, Conaway, Stargatt & Taylor · Rodney Square North, 11th Floor · P.O. Box 391 · Wilmington, DE 19899-0391 · 302-571-6600

TAX AND EMPLOYEE BENEFITS LAW

Paul H. Boswell, Jr. · Schmittinger & Rodriguez · 414 South State Street · P.O. Box 497 · Dover, DE 19903-0497 · 302-674-0140

David J. Garrett · Potter Anderson & Corroon · 350 Delaware Trust Building · 902 Market Street · P.O. Box 951 · Wilmington, DE 19899-0951 · 302-658-6771

Johannes R. Krahmer · (Corporate & Partnership Transactions, State Tax, Tax Disputes) · Morris, Nichols, Arsht & Tunnell · 1201 North Market Street · P.O. Box 1347 · Wilmington, DE 19899-1347 · 302-658-9200

Robert Meyer · Bayard, Handelman & Murdoch · 902 Market Street · P.O. Box 25130 · Wilmington, DE 19899 · 302-655-5000

Thomas P. Sweeney · Richards, Layton & Finger · One Rodney Square · P.O. Box 551 · Wilmington, DE 19899 · 302-658-6541

Leonard S. Togman · Potter Anderson & Corroon · 350 Delaware Trust Building 902 Market Street · P.O. Box 951 · Wilmington, DE 19899-0951 · 302-658-6771

Norris P. Wright · Morris, James, Hitchens & Williams · 222 Delaware Avenue · P.O. Box 2306 · Wilmington, DE 19899-2306 · 302-888-6800

TRUSTS AND ESTATES

Paul H. Boswell, Jr. · Schmittinger & Rodriguez · 414 South State Street · P.O. Box 497 · Dover, DE 19903-0497 · 302-674-0140

Richard G. Bacon · Richards, Layton & Finger · One Rodney Square · P.O. Box 551 · Wilmington, DE 19899 · 302-658-6541

Robert W. Crowe · Cooch and Taylor · 824 Market Street Mall · P.O. Box 1680 Wilmington, DE 19899 · 302-652-3641

David J. Garrett · Potter Anderson & Corroon · 350 Delaware Trust Building · 902 Market Street · P.O. Box 951 · Wilmington, DE 19899-0951 · 302-658-6771

Joseph H. Geoghegan · Potter Anderson & Corroon · 350 Delaware Trust Building · 902 Market Street · P.O. Box 951 · Wilmington, DE 19899-0951 · 302-658-6771

Peter S. Gordon · (General Tax Practice) · Williams, Gordon & Martin · One Commerce Center, Suite 600 · 12th & Orange Streets · P.O. Box 511 · Wilmington, DE 19899-0511 · 302-575-0873

Henry N. Herndon, Jr. · Morris, James, Hitchens & Williams · 222 Delaware Avenue · P.O. Box 2306 · Wilmington, DE 19899-2306 · 302-888-6800

Johannes R. Krahmer · (Estate Planning) · Morris, Nichols, Arsht & Tunnell · 1201 North Market Street · P.O. Box 1347 · Wilmington, DE 19899-1347 · 302-658-9200

F. Edmund Lynch · Ament Evans Lynch & Carr · Three Christina Centre, 14th Floor · 201 North Walnut Street · P.O. Box 2328 · Wilmington, DE 19899 · 302-655-2599

Joanna Reiver · Schlusser, Reiver, Hughes & Sisk · 1700 West 14th Street · Wilmington, DE 19806 · 302-655-8181

Thomas P. Sweeney · Richards, Layton & Finger · One Rodney Square · P.O. Box 551 · Wilmington, DE 19899 · 302-658-6541

Norris P. Wright · Morris, James, Hitchens & Williams · 222 Delaware Avenue · P.O. Box 2306 · Wilmington, DE 19899-2306 · 302-888-6800

DISTRICT OF COLUMBIA

BANKRUPTCY LAW

Nelson Deckelbaum · Deckelbaum, Ogens & Fisher · 1140 Connecticut Avenue, NW · Washington, DC 20036 · 202-223-1474

Francis P. Dicello · Hazel & Thomas · 2001 Pennsylvania Avenue, NW, Suite 400 Washington, DC 20006 · 202-659-7000

Charles A. Docter · (Business Reorganization, Debtors' Rights, Bankruptcy Litigation) · Docter & Docter · 1325 G Street, NW, Suite 700 · Washington, DC 20005 · 202-628-6800

Murray Drabkin · Cadwalader, Wickersham & Taft · 1333 New Hampshire Avenue, NW, Suite 700 · Washington, DC 20036 · 202-862-2200

Nathan B. Feinstein · Piper & Marbury · 1200 Nineteenth Street, NW · Washington, DC 20036 · 202-861-3900

Roger Frankel · Arent, Fox, Kintner, Plotkin & Kahn · 1050 Connecticut Avenue, NW · Washington, DC 20036-5339 · 202-857-6126

Richard H. Gins · Gins & Seeber · 2021 L Street, NW, Suite 200 · Washington, DC 20036 · 202-785-9123

Bruce Goldstein · Zuckerman, Spaeder, Goldstein, Taylor & Kolker · 1201 Connecticut Avenue, NW, Suite 1200 · Washington, DC 20036 · 202-778-1800

William J. Perlstein · Wilmer, Cutler & Pickering · 2445 M Street, NW · Washington, DC 20037-1420 · 202-663-6000

Richard P. Schifter · Arnold & Porter · Thurman Arnold Building · 1200 New Hampshire Avenue, NW · Washington, DC 20036 · 202-872-6700

William Daniel Sullivan · Melrod, Redman & Gartlan · 1801 K Street, NW, Suite 1100 · Washington, DC 20006 · 202-822-5300

Roger M. Whelan* · (Business Reorganization, Creditors' Rights, Debtors' Rights, Bankruptcy Litigation) · Shaw, Pittman, Potts & Trowbridge · 2300 N Street, NW · Washington, DC 20037 · 202-663-8963

BUSINESS LITIGATION

Howard Adler, Jr. · (Antitrust) · Davis, Graham & Stubbs · 1200 Nineteenth Street, NW, Suite 500 · Washington, DC 20036-2402 · 202-822-8660

Harvey M. Applebaum · (Antitrust, International Trade) · Covington & Burling 1201 Pennsylvania Avenue, NW · P.O. Box 7566 · Washington, DC 20044 · 202-662-6000

Donald I. Baker · (Antitrust, Arbitration) · Sutherland, Asbill & Brennan · 1275 Pennsylvania Avenue, NW, Suite 800 · Washington, DC 20004-2404 · 202-383-0100

John W. Barnum · (Antitrust, Securities, Transportation) · White & Case · 1747 Pennsylvania Avenue, NW · Washington, DC 20006 · 202-872-0013

Robert T. Basseches* · (Administrative, Transportation) · Shea & Gardner · 1800 Massachusetts Avenue, NW, Suite 800 · Washington, DC 20036 · 202-828-2000

Richard W. Beckler* · (Antitrust, RICO, Securities) · Fulbright & Jaworski · 801 Pennsylvania Avenue, NW · Washington, DC 20004-2604 · 202-662-0200

David Booth Beers · Shea & Gardner · 1800 Massachusetts Avenue, NW, Suite 800 · Washington, DC 20036 · 202-828-2000

Alexander E. Bennett · (Government Contract) · Arnold & Porter · Thurman Arnold Building · 1200 New Hampshire Avenue, NW · Washington, DC 20036 · 202-872-6700

Robert S. Bennett · Skadden, Arps, Slate, Meagher & Flom · 1440 New York Avenue, NW · Washington, DC 20005 · 202-371-7000

Judah Best · (Appellate, Securities) · Debevoise & Plimpton · 555 Thirteenth Street, NW, Suite 1100 East · Washington, DC 20004 · 202-383-8000

Peter K. Bleakley · Arnold & Porter · Thurman Arnold Building · 1200 New Hampshire Avenue, NW · Washington, DC 20036 · 202-872-6700

Timothy J. Bloomfield · (Antitrust) · Dunnells, Duvall & Porter · 2100 Pennsylvania Avenue, NW, Fourth Floor · Washington, DC 20037 · 202-861-1400

John Bodner, Jr.* · (Administrative, Antitrust, Appellate, Commercial) · Howrey & Simon · 1730 Pennsylvania Avenue, NW, Suite 900 · Washington, DC 20006-4793 · 202-783-0800

Charles N. Brower · (International) · White & Case · 1747 Pennsylvania Avenue, NW, Suite 500 · Washington, DC 20006 · 202-872-0013

Thomas W. Brunner* · (Antitrust, Insurance) · Wiley, Rein & Fielding · 1776 K Street, NW · Washington, DC 20006-2359 · 202-429-7000

Donald T. Bucklin* · Squire, Sanders & Dempsey · 1201 Pennsylvania Avenue, NW · P.O. Box 407 · Washington, DC 20044 · 202-626-6600

Plato Cacheris* · (RICO) · Cacheris & Towey · 1914 Sunderland Place, NW · Washington, DC 20036 · 202-452-9886

Vincent H. Cohen · Hogan & Hartson · Columbia Square · 555 Thirteenth Street, NW · Washington, DC 20004-1109 · 202-637-5600

Richard T. Colman · Howrey & Simon · 1730 Pennsylvania Avenue, NW, Suite 900 · Washington, DC 20006-4793 · 202-783-0800

Aubrey M. Daniel III · (Antitrust, Products Liability) · Williams & Connolly · Hill Building · 839 Seventeenth Street, NW · Washington, DC 20006 · 202-331-5000

Sidney Dickstein · Dickstein, Shapiro & Morin · 2101 L Street, NW, Suite 900 · Washington, DC 20037 · 202-785-9700

Richard O. Duvall* · Dunnells, Duvall & Porter · 2100 Pennsylvania Avenue NW, Fourth Floor · Washington, DC 20037 · 202-861-1400

Timothy B. Dyk · (FCC, First Amendment) · Jones, Day, Reavis & Pogue · 1450 G Street, NW · Washington, DC 20005-2088 · 202-879-7600

Milton Eisenberg · (Government Contract) · Fried, Frank, Harris, Shriver & Jacobson · 1001 Pennsylvania Avenue, NW, Suite 800 · Washington, DC 20004-3505 · 202-639-7000

Richard J. Favretto · (Antitrust, RICO, Securities) · Mayer, Brown & Platt · 2000 Pennsylvania Avenue, NW, Suite 6500 · Washington, DC 20006 · 202-463-2000

Donald L. Flexner · Crowell & Moring · 1001 Pennsylvania Avenue, NW · Washington, DC 20004-2505 · 202-624-2500

Richard J. Flynn · (Antitrust, Regulated Industries) · Sidley & Austin · 1722 I Street, NW, Ninth Floor · Washington, DC 20006 · 202-429-4000

Paul L. Friedman · (Appellate, Commercial, RICO, Securities) · White & Case · 1747 Pennsylvania Avenue, NW · Washington, DC 20006 · 202-872-0013

Vincent J. Fuller · Williams & Connolly · Hill Building · 839 Seventeenth Street, NW · Washington, DC 20006 · 202-331-5000

William L. Gardner · Morgan, Lewis & Bockius · 1800 M Street, NW, Suite 800N · Washington, DC 20036 · 202-467-7000

Robert J. Geniesse · (Administrative) · Debevoise & Plimpton · 555 Thirteenth Street, NW, Suite 1100 East · Washington, DC 20004 · 202-383-8000

Jamie S. Gorelick* · (Antitrust, Finance) · Miller, Cassidy, Larroca & Lewin · 2555 M Street, NW, Suite 500 · Washington, DC 20037 · 202-293-6400

Joseph M. Hassett · Hogan & Hartson · Columbia Square · 555 Thirteenth Street, NW · Washington, DC 20004-1109 · 202-637-5600

John D. Hawke, Jr. · (Banking) · Arnold & Porter · Thurman Arnold Building · 1200 New Hampshire Avenue, NW · Washington, DC 20036 · 202-872-6700

Michael J. Henke* · (Administrative, Antitrust, Energy) · Vinson & Elkins · Willard Office Building, Suite 800 · 1455 Pennsylvania Avenue, NW · Washington, DC 20004-1007 · 202-639-6500

Richard A. Hibey · Anderson, Hibey, Nauheim & Blair · 1708 New Hampshire Avenue, NW · Washington, DC 20009 · 202-483-1900

Harry Huge · (Securities) · Donovan Leisure · 1250 Twenty-Fourth Street, NW, Suite 700 · Washington, DC 20037-1124 · 202-467-8300

David B. Isbell · (Accounting) · Covington & Burling · 1201 Pennsylvania Avenue, NW · P.O. Box 7566 · Washington, DC 20044 · 202-662-6000

William H. Jeffress, Jr.* · (Banking, Securities) · Miller, Cassidy, Larroca & Lewin · 2555 M Street, NW, Suite 500 · Washington, DC 20037 · 202-293-6400

Robert E. Jordan, Jr.* · (Antitrust, Energy) · Steptoe & Johnson · 1330 Connecticut Avenue, NW · Washington, DC 20036-1795 · 202-429-3000

Joel I. Klein · Onek, Klein & Farr · 2550 M Street, NW, Suite 350 · Washington, DC 20037 · 202-775-0184

Abe Krash · (Antitrust) · Arnold & Porter · Thurman Arnold Building · 1200 New Hampshire Avenue, NW · Washington, DC 20036 · 202-872-6700

Lawrence J. Latto* · (Appellate, Securities) · Shea & Gardner · 1800 Massachusetts Avenue, NW, Suite 800 · Washington, DC 20036 · 202-828-2000

Nathan Lewin* · (Appellate) · Miller, Cassidy, Larroca & Lewin · 2555 M Street, NW, Suite 500 · Washington, DC 20037 · 202-293-6400

Richard C. Lowery · Wiley, Rein & Fielding · 1776 K Street, NW · Washington, DC 20006-2359 · 202-429-7000

Michael J. Madigan* · (Banking, Commercial, Representation Before Congressional Investigations) · Akin, Gump, Strauss, Hauer & Feld · 1333 New Hampshire Avenue, NW, Suite 400 · Washington, DC 20036 · 202-887-4000

Arthur F. Mathews · (Commodities, Foreign Corrupt Practices Act, RICO, Securities) · Wilmer, Cutler & Pickering · 2445 M Street, NW · Washington, DC 20037-1420 · 202-663-6000

Daniel K. Mayers* · (Antitrust, Appellate, International) · Wilmer, Cutler & Pickering · 2445 M Street, NW · Washington, DC 20037-1420 · 202-663-6000

William E. McDaniels · (Libel & Slander, Medical Malpractice, Products Liability) · Williams & Connolly · Hill Building · 839 Seventeenth Street, NW · Washington, DC 20006 · 202-331-5000

Bruce L. McDonald · Wiley, Rein & Fielding · 1776 K Street, NW · Washington, DC 20006-2359 · 202-429-7000

Hugh M. McIntosh · (Energy, Commercial, Corporate Finance, Real Estate Finance) · Vinson & Elkins · Willard Office Building, Suite 800 · 1455 Pennsylvania Avenue · Washington, DC 20004-1007 · 202-639-6730

R. Bruce McLean · (Energy) · Akin, Gump, Strauss, Hauer & Feld · 1333 New Hampshire Avenue, NW, Suite 400 · Washington, DC 20036 · 202-887-4000

Charles A. Miller · (Administrative, Health & Welfare, Transportation) · Covington & Burling · 1201 Pennsylvania Avenue, NW · P.O. Box 7566 · Washington, DC 20044 · 202-662-6000

Herbert J. Miller, Jr.* · Miller, Cassidy, Larroca & Lewin · 2555 M Street, NW, Suite 500 · Washington, DC 20037 · 202-293-6400

Ralph J. Moore, Jr. · (Railway) · Shea & Gardner · 1800 Massachusetts Avenue, NW, Suite 800 · Washington, DC 20036 · 202-828-2000

Hugh P. Morrison, Jr. · (Antitrust) · Cahill Gordon & Reindel · 1990 K Street, NW · Washington, DC 20006 · 202-862-8900

David C. Murchison · (Antitrust) · Howrey & Simon · 1730 Pennsylvania Avenue, NW, Suite 900 · Washington, DC 20006-4793 · 202-783-0800

Irvin B. Nathan · (Antitrust, RICO, Securities) · Arnold & Porter · Thurman Arnold Building · 1200 New Hampshire Avenue, NW · Washington, DC 20036 · 202-872-6700

Peter J. Nickles · Covington & Burling · 1201 Pennsylvania Avenue, NW · P.O. Box 7566 · Washington, DC 20044 · 202-662-6000

John E. Nolan, Jr. · Steptoe & Johnson · 1330 Connecticut Avenue, NW · Washington, DC 20036-1795 · 202-429-3000

Michael Nussbaum · (Appellate, Commercial, International, Securities) · Nussbaum & Wald · One Thomas Circle, Suite 200 · Washington, DC 20005-5802 · 202-833-8900

Theodore B. Olson · (Appellate, Commercial, Constitutional, Media) · Gibson, Dunn & Crutcher · 1050 Connecticut Avenue, NW, Suite 900 · Washington, DC 20036 · 202-955-8500

Roberts B. Owen* · (Antitrust, Appellate, International, Securities) · Covington & Burling · 1201 Pennsylvania Avenue, NW · P.O. Box 7566 · Washington, DC 20044 · 202-662-6000

Thomas E. Patton* · (Antitrust, Securities) · Schnader, Harrison, Segal & Lewis · 1111 Nineteenth Street, NW, Suite 1000 · Washington, DC 20036 · 202-463-2900

Richard M. Phillips · (Securities) · Kirkpatrick & Lockhart · 1800 M Street, NW, South Lobby, Suite 900 · Washington, DC 20036 · 202-778-9000

Harvey L. Pitt · (Securities) · Fried, Frank, Harris, Shriver & Jacobson · 1001 Pennsylvania Avenue, NW, Suite 800 · Washington, DC 20004-2505 · 202-639-7000

Stephen J. Pollak · (Antitrust, Appellate, Civil Rights, Government Regulations, Labor) · Shea & Gardner · 1800 Massachusetts Avenue, NW, Suite 800 · Washington, DC 20036 · 202-828-2000

E. Barrett Prettyman, Jr. · (Administrative, Appellate) · Hogan & Hartson · Columbia Square · 555 Thirteenth Street, NW · Washington, DC 20004-1109 · 202-637-5600

Bert W. Rein* · (Administrative, Antitrust, Commercial, Transportation) · Wiley, Rein & Fielding · 1776 K Street, NW · Washington, DC 20006-2359 · 202-429-7000

Daniel A. Rezneck · (Appellate) · Arnold & Porter · Thurman Arnold Building · 1200 New Hampshire Avenue, NW · Washington, DC 20036 · 202-872-6700

James Robertson · (Commercial, Products Liability) · Wilmer, Cutler & Pickering · 2445 M Street, NW · Washington, DC 20037-1420 · 202-663-6000

Charles F. C. Ruff · (RICO, Securities) · Covington & Burling · 1201 Pennsylvania Avenue, NW · P.O. Box 7566 · Washington, DC 20044 · 202-662-6000

Stephen H. Sachs* · (Securities) · Wilmer, Cutler & Pickering · 2445 M Street, NW · Washington, DC 20037-1420 · 202-663-6000

Stephen M. Sacks · Arnold & Porter · Thurman Arnold Building · 1200 New Hampshire Avenue, NW · Washington, DC 20036 · 202-872-6700

Robert N. Sayler* · (Antitrust, Insurance Coverage) · Covington & Burling · 1201 Pennsylvania Avenue, NW · P.O. Box 7566 · Washington, DC 20044 · 202-662-6000

John H. Schafer III · (Antitrust, Securities) · Covington & Burling · 1201 Pennsylvania Avenue, NW · P.O. Box 7566 · Washington, DC 20044 · 202-662-6000

Lawrence H. Schwartz · Cooter & Gell · 1201 New York Avenue, NW, Suite 900 Washington, DC 20005 · 202-289-5638

William H. Schweitzer · (Election) · Baker & Hostetler · 1050 Connecticut Avenue, NW, Suite 1100 · Washington, DC 20036 · 202-861-1500

David I. Shapiro · Dickstein, Shapiro & Morin · 2101 L Street, NW, Suite 900 · Washington, DC 20037 · 202-785-9700

James E. Sharp · Sharp & Lankford · 1785 Massachusetts Avenue, NW, Fourth Floor · Washington, DC 20036 · 202-745-1700

John H. Shenefield · (Antitrust) · Morgan, Lewis & Bockius · 800 M Street, NW, Suite 800N · Washington, DC 20036 · 202-467-7000

Stephen N. Shulman* · (Commercial, International, Securities) · Cadwalader, Wickersham & Taft · 1333 New Hampshire Avenue, NW, Suite 700 · Washington, DC 20036 · 202-862-2200

Deanne C. Siemer · Pillsbury Madison & Sutro · 1667 K Street, NW, Suite 1100 · Washington, DC 20006 · 202-463-2392

Earl J. Silbert* · Schwalb, Donnenfeld, Bray & Silbert · 1025 Thomas Jefferson Street, NW, Suite 300 East · Washington, DC 20007 · 202-965-7910

Joe Sims · (Administrative, Antitrust) · Jones, Day, Reavis & Pogue · Metropolitan Square · 1450 G Street, NW · Washington, DC 20005-2088 · 202-879-3939

Allen R. Snyder* · (Appellate, Commercial, Constitutional) · Hogan & Hartson · Columbia Square · 555 Thirteenth Street, NW · Washington, DC 20004-1109 · 202-637-5600

Jacob A. Stein · Stein, Mitchell & Mezines · 1100 Connecticut Avenue, NW, Suite 1130 · Washington, DC 20036 · 202-737-7777

William W. Taylor III* · Zuckerman, Spaeder, Goldstein, Taylor & Kolker · 1201 Connecticut Avenue, NW, Suite 1200 · Washington, DC 20036 · 202-778-1800

Steven M. Umin · Williams & Connolly · Hill Building · 839 Seventeenth Street, NW · Washington, DC 20006 · 202-331-5000

John Vanderstar · (Antitrust, Appellate, Constitutional) · Covington & Burling · 1201 Pennsylvania Avenue, NW · P.O. Box 7566 · Washington, DC 20044 · 202-662-6000

John W. Vardaman, Jr. · (Environmental) · Williams & Connolly · Hill Building · 839 Seventeenth Street, NW · Washington, DC 20006 · 202-331-5000

James H. Wallace, Jr.* · (Antitrust, International, RICO, Patents) · Wiley, Rein & Fielding · 1776 K Street, NW · Washington, DC 20006-2359 · 202-429-7000

David N. Webster* · (RICO, Securities) · Caplin & Drysdale · One Thomas Circle, NW, Suite 1100 · Washington, DC 20005 · 202-862-8850

Robert L. Weinberg* · (Administrative, Commercial, Energy, RICO) · Williams & Connolly · Hill Building · 839 Seventeenth Street, NW · Washington, DC 20006 · 202-331-5000

Richard J. Wertheimer · (Antitrust, Securities) · Arnold & Porter · Thurman Arnold Building · 1200 New Hampshire Avenue, NW · Washington, DC 20036 · 202-872-6700

Howard P. Willens · Wilmer, Cutler & Pickering · 2445 M Street, NW · Washington, DC 20037-1420 · 202-663-6000

Elroy H. Wolff · (Antitrust, Trade Regulations) · Sidley & Austin · 1722 I Street, NW, Sixth Floor · Washington, DC 20006 · 202-429-4000

Paul Martin Wolff · (Banking, First Amendment, Securities) · Williams & Connolly · Hill Building · 839 Seventeenth Street, NW · Washington, DC 20006 · 202-331-5000

CORPORATE LAW

Clifford J. Alexander · (Banking, Broker-Dealer, Investment Adviser, Investment Companies, Securities) · Kirkpatrick & Lockhart · 1800 M Street, NW, South Lobby, Suite 900 · Washington, DC 20036 · 202-778-9000

Charles E. Allen · Hogan & Hartson · Columbia Square · 555 Thirteenth Street, NW · Washington, DC 20004-1109 · 202-637-5600

Robert A. Altman · (Banking, Finance, Food & Drug) · Clifford & Warnke · 815 Connecticut Avenue, NW, 12th Floor · Washington, DC 20006 · 202-828-4200

Donald I. Baker · (Antitrust, Banking) · Sutherland, Asbill & Brennan · 1275 Pennsylvania Avenue, NW, Suite 800 · Washington, DC 20004-2404 · 202-383-0100

Alan J. Berkeley · (Securities) · Kirkpatrick & Lockhart · 1800 M Street, NW, South Lobby, Suite 900 · Washington, DC 20036 · 202-778-9000

Robert L. Bevan · (Banking, Financial Institutions, International Banking, Securities Regulation) · Hopkins & Sutter · 888 Sixteenth Street, NW · Washington, DC 20006 · 202-835-8000

John Bodner, Jr.* · (Administrative, Antitrust, International Trade, Mergers & Acquisitions) · Howrey & Simon · 1730 Pennsylvania Avenue, NW, Suite 900 · Washington, DC 20006-4793 · 202-783-0800

Brooksley Born · Arnold & Porter · Thurman Arnold Building · 1200 New Hampshire Avenue, NW · Washington, DC 20036 · 202-872-6700

Charles N. Brower · (International) · White & Case · 1747 Pennsylvania Avenue, NW, Suite 500 · Washington, DC 20006 · 202-872-0013

David N. Brown · (Mergers & Acquisitions, Securities) · Covington & Burling · 1201 Pennsylvania Avenue, NW · P.O. Box 7566 · Washington, DC 20044 · 202-662-6000

Joseph A. Califano, Jr. · Dewey Ballantine · 1775 Pennsylvania Avenue, NW · Washington, DC 20006 · 202-862-1000

Stuart F. Carwile · (Banking, Corporate Finance, Mergers & Acquisitions) · Wiley, Rein & Fielding · 1776 K Street, NW · Washington, DC 20006-2359 · 202-429-7000

Richard W. Cass · Wilmer, Cutler & Pickering · 2445 M Street, NW · Washington, DC 20037-1420 · 202-663-6000

George L. Christopher · Kirkpatrick & Lockhart · 1800 M Street, NW, South Lobby, Suite 900 · Washington, DC 20036 · 202-778-9000

Clark M. Clifford · Clifford & Warnke · 815 Connecticut Avenue, NW, 12th Floor · Washington, DC 20006 · 202-828-4200

Calvin H. Cobb, Jr.* · (Corporate Finance, Securities & Related Litigation) · Steptoe & Johnson · 1330 Connecticut Avenue, NW · Washington, DC 20036-1795 · 202-429-3000

Louis R. Cohen · Wilmer, Cutler & Pickering · 2445 M Street, NW · Washington, DC 20037-1420 · 202-663-6000

William T. Coleman, Jr. · (Antitrust, International Trade, Mergers & Acquisitions) · O'Melveny & Myers · 555 Thirteenth Street, NW, Suite 500 West · Washington, DC 20004 · 202-383-5300

Myron P. Curzan · Arnold & Porter · Thurman Arnold Building · 1200 New Hampshire Avenue, NW · Washington, DC 20036 · 202-872-6700

Lloyd N. Cutler · (Antitrust, International) · Wilmer, Cutler & Pickering · 2445 M Street, NW · Washington, DC 20037-1420 · 202-663-6000

Nelson Deckelbaum · (Business Reorganization) · Deckelbaum, Ogens & Fisher 1140 Connecticut Avenue, NW · Washington, DC 20036 · 202-223-1474

Edward E. Dyson · (International) · Baker & McKenzie · 815 Connecticut Avenue, NW, Suite 1100 · Washington, DC 20006 · 202-452-7000

Peter D. Ehrenhaft · (Antitrust, International, International Trade, Technology Transfers) · Bryan, Cave, McPheeters & McRoberts · 700 Thirteenth Street, NW, Suite 700 · Washington, DC 20005-3960 · 202-508-6000

Anthony F. Essaye · (International Banking) · Rogers & Wells · 1737 H Street, NW · Washington, DC 20006 · 202-331-7760

Kenneth R. Feinberg · (Administrative) · Kaye, Scholer, Fierman, Hays & Handler · 901 Fifteenth Street, NW, Suite 1100 · Washington, DC 20005 · 202-682-3500

Lloyd H. Feller · (Securities) · Morgan, Lewis & Bockius · 1800 M Street, NW, Suite 800N · Washington, DC 20036 · 202-467-7000

Ralph C. Ferrara · (Securities) · Debevoise & Plimpton · 555 Thirteenth Street, NW, Suite 1100 East · Washington, DC 20004 · 202-383-8000

James F. Fitzpatrick · (Administrative, Legislative Proceedings) · Arnold & Porter · Thurman Arnold Building · 1200 New Hampshire Avenue, NW · Washington, DC 20036 · 202-872-6700

Howard I. Flack · Hogan & Hartson · Columbia Square · 555 Thirteenth Street, NW · Washington, DC 20004-1109 · 202-637-5600

George C. Freeman, Jr. · (Administrative, Energy, Environmental) · Hunton & Williams · 2000 Pennsylvania Avenue, NW · P.O. Box 19230 · Washington, DC 20036 · 202-955-1500

Milton V. Freeman · (Securities) · Arnold & Porter · Thurman Arnold Building · 1200 New Hampshire Avenue, NW · Washington, DC 20036 · 202-872-6700

J. Warren Gorrell, Jr. · Hogan & Hartson · Columbia Square · 555 Thirteenth Street, NW · Washington, DC 20004-1109 · 202-637-5600

Daniel M. Gribbon · (Antitrust, International) · Covington & Burling · 1201 Pennsylvania Avenue, NW · P.O. Box 7566 · Washington, DC 20044 · 202-662-5310

Stephen W. Hamilton · Skadden, Arps, Slate, Meagher & Flom · 1440 New York Avenue, NW · Washington, DC 20005-2107 · 202-371-7000

Robert A. Hammond II · (Antitrust) · Wilmer, Cutler & Pickering · 2445 M Street, NW · Washington, DC 20037-1420 · 202-663-6000

John D. Hawke, Jr. · (Banking) · Arnold & Porter · Thurman Arnold Building · 1200 New Hampshire Avenue, NW · Washington, DC 20036 · 202-872-6700

Michael S. Helfer · (Banking) · Wilmer, Cutler & Pickering · 2445 M Street, NW Washington, DC 20037-1420 · 202-663-6000

Robert E. Herzstein · (International, Trade Investment) · Shearman & Sterling 1001 Thirtieth Street, NW · Washington, DC 20007 · 202-298-6402

John J. Huber · Latham & Watkins · 1001 Pennsylvania Avenue, NW, Suite 1300 Washington, DC 20004 · 202-637-2200

William M. Isaac · (Banking) · Arnold & Porter · Three Lafayette Centre, Suite 850 · 1155 Twenty-First Street, NW · Washington, DC 20036 · 202-872-6700

Robert E. Jordan III* · (Antitrust) · Steptoe & Johnson · 1330 Connecticut Avenue, NW · Washington, DC 20036-1795 · 202-429-3000

Miles W. Kirkpatrick · (Antitrust) · Morgan, Lewis & Bockius · 1800 M Street, NW, Suite 800N · Washington, DC 20036 · 202-467-7000

Michael R. Klein · (SEC Investigations, Securities) · Wilmer, Cutler & Pickering 2445 M Street, NW · Washington, DC 20037-1420 · 202-663-6000

Abe Krash · (Antitrust) · Arnold & Porter · Thurman Arnold Building · 1200 New Hampshire Avenue, NW · Washington, DC 20036 · 202-872-6700

Stuart J. Land · (Food & Drug) · Arnold & Porter · Thurman Arnold Building · 1200 New Hampshire Avenue, NW · Washington, DC 20036 · 202-872-6700

Lawrence J. Latto* · (Securities, Securities Regulation) · Shea & Gardner · 1800 Massachusetts Avenue, NW, Suite 800 · Washington, DC 20036 · 202-828-2000

Dennis J. Lehr · (Banking) · Hogan & Hartson · Columbia Square · 555 Thirteenth Street, NW · Washington, DC 20004-1109 · 202-637-5600

Arnold M. Lerman · (Administrative, Antitrust, Banking) · Wilmer, Cutler & Pickering · 2445 M Street, NW · Washington, DC 20037-1420 · 202-663-6000

Alan B. Levenson · (Financial Institutions, Securities, Securities Regulation) · Fulbright & Jaworski · 801 Pennsylvania Avenue, NW · Washington, DC 20004-2604 · 202-662-4600

Robert A. Lipstein · (Antitrust, International) · Coudert Brothers · 1627 I Street, NW, Suite 1200 · Washington, DC 20006 · 202-775-5100

Dennis G. Lyons · Arnold & Porter · Thurman Arnold Building · 1200 New Hampshire Avenue, NW · Washington, DC 20036 · 202-872-6700

Stanley J. Marcuss · (International) · Milbank, Tweed, Hadley & McCloy · 1825 I Street, NW, Suite 900 · Washington, DC 20006 · 202-835-7500

Daniel H. Margolis · (Antitrust) · Patton, Boggs & Blow · 2550 M Street, NW, Suite 800 · Washington, DC 20037 · 202-457-6000

David B. H. Martin, Jr. · (Banking, Mergers & Acquisitions, Securities) · Hogan & Hartson · Columbia Square · 555 Thirteenth Street, NW · Washington, DC 20004-1109 · 202-637-5600 6858

Paul J. Mason · (Securities) · Sutherland, Asbill & Brennan · 1275 Pennsylvania Avenue, NW, Suite 800 · Washington, DC 20004-2404 · 202-383-0100

Neal S. McCoy · (Securities) · Skadden, Arps, Slate, Meagher & Flom · 1440 New York Avenue, NW · Washington, DC 20005-2107 · 202-371-7000

Allan S. Mostoff · (Financial Institutions, Investment Companies & Advisers, Securities) · Dechert Price & Rhoads · 1500 K Street, NW, Suite 500 · Washington, DC 20005 · 202-626-3300

Cantwell Faulkner Muckenfuss III · (Banking, Financial Institutions) · Gibson, Dunn & Crutcher · 1050 Connecticut Avenue, NW, Suite 900 · Washington, DC 20036 · 202-955-8500

John F. Olson · (Securities) · Gibson, Dunn & Crutcher · 1050 Connecticut Avenue, NW, Suite 900 · Washington, DC 20036 · 202-955-8500

Richard M. Phillips · (Securities) · Kirkpatrick & Lockhart · 1800 M Street, NW, South Lobby, Suite 900 · Washington, DC 20036 · 202-778-9000

Robert Pitofsky · (Antitrust) · Arnold & Porter · Thurman Arnold Building · 1200 New Hampshire Avenue, NW · Washington, DC 20036 · 202-872-6700

Harvey L. Pitt · (Securities) · Fried, Frank, Harris, Shriver & Jacobson · 1001 Pennsylvania Avenue, NW, Suite 800 · Washington, DC 20004-2505 · 202-639-7000

George B. Reid, Jr. · (Mergers & Acquisitions, Securities) · Covington & Burling 1201 Pennsylvania Avenue, NW · P.O. Box 7566 · Washington, DC 20044 · 202-662-6000

William D. Rogers · (International) · Arnold & Porter · Thurman Arnold Building 1200 New Hampshire Avenue, NW · Washington, DC 20036 · 202-872-6700

William P. Rogers · (International) · Rogers & Wells · 1737 H Street, NW · Washington, DC 20006 · 202-331-7760

Peter J. Romeo · (Securities) · Hogan & Hartson · Columbia Square · 555 Thirteenth Street, NW · Washington, DC 20004-1109 · 202-637-5600

James J. Rosenhauer · Hogan & Hartson · Columbia Square · 555 Thirteenth Street, NW · Washington, DC 20004-1109 · 202-637-5600

Douglas E. Rosenthal · (Antitrust, International) · Coudert Brothers · 1627 I Street, NW · Washington, DC 20006 · 202-775-5100

Eugene T. Rossides · (International Trade, Legislative) · Rogers & Wells · 1737 H Street, NW · Washington, DC 20006 · 202-331-7760

Marcus A. Rowden · (Energy, High Technology, International) · Fried, Frank, Harris, Shriver & Jacobson · 1001 Pennsylvania Avenue, NW, Suite 800 · Washington, DC 20004-2505 · 202-639-7000

Richard H. Rowe · (Corporate Finance, International Finance, Securities, Securities Regulation) · Proskauer Rose Goetz & Mendelsohn · 2001 L Street, NW, Suite 400 · Washington, DC 20036 · 202-416-6820

Henry P. Sailer · (Trade Regulation) · Covington & Burling · 201 Pennsylvania Avenue, NW · P.O. Box 7566 · Washington, DC 20044 · 202-662-6000

Frank P. Saponaro, Jr. · (Energy, Oil & Gas) · Arent, Fox, Kintner, Plotkin & Kahn · 1050 Connecticut Avenue, NW · Washington, DC 20036-5339 · 202-857-6080

James H. Schropp · (Securities) · Fried, Frank, Harris, Shriver & Jacobson · 1001 Pennsylvania Avenue, NW, Suite 800 · Washington, DC 20004-2505 · 202-639-7000

Joe Sims · (Administrative, Antitrust) · Jones, Day, Reavis & Pogue · Metropolitan Square · 1450 G Street, NW · Washington, DC 20005-2088 · 202-879-3939

Michael N. Sohn · (Administrative, Antitrust, Trade Regulations) · Arnold & Porter · Thurman Arnold Building · 1200 New Hampshire Avenue, NW · Washington, DC 20036 · 202-872-6700

A. A. Sommer, Jr. · (Corporate Finance, Mergers & Acquisitions, Securities, Securities Regulation)) · Morgan, Lewis & Bockius · 1800 M Street, NW, Suite 9800N · Washington, DC 20036 · 202-467-7000

Richard A. Steinwurtzel · Fried, Frank, Harris, Shriver & Jacobson · 1001 Pennsylvania Avenue, NW, Suite 800 · Washington, DC 20004-2505 · 202-639-7000

Samuel A. Stern · (International) · Dickstein, Shapiro & Morin · 2101 L Street, NW, Suite 900 · Washington, DC 20037 · 202-785-9700

John R. Stevenson · (International Arbitration) · Sullivan & Cromwell · 1701 Pennsylvania Avenue, NW · Washington, DC 20006 · 202-956-7500

William E. Swope · Jones, Day, Reavis & Pogue · Metropolitan Square · 1450 G Street, NW · Washington, DC 20005-2088 · 202-879-3939

Thomas P. Vartanian · (Financial Institutions Transactions, Mergers & Acquisitions) · Fried, Frank, Harris, Shriver & Jacobson · 1001 Pennsylvania Avenue, NW, Suite 800 · Washington, DC 20004-2505 · 202-639-7000

G. Duane Vieth · Arnold & Porter · Thurman Arnold Building · 1200 New Hampshire Avenue, NW · Washington, DC 20036 · 202-872-6700

Robert L. Wald · (Antitrust, Administrative Law) · Nussbaum & Wald · One Thomas Circle, Suite 200 · Washington, DC 20005-5802 · 202-833-8900

Peter J. Wallison · Gibson, Dunn & Crutcher · 1050 Connecticut Avenue, NW, Suite 900 · Washington, DC 20036 · 202-955-8500

Alan S. Ward · Baker & Hostetler · 1050 Connecticut Avenue, NW, Suite 1100 Washington, DC 20036 · 202-861-1500

Paul C. Warnke · (Administrative, Antitrust, International Trade) · Clifford & Warnke · 815 Connecticut Avenue, NW, 12th Floor · Washington, DC 20006 · 202-828-4200

Mark A. Weiss · (Banking, Financial Institutions) · Covington & Burling · 1201 Pennsylvania Avenue, NW · P.O. Box 7566 · Washington, DC 20044 · 202-662-6000

Richard E. Wiley · (Administrative, Telecommunications) · Wiley, Rein & Fielding · 1776 K Street, NW · Washington, DC 20006-2359 · 202-429-7000

Wesley S. Williams, Jr. · (Banking) · Covington & Burling · 1201 Pennsylvania Avenue, NW · P.O. Box 7566 · Washington, DC 20044 · 202-662-6000

J. Roger Wollenberg · (Telecommunications) · Wilmer, Cutler & Pickering · 2445 M Street, NW · Washington, DC 20037-1420 · 202-663-6000

CRIMINAL DEFENSE

Raymond Banoun · (Environmental Crimes, White Collar Crimes) · Arent, Fox, Kintner, Plotkin & Kahn · Washington Square · 1050 Connecticut Avenue, NW · Washington, DC 20036-5339 · 202-857-6424

Richard W. Beckler* · (Non-Violent Crimes, Federal Court, State Court, White Collar Crimes) · Fulbright & Jaworski · 801 Pennsylvania Avenue, NW · Washington, DC 20004-2604 · 202-662-0200

Richard L. Beizer · Crowell & Moring · 1001 Pennsylvania Avenue, NW · Washington, DC 20004-2505 · 202-624-2500

Richard Ben-Veniste · Ben-Veniste & Shernoff · 1667 K Street, NW, Suite 405 · Washington, DC 20006 · 202-331-8700

Robert S. Bennett · Skadden, Arps, Slate, Meagher & Flom · 1440 New York Avenue, NW · Washington, DC 20005 · 202-371-7000

Judah Best · (also Appellate) · Debevoise & Plimpton · 555 Thirteenth Street, NW, Suite 1100 East · Washington, DC 20004 · 202-383-8000

John M. Bray* · Schwalb, Donnenfeld, Bray & Silbert · 1025 Thomas Jefferson Street, NW, Suite 300 East · Washington, DC 20007 · 202-965-7910

Donald T. Bucklin* · Squire, Sanders & Dempsey · 1201 Pennsylvania Avenue, NW · P.O. Box 407 · Washington, DC 20044 · 202-626-6600

Plato Cacheris* · (Federal Court, State Court) · Cacheris & Towey · 1914 Sunderland Place, NW · Washington, DC 20036 · 202-452-9886

Aubrey M. Daniel III · Williams & Connolly · Hill Building · 839 Seventeenth Street, NW · Washington, DC 20006 · 202-331-5000

John M. Dowd · Akin, Gump, Strauss, Hauer & Feld · 1333 New Hampshire Avenue, NW, Suite 400 · Washington, DC 20036 · 202-887-4386

Gerald A. Feffer* · (Non-Violent Crimes) · Williams & Connolly · Hill Building 839 Seventeenth Street, NW · Washington, DC 20006 · 202-331-5007

Hamilton P. Fox III · Sutherland, Asbill & Brennan · 1275 Pennsylvania Avenue, NW, Suite 700 · Washington, DC 20004 · 202-383-0666

Paul L. Friedman · (Federal Court, White Collar Crimes) · White & Case · 1747 Pennsylvania Avenue, NW · Washington, DC 20006 · 202-872-0013

Vincent J. Fuller · Williams & Connolly · Hill Building · 839 Seventeenth Street, NW · Washington, DC 20006 · 202-331-5000

William J. Garber · 301 I Street, NW · Washington, DC 20001-2524 · 202-638-4667

Seymour Glanzer · Dickstein, Shapiro & Morin · 2101 L Street, NW, Suite 900 · Washington, DC 20037 · 202-785-9700

Jamie S. Gorelick* · (Federal Court, Environmental Crimes) · Miller, Cassidy, Larroca & Lewin · 2555 M Street, NW, Suite 500 · Washington, DC 20037 · 202-293-6400

Thomas C. Green · 22 I Street, NW, Seventh Floor · Washington, DC 20006 · 202-429-4069

Richard A. Hibey · Anderson, Hibey, Nauheim & Blair · 1708 New Hampshire Avenue, NW · Washington, DC 20009 · 202-483-1900

William G. Hundley · Akin, Gump, Strauss, Hauer & Feld · 1333 New Hampshire Avenue, NW, Suite 400 · Washington, DC 20036 · 202-887-4000

William H. Jeffress, Jr.* · (Federal Court, White-Collar) · Miller, Cassidy, Larroca & Lewin · 2555 M Street, NW, Suite 500 · Washington, DC 20037 · 202-293-6400

John T. Kotelly · Dickstein, Shapiro & Morin · 2101 L Street, NW · Washington, DC 20037 · 202-828-2237

Nathan Lewin* · (Non-Violent Crimes, Federal Court) · Miller, Cassidy, Larroca & Lewin · 2555 M Street, NW, Suite 500 · Washington, DC 20037 · 202-293-6400

Arthur F. Mathews · Wilmer, Cutler & Pickering · 2445 M Street, NW · Washington, DC 20037-1420 · 202-663-6000

William E. McDaniels · Williams & Connolly · Hill Building · 839 Seventeenth Street, NW · Washington, DC 20006 · 202-331-5000

Herbert J. Miller, Jr.* · (Federal Court) · Miller, Cassidy, Larroca & Lewin · 2555 M Street, NW, Suite 500 · Washington, DC 20037 · 202-293-6400

R. Stan Mortenson* · (Federal Court, State Court) · Miller, Cassidy, Larroca & Lewin · 2555 M Street, NW, Suite 500 · Washington, DC 20037 · 202-833-5121

R. Kenneth Mundy · Reynolds & Mundy · 1155 Fifteenth Street, NW, Suite 1004 Washington, D. C. 20005 · 202-223-4470

Robert F. Muse* · Stein, Mitchell & Mezines · 1100 Connecticut Avenue, NW, 11th Floor · Washington, DC 20036 · 202-737-7777

Irvin B. Nathan · Arnold & Porter · Thurman Arnold Building · 1200 New Hampshire Avenue, NW · Washington, DC 20036 · 202-872-6700

David Povich* · Williams & Connolly · Hill Building · 839 Seventeenth Street, NW · Washington, DC 20006 · 202-331-5000

Carl S. Rauh · Skadden, Arps, Slate, Meagher & Flom · 1440 New York Avenue, NW · Washington, DC 20005-2107 · 202-371-7000

Daniel A. Rezneck · Arnold & Porter · Thurman Arnold Building · 1200 New Hampshire Avenue, NW · Washington, DC 20036 · 202-872-6700

Kenneth M. Robinson* · (Violent Crimes, Non-Violent Crimes, Federal State, Complex White-Collar Crimes) · Robinson & Grimm · Judiciary Manor · 301 I Street, NW · Washington, DC 20001 · 202-347-6100

Charles F. C. Ruff · Covington & Burling · 1201 Pennsylvania Avenue, NW · P.O. Box 7566 · Washington, DC 20044 · 202-662-6000

James E. Sharp · Sharp & Lankford · 1785 Massachusetts Avenue, NW, Fourth Floor · Washington, DC 20036 · 202-745-1700

Earl J. Silbert* · Schwalb, Donnenfeld, Bray & Silbert · 1025 Thomas Jefferson Street, Third Floor · Washington, DC 20007 · 202-965-7910

Roger C. Spaeder · (Non-Violent Crimes) · Zuckerman, Spaeder, Goldstein, Taylor & Kolker · 1201 Connecticut Avenue, NW, Suite 1200 · Washington, DC 20036 · 202-778-1800

Jacob A. Stein · (also Appellate) · Stein, Mitchell & Mezines · 1100 Connecticut Avenue, NW, Suite 1130 · Washington, DC 20036 · 202-737-7777

Brendan V. Sullivan, Jr. · Williams & Connolly · Hill Building · 839 Seventeenth Street, NW · Washington, DC 20006 · 202-331-5000

William W. Taylor III* · Zuckerman, Spaeder, Goldstein, Taylor & Kolker · 1201 Connecticut Avenue, NW, Suite 1200 · Washington, DC 20036 · 202-778-1800

Gerard F. Treanor, Jr. · Venable, Baetjer, Howard & Civiletti · 1201 New York Avenue, NW, Suite 1000 · Washington, DC 20005 · 202-962-4867

John W. Vardaman, Jr. · Williams & Connolly · Hill Building · 839 Seventeenth Street, NW · Washington, DC 20006 · 202-331-5000

Robert L. Weinberg* · (Federal Court, State Court, Grand Jury Litigation) · Williams & Connolly · Hill Building · 839 Seventeenth Street, NW · Washington, DC 20006 · 202-331-5000

Roger E. Zuckerman* · Zuckerman, Spaeder, Goldstein, Taylor & Kolker · 1201 Connecticut Avenue, NW, Suite 1200 · Washington, DC 20036 · 202-778-1800

FAMILY LAW

Sanford K. Ain · Sherman, Meehan & Curtin · 1900 M Street, NW, Suite 601 · Washington, DC 20036 · 202-331-7120

Rita M. Bank · Feldesman, Leifer, Fidell & Bank · 2001 L Street, NW, Suite 300 Washington, DC 20036 · 202-466-8960

Pamela Borland Forbes · Feldesman, Leifer, Fidell & Bank · 2001 L Street, NW, Suite 300 · Washington, DC 20036 · 202-466-8960

Daniel G. Grove · Keck, Mahin & Cate · 1201 New York Avenue, NW, Penthouse · Washington, DC 20005 · 202-347-7006

Armin U. Kuder* · Kuder, Smollar & Friedman · 1015 Twentieth Street, NW, Suite 200 · Washington, DC 20036 · 202-331-7522

Sidney S. Sachs · Sachs, Greenebaum & Tayler · 1140 Connecticut Avenue, NW, Suite 900 · Washington, DC 20036 · 202-828-8200

Daniel E. Schultz · Daniel E. Schultz & Associates · 1825 K Street, NW, Suite 901 · Washington, DC 20006 · 202-452-1120

Peter R. Sherman · Sherman, Meehan & Curtin · 1900 M Street, NW, Suite 601 Washington, DC 20036 · 202-331-7120

Marna Susan Tucker* · Feldesman, Tucker, Leifer, Fidell & Bank · 2001 L Street, NW, Suite 300 · Washington, DC 20036 · 202-466-8960

FIRST AMENDMENT LAW

Kevin T. Baine · Williams & Connolly · Hill Building · 839 Seventeenth Street, NW · Washington, DC 20006 · 202-331-5000

Timothy B. Dyk · Jones, Day, Reavis & Pogue · 1450 G Street, NW · Washington, DC 20005-2088 · 202-879-7600

David E. Kendall · Williams & Connolly · Hill Building · 839 Seventeenth Street, NW · Washington, DC 20006 · 202-331-5000

Nathan Lewin* · (Religion) · Miller, Cassidy, Larroca & Lewin · 2555 M Street, NW, Suite 500 · Washington, DC 20037 · 202-293-6400

Mark H. Lynch · Covington & Burling · 1201 Pennsylvania Avenue, NW · P.O. Box 7566 · Washington, DC 20044 · 202-662-5544

E. Barrett Prettyman, Jr. · Hogan & Hartson · Columbia Square · 555 Thirteenth Street, NW · Washington, DC 20004-1109 · 202-637-5600

Bruce W. Sanford · Baker & Hostetler · 1050 Connecticut Avenue, NW, Suite 1100 · Washington, DC 20036 · 202-861-1500

Richard M. Schmidt, Jr. · Cohen & Marks · 1333 New Hampshire Avenue, NW, Suite 600 · Washington, DC 20036 · 202-293-3860

HEALTH CARE LAW

Earl M. (Duke) Collier, Jr. · Hogan & Hartson · Columbia Square · 555 Thirteenth Street, NW · Washington, DC 20004-1109 · 202-637-5600

Raymond D. Cotton · Ross, Marsh, Foster, Myers & Quiggle · 888 Sixteenth Street, NW, Suite 400 · Washington, DC 20006 · 202-822-8888

Thomas C. Fox · Reed Smith Shaw & McClay · Ring Building · 1200 Eighteenth Street, NW · Washington, DC 20036 · 202-457-8623

Gregory M. Luce · Fulbright & Jaworski · 801 Pennsylvania Avenue, NW · Washington, DC 20004-2604 · 202-662-0200

Barbara Mishkin · Hogan & Hartson · Columbia Square · 555 Thirteenth Street, NW · Washington, DC 20004-1109 · 202-637-5600

Galen D. Powers · Powers, Pyle & Sutter · 1015 Eighteenth Street, NW, Suite 900 · Washington, DC 20036 · 202-466-6550

Phillip Proger · Jones, Day, Reavis & Pogue · Metropolitan Square · 1450 G Street, NW · Washington, DC 20005-2088 · 202-879-3939

Ronald N. Sutter · Powers, Pyle & Sutter · 1015 Eighteenth Street, NW, Suite 900 · Washington, DC 20036 · 202-296-9243

IMMIGRATION LAW

Sam Bernsen · Fragomen, DelRey & Bernsen · 1140 Connecticut Avenue, NW, Suite 1000 · Washington, DC 20036 · 202-223-5515

David Carliner · Carliner & Remes · 1511 K Street, NW, Suite 931 · Washington, DC 20005 · 202-783-5353

Thomas A. Elliott · Law Office of Thomas A. Elliott · 1725 K Street, NW · Washington, DC 20006 · 202-429-1725

Charles Gordon · 1511 K Street, NW, Suite 931 · Washington, DC 20005 · 202-783-1330

Michael Maggio · Maggio & Kattar · 11 Dupont Circle, NW, Suite 775 · Washington, DC 20036 · 202-483-0053

Mark A. Mancini · Wasserman, Mancini & Chang · 1724 H Street, NW, Second Floor · Washington, DC 20006 · 202-783-8905

Jan Pedersen · Pedersen & Luketina · 1000 Sixteenth Street, Suite 601 · Washington, DC 20036 · 202-785-1960

Paul W. Schmidt · Jones, Day, Reavis & Pogue · 1450 G Street, NW · Washington, DC 20005-2088 · 202-879-7600

INTELLECTUAL PROPERTY LAW

Donald W. Banner · Banner, Birch, McKie & Beckett · One Thomas Circle, NW Washington, DC 20005 · 202-296-5500

Jon A. Baumgarten · Proskauer Rose Goetz & Mendelsohn · 2001 L Street, NW, Suite 300 · Washington, DC 20036 · 202-416-6810

James F. Davis · Howrey & Simon · 1730 Pennsylvania Avenue, NW, Suite 900 Washington, DC 20006-4793 · 202-783-0800

Donald R. Dunner · Finnegan, Henderson, Farabow, Garrett & Dunner · 1300 I Street, NW, Suite 700 · Washington, DC 20001 · 202-408-4000

Ford F. Farabow · Finnegan, Henderson, Farabow, Garrett & Dunner · 1300 I Street, NW, Suite 700 · Washington, DC 20001 · 202-408-4000

Jorge A. Goldstein · (Bio-Technology) · Sterne, Kessler, Goldstein & Fox · 1225 Connecticut Avenue, NW, Suite 300 · Washington, DC 20036 · 202-833-7533

Laurence R. Hefter · Finnegan, Henderson, Farabow, Garrett & Dunner · 1300 I Street, NW, Suite 700 · Washington, DC 20001 · 202-408-4000

Arthur J. Levine · (Computer) · Finnegan, Henderson, Farabow, Garrett & Dunner · 1300 I Street, NW, Suite 700 · Washington, DC 20001 · 202-408-4000

Charles E. Lipsey · Finnegan, Henderson, Farabow, Garrett & Dunner · 1300 I Street, NW, Suite 700 · Washington, DC 20001 · 202-408-4000

Edward F. McKie, Jr. · Banner, Birch, McKie & Beckett · One Thomas Circle, NW · Washington, DC 20005 · 202-296-5500

George M. Sirilla · Cushman, Darby & Cushman · 1615 L Street, NW, 11th Floor Washington, DC 20036-5601 · 202-861-3000

William K. West · Cushman, Darby & Cushman · 1615 L Street, NW, 11th Floor Washington, DC 20036-5601 · 202-861-3000

LABOR AND EMPLOYMENT LAW

Robert M. Baptiste · (Labor) · Baptiste & Wilder · 1919 Pennsylvania Avenue, NW, Suite 505 · Washington, DC 20006 · 202-223-0723

Edith Barnett · (Individuals) · Barnett & Weiss · 1300 Nineteenth Street, NW, Suite 240 · Washington, DC 20036 · 202-828-1738

David S. Barr · (Labor) · Barr, Peer & Cohen · 1620 I Street, NW, Suite 603 · Washington, DC 20006 · 202-223-1900

Hugh J. Beins · (Labor) · Beins, Axelrod, Osborne & Mooney · 2033 K Street, NW, Suite 300 · Washington, DC 20006 · 202-429-1900

Elliot Bredhoff · (Labor) · Bredhoff & Kaiser · 1000 Connecticut Avenue, NW, Suite 1300 · Washington, DC 20036 · 202-833-9340

Charles I. Cohen · (Management) · Ogletree, Deakins, Nash, Smoak & Stewart 2400 N Street, Fifth Floor · Washington, DC 20037 · 202-887-0855

George H. Cohen · (Labor) · Bredhoff & Kaiser · 1000 Connecticut Avenue, NW, Suite 1300 · Washington, DC 20036 · 202-833-9340

Laurence J. Cohen · (Labor) · Sherman, Dunn, Cohen, Leifer & Yellig · 1125 Fifteenth Street, NW, Suite 801 · Washington, DC 20005 · 202-785-9300

Robert J. Connerton · (Labor) · Connerton, Ray & Simon · 1920 L Street, NW, Fourth Floor · Washington, DC 20036 · 202-466-6790

William J. Curtin · (Management) · Morgan, Lewis & Bockius · 1800 M Street, NW, Suite 800N · Washington, DC 20036 · 202-467-7000

Zachary D. Fasman · (Management) · Paul, Hastings, Janofsky & Walker · 1050 Connecticut Avenue, NW, 12th Floor · Washington, DC 20036-5331 · 202-223-9000

Robert B. Fitzpatrick · (Individuals) · Fitzpatrick & Verstegen · Spring Valley Center, Suite 400 · 4801 Massachusetts Avenue, NW · Washington, DC 20016-2087 · 202-364-8710

Laurence E. Gold · (Labor) · Connerton, Ray & Simon · 1920 L Street, NW, Fourth Floor · Washington, DC 20036 · 202-466-6790

Robert C. Gombar · (Management) · Jones, Day, Reavis & Pogue · Metropolitan Square, Suite 600 · 1450 G Street, NW · Washington, DC 20005-2088 · 202-879-3939

Michael H. Gottesman · (Labor) · Bredhoff & Kaiser · 1000 Connecticut Avenue, NW, Suite 1300 · Washington, DC 20036 · 202-833-9340

Isaac N. Groner · (Labor) · 1050 Connecticut Avenue, NW, Suite 1230 · Washington, DC 20036-5310 · 202-331-8888

Richard C. Hotvedt · (Management) · Morgan, Lewis & Bockius · 1800 M Street, NW, Suite 800N · Washington, DC 20036 · 202-467-7000

Harry Huge · (Individuals) · Donovan Leisure · 1250 Twenty-Fourth Street, NW, Suite 700 · Washington, DC 20037-1124 · 202-467-8300

John S. Irving, Jr. · (Management) · Kirkland & Ellis · 655 Fifteenth Street, NW, Suite 1200 · Washington, DC 20005 · 202-879-5000

George W. Johnston · (Management) · Venable, Baetjer, Howard & Civiletti · 1301 New York Avenue, NW, Suite 1000 · Washington, DC 20005 · 202-962-4800

William J. Kilberg* · (Management, EEO, OSHA) · Gibson, Dunn & Crutcher 1050 Connecticut Avenue, NW, Suite 900 · Washington, DC 20036 · 202-955-8500

Richard Kirschner · (Labor) · Kirschner, Weinberg & Dempsey · 1615 L Street, NW, Suite 1360 · Washington, DC 20036 · 202-775-5900

Andrew M. Kramer · (Management) · Jones, Day, Reavis & Pogue · Metropolitan Square · 1450 G Street, NW · Washington, DC 20005-2088 · 202-879-3939

Ian D. Lanoff · Bredhoff & Kaiser · 1000 Connecticut Avenue, NW, Suite 1300 Washington, DC 20036 · 202-833-9340

John A. McGuinn · (Management) · Porter, Wright, Duff & Hasley · International Square · 1825 I Street, NW, Suite 300 · Washington, DC 20006-5486 · 202-333-8000

Peter G. Nash · (Management) · Ogletree, Deakins, Nash, Smoak & Stewart · 2400 N Street, NW, Fifth Floor · Washington, DC 20037 · 202-887-0855

Charles P. O'Connor · (Management) · Morgan, Lewis & Bockius · 1800 M Street, NW, Suite 800N · Washington, DC 20036 · 202-467-7000

William W. Osborne, Jr.* · (Labor) · Beins, Axelrod, Osborne & Mooney · 2033 K Street, NW, Suite 300 · Washington, DC 20006 · 202-429-1900

Frank Petramalo, Jr. · (Labor) · Gordon & Barnett · 1133 Twenty-First Street, NW, Suite 450 · Washington, DC 20036 · 202-833-3400

Thomas J. Quigley · (Management) · Squire, Sanders & Dempsey · 1201 Pennsylvania Avenue, NW · P.O. Box 407 · Washington, DC 20004 · 202-626-6600

Harry A. Rissetto · Morgan, Lewis & Bockius · 1800 M Street, NW, Suite 800N Washington, DC 20036 · 202-467-7000

Steven J. Sacher · (Management) · Johnson & Gibbs · 1301 K Street, NW, Suite 800 East · Washington, DC 20005 · 202-682-4505

Arthur M. Schiller* · (Labor, Individuals) · Newman & Newell · 1920 N Street, NW, Suite 430 · Washington, DC 20036 · 202-857-5658

Stanley R. Strauss · (Management) · Ogletree, Deakins, Nash, Smoak & Stewart 2400 N Street, NW, Fifth Floor · Washington, DC 20037 · 202-887-0855

Stephen E. Tallent · (Management) · Gibson, Dunn & Crutcher · 1050 Connecticut Avenue, NW, Suite 900 · Washington, DC 20036 · 202-955-8500

Carl L. Taylor* · (Management) · Johnson & Gibbs · 1301 K Street, NW, Suite 800 East · Washington, DC 20005-3307 · 202-682-4503

Michael A. Taylor · (Management) · Ogletree, Deakins, Nash, Smoak & Stewart 2400 N Street, NW, Fifth Floor · Washington, DC 20037 · 202-887-0855

Robert T. Thompson · (Management) · Thompson, Mann and Hutson · 3000 K Street, NW, Suite 600 · Washington, DC 20007 · 202-783-1900

E. Carl Uehlein , Jr. · Morgan, Lewis & Bockius · 1800 M Street, NW, Suite 800N · Washington, DC 20036 · 202-467-7000

Dennis H. Vaughn · (Management) · Paul, Hastings, Janofsky & Walker · 1050 Connecticut Avenue, NW, 12th Floor · Washington, DC 20036-5331 · 202-223-9000

Carl W. Vogt · (Management) · Fulbright & Jaworski · 801 Pennsylvania Avenue, NW · Washington, DC 20004-2604 · 202-662-4600

Lawrence T. Zimmerman · (Management) · Law Offices of Lawrence T. Zimmerman · 2300 N Street, NW, Suite 600 · Washington, DC 20037 · 202-663-9013

NATURAL RESOURCES AND ENVIRONMENTAL LAW

James R. Bieke, Jr. · Shea & Gardner · 1800 Massachusetts Avenue, NW, Suite 800 · Washington, DC 20036 · 202-828-2000

Lynn R. Coleman · Skadden, Arps, Slate, Meagher & Flom · 1440 New York Avenue, NW · Washington, DC 20005-2107 · 202-371-7000

Andrea Bear Field · Hunton & Williams · 2000 Pennsylvania Avenue, NW, Suite 9000 · P.O. Box 19230 · Washington, DC 20036 · 202-955-1500

Theodore L. Garrett* · (Water, Air, Hazardous Waste) · Covington & Burling · 1201 Pennsylvania Avenue, NW · P.O. Box 7566 · Washington, DC 20044 · 202-662-6000

Carroll L. Gilliam · (Natural Gas) · Katten Muchin & Zavis · 1025 Thomas Jefferson, NW, East Lobby, Suite 700 · Washington, DC 20007 · 202-625-3500

J. Hovey Kemp · (Oil & Gas) · Davis, Graham & Stubbs · 1200 Nineteenth Street, NW, Suite 500 · Washington, DC 20036-2402 · 202-822-8660

Angus Macbeth · Sidley & Austin · 1722 I Street, NW, Fifth Floor · Washington, DC 20006 · 202-429-4000

Hugh M. McIntosh · (Oil & Gas) · Vinson & Elkins · Willard Office Building, Suite 800 · 1455 Pennsylvania Avenue · Washington, DC 20004-1007 · 202-639-6730

David E. Menotti · Perkins Coie · 1110 Vermont Avenue, NW, Suite 1200 · Washington, DC 20005 · 202-887-9030

Rush Moody, Jr. · (Gas Pipelines) · Andrews & Kurth · 1701 Pennsylvania Avenue, NW, Suite 200 · Washington, DC 20006 · 202-662-2700

James W. Moorman · Cadwalader, Wickersham & Taft · 1333 New Hampshire Avenue, NW, Suite 700 · Washington, DC 20036 · 202-862-2200

Frederick Moring · (Natural Gas) · Crowell & Moring · 1001 Pennsylvania Avenue, NW · Washington, DC 20004-2505 · 202-624-2500

Jerome C. Muys · (Public Lands, Water) · Will & Muys · 1015 Eighteenth Street, NW, Suite 600 · Washington, DC 20036 · 202-429-4344

William F. Pedersen, Jr. · Perkins Coie · 1110 Vermont Avenue, NW, Suite 1200 Washington, DC 20005 · 202-887-9030

John R. Quarles, Jr. · Morgan, Lewis & Bockius · 1800 M Street, NW, Suite 800N · Washington, DC 20036 · 202-467-7000

James A. Rogers · Skadden, Arps, Slate, Meagher & Flom · 1440 New York Avenue, NW · Washington, DC 20005-2107 · 202-371-7000

Steven Schatzow · Morgan, Lewis & Bockius · 1800 M Street, NW, Suite 800N Washington, DC 20036 · 202-467-7000

Jay T. Smith II · Covington & Burling · 201 Pennsylvania Avenue, NW · P.O. Box 7566 · Washington, DC 20044 · 202-662-6000

Richard G. Stoll, Jr. · Freedman, Levy, Kroll & Simonds · 1050 Connecticut Avenue, NW, Suite 825 · Washington, DC 20036-5366 · 202-457-5100

Steven A. Tasher* · (Water, Solid Waste, Hazardous Waste, Impact of Environmental Law on Real Estate & Business Transactions) · Willkie Farr & Gallagher Three Lafayette Centre · 1155 Twenty-First Street, NW · Washington, DC 20036-3302 · 202-328-8000

Thomas H. Truitt · Piper & Marbury · 1200 Nineteenth Street, NW · Washington, DC 20036 · 202-861-3900

PERSONAL INJURY LITIGATION

Vincent H. Cohen · (Defendants) · Hogan & Hartson · Columbia Square · 555 Thirteenth Street, NW · Washington, DC 20004-1109 · 202-637-5600

Milton Heller* · (Plaintiffs, Medical Malpractice, Products Liability, Automobile Collision) · Solar Building, Suite 300 · 1000 Sixteenth Street, NW · Washington, DC 20036 · 202-737-4300

John F. Mahoney, Jr. · (Defendants) · Mahoney, Hogan, Heffler & Heald · 777 Fourteenth Street, NW, Suite 600 · Washington, DC 20005 · 202-347-6161

Nicholas S. McConnell · (Defendants, Medical Malpractice) · Jackson and Campbell · 1120 Twentieth Street, NW, Suite 300S · Washington, DC 20036 · 202-457-1600

Gerard E. Mitchell* · (Plaintiffs) · Stein, Mitchell & Mezines · 1100 Connecticut Avenue, NW, 11th Floor · Washington, DC 20036 · 202-737-7777

Joseph D. Montedonico* · (Defendants) · Montedonico and Mason · 1605 New Hampshire Avenue, NW · Washington, DC 20009 · 202-797-0700

Robert F. Muse · (Plaintiffs) · Stein, Mitchell & Mezines · 1100 Connecticut Avenue, NW, Suite 1130 · Washington, DC 20036 · 202-737-7777

Jack H. Olender* · (Plaintiffs, Medical Malpractice, Products Liability, Automobile Collision) · Jack H. Olender and Associates · One Farragut Square South, 11th Floor · 1634 I Street, NW · Washington, DC 20006 · 202-879-7777

Jacob A. Stein · (Plaintiffs) · Stein, Mitchell & Mezines · 1100 Connecticut Avenue, NW, Suite 1130 · Washington, DC 20036 · 202-737-7777

David N. Webster* · (Products Liability) · Caplin & Drysdale · One Thomas Circle, NW, Suite 1100 · Washington, DC 20005 · 202-862-8850

PUBLIC UTILITY LAW

George A. Avery · (Natural Gas, Electric) · Cadwalader, Wickersham & Taft · 1333 New Hampshire Avenue, NW, Suite 700 · Washington, DC 20036 · 202-862-2365

J. Alonzo Bauknight · (Electric) · Newman & Holtzinger · 1615 L Street, NW, Suite 1000 · Washington, DC 20036 · 202-955-6600

Clark E. Downs · (Electric) · Jones, Day, Reavis & Pogue · Metropolitan Square 1450 G Street, NW · Washington, DC 20005-2088 · 202-879-3939

Reinier H. J. H. Lock · (Electric Power Regulation, Electric Cogeneration, Independent Power Production) · LeBoeuf, Lamb, Leiby & MacRae · 1333 New Hampshire Avenue, NW, Suite 1100 · Washington, DC 20036 ·

Richard M. Merriman* · (Natural Gas, Electric) · Reid & Priest · 701 Pennsylvania, NW · Washington, DC 20004 · 202-508-4001

Nicholas S. Reynolds · (Nuclear) · Winston & Strawn · 1400 L Street, NW, 12th Floor · Washington, DC 20005 · 202-371-5700

Raymond N. Shibley · (Natural Gas) · LeBoeuf, Lamb, Leiby & MacRae · 1333 New Hampshire Avenue, NW, Suite 1100 · Washington, DC 20036 · 202-457-7500

REAL ESTATE LAW

Sanford K. Ain · Sherman, Meehan & Curtin · 1900 M Street, NW, Suite 601 · Washington, DC 20036 · 202-331-7120

George H. Beuchert, Jr. · Stohlman, Beuchert, Egan & Smith · 1775 Pennsylvania Avenue, NW, Suite 400 · Washington, DC 20006 · 202-452-1775

C. Richard Beyda · Grossberg, Yochelson, Fox & Beyda · 2100 Pennsylvania Avenue, NW, Suite 770 · Washington, DC 20037 · 202-296-9696

Earl M. Colson · (Commercial Transactions) · Arent, Fox, Kintner, Plotkin & Kahn · Washington Square · 1050 Connecticut Avenue, NW · Washington, DC 20036-5339 · 202-857-6000

Myron P. Curzan · Arnold & Porter · Thurman Arnold Building · 1200 New Hampshire Avenue, NW · Washington, DC 20036 · 202-872-6700

Jeffry R. Dwyer · Morrison & Foerster · 2000 Pennsylvania Avenue, NW, Suite 5500 · Washington, DC 20006 · 202-887-1500

Stanley J. Fineman · Wilkes, Artis, Hedrick & Lane · 1666 K Street, NW, Suite 1100 · Washington, DC 20006-2359 · 202-457-7800

Joseph M. Fries · Arent, Fox, Kintner, Plotkin & Kahn · Washington Square · 1050 Connecticut Avenue, NW · Washington, DC 20036-5339 · 202-857-6000

Norman M. Glasgow, Sr. · Wilkes, Artis, Hedrick & Lane · 1666 K Street, NW, Suite 1100 · Washington, DC 20006-2359 · 202-457-7800

Solomon Grossberg · Grossberg, Yochelson, Fox & Beyda · 2100 Pennsylvania Avenue, NW, Suite 770 · Washington, DC 20037 · 202-296-9696

Albert L. Ledgard, Jr. · Wilkes, Artis, Hedrick & Lane · 1666 K Street, NW, Suite 1100 · Washington, DC 20006-2359 · 202-457-7800

R. Robert Linowes · Linowes & Blocher · 800 K Street, NW, Suite 840 · Washington, DC 20001 · 202-408-3220

Leonard S. Melrod · Melrod, Redman & Gartlan · 1801 K Street, NW, Suite 1100 Washington, DC 20006 · 202-822-5300

David M. Osnos · Arent, Fox, Kintner, Plotkin & Kahn · Washington Square · 1050 Connecticut Avenue, NW · Washington, DC 20036-5339 · 202-857-6000

Stephen W. Porter · Dunnells, Duvall & Porter · 2100 Pennsylvania Avenue, NW, Fourth Floor · Washington, DC 20037 · 202-861-1400

Whayne S. Quin · Wilkes, Artis, Hedrick & Lane · 1666 K Street, NW, Suite 1100 · Washington, DC 20006-2359 · 202-457-7800

Stefan F. Tucker · Tucker, Flyer, Sanger & Lewis · 1615 L Street, NW, Suite 400 Washington, DC 20036 · 202-452-8600

TAX AND EMPLOYEE BENEFITS LAW

Donald C. Alexander* · Cadwalader, Wickersham & Taft · 1333 New Hampshire Avenue, NW, Suite 700 · Washington, DC 20036 · 202-862-2200

Mac Asbill, Jr.* · (Employee Benefits, Tax Disputes) · Sutherland, Asbill & Brennan · 1275 Pennsylvania Avenue, Suite 800 · Washington, DC 20004-2404 · 202-383-0100

Dennis P. Bedell · Miller & Chevalier · Metropolitan Square, Suite 900 · 655 Fifteenth Street, NW · Washington, DC 20005 · 202-626-5800

Herbert N. Beller · Bryan, Cave, McPheeters & McRoberts · 700 Thirteenth Street, NW, Suite 700 · Washington, DC 20005-3960 · 202-508-6000

Mortimer M. Caplin · (Tax Disputes) · Caplin & Drysdale · One Thomas Circle, NW, Suite 1100 · Washington, DC 20005 · 202-862-5000

John E. Chapoton · Vinson & Elkins · Willard Office Building, Suite 800 · 1455 Pennsylvania Avenue · Washington, DC 20004-1007 · 202-639-6500

Sheldon S. Cohen · Morgan, Lewis & Bockius · 1800 M Street, NW, Suite 800N Washington, DC 20036 · 202-467-7000

D. Kevin Dolan · Weil, Gotshal & Manges · 1615 L Street, NW, Suite 700 · Washington, DC 20036 · 202-682-7000

H. Stewart Dunn, Jr. · Ivins, Phillips & Barker · 1700 Pennsylvania Avenue, NW, Suite 600 · Washington, DC 20006 · 202-393-7600

Gerald A. Feffer* · (Tax Disputes) · Williams & Connolly · Hill Building · 839 Seventeenth Street, NW · Washington, DC 20006 · 202-331-5007

Lawrence B. Gibbs · Johnson & Gibbs · 1301 K Street, NW, Suite 800 East · Washington, DC 20005 · 202-682-4501

Martin D. Ginsburg* · (Corporate & Partnership Transactions, Tax Disputes) · Fried, Frank, Harris, Shriver & Jacobson · 1001 Pennsylvania Avenue, NW, Suite 800 · Washington, DC 20004-2505 · 202-639-7000

Jay W. Glasmann · Ivins, Phillips & Barker · 1700 Pennsylvania Avenue, NW, Suite 600 · Washington, DC 20006 · 202-393-7600

Michael S. Gordon · (Employee Benefits) · Law Offices of Michael S. Gordon · 747 Pennsylvania Avenue, NW · Washington, DC 20006 · 202-223-8576

Erwin N. Griswold · Jones, Day, Reavis & Pogue · Metropolitan Square · 1450 G Street, NW · Washington, DC 20005-2088 · 202-879-3939

Theodore R. Groom · Groom and Nordberg · 1701 Pennsylvania Avenue, NW · Washington, DC 20006 · 202-857-0620

Don V. Harris, Jr. · Covington & Burling · 1201 Pennsylvania Avenue, NW · P.O. Box 7566 · Washington, DC 20044 · 202-662-6000

Lawrence J. Hass · (Employee Benefits) · Akin, Gump, Strauss, Hauer & Feld 1333 New Hampshire Avenue, NW, Suite 400 · Washington, DC 20036 · 202-887-4000

Edward J. Hawkins · Squire, Sanders & Dempsey · 1201 Pennsylvania Avenue, NW · P.O. Box 407 · Washington, DC 20044 · 202-626-6830

James P. Holden · Steptoe & Johnson · 1330 Connecticut Avenue, NW · Washington, DC 20036-1795 · 202-429-3000

John B. Jones, Jr. · Covington & Burling · 1201 Pennsylvania Avenue, NW · P.O. Box 7566 · Washington, DC 20044 · 202-662-6000

A. Carl Kaseman III · Piper & Marbury · 1200 Nineteenth Street, NW · Washington, DC 20036 · 202-861-3900

William J. Kilberg · (Employee Benefits) · Gibson, Dunn & Crutcher · 1050 Connecticut Avenue, NW, Suite 900 · Washington, DC 20036 · 202-955-8500

Jerome Kurtz · Paul Weiss Rifkind Wharton & Garrison · 1615 L Street, NW, Suite 1300 · Washington, DC 20036 · 202-223-7300

F. David Lake, Jr. · Wilmer, Cutler & Pickering · 2445 M Street, NW · Washington, DC 20037-1420 · 202-663-6000

Stuart M. Lewis · (Employee Benefits) · Silverstein and Mullens · 1776 K Street, NW · Washington, DC 20006 · 202-452-7900

Jerome B. Libin · Sutherland, Asbill & Brennan · 1275 Pennsylvania Avenue, NW, Suite 800 · Washington, DC 20004-2404 · 202-383-0100

Jerome B. Libin · Sutherland, Asbill & Brennan · 1275 Pennsylvania Avenue, NW, Suite 800 · Washington, DC 20004-2404 · 202-383-0100

Phillip L. Mann · Miller & Chevalier · Metropolitan Square, Suite 900 · 655 Fifteenth Street · Washington, DC 20005 · 202-626-5800

Richard E. May · Hunton & Williams · 2000 Pennsylvania Avenue, NW · P.O. Box 19230 · Washington, DC 20036 · 202-955-1578

Louis T. Mazawey · (Employee Benefits) · Groom and Nordberg · 1701 Pennsylvania Avenue, NW · Washington, DC 20006 · 202-857-0620

William S. McKee · King & Spalding · 1730 Pennsylvania Avenue, NW, Suite 1200 · Washington, DC 20006 · 202-737-0500

Ralph J. Moore, Jr. · Shea & Gardner · 1800 Massachusetts Avenue, NW · Washington, DC 20036 · 202-828-2000

Cono R. Namorato · Caplin & Drysdale · One Thomas Circle, NW, Suite 1100 · Washington, DC 20005 · 202-862-5000

John S. Nolan · Miller & Chevalier · Metropolitan Square, Suite 900 · 655 Fifteenth Street, NW · Washington, DC 20005-5701 · 202-626-5800

Carl A. Nordberg · Groom and Nordberg · 1701 Pennsylvania Avenue, NW · Washington, DC 20006 · 202-857-0620

James T. O'Hara · Jones, Day, Reavis & Pogue · Metropolitan Square · 1450 G Street, NW · Washington, DC 20005-2088 · 202-879-3939

C. Frederick Oliphant III · (Employee Benefits) · Miller & Chevalier · Metropolitan Square, Suite 900 · 655 Fifteenth Street, NW · Washington, DC 20005 · 202-626-5800

Jerry L. Oppenheimer · Mayer, Brown & Platt · 2000 Pennsylvania Avenue, NW, Suite 6500 · Washington, DC 20006 · 202-463-2000

Gary G. Quintiere · (Employee Benefits) · Morgan, Lewis & Bockius · 1800 M Street, NW, Suite 800N · Washington, DC 20036 · 202-467-7290

Lipman Redman · Melrod, Redman & Gartlan · 1801 K Street, NW, Suite 1100 Washington, DC 20006 · 202-822-5300

Theodore E. Rhodes · (Employee Benefits) · Steptoe & Johnson · 1330 Connecticut Avenue, NW · Washington, DC 20036-1795 · 202-429-3000

Mikel M. Rollyson · Davis Polk & Wardwell · 1575 I Street, NW, Suite 400 · Washington, DC 20005 · 202-789-7100

H. David Rosenbloom · Caplin & Drysdale · One Thomas Circle, NW, Suite 1100 · Washington, DC 20005 · 202-862-5000

Stanford G. Ross · Arnold & Porter · Thurman Arnold Building · 1200 New Hampshire Avenue, NW · Washington, DC 20036 · 202-872-6700

Steven J. Sacher · (Employee Benefits) · Johnson & Gibbs · 1301 K Street, NW, Suite 800 East · Washington, DC 20005-3307 · 202-383-8760

K. Peter Schmidt · (Employee Benefits) · Arnold & Porter · Thurman Arnold Building · 1200 New Hampshire Avenue, NW · Washington, DC 20036 · 202-872-6700

Larry E. Shapiro · (Employee Benefits) · Lee, Toomey & Kent · 1200 Eighteenth Street, NW, Eighth Floor · Washington, DC 20036 · 202-457-8500

Leonard L. Silverstein · Silverstein and Mullens · 1776 K Street, NW, Suite 800 Washington, DC 20006 · 202-452-7920

Richard W. Skillman · (Employee Benefits) · Caplin & Drysdale · One Thomas Circle, NW, Suite 1100 · Washington, DC 20005 · 202-862-5000

William L. Sollee · (Employee Benefits) · Ivins, Phillips & Barker · 1700 Pennsylvania Avenue, NW, Suite 600 · Washington, DC 20006 · 202-393-7600

Thomas A. Troyer · Caplin & Drysdale · One Thomas Circle, NW, Suite 1100 · Washington, DC 20005 · 202-862-5000

Stefan F. Tucker · Tucker, Flyer, Sanger & Lewis · 1615 L Street, NW, Suite 400 Washington, DC 20036 · 202-452-8600

John M. Vine · (Employee Benefits) · Covington & Burling · 1201 Pennsylvania Avenue, NW · P.O. Box 7566 · Washington, DC 20044 · 202-662-6000

B. John Williams, Jr. · Morgan, Lewis & Bockius · 1800 M Street, NW, Suite 700N · Washington, DC 20036 · 202-467-7184

TRUSTS AND ESTATES

Doris D. Blazek · Covington & Burling · 1201 Pennsylvania Avenue, NW · P.O. Box 7566 · Washington, DC 20044 · 202-662-6000

Earl M. Colson · (Estate Planning) · Arent, Fox, Kintner, Plotkin & Kahn · Washington Square · 1050 Connecticut Avenue, NW · Washington, DC 20036-5339 · 202-857-6000

Michael F. Curtin · Sherman, Meehan & Curtin · 1900 M Street, NW, Suite 601 Washington, DC 20036 · 202-331-7120

Sara-Ann Determan · Hogan & Hartson · Columbia Square · 555 Thirteenth Street, NW · Washington, DC 20004-1109 · 202-637-5600

Richard H. Mayfield · Craighill, Mayfield & McCally · 4910 Massachusetts Avenue, NW, Suite 215 · Washington, DC 20016 · 202-364-4242

Jerry J. McCoy · Silverstein and Mullens · 1776 K Street, NW · Washington, DC 20006 · 202-452-7989

Nancy K. Mintz · Arnold & Porter · Thurman Arnold Building · 1200 New Hampshire Avenue, NW · Washington, DC 20036 · 202-872-6700

Ralph J. Moore, Jr. · Shea and Gardner · 1800 Massachusetts Avenue, NW · Washington, DC 20036 · 202-828-2000

FLORIDA

BANKRUPTCY LAW

Patrick A. Barry · Dykema Gossett · 200 East Las Olas Boulevard, 19th Floor · P.O. Box 1629 · Fort Lauderdale, FL 33302 · 305-728-3400

Chad P. Pugatch · Law Office of Chad P. Pugatch · 6700 North Andrews Avenue, Suite 407 · Fort Lauderdale, FL 33309 · 305-776-2055

Raymond B. Ray · Law Office of Raymond B. Ray · One Financial Plaza, Suite 2602 · Fort Lauderdale, FL 33394 · 305-763-6006

Reggie David Sanger · (Business Reorganization, Creditors' Rights, Debtors' Rights, Bankruptcy Litigation) · 208 Southeast Ninth Street · Fort Lauderdale, FL 33316 · 305-463-8547

Stephen D. Busey* · Smith & Hulsey · 1800 First Union National Bank Tower · 225 Water Street · P.O. Box 53315 · Jacksonville, FL 32201-3315 · 904-359-7700

Scott L. Baena · Stroock & Stroock & Lavan · Southeast Financial Center, Suite 3300 · 200 South Biscayne Boulevard · Miami, FL 33131-2385 · 305-358-9900

Francis L. Carter · Coll Davidson Carter Smith Salter & Barkett · 3200 Miami Center · 201 South Biscayne Boulevard · Miami, FL 33131 · 305-373-5200

John H. Genovese · Holland & Knight · 1200 Brickell Avenue, 14th Floor · Miami, FL 33109 · 305-374-8500

John W. Kozyak · Kozyak Tropin Throckmorton & Humphreys · Southeast Financial Center, Suite 2850 · 200 South Biscayne Boulevard · Miami, FL 33131-2335 · 305-372-1800

Timothy J. Norris* · (Business Reorganization, Creditors' Rights, Debtors' Rights, Bankruptcy Litigation) · Mershon, Sawyer, Johnston, Dunwody & Cole · Southeast Financial Center, Suite 4500 · 200 South Biscayne Boulevard · Miami, FL 33131-2387 · 305-358-5100

Lawrence M. Schantz · (Business Reorganization, Creditors' Rights, Debtors' Rights, Bankruptcy Litigation) · Schantz, Schatzman & Aaronson · Southeast Financial Center, Suite 3650 · 200 South Biscayne Boulevard · Miami, FL 33131-2394 · 305-371-3100

Robert A. Schatzman · Schantz, Schatzman & Aaronson · Southeast Financial Center, Suite 3650 · 200 South Biscayne Boulevard · Miami, FL 33131-2394 · 305-371-3100

Jules S. Cohen · (Business Reorganization, Creditors' Rights, Bankruptcy Litigation) · 808 North Mills Avenue · Orlando, FL 32803 · 407-896-4493

Michael G. Williamson · (Business Reorganization, Creditors' Rights) · Maguire, Voorhis & Wells · Two South Orange Plaza · P.O. Box 633 · Orlando, FL 32802 407-843-4421

Samuel J. Zusmann, Jr.* · (Business Reorganization, Creditors' Rights, Debtors' Rights, Bankruptcy Litigation) · Maguire, Voorhis & Wells · Two South Orange Avenue, Suite 3000 · P.O. Box 633 · Orlando, FL 32802 · 407-423-4421

Leonard H. Gilbert* · (Business Reorganization, Creditors' Rights) · Carlton, Fields, Ward, Emmanuel, Smith & Cutler · One Harbor Place · 777 South Harbour Island Drive · P.O. Box 3239 · Tampa, FL 33601 · 813-223-7000

Robert B. Glenn, Jr. · Glenn, Rasmussen, Fogarty, Merryday & Russo · Ashley Tower, Suite 1300 · 100 South Ashley Drive · P.O. Box 3333 · Tampa, FL 33601-3333 · 813-229-3333

Douglas P. McClurg* · Holland & Knight · 400 North Ashley Drive, Suite 2300 P.O. Box 1288 · Tampa, FL 33601-1288 · 813-227-8500

Harley E. Riedel II · Stichter, Riedel, Blain & Prosser · 100 Madison Street, Suite 300 · P.O. Drawer 2802 · Tampa, FL 33601 · 813-229-0144

Don M. Stichter · Stichter, Riedel, Blain & Prosser · 100 East Madison Street, Suite 300 · P.O. Drawer 2802 · Tampa, FL 33601 · 813-229-0144

Charles M. Tatelbaum* · (Business Reorganization, Creditors' Rights, Debtors' Rights, Bankruptcy Litigation) · Johnson, Blakely, Pope, Bokor, Ruppel & Burns 201 East Kennedy Boulevard, Suite 1700 · P.O. Box 1100 · Tampa, FL 33601 · 813-225-2500

William Knight Zewadski · (Business Reorganization, Creditors' Rights, Bankruptcy Litigation) · Trenam, Simmons, Kemker, Scharf, Barkin, Frye & O'Neill Barnett Plaza, Suite 2700 · 101 East Kennedy Boulevard · P.O. Box 1102 · Tampa, FL 33601-1102 · 813-223-7474

Daniel L. Bakst* · (Business Reorganization, Creditors' Rights, Debtors' Rights, Bankruptcy Litigation) · Ackerman, Bakst, Lauer and Scherer · Northbridge Centre, 15th Floor · 515 North Flagler Drive · P.O. Drawer 3948 · West Palm Beach, FL 33402-3948 · 407-655-4500

BUSINESS LITIGATION

F. Wallace Pope, Jr. · Johnson, Blakely, Pope, Bokor, Ruppel & Burns · 911 Chestnut Street · P.O. Box 1368 · Clearwater, FL 34617 · 813-461-1818

Ruben M. Garcia · 110 Southeast Sixth Street, Suite 1220 · Fort Lauderdale, FL 33301 · 305-462-4600

John F. Corrigan* · (Commercial) · 500 North Ocean Street · Jacksonville, FL 32202 · 904-353-8295

John A. De Vault III* · Bedell, Dittmar, De Vault & Pillans · The Bedell Building · 101 East Adams Street · Jacksonville, FL 32202 · 904-353-0211

C. Harris Dittmar · Bedell, Dittmar, De Vault & Pillans · The Bedell Building · 101 East Adams Street · Jacksonville, FL 32202 · 904-353-0211

James C. Rinaman, Jr.* · (Appellate, Banking, Commercial, RICO) · Marks, Gray, Conroy & Gibbs · 800 Southeast Bank Building · 1200 Gulf Life Drive · P.O. Box 447 · Jacksonville, FL 32201 · 904-398-0900

Steven A. Werber · Foley & Lardner, Legler & Commander · The Greenleaf Building · 200 Laura Street · P.O. Box 240 · Jacksonville, FL 32202-0240 · 904-359-2000

James L. Armstrong III* · Kelley, Drye & Warren · 2400 Miami Center · 201 South Biscayne Boulevard · Miami, FL 33131-2399 · 305-372-2400

Richard Alan Arnold · Kenny Nachwalter, Seymour & Arnold · 400 Miami Center · 201 South Biscayne Boulevard · Miami, FL 33131-2305 · 305-358-8151

Hugo L. Black, Jr. · Kelly, Black, Black, Byrne, Beasley & Bales · 1400 Alfred I. du Pont Building · 169 East Flagler Street · Miami, FL 33131 · 305-358-5700

Sam Daniels · (Appellate) · Daniels and Talisman · 100 North Biscayne Boulevard, 24th Floor · Miami, FL 33132 · 305-381-7720

Barry R. Davidson* · (Antitrust, Commercial, Securities, Transportation) · Coll Davidson Carter Smith Salter & Barkett · 3200 Miami Center · 201 South Biscayne Boulevard · Miami, FL 33131 · 305-373-5200

Alvin B. Davis · Steel Hector & Davis · 4000 Southeast Financial Center · 200 South Biscayne Boulevard · Miami, FL 33131-2398 · 305-577-2800

Joel D. Eaton* · (Appellate) · Podhurst Orseck Parks Josefsberg Eaton Meadow Olin & Perwin · City National Bank Building, Suite 800 · 25 West Flagler Street · Miami, FL 33130 · 305-358-2800

Arthur J. England, Jr. · Fine Jacobson Schwartz Nash Block & England · 100 Southeast Second Street · Miami, FL 33131-2112 · 305-577-4075

Bruce W. Greer · Greer, Homer & Bonner · 100 Southeast Second Street, Suite 3400 · Miami, FL 33131 · 305-350-5100

Mark Hicks · (Appellate) · Hicks, Anderson & Blum · 100 North Biscayne Boulevard, 24th Floor · Miami, FL 33132 · 305-374-8171

Robert C. Josefsberg* · Podhurst Orseck Josefsberg Eaton Meadow Olin & Perwin · City National Bank Building, Suite 800 · 25 West Flagler Street · Miami, FL 33130-1780 · 305-358-2800

James J. Kenny* · (Antitrust) · Kenny Nachwalter Seymour & Arnold · 400 Miami Center · 201 South Biscayne Boulevard · Miami, FL 33131-2305 · 305-358-8151

Michael Nachwalter* · (Antitrust, Banking, Commercial, Securities) · Kenny Nachwalter, Seymour & Arnold · 400 Miami Center · 201 South Biscayne Boulevard · Miami, FL 33131-2305 · 305-358-8151

Aaron Podhurst · Podhurst Orseck Josefsberg Eaton Meadow Olin & Perwin · City National Bank Building, Suite 800 · 25 West Flagler Street · Miami, FL 33130 · 305-358-2800

Daniel S. Pearson · Holland & Knight · 1200 Brickell Avenue, 14th Floor · Miami, FL 33109 · 305-374-8500

Gerald F. Richman* · (Antitrust, Commercial, RICO, Securities) · Floyd Pearson Richman Greer Weil Zack & Brumbaugh · 175 Northwest First Avenue, 26th Floor · Miami, FL 33128 · 305-373-4000

David L. Ross · Greenberg, Traurig, Hoffman, Lipoff, Rosen & Quentel · 1221 Brickell Avenue · Miami, FL 33131 · 305-579-0500

Richard Caldwell Smith* · Coll Davidson Carter Smith Salter & Barkett · 3200 Miami Center · 201 South Biscayne Boulevard · Miami, FL 33131-2312 · 305-373-5200

Herbert Stettin · AmeriFirst Building, Suite 2215 · One Southeast Third Avenue Miami, FL 33131 · 305-373-3353

Parker Davidson Thomson · (Appellate) · Thomson Bohrer Werth & Razook · 1700 Amerifirst Building · One East Third Avenue · Miami, FL 33131-2363 · 305-350-7200

Michael J. Burman · Slawson, Burman & Critton · 712 U.S. Highway One, Suite 300 · North Palm Beach, FL 33408 · 407-842-2820

Darryl M. Bloodworth* · Dean, Mead, Egerton, Bloodworth, Capouano & Bozarth · 800 North Magnolia Avenue, Suite 1500 · P.O. Box 2346 · Orlando, FL 32802-2346 · 407-841-1200

David B. King · King & Blackwell · P.O. Box 1631 · Orlando, FL 32802-1631 · 407-422-2472

Gregory A. Presnell* · Akerman, Senterfitt & Eidson · CNA Tower, 17th Floor 255 South Orange Avenue · P.O. Box 231 · Orlando, FL 32802 · 407-843-7860

H. Edward Moore, Jr. · Moore, Hill & Westmoreland · Sun Bank Tower, Ninth Floor · 220 West Garden Street · P.O. Box 1792 · Pensacola, FL 32598-1792 · 904-434-3541

Anthony S. Battaglia* · Battaglia, Ross, Hastings and Dicus · 980 Tyrone Boulevard · P.O. Box 41100 · Saint Petersburg, FL 33743 · 813-381-2300

Julian D. Clarkson · (Appellate) · Holland & Knight · Barnett Bank Building, Suite 600 · P.O. Drawer 810 · Tallahassee, FL 32302 · 904-224-7000

W. Dexter Douglass · Douglass, Cooper, Coppins & Powell · 211 East Call Street P.O. Box 1674 · Tallahassee, FL 32302 · 904-224-6191

Robert R. Feagin · (Antitrust) · Holland & Knight · Barnett Bank Building, Suite 600 · P.O. Drawer 810 · Tallahassee, FL 32302 · 904-224-7000

Carl Pennington · Pennington, Wilkinson, Dunlap, Bateman & Camp · 3375A Capital Circle, NE · P.O. Box 13527 · Tallahassee, FL 32317-3527 · 904-385-1103

Marvin E. Barkin* · (Banking, Securities, Corporate/Derivative) · Trenam, Simmons, Kemker, Scharf, Barkin, Frye & O'Neill · Barnett Plaza, Suite 2700 · 101 East Kennedy Boulevard · P.O. Box 1102 · Tampa, FL 33601-1102 · 813-223-7474

Michael A. Fogarty · Glenn, Rasmussen, Fogarty, Merryday & Russo · First Union Center, Suite 1300 · 100 South Ashley Drive · P.O. Box 3333 · Tampa, FL 33601-3333 · 813-229-3333

William C. Frye · Trenam, Simmons, Kemker, Scharf, Barkin, Frye & O'Neill · Barnett Plaza, Suite 2700 · 101 East Kennedy Boulevard · P.O. Box 1102 · Tampa, FL 33601-1102 · 813-223-7474

Thomas C. MacDonald, Jr.* · (Administrative, Appellate, Commercial, RICO) · Shackleford, Farrior, Stallings & Evans · 501 East Kennedy Boulevard, Suite 1400 P.O. Box 3324 · Tampa, FL 33601 · 813-273-5000

Sylvia H. Walbolt · Carlton, Fields, Ward, Emmanuel, Smith & Cutler · One Harbor Place · 777 South Harbour Island Drive · P.O. Box 3239 · Tampa, FL 33601 · 813-223-7000

Leigh E. Dunston · Gunster, Yoakley & Stewart · Phillips Point · 777 South Flagler Drive, Suite 500 · West Palm Beach, FL 33401-6194 · 407-655-1980

Larry A. Klein · (Appellate) · Klein & Walsh · Flagler Center, Suite 503 · 501 South Flagler Drive · West Palm Beach, FL 33401 · 407-659-5455

Robert T. Scott · Gunster, Yoakley & Stewart · Phillips Point · 777 South Flagler Drive, Suite 500 · West Palm Beach, FL 33401-6194 · 407-655-1980

Sidney A. Stubbs, Jr. · Jones, Foster, Johnston & Stubbs · Flagler Center Tower 505 South Flagler Drive · P.O. Drawer E · West Palm Beach, FL 33402-3475 · 407-659-3000

CORPORATE LAW

Kenneth M. Kirschner · Kirschner, Main, Petrie, Graham & Tanner · 10 West Adams Street · Jacksonville, FL 32202 · 904-354-4141

Mitchell W. Legler · Foley & Lardner · The Greenleaf Building · 200 Laura Street · P.O. Box 240 · Jacksonville, FL 32202-0240 · 904-359-2000

Luther F. Sadler, Jr. · Foley & Lardner, Legler & Commander · The Greenleaf Building · 200 Laura Street · P.O. Box 240 · Jacksonville, FL 32202-0240 · 904-359-2000

E. Ellis Zahra, Jr. · LeBoeuf, Lamb, Leiby & MacRae · 200 Laura Street, Suite 1200 · Jacksonville, FL 32202 · 904-354-8000

Cesar L. Alvarez · Greenberg, Traurig, Hoffman, Lipoff, Rosen & Quentel · 1221 Brickell Avenue · Miami, FL 33131 · 305-579-0500

Bowman Brown · (Banking, Financial Institutions, International Banking, Mergers & Acquisitions) · Shutts & Bowen · 1500 Miami Center · 100 Chopin Plaza · Miami, FL 33131 · 305-379-9107

Jerry B. Crockett · Steel Hector & Davis · 4000 Southeast Financial Center · 200 South Biscayne Boulevard · Miami, FL 33131-2398 · 305-577-2800

Larry J. Hoffman · Greenberg, Traurig, Hoffman, Lipoff, Rosen & Quentel · 1221 Brickell Avenue · Miami, FL 33131 · 305-579-0500

Thomas R. McGuigan · Steel Hector & Davis · 4000 Southeast Financial Center · 200 South Biscayne Boulevard · Miami, FL 33131-2398 · 305-577-2800

Noel H. Nation · Baker & McKenzie · Barnett Tower, Suite 1600 · 701 Brickell Avenue · Miami, FL 33131 · 305-789-8900

William O. E. Henry · Holland & Knight · 800 North Magnolia Avenue, Penthouse A · P.O. Box 1526 · Orlando, FL 32802 · 407-425-8500

James W. Beasley, Jr. · Cadwalader, Wickersham & Taft · 440 Royal Palm Way, Suite 200 · Palm Beach, FL 33480 · 407-655-9500

Warren J. Frazier · Shackleford, Farrior, Stallings & Evans · 501 East Kennedy Boulevard, Suite 1400 · P.O. Box 3324 · Tampa, FL 33601 · 813-273-5000

Michael L. Jamieson · (Corporate Finance, International Finance, Mergers & Acquisitions, Securities) · Holland & Knight · 400 North Ashley Drive, Suite 2300 · P.O. Box 1288 · Tampa, FL 33601-1288 · 813-227-8500

Richard M. Leisner · Trenam, Simmons, Kemker, Scharf, Barkin, Frye & O'Neill · Barnett Plaza, Suite 2700 · 101 East Kennedy Boulevard · P.O. Box 1102 Tampa, FL 33601-1102 · 813-223-7474

Robert C. Rasmussen · (Corporate Finance, Mergers & Acquisitions, Securities Regulation) · Glenn, Rasmussen, Fogarty, Merryday & Russo · 100 South Ashley Drive, Suite 1300 · Tampa, FL 33602 · 813-229-3333

John B. McCracken · Jones, Foster, Johnston & Stubbs · Flagler Center Tower 505 South Flagler Drive · P.O. Drawer E · West Palm Beach, FL 33402-3475 · 407-659-3000

Michael V. Mitrione · Gunster, Yoakley & Stewart · Phillips Point · 777 South Flagler Drive, Suite 500 · West Palm Beach, FL 33401-6194 · 407-655-1980

CRIMINAL DEFENSE

Joseph G. Donahey, Jr. · Tanney, Forde, Donahey, Eno & Tanney · 2454 McMullen Booth Road, Suite 501-A · Clearwater, FL 34619 · 813-726-4781

Edward A. Carhart · Bailey Gerstein Carhart Rashkind Dresnick & Rippingille · 40770 Biscayne Boulevard, Suite 950 · Coral Gables, FL 33137 · 305-445-1122

J. David Bogenschutz* · Kay and Bogenschutz · 633 Southeast Third Avenue, Suite 4F · Fort Lauderdale, FL 33301 · 305-764-0033

Bruce M. Lyons · Lyons and Sanders · 600 Northeast Third Avenue · Fort Lauderdale, FL 33304-2689 · 305-467-8700

Bruce S. Rogow · Nova University Law Center · 3100 Southwest Ninth Avenue Fort Lauderdale, FL 33315 · 305-524-2465

Bruce E. Wagner · 1520 Southeast Third Avenue · Fort Lauderdale, FL 33316 · 305-467-2602

Bruce A. Zimet* · One Financial Plaza, Suite 2612 · Fort Lauderdale, FL 33394 305-764-7081

Larry G. Turner* · (Violent Crimes, Non-Violent Crimes, Federal Court, State Court) · Turner, Kurrus & Griscti · 204 West University Avenue, Suite 6 · P.O. Box 508 · Gainesville, FL 32602 · 904-375-4460

Edward M. Booth · Booth and Arnold · 1301 Gulf Life Drive · Jacksonville, FL 32207 · 904-399-5400

Henry M. Coxe III* · (Violent Crimes, Non-Violent Crimes, State Court) · Coxe & Schemer · 424 East Monroe Street · Jacksonville, FL 32202 · 904-356-2389

Albert J. Datz · Datz, Jacobson & Lembcke · Independent Square, Suite 2902 · One Independent Drive · Jacksonville, FL 32202 · 904-355-5467

C. Harris Dittmar · Bedell, Dittmar, De Vault & Pillans · The Bedell Building · 101 East Adams Street · Jacksonville, FL 32202 · 904-353-0211

William J. Sheppard · Sheppard & White · 215 Washington Street · Jacksonville, FL 32202 · 904-356-9661

F. Lee Bailey · Bailey Gerstein Cathcart Rashkind Dresnick & Rippingille · 4770 Biscayne Boulevard, Suite 950 · Miami, FL 33137 · 305-573-4400

Donald I. Bierman · (Non-Violent Crimes, Federal Court, State Court, White-Collar Tax) · Bierman, Shohat & Loewy · Courthouse Center, Suite 1730 · 175 Northwest Avenue · Miami, FL 33128-1817 · 305-358-7000

Roy E. Black · Black & Furci · Miami Center, Suite 1300 · 201 South Biscayne Boulevard · Miami, FL 33131 · 305-371-6421

Irwin J. Block · Fine Jacobson Schwartz Nash Block & England · One CenTrust Financial Center · 100 Southeast Second Street · Miami, FL 33131-2130 · 305-577-4050

Jack M. Denaro* · (Violent Crimes, Non-Violent Crimes, Federal Court, State Court) · Dadeland Square, Suite 504 · 7700 North Kendall Drive · Miami, FL 33156 · 305-274-9550

Richard E. Gerstein* · (Violent Crimes, Federal Court, State Court, Grand Jury Representation) · Bailey Gerstein Cathcart Rashkind Dresnick & Rippingille · 4770 Biscayne Boulevard, Suite 950 · Miami, FL 33137 · 305-573-4400

Joel Hirschhorn · 2766 Douglas Road · Miami, FL 33133 · 305-445-5320

James J. Hogan · (Federal Court, State Court) · Hogan, Greer & Shapiro · 2400 South Dixie Highway, Suite 200 · Miami, FL 33133 · 305-854-8989

Robert C. Josefsberg* · Podhurst Orseck Josefsberg Eaton Meadow Olin & Perwin · City National Bank Building, Suite 800 · 25 West Flagler Street · Miami, FL 33130-1780 · 305-358-2800

Theodore Klein* · Fine Jacobson Schwartz Nash Block & England · One Cen-Trust Financial Center · 100 Southeast Second Street · Miami, FL 33131-2112 · 305-577-4050

Albert J. Krieger · 1899 South Bayshore Drive · Miami, FL 33133 · 305-854-0050

E. David Rosen* · New World Tower, Suite 2910 · 100 North Biscayne Boulevard
Miami, FL 33132-2305 · 305-377-3737

Edward R. Shohat* · Bierman, Shohat & Loewy · Courthouse Center, Suite 1730
175 Northwest Avenue · Miami, FL 33128-1817 · 305-358-7000

Neal R. Sonnett · Sonnett, Sale & Kuehne · Two Southeast Biscayne Boulevard,
Suite 2600 · Miami, FL 33131-1802 · 305-358-2000

James M. Russ* · (Federal Court, State Court, Federal Crimes) · Tinker Building
18 West Pine Street · Orlando, FL 32801-2697 · 407-849-6050

E. C. Deeno Kitchen* · Kitchen & High · 1102 North Gadsden Street · P.O. Box
1854 · Tallahassee, FL 32302 · 904-561-6219

Murray M. Wadsworth* · Wadsworth & Davis · 203 North Gadsden Street, Suite
One · P.O. Box 10529 · Tallahassee, FL 32302-2529 · 904-224-9037

Ronald K. Cacciatore* · (Violent Crimes, Non-Violent Crimes, Federal Court,
State Court) · 600 North Florida Avenue, Suite 1535 · Tampa, FL 33602 · 813-
223-4831

Barry A. Cohen · Law Offices of Barry Cohen · 100 Twiggs Street, Suite 4000 ·
Tampa, FL 33602 · 813-225-1655

Bennie Lazzara, Jr. · Lazzara, Caskey, Polli & Paul · 606 Madison Street, Suite
2001 · Tampa, FL 33602 · 813-229-2224

Gary R. Trombley* · Winkles, Trombley, Kynes & Markman · Tampa Theatre
Building, 10th Floor · 707 North Franklin Street · P.O. Box 3356 · Tampa, FL
33601 · 813-229-7918

D. Frank Winkles, Jr. · Winkles, Trombley & Kynes · 707 North Franklin Street,
10th Floor · P.O. Box 3356 · Tampa, FL 33601 · 813-229-7918

Richard G. Lubin · Lubin and Gano · 1217 South Flagler · West Palm Beach, FL
33401 · 407-655-2040

FAMILY LAW

Alan J. Rubinstein* · (Child Custody, Divorce, Marital Settlement Agreements,
Equitable Division) · Rubinstein & Devine · 2126 First Street · P.O. Box 368 ·
Fort Myers, FL 33902 · 813-332-3400

A. Matthew Miller · Miller, Schwartz & Miller · 4040 Sheridan Street · Hollywood, FL 33021 · 305-962-2000

James Fox Miller · Miller, Schwartz & Miller · 4040 Sheridan Street · P.O. Box 7259 · Hollywood, FL 33081-1259 · 305-962-2000

Edward M. Booth · Booth and Arnold · 1301 Gulf Life Drive, Suite 2440 · Jacksonville, FL 32207 · 904-399-5400

Albert J. Datz · Datz, Jacobson & Lembcke · Independent Square, Suite 2902 · Jacksonville, FL 32202 · 904-355-5467

Elliot Zisser · Zisser, Robison, Spohrer & Wilner · 624 Ocean Street · Jacksonville, FL 32202 · 904-354-8455

Brenda M. Abrams* · Abrams & Abrams · 3341 Cornelia Drive · Miami, FL 33133 · 305-858-8828

Marsha B. Elser · Elser & Hodor · 1575 Courthouse Tower · 44 West Flagler Street · Miami, FL 33130 · 305-577-0090

Melvyn B. Frumkes · Frumkes & Associates · 100 North Biscayne Boulevard, Suite 1607 · Miami, FL 33132 · 305-371-5600

Maurice Jay Kutner* · Roberts Building, 12th Floor · 28 West Flagler Street · Miami, FL 33130-1801 · 305-377-9411

Ray H. Pearson* · (Child Custody, Divorce, Marital Settlement Agreements, Equitable Division) · Floyd Pearson Richman Greer Weil Zack & Brumbaugh · 175 Northwest First Avenue, 26th Floor · Miami, FL 33128 · 305-373-4000

T. Sol Johnson · Johnson, Green & Locklin · 800 Southeast Caroline Street · P.O. Box 605 · Milton, FL 32572 · 904-623-3841

Burton Young* · Young, Stern & Tannenbaum · 17071 West Dixie Highway · P.O. Box 600 550 · North Miami Beach, FL 33160 · 305-945-1851

Michael R. Walsh · 326 North Fern Creek Avenue · Orlando, FL 32803 · 407-896-9431

David H. Levin* · (Plaintiffs) · Levin, Middlebrooks, Mabie, Thomas, Mayes & Mitchell · Seville Tower · 226 South Palafox Street · P.O. Box 12308 · Pensacola, FL 32581 · 904-435-7000

Arthur D. Ginsburg* · Icard, Merrill, Cullis, Timm, Furen & Ginsburg · 2033 Main Street, Suite 600 · P.O. Drawer 4195 · Sarasota, FL 34230 · 813-366-8100

G. Robert Schultz · Law Offices of G. Robert Schultz · 696 First Avenue North, Suite 305 · St. Petersburg, FL 33701 · 813-822-5718

Robert W. Fields* · Garcia & Fields · Barnett Plaza, Suite 2560 · 101 East Kennedy Boulevard · Tampa, FL 33602 · 813-222-8500

Stephen W. Sessums* · (Divorce, Marital Settlement, Equitable Division) · Sessums & Mason · 307 South Magnolia Avenue · P.O. Box 2409 · Tampa, FL 33601-2409 · 813-251-9200

James P. O'Flarity* · 215 Fifth Street, Suite 108 · West Palm Beach, FL 33401 407-659-4666

Donald J. Sasser · 1800 Australian Avenue South, Suite 203 · P.O. Drawer M · West Palm Beach, FL 33402 · 407-689-4378

FIRST AMENDMENT LAW

Bruce S. Rogow* · Nova University Law Center · 3100 Southwest Ninth Avenue Fort Lauderdale, FL 33315 · 305-524-2465

George D. Gabel, Jr. · Gabel, Taylor & Dees · 76 South Laura Street, Suite 1600 Jacksonville, FL 32202-5450 · 904-353-7329

Talbot D'Alemberte · Steel Hector & Davis · 4000 Southeast Financial Center · 200 South Biscayne Boulevard · Miami, FL 33131-2398 · 305-577-2800

Richard J. Ovelman · Baker & McKenzie · Barnett Tower, Suite 1600 · 701 Brickell Avenue · Miami, FL 33131 · 305-789-8900

Daniel P. S. Paul · Jorden Schulte & Burchette · 701 Brickell Avenue, Suite 2400 Miami, FL 33131 · 305-347-6819

George Karl Rahdert · Rahdert & Anderson · 535 Central Avenue · St. Petersburg, FL 33701 · 813-823-4191

Gregg D. Thomas · Holland & Knight · 400 North Ashley Drive, Suite 2300 · P.O. Box 1288 · Tampa, FL 33601-1288 · 813-227-8500

HEALTH CARE LAW

Robert P. Macina · Greenberg, Traurig, Hoffman, Lipoff, Rosen & Quentel · 500 East Broward Boulevard, 13th Floor · Fort Lauderdale, FL 33394 · 305-765-0500

Barry G. Craig · Mershon, Sawyer, Johnston, Dunwody & Cole · Southeast Financial Center, Suite 4500 · 200 South Biscayne Boulevard · Miami, FL 33131-2387 · 305-358-5100

Gary S. Davis · Steel Hector & Davis · 4000 Southeast Financial Center · 200 South Biscayne Boulevard · Miami, FL 33131-2398 · 305-577-7000

Joel L. Stocker · Greenberg, Traurig, Hoffman, Lipoff, Rosen & Quentel · 1221 Brickell Avenue · Miami, FL 33131 · 305-579-0500

Christopher D. Rolle · (Bio-Ethics) · Foley & Lardner · 111 North Orange Avenue · P.O. Box 2193 · Orlando, FL 32802-2193 · 407-423-7656

Daniel N. Burton · Foley & Lardner · One Tampa City Center, Suite 2900 · P.O. Box 3391 · Tampa, FL 33601-3391 · 813-229-2300

Ralph C. Dell · Allen, Dell, Frank & Trinkle · 101 East Kennedy Boulevard, Suite 1240 · P.O. Box 2111 · Tampa, FL 33601 · 813-223-5351

Barbara R. Pankau · Morrison, Morrison & Gregory · 600 North Florida Avenue, Suite 1700 · Tampa, FL 33602 · 813-224-0739

IMMIGRATION LAW

Michael A. Bander · 444 Brickell Avenue, Suite 300 · Miami, FL 33131 · 305-358-5800

Ira J. Kurzban · Kurzban, Kurzbam & Weinger · 2650 Southwest 27th Avenue, Second Floor · Miami, FL 33133 · 305-444-0060

Michael N. Weiss · Weiss & Hernandez · 44 West Flagler Street, Suite 1600 · Miami, FL 33130 · 305-358-1500

Philip M. Zyne · The AmeriFirst Building, Suite 1240 · One Southeast Third Avenue · Miami, FL 33131 · 305-379-2661

INTELLECTUAL PROPERTY LAW

Jack E. Dominik · Dominik, Stein, Saccocio, Reese, Colitz & Van Der Wall · 6175 Northwest 153rd Street, Suite 225 · Miami, FL 33014 · 305-556-7000

Sybil Meloy · (Estate Administration, Estate Litigation) · Ruden, Barnett, McClosky, Smith, Schuster & Russell · Barnett Bank Tower, Suite 1900 · 701 Brickell Avenue · Miami Beach, FL 33131 · 305-789-2700

Robert W. Duckworth · Duckworth, Allen, Dyer & Doppelt · One South Orange Avenue, Suite 600 · P.O. Box 3791 · Orlando, FL 32802-3791 · 407-841-2330

LABOR AND EMPLOYMENT LAW

Rodney W. Smith · (Labor, Individuals) · 401 Northeast First Street · P.O. Box 628 · Alachua, FL 32615 · 904-462-4005

Robert E. Weisberg* · (Individuals) · 1450 Madruga Avenue, Suite 209 · Coral Gabels, FL 33146 · 305-666-6095

Neil Chonin · (Individuals) · Chonin & Sher · 304 Palermo Avenue · Coral Gables, FL 33134 · 305-443-5125

William H. Andrews* · (Management) · Coffman, Coleman, Andrews & Grogan 2065 Herschel Street · P.O. Box 40089 · Jacksonville, FL 32203 · 904-389-5161

Daniel R. Coffman, Jr. · (Management) · Coffman, Coleman, Andrews & Grogan 2065 Herschel Street · P.O. Box 40089 · Jacksonville, FL 32203 · 904-389-5161

Patrick D. Coleman · (Management) · Coffman, Coleman, Andrews & Grogan · 2065 Herschel Street · P.O. Box 40089 · Jacksonville, FL 32203 · 904-389-5161

Guy O. Farmer II* · (Management) · Foley & Lardner · The Greenleaf Building 200 Laura Street · P.O. Box 240 · Jacksonville, FL 32202-0240 · 904-359-2000

Michael K. Grogan · (Management) · Coffman, Coleman, Andrews & Grogan · 2065 Herschel Street · P.O. Box 40089 · Jacksonville, FL 32203 · 904-389-5161

Eric J. Holshouser · (Management) · Coffman, Coleman, Andrews & Grogan · 2065 Herschel Street · P.O. Box 40089 · Jacksonville, FL 32203 · 904-389-5161

John F. Kattman · (Labor, Individuals) · Kattman, Eshelman & MacLennan · 1920 San Marco Boulevard · Jacksonville, FL 32207 · 904-398-1229

Thomas J. Pilacek · (Labor, Individuals) · Law Offices of Thomas J. Pilacek · 2101 West State Road, Suite 105 · Longwood, FL 32779 · 407-774-9500

Michael W. Casey III* · (Management) · Muller, Mintz, Kornreich, Caldwell, Casey, Crosland & Bramnick · Southeast Financial Center, Suite 3600 · 200 South Biscayne Boulevard · Miami, FL 33131-2338 · 305-358-5500

Elizabeth J. du Fresne · (Individuals) · Steel Hector & Davis · 4000 Southeast Financial Center, 41st Floor · Miami, FL 33131 · 305-577-2855

Joseph Z. Fleming* · (Management) · 620 Ingraham Building · 25 Southeast Second Avenue · Miami, FL 33131 · 305-373-0791

Jesse S. Hogg* · (Management, Individuals) · Hogg, Allen, Norton & Blue · 121 Majorca, Third Floor · Miami, FL 33134 · 305-445-7801

Peter J. Hurtgen · (Management) · Morgan, Lewis & Bockius · 5300 Southeast Financial Center · 200 South Biscayne Boulevard · Miami, FL 33131-2339 · 305-579-0300

Joseph H. Kaplan · (Labor) · Kaplan & Bloom · 1951 Northwest 17th Avenue · P.O. Box 520337 · Miami, FL 33152 · 305-325-1661

David V. Kornreich · (Management) · Muller, Mintz, Kornreich, Caldwell, Casey, Crosland & Bramnick · Southeast Financial Center, Suite 3600 · 200 South Biscayne Boulevard · Miami, FL 33131-2338 · 305-358-5500

Ira J. Kurzban* · (Individuals) · Kurzban Kurzban and Weinger · Plaza 2650, Second Floor · 2650 Southwest 27th Avenue · Miami, FL 33133 · 305-444-0060

David M. Lipman* · (Individuals) · Lipman & Weisberg · 5901 Southwest 74th Street, Suite 304 · Miami, FL 33143 · 305-662-2600

George F. Lynch · (Management) · Squire, Sanders & Dempsey · 3000 Miami Center · 201 South Biscayne Boulevard · Miami, FL 33131 · 305-577-8700

Robert L. Norton · Hogg, Allen, Norton & Blue · 121 Majorca, Third Floor · Miami, FL 33134 · 305-445-7801

Robert A. Sugarman* · (Labor, Individuals) · Sugarman & Susskind · 5959 Blue Lagoon Drive, Suite 150 · Miami, FL 33126 · 305-264-2121

Howard S. Susskind · (Labor) · Sugar & Susskind · 5959 Blue Lagoon Drive, Suite 150 · Miami, FL 33126 · 305-264-2121

James G. Brown · (Management) · Richeson and Brown · 135 North Magnolia Avenue · P.O. Box 3006 · Orlando, FL 32802 · 407-425-7755

Norman F. Burke · (Management) · Foley & Lardner · 111 North Orange Avenue P.O. Box 2193 · Orlando, FL 32802-2193 · 407-423-7656

Joseph Egan, Jr. · (Labor) · Egan, Lev & Siwica · 918 Lucerne Terrace · Orlando, FL 32806 · 407-422-1400

Thomas C. Garwood, Jr. · (Management) · Garwood & McKenna · 322 East Pine Street · P.O. Box 60 · Orlando, FL 32802 · 407-841-9496

Tobe M. Lev · Egan, Lev & Siwica · 918 Lucerne Terrace · Orlando, FL 32806 407-422-1400

Leo P. Rock, Jr. · (Management) · Gray, Harris & Robinson · Southeast Bank Building, Suite 1200 · 201 East Pine Street · P.O. Box 3068 · Orlando, FL 32802-3068 · 407-843-8880

John-Edward Alley* · (Management) · Alley and Alley · 205 Brush Street · P.O. Box 1427 · Tampa, FL 33601 · 813-229-6481

James M. Blue · (Management) · Hogg, Allen, Norton & Blue · 224 South Hyde Park, Suite 350 · Tampa, FL 33609 · 813-251-1210

John J. Chamblee, Jr.* · (Labor, Individuals) · Chamblee, Miles & Grizzard · 202 Cardy Street · Tampa, FL 33606 · 813-251-4542

John E. Dinkel III · (Management) · Macfarlane, Ferguson, Allison & Kelly · 215 Madison Street · P.O. Box 1531 · Tampa, FL 33602 · 813-223-2411

Thomas M. Gonzalez* · (Management) · Thompson, Sizemore & Gonzalez · The Plaza on the Mall, Suite 838 · 201 East Kennedy Boulevard · P.O. Box 639 · Tampa, FL 33601 · 813-273-0050

Robert D. Hall, Jr. · (Management) · Alley and Alley · 205 Brush Street · P.O. Box 1427 · Tampa, FL 33601-1427 · 813-229-6481

Frank E. Hamilton, Jr. · (Labor) · Frank Hamilton & Associates · 2620 West Kennedy Boulevard · Tampa, FL 33609-3294 · 813-879-9842

Paul A. Saad · (Management) · Hogg, Allen, Norton & Blue · 224 South Hyde Park, Suite 350 · Tampa, FL 33609 · 813-251-1210

William E. Sizemore · (Management) · Thompson, Sizemore & Gonzalez · 109 North Brush Street, Suite 200 · P.O. Box 639 · Tampa, FL 33602 · 813-273-0050

Harrison C. Thompson, Jr. · (Management) · Thompson, Sizemore & Gonzalez 109 North Brush Street, Suite 200 · P.O. Box 639 · Tampa, FL 33602 · 813-273-0050

Peter W. Zinober · (Management) · Zinober & Burr · Enterprise Plaza, Suite 1750 201 East Kennedy Boulevard · Tampa, FL 33602 · 813-224-9004

MARITIME LAW

James F. Moseley, Sr.* · (Personal Injury, General) · Taylor, Moseley & Joyner 501 West Bay Street · Jacksonville, FL 32202 · 904-356-1306

G. Morton Good · Kelley Drye and Warren · Miami Center, Suite 2400 · 201 South Biscayne Boulevard · Miami, FL 33131 · 305-379-6523

Frank J. Marston* · Fowler, White, Burnett, Hurley, Banick & Strickroot · Courthouse Center, 11th Floor · 175 Northwest First Avenue · Miami, FL 33128-1817 · 305-358-6550

David G. Hanlon · Shackleford, Farrior, Stallings & Evans · East Kennedy Boulevard, Suite 1400 · P.O. Box 3324 · Tampa, FL 33601 · 813-273-5000

Brendan P. O'Sullivan* · Fowler, White, Gillen, Boggs, Villareal and Banker · 501 East Kennedy Boulevard, Suite 1700 · P.O. Box 1438 · Tampa, FL 33601 · 813-228-7411

Nathaniel G. W. Pieper · Lau, Lane, Pieper & Asti · 100 South Ashley Drive · Tampa, FL 33601-0838 · 813-229-2121

Roger A. Vaughan, Jr.* · (Plaintiffs Personal Injury) · Wagner, Cunningham, Vaughan & McLaughlin · 708 Jackson Street (Corner of Jefferson) · Tampa, FL 33602 · 813-223-7421

Dewey R. Villareal, Jr.* · Fowler, White, Gillen, Boggs, Villareal and Banker · 501 East Kennedy Boulevard, Suite 1700 · P.O. Box 1438 · Tampa, FL 33601 · 813-228-7411

NATURAL RESOURCES AND ENVIRONMENTAL LAW

Donald C. McClosky · Ruden, Barnett, McClosky, Smith, Schuster & Russell · NCNB Building, Penthouse B · 110 East Broward Boulevard · P.O. Box 1900 · Fort Lauderdale, FL 33302 · 305-764-6660

Frank X. Friedmann, Jr. · Rogers, Towers, Bailey, Jones & Gay · 1300 Gulf Life Drive · Jacksonville, FL 32207 · 904-398-3911

Joseph Z. Fleming* · (Water, Hazardous Waste, Land Use) · 620 Ingraham Building · 25 Southeast Second Avenue · Miami, FL 33131 · 305-373-0791

John G. Fletcher II* · 7600 Red Road, Suite 304 · Miami, FL 33143 · 305-665-7521

Alan S. Gold · Greenberg, Traurig, Hoffman, Lipoff, Rosen & Quentel · 1221 Brickell Avenue · Miami, FL 33131 · 305-579-0500

Anthony J. O'Donnell, Jr. · (Plaintiffs) · Baker & McKenzie · 701 Brickell Avenue, Suite 1600 · Miami, FL 33131 · 305-789-7999

Stanley B. Price · Fine Jacobson Schwartz Nash Block & England · One Cen-Trust Financial Center · 100 Southeast Second Street · Miami, FL 33131-2130 · 305-577-4000

Clifford A. Schulman · Greenberg, Traurig, Hoffman, Lipoff, Rosen & Quentel 1221 Brickell Avenue · Miami, FL 33131 · 305-579-0500

Robert H. Traurig · Greenberg, Traurig, Hoffman, Lipoff, Rosen & Quentel · 1221 Brickell Avenue · Miami, FL 33131 · 305-579-0500

Robert J. Pleus, Jr. · Pleus, Adams & Spears · 940 Highland Avenue · Orlando, FL 32803 · 407-422-8116

Wade L. Hopping · (Water, Air) · Hopping Boyd Green & Sams · 123 South Calhoun · P.O. Box 6526 · Tallahassee, FL 32301 · 904-222-7500

Joseph W. Landers, Jr.* · (Water, Air, Hazardous Waste, Wetlands) · Landers & Parsons · 310 West College Avenue, Third Floor · P.O. Box 271 · Tallahassee, FL 32302 · 904-681-0311

Philip S. Parsons · (Water, Air, Hazardous Waste, Wetlands) · Landers & Parsons 310 West College Avenue, Third Floor · P.O. Box 271 · Tallahassee, FL 32302 · 904-681-0311

William D. Preston · (Solid Waste, Hazardous Waste) · Hopping Boyd Green & Sams · First Florida Bank Building, Suite 420 · 123 South Calhoun · P.O. Box 6526 · Tallahassee, FL 32314 · 904-222-7500

Robert M. Rhodes · Steel, Hector & Davis · 215 South Monroe Street, Suite 601 Tallahassee, FL 32301 · 904-222-2300

Gary P. Sams* · Hopping Boyd Green & Sams · First Florida Bank Building, Suite 420 · P.O. Box 6526 · Tallahassee, FL 32314 · 904-222-7500

Roger D. Schwenke · (Water, Air, Solid Waste, Hazardous Waste) · Carlton, Fields, Ward, Emmanuel, Smith & Cutler · One Harbor Place · 777 South Harbour Island Drive · P.O. Box 3239 · Tampa, FL 33601 · 813-223-7000

Theodore C. Taub · Taub & Williams · 100 South Ashley Drive, Suite 2100 · P.O. Box 3430 · Tampa, FL 33601 · 813-228-8000

PERSONAL INJURY LITIGATION

Rex Conrad · (Defendants) · Conrad, Scherer & James · 633 South Federal Highway · P.O. Box 14723 · Fort Lauderdale, FL 33302 · 305-462-5500

Joseph S. Kashi · (Defendants) · Conrad, Scherer & James · 633 South Federal Highway · P.O. Box 14723 · Fort Lauderdale, FL 33302 · 305-462-5500

Jon E. Krupnick · (Plaintiffs) · Krupnick, Campbell, Malone and Roselli · 700 Southeast Third Avenue, Suite 100 · Fort Lauderdale, FL 33316 · 305-763-8181

Sheldon J. Schlesinger · (Plaintiffs) · 1212 Southeast Third Avenue · Fort Lauderdale, FL 33316 · 305-467-8800

Dianne Jay Weaver* · (Plaintiffs) ·· Weaver, Weaver & Petrie · 500 Southeast Sixth Street · P.O. Box 14663 · Fort Lauderdale, FL 33302-4663 · 305-763-2511

Robert J. Beckham* · (Plaintiffs, Professional Malpractice) · Beckham & McAliley · Independent Square, Suite 3131 · One Independent Drive · Jacksonville, FL 32202 · 904-354-9022

James E. Cobb · (Defendants) · Osborne, McNatt & Cobb · 225 Water Street, Suite 1400 · Jacksonville, FL 32202 · 904-354-0624

William C. Gentry · (Plaintiffs) · Gentry & Phillips · Six East Bay Street, Suite 400 · P.O. Box 837 · Jacksonville, FL 32201 · 904-356-4100

James C. Rinaman, Jr.* · (Defendants, Products Liability, Professional Malpractice, Appellate) · Marks, Gray, Conroy & Gibbs · 800 Southeast Bank Building · 1200 Gulf Life Drive · P.O. Box 447 · Jacksonville, FL 32201 · 904-398-0900

Sammy Cacciatore · (Plaintiffs) · Nance, Cacciatore, Sisserson & Duryea · 525 North Harbor City Boulevard · Melbourne, FL 32935 · 407-254-8416

Henry Burnett · (Defendants) · Fowler, White, Burnett, Hurley, Banick & Strickroot · Courthouse Center, 11th Floor · 175 West North First Avenue · Miami, FL 33128 · 305-358-6550

Bill Colson* · (Plaintiffs) · Colson, Hicks, Eidson, Colson & Matthews · Southeast Financial Center, 47th Floor · 200 South Biscayne Boulevard · Miami, FL 33131-2310 · 305-373-5400

Joel D. Eaton* · (Appellate) · Podhurst Orseck Parks Josefsberg Eaton Meadow Olin & Perwin · City National Bank Building, Suite 800 · 25 West Flagler Street Miami, FL 33130-1780 · 305-358-2800

David C. Goodwin* · (Defendants) · Morgan Lewis & Bockius · 5300 Southeast Financial Center · 200 South Biscayne Boulevard · Miami, FL 33131-2339 · 305-579-0300

William M. Hicks* · (Plaintiffs) · Colson, Hicks, Eidson, Colson & Matthews · Southeast Financial Center, 47th Floor · 200 South Biscayne Boulevard · Miami, FL 33131-2310 · 305-373-5400

Edward A. Moss · Anderson, Moss, Parks & Russo · New World Tower, Suite 2500 · 100 North Biscayne Boulevard · Miami, FL 33132 · 305-358-5171

Robert L. Parks* · (Plaintiffs, Products Liability, Airplane Collision) · Anderson, Moss, Parks & Russo · New World Tower, 25th Floor · 100 North Biscayne Boulevard · Miami, FL 33132 · 305-358-5171

Aaron Podhurst · Podhurst Orseck Josefsberg Eaton Meadow Olin & Perwin · City National Bank Building, Suite 800 · 25 West Flagler Street · Miami, FL 33130 · 305-358-2800

Stanley M. Rosenblatt* · (Plaintiffs, Professional Malpractice, Airplane Collision) Concord Building, 11th & 12th Floors · 66 West Flagler Street · Miami, FL 33130 305-374-6131

Murray Sams, Jr.* · (Plaintiffs) · Sams, Donato & Flynn · 700 Concord Building 66 West Flagler Street · Miami, FL 33130 · 305-374-3181

J. B. Spence · (Plaintiffs) · Spence, Payne, Masington, Needle & Eversole · 2950 Southwest 27th Avenue, Suite 300 · Miami, FL 33133 · 305-447-0641

Larry S. Stewart* · (Plaintiffs) · Stewart Tilghman Fox & Bianchi · 44 West Flagler Street, Suite 1900 · Miami, FL 33130-1808 · 305-358-6644

Joe N. Unger · (Appellate) · Concord Building, 11th Floor · 66 West Flagler Street Miami, FL 33130 · 305-374-5500

Richard W. Slawson · (Plaintiffs) · Slawson, Burman & Critton · 712 U.S. Highway One, Suite 300 · North Palm Beach, FL 33408 · 407-842-2820

Michael Maher* · (Plaintiffs) · Maher, Gibson and Guiley · 90 East Livingston Street, Suite 200 · Orlando, FL 32801 · 407-839-0866

Fredric G. Levin* · (Plaintiffs) · Levin, Middlebrooks, Mabie, Thomas, Mayes & Mitchell · Seville Tower · 226 South Palafox Street · P.O. Box 12308 · Pensacola, FL 32581 · 904-435-7000

Lefferts L. Mabie, Jr. · (Plaintiffs) · Levin, Middlebrooks, Mabie, Thomas, Mayes & Mitchell · Seville Tower · 226 South Palafox Street · P.O. Box 12308 · Pensacola, FL 32581 · 904-435-7000

Glenn M. Woodworth · (Plaintiffs) · Woodworth & Lamb · 5999 Central Avenue St. Petersburg, FL 33710 · 813-345-2499

John R. Beranek · (Appellate) · Aurell, Radey, Hinkle & Thomas · Monroe Tower, Suite 1000 · 101 North Monroe Street · Tallahassee, FL 32301 · 904-681-7766

Julian D. Clarkson · (Appellate) · Holland & Knight · Barnett Bank Building, Suite 600 · P.O. Drawer 810 · Tallahassee, FL 32302 · 904-224-7000

W. Dexter Douglass · Douglass, Cooper, Coppins & Powell · 211 East Call Street P.O. Box 1674 · Tallahassee, FL 32302 · 904-224-6191

Robert E. Banker* · (Defendants, Medical Malpractice, Professional Malpractice, Airplane Collision) · Fowler, White, Gillen, Boggs, Villareal and Banker · 501 East Kennedy Boulevard, Suite 1700 · P.O. Box 1438 · Tampa, FL 33601 · 813-228-7411

Daniel N. Burton · (Defendants) · Foley & Lardner · One Tampa City Center, Suite 2900 · P.O. Box 3391 · Tampa, FL 33601-3391 · 813-229-2300

Anthony W. Cunningham* · (Plaintiffs, Products Liability, Professional Malpractice, Airplane Collision) · Wagner, Cunningham, Vaughan & McLaughlin · 708 Jackson Street (Corner of Jefferson) · Tampa, FL 33602 · 813-223-7421

T. Paine Kelly, Jr.* · (Defendants, Medical Malpractice, Products Liability) · Macfarlane, Ferguson, Allison & Kelly · 215 Madison Street · P.O. Box 1531 · Tampa, FL 33602 · 813-223-2411

Alan C. Sundberg · (Appellate) · Carlton, Fields, Ward, Emmanuel, Smith & Cutler · One Harbor Place · 777 South Harbour Island Drive · P.O. Box 3239 · Tampa, FL 33601 · 813-223-7000

Roger A. Vaughan, Jr.* · (Plaintiffs) · Wagner, Cunningham, Vaughan & McLaughlin · 708 Jackson Street (Corner of Jefferson) · Tampa, FL 33602 · 813-223-7421

F. William Wagner · (Plaintiffs) · Wagner, Cunningham, Vaughan & McLaughlin 708 Jackson Street (Corner of Jefferson) · Tampa, FL 33602 · 813-223-7421

C. Steven Yerrid* · Yerrid, Knopik & Valenzuela · 101 East Kennedy Boulevard Barnett Plaza, Suite 2160 · Tampa, FL 33602 · 813-222-8222

Theodore Babbitt* · (Plaintiffs, Medical Malpractice, Products Liability, Automobile Collision) · Babbitt and Hazouri · 1801 Australian Avenue South · P.O. Drawer 024426 · West Palm Beach, FL 33402-4426 · 407-684-2500

Edna L. Caruso · (Plaintiffs, Appellate) · Barrister's Building, Suite 4B · 1615 Forum Place · West Palm Beach, FL 33401 · 407-686-8010

Fred A. Hazouri* · (Plaintiffs, Medical Malpractice, Products Liability, Automobile Collision) · Babbitt and Hazouri · 1801 Australian Avenue South · P.O. Drawer 024426 · West Palm Beach, FL 33402-4426 · 407-684-2500

Larry A. Klein · (Appellate) · Klein & Walsh · Flagler Center, Suite 503 · 501 South Flagler Drive · West Palm Beach, FL 33401 · 407-659-5455

Lake Lytal, Jr.* · (Plaintiffs, Medical Malpractice, Products Liability, Automobile Collision) · Lytal & Reiter · 515 North Flagler Drive, 10th Floor · P.O. Box 024466 · West Palm Beach, FL 33402-4466 · 407-655-1990

Robert M. Montgomery, Jr.* · (Plaintiffs) · Montgomery & Larmoyeux · 1016 Clearwater Place · P.O. Drawer 3086 · West Palm Beach, FL 33402-3086 · 407-686-6300

Justus W. Reid · Reid, Ricca & Rigell · 500 South Australian Avenue · P.O. Drawer 2926 · West Palm Beach, FL 33402 · 407-659-7700

Joseph J. Reiter* · (Plaintiffs) · Lytal & Reiter · 515 North Flagler Drive, 10th Floor · P.O. Box 024466 · West Palm Beach, FL 33402-4466 · 407-655-1990

Christian D. Searcy, Sr.* · (Plaintiffs, Products Liability, Automobile Collision, Brain Injury, Wrongful Death) · Searcy and Denney · 2139 Palm Beach Lakes Boulevard · P.O. Drawer 3626 · West Palm Beach, FL 33402 · 407-686-6300

PUBLIC UTILITY LAW

Matthew M. Childs · Steel, Hector & Davis · 215 South Monroe Street, Suite 601 Tallahassee, FL 32301 · 904-222-2300

Bruce D. May · Holland & Knight · Barnett Bank Building, Suite 600 · P.O. Drawer 810 · Tallahassee, FL 32302 · 904-224-7000

Bruce W. Renard · (Telephone Utilities) · Messer, Vickers, Caparello, Madsen & Lewis · 215 South Monroe Street, Suite 701 · P.O. Box 1876 · Tallahassee, FL 32302 · 904-222-0720

Lee L. Willis · Ausley, McMullen, McGehee, Carothers & Proctor · Washington Square Building · 227 South Calhoun Street · P.O. Box 391 · Tallahassee, FL 32302 · 904-224-9115

REAL ESTATE LAW

Timothy A. Johnson, Jr. · Johnson, Blakely, Pope, Bokor, Ruppel & Burns · 911 Chestnut Street · P.O. Box 1368 · Clearwater, FL 34617 · 813-461-1818

Donald C. McClosky · Ruden, Barnett, McClosky, Smith, Schuster & Russell · The North Carolina National Bank Building · 110 East Broward Boulevard · P.O. Box 1900 · Fort Lauderdale, FL 33302 · 305-764-6660

W. O. Birchfield · (Eminent Domain) · Martin, Ade, Birchfield & Mickler · 3000 Independent Square · One Independent Drive · P.O. Box 59 · Jacksonville, FL 32201 · 904-354-2050

Charles E. Commander III · Foley & Lardner, Legler & Commander · The Greenleaf Building · 200 Laura Street · P.O. Box 240 · Jacksonville, FL 32202-0240 · 904-359-2000

David M. Foster · Rogers, Towers, Bailey, Jones & Gay · 1300 Gulf Life Drive Jacksonville, FL 32207 · 904-398-3911

Robert O. Mickler · Martin, Ade, Birchfield & Mickler · 3000 Independent Square · One Independent Drive · P.O. Box 59 · Jacksonville, FL 32201 · 904-354-2050

William E. Scheau · Ulmer, Murchison, Ashby & Taylor · First Union Bank Building, Suite 1600 · 200 West Forsyth Street · P.O. Box 479 · Jacksonville, FL 32201 · 904-354-5652

James S. Taylor · Ulmer, Murchison, Ashby & Taylor · First Union Bank Building, Suite 1600 · 200 West Forsyth Street · P.O. Box 479 · Jacksonville, FL 32201 904-354-5652

Henry M. Kittleson · Holland & Knight · 92 Lake Wire Drive · P.O. Box 32092 Lakeland, FL 33802 · 813-682-1161

Lawrence Godofsky · Greenberg, Traurig, Hoffman, Lipoff, Rosen & Quentel · 1221 Brickell Avenue · Miami, FL 33131 · 305-579-0500

Matthew B. Gorson · Greenberg, Traurig, Hoffman, Lipoff, Rosen & Quentel · 1221 Brickell Avenue · Miami, FL 33131 · 305-579-0500

Burton A. Hartman · Squire, Sanders & Dempsey · 3000 Miami Center · 201 South Biscayne Boulevard · Miami, FL 33131 · 305-577-8700

David S. Kenin · Greenberg, Traurig, Hoffman, Lipoff, Rosen & Quentel · 1221 Brickell Avenue · Miami, FL 33131 · 305-579-0500

Robert E. Livingston · Patton & Kanner · 150 Southeast Second Avenue, Third Floor · Miami, FL 33131 · 305-373-5761

Albert D. Quentel · Greenberg, Traurig, Hoffman, Lipoff, Rosen & Quentel · 1221 Brickell Avenue · Miami, FL 33131 · 305-579-0500

Donald S. Rosenberg · Rosenberg, Reisman & Stein · 2600 AmeriFirst Building One Southeast Third Avenue · Miami, FL 33131 · 305-358-2600

Morris Rosenberg · Rosenberg, Reisman & Stein · 2600 AmeriFirst Building · One Southeast Third Avenue · Miami, FL 33131 · 305-358-2600

Robert H. Traurig · Greenberg, Traurig, Hoffman, Lipoff, Rosen & Quentel · 1221 Brickell Avenue · Miami, FL 33131 · 305-579-0500

Leo Rose, Jr. · Therrel Baisden & Meyer Weiss · Sun Bank/Miami, Suite 500 · 1111 Lincoln Road · Miami Beach, FL 33139 · 305-672-1921

Harry B. Smith · Ruden, Barnett, McClosky, Smith, Schuster & Russell · Barnett Bank Tower, Suite 1900 · 701 Brickell Avenue · Miami Beach, FL 33131 · 305-789-2700

William E. Doster · Lowndes, Drosdick, Doster, Kantor & Reed · 215 North Eola Drive · P.O. Box 2809 · Orlando, FL 32802 · 407-843-4600

John F. Lowndes · Lowndes, Drosdick, Doster, Kantor & Reed · 215 North Eola Drive · P.O. Box 2809 · Orlando, FL 32802 · 407-843-4600

James K. Rush · Anderson & Rush · 322 East Central Boulevard · P.O. Box 2288 Orlando, FL 32802 · 305-849-0020

Patrick G. Emmanuel · Emmanuel, Sheppard & Condon · 30 South Spring Street P.O. Box 1271 · Pensacola, FL 32596 · 904-433-6581

Anthony S. Battaglia* · (Commercial) · Battaglia, Ross, Hastings and Dicus · 980 Tyrone Boulevard · P.O. Box 41100 · Saint Petersburg, FL 33743 · 813-381-2300

Wade L. Hopping · (Zoning, Land Use) · Hopping Boyd Green & Sams · 123 South Calhoun · P.O. Box 6526 · Tallahassee, FL 32301 · 904-222-7500

Joseph B. Cofer · Carlton, Fields, Ward, Emmanuel, Smith & Cutler · One Harbor Place · 777 South Harbour Island Drive · P.O. Box 3239 · Tampa, FL 33601 · 813-223-7000

Thomas N. Henderson III · Hill, Ward & Henderson · 101 East Kennedy Boulevard, Suite 3700 · P.O. Box 2231 · Tampa, FL 33601 · 813-221-3900

Stephen J. Mitchell · Annis, Mitchell, Cockey, Edwards & Roehn · One Tampa City Center Building, Suite 2100 · P.O. Box 3433 · Tampa, FL 33601 · 813-229-3321

James M. Reed · Taub & Williams · 100 South Ashley Drive, Suite 2100 · P.O. Box 3430 · Tampa, FL 33601 · 813-228-8000

Leslie D. Scharf · Trenam, Simmons, Kemker, Scharf, Barkin, Frye & O'Neill · Barnett Plaza, Suite 2700 · 101 East Kennedy Boulevard · P.O. Box 1102 · Tampa, FL 33601-1102 · 813-223-7474

William R. Boose III · (Zoning, Land Use) · Boose Casey Ciklin Lubitz Martens McBane & O'Connell · Northbridge Tower I, 19th Floor · 515 North Flagler Drive · P.O. Drawer 024626 · West Palm Beach, FL 33402-4626 · 407-832-5900

Peter A. Nathan · Jacob & Weingarten · 1555 Palm Beach Lakes Boulevard, Suite 1510 · West Palm Beach, FL 33401 · 407-640-5600

Marvin S. Rosen · Honigman Miller Schwartz and Cohn · 222 Lakeview Avenue, Suite 800 · West Palm Beach, FL 33401 · 407-683-4500

TAX AND EMPLOYEE BENEFITS LAW

Bruce H. Bokor · Johnson, Blakely, Pope, Bokor, Ruppel & Burns · 911 Chestnut Street · P.O. Box 1368 · Clearwater, FL 34617 · 813-461-1818

Charles P. Sacher · (Employee Benefits) · Walton Lantaff Schroeder & Carson · Gables International Plaza, Suite 1101 · 2655 Le Jeune Road · Coral Gables, FL 33134 · 305-379-6411

James B. Davis · (Employee Benefits) · Greaton and Davis · 2601 East Oakland Park Boulevard, Suite 601 · P.O. Box 9027 · Fort Lauderdale, FL 33310 · 305-561-0313

Louis J. Dereuil · Isley & Dereuil · 1040 Bayview Drive, Suite 424 · Fort Lauderdale, FL 33304 · 305-564-7525

Michael L. Trop · (Employee Benefits) · Atlas, Pearlman & Trop · 700 Southeast Third Avenue, Suite 300 · Fort Lauderdale, FL 33316 · 305-463-3173

Kenneth G. Anderson · Gulf Life Tower, Suite 2540 · Jacksonville, FL 32207 · 904-399-8000

Michael W. Fisher · Fisher, Towsey, Leas & Ball · 2600 Independent Square · One Independent Drive · Jacksonville, FL 32202 · 904-356-2600

Fred H. Steffey · Southpoint Building, Suite 300 · 6620 Southpoint Drive South · Jacksonville, FL 32216 · 904-296-0037

John D. Armstrong · Mershon, Sawyer, Johnston, Dunwody & Cole · Southeast Financial Center, Suite 4500 · 200 South Biscayne Boulevard · Miami, FL 33131-2387 · 305-358-5100

Michael J. Canan · (Employee Benefits) · Steel Hector & Davis · 4000 Southeast Financial Center · 200 South Biscayne Boulevard · Miami, FL 33131-2398 · 305-577-2800

K. Lawrence Gragg · White & Case · Southeast Financial Center, Suite 4900 · 200 South Biscayne Boulevard · Miami, FL 33131 · 305-371-2700

Edward Heilbronner · (Employee Benefits) · Paul, Landy, Beily & Harper · 200 Southeast First Street, 12th Floor · Miami, FL 33131 · 305-995-9493

Robert F. Hudson, Jr. · Baker & McKenzie · Barnett Tower, Suite 1600 · 701 Brickell Avenue · Miami, FL 33131 · 305-789-8900

Martin Kalb · Greenberg, Traurig, Hoffman, Lipoff, Rosen & Quentel · 1221 Brickell Avenue · Miami, FL 33131 · 305-579-0500

Joel J. Karp · Paul, Landy, Beiley & Harper · 200 Southeast First Street, 12th Floor · Miami, FL 33131 · 305-358-9300

Shepard King · Steel Hector & Davis · 4000 Southeast Financial Center · 200 South Biscayne Boulevard · Miami, FL 33131-2398 · 305-577-2865

Martin J. Nash · Fine Jacobson Schwartz Nash Block & England · One CenTrust Financial Center · 100 Southeast Second Street · Miami, FL 33131-2130 · 305-577-4000

Henry H. Raattama, Jr. · Mershon, Sawyer, Johnston, Dunwody & Cole · Southeast Financial Center, Suite 4500 · 200 South Biscayne Boulevard · Miami, FL 33131-2387 · 305-358-5100

Benjamin S. Schwartz · Fine Jacobson Schwartz Nash Block & England · One CenTrust Financial Center · 100 Southeast Second Street · Miami, FL 33131-2130 · 305-577-4000

Byron L. Sparber · Squire, Sanders & Dempsey · 3000 Miami Center · 201 South Biscayne Boulevard · Miami, FL 33131 · 305-577-8700

Donald R. Tescher · Tescher, Chaves & Hochman · 9100 South Dadeland Boulevard, Suite 1707, Penthouse One · Miami, FL 33156 · 305-670-0444

Samuel C. Ullman · (Corporate & Partnership Transactions, State Tax, Tax Disputes) · Kelley Drye & Warren · 2400 Miami Center · 201 South Biscayne Boulevard · Miami, FL 33131-2399 · 305-372-2400

Andrew H. Weinstein* · (Tax Disputes, Foreign Tax) · Holland & Knight · 1200 Brickell Avenue · P.O. Box 015441 · Miami, FL 33131 · 305-374-8500

Charles H. Egerton · Dean, Mead, Egerton, Bloodworth, Capouano & Bozarth · 800 North Magnolia Avenue, Suite 1500 · Orlando, FL 32803-2346 · 407-841-1200

Robert W. Mead, Jr. · Dean, Mead, Egerton, Bloodworth, Capouano & Bozarth · 800 North Magnolia Avenue, Suite 1500 · Orlando, FL 32802-2346 · 407-841-1200

Michael D. Annis · Annis, Mitchell, Cockey, Edwards & Roehn · One Tampa City Center Building, Suite 2100 · P.O. Box 3433 · Tampa, FL 33601 · 813-229-3321

Leslie J. Barnett · Barnett, Bolt & Kirkwood · 601 Bayshore Place, Suite 700 · P.O. Box 3287 · Tampa, FL 33601 · 813-253-2020

E. Jackson Boggs · Fowler, White, Gillen, Boggs, Villareal and Banker · 501 East Kennedy Boulevard, Suite 1700 · P.O. Box 1438 · Tampa, FL 33601 · 813-228-7411

Joseph D. Edwards · (Employee Benefits) · Annis, Mitchell, Cockey, Edwards & Roehn · One Tampa City Center Building, Suite 2100 · P.O. Box 3433 · Tampa, FL 33601 · 813-229-3321

Albert C. O'Neill, Jr. · Trenam, Simmons, Kemker, Scharf, Barkin, Frye & O'Neill · Barnett Plaza, Suite 2700 · 101 East Kennedy Boulevard · P.O. Box 1102 Tampa, FL 33601-1102 · 813-223-7474

Stanley W. Rosenkranz · Shear, Newman, Hahn & Rosenkranz · 201 East Kennedy Boulevard, Suite 1000 · P.O. Box 2378 · Tampa, FL 33601 · 813-228-8530

Frederick M. Rothenberg · (Employee Benefits) · Fowler, White, Gillen, Boggs, Villareal and Banker · 501 East Kennedy Boulevard, Suite 1700 · P.O. Box 1438 Tampa, FL 33601 · 813-228-7411

Ronald J. Russo · (Tax, Employee Benefits) · Glenn, Rasmussen, Fogarty, Merryday & Russo · Ashley Tower, Suite 1300 · 100 South Ashley Drive · P.O. Box 3333 · Tampa, FL 33601-3333 · 813-229-3333

Sherwin P. Simmons · Trenam, Simmons, Kemker, Scharf, Barkin, Frye & O'Neill · Barnett Plaza, Suite 2700 · 101 East Kennedy Boulevard · P.O. Box 1102 Tampa, FL 33601-1102 · 813-223-7474

Jerald David August · August & Comter · One Clearlake Centre, Suite 1111 · 250 Australian Avenue South · West Palm Beach, FL 33401 · 407-835-9600

Jerald David August · August & Comiter · One Clearlake Centre, Suite 1111 · 250 Australian Avenue South · West Palm Beach, FL 33401 · 407-835-9600

TRUSTS AND ESTATES

Robert D. Chapin · Chapin & Armstrong · 1201 Northeast Eighth Street · Delray Beach, FL 33483-7203 · 407-272-1225

Rohan Kelley* · (Estate Litigation) · 3365 Galt Ocean Drive · Fort Lauderdale, FL 33308 · 305-563-1400

John G. Grimsley · Mahoney Adams Milam Surface & Grimsley · Barnett Bank Building · 100 Laura Street · P.O. Box 4099 · Jacksonville, FL 32201 · 904-354-1100

Fred H. Steffey · Southpoint Building, Suite 300 · 6620 Southpoint Drive South Jacksonville, FL 32216 · 904-296-0037

Norman J. Benford · Greenberg, Traurig, Hoffman, Lipoff, Rosen & Quentel · 1221 Brickell Avenue · Miami, FL 33131 · 305-579-0500

Robert D. W. Landon II · Mershon, Sawyer, Johnston, Dunwody & Cole · Southeast Financial Center, Suite 4500 · 200 South Biscayne Boulevard · Miami, FL 33131-2387 · 305-358-5100

Wilson Smith* · (Probate & Trust Litigation) · Two Datran Center, Suite 515 · 9130 South Dadeland Boulevard · Miami, FL 33156 · 305-670-3005

Paul M. Stokes · (Estate Planning, Estate Administration, Probate/Trust Litigation) · Kelley Drye & Warren · 2400 Miami Center · 201 South Biscayne Boulevard Miami, FL 33131-2399 · 305-379-6523

Bruce Stone · Holland & Knight · 1200 Brickell Avenue · P.O. Box 015441 · Miami, FL 33101 · 305-374-8500

Robert A. White · Mershon, Sawyer, Johnston, Dunwody & Cole · Southeast Financial Center, Suite 4500 · 200 South Biscayne Boulevard · Miami, FL 33131-2387 · 305-358-5100

Samuel S. Smith* · (Estate Administration, Estate Litigation) · Ruden, Barnett, McClosky, Smith, Schuster & Russell · Barnett Bank Tower, Suite 1900 · 701 Brickell Avenue · Miami Beach, FL 33131 · 305-789-2700

Robert D. W. Landon II · Mershon, Sawyer, Johnston, Dunwody & Cole · 5551 Ridgeway Drive, Suite 501 · Naples, FL 33963 · 813-598-1055

Charles E. Early · Early & Early · 1390 Main Street, Suite 920 · Sarasota, FL 34236 · 813-366-2707

William S. Belcher · Belcher & Fleece · Courthouse Square, Suite 301 · 600 First Avenue North · P.O. Box 330 · St. Petersburg, FL 33731 · 813-822-3941

Leslie J. Barnett · Barnett, Bolt & Kirkwood · 601 Bayshore Place, Suite 700 · P.O. Box 3287 · Tampa, FL 33601 · 813-253-2020

John Arthur Jones · Holland & Knight · 400 North Ashley Drive, Suite 2300 · P.O. Box 1288 · Tampa, FL 33601-1288 · 813-227-8500

Edward F. Koren · Holland & Knight · 400 North Ashley Drive, Suite 2300 · P.O. Box 1288 · Tampa, FL 33601-1288 · 813-227-8500

Roger O. Isphording · (Estate Planning, Estate Administration) · Isphording, Korp, Payne, Muirhead, White & Horlick · 333 South Tamiami Trail · P.O Box 1614 · Venice, FL 33595 · 813-488-7751

James G. Pressly, Jr. · (Estate Planning, Estate Administration, Estate Litigation) · Pressly & Pressly · Esperante Building, Suite 910 · 222 Lakeview Avenue West Palm Beach, FL 33401-6112 · 407-659-4040

A. Obie Stewart · Gunster, Yoakley & Stewart · Phillips Point · 777 South Flagler Drive, Suite 500 East · West Palm Beach, FL 33401-6194 · 407-655-1980

GEORGIA

BANKRUPTCY LAW

R. Neal Batson · Alston & Bird · One Atlantic Center · 1201 West Peachtree Street · Atlanta, GA 30309-3424 · 404-881-7267

C. David Butler* · (Business Reorganization, Creditors' Rights, Debtors' Rights, Bankruptcy Litigation) · Alston & Bird · One Atlantic Center · 1201 West Peachtree Street · Atlanta, GA 30309-3424 · 404-881-7158

Charles E. Campbell* · (Business Reorganization, Creditors' Rights, Debtors' Rights, Bankruptcy Litigation) · Hicks, Maloof & Campbell · Marquis Two Tower, Suite 2200 · 285 Peachtree Center Avenue, NE · Atlanta, GA 30303-1234 404-588-1100

Christopher L. Carson · Jones, Day, Reavis & Pogue · First Atlanta Tower, 33rd Floor · Atlanta, GA 30383-3101 · 404-521-3939

Ezra H. Cohen · Troutman, Sanders, Lockerman & Ashmore · Candler Building, Suite 1400 · 127 Peachtree Street, NE · Atlanta, GA 30303-1810 · 404-658-8000

C. Edward Dobbs* · (Creditors' Rights) · Parker, Hudson, Rainer & Dobbs · 1200 Carnegie Building · 133 Carnegie Way · Atlanta, GA 30303 · 404-523-5300

David G. Epstein · King & Spalding · 2500 Trust Company Tower · Atlanta, GA 30303 · 404-572-4600

James C. Frenzel · Smith, Gambrell & Russell · 2400 First Atlanta Tower · Two Peachtree Street, NW · Atlanta, GA 30383-2501 · 404-656-1800

Robert E. Hicks · Hicks, Maloof & Campbell · Marquis Two Tower, Suite 2200 285 Peachtree Center Avenue, NE · Atlanta, GA 30303-1234 · 404-588-1100

Alfred S. Lurey · (Business Reorganization) · Kilpatrick & Cody · 100 Galleria Parkway, Suite 1750 · Atlanta, GA 30339 · 404-956-2600

Joel B. Piassick · Kilpatrick & Cody · The Equitable Building, Suite 3100 · 100 Peachtree Street · Atlanta, GA 30043 · 404-572-6500

Jerome L. Kaplan · Arnall Golden & Gregory · 582 Walnut Street · Macon, GA 30201 · 912-745-3344

BUSINESS LITIGATION

Byron R. Attridge · King & Spalding · 2500 Trust Company Tower · Atlanta, GA 30303 · 404-572-4600

Griffin B. Bell · King & Spalding · 2500 Trust Company Tower · Atlanta, GA 30303 · 404-572-4600

Emmet J. Bondurant II · Bondurant, Mixson & Elmore · 3900 IBM Tower · 1201 West Peachtree Street, NW · Atlanta, GA 30309 · 404-881-4100

Nickolas P. Chilivis · Chilivis & Grindler · 3127 Maple Drive, NE · Atlanta, GA 30305 · 404-233-4171

John J. Dalton · Troutman, Sanders, Lockerman & Ashmore · Candler Building, Suite 1400 · 127 Peachtree Street, NE · Atlanta, GA 30303-1810 · 404-658-8000

J. D. Fleming, Jr.* · Sutherland, Asbill & Brennan · 999 Peachtree Street, NE · Atlanta, GA 30309-3996 · 404-853-8062

Robert E. Hicks · (Bankruptcy, Workouts) · Hicks, Maloof & Campbell · Marquis Two Tower, Suite 2200 · 285 Peachtree Center Avenue, NE · Atlanta, GA 30303-1234 · 404-588-1100

G. Conley Ingram* · (Appellate, Commercial, Zoning, Eminent Domain, State Tax) · Alston & Bird · 100 Galleria Parkway, Suite 1200 · Atlanta, GA 30339-3195 404-881-7649

G. Conley Ingram* · Alston & Bird · 100 Galleria Parkway, Suite 1200 · Atlanta, GA 30339-3195 · 404-881-7649

Frank C. Jones* · King & Spalding · 2500 Trust Company Tower · Atlanta, GA 30303 · 404-572-4600

Dorothy Y. Kirkley · Paul, Hastings, Janofsky & Walker · Georgia Pacific Center, 42nd Floor · 133 Peachtree Street, NE · Atlanta, GA 30303 · 404-527-8211

Frank Love, Jr.* · (Antitrust, Appellate, Commercial, Patent Litigation) · Powell, Goldstein, Frazer & Murphy · 191 Peachtree Tower, 16th Floor · Atlanta, GA 30303 · 404-572-6600

William H. Major* · Heyman and Sizemore · 1940 The Equitable Building · 100 Peachtree Street, NE · Atlanta, GA 30303 · 404-521-2268

John T. Marshall* · (Banking, Commercial, Securities) · Powell, Goldstein, Frazer & Murphy · 191 Peachtree Tower, 16th Floor · Atlanta, GA 30303 · 404-572-6600

Earle B. May, Jr. · Alston & Bird · 100 Galleria Parkway, Suite 1200 · Atlanta, GA 30339-3195 · 404-881-7000

Eugene G. Partain* · Powell, Goldstein, Frazer & Murphy · 191 Peachtree Tower, 16th Floor · Atlanta, GA 30303 · 404-572-6600

Ronald L. Reid · Alston & Bird · One Atlantic Center · 1201 West Peachtree Street · Atlanta, GA 30339-3195 · 404-881-7246

C. B. Rogers · Rogers & Hardin · Peachtree Center, 2700 Cain Tower · 229 Peachtree Street, NE · Atlanta, GA 30303 · 404-522-4700

Sidney O. Smith, Jr.* · Alston & Bird · One Atlantic Center · 1201 West Peachtree Street · Atlanta, GA 30309-3424 · 404-881-7173

Trammell E. Vickery · Troutman, Sanders, Lockerman & Ashmore · Candler Building, Suite 1400 · 127 Peachtree Street, NE · Atlanta, GA 30303-1810 · 404-658-8000

Wyck A. Knox, Jr.* · Knox & Zacks · First Union Bank Building, Suite 1400 · 699 Broad Street · P.O. Box 2043 · Augusta, GA 30903 · 404-724-2622

David H. Tisinger* · (Commercial) · Tisinger, Tisinger, Vance & Greer · 100 Wagon Yard Plaza · P.O. Box 2069 · Carrollton, GA 30117 · 404-834-4467

W. G. Scrantom, Jr. · Page, Scrantom, Harris & Chapman · 1043 Third Avenue P.O. Box 1199 · Columbus, GA 31994 · 404-324-0251

E. Freeman Leverett · Heard, Leverett & Phelps · 25 Thomas Street · P.O. Drawer 399 · Elberton, GA 30635 · 404-283-2651

H. Jerome Strickland · Jones, Cork & Miller · Trust Company Bank Building, Suite 500 · 606 Cherry Street · P.O. Box 6437 · Macon, GA 31208-6437 · 912-745-2821

Walter C. Hartridge · Bouhan, Williams & Levy · The Armstrong House · 447 Bull Street · P.O. Box 2139 · Savannah, GA 31498 · 912-236-2491

Malcolm R. Maclean · Hunter, Maclean, Exley & Dunn · 200 East St. Julian Street · P.O. Box 9848 · Savannah, GA 31412-0048 · 912-236-0261

John B. Miller · (Banking, RICO) · Miller, Simpson & Tatum · Trust Company Bank Building, Suite 400 · 33 Bull Street · P.O. Box 1567 · Savannah, GA 31498 912-233-5722

CORPORATE LAW

H. H. Perry, Jr. · Perry, Walters & Lippitt · 409 North Jackson Street · P.O. Box 469 · Albany, GA 31703-8401 · 912-432-7438

Miles J. Alexander · Kilpatrick & Cody · The Equitable Building, Suite 3100 · 100 Peachtree Street · Atlanta, GA 30043 · 404-572-6500

David S. Baker · (Banking-RTC/FDIC, Corporate Finance, Financial Institutions-RTC/FDIC, Mergers & Acquisitions) · Powell, Goldstein, Frazer & Murphy · 191 Peachtree Tower, 16th Floor · Atlanta, GA 30303 · 404-572-6600

George L. Cohen · Sutherland, Asbill & Brennan · 999 Peachtree Street, NE · Atlanta, GA 30309-3996 · 404-853-8000

F. Dean Copeland · (Banking, Financial Institutions, Mergers & Acquisitions, Securities) · Alston & Bird · One Atlantic Center · 1201 West Peachtree Street · Atlanta, GA 30309-3424 · 404-881-7443

Tench C. Coxe · Troutman, Sanders, Lockerman & Ashmore · Candler Building, Suite 1400 · 127 Peachtree Street, NE · Atlanta, GA 30303-1810 · 404-658-8000

F. T. Davis, Jr. · Long, Aldridge & Norman · 1500 Marquis Two Tower, NW · 285 Peachtree Center Avenue · Atlanta, GA 30303 · 404-527-4000

William E. Eason, Jr. · Paul, Hasting, Janofsky & Walker · Georgia Pacific Center, 42nd Floor · 133 Peachtree Street, NE · Atlanta, GA 30303 · 404-527-7894

Elliott Goldstein · Powell, Goldstein, Frazer & Murphy · 191 Peachtree Tower, 16th Floor · Atlanta, GA 30303 · 404-572-6600

Bradley Hale · King & Spalding · 2500 Trust Company Tower · Atlanta, GA 30303 · 404-572-4600

Edward J. Hardin · Rogers & Hardin · Peachtree Center, 2700 Cain Tower · 229 Peachtree Street, NE · Atlanta, GA 30303 · 404-522-4700

Edward J. Hawie · King & Spalding · 2500 Trust Company Tower · Atlanta, GA 30303 · 404-572-4600

John D. Hopkins · King & Spalding · 2500 Trust Company Tower · Atlanta, GA 30303 · 404-572-4600

Harry C. Howard · King & Spalding · 2500 Trust Company Tower · Atlanta, GA 30303 · 404-572-4600

Paul L. Hudson, Jr. · Parker, Hudson, Rainer & Dobbs · 1200 Carnegie Building 133 Carnegie Way · Atlanta, GA 30303 · 404-523-5300

William S. Jacobs · Trotter, Smith & Jacobs · 400 Colony Square, Suite 2200 · 1201 Peachtree Street · Atlanta, GA 30361 · 404-881-0500

McChesney Hill Jeffries · Jones, Day, Reavis & Pogue · 3300 First Atlanta Tower Atlanta, GA 30383-3101 · 404-581-8000

Clay C. Long · Long, Aldridge & Norman · 1500 Marquis Two Tower · 285 Peachtree Center Avenue, NE · Atlanta, GA 30303-1257 · 404-527-4000

Sidney J. Nurkin · Powell, Goldstein, Frazer & Murphy · 191 Peachtree Tower, 16th Floor · Atlanta, GA 30303 · 404-572-6600

Barry Phillips · Kilpatrick & Cody · The Equitable Building, Suite 3100 · 100 Peachtree Street · Atlanta, GA 30043 · 404-572-6500

Robert M. Royalty · Sutherland, Asbill & Brennan · 999 Peachtree Street, NE · Atlanta, GA 30309-3996 · 404-853-8000

Harold L. Russell* · (Financial Institutions) · Smith, Gambrell & Russell · 2400 First Atlanta Tower · Two Peachtree Street, NW · Atlanta, GA 30383-2501 · 404-656-1800

James M. Sibley · King & Spalding · 2500 Trust Company Tower · Atlanta, GA 30303 · 404-572-4600

Nathaniel G. Slaughter III · Slaughter & Virgin · 400 Colony Square, Suite 1110 1201 Peachtree Street, NE · Atlanta, GA 30361 · 404-897-1110

James L. Smith III · Trotter, Smith & Jacobs · 400 Colony Square, Suite 2200 · 1201 Peachtree Street · Atlanta, GA 30361 · 404-881-0500

Michael H. Trotter · Trotter, Smith & Jacobs · 400 Colony Square, Suite 2200 · 1201 Peachtree Street · Atlanta, GA 30361 · 404-881-0500

L. Neil Williams, Jr. · Alston & Bird · One Atlantic Center · 1201 West Peachtree Street · Atlanta, GA 30309-3424 · 404-881-7000

James H. Wilson, Jr. · Sutherland, Asbill & Brennan · 999 Peachtree Street, NE Atlanta, GA 30309-3996 · 404-853-8158

Forrest L. Champion, Jr. · Champion & Champion · 1030 Second Avenue · Columbus, GA 31901 · 404-324-4477

Albert W. Stubbs · Hatcher, Stubbs, Land, Hollis & Rothschild · 500 The Corporate Center · P.O. Box 2707 · Columbus, GA 31993-5699 · 404-324-0201

John D. Comer · Sell & Melton · 1414 Charter Medical Building · P.O. Box 229 Macon, GA 31297-2899 · 912-746-8521

Edward J. Harrell · (Banking, Financial Institutions, Mergers & Acquisitions, Securities) · Martin, Snow, Grant & Napier · 240 Third Street · P.O. Box 1606 · Macon, GA 31202-1606 · 912-743-7051

Albert P. Reichert · Anderson, Walker & Reichert · Trust Company Bank Building, Suite 404 · Macon, GA 31298-0399 · 912-743-8651

G. Boone Smith III · Smith & Hawkins · 230 Third Avenue · P.O. Box 6495 · Macon, GA 31208 · 912-743-4436

Thomas S. Gray, Jr. · Oliver Maner & Gray · 218 West State Street · P.O. Box 10186 · Savannah, GA 31412 · 912-236-3311

CRIMINAL DEFENSE

Edward D. Tolley* · Cook, Noell, Tolley & Aldridge · 304 East Washington Street · P.O. Box 1927 · Athens, GA 30603 · 404-549-6111

Nickolas P. Chilivis · Chilivis & Grindler · 3127 Maple Drive, NE · Atlanta, GA 30305 · 404-233-4171

Jerome J. Froelich, Jr. · McKenney & Froelich · 1349 West Peachtree Street, Suite 1680 · Atlanta, GA 30309-2920 · 404-881-1111

Edward T. M. Garland* · Garland & Samuel · 3151 Maple Drive · Atlanta, GA 30305 · 404-262-2225

John R. Martin* · (Violent Crimes, Non-Violent Crimes, Federal Court, State Court) · Martin Brothers · The Grant Building, Suite 500 · 44 Broad Street · Atlanta, GA 30303 · 404-522-0400

Donald F. Samuel · Garland & Samuel · 3151 Maple Drive · Atlanta, GA 30305 404-262-2225

Frank K. Martin · (Federal Court, State Court, Environmental Crimes) · The Joseph House · 828 Broadway · P.O. Box 1436 · Columbus, GA 31902-1436 · 404-324-7371

John Wright Jones · Jones & Boykin & Associates · 701 Abercorn Street · Savannah, GA 31401 · 912-236-6161

William T. Moore, Jr.* · (Non-Violent Crimes, Federal Court, State Court, Environmental Crimes) · Oliver Maner & Gray · 218 West State Street · P.O. Box 10186 · Savannah, GA 31412 · 912-236-3311

Bobby Lee Cook · Cook & Palmour · 128 South Commerce Street · P.O. Box 370 Summerville, GA 30747 · 404-857-3421

J. Converse Bright · Blackburn, Bright, Edwards & Tumison · 1008 North Patterson Street · P.O. Box 579 · Valdosta, GA 31603-0579 · 912-247-0800

ENTERTAINMENT LAW

Joel A. Katz · Katz & Cherry · 3423 Piedmont Road, NE, Suite 200 · Atlanta, GA 30305 · 404-237-7700

FAMILY LAW

Edward E. Bates, Jr. · Warner, Mayoue & Bates · 100 Galleria Parkway, NW, Suite 1300 · Atlanta, GA 30339 · 404-951-2700

A. Paul Cadenhead* · (Divorce, Marital Settlement Agreements, Mediation) · Hurt, Richardson, Garner, Todd & Cadenhead · First Union Tower, Suite 1400 999 Peachtree Street, NE · Atlanta, GA 30309-3999 · 404-870-6000

Harry L. Cashin, Jr. · Cashin & Morton · Two Midtown Plaza, Suite 1900 · 1360 Peachtree Street, NE · Atlanta, GA 30309 · 404-870-1500

Baxter L. Davis · Davis, Matthews & Quigley · Lenox Towers II, 14th Floor · 3400 Peachtree Road, NE · Atlanta, GA 30326 · 404-261-3900

Harry P. Hall, Jr.* · Westmoreland & Hall · 10 Piedmont Center, Suite 500 · 3495 Piedmont Road, NE · Atlanta, GA 30305 · 404-365-9090

Barry B. McGough* · (Child Custody, Divorce, Marital Settlement Agreements, Equitable Division) · Frankel, Hardwick, Tanenbaum & Fink · 359 East Paces Ferry Road, Suite 400 · Atlanta, GA 30305 · 404-266-2930

C. Wilbur Warner, Jr.* · Warner, Mayoue & Ryals · 100 Galleria Parkway, NW, Suite 1300 · Atlanta, GA 30339-3183 · 404-951-2700

Joseph T. Tuggle, Jr. · McCamy Law Firm · 411 West Crawford Street · P.O. Box 1105 · Dalton, GA 30722-1105 · 404-278-4499

M. T. Simmons, Jr. · Simmons, Warren & Szczecko · First National Bank Building, Suite 850 · 315 West Ponce DeLeon Street · Decatur, GA 30030 · 404-378-1711

Kice H. Stone* · Stone, Christian & Raymond · Great Southern Federal Building, Suite 230 · 484 Mulberry Street · P.O. Box 107 · Macon, GA 31202-0107 · 912-741-0060

Lawrence B. Custer · Custer & Hill · 241 Washington Avenue · P.O. Box 1224 Marietta, GA 30061 · 404-429-8300

Roger J. Dodd · Dodd & Turner · 613 North Patterson Street · P.O. Box 1066 · Valdosta, GA 31603-1066 · 912-242-4470

FIRST AMENDMENT LAW

Terrence B. Adamson · Dow, Lohnes & Albertson · One Ravinia Drive, Suite 1300 · Atlanta, GA 30346 · 404-395-8846

Joseph R. Bankoff · King & Spalding · 2500 Trust Company Tower · Atlanta, GA 30303 · 404-572-4600

Albert G. Norman, Jr. · Long, Aldridge & Norman · 1500 Marquis Two Tower, NW · 285 Peachtree Center Avenue · Atlanta, GA 30303 · 404-527-4000

James C. Rawls · Powell, Goldstein, Frazer & Murphy · 191 Peachtree Tower, 16th Floor · Atlanta, GA 30303 · 404-572-6600

David E. Hudson · Hull, Towill, Norman & Barrett · Trust Company Bank Building, Seventh Floor · P.O. Box 1564 · Augusta, GA 30913 · 404-722-4481

HEALTH CARE LAW

Larry V. McLeod · Erwin, Epting, Gibson & McLeod · Citizens & Southern National Bank Building, Eighth Floor · P.O. Box 8108 · Athens, GA 30603 · 404-549-9400

Robert W. Miller · King & Spalding · 2500 Trust Company Tower · Atlanta, GA 30303 · 404-572-4600

John H. Parker, Jr. · Parker, Hudson, Rainer & Dobbs · 1200 Carnegie Building 133 Carnegie Way · Atlanta, GA 30303 · 404-523-5300

Glen A. Reed · King & Spalding · 2500 Trust Company Tower · Atlanta, GA 30303 · 404-572-4600

Kim H. Roeder · Powell, Goldstein, Frazer & Murphy · 191 Peachtree Tower, 16th Floor · Atlanta, GA 30303 · 404-572-6600

Jack S. Schroder, Jr. · Alston & Bird · 100 Galleria Parkway, Suite 1200 · Atlanta, GA 30339-3195 · 404-881-7000

Wyck A. Knox, Jr.* · Knox & Zacks · First Union Bank Building, Suite 1400 · 699 Broad Street · P.O. Box 2043 · Augusta, GA 30903 · 404-724-2622

David M. Zacks, Jr. · Knox & Zacks · First Union Bank Building, Suite 1400 · 699 Broad Street · P.O. Box 2043 · Augusta, GA 30903 · 404-724-2622

John D. Comer · Sell & Melton · 1414 Charter Medical Building · P.O. Box 229 Macon, GA 31297-2899 · 912-746-8521

IMMIGRATION LAW

Robert E. Banta · Kilpatrick & Cody · The Equitable Building, Suite 3100 · 100 Peachtree Street · Atlanta, GA 30043 · 404-572-6500

Daryl R. Buffenstein · Paul, Hastings, Janofsky & Walker · Georgia Pacific Center, 42nd Floor · 133 Peachtree Street, NE · Atlanta, GA 30303 · 404-588-9900

Myron N. Kramer · Brent & Kramer · One Buckhead Plaza, Suite 875 · 3060 Peachtree Road, NW · Atlanta, GA 30305 · 404-364-2020

Dale M. Schwartz · Troutman, Sanders, Lockerman & Ashmore · Candler Building, Suite 1400 · 127 Peachtree Street, NE · Atlanta, GA 30303-1810 · 404-658-8097

INTELLECTUAL PROPERTY LAW

Miles J. Alexander · Kilpatrick & Cody · The Equitable Building, Suite 3100 · 100 Peachtree Street · Atlanta, GA 30043 · 404-572-6500

Anthony B. Askew · Jones, Askew & Lunsford · 230 Peachtree Street, Suite 2000 · Atlanta, GA 30303 · 404-688-7500

Todd Deveau, Jr. · Hurt, Richardson, Garner, Todd & Cadenhead · First Union Tower, Suite 1400 · 999 Peachtree Street, NE · Atlanta, GA 30309-3999 · 404-870-6461

Martin J. Elgison · Alston & Bird · One Atlantic Center · 1201 West Peachtree Street · Atlanta, GA 30309-3424 · 404-881-7000

William H. Needle · Needle & Rosenberg · 133 Carnegie Way, NW, Suite 400 · Atlanta, GA 30303 · 404-688-0770

John S. Pratt · Kilpatrick & Cody · The Equitable Building, Suite 3100 · 100 Peachtree Street · Atlanta, GA 30043 · 404-572-6500

Jerre B. Swann · (Copyright, Litigation) · Kilpatrick & Cody · The Equitable Building, Suite 3100 · 100 Peachtree Street · Atlanta, GA 30303 · 404-572-6540

Virginia S. Taylor · Kilpatrick & Cody · The Equitable Building, Suite 3100 · 100 Peachtree Street · Atlanta, GA 30043 · 404-572-6514

LABOR AND EMPLOYMENT LAW

Duane C. Aldrich* · (Management) · Kilpatrick & Cody · The Equitable Building, Suite 3100 · 100 Peachtree Street · Atlanta, GA 30043 · 404-572-6500

R. Lawrence Ashe, Jr. · (Employment Discrimination Defense) · Paul, Hastings, Janofsky & Walker · Georgia Pacific Center, 42nd Floor · 133 Peachtree Street, NE · Atlanta, GA 30303 · 404-588-9900

Lovic A. Brooks, Jr. · (Management) · Constangy, Brooks & Smith · The 230 Building, Suite 2400 · 230 Peachtree Street, NW · Atlanta, GA 30303-1537 · 404-525-8622

Thomas H. Christopher · (Management) · Kilpatrick & Cody · The Equitable Building, Suite 3100 · 100 Peachtree Street · Atlanta, GA 30043 · 404-572-6500

Homer L. Deakins* · (Management) · Ogletree, Deakins, Nash, Smoak & Stewart · IBM Tower, Suite 3800 · 1201 West Peachtree Street · Atlanta, GA 30309 · 404-881-1300

James D. Fagan · (Labor) · Stanford, Fagan & Giolito · 1401 Peachtree Street, NE, Suite 238 · Atlanta, GA 30309 · 404-897-1000

C. Lash Harrison · (Management) · Ford & Harrison · 600 Peachtree at the Circle Building · 1275 Peachtree Street, NE · Atlanta, GA 30309 · 404-888-3800

Harris Jacobs* · (Labor) · Jacobs and Langford · The Equitable Building, Suite 1000 · 100 Peachtree Street, NW · Atlanta, GA 30303 · 404-522-4280

Mary Ann B. Oakley* · (Individuals) · 133 Carnegie Way, Suite 508 · Atlanta, GA 30303 · 404-223-5250

William B. Paul · (Management) · Clark, Paul, Hoover & Mallard · One Midtown Plaza, Suite 900 · 1360 Peachtree Street, NE · Atlanta, GA 30309-3214 · 404-874-7500

Frank Barry Shuster* · (Labor, Individuals) · Blackburn, Shuster, King & King 6735 Peachtree Industrial Boulevard, Suite 235 · Atlanta, GA 30360 · 404-441-1526

James W. Wimberly, Jr. · (Management) · Wimberly & Lawson · Lenox Towers, Suite 1750 · 3400 Peachtree Road, NE · Atlanta, GA 30326 · 404-365-0900

NATURAL RESOURCES AND ENVIRONMENTAL LAW

David S. Baker · (Water, Air, Solid Waste, Hazardous Waste) · Powell, Goldstein, Frazer & Murphy · 191 Peachtree Tower, 16th Floor · Atlanta, GA 30303 · 404-572-6600

J. D. Fleming, Jr.* · Sutherland, Asbill & Brennan · 999 Peachtree Street, NE · Atlanta, GA 30309-3996 · 404-853-8062

James S. Stokes · Alston & Bird · One Atlantic Center · 1201 West Peachtree Street · Atlanta, GA 30309-3424 · 404-881-7294

PERSONAL INJURY LITIGATION

Gary B. Blasingame · (Defendants) · Blasingame, Burch, Garrard & Bryant · 440 College Avenue North · P.O. Box 832 · Athens, GA 30603 · 404-354-4000

William Q. Bird · (Plaintiffs) · Bird & Associates · 14 Seventeenth Street, Suite Five · Atlanta, GA 30309 · 404-873-4696

Thomas S. Carlock · (Defendants) · Webb, Carlock, Copeland, Semler & Stair · 2302 Peachtree Street, NW, Suite 2500 · P.O. Box 56770 · Atlanta, GA 30343 · 404-522-8220

Nickolas P. Chilivis · Chilivis & Grindler · 3127 Maple Drive, NE · Atlanta, GA 30305 · 404-233-4171

Foy R. Devine* · (Plaintiffs, Products Liability) · 2931 Piedmont Road, NE · Atlanta, GA 30305 · 404-233-4141

Joe C. Freeman, Jr. · Freeman & Hawkins · 2800 First Atlanta Tower · Atlanta, GA 30383 · 404-522-0856

George W. Hart · (Defendants) · Hart & McIntyre · 1230 Peachtree Street, NE, Suite 3775 · Atlanta, GA 30309 · 404-876-3775

Paul M. Hawkins · (Plaintiffs) · Freeman & Hawkins · 2800 First Atlanta Tower Atlanta, GA 30383 · 404-522-0856

William C. Lanham · (Plaintiffs) · Johnson & Ward · 2100 The Equitable Building 100 Peachtree Street, NE · Atlanta, GA 30303 · 404-524-5626

Daryll Love · Love and Willingham · The Candler Building, Suite 500 · 127 Peachtree Street · Atlanta, GA 30303 · 404-581-0101

Frank Love, Jr.* · Powell, Goldstein, Frazer & Murphy · 191 Peachtree Tower, 16th Floor · Atlanta, GA 30303 · 404-572-6600

William H. Major* · (Plaintiffs, Defendants) · Heyman and Sizemore · 1940 The Equitable Building · 100 Peachtree Street, NE · Atlanta, GA 30303 · 404-521-2268

Thomas William Malone* · (Plaintiffs, Medical Malpractice, Products Liability, Automobile Collision) · 2957 Clairmont Road, Suite 250 · P.O. Box 49406 · Atlanta, GA 30359 · 404-325-8855

John T. Marshall* · (Plaintiffs, Products Liability, Professional Malpractice) · Powell, Goldstein, Frazer & Murphy · 191 Peachtree Tower, 16th Floor · Atlanta, GA 30303 · 404-572-6600

Edgar A. Neely, Jr. · (Defendants) · Neely & Player · Marquis Two, Suite 2600 285 Peachtree Center Avenue · Atlanta, GA 30303-1270 · 404-681-2600

Albert H. Parnell · (Defendants) · Freeman & Hawkins · 2800 First Atlanta Tower · Atlanta, GA 30383 · 404-522-0856

Andrew M. Scherffius · (Plaintiffs) · 3166 Mathieson Drive · P.O. Box 7890 · Atlanta, GA 30357 · 404-261-3562

Ben L. Weinberg, Jr.* · (Defendants) · Long, Weinberg, Ansley and Wheeler · 999 Peachtree Street, NE, Suite 2700 · Atlanta, GA 30309 · 404-876-2700

Sidney F. Wheeler* · (Defendants) · Long, Weinberg, Ansley and Wheeler · 999 Peachtree Street, NE, Suite 2700 · Atlanta, GA 30309 · 404-876-2700

Thomas R. Burnside, Jr.* · (Plaintiffs) · Burnside, Wall & Daniel · 454 Greene Street · P.O. Box 2125 · Augusta, GA 30903 · 404-722-0768

Patrick J. Rice · Hull, Towill, Norman & Barrett · Trust Company Bank Building, Seventh Floor · P.O. Box 1564 · Augusta, GA 30913 · 404-722-4481

Wallace E. Harrell · (Defendants) · Gilbert, Harrell, Skelton, Gilbert, Sumerford & Martin · First Federal Plaza, Suite 200 · Brunswick, GA 31521 · 912-265-6700

David H. Tisinger* · (Defendants, Medical Malpractice) · Tisinger, Tisinger, Vance & Greer · 100 Wagon Yard Plaza · P.O. Box 2069 · Carrollton, GA 30117 · 404-834-4467

James E. Butler, Jr.* · (Plaintiffs, Medical Malpractice, Products Liability, Automobile Collision) · Butler, Wooten, Overby & Cheeley · 1500 Second Avenue P.O. Box 2766 · Columbus, GA 31902 · 404-322-1990

John W. Denney · Kelley, Denney, Pease & Allison · 318 Eleventh Street · P.O. Box 2648 · Columbus, GA 31994-0499 · 404-324-3711

C. Neal Pope · (Plaintiffs) · Pope, McGlamry, Kilpatrick & Morrison · 720 Broadway · P.O. Box 2128 · Columbus, GA 31902-2128 · 404-324-0050

W. G. Scrantom, Jr. · Page, Scrantom, Harris & Chapman · 1043 Third Avenue P.O. Box 1199 · Columbus, GA 31994 · 404-324-0251

Charles H. Hyatt · (Plaintiffs) · 201 Trust Building · 545 North McDonough Street · Decatur, GA 30030 · 404-378-3635

Charles M. Jones* · (Plaintiffs, Medical Malpractice, Products Liability, Automobile Collision, Airplane Collision, Appellate) · Jones, Osteen, Jones & Arnold 206 East Court Street · P.O. Box 800 · Hinesville, GA 31313-0800 · 912-876-0111

Manley F. Brown · (Plaintiffs, Products Liability) · O'Neal, Brown & Sizemore · 1001 Fulton Federal Building · Macon, GA 31201 · 912-742-8981

W. Carl Reynolds · (Plaintiffs) · Reynolds & McArthur · 850 Walnut Street · P.O. Box 6897 · Macon, GA 31208-6897 · 912-741-6000

Cubbedge Snow, Jr.* · (Defendants, Products Liability, Automobile Collision, Insurance Coverage) · Martin, Snow, Grant & Napier · 240 Third Street · P.O. Box 1606 · Macon, GA 31202-1606 · 912-743-7051

Robert M. Brinson · (Defendants) · Brinson, Askew & Berry · Omberg House · 615 West First Street · P.O. Box 5513 · Rome, GA 30161 · 404-291-8853

John Wright Jones · 701 Abercorn Street · Savannah, GA 31401 · 912-236-6161

Frank W. Seiler* · (Plaintiffs, Defendants, Medical Malpractice, Products Liability) · Bouhan, Williams & Levy · The Armstrong House · 447 Bull Street · P.O. Box 2139 · Savannah, GA 31498 · 912-236-2491

PUBLIC UTILITY LAW

Michael S. Bradley · Hicks, Maloof & Campbell · Marquis Two Tower, Suite 2200 · 285 Peachtree Center Avenue, NE · Atlanta, GA 30303-1234 · 404-588-1100

Charles E. Campbell · Hicks, Maloof & Campbell · Marquis Two Tower, Suite 2200 · 285 Peachtree Center Avenue, NE · Atlanta, GA 30303-1234 · 404-588-1100

Gordon D. Giffin · Long, Aldridge & Norman · 1500 Marquis Two Tower · 285 Peachtree Center Avenue, NE · Atlanta, GA 30303-1257 · 404-527-4000

Christopher C. Hagy · Sutherland, Asbill & Brennan · 999 Peachtree Street, NE, 21st Floor · Atlanta, GA 30309-3996 · 404-853-8000

Douglas L. Miller · Troutman, Sanders, Lockerman & Ashmore · Candler Building, Suite 1400 · 127 Peachtree Street, NE · Atlanta, GA 30303-1810 · 404-658-8000

Albert G. Norman, Jr. · Long, Aldridge & Norman · 1500 Marquis Two Tower 285 Peachtree Center Avenue, NE · Atlanta, GA 30303-1257 · 404-527-4000

REAL ESTATE LAW

John G. Aldridge · Long, Aldridge & Norman · Two Concourse Parkway, Suite 750 · Atlanta, GA 30328-5347 · 404-527-8510

L. Travis Brannon, Jr. · Jones, Day, Reavis & Pogue · 3300 First Atlanta Tower Atlanta, GA 30383-3101 · 404-581-8000

David Lee Coker · King & Spalding · 2500 Trust Company Tower · Atlanta, GA 30303 · 404-572-4600

A. James Elliott · Alston & Bird · 100 Galleria Parkway, Suite 1200 · Atlanta, GA 30339-3195 · 404-881-7749

Robert G. Holt · Holt, Ney, Zatcoff & Wasserman · 100 Galleria Parkway, Suite 600 · Atlanta, GA 30339 · 404-956-9600

James H. Keaten · Powell, Goldstein, Frazer & Murphy · 191 Peachtree Tower, 16th Floor · Atlanta, GA 30303 · 404-572-6600

Clay C. Long · Long, Aldridge & Norman · 1500 Marquis Two Tower · 285 Peachtree Center Avenue, NE · Atlanta, GA 30303-1257 · 404-527-4000

Julian D. Nealey · Paul, Hastings, Janofsky & Walker · Georgia Pacific Center, 42nd Floor · 133 Peachtree Street, NE · Atlanta, GA 30303 · 404-588-9900

James M. Ney · (Zoning, Land Use, Commercial Transactions) · Holt, Ney, Zatcoff & Wasserman · 100 Galleria Parkway, Suite 600 · Atlanta, GA 30339 · 404-956-9600

William R. Patterson · Sutherland, Asbill & Brennan · 999 Peachtree Street, NE Atlanta, GA 30309-3996 · 404-853-8000

Mason W. Stephenson · King & Spalding · 2500 Trust Company Tower · Atlanta, GA 30303 · 404-572-4600

William F. Stevens · Long, Aldridge & Norman · Two Concourse Parkway, Suite 750 · Atlanta, GA 30328-5347 · 404-527-8510

W. Joseph Thompson · (Commercial Transactions) · Powell, Goldstein, Frazer & Murphy · 191 Peachtree Tower, 16th Floor · Atlanta, GA 30303 · 404-572-6600

James H. Wildman · King & Spalding · 2500 Trust Company Tower · Atlanta, GA 30303 · 404-572-4600

Sanford H. Zatcoff · Holt, Ney, Zatcoff & Wasserman · 100 Galleria Parkway, Suite 600 · Atlanta, GA 30339 · 404-956-9600

V. J. Adams · Adams & Adams · 155 College Street, Suite A · Macon, GA 31201 912-745-4252

William W. Shearouse, Jr. · Weiner, Shearouse, Weitz, Greenberg & Shawe · 14 East State Street · P.O. Box 10105 · Savannah, GA 31412-0305 · 912-233-2251

Charles L. Sparkman · Oliver Maner & Gray · 218 West State Street · P.O. Box 10186 · Savannah, GA 31412 · 912-236-3311

TAX AND EMPLOYEE BENEFITS LAW

Harold E. Abrams · (Corporate & Partnership Transactions) · Kilpatrick & Cody 100 Galleria Parkway, Suite 1750 · Atlanta, GA 30339 · 404-956-2600

Herschel M. Bloom · King & Spalding · 2500 Trust Company Tower · Atlanta, GA 30303 · 404-572-4600

N. Jerold Cohen* · (Corporate & Partnership Transactions, State Tax, Tax Disputes, International Tax) · Sutherland, Asbill & Brennan · 999 Peachtree Street, NE · Atlanta, GA 30309-3996 · 404-853-8000

Philip C. Cook · (State Tax, Employee Benefits, Tax Disputes) · Alston & Bird One Atlantic Center · 1201 West Peachtree Street · Atlanta, GA 30309-3424 · 404-881-7491

Frazer Durrett, Jr. · (Corporate & Partnership Transactions) · Alston & Bird · 100 Galleria Parkway, Suite 1200 · Atlanta, GA 30339-3195 · 404-881-7664

Michael J. Egan · Sutherland, Asbill & Brennan · 999 Peachtree Street, NE · Atlanta, GA 30309-3996 · 404-853-8000

Charles E. Elrod, Jr. · (Employee Benefits) · Elrod & Thompson · 1500 Peachtree Center, South Tower · 225 Peachtree Street, NE · Atlanta, GA 30303 404-659-1500

Robert M. Fink · Troutman, Sanders, Lockerman & Ashmore · One Ravinia Drive, Suite 1600 · Atlanta, GA 30046 · 404-658-8300

Stephen F. Gertzman · Sutherland, Asbill & Brennan · 999 Peachtree Street, NE Atlanta, GA 30309-3996 · 404-853-8000

James K. Hasson, Jr. · Sutherland, Asbill & Brennan · 999 Peachtree Street, NE Atlanta, GA 30309-3996 · 404-853-8000

Robert H. Hishon* · (Corporate & Partnership Transactions, Tax Disputes) · Hishon & Burbage · Eleven Hundred Peachtree Building, Suite 2000 · 1100 Peachtree Street · Atlanta, GA 30309 · 404-984-4000

William L. Kinzer · Powell, Goldstein, Frazer & Murphy · 191 Peachtree Tower, 16th Floor · Atlanta, GA 30303 · 404-572-6600

Donald S. Kohla · (Employee Benefits) · King & Spalding · 2500 Trust Company Tower · Atlanta, GA 30303 · 404-572-4600

James H. Landon · (Employee Benefits) · Jones, Day, Reavis & Pogue · 3300 First Atlanta Tower · Atlanta, GA 30383-3101 · 404-581-8000

Oliver C. Murray, Jr. · Murray & Erck · 219 Perimeter Center Parkway, Suite 100 Atlanta, GA 30346 · 404-671-9400

William F. Nelson · King & Spalding · 2500 Trust Company Tower · Atlanta, GA 30303 · 404-572-4600

William R. Patterson · Sutherland, Asbill & Brennan · 999 Peachtree Street, NE Atlanta, GA 30309-3996 · 404-853-8000

Randolph W. Thrower · Sutherland, Asbill & Brennan · 999 Peachtree Street, NE · Atlanta, GA 30309-3996 · 404-853-8000

John A. Wallace · King & Spalding · 2500 Trust Company Tower · Atlanta, GA 30303 · 404-572-4600

Michael G. Wasserman · Holt, Ney, Zatcoff & Wasserman · 100 Galleria Parkway, Suite 600 · Atlanta, GA 30339 · 404-956-9600

James H. Wilson, Jr. · Sutherland, Asbill & Brennan · 999 Peachtree Street, NE Atlanta, GA 30309-3996 · 404-853-8158

Walter H. Wingfield · (Employee Benefits) · Sutherland, Asbill & Brennan · 999 Peachtree Street, NE · Atlanta, GA 30309-3996 · 404-853-8000

Robert G. Woodward · King & Spalding · 2500 Trust Company Tower · Atlanta, GA 30303 · 404-572-4600

J. Quentin Davidson, Jr. · Davidson, Calhoun & Miller · The Joseph House · 828 Broadway · P.O. Box 2828 · Columbus, GA 31994-1599 · 404-327-2552

Morton A. Harris · (Corporate & Partnership Transactions, Employee Benefits, Tax Disputes) · Page, Scrantom, Harris & Chapman · 1043 Third Avenue · P.O. Box 1199 · Columbus, GA 31994 · 404-324-0251

Albert P. Reichert, Jr. · Anderson, Walker & Reichert · Trust Company Bank Building, Suite 404 · Macon, GA 31298-0399 · 912-743-8651

David H. Dickey · Oliver Maner & Gray · 218 West State Street · P.O. Box 10186 Savannah, GA 31412 · 912-236-3311

Henry M. Dunn, Jr. · (Corporate & Partnership Transactions) · Hunter, Maclean, Exley & Dunn · 200 East St. Julian Street · P.O. Box 9848 · Savannah, GA 31412-0048 · 912-236-0261

Julian R. Friedman · Oliver Maner & Gray · 218 West State Street · P.O. Box 10186 · Savannah, GA 31412 · 912-236-3311

Mark M. Silvers, Jr. · Hunter, Maclean, Exley & Dunn · Castle Building, Third Floor · 200 East St. Julian Street · P.O. Box 9848 · Savannah, GA 31412-0048 · 912-236-0261

Donald L. Waters · Hunter, Maclean, Exley & Dunn · 200 East St. Julian Street P.O. Box 9848 · Savannah, GA 31412-0048 · 912-236-0261

TRUSTS AND ESTATES

Larry V. McLeod · Erwin, Epting, Gibson & McLeod · Citizens & Southern National Bank Building, Eighth Floor · P.O. Box 8108 · Athens, GA 30603 · 404-549-9400

Harold E. Abrams · (Estate Planning) · Kilpatrick & Cody · 100 Galleria Parkway, Suite 1750 · Atlanta, GA 30339 · 404-956-2600

Henry L. Bowden, Jr. · King & Spalding · 2500 Trust Company Tower · Atlanta, GA 30303 · 404-572-4600

Frazer Durrett, Jr. · (Estate Planning) · Alston & Bird · 100 Galleria Parkway, Suite 1200 · Atlanta, GA 30339-3195 · 404-881-7664

Robert G. Edge · Alston & Bird · One Atlantic Center · 1201 West Peachtree Street · Atlanta, GA 30309 · 404-881-7470

Michael J. Egan · Sutherland, Asbill & Brennan · 999 Peachtree Street, NE · Atlanta, GA 30309-3996 · 404-853-8000

William Joseph Linkous, Jr. · Powell, Goldstein, Frazer & Murphy · 191 Peachtree Tower, 16th Floor · Atlanta, GA 30303 · 404-572-6600

Joseph C. Miller · Rogers & Hardin · Peachtree Center, 2700 Cain Tower · 229 Peachtree Street, NE · Atlanta, GA 30303 · 404-522-4700

Wayne R. Vason · (Estate Planning, Estate Administration, Charitable Trusts) · Troutman, Sanders, Lockerman & Ashmore · Candler Building, Suite 1400 · 127 Peachtree Street, NE · Atlanta, GA 30303-1810 · 404-658-8000

John A. Wallace · King & Spalding · 2500 Trust Company Tower · Atlanta, GA 30303 · 404-572-4600

Benjamin T. White · Alston & Bird · One Atlantic Center · 1201 West Peachtree Street · Atlanta, GA 30309-3424 · 404-881-7488

Larry J. White · Sutherland, Asbill & Brennan · 999 Peachtree Street, NE · Atlanta, GA 30309-3996 · 404-853-8000

John D. Comer · Sell & Melton · 1414 Charter Medical Building · P.O. Box 229 Macon, GA 31297-2899 · 912-746-8521

Albert P. Reichert · Anderson, Walker & Reichert · Trust Company Bank Building, Suite 404 · Macon, GA 31298-0399 · 912-743-8651

David H. Dickey · Oliver Maner & Gray · 218 West State Street · P.O. Box 10186 Savannah, GA 31412 · 912-236-3311

Julian R. Friedman · Oliver Maner & Gray · 218 West State Street · P.O. Box 10186 · Savannah, GA 31412 · 912-236-3311

John E. Simpson · Miller, Simpson & Tatum · Trust Company Bank Building, Suite 400 · 33 Bull Street · P.O. Box 1567 · Savannah, GA 31498 · 912-233-5722

HAWAII

BANKRUPTCY LAW

R. Charles Bocken · Damon Key Bocken Leong Kupchak · Pauahi Tower, Suite 1600 · 1001 Bishop Street · Honolulu, HI 96813 · 808-531-8031

Gregory P. Conlan · Chun, Kerr, Dodd & Kaneshige · Amfac Building, 14th Floor · 700 Bishop Street · Honolulu, HI 96813-4188 · 808-531-6575

Nicholas C. Dreher · Cades Schutte Fleming & Wright · Bishop Trust Building 1000 Bishop Street · P.O. Box 939 · Honolulu, HI 96808 · 808-521-9223

James N. Duca* · Kessner, Duca & Maki · Central Pacific Plaza, 19th Floor · 220 South King Street · Honolulu, HI 96813 · 808-522-1900

Don Jeffrey Gelber · (Business Reorganization, Creditors' Rights, Bankruptcy Litigation) · Gelber, Gelber & Ingersoll · Hawaii Building, Suite 1400 · 745 Fort Street · Honolulu, HI 96813 · 808-524-0155

Ronald K. Sakimura · Goodsill Anderson Quinn & Stifel · Bancorp Tower · Financial Plaza of the Pacific · P.O. Box 3196 · Honolulu, HI 96801 · 808-547-5600

James A. Wagner · Wagner & Watson · Mauka Tower, Suite 2480 · 737 Bishop Street · Honolulu, HI 96813 · 808-533-1872

BUSINESS LITIGATION

Martin Anderson · Goodsill Anderson Quinn & Stifel · Bancorp Tower · Financial Plaza of the Pacific · P.O. Box 3196 · Honolulu, HI 96801 · 808-547-5600

James S. Campbell · Cades Schutte Fleming & Wright · Bishop Trust Building 1000 Bishop Street · P.O. Box 939 · Honolulu, HI 96808 · 808-521-9200

William H. Dodd · Chun, Kerr, Dodd & Kaneshige · Amfac Building, 14th Floor 700 Bishop Street · Honolulu, HI 96813-4188 · 808-531-6575

Wallace S. Fujiyama · Fujiyama, Duffy & Fujiyama · Pauahi Tower, Suite 2700 Bishop Square · 1001 Bishop Street · Honolulu, HI 96813 · 808-536-0802

Edward A. Jaffe* · (Appellate, Banking, Commercial, Securities) · Torkildson, Katz, Jossem, Fonseca, Jaffe & Moore · AMFAC Building, 15th Floor · 700 Bishop Street · Honolulu, HI 96813-4187 · 808-521-1051

Bert T. Kobayashi, Jr.* · (Antitrust, Commercial) · Kobayashi, Sugita, Goda · 745 Fort Street, Fifth Floor · Honolulu, HI 96813 · 808-544-8300

Paul A. Lynch · Case & Lynch · 2600 Grosvenor Center, Mauka Tower · 737 Bishop Street · P.O. Box 494 · Honolulu, HI 96809-0494 · 808-547-5400

Dennis E. W. O'Connor* · (Commercial, Securities) · Reinwald, O'Connor Marrack Hoskins & Playdon · 2400 PRI Tower, Grosvenor Center · P.O. Box 3199 · Honolulu, HI 96801 · 808-524-8350

CORPORATE LAW

James W. Boyle · Carlsmith Ball Wichman Murray Case Mukai & Ichiki · Pacific Tower, Suite 2200 · 1001 Bishop Street · P.O. Box 656 · Honolulu, HI 96809 · 808-523-2500

Daniel H. Case · Case & Lynch · 2600 Grosvenor Center, Mauka Tower · 737 Bishop Street · P.O. Box 494 · Honolulu, HI 96809-0494 · 808-547-5400

James H. Case · Carlsmith Ball Wichman Murray Case Mukai & Ichiki · Pacific Tower, Suite 2200 · 1001 Bishop Street · P.O. Box 656 · Honolulu, HI 96809 · 808-523-2500

Marshall M. Goodsill · Goodsill Anderson Quinn & Stifel · Bancorp Tower · Financial Plaza of the Pacific · P.O. Box 3196 · Honolulu, HI 96801-3196 · 808-547-5600

Michael P. Porter · Cades Schutte Fleming & Wright · Bishop Trust Building · 1000 Bishop Street · P.O. Box 939 · Honolulu, HI 96808 · 808-521-9214

David J. Reber · Goodsill Anderson Quinn & Stifel · Bancorp Tower · Financial Plaza of the Pacific · P.O. Box 3196 · Honolulu, HI 96801 · 808-547-5600

E. Gunner Schull · Cades Schutte Fleming & Wright · Bishop Trust Building · 1000 Bishop Street · P.O. Box 939 · Honolulu, HI 96808 · 808-521-9200

Hugh Shearer · Goodsill Anderson Quinn & Stifel · Bancorp Tower · Financial Plaza of the Pacific · P.O. Box 3196 · Honolulu, HI 96801 · 808-547-5600

CRIMINAL DEFENSE

John S. Edmunds* · Edmunds, Verga & O'Brien · Davies Pacific Center, Suite 2104 · 841 Bishop Street · Honolulu, HI 96813-3945 · 808-524-2000

Brook Hart · Hart & Wolff · Melim Building, Suite 610 · 333 Queen Street · Honolulu, HI 96813 · 808-526-0811

Matthew S. K. Pyun, Jr.* · 615 Piikoi Street, Suite 1601 · Honolulu, HI 96814 · 808-524-1633

Philip H. Lowenthal · Lowenthal, August & Graham · 2261 Aupuni Street · Wailuku, HI 96793 · 808-242-5000

FAMILY LAW

William C. Darrah · (Divorce, Marital Settlement Agreements, Equitable Division) · Law Offices of William C. Darrah · 547 Halekauwila Street, Suite 105 · Honolulu, HI 96813 · 808-531-7232

Durell Douthit* · Durell Douthit—Lawyer · Kendall Building, Suite 700 · 888 Mililani Street Mall · Honolulu, HI 96813 · 808-537-2776

Geoffrey Hamilton* · Char Hamilton Campbell & Thom · Grosvenor Center, Mauka Tower, Suite 2100 · 737 Bishop Street · Honolulu, HI 96813 · 808-524-3800

Charles T. Kleintop · Stirling & Kleintop · 1650 Pioneer Plaza · 900 Fort Street Honolulu, HI 96813 · 808-524-5183

Thomas L. Stirling, Jr.* · (Divorce, Marital Settlement Agreements, Equitable Division) · Stirling & Kleintop · 1650 Pioneer Plaza · 900 Fort Street · Honolulu, HI 96813 · 808-524-5183

FIRST AMENDMENT LAW

Paul D. Alston · Alston, Hunt, Floyd & Ing · 1300 Pacific Tower · 1001 Bishop Street · Honolulu, HI 96813 · 808-524-1212

David J. Dezzani · Goodsill Anderson Quinn & Stifel · Bancorp Tower · Financial Plaza of the Pacific · P.O. Box 3196 · Honolulu, HI 96801-3196 · 808-547-5600

Jeffrey S. Portnoy* · Cades Schutte Fleming & Wright · Bishop Trust Building 1000 Bishop Street · P.O. Box 939 · Honolulu, HI 96808 · 808-521-9200

HEALTH CARE LAW

Wesley Y. S. Chang · Foley Maehara Judge Nip & Chang · 737 Bishop Street, Suite 2700 · Honolulu, HI 96813 · 808-526-3011

Robert S. Katz · Torkildson, Katz, Jossem, Fonseca, Jaffe & Moore · Amfac Building, 15th Floor · 700 Bishop Street · Honolulu, HI 96813-4187 · 808-521-1051

Michael A. Shea · Goodsill Anderson Quinn & Stifel · Bancorp Tower · Financial Plaza of the Pacific · P.O. Box 3196 · Honolulu, HI 96801-3196 · 808-547-5600

IMMIGRATION LAW

Peter T. Kashiwa , Jr. · Goodsill Anderson Quinn & Stifel · Bancorp Tower · Financial Plaza of the Pacific · P.O. Box 3196 · Honolulu, HI 96801-3196 · 808-547-5600

Ronald T. Oldenburg · Law Office of Ronald T. Oldenburg · Gold Bond Building, Suite 602 · 677 Ala Moana Boulevard · Honolulu, HI 96813 · 808-536-2347

William F. (Buzz) Thompson II · Blackfield Hawaii Building · 1221 Kapiolani Boulevard, Penthouse 10 · Honolulu, HI 96814 · 808-523-0911

INTELLECTUAL PROPERTY LAW

Edward R. Bendet · Bendet Fidell & Sakai · 1500 Davies Pacific Center · 841 Bishop Street · Honolulu, HI 96813 · 808-524-0544

Martin H. Hsia · Cades Schutte Fleming & Wright · Bishop Trust Building · 1000 Bishop Street · P.O. Box 939 · Honolulu, HI 96808 · 808-521-9200

LABOR AND EMPLOYMENT LAW

Jared H. Jossem · (Management) · Torkildson, Katz, Jossem, Fonseca, Jaffe & Moore · Amfac Building, 15th Floor · 700 Bishop Street · Honolulu, HI 96813-4187 · 808-521-1051

Robert S. Katz · (Management) · Torkildson, Katz, Jossem, Fonseca, Jaffe & Moore · Amfac Building, 15th Floor · 700 Bishop Street · Honolulu, HI 96813-4187 · 808-521-1051

James A. King · (Labor) · King, Nakamura & Chun-Hoon · 928 Nuuanu Avenue, Suite 208 · Honolulu, HI 96817 · 808-521-8041

Barry W. Marr · Carlsmith Ball Wichman Murray Case Mukai & Ichiki · Pacific Tower, Suite 2200 · 1001 Bishop Street · P.O. Box 656 · Honolulu, HI 96809 · 808-523-2678

Herbert R. Takahashi · (Labor, Individuals) · Takahashi & Masui · 547 Halekauwila Street, Room 206 · Honolulu, HI 96813 · 808-526-3003

Raymond M. Torkildson · (Management) · Torkildson, Katz, Jossem, Fonseca, Jaffe & Moore · Amfac Building, 15th Floor · 700 Bishop Street · Honolulu, HI 96813-4187 · 808-521-1051

PERSONAL INJURY LITIGATION

Edmund Burke* · (Medical Malpractice, Products Liability, Airplane Collision) · Burke, Sakai, McPheeters, Bordner & Gilardy · 3100 Mauka Tower · Grosvenor Center · 737 Bishop Street · Honolulu, HI 96813 · 808-523-9833

Mark S. Davis · Davis & Levin · Merchant Square · 10 Marin Street · Honolulu, HI 96817 · 808-524-7500

David J. Dezzani · Goodsill Anderson Quinn & Stifel · Bancorp Tower · Financial Plaza of the Pacific · P.O. Box 3196 · Honolulu, HI 96801 · 808-547-5600

James E. Duffy, Jr. · Fujiyama, Duffy & Fujiyama · Pauahi Tower, Suite 2700 · Bishop Square · 1001 Bishop Street · Honolulu, HI 96813 · 808-536-0802

John S. Edmunds* · (Plaintiffs) · Edmunds, Verga & O'Brien · Davies Pacific Center, Suite 2104 · 841 Bishop Street · Honolulu, HI 96813 · 808-524-2000

David L. Fairbanks* · (Plaintiffs) · Cronin, Fried, Sekiya, Kekina & Fairbanks · 1900 Davies Pacific Center · 841 Bishop Street · Honolulu, HI 96813 · 808-524-1433

Wallace S. Fujiyama · Fujiyama, Duffy & Fujiyama · Pauahi Tower, Suite 2700 Bishop Square · 1001 Bishop Street · Honolulu, HI 96813 · 808-536-0802

Burnham H. Greeley · (Defendants) · Greeley, Walker & Kowen · Pauahi Tower, Suite 1300 · 1001 Bishop Street · Honolulu, HI 96813 · 808-526-2211

James Kawashima · Watanabe, Ing & Kawashima · Hawaii Building, Suite 500 · 745 Fort Street · Honolulu, HI 96813 · 808-544-8300

Bert T. Kobayashi, Jr.* · (Defendants) · Kobayashi, Sugita, Goda · 745 Fort Street, Fifth Floor · Honolulu, HI 96813 · 808-544-8300

Ronald D. Libkuman · Libkuman, Ventura, Ayabe, Chong & Nishimoto · 3000 Grosvenor Center · 737 Bishop Street · Honolulu, HI 96813 · 808-537-6119

Dennis E. W. O'Connor · Reinwald, O'Connor Marrack Hoskins & Playdon · 2400 PRI Tower, Grosvenor Center · P.O. Box 3199 · Honolulu, HI 96801 · 808-524-8350

David C. Schutter · (Plaintiffs) · Schutter & Glickstein · Kawaiahao Plaza, Penthouse Suite 618 · 567 South King Street · Honolulu, HI 96813 · 808-524-4600

Gerald Y. Sekiya · (Plaintiffs) · Cronin, Fried, Sekiya, Kekina & Fairbanks · 1900 Davies Pacific Center · 841 Bishop Street · Honolulu, HI 96813 · 808-524-1433

Raymond J. Tam · (Plaintiffs) · Shim, Tam & Kirimitsu · 333 Queen Street, Suite 900 · Honolulu, HI 96813 · 808-524-5803

James F. Ventura · Libkuman, Ventura, Ayabe, Chong & Nishimoto · 3000 Grosvenor Center · 737 Bishop Street · Honolulu, HI 96813 · 808-537-6119

James Krueger* · (Plaintiffs) · 2065 Main Street · P.O. Box T · Wailuku, HI 96793 · 808-244-7444

PUBLIC UTILITY LAW

Thomas S. Williams, Jr. · Goodsill Anderson Quinn & Stifel · Bancorp Tower · Financial Plaza of the Pacific · P.O. Box 3196 · Honolulu, HI 96801-3196 · 808-547-5600

REAL ESTATE LAW

Clinton R. Ashford* · Ashford & Wriston · Title Guaranty Building, Sixth Floor 235 Queen Street · P.O. Box 131 · Honolulu, HI 96810 · 808-524-4787

Robert B. Bunn · (Eminent Domain, Commercial Transactions, Real Estate Taxation, Water Rights) · Cades Schutte Fleming & Wright · Bishop Trust Building · 1000 Bishop Street · P.O. Box 939 · Honolulu, HI 96808 · 808-521-9207

Daniel H. Case · Case, Kay & Lynch · 2600 Grosvenor Center, Mauka Tower · 737 Bishop Street · P.O. Box 494 · Honolulu, HI 96809-0494 · 808-547-5400

Edward Y. C. Chun · Chun, Kerr, Dodd & Kaneshige · Amfac Building, 14th Floor · 700 Bishop Street · Honolulu, HI 96813-4188 · 808-531-6575

C. Jepson Garland · Goodsill Anderson Quinn & Stifel · Bancorp Tower · Financial Plaza of the Pacific · P.O. Box 3196 · Honolulu, HI 96801 · 808-547-5600

John Jubinsky* · Title Guaranty Building, Sixth Floor · 235 Queen Street · P.O. Box 3595 · Honolulu, HI 96811 · 808-532-1818

Ronald H. W. Lum · Goodsill Anderson Quinn & Stifel · Bancorp Tower · Financial Plaza of the Pacific · P.O. Box 3196 · Honolulu, HI 96801 · 808-547-5600

Douglas E. Prior · Cades Schutte Fleming & Wright · Bishop Trust Building · 1000 Bishop Street · P.O. Box 939 · Honolulu, HI 96808 · 808-521-9200

Dwight M. Rush · Rush, Moore, Craven, Sutton, Morri & Beh · Hawaii Building, 20th Floor · 745 Fort Street · Honolulu, HI 96813 · 808-521-0400

Donald E. Scearce · Cades Schutte Fleming & Wright · Bishop Trust Building · 1000 Bishop Street · P.O. Box 939 · Honolulu, HI 96808 · 808-521-9200

A. James Wriston, Jr. · Ashford & Wriston · Title Guaranty Building, Sixth Floor 235 Queen Street · P.O. Box 131 · Honolulu, HI 96810 · 808-524-4787

TAX AND EMPLOYEE BENEFITS LAW

H. Mitchell D'Olier · Goodsill Anderson Quinn & Stifel · Bancorp Tower · Financial Plaza of the Pacific · P.O. Box 3196 · Honolulu, HI 96801-3196 · 808-547-5600

Roger H. Epstein · (Corporate & Partnership Transactions, Tax Disputes, International Tax) · Cades Schutte Fleming & Wright · Bishop Trust Building · 1000 Bishop Street · P.O. Box 939 · Honolulu, HI 96808 · 808-521-9200

Roger W. Fonseca · (Employee Benefits) · Torkildson, Katz, Jossem, Fonseca, Jaffe & Moore · Amfac Building, 15th Floor · 700 Bishop Street · Honolulu, HI 96813-4187 · 808-521-1051

Stephen M. Gelber · (Corporate & Partnership Transactions, State Tax, Tax Disputes) · Gelber, Gelber & Ingersoll · Hawaii Building, Suite 1400 · 745 Fort Street · Honolulu, HI 96813 · 808-524-0155

Mervyn S. Gerson · (Corporate & Partnership Transactions, Tax Disputes) · Gerson, Grekin & Wynhoff · Pacific Tower, Suite 780 · 1001 Bishop Street · Honolulu, HI 96813 · 808-524-4800

George G. Grubb · Carlsmith Ball Wichman Murray Case Mukai & Ichiki · Pacific Tower, Suite 2200 · 1001 Bishop Street · P.O. Box 656 · Honolulu, HI 96809 · 808-523-2500

Michael A. Shea · Goodsill Anderson Quinn & Stifel · Bancorp Tower · Financial Plaza of the Pacific · P.O. Box 3196 · Honolulu, HI 96801-3196 · 808-547-5600

James L. Starshak · (Employee Benefits) · Carlsmith Ball Wichman Murray Case Mukai & Ichiki · Pacific Tower, Suite 2200 · 1001 Bishop Street · P.O. Box 656 Honolulu, HI 96809 · 808-523-2500

TRUSTS AND ESTATES

John R. Conrad · Cades Schutte Fleming & Wright · Bishop Trust Building · 1000 Bishop Street · P.O. Box 939 · Honolulu, HI 96808 · 808-521-9200

C. F. Damon, Jr. · Damon Key Bocken Leong Kupchak · Pauahi Tower, Suite 1600 · 1001 Bishop Street · Honolulu, HI 96813 · 808-531-8031

Robert G. Hite · Goodsill Anderson Quinn & Stifel · Bancorp Tower · Financial Plaza of the Pacific · P.O. Box 3196 · Honolulu, HI 96801-3196 · 808-547-5600

David C. Larsen · Cades Schutte Fleming & Wright · Bishop Trust Building · 1000 Bishop Street · P.O. Box 939 · Honolulu, HI 96808 · 808-521-9200

Elliot H. Loden · (Estate Planning, Estate Administration, Estate Taxation, Estate Tax Matters before the IRS) · 2990 Grosvenor Center · 737 Bishop Street · Honolulu, HI 96813 · 808-524-8099

Arthur B. Reinwald* · Hoddick, Reinwald, O'Connor & Marrack · 2400 PRI Tower, Grosvenor Center · P.O. Box 3199 · Honolulu, HI 96801 · 808-524-8350

James L. Starshak · (Estate Planning, Charitable Trusts) · Carlsmith Ball Wichman Murray Case Mukai & Ichiki · Pacific Tower, Suite 2200 · 1001 Bishop Street P.O. Box 656 · Honolulu, HI 96809 · 808-523-2500

Robert Williams Hastings II · Torkildson, Katz, Jossem, Fonseca, Jaffe & Moore Hanama Place, Suite 105 · 75-5706 Kuakini Highway · Kailua-Kona, HI 96740 · 808-329-8581

IDAHO

BANKRUPTCY LAW

Terry L. Myers* · (Business Reorganization, Creditors' Rights, Bankruptcy Litigation) · Givens, Pursley, Webb & Huntley · Park Place, Suite 200 · 277 North Sixth Street · P.O. Box 2720 · Boise, ID 83701 · 208-342-6571

R. Michael Southcombe* · (Business Reorganization, Creditors' Rights, Debtors' Rights, Bankruptcy Litigation) · Cosho, Humphrey, Greener & Welsh · Carnegie Building · 815 West Washington Street · Boise, ID 83702 · 208-344-7811

BUSINESS LITIGATION

Carl P. Burke · Elam, Burke and Boyd · Key Financial Center, 10th Floor · 702 West Idaho Street · Boise, ID 83701 · 208-343-5454

Jess B. Hawley, Jr. · Hawley Troxell Ennis & Hawley · First Interstate Building, Suite 1000 · 877 Main Street · Boise, ID 83701 · 208-344-6000

Louis F. Racine, Jr. · Racine, Olson, Nye, Cooper & Budge · Center Plaza · P.O. Box 1391 · Pocatello, ID 83204 · 208-232-6101

CORPORATE LAW

Carl P. Burke · Elam, Burke and Boyd · Key Financial Center, 10th Floor · 702 West Idaho Street · Boise, ID 83701 · 208-343-5454

Jess B. Hawley, Jr. · Hawley Troxell Ennis & Hawley · First Interstate Building, Suite 1000 · 877 Main Street · Boise, ID 83701 · 208-344-6000

Louis F. Racine, Jr. · Racine, Olson, Nye, Cooper & Budge · Center Plaza · P.O. Box 1391 · Pocatello, ID 83201 · 208-232-6101

CRIMINAL DEFENSE

Thomas A. Mitchell · Mitchell Law Firm · 316 Elder Building · Coeur d'Alene, ID 83814 · 208-664-8111

FAMILY LAW

Louis H. Cosho* · Cosho, Humphrey, Greener & Welsh · Carnegie Building · 815 West Washington Street · Boise, ID 83702 · 208-344-7811

Stanley W. Welsh · Cosho, Humphrey, Greener & Welsh · Carnegie Building · 815 West Washington Street · Boise, ID 83702 · 208-344-7811

LABOR AND EMPLOYMENT LAW

Fred Joseph Hahn · (Management) · Holden, Kidwell, Hahn & Crapo · West One Bank Building, Third Floor · 330 Shoup Avenue · P.O. Box 50130 · Idaho Falls, ID 83405 · 208-523-0620

NATURAL RESOURCES AND ENVIRONMENTAL LAW

Roy L. Eiguren · Davis Wright Tremaine · 350 North Ninth Street, Suite 400 · Boise, ID 83702 · 208-336-8844

Kent W. Foster* · (Mining, Water) · Holden, Kidwell, Hahn & Crapo · Idaho First National Bank Building, Third Floor · 330 Shoup Avenue · P.O. Box 50130 Idaho Falls, ID 83405 · 208-523-0620

John A. Rosholt · (Water) · Nelson, Rosholt, Robertson, Tolman & Tucker · 142 Third Avenue North · P.O. Box 1906 · Twin Falls, ID 83303 · 208-734-0700

PERSONAL INJURY LITIGATION

Peter J. Boyd* · (Products Liability, Professional Malpractice, Automobile Collision, Airplane Collision) · Elam, Burke and Boyd · First Interstate Bank Building, Suite 1010 · 702 West Idaho Street · P.O. Box 1539 · Boise, ID 83701 · 208-343-5454

Carl P. Burke · (Defendants) · Elam, Burke and Boyd · Key Financial Center, 10th Floor · 702 West Idaho Street · Boise, ID 83701 · 208-343-5454

Louis F. Racine, Jr. · Racine, Olson, Nye, Cooper & Budge · Center Plaza · P.O. Box 1391 · Pocatello, ID 83201 · 208-232-6101

John C. Hepworth · (Plaintiffs) · Hepworth, Nungester, Felton & Lezamiz · 133 Shoshone Street North · P.O. Box 389 · Twin Falls, ID 83303-0389 · 208-734-7510

PUBLIC UTILITY LAW

Larry D. Ripley · Evans, Keane, Koontz, Boyd, Simko & Ripley · West One Plaza, Suite 1701 · P.O. Box 959 · Boise, ID 83701 · 208-384-1800

Conley Ward, Jr. · Givens, Pursley, Webb & Huntley · Park Place, Suite 200 · 277 North Sixth Street · P.O. Box 2720 · Boise, ID 83701 · 208-342-6571

REAL ESTATE LAW

M. Neil Newhouse · Hawley Troxell Ennis & Hawley · First Interstate Building, Suite 1000 · 877 Main Street · Boise, ID 83701 · 208-344-6000

Kenneth L. Pursley · Givens, Pursley, Webb & Huntley · Park Place, Suite 200 277 North Sixth Street · P.O. Box 2720 · Boise, ID 83701 · 208-342-6571

TAX AND EMPLOYEE BENEFITS LAW

Robert S. Erickson · Hawley Troxell Ennis & Hawley · First Interstate Building, Suite 1000 · 877 Main Street · Boise, ID 83701 · 208-344-6000

Stephen E. Martin · Holden, Kidwell, Hahn & Crapo · West One Bank Building, Third Floor · 330 Shoup Avenue · P.O. Box 50130 · Idaho Falls, ID 83405 · 208-523-0620

Gayle A. Sorenson · (Employee Benefits) · Holden, Kidwell, Hahn & Crapo · Idaho First National Bank Building, Third Floor · 330 Shoup Avenue · P.O. Box 50130 · Idaho Falls, ID 83405 · 208-523-0620

Philip E. Peterson · 318 Fifth Street · Lewiston, ID 83501 · 208-885-6422

TRUSTS AND ESTATES

Stephen E. Martin · Holden, Kidwell, Hahn & Crapo · West One Bank Building, Third Floor · 330 Shoup Avenue · P.O. Box 50130 · Idaho Falls, ID 83405 · 208-523-0620

Philip E. Peterson · 318 Fifth Street · Lewiston, ID 83501 · 208-885-6422

ILLINOIS

BANKRUPTCY LAW

H. Bruce Bernstein · Sidley & Austin · One First National Plaza · Chicago, IL 60603 · 312-853-7000

Milton L. Fisher · (Business Reorganization, Creditors' Rights, Debtors' Rights, Debtor In-Possession Financing) · Mayer, Brown & Platt · 190 South La Salle Street · Chicago, IL 60603-3441 · 312-782-0600

Malcolm M. Gaynor · Schwartz Cooper Kolb & Gaynor · 20 South Clark Street · Chicago, IL 60603 · 312-726-0845

Louis W. Levit · Ross & Hardies · 150 North Michigan Avenue, Suite 2500 · Chicago, IL 60601 · 312-558-1000

David N. Missner · Rudnick & Wolfe · 203 North La Salle Street, Suite 1500 · Chicago, IL 60601 · 312-368-4000

Gerald F. Munitz · Winston & Strawn · 35 West Wacker Drive, Suite 4200 · Chicago, IL 60601 · 312-558-5600

Norman H. Nachman · Winston & Strawn · 35 West Wacker Drive, Suite 4200 · Chicago, IL 60601 · 312-558-5600

A. Bruce Schimberg · (Business Reorganization, Creditors' Rights) · Sidley & Austin · One First National Plaza · Chicago, IL 60603 · 312-853-7000

James E. Spiotto · Chapman and Cutler · 111 West Monroe Street, Suite 1300 · Chicago, IL 60603 · 312-845-3000

J. Robert Stoll · Mayer, Brown & Platt · 190 South La Salle Street, Suite 3900 · Chicago, IL 60603-3441 · 312-782-0600

Allan G. Sweig · Altheimer & Gray · 10 South Wacker Drive, Suite 4000 · Chicago, IL 60606 · 312-715-4000

Neal L. Wolf* · (Business Reorganization, Creditors' Rights, Debtors' Rights, Bankruptcy Litigation) · Winston & Strawn · 35 West Wacker Drive · Chicago, IL 60601 · 312-558-5232

Joel A. Kunin · (Business Reorganization, Creditors' Rights, Debtors' Rights, Bankruptcy Litigation) · Carr, Korein, Tillery, Kunin, Montroy, Glass & Bogard 412 Missouri Avenue · East St. Louis, IL 62201 · 618-274-0434

BUSINESS LITIGATION

Fred H. Bartlit, Jr. · Kirkland & Ellis · 200 East Randolph Drive · Chicago, IL 60601 · 312-861-2000

Frank Cicero, Jr.* · Kirkland & Ellis · 200 East Randolph Drive · Chicago, IL 60601 · 312-861-2000

Michael W. Coffield · Coffield Ungaretti Harris & Slavin · 3500 Three First National Plaza · Chicago, IL 60602 · 312-977-4400

Tyrone C. Fahner · Mayer, Brown & Platt · 190 South La Salle Street · Chicago, IL 60603-3441 · 312-701-7062

Edward L. Foote · Winston & Strawn · 35 West Wacker Drive, Suite 4200 · Chicago, IL 60601 · 312-558-5600

Thomas A. Foran* · (Antitrust, Commercial) · Foran, Wiss & Schultz · 30 North La Salle Street, Suite 3000 · Chicago, IL 60602 · 312-368-8330

Kevin M. Forde* · (Appellate, Commercial, Class Actions) · 111 West Washington Street, Suite 1100 · Chicago, IL 60602-2768 · 312-726-5015

William J. Harte · 111 West Washington Street, Suite 1100 · Chicago, IL 60602 312-726-5015

Reuben L. Hedlund* · (Commercial, Securities, Construction Disputes) · Latham & Watkins · Sears Tower, Suite 5800 · Chicago, IL 60606 · 312-876-7700

William R. Jentes* · (Antitrust, Commercial, International, Securities) · Kirkland & Ellis · 200 East Randolph Drive · Chicago, IL 60601 · 312-861-2000

Donald G. Kempf, Jr. · Kirkland & Ellis · 200 East Randolph Drive · Chicago, IL 60601 · 312-861-2000

Kael B. Kennedy · Schuyler, Roche & Zwirner · One Prudential Plaza, Suite 3800 130 East Randolph Street · Chicago, IL 60601 · 312-565-2400

Francis J. McConnell* · (Antitrust, Appellate, Commercial, Securities) · McConnell & Mendelson · 140 South Dearborn Street, Suite 500 · Chicago, IL 60603 · 312-263-1212

Francis D. Morrissey · (Appellate) · Baker & McKenzie · One Prudential Plaza, Suite 2700 · 130 East Randolph Drive · Chicago, IL 60601 · 312-861-8000

Stephen C. Neal · Kirkland & Ellis · 200 East Randolph Drive · Chicago, IL 60601 · 312-861-2284

Patrick W. O'Brien* · (Antitrust) · Mayer, Brown & Platt · 190 South La Salle Street · Chicago, IL 60603-3441 · 312-782-0600

Earl E. Pollock · Sonnenschein Nath & Rosenthal · Sears Tower, Suite 8000 · 233 South Wacker Drive · Chicago, IL 60606-6404 · 312-876-8000

Richard J. Prendergast · 111 West Washington Street, Suite 1100 · Chicago, IL 60602-2768 · 312-641-0881

Lowell E. Sachnoff · Sachnoff & Weaver · 30 South Wacker Drive, Suite 2900 · Chicago, IL 60606 · 312-207-1000

Jerold S. Solovy · Jenner & Block · One IBM Plaza · 330 North Wabash Avenue Chicago, IL 60611 · 312-222-9350

Thomas P. Sullivan* · Jenner & Block · One IBM Plaza · 330 North Wabash Avenue · Chicago, IL 60611 · 312-222-9350

Philip W. Tone · (Antitrust, Appellate, Commercial, Securities) · Jenner & Block One IBM Plaza · 330 North Wabash Avenue · Chicago, IL 60611 · 312-222-9350

Howard J. Trienens* · Sidley & Austin · One First National Plaza · Chicago, IL 60603 · 312-853-7417

Dan K. Webb · Winston & Strawn · 35 West Wacker Drive, Suite 4200 · Chicago, IL 60601 · 312-558-5600

H. Blair White* · Sidley & Austin · One First National Plaza · Chicago, IL 60603 312-853-7000

Max E. Wildman* · Wildman, Harrold, Allen & Dixon · 225 West Wacker Drive Chicago, IL 60606 · 312-201-2627

CORPORATE LAW

Jean Allard · Sonnenschein Nath & Rosenthal · Sears Tower, Suite 8000 · 233 South Wacker Drive · Chicago, IL 60606-6404 · 312-876-8000

J. Trent Anderson · Mayer, Brown & Platt · 190 South La Salle Street · Chicago, IL 60603-3441 · 312-782-0600

James G. Archer · Sidley & Austin · One First National Plaza · Chicago, IL 60603 312-853-7000

Cameron S. Avery · (Mutual Funds, Securities, Corporate Finance, Financial Institutions) · Bell, Boyd & Lloyd · Three First National Plaza, Suite 3200 · 70 West Madison Street · Chicago, IL 60602-4207 · 312-372-1121

Frank E. Babb · McDermott, Will & Emery · 227 West Monroe Street · Chicago, IL 60606 · 312-372-2000

Harold S. Barron · Seyfarth, Shaw, Fairweather & Geraldson · 55 East Monroe Street, Suite 4200 · Chicago, IL 60603 · 312-346-8000

Robert L. Berner, Jr. · Baker & McKenzie · One Prudential Plaza, Suite 2800 · 130 East Randolph Drive · Chicago, IL 60601 · 312-861-8000

H. Bruce Bernstein · Sidley & Austin · One First National Plaza · Chicago, IL 60603 · 312-853-7000

John H. Bitner · (Corporate Finance, Mergers & Acquisitions, Securities, Securities Regulation) · Bell, Boyd & Lloyd · Three First National Plaza, Suite 3200 70 West Madison Street · Chicago, IL 60602-4207 · 312-372-1121

John C. Blew · Bell, Boyd & Lloyd · Three First National Plaza, Suite 3200 · 70 West Madison Street · Chicago, IL 60602-4207 · 312-372-1121

Bruce L. Bower · Winston & Strawn · 35 West Wacker Drive, Suite 4200 · Chicago, IL 60601 · 312-558-5600

James J. Brennan · Sidley & Austin · One First National Plaza · Chicago, IL 60603 · 312-853-7000

Milton H. Cohen · Schiff Hardin & Waite · 7200 Sears Tower · 233 South Wacker Drive · Chicago, IL 60606-6473 · 312-876-1000

Peter P. Coladarci · (Corporate Finance, Financial Institutions, Securities) · Chapman and Cutler · 111 West Monroe Street, Suite 1400 · Chicago, IL 60603 312-845-3712

Thomas A. Cole · Sidley & Austin · One First National Plaza · Chicago, IL 60603 312-853-7000

Dewey B. Crawford · Gardner, Carton & Douglas · Quaker Tower, Suite 3400 · 321 North Clark Street · Chicago, IL 60610-4795 · 312-644-3000

Charles F. Custer · (Mutual Funds) · Vedder, Price, Kaufman & Kammholz · 222 North La Salle Street, 26th Floor · Chicago, IL 60601-1003 · 312-609-7545

Wilbur C. Delp, Jr. · Sidley & Austin · One First National Plaza · Chicago, IL 60603 · 312-853-7000

Edwin R. Dunn · Baker & McKenzie · One Prudential Plaza, Suite 2800 · 130 East Randolph Drive · Chicago, IL 60601 · 312-861-8000

Paul H. Dykstra · (Mutual Funds, Securities) · Gardner, Carton & Douglas · Quaker Tower, Suite 3400 · 321 North Clark Street · Chicago, IL 60610-4795 · 312-644-3000

Joseph S. Ehrman · Sidley & Austin · One First National Plaza · Chicago, IL 60603 · 312-853-7000

Carter W. Emerson · Kirkland & Ellis · 200 East Randolph Drive · Chicago, IL 60601 · 312-861-2052

Jay Erens · Hopkins & Sutter · Three First National Plaza, Suite 4300 · Chicago, IL 60602 · 312-558-6600

C. Curtis Everett · (Corporate Finance, Mergers & Acquisitions, Securities, Securities Regulation) · Bell, Boyd & Lloyd · Three First National Plaza, Suite 3200 · 70 West Madison Street · Chicago, IL 60602-4207 · 312-372-1121

Ronald H. Filler · (Securities, Securities Regulation, Commodities) · Vedder, Price, Kaufman & Kammholz · 222 North La Salle Street, Suite 2600 · Chicago, IL 60601-1003 · 312-609-7500

Neil Flanagin · Sidley & Austin · One First National Plaza · Chicago, IL 60603 · 312-853-7000

Raymond I. Geraldson · Seyfarth, Shaw, Fairweather & Geraldson · 55 East Monroe Street, Suite 4200 · Chicago, IL 60603 · 312-346-8000

Francis J. Gerlits · Kirkland & Ellis · 200 East Randolph Drive · Chicago, IL 60601 · 312-861-2000

Norman M. Gold · Altheimer & Gray · 10 South Wacker Drive, Suite 4000 · Chicago, IL 60606 · 312-715-4000

Stanford J. Goldblatt · Hopkins & Sutter · Three First National Plaza, Suite 4300 · Chicago, IL 60602 · 312-558-6600

Stuart L. Goodman · Schiff Hardin & Waite · 7200 Sears Tower · 233 South Wacker Drive · Chicago, IL 60606-6473 · 312-876-1000

R. James Gormley · Bell, Boyd & Lloyd · Three First National Plaza, Suite 3200 · 70 West Madison Street · Chicago, IL 60602-4207 · 312-372-1121

Milton H. Gray · Altheimer & Gray · 10 South Wacker Drive, Suite 4000 · Chicago, IL 60606 · 312-715-4000

Victor E. Grimm* · (Antitrust) · Bell, Boyd & Lloyd · Three First National Plaza, Suite 3200 · 70 West Madison Street · Chicago, IL 60602-4207 · 312-372-1121

Arthur W. Hahn · (Commodities, Futures) · Katten Muchin & Zavis · 525 West Monroe Street, Suite 1600 · Chicago, IL 60606-3693 · 312-902-5200

Frederick Hartmann · (Corporate Finance, Leveraged Buyouts, Mergers & Acquisitions, Securities) · Schiff Hardin & Waite · 7200 Sears Tower · 233 South Wacker Drive · Chicago, IL 60606-6473 · 312-876-1000

Robert A. Helman · Mayer, Brown & Platt · 190 South La Salle Street · Chicago, IL 60603-3441 · 312-782-0600

James P. Hemmer · Bell, Boyd & Lloyd · Three First National Plaza, Suite 3200 · 70 West Madison Street · Chicago, IL 60602-4207 · 312-372-1121

Leo Herzel · Mayer, Brown & Platt · 190 South La Salle Street, Suite 3900 · Chicago, IL 60603-3441 · 312-782-0600

Glen E. Hess · Kirkland & Ellis · 200 East Randolph Drive · Chicago, IL 60601 312-861-2000

Elmer W. Johnson · Kirkland & Ellis · 200 East Randolph Drive · Chicago, IL 60601 · 312-861-2010

James D. Johnson · (Corporate Finance, Leveraged Buyouts, Mergers & Acquisitions, Securities).. · ..Sidley & Austin · One First National Plaza · Chicago, IL 60603 · 312-853-7000

Andrew R. Laidlaw · Seyfarth, Shaw, Fairweather & Geraldson · 55 East Monroe Street, Suite 4200 · Chicago, IL 60603 · 312-346-8000

Jack S. Levin · (Leveraged Buyouts, Mergers & Acquisitions, Venture Capital) · Kirkland & Ellis · 200 East Randolph Drive · Chicago, IL 60601 · 312-861-2000

Julius Lewis · Sonnenschein Nath & Rosenthal · Sears Tower, Suite 8000 · 233 South Wacker Drive · Chicago, IL 60606-6404 · 312-876-8000

Donald G. Lubin · Sonnenschein Nath & Rosenthal · Sears Tower, Suite 8000 · 233 South Wacker Drive · Chicago, IL 60606-6404 · 312-876-8000

H. George Mann · McDermott, Will & Emery · 227 West Monroe Street · Chicago, IL 60606 · 312-372-2000

Charles R. Manzoni, Jr. · Gardner, Carton & Douglas · Quaker Tower, Suite 3400 · 321 North Clark Street · Chicago, IL 60610-4795 · 312-644-3000

Jeremiah Marsh · Hopkins & Sutter · Three First National Plaza, Suite 4300 · Chicago, IL 60602 · 312-558-6600

John T. McCarthy · Bell, Boyd & Lloyd · Three First National Plaza, Suite 3200 70 West Madison Street · Chicago, IL 60602-4207 · 312-372-1121

John H. McDermott · McDermott, Will & Emery · 227 West Monroe Street · Chicago, IL 60606 · 312-372-2000

Harrold E. McKee · Mayer, Brown & Platt · 190 South La Salle Street, Suite 3900 Chicago, IL 60603-3441 · 312-782-0600

Stanley H. Meadows · McDermott, Will & Emery · 227 West Monroe Street · Chicago, IL 60606 · 312-372-2000

Peter H. Merlin · Gardner, Carton & Douglas · Quaker Tower, Suite 3400 · 321 North Clark Street · Chicago, IL 60610-4795 · 312-644-3000

Michael L. Meyer · (Mutual Funds, Mergers & Acquisitions, Securities Regulation) · Schiff Hardin & Waite · 7200 Sears Tower · 233 South Wacker Drive · Chicago, IL 60606-6473 · 312-876-1000

Howard C. Michaelsen, Jr. · McDermott, Will & Emery · 227 West Monroe Street · Chicago, IL 60606 · 312-372-2000

Maurice J. Miller · Sidley & Austin · One First National Plaza · Chicago, IL 60603 · 312-853-7000

Paul J. Miller · Sonnenschein Nath & Rosenthal · Sears Tower, Suite 8000 · 233 South Wacker Drive · Chicago, IL 60606-6404 · 312-876-8000

Allan B. Muchin · Katten Muchin & Zavis · 525 West Monroe Street, Suite 1600 Chicago, IL 60606-3693 · 312-902-5200

Charles W. Mulaney, Jr. · Skadden, Arps, Slate, Meagher & Flom · 333 West Wacker Drive, Suite 1900 · Chicago, IL 60606 · 312-407-0700

Cordell J. Overgaard · Hopkins & Sutter · Three First National Plaza, Suite 4300 Chicago, IL 60602 · 312-558-6600

Gerald M. Penner · Katten Muchin & Zavis · 525 West Monroe Street, Suite 1600 Chicago, IL 60606-3693 · 312-902-5200

William O. Petersen · Vedder, Price, Kaufman & Kammholz · 222 North La Salle Street, Suite 2500 · Chicago, IL 60601-1003 · 312-609-7500

Michael E. Phenner · Hopkins & Sutter · Three First National Plaza, Suite 4300 Chicago, IL 60602 · 312-558-6600

Edward G. Proctor · Hinshaw & Culbertson · 222 North La Salle Street, Suite 300 · Chicago, IL 60601-1081 · 312-704-3000

James M. Reum · (Corporate Finance, International Banking, Mergers & Acquisitions, Securities) · Hopkins & Sutter · Three First National Plaza · Chicago, IL 60602 · 312-558-6600

Thomas A. Reynolds, Jr. · Winston & Strawn · 35 West Wacker Drive, Suite 4200 Chicago, IL 60601 · 312-558-5600

James T. Rhind · Bell, Boyd & Lloyd · Three First National Plaza, Suite 3200 · 70 West Madison Street · Chicago, IL 60602-4207 · 312-372-1121

Burton R. Rissman · Schiff Hardin & Waite · 7200 Sears Tower · 233 South Wacker Drive · Chicago, IL 60606-6473 · 312-876-1000

Richard M. Rosenberg · Mayer, Brown & Platt · 190 South La Salle Street, Suite 3900 · Chicago, IL 60603-3441 · 312-782-0600

Peter L. Rossiter · Schiff Hardin & Waite · 7200 Sears Tower · 233 South Wacker Drive · Chicago, IL 60606-6473 · 312-876-1000

David S. Ruder · Baker & McKenzie · One Prudential Plaza, 28th Floor · 130 East Randolph Drive · Chicago, IL 60601 · 312-861-8000

A. Bruce Schimberg · (Banking) · Sidley & Austin · One First National Plaza · Chicago, IL 60603 · 312-853-7000

Harold D. Shapiro · (International, International Banking, International Finance, International Trade) · Sonnenschein Nath & Rosenthal · Sears Tower, Suite 8000 233 South Wacker Drive · Chicago, IL 60606-6404 · 312-876-8000

Keith Shay · (Banking, Corporate Finance, Mergers & Acquisitions, Securities) · Schiff Hardin & Waite · 7200 Sears Tower · 233 South Wacker Drive · Chicago, IL 60606-6473 · 312-876-1000

Frederick B. Thomas · Mayer, Brown & Platt · 190 South La Salle Street, Suite 3900 · Chicago, IL 60603-3441 · 312-782-0600

Kenneth I. Vaughan · Chapman and Cutler · 111 West Monroe Street, Suite 1400 Chicago, IL 60603 · 312-845-3000

Norman Waite, Jr. · Winston & Strawn · 35 West Wacker Drive, Suite 4200 · Chicago, IL 60601 · 312-558-5600

Priscilla A. Walter · Gardner, Carton & Douglas · Quaker Tower, Suite 3400 · 321 North Clark Street · Chicago, IL 60610-4795 · 312-644-3000

Herbert S. Wander · Katten Muchin & Zavis · 525 West Monroe Street, Suite 1600 · Chicago, IL 60606-3693 · 312-902-5267

Wayne W. Whalen · Skadden, Arps, Slate, Meagher & Flom · 333 West Wacker Drive · Chicago, IL 60606 · 312-407-0700

Joseph E. Wyse · (Mergers & Acquisitions) · Seyfarth, Shaw, Fairweather & Geraldson · 55 East Monroe Street, Suite 4200 · Chicago, IL 60603-5803 · 312-346-8000

Robert A. Yolles · Jones, Day, Reavis & Pogue · 225 West Washington Street, 26th Floor · Chicago, IL 60606 · 312-782-3939

CRIMINAL DEFENSE

Samuel Forbes Adam · 53 West Jackson Street, Suite 1430 · Chicago, IL 60604 · 312-236-5543

William A. Barnett* · (Non-Violent Crimes, Federal Court, State Court) · 135 South La Salle Street, Suite 808 · Chicago, IL 60603 · 312-726-4480

Thomas M. Breen · Martin & Breen · 221 North La Salle Street, Suite 2100 · Chicago, IL 60601 · 312-346-2550

George J. Cotsirilos · Cotsirilos, Stephenson, Tighe & Streicker · 33 North Dearborn Street · Chicago, IL 60602 · 312-263-0345

Thomas D. Decker · Thomas D. Decker & Associates · 135 South La Salle Street, Suite 1527 · Chicago, IL 60603 · 312-263-4180

Edward M. Genson · Genson, Steinback and Gillespie · 53 West Jackson Boulevard, Suite 1420 · Chicago, IL 60604 · 312-726-9015

William Joseph Linklater · Baker & McKenzie · One Prudential Plaza · 130 East Randolph Drive · Chicago, IL 60601 · 312-861-8000

Royal B. Martin, Jr.* · (Federal Court) · Silets and Martin · The Marquette Building, 15th Floor · 140 South Dearborn Street · Chicago, IL 60603 · 312-263-5800

Michael D, Monico · Monico, Pavich & Spevack · Barrister Hall, Suite 720 · 29 South LaSalle · Chicago, IL 60603 · 312-782-8500

George J. Murtaugh, Jr. · 100 West Monroe Street, Suite 1800 · Chicago, IL 60603 · 312-781-0940

Michael B. Nash · 53 West Jackson Boulevard, Suite 615 · Chicago, IL 60604 · 312-922-8980

Harvey M. Silets* · (Federal Court, Environmental Crimes) · Silets and Martin · The Marquette Building, 15th Floor · 140 South Dearborn Street · Chicago, IL 60603 · 312-263-5800

Robert M. Stephenson* · (also Appellate) · Cotsirilos, Stephenson, Tighe & Streicker · 33 North Dearborn Street · Chicago, IL 60602 · 312-263-0345

James R. Streicker · Cotsirilos, Stephenson, Tighe & Streicker · 33 North Dearborn Street · Chicago, IL 60602 · 312-263-0345

Thomas P. Sullivan* · Jenner & Block · One IBM Plaza · 330 North Wabash Avenue · Chicago, IL 60611 · 312-222-9350

Patrick A. Tuite* · (Non-Violent Crimes, Federal Court, State Court, Environmental Crimes) · The Law Offices of Patrick A. Truite · 105 West Adams Street, 31st Floor · Chicago, IL 60603 · 312-641-1022

Dan K. Webb · Winston & Strawn · 35 West Wacker Drive, Suite 4200 · Chicago, IL 60601 · 312-558-5600

William J. Martin · Martin & Breen · 1010 Lake Street · Oak Park, IL 60301 · 708-848-2100

FAMILY LAW

Miles N. Beermann* · (Child Custody, Divorce, Marital Settlement Agreements, Equitable Division) · Beermann, Swerdlove, Woloshin & Barezky · 69 West Washington Street, Room 600 · Chicago, IL 60602-3016 · 312-621-9700

Arthur M. Berman* · Kirsh, Berman & Hoffenberg · 120 West Madison Street · Chicago, IL 60602 · 312-782-3020

Muller Davis* · Davis, Friedman, Zavett, Kane & MacRae · The Marquette Building, Suite 1600 · 140 South Dearborn Street · Chicago, IL 60603 · 312-782-2220

Joseph N. Du Canto* · (Divorce, Marital Settlement Agreement, Equitable Division, Tax) · Schiller, Du Canto and Fleck · 200 North La Salle Street, Suite 2700 Chicago, IL 60601-1089 · 312-641-5560

James H. Feldman* · (Child Custody, Divorce, Marital Settlement Agreements, Equitable Division) · Jenner & Block · One IBM Plaza · 330 North Wabash Avenue · Chicago, IL 60611 · 312-222-9350

Charles J. Fleck* · Schiller, Du Canto and Fleck · 200 North La Salle Street, Suite 2700 · Chicago, IL 60601-1089 · 312-641-5560

James T. Friedman* · Davis, Friedman, Zavett, Kane & MacRae · The Marquette Building, Suite 1600 · 140 South Dearborn Street · Chicago, IL 60603 · 312-782-2220

Sanford Kirsh* · Kirsh, Berman & Hoffenberg · 120 West Madison Street · Chicago, IL 60602 · 312-782-3020

Bernard B. Rinella* · (Child Custody, Divorce, Marital Settlement Agreements, Equitable Division) · Rinella and Rinella · One North La Salle Street, Suite 3400 Chicago, IL 60602-4094 · 312-236-5454

Howard H. Rosenfeld · Rosenfeld, Rotenberg, Schwartzman, Hafron & Shapiro 221 North LaSalle Street, Suite 1763 · Chicago, IL 60601 · 312-372-6058

Donald C. Schiller* · Schiller, Du Canto and Fleck · 200 North La Salle Street, Suite 2700 · Chicago, IL 60601-1089 · 312-641-5560

Arnold B. Stein · (Divorce) · Schiller, Du Canto and Fleck · 200 North La Salle Street, Suite 2700 · Chicago, IL 60601-1089 · 312-641-5510

Errol Zavett* · (Divorce, Marital Settlement Agreements, Equitable Division) · Davis, Friedman, Zavett, Kane & MacRae · The Marquette Building, Suite 1600 140 South Dearborn Street · Chicago, IL 60603 · 312-782-2220

Steven H. Katz · (Divorce) · 325 Washington Street, Suite 401 · Waukegan, IL 60085 · 708-623-8300

Harold G. Field* · Harold G. Field & Associates · 126 South County Farm Road, Suite 2B · Wheaton, IL 60187 · 708-665-5800

H. Joseph Gitlin · (Adoption, Child Custody, Divorce, Marital Settlement Agreements, Equitable Division) · Gitlin & Burns · 111 Dean Street · Woodstock, IL 60098 · 815-338-0021

FIRST AMENDMENT LAW

Michael M. Conway · Hopkins & Sutter · Three First National Plaza · Chicago, IL 60602 · 312-558-6600

Samuel Fifer · Sonnenschein Nath & Rosenthal · Sears Tower, Suite 8000 · 233 South Wacker Drive · Chicago, IL 60606-6404 · 312-876-8000

Burton Joseph · Barsy, Joseph & Lichstenstein · 134 North LaSalle, Suite 400 · Chicago, IL 60602 · 312-346-9270

James Klenk · Sonnenschein Nath & Rosenthal · Sears Tower, Suite 8000 · 233 South Wacker Drive · Chicago, IL 60606-6404 · 312-876-8000

HEALTH CARE LAW

Bernadette Muller Broccolo · Gardner, Carton & Douglas · Quaker Tower, Suite 3400 · 321 North Clark Street · Chicago, IL 60610-4795 · 312-245-8432

Edward L. Bryant, Jr. · Gardner, Carton & Douglas · Quaker Tower, Suite 3400 321 North Clark Street · Chicago, IL 60610-4795 · 312-245-8420

Michael R. Callahan · Katten Muchin & Zavis · 525 West Monroe, Suite 1600 · Chicago, IL 60606-3693 · 312-902-5200

Thomas M. Fahey · Coffield Ungaretti Harris & Slavin · 3500 Three First National Plaza · Chicago, IL 60602 · 312-977-4400

Gerald J. Neal · Foley & Lardner · Three First National Plaza, Suite 4950 · 70 West Madison Street · Chicago, IL 60602-4208 · 312-444-9500

William Roach · Gardner, Carton & Douglas · Quaker Tower, Suite 3400 · 321 North Clark Street · Chicago, IL 60610-4795 · 312-245-8432

Richard H. Sanders · Vedder, Price, Kaufman & Kammholz · 222 North La Salle Street, Suite 2600 · Chicago, IL 60601-1003 · 312-609-7500

Thomas O. Shields · Hopkins & Sutter · Three First National Plaza · Chicago, IL 60602 · 312-558-6660

Robert J. Zimmerman · Foley & Lardner · Three First National Plaza, Suite 4950 70 West Madison Street · Chicago, IL 60602-4208 · 312-444-9500

IMMIGRATION LAW

Robert D. Ahlgren · Ahlgren & Blumenfeld · 105 West Madison, Suite 800 · Chicago, IL 60602 · 312-782-1804

Terry Yale Feiertag · Mandel, Lipton and Stevenson · 33 North Dearborn Street, Suite 2400 · Chicago, IL 60602 · 312-236-7080

Donald B. Kempster · Donald B. Kempster & Associates · 332 South Michigan Avenue, Suite 860 · Chicago, IL 60604 · 312-341-9730

Margaret H. McCormick · Minsky, McCormick & Hallagan · 122 South Michigan Avenue, Suite 1800 · Chicago, IL 60603 · 312-427-6163

Joseph Minsky · Minsky, McCormick & Hallagan · 122 South Michigan Avenue, Suite 1800 · Chicago, IL 60603 · 312-427-6163

Paul L. Zulkie · Witman, Goldberg & Zulkie · 222 South Riverside Plaza, Suite 2300 · Chicago, IL 60606-6101 · 312-648-2244

INTELLECTUAL PROPERTY LAW

John W. Chestnut · Tilton, Fallon, Lungmus & Chestnut · 100 South Wacker Drive · Chicago, IL 60606 · 312-263-1841

Ronald B. Coolley · Arnold, White & Durkee · 800 Quaker Tower · 321 North Clark Street · Chicago, IL , 60610 · 312-744-0090

Jerome Gilson · Willian Brinks Olds Hofer Gilson & Lione · NBC Tower, Suite 3600 · 455 North Cityfront Plaza Drive · Chicago, IL 60611-5599 · 312-321-4200

David Craig Hilliard · Pattishall, McAuliffe, Newbury, Hilliard & Geraldson · 311 South Wacker Drive, Suite 5000 · Chicago, IL 60606 · 312-554-8000

Roy E. Hofer · Willian Brinks Olds Hofer Gilson & Lione · NBC Tower, Suite 3600 · 455 North Cityfront Plaza Drive · Chicago, IL 60611-5599 · 312-321-4200

Robert G. Krupka · Kirkland & Ellis · 200 East Randolph Drive · Chicago, IL 60601 · 312-861-2418

Wm. Marshall Lee, Sr. · Lee, Mann, Smith, McWilliams & Sweeney · 105 West Adams Street, Suite 300 · Chicago, IL 60603 · 312-368-1300

Henry L. Mason · Sidley & Austin · One First National Plaza · Chicago, IL 60603 312-853-7000

Robert M. Newbury · Pattishall, McAuliffe, Newbury, Hilliard & Geraldson · 311 South Wacker Drive, Suite 5000 · Chicago, IL 60606 · 312-554-8000

Dean A. Olds · Willian Brinks Olds Hofer Gilson & Lione · NBC Tower, Suite 3600 · 455 North Cityfront Plaza Drive · Chicago, IL 60611-5599 · 312-321-4200

Beverly W. Pattishall · Pattishall, McAuliffe, Newbury, Hilliard & Geraldson · 311 South Wacker Drive, Suite 5000 · Chicago, IL 60606 · 312-554-8000

Daniel W. Vittum, Jr. · Kirkland & Ellis · 200 East Randolph Drive · Chicago, IL 60601 · 312-861-2418

LABOR AND EMPLOYMENT LAW

Sherman M. Carmell · (Labor) · Carmell, Charone, Widmer, Mathews & Moss 225 West Washington Street · Chicago, IL 60606 · 312-236-8033

Sheldon M. Charone · (Labor) · Carmell, Charone, Widmer, Mathews & Moss · 225 West Washington Street · Chicago, IL 60606 · 312-236-8033

R. Theodore Clark, Jr. · (Management) · Seyfarth, Shaw, Fairweather & Geraldson · 55 East Monroe Street, Suite 4200 · Chicago, IL 60603 · 312-346-8000

Gilbert A. Cornfield* · (Labor) · Cornfield and Feldman · 343 South Dearborn Street, 13th Floor · Chicago, IL 60604-3852 · 312-922-2800

Eugene Cotton · (Labor) · Cotton, Watt, Jones & King · 122 South Michigan Avenue, Suite 2050 · Chicago, IL 60603 · 312-427-5100

Lawrence D. Ehrlich · (Management) · Borovsky & Ehrlich · 205 North Michigan Avenue, 41st Floor · Chicago, IL 60601 · 312-861-0800

Gilbert Feldman · (Labor) · Cornfield and Feldman · 343 South Dearborn Street, 13th Floor · Chicago, IL 60604-3852 · 312-922-2800

James C. Franczek, Jr. · (Management) · Vedder, Price, Kaufman & Kammholz 222 North La Salle Street, Suite 2600 · Chicago, IL 60601-1003 · 312-609-7660

Irving M. Friedman · (Labor) · Katz, Friedman, Schur & Eagle · Seven South Dearborn, Suite 1700 · Chicago, IL 60603 · 312-263-6330

Marvin Gittler · (Labor) · Asher, Pavalon, Gittler & Greenfield · Two North La Salle Street, Suite 1200 · Chicago, IL 60602 · 312-263-1500

Barbara J. Hillman · (Labor) · Cornfield and Feldman · 343 South Dearborn Street, 13th Floor · Chicago, IL 60604-3852 · 312-922-2800

Theophil C. Kammholz · (Management) · Vedder, Price, Kaufman & Kammholz 222 North La Salle Street, Suite 2600 · Chicago, IL 60601-1003 · 312-609-7500

Harold A. Katz · (Labor) · Katz, Friedman, Schur & Eagle · Seven South Dearborn Street, Suite 1700 · Chicago, IL 60603 · 312-263-6330

Richard W. Laner · (Management) · Laner, Muchin, Dombrow, Becker, Levin and Tominberg · 350 North Clark Street, Suite 400 · Chicago, IL 60610-4798 · 312-467-9800

Kenneth T. Lopatka* · (Management) · Lopatka, Nohlgren & Martin · 1415 North Dayton Street · Chicago, IL 60622 · 312-337-4200

Richard L. Marcus* · (Management) · Sonnenschein Nath & Rosenthal · Sears Tower, Suite 8000 · 233 South Wacker Drive · Chicago, IL 60606-6404 · 312-876-7394

George J. Matkov, Jr. · (Management) · Matkov, Salzman, Madoff & Gunn · 100 West Monroe Street, Suite 1500 · Chicago, IL 60603-1906 · 312-332-0777

Edward B. Miller* · (Management) · Pope, Ballard, Shepard & Fowle · 69 West Washington Street · Chicago, IL 60602-3069 · 312-630-4200

Richard D. Ostrow · (Management) · Seyfarth, Shaw, Fairweather & Geraldson 55 East Monroe Street, Suite 4200 · Chicago, IL 60603 · 312-346-8000

MARITIME LAW

Warren J. Marwedel* · Keck, Mahin & Cate · 8300 Sears Tower · 233 South Wacker Drive · Chicago, IL 60606-6589 · 312-876-3400

Theodore C. Robinson · Ray, Robinson, Hanninen & Carle · 135 South La Salle Street, Suite 1916 · Chicago, IL 60603-4233 · 312-726-2905

Michael A. Snyder · Michael A. Snyder & Associates · 850 West Jackson Boulevard, Suite 310 · Chicago, IL 60607 · 312-421-3110

NATURAL RESOURCES AND ENVIRONMENTAL LAW

Percy L. Angelo · Mayer, Brown & Platt · 190 South La Salle Street, Suite 3900 Chicago, IL 60603-3441 · 312-782-0600

Thomas M. McMahon · Sidley & Austin · One First National Plaza · Chicago, IL 60603 · 312-853-7000

Sheldon A. Zabel · Schiff Hardin & Waite · 7200 Sears Tower · 233 South Wacker Drive · Chicago, IL 60606-6473 · 312-876-1000

PERSONAL INJURY LITIGATION

William C. Murphy* · Murphy, Hupp, Foote, Mielke and Kinnally · North Island Center · P.O. Box 5030 · Aurora, IL 60507 · 312-844-0056

Thomas F. Bridgman · (Defendants) · Baker & McKenzie · One Prudential Plaza, Suite 2600 · 130 East Randolph Drive · Chicago, IL 60601 · 312-861-8000

Robert J. Cooney, Sr. · (Plaintiffs) · Cooney and Conway · 77 West Washington Street · Chicago, IL 60602 · 312-236-6166

Philip H. Corboy · (Plaintiffs) · Corboy & Demetrio · 33 North Dearborn Street, 21st Floor · Chicago, IL 60602 · 312-346-3191

Thomas A. Demetrio* · (Plaintiffs, Medical Malpractice, Airplane Collision) · Corboy & Demetrio · 33 North Dearborn Street, 21st Floor · Chicago, IL 60602 312-346-3191

James T. Demos · (Plaintiffs) · Demos & Burke · 33 North Dearborn Street, Suite 826 · Chicago, IL 60602 · 312-263-4388

Richard G. French* · (Defendants, Medical Malpractice, Products Liability, Professional Malpractice, Automobile Collision, Appellate) · French Kezelis & Kominiarek · 33 North Dearborn Street, Suite 1800 · Chicago, IL 60602 · 312-782-0634

Al Hofeld* · (Plaintiffs) · Hofeld and Schaffner · 33 North Dearborn Street, Suite 1600 · Chicago, IL 60602 · 312-372-4250

Harold L. Jacobson* · (Defendants) · Lord, Bissell & Brook · Harris Bank Building, Suites 3200-3600 · 115 South La Salle Street · Chicago, IL 60603 · 312-443-0700

William V. Johnson · (Defendants) · Johnson & Bell · 222 North La Salle Street, Suite 2200 · Chicago, IL 60601 · 312-372-0770

William D. Maddux · (Plaintiffs) · William D. Maddux & Associates · One North La Salle Street, Suite 3800 · Chicago, IL 60602 · 312-782-2525

Jerome Mirza* · (Plaintiffs) · Jerome Mirza and Associates · Three First National Plaza · Chicago, IL 60602 · 312-368-1903

C. Barry Montgomery* · (Defendants) · Williams & Montgomery · 2100 Civic Opera Building · 20 North Wacker Drive · Chicago, IL 60606-3094 · 312-443-3200

Eugene I. Pavalon · (Plaintiffs) · Pavalon & Gifford · Two North La Salle Street, Suite 1600 · Chicago, IL 60602 · 312-419-7400

Joseph A. Power, Jr.* · (Plaintiffs) · Hayes & Power · Three First National Plaza, Suite 3910 · Chicago, IL 60602 · 312-236-9381

Neil K. Quinn* · (Defendants, Medical Malpractice, Products Liability, Professional Malpractice) · Pretzel & Stouffer · One South Wacker Drive, Suite 2500 · Chicago, IL 60606-4673 · 312-346-1973

Leonard M. Ring · (Plaintiffs) · Leonard M. Ring and Associates · 111 West Washington Street, Suite 1333 · Chicago, IL 60602 · 312-332-1765

Thomas F. Tobin · (Defendants) · Baker & McKenzie · One Prudential Plaza, Suite 2700 · 130 East Randolph Drive · Chicago, IL 60601 · 312-861-8000

Rex Carr* · (Plaintiffs, Medical Malpractice, Products Liability, Professional Malpractice, Automobile Collision) · Carr, Korein, Tillery, Kunin, Montroy, Glass & Bogard · 412 Missouri Avenue · East St. Louis, IL 62201 · 618-274-0434

Thomas F. Londrigan* · (Plaintiffs, Medical Malpractice, Products Liability) · Londrigan, Potter & Randle · 1227 South Seventh Street · P.O. Box 62705 · Springfield, IL 62703 · 217-544-9823

PUBLIC UTILITY LAW

Peter V. Fazio, Jr. · Schiff Hardin & Waite · 7200 Sears Tower · 233 South Wacker Drive · Chicago, IL 60606-6473 · 312-876-1000

Robert A. Helman · Mayer, Brown & Platt · 190 South La Salle Street · Chicago, IL 60603-3441 · 312-782-0600

REAL ESTATE LAW

Robert M. Berger · Mayer, Brown & Platt · 190 South La Salle Street · Chicago, IL 60603-3441 · 312-782-0600

Frank C. Bernard · Sonnenschein Nath & Rosenthal · Sears Tower, Suite 8000 233 South Wacker Drive · Chicago, IL 60606-6404 · 312-876-8000

Martin K. Blonder · Rosenthal and Schanfield · Mid Continental Plaza, Suite 4620 · 55 East Monroe Street · Chicago, IL 60603 · 312-236-5622

Charles L. Edwards · (Commercial Transactions, Industrial Transactions) · Rudnick & Wolfe · 203 North La Salle Street, 18th Floor · Chicago, IL 60601-1293 · 312-368-4010

Livingston Fairbank, Jr. · Rudnick & Wolfe · 203 North La Salle Street, Suite 1500 · Chicago, IL 60602 · 312-368-4000

Fred I. Feinstein · McDermott, Will & Emery · 227 West Monroe Street · Chicago, IL 60606 · 312-372-2000

Norman Geis · Greenberger, Krauss & Jacobs · 180 North La Salle Street, Suite 2700 · Chicago, IL 60601 · 312-346-1300

Jerome H. Gerson · Winston & Strawn · 35 West Wacker Drive, Suite 4200 · Chicago, IL 60601 · 312-558-5467

David Glickstein · Greenberger, Krauss & Jacobs · 180 North La Salle Street, Suite 2700 · Chicago, IL 60601 · 312-346-1300

Robert H. Goldman · Rudnick & Wolfe · 203 North La Salle Street, Suite 1500 Chicago, IL 60602 · 312-368-4000

Donald J. Gralen · Sidley & Austin · One First National Plaza · Chicago, IL 60603 · 312-853-7000

Ernest Greenberger · Greenberger, Krauss & Jacobs · 180 North La Salle Street, Suite 2700 · Chicago, IL 60601 · 312-346-1300

Wayne R. Hannah, Jr. · Sonnenschein Nath & Rosenthal · Sears Tower, Suite 8000 · 233 South Wacker Drive · Chicago, IL 60606-6404 · 312-876-8000

Thomas C. Homburger · (Commercial Transactions, Financial) · Bell, Boyd & Lloyd · Three First National Plaza, Suite 3200 · 70 West Madison Street · Chicago, IL 60602-4207 · 312-807-4267

Paul Homer · Rudnick & Wolfe · 203 North La Salle Street, Suite 1500 · Chicago, IL 60202 · 312-368-4000

Maurice Jacobs · Greenberger, Krauss & Jacobs · 180 North La Salle Street, Suite 2700 · Chicago, IL 60601 · 312-346-1300

Howard E. Kane · Rudnick & Wolfe · 203 North La Salle Street, Suite 1500 · Chicago, IL 60602 · 312-368-4000

Michael S. Kurtzon · Miller, Shakman, Hamilton & Kurtzon · 208 South La Salle Street, Suite 1200 · Chicago, IL 60604 · 312-263-3700

David E. Malfar · David E. Malfar & Associates · 77 West Washington Street, Suite 619 · Chicago, IL 60602 · 312-726-8200

Nina B. Matis · Katten Muchin & Zavis · 525 West Monroe Street, Suite 1600 · Chicago, IL 60606-3693 · 312-902-5200

Ronald S. Miller · Miller, Shakman, Hamilton & Kurtzon · 208 South La Salle Street, Suite 1200 · Chicago, IL 60604 · 312-263-3700

Patrick G. Moran · Sonnenschein Nath & Rosenthal · Sears Tower, Suite 8000 · 233 South Wacker Drive · Chicago, IL 60606-6404 · 312-876-8000

Benjamin J. Randall · Katz Randall & Weinberg · 200 North LaSalle Street, Suite 2300 · Chicago, IL 60601 · 312-807-3800

Frank A. Reichelderfer · Burke, Wilson & McIlvaine · 500 West Madison Street, Suite 3700 · Chicago, IL 60606 · 312-715-5000

Lester Rosen · Rosenthal and Schanfield · Mid Continental Plaza, Suite 4620 · 55 East Monroe Street · Chicago, IL 60603 · 312-236-5622

Paul D. Rudnick · Rudnick & Wolfe · 203 North La Salle Street, Suite 1500 · Chicago, IL 60602 · 312-368-4000

Stanton Schuman · Gottlieb & Swchartz · 200 East Randolph · Chicago, IL 60601 312-819-1000

William R. Theiss · Kirkland & Ellis · 200 East Randolph Drive · Chicago, IL 60601 · 312-861-2000

Brian Meltzer · Keck, Mahin & Cate · 1515 East Woodfield Road, Suite 250 · Schaumburg, IL 60173 · 708-330-1200

TAX AND EMPLOYEE BENEFITS LAW

Melvin S. Adess · Kirkland & Ellis · 200 East Randolph Drive · Chicago, IL 60601 312-861-2000

Robert H. Aland · Baker & McKenzie · One Prudential Plaza, Suite 3200 · 130 East Randolph Drive · Chicago, IL 60601 · 312-861-8000

Sheldon I. Banoff · Katten Muchin & Zavis · 525 West Monroe, Suite 1600 · Chicago, IL 60606-3693 · 312-902-5200

Frank V. Battle, Jr. · Sidley & Austin · One First National Plaza · Chicago, IL 60603 · 312-853-7000

Michael G. Beemer · Vedder, Price, Kaufman & Kammholz · 222 North La Salle Street, Suite 2600 · Chicago, IL 60601-1003 · 312-609-7500

Theodore Berger · Miller, Shakman, Hamilton & Kurtzon · 208 South La Salle Street, Suite 1200 · Chicago, IL 60604 · 312-263-3700

Stephen S. Bowen · Latham & Watkins · Sears Tower, Suite 5800 · Chicago, IL 60606 · 312-876-7700

Edward J. Buchholz · (Corporate & Partnership Transactions) · Winston & Strawn · 35 West Wacker Drive · Chicago, IL 60601 · 312-558-6327

Patrick J. Caraher · (Employee Benefits) · McDermott, Will & Emery · 227 West Monroe Street · Chicago, IL 60606 · 312-372-2000

Lawrence M. Dubin · Hopkins & Sutter · Three First National Plaza, Suite 4300 Chicago, IL 60602 · 312-558-6600

Marshall E. Eisenberg · Neal, Gerber & Eisenberg · Two North La Salle Street, Suite 2200 · Chicago, IL 60602 · 312-269-8000

Glenn E. Ferencz · Gardner, Carton & Douglas · Quaker Tower, Suite 3400 · 321 North Clark Street · Chicago, IL 60610-4795 · 312-245-8679

Bradford L. Ferguson · Hopkins & Sutter · Three First National Plaza, Suite 4300 · Chicago, IL 60602 · 312-558-6600

Sheldon I. Fink · Sonnenschein Nath & Rosenthal · Sears Tower, Suite 8000 · 233 South Wacker Drive · Chicago, IL 60606-6404 · 312-876-8000

Louis S. Freeman · Sonnenschein Nath & Rosenthal · Sears Tower, Suite 8000 233 South Wacker Drive · Chicago, IL 60606-6404 · 312-876-8000

William C. Golden · Sidley & Austin · One First National Plaza · Chicago, IL 60603 · 312-853-7000

Arthur I. Gould · Mayer, Brown & Platt · 190 South La Salle Street, Suite 3900 Chicago, IL 60603-3441 · 312-782-0600

Thomas M. Haderlein · Baker & McKenzie · One Prudential Plaza, Suite 2800 · 130 East Randolph Drive · Chicago, IL 60601 · 312-861-8000

Frederic W. Hickman · Hopkins & Sutter · Three First National Plaza, Suite 4300 · Chicago, IL 60602 · 312-558-6600

George B. Javaras · Kirkland & Ellis · 200 East Randolph Drive · Chicago, IL 60601 · 312-861-2000

Burton W. Kanter* · Neal, Gerber & Eisenberg · Two North La Salle Street , Suite 2200 · Chicago, IL 60602 · 312-269-8000

Jared Kaplan · Keck, Mahin & Cate · 8300 Sears Tower · 233 South Wacker Drive · Chicago, IL 60606-6589 · 312-876-3400

Stanton A. Kessler · Mayer, Brown & Platt · 190 South La Salle Street, Suite 3900 Chicago, IL 60603-3441 · 312-782-0600

Howard G. Krane · Kirkland & Ellis · 200 East Randolph Drive · Chicago, IL 60601 · 312-861-2000

Herbert W. Krueger · (Employee Benefits) · Mayer, Brown & Platt · 190 South La Salle Street, Suite 3900 · Chicago, IL 60603-3441 · 312-782-0600

Milton A. Levenfeld · Levenfeld, Eisenberg, Janger, Glassberg, Samotny & Halper · 33 West Monroe Street, 21st Floor · Chicago, IL 60603 · 312-346-8380

Jack S. Levin · (Corporate & Partnership Transactions) · Kirkland & Ellis · 200 East Randolph Drive · Chicago, IL 60601 · 312-861-2000

Richard L. Menson · (Employee Benefits) · Gardner, Carton & Douglas · Quaker Tower, Suite 3400 · 321 North Clark Street · Chicago, IL 60610-4795 · 312-644-3000

Timothy M. Mlsna · (Employee Benefits) · Kirkland & Ellis · 200 East Randolph Drive · Chicago, IL 60601 · 312-861-2000

William L. Morrison · Gardner, Carton & Douglas · Quaker Tower, Suite 3400 321 North Clark Street · Chicago, IL 60610-4795 · 312-644-3000

Alan D. Nesburg · (Employee Benefits) · McDermott, Will & Emery · 227 West Monroe Street · Chicago, IL 60606 · 312-372-2000

John K. O'Connor · Lord, Bissell & Brook · Harris Bank Building, Suites 3400 · 115 South La Salle Street · Chicago, IL 60603 · 312-443-0700

Arthur S. Rollin · Skadden, Arps, Slate, Meagher & Flom · 333 West Wacker Drive · Chicago, IL 60606 · 312-407-0700

Jeffrey T. Sheffield · Kirkland & Ellis · 200 East Randolph Drive · Chicago, IL 60601 · 312-861-2000

Roger C. Siske · (Employee Benefits) · Sonnenschein Nath & Rosenthal · Sears Tower, Suite 8000 · 233 South Wacker Drive · Chicago, IL 60606-6404 · 312-876-8000

Samuel C. Thompson, Jr. · Schiff Hardin & Waite · 7200 Sears Tower · 233 South Wacker Drive · Chicago, IL 60606-6473 · 312-876-1000

Douglas H. Walter · Bell, Boyd & Lloyd · Three First National Plaza, Suite 3200 70 West Madison Street · Chicago, IL 60602-4207 · 312-782-3939

Raymond P. Wexler · Kirkland & Ellis · 200 East Randolph Drive · Chicago, IL 60601 · 312-861-2418

TRUSTS AND ESTATES

Ivan A. Elliott, Jr. · (Estate Planning, Estate Administration) · Conger & Elliott Farm Bureau Building · Carmi, IL 62821-0220 · 618-382-4187

Frederick G. Acker · McDermott, Will & Emery · 227 West Monroe Street · Chicago, IL 60606 · 312-372-2000

Roy M. Adams · Schiff Hardin & Waite · 7200 Sears Tower · 233 South Wacker Drive · Chicago, IL 60606-6473 · 312-876-1000

W. Timothy Baetz · McDermott, Will & Emery · 227 West Monroe Street · Chicago, IL 60606 · 312-372-2000

Larry D. Berning · (Estate Planning, Estate Administration, Charitable Trusts) · Sidley & Austin · One First National Plaza · Chicago, IL 60603 · 312-853-7000

Arthur W. Brown, Jr. · Altheimer & Gray · 10 South Wacker Drive, Suite 4000 Chicago, IL 60606 · 312-715-4000

Donald A. Gillies · Altheimer & Gray · 10 South Wacker Drive, Suite 4000 · Chicago, IL 60606 · 312-715-4000

Donald A. Glassberg · Levenfeld, Eisenberg, Janger, Glassberg, Samotny & Halper · 33 West Monroe Street, 21st Floor · Chicago, IL 60603-5448 · 312-346-8380

Howard M. McCue III · Mayer, Brown & Platt · 190 South La Salle Street, Suite 3900 · Chicago, IL 60603-3441 · 312-782-0600

Franklin W. Nitikman · McDermott, Will & Emery · 227 West Monroe Street · Chicago, IL 60606 · 312-372-2000

James M. Trapp · McDermott, Will & Emery · 227 West Monroe Street · Chicago, IL 60606 · 312-372-2000

William C. Weinsheimer · Hopkins & Sutter · Three First National Plaza · Chicago, IL 60602 · 312-558-6600

James N. Zartman · Chapman and Cutler · 111 West Monroe Street, Suite 1300 · Chicago, IL 60603 · 312-845-3000

Jerold I. Horn · 515 Jefferson Bank Building · Peoria, IL 61602 · 309-676-2778

INDIANA

BANKRUPTCY LAW

William A. Thorne · (Business Reorganization, Creditors' Rights) · Thorne, Grodnik & Ransel · 228 West High Street · Elkhart, IN 46516-3176 · 219-294-7473

Howard B. Sandler · Beckman, Lawson, Sandler, Snyder & Federoff · 800 Standard Federal Plaza · P.O. Box 800 · Fort Wayne, IN 46801-0800 · 219-422-0800

Jerald I. Ancel · Sommer & Barnard · 4000 Bank One Tower · 111 Monument Circle · P.O. Box 44363 · Indianapolis, IN 46244-0363 · 317-630-4000

Steven H. Ancel · Ancel & Dunlap · Market Square Center, Suite 1770 · 151 North Delaware · Indianapolis, IN 46204 · 317-634-9052

Sigmund J. Beck · (Business Reorganization, Creditors' Rights, Debtors' Rights, Bankruptcy Litigation) · Bamberger & Feibleman · 500 Union Federal Building · 45 North Pennsylvania Street · Indianapolis, IN 46204 · 317-639-5151

James E. Carlberg · Klineman, Rose, Wolf and Wallack · 135 North Pennsylvania Street, Suite 2100 · Indianapolis, IN 46204 · 317-264-5000

James M. Carr · Baker & Daniels · 300 North Meridian Street, Suite 2700 · Indianapolis, IN 46204 · 317-237-0300

John R. Carr, Jr. · Buschmann, Carr & Shanks · 1020 Market Tower · 10 West Market Street · Indianapolis, IN 46204 · 317-636-5511

David H. Kleiman · Dann Pecar Newman Talesnick & Kleiman · One American Square, Suite 2300 · P.O. Box 82008 · Indianapolis, IN 46282 · 317-632-3232

James A. Knauer · (Business Reorganization, Creditors' Rights, Debtors' Rights, Bankruptcy Litigation) · Kroger, Gardis & Regas · 700 Guaranty Building · 20 North Meridian Street · Indianapolis, IN 46204-3059 · 317-634-6328

Elliott D. Levin · Rubin & Levin · 500 Marott Center · 342 Massachusetts Avenue Indianapolis, IN 46204-2161 · 317-634-0300

Stanley Talesnick · Dann Pecar Newman Talesnick & Kleiman · One American Square, Suite 2300 · P.O. Box 82008 · Indianapolis, IN 46282 · 317-632-3232

Thomas D. Titsworth · Bamberger & Feibleman · 500 Union Federal Building · 45 North Pennsylvania Street · Indianapolis, IN 46204 · 317-639-5151

BUSINESS LITIGATION

John L. Carroll · Johnson, Carroll & Griffith · 2230 West Franklin Street · P.O. Box 6016 · Evansville, IN 47719-0016 · 812-425-4466

Leonard E. Eilbacher · Hunt, Suedhoff, Borror & Eilbacher · 900 Paine Webber Building · 803 South Calhoun Street · Fort Wayne, IN 46802-2399 · 219-423-1311

Milford M. Miller · Miller Carson & Boxberger · 1400 One Summit Square · Fort Wayne, IN 46802-3173 · 219-423-9411

Edward L. Murphy, Jr. · Miller Carson & Boxberger · 1400 One Summit Square Fort Wayne, IN 46802 · 219-423-9411

Richard E. Steinbronn · Barnes & Thornburg · One Summit Square, Suite 600 Fort Wayne, IN 46802 · 219-423-9440

Frederick F. Eichhorn, Jr. · Eichhorn, Eichhorn & Link · 200 Russell Street · P.O. Box 6328 · Hammond, IN 46325-6328 · 219-931-0560

David C. Jensen · Eichhorn, Eichhorn & Link · 200 Russell Street · P.O. Box 6328 · Hammond, IN 46325-6328 · 219-931-0560

Frederick H. Link* · Eichhorn, Eichhorn & Link · 200 Russell Street · P.O. Box 6328 · Hammond, IN 46325-6328 · 219-931-0560

Terrill Albright · Baker & Daniels · 300 North Meridian Street, Suite 2700 · Indianapolis, IN 46204 · 317-237-0300

William C. Barnard · (also Appellate) · Sommer & Barnard · 4000 Bank One Tower · 111 Monument Circle · P.O. Box 44363 · Indianapolis, IN 46244-0363 · 317-630-4000

Virgil L. Beeler* · (Administrative, Appellate, Commercial, Government Regulation) · Baker & Daniels · 300 North Meridian Street, Suite 2700 · Indianapolis, IN 46204 · 317-237-0300

Joe C. Emerson* · (Antitrust, Appellate, Securities, Derivative Shareholder) · Baker & Daniels · 300 North Meridian Street, Suite 2700 · Indianapolis, IN 46204 317-237-1257

Arthur P. Kalleres* · (Construction Law) · Ice Miller Donadio & Ryan · One American Square · P.O. Box 82001 · Indianapolis, IN 46282-0002 · 317-236-2100

Donald E. Knebel* · Barnes & Thornburg · 1313 Merchants Bank Building · 11 South Meridian Street · Indianapolis, IN 46204 · 317-638-1313

James A. McDermott* · (also Appellate) · Barnes & Thornburg · 1313 Merchants Bank Building · 11 South Meridian Street · Indianapolis, IN 46204 · 317-638-1313

Lee B. McTurnan* · McTurnan & Turner · 2070 Market Tower · 10 West Market Street · Indianapolis, IN 46204 · 317-464-8181

Hugh E. Reynolds, Jr. · Locke, Reynolds, Boyd & Weisell · 1000 Capital Center South, 10th Floor · 201 North Illinois Street · Indianapolis, IN 46204 · 317-237-3800

Christopher G. Scanlon · Baker & Daniels · 300 North Meridian Street, Suite 2700 · Indianapolis, IN 46204 · 317-237-0300

Evan E. Steger · (Commercial, Finance, RICO, Securities) · Ice Miller Donadio & Ryan · One American Square · P.O. Box 82001 · Indianapolis, IN 46282-0002 317-236-2100

Stephen W. Terry, Jr.* · (Administrative/Environmental, Antitrust, Appellate, Commercial) · Baker & Daniels · 300 North Meridian Street, Suite 2700 · Indianapolis, IN 46204 · 317-237-0300

William P. Wooden · Wooden McLaughlin & Sterner · 201 Capitol Center South 201 North Illinois Street · Indianapolis, IN 46204 · 317-639-6151

Russell H. Hart · Stuart & Branigin · 801 The Life Building · P.O. Box 1010 · Lafayette, IN 47902 · 317-423-1561

James V. McGlone · Stuart & Branigin · 801 The Life Building · P.O. Box 1010 Lafayette, IN 47902 · 317-423-1561

J. Lee McNeely* · McNeely, Sanders, Stephenson & Thopy · 30 East Washington Street, Suite 400 · P.O. Box 457 · Shelbyville, IN 46176 · 317-392-3619

Robert J. Konopa · (Commercial, Transportation) · Kramer, Butler, Simeri, Konopa and Laderer · One Michiana Square, Suite 300 · 100 East Wayne Street P.O. Box 1438 · South Bend, IN 46624-1438 · 219-233-3303

Richard W. Morgan · Barnes & Thornburg · 600 First Source Bank Center · 100 North Michigan Street · South Bend, IN 46601 · 219-233-1171

Franklin A. Morse II · Barnes & Thornburg · 600 First Source Bank Center · 100 North Michigan Street · South Bend, IN 46601 · 219-233-1171

John T. Mulvihill · Barnes & Thornburg · 600 First Source Bank Center · 100 North Michigan Street · South Bend, IN 46601 · 219-233-1171

James H. Pankow · Jones, Obenchain, Ford, Pankow & Lewis · 1800 Valley American Bank Building · P.O. Box 4577 · South Bend, IN 46634-4577 · 219-233-1194

Thomas H. Singer* · (Plaintiffs) · Nickle and Piasecki · 205 West Jefferson, Suite 413 · South Bend, IN 46601 · 219-232-4747

CORPORATE LAW

Philip L. Carson · Miller Carson & Boxberger · 1400 One Summit Square · Fort Wayne, IN 46802-3173 · 219-423-9411

Miles C. Gerberding · Barnes & Thornburg · One Summit Square, Suite 600 · Fort Wayne, IN 46802 · 219-423-9440

David Haist · Barnes & Thornburg · 600 One Summit Square · Fort Wayne, IN 46802 · 219-423-9440

Robert T. Hoover · Baker & Daniels · 2400 Fort Wayne National Bank Building P.O. Box 12709 · Fort Wayne, IN 46864 · 219-424-8000

John P. Martin · Barrett & McNagny · Lincoln Bank Tower, Third Floor · 216 East Barry Street · P.O. Box 2263 · Fort Wayne, IN 46801-2263 · 219-423-9551

Thomas M. Shoaff · Baker & Daniels · 2400 Fort Wayne National Bank Building P.O. Box 12709 · Fort Wayne, IN 46864 · 219-424-8000

N. Reed Silliman · Baker & Daniels · 2400 Fort Wayne National Bank Building Fort Wayne, IN 46802 · 219-424-8000

James A. Aschleman · (Corporate Finance, Leveraged Buyouts, Mergers & Acquisitions, Securities) · Baker & Daniels · 300 North Meridian Street, Suite 2700 Indianapolis, IN 46204 · 317-237-0300

Leonard J. Betley · Ice Miller Donadio & Ryan · One American Square · P.O. Box 82001 · Indianapolis, IN 46282-0002 · 317-236-2100

John D. Cochran · Baker & Daniels · 300 North Meridian Street, Suite 2700 · Indianapolis, IN 46204 · 317-237-0300

Richard E. Deer · Barnes & Thornburg · 1313 Merchants Bank Building · 11 South Meridian Street · Indianapolis, IN 46204 · 317-638-1313

Richard M. Leagre · (Banking, Corporate Finance, International Trade, Securities) · Leagre & Barnes · 9100 Keystone Crossing, Suite 800 · P.O. Box 40609 · Indianapolis, IN 46240-0609 · 317-843-1655

Thomas M. Lofton · Baker & Daniels · 300 North Meridian Street, Suite 2700 · Indianapolis, IN 46204 · 317-237-0300

Michael P. Lucas · (Municipal Finance) · Barnes & Thornburg · 1313 Merchants Bank Building · 11 South Meridian Street · Indianapolis, IN 46204 · 317-638-1313

Bruce A. Polizotto · Ice Miller Donadio & Ryan · One American Square · P.O. Box 82001 · Indianapolis, IN 46282-0002 · 317-236-2100

Robert H. Reynolds · (Corporate Finance, International, Mergers & Acquisitions) Barnes & Thornburg · 1313 Merchants Bank Building · 11 South Meridian Street Indianapolis, IN 46204 · 317-638-1313

Jack R. Snyder · Ice Miller Donadio & Ryan · One American Square · P.O. Box 82001 · Indianapolis, IN 46282-0002 · 317-236-2100

James A. Strain · Barnes & Thornburg · 1313 Merchants Bank Building · 11 South Meridian Street · Indianapolis, IN 46204 · 317-638-1313

John A. Burgess · Barnes & Thornburg · 600 First Source Bank Center · 100 North Michigan Street · South Bend, IN 46601 · 219-233-1171

G. Burt Ford · Jones, Obenchain, Ford, Pankow & Lewis · 1800 Valley American Bank Building · P.O. Box 4577 · South Bend, IN 46634-4577 · 219-233-1194

Edward J. Gray · Barnes & Thornburg · 600 First Source Bank Center · 100 North Michigan Street · South Bend, IN 46601 · 219-233-1171

Nelson J. Vogel, Jr. · (Mergers & Acquisitions) · Barnes & Thornburg · 600 First Source Bank Center · 100 North Michigan Street · South Bend, IN 46601 · 219-233-1171

CRIMINAL DEFENSE

Jeffrey A. Lockwood · Schuyler, Eisele & Lockwood · 200 East 11th Street, Suite 100 · Anderson, IN 46016 · 317-643-3300

Tom G. Jones · Jones, Loveall & Johnson · 150 North Main Street · Franklin, IN 46131 · 317-736-7174

Robert W. Hammerle · Allen, Baratt, & Hammerle · 136 East Market Street, Suite 800 · Indianapolis, IN 46204 · 317-635-6567

Richard Kammen* · McClure, McClure & Kammen · 235 North Delaware · Indianapolis, IN 46204 · 317-632-6341

J. Richard Kiefer · Safrin, Kiefer & McGoff · 8880 Keystone Crossing, Suite 750 Indianapolis, IN 46240 · 317-848-1000

Owen M. Mullin* · 116 North Delaware Street · Indianapolis, IN 46204 · 317-639-1391

Don A. Tabbert* · (Non-Violent Crimes, Federal Court, State Court) · Tabbert & Ford · Indiana National Bank Tower, Suite 2100 · One Indiana Square · Indianapolis, IN 46204 · 317-639-5444

James H. Voyles, Jr.* · Ober, Symmes, Cardwell, Voyles & Zahn · 300 Consolidated Building · 115 North Pennsylvania Street · Indianapolis, IN 46204 · 317-632-4463

Nick J. Thiros · Cohen & Thiros · Gainer Bank Center, Suite 899 · 8585 Broadway · Merrillville, IN 46410 · 219-769-1600

FAMILY LAW

Andrew C. Mallor · Mallor, Grodner & Bohrer · 1011 North Walnut Street · P.O. Box 1848 · Bloomington, IN 47402 · 812-336-0200

John D. Proffitt* · Campbell, Kyle & Proffitt · 650 East Carmel Drive, Suite 400 Carmel, IN 46032 · 317-846-6514

John M. Howard, Jr. · Howard, Lawson & Wood · 110 South Washington Street Danville, IN 46122 · 317-745-6471

James A. Buck* · Buck, Berry, Landau & Breunig · 302 North Alabama Street · Indianapolis, IN 46204 · 317-638-3333

Franklin I. Miroff* · (Adoption, Child Custody, Divorce, Equitable Division) · Ancel, Miroff & Frank · Two Market Square Center, Suite 1000 · 251 East Ohio Street · P.O. Box 44219 · Indianapolis, IN 46244 · 317-634-1245

Marvin H. Mitchell* · Mitchell Hurst Jacobs & Dick · 152 East Washington Street Indianapolis, IN 46204-3615 · 317-636-0808

Molly P. Rucker* · Rucker, Bennett & Kertis · 520 Merchants Bank Building · Indianapolis, IN 46204 · 317-634-6173

James P. Seidensticker, Jr. · Bose McKinney & Evans · 2700 First Indiana Plaza Indianapolis, IN 46204 · 317-684-5000

Wilson S. Stober* · (Divorce, Marital Settlement Agreements, Equitable Division) · Baker & Daniels · 300 North Meridian Street, Suite 2700 · Indianapolis, IN 46204 · 317-237-0300

Edward O. DeLaney · Barnes & Thornburg · 1313 Merchants Bank Building · 11 South Meridian Street · Indianapolis, IN 46204 · 317-638-1313

FIRST AMENDMENT LAW

Richard Kammen · McClure, McClure & Kammen · 235 North Delaware · Indianapolis, IN 46204 · 317-632-6341

HEALTH CARE LAW

Thomas D. Logan · Rothberg, Gallmeyer, Fruechtenicht & Logan · 915 South Clinton Street, Suite 800 · P.O. Box 11647 · Fort Wayne, IN 46859-1647 · 219-422-9454

Brian J. Deppe · La Grange, Fredbeck & Deppe · Nine East Court · Franklin, IN 46131 · 317-736-5138

Rex P. Killian · Hall, Render, Killian, Heath & Lyman · 8402 Harcourt Road, Suite 820 · Indianapolis, IN 46260 · 317-871-6222

John C. Render · Hall, Render, Killian, Heath & Lyman · 1100 One American Square · Indianapolis, IN 46282 · 317-633-4884

Myra C. Selby · Ice Miller Donadio & Ryan · One American Square · P.O. Box 82001 · Indianapolis, IN 46282-0002 · 317-236-2100

Glenn T. Troyer · Locke, Reynolds, Boyd & Weisell · 1000 Capital Center South, 10th Floor · 201 North Illinois Street · Indianapolis, IN 46204 · 317-237-3800

Thomas F. Lewis, Jr. · Jones, Obenchain, Ford, Pankow & Lewis · 1800 Valley American Bank Building · P.O. Box 4577 · South Bend, IN 46634-4577 · 219-233-1194

IMMIGRATION LAW

Paul D. Gresk · Johnson, Smith, Densborn, Wright & Heath · 1800 INB Tower One Indiana Square · Indianapolis, IN 46204 · 317-634-9777

Richard E. Parker · Ice Miller Donadio & Ryan · One American Square · P.O. Box 82001 · Indianapolis, IN 46282-0002 · 317-236-2278

Catherine A. Singleton · Johnson, Smith, Densborn, Wright & Heath · One Indiana Square, Suite 1800 · Indianapolis, IN 46204 · 317-634-9777

INTELLECTUAL PROPERTY LAW

John F. Hoffman · Jeffers, Hoffman & Niewyk · Fort Wayne, IN 46802 · 219-426-1700

William R. Coffey · Barnes & Thornburg · 1313 Merchants Bank Building · 11 South Meridian Street · Indianapolis, IN 46204 · 317-638-1313

Charles David Emhardt · Moriarty & McNett · Bank One Center Tower, Suite 3700 · 11 South Meridian Street · Indianapolis, IN 46204 · 317-634-3456

Jay G. Taylor · Ice Miller Donadio & Ryan · One American Square · P.O. Box 82001 · Indianapolis, IN 46282-0002 · 317-236-2150

LABOR AND EMPLOYMENT LAW

Ernest M. Beal, Jr. · (Management, Individuals, EEO) · 9025 Coldwater Road, Suite 400 · Fort Wayne, IN 46825 · 219-489-2833

Herbert C. Snyder, Jr. · (Management) · Barnes & Thornburg · One Summit Square, Suite 600 · Fort Wayne, IN 46802 · 219-423-9440

Robert K. Bellamy* · (Management) · Barnes & Thornburg · 1313 Merchants Bank Building · 11 South Meridian Street · Indianapolis, IN 46204 · 317-638-1313

S. R. Born II · (Management) · Ice Miller Donadio & Ryan · One American Square · P.O. Box 82001 · Indianapolis, IN 46282-0002 · 317-236-2100

Belle Choate · (Individuals) · Choate Visher & Haith · 151 North Delaware Street, Suite 740 · Indianapolis, IN 46204 · 317-634-3113

Leland B. Cross, Jr. · (Management) · Ice Miller Donadio & Ryan · One American Square · P.O. Box 82001 · Indianapolis, IN 46282-0002 · 317-236-2233

Frederick W. Dennerline III · (Labor) · Fillenwarth, Dennerline, Groth & Baird 1213 North Arlington Avenue, Suite 204 · Indianapolis, IN 46219 · 317-353-9363

Edward J. Fillenwarth, Jr. · (Labor) · Fillenwarth, Dennerline, Groth & Baird · 1213 North Arlington Avenue, Suite 204 · Indianapolis, IN 46219 · 317-353-9363

William R. Groth* · (Labor) · Fillenwarth, Dennerline, Groth & Baird · 1213 North Arlington Avenue, Suite 204 · Indianapolis, IN 46219 · 317-353-9363

Raymond J. Hafsten, Jr. · (Individuals) · 615 Merchants Bank Building · 11 South Meridian Street · Indianapolis, IN 46204 · 317-635-2244

Robert E. Highfield · (Management) · Barnes & Thornburg · 1313 Merchants Bank Building · 11 South Meridian Street · Indianapolis, IN 46204 · 317-638-1313

Martin J. Klaper · (Management) · Ice Miller Donadio & Ryan · One American Square · P.O. Box 82001 · Indianapolis, IN 46282-0002 · 317-236-2100

Barry A. Macey · (Labor, Individuals) · Segal & Macey · 445 North Pennsylvania Street, Suite 401 · Indianapolis, IN 46204-1800 · 317-637-2345

Michael R. Maine · (Management) · Baker & Daniels · 300 North Meridian Street, Suite 2700 · Indianapolis, IN 46204 · 317-237-1319

David W. Miller* · (Management) · Baker & Daniels · 300 North Meridian Street, Suite 2700 · Indianapolis, IN 46204 · 317-237-0300

Alan T. Nolan · (Management) · Ice Miller Donadio & Ryan · One American Square · P.O. Box 82001 · Indianapolis, IN 46282-0002 · 317-236-2100

Richard E. Parker · (Management) · Ice Miller Donadio & Ryan · One American Square · P.O. Box 82001 · Indianapolis, IN 46282-0002 · 317-236-2100

William E. Roberts · (Management) · Barnes & Thornburg · 1313 Merchants Bank Building · 11 South Meridian Street · Indianapolis, IN 46204 · 317-638-1313

Jack H. Rogers* · (Management) · Barnes & Thornburg · 1313 Merchants Bank Building · 11 South Meridian Street · Indianapolis, IN 46204 · 317-638-1313

Susan B. Tabler · (Management) · Ice Miller Donadio & Ryan · One American Square · P.O. Box 82001 · Indianapolis, IN 46282-0002 · 317-236-2100

Daniel W. Rudy · (Management) · Barnes & Thornburg · 600 First Source Bank Center · 100 North Michigan Street · South Bend, IN 46601 · 219-233-1171

NATURAL RESOURCES AND ENVIRONMENTAL LAW

W. C. Blanton* · (Coal, Air, Hazardous Waste) · Ice Miller Donadio & Ryan · One American Square · P.O. Box 82001 · Indianapolis, IN 46282-0002 · 317-236-2100

G. Daniel Kelley, Jr. · (also Coal) · Ice Miller Donadio & Ryan · One American Square · P.O. Box 82001 · Indianapolis, IN 46282-0002 · 317-236-2100

Bryan G. Tabler* · (Water, Air, Solid Waste, Hazardous Waste) · Barnes & Thornburg · 1313 Merchants Bank Building · 11 South Meridian Street · Indianapolis, IN 46204 · 317-231-7226

PERSONAL INJURY LITIGATION

Charles L. Berger · (Plaintiffs) · Berger and Berger · 313 Main Street · Evansville, IN 47708 · 812-425-8101

John M. Clifton, Jr.* · (Plaintiffs—other than malpractice, Defendants, Medical Malpractice, Professional Malpractice) · Barrett & McNagny · Lincoln Bank Tower, Third Floor · 215 East Barry Street · P.O. Box 2263 · Fort Wayne, IN 46801-2263 · 219-423-9551

Sherrill Wm. Colvin* · (Plaintiffs, Medical Malpractice, Products Laibility, Automobile Collision) · Haller & Colvin · 444 East Main Street · Fort Wayne, IN 46802 · 219-426-0444

Leonard E. Eilbacher · Hunt, Suedhoff, Borror & Eilbacher · 900 Paine Webber Building · 803 South Calhoun Street · Fort Wayne, IN 46802-2399 · 219-423-1311

Edward L. Murphy, Jr. · (Defendants) · Miller Carson & Boxberger · 1400 One Summit Square · Fort Wayne, IN 46802 · 219-423-9411

Tom G. Jones · (Plaintiffs) · Jones, Loveall & Johnson · 150 North Main Street Franklin, IN 46131 · 317-736-7174

Frederick H. Link* · (Defendants) · Eichhorn, Eichhorn & Link · 200 Russell Street · P.O. Box 6328 · Hammond, IN 46325-6328 · 219-931-0560

Ted S. Miller · Barrett & McNagny · 429 Jefferson Park Mall · P.O. Box 5156 · Huntington, IN 46750 · 219-356-7766

Ralph A. Cohen · (Defendants) · Ice Miller Donadio & Ryan · One American Square · P.O. Box 82001 · Indianapolis, IN 46282-0002 · 317-236-2100

James R. Fisher* · (Plaintiffs, Defendants, Products Liability, Appellate) · Ice Miller Donadio & Ryan · One American Square · One American Square · P.O. Box 82001 · Indianapolis, IN 46282-0002 · 317-236-2100

F. Boyd Hovde* · (Plaintiffs, Medical Malpractice, Products Liability, Automobile Collision, Airplane Collision) · Townsend, Hovde & Montross · 230 East Ohio Street · Indianapolis, IN 46204 · 317-637-1521

William W. Hurst · (Plaintiffs) · Mitchell Hurst Jacobs & Dick · 152 East Washington Street · Indianapolis, IN 46204-3615 · 317-636-0808

William V. Hutchens · (Defendants) · Locke, Reynolds, Boyd & Weisell · 1000 Capital Center South, 10th Floor · 201 North Illinois Street · Indianapolis, IN 46204 · 317-237-3800

Lloyd H. Milliken, Jr. · (Defendants, Products Liability, Appellate) · Locke, Reynolds, Boyd & Weisell · 1000 Capital Center South, 10th Floor · 201 North Illinois Street · Indianapolis, IN 46204 · 317-237-3800

W. Scott Montross* · (Plaintiffs) · Townsend, Hovde & Montross · 230 East Ohio Street · Indianapolis, IN 46204 · 317-642-4444

Gordon E. Tabor · (Plaintiffs) · Tabor, Fels & Tabor · 141 East Ohio Street, Suite 200 · Indianapolis, IN 46204 · 317-236-9000

John F. Townsend, Jr. · (Plaintiffs) · Townsend, Hovde & Montross · 230 East Ohio Street · Indianapolis, IN 46204 · 317-637-1521

Harry A. Wilson, Jr. · (Plaintiffs) · Wilson, Kehoe & Winingham · 850 Fort Wayne Avenue · P.O. Box 1317 · Indianapolis, IN 46206 · 317-632-7393

Louis Buddy Yosha · (Plaintiffs) · Townsend, Yosha & Cline · 2220 North Meridian Street · Indianapolis, IN 46208 · 317-925-9200

John A. Young · (Defendants) · Young, Cochran & Reese · 630 Century Building 36 South Pennsylvania Street · Indianapolis, IN 46204 · 317-633-4200

Edgar W. Bayliff · Bayliff, Harrigan, Cord & Maugans · The Security Building · 123 North Buckeye Street · P.O. Box 2249 · Kokomo, IN 46904-2249 · 317-459-3941

Charles R. Vaughan · Vaughan and Vaughan · 909 Bank One Building · P.O. Box 498 · Lafayette, IN 47902 · 317-742-0056

Roger L. Pardieck · (Plaintiffs) · Pardieck, Gill & Vargo · 100 North Chestnut Street · P.O. Box 608 · Seymour, IN 47274 · 812-523-8686

John E. Doran · (Defendants) · Doran, Blackmond, Ready, Hamilton & Williams 205 West Jefferson Boulevard, Suite 515 · South Bend, IN 46601 · 219-288-1800

Robert J. Konopa · (Defendants, Products Liability, Automobile Collision) · Kramer, Butler, Simeri, Konopa and Laderer · One Michiana Square, Suite 300 · 100 East Wayne Street · P.O. Box 1438 · South Bend, IN 46624-1438 · 219-233-3303

James H. Pankow · (Defendants) · Jones, Obenchain, Ford, Pankow & Lewis · 1800 Valley American Bank Building · P.O. Box 4577 · South Bend, IN 46634-4577 · 219-233-1194

Thomas H. Singer* · (Plaintiffs) · Nickle and Piasecki · 205 West Jefferson, Suite 413 · South Bend, IN 46601 · 219-232-4747

Max E. Goodwin · (Plaintiffs) · Mann, Chaney, Johnson, Goodwin & Williams · Sixth and Ohio Streets, NW · P.O. Box 1643 · Terre Haute, IN 47808 · 812-232-0107

PUBLIC UTILITY LAW

George A. Porch · Bamberger, Foreman, Oswald and Hahn · 708 Hulman Building · P.O. Box 657 · Evansville, IN 47704 · 812-425-1591

Robert L. Hartley, Jr. · Martin, Wade, Hartley & Hollingsworth · 3590 North Meridian Street · P.O. Box 88676 · Hammond, IN 46208-0676 · 317-924-6700

Michael G. Banta · Barnes & Thornburg · 1313 Merchants Bank Building · 11 South Meridian Street · Indianapolis, IN 46204 · 317-638-1313

Daniel W. McGill · Barnes & Thornburg · 1313 Merchants Bank Building · 11 South Meridian Street · Indianapolis, IN 46204 · 317-638-1313

Fred E. Schlegel · Baker & Daniels · 300 North Meridian Street, Suite 2700 · Indianapolis, IN 46204 · 317-237-0300

REAL ESTATE LAW

W. Jack Schroeder · W. Jack Schroeder Law Office · 307 Union Federal Building Evansville, IN 47708-1692 · 812-423-0073

Robert T. Hoover · Baker & Daniels · 2400 Fort Wayne National Bank Building Fort Wayne, IN 46802 · 219-424-8000

Douglas E. Miller · Barrett & McNagny · Lincoln Bank Tower, Third Floor · 215 East Barry Street · P.O. Box 2263 · Fort Wayne, IN 46801-2263 · 219-423-9551

Jean S. Blackwell · Bose McKinney & Evans · 2700 First Indiana Building · Indianapolis, IN 46204 · 317-684-5109

John A. Grayson · Ice Miller Donadio & Ryan · One American Square · P.O. Box 82001 · Indianapolis, IN 46282-0002 · 317-236-2100

Tom Charles Huston · Barnes & Thornburg · 1313 Merchants Bank Building · 11 South Meridian Street · Indianapolis, IN 46204 · 317-638-1313

William F. LeMond · LeMond, Carson, Yockey, Pehler, Caplin & Associates · 600 Union Federal Building · 45 North Pennsylvania Street · Indianapolis, IN 46204 · 317-236-6300

Norman R. Newman · Dann Pecar Newman Talesnick & Kleiman · One American Square, Suite 2300 · P.O. Box 82008 · Indianapolis, IN 46282 · 317-632-3232

Philip A. Nicely · Bose McKinney & Evans · 8888 Keystone Crossing, Suite 1201 Indianapolis, IN 46240 · 317-574-3701

Philip D. Pecar · (Land Use, Commercial Transactions, Industrial Transactions) Dann Pecar Newman Talesnick & Kleiman · One American Square, Suite 2300 · P.O. Box 82008 · Indianapolis, IN 46282 · 317-632-3232

Charles E. Wilson · (Zoning, Land Use, Commercial Transactions, Industrial Transactions, Real Estate Taxation) · Ice Miller Donadio & Ryan · One American Square · P.O. Box 82001 · Indianapolis, IN 46282-0002 · 317-236-2100

Thomas R. McCully · Stuart & Branigin · 801 The Life Building · P.O. Box 1010 Lafayette, IN 47902 · 317-423-1561

Bruce R. Bancroft · Barnes & Thornburg · 600 First Source Bank Center · 100 North Michigan Street · South Bend, IN 46601 · 219-233-1171

Richard W. Morgan · Barnes & Thornburg · 600 First Source Bank Center · 100 North Michigan Street · South Bend, IN 46601 · 219-233-1171

TAX AND EMPLOYEE BENEFITS LAW

George N. Bewley, Jr. · (Employee Benefits) · Bewley & Koday · 2006 Fort Wayne National Bank Building · 110 West Berry Street · Fort Wayne, IN 46802 219-424-0566

Miles C. Gerberding · Barnes & Thornburg · One Summit Square, Suite 600 · Fort Wayne, IN 46802 · 219-423-9440

David Haist · Barnes & Thornburg · 600 One Summit Square · Fort Wayne, IN 46802 · 219-423-9440

N. Thomas Horton II · (Employee Benefits) · Barrett & McNagny · Lincoln Bank Tower, Third Floor · 215 East Berry Street · P.O. Box 2263 · Fort Wayne, IN 46801-2263 · 219-423-9551

Stephen J. Williams · (Tax Disputes) · Shambaugh, Kast, Beck & Williams · 1900 Lincoln Bank Tower · Fort Wayne, IN 46802-2405 · 219-423-1430

Toni Sue Ax · (Employee Benefits) · Barnes & Thornburg · 1313 Merchants Bank Building · 11 South Meridian Street · Indianapolis, IN 46204 · 317-638-1313

Donald P. Bennett · Baker & Daniels · 300 North Meridian Street, Suite 2700 · Indianapolis, IN 46204 · 317-237-0300

Leonard J. Betley · Ice Miller Donadio & Ryan · One American Square · P.O. Box 82001 · Indianapolis, IN 46282-0002 · 317-236-2100

Mary Beth Braitman · (Employee Benefits) · Ice Miller Donadio & Ryan · One American Square · P.O. Box 82001 · Indianapolis, IN 46282-0002 · 317-236-2100

Donald W. Buttrey · McHale, Cook & Welch · 1100 Chamber of Commerce Building · Indianapolis, IN 46204 · 317-634-7588

Francina A. Dlouhy · Baker & Daniels · 300 North Meridian Street, Suite 2700 Indianapolis, IN 46204 · 317-237-0300

John L. Egloff · Riley, Bennett & Egloff · 1810 One American Square · Indianapolis, IN 46282 · 317-636-8000

Daniel H. FitzGibbon · (Corporate & Partnership Transactions) · Barnes & Thornburg · 1313 Merchants Bank Building · 11 South Meridian Street · Indianapolis, IN 46204 · 317-638-1313

Robert E. Johnson · Krieg DeVault Alexander & Capehart · 2800 Indiana National Bank Tower · One Indiana Square · Indianapolis, IN 46204 · 317-636-4341

James D. Kemper · (Employee Benefits) · Ice Miller Donadio & Ryan · One American Square · P.O. Box 82001 · Indianapolis, IN 46282-0002 · 317-236-2100

Marc W. Sciscoe · (Employee Benefits) · Ice Miller Donadio & Ryan · One American Square · P.O. Box 82001 · Indianapolis, IN 46282-0002 · 317-236-2100

Barton T. Sprunger · Ice Miller Donadio & Ryan · One American Square · P.O. Box 82001 · Indianapolis, IN 46282-0002 · 317-236-2100

Larry J. Stroble · Barnes & Thornburg · 1313 Merchants Bank Building · 11 South Meridian Street · Indianapolis, IN 46204 · 317-638-1313

Donald G. Sutherland · Ice Miller Donadio & Ryan · One American Square · P.O. Box 82001 · Indianapolis, IN 46282-0002 · 317-236-2100

Brian J. Lake · (Employee Benefits) · Barnes & Thornburg · 600 First Source Bank Center · 100 North Michigan Street · South Bend, IN 46601 · 219-233-1171

Richard B. Urda, Jr. · (Employee Benefits) · The Urda Professional Corporation 311 First Interstate Bank Building · South Bend, IN 46601 · 219-234-2161

Nelson J. Vogel, Jr. · (Corporate & Partnership Transactions) · Barnes & Thornburg · 600 First Source Bank Center · 100 North Michigan Street · South Bend, IN 46601 · 219-233-1171

TRUSTS AND ESTATES

Donald W. Jurgemeyer · P.O. Box 624 · Columbus, IN 47201-0624 · 812-372-0205

James M. Barrett III · Barrett & McNagny · Lincoln Bank Tower, Third Floor · 215 East Berry Street · P.O. Box 2263 · Fort Wayne, IN 46801-2263 · 219-423-9551

Miles C. Gerberding · Barnes & Thornburg · One Summit Square, Suite 800 · Fort Wayne, IN 46802 · 219-423-9440

Stephen J. Williams · Shambaugh, Kast, Beck & Williams · 1900 Lincoln Bank Tower · Fort Wayne, IN 46802-2405 · 219-423-1430

Arthur W. Banta · Krieg DeVault Alexander & Capehart · 2800 Indiana National Bank Tower · One Indiana Square · Indianapolis, IN 46204 · 317-636-4341

Charles F. Cremer, Jr.* · (Estate & Trust Litigation) · Law Offices of Charles F. Cremer, Jr. · Two Market Square Center, Suite 915 · 251 East Ohio Street · Indianapolis, IN 46204 · 317-636-8182

Francis J. Feeney, Jr.* · Feeney & Ward · 1014 Circle Tower Building · Indianapolis, IN 46204 · 317-639-9501

Kristin G. Fruehwald · Barnes & Thornburg · 1313 Merchants Bank Building · 11 South Meridian Street · Indianapolis, IN 46204 · 317-638-1313

G. Weldon Johnson · (Estate Planning, Estate Administration, Charitable Trusts) Johnson, Hall and Lawhead · 8900 Keystone Crossing, Suite 940 · Indianapolis, IN 46240-2162 · 317-848-5808

Robert A. Lichtenauer · 8140 Knue Road, Suite 110 · Indianapolis, IN 46250 · 317-845-1988

James F. Matthews · Hill, Fulwider, McDowell, Funk & Matthews · One Indiana Square, Suite 2335 · Indianapolis, IN 46204 · 317-634-2955

Russell Jay Ryan, Jr. · Hackman, McClarnon, Hulett & Cracraft · One Indiana Square, Suite 2400 · Indianapolis, IN 46204 · 317-636-5401

Lisa Stone Sciscoe · (Estate Planning, Estate Administration, Charitable Trusts) Ice Miller Donadio & Ryan · One American Square · One American Square · P.O. Box 82001 · Indianapolis, IN 46282-0002 · 317-236-2315

Shirley A. Shideler · Barnes & Thornburg · 1313 Merchants Bank Building · 11 South Meridian Street · Indianapolis, IN 46204 · 317-638-1313

Jerome M. Strauss · (Estate Planning, Estate Administration, Charitable Trusts, Estate Taxes) · Ice Miller Donadio & Ryan · One American Square · P.O. Box 82001 · Indianapolis, IN 46282-0002 · 317-236-2100

Gordon D. Wishard · (Estate Planning, Estate Administration, Charitable Trusts) Ice Miller Donadio & Ryan · One American Square · One American Square · P.O. Box 82001 · Indianapolis, IN 46282-0002 · 317-236-2476

John A. Burgess · Barnes & Thornburg · 600 First Source Bank Center · 100 North Michigan Street · South Bend, IN 46601 · 219-233-1171

G. Burt Ford · Jones, Obenchain, Ford, Pankow & Lewis · 1800 Valley American Bank Building · P.O. Box 4577 · South Bend, IN 46634-4577 · 219-233-1194

Edward J. Gray · Barnes & Thornburg · 600 First Source Bank Center · 100 North Michigan Street · South Bend, IN 46601 · 219-233-1171

Charles Roemer · Roemer and Mintz · 1400 Society Bank Building · South Bend, IN 46601 · 219-234-1234

IOWA

BANKRUPTCY LAW

Larry G. Gutz · Moyer & Bergman · Commerce Exchange Building, Suite 315 · 2720 First Avenue, NE · P.O. Box 1943 · Cedar Rapids, IA 52406-1943 · 319-366-7331

Carroll J. Reasoner · (Creditors' Rights) · Shuttleworth & Ingersoll · 500 Merchants National Bank Building · P.O. Box 2107 · Cedar Rapids, IA 52406-2107 · 319-365-9461

Harry R. Terpstra · Terpstra Law Offices · 830 Higley Building · Cedar Rapids, IA 52401 · 319-364-2467

C. R. Hannan · Perkins, Sacks, Hannan, Reilly & Petersen · 215 South Main Street · P.O. Box 1016 · Council Bluffs, IA 51502-1016 · 712-328-1575

Thomas L. Flynn · (Creditors' Rights, Debtors' Rights) · Belin Harris Helmick Lamson McCormick · 2000 Financial Center · Des Moines, IA 50309 · 515-243-7100

Donald F. Neiman · Neiman, Neiman, Stone & Spellman · 1119 High Street · Des Moines, IA 50308-2674 · 515-282-9247

A. Frank Baron · (Business Reorganization, Creditors' Rights, Debtors' Rights, Bankruptcy Litigation) · Baron, Sar, Goodwin, Gill, Lohr & Jarman · 750 Pierce Street · P.O. Box 717 · Sioux City, IA 51102 · 712-277-1015

BUSINESS LITIGATION

David M. Elderkin* · Elderkin & Pirnie · 700 Higley Building · P.O. Box 1968 Cedar Rapids, IA 52406-1968 · 319-362-2137

Patrick M. Roby* · (Banking, Commercial) · Shuttleworth & Ingersoll · 500 Merchants National Bank Building · P.O. Box 2107 · Cedar Rapids, IA 52406-2107 319-365-9461

Steven H. Krohn · Smith, Peterson, Beckman & Willson · 33 Main Place, Suite 300 · P.O. Box 249 · Council Bluffs, IA 51502 · 712-328-1833

Robert V. P. Waterman* · Lane & Waterman · 600 Davenport Bank Building · Davenport, IA 52801 · 319-324-3246

Lex Hawkins · Hawkins & Norris · 2801 Fleur Drive · Des Moines, IA 50321 · 515-288-6532

H. Richard Smith* · Ahlers, Cooney, Dorweiler, Haynie, Smith & Allbee · 100 Court Avenue, Suite 600 · Des Moines, IA 50309-2231 · 515-243-7611

LeRoy R. Voigts* · (Securities) · Nyemaster, Goode, McLaughlin, Voigts, West, Hansell & O'Brien · 1900 Hub Tower · Des Moines, IA 50309 · 515-283-3100

Maurice B. Nieland* · (Commercial) · Rawlings, Nieland, Probasco, Killinger, Ellwanger, Jacobs & Mohrhauser · Toy Building, Suite 300 · Sioux City, IA 51101 712-277-2373

William J. Rawlings* · (Commercial) · Rawlings, Nieland, Probasco, Killinger, Ellwanger, Jacobs & Mohrhauser · Toy Building, Suite 300 · Sioux City, IA 51101 712-277-2373

David J. Dutton* · (Antitrust, Banking, Commercial, Finance) · Mosier, Thomas, Beatty, Dutton, Braun & Staack · 3151 Brockway Road · P.O. Box 810 · Waterloo, IA 50704 · 319-234-4471

CORPORATE LAW

F. James Bradley · Bradley & Riley · First Corporate Place · 100 First Street, SW Cedar Rapids, IA 52404 · 319-363-0101

Thomas M. Collins · Shuttleworth & Ingersoll · 500 Merchants National Bank Building · P.O. Box 2107 · Cedar Rapids, IA 52406-2107 · 319-365-9461

Darrel A. Morf · Simmons, Perrine, Albright & Ellwood · 1200 Merchants National Bank Building · Cedar Rapids, IA 52401 · 319-366-7641

Carroll J. Reasoner · Shuttleworth & Ingersoll · 500 Merchants National Bank Building · P.O. Box 2107 · Cedar Rapids, IA 52406-2107 · 319-365-9461

David W. Belin · Belin Harris Helmick Tesdell Lamson McCormick · 2000 Financial Center · Seventh & Walnut Streets · Des Moines, IA 50309 · 515-243-7100

Donald J. Brown · Davis, Hockenberg, Wine, Brown, Koehn & Shors · 2300 Financial Center · 666 Walnut Street · Des Moines, IA 50309 · 515-243-2300

A. Arthur Davis · Davis, Hockenberg, Wine, Brown, Koehn & Shors · 2300 Financial Center · 666 Walnut Street · Des Moines, IA 50309 · 515-243-2300

L. Call Dickinson, Jr. · Dickinson, Throckmorton, Parker, Mannheimer & Raife 1600 Hub Tower · 699 Walnut Street · Des Moines, IA 50309-3929 · 515-244-2600

Edgar F. Hansell · Nyemaster, Goode, McLaughlin, Voigts, West, Hansell & O'Brien · 1900 Hub Tower · 699 Walnut Street · Des Moines, IA 50309 · 515-283-3100

Jeffrey E. Lamson · Belin Harris Helmick Tesdell Lamson McCormick · 2000 Financial Center · Seventh & Walnut Streets · Des Moines, IA 50309 · 515-243-7100

Marvin S. Berenstein · Berenstein, Vriezelaar, Moore, Moser & Tigges · 300 Commerce Building · P.O. Box 1557 · Sioux City, IA 51102 · 712-252-3226

Marvin J. Klass · Klass, Hanks, Stoos & Carter · Jackson Plaza, Suite 300 · Fourth and Jackson Streets · P.O. Box 327 · Sioux City, IA 51102 · 712-252-1866

W. Louis Beecher · Beecher, Rathert, Field, Fister, Walker & Morris · Court Square Building, Suite 300 · 620 Lafayette Street · P.O. Box 178 · Waterloo, IA 50704 · 319-234-1766

Steven A. Weidner · Swisher & Cohrt · 528 West Fourth Street · P.O. Box 1200 Waterloo, IA 50704 · 319-232-6555

CRIMINAL DEFENSE

William L. Kutmus · Kutmus & Pennington · 620 Fleming Building · 218 Sixth Avenue · Des Moines, IA 50309 · 515-288-3339

Raymond Rosenberg · The Rosenberg Law Firm · 1010 Insurance Exchange Building · 505 Fifth Avenue · Des Moines, IA 50309 · 515-243-7600

Lawrence F. Scalise · Scalise, Scism, Sandre, Uhl, McConville, Miller & Holliday · 2910 Grand Avenue · Des Moines, IA 50312 · 515-282-2910

Leon F. Spies* · (Federal Court, State Court) · Mellon & Spies · 411 Iowa State Bank & Trust Building · Iowa City, IA 52240 · 319-337-4193

FAMILY LAW

Robert M. Jilek · Simmons, Perrine, Albright & Ellwood · 1200 Merchants National Bank Building · Cedar Rapids, IA 52401 · 319-366-7641

Harlan Hockett · Harlan Hockett Law Firm · 300 Walnut Street, Suite 270 · Des Moines, IA 50309 · 515-244-7820

Roger J. Hudson · Smith, Schneider, Stiles, Mumford, Schrage, Zurek, Wilmer & Hudson · 1000 Equitable Building · Des Moines, IA 50309 · 515-245-6789

Thomas P. Hyland · Hyland, Laden & Pearson · 3232 Hubbell Avenue · Des Moines, IA 50317 · 515-262-9595

James M. Meade* · (Adoption, Divorce) · Kirkwood & Meade · 6963 University Avenue · Des Moines, IA 50311 · 515-274-1429

Patricia A. Shoff* · Davis, Hockenberg, Wine, Brown, Koehn & Shors · 2300 Financial Center · 666 Walnut Street · Des Moines, IA 50309 · 515-243-2300

Philip A. Leff · Leff, Leff, Leff, Haupert & Traw · 222 South Linn Street · P.O. Box 2447 · Iowa City, IA 52244 · 319-338-7551

Sharon A. Mellon* · Mellon & Spies · 411 Iowa State Bank & Trust Building · Iowa City, IA 52240 · 319-337-4193

Patricia A. McGivern · Clark, Butler, Walsh & McGivern · River Plaza Building, Suite 400 · 10 West Fourth Street · P.O. Box 596 · Waterloo, IA 50704 · 319-234-5701

HEALTH CARE LAW

Diane Kutzko · Shuttleworth & Ingersoll · 500 Merchants National Bank Building
P.O. Box 2107 · Cedar Rapids, IA 52406-2107 · 319-365-9461

Ralph H. Heninger · Heninger and Heninger · 101 West Second Street, Suite 501
Davenport, IA 52801 · 319-324-0418

Norene D. Jacobs · Davis, Hockenberg, Wine, Brown, Koehn & Shors · 2300
Financial Center · 666 Walnut Street · Des Moines, IA 50309 · 515-243-2300

John D. Shors · Davis, Hockenberg, Wine, Brown, Koehn & Shors · 2300 Financial Center · 666 Walnut Street · Des Moines, IA 50309 · 515-243-2300

Cynthia C. Moser · Berenstein, Vriezelaar, Moore, Moser & Tigges · 300 Commerce Building · P.O. Box 1557 · Sioux City, IA 51102 · 712-252-3226

INTELLECTUAL PROPERTY LAW

James C. Nemmers · Shuttleworth & Ingersoll · 500 Merchants National Bank
Building · P.O. Box 2107 · Cedar Rapids, IA 52406-2107 · 319-365-9461

Bruce W. McKee · Zarley, McKee, Thomte, Voorhees & Sease · 801 Grand, Suite
3200 · Des Moines, IA 50309-2721 · 515-288-3667

Edmund J. Sease · Zarley, McKee, Thomte, Voorhees & Sease · 801 Grand,
Suite 3200 · Des Moines, IA 50309-2721 · 515-288-3667

Michael G. Voorhees · Zarley, McKee, Thomte, Voorhees & Sease · 801 Grand,
Suite 3200 · Des Moines, IA 50309-2721 · 515-288-3667

Donald H. Zarley · Zarley, McKee, Thomte, Voorhees & Sease · 801 Grand,
Suite 3200 · Des Moines, IA 50309-2721 · 515-288-3667

G. Brian Pingel · Shearer, Templer & Pingel · 437 Colony Park Building · 3737
Woodland Avenue · West Des Moines, IA 50265 · 515-225-3737

LABOR AND EMPLOYMENT LAW

John R. Carpenter · (Management) · Simmons, Perrine, Albright & Ellwood ·
1200 Merchants National Bank Building · Cedar Rapids, IA 52401 · 319-366-7641

Iris E. Muchmore · Simmons, Perrine, Albright & Ellwood · 1200 Merchants
National Bank Building · Cedar Rapids, IA 52401 · 319-366-7641

John C. Barrett* · (Individuals) · The Barrett Law Offices · 910 Equitable Building · Des Moines, IA 50309 · 515-244-4474

Mark W. Bennett* · (Management, Individuals, Employment Discrimination, Wrongful Discharge) · Babich, Bennett & Nickerson · 100 Court Avenue, Suite 403 · Des Moines, IA 50309 · 515-244-4300

John R. Phillips · (Management) · Nyemaster, Goode, McLaughlin, Voigts, West, Hansell & O'Brien · 1900 Hub Tower · Des Moines, IA 50309 · 515-283-3100

Charles W. McManigal · (Management) · Laird, Heiny, McManigal, Winga, Duffy & Stambaugh · 300 American Federal Building · 10 First Street, NW · P.O. Box 1567 · Mason City, IA 50401-8567 · 515-423-5154

Harry H. Smith · Smith & Smith · 632-640 Badgerow Building · Sioux City, IA 51101 · 712-255-8094

MacDonald Smith · (Labor) · Smith & Smith · 632-640 Badgerow Building · Sioux City, IA 51101 · 712-255-8094

Leon R. Shearer* · (Management) · Shearer, Templer & Pingel · 437 Colony Park Building · 3737 Woodland Avenue · West Des Moines, IA 50265 · 515-225-3737

PERSONAL INJURY LITIGATION

David M. Elderkin* · Elderkin, Pirnie, von Lackum & Elderkin · 700 Higley Building · P.O Box 1968 · Cedar Rapids, IA 52406-1968 · 319-362-2137

Ralph W. Gearhart · (Defendants) · Shuttleworth & Ingersoll · 500 Merchants National Bank Building · P.O. Box 2107 · Cedar Rapids, IA 52406 · 319-365-9461

Patrick M. Roby* · (Plaintiffs, Defendants) · Shuttleworth & Ingersoll · 500 Merchants National Bank Building · P.O. Box 2107 · Cedar Rapids, IA 52406-2107 319-365-9461

James R. Snyder · (Defendants) · Simmons, Perrine, Albright & Ellwood · 1200 Merchants National Bank Building · Cedar Rapids, IA 52401 · 319-366-7641

Peter J. Peters · 233 Pearl Street · P.O. Box 938 · Council Bluffs, IA 51502 · 712-328-3157

Philip J. Willson · (Defendants) · Smith, Peterson, Beckman & Willson · 35 Main Place, Suite 300 · P.O. Box 249 · Council Bluffs, IA 51502 · 712-328-1833

Robert A. Van Vooren · Lane & Waterman · 600 Davenport Bank Building · Davenport, IA 52801 · 319-324-3246

Robert V. P. Waterman, Sr.* · (Defendants) · Lane & Waterman · 700 Davenport Bank Building · Davenport, IA 52801 · 319-324-3246

Kent M. Forney · (Defendants) · Bradshaw, Fowler, Proctor & Fairgrave · 801 Grand Avenue · Des Moines, IA 50309-2727 · 515-243-4191

Lex Hawkins · (Plaintiffs) · Hawkins & Norris · 2801 Fleur Drive · Des Moines, IA 50321 · 515-288-6532

Verne Lawyer · (Plaintiffs) · Law Offices of Verne Lawyer · Fleming Building, Fourth Floor · Des Moines, IA 50309 · 515-288-2213

Ross H. Sidney · (Defendants) · Grefe & Sidney · 2222 Grand Avenue · P.O. Box 10434 · Des Moines, IA 50306 · 515-245-4300

H. Richard Smith* · (Defendants) · Ahlers, Cooney, Dorweiler, Haynie, Smith & Allbee · 100 Court Avenue, Suite 600 · Des Moines, IA 50309-2231 · 515-243-7611

LeRoy R. Voigts* · (Medical Malpractice, Products Liability, Professional Malpractice, Automobile Collision) · Nyemaster, Goode, McLaughlin, Voigts, West, Hansell & O'Brien · 1900 Hub Tower · Des Moines, IA 50309 · 515-283-3100

William C. Fuerste* · (Plaintiffs, Defendants, Medical Malpractice, Products Liability) · Fuerste, Carew, Coyle, Juergens & Sudmeier · 200 Security Building · Dubuque, IA 52001 · 319-556-4011

Francis Fitzgibbons · (Plaintiffs, Defendants, Medical Malpractice) · Fitzgibbons Brothers · 108 North Seventh Street · P.O. Box 496 · Estherville, IA 51334 · 712-362-7215

James P. Hayes · (Plaintiffs) · Meardon, Sueppel, Downer & Hayes · 122 South Linn Street · Iowa City, IA 52240 · 319-338-9222

David E. Funkhouser · (Defendants) · Brown, Kinsey & Funkhouser · 214 North Adams Avenue · P.O. Box 679 · Mason City, IA 50401 · 515-423-6223

Thomas J. Vilsack* · (Defendants) · Bell & Vilsack · 111 East Washington Street · Mt. Pleasant, IA 52641 · 319-385-2511

Marvin F. Heidman* · (Defendants, Medical Malpractice, Products Liabiity, Professional Malpractice) · Eidsmoe, Heidman, Redmond, Fredregill, Patterson & Schatz · Home Federal Building, Suite 200 · 701 Pierce Street · P.O. Box 3086 · Sioux City, IA 51102 · 712-255-8838

William J. Rawlings* · Rawlings, Nieland, Probasco, Killinger, Ellwanger, Jacobs & Mohrhauser · Toy Building, Suite 300 · Sioux City, IA 51101 · 712-277-2373

John J. Greer · Greer, Montgomery, Barry & Bovee · 316 Eleventh Southwest Plaza · P.O. Box 7038 · Spencer, IA 51301 · 712-262-1150

David J. Dutton* · (Products Liability, Professional Malpractice, Automobile Collision) · Mosier, Thomas, Beatty, Sutton, Braun & Staack · 3151 Brockway Road · P.O. Box 810 · Waterloo, IA 50704 · 319-234-4471

Edward J. Gallagher, Jr.* · (Plaintiffs, Medical Malpractice, Products Liability, Automobile Collision) · Gallagher, Langlas & Gallagher · Law Building · 405 East Fifth Street · P.O. Box 2615 · Waterloo, IA 50704 · 319-233-6163

Eldon R. McCann · (Defendants) · Swisher & Cohrt · 528 West Fourth Street · P.O. Box 1200 · Waterloo, IA 50704 · 319-232-6555

PUBLIC UTILITY LAW

Robert F. Holz · (Telecommunications) · Davis, Hockenberg, Wine, Brown, Koehn & Shors · 2300 Financial Center · 666 Walnut Street · Des Moines, IA 50309 · 515-243-2300

Philip E. Stoffregen · (Telecommunications) · Dickinson, Throckmorton, Parker, Mannheimer & Raife · 1600 Hub Tower · 699 Walnut Street · Des Moines, IA 50309-3929 · 515-244-2600

Sheila K. Tipton · (Electric) · Bradshaw, Fowler, Proctor & Fairgrave · 801 Grand Avenue · Des Moines, IA 50309-2727 · 515-243-4191

REAL ESTATE LAW

LeRoy H. Redfern · Redfern, Dieter, Larsen & Moore · 315 Clay Street · P.O. Box 627 · Cedar Falls, IA 50613 · 319-277-6830

David W. Kubicek · Simmons, Perrine, Albright & Ellwood · 1200 Merchants National Bank Building · Cedar Rapids, IA 52401 · 319-366-7641

William R. Shuttleworth · Shuttleworth & Ingersoll · 500 Merchants National Bank Building · P.O. Box 2107 · Cedar Rapids, IA 52406-2107 · 319-365-9461

Richard E. Ramsay · Davis, Hockenberg, Wine, Brown, Koehn & Shors · 2300 Financial Center · 666 Walnut Street · Des Moines, IA 50309 · 515-243-2300

John B. Anderson · Corbett, Anderson, Corbett, Poulson, Flom & Vellinga · 400 Security Bank Building · P.O. Box 3527 · Sioux City, IA 51102 · 712-277-1261

George F. Madsen · Marks & Madsen · United Federal Plaza Building, Suite 303 700 Fourth Street · P.O. Box 3226 · Sioux City, IA 51102-3226 · 712-258-1200

W. Louis Beecher · Beecher, Rathert, Field, Fister, Walker & Morris · Court Square Building, Suite 300 · 620 Lafayette Street · P.O. Box 178 · Waterloo, IA 50704 · 319-234-1766

George D. Keith · Martin, Nutting, Miller, Keith & Pedersen · Sycamore 501 Building, Suite 710 · P.O. Box 2158 · Waterloo, IA 50704 · 319-235-9212

Stephen C. Nelson · Moyer & Bergman · Commerce Exchange Building, Third Floor · 2720 First Avenue, NE · P.O. Box 1943 · Cedar Rapids, IA 52406-1943 · 319-366-7331

TAX AND EMPLOYEE BENEFITS LAW

J. Scott Bogguss · (Tax, Employee Benefits) · Moyer & Bergman · Commerce Exchange Building, Third Floor · 2720 First Avenue, NE · P.O. Box 1943 · Cedar Rapids, IA 52406-1943 · 319-366-7331

Michael P. Donohue · Moyer & Bergman · Commerce Exchange Building, Third Floor · 2720 First Avenue, NE · P.O. Box 1943 · Cedar Rapids, IA 52406-1943 · 319-366-7331

Gary J. Streit · (Tax, Employee Benefits) · Shuttleworth & Ingersoll · 500 Merchants National Bank Building · P.O. Box 2107 · Cedar Rapids, IA 52406-2107 · 319-365-9461

Gene H. Snapp, Jr. · (Employee Benefits) · 525 Davenport Bank Building · Davenport, IA 52801 · 319-322-7917

Donald J. Brown · (Corporate & Partnership Transactions) · Davis, Hockenberg, Wine, Brown, Koehn & Shors · 2300 Financial Center · 666 Walnut Street · Des Moines, IA 50309 · 515-243-2300

Bruce I. Campbell · Davis, Hockenberg, Wine, Brown, Koehn & Shors · 2300 Financial Center · 666 Walnut Street · Des Moines, IA 50309 · 515-243-2300

Frank J. Carroll · Davis, Hockenberg, Wine, Brown, Koehn & Shors · 2300 Financial Center · 666 Walnut Street · Des Moines, IA 50309 · 515-243-2300

David C. Craig · (Employee Benefits) · Brown, Winick, Graves, Donnelly, Baskerville and Schoenebaum · Two Ruan Center, Suite 1100 · 601 Locust Street · Des Moines, IA 50309 · 515-283-2076

John V. Donnelly* · (Corporate & Partnership Transactions, State Tax, Tax Disputes) · Brown, Winick, Graves, Donnelly, Baskerville and Schoenebaum · Two Ruan Center, Suite 1100 · 601 Locust Street · Des Moines, IA 50309 · 515-283-2076

Burns Mossman* · (State Tax, Tax Disputes) · Nyemaster, Goode, McLaughlin, Voigts, West, Hansell & O'Brien · 1900 Hub Tower · Des Moines, IA 50309 · 515-283-3100

John H. Raife · Dickinson, Throckmorton, Parker, Mannheimer & Raife · 1600 Hub Tower · 699 Walnut Street · Des Moines, IA 50309-3929 · 515-244-2600

R. Craig Shives · (Employee Benefits) · Nyemaster, Goode, McLaughlin, Voigts, West, Hansell & O'Brien · 1900 Hub Tower · Des Moines, IA 50309 · 515-283-3100

William S. Smith · Smith, Schneider, Stiles, Mumford, Schrage, Zurek, Wimer & Hudson · Equitable Building, 10th Floor · Des Moines, IA 50309 · 515-245-6789

Jon L. Staudt · Belin Harris Helmick Tesdell Lamson McCormick · 2000 Financial Center · Seventh & Walnut Streets · Des Moines, IA 50309 · 515-243-7100

Margaret D. Van Houten · Bradshaw, Fowler, Proctor & Fairgrave · 801 Grand Avenue · Des Moines, IA 50309-2727 · 515-243-4191

Marvin Winick · Brown, Winick, Graves, Donnelly, Baskerville and Schoenebaum · Two Ruan Center, Suite 1100 · 601 Locust Street · Des Moines, IA 50309 515-283-2076

David D. Crumley · Stark, Crumley & Jacobs · Warden Plaza · Fort Dodge, IA 50501-4744 · 515-576-7558

William V. Phelan · Phelan, Tucker, Boyle & Mullen · 321 East Market · P.O. Box 2150 · Iowa City, IA 52244 · 319-354-1104

James A. Nepple · Stanley, Rehling, Lande & Van Der Kamp · 300 First National Bank Building · P.O. Box 619 · Muscatine, IA 52761-0619 · 319-264-5000

Marvin S. Berenstein · Berenstein, Vriezelaar, Moore, Moser & Tigges · 300 Commerce Building · P.O. Box 1557 · Sioux City, IA 51102 · 712-252-3226

Gene A. Probasco · Rawlings, Nieland, Probasco, Killinger, Ellwanger, Jacobs & Mohrhauser · Toy Building, Suite 300 · Sioux City, IA 51101 · 712-277-2373

Orville W. Bloethe · Bloethe-Vanzee Law Office · 702 Third Street · Victor, IA 52347 · 319-647-3121

TRUSTS AND ESTATES

LeRoy H. Redfern · Redfern, Dieter, Larsen & Moore · 315 Clay Street · P.O. Box 627 · Cedar Falls, IA 50613 · 319-277-6830

F. James Bradley · Bradley & Riley · First Corporate Place · 100 First Street, SW Cedar Rapids, IA 52404 · 319-363-0101

Michael O. McDermott · Shuttleworth & Ingersoll · 500 Merchants National Bank Building · P.O. Box 2107 · Cedar Rapids, IA 52406-2107 · 319-365-9461

Darrel A. Morf · Simmons, Perrine, Albright & Ellwood · 1200 Merchants National Bank Building · Cedar Rapids, IA 52401 · 319-366-7641

Jack W. Peters · Stuart, Tinley, Peters, Thorn, Smits, French & Hughes · 310 West Kanesville Boulevard, Second Floor · P.O. Box 398 · Council Bluffs, IA 51502 · 712-322-4033

Robert C. Reimer · Reimer, Lohman & Reitz · 25 South Main Street · Denison, IA 51442 · 712-263-4627

Donald J. Brown · (Estate Planning) · Davis, Hockenberg, Wine, Brown, Koehn & Shors · 2300 Financial Center · 666 Walnut Street · Des Moines, IA 50309 · 515-243-2300

Bruce I. Campbell · Davis, Hockenberg, Wine, Brown, Koehn & Shors · 2300 Financial Center · 666 Walnut Street · Des Moines, IA 50309 · 515-243-2300

Charles E. Harris · Belin Harris Helmick Lamson McCormick · 2000 Financial Center · Des Moines, IA 50309 · 515-243-7100

J. Edward Power · (Estate Planning, Estate Administration, Charitable Trusts) · Bradshaw, Fowler, Proctor & Fairgrave · 801 Grand Avenue · Des Moines, IA 50309-2727 · 515-243-4191

William V. Phelan · Phelan, Tucker, Boyle & Mullen · 321 East Market · P.O. Box 2150 · Iowa City, IA 52244 · 319-354-1104

Socrates G. Pappajohn · Pappajohn, Shriber, Eide & Nicholas · 800 Brick and Tile Building · 119 Second Street, NW · Mason City, IA 50401 · 515-423-4264

Harold R. Winston · Winston, Reuber, Swanson & Byrne · 119 Second Street, NW · Mason City, IA 50401 · 515-423-1913

John B. Anderson · Corbett, Anderson, Corbett & Daniels · 400 Security Bank Building · P.O. Box 3527 · Sioux City, IA 51102 · 712-277-1261

Marvin S. Berenstein · Berenstein, Vriezelaar, Moore, Moser & Tigges · 300 Commerce Building · P.O. Box 1557 · Sioux City, IA 51102 · 712-252-3226

Bernard B. Marks · Marks & Madsen · United Federal Plaza Building, Suite 303 700 Fourth Street · P.O. Box 3226 · Sioux City, IA 51102-3226 · 712-258-1200

Orville W. Bloethe · Bloethe-Vanzee Law Office · 702 Third Street · Victor, IA 52347 · 319-647-3121

Orville W. Bloethe · 702 Third Street · Victor, IA 52347 · 319-647-3121

Richard G. Zellhoefer · Zellhoefer Law Firm · The Chicago Central Building, Suite 507 · P.O. Box 477 · Waterloo, IA 50704 · 319-291-4045

KANSAS

BANKRUPTCY LAW

Chris W. Henry · McDowell, Rice & Smith · 600 Security Bank Building · Kansas City, KS 66101 · 913-621-5400

Thomas M. Mullinix III · Evans & Mullinix · Country Hill Bank Building, Suite 220 · 15301 West 87th Street · Lenexa, KS 66219 · 913-541-1200

F. Stannard Lentz · Lentz & Clark · 5818 Reeds Road · P.O. Box 1704 · Mission, KS 66222-0704 · 913-384-2464

Michael H. Berman · Berman & Singer · 4121 West 83rd Street, Suite 265 · P.O. Box 8010 · Prairie Village, KS 66208 · 913-649-1555

Robert L. Baer* · (Business Reorganization, Bankruptcy Litigation) · Cosgrove, Webb & Oman · Bank IV Tower, Suite 1100 · 534 Kansas Avenue · Topeka, KS 66603 · 913-235-9511

Jan Hamilton* · (Business Reorganization, Creditors' Rights, Debtors' Rights, Bankruptcy Litigation) · Hamilton, Peterson, Tipton & Keeshan · 1206 West 10th Street · Topeka, KS 66604-1291 · 913-233-1903

Dale L. Somers · (Business Reorganization, Creditors' Rights, Debtors' Rights, Bankruptcy Litigation) · Davis, Wright, Unrein, Hummer & McCallister · The Davis Building · 100 East Ninth Street · Topeka, KS 66612 · 913-232-2200

David C. Adams · (Business Reorganization) · Morris, Laing, Evans, Brock & Kennedy · 200 West Douglas Street, Fourth Floor · Wichita, KS 67202-3084 · 316-262-2671

Donald W. Bostwick · Adams, Jones, Robinson and Malone · 600 Market Centre 155 North Market Street · P.O. Box 1034 · Wichita, KS 67201 · 316-265-8591

J. Eric Engstrom · (Business Reorganization, Creditors' Rights, Debtors' Rights, Bankruptcy Litigation) · Fleeson, Gooing, Coulson & Kitch · 1600 Kansas State Bank Building · 125 North Market Street · P.O. Box 997 · Wichita, KS 67201-0997 316-267-7361

Christopher J. Redmond · Redmond, Redmond & Nazar · 200 West Douglas Street, Ninth Floor · Wichita, KS 67202 · 316-262-8361

BUSINESS LITIGATION

John J. Jurcyk, Jr. · McAnany, Van Cleave & Phillips · 707 Minnesota Avenue, Fourth Floor · P.O. Box 1300 · Kansas City, KS 66117 · 913-371-3838

George A. Lowe* · Lowe, Farmer, Bacon & Roe · Colonial Building · 110 West Loula · P.O. Box 580 · Olathe, KS 66061-0580 · 913-782-0422

Charles D. McAtee · Schroer, Rice · 115 East Seventh Street · P.O. Box 2667 · Topeka, KS 66601-2667 · 913-233-1235

Donald Patterson* · Fisher, Patterson, Sayler & Smith · 400 Bank IV Tower · P.O. Box 949 · Topeka, KS 66601 · 913-232-7761

Donald W. Bostwick · Adams, Jones, Robinson and Malone · 600 Market Centre 155 North Market Street · P.O. Box 1034 · Wichita, KS 67201 · 316-265-8591

Richard C. Hite · Kahrs, Nelson, Fanning, Hite & Kellogg · 200 West Douglas Street, Suite 630 · Wichita, KS 67202-3089 · 316-265-7761

Robert L. Howard · Foulston & Siefkin · 700 Fourth Financial Center · Broadway at Douglas · Wichita, KS 67202-2212 · 316-267-6371

Joseph W. Kennedy · Morris, Laing, Evans, Brock & Kennedy · 200 West Douglas Street, Fourth Floor · Wichita, KS 67202 · 316-262-2671

Thomas D. Kitch · Fleeson, Gooing, Coulson & Kitch · 1600 Kansas State Bank Building · 125 North Market Street · P.O. Box 997 · Wichita, KS 67201-0997 · 316-267-7361

W. Robert Martin · Martin, Pringle, Oliver, Wallace & Swartz · 300 Page Court 220 West Douglas Street · Wichita, KS 67202 · 316-265-9311

Donald R. Newkirk* · Fleeson, Gooing, Coulson & Kitch · 1600 Kansas State Bank Building · 125 North Market Street · P.O. Box 997 · Wichita, KS 67201-0997 316-267-7361

Gerald Sawatzky · Foulston & Siefkin · 700 Fourth Financial Center · Broadway at Douglas · Wichita, KS 67202-2212 · 316-267-6371

Mikel L. Stout* · Foulston & Siefkin · 700 Fourth Financial Center · Broadway at Douglas · Wichita, KS 67202-2212 · 316-267-6371

John P. Woolf* · Triplett, Woolf & Garretson · 800 Centre City Plaza · 151 North Main Street · Wichita, KS 67202-1409 · 316-265-5700

CORPORATE LAW

William P. Trenkle, Jr. · Mangan, Dalton, Trenkle, Rebein and Doll · 208 West Spruce Street · Dodge City, KS 67801-4425 · 316-227-8126

Webster L. Golden · Stevens, Brand, Lungstrum, Golden & Winter · 502 First National Bank Tower · P.O. Box 189 · Lawrence, KS 66044 · 913-843-0811

Charles S. (Terry) Arthur III · Arthur, Green, Arthur, Conderman & Stutzman 201-203 Union National Bank Tower · P.O. Box 248 · Manhattan, KS 66502 · 913-537-1345

Alson R. Martin · Shook, Hardy & Bacon · 40 Corporate Woods, Suite 650 · 9401 Indian Creek Parkway · P.O. Box 25128 · Overland Park, KS 66225 · 913-451-6060

Thomas W. Van Dyke · Linde Thomson Langworthy Kohn & Van Dyke · 7101 College Boulevard, Suite 1500 · Overland Park, KS 66210 · 913-649-4900

Robert E. Edmonds · (Banking, Mergers & Acquisitions, Securities, Securities Regulation) · Goodell, Stratton, Edmonds & Palmer · 515 South Kansas Avenue Topeka, KS 66603-3999 · 913-233-0593

H. Philip Elwood · Goodell, Stratton, Edmonds & Palmer · 515 South Kansas Avenue · Topeka, KS 66603-3999 · 913-233-0593

James D. Waugh · Cosgrove, Webb & Oman · Bank IV Tower, Suite 1100 · 534 Kansas Avenue · Topeka, KS 66603 · 913-235-9511

Stanley G. Andeel · Foulston & Siefkin · 700 Fourth Financial Center · Broadway at Douglas · Wichita, KS 67202-2212 · 316-267-6371

William M. Cobb · Bever, Dye, Mustard & Belin · 700 First National Bank Building · 106 West Douglas Street · Wichita, KS 67202 · 316-263-8294

Spencer L. Depew · Depew Gillen & Rathbun · 621 First National Bank Building Wichita, KS 67202-3308 · 316-265-9621

Benjamin C. Langel · Foulston & Siefkin · 700 Fourth Financial Center · Broadway at Douglas · Wichita, KS 67202-2212 · 316-267-6371

Willard B. Thompson · Fleeson, Gooing, Coulson & Kitch · 1600 Kansas State Bank Building · 125 North Market Street · P.O. Box 997 · Wichita, KS 67201-0997 316-267-7361

Thomas C. Triplett · Triplett, Woolf & Garretson · 800 Centre City Plaza · 151 North Main Street · Wichita, KS 67202-1409 · 316-265-5700

Gerrit H. Wormhoudt · Fleeson, Gooing, Coulson & Kitch · 1600 Kansas State Bank Building · 125 North Market Street · P.O. Box 997 · Wichita, KS 67201-0997 316-267-7361

CRIMINAL DEFENSE

James L. Eisenbrandt · Morris & Larson · 6900 College Boulevard, Suite 800 · Overland Park, KS 66211 · 913-345-1233

Mark L. Bennett, Jr. · Bennett, Dillon & Callahan · 1605 Southwest 37th Street Topeka, KS 66611 · 913-267-5063

Robert D. Hecht · Scott, Quinlan & Hecht · 3301 Van Buren · Topeka, KS 66611 913-267-0040

Jack Focht* · Focht, Hughey, Hund & Calvert · Brooker Plaza, Suite 300 · 807 North Waco · Wichita, KS 67203 · 316-269-9055

Stephen M. Joseph* · (Federal Court, State Court, White Collar) · Joseph, Robison & Anderson · 800 Sutton Place · 209 East William Street · Wichita, KS 67202-4013 · 316-262-0667

Daniel E. Monnat · Monnat & Spurrier · 512 Petroleum Building · 221 South Broadway · Wichita, KS 67202 · 316-264-2800

Charles A. O'Hara · O'Hara, O'Hara & Tousley · 1502 North Broadway · Wichita, KS 67214 · 316-263-5601

Stephen E. Robison* · (Non-Violent Crimes, Federal Court, State Court, White Collar Crimes) · Joseph, Robison & Anderson · 209 East William Street, Suite 800 · Wichita, KS 67202 · 316-262-0667

FAMILY LAW

J. Bradley Short · Cooke, Johnston, Baallweg, Christlieb, Tuley & Moore · 5401 College Boulevard, Suite 106 · Leawood, KS 66211 · 913-491-4400

Joe L. Norton* · Watson, Ess, Marshall & Enggas · 130 North Cherry Street · P.O. Box 550 · Olathe, KS 66061-0550 · 913-782-2350

Ray L. Borth · Borth & Borth · 9260 Glenwood · Overland Park, KS 66212 · 913-649-8989

John H. Johntz, Jr.* · (Child Custody, Divorce, Marital Settlement Agreements, Equitable Division) · Payne & Jones · Commerce Terrace, Suite 200 · College Boulevard at King · P.O. Box 25625 · Overland Park, KS 66225-5625 · 913-469-4100

T. Bradley Manson* · Payne & Jones · Commerce Terrace, Suite 200 · College Boulevard at King · P.O. Box 25625 · Overland Park, KS 66225-5625 · 913-469-4100

Linda D. Elrod · Washburn University Law School · 1700 College Avenue · Topeka, KS 66621 · 913-295-6300

Stephen J. Blaylock* · Woodard, Blaylock, Hernandez, Pilgreen & Roth · Riverfront Place · 833 North Waco · P.O. Box 127 · Wichita, KS 67201-0127 · 316-263-4958

Donald E. Lambdin* · Lambdin, Kluge & Zacharias · 830 North Main · P.O. Box 454 · Wichita, KS 67201-0454 · 316-265-3285

FIRST AMENDMENT LAW

Dan Biles · Gates & Glyde · 10990 Quivira, Suite 200 · Overland Park, KS 66210 913-661-0222

Michael W. Merriam · Goodell, Stratton, Edmonds & Palmer · 515 South Kansas Avenue · Topeka, KS 66603-3999 · 913-233-0593

Gerrit H. Wormhoudt · Fleeson, Gooing, Coulson & Kitch · 1600 Kansas State Bank Building · 125 North Market Street · P.O. Box 997 · Wichita, KS 67201-0997 316-267-7361

HEALTH CARE LAW

Charles R. Hay · Goodell, Stratton, Edmonds & Palmer · 515 South Kansas Avenue · Topeka, KS 66603-3999 · 913-233-0593

Marla J. Luckert · Goodell, Stratton, Edmonds & Palmer · 515 South Kansas Avenue · Topeka, KS 66603-3999 · 913-233-0593

Wayne T. Stratton · Goodell, Stratton, Edmonds & Palmer · 515 South Kansas Avenue · Topeka, KS 66603-3999 · 913-233-0593

Stephen M. Blaes · Foulston & Siefkin · 700 Fourth Financial Center · Broadway at Douglas · Wichita, KS 67202-2212 · 316-267-6371

Robert L. Heath · Foulston & Siefkin · 700 Fourth Financial Center · Broadway at Douglas · Wichita, KS 67202-2212 · 316-267-6371

INTELLECTUAL PROPERTY LAW

D. A. N. Chase · Linde Thomson Langworthy Kohn & Van Dyke · 7101 College Boulevard, Suite 1500 · Overland Park, KS 66210 · 913-649-4900

LABOR AND EMPLOYMENT LAW

John J. Blake · (Labor) · Blake & Uhlig · 475 New Brotherhood Building · 753 State Avenue · Kansas City, KS 66101 · 913-321-8884

Joseph W. Moreland · (Labor) · Blake & Uhlig · 475 New Brotherhood Building 753 State Avenue · Kansas City, KS 66101 · 913-321-8884

William G. Haynes · (Management) · Frieden, Haynes & Forbes · P.O. Box 639 Topeka, KS 66601 · 913-232-7266

Arthur E. Palmer · (Management) · Goodell, Stratton, Edmonds & Palmer · 515 South Kansas Avenue · Topeka, KS 66603-3999 · 913-233-0593

W. Stanley Churchill · (Management) · Martin, Churchill, Overman, Hill & Cole 500 North Market Street · Wichita, KS 67214 · 316-263-3200

William H. Dye · (Management) · Foulston & Siefkin · 700 Fourth Financial Center · Broadway at Douglas Street · Wichita, KS 67202-2212 · 316-267-6371

Thomas E. Hammond · (Labor) · Render, Kamas & Hammond · 700 Riverview Building · 345 Riverview Street · P.O. Box 47370 · Wichita, KS 67201 · 316-267-2212

Marvin J. Martin · (Management) · Martin, Churchill, Overman, Hill & Cole · 500 North Market Street · Wichita, KS 67214 · 316-263-3200

Robert N. Partridge · (Management) · Foulston & Siefkin · 700 Fourth Financial Center · Broadway at Douglas Street · Wichita, KS 67202-2212 · 316-267-6371

Stephen B. Plummer* · (Individuals) · Rumsey, Richey & Plummer · 1041 North Waco Street · Wichita, KS 67203 · 316-262-4481

NATURAL RESOURCES AND ENVIRONMENTAL LAW

Ralph R. Brock · (Oil & Gas) · Morris, Laing, Evans, Brock & Kennedy · 200 West Douglas Street, Fourth Floor · Wichita, KS 67202 · 316-262-2671

Kenneth W. Pringle · Martin, Pringle, Oliver, Wallace & Swartz · 300 Page Court 220 West Douglas Street · Wichita, KS 67202 · 316-265-9311

Randall K. Rathbun* · (Plaintiffs, Environmental Litigation) · Depew Gillen & Rathbun · 621 First National Bank Building · Wichita, KS 67202-3308 · 316-265-9621

Gerald Sawatzky · Foulston & Siefkin · 700 Fourth Financial Center · Broadway at Douglas · Wichita, KS 67202-2212 · 316-267-6371

PERSONAL INJURY LITIGATION

Jack E. Dalton* · Mangan, Dalton, Trenkle, Rebein and Doll · 208 West Spruce Street · Dodge City, KS 67801-4425 · 316-227-8126

Donald W. Vasos* · (Plaintiffs) · Vasos, Kugler & Dickerson · 10 Cambridge Place, Suite 200 · 10 East Cambridge Circle Drive · Kansas City, KS 66103 · 913-342-3100

Kerry E. McQueen · Neubauer, Sharp, McQueen, Dreiling & Morain · 419 North Kansas Street · P.O. Box 2619 · Liberal, KS 67905-2619 · 316-624-2548

Gene H. Sharp · Neubauer, Sharp, McQueen, Dreiling & Morain · 419 North Kansas Street · P.O. Box 2619 · Liberal, KS 67905-2619 · 316-624-2548

Victor A. Bergman · (Plaintiffs) · Shamberg, Johnson, Bergman & Morris · 4551 West 107th Street, Suite 355 · Overland Park, KS 66207 · 913-642-0600

Lynn R. Johnson* · (Plaintiffs, Medical Malpractice, Products Liability, Professional Malpractice) · Shamberg, Johnson, Bergman & Goldman & Morris · Foxhill Place Building · 4551 West 107th Street, Suite 355 · Overland Park, KS 66207 · 913-642-0600

Frank Saunders, Jr. · (Defendants) · Wallace, Saunders, Austin, Brown & Enochs · 10111 Santa Fe Drive · P.O. Box 12290 · Overland Park, KS 66212 · 913-888-1000

John E. Shamberg* · (Plaintiffs, Products Liability, Professional Malpractice, Automobile Collision) · Shamberg, Johnson, Bergman & Morris · 4551 West 107th Street, Suite 355 · Overland Park, KS 66207 · 913-642-0600

Thomas E. Sullivan* · (Plaintiffs) · Law Offices of Thomas E. · 10990 Quivira Street, Suite 280 · Overland Park, KS 66210 · 913-451-1981

Aubrey G. Linville · Clark, Mize & Linville · 129 South Eighth · P.O. Box 380 Salina, KS 67402-0380 · 913-823-6325

Charles S. Fisher, Jr. · (Plaintiffs) · Fisher, Cavanaugh & Smith · Bank IV Tower, Suite 1035 · 534 Kansas Avenue · Topeka, KS 66603 · 913-354-7622

Jerry R. Palmer* · (Plaintiffs, Medical Malpractice, Professional Malpractice, Automobile Collision) · Palmer & Marquardt · Columbian Building, Suite 102 · 112 West Sixth · Topeka, KS 66603-3862 · 913-233-1836

Donald Patterson* · (Defendants) · Fisher, Patterson, Sayler & Smith · 400 Bank IV Tower · P.O. Box 949 · Topeka, KS 66601 · 913-232-7761

Eugene B. Ralston · (Plaintiffs) · Ralston, Buck & Associates · 2913 Southwest Maupin Lane · Topeka, KS 66614 · 913-273-8002

Gene E. Schroer · (Plaintiffs) · Schroer, Rice · 115 East Seventh Street · Topeka, KS 66603 · 913-357-0333

Edwin Dudley Smith · (Defendants) · Fisher, Patterson, Sayler & Smith · 400 Bank IV Tower · P.O. Box 949 · Topeka, KS 66601 · 913-232-7761

Wayne T. Stratton* · (Defendants, Medical Malpractice, Professional Malpractice) · Goodell, Stratton, Edmonds & Palmer · 515 South Kansas Avenue · Topeka, KS 66603-3999 · 913-233-0593

Wesley A. Weathers* · (Products Liability, Toxic Tort) · Weathers & Riley · 4848 Southwest 21st Street, Suite 202 · P.O. Box 67209 · Topeka, KS 66667 · 913-273-2020

Arden J. Bradshaw* · (Plaintiffs, Medical Malpractice Products Liability, Airplane Collision) · Michaud, Hutton & Bradshaw · 8100 East 22nd Street North, Building 1200 · Wichita, KS 67226-2312 · 316-686-3404

Richard C. Hite · (Defendants) · Kahrs, Nelson, Fanning, Hite & Kellogg · 200 West Douglas Street, Suite 630 · Wichita, KS 67202-3089 · 316-265-7761

H. E. Jones · (Defendants) · Herschberger, Patterson, Jones & Roth · 100 South Main Street, Suite 600 · Wichita, KS 67202 · 316-263-7583

Albert L. Kamas · (Plaintiffs) · Render, Kamas & Hammond · 700 Riverview Building · 345 Riverview · P.O. Box 47370 · Wichita, KS 67201 · 316-267-2212

Darrell D. Kellogg* · (Defendants, Medical Malpractice, Professional Malpractice, Airplane Collision) · Kahrs, Nelson, Fanning, Hite & Kellogg · 200 West Douglas Street, Suite 630 · Wichita, KS 67202-3089 · 316-265-7761

Gerald L. Michaud · (Plaintiffs) · Michaud, Hutton & Bradshaw · Building 1200 8100 East 22nd Street North · P.O. Box 2757 · Wichita, KS 67226-2312 · 316-686-3404

Ken M. Peterson · Morris, Laing, Evans, Brock & Kennedy · 200 West Douglas Street, Fourth Floor · Wichita, KS 67202-3084 · 316-262-2671

Bradley Post* · (Plaintiffs, Medical Malpractice, Products Liability, Professional Malpractice) · Post, Syrios & Kinch · Occidental Plaza, Suite 204 · 300 North Main Street · Wichita, KS 67202-2078 · 316-267-6391

Mikel L. Stout* · (Defendants) · Foulston & Siefkin · 700 Fourth Financial Center · Broadway at Douglas · Wichita, KS 67202-2212 · 316-267-6371

Darrell L. Warta* · (Defendants) · Foulston & Siefkin · 700 Fourth Financial Center · Broadway at Douglas · Wichita, KS 67202-2212 · 316-267-6371

PUBLIC UTILITY LAW

James P. Zakoura · Smithyman & Zakoura · 650 Commerce Plaza · 7300 West 110th Street · Overland Park, KS 66210 · 913-661-9800

James L. Grimes · (Natural Gas, Telephone) · Cosgrove, Webb & Oman · Bank IV Tower, Suite 1100 · 534 Kansas Avenue · Topeka, KS 66603 · 913-235-9511

REAL ESTATE LAW

Stephen T. Adams · Blackwell Sanders Matheny Weary & Lombardi · 40 Corporate Woods, Suite 1200 · 9401 Indian Creek Parkway · Overland Park, KS 66210 913-345-8400

Jack N. Fingersh · Lewis, Price & Fingersh · Corporate Woods, Building 40, Suite 1100 · 9401 Indian Creek Parkway · P.O. Box 25550 · Overland Park, KS 66225 · 913-451-8500

Gerald L. Goodell · Goodell, Stratton, Edmonds & Palmer · 515 South Kansas Avenue · Topeka, KS 66603-3999 · 913-233-0593

Philip L. Bowman · Adams, Jones, Robinson and Malone · Market Center, Suite 600 · 155 North Market Street · P.O. Box 1034 · Wichita, KS 67201 · 316-265-8591

Phillip S. Frick · Foulston & Siefkin · 700 Fourth Financial Center · Broadway at Douglas · Wichita, KS 67202-2212 · 316-267-6371

Willard B. Thompson · Fleeson, Gooing, Coulson & Kitch · 1600 Kansas State Bank Building · 125 North Market Street · P.O. Box 997 · Wichita, KS 67201-0997 316-267-7361

TAX AND EMPLOYEE BENEFITS LAW

Philip D. Ridenour* · Ridenour and Knobbe · 109 West Avenue A · P.O. Box 808 Cimarron, KS 67835 · 316-855-3492

William P. Trenkle, Jr. · Mangan, Dalton, Trenkle, Rebein and Doll · 208 West Spruce Street · Dodge City, KS 67801-4425 · 316-227-8126

Martin B. Dickinson, Jr. · (Corporate & Partnership Transactions) · Barber, Emerson, Springer, Zinn & Murray · Massachusetts Street at South Park · P.O. Box 666 · Lawrence, KS 66044 · 913-843-6600

Richard L. Zinn · Barber, Emerson, Springer, Zinn & Murray · Massachusetts Street at South Park · P.O. Box 666 · Lawrence, KS 66044 · 913-843-6600

Charles S. (Terry) Arthur III · Arthur, Green, Arthur, Conderman & Stutzman 201-203 Union National Bank Tower · P.O. Box 248 · Manhattan, KS 66502 · 913-537-1345

George F. Crawford · Morrison, Hecker, Curtis, Kuder & Parrish · Corporate Woods, Building 14, Suite 520 · 8717 West 110th Street · Overland Park, KS 66210-2192 · 913-345-2700

Thomas K. Jones · Payne & Jones · Commerce Terrace, Suite 200 · College Boulevard at King · P.O. Box 25625 · Overland Park, KS 66225-5625 · 913-469-4100

Alson R. Martin · (Tax, Employee Benefits) · Shook, Hardy & Bacon · 40 Corporate Woods, Suite 650 · 9401 Indian Creek Parkway · P.O. Box 25128 · Overland Park, KS 66225 · 913-451-6060

William K. Waugh III · Lathrop Norquist & Miller · 40 Corporate Woods, Suite 1050 · 9401 Indian Creek Parkway · Overland Park, KS 66210 · 913-451-0820

Thomas J. Kennedy · Kennedy Berkley Yarnevich & Williamson · United Building, Seventh Floor · P.O. Box 2567 · Salina, KS 67402-2567 · 913-825-4674

Peter L. Peterson · (Tax, Employee Benefits) · Clark, Mize & Linville · 129 South Eighth Street · P.O. Box 380 · Salina, KS 67402-0380 · 913-823-6325

Donald J. Horttor* · (Corporate & Partnership Transactions, State Tax, Tax Disputes) · Cosgrove, Webb & Oman · Bank IV Tower, Suite 1100 · 534 Kansas Avenue · Topeka, KS 66603 · 913-235-9511

R. Austin Nothern · Schroeder, Heeney, Groff & Coffman · 400 Southwest Eighth Avenue, Suite 408 · Topeka, KS 66603-3956 · 913-234-3461

Jeffrey L. Ungerer · 2231 Southwest Wanamaker Road, Suite 101 · Topeka, KS 66614 · 913-273-5250

Stanley G. Andeel · Foulston & Siefkin · 700 Fourth Financial Center · Broadway at Douglas Street · Wichita, KS 67202-2212 · 316-267-6371

William M. Cobb · Bever, Dye, Mustard & Belin · 700 First National Bank Building · 106 West Douglas Street · Wichita, KS 67202 · 316-263-8294

James P. Rankin · (Employee Benefits) · Foulston & Siefkin · 700 Fourth Financial Center · Broadway at Douglas Street · Wichita, KS 67202-2212 · 316-267-6371

R. Chris Robe · (Employee Benefits) · Bever, Dye, Mustard & Belin · 700 First National Bank Building · 106 West Douglas Street · Wichita, KS 67202 · 316-263-8294

Harvey Sorensen · (Corporate & Partnership Transactions, State Tax, Tax Disputes) · Foulston & Siefkin · 700 Fourth Financial Center · Broadway at Douglas Street · Wichita, KS 67202-2212 · 316-267-6371

Willard B. Thompson · Fleeson, Gooing, Coulson & Kitch · 1600 Kansas State Bank Building · 125 North Market Street · P.O. Box 997 · Wichita, KS 67201-0997 316-267-7361

Thomas C. Triplett · Triplett, Woolf & Garretson · 800 Centre City Plaza · 151 North Main Street · Wichita, KS 67202-1409 · 316-265-5700

TRUSTS AND ESTATES

Philip D. Ridenour* · (Estate Planning) · Ridenour and Knobbe · 109 West Avenue A · P.O. Box 808 · Cimarron, KS 67835 · 316-855-3492

William P. Trenkle, Jr. · Mangan, Dalton, Trenkle, Rebein and Doll · 208 West Spruce Street · Dodge City, KS 67801-4425 · 316-227-8126

Martin B. Dickinson, Jr. · (Estate Planning, Estate Administration) · Barber, Emerson, Springer, Zinn & Murray · Massachusetts Street at South Park · P.O. Box 666 · Lawrence, KS 66044 · 913-843-6600

Webster L. Golden · Stevens, Brand, Lungstrum, Golden & Winter · 502 First National Bank Tower · P.O. Box 189 · Lawrence, KS 66044 · 913-843-0811

Charles S. (Terry) Arthur III · Arthur, Green, Arthur, Conderman & Stutzman 201-203 Union National Bank Tower · P.O. Box 248 · Manhattan, KS 66502 · 913-537-1345

Nancy Schmidt Roush · (Estate Planning, Estate Administration) · Shook, Hardy & Bacon · 40 Corporate Woods, Suite 650 · 9401 Indian Creek Parkway · P.O. Box 25128 · Overland Park, KS 66225 · 913-451-6060

Peter L. Peterson · Clark, Mize & Linville · 129 South Eighth Street · P.O. Box 380 · Salina, KS 67402-0380 · 913-823-6325

Donald J. Horttor* · (Estate Planning, Estate Administration, Charitable Trusts) Cosgrove, Webb & Oman · Bank IV Tower, Suite 1100 · 534 Kansas Avenue · Topeka, KS 66603 · 913-235-9511

E. Gene McKinney · McKinney & McKinney · 517 Capitol Federal Building · 700 Kansas Avenue · Topeka, KS 66603 · 913-233-1321

R. Austin Nothern · Schroeder, Heeney, Groff & Coffman · 400 Southwest Eighth Avenue, Suite 408 · Topeka, KS 66603-3956 · 913-234-3461

Stanley G. Andeel · Foulston & Siefkin · 700 Fourth Financial Center · Broadway at Douglas Street · Wichita, KS 67202-2212 · 316-267-6371

Linda K. Constable · Foulston & Siefkin · 700 Fourth Financial Center · Broadway at Douglas Street · Wichita, KS 67202-2212 · 316-267-6371

Richard C. Harris* · Foulston & Siefkin · 700 Fourth Financial Center · Broadway at Douglas Street · Wichita, KS 67202-2212 · 316-267-6371

Willard B. Thompson* · Fleeson, Gooing, Coulson & Kitch · 1600 Kansas State Bank Building · 125 North Market Street · P.O. Box 997 · Wichita, KS 67201-0997 316-267-7361

Thomas C. Triplett · Triplett, Woolf & Garretson · 800 Centre City Plaza · 151 North Main Street · Wichita, KS 67202-1409 · 316-265-5700

KENTUCKY

BANKRUPTCY LAW

W. Thomas Bunch · Bunch & Brock · Security Trust Building, Suite 805 · P.O. Box 2086 · Lexington, KY 40594 · 606-254-5522

Joseph M. Scott, Jr. · Stoll, Keenon & Park · 1000 First Security Plaza · Lexington, KY 40507-1380 · 606-231-3000

Jerry D. Truitt · Ogden, Sturgill, & Welch · 155 East Main Street · Lexington, KY 40507 · 606-255-8581

John W. Ames* · (Business Reorganization, Creditors' Rights, Debtors' Rights, Bankruptcy Litigation) · Greenebaum Doll & McDonald · 3300 First National Tower · Louisville, KY 40202-3197 · 502-589-4200

John P. Reisz · Wyatt, Tarrant & Combs · 2700 Citizens Plaza · Louisville, KY 40202 · 502-589-5235

BUSINESS LITIGATION

John David Cole* · Cole, Broderick, Minton, Moore & Thornton · Phoenix Place 921 College Street · P.O. Box 1869 · Bowling Green, KY 42102-1869 · 502-781-6650

Donald Duff · 212 Washington Street · P.O. Box 1160 · Frankfort, KY 40602 · 502-223-7656

William E. Johnson · Johnson, Judy, Stoll, Keenon & Park · 326 West Main Street · Frankfort, KY 40601 · 502-875-6000

William D. Kirkland · McBrayer, McGinnis, Leslie & Kirkland · State National Bank Building, Suite 300 · Frankfort, KY 40602 · 502-223-1200

W. Terry McBrayer · McBrayer, McGinnis, Leslie & Kirkland · State National Bank Building, Suite 300 · Frankfort, KY 40602 · 502-223-1200

Charles L. Calk* · Gess Mattingly & Atchison · 201 West Short Street · Lexington, KY 40507-1269 · 606-255-2344

C. Kilmer Combs · Wyatt, Tarrant & Combs · 1700 Lexington Financial Center 250 West Main Street · Lexington, KY 40507 · 606-233-2012

C. Gibson Downing* · 1999 Richmond Road, Suite 2-B · Lexington, KY 40502 606-268-2869

Harry B. Miller, Jr. · Miller, Griffin & Marks · Security Trust Building, Suite 700 271 West Short Street · Lexington, KY 40507 · 606-255-6676

James Park, Jr. · Brown, Todd & Heyburn · 2700 Lexington Financial Center · Lexington, KY 40507-1634 · 606-233-4068

Charles J. Cronan IV* · (Commercial) · Stites & Harbison · 600 West Main Street Louisville, KY 40202 · 502-587-3400

William D. Grubbs* · (Commercial) · Woodward, Hobson & Fulton · 2500 First National Tower · Louisville, KY 40202-3175 · 502-585-3321

K. Gregory Haynes* · Wyatt, Tarrant & Combs · 2600 Citizens Plaza · Louisville, KY 40202 · 502-589-5235

Marvin J. Hirn* · Hirn Reed Harper & Eisinger · 2450 Meidinger Tower · Louisville, KY 40202 · 502-585-2450

John R. McCall · Brown, Todd & Heyburn · 1600 Citizens Plaza · Louisville, KY 40202-2873 · 502-589-5400

Kenneth J. Tuggle* · (Antitrust, Computer Hardware & Software) · Brown, Todd & Heyburn · 1600 Citizens Plaza · Louisville, KY 40202-2873 · 502-589-5400

Lively M. Wilson · Stites & Harbison · 600 West Main Street · Louisville, KY 40202 · 502-587-3400

Edgar A. Zingman · Wyatt, Tarrant & Combs · 2600 Citizens Plaza · Louisville, KY 40202 · 502-589-5235

Morton J. Holbrook, Jr. · Holbrook, Wible, Sullivan & Mountjoy · 100 Saint Ann Building · P.O. Box 727 · Owensboro, KY 42302 · 502-926-4000

CORPORATE LAW

Bruce F. Clark · Stites & Harbison · 421 West Main Street · Frankfort, KY 40601 502-223-3477

William E. Johnson · Johnson, Judy, Stoll, Keenon & Park · 326 West Main Street · Frankfort, KY 40601 · 502-875-5544

John G. Atchison, Jr. · Gess Mattingly & Atchison · 201 West Short Street · Lexington, KY 40507-1269 · 606-255-2344

Lawrence K. Banks · Greenebaum Doll & McDonald · 1400 Vine Center Tower P.O. Box 1808 · Lexington, KY 40593 · 606-231-8500

C. Gibson Downing* · 1999 Richmond Road, Suite 2B · Lexington, KY 40502 · 606-268-2869

Lawrence E. Forgy, Jr. · Stoll, Keenon & Park · 1000 First Security Plaza · Lexington, KY 40507-1380 · 606-231-3000

James A. Kegley · Greenebaum Doll & McDonald · 1400 Vine Center Tower · P.O. Box 1808 · Lexington, KY 40593 · 606-231-8500

William L. Montague · Stoll, Keenon & Park · 1000 First Security Plaza · Lexington, KY 40507-1380 · 606-231-3000

James Park, Jr. · Brown, Todd & Heyburn · 2700 Lexington Financial Center · Lexington, KY 40507-1634 · 606-233-4068

Stewart E. Conner · Wyatt, Tarrant & Combs · 2800 Citizens Plaza · Louisville, KY 40202 · 502-589-5235

Gordon B. Davidson · Wyatt, Tarrant & Combs · 2700 Citizens Plaza · Louisville, KY 40202 · 502-589-5235

Ivan M. Diamond · Greenebaum Doll & McDonald · 3300 First National Tower Louisville, KY 40202-3197 · 502-589-4200

A. Robert Doll · (Mergers & Acquisitions) · Greenebaum Doll & McDonald · 3300 First National Tower · Louisville, KY 40202-3197 · 502-589-4200

Irwin J. Eisinger · (Corporate Finance, Mutual Funds, Securities, Securities Regulation) · Hirn Reed Harper & Eisinger · 2450 Meidinger Tower · Louisville, KY 40202 · 502-585-2450

C. Edward Glasscock · Brown, Todd & Heyburn · 1600 Citizens Plaza · Louisville, KY 40202-2873 · 502-589-5400

Edwin H. Perry · Greenebaum Doll & McDonald · 3300 First National Tower · Louisville, KY 40202-3197 · 502-589-4200

R. James Straus · Brown, Todd & Heyburn · 1600 Citizens Plaza · Louisville, KY 40202-2873 · 502-589-5400

Rucker Todd · Brown, Todd & Heyburn · 1600 Citizens Plaza · Louisville, KY 40202-2873 · 502-589-5400

James S. Welch · Ogden, Sturgill & Welch · 1200 One Riverfront Plaza · Louisville, KY 40202-2973 · 502-582-1601

CRIMINAL DEFENSE

William E. Johnson · Johnson, Judy, Stoll, Keenon & Park · 326 West Main Street · Frankfort, KY 40601 · 502-875-6000

James A. Shuffett* · Shuffett and Paris · 403 Security Trust Building · 271 West Short Street · Lexington, KY 40507-1292 · 606-252-5794

Frank E. Haddad, Jr. · Kentucky Home Life Building, Fifth Floor · 239 South Fifth Street · Louisville, KY 40202 · 502-583-4881

FAMILY LAW

Glen S. Bagby* · Brock, Brock & Bagby · 190 Market Street · Lexington, KY 40507 · 606-255-7795

Sandra Mendez-Dawahare · Landrum & Shouse · 106 West Vine Street · P.O. Box 951 · Lexington, KY 40588-0951 · 606-255-2424

Harry B. Miller, Jr. · Miller, Griffin & Marks · Security Trust Building, Suite 700 271 West Short Street · Lexington, KY 40507 · 606-255-6676

Natalie S. Wilson* · Gess Mattingly & Atchison · 201 West Short Street · Lexington, KY 40507-1269 · 606-255-2344

Virginia C. Burbank* · Burbank and Burbank · First Trust Centre, Suite 600 North · Fifth and Market Streets · Louisville, KY 40202 · 502-585-5100

William P. Mulloy, Sr.* · (Adoption, Child Custody, Divorce, Marital Settlement Agreements) · Mulloy, Walz, Wetterer, Fore & Schwartz · First Trust Centre, Suite 700 North · 200 South Fifth Street · Louisville, KY 40202 · 502-589-5250

FIRST AMENDMENT LAW

Jon L. Fleischaker* · Wyatt, Tarrant & Combs · 2600 Citizens Plaza · Louisville, KY 40202 · 502-589-5235

HEALTH CARE LAW

Robert G. Stevens · Deters, Benzinger & LaVelle · Thomas More Park · 2701 Turkeyfoot Road · Covington, KY 41017 · 606-341-1881

R. Thomas Carter · Goldberg & Simpson · 2800 First National Tower · Louisville, KY 40202 · 502-589-4440

J. Larry Cashen · Wyatt, Tarrant & Combs · 2800 Citizens Plaza · Louisville, KY 40202 · 502-589-5235

John R. Cummins · Greenebaum Doll & McDonald · 3300 First National Tower Louisville, KY 40202-3197 · 502-589-4200

Susan B. Turner · Wyatt, Tarrant & Combs · 2700 Citizens Plaza · Louisville, KY 40202 · 502-589-5235

IMMIGRATION LAW

Glen M. Krebs · Greenebaum Doll & McDonald · 1400 Vine Center Tower · P.O. Box 1808 · Lexington, KY 40593 · 606-231-8500

INTELLECTUAL PROPERTY LAW

J. Ralph King · King and Schickli · Corporate Gateway, Suite 210 · 3070 Harrodsburg Road · Lexington, KY 40503 · 606-223-4050

James R. Higgins, Jr. · Middleton & Reutlinger · 2500 Brown & Williamson Tower · Louisville, KY 40202-3410 · 502-584-1135

Charles G. Lamb, Jr. · Middleton & Reutlinger · 2500 Brown & Williamson Tower · Louisville, KY 40202-3410 · 502-584-1135

LABOR AND EMPLOYMENT LAW

Jon L. Fleischaker* · (Management) · Wyatt, Tarrant & Combs · 2600 Citizens Plaza · Louisville, KY 40202 · 502-589-5235

James C. Hickey · (Individuals) · MacKenzie & Peden · 650 Starks Building · Louisville, KY 40202 · 502-589-1110

D. Patton Pelfrey · (Management) · Brown, Todd & Heyburn · 1600 Citizens Plaza · Louisville, KY 40202-2873 · 502-589-5400

Alton D. Priddy · (Labor) · Hardy, Logan, Priddy & Cotton · 604 Republic Building · 429 West Muhammad Ali Boulevard · Louisville, KY 40202 · 502-569-2740

Raymond L. Sales · (Labor) · Segal, Isenberg, Sales, Stewart & Cutler · Marion E. Taylor Building, Third Floor · 312 Fourth Avenue · Louisville, KY 40202 · 502-568-5600

Herbert L. Segal · (Labor) · Segal, Isenberg, Sales, Stewart & Cutler · Marion E. Taylor Building, Third Floor · 312 Fourth Avenue · Louisville, KY 40202 · 502-568-5600

James U. Smith III · (Management) · Smith and Smith · 400 North First Trust Centre · 200 South Fifth Street · Louisville, KY 40202 · 502-587-0761

Matthew R. Westfall · (Management) · Westfall, Talbott & Woods · 501 South Second Street · Louisville, KY 40202 · 502-584-7722

NATURAL RESOURCES AND ENVIRONMENTAL LAW

George L. Seay, Jr. · Wyatt, Tarrant & Combs · McClure Building, Suite 200 · 308 West Main Street · P.O. Box 495 · Frankfort, KY 40602 · 502-223-2104

Joseph J. Zaluski* · (Coal, Mining, Solid Waste, Hazardous Waste) · Wyatt, Tarrant & Combs · McClure Building, Suite 200 · 308 West Main Street · P.O. Box 495 · Frankfort, KY 40602 · 502-223-2104

Maxwell P. Barret, Jr. · Stoll, Keenon & Park · 1000 First Security Plaza · Lexington, KY 40507-1380 · 606-231-3000

Lloyd R. Cress · Greenebaum Doll & McDonald · 1400 Vine Center Tower · P.O. Box 1808 · Lexington, KY 40593 · 606-231-8500

Marcus P. McGraw · Greenebaum Doll & McDonald · 1400 Vine Center Tower P.O. Box 1808 · Lexington, KY 40593 · 606-231-8500

PERSONAL INJURY LITIGATION

Reginald L. Ayers · Bell, Orr, Ayers & Moore · 1010 College Street · P.O. Box 738 · Bowling Green, KY 42102-0738 · 502-781-8111

John David Cole* · (Defendants) · Cole, Broderick, Minton, Moore & Thornton Phoenix Place · 921 College Street · P.O. Box 1869 · Bowling Green, KY 42102-1869 · 502-781-6650

Mark G. Arnzen* · (Defendants) · Arnzen, Parry & Wentz · 600 Greenup Street Covington, KY 41012-0472 · 606-431-6100

John L. Spalding* · (Defendants) · Spalding, Hannah & Rouse · Professional Arts Building · 333 Madison Avenue · Covington, KY 41011 · 606-291-4646

Philip Taliaferro III · (Plaintiffs) · Taliaferro & Mann · 1005 Madison Avenue · P.O. Box 468 · Covington, KY 41012-0468 · 606-291-9900

E. Andre Busald* · (Plaintiffs, Products Liability, Professional Malpractice, Automobile Collision) · Busald Funk Zevely · 226 Main Street · Florence, KY 41042-6910 · 606-371-3600

Uhel O. Barrickman · (Defendants) · Richardson, Barrickman, Dickinson & Ropp · 118 East Public Square · P.O. Box 358 · Glasgow, KY 42142-0358 · 502-651-2116

W. T. Adkins · (Defendants) · Boehl Stopher Graves & Deindoerfer · 444 West Second Street · Lexington, KY 40507 · 606-252-6721

William R. Garmer* · (Plaintiffs) · Savage, Garmer & Elliott · 141 North Broadway · Lexington, KY 40507 · 606-254-9351

D. G. Lynn · (Defendants, Medical Malpractice, Products Liability, Professional Malpractice) · Hays, Moss and Lynn · 267 West Short Street · Lexington, KY 40507 · 606-253-0523

Peter Perlman · (Plaintiffs) · Law Offices of Peter Perlman · 388 South Broadway Lexington, KY 40508 · 606-253-3919

Joe C. Savage · (Plaintiffs) · Savage, Garmer & Elliott · 141 North Broadway · Lexington, KY 40507 · 606-254-9351

Robert J. Turley · (Plaintiffs) · Turley & Moore · Limestone Building, First Floor 134 North Limestone Street · Lexington, KY 40507 · 606-252-1705

John T. Ballantine* · (Defendants, Medical Malpractice, Professional Malpractice) · Ogden, Sturgill & Welch · 1200 One Riverfront Plaza · Louisville, KY 40202-2973 · 502-582-1601

F. Thomas Conway · Conway & Adams · 621 West Main Street · Louisville, KY 40202 · 502-583-4433

Charles J. Cronan IV* · (Defendants, Products Liability) · Stites & Harbison · 600 West Main Street · Louisville, KY 40202 · 502-587-3400

Frank P. Doheny, Jr.* · (Defendants) · Woodward, Hobson & Fulton · 2500 First National Tower · Louisville, KY 40202-3175 · 502-585-3321

Frederick C. Dolt* · (Plaintiffs) · Dolt, Furkin & Thompson · 310 Starks Building Louisville, KY 40202 · 502-587-6554

Larry B. Franklin · (Plaintiffs) · Franklin and Hance · First National Tower, 23rd Floor · 101 South Fifth Street · Louisville, KY 40202 · 502-582-2270

William D. Grubbs* · (Defendants) · Woodward, Hobson & Fulton · 2500 First National Tower · Louisville, KY 40202-3175 · 502-585-3321

William O. Guethlein* · (Defendants, Medical Malpractice, Products Liability, Professional Malpractice, Automobile Collision) · Boehl Stopher Graves & Deindoerfer · One Riverfront Plaza, Suite 2300 · Louisville, KY 40202 · 502-589-5980

Armer H. Mahan, Jr. · (Defendants) · Lynch, Cox, Gilman & Mahan · 500 Meidinger Tower · Louisville, KY 40202 · 502-589-4215

William R. Patterson, Jr. · (Plaintiffs) · Law Offices of William R. Patterson · 816 East Chestnut Street · Louisville, KY 40204 · 502-583-1122

Edward H. Stopher* · (Defendants, Products Liability, Professional Malpractice) Boehl Stopher Graves & Deindoerfer · One Riverfront Plaza, Suite 2300 · Louisville, KY 40202 · 502-589-5980

Gary M. Weiss* · (Plaintiffs) · Weiss & Roseberry · Bank of Louisville Building 510 West Broadway · Louisville, KY 40202 · 502-587-1000

Lively M. Wilson · (Defendants) · Stites & Harbison · 600 West Main Street · Louisville, KY 40202 · 502-587-3400

Frank V. Benton III* · (Plaintiffs, Defendants, Medical Malpractice, Automobile Collision) · Benton, Benton & Luedeke · 18 North Fort Thomas Avenue · Newport, KY 41075 · 606-781-2345

PUBLIC UTILITY LAW

O. Grant Bruton* · Middleton & Reutlinger · 2500 Brown & Williamson Tower Louisville, KY 40202-3410 · 502-584-1135

C. Kent Hatfield · Middleton & Reutlinger · 2500 Brown & Williamson Tower · Louisville, KY 40202-3410 · 502-584-1135

Richard F. Newell · Ogden, Sturgill & Welch · 1200 One Riverfront Plaza · Louisville, KY 40202-2973 · 502-582-1601

REAL ESTATE LAW

Michael L. Ades · Greenebaum Doll & McDonald · 1400 Vine Center Tower · P.O. Box 1808 · Lexington, KY 40593 · 606-231-8500

Gary W. Barr · Stoll, Keenon & Park · 1000 First Security Plaza · Lexington, KY 40507-1380 · 606-231-3000

James T. Hodge · Wyatt, Tarrant & Combs · 1700 Lexington Financial Center · 250 West Main Street · Lexington, KY 40507 · 606-233-2012

William M. Lear, Jr.* · Stoll, Keenon & Park · 1000 First Security Plaza · Lexington, KY 40507-1380 · 606-231-3000

Foster Ockerman · Martin, Ockerman & Brabant · 200 North Upper Street · Lexington, KY 40507 · 606-254-4401

Mark B. Davis* · (Land Use, Commercial Transactions, Industrial Transactions) Brown, Todd & Heyburn · 1600 Citizens Plaza · Louisville, KY 40202-2873 · 502-589-5400

David C. Fannin · Wyatt, Tarrant & Combs · 2700 Citizens Plaza · Louisville, KY 40202 · 502-589-5235

Michael M. Fleishman · (Commercial Transactions) · Greenebaum Doll & McDonald · 3300 First National Tower · Louisville, KY 40202-3197 · 502-589-4200

Alfred S. Joseph III · (Zoning, Commercial Transactions, Industrial Transactions) · Stites & Harbison · 600 West Main Street · Louisville, KY 40202 · 502-587-3400

John S. Osborn, Jr. · Wyatt, Tarrant & Combs · 2700 Citizens Plaza · Louisville, KY 40202 · 502-589-5235

Michael G. Shaikun · Greenebaum Doll & McDonald · 3300 First National Tower · Louisville, KY 40202-3197 · 502-589-4200

TAX AND EMPLOYEE BENEFITS LAW

Charles R. Hembree · Kincaid, Wilson, Schaeffer, Hembree, Van Inwegen & Kinser · Kincaid Towers, Suite 650 · Lexington, KY 40507 · 606-253-6411

Charles Fassler · Greenebaum Doll & McDonald · 3300 First National Tower · Louisville, KY 40202-3197 · 502-589-4200

G. Alexander Hamilton · (Employee Benefits) · Wyatt, Tarrant & Combs · 2800 Citizens Plaza · Louisville, KY 40202 · 502-589-5235

Laramie L. Leatherman · Greenebaum Doll & McDonald · 3300 First National Tower · Louisville, KY 40202-3197 · 502-589-4200

Thomas J. Luber* · (Corporate & Partnership Transactions, State Tax, Tax Disputes) · Wyatt, Tarrant & Combs · 2800 Citizens Plaza · Louisville, KY 40202 502-589-5235

Joseph C. Oldham · (Employee Benefits) · Ogden, Sturgill & Welch · 1200 One Riverfront Plaza · Louisville, KY 40202-2973 · 502-582-1601

Ivan J. Schell · (Employee Benefits) · Hirn Reed Harper & Eisinger · 2450 Meidinger · Louisville, KY 40202 · 502-585-2450

TRUSTS AND ESTATES

John G. Atchison, Jr. · Gess Mattingly & Atchison · 201 West Short Street · Lexington, KY 40507-1269 · 606-255-2344

John T. Bondurant · (Estate Planning, Estate Administration) · Brown, Todd & Heyburn · 1600 Citizens Plaza · Louisville, KY 40202-2873 · 502-589-5400

James L. Coorssen · (Estate Planning, Estate Administration, Charitable Trusts) Ogden, Sturgill & Welch · 1200 One Riverfront Plaza · Louisville, KY 40202-2973 502-582-1601

John R. Cummins · Greenebaum Doll & McDonald · 3300 First National Tower Louisville, KY 40202-3197 · 502-589-4200

F. Gerald Greenwell · Brown, Todd & Heyburn · 1600 Citizens Plaza · Louisville, KY 40202-2873 · 502-589-5400

Martin S. Weinberg · Greenebaum Doll & McDonald · 3300 First National Tower · Louisville, KY 40202-3197 · 502-589-4200

LOUISIANA

BANKRUPTCY LAW

David S. Rubin* · Kantrow, Spaht, Weaver & Blitzer · City Plaza, Suite 300 · 445 North Boulevard · P.O. Box 2997 · Baton Rouge, LA 70821-2997 · 504-383-4703

William E. Steffes · Steffes & Macmurdo · 2237 South Acadian Thruway, Suite 600 · Baton Rouge, LA 70808 · 504-927-6590

Douglas S. Draper* · (Business Reorganization, Creditors' Rights, Debtors' Rights, Bankruptcy Litigation) · Friend, Wilson & Draper · LL&E Tower, Suite 2600 · 909 Poydras Street · New Orleans, LA 70112-4002 · 504-581-9595

Edward M. Heller · Bronfin, Heller, Steinberg & Berins · 2500 Poydras Center · 650 Poydras Street · New Orleans, LA 70130-6010 · 504-568-1888

R. Patrick Vance* · (Business Reorganization, Creditors' Rights, Debtors' Rights, Bankruptcy Litigation) · Jones, Walker, Waechter, Poitevent, Carrere & Denegre Place St. Charles, Suite 5100 · 201 St. Charles Avenue · New Orleans, LA 70170-5100 · 504-582-8000

James Robert Jeter · Cook, Yancey, King & Galloway · Commercial National Tower, Suite 1700 · 333 Texas Street · P.O. Box 22260 · Shreveport, LA 71120-2260 · 318-221-6277

BUSINESS LITIGATION

John B. Scofield* · (Commercial) · Scofield, Gerard, Veron, Hoskins & Soileau 1114 Ryan Street · P.O. Drawer 3028 · Lake Charles, LA 70602 · 318-433-9436

Robert E. Barkley, Jr. · Barkley & White · 2401 Pan American Life Centre · 601 Poydras Street · New Orleans, LA 70130-6036 · 504-595-3350

Curtis R. Boisfontaine · Sessions & Fishman · Place St. Charles, 35th Floor · 201 St. Charles Avenue · New Orleans, LA 70170 · 504-582-1500

Gene W. Lafitte · Liskow & Lewis · One Shell Square, 50th Floor · New Orleans, LA 70139 · 504-581-7979

Charles W. Lane III* · (Antitrust, Commercial, Securities) · Jones, Walker, Waechter, Poitevent, Carrere & Denegre · Place St. Charles, Suite 5100 · 201 St. Charles Avenue · New Orleans, LA 70170-5100 · 504-582-8000

John M. McCollam* · (Commercial, Energy, RICO) · Gordon, Arata, McCollam & Duplantis · Place St. Charles, Suite 4000 · 201 St. Charles Avenue · New Orleans, LA 70170-4000 · 504-582-1111

Benjamin R. Slater, Jr. · Monroe & Lemann · Place St. Charles, Suite 3300 · 201 St. Charles Avenue · New Orleans, LA 70170-3300 · 504-586-1900

Walter C. Thompson, Jr. · Sessions & Fishman · Place St. Charles, 35th Floor · 201 St. Charles Avenue · New Orleans, LA 70170-3500 · 504-582-1500

Phillip A. Wittmann · Stone, Pigman, Walther, Wittmann & Hutchinson · 546 Carondelet Street · New Orleans, LA 70130-3588 · 504-581-3200

Billy R. Pesnell · Hargrove, Guyton, Ramey and Barlow · Louisiana Tower, 10th Floor · 401 Edwards Street · P.O. Box B · Shreveport, LA 71161-0010 · 318-227-1113

Robert G. Pugh, Sr. · Pugh, Pugh & Pugh · Commercial National Tower, Suite 2100 · 333 Texas Street, Suite 2100 · Shreveport, LA 71101-5302 · 318-227-2270

CORPORATE LAW

Michael H. Rubin* · (Commercial Transactions) · Rubin, Curry, Colvin & Joseph One American Place, Ninth Floor · Baton Rouge, LA 70825 · 504-383-9000

Anthony J. Correro III · Jones, Walker, Waechter, Poitevent, Carrere & Denegre Place St. Charles, Suite 5100 · 201 St. Charles Avenue · New Orleans, LA 70170-5100 · 504-582-8000

George Denegre · Jones, Walker, Waechter, Poitevent, Carrere & Denegre · Place St. Charles, Suite 5100 · 201 St. Charles Avenue · New Orleans, LA 70170-5100 · 504-582-8000

Louis Y. Fishman · Sessions & Fishman · Place St. Charles, 35th Floor · 201 St. Charles Avenue · New Orleans, LA 70170 · 504-582-1500

Paul M. Haygood · (Corporate Finance, Financial Institutions, Mergers & Acquisitions, Securities) · Stone, Pigman, Walther, Wittmann & Hutchinson · 546 Carondelet Street · New Orleans, LA 70130-3588 · 504-581-3200

Campbell C. Hutchinson* · (Mergers & Acquisitions, Securities Regulation) · Stone, Pigman, Walther, Wittmann & Hutchinson · 546 Carondelet Street · New Orleans, LA 70130-3588 · 504-581-3200

Guy C. Lyman, Jr. · Milling, Benson, Woodward, Hillyer, Pierson & Miller · LL&E Tower, Suite 2300 · 909 Poydras Street · New Orleans, LA 70112-1017 · 504-569-7000

L. Richards McMillan II · (Corporate Finance, Mergers & Acquisitions, Securities Regulation) · Jones, Walker, Waechter, Poitevent, Carrere & Denegre · Place St. Charles, Suite 5100 · 201 St. Charles Avenue · New Orleans, LA 70170-5100 504-582-8000

Charles A. Snyder · Milling, Benson, Woodward, Hillyer, Pierson & Miller · LL&E Tower, Suite 2300 · 909 Poydras Street · New Orleans, LA 70112-1017 · 504-569-7000

Robert M. Walmsley, Jr. · Stone, Pigman, Walther, Wittmann & Hutchinson · 546 Carondelet Street · New Orleans, LA 70130-3588 · 504-581-3200

John D. Wogan · Monroe & Lemann · Place St. Charles, Suite 3300 · 201 St. Charles Avenue · New Orleans, LA 70170-3300 · 504-586-1900

Richard P. Wolfe · Monroe & Lemann · Place St. Charles, Suite 3300 · 201 St. Charles Avenue · New Orleans, LA 70170-3300 · 504-586-1900

CRIMINAL DEFENSE

Camille F. Gravel* · (Federal Court, State Court) · Gravel, Brady & Berrigan · 711 Washington Street · P.O. Box 1792 · Alexandria, LA 71309-1792 · 318-487-4501

J. Michael Small* · (Violent Crimes, Federal Court, State Court, Death Penalty) One Centre Court, Suite 201 · P.O. Box 1470 · Alexandria, LA 71309 · 318-487-8963

James E. Boren · 343 Riverside Mall, Suite 400 · Baton Rouge, LA 70801 · 504-387-5786

Lewis O. Unglesby* · (Plaintiffs) · Unglesby & Barrios · 246 Napoleon Street · Baton Rouge, LA 70802 · 504-387-0120

Risley C. Triche · Law Office of Risley C. Triche · 4759 Highway One · P.O. Drawer 339 · Napoleonville, LA 70390 · 504-369-6168

F. Irvin Dymond · Dymond, Crull & Castaing · First National Bank of Commerce Building, Suite 707 · New Orleans, LA 70112 · 504-581-7700

Robert Glass · Glass & Reed · 338 Lafayette Street · New Orleans, LA 70130 · 504-581-9065

John R. Martzell* · (Federal Court) · Martzell, Thomas & Bickford · 338 Lafayette Street · New Orleans, LA 70130 · 504-581-9065

Julian R. Murray, Jr. · Murray, Braden, Gonzalez & Richardson · 612 Gravier Street · New Orleans, LA 70130 · 504-581-2000

John Wilson Reed · Glass & Reed · 338 Lafayette Street · New Orleans, LA 70130 · 504-581-9065

L. Edwin Greer · Peatross, Greer & Frazier · Hutchinson Building, Suite 404 · P.O. Box 404 · Shreveport, LA 71162 · 318-222-0202

Wellborn Jack, Jr. · 101 Milam Street · Shreveport, LA 71101 · 318-227-9637

FAMILY LAW

Robert L. Cole* · Cole & Guidry · 405 West Main Street · Lafayette, LA 70501 318-232-6183

Robert C. Lowe* · Lowe, Stein, Hoffman & Allweiss · Poydras Center, Suite 2450 · 650 Poydras Street · New Orleans, LA 70130 · 504-581-2450

Philip R. Riegel, Jr. · Parlongue & Riegel · First National Bank of Commerce Building · 210 Baronne Street, Suite 620 · New Orleans, LA 70112 · 504-522-0126

Hani E. Dehan · Love, Rigby, Dehan, McDaniel & Goode · Johnson Building, Sixth Floor · P.O. Box 1835 · Shreveport, LA 71166-1835 · 318-226-1880

Kenneth Rigby* · Love, Rigby, Dehan, McDaniel & Goode · Johnson Building, Sixth Floor · P.O. Box 1835 · Shreveport, LA 71166-1835 · 318-226-1880

H. F. Sockrider, Jr. · Sockrider, Bolin & Anglin · 327 Crockett Street · Shreveport, LA 71101 · 318-221-5503

FIRST AMENDMENT LAW

Stephen B. Lemann · Monroe & Lemann · Place St. Charles, Suite 3300 · 201 St. Charles Avenue · New Orleans, LA 70170-3300 · 504-586-1900

Jack M. Weiss · Stone, Pigman, Walther, Wittmann & Hutchinson · 546 Carondelet Street · New Orleans, LA 70130-3588 · 504-581-3200

HEALTH CARE LAW

Robert W. Clements · Stockwell, Sievert, Viccellio, Clements & Shaddock · One Lakeside Plaza · P.O. Box 2900 · Lake Charles, LA 70601 · 504-436-9491

Gail B. Agrawal · Monroe & Lemann · Place St. Charles, Suite 3300 · 201 St. Charles Avenue · New Orleans, LA 70170-3300 · 504-586-1900

William F. Banta · Coleman, Dutry & Thomson · 321 St. Charles Avenue, 10th Floor · New Orleans, LA 70130 · 504-586-1979

Donna G. Klein · McGlinchey, Stafford, Cellini & Lang · 643 Magazine Street · P.O. Box 60643 · New Orleans, LA 70160-0643 · 504-586-1200

Byron A. Richie · Richie & Richie · 1800 Creswell Avenue · P.O. Box 44065 · Shreveport, LA 71134-4065 · 318-222-8305

Charles W. Salley* · Lunn, Irion, Johnson, Salley & Carlisle · 500 Slattery Building · P.O. Box 1534 · Shreveport, LA 71165-1534 · 318-222-0665

IMMIGRATION LAW

Lawrence B. Fabacher II · Gill & Fabacher · 833 Baronne Street · New Orleans, LA 70113 · 504-522-2800

Mark G. Murov · Murov & Ward · One Poydras Plaza, Suite 1250 · 639 Loyola Avenue · New Orleans, LA 70113 · 504-523-6100

LABOR AND EMPLOYMENT LAW

William R. D'Armond* · (Management) · Kean, Miller, Hawthorne, D'Armond, McCowan & Jarman · One American Place, 22nd Floor · P.O. Box 3513 · Baton Rouge, LA 70821 · 504-387-0999

G. Michael Pharis · (Management) · Taylor, Porter, Brooks & Phillips · Premier Centre, Eighth Floor · 451 Florida Boulevard · P.O. Box 2471 · Baton Rouge, LA 70821-2471 · 504-387-3221

Jerry L. Gardner, Jr.* · (Labor) · Gardner, Robein and Urann · 2540 Severn Avenue, Suite 400 · Metairie, LA 70002 · 504-885-9994

Louis L. Robein, Jr. · (Labor, Individuals) · Gardner, Robein and Urann · 2540 Severn Avenue, Suite 400 · Metairie, LA 70002 · 504-885-9994

Steven Hymowitz · (Management) · McCalla, Thompson, Pyburn & Ridley · Poydras Center, Suite 2800 · 650 Poydras Street · P.O. Box 50639 · New Orleans, LA 70130 · 504-524-2499

Leslie L. Inman · (Management) · Kullman, Inman, Bee, Downing & Banta · 1600 Energy Centre · 1100 Poydras Street · P.O. Box 60118 · New Orleans, LA 70160 · 504-524-4162

Frederick S. Kullman · (Management) · Kullman, Inman, Bee, Downing & Banta · 1600 Energy Centre · 1100 Poydras Street · P.O. Box 60118 · New Orleans, LA 70160 · 504-524-4162

D. Andrew Lang · (Management) · McGlinchy, Stafford, Cellini & Lang · 643 Magazine Street · P.O. Box 60643 · New Orleans, LA 70160-3477 · 504-586-1200

Robert K. McCalla · (Management) · McCalla, Thompson, Pyburn & Ridley · Poydras Center, Suite 2800 · 650 Poydras Street · P.O. Box 50639 · New Orleans, LA 70130 · 504-524-2499

A. Richard Gear* · (Management) · Cook, Yancey, King & Galloway · Commercial National Tower, Suite 1700 · 333 Texas Street · P.O. Box 22260 · Shreveport, LA 71120-2260 · 318-221-6277

MARITIME LAW

Leonard Fuhrer · (Plaintiffs) · Fuhrer, Flournoy, Hunter & Morton · 900 Foisy Avenue · P.O. Box 1270 · Alexandria, LA 71309 · 318-487-9858

Paul H. Due* · (Plaintiffs, Personal Injury) · Due, Smith, Caballero & Price · 8201 Jefferson Highway · Baton Rouge, LA 70809 · 504-929-7481

John Allen Bernard · Onebane, Donohoe, Bernard, Torian, Diaz, McNamara & Abell · 102 Versailles Boulevard, Suite 600 · P.O. Drawer 3507 · Lafayette, LA 70502 · 318-237-2660

James R. Nieset · Plauche, Smith & Nieset · 1123 Pithon Street · P.O. Drawer 1705 · Lake Charles, LA 70602 · 318-436-0522

Allen L. Smith, Jr. · Plauche, Smith & Nieset · 1123 Pithon Street · P.O. Drawer 1705 · Lake Charles, LA 70602 · 318-436-0522

Donald R. Abaunza* · Liskow & Lewis · One Shell Square, 50th Floor · New Orleans, LA 70139 · 504-581-7979

Robert B. Acomb, Jr.* · (Charter Parties, Ship Financing, Personal Injury, Collision) Jones, Walker, Waechter, Poitevent, Carrere & Denegre · Place St. Charles, Suite 5100 · 201 St. Charles Avenue · New Orleans, LA 70170-5100 · 504-582-8000

John A. Bolles · Terriberry, Carroll & Yancey · 3100 Energy Centre · 1100 Poydras Street · New Orleans, LA 70163 · 504-523-6451

Wood Brown III* · (Personal Injury) · Montgomery, Barnett, Brown, Read, Hammond & Mintz · 3200 Energy Centre · 1100 Poydras Street · New Orleans, LA 70163-3200 · 504-585-3200

Eldon E. Fallon · Gainsburgh, Benjamin, Fallon, David & Ates · 2800 Energy Centre · 1100 Poydras · New Orleans, LA 70163-2800 · 504-522-2304

Warren M. Faris · Faris, Ellis, Cutrone & Gilmore · Whitney Building, Suite 1207 228 St. Charles Avenue · New Orleans, LA 70130 · 504-581-6373

George A. Frilot III · Lemle & Kelleher · Pan-American Life Center, 21st Floor 601 Poydras Street · New Orleans, LA 70130-6097 · 504-586-1241

Samuel C. Gainsburgh · (Plaintiffs) · Gainsburgh, Benjamin, Fallon, David & Ates · 2800 Energy Centre · 1100 Poydras Street · New Orleans, LA 70163-2800 504-522-2304

John B. Gooch, Jr. · Montgomery, Barnett, Brown, Read, Hammond & Mintz · 3200 Energy Centre · 1100 Poydras Street · New Orleans, LA 70163 · 504-585-3200

John Phelps Hammond · Montgomery, Barnett, Brown, Read, Hammond & Mintz · 3200 Energy Centre · 1100 Poydras Street · New Orleans, LA 70163 · 504-585-3200

George W. Healy III · Phelps Dunbar · Texaco Center, 30th Floor · 400 Poydras Street · New Orleans, LA 70130-3245 · 504-566-1311

John W. Sims · Phelps Dunbar · Texaco Center, 30th Floor · 400 Poydras Street New Orleans, LA 70130-3245 · 504-566-1311

NATURAL RESOURCES AND ENVIRONMENTAL LAW

Lawrence E. Donohoe, Jr. · Onebane, Donohoe, Bernard, Torian, Diaz, McNamara & Abell · 102 Versailles Boulevard, Suite 600 · P.O. Drawer 3507 · Lafayette, LA 70502 · 318-237-2660

Daniel Ryan Sartor, Jr. · Snellings, Breard, Sartor, Inabnett & Trascher · 1503 North 19th Street · P.O. Box 2055 · Monroe, LA 71207-2055 · 318-387-8000

Gene W. Lafitte · Liskow & Lewis · One Shell Square, 50th Floor · New Orleans, LA 70139 · 504-581-7979

John M. McCollam* · (Oil & Gas) · Gordon, Arata, McCollam & Duplantis · Place St. Charles, Suite 4000 · 201 St. Charles Avenue · New Orleans, LA 70170-0000 · 504-582-1111

Ray A. Barlow* · (Oil & Gas) · Hargrove, Guyton, Ramey & Barlow · Louisiana Tower, 10th Floor · 401 Edwards Street · P.O. Box B · Shreveport, LA 71161-0010 318-227-1113

Robert Roberts III · Blanchard, Walker, O'Quinn & Roberts · Premier Bank Tower · P.O. Drawer 1126 · Shreveport, LA 71163-1126 · 318-221-6858

PERSONAL INJURY LITIGATION

Leonard Fuhrer · (Plaintiffs) · Fuhrer, Flournoy, Hunter & Morton · 900 Foisy Avenue · P.O. Box 1270 · Alexandria, LA 71309 · 318-487-9858

Howard B. Gist, Jr. · (Defendants) · Gist, Methvin, Hughes & Munsterman · 803 Johnston Street · P.O. Box 1871 · Alexandria, LA 71309-1871 · 318-448-1632

LeDoux R. Provosty, Jr.* · (Defendants, Medical Malpractice, Products Liability) · Provosty, Sadler & deLaunay · Hibernia Bank Building, Eighth Floor · P.O. Drawer 1791 · Alexandria, LA 71309-1791 · 318-445-3631

Paul H. Due* · (Plaintiffs, Products Liability, Airplane Collision) · Due, Smith, Caballero & Price · 8201 Jefferson Highway · Baton Rouge, LA 70809 · 504-929-7481

James E. Diaz, Sr. · (Defendants) · Onebane, Donohoe, Bernard, Torian, Diaz, McNamara & Abell · 102 Versailles Boulevard, Suite 600 · P.O. Drawer 3507 · Lafayette, LA 70502 · 318-237-2660

Patrick A. Juneau, Jr.* · (Defendants, Products Liability) · Juneau, Judice, Hill & Adley · 926 Coolidge Boulevard · Lafayette, LA 70503-2434 · 318-235-2405

John G. Torian · (Defendants) · Onebane, Donohoe, Bernard, Torian, Diaz, McNamara & Abell · 102 Versailles Boulevard, Suite 600 · P.O. Drawer 3507 · Lafayette, LA 70502 · 318-237-2660

Bob F. Wright · (Plaintiffs) · Domengeaux & Wright · 556 Jefferson Street, Suite 500 · P.O. Box 3668 · Lafayette, LA 70501-3668 · 318-233-3033

William B. Baggett, Sr. · (Plaintiffs) · Baggett, McCall & Burgess · 3006 Country Club Road · Lake Charles, LA 70605 · 318-478-8888

Thomas M. Bergstedt · (Defendants) · Bergstedt & Mount · 1101 Lake Shore Drive, Suite 200 · Lake Charles, LA 70602 · 318-433-3004

A. Lane Plauche · (Defendants) · Plauche, Smith & Nieset · 1123 Pithon Street P.O. Drawer 1705 · Lake Charles, LA 70602-1705 · 318-436-0522

John B. Scofield* · (Defendants) · Scofield, Gerard, Veron, Hoskins & Soileau · 1114 Ryan Street · P.O. Drawer 3028 · Lake Charles, LA 70602 · 318-433-9436

Allen L. Smith, Jr. · Plauche, Smith & Nieset · 1123 Pithon Street · P.O. Drawer 1705 · Lake Charles, LA 70602 · 318-436-0522

Lawrence K. Burleigh* · (Plaintiffs) · Guarisco Shopping Center · 907 Seventh Street · P.O. Box 2625 · Morgan City, LA 70381 · 504-384-1910

Gerard F. Thomas, Jr. · Thomas & Dunahoe · 137 Trudeau Street · P.O. Box 548 Natchitoches, LA 71457 · 318-352-6455

Robert B. Acomb, Jr.* · (Defendants) · Jones, Walker, Waechter, Poitevent, Carrere & Denegre · Place St. Charles, Suite 5100 · 201 St. Charles Avenue · New Orleans, LA 70170-5100 · 504-582-8000

Henry B. Alsobrook, Jr.* · (Defendants, Medical Malpractice, Products Liability, Appellate) · Adams and Reese · 4500 One Shell Square · New Orleans, LA 70139 · 504-581-3234

Wood Brown III* · (Defendants) · Montgomery, Barnett, Brown, Read, Hammond & Mintz · 3200 Energy Centre · 1100 Poydras Street · New Orleans, LA 70163 · 504-585-3200

Alvin R. Christovich, Jr. · (Defendants) · Christovich and Kearney · Pan American Life Center, Suite 2300 · 601 Poydras Street · New Orleans, LA 70130 · 504-561-5700

William K. Christovich* · (Defendants, Products Liability, Professional Malpractice) · Christovich and Kearney · Pan American Life Center, Suite 2300 · 601 Poydras Street · New Orleans, LA 70130-6078 · 504-561-5700

Robert M. Contois, Jr.* · (Defendants) · Jones, Walker, Waechter, Poitevent, Carrere & Denegre · Place St. Charles, Suite 5100 · 201 St. Charles Avenue · New Orleans, LA 70170-5100 · 504-582-8000

Eldon E. Fallon · Gainsburgh, Benjamin, Fallon, David & Ates · 2800 Energy Centre · 1100 Poydras · New Orleans, LA 70163-2800 · 504-522-2304

Samuel C. Gainsburgh · (Plaintiffs) · Gainsburgh, Benjamin, Fallon, David & Ates · 2800 Energy Centre · 1100 Poydras Street · New Orleans, LA 70163-2800 504-522-2304

Russ M. Herman · (Plaintiffs) · Herman, Herman, Katz & Cotlar · 820 O'Keefe Avenue · New Orleans, LA 70113 · 504-581-4892

H. Martin Hunley, Jr. · (Defendants) · Lemle & Kelleher · Pan-American Life Center, 21st Floor · 601 Poydras Street · New Orleans, LA 70130-6097 · 504-586-1241

Frank E. Lamothe III* · (Plaintiffs) · Lamothe, Hamilton & Odom · Pan American Life Center, Suite 2750 · 601 Poydras Street · New Orleans, LA 70130 · 504-566-1805

Robert E. Leake, Jr.* · (Defendants, Professional Malpractice) · Leake & Andersson · 1700 Energy Centre · 1100 Poydras Street · New Orleans, LA 70163 504-585-7500

Harvey J. Lewis · (Plaintiffs) · Lewis & Kullman · 2615 Pan American Life Center 601 Poydras Street · New Orleans, LA 70130 · 504-588-1500

John R. Martzell* · (Products Liability, Maritime) · Martzell, Thomas & Bickford 338 Lafayette Street · New Orleans, LA 70130 · 504-581-9065

Dermot S. McGlinchey* · (Defendants, Directors-Officer Liability) · McGlinchey, Stafford, Cellini & Lang · 643 Magazine Street · P.O. Box 60643 · New Orleans, LA 70160-0643 · 504-586-1200

Stephen B. Murray · (Plaintiffs) · Murray Law Firm · 650 Poydras Street, Suite 1450 · New Orleans, LA 70130 · 504-525-8100

John J. Weigel* · (Defendants, Products Liability, Professional Malpractice) · Jones, Walker, Waechter, Poitevent, Carrere & Denegre · Place St. Charles, Suite 5100 · 201 St. Charles Avenue · New Orleans, LA 70170-5100 · 504-582-8000

Lawrence D. Wiedemann · (Plaintiffs) · Wiedemann & Wiedemann · 821 Baronne Street · P.O. Box 30648 · New Orleans, LA 70190-0648 · 504-581-6180

Thomas J. Wyllie · (Defendants) · Adams and Reese · 4500 One Shell Square · New Orleans, LA 70139 · 504-581-3234

Leslie J. Schiff · Sandoz, Sandoz & Schiff · 137 West Landry Street · P.O. Drawer 900 · Opelousas, LA 70570 · 318-942-9771

A. Kennon Goff III · Goff and Goff · 612 North Vienna Street · P.O. Box 2050 · Ruston, LA 71273-2050 · 318-255-1760

Troy E. Bain* · (Plaintiffs, Medical Malpractice, Products Liability, Automobile Collision, Appellate) · 1540 Irving Place · Shreveport, LA 71101 · 318-221-0076

Herschel E. Richard, Jr.* · (Defendants, Medical Malpractice, Products Liability, Professional Malpractice) · Cook, Yancey, King & Galloway · Commercial National Tower, Suite 1700 · 333 Texas Street · P.O. Box 22260 · Shreveport, LA 71120-2260 · 318-221-6277

Charles W. Salley* · (Defendants) · Lunn, Irion, Johnson, Salley & Carlisle · 500 Slattery Building · P.O. Box 1534 · Shreveport, LA 71165-1534 · 318-222-0665

PUBLIC UTILITY LAW

Tom F. Pillips · Taylor, Porter, Brooks & Phillips · Premier Centre, Eighth Floor 451 Florida Boulevard · P.O. Box 2471 · Baton Rouge, LA 70821-2471 · 504-387-3221

J. Wayne Anderson · Monroe & Lemann · Place St. Charles, Suite 3300 · 201 St. Charles Avenue · New Orleans, LA 70170-3300 · 504-586-1900

Michael R. Fontham · Stone, Pigman, Walther, Wittmann & Hutchinson · 546 Carondelet Street · New Orleans, LA 70130-3588 · 504-581-3200

REAL ESTATE LAW

Donald E. Bradford · Gary Field Landry & Bradford · Four United Plaza, Suite 500 · 8555 United Plaza Boulevard · Baton Rouge, LA 70809-7000 · 504-922-5000

H. Edwin McGlasson, Jr. · (Commercial Transactions) · Voorhies & Labbe · Acadiana National Bank Building, Fourth Floor · 700 St. John Street · P.O. Box 3527 · Lafayette, LA 70502-3527 · 318-232-9700

Philip deV. Claverie · Phelps Dunbar · Texaco Center, 30th Floor · 400 Poydras Street · New Orleans, LA 70130-3245 · 504-566-1311

Julian H. Good · (Commercial Transactions, Industrial Transactions, Financing) Lemle & Kelleher · Pan-American Life Center, 21st Floor · 601 Poydras Street · New Orleans, LA 70130-6097 · 504-584-9436

Mitchell W. Herzog · Herzog & Mouton · 1515 Poydras Street, Suite 1840 · New Orleans, LA 70112 · 504-585-2615

Henry F. O'Connor, Jr. · Steeg and O'Connor · Place St. Charles · 201 St. Charles Avenue, Suite 3201 · New Orleans, LA 70170 · 504-582-1199

Louis G. Shushan · Shushan, Meyer, Jackson & McPherson · 1010 Common Street, Suite 1500 · New Orleans, LA 70112 · 504-581-9444

Moise S. Steeg, Jr.* · Steeg and O'Connor · Place St. Charles · 201 St. Charles Avenue, Suite 3201 · New Orleans, LA 70170 · 504-582-1199

Hugh T. Ward · Peters, Ward, Bright & Hennessy · The Premier Bank Tower, Suite 1000 · 400 Texas Street · P.O. Box 91 · Shreveport, LA 71161 · 318-221-0684

TAX AND EMPLOYEE BENEFITS LAW

John C. Blackman IV · (Tax, Employee Benefits) · Jones, Walker, Waechter, Poitevent, Carrere & Denegre · Place St. Charles, Suite 1700 · One American Place · Baton Rouge, LA 70825 · 504-346-5505

Robert R. Casey · Jones, Walker, Waechter, Poitevent, Carrere & Denegre · Place St. Charles, Suite 5100 · 201 St. Charles Avenue, Suite 5100 · P.O. Box 1267 Baton Rouge, LA 70170-5100 · 504-343-4465

Carey J. Messina · Kean, Miller, Hawthorne, D'Armond, McCowan & Jarman · One American Place, 22nd Floor · P.O. Box 3513 · Baton Rouge, LA 70821 · 504-387-0999

Robert C. Schmidt · (Employee Benefits) · Law Office of Robert C. Schmidt · 10935 Perkins Road · P.O. Box 80317 · Baton Rouge, LA 70898 · 504-767-7093

Robert Lee Curry III · Theus, Grisham, Davis & Leigh · 1600 Lamy Lane · P.O. Drawer 4768 · Monroe, LA 71211-4768 · 318-388-0100

Paul K. Kirkpatrick, Jr. · Hudson, Potts & Bernstein · Premier Bank Tower, 10th Floor · P.O. Drawer 3008 · Monroe, LA 71210 · 318-388-4400

Jane E. Armstrong · (Employee Benefits) · Phelps Dunbar · Texaco Center, 30th Floor · 400 Poydras Street · New Orleans, LA 70130-3245 · 504-566-1311

Hilton S. Bell · (Corporate & Partnership Transactions, State Tax, Employee Benefits) · Milling, Benson, Woodward, Hillyer, Pierson & Miller · LL&E Tower, Suite 2300 · 909 Poydras Street · New Orleans, LA 70112-1017 · 504-569-7000

Edward B. Benjamin, Jr. · Jones, Walker, Waechter, Poitevent, Carrere & Denegre · Place St. Charles, 51st Floor · 201 St. Charles Avenue · New Orleans, LA 70170-5100 · 504-582-8000

William C. Gambel · Milling, Benson, Woodward, Hillyer, Pierson & Miller · LL&E Tower, Suite 2300 · 909 Poydras Street · New Orleans, LA 70112-1017 · 504-569-7000

Michael E. Guarisco* · (Corporate & Partnership Transactions, Employee Benefits, Tax Disputes, Estate Planning) · Guarisco, Weiler & Cordes · 2660 Poydras Center · 650 Poydras Street · New Orleans, LA 70130-6196 · 504-524-2944

Thomas C. Keller · Jones, Walker, Waechter, Poitevent, Carrere & Denegre · Place St. Charles · 201 St. Charles Avenue, Suite 5100 · New Orleans, LA 70170-5100 · 504-582-8000

Thomas B. Lemann · (Tax Disputes) · Monroe & Lemann · Place St. Charles, Suite 3300 · 201 St. Charles Avenue · New Orleans, LA 70170-3300 · 504-586-1900

Edward F. Martin · (Employee Benefits) · Jones, Walker, Waechter, Poitevent, Carrere & Denegre · Place St. Charles · 201 St. Charles Avenue, Suite 5100 · New Orleans, LA 70170-5100 · 504-582-8000

Max Nathan, Jr. · Sessions & Fishman · Place St. Charles, 35th Floor · 201 St. Charles Avenue · New Orleans, LA 70170 · 504-582-1500

Rudolph R. Ramelli · (Employee Benefits) · Jones, Walker, Waechter, Poitevent, Carrere & Denegre · Place St. Charles · 201 St. Charles Avenue, Suite 5100 · New Orleans, LA 70170-5100 · 504-582-8000

Jerome J. Reso, Jr. · Baldwin & Haspel · 1100 Poydras Street, 22nd Floor · New Orleans, LA 70163-2200 · 504-585-7711

H. Paul Simon* · (Corporate & Partnership Transactions,Tax Disputes) · Simon, Peragine, Smith & Redfearn · Energy Centre, 30th Floor · 1100 Poydras Street · New Orleans, LA 70163-3000 · 504-569-2030

Quintin T. Hardtner III · Hargrove, Guyton, Ramey and Barlow · Louisiana Tower, 10th Floor · 401 Edwards Street · P.O. Box B · Shreveport, LA 71161-0010 318-227-1113

J. Edgerton Pierson, Jr. · (State Tax) · Blanchard, Walker, O'Quinn & Roberts Premier Bank Tower · P.O. Drawer 1126 · Shreveport, LA 71163-1126 · 318-221-6858

Cecil E. Ramey, Jr. · Hargrove, Guyton, Ramey and Barlow · Louisiana Tower, 10th Floor · 401 Edwards Street · P.O. Box B · Shreveport, LA 71161-0010 · 318-227-1113

Donald P. Weiss · Wiener, Weiss, Madison & Howell · CNB Tower, 23rd Floor 333 Texas Street · P.O. Box 21990 · Shreveport, LA 71120-1990 · 318-226-9100

TRUSTS AND ESTATES

John C. Blackman IV · Jones, Walker, Waechter, Poitevent, Carrere & Denegre One American Place, Suite 1700 · Baton Rouge, LA 70825 · 504-346-5505

Sidney M. Blitzer, Jr. · Kantrow, Spaht, Weaver & Blitzer · City Plaza, Suite 300 445 North Boulevard · P.O. Box 2997 · Baton Rouge, LA 70821-2997 · 504-383-4703

Gerald Le Van · Kean, Miller, Hawthorne, D'Armond, McCowan & Jarman · One American Place, 22nd Floor · P.O. Box 3513 · Baton Rouge, LA 70821 · 504-387-0999

Ben R. Miller, Jr. · Kean, Miller, Hawthorne, D'Armond, McCowan & Jarman · One American Place, 22nd Floor · P.O. Box 3513 · Baton Rouge, LA 70821 · 504-387-0999

H. Edwin McGlasson, Jr. · Voorhies & Labbe · Acadiana National Bank Building, Fourth Floor · 700 St. John Street · P.O. Box 3527 · Lafayette, LA 70502-3527 · 318-232-9700

William E. Shaddock · Stockwell, Sievert, Viccellio, Clements & Shaddock · One Lakeside Plaza, Fourth Floor · P.O. Box 2900 · Lake Charles, LA 70602 · 318-436-9491

Robert Lee Curry III · Theus, Grisham, Davis & Leigh · 1600 Lamy Lane · P.O. Drawer 4768 · Monroe, LA 71211-4768 · 318-388-0100

Paul K. Kirkpatrick, Jr. · Hudson, Potts & Bernstein · Premier Bank Tower, 10th Floor · P.O. Drawer 3008 · Monroe, LA 71210 · 318-388-4400

Daniel Ryan Sartor, Jr. · Snellings, Breard, Sartor, Inabnett & Trascher · 1503 North 19th Street · P.O. Box 2055 · Monroe, LA 71207-2055 · 318-387-8000

Edward B. Benjamin, Jr. · Jones, Walker, Waechter, Poitevent, Carrere & Denegre · Place St. Charles, Suite 5100 · 201 St. Charles Avenue · New Orleans, LA 70170-5100 · 504-582-8000

David F. Edwards · Jones, Walker, Waechter, Poitevent, Carrere & Denegre · Place St. Charles, Suite 5100 · 201 St. Charles Avenue · New Orleans, LA 70170-5100 · 504-582-8184

Thomas B. Lemann · (Estate Planning) · Monroe & Lemann · Place St. Charles, Suite 3300 · 201 St. Charles Avenue · New Orleans, LA 70170-3300 · 504-586-1900

Edward F. Martin · Jones, Walker, Waechter, Poitevent, Carrere & Denegre · Place St. Charles, Suite 5100 · 201 St. Charles Avenue · New Orleans, LA 70170-5100 · 504-582-8000

Joel A. Mendler · (Estate Planning, Charitable Trusts) · Baldwin & Haspel · 2200 Energy Centre · 1100 Poydras Street, 22nd Floor · New Orleans, LA 70163-2200 504-585-7711

Max Nathan, Jr. · Sessions & Fishman · Place St. Charles, 35th Floor · 201 St. Charles Avenue · New Orleans, LA 70170 · 504-582-1500

Paul O. H. Pigman · Stone, Pigman, Walther, Wittmann & Hutchinson · 546 Carondelet Street · New Orleans, LA 70130-3588 · 504-581-3200

Jerome J. Reso, Jr. · Baldwin & Haspel · 1100 Poydras Street, 22nd Floor · New Orleans, LA 70163-2200 · 504-585-7711

H. Paul Simon* · (Estate Planning, Estate Administration) · Simon, Peragine, Smith & Redfearn · Energy Centre, 30th Floor · 1100 Poydras Street · New Orleans, LA 70163-3000 · 504-569-2030

Quintin T. Hardtner III · Hargrove, Guyton, Ramey & Barlow · Louisiana Tower, 10th Floor · 401 Edwards Street · P.O. Box B · Shreveport, LA 71161-0010 318-227-1113

T. Haller Jackson, Jr. · Tucker, Jeter, Jackson and Hickman · 405 Edwards Street, Suite 905 · Shreveport, LA 71101-3146 · 318-425-7764

Stuart D. Lunn · Smitherman, Lunn, Chastain & Hill · Commercial National Bank Building, Eighth Floor · 333 Texas Street · Shreveport, LA 71101-3673 · 318-227-1990

J. Edgerton Pierson, Jr. · (Estate Administration) · Blanchard, Walker, O'Quin & Roberts · Premier Bank Tower · P.O. Drawer 1126 · Shreveport, LA 71163-1126 · 318-221-6858

Cecil E. Ramey, Jr. · Hargrove, Guyton, Ramey & Barlow · Louisiana Tower, 10th Floor · 401 Edwards Street · P.O. Box B · Shreveport, LA 71161-0010 · 318-227-1113

Donald P. Weiss · Wiener, Weiss, Madison & Howell · CNB Tower, 23rd Floor 333 Texas Street · P.O. Box 21990 · Shreveport, LA 71120-1990 · 318-226-9100

MAINE

BANKRUPTCY LAW

Louis H. Kornreich · Gross, Minsky, Mogul & Singal · 23 Water Street · P.O. Box 917 · Bangor, ME 04401 · 207-942-4644

Daniel Amory · (Business Reorganization, Creditors' Rights, Debtors' Rights, Bankruptcy Litigation) · Drummond Woodsum Plimpton & MacMahon · 245 Commercial Street · Portland, ME 04101-1117 · 207-772-1941

Andrew A. Cadot · (Business Reorganization, Creditors' Rights, Bankruptcy Litigation) · Perkins, Thompson, Hinckley & Keddy · One Canal Plaza · P.O. Box 426 · Portland, ME 04112-0426 · 207-774-2635

Gerald S. Cope · Cope and Cope · One Union Street · Portland, ME 04101 · 207-772-7491

Robert J. Keach · Verrill & Dana · One Portland Square · P.O. Box 586 · Portland, ME 04112-0586 · 207-774-4000

George J. Marcus · Pierce, Atwood, Scribner, Allen, Smith & Lancaster · One Monument Square · Portland, ME 04101 · 207-773-6411

Gregory A. Tselikis · Bernstein, Shur, Sawyer and Nelson · 100 Middle Street, Sixth Floor · P.O. Box 9729 · Portland, ME 04104-5029 · 207-774-1200

P. Benjamin Zuckerman · Verrill & Dana · One Portland Square · P.O. Box 586 Portland, ME 04112-0586 · 207-774-4000

BUSINESS LITIGATION

Charles H. Abbott* · Skelton, Taintor & Abbott · 95 Main Street · P.O. Box 3200 Auburn, ME 04212-3200 · 207-784-3200

Lewis V. Vafiades* · Vafiades, Brountas & Kominsky · Key Plaza · 23 Water Street · P.O. Box 919 · Bangor, ME 04402-0919 · 207-947-6915

Jack H. Simmons* · Berman, Simmons & Goldberg · 129 Lisbon Street · P.O. Box 961 · Lewiston, ME 04243-0961 · 207-784-3576

Ralph I. Lancaster, Jr. · Pierce, Atwood, Scribner, Allen, Smith & Lancaster · One Monument Square · Portland, ME 04101 · 207-773-6411

Gerald F. Petruccelli · Petruccelli, Cox & Martin · 50 Monument Square · P.O. Box 9733 · Portland, ME 04104-5033 · 207-775-0200

Jotham D. Pierce, Jr.* · Pierce, Atwood, Scribner, Allen, Smith & Lancaster · One Monument Square · Portland, ME 04101 · 207-773-6411

Peter J. Rubin* · (Commercial, Construction) · Bernstein, Shur, Sawyer and Nelson · 100 Middle Street, Sixth Floor · P.O. Box 9729 · Portland, ME 04104-5029 · 207-774-1200

CORPORATE LAW

Bruce A. Coggeshall · Pierce, Atwood, Scribner, Allen, Smith & Lancaster · One Monument Square · Portland, ME 04101 · 207-773-6411

Joseph L. Delafield III · (Corporate Finance, Mergers & Acquisitions, Securities) Drummond Woodsum Plimpton & MacMahon · 245 Commercial Street · Portland, ME 04101-1117 · 207-772-1941

Gordon F. Grimes · Bernstein, Shur, Sawyer and Nelson · 100 Middle Street, Sixth Floor · P.O. Box 9729 · Portland, ME 04104-5029 · 207-774-1200

Leonard M. Nelson · Bernstein, Shur, Sawyer and Nelson · 100 Middle Street, Sixth Floor · P.O. Box 9729 · Portland, ME 04104-5029 · 207-774-1200

Jeremiah D. Newbury · Pierce, Atwood, Scribner, Allen, Smith & Lancaster · One Monument Square · Portland, ME 04101 · 207-773-6411

Peter B. Webster · Verrill & Dana · One Portland Square · P.O. Box 586 · Portland, ME 04112-0586 · 207-774-4000

Owen W. Wells · Perkins, Thompson, Hinckley & Keddy · One Canal Plaza · P.O. Box 426 · Portland, ME 04112-0426 · 207-774-2635

James B. Zimpritch · Pierce, Atwood, Scribner, Allen, Smith & Lancaster · One Monument Square · Portland, ME 04101 · 207-773-6411

CRIMINAL DEFENSE

George Z. Singal · Gross, Minsky, Mogul & Singal · 23 Water Street · P.O. Box 917 · Bangor, ME 04401 · 207-942-4644

Jack H. Simmons* · (Federal Court, State Court) · Berman, Simmons & Goldberg 129 Lisbon Street · P.O. Box 961 · Lewiston, ME 04243-0961 · 207-784-3576

Peter J. DeTroy III · Norman, Hanson & DeTroy · 415 Congress Street, Fifth Floor · P.O. Box 4600 DTS · Portland, ME 04112 · 207-774-7000

Ralph I. Lancaster, Jr. · Pierce, Atwood, Scribner, Allen, Smith & Lancaster · One Monument Square · Portland, ME 04101 · 207-773-6411

Daniel G. Lilley · 39 Portland Pier Street · P.O. Box 4803 DTS · Portland, ME 04112 · 207-774-6206

Peter J. Rubin* · Bernstein, Shur, Sawyer and Nelson · 100 Middle Street, Sixth Floor · P.O. Box 9729 · Portland, ME 04104-5029 · 207-774-1200

FAMILY LAW

Roger J. Katz* · Lipman and Katz · 72 Winthrop Street · P.O. Box 1051 · Augusta, ME 04332-1051 · 207-622-3711

Susan R. Kominsky · Vafiades, Brountas & Kominsky · 23 Water Street · P.O. Box 919 · Bangor, ME 04402-0919 · 207-947-6915

Robert A. Laskoff* · Robert A. Laskoff Attorneys-at-Law · 103 Park Street · P.O. Box 7206 · Lewiston, ME 04243-7206 · 207-786-3173

Michael P. Asen · Mittel, Asen, Eggert & Hunter · 97 State Street · P.O. Box 427 Portland, ME 04112 · 207-775-3101

Sumner Thurman Bernstein · Bernstein, Shur, Sawyer and Nelson · 100 Middle Street, Sixth Floor · P.O. Box 9729 · Portland, ME 04104-5029 · 207-774-1200

Phyllis G. Givertz* · Givertz, Lunt & Hambley · 10 Moulton Street · P.O. Box 4801 · Portland, ME 04112-4801 · 207-772-8373

Barry Zimmerman · Kelly, Remmel & Zimmerman · 53 Exchange Street · P.O. Box 597 · Portland, ME 04112 · 207-775-1020

FIRST AMENDMENT LAW

Bernard J. Kubetz · Eaton, Peabody, Bradford & Veague · Fleet Center-Exchange Street · P.O. Box 1210 · Bangor, ME 04402-1210 · 207-947-0110

John M. R. Paterson · Bernstein, Shur, Sawyer and Nelson · 100 Middle Street, Sixth Floor · P.O. Box 9729 · Portland, ME 04104-5029 · 207-774-1200

Jonathan Piper · Preti, Flaherty, Beliveau & Pachios · 443 Congress Street · Portland, ME 04101 · 207-775-5831

HEALTH CARE LAW

Joseph M. Kozak · Pierce, Atwood, Scribner, Allen, Smith & Lancaster · 77 Winthrop Street · Augusta, ME 04330 · 207-622-6311

John P. Doyle, Jr. · Preti, Flaherty, Beliveau & Pachios · 443 Congress Street · Portland, ME 04101 · 207-775-5831

INTELLECTUAL PROPERTY LAW

Robert H. Stier, Jr. · Bernstein, Shur, Sawyer and Nelson · 100 Middle Street, Sixth Floor · P.O. Box 9729 · Portland, ME 04104-5029 · 207-774-1200

LABOR AND EMPLOYMENT LAW

Herbert H. Bennett · (Management) · Herbert H. Bennett and Associates · 121 Middle Street, Suite 300 · Portland, ME 04101-4104 · 207-773-4775

Peter H. Jacobs* · (Management) · Pierce, Atwood, Scribner, Allen, Smith & Lancaster · One Monument Square · Portland, ME 04101 · 207-773-6411

Hugh G. E. MacMahon · Drummond Woodsum Plimpton & MacMahon · 245 Commercial Street · Portland, ME 04101 · 207-772-1941

S. Mason Pratt, Jr.* · (Management) · Pierce, Atwood, Scribner, Allen, Smith & Lancaster · One Monument Square · Portland, ME 04101 · 207-773-6411

Howard T. Reben* · (Individuals, Labor) · Sunenblick, Reben, Benjamin & March · 97 India Street · Portland, ME 04101 · 207-772-5496

Patrick N. McTeague · (Labor) · McTeague, Higbee, Libner, MacAdam, Case & Watson · Four Union Park · P.O. Box 5000 · Topsham, ME 04086 · 207-725-5581

NATURAL RESOURCES AND ENVIRONMENTAL LAW

Clifford H. Goodall · Dyer, Goodall & Larouche · 45 Memorial Circle · Augusta, ME 04330 · 207-622-3693

Jeffrey A. Thaler* · (Plaintiffs) · Berman, Simmons & Goldberg · 129 Lisbon Street · P.O. Box 961 · Lewiston, ME 04243-0961 · 207-784-3576

Daniel E. Boxer · (Water, Air, Solid Waste, Hazardous Waste) · Pierce, Atwood, Scribner, Allen, Smith & Lancaster · One Monument Square · Portland, ME 04101 · 207-773-6411

E. Stephen Murray* · Murray, Plumb & Murray · 75 Pearl Street · Portland, ME 04101 · 207-773-5651

PERSONAL INJURY LITIGATION

George Z. Singal · Gross, Minsky, Mogul & Singal · 23 Water Street · P.O. Box 917 · Bangor, ME 04401 · 207-942-4644

Lewis V. Vafiades* · (Defendants) · Vafiades, Brountas & Kominsky · 23 Water Street · P.O. Box 919 · Bangor, ME 04402-0919 · 207-947-6915

Jack H. Simmons* · (Plaintiffs, Medical Malpractice, Products Liability, Automobile Collision) · Berman, Simmons & Goldberg · 129 Lisbon Street · P.O. Box 961 · Lewiston, ME 04243-0961 · 207-784-3576

Peter W. Culley · Pierce, Atwood, Scribner, Allen, Smith & Lancaster · One Monument Square · Portland, ME 04101 · 207-773-6411

Peter J. DeTroy II · Norman, Hanson & DeTroy · 415 Congress Street, Fifth Floor · P.O. Box 4600 DTS · Portland, ME 04112 · 207-774-7000

Ralph I. Lancaster, Jr. · Pierce, Atwood, Scribner, Allen, Smith & Lancaster · One Monument Square · Portland, ME 04101 · 207-773-6411

Peter J. Rubin* · (Products Liability) · Bernstein, Shur, Sawyer and Nelson · 100 Middle Street, Sixth Floor · P.O. Box 9729 · Portland, ME 04104-5029 · 207-774-1200

PUBLIC UTILITY LAW

Anthony W. Buxton · Preti, Flaherty, Beliveau & Pachios · 45 Memorial Circle Augusta, ME 04332-1058 · 207-623-5167

Mark L. Haley · Conley, Haley, O'Neil & Kaplan · 30 Front Street · P.O. Box 651 Bath, ME 04530 · 207-443-5576

Gerald M. Amero · Pierce, Atwood, Scribner, Allen, Smith & Lancaster · One Monument Square · Portland, ME 04101 · 207-773-6411

John W. Gulliver · Pierce, Atwood, Scribner, Allen, Smith & Lancaster · One Monument Square · Portland, ME 04101 · 207-773-6411

REAL ESTATE LAW

Donald A. Fowler, Jr. · Pierce, Atwood, Scribner, Allen, Smith & Lancaster · One Monument Square · Portland, ME 04101 · 207-773-6411

David Plimpton · Drummond Woodsum Plimpton & MacMahon · 245 Commercial Street · Portland, ME 04101-1117 · 207-772-1941

Walter E. Webber · Jensen Baird Gardner & Henry · 10 Free Street · P.O. Box 4510 · Portland, ME 04112 · 207-775-7271

Louis A. Wood · Verrill & Dana · One Portland Square · P.O. Box 586 · Portland, ME 04112-0586 · 207-774-4000

TAX AND EMPLOYEE BENEFITS LAW

Craig W. Friedrich · (Corporate & Partnership Transactions, State Tax, Tax Disputes, International) · Bernstein, Shur, Sawyer and Nelson · 100 Middle Street, Sixth Floor · P.O. Box 9729 · Portland, ME 04104-5029 · 207-774-1200

William C. Smith · Pierce, Atwood, Scribner, Allen, Smith & Lancaster · One Monument Square · Portland, ME 04101 · 207-773-6411

Thomas J. Van Meer · Van Meer & Belanger · 100 Commercial Street, Suite 210 Portland, ME 04101 · 207-871-7500

TRUSTS AND ESTATES

Richard P. LeBlanc · Bernstein, Shur, Sawyer and Nelson · 100 Middle Street, Sixth Floor · P.O. Box 9729 · Portland, ME 04104-5029 · 207-774-1200

William C. Smith · Pierce, Atwood, Scribner, Allen, Smith & Lancaster · One Monument Square · Portland, ME 04101 · 207-773-6411

Thomas J. Van Meer · Van Meer & Belanger · 100 Commercial Street, Suite 210 Portland, ME 04101 · 207-871-7500

Robert B. Williamson, Jr. · Verrill & Dana · One Portland Square · P.O. Box 586 Portland, ME 04112-0586 · 207-774-4000

MARYLAND

BANKRUPTCY LAW

Lawrence David Coppel · Gordon, Feinblatt, Rothman, Hoffberger & Hollander Garrett Building · 233 East Redwood Street · Baltimore, MD 21202 · 301-576-4000

Richard M. Kremen · Piper & Marbury · 1100 Charles Center · 35 South Charles Street · Baltimore, MD 21201-3010 · 301-539-2530

Harvey M. Lebowitz · Frank, Bernstein, Conaway & Goldman · 300 East Lombard Street · Baltimore, MD 21202 · 301-625-3500

George W. Liebmann* · (Business Reorganization, Creditors' Rights) · Law Offices of George W. Liebmann · Eight West Hamilton Street · Baltimore, MD 21201-5008 · 301-752-5887

Roger Frankel · Arent, Fox, Kintner, Plotkin & Kahn · 7475 Wisconsin Avenue, Suite 900 · Bethesda, MD 20814 · 301-657-4800

Alan S. Kerxton · 4550 Montgomery Avenue, Suite 775N · Bethesda, MD 20814 301-951-1500

Richard H. Gins · Gins & Seeber · 451 Hungerford Drive, Suite 505 · Rockville, MD 20850 · 301-762-9123

BUSINESS LITIGATION

George Beall* · (Commercial, Securities) · Hogan & Hartson · 111 South Calvert Street, 16th Floor · Baltimore, MD 21202 · 301-659-2700

Francis B. Burch, Jr.* · (Commercial, Finance, Securities) · Piper & Marbury · 1100 Charles Center South · 36 South Charles Street · Baltimore, MD 21201-3010 301-539-2530

Benjamin R. Civiletti · Venable, Baetjer and Howard · 1800 Mercantile Bank & Trust Building · Two Hopkins Plaza · Baltimore, MD 21201-2978 · 301-244-7400

George A. Nilson · Piper & Marbury · 1100 Charles Center South · 36 South Charles Street · Baltimore, MD 21201-3010 · 301-539-2530

Wilbur D. Preston, Jr.* · Whiteford, Taylor & Preston · Signet Tower, Suite 1400 · Seven Saint Paul Street · Baltimore, MD 21202-1626 · 301-347-8700

Kieron F. Quinn* · (RICO, Class Actions) · Quinn, Ward and Kershaw · 113 West Monument Street · Baltimore, MD 21201 · 301-685-6700

Shale D. Stiller* · Frank, Bernstein, Conaway & Goldman · 300 East Lombard Street · Baltimore, MD 21202 · 301-625-3500

James J. Cromwell · Frank, Bernstein, Conaway & Goldman · 6701 Democracy Boulevard, Suite 600 · Bethesda, MD 20817 · 301-897-8282

CORPORATE LAW

Lowell R. Bowen · Miles & Stockbridge · 10 Light Street · Baltimore, MD 21202 301-727-6464

Andre W. Brewster · Piper & Marbury · 1100 Charles Center South · 36 South Charles Street · Baltimore, MD 21201-3010 · 301-539-2530

Edward Owen Clarke, Jr. · Piper & Marbury · 1100 Charles Center South · 36 South Charles Street · Baltimore, MD 21201-3010 · 301-539-2530

Bryson L. Cook · (Corporate Finance, International Finance, Leveraged Buy-outs, Mergers & Acquisitions) · Venable, Baetjer and Howard · 1800 Mercantile Bank & Trust Building · Two Hopkins Plaza · Baltimore, MD 21201-2978 · 301-244-7400

Decatur H. Miller · Piper & Marbury · 1100 Charles Center South · 36 South Charles Street · Baltimore, MD 21201-3010 · 301-539-2530

Larry P. Scriggins · Piper & Marbury · 1100 Charles Center South · 36 South Charles Street · Baltimore, MD 21201-3010 · 301-539-2530

George P. Stamas · Piper & Marbury · 1100 Charles Center South · 36 South Charles Street · Baltimore, MD 21201-3010 · 301-539-2530

Shale D. Stiller* · Frank, Bernstein, Conaway & Goldman · 300 East Lombard Street · Baltimore, MD 21202 · 301-625-3500

Alan D. Yarbro · Venable, Baetjer and Howard · 1800 Mercantile Bank & Trust Building · Two Hopkins Plaza · Baltimore, MD 21201-2978 · 301-244-7400

CRIMINAL DEFENSE

Benjamin R. Civiletti · Venable, Baetjer and Howard · 1800 Mercantile Bank & Trust Building · Two Hopkins Plaza · Baltimore, MD 21201-2978 · 301-244-7400

Ty Cobb · (White Collar) · Hogan & Hartson · 111 South Calvert Street, 16th Floor · Baltimore, MD 21202 · 301-659-2700

Andrew Jay Graham* · Kramon & Graham · Sun Life Building, Charles Center 20 South Charles Street · Baltimore, MD 21201 · 301-752-6030

James P. Ulwick · Kramon & Graham · Sun Life Building, Charles Center · 20 South Charles Street · Baltimore, MD 21201 · 301-752-6030

Arnold M. Weiner · (Environmental Crimes, White Collar Crimes) · Hazel & Thomas · Bank of Baltimore Building, Suite 2100 · 120 East Baltimore Street · Baltimore, MD 21202 · 301-783-3500

Russell J. White · White & Karceski · 305 West Chesapeake Avenue Suite 100 · Towson, MD 21204 · 301-583-1325

FAMILY LAW

Bruce A. Kaufman · Rosenthal, Kaufman & Reis · 1212 Blaustein Building · One North Charles Street · Baltimore, MD 21201 · 301-752-5678

Beverly Anne Groner* · Groner and Groner · Air Rights Plaza III, Suite 403N · 4550 Montgomery Avenue · Bethesda, MD 20814 · 301-657-2828

Walter W. Johnson, Jr. · 8701 Georgia Avenue, Suite 700 · Silver Spring, MD 20910 · 301-587-2090

FIRST AMENDMENT LAW

Peter F. Axelrod · Frank, Bernstein, Conaway & Goldman · 300 East Lombard Street · Baltimore, MD 21202 · 301-625-3500

C. Christopher Brown · Brown, Goldstein & Levy · Maryland Bar Center, Suite 300 · 520 West Fayette Street · Baltimore, MD 21201 · 301-659-0717

Douglas D. Connah, Jr. · Venable, Baetjer and Howard · 1800 Mercantile Bank & Trust Building · Two Hopkins Plaza · Baltimore, MD 21201-2978 · 301-244-7400

Mary R. Craig · Doyle & Craig · 25 South Charles Street · Baltimore, MD 21201 301-332-0520

Theodore Sherbow · Weisberg and Green · 100 South Charles Street · Baltimore, MD 21202 · 301-332-8675

HEALTH CARE LAW

Eugene M. Feinblatt · Gordon, Feinblatt, Rothman, Hoffberger & Hollander · Garrett Building · 233 East Redwood Street · Baltimore, MD 21202 · 301-576-4000

Leonard C. Homer · Ober, Kaler, Grimes & Shriver · 120 East Baltimore Street Baltimore, MD 20202-1111643 · 301-685-1120

Joanne E. Pollak · Piper & Marbury · 1100 Charles Center South · 36 South Charles Street · Baltimore, MD 21201-3010 · 301-539-2530

Sanford V. Teplitzky · Ober, Kaler, Grimes & Shriver · 120 East Baltimore Street Baltimore, MD 20202-1643 · 301-685-1120

Jack C. Tranter · Piper & Marbury · 1100 Charles Center South · 36 South Charles Street · Baltimore, MD 21201-3010 · 301-539-2530

Robert G. Brewer, Jr. · Lerch, Early, Roseman & Frankel · Three Bethesda Metro Center, 10th Floor · Bethesda, MD 20814-5367 · 301-986-1300

IMMIGRATION LAW

Mary E. Pivec · (Business Visas, Consular Processing, Employer Sanctions/Antidiscrimination Defense) · Venable, Baetjer and Howard · 1800 Mercantile Bank & Trust Building · Two Hopkins Plaza · Baltimore, MD 21201-2978 · 301-244-7400

LABOR AND EMPLOYMENT LAW

Jana Howard Carey* · (Management) · Venable, Baetjer and Howard · 1800 Mercantile Bank & Trust Building · Two Hopkins Plaza · Baltimore, MD 21201-2978 · 301-244-7636

Leonard E. Cohen · (Management) · Frank, Bernstein, Conaway & Goldman · 300 East Lombard Street · Baltimore, MD 21202 · 301-625-3500

A. Samuel Cook · (Management) · Venable, Baetjer and Howard · 1800 Mercantile Bank & Trust Building · Two Hopkins Plaza · Baltimore, MD 21201-2978 · 301-244-7400

Warren M. Davison* · (Management) · Littler, Mendelson, Fastiff & Tichy · The World Trade Center, Suite 1653 · Baltimore, MD 21202 · 301-528-9545

Stephen W. Godoff · (Individuals) · Godoff & Zimmerman · 14 West Madison Street · Baltimore, MD 21201 · 301-539-0717

Robert S. Hillman · Whiteford, Taylor & Preston · Seven Saint Paul Street, Suite 1400 · Baltimore, MD 21202-1626 · 301-347-8700

Stephen D. Langhoff · (Individuals) · Langhoff & Wacker · 207 East Redwood Street · Baltimore, MD 21202 · 301-332-1010

N. Peter Lareau · (Management) · Venable, Baetjer and Howard · 1800 Mercantile Bank & Trust Building · Two Hopkins Plaza · Baltimore, MD 21201-2978 · 301-244-7400

Stanley Mazaroff · (Management) · Venable, Baetjer and Howard · 1800 Mercantile Bank & Trust Building · Two Hopkins Plaza · Baltimore, MD 21201-2978 301-244-7400

Joseph K. Pokempner · (Management) · Whiteford, Taylor & Preston · Seven Saint Paul Street, Suite 1400 · Baltimore, MD 21202-1626 · 301-347-8700

William J. Rosenthal* · (Management) · Shawe & Rosenthal · Sun Life Building, Charles Center · 20 South Charles Street · Baltimore, MD 21201 · 301-752-1040

Earle K. Shawe · (Management) · Shawe & Rosenthal · Sun Life Building, Charles Center · 20 South Charles Street · Baltimore, MD 21201 · 301-752-1040

Larry M. Wolf* · (Management) · Whiteford, Taylor & Preston · Seven Saint Paul Street, Suite 1400 · Baltimore, MD 21202-1626 · 301-347-8700

Cosimo C. Abato · (Labor) · Abato, Rubenstein, Abato & Smith · 2360 West Joppa Road, Suite 308 · Lutherville, MD 21093 · 301-321-0990

Bernard W. Rubenstein · (Labor) · Abato, Rubenstein, Abato & Smith · 2360 West Joppa Road, Suite 308 · Lutherville, MD 21093 · 301-321-0990

Joel A. Smith · (Labor) · Abato, Rubenstein, Abato & Smith · 2360 West Joppa Road, Suite 308 · Lutherville, MD 21093 · 301-321-0990

MARITIME LAW

William R. Dorsey III* · Semmes, Bowen & Semmes · 250 West Pratt Street · Baltimore, MD 21201 · 301-539-5040

Francis J. Gorman* · Semmes, Bowen & Semmes · 250 West Pratt Street · Baltimore, MD 21201 · 301-539-5040

Donald C. Greenman · Ober, Kaler, Grimes & Shriver · 120 East Baltimore Street Baltimore, MD 21202-1643 · 301-685-1120

Manfred W. Leckszas* · Ober, Kaler, Grimes & Shriver · 120 East Baltimore Street · Baltimore, MD 21202-1643 · 301-685-1120

Kieron F. Quinn* · Quinn, Ward and Kershaw · 113 West Monument Street · Baltimore, MD 21201 · 301-685-6700

David W. Skeen · Wright, Constable & Skeen · 250 West Pratt Street, 13th Floor l Baltimore, MD 21201-2423 · 301-539-5541

M. Hamilton Whitman, Jr. · Ober, Kaler, Grimes & Shriver · 120 East Baltimore Street · Baltimore, MD 21202-1643 · 301-685-1120

NATURAL RESOURCES AND ENVIRONMENTAL LAW

Robert G. Smith · Venable, Baetjer and Howard · 1800 Mercantile Bank & Trust Building · Two Hopkins Plaza · Baltimore, MD 21201-2978 · 301-244-7400

Thomas H. Truitt · Piper & Marbury · 1100 Charles Center South · 36 South Charles Street · Baltimore, MD 21201-3010 · 301-539-2530

PERSONAL INJURY LITIGATION

William A. Ehrmantraut · (Defendants) · Wharton, Levin & Ehrmantraut · 225 Duke of Gloucester Street · Annapolis, MD 21404-0551 · 301-263-5900

Paul D. Bekman* · (Plaintiffs, Medical Malpractice, Products Liability, Automobile Collision) · Israelson, Salsbury, Clements & Bekman · Jefferson Building, Suite 600 · Two East Fayette Street · Baltimore, MD 21202 · 301-539-6633

Marvin Ellin · (Plaintiffs) · Ellin and Baker · 1101 St. Paul Street, Second Floor Baltimore, MD 21202 · 301-727-1787

James M. Gabler* · (Plaintiffs) · Sandbower, Gabler & O'Shaughnessy · 22 East Fayette Street, Fifth Floor · Baltimore, MD 21202-1706 · 301-576-0762

M. King Hill, Jr. · (Defendants) · Smith, Somerville & Case · 100 Light Street, Third Floor · Baltimore, MD 21202-1084 · 301-727-1164

Max R. Israelson* · (Plaintiffs) · Israelson, Salsbury, Clements & Bekman · Jefferson Building, Suite 600 · Two East Fayette Street · Baltimore, MD 21202 · 301-539-6633

Stuart M. Salsbury · Israelson, Salsbury, Clements & Bekman · Jefferson Building, Suite 600 · Two East Fayette Street · Baltimore, MD 21202 · 301-539-6633

John E. Sandbower III · Sandbower, Gabler & O'Shaughnessy · 22 East Fayette Street, Fifth Floor · Baltimore, MD 21202-1706 · 301-576-0762

Paul Mark Sandler · Freishtat & Sandler · One Calvert Plaza, Suite 1500 · 201 East Baltimore Street · Baltimore, MD 21202 · 301-727-7740

Donald E. Sharpe* · (Defendants, Products Liability) · Piper & Marbury · 1100 Charles Center South · 36 South Charles Street · Baltimore, MD 21201-3010 · 301-539-2530

James J. Cromwell · (Defendants) · Frank, Bernstein, Conaway & Goldman · 6701 Democracy Boulevard, Suite 600 · Bethesda, MD 20817 · 301-897-8282

Thomas A. Farrington · (Defendants) · 9200 Basil Court, Suite 204 · Landover, MD 20785 · 301-322-4000

Albert D. Brault · (Defendants) · Brault, Graham, Scott & Brault · 101 South Washington Street · Rockville, MD 20850 · 301-424-1060

Francis J. Ford · (Defendants) · Ford, Chervenak & Foote · One Church Street, Suite 303 · Rockville, MD 20850 · 301-279-2000

Robert R. Michael · (Plaintiffs) · Shadoan and Michael · 108 Park Avenue · Rockville, MD 20850 · 301-762-5150

George W. Shadoan* · (Plaintiffs, Medical Malpractice, Products Liability, Professional Malpractice, Automobile Collision) · Shadoan and Michael · 108 Park Avenue · Rockville, MD 20850 · 301-762-5150

Bayard Z. Hochberg* · (Plaintiffs) · Hochberg, Chiarello, Costello & Dowell · 528 East Joppa Road · Towson, MD 21204-5403 · 301-823-2922

George W. White, Jr.* · (Plaintiffs, Medical Malpractice, Products Liability, Professional Malpractice, Automobile Collision) · White, Mindel, Clarke & Hill · 40 West Chesapeake Avenue, 3rd Floor · Towson, MD 21204 · 301-828-1050

William B. Whiteford · (Defendants) · Whiteford, Taylor & Preston · 210 West Pennsylvania Avenue · Towson, MD 21204 · 301-832-2000

Charles E. Channing, Jr. · (Defendants) · Sasscer, Clagett, Channing & Bucher 14803 Pratt Street · P.O. Box 550 · Upper Marlboro, MD 20772 · 301-627-5500

PUBLIC UTILITY LAW

Roger D. Redden · Piper & Marbury · 1100 Charles Center South · 36 South Charles Street · Baltimore, MD 21201-3010 · 301-539-2530

Edward F. Shea, Jr., Jr. · Kaplan, Heyman, Greenberg, Engelman & Belgrad · Charles & Redwood Streets · 20 South Charles Street · Baltimore, MD 21201 · 301-539-6967

REAL ESTATE LAW

Charles T. Albert · Piper & Marbury · 1100 Charles Center South · 36 South Charles Street · Baltimore, MD 21201-3010 · 301-539-2530

Ronald P. Fish · Frank, Bernstein, Conaway & Goldman · 300 East Lombard Street · Baltimore, MD 21202 · 301-625-3500

Morton P. Fisher, Jr. · (Commercial Transactions, Industrial Transactions, Public/Private Partnerships, Workouts) · Frank, Bernstein, Conaway & Goldman · 300 East Lombard Street · Baltimore, MD 21202 · 301-625-3500

David H. Fishman · (Commercial Transactions, Industrial Transactions) · Gordon, Feinblatt, Rothman, Hoffberger & Hollander · Garrett Building · 233 East Redwood Street · Baltimore, MD 21202 · 301-576-4000

Edward J. Levin · Piper & Marbury · 1100 Charles Center South · 36 South Charles Street · Baltimore, MD 21201-3010 · 301-539-2530

Russell Ronald Reno, Jr. · Venable, Baetjer and Howard · 1800 Mercantile Bank & Trust Building · Two Hopkins Plaza · Baltimore, MD 21201-2978 · 301-244-7400

TAX AND EMPLOYEE BENEFITS LAW

Bryson L. Cook · (Corporate & Partnership Transactions) · Venable, Baetjer and Howard · 1800 Mercantile Bank & Trust Building · Two Hopkins Plaza · Baltimore, MD 21201-2978 · 301-244-7400

Lawrence M. Katz · Piper & Marbury · 1100 Charles Center South · 36 South Charles Street · Baltimore, MD 21201-3010 · 301-539-2530

L. Paige Marvel · Venable, Baetjer and Howard · 1800 Mercantile Bank & Trust Building · Two Hopkins Plaza · Baltimore, MD 21201-2978 · 301-244-7400

Stephen L. Owen · Venable, Baetjer and Howard · 1800 Mercantile Bank & Trust Building · Two Hopkins Plaza · Baltimore, MD 21201-2978 · 301-244-7400

Shale D. Stiller* · Frank, Bernstein, Conaway & Goldman · 300 East Lombard Street · Baltimore, MD 21202 · 301-625-3500

TRUSTS AND ESTATES

Albert S. Barr III · (Estate Planning, Estate Administration, Planning for Elderly & Disabled) · Barr & Testa · Village Square I, Suite 127 · Village of Cross Keys Baltimore, MD 21210 · 301-435-8787

Max E. Blumenthal · Frank, Bernstein, Conaway & Goldman · 300 East Lombard Street · Baltimore, MD 21202 · 301-625-3500

Stanard T. Klinefelter · Piper & Marbury · 1100 Charles Center South · 36 South Charles Street · Baltimore, MD 21201-3010 · 301-539-2530

Alexander I. Lewis III · Venable, Baetjer and Howard · 1800 Mercantile Bank & Trust Building · Two Hopkins Plaza · Baltimore, MD 21201-2978 · 301-244-7400

A. MacDonough Plant · Semmes, Bowen & Semmes · 250 West Pratt Street · Baltimore, MD 21201 · 301-539-5040

C. Van Leuven Stewart · Venable, Baetjer and Howard · 1800 Mercantile Bank & Trust Building · Two Hopkins Plaza · Baltimore, MD 21201-2978 · 301-244-7400

Robert M. Thomas · Venable, Baetjer and Howard · 1800 Mercantile Bank & Trust Building · Two Hopkins Plaza · Baltimore, MD 21201-2978 · 301-244-7400

George E. Thomsen · McKenney, Thomsen and Burke · 1723 Munsey Building Baltimore, MD 21202 · 301-539-2595

W. Shepherdson Abell · Furey, Doolan & Abell · Penthouse One · 8401 Connecticut Avenue · Chevy Chase, MD 20815 · 301-652-6880

MASSACHUSETTS

BANKRUPTCY LAW

Mark N. Berman · (Business Reorganization, Creditors' Rights, Debtors' Rights, Bankruptcy Litigation) · Hutchins & Wheeler · 101 Federal Street · Boston, MA 02110 · 617-951-6600

Stanley B. Bernstein · Foley, Hoag & Elliot · One Post Office Square, 17th Floor Boston, MA 02109 · 617-482-1390

Henry J. Boroff* · (Business Reorganization, Creditors' Rights, Debtors' Rights, Bankruptcy Litigation) · Boroff & Associates · 55 Summer Street · Boston, MA 02110 · 617-482-2626

Daniel C. Cohn · (Debtors' Rights) · Cohn, Roitman & Kelakos · 265 Franklin Street · Boston, MA 02110 · 617-951-22505

Paul P. Daley · Hale and Dorr · 60 State Street · Boston, MA 02109 · 617-742-9100

Peter A. Fine · (Business Reorganization, Creditors' Rights, Debtors' Rights) · Choate, Hall & Stewart · Exchange Place · 53 State Street · Boston, MA 02109 · 617-227-5020

Robert M. Gargill · Choate, Hall & Stewart · Exchange Place · 53 State Street · Boston, MA 02109 · 617-227-5020

Daniel M. Glosband · (Business Reorganization, Creditors' Rights, Bankruptcy Litigation) · Goodwin, Procter & Hoar · Exchange Place · Boston, MA 02109-2881 617-570-1000

Richard L. Levine · Hill & Barlow · One International Place · 100 Oliver Street Boston, MA 02110-2607 · 617-439-3555

William F. Macauley* · (Business Reorganization, Creditors' Rights, Debtors' Rights, Bankruptcy Litigation) · Craig and Macauley · 600 Atlantic Avenue · Boston, MA 02210 · 617-367-9500

William F. McCarthy · Ropes & Gray · One International Place · Boston, MA 02110-2624 · 617-951-7000

Richard E. Mikels · Mintz, Levin, Cohn, Ferris, Glovsky and Popeo · One Financial Center · Boston, MA 02111 · 617-542-6000

Charles P. Normandin · Ropes & Gray · One International Place · Boston, MA 02110-2624 · 617-951-7000

Michael J. Pappone · Goodwin, Procter & Hoar · Exchange Place · Boston, MA 02109-2881 · 617-570-1000

Mark N. Polebaum · Hale and Dorr · 60 State Street · Boston, MA 02109 · 617-742-9100

Jon D. Schneider · (Business Reorganization, Creditors' Rights, Debtors' Rights, Bankruptcy Litigation) · Goodwin, Procter & Hoar · Exchange Place · Boston, MA 02109-2881 · 617-570-1000

Robert Somma · Goldstein & Manello · 265 Franklin Street · Boston, MA 02110 617-439-8900

C. Hall Swaim · Hale and Dorr · 60 State Street · Boston, MA 02109 · 617-742-9100

John L. Whitlock · Palmer & Dodge · One Beacon Street, 23nd Floor · Boston, MA 02108 · 617-573-0100

Eugene B. Berman · Kamberg, Berman · 31 Elm Street · P.O. Box 2439 · Springfield, MA 01101-2439 · 413-781-1300

Joseph B. Collins · (Business Reorganization, Creditors' Rights, Debtors' Rights) Hendel, Collins & Newton · 101 State Street · Springfield, MA 01103 · 413-734-6411

Philip J. Hendel · Hendel, Collins & Newton · 101 State Street · Springfield, MA 01103 · 413-734-6411

Irving D. Labovitz · Cooley, Shrair, Alpert, Labovitz and Dambrov · 1380 Main Street, Fifth Floor · Springfield, MA 01103 · 413-781-0750

J. Robert Seder · Seder & Chandler · Burnside Building · 339 Main Street · Worcester, MA 01608 · 508-757-7721

Richard A. Sheils, Jr. · (Creditors' Rights) · Bowditch & Dewey · 311 Main Street Worcester, MA 01608-1552 · 508-791-3511

George W. Tetler III · Bowditch & Dewey · 311 Main Street · Worcester, MA 01608-1552 · 508-791-3511

BUSINESS LITIGATION

Samuel Adams* · (Commercial, Finance) · Warner & Stackpole · 75 State Street Boston, MA 02109 · 617-951-9000

Edward J. Barshak · Sugarman, Rogers, Barshak & Cohen · 33 Union Street · Boston, MA 02108-2406 · 617-227-3030

Thomas D. Burns · Burns & Levinson · 125 Summer Street · Boston, MA 02110 617-345-3000

Robert A. Cesari · Cesari & McKenna · 30 Rowes Wharf · Boston, MA 02110 · 617-261-6800

Earle C. Cooley · Cooley, Manion, Moore & Jones · 21 Custom House Street · Boston, MA 02110 · 617-737-3100

John J. Curtin, Jr.* · Bingham, Dana & Gould · 150 Federal Street · Boston, MA 02110 · 617-951-8000

Harry T. Daniels · Hale and Dorr · 60 State Street · Boston, MA 02109 · 617-742-9100

Charles Donelan · (Antitrust) · Day, Berry & Howard · 260 Franklin Street · Boston, MA 02109 · 617-345-4600

Jerome P. Facher · Hale and Dorr · 60 State Street · Boston, MA 02109 · 617-742-9100

Robert E. Fast · Hale and Dorr · 60 State Street · Boston, MA 02109 · 617-742-9100

Albert M. Fortier, Jr. · (Estate Planning) · Rackemann, Sawyer & Brewster · One Financial Center · Boston, MA 02111-2659 · 617-542-2300

Francis H. Fox · Bingham, Dana & Gould · 150 Federal Street · Boston, MA 02110 · 617-951-8000

Paul B. Galvani* · (Securities, Environmental) · Ropes & Gray · One International Place · Boston, MA 02110-2624 · 617-951-7000

David A. Garbus · Brown, Rudnick, Freed & Gesmer · One Financial Center, 18th Floor · Boston, MA 02111 · 617-330-9000

Jerome Gotkin* · (Antitrust, Commercial, Securities, Shareholder Disputes/ Close Corporations) · Mintz, Levin, Cohn, Ferris, Glovsky and Popeo · One Financial Center · Boston, MA 02111 · 617-542-6000

John M. Harrington, Jr.* · (Antitrust, Appellate, Securities) · Ropes & Gray · One International Place · Boston, MA 02110-2624 · 617-951-7000

Samuel Hoar* · (Commercial, Tax Abatement) · Goodwin, Procter & Hoar · Exchange Place · Boston, MA 02109-2881 · 617-570-1000

Michael B. Keating · Foley, Hoag & Eliot · One Post Office Square, 17th Floor Boston, MA 02109 · 617-482-1390

Joel A. Kozol · Friedman & Atherton · 28 State Street, 19th Floor · Boston, MA 02109 · 617-227-5540

James B. Lampert · Hale and Dorr · 60 State Street · Boston, MA 02109 · 617-742-9100

Daniel O. Mahoney · Palmer & Dodge · One Beacon Street · Boston, MA 02108 617-573-0100

Gael Mahony · Hill & Barlow · One International Place · 100 Oliver Street · Boston, MA 02110-2607 · 617-439-3555

A. Lane McGovern · Ropes & Gray · One International Place · Boston, MA 02110-2624 · 617-951-7000

George A. McLaughlin, Jr.* · The McLaughlin Brothers · 44 School Street · Boston, MA 02108 · 617-523-7165

William G. Meserve · Ropes & Gray · One International Place · Boston, MA 02110-2624 · 617-951-7000

Robert J. Muldoon, Jr.* · Sherin and Lodgen · 100 Summer Street · Boston, MA 02110 · 617-426-5720

Martin J. O'Donnell · Cesari & McKenna · 30 Rowes Wharf · Boston, MA 02110 617-261-6800

Blair L. Perry · Fish & Richardson · One Financial Center · Boston, MA 02111 617-542-5070

R. Robert Popeo · Mintz, Levin, Cohn, Ferris, Glovsky and Popeo · One Financial Center · Boston, MA 02111 · 617-542-6000

Richard W. Renehan · Hill & Barlow · One International Place · 100 Oliver Street Boston, MA 02110-2607 · 617-439-3555

Jeffrey B. Rudman · Hale and Dorr · 60 State Street · Boston, MA 02109 · 617-742-9100

Stanley H. Rudman · Rubin and Rudman · 50 Rose Wharf · Boston, MA 02110 617-330-7000

Thomas J. Sartory* · (Banking, Commercial, Finance, Employment) · Goulston & Storrs · 400 Atlantic Avenue · Boston, MA 02110-3333 · 617-482-1776

Marshall Simonds · Goodwin, Procter & Hoar · Exchange Place · Boston, MA 02109-2881 · 617-570-1000

James D. St. Clair · Hale and Dorr · 60 State Street · Boston, MA 02109 · 617-742-9100

Joseph D. Steinfield* · (First Amendment) · Hill & Barlow · One International Place · 100 Oliver Street · Boston, MA 02110-2607 · 617-439-3555

Allan van Gestel* · Goodwin, Procter & Hoar · Exchange Place · Boston, MA 02109-2881 · 617-570-1000

Charles K. Bergin, Jr. · Robinson Donovan Madden & Barry · Valley Bank Tower, Suite 1400 · 1500 Main Street · P.O. Box 15609 · Springfield, MA 01115 413-732-2301

John D. Ross, Jr. · Ross & Ross · 101 State Street, Suite 701-705 · Springfield, MA 01103 · 413-736-2725

Michael P. Angelini* · Bowditch & Dewey · 311 Main Street · Worcester, MA 01608-1552 · 508-791-3511

Burton Chandler* · Seder & Chandler · 300 Burnside Building · 339 Main Street Worcester, MA 01608-1585 · 508-757-7721

John O. Mirick · Mirick, O'Connell, DeMallie & Lougee · 1700 Mechanics Bank Tower · Worcester Center · Worcester, MA 01608-1477 · 508-799-0541

Charles B. Swartwood III · Mountain, Dearborn & Whiting · 370 Main Street, Seventh Floor · Worcester, MA 01608 · 508-756-2423

Seymour Weinstein · Weinstein, Bernstein & Burwick · 370 Main Street, Suite 1150 · Worcester, MA 01608 · 508-756-4393

CORPORATE LAW

Constantine Alexander · Nutter, McClennen & Fish · One International Place · Boston, MA 02110-2699 · 617-439-2000

Norman B. Asher · Hale and Dorr · 60 State Street · Boston, MA 02109 · 617-742-9100

John E. Beard · Ropes & Gray · One International Place · Boston, MA 02110-2624 · 617-951-7000

Edward A. Benjamin · (Securities) · Ropes & Gray · One International Place · Boston, MA 02110-2624 · 617-951-7000

Norman A. Bikales · (Corporate Finance, Financial Institutions, Mergers & Acquisitions, Securities) · Sullivan & Worcester · One Post Office Square · Boston, MA 02109 · 617-338-2800

Michael J. Bohnen · Nutter, McClennen & Fish · One International Place · Boston, MA 02110-2699 · 617-439-2000

Mark G. Borden · Hale and Dorr · 60 State Street · Boston, MA 02109 · 617-742-9100

Paul P. Brountas · Hale and Dorr · 60 State Street · Boston, MA 02109 · 617-742-9100

Truman S. Casner · Ropes & Gray · One International Place · Boston, MA 02110-2624 · 617-951-7000

F. Douglas Cochrane · Ropes & Gray · One International Place · Boston, MA 02110-2624 · 617-951-7000

John F. Cogan, Jr. · Hale and Dorr · 60 State Street · Boston, MA 02109 · 617-742-9100

Donald J. Evans · (Corporate Finance, International, Leveraged Buyouts, Mergers & Acquisitions) · Goodwin, Procter & Hoar · Exchange Place · Boston, MA 02109-2881 · 617-570-1000

Champe A. Fisher · Ropes & Gray · One International Place · Boston, MA 02110-2624 · 617-951-7000

Richard E. Floor · Goodwin, Procter & Hoar · Exchange Place · Boston, MA 02109-2881 · 617-570-1000

Donald W. Glazer · (Corporate Finance, Emerging Companies, Executive Compensation & Stock Plans) · Ropes & Gray · One International Place · Boston, MA 02110-2624 · 617-951-7000

Gordon B. Greer · Bingham, Dana & Gould · 150 Federal Street · Boston, MA 02110 · 617-951-8000

Irving J. Helman · Nutter, McClennen & Fish · One International Place, 15th Floor · Boston, MA 02110-2699 · 617-439-2000

Stanley Keller · Palmer & Dodge · One Beacon Street · Boston, MA 02108 · 617-573-0100

Anthony J. Medaglia, Jr. · (Corporate Finance, Financial Institutions, Securities Regulation) · Hutchins & Wheeler · 101 Federal Street · Boston, MA 02110 · 617-951-6600

Andrew L. Nichols · Choate, Hall & Stewart · Exchange Place · 53 State Street · Boston, MA 02109 · 617-227-5020

Kenneth J. Novack · (Corporate Finance, International, Mergers & Acquisitions, Securities) · Mintz, Levin, Cohn, Ferris, Glovsky and Popeo · One Financial Center · Boston, MA 02111 · 617-542-6000

Robert L. Nutt · Ropes & Gray · One International Place · Boston, MA 02110-2624 · 617-951-7000

Paul R. Rugo · Goodwin, Procter & Hoar · Exchange Place · Boston, MA 02109-2881 · 617-570-1000

Ernest J. Sargeant · Ropes & Gray · One International Place · Boston, MA 02110-2624 · 617-951-7000

Richard W. Southgate · Ropes & Gray · One International Place · Boston, MA 02110-2624 · 617-951-7000

Richard J. Testa · Testa, Hurwitz & Thibeault · Exchange Place · 53 State Street Boston, MA 02109 · 617-367-7500

George W. Thibeault · Testa, Hurwitz & Thibeault · Exchange Place · 53 State Street · Boston, MA 02109 · 617-367-7500

Paul S. Doherty · Doherty, Wallace, Pillsbury and Murphy · One Monarch Place, 19th Floor · 1414 Main Street · Springfield, MA 01144-1002 · 413-733-3111

J. Nicholas Filler · (Finance) · Bulkley, Richardson and Gelinas · BayBank Tower, Suite 2700 · 1500 Main Street · P.O. Box 15507 · Springfield, MA 01115-5507 · 413-781-2820

Ronald P. Weiss · Bulkley, Richardson and Gelinas · BayBank Tower, Suite 2700 1500 Main Street · P.O. Box 15507 · Springfield, MA 01115-5507 · 413-781-2820

Michael P. Angelini* · Bowditch & Dewey · 311 Main Street · Worcester, MA 01608-1552 · 508-791-3511

Burton Chandler* · Seder & Chandler · 300 Burnside Building · 339 Main Street Worcester, MA 01608-1585 · 508-757-7721

Phillip S. Davis · Fletcher, Tilton & Whipple · 370 Main Street · Worcester, MA 01608 · 508-798-8621

David L. Lougee · (Corporate Finance, Leveraged Buyouts, Mergers & Acquisitions, Securities) · Mirick, O'Connell, DeMallie & Lougee · 1700 Mechanics Bank Tower · Worcester Center · Worcester, MA 01608-1477 · 508-799-0541

Robert J. Martin · Mirick, O'Connell, DeMallie & Lougee · 1700 Mechanics Bank Tower · Worcester Center · Worcester, MA 01608-1477 · 508-799-0541

Thomas R. Mountain · Mountain, Dearborn & Whiting · 370 Main Street, Seventh Floor · Worcester, MA 01608 · 508-756-2423

J. Robert Seder · Seder & Chandler · Burnside Building · 339 Main Street · Worcester, MA 01608 · 508-757-7721

CRIMINAL DEFENSE

F. Lee Bailey · Bailey, Fishman & Leonard · 66 Long Wharf · Boston, MA 02110 617-723-1980

Joseph J. Balliro, Sr. · Balliro, Mondano & Balliro · Three Arlington Street · Boston, MA 02116 · 617-227-5822

Earle C. Cooley · Cooley, Manion, Moore & Jones · 21 Custom House Street · Boston, MA 02110 · 617-737-3100

Albert F. Cullen, Jr.* · (Federal Court) · Cullen & Butters · 160 Federal Street, 22nd Floor · Boston, MA 02110 · 617-439-0222

Francis J. DiMento · DiMento & Sullivan · 100 State Street · Boston, MA 02109 617-523-5253

Thomas E. Dwyer, Jr. · Dwyer, Collora & Gertner · 400 Atlantic Avenue · Boston, MA 02110 · 617-357-9202

Richard M. Egbert · 125 Summer Street · Boston, MA 02110 · 617-439-6020

Nancy Gertner · Dwyer Collora & Gertner · 400 Atlantic Avenue · Boston, MA 02110 · 617-357-9202

Andrew H. Good* · Silverglate & Good · The Batterymarch Building · 89 Broad Street, 14th Floor · Boston, MA 02110-3511 · 617-542-6663

William P. Homans, Jr.* · (Violent Crimes, Non-Violent Crimes, Federal Court, State Court) · Homans, Hamilton & Dahmen · One Court Street · Boston, MA 02108 · 617-523-3716

Albert L. Hutton, Jr. · Six Beacon Street · Boston, MA 02108 · 617-227-1111

J. Albert Johnson · Johnson, Mee & May · Eight Whittier Place · Boston, MA 02114 · 617-227-8900

Robert D. Keefe · Hale and Dorr · 60 State Street · Boston, MA 02109 · 617-742-9100

James W. Lawson · Oteri, Weinberg & Lawson · 20 Park Plaza, Suite 905 · Boston, MA 02116 · 617-227-3700

Joseph S. Oteri* · Oteri, Weinberg & Lawson · 20 Park Plaza, Suite 905 · Boston, MA 02116 · 617-227-3700

R. Robert Popeo · Mintz, Levin, Cohn, Ferris, Glovsky and Popeo · One Financial Center · Boston, MA 02111 · 617-542-6000

Charles W. Rankin, Jr. · (Appellate) · Rankin & Sultan · One Commercial Wharf North, Second Floor · Boston, MA 02110 · 617-720-0011

Jonathan Shapiro · Stern & Shapiro · 80 Boylston Street, Suite 910 · Boston, MA 02116 · 617-542-0663

Harvey A. Silverglate* · Silverglate & Good · The Batterymarch Building · 89 Broad Street, 14th Floor · Boston, MA 02110-3511 · 617-542-6663

James D. St. Clair · Hale and Dorr · 60 State Street · Boston, MA 02109 · 617-742-9100

Max D. Stern* · Stern & Shapiro · 80 Boylston Street, Suite 910 · Boston, MA 02116 · 617-542-0663

James L. Sultan · (Appellate) · Rankin & Sultan · One Commercial Wharf North, Second Floor · Boston, MA 02110 · 617-720-0011

John Wall* · Law Office of John Wall · 141 Tremont Street, Seventh Floor · Boston, MA 02111 · 617-482-8650

Martin G. Weinberg · Oteri, Weinberg & Lawson · 20 Park Plaza, Suite 905 · Boston, MA 02116 · 617-227-3700

Thomas F. McEvilly* · (Violent Crimes, Non-Violent Crimes, Federal Court, State Court) · McEvilly & Curley · 48 West Street · Leominster, MA 01453 · 508-534-3556

Barry M. Haight · Buckley, Haight, Muldoon, Jubinville & Gilligan · 480 Adams Street · Milton, MA 01286 · 617-698-5700

Martin Kenneth Leppo* · (Violent Crimes, Non-Violent Crimes, Federal Court, State Court) · The Belcher Mansion · 490 North Main Street at Grove · Randolph, MA 02368 · 617-961-3344

Anthony M. Traini* · 500 North Main Street, Suite D · Randolph, MA 02368 · 617-961-5400

Efrem A. Gordon · 101 State Street, Room 410 · Springfield, MA 01103 · 413-737-4316

Michael O. Jennings · 73 State Street · Springfield, MA 01103 · 413-737-7349

Samuel A. Marsella* · (Federal Court) · Doherty, Wallace, Pillsbury and Murphy One Monarch Place, 19th Floor · 1414 Main Street · Springfield, MA 01144-1002 413-733-3111

John M. Thompson · Salomone & Thompson · 175 State Street, Suite 200 · Springfield, MA 01103 · 413-737-7783

Peter L. Ettenberg* · (Violent Crimes, Non-Violent Crimes, Federal Court, State Court) · Gould & Ettenberg · 370 Main Street, Suite 850 · Worcester, MA 01608 508-752-6733

Conrad W. Fisher · (Violent Crimes, Non-Violent Crimes, State Court) · Fisher, Mandell & Newlands · 47 Harvard Street · Worcester, MA 01609-2876 · 508-791-3466

Andrew L. Mandell · Fisher, Mandell & Newlands · 47 Harvard Street · Worcester, MA 01609-2876 · 508-791-3466

Michael M. Monopoli · 94 Highland Street · Worcester, MA 01609 · 508-754-2229

James G. Reardon* · Reardon & Reardon · One Exchange Place · Worcester, MA 01608 · 508-754-1111

ENTERTAINMENT LAW

Bob Woolf · Bob Woolf Associates · 4575 Prudential Tower · Boston, MA 02199 617-437-1212

FAMILY LAW

Jacob M. Atwood* · Atwood & Cherny · Mason House · 211 Commonwealth Avenue · Boston, MA 02116 · 617-262-6400

Ruth R. Budd · Hemenway & Barnes · 60 State Street · Boston, MA 02109-1899 617-227-7940

Barry J. Connelly · Connelly & Norton · 204 Union Wharf · Boston, MA 02109 617-367-0600

James R. DeGiacomo · Roche, Carens & DeGiacomo · One Post Office Square Boston, MA 02109 · 617-451-9300

George M. Ford · Bingham, Dana & Gould · 150 Federal Street · Boston, MA 02110 · 617-951-8000

Weld S. Henshaw · Choate, Hall & Stewart · Exchange Place · 53 State Street · Boston, MA 02109 · 617-227-7566

Monroe L. Inker · White, Inker, Aronson · One Washington Mall · Boston, MA 02108 · 617-367-7700

Norman I. Jacobs* · Esdaile, Barrett & Esdaile · 75 Federal Street · Boston, MA 02110 · 617-482-0333

Paul M. Kane · McGrath & Kane · Four Longfellow Place · Boston, MA 02114-2832 · 617-523-5600

Haskell A. Kassler* · (Divorce, Marital Settlement Agreements, Equitable Division) · Kassler & Feuer · 85 Devonshire Street · Boston, MA 02109 · 617-227-4800

Robert J. Kates* · Widett, Slater & Goldman · 60 State Street · Boston, MA 02109 · 617-227-7200

David H. Lee · Lee & Levine · 399 Boylston Street, Suite 1200 · Boston, MA 02116 · 617-266-6262

Robert F. McGrath · McGrath & Kane · Four Longfellow Place · Boston, MA 02114-2832 · 617-523-5600

W. Hugh M. Morton · Hill & Barlow · One International Place · 100 Oliver Street Boston, MA 02110-2607 · 617-439-3555

John J. Norton* · Connelly & Norton · 343 Commercial Street · 204 Union Wharf Boston, MA 02109 · 617-367-0600

Lawrence T. Perera · Hemenway & Barnes · 60 State Street, Eighth Floor · Boston, MA 02109 · 617-227-7940

Paul P. Perocchi · Brown, Rudnick, Freed & Gesmer · One Financial Center, 18th Floor · Boston, MA 02111 · 617-330-9000

Samuel S. Robinson · Peabody & Arnold · 50 Rowes Wharf · Boston, MA 02110 617-951-2100

Margaret S. Travers* · Taylor, Anderson & Travers · 75 Federal Street · Boston, MA 02110 · 617-654-8200

John P. White, Jr. · White, Inker, Aronson · One Washington Mall · Boston, MA 02108 · 617-367-7700

Ronald A. Witmer · Witmer & Associates · One Joy Street · Boston, MA 02108 617-248-0550

Jason J. Cohen* · Cohen & Gaffin · Court Square Building · 615 Concord Street P.O. Box 886 · Framingham, MA 01701 · 508-872-6565

Paul A. Cataldo* · Bachner, Roche & Cataldo · 55 West Central Street · P.O. Box 267 · Franklin, MA 02038-0267 · 508-528-2400

Efrem A. Gordon · 101 State Street, Room 410 · Springfield, MA 01103 · 413-737-4316

Samuel A. Marsella* · Doherty, Wallace, Pillsbury and Murphy · One Monarch Place, 19th Floor · 1414 Main Street · Springfield, MA 01144-1002 · 413-733-3111

Peter Roth · Bulkley, Richardson and Gelinas · BayBank Tower, Suite 2700 · 1500 Main Street · P.O. Box 15507 · Springfield, MA 01115-5507 · 413-781-2820

Gerald E. Norman · Norman & Ricci · 37 Harvard Street · Worcester, MA 01608 508-752-7548

FIRST AMENDMENT LAW

M. Robert Dushman · Brown, Rudnick, Freed & Gesmer · One Financial Center, 18th Floor · Boston, MA 02111 · 617-330-9000

E. Susan Garsh · Bingham, Dana & Gould · 150 Federal Street · Boston, MA 02110 · 617-951-8000

Joseph D. Steinfield* · Hill & Barlow · One International Place · 100 Oliver Street · Boston, MA 02110-2607 · 617-439-3555

John Taylor Williams · Palmer & Dodge · One Beacon Street · Boston, MA 02108 617-573-0100

HEALTH CARE LAW

Paul W. Allison · Choate, Hall & Stewart · Exchange Place · 53 State Street · Boston, MA 02109 · 617-227-5020

Kenneth A. Behar · Behar & Kalman · Six Beacon Street, Suite 312 · Boston, MA 02108 · 617-227-7660

Harvey W. Freishtat · McDermott, Will & Emery · 75 State Street, Suite 1700 · Boston, MA 02109-1807 · 617-345-5000

Jeffrey L. Heidt · Choate, Hall & Stewart · Exchange Place · 53 State Street · Boston, MA 02109 · 617-227-5020

Nancy R. Rice · Ropes & Gray · One International Place · Boston, MA 02110-2624 617-951-7000

Daniel T. Roble · Ropes & Gray · One International Place · Boston, MA 02110-2624 · 617-951-7000

Regina S. Rockefeller · Hutchins & Wheeler · 101 Federal Street · Boston, MA 02110 · 617-951-6600

David W. Rosenberg · Hill & Barlow · One International Place · 100 Oliver Street Boston, MA 02110-2607 · 617-439-3555

Ronald B. Schram · Ropes & Gray · One International Place · Boston, MA 02110-2624 · 617-951-7000

Richard P. Ward · Ropes & Gray · One International Place · Boston, MA 02110-2624 · 617-951-7000

Stephen M. Weiner · Mintz, Levin, Cohn, Ferris, Glovsky and Popeo · One Financial Center · Boston, MA 02111 · 617-542-6000

IMMIGRATION LAW

Lawrence D. Bastone · Bastone & Associates · 85 Devonshire Street, Seventh Floor · Boston, MA 02109 · 617-227-3535

Francis E. Chin · Watson Law Offices · Two Liberty Square · Boston, MA 02109 617-482-1775

Harvey Kaplan · Kaplan, O'Sullivan & Friedman · 114 State Street, Suite 300 · Boston, MA 02109 · 617-523-3049

Gary A. Pappas · Pappas & Lenzo · 114 Union Wharf · Boston, MA 02109 · 617-742-0080

Roy J. Watson · Watson Law Offices · 85 Devonshire Street · Boston, MA 02109 617-227-0300

Stephen A. Clark · Flynn & Clark · Two Liberty Square · Cambridge, MA 02139 617-354-1550

INTELLECTUAL PROPERTY LAW

Robert A. Cesari · Cesari & McKenna · 30 Rowes Wharf · Boston, MA 02110 · 617-261-6800

David G. Conlin · Dike, Bronstein, Roberts & Cushman · 130 Water Street · Boston, MA 02109 · 617-523-3400

James B. Lampert · Hale and Dorr · 60 State Street · Boston, MA 02109 · 617-742-9100

Gary A. Walpert · Hale and Dorr · 60 State Street · Boston, MA 02109 · 617-742-9100

David Wolf · Wolf, Greenfield & Sacks · 600 Atlantic Avenue · Boston, MA 02109 617-720-3500

LABOR AND EMPLOYMENT LAW

Michael R. Brown · (Management) · Palmer & Dodge · One Beacon Street · Boston, MA 02110 · 617-573-0472

Richard W. Coleman · (Labor) · Segal, Roitman & Coleman · 11 Beacon Street Boston, MA 02108 · 617-742-0208

Glenn E. Dawson · (Management) · 101 Tremont Street · Boston, MA 02108 · 617-338-9828

Allan W. Drachman · (Management) · Deutsch Williams Brooks DeRensis Holland & Drachman · 99 Summer Street · Boston, MA 02110-1235 · 617-951-2300

David B. Ellis · (Management) · Foley, Hoag & Eliot · One Post Office Square, 17th Floor · Boston, MA 02109 · 617-482-1390

Michael A. Feinberg · (Labor) · Feinberg, Charnas & Schwartz · 33 Broad Street, Suite 1100 · Boston, MA 02109 · 617-227-1976

Arthur J. Flamm · (Labor) · Flamm & Birmingham · 50 Congress Street · Boston, MA 02109 · 617-720-3888

Murray S. Freeman · (Management) · Nutter, McClennen & Fish · One International Place, 15th Floor · Boston, MA 02110-2699 · 617-439-2000

Alvin M. Glazerman · (Management) · Edwards & Angell · 101 Federal Street · Boston, MA 02110 · 617-439-4444

Albert L. Goldman · (Labor) · Angoff, Goldman, Manning, Pyle, Wanger & Hiatt 44 School Street · Boston, MA 02108 · 617-723-5500

James T. Grady* · (Labor) · Grady and Dwyer · Two Center Plaza, Suite 430 · Boston, MA 02108 · 617-723-9777

Jonathan P. Hiatt · (Labor) · Angoff, Goldman, Manning, Pyle, Wanger & Hiatt 44 School Street · Boston, MA 02108 · 617-723-5500

Alan Kaplan · (Management) · Morgan, Brown & Joy · One Boston Place, 16th Floor · Boston, MA 02108 · 617-523-6666

Henry M. Kelleher · (Management) · Foley, Hoag & Eliot · One Post Office Square, 17th Floor · Boston, MA 02109 · 617-482-1390

Joan A. Lukey · (Individuals) · Hale and Dorr · 60 State Street · Boston, MA 02109 · 617-742-9100

Robert D. Manning · (Labor) · Angoff, Goldman, Manning, Pyle, Wanger & Hiatt · 44 School Street · Boston, MA 02108 · 617-723-5500

John F. McMahon, Jr.* · (Labor, ERISA Issues) · Angoff, Goldman, Manning, Pyle, Wanger & Hiatt · 44 School Street · Boston, MA 02108 · 617-723-5500

Alan S. Miller · (Management) · Stoneman, Chandler & Miller · 99 High Street Boston, MA 02110 · 617-542-6789

Thomas L. P. O'Donnell · (Management) · Ropes & Gray · One International Place · Boston, MA 02110-2624 · 617-951-7000

Stephen B. Perlman · (Management) · Ropes & Gray · One International Place Boston, MA 02110-2624 · 617-951-7000

Warren H. Pyle · (Labor, Individuals) · Angoff, Goldman, Manning, Pyle, Wanger & Hiatt · 44 School Street · Boston, MA 02108 · 617-723-5500

Nelson G. Ross · (Management) · Ropes & Gray · One International Place · Boston, MA 02110-2624 · 617-951-7000

Mark E. Schreiber* · (Individuals) · Schreiber & McKelway · 11 Beacon Street · Boston, MA 02108 · 617-720-1310

Donald J. Siegel · (Labor) · Segal, Roitman & Coleman · 11 Beacon Street · Boston, MA 02108 · 617-742-0208

Ira Sills · (Labor) · Segal, Roitman & Coleman · 11 Beacon Street · Boston, MA 02108 · 617-742-0208

Jerome H. Somers · (Management) · Goodwin, Procter & Hoar · Exchange Place Boston, MA 02109-2881 · 617-570-1000

E. David Wanger · (Labor) · Angoff, Goldman, Manning, Pyle, Wanger & Hiatt 44 School Street · Boston, MA 02108 · 617-723-5500

Arthur P. Menard · (Management) · 29 Admiral's Way · Chelsea, MA 02150 · 617-889-2200

John D. O'Reilly III · (Management) · O'Reilly & Grosso · 1300A Worcester Road Framingham, MA 01701 · 508-875-1220

Mark G. Kaplan · (Labor) · Kaplan & Lenow · The Chatham Center · 29 Crafts Street · Newton, MA 02108 · 617-630-9300

Alan J. McDonald · (Labor) · McDonald, Noonan & Lamond · One Gateway Center · Newton, MA 02158 · 617-965-8116

Nathan S. Paven · (Labor) · Nathan S. Paven & Associates · 40 Wollaston Avenue P.O. Box 88 · Quincy, MA 02170 · 617-472-0480

Ralph F. Abbott, Jr. · (Management) · Skoler, Abbott & Presser · One Monarch Place, Suite 2000 · Springfield, MA 01144 · 413-737-4753

Richard D. Hayes · Sullivan & Hayes · Baystate West, Suite 1712 · 1500 Main Street · P.O. Box 15668 · Springfield, MA 01115 · 413-736-4538

Jay M. Presser · Skoler, Abbott & Presser · One Monarch Place, Suite 2000 · Springfield, MA 01144 · 413-737-4753

Frederick L. Sullivan · (Management) · Sullivan & Hayes · Baystate West, Suite 1712 · 1500 Main Street · P.O. Box 15668 · Springfield, MA 01115 · 413-736-4538

Michael P. Angelini* · (Management) · Bowditch & Dewey · 311 Main Street · Worcester, MA 01608-1552 · 508-791-3511

Demitrios M. Moschos · Mirick, O'Connell, DeMallie & Lougee · 1700 Mechanics Bank Tower · Worcester Center · Worcester, MA 01608-1477 · 508-799-0541

Duane T. Sargisson · (Management) · Bowditch & Dewey · 311 Main Street · Worcester, MA 01608-1552 · 508-791-3511

James E. Wallace, Jr. · (Management) · Bowditch & Dewey · 311 Main Street · Worcester, MA 01608-1552 · 508-791-3511

Robert Weihrauch* · (Management) · Weihrauch & Coblentz · 19 Norwich Street, Suite 302 · Worcester, MA 01608 · 508-752-7549

NATURAL RESOURCES AND ENVIRONMENTAL LAW

Laurie Burt · Foley, Hoag & Eliot · One Post Office Square, 17th Floor · Boston, MA 02109 · 617-482-1390

Susan M. Cooke · Goodwin, Procter & Hoar · Exchange Place · Boston, MA 02109-2881 · 617-570-1000

Michael P. Last · Gaston & Snow · One Federal Street · Boston, MA 02110-2099 617-426-4600

Gregor I. McGregor · (Plaintiffs) · McGregor, Shea & Doliner · 18 Tremont Street, Suite 900 · Boston, MA 02108 · 617-227-7289

Anton T. Moehrke · Wright & Moehrke · 283 Dartmouth Street · Boston, MA 02116 · 617-266-5700

Mary K. Ryan · Nutter, McClennen & Fish · One International Place, 15th Floor Boston, MA 02110-2699 · 617-439-2000

Jan R. Schlichtmann · (Plaintiffs) · Schlichtmann, Conway, Crowley & Hugo · Four Faneuil Hall Marketplace · Boston, MA 02109 · 617-973-9777

Christopher B. Myhrum · (Hazardous Waste) · Bulkley, Richardson and Gelinas BayBank Tower, Suite 2700 · 1500 Main Street · P.O. Box 15507 · Springfield, MA 01115-5507 · 413-781-2820

PERSONAL INJURY LITIGATION

J. Norman O'Connor, Sr.* · (Plaintiffs, Defendants, Products Liability, Professional Malpractice) · Donovan & O'Connor · One Commercial Place · P.O. Box 230 · Adams, MA 01220-0230 · 413-743-3200

Samuel Adams* · (Defendants, Products Liability) · Warner & Stackpole · 75 State Street · Boston, MA 02109 · 617-951-9000

Charles W. Barrett, Jr. · (Plaintiffs) · Esdaile, Barrett & Esdaile · 75 Federal Street · Boston, MA 02110 · 617-482-0333

Edward J. Barshak · (Defendants) · Sugarman, Rogers, Barshak & Cohen · 33 Union Street · Boston, MA 02108-2406 · 617-227-3030

Leo V. Boyle · (Plaintiffs) · Meehan, Boyle & Cohen · 85 Devonshire Street · Boston, MA 02109 · 617-523-8300

Thomas D. Burns · (Defendants) · Burns & Levinson · 125 Summer Street · Boston, MA 02110 · 617-345-3000

Thomas E. Cargill, Jr. · (Plaintiffs) · Cargill & Associates · One Lewis Wharf · Boston, MA 02110 · 617-227-0400

Cynthia J. Cohen · (Appellate) · Meehan, Boyle & Cohen · 85 Devonshire Street, Fifth Floor · Boston, MA 02109 · 617-523-8300

Earle C. Cooley · Cooley, Manion, Moore & Jones · 21 Custom House Street · Boston, MA 02110 · 617-737-3100

William J. Dailey, Jr. · (Defendants) · Sloane & Walsh · 10 Tremont Street · Boston, MA 02108 · 617-523-6010

James N. Esdaile, Jr. · (Plaintiffs) · Esdaile, Barrett & Esdaile · 75 Federal Street Boston, MA 02110 · 617-482-0333

John J. C. Herlihy* · Herlihy and Associates · 133 Federal Street · Boston, MA 02110 · 617-426-6100

Samuel Hoar* · (Plaintiffs) · Goodwin, Procter & Hoar · Exchange Place · Boston, MA 02109-2881 · 617-570-1000

Raymond J. Kenney, Jr.* · (Defendants, Medical Malpractice, Products Liability, Professional Malpractice, Automobile Collision) · Martin, Magnuson, McCarthy & Kenney · 133 Portland Street · Boston, MA 02114 · 617-227-3240

John E. Lecomte · (Defendants, Insurance Solvency) · Lecomte, Emanuelson, Tick & Doyle · 75 Federal Street · Boston, MA 02110 · 617-695-0100

James F. Meehan* · Meehan, Boyle & Cohen · 85 Devonshire Street, Fifth Floor Boston, MA 02109 · 617-523-8300

Michael E. Mone · (Plaintiffs) · Esdaile, Barrett & Esdaile · 75 Federal Street · Boston, MA 02110 · 617-482-0333

Lionel H. Perlo · (Defendants) · Ficksman & Conley · 28 State Street, Suite 2015 Boston, MA 02109 · 617-720-1515

Charles P. Reidy III* · (Defendants, Medical Malpractice, Products Liability, Professional Malpractice) · Martin, Magnuson, McCarthy & Kenney · 133 Portland Street · Boston, MA 02114 · 617-227-3240

Camille Francis Sarrouf · (Plaintiffs) · Sarrouf, Tarricone & Flemming · 95 Commercial Wharf · Boston, MA 02110 · 617-227-5800

Marshall Simonds · (Defendants) · Goodwin, Procter & Hoar · Exchange Place Boston, MA 02109-2881 · 617-570-1000

Neil Sugarman* · (Plaintiffs, Medical Malpractice, Products Liability, Automobile Collision, Airplane Collision) · Sugarman and Sugarman · 141 Tremont Street, 11th Floor · Boston, MA 02111 · 617-542-1000

Edward M. Swartz · (Plaintiffs) · Swartz & Swartz · 10 Marshall Street · Boston, MA 02108 · 617-742-1900

Albert P. Zabin · (Plaintiffs) · Schneider, Reilly, Zabin & Costello · Three Center Plaza, Suite 430 · Boston, MA 02108 · 617-227-7500

Thomas F. Burke* · (Plaintiffs) · Burke and Smith · 49 Slocum Road · Dartmouth, MA 02747 · 508-993-1743

Charles R. Desmarais · (Defendants) · Law Offices of Charles R. Desmarais · 446 County Street · New Bedford, MA 02740 · 508-999-2341

David A. McLaughlin* · McLaughlin & Folan · 448 County Street · P.O. Box A-2095 · New Bedford, MA 02740 · 508-992-9800

Ronald E. Oliveira · Cain, Hibbard, Myers & Cook · 66 West Street · Pittsfield, MA 01201 · 413-443-4771

James L. Allen* · Ely & King · One Financial Plaza · 1350 Main Street · Springfield, MA 01103 · 413-781-1920

Charles K. Bergin, Jr. · Robinson Donovan Madden & Barry · Valley Bank Tower, Suite 1400 · 1500 Main Street · P.O. Box 15609 · Springfield, MA 01115 413-732-2301

Edward L. Donnellan · (Defendants) · Keyes and Donnellan · Northeast Savings Building · 1243 Main Street · Springfield, MA 01103 · 413-781-6540

Gerard L. Pelligrini · Pelligrini & Seely · 1145 Main Street · P.O. Box 30009 · Springfield, MA 01103 · 413-785-5307

John D. Ross, Jr. · Ross & Ross · 101 State Street, Suite 701-705 · Springfield, MA 01103 · 413-736-2725

William E. Bernstein · (Plaintiffs) · Weinstein, Bernstein & Burwick · 370 Main Street, Suite 1150 · Worcester, MA 01608 · 508-756-4393

John F. Keenan* · (Plaintiffs) · Wolfson, Dodson, Keenan & Cotton · 390 Main Street, Suite 1000 · Worcester, MA 01608-2575 · 508-791-8181

Gerard R. Laurence* · (Defendants) · Milton, Laurence & Dixon · 825 Mechanics Bank Tower · 100 Front Street · Worcester, MA 01608 · 508-791-6386

Philip J. MacCarthy · (Defendants) · MacCarthy Pojani and Hurley · 446 Main Street · Worcester, MA 01608 · 508-798-2480

James G. Reardon* · (Plaintiffs) · Reardon & Reardon · One Exchange Place · Worcester, MA 01608 · 508-754-1111

Berge C. Tashjian* · (Defendants) · Tashjian, Simsarian & Wickstrom · 370 Main Street · Worcester, MA 01608 · 508-756-1578

Seymour Weinstein · (Plaintiffs) · Weinstein, Bernstein & Burwick · 370 Main Street, Suite 1150 · Worcester, MA 01608 · 508-756-4393

John A. Wickstrom · (Defendants) · Tashjian, Simsarian & Wickstrom · 370 Main Street · Worcester, MA 01608 · 508-756-1578

PUBLIC UTILITY LAW

Richard W. Benka · Foley, Hoag & Eliot · One Post Office Square, 17th Floor · Boston, MA 02109 · 617-482-1390

Jon N. Bonsall · Keohane, DeTore & Keegan · 21 Custom House Street · Boston, MA 02110 · 617-951-1400

James K. Brown · Foley, Hoag & Eliot · One Post Office Square, 17th Floor · Boston, MA 02109 · 617-482-1390

Paul K. Connolly, Jr. · LeBoeuf, Lamb, Leiby & MacRae · 260 Franklin Street Boston, MA 02110 · 617-439-9500

Robert S. Cummings · Peabody & Brown · 101 Federal Street · Boston, MA 02110 · 617-345-1000

Robert K. Gad III · Ropes & Gray · One International Place · Boston, MA 02110-2624 · 617-951-7000

Lindsay Johnson · Selgrade & Johnson · One Boston Place, Suite 1210 · Boston, MA 02108 · 617-523-8260

Robert J. Keegan · Keohane, DeTore & Keegan · 21 Custom House Street · Boston, MA 02110 · 617-951-1400

Harold J. Keohane · Keohane, DeTore & Keegan · 21 Custom House Street · Boston, MA 02110 · 617-951-1400

Reginald C. Lindsay · Hill & Barlow · One International Place · 100 Oliver Street Boston, MA 02110-2607 · 617-439-3555

Michael B. Meyer · Meyer, Connolly, Sloman & MacDonald · 12 Post Office Square · Boston, MA 02109 · 617-423-2254

Roscoe Trimmier, Jr. · Ropes & Gray · One International Place · Boston, MA 02110-2624 · 617-951-7000

REAL ESTATE LAW

Stephen Carr Anderson · Rackemann, Sawyer & Brewster · One Financial Center · Boston, MA 02111-2659 · 617-542-2300

John F. Bok · Gaston & Snow · One Federal Street · Boston, MA 02110-2099 · 617-426-4600

Howard E. Cohen · Mintz, Levin, Cohn, Ferris, Glovsky and Popeo · One Financial Center · Boston, MA 02111 · 617-542-6000

A. Jeffrey Dando · Goodwin, Procter & Hoar · Exchange Place · Boston, MA 02109-2881 · 617-570-1000

Robert C. Davis · Goulston & Storrs · 400 Atlantic Avenue · Boston, MA 02110-3333 · 617-482-1776

Steven S. Fischman · Goulston & Storrs · 400 Atlantic Avenue · Boston, MA 02110-3333 · 617-482-1776

Peter D. Gens · Brown, Rudnick, Freed & Gesmer · One Financial Center, 18th Floor · Boston, MA 02111 · 617-330-9000

Joseph W. Haley · Goodwin, Procter & Hoar · Exchange Place · Boston, MA 02109-2881 · 617-570-1000

John D. Hamilton, Jr. · (Zoning, Land Use, Commercial Transactions, Industrial Transactions) · Hale and Dorr · 60 State Street · Boston, MA 02109 · 617-742-9100

Thomas Kaplan · Goulston & Storrs · 400 Atlantic Avenue · Boston, MA 02110-3333 · 617-482-1776

Jordon P. Krasnow · Goulston & Storrs · 400 Atlantic Avenue · Boston, MA 02110-3333 · 617-482-1776

Stephen P. Lindsay · Ropes & Gray · One International Place · Boston, MA 02110-2624 · 617-951-7000

Vincent P. McCarthy · (Land Use, Commercial Transactions, Industrial Transactions) · Hale and Dorr · 60 State Street · Boston, MA 02109 · 617-742-9100

Phillip J. Nexon · Goulston & Storrs · 400 Atlantic Avenue · Boston, MA 02110-3333 · 617-482-1776

John A. Pike · Ropes & Gray · One International Place · Boston, MA 02110-2624 617-951-7000

David P. Ries · Goodwin, Procter & Hoar · Exchange Place · Boston, MA 02109-2881 · 617-570-1000

Alan W. Rottenberg · Goulston & Storrs · 400 Atlantic Avenue · Boston, MA 02110-3333 · 617-482-1776

Philip D. Stevenson · Hale and Dorr · 60 State Street · Boston, MA 02109 · 617-742-9100

Elliot M. Surkin · Hill & Barlow · One International Place · 100 Oliver Street · Boston, MA 02110-2607 · 617-439-3555

Robert Tuchmann · Hale and Dorr · 60 State Street · Boston, MA 02109 · 617-742-9100

Peter Van · Mintz, Levin, Cohn, Ferris, Glovsky and Popeo · One Financial Center · Boston, MA 02111 · 617-542-6000

Herbert W. Vaughan · Hale and Dorr · 60 State Street · Boston, MA 02109 · 617-742-9100

A. Craig Brown · Doherty, Wallace, Pillsbury and Murphy · One Monarch Place, 19th Floor · 1414 Main Street · Springfield, MA 01144-1002 · 413-733-3111

Michael S. Ratner · Bacon, Wilson, Ratner, Cohen, Salvage, Fialky & Fitzgerald 95 State Street, Suite 1100 · Springfield, MA 01103 · 413-781-0560

Stephen A. Shatz · Shatz, Schwartz and Fentin · 1441 Main Street, Suite 1100 · Springfield, MA 01103 · 413-737-1131

Austin W. Keane · (Zoning, Land Use, Commercial Transactions, Industrial Transactions) · Bowditch & Dewey · 311 Main Street · Worcester, MA 01608-1552 508-791-3511

TAX AND EMPLOYEE BENEFITS LAW

David R. Andelman · Lourie & Cutler · 60 State Street · Boston, MA 02109 · 617-742-6720

Thomas W. Anninger · (Employee Benefits) · William M. Mercer · 200 Clarendon Street · Boston, MA 02116 · 617-421-5338

Fred R. Becker · Ropes & Gray · One International Place · Boston, MA 02110-2624 · 617-951-7000

David J. Blattner, Jr. · Ropes & Gray · One International Place · Boston, MA 02110-2624 · 617-951-7000

John S. Brown · Bingham, Dana & Gould · 150 Federal Street · Boston, MA 02110 · 617-951-8000

Kingsbury Browne, Jr. · Hill & Barlow · One International Place · 100 Oliver Street · Boston, MA 02110-2607 · 617-439-3555

John J. Cleary · (Employee Benefits) · Goodwin, Procter & Hoar · Exchange Place · Boston, MA 02109-2881 · 617-570-1000

Frederic G. Corneel · Sullivan & Worcester · One Post Office Square · Boston, MA 02109 · 617-338-2800

Howard A. Cubell · Goodwin, Procter & Hoar · Exchange Place · Boston, MA 02109-2881 · 617-570-1000

Michael M. Davis · Sullivan & Worcester · One Post Office Square · Boston, MA 02109 · 617-338-2800

David M. Donaldson · Ropes & Gray · One International Place · Boston, MA 02110-2624 · 617-951-7000

M. Gordon Ehrlich · Bingham, Dana & Gould · 150 Federal Street · Boston, MA 02110 · 617-951-8000

Marion R. Fremont-Smith · Choate, Hall & Stewart · Exchange Place · 53 State Street · Boston, MA 02109 · 617-227-5020

Russell A. Gaudreau, Jr. · (Employee Benefits) · Ropes & Gray · One International Place · Boston, MA 02110-2624 · 617-951-7000

Richard W. Giuliani · Hale and Dorr · 60 State Street · Boston, MA 02109 · 617-742-9100

Edward L. Glazer · Goodwin, Procter & Hoar · Exchange Place · Boston, MA 02109-2881 · 617-570-1170

Ronald L. Groves · (Municipal Obligations, Employee Stock Ownership Plans, Executive Compensation) · Ropes & Gray · One International Place · Boston, MA 02110-2624 · 617-951-7000

Richard M. Harter · (Employee Benefits) · Bingham, Dana & Gould · 150 Federal Street · Boston, MA 02110 · 617-951-8000

Frederick D. Herberich · Gaston & Snow · One Federal Street · Boston, MA 02110-2099 · 617-426-4600

Jerome S. Hertz · Mintz, Levin, Cohn, Ferris, Glovsky and Popeo · One Financial Center · Boston, MA 02111 · 617-542-6000

Edward F. Hines, Jr. · (State Tax, Tax Disputes) · Choate, Hall & Stewart · Exchange Place · 53 State Street · Boston, MA 02109 · 617-227-5020

James R. Hopkins · Perkins, Smith & Cohen · One Federal Street · Boston, MA 02110 · 617-426-8900

Daniel D. Levenson · Lourie & Cutler · 60 State Street · Boston, MA 02109 · 617-742-6720

Paul R. McDaniel · (Corporate & Partnership Transactions, International Taxation) · Hill & Barlow · One International Place · 100 Oliver Street · Boston, MA 02110-2607 · 617-439-3555

Robert J. McGee · Palmer & Dodge · One Beacon Street · Boston, MA 02108 · 617-573-0100

Michael E. Mooney · Nutter, McClennen & Fish · One International Place · Boston, MA 02210-2699 · 617-439-2000

David L. Raish · (Employee Benefits) · Ropes & Gray · One International Place Boston, MA 02110-2624 · 617-951-7000

Leonard Schneidman · Foley, Hoag & Eliot · One Post Office Square, 17th Floor Boston, MA 02109 · 617-482-1390

Stephen E. Shay · (International Tax Law) · Ropes & Gray · One International Place · Boston, MA 02110-2624 · 617-951-7000

Walter G. Van Dorn · Powers & Hall · 100 Franklin Street · Boston, MA 02110 617-728-9600

Paul S. Doherty · Doherty, Wallace, Pillsbury and Murphy · One Monarch Place, 19th Floor · 1414 Main Street · Springfield, MA 01144-1002 · 413-733-3111

Richard M. Gaberman · Gaberman & Parish · 32 Hampden Street · Springfield, MA 01103 · 413-781-5066

Robert E. Murphy · Doherty, Wallace, Pillsbury and Murphy · One Monarch Place, 19th Floor · 1414 Main Street · Springfield, MA 01144-1002 · 413-733-3111

Ronda G. Parish · (Employee Benefits) · Gaberman & Parish · 32 Hampden Street · Springfield, MA 01103 · 413-781-5066

Stuart A. Hammer · Fletcher, Tilton & Whipple · 370 Main Street · Worcester, MA 01608 · 508-798-8621

Raymond T. Mahon · Bowditch & Dewey · 311 Main Street · Worcester, MA 01608-1552 · 508-791-3511

Andrew B. O'Donnell · Mirick, O'Connell, DeMallie & Lougee · 1700 Mechanics Bank Tower · Worcester Center · Worcester, MA 01608-1477 · 508-799-0541

TRUSTS AND ESTATES

Thomas H. Belknap · Hill & Barlow · One International Place · 100 Oliver Street Boston, MA 02110-2607 · 617-439-3555

W. Lincoln Boyden · Ropes & Gray · One International Place · Boston, MA 02110-2624 · 617-951-7000

Virginia F. Coleman · Ropes & Gray · One International Place · Boston, MA 02110-2624 · 617-951-7000

Marion R. Fremont-Smith · (Estate Planning, Estate Administration, Charitable Trusts) · Choate, Hall & Stewart · Exchange Place · 52 State Street · Boston, MA 02109 · 617-227-5020

Alfred W. Fuller · Ropes & Gray · One International Place · Boston, MA 02110-2624 · 617-951-7000

Louis H. Hamel, Jr. · Hale and Dorr · 60 State Street · Boston, MA 02109 · 617-742-9100

William F. Kehoe · Gaston & Snow · One Federal Street · Boston, MA 02110-2099 · 617-426-4600

George H. Kidder · Hemenway & Barnes · 60 State Street · Boston, MA 02109 617-227-7940

William J. Pechilis · Goodwin, Procter & Hoar · Exchange Place · Boston, MA 02109-2881 · 617-570-1000

Lawrence T. Perera* · (Estate Planning, Estate Administration) · Hemenway & Barnes · 60 State Street · Boston, MA 02109 · 617-227-7940

Robert C. Pomeroy · Goodwin, Procter & Hoar · Exchange Place · Boston, MA 02109-2881 · 617-570-1150

Hanson S. Reynolds* · Foley, Hoag & Eliot · One Post Office Square, 17th Floor Boston, MA 02109 · 617-482-1390

George T. Shaw · Hemenway & Barnes · 60 State Street · Boston, MA 02109 · 617-227-7940

Nicholas U. Sommerfeld · Gaston & Snow · One Federal Street · Boston, MA 02110-2099 · 617-426-4600

Augustus W. Soule, Jr. · (Estate Planning, Estate Administration) · Sullivan & Worcester · One Post Office Square · Boston, MA 02109 · 617-338-2800

Jonathan Strong · Hill & Barlow · One International Place · 100 Oliver Street · Boston, MA 02110-2607 · 617-439-3555

Philip H. Suter · Sullivan & Worcester · One Post Office Square · Boston, MA 02109 · 617-338-2800

James G. Wheeler · Hutchins & Wheeler · 101 Federal Street · Boston, MA 02110 617-951-6600

Raymond H. Young · Young & Bayle · 60 State Street · Boston, MA 02109 · 617-227-9490

Christopher T. Carlson · Gilmore, Rees & Carlson · 1000 Franklin Village Drive Franklin, MA 02038 · 508-520-2200

Paul S. Doherty · Doherty, Wallace, Pillsbury and Murphy · One Monarch Place, 19th Floor · 1414 Main Street · Springfield, MA 01144-1002 · 413-733-3111

Richard M. Gaberman · Garberman & Parish · 32 Hampden Street · Springfield, MA 01103 · 413-781-5066

Robert E. Murphy · Doherty, Wallace, Pillsbury and Murphy · One Monarch Place, 19th Floor · 1414 Main Street · Springfield, MA 01144-1002 · 413-733-3111

Jeffrey W. Roberts · Robinson Donovan Madden & Barry · Valley Bank Tower, Suite 1400 · 1500 Main Street · P.O. Box 15609 · Springfield, MA 01115 · 413-732-2301

Gordon H. Wentworth · Robinson Donovan Madden & Barry · Valley Bank Tower, Suite 1400 · 1500 Main Street · P.O. Box 15609 · Springfield, MA 01115 413-732-2301

Richard W. Dearborn · Mountain, Dearborn & Whiting · 370 Main Street, Seventh Floor · Worcester, MA 01608 · 508-756-2423

Thomas R. Mountain · Mountain, Dearborn & Whiting · 370 Main Street, Seventh Floor · Worcester, MA 01608 · 508-756-2423

Sumner B. Tilton, Jr. · Fletcher, Tilton & Whipple · 370 Main Street · Worcester, MA 01608 · 508-798-8621

MICHIGAN

BANKRUPTCY LAW

I. William Cohen · Pepper, Hamilton & Scheetz · 100 Renaissance Center, Suite 3600 · Detroit, MI 48243-1157 · 313-259-7110

Jonathan S. Green · Jaffe, Snider, Raitt & Heuer · One Woodward Avenue, Suite 2400 · Detroit, MI 48226 · 313-961-8380

Stuart E. Hertzberg · Pepper, Hamilton & Scheetz · 100 Renaissance Center, Suite 3600 · Detroit, MI 48243-1157 · 313-259-7110

Dennis S. Kayes · Pepper, Hamilton & Scheetz · 100 Renaissance Center, Suite 3600 · Detroit, MI 48243-1157 · 313-259-7110

Louis P. Rochkind · Jaffe, Snider, Raitt & Heuer · One Woodward Avenue, Suite 2400 · Detroit, MI 48226 · 313-961-8380

Barbara Rom · Pepper, Hamilton & Scheetz · 100 Renaissance Center, Suite 3600 · Detroit, MI 48243-1157 · 313-259-7110

Ronald L. Rose* · Dykema Gossett · 400 Renaissance Center, 35th Floor · Detroit, MI 48243 · 313-568-6800

Lawrence K. Snider · Jaffe, Snider, Raitt & Heuer · One Woodward Avenue, Suite 2400 · Detroit, MI 48226 · 313-961-8380

Sheldon S. Toll · Honigman Miller Schwartz and Cohn · 2290 First National Building · Detroit, MI 48226-3583 · 313-256-7800

Timothy J. Curtin · Varnum, Riddering, Schmidt & Howlett · 171 Monroe Avenue, NW, Suite 800 · Grand Rapids, MI 49503 · 616-459-4186

James A. Engbers · Miller, Johnson, Snell & Cummiskey · 800 Calder Plaza Building · Grand Rapids, MI 49503 · 616-459-8311

James B. Frakie · Day, Sawdey & Flaggert · Old Kent Center · 200 Monroe Avenue, Suite 300 · Grand Rapids, MI 49503 · 616-774-8121

Jeffrey R. Hughes · (Creditors' Rights, Bankruptcy Litigation) · Varnum, Riddering, Schmidt & Howlett · 171 Monroe Avenue, NW, Suite 800 · Grand Rapids, MI 49503 · 616-459-4186

Patrick E. Mears · Warner, Norcross & Judd · 900 Old Kent Building · 111 Lyon Street, NW · Grand Rapids, MI 49503-2489 · 616-459-6121

Robert W. Sawdey · Day, Sawdey & Flaggert · Old Kent Center · 200 Monroe Avenue, Suite 300 · Grand Rapids, MI 49503 · 616-774-8121

Wallace M. Handler · Snyder and Handler · 1365 American Center · 27777 Frank Road · Southfield, MI 48034 · 313-352-1900

Thomas W. Schouten · Dunn, Schouten & Snoap · 2745 DeHoop Avenue, SW · Wyoming, MI 49509 · 616-538-6380

BUSINESS LITIGATION

Richard G. Smith* · Smith & Brooker · 703 Washington Avenue · P.O. Box X-921 Bay City, MI 48707-0921 · 517-892-2595

Lawrence G. Campbell · Dickinson, Wright, Moon, Van Dusen & Freeman · 800 First National Building · P.O. Box 509 · Detroit, MI 48226-3555 · 313-223-3500

Laurence D. Connor* · Dykema Gossett · 400 Renaissance Center, 35th Floor · Detroit, MI 48243 · 313-568-6800

Robert G. Cutler · Dykema Gossett · 400 Renaissance Center, 35th Floor · Detroit, MI 48243 · 313-568-6800

Eugene Driker · Barris, Sott, Denn & Driker · 211 West Fort Street, 15th Floor Detroit, MI 48226-3281 · 313-965-9725

Robert A. Fineman · Honigman Miller Schwartz and Cohn · 2290 First National Building · Detroit, MI 48226-3583 · 313-256-7800

Norman Hyman* · Honigman Miller Schwartz and Cohn · 2290 First National Building · Detroit, MI 48226-3583 · 313-256-7800

Philip J. Kessler* · (Antitrust, Commercial, Finance, Securities) · Butzel Long · 150 West Jefferson, Suite 900 · Detroit, MI 48226-4430 · 313-225-7000

Richard J. McClear* · (Commercial) · Dykema Gossett · 400 Renaissance Center, 35th Floor · Detroit, MI 48243 · 313-568-6800

Kenneth J. McIntyre* · Dickinson, Wright, Moon, Van Dusen & Freeman · 800 First National Building · P.O. Box 509 · Detroit, MI 48226-3555 · 313-223-3500

Richard E. Rassel · Butzel Long · 150 West Jefferson, Suite 900 · Detroit, MI 48226-4430 · 313-225-7000

James K. Robinson · Honigman Miller Schwartz and Cohn · 2290 First National Building · Detroit, MI 48226-3583 · 313-256-7800

William A. Sankbeil* · (Antitrust, Commercial) · Kerr, Russell and Weber · Comerica Building, Suite 2100 · Detroit, MI 48226-3271 · 313-961-0200

William M. Saxton* · Butzel Long · 150 West Jefferson, Suite 900 · Detroit, MI 48226-4430 · 313-225-7000

Theodore Souris* · Bodman, Longley & Dahling · 100 Renaissance Center, 34th Floor · Detroit, MI 48243 · 313-259-7777

Carl H. von Ende* · (Banking, Commercial, Securities) · Miller, Canfield, Paddock and Stone · 150 West Jefferson, Suite 2500 · Detroit, MI 48226 · 313-963-6420

W. Gerald Warren* · Dickinson, Wright, Moon, Van Dusen & Freeman · 800 First National Building · P.O. Box 509 · Detroit, MI 48226-3555 · 313-223-3500

Sharon M. Woods · Barris, Sott, Denn & Driker · 211 West Fort Street, 15th Floor · Detroit, MI 48226-3281 · 313-965-9725

Donald S. Young* · Dykema Gossett · 400 Renaissance Center, 35th Floor · Detroit, MI 48243 · 313-568-6800

Richard B. Baxter* · (Commercial) · Dykema Gossett · 200 Oldtown Riverfront Building · 248 Louis Campau Promenade, NW · Grand Rapids, MI 49503-0321 · 616-776-7500

Grant J. Gruel* · Gruel, Mills, Nims and Pylman · 50 Monroe Place, Suite 700 West · Grand Rapids, MI 49503 · 616-235-5500

William K. Holmes* · Warner, Norcross & Judd · 900 Old Kent Building · 111 Lyon Street, NW · Grand Rapids, MI 49503-2489 · 616-459-6121

Jon G. March · Miller, Johnson, Snell & Cummiskey · 800 Calder Plaza Building Grand Rapids, MI 49503 · 616-459-8311

L. Roland Roegge* · Smith, Haughey, Rice & Roegge · 200 Calder Plaza Building · 250 Monroe Avenue, NW · Grand Rapids, MI 49503-2251 · 616-774-8000

Michael E. Cavanaugh* · (Administrative, Commercial) · Fraser Trebilcock Davis & Foster · 1000 Michigan National Tower · Lansing, MI 48933 · 517-482-5800

John L. Collins* · Foster, Swift, Collins & Smith · 313 South Washington Square Lansing, MI 48933-2193 · 517-372-8050

Webb A. Smith* · Foster, Swift, Collins & Smith · 313 South Washington Square Lansing, MI 48933-2193 · 517-372-8050

Theodore W. Swift* · (Administrative, Commercial) · Foster, Swift, Collins & Smith · 313 South Washington Square · Lansing, MI 48933-2193 · 517-372-8050

Irwin M. Alterman · Kemp, Klein, Umphrey & Endelman · Columbia Center, Suite 600 · 201 West Big Beaver · Troy, MI 48084 · 313-528-1111

CORPORATE LAW

Chris L. McKenney · Conlin, McKenney & Philbrick · 700 City Center Building Ann Arbor, MI 48104-1994 · 313-761-9000

Bruce D. Birgbauer · (International, Leveraged Buyouts, Mergers & Acquisitions) · Miller, Canfield, Paddock and Stone · 150 West Jefferson, Suite 2500 · Detroit, MI 48226 · 313-963-6420

Fred W. Freeman · Dickinson, Wright, Moon, Van Dusen & Freeman · 800 First National Building · P.O. Box 509 · Detroit, MI 48226-3555 · 313-223-3500

Richard B. Gushee · Miller, Canfield, Paddock and Stone · 150 West Jefferson, Suite 2500 · Detroit, MI 48226 · 313-963-6420

Verne C. Hampton II · Dickinson, Wright, Moon, Van Dusen & Freeman · 800 First National Building · P.O. Box 509 · Detroit, MI 48226-3555 · 313-223-3500

Edward C. Hanpeter · Dykema Gossett · 400 Renaissance Center, 35th Floor · Detroit, MI 48243 · 313-568-6800

Ira J. Jaffe · Jaffe, Snider, Raitt & Heuer · One Woodward Avenue, Suite 2400 · Detroit, MI 48226 · 313-961-8380

Patrick J. Ledwidge · (Banking) · Dickinson, Wright, Moon, Van Dusen & Freeman · 800 First National Building · P.O. Box 509 · Detroit, MI 48226-3555 313-223-3500

Cyril Moscow · Honigman Miller Schwartz and Cohn · 2290 First National Building · Detroit, MI 48226-3583 · 313-256-7800

Martin C. Oetting · Hill Lewis · 100 Renaissance Center, 32nd Floor · Detroit, MI 48243 · 313-259-3232

George E. Parker III · (Banking, Financial Institutions) · Miller, Canfield, Paddock and Stone · 150 West Jefferson, Suite 2500 · Detroit, MI 48226 · 313-963-6420

Richard D. Rohr · Bodman, Longley & Dahling · 100 Renaissance Center, 34th Floor · Detroit, MI 48243 · 313-259-7777

Alan E. Schwartz · Honigman Miller Schwartz and Cohn · 2290 First National Building · Detroit, MI 48226-3583 · 313-256-7800

Brian Sullivan · Dykema Gossett · 400 Renaissance Center, 35th Floor · Detroit, MI 48243 · 313-568-6800

Richard C. Van Dusen · Dickinson, Wright, Moon, Van Dusen & Freeman · 800 First National Building · P.O. Box 509 · Detroit, MI 48226-3555 · 313-223-3500

Frank K. Zinn · Dykema Gossett · 400 Renaissance Center, 35th Floor · Detroit, MI 48243 · 313-568-6800

Conrad A. Bradshaw · Warner, Norcross & Judd · 900 Old Kent Building · 111 Lyon Street, NW · Grand Rapids, MI 49503-2489 · 616-459-6121

James H. Breay · (Banking) · Warner, Norcross & Judd · 900 Old Kent Building 111 Lyon Street, NW · Grand Rapids, MI 49503-2489 · 616-459-6121

R. Malcolm Cumming · Warner, Norcross & Judd · 900 Old Kent Building · 111 Lyon Street, NW · Grand Rapids, MI 49503-2489 · 616-459-6121

James N. DeBoer, Jr. · Varnum, Riddering, Schmidt & Howlett · 171 Monroe Avenue, NW, Suite 800 · Grand Rapids, MI 49503 · 616-459-4186

Paul K. Gaston · Warner, Norcross & Judd · 900 Old Kent Building · 111 Lyon Street, NW · Grand Rapids, MI 49503-2489 · 616-459-6121

David M. Hecht · Dickinson, Wright, Moon, Van Dusen & Freeman · 300 Ottawa Avenue, NW, Suite 650 · Grand Rapids, MI 49503 · 616-458-1300

Donald L. Johnson · Varnum, Riddering, Schmidt & Howlett · 171 Monroe Avenue, NW, Suite 800 · Grand Rapids, MI 49503 · 616-459-4186

Hugh H. Makens · Warner, Norcross & Judd · 900 Old Kent Building · 111 Lyon Street, NW · Grand Rapids, MI 49503-2489 · 616-459-6121

Charles E. McCallum · (Corporate Finance, International, Mergers & Acquisitions, Securities Regulation) · Warner, Norcross & Judd · 900 Old Kent Building 111 Lyon Street, NW · Grand Rapids, MI 49503-2489 · 616-459-6121

Daniel C. Molhoek · Varnum, Riddering, Schmidt & Howlett · 171 Monroe Avenue, NW, Suite 800 · Grand Rapids, MI 49503 · 616-459-4186

John R. Nichols · (Corporate Finance, Leveraged Buyouts, Mergers & Acquisitions) · Law, Weathers & Richardson · 200 Ottawa Avenue, NW, Suite 500 · Grand Rapids, MI 49503 · 616-459-1171

Gordon J. Quist* · (Commercial) · Miller, Johnson, Snell & Cummiskey · 800 Calder Plaza Building · Grand Rapids, MI 49503 · 616-459-8311

David W. McKeague · (Banking, Financial Institutions) · Foster, Swift, Collins & Smith · 313 South Washington Square · Lansing, MI 48933-2193 · 517-372-8050

Ronald R. Pentecost* · (Banking, Financial Institutions, Mergers & Acquisitions, Securities) · Fraser Trebilcock Davis & Foster · 1000 Michigan National Tower · Lansing, MI 48933 · 517-482-5800

Peter S. Sheldon · Dickinson, Wright, Moon, Van Dusen & Freeman · 215 South Washington Square, Suite 200 · Lansing, MI 48933 · 517-371-1730

John J. Slavin · Freud, Markus, Slavin & Galgan · 100 East Big Beaver Road, Suite 900 · Troy, MI 48083 · 313-528-3223

CRIMINAL DEFENSE

Robert S. Harrison · Robert S. Harrison & Associates · 6735 Telegraph Road, Suite 350 · Birmingham, MI 48010 · 313-540-5900

David F. DuMouchel · DuMouchel Law Office · 150 West Jefferson, Suite 900 · Detroit, MI 48226-4430 · 313-962-0100

Neil H. Fink* · (Federal Court, State Court) · Evans & Luptak · 2500 Buhl Building · Detroit, MI 48226 · 313-963-9625

James K. Robinson · Honigman Miller Schwartz and Cohn · 2290 First National Building · Detroit, MI 48226-3583 · 313-256-7800

Leo A. Farhat · Farhat, Story & Kraus · 4572 South Hagadorn Road · East Lansing, MI 48823 · 517-351-3700

FAMILY LAW

Henry Baskin · Baskin & Feldstein · 30200 Telegraph Road, Suite 444 · Birmingham, MI 48010 · 313-642-5500

Robert Z. Feldstein · Baskin & Feldstein · 30200 Telegraph Road, Suite 444 · Birmingham, MI 48010-3079 · 313-646-3300

Hanley M. Gurwin* · (Divorce, Marital Settlement Agreements, Mediation & Arbitration) · Hill Lewis · 255 South Woodward Avenue, Suite 301 · Birmingham, MI 48009 · 313-642-9692

Norman N. Robbins* · (Child Custody, Divorce, Marital Settlement Agreements, Mediation of Marital Disputes) · 30400 Telegraph Road · Birmingham, MI 48010 · 313-647-5530

John F. Schaefer · Williams, Schaefer, Ruby & Williams · 380 North Woodward Avenue, Suite 300 · Birmingham, MI 48009 · 313-642-0333

Frederick G. Buesser, Jr.* · Buesser, Buesser, Blank, Lynch, Fryhoff & Graham 4190 Telegraph Road, Suite 2000 · Bloomfield Hills, MI 48302-3426 · 313-642-7880

Frederick G. Buesser III · (Child Custody, Divorce, Marital Settlement Agreements, Equitable Division) · Buesser, Buesser, Blank, Lynch, Fryhoff & Graham 4190 Telegraph Road, Suite 2000 · Bloomfield Hills, MI 48302-3426 · 313-642-7880

Carole L. Chiamp* · (Divorce) · Chiamp & Associates · 3610 Cadillac Tower · Detroit, MI 48226 · 313-961-5660

Kenneth E. Prather · Prather and Foley · 3800 Penobscot Building · Detroit, MI 48226-4220 · 313-962-7722

Jeptha W. Schureman · Schureman, Frakes, Glass & Wulfmeier · 440 East Congress, Fourth Floor · Detroit, MI 48226 · 313-961-1500

Bruce A. Barnhart · Varnum, Riddering, Schmidt & Howlett · 171 Monroe Avenue, NW, Suite 800 · Grand Rapids, MI 49503 · 616-459-4186

James W. Zerrenner · 72 Ransom, NE · Grand Rapids, MI 49503 · 616-774-4414

Robert J. Barnard, Jr. · Barnard, Smith & Burness · 249 Cooley Street · Kalamazoo, MI 49007 · 616-349-3700

FIRST AMENDMENT LAW

Gregory L. Curtner · Miller, Canfield, Paddock and Stone · 150 West Jefferson, Suite 2500 · Detroit, MI 48226 · 313-963-6420

Herschel P. Fink · Honigman Miller Schwartz and Cohn · 2290 First National Building · Detroit, MI 48226-3583 · 313-256-7546

Richard E. Rassel · Butzel Long · 150 West Jefferson, Suite 900 · Detroit, MI 48226-4430 · 313-225-7000

John J. Ronayne III · Kasiborski, Ronayne & Flaska · 3066 Penobscot Building Detroit, MI 48226 · 313-961-1900

James E. Stewart · Butzel Long · 150 West Jefferson Street, Suite 900 · Detroit, MI 48226 · 313-225-7022

J. A. Cragwall, Jr. · Warner, Norcross & Judd · 900 Old Kent Building · 111 Lyon Street, NW · Grand Rapids, MI 49503-2489 · 616-459-6121

Michael E. Cavanaugh* · Fraser Trebilcock Davis & Foster · 1000 Michigan National Tower · Lansing, MI 48933 · 517-482-5800

HEALTH CARE LAW

John B. DeVine · Miller, Canfield, Paddock and Stone · 101 North Main Street, Seventh Floor · Ann Arbor, MI 48104-1400 · 313-663-2445

Bettye S. Elkins · Dykema Gossett · 315 East Eisenhower Parkway, Suite 100 · Ann Arbor, MI 48108 · 313-747-7673

J. Kay Felt · Dykema Gossett · 400 Renaissance Center, 35th Floor · Detroit, MI 48243 · 313-568-6800

Timothy M. Guerriero · Brady Hathaway · 1100 Penobscot Building · Detroit, MI 48226-4012 · 313-965-3700

William O. Hochkammer · Honigman Miller Schwartz and Cohn · 2290 First National Building · Detroit, MI 48226-3583 · 313-256-7661

Charles R. Kinnaird · Dickinson, Wright, Moon, Van Dusen & Freeman · 800 First National Building · P.O. Box 509 · Detroit, MI 48226-3555 · 313-223-3500

Seth M. Lloyd · Dykema Gossett · 400 Renaissance Center, 35th Floor · Detroit, MI 48243 · 313-568-6800

Stuart M. Lockman · Honigman Miller Schwartz and Cohn · 2290 First National Building · Detroit, MI 48226-3583 · 313-256-7800

Chris E. Rossman · Honigman Miller Schwartz and Cohn · 2290 First National Building · Detroit, MI 48226-3583 · 313-256-7800

Margaret Shannon · Honigman Miller Schwartz and Cohn · 2290 First National Building · Detroit, MI 48226-3583 · 313-256-7800

John N. Logie · Warner, Norcross & Judd · 900 Old Kent Building · 111 Lyon Street, NW · Grand Rapids, MI 49503-2489 · 616-459-6121

IMMIGRATION LAW

William H. Dance · 3685 Penobscot Building · Detroit, MI 48226 · 313-963-3412

John E. English · English & van Horne · 4472 Penobscot Building · Detroit, MI 48226 · 313-961-5100

LABOR AND EMPLOYMENT LAW

Philip Green · (Individuals) · Green & Green · 475 Market Place, Suite D · Ann Arbor, MI 48108 · 313-665-4036

J. Douglas Korney* · (Labor) · Korney & Heldt · 30700 Telegraph Road, Suite 1551 · Birmingham, MI 48010 · 313-646-1050

Charles E. Keller · (Management) · Keller, Thoma, Schwarze, Schwarze, DuBay & Katz · 100 West Long Lake Road, Suite 122 · Bloomfield Hills, MI 48304 · 313-647-3114

Brian S. Ahearn* · (Management) · Stringari, Fritz, Kreger, Ahearn, Hunsinger, Bennett & Crandall · 650 First National Building · Detroit, MI 48226 · 313-961-6474

Robert J. Battista · (Management) · Butzel Long · 150 West Jefferson, Suite 900 Detroit, MI 48226-4430 · 313-225-7000

Kathleen L. Bogas* · (Individuals) · Sachs, Nunn, Kates, Kadushin, O'Hare, Helveston & Waldman · 1000 Farmer Street · Detroit, MI 48226 · 313-965-3464

John F. Brady · (Management) · Brady Hathaway · 1100 Penobscot Building · Detroit, MI 48226-4012 · 313-965-3700

Richard J. Fritz · (Management) · Stringari, Fritz, Kreger, Ahearn, Hunsinger, Bennett & Crandall · 650 First National Building · Detroit, MI 48226 · 313-961-6474

Deborah L. Gordon* · (Individuals) · Stark & Gordon · 1600 Ford Building · Detroit, MI 48226 · 313-962-3784

Gordon A. Gregory · (Labor) · Gregory, Van Lopik, Moore & Jeakle · 3727 Cadillac Tower · Detroit, MI 48226 · 313-964-5600

Ronald R. Helveston · (Labor) · Sachs, Nunn, Kates, Kadushin, O'Hare, Helveston & Waldman · 1000 Farmer Street · Detroit, MI 48226 · 313-965-3464

Dennis D. James · (Individuals) · Lopapin, Miller, Freedman, Bluestone, Erlich, Rosen & Bartnick · 1301 East Jefferson Street · Detroit, MI 48207-3197 · 313-259-7800

Thomas G. Kienbaum* · (Management) · Dickinson, Wright, Moon, Van Dusen & Freeman · 800 First National Building · P.O. Box 509 · Detroit, MI 48226-3555 313-223-3500

Conrad W. Kreger · Stringari, Fritz, Kreger, Ahearn, Hunsinger, Bennett & Crandall · 650 First National Building · Detroit, MI 48226 · 313-961-6474

John Corbett O'Meara* · (Management) · Dickinson, Wright, Moon, Van Dusen & Freeman · 800 First National Building · P.O. Box 509 · Detroit, MI 48226-3555 313-223-3500

Michael L. Pitt* · (Labor, Individuals) · Kelman, Loria, Downing, Schneider & Simpson · 2300 First National Building · 660 Woodward Avenue · Detroit, MI 48226-3521 · 313-961-7363

Ronald J. Reosti · (Individuals) · Reosti & Hayes · 925 Ford Building · Detroit, MI 48226 · 313-962-2770

John R. Runyan, Jr. · (Individuals) · Sachs, Nunn, Kates, Kadushin, O'Hare, Helveston & Waldman · 1000 Farmer Street · Detroit, MI 48226 · 313-965-3464

Theodore Sachs* · (Labor) · Sachs, Nunn, Kates, Kadushin, O'Hare, Helveston & Waldman · 1000 Farmer Street · Detroit, MI 48226 · 313-965-3464

Ronald J. Santo · (Management) · Dykema Gossett · 400 Renaissance Center, 35th Floor · Detroit, MI 48243 · 313-568-6800

William M. Saxton · (Management) · Butzel Long · 150 West Jefferson, Suite 900 Detroit, MI 48226-4430 · 313-225-7000

Sheldon J. Stark* · (Individuals) · Stark & Gordon · 1600 Ford Building · Detroit, MI 48226 · 313-962-3784

Robert M. Vercruysse* · (Management) · Butzel Long · 150 West Jefferson, Suite 900 · Detroit, MI 48226-4430 · 313-225-7013

Eugene Alkema · (Management) · Varnum, Riddering, Schmidt & Howlett · 171 Monroe Avenue, NW, Suite 800 · Grand Rapids, MI 49503 · 616-459-4186

Jack R. Clary · (Management) · Clary, Nantz, Wood, Hoffius, Rankin & Cooper 500 Calder Plaza, Suite 500 · 250 Monroe Avenue, NW · Grand Rapids, MI 49503 616-459-9487

Michael L. Fayette · (Labor) · Pinsky, Smith, Fayette & Hulswit · 1515 McKay Tower · Grand Rapids, MI 49503 · 616-451-8496

Norman E. Jabin · (Management) · Miller, Johnson, Snell & Cummiskey · 800 Calder Plaza Building · Grand Rapids, MI 49503 · 616-459-8311

H. Rhett Pinsky · (Individuals) · Pinsky, Smith, Fayette & Hulswit · 1515 McKay Tower · Grand Rapids, MI 49503 · 616-451-8496

Edward M. Smith · (Labor, Individuals) · Pinsky, Smith, Fayette & Hulswit · 1515 McKay Tower · Grand Rapids, MI 49503 · 616-451-8496

Kent J. Vana · (Management) · Varnum, Riddering, Schmidt & Howlett · 171 Monroe Avenue, NW, Suite 800 · Grand Rapids, MI 49503 · 616-459-4186

Carl E. Ver Beek · (Management) · Varnum, Riddering, Schmidt & Howlett · 171 Monroe Avenue, NW, Suite 800 · Grand Rapids, MI 49503 · 616-459-4186

Thomas P. Hustoles · (Management) · Miller, Canfield, Paddock and Stone · 444 West Michigan Avenue · Kalamazoo, MI 49007 · 616-381-7030

Darryl R. Cochrane · (Labor) · McCroskey, Feldman, Cochrane & Brock · 1440 Peck Street · P.O. Box 27 · Muskegon, MI 49443 · 616-726-4861

Donald J. Veldman · (Management) · Warner, Norcross & Judd · Comerica Bank Building · 801 West Norton Avenue · P.O. Box 0417 · Muskegon, MI 49443-0417 616-739-2297

James A. White · (Labor) · White, Beekman, Przybylowicz, Schneider & Baird · 2214 University Park Drive, Suite 200 · Okemos, MI 48864 · 517-349-7744

Joseph A. Golden · (Individuals) · Sommers, Schwartz, Silver & Schwartz · 2000 Town Center, Suite 900 · Southfield, MI 48075 · 313-355-0300

Charles Gottlieb · Gottlieb & Goren · 26261 Evergreen, Suite 460 · Southfield, MI 48076 · 313-352-1880

Samuel C. McKnight · (Labor) · Klimist, McKnight, Sale, McClow & Canzano · 400 Galleria, Suite 117 · Southfield, MI 48034 · 313-354-9650

Bruce A. Miller · (Labor) · Miller, Cohen, Martens & Ice · 17117 West Nine Mile, Suite 1400 · Southfield, MI 48075 · 313-559-2110

NATURAL RESOURCES AND ENVIRONMENTAL LAW

Jeffrey K. Haynes* · (Plaintiffs) · VanderKloot & Haynes · 860 West Long Lake Road, Suite 200 · P.O. Box 980 · Bloomfield Hills, MI 48303-0980 · 313-540-8388

Philip A. Grashoff, Jr. · Honigman Miller Schwartz and Cohn · 2290 First National Building · Detroit, MI 48226-3583 · 313-256-7973

Steven C. Nadeau · (Environmental) · Dickinson, Wright, Moon, Van Dusen & Freeman · 800 First National Building · P.O. Box 509 · Detroit, MI 48226-3555 313-223-3500

Joseph M. Polito · Honigman Miller Schwartz and Cohn · 2290 First National Building · Detroit, MI 48226-3583 · 313-256-7800

Herbert G. Sparrow III* · Dickinson, Wright, Moon, Van Dusen & Freeman · 800 First National Building · P.O. Box 509 · Detroit, MI 48226-3555 · 313-223-3500

David L. Tripp · Dykema Gossett · 400 Renaissance Center, 35th Floor · Detroit, MI 48243 · 313-568-6800

Eugene E. Smary · (Environmental) · Warner, Norcross & Judd · 900 Old Kent Building · 111 Lyon Street, NW · Grand Rapids, MI 49503-2489 · 616-459-6121

Peter W. Steketee · Law Office of Peter W. Steketee · 660 Cascade West Parkway, SE, Suite 65 · Grand Rapids, MI 49546 · 616-949-6551

Michael L. Robinson · Warner, Norcross & Judd · Comerica Bank Building · 801 West Norton Avenue · P.O. Box 0417 · Muskegon, MI 49443-0417 · 616-739-2297

John W. Voelpel · Honigman Miller Schwartz and Cohn · 2290 First National Building · Detroit, MI 48226-3583 · 313-256-7800

PERSONAL INJURY LITIGATION

Richard G. Smith* · (Defendants, Professional Malpractice) · Smith & Brooker · 703 Washington Avenue · P.O. Box X-921 · Bay City, MI 48707-0921 · 517-892-2595

George A. Googasian · (Plaintiffs) · Googasian, Hopkins, Hohauser & Forhan · 6895 Telegraph Road · Birmingham, MI 48010 · 313-540-3333

Kenneth B. McConnell · (Plaintiffs) · 2000 North Woodward Avenue, Suite 100 Bloomfield Hills, MI 48013 · 313-645-1710

George J. Bedrosian · (Plaintiffs) · Goodman, Eden, Millender & Bedrosian · 3000 Cadillac Tower · Detroit, MI 48226 · 313-965-0050

William D. Booth · (Defendants) · Plunkett & Cooney · 900 Marquette Building Detroit, MI 48226-3260 · 313-965-3900

Lawrence S. Charfoos* · (Plaintiffs) · Charfoos & Christensen · Penobscot Building, 40th Floor · Detroit, MI 48226 · 313-963-8080

David W. Christensen* · (Plaintiffs, Medical Malpractice, Products Liability, Professional Malpractice) · Charfoos & Christensen · Penobscot Building, 40th Floor · Detroit, MI 48226 · 313-963-8080

David J. Cooper* · (Defendants, Medical Malpractice, Products Liability) · Garan, Lucow, Miller, Seward, Cooper & Becker · Woodbridge Place · 1000 Woodbridge Street · Detroit, MI 48207-3192 · 313-446-1530

Daniel L. Garan · (Defendants, Products Liability) · Garan, Lucow, Miller, Seward, Cooper & Becker · Woodbridge Place · 1000 Woodbridge Street · Detroit, MI 48207-3192 · 313-446-1530

Richard M. Goodman* · (Plaintiffs, Medical Malpractice, Products Liability) · Goodman, Lister, Seikaly & Peters · 1394 East Jefferson Street · Detroit, MI 48207 · 313-567-6165

John A. Kruse* · (Defendants) · Harvey, Kruse, Westen & Milan · 1590 First National Bank Building · Detroit, MI 48226 · 313-964-3100

Richard J. McClear* · (Defendants) · Dykema Gossett · 400 Renaissance Center, 35th Floor · Detroit, MI 48243 · 313-568-6800

John E. S. Scott* · (Defendants, Products Liability) · Dickinson, Wright, Moon, Van Dusen & Freeman · 800 First National Building · P.O. Box 509 · Detroit, MI 48226-3555 · 313-223-3500

Barry P. Waldman · (Plaintiffs) · Sachs, Nunn, Kates, Kadushin, O'Hare, Helveston & Waldman · 1000 Farmer Street · Detroit, MI 48226 · 313-965-3464

David J. Watters · (Defendants, Medical Malpractice) · Plunkett & Cooney · 900 Marquette Building · Detroit, MI 48226-3260 · 313-965-3900

Richard B. Baxter* · (Plaintiffs, Defendants) · Dykema Gossett · 200 Oldtown Riverfront Building · 248 Louis Campau Promenade, NW · Grand Rapids, MI 49503-0321 · 616-776-7500

Grant J. Gruel* · Gruel, Mills, Nims and Pylman · 50 Monroe Place, Suite 700 West · Grand Rapids, MI 49503 · 616-235-5500

William G. Reamon, Sr. · (Plaintiffs) · Waters Building, Suite 200-C · Grand Rapids, MI 49503 · 616-774-2377

William J. Waddell · 180 Monroe Avenue, NW, Suite 4000 · Grand Rapids, MI 49503 · 616-235-7737

Barry D. Boughton · Sinas, Dramis, Brake, Boughton & McIntyre · 520 Seymour Avenue · Lansing, MI 48933-1192 · 517-372-7780

John L. Collins* · (Defendants, Medical Malpractice, Products Liability, Professional Malpractice) · Foster, Swift, Collins & Smith · 313 South Washington Square · Lansing, MI 48933-2193 · 517-372-8050

William N. Kritselis* · (Plaintiffs, Medical Malpractice, Products Liability, Automobile Collision, Highway Defect) · Church, Kritselis, Wyble & Robinson · 3939 Capitol City Boulevard · Lansing, MI 48906-9962 · 517-323-4770

George T. Sinas* · (Plaintiffs) · Sinas, Dramis, Brake, Boughton & McIntyre · 520 Seymour Avenue · Lansing, MI 48933-1192 · 517-372-7780

Cassius E. Street, Jr. · (Plaintiffs) · Street & Grua · 2401 East Grand River · Lansing, MI 48912 · 517-487-8300

Stanley S. Schwartz · (Plaintiffs) · Sommers, Schwartz, Silver & Schwartz · 2000 Town Center, Suite 900 · Southfield, MI 48075 · 313-355-0300

William J. Weinstein* · (Plaintiffs) · Weinstein, Gordon and Hoffman · 18411 West Twelve Mile Road · Southfield, MI 48076 · 313-443-1500

Dean A. Robb · (Plaintiffs) · Robb, Messing & Palmer · 420 East Front Street · P.O. Box 1132 · Traverse City, MI 49684 · 616-947-2462

PUBLIC UTILITY LAW

Roderick S. Coy · Hill Lewis · 200 North Capitol Avenue, Suite 600 · Lansing, MI 48933 · 517-484-4481

Albert Ernst · Dykema Gossett · 800 Michigan National Tower · Lansing, MI 48933 · 517-374-9100

Harvey J. Messing · Loomis Ewert · 232 South Capitol Avenue, Suite 1000 · Lansing. MI 48933 · 517-482-2400

REAL ESTATE LAW

Robert E. Gilbert · (Commercial Transactions) · Miller, Canfield, Paddock and Stone · 101 North Main Street, Seventh Floor · Ann Arbor, MI 48104-1400 · 313-663-2445

Stephen A. Bromberg · Butzel Long · 32270 Telegraph Road, Suite 200 · Birmingham, MI 48010-4996 · 313-258-1616

Stephen E. Dawson · Dickinson, Wright, Moon, Van Dusen & Freeman · 525 North Woodward Avenue · P.O. Box 509 · Bloomfield Hills, MI 48303-0509 · 313-646-4300

William T. Myers · Dykema Gossett · 505 North Woodward Avenue, Suite 3000 Bloomfield Hills, MI 48304 · 313-540-0700

John E. Amerman · Honigman Miller Schwartz and Cohn · 2290 First National Building · Detroit, MI 48226-3583 · 313-256-7800

William G. Barris · Barris, Sott, Denn & Driker · 211 West Fort Street, 15th Floor Detroit, MI 48226-3281 · 313-965-9725

Maurice S. Binkow · Honigman Miller Schwartz and Cohn · 2290 First National Building · Detroit, MI 48226-3583 · 313-256-7800

Robert S. Bolton · Jaffe, Snider, Raitt & Heuer · One Woodward Avenue, Suite 2400 · Detroit, MI 48226 · 313-961-7900

James W. Draper · (Land Use, Eminent Domain, Commercial Transactions, Industrial Transactions) · Dykema Gossett · 400 Renaissance Center, 35th Floor Detroit, MI 48243 · 313-568-6800

William B. Dunn · Clark, Klein & Beaumont · 1600 First Federal Building · 1001 Woodward Avenue · Detroit, MI 48226 · 313-965-8300

Norman Hyman* · (Zoning) · Honigman Miller Schwartz and Cohn · 2290 First National Building · Detroit, MI 48226-3583 · 313-256-7800

Lawrence D. McLaughlin · Honigman Miller Schwartz and Cohn · 2290 First National Building · Detroit, MI 48226-3583 · 313-256-7800

Russell A. McNair, Jr. · Dickinson, Wright, Moon, Van Dusen & Freeman · 800 First National Building · P.O. Box 509 · Detroit, MI 48226-3555 · 313-223-3500

Robert R. Nix II · Kerr, Russell & Weber · 2100 Commerce Building · Detroit, MI 48226 · 313-961-0200

Stephen G. Palms · Miller, Canfield, Paddock and Stone · 150 West Jefferson, Suite 2500 · Detroit, MI 48226 · 313-963-6420

Richard E. Rabbideau · Dykema Gossett · 400 Renaissance Center, 35th Floor · Detroit, MI 48243 · 313-568-6800

Allen Schwartz · Miller, Canfield, Paddock and Stone · 150 West Jefferson, Suite 2500 · Detroit, MI 48226 · 313-963-6420

James M. Tervo · Dickinson, Wright, Moon, Van Dusen & Freeman · 800 First National Building · P.O. Box 509 · Detroit, MI 48226-3555 · 313-223-3500

Sheldon P. Winkelman · Honigman Miller Schwartz and Cohn · 2290 First National Building · Detroit, MI 48226-3583 · 313-256-7800

William J. Zousmer · Honigman Miller Schwartz and Cohn · 2290 First National Building · Detroit, MI 48226-3583 · 313-256-7800

Jack M. Bowie · McShane & Bowie · 540 Old Kent Building · Grand Rapids, MI 49503 · 616-774-0641

James R. Brown · Mika, Meyers, Beckett & Jones · 200 Ottawa Street, NW, Suite 700 · Grand Rapids, MI 49503 · 616-459-3200

John G. Cameron, Jr. · Warner, Norcross & Judd · 900 Old Kent Building · 111 Lyon Street, NW · Grand Rapids, MI 49503-2489 · 616-459-6121

Nyal D. Deems · Varnum, Riddering, Schmidt & Howlett · 171 Monroe Avenue, NW, Suite 800 · Grand Rapids, MI 49503 · 616-459-4186

Robert L. Nelson · Dykema Gossett · 200 Oldtown Riverfront Building · 248 Louis Campau Promenade, NW · Grand Rapids, MI 49503-0321 · 616-776-7500

William K. Van't Hof · (Condominium Law) · Varnum, Riddering, Schmidt & Howlett · 171 Monroe Avenue, NW, Suite 800 · Grand Rapids, MI 49503 · 616-459-4186

Douglas J. Austin · Fraser Trebilcock Davis & Foster · 1000 Michigan National Tower · Lansing, MI 48933 · 517-482-5800

Robert J. McCullen · Foster, Swift, Collins & Smith · 313 South Washington Square · Lansing, MI 48933-2193 · 517-372-8050

Gary A. Taback · Somers, Schwartz, Silver & Schwartz · 2000 Town Center, Suite 900 · Southfield, MI 48075-1100 · 313-355-0300

TAX AND EMPLOYEE BENEFITS LAW

Robert B. Stevenson · (Employee Benefits) · Stevenson Keppelman Associates · First National Bank Building, Suite 700 · 201 South Main Street · Ann Arbor, MI 48104-2105 · 313-747-7050

Louis W. Kasischke · Dykema Gossett · 505 North Woodward Avenue, Suite 3000 · Bloomfield Hills, MI 48304 · 313-540-0700

Ward Randol, Jr. · (Employee Benefits) · Dickinson, Wright, Moon, Van Dusen & Freeman · 525 North Woodward Avenue · P.O. Box 509 · Bloomfield Hills, MI 48303-0509 · 313-646-4300

David M. Rosenberger · (Employee Benefits) · Dykema Gossett · 505 North Woodward Avenue, Suite 3000 · Bloomfield Hills, MI 48304 · 313-540-0758

Robert G. Buydens · (Employee Benefits) · Clark, Klein & Beaumont · 1600 First Federal Building · 1001 Woodward Avenue · Detroit, MI 48226 · 313-965-8300

Roger Cook · Honigman Miller Schwartz and Cohn · 2290 First National Building Detroit, MI 48226-3583 · 313-256-7800

Joseph F. Dillon · (Tax Disputes) · Raymond & Dillon · 400 Renaissance Center, Suite 2370 · Detroit, MI 48243 · 313-259-7700

John H. Eggertsen · (Employee Benefits) · Honigman Miller Schwartz and Cohn 2290 First National Building · Detroit, MI 48226-3583 · 313-256-7800

E. James Gamble · Dykema Gossett · 400 Renaissance Center, 35th Floor · Detroit, MI 48243 · 313-568-6800

Eugene A. Gargaro, Jr. · Dykema Gossett · 400 Renaissance Center, 35th Floor Detroit, MI 48243 · 313-568-6800

Joseph F. Maycock, Jr. · (Employee Benefits) · Miller, Canfield, Paddock and Stone · 150 West Jefferson, Suite 2500 · Detroit, MI 48226 · 313-963-6420

Samuel J. McKim III · Miller, Canfield, Paddock and Stone · 150 West Jefferson, Suite 2500 · Detroit, MI 48226 · 313-963-6420

Sherill Siebert · (Employee Benefits) · Honigman Miller Schwartz and Cohn · 2290 First National Building · Detroit, MI 48226-3583 · 313-256-7800

Stevan Uzelac · Miller, Canfield, Paddock and Stone · 150 West Jefferson, Suite 2500 · Detroit, MI 48226 · 313-963-6420

Lawrence R. Van Til* · (Eminent Domain, State Tax) · Van Til & Associates · 400 Renaissance Center, Suite 500 · Detroit, MI 48243 · 313-259-2250

James C. Bruinsma · (Employee Benefits) · Miller, Johnson, Snell & Cummiskey 800 Calder Plaza Building · Grand Rapids, MI 49503 · 616-459-8311

William R. Hineline · Law, Weathers & Richardson · 200 Ottawa, NW, Suite 500 Grand Rapids, MI 49503 · 616-459-1171

Stephen R. Kretschman · Warner, Norcross & Judd · 900 Old Kent Building · 111 Lyon Street, NW · Grand Rapids, MI 49503-2489 · 616-459-6121

John W. McNeil · Miller, Johnson, Snell & Cummiskey · 800 Calder Plaza Building · Grand Rapids, MI 49503 · 616-459-8311

J. Lee Murphy · Miller, Johnson, Snell & Cummiskey · 800 Calder Plaza Building Grand Rapids, MI 49503 · 616-459-8311

Roger H. Oetting · Warner, Norcross & Judd · 900 Old Kent Building · 111 Lyon Street, NW · Grand Rapids, MI 49503-2489 · 616-459-6121

Vernon P. Saper · (Employee Benefits) · Warner, Norcross & Judd · 900 Old Kent Building · 111 Lyon Street, NW · Grand Rapids, MI 49503-2489 · 616-459-6121

George L. Whitfield · (Employee Benefits) · Warner, Norcross & Judd · 900 Old Kent Building · 111 Lyon Street, NW · Grand Rapids, MI 49503-2489 · 616-459-6121

Allan J. Claypool · Foster, Swift, Collins & Smith · 313 South Washington Square Lansing, MI 48933-2193 · 517-372-8050

Stephen I. Jurmu · (Employee Benefits) · Foster, Swift, Collins & Smith · 313 South Washington Square · Lansing, MI 48933-2193 · 517-372-8050

Peter S. Sheldon · Dickinson, Wright, Moon, Van Dusen & Freeman · 215 South Washington Square, Suite 200 · Lansing, MI 48933 · 517-371-1730

Marcus Plotkin · Plotkin, Yolles, Siegel, Schultz & Bergh · 2000 Town Center, Suite 600 · Southfield, MI 48075 · 313-354-3200

J. D. Hartwig · Hartwig, Crow & Jones · 206 Court Street · P.O. Box 6 · St. Joseph, MI 49085 · 616-983-0615

TRUSTS AND ESTATES

Raymond T. Huetteman, Jr. · (Estate Planning, Estate Administration) · Dykema Gossett · 315 East Eisenhower Parkway, Suite 100 · Ann Arbor, MI 48108 · 313-747-7663

Susan S. Westerman · Stein, Moran & Westerman · 320 North Main Street · Ann Arbor, MI 48104 · 313-769-6838

E. James Gamble · Dykema Gossett · 400 Renaissance Center, 35th Floor · Detroit, MI 48243 · 313-568-6800

Robert B. Joslyn · (Estate Planning, Estate Administration, Trust Administration) · Joslyn, Keydel, Wallace & Carney · 2211 Comerica Building · Detroit, MI 48226 · 313-964-4181

Frederick R. Keydel · (Estate Planning Trust Administration) · Joslyn, Keydel, Wallace & Carney · 2211 Comerica Building · Detroit, MI 48226 · 313-964-4181

John D. Mabley · Hill Lewis · 100 Renaissance Center, Suite 3200 · Detroit, MI 48243 · 313-259-3232

George D. Miller, Jr. · Bodman, Longley & Dahling · 100 Renaissance Center, 34th Floor · Detroit, MI 48243 · 313-393-7510

Douglas J. Rasmussen · Clark, Klein & Beaumont · 1600 First Federal Building 1001 Woodward Avenue · Detroit, MI 48226 · 313-965-8300

Robert Donald Brower, Jr. · Miller, Johnson, Snell & Cummiskey · 800 Calder Plaza Building · Grand Rapids, MI 49503 · 616-459-8311

Dirk C. Hoffius · Varnum, Riddering, Schmidt & Howlett · 171 Monroe Avenue, NW, Suite 800 · Grand Rapids, MI 49503 · 616-459-4186

Fredric A. Sytsma · Varnum, Riddering, Schmidt & Howlett · 171 Monroe Avenue, NW, Suite 800 · Grand Rapids, MI 49503 · 616-459-4186

W. Michael Van Haren · (Estate Planning, Estate Administration, Charitable Trusts) · Warner, Norcross & Judd · 900 Old Kent Building · 111 Lyon Street, NW Grand Rapids, MI 49503-2489 · 616-459-6121

Allan J. Claypool · Foster, Swift, Collins & Smith · 313 South Washington Square Lansing, MI 48933-2193 · 517-372-8050

Joe C. Foster, Jr. · Fraser Trebilcock Davis & Foster · 1000 Michigan National Tower · Lansing, MI 48933 · 517-482-5800

Everett R. Zack · Fraser Trebilcock Davis & Foster · 1000 Michigan National Tower · Lansing, MI 48933 · 517-482-5800

James A. Kendall · (Estate Planning, Estate Administration, Charitable Trusts, Estate & Gift Tax) · Currie & Kendall · 6024 Eastman Road · P.O. Box 1846 · Midland, MI 48641 · 517-839-0300

Michael W. Irish · Culver, Lague & McNally · 600 Terrace Plaza · P.O. Box 389 Muskegon, MI 49443 · 616-725-8148

John Harvey Martin · Landman, Latimer, Clink & Robb · 400 Terrace Plaza · P.O. Box 1488 · Muskegon, MI 49443 · 616-722-2671

J. D. Hartwig · Hartwig, Crow & Jones · 206 Court Street · P.O. Box 6 · St. Joseph, MI 49085 · 616-983-0615

James E. Beall · Stark, Reagan & Finnerty · 1111 West Long Lake Road, Suite 202 · Troy, MI 48098-6310 · 313-641-9955

MINNESOTA

BANKRUPTCY LAW

James L. Baillie · Fredrikson & Byron · 1100 International Centre · 900 Second Avenue South · Minneapolis, MN 55402-3397 · 612-347-7000

Richard D. Holper · Robins, Kaplan, Miller & Ciresi · 1800 International Centre 900 Second Avenue South · Minneapolis, MN 55402-3394 · 612-349-8500

William I. Kampf · Fredrikson & Byron · 1100 International Centre · 900 Second Avenue South · Minneapolis, MN 55402-3397 · 612-347-7000

Melvin I. Orenstein · Lindquist & Vennum · 4200 IDS Center · 80 South Eighth Street · Minneapolis, MN 55402 · 612-371-3211

Howard A. Patrick · Robins, Kaplan, Miller & Ciresi · 1800 International Centre 900 Second Avenue South · Minneapolis, MN 55402-3394 · 612-349-8500

Paul J. Scheerer · Dorsey & Whitney · 2200 First Bank Place East · Minneapolis, MN 55402 · 612-340-2600

BUSINESS LITIGATION

Raymond L. Erickson · Hanft, Fride, O'Brien, Harries, Swelbar & Burns · 1000 First Bank Place · 130 West Superior Street · Duluth, MN 55802-2994 · 218-722-4766

John J. Killen* · Johnson, Killen, Thibodeau & Seiler · 811 Norwest Center · 230 West Superior Street · Duluth, MN 55802 · 218-722-6331

Lawrence C. Brown · Faegre & Benson · 2200 Norwest Center · 90 South Seventh Street · Minneapolis, MN 55402-3901 · 612-336-3000

Tyrone P. Bujold* · Robins, Kaplan, Miller & Ciresi · 1800 International Centre 900 Second Avenue South · Minneapolis, MN 55402-3394 · 612-349-8500

Gordon G. Busdicker* · (Antitrust, Commercial, Securities) · Faegre & Benson 2200 Norwest Center · 90 South Seventh Street · Minneapolis, MN 55402-3117 · 612-336-3000

Peter Dorsey · Dorsey & Whitney · 2200 First Bank Place East · Minneapolis, MN 55402 · 612-340-2600

Harold D. Field, Jr. · (Commercial, Securities, Fiduciary Duties) · Leonard, Street and Deinard · 150 South Fifth Street, Suite 2300 · Minneapolis, MN 55402 612-335-1500

John D. French* · (Administrative, Antitrust) · Faegre & Benson · 2200 Norwest Center · 90 South Seventh Street · Minneapolis, MN 55402-3901 · 612-336-3000

Terence M. Fruth · Fruth & Anthony · 1350 International Centre · 900 Second Avenue South · Minneapolis, MN 55402 · 612-349-6969

Craig W. Gagnon* · Oppenheimer Wolff and Donnelly · Plaza VII · 45 South Seventh Street, Suite 3400 · Minneapolis, MN 55402 · 612-344-9300

Edward M. Glennon · Lindquist & Vennum · 4200 IDS Center · 80 South Eighth Street · Minneapolis, MN 55402 · 612-371-3211

Elliot S. Kaplan* · Robins, Kaplan, Miller & Ciresi · 1800 International Centre · 900 Second Avenue South · Minneapolis, MN 55402-3394 · 612-349-8500

Timothy D. Kelly* · Kelly & Berens · 3720 IDS Center · 80 South Eight Street Minneapolis, MN 55402 · 612-349-6171

Dale I. Larson · Zelle & Larson · City Center, Suite 4400 · 33 South Sixth Street Minneapolis, MN 55402 · 612-339-2020

John D. Levine · Dorsey & Whitney · 2200 First Bank Place East · Minneapolis, MN 55402 · 612-340-2600

George F. McGunnigle · (Securities) · Leonard, Street and Deinard · 150 South Fifth Street, Suite 2300 · Minneapolis, MN 55402 · 612-335-1500

Clay R. Moore* · (Antitrust, Appellate, Commercial, Finance) · Mackall, Crounse & Moore · 1600 TCF Tower · 121 South Eighth Street · Minneapolis, MN 55402 612-333-1341

Jerome B. Pederson · (Antitrust, Commercial) · Fredrikson & Byron · 1100 International Centre · 900 Second Avenue South · Minneapolis, MN 55402-3397 612-347-7006

Charles W. Quaintance, Jr.* · Maslon Edelman Borman & Brand · 1800 Midwest Plaza · 801 Nicollet Mall · Minneapolis, MN 55402-2591 · 612-339-8015

Robert A. Schwartzbauer · (Antitrust) · Dorsey & Whitney · 2200 First Bank Place East · Minneapolis, MN 55402 · 612-340-2782

Daniel R. Shulman* · (Antitrust, Commercial) · Gray, Plant, Mooty, Mooty & Bennett · 3400 City Center · 33 South Sixth Street · Minneapolis, MN 55402-3796 612-343-2800

James S. Simonson · Gray, Plant, Mooty, Mooty & Bennett · 3400 City Center 33 South Sixth Street · Minneapolis, MN 55402-3796 · 612-343-2800

Richard B. Solum* · Dorsey & Whitney · 2200 First Bank Place East · Minneapolis, MN 55402 · 612-340-2600

Jan Stuurmans* · (Commercial, Securities) · Stuurmans & Karan · 600 Title Insurance Building · 400 Second Avenue South · Minneapolis, MN 55401 · 612-339-5581

Thomas W. Tinkham* · Dorsey & Whitney · 2200 First Bank Place East · Minneapolis, MN 55402 · 612-340-2600

Robert R. Dunlap · Dunlap, Finseth, Berndt & Sandberg · 505 Marquette Bank Building · P.O. Box 549 · Rochester, MN 55903 · 507-288-9111

Ronald L. Seeger* · Michaels Seeger Rosenblad & Arnold · Norwest Bank Building, Suite 550 · 21 First Street Southwest · Rochester, MN 55902 · 507-288-7755

John A. Cochrane · Cochrane & Bresnahan · 24 East Fourth Street · St. Paul, MN 55101-1099 · 612-298-1950

David C. Forsberg · Briggs and Morgan · 2200 First National Bank Building · St. Paul, MN 55101 · 612-291-1215

Elmer B. Trousdale · Oppenheimer Wolff and Donnelly · First Bank Building, Suite 1700 · St. Paul, MN 55101 · 612-223-2500

Eugene M. Warlich · Doherty, Rumble & Butler · 2800 Minnesota World Trade Center · 30 East Seventh Street · St. Paul, MN 55101-4999 · 612-291-9333

Robert R. Weinstine · Winthrop & Weinstine · 3200 World Trade Center · 30 East Seventh Street · St. Paul, MN 55101 · 612-290-8400

CORPORATE LAW

Paul T. Birkeland · (Banking) · Faegre & Benson · 2200 Norwest Center · 90 South Seventh Street · Minneapolis, MN 55402-3901 · 612-336-3000

Michael E. Bress · Dorsey & Whitney · 2200 First Bank Place East · Minneapolis, MN 55402 · 612-340-2600

Kenneth L. Cutler · Dorsey & Whitney · 2200 First Bank Place East · Minneapolis, MN 55402 · 612-340-2600

Stanley Efron · (Corporate Finance, Mergers & Acquisitions, Securities) · Henson & Efron · 1200 Title Insurance Building · 400 Second Avenue South · Minneapolis, MN 55401 · 612-339-2500

Gerald T. Flom · Faegre & Benson · 2200 Norwest Center · 90 South Seventh Street · Minneapolis, MN 55402-3901 · 612-336-3000

John D. French* · (Antitrust, Mergers & Acquisitions) · Faegre & Benson · 2200 Norwest Center · 90 South Seventh Street · Minneapolis, MN 55402-3901 · 612-336-3000

Philip S. Garon · Faegre & Benson · 2200 Norwest Center · 90 South Seventh Street · Minneapolis, MN 55402-3901 · 612-336-3000

John S. Hibbs · Dorsey & Whitney · 2200 First Bank Place East · Minneapolis, MN 55402 · 612-340-2600

Samuel L. Kaplan · Kaplan, Strangis and Kaplan · 5500 Norwest Center · 90 South Seventh Street · Minneapolis, MN 55402 · 612-375-1138

Richard G. Lareau · Oppenheimer Wolff and Donnelly · 45 South Seventh Street Minneapolis, MN 55402 · 612-344-9300

Keith A. Libbey · (Banking, Corporate Finance, Mergers & Acquisitions) · Fredrikson & Byron · 1100 International Centre · 900 Second Avenue South · Minneapolis, MN 55402-3397 · 612-347-7000

Gerald E. Magnuson · Lindquist & Vennum · 4200 IDS Center · 80 South Eighth Street · Minneapolis, MN 55402 · 612-371-3211

Lee R. Mitau · Dorsey & Whitney · 2200 First Bank Place East · Minneapolis, MN 55402 · 612-340-2600

Morris M. Sherman · Leonard, Street and Deinard · 150 South Fifth Street, Suite 2300 · Minneapolis, MN 55402 · 612-335-1500

Roger V. Stageberg · Lommen, Nelson, Cole & Stageberg · 1800 IDS Center · 80 South Eighth Street · Minneapolis, MN 55402 · 612-339-8131

Ralph Strangis · Kaplan, Strangis and Kaplan · 5500 Norwest Center · 90 South Seventh Street · Minneapolis, MN 55402 · 612-375-1138

Burt E. Swanson · Briggs and Morgan · 2400 IDS Center · 80 South Eighth Street Minneapolis, MN 55402 · 612-339-0661

Richard G. Swanson · Dorsey & Whitney · 2200 First Bank Place East · Minneapolis, MN 55402 · 612-340-2600

William A. Whitlock · Dorsey & Whitney · 2200 First Bank Place East · Minneapolis, MN 55402 · 612-340-2669

Alan J. Wilensky · Dorsey & Whitney · 2200 First Bank Place East · Minneapolis, MN 55402 · 612-340-2600

Lawrence J. Hayes · Maun, Green, Hayes, Simon, Johanneson and Brehl · 332 Hamm Building · St. Paul, MN 55102 · 612-224-7300

Thomas E. Rohricht · Doherty, Rumble & Butler · 2800 Minnesota World Trade Center · 30 East Seventh Street · St. Paul, MN 55101-4999 · 612-291-9333

Eugene M. Warlich · Doherty, Rumble & Butler · 2800 Minnesota World Trade Center · 30 East Seventh Street · St. Paul, MN 55101-4999 · 612-291-9333

Sherman Winthrop · Winthrop & Weinstine · 3200 Minnesota World Trade Center · 30 East Seventh Street · St. Paul, MN 55101 · 612-292-8110

CRIMINAL DEFENSE

Robert E. Lucas · 128 West First Street · Duluth, MN 55802 · 218-727-2810

Joseph S. Friedberg · Commerce-at-the-Crossings, Suite 205 · 250 Second Avenue, South · Minneapolis, MN 55401 · 612-339-8626

William J. Mauzy · Mauzy & Short · 2885 Norwest Center · 90 South Seventh Street · Minneapolis, MN 55402 · 612-340-9108

Ronald I. Meshbesher · Meshbesher & Spence · 1616 Park Avenue · Minneapolis, MN 55404 · 612-339-9121

Jack S. Nordby · Meshbesher & Spence · 2600 Minnesota World Trade Center 30 East Seventh Street · Minneapolis, MN 55501 · 612-339-9121

Phillip S. Resnick · Phillip S. Resnick & Associates · 701 Fourth Avenue South, Suite 1710 · Minneapolis, MN 55415 · 612-339-0411

Douglas W. Thomson · Thomson & Ellis · 345 St. Peter Street, Suite 300 · St. Paul, MN 55102 · 612-227-0856

FAMILY LAW

Jack S. Jaycox* · 400 Southgate Office Plaza · 5001 West 80th Street · Bloomington, MN 55437 · 612-835-6300

James H. Hennessy · (Divorce, Marital Settlement Agreements, Equitable Division) · Moss & Barnett · 4800 Norwest Center · 90 South Seventh Street · Minneapolis, MN 55402-4119 · 612-347-0300

Robert F. Henson · Henson & Efron · 1200 Title Insurance Building · 400 Second Avenue South · Minneapolis, MN 55401 · 612-339-2500

A. Larry Katz · Katz & Manka · 4830 IDS Center · 80 South Eighth Street · Minneapolis, MN 55402 · 612-333-1671

Edward L. Winer* · (Child Custody, Divorce, Marital Settlement Agreements, Premarital Agreements) · Moss & Barnett · 4800 Norwest Center · 90 South Seventh Street · Minneapolis, MN 55402-4119 · 612-347-0300

Robert H. Zalk · Fredrikson & Byron · 1100 International Centre · 900 Second Avenue South · Minneapolis, MN 55402-3397 · 612-347-7000

Lawrence D. Downing · Lawrence D. Downing & Associates · 330 Norwest Center · 21 First Street SW · Rochester, MN 55902 · 507-288-8432

Richard D. Goff · Goff, Kaplan, Wolf & Shapiro · 900 Capitol Centre · 386 North Wabasha · St. Paul, MN 55102 · 612-222-6341

William E. Haugh, Jr. · Collins, Buckley, Sauntry and Haugh · West 1100 First National Bank Building · 332 Minnesota Street · St. Paul, MN 55101 · 612-227-0611

FIRST AMENDMENT LAW

John P. Borger · Faegre & Benson · 2200 Norwest Center · 90 South Seventh Street · Minneapolis, MN 55402-3901 · 612-336-3000

Paul R. Hannah · Hannah & Zenner · 1122 Pioneer Building · 336 Roberts Street St. Paul, MN 55101 · 612-223-5525

HEALTH CARE LAW

Jay Christiansen · Faegre & Benson · 2200 Norwest Center · 90 South Seventh Street · Minneapolis, MN 55402-3901 · 612-336-3000

Konrad J. Friedemann · Fredrikson & Byron · 1100 International Centre · 900 Second Avenue South · Minneapolis, MN 55402-3397 · 612-347-7034

John S. Hibbs · Dorsey & Whitney · 2200 First Bank Place East · Minneapolis, MN 55402 · 612-340-8700

Margo S. Struthers · Moss & Barnett · 4800 Norwest Center · 90 South Seventh Street · Minneapolis, MN 55402-4119 · 612-347-0300

Paul M. Torgerson · Dorsey & Whitney · 2200 First Bank Place East · Minneapolis, MN 55402 · 612-340-8700

Bruce E. Hanson · Doherty, Rumble & Butler · 2800 Minnesota World Trade Center · 30 East Seventh Street · St. Paul, MN 55101-4999 · 612-291-9333

IMMIGRATION LAW

Jerome B. Ingber · Ingber & Aronson · 1221 Nicollet Mall, Suite 225 · Minneapolis, MN 55403 · 612-339-0517

Howard S. (Sam) Myers III · Popham, Haik, Schnobrich & Kaufman · 3300 Piper Jaffray Tower · 222 South Ninth Street · Minneapolis, MN 55402 · 612-333-4800

INTELLECTUAL PROPERTY LAW

Alan G. Carlson · Merchant & Gould · 3100 Norwest Center · Minneapolis, MN 55402 · 612-332-5300

Robert T. Edell · Merchant & Gould · 3100 Norwest Center · Minneapolis, MN 55402 · 612-332-5300

John D. Gould · Merchant & Gould · 3100 Norwest Center · Minneapolis, MN 55402 · 612-332-5300

Eugene L. Johnson · Dorsey & Whitney · 2200 First Bank Place East · Minneapolis, MN 55402 · 612-340-2625

Malcolm L. Moore · Moore & Hansen · 3000 Norwest Center · 90 South Seventh Street · Minneapolis, MN 55402 · 612-332-8200

Phillip H. Smith · Merchant & Gould · 3100 Norwest Center · Minneapolis, MN 55402 · 612-332-5300

LABOR AND EMPLOYMENT LAW

Don L. Bye · (Labor, Individuals) · Halverson Watters Bye Downs Reyelts & Bateman · 700 Providence Building · Duluth, MN 55802 · 218-727-6833

Emery W. Bartle* · (Management) · Dorsey & Whitney · 2200 First Bank Place East · Minneapolis, MN 55402 · 612-340-2600

Dale E. Beihoffer · (Management) · Faegre & Benson · 2200 Norwest Center · 90 South Seventh Street · Minneapolis, MN 55402-3901 · 612-336-3000

Gregg M. Corwin* · (Labor, Individuals) · West Parkdale Plaza Building, Suite 430 · 1660 South Highway 100 · Minneapolis, MN 55416-1506 · 612-544-7774

R. Scott Davies · Briggs and Morgan · 2400 IDS Center · 80 South Eighth Street · Minneapolis, MN 55402 · 612-339-0661

Terence M. Fruth · (Management) · Fruth & Anthony · 1350 International Centre · 900 Second Avenue South · Minneapolis, MN 55402 · 612-349-6969;

Stephen D. Gordon · (Labor) · Gordon-Miller-O'Brien · 1208 Plymouth Building · 12 South Sixth Street · Minneapolis, MN 55402 · 612-333-5831

Kathleen M. Graham · (Individuals) · Leonard, Street and Deinard · 150 South Fifth Street, Suite 2300 · Minneapolis, MN 55402 · 612-335-1500

Robert L. Hobbins · Dorsey & Whitney · 2200 First Bank Place East · Minneapolis, MN 55402 · 612-340-2600

David R. Hols · (Management) · Felhaber, Larson, Fenlon and Vogt · 1935 Piper Jaffray Tower · 220 Ninth Street · Minneapolis, MN 55402 · 612-339-6321

Richard A. Miller · (Labor) · Gordon-Miller-O'Brien · 1208 Plymouth Building · 12 South Sixth Street · Minneapolis, MN 55402 · 612-333-5831

Roger A. Peterson · (Labor) · Peterson, Engberg & Peterson · 700 Title Insurance Building · Minneapolis, MN 55401 · 612-338-6743

Robert R. Reinhardt · Oppenheimer Wolff and Donnelly · The Plaza VII Building, Suite 3400 · 45 South Seventh Street · Minneapolis, MN 55402 · 612-223-2500

James M. Samples* · (Management) · Faegre & Benson · 2200 Norwest Center 90 South Seventh Street · Minneapolis, MN 55402-3901 · 612-336-3000

Paul C. Sprenger* · (Individuals) · Sprenger, Olson & Shutes · 325 Ridgewood Avenue · Minneapolis, MN 55403 · 612-871-8910

Thomas M. Vogt · (Management) · Felhaber, Larson, Fenlon and Vogt · 1930 Piper Jaffray Tower · 222 South Ninth Street · Minneapolis, MN 55402 · 612-339-6321

John C. Zwakman · (Management) · Dorsey & Whitney · 2200 First Bank Place East · Minneapolis, MN 55402 · 612-340-2600

Ronald L. Seeger* · (Management) · Michaels Seeger Rosenblad & Arnold · Norwest Bank Building, Suite 550 · 21 First Street Southwest · Rochester, MN 55902 · 507-288-7755

Edward J. Bohrer · (Management) · Felhaber, Larson, Fenlon and Vogt · 900 Meritor Tower · 444 Cedar Street · St. Paul, MN 55101 · 612-222-6321

Michael J. Galvin, Jr.* · (Management) · Briggs and Morgan · 2200 First National Bank Building · St. Paul, MN 55101 · 612-291-1215

Roger A. Jensen* · (Labor) · Peterson, Bell, Converse & Jensen · 2100 American National Bank Building · St. Paul, MN 55101 · 612-224-4703

Thomas P. Kane* · (Management) · Oppenheimer Wolff and Donnelly · First Bank Building, Suite 1700 · St. Paul, MN 55101 · 612-223-2500

Eric R. Miller* · (Labor, Individuals) · Oppenheimer Wolff & Donnelly · First Bank Building, Suite 1700 · St. Paul, MN 55101 · 612-223-2500

James C. O'Neill · (Individuals) · Law Office of James C. O'Neill · 425 Hamm Building · St. Paul, MN 55102 · 612-222-7463

NATURAL RESOURCES AND ENVIRONMENTAL LAW

Charles K. Dayton* · (Logging) · Leonard, Street and Deinard · 150 South Fifth Street, Suite 2300 · Minneapolis, MN 55402 · 612-335-1500

Raymond A. Haik · Popham, Haik, Schnobrich & Kaufman · 3300 Piper Jaffray Tower · 222 South Ninth Street · Minneapolis, MN 55402 · 612-333-4800

John H. Herman · (Environmental Review & Permitting) · Leonard, Street and Deinard · 150 South Fifth Street, Suite 2300 · Minneapolis, MN 55402 · 612-335-1500

Brian B. O'Neill* · (Plaintiffs) · Faegre & Benson · 2200 Norwest Center · 90 South Seventh Street · Minneapolis, MN 55402-3901 · 612-336-3000

James A. Payne · (Air, Water, Hazardous Waste) · Popham, Haik, Schnobrich & Kaufman · 3300 Piper Jaffray Tower · 222 South Ninth Street · Minneapolis, MN 55402 · 612-333-4800

Byron E. Starns · (Resources, Air and Water) · Leonard, Street and Deinard · 150 South Fifth Street, Suite 2300 · Minneapolis, MN 55402 · 612-335-1500

PERSONAL INJURY LITIGATION

Romaine R. Powell* · Powell, Lang & Schueppert · 713 Beltrami Avenue · P.O. Box 908 · Bemidji, MN 56601-0908 · 218-751-5650

Elton A. Kuderer · (Defendants) · Erickson, Zierke, Kuderer, Madsen & Wollschalger · 114 West Second Street · P.O. Box 571 · Fairmont, MN 56031 · 507-238-4711

Richard L. Pemberton* · Hefte, Pemberton, Sorlie & Rufer · Law Office Building · 110 North Mill Street · P.O. Box 866 · Fergus Falls, MN 56538-0866 · 218-736-5493

Edward J. Matonich · (Plaintiffs) · Matonich & Persson · 2031 Second Avenue East · P.O. Box 127 · Hibbing, MN 55746 · 218-263-8881

Robert M. Austin · (Defendants) · Austin & Roth · 715 Cargill Building · Northstar Center · Minneapolis, MN 55402 · 612-332-4273

Richard A. Bowman · (Defendants) · Bowman and Brooke · Midwest Plaza West, Suite 600 · 801 Nicollet Mall · Minneapolis, MN 55402 · 612-339-8682

Tyrone P. Bujold* · (Plaintiffs) · Robins, Kaplan, Miller & Ciresi · 1800 International Centre · 900 Second Avenue South · Minneapolis, MN 55402-3394 · 612-349-8500

Michael V. Ciresi* · (Products Liability) · Robins, Kaplan, Miller & Ciresi · 1800 International Centre · 900 Second Avenue South · Minneapolis, MN 55402-3394 612-349-8500

Phillip A. Cole · (Defendants) · Lommen, Nelson, Cole & Stageberg · 1800 IDS Center · 80 South Eighth Street · Minneapolis, MN 55402 · 612-339-8131

James L. Fetterly* · (Plaintiffs, Products Liability, Professional Malpractice) · Fetterly & Gordon · 808 Nicollet Mall, Suite 800 · Minneapolis, MN 55402 · 612-333-2003

David F. Fitzgerald* · (Plaintiffs, Defendants, Products Liability, Airplane Collision) · Rider, Bennett, Egan & Arundel · 2000 Lincoln Centre · 333 South Seventh Street · Minneapolis, MN 55402 · 612-340-7951

James Fitzmaurice · (Defendants) · Faegre & Benson · 2200 Norwest Center · 90 South Seventh Street · Minneapolis, MN 55402-3901 · 612-336-3000

William D. Flaskamp · (Defendants) · Meagher & Geer · 4200 Multifoods Tower 33 South Sixth Street · Minneapolis, MN 55402 · 612-338-0661

Ludwig B. Gartner, Jr.* · (Defendants, Products Liability, Professional Malpractice, Airplane Collision) · Faegre & Benson · 2200 Norwest Center · 90 South Seventh Street · Minneapolis, MN 55402-3901 · 612-336-3000

Richard G. Hunegs* · (Medical Malpractice, Products Liability, Automobile Collision, Airplane Collision) · DeParcq, Hunegg, Stone, Koenig & Reid · 565 Northstar East · 608 Second Avenue South · Minneapolis, MN 55402 · 612-339-4511

Lewis A. Remele · Bassford, Heckt, Lockhart, Truesdell & Briggs · 3550 Multifoods Tower · 33 South Sixth Street, Suite 3550 · Minneapolis, MN 55402-3787 612-333-3000

Roger R. Roe · (Defendants) · Rider, Bennett, Egan & Arundel · 2000 Lincoln Centre · 333 South Seventh Street · Minneapolis, MN 55402 · 612-340-7951

James R. Schwebel* · (Plaintiffs) · Schwebel, Goetz & Sieben · 5120 IDS Center · 80 South Eighth Street · Minneapolis, MN 55402-2246 · 612-333-8361

Mark N. Stageberg · (Defendants) · Lommen, Nelson, Cole & Stageberg · 1800 IDS Center · 80 South Eighth Street · Minneapolis, MN 55402 · 612-339-8131

Lynn G. Truesdell III* · (Defendants) · Bassford, Heckt, Lockhart, Truesdell & Briggs · 3550 Multifoods Tower · Minneapolis, MN 55402-3787 · 612-333-3000

Donald F. Hunter · (Defendants) · Gislason, Dosland, Hunter & Malecki · 9900 Bren Road East · P.O. Box 5297 · Minnetonka, MN 55343-2297 · 612-933-9900

Gunder D. Gunhus* · (Defendants) · Gunhus, Grinnell, Klinger, Swenson & Guy · 512 Center Avenue · P.O. Box 1077 · Moorhead, MN 56561-1077 · 218-236-6462

C. Allen Dosland* · (Medical Malpractice, Professional Malpractice) · Gislason, Dosland, Hunter and Malecki · State and Center Streets · P.O. Box 458 · New Ulm, MN 56073 · 507-354-3111

Robert R. Dunlap · (Defendants) · Dunlap, Finseth, Berndt & Sandberg · 505 Marquette Bank Building · P.O. Box 549 · Rochester, MN 55903 · 507-288-9111

Gene P. Bradt · Hansen, Dordell, Bradt, Odlaug & Bradt · 1200 Meritor Tower · 444 Cedar Street · St. Paul, MN 55101 · 612-227-8056

Thomas M. Conlin · (Defendants) · Murnane, Conlin, White, Brandt & Hoffman · 18 Marquette Tower · 444 Cedar Street · St. Paul, MN 55101 · 612-227-9411

John F. Eisberg* · (Plaintiffs) · Robins, Kaplan, Miller & Ciresi · 1500 Landmark Towers · 345 Saint Peter Street · St. Paul, MN 55102-1638 · 612-224-5884

Boyd H. Ratchye · (Defendants, Products Liability, Airplane Collision) · Doherty, Rumble & Butler · 2800 Minnesota World Trade Center · 30 East Seventh Street · St. Paul, MN 55101-4999 · 612-291-9333

Russell M. Spence · (Plaintiffs) · Meshbesher & Spence · 2600 Minnesota World Trade Center · 30 East Seventh Street · St. Paul, MN 55501 · 612-227-0799

Robert T. White · (Defendants) · Murnane, Conlin, White, Brandt & Hoffman · 18 Marquette Tower · 444 Cedar Street · St. Paul, MN 55101 · 612-227-9411

PUBLIC UTILITY LAW

Samuel L. Hanson · Briggs and Morgan · 2400 IDS Center · 80 South Eighth Street · Minneapolis, MN 55402 · 612-339-0661

Robert S. Lee · Mackall, Crounse & Moore · 1600 TCF Tower · 121 South Eighth Street · Minneapolis, MN 55402 · 612-333-1341

James A. Gallagher · (Telecommunications) · Maun & Simon · 2300 World Trade Center · 30 East Seventh Street · St. Paul, MN 55101-4904 · 612-229-2900

Harold LeVander, Jr. · Maun & Simon · 2300 World Trade Center · 30 West Seventh Street · St. Paul, MN 55101 · 612-229-2900

REAL ESTATE LAW

Allan E. Mulligan · Larkin, Hoffman, Daly & Lindgren · Northwestern Financial Center, Suite 1500 · 7900 Xerxes Avenue South · Bloomington, MN 55431 · 612-835-3800

William M. Burns · Hanft, Fride, O'Brien, Harries, Swelbar & Burns · 1000 First Bank Place · 130 West Superior Street · Duluth, MN 55802-2994 · 218-722-4766

Philip F. Boelter · Dorsey & Whitney · 2200 First Bank Place East · Minneapolis, MN 55402 · 612-340-2600

John R. Carroll · Best and Flanagan · 3500 IDS Center · Minneapolis, MN 55402 612-339-7121

John S. Crouch · Gray, Plant, Mooty, Mooty & Bennett · 3400 City Center · 33 South Sixth Street · Minneapolis, MN 55402-3796 · 612-343-2800

Stephen J. Davis · 3910 Multifoods Tower · 33 South Sixth Street · Minneapolis, MN 55402 · 612-341-0300

James B. Druck · Popham Haik Schnobrich & Kaufman · 3300 Piper Jaffray Tower · 222 South Ninth Street · Minneapolis, MN 55402 · 612-333-4800

James A. Dueholm · Faegre & Benson · 2200 Norwest Center · 90 South Seventh Street · Minneapolis, MN 55402-3901 · 612-336-3000

Mark F. Engebretson · Faegre & Benson · 2200 Norwest Center · 90 South Seventh Street · Minneapolis, MN 55402-3901 · 612-336-3000

Thomas S. Erickson · (Zoning, Land Use, Commercial Transactions, Industrial Transactions) · Dorsey & Whitney · 2200 First Bank Place East · Minneapolis, MN 55402 · 612-340-2600

Charles S. Ferrell · Faegre & Benson · 2200 Norwest Center · 90 South Seventh Street · Minneapolis, MN 55402-3901 · 612-336-3000

Charles R. Haynor · Briggs and Morgan · 2400 IDS Center · 80 South Eighth Street · Minneapolis, MN 55402 · 612-334-8512

Robert A. Heiberg · Dorsey & Whitney · 2200 First Bank Place East · Minneapolis, MN 55402 · 612-340-2600

Duane E. Joseph · Dorsey & Whitney · 2200 First Bank Place East · Minneapolis, MN 55402 · 612-340-2600

Richard H. Massopust · Oppenheimer Wolff and Donnelly · 45 South Seventh Street, Suite 3400 · Minneapolis, MN 55402 · 612-344-9300

Thomas M. Mayerle · Faegre & Benson · 2200 Norwest Center · 90 South Seventh Street · Minneapolis, MN 55402-3901 · 612-336-3000

Melvin R. Mooty · Gray, Plant, Mooty, Mooty & Bennett · 3400 City Center · 33 South Sixth Street · Minneapolis, MN 55402-3796 · 612-343-2800

Donald P. Norwich · Oppenheimer Wolff and Donnelly · The Plaza VII Building, Suite 3400 · 45 South Seventh Street · Minneapolis, MN 55402 · 612-344-9300

Paul H. Ravich · Robins, Kaplan, Miller & Ciresi · 1800 International Centre · 900 Second Avenue South · Minneapolis, MN 55402-3394 · 612-349-8500

Frederic T. Rosenblatt · Leonard, Street and Deinard · 150 South Fifth Street, Suite 2300 · Minneapolis, MN 55402 · 612-335-1500

Robert J. Silverman · (Eminent Domain, Commercial Transactions, Industrial Transactions) · Dorsey & Whitney · 2200 First Bank Place East · Minneapolis, MN 55402 · 612-340-2600

John W. Thiel · Gray, Plant, Mooty, Mooty & Bennett · 3400 City Center · 33 South Sixth Street · Minneapolis, MN 55402-3796 · 612-343-2800

Mark W. Westra · (Commercial Transactions, Finance, Workouts) · Fabyanske, Svoboda, Westra, Davis & Hart · International Centre II, Suite 1150 · 920 Second Avenue South · Minneapolis, MN 55402 · 612-338-0115

John R. Wheaton · Faegre & Benson · 2200 Norwest Center · 90 South Seventh Street · Minneapolis, MN 55402-3901 · 612-336-3000

TAX AND EMPLOYEE BENEFITS LAW

Gene N. Fuller · Larkin, Hoffman, Daly & Lindgren · Northwestern Financial Center, Suite 1500 · 7900 Xerxes Avenue South · Bloomington, MN 55431 · 612-835-3800

James H. Stewart · Fryberger, Buchanan, Smith & Frederick · 700 Lonsdale Building · 302 West Superior Street · Duluth, MN 55802-1863 · 218-722-0861

David R. Brennan · Faegre & Benson · 2200 Norwest Center · 90 South Seventh Street · Minneapolis, MN 55402-3901 · 612-336-3000

Don D. Carlson · (Employee Benefits) · Dorsey & Whitney · 2200 First Bank Place East · Minneapolis, MN 55402 · 612-340-2600

Jack W. Carlson · Thomsen & Nybeck · Edinborough Corporate Center East, Suite 600 · 3300 Edinborough Way · Minneapolis, MN 55435 · 612-835-7000

Hubert V. Forsier · (Employee Benefits) · Faegre & Benson · 2200 Norwest Center · 90 South Seventh Street · Minneapolis, MN 55402-3901 · 612-336-3000

Bruce D. Grussing · (Employee Benefits) · Gray, Plant, Mooty, Mooty & Bennett 3400 City Center · 33 South Sixth Street · Minneapolis, MN 55402-3796 · 612-343-2800

Richard A. Hackett · Gray, Plant, Mooty, Mooty & Bennett · 3400 City Center 33 South Sixth Street · Minneapolis, MN 55402-3796 · 612-343-2800

George E. Harding · (Employee Benefits) · Faegre & Benson · 2200 Norwest Center · 90 South Seventh Street · Minneapolis, MN 55402-3901 · 612-336-3000

William H. Hippee, Jr. · Dorsey & Whitney · 2200 First Bank Place East · Minneapolis, MN 55402 · 612-340-2600

John S. Jagiela · Lindquist & Vennum · 4200 IDS Center · 80 South Eighth Street · Minneapolis, MN 55402 · 612-371-3211

Phillip H. Martin · Dorsey & Whitney · 2200 First Bank Place East · Minneapolis, MN 55402 · 612-340-2600

John M. Nichols · (Employee Benefits) · Gray, Plant, Mooty, Mooty & Bennett 3400 City Center · 33 South Sixth Street · Minneapolis, MN 55402-3796 · 612-343-2800

Burton G. Ross · Ross, Rosenblatt & Wilson · 4000 Piper Jaffray Tower · 222 South Ninth Street · Minneapolis, MN 55402 · 612-339-4141

Clinton A. Schroeder · (Tax Disputes) · Gray, Plant, Mooty, Mooty & Bennett 3400 City Center · 33 South Sixth Street · Minneapolis, MN 55402-3796 · 612-343-2800

Bruce J. Shnider · Dorsey & Whitney · 2200 First Bank Place East · Minneapolis, MN 55402 · 612-340-2600

John K. Steffen · Faegre & Benson · 2200 Norwest Center · 90 South Seventh Street · Minneapolis, MN 55402-3901 · 612-336-3000

John W. Windhorst, Jr.* · (State Tax, Tax Disputes) · Dorsey & Whitney · 2200 First Bank Place East · Minneapolis, MN 55402 · 612-340-2645

Kimball J. Devoy · (Corporate & Partnership Transactions, Cooperative Taxation) · Doherty, Rumble & Butler · 2800 Minnesota World Trade Center · 30 East Seventh Street · St. Paul, MN 55101-4999 · 612-291-9333

Jerome A. Geis* · (Corporate & Partnership Transactions, State Tax, Tax Disputes) · Briggs and Morgan · 2200 First National Bank Building · St. Paul, MN 55101 · 612-291-1215

John P. Schmidtke · (Employee Benefits) · Oppenheimer Wolff and Donnelly · First Bank Building, Suite 1700 · St. Paul, MN 55101 · 612-223-2500

TRUSTS AND ESTATES

Richard R. Burns · Hanft, Fride, O'Brien, Harries, Swelbar & Burns · 1000 First Bank Place · 130 West Superior Street · Duluth, MN 55802-2994 · 218-722-4766

Mark T. Signorelli · Brown, Andrew, Hallenbeck, Signorelli & Zallar · Alworth Building, Suite 300 · Duluth, MN 55802 · 218-722-1764

James H. Stewart · (Estate Planning) · Fryberger, Buchanan, Smith & Frederick 700 Lonsdale Building · 302 West Superior Street · Duluth, MN 55802-1863 · 218-722-0861

Edward M. Arundel · Rider, Bennett, Egan & Arundel · 2000 Lincoln Centre · 333 South Seventh Street · Minneapolis, MN 55402 · 612-340-7905

William J. Brody · Fredrikson & Byron · 1100 International Centre · 900 Second Avenue South · Minneapolis, MN 55402-3397 · 612-347-7000

John P. Byron · (Estate Planning, Estate Administration) · Fredrikson & Byron · 1100 International Centre · 900 Second Avenue South · Minneapolis, MN 55402-3397 · 612-347-7000

Robert L. Crosby · Best and Flanagan · 3500 IDS Center · Minneapolis, MN 55402 · 612-339-7121

Patrick F. Flaherty* · (Estate Planning, Estate Administration, Charitable Trusts, Foundations) · Moss & Barnett · 4800 Norwest Center · 90 South Seventh Street Minneapolis, MN 55402-4119 · 612-347-0300

John E. Harris · Faegre & Benson · 2200 Norwest Center · 90 South Seventh Street · Minneapolis, MN 55402-3901 · 612-336-3000

Edward G. Heilman · Faegre & Benson · 2200 Norwest Center · 90 South Seventh Street · Minneapolis, MN 55402-3901 · 612-336-3000

Larry R. Henneman · Rider, Bennett, Egan & Arundel · 2000 Lincoln Centre · 333 South Seventh Street · Minneapolis, MN 55402 · 612-340-7951

Larry W. Johnson · Dorsey & Whitney · 2200 First Bank Place East · Minneapolis, MN 55402 · 612-340-2600

Sidney Kaplan · (Estate Planning, Estate Administration, Charitable Trusts) · Mackall, Crounse & Moore · 1600 TCF Tower · 121 South Eighth Street · Minneapolis, MN 55402 · 612-333-1341

Gene C. Olson · Rider, Bennett, Egan & Arundel · 2000 Lincoln Centre · 333 South Seventh Street · Minneapolis, MN 55402 · 612-340-7905

John L. Powers · Fredrikson & Byron · 1100 International Centre · 900 Second Avenue South · Minneapolis, MN 55402-3397 · 612-347-7000

Raymond A. Reister · Dorsey & Whitney · 2200 First Bank Place East · Minneapolis, MN 55402 · 612-340-2600

Richard C. Schmoker · Faegre & Benson · 2200 Norwest Center · 90 South Seventh Street · Minneapolis, MN 55402-3901 · 612-336-3000

Clinton A. Schroeder · (Charitable Trusts) · Gray, Plant, Mooty, Mooty & Bennett · 3400 City Center · 33 South Sixth Street · Minneapolis, MN 55402-3796 · 612-343-2800

Robert A. Stein · Gray, Plant, Mooty, Mooty & Bennett · 3400 City Center · 33 South Sixth Street · Minneapolis, MN 55402-3796 · 612-343-2800

Robert J. Struyk · Dorsey & Whitney · 2200 First Bank Place East · Minneapolis, MN 55402 · 612-340-2600

Robert G. Weber · Fredrikson & Byron · 1100 International Centre · 900 Second Avenue South · Minneapolis, MN 55402-3397 · 612-347-7000

John R. Wicks · Dorsey & Whitney · 201 First Avenue, SW, Suite 340 · Rochester, MN 55902 · 507-288-3156

Steve A. Brand · Briggs and Morgan · 2200 First National Bank Building · St. Paul, MN 55101 · 612-223-6577

Robert L. Bullard · Oppenheimer Wolff and Donnelly · First Bank Building, Suite 1700 · St. Paul, MN 55101 · 612-223-2500

Terence N. Doyle · Briggs and Morgan · 2200 First National Bank Building · St. Paul, MN 55101 · 612-291-1215

John C. Johanneson · Maun, Green, Hayes, Simon, Johanneson and Brehl · 332 Hamm Building · St. Paul, MN 55102 · 612-224-7300

John J. McNeely · Briggs and Morgan · 2200 First National Bank Building · St. Paul, MN 55101 · 612-291-1215

Cole Oehler · Briggs and Morgan · 2200 First National Bank Building · St. Paul, MN 55101 · 612-291-1215

Lehan J. Ryan · Oppenheimer Wolff and Donnelly · First Bank Building, Suite 1700 · St. Paul, MN 55101 · 612-223-2500

McNeil V. Seymour · Briggs and Morgan · 2200 First National Bank Building · St. Paul, MN 55101 · 612-291-1215

Richard A. Wilhoit · Doherty, Rumble & Butler · 2800 Minnesota World Trade Center · 30 East Seventh Street · St. Paul, MN 55101-4999 · 612-291-9333

MISSISSIPPI

BANKRUPTCY LAW

Robert A. Byrd · Robert A. Byrd & Associates · 157 Reynoir Street · P.O. Box 1939 · Biloxi, MS 39533 · 601-432-8123

Jefferson C. Bell · 216 West Pine Street · Hattiesburg, MS 39401 · 601-582-5011

Richard T. Bennett · (Business Reorganization, Creditors' Rights, Debtors' Rights, Bankruptcy Litigation) · Bennett, Lotterhos, Sulser & Wilson · 200 North State Street · P.O. Box 98 · Jackson, MS 39205-0098 · 601-944-0466

Robert W. King* · (Creditors' Rights) · King & Spencer · Court Square South Building · 429 Tombigbee Street · P.O. Box 123 · Jackson, MS 39205-0123 · 601-948-1547

Robert G. Nichols, Jr. · Law Offices of Robert G. Nichols · Five Old River Place, Suite 204 · P.O. Box 1526 · Jackson, MS 39215-1526 · 601-353-9522

James W. O'Mara · (Business Reorganization, Creditors' Rights, Bankruptcy Litigation) · Butler, Snow, O'Mara, Stevens & Cannada · Deposit Guaranty Plaza, 17th Floor · P.O. Box 22567 · Jackson, MS 39225-2567 · 601-948-5711

Pat H. Scanlon* · Young, Scanlon and Sessums · 2000 Deposit Guaranty Plaza · P.O. Box 23059 · Jackson, MS 39225-3059 · 601-948-6100

BUSINESS LITIGATION

Fred C. DeLong, Jr. · Campbell, DeLong, Hagwood, Wade & Stuart · 923 Washington Avenue · P.O. Box 1856 · Greenville, MS 38702-1856 · 601-335-6011

W. Joel Blass · Mize, Thompson & Blass · Gulf National Bank Building, Suite 310 · P.O. Box 160 · Gulfport, MS 39502 · 601-863-2612

Rowland W. Heidelberg · Heidelberg, Sutherland and McKenzie · The 301 West Pine Building · P.O. Box 1070 · Hattiesburg, MS 39403 · 601-545-8180

Frank D. Montague, Jr. · Montague, Pittman, Rogers & Schwartz · 525 Main Street · P.O. Drawer 1975 · Hattiesburg, MS 39403-1975 · 601-544-1234

Alex A. Alston, Jr.* · Thomas, Price, Alston, Jones & Davis · 121 North State Street · P.O. Drawer 1532 · Jackson, MS 39215-1532 · 601-948-6882

Lawrence J. Franck · Butler, Snow, O'Mara, Stevens & Cannada · 1700 Deposit Guaranty Plaza, 17th Floor · P.O. Box 22567 · Jackson, MS 39225-2567 · 601-948-5711

William F. Goodman, Jr.* · (Banking, Commercial) · Watkins & Eager · The Emporium Building · 400 East Capitol Street · Jackson, MS 39201 · 601-948-6470

George P. Hewes III · Brunini, Grantham, Grower & Hewes · 1400 Trustmark Building · P.O. Drawer 119 · Jackson, MS 39205 · 601-948-3101

Alan W. Perry* · Forman, Perry, Watkins & Krutz · One Jackson Place, Suite 1200 · P.O. Box 22608 · Jackson, MS 39225-2608 · 601-969-6011

Thomas D. Bourdeaux* · (Commercial) · Bourdeaux & Jones · 505 Twenty-First Avenue · P.O. Box 2009 · Meridian, MS 39302-2009 · 601-693-2393

Fred C. DeLong, Jr.* · Campbell, DeLong, Hagwood, Wade & Stuart · 923 Washington Avenue · P.O. Box 1856 · Greenville, MS 38702-1856 · 601-335-6011

W. Joel Blass · Mize, Thompson & Blass · Gulf National Bank Building, Suite 310 · P.O. Box 160 · Gulfport, MS 39501 · 601-863-2612

Charles R. Galloway · Galloway & Galloway · 1300 Twenty-Fifth Avenue, Suite 204 · P.O. Drawer 4248 · Gulfport, MS 39502 · 601-864-1170

George E. Morse · White & Morse · One Hancock Plaza, Suite 1209 · P.O. Drawer 100 · Gulfport, MS 39502 · 601-863-9821

James F. McKenzie · Heidelberg, Sutherland and McKenzie · The 301 West Pine Building · P.O. Box 1070 · Hattiesburg, MS 39403 · 601-545-8180

Frank D. Montague, Jr. · Montague, Pittman, Rogers & Schwartz · 525 Main Street · P.O. Drawer 1975 · Hattiesburg, MS 39403-1975 · 601-544-1234

Leigh B. Allen III · Brunini, Grantham, Grower & Hewes · 1400 Trustmark Building · P.O. Drawer 119 · Jackson, MS 39205 · 601-948-3101

William O. Carter, Jr. · Wise Carter Child & Caraway · 600 Heritage Building · Congress at Capitol · P.O. Box 651 · Jackson, MS 39205 · 601-354-2385

George R. Fair · Watkins & Eager · The Emporium Building · 400 East Capitol Street · Jackson, MS 39201 · 601-948-6470

E. Clifton Hodge, Jr. · (Banking, Financial Institutions, Mergers & Acquisitions, Securities Regulation) · Phelps Dunbar · Mirror Lake Plaza, Suite 1400 · 2829 Lakeland Drive · P.O. Box 55507 · Jackson, MS 39296-5507 · 601-939-3895

William Steene Painter · Watkins Ludlam & Stennis · 633 North State Street · P.O. Box 427 · Jackson, MS 39205-0427 · 601-949-4848

Edward A. Wilmesherr · (Administrative, Banking, Financial Institutions, Mergers & Acquisitions) · Butler, Snow, O'Mara, Stevens & Cannada · Deposit Guaranty Plaza, 17th Floor · P.O. Box 22567 · Jackson, MS 39225-2567 · 601-948-5711

Thomas D. Bourdeaux* · Bourdeaux & Jones · 505 Twenty-First Avenue · P.O. Box 2009 · Meridian, MS 39302-2009 · 601-693-2393

F. M. Bush III · Phelps Dunbar · One Mississippi Plaza, Suite 700 · P.O. Box 1220 Tupelo, MS 38802-1220 · 601-842-7907

Fred M. Bush, Jr. · Phelps Dunbar · One Mississippi Plaza, Suite 700 · P.O. Box 1220 · Tupelo, MS 38802-1220 · 601-842-7907

CRIMINAL DEFENSE

John Booth Farese* · (Federal Court, State Court) · Farese, Farese & Farese · P.O. Box 98 · Ashland, MS 38603 · 601-224-6211

Boyce Holleman · 1913 Fifteenth Street · P.O. Drawer 1030 · Gulfport, MS 39502 · 601-863-3142

Joe Sam Owen · Owen, Galloway and Clark · The Merchants Bank Building · 1300 Twenty-Fifth Avenue · P.O. Box 218 · Gulfport, MS 39501 · 601-868-2821

Weaver E. Gore, Jr.* · Eastover Bank Building, Suite 820 · 120 North Congress Street · P.O. Box 186 · Jackson, MS 39205 · 601-354-4057

Thomas E. Royals* · Royals & Hartung · Eastover Bank Building, Suite 600 · P.O. Box 22909 · Jackson, MS 39225-2909 · 601-948-7777

FAMILY LAW

Joseph R. Meadows* · Meadows, Riley, Koenenn & Teel · 1720 Twenty-Third Avenue · P.O. Drawer 550 · Gulfport, MS 39501 · 601-864-4511

James A. Becker, Jr. · Watkins & Eager · The Emporium Building · 400 East Capitol Street · Jackson, MS 39201 · 601-948-6470

L. C. James · L. C. James & Associates · 105 North State Street · P.O. Box 897 · Jackson, MS 39205 · 601-354-0797

Robert W. King* · (Divorce) · King & Spencer · Court Square South Building · 429 Tombigbee Street · P.O. Box 123 · Jackson, MS 39205-0123 · 601-948-1547

FIRST AMENDMENT LAW

W. Joel Blass · Mize, Thompson & Blass · Gulf National Bank Building, Suite 310 · P.O. Box 160 · Gulfport, MS 39502 · 601-863-2612

John C. Henegan · Butler, Snow, O'Mara, Stevens & Cannada · Deposit Guaranty Plaza, 17th Floor · P.O. Box 22567 · Jackson, MS 39225-2567 · 601-948-5711

Luther T. Munford · Phelps Dunbar · Mirror Lake Plaza, Suite 1400 · 2829 Lakeland Drive · P.O. Box 55507 · Jackson, MS 39296-5507 · 601-939-3895

Leonard D. Van Slyke · Thomas, Price, Alston, Jones & Davis · 121 North State Street · P.O. Drawer 1532 · Jackson, MS 39215-1532 · 601-948-6882

HEALTH CARE LAW

Richard G. Cowart · Watkins Ludlam & Stennis · 633 North State Street · P.O. Box 427 · Jackson, MS 39205-0427 · 601-949-4848

George Q. Evans · Wise Carter Child & Caraway · 600 Heritage Building · Congress at Capitol · P.O. Box 651 · Jackson, MS 39205 · 601-354-2385

LABOR AND EMPLOYMENT LAW

Danny E. Cupit · (Labor, Individuals) · Cupit, Jones & Fairbank · 304 North Congress Street · P.O. Box 22929 · Jackson, MS 39225 · 601-355-2099

Louis A. Fuselier · (Management) · Fuselier, Ott, McKee & Shivers · 2100 Deposit Guaranty Plaza · Jackson, MS 39201 · 601-948-2226

John L. Maxey II · (Labor, Individuals) · Maxey, Pigott, Wann & Begley · Heritage Building, Suite 410 · 401 East Capitol Street · P.O. Box 3977 · Jackson, MS 39207 · 601-355-8855

M. Curtiss McKee* · (Management) · Fuselier, Ott, McKee & Shivers · 2100 Deposit Guaranty Plaza · Jackson, MS 39201-2376 · 601-948-2226

Kenneth E. Milam · (Management) · Phelps Dunbar · Mirror Lake Plaza, Suite 1400 · 2829 Lakeland Drive · P.O. Box 55507 · Jackson, MS 39296-5507 · 601-939-3895

Armin J. Moeller · (Management) · Phelps Dunbar · Mirror Lake Plaza, Suite 1400 · 2829 Lakeland Drive · P.O. Box 55507 · Jackson, MS 39296-5507 · 601-939-3895

Emile C. Ott · (Management) · Fuselier, Ott, McKee & Shivers · 2100 Deposit Guaranty Plaza · Jackson, MS 39201 · 601-948-2226

NATURAL RESOURCES AND ENVIRONMENTAL LAW

Alex A. Alston, Jr.* · (Plaintiffs) · Thomas, Price, Alston, Jones & Davis · 121 North State Street · P.O. Drawer 1532 · Jackson, MS 39215-1532 · 601-948-6882

Edmund L. Brunini, Jr. · Brunini, Grantham, Grower & Hewes · 1400 Trustmark Building · P.O. Drawer 119 · Jackson, MS 39205 · 601-948-3101

Thomas R. Crews · Thompson, Alexander & Crews · Thompson Building · 118 North Congress Street · P.O. Box 410 · Jackson, MS 39205 · 601-948-4831

Martha W. Gerald · Gerald & Brand · One Jackson Place, Suite 900 · P.O. Box 158 · Jackson, MS 39205-0158 · 601-948-3030

John M. Grower · Brunini, Grantham, Grower & Hewes · 1400 Trustmark Building · P.O. Drawer 119 · Jackson, MS 39205 · 601-948-3101

Scott P. Hemleben* · (Oil & Gas, Water, Air, Solid Waste) · Gerald & Brand · One Jackson Place, Suite 900 · P.O. Box 158 · Jackson, MS 39205-0158 · 601-948-3030

Otis Johnson, Jr. · (Oil & Gas) · Heidelberg & Woodliff · Capital Towers, Suite 1400 · P.O. Box 23040 · Jackson, MS 39225 · 601-948-3800

John Land McDavid* · (Oil & Gas) · McDavid, Noblin & West · 200 Security Centre North, Suite 1000 · 210 South Lamar Street · Jackson, MS 39201 · 601-948-3305

Jefferson D. Stewart* · (Oil & Gas, Water) · Brunini, Grantham, Grower & Hewes · 1400 Trustmark Building · P.O. Drawer 119 · Jackson, MS 39205 · 601-948-3101

Glenn G. Taylor* · (Oil & Gas, Hazardous Waste) · Copeland Cook Taylor & Bush · 1700 Capital Towers · Jackson, MS 39225-2132 · 601-354-0123

Luther M. Thompson · (Oil & Gas) · Heidelberg & Woodliff · Capital Towers, Suite 1400 · P.O. Box 23040 · Jackson, MS 39225 · 601-948-3800

Walker L. Watters · Gerald & Brand · One Jackson Place, Suite 900 · P.O. Box 158 · Jackson, MS 39205-0158 · 601-948-3030

William Marion Smith · Adams, Forman, Truly, Smith & Bramlette · 409 Franklin Street · P.O. Box 1307 · Natchez, MS 39120-1307 · 601-442-6495

PERSONAL INJURY LITIGATION

Charles M. Merkel · (Plaintiffs) · Merkel & Cocke · 30 Delta Avenue · P.O. Box 1388 · Clarksdale, MS 38614 · 601-627-9641

William J. Threadgill · (Defendants) · Mitchell, McNutt, Threadgill, Smith & Sams · 215 Fifth Street North · P.O. Box 1366 · Columbus, MS 39703 · 601-328-2316

Fred C. DeLong, Jr. · (Defendants) · Campbell, DeLong, Hagwood, Wade & Stuart · 923 Washington Avenue · P.O. Box 1856 · Greenville, MS 38702-1856 · 601-335-6011

Harry R. Allen* · (Defendants, Medical Malpractice, Products Liability, Fire & Casualty Litigation-Insurance) · Bryan, Nelson, Allen, Schroeder, Cobb & Hood 1201 Thirty-First Avenue · P.O. Drawer 4108 · Gulfport, MS 39502-4108 · 601-864-4011

Rae Bryant* · (Defendants) · Bryant, Colingo, Williams & Clark · 2223 Fourteenth Street · P.O. Box 10 · Gulfport, MS 39502-0010 · 601-863-6101

Roger T. Clark · (Defendants) · Bryant, Colingo, Williams & Clark · 2223 Fourteenth Street · P.O. Box 10 · Gulfport, MS 39502-0010 · 601-863-6101

Boyce Holleman · 1913 Fifteenth Street · P.O. Drawer 1030 · Gulfport, MS 39502 601-863-3142

Joe Sam Owen · Owen, Galloway and Clark · The Merchants Bank Building · 1300 25th Avenue · P.O. Box 218 · Gulfport, MS 39502 · 601-868-2821

Thomas L. Stennis III · (Defendants) · Stennis & McDonald · 2301 Fourteenth Street, Suite 600 · Gulfport, MS 39502 · 601-867-6230

Rowland W. Heidelberg · (Defendants) · Heidelberg, Sutherland and McKenzie The 301 West Pine Building · P.O. Box 1070 · Hattiesburg, MS 39403 · 601-545-8180

Curtis E. Coker · (Defendants) · Daniel, Coker, Horton and Bell · 111 East Capitol Building, Suite 600 · P.O. Box 1084 · Jackson, MS 39215 · 601-969-7607

James P. Cothren · (Plaintiffs) · Cothren & Pittman · 410 South Presidents Street P.O. Box 22985 · Jackson, MS 39225-2985 · 601-948-6151

Joe H. Daniel · (Defendants) · Daniel, Coker, Horton and Bell · 111 East Capitol Building, Suite 600 · P.O. Box 1084 · Jackson, MS 39215 · 601-969-7607

Lawrence J. Franck · (Defendants) · Butler, Snow, O'Mara, Stevens & Cannada Deposit Guaranty Plaza, 17th Floor · P.O. Box 22567 · Jackson, MS 39225-2567 601-948-5711

William F. Goodman, Jr.* · (Defendants) · Watkins & Eager · The Emporium Building · 400 East Capitol Street · Jackson, MS 39201 · 601-948-6470

Lee Davis Thames* · (Products Liability, Toxic Tort) · Butler, Snow, O'Mara, Stevens & Cannada · Deposit Guaranty Plaza, 17th Floor · P.O. Box 22567 · Jackson, MS 39225-2567 · 601-948-5711

Ernest W. Graves* · (Defendants) · Gibbes, Graves, Mullins, Bullock & Ferris · 1107 West Sixth Street · P.O. Box 1409 · Laurel, MS 39441-1409 · 601-649-8611

Leonard B. Melvin, Jr. · (Plaintiffs) · Melvin & Melvin · 424 Sawmill Road · P.O. Box 142 · Laurel, MS 39441 · 601-426-6306

Thomas D. Bourdeaux* · (Defendants, Products Liability) · Bourdeaux & Jones 505 Twenty-First Avenue · P.O. Box 2009 · Meridian, MS 39302-2009 · 601-693-2393

Walter W. Eppes, Jr.* · (Defendants, Medical Malpractice, Products Liability, Professional Malpractice) · Eppes, Watts & Shannon · 4805 Poplar Springs Drive P.O. Box 3787 · Meridian, MS 39303-3787 · 601-483-3968

Jack F. Dunbar · Holcomb, Dunbar, Connell, Chaffin & Willard · Courthouse Square · 1217 Jackson Avenue · P.O. Box 707 · Oxford, MS 38655 · 601-234-8775

Grady F. Tollison, Jr.* · (Plaintiffs) · Tollison Austin & Twiford · 103 North Lamar Avenue · P.O. Box 1216 · Oxford, MS 38655 · 601-234-7070

L. F. Sams, Jr.* · (Defendants, Medical Malpractice, Products Liability, Professional Malpractice) · Mitchell, McNutt, Threadgill, Smith & Sams · 105 South Front Street · P.O. Box 7120 · Tupelo, MS 38802-7120 · 601-842-3871

William H. Liston · (Plaintiffs) · Liston/Lancaster · 128 North Quitman Avenue P.O. Box 645 · Winona, MS 38967 · 601-283-2132

PUBLIC UTILITY LAW

James K. Child, Jr. · Wise Carter Child & Caraway · 600 Heritage Building · Congress at Capitol · P.O. Box 651 · Jackson, MS 39205 · 601-968-5500

Newt P. Harrison · Brunini, Grantham, Grower & Hewes · 1400 Trustmark Building · P.O. Drawer 119 · Jackson, MS 39205 · 601-948-3101

Harold D. Miller · Butler, Snow, O'Mara, Stevens & Cannada · Deposit Guaranty Plaza, 17th Floor · P.O. Box 22567 · Jackson, MS 39225-2567 · 601-948-5711

REAL ESTATE LAW

Charles K. Pringle · 833 Vieux Marche · P.O. Box 211 · Biloxi, MS 39533 · 601-374-1747

Walter Rayford Jones · Jones, Jones & Jones · 1605 Twenty-Third Avenue · P.O. Box 4227 · Gulfport, MS 39502 · 601-864-8965

James F. McKenzie · Heidelberg, Sutherland and McKenzie · The 301 West Pine Building · P.O. Box 1070 · Hattiesburg, MS 39403 · 601-545-8180

Bobby L. Covington · Taylor, Covington, Smith, Lambert & Bailey · 315 Tombigee Street · Jackson, MS 39201 · 601-961-4861

Henry M. Kendall · Trustmark National Bank, Suite 537 · 248 East Capitol Street P.O. Box 330 · Jackson, MS 39205 · 601-353-2797

William C. Smith, Jr. · Taylor, Covington, Smith, Lambert & Bailey · 315 Tombigee Street · Jackson, MS 39201 · 601-961-4861

Jim B. Tohill · Watkins, Ludlam & Stennis · 633 North State Street · P.O. Box 427 · Jackson, MS 39205-0427 · 601-949-4900

TAX AND EMPLOYEE BENEFITS LAW

Paul M. Newton · Newton and Hoff · 2416 Fourteenth Street · P.O. Box 910 · Gulfport, MS 39502 · 601-863-8827

D. Carl Black, Jr. · (Tax, Employee Benefits) · Butler, Snow, O'Mara, Stevens & Cannada · Deposit Guaranty Plaza, 17th Floor · P.O. Box 22567 · Jackson, MS 39225-2567 · 601-948-5711

James K. Dossett, Jr. · Dossett, Goode, Barnes and Broom · Security Centre North, Suite 900 · 200 Lamar Street · P.O. Box 2449 · Jackson, MS 39225-2449 · 601-948-3160

David B. Grishman · (Corporate & Partnership Transactions, State Tax, Tax Disputes) · Watkins Ludlam & Stennis · 633 North State Street · P.O. Box 427 · Jackson, MS 39205 · 601-949-4900

C. Delbert Hosemann, Jr. · (Employee Benefits) · Phelps Dunbar · Mirror Lake Plaza, Suite 1400 · 2829 Lakeland Drive · P.O. Box 55507 · Jackson, MS 39296-5507 · 601-939-3895

Lauch M. Magruder, Jr. · (State Tax, Tax Disputes) · Butler, Snow, O'Mara, Stevens & Cannada · P.O. Box 22567 · Jackson, MS 39225-2567 · 601-948-5711

Hugh C. Montgomery, Jr.* · (State Tax, Tax Disputes) · Butler, Snow, O'Mara, Stevens & Cannada · 1700 Deposit Guaranty Plaza · Jackson, MS 39201 · 601-354-5504

TRUSTS AND ESTATES

Edward P. Connell · Holcomb, Dunbar, Connell, Chaffin & Willard · 152 Delta Avenue · P.O. Box 368 · Clarksdale, MS 38614 · 601-627-2241

Hunter M. Gholson · Gholson Hicks & Nichols · P.O. Box 1111 · Columbus, MS 39703-1111 · 601-327-0662

Paul M. Newton · Newton and Hoff · 2416 Fourteenth Street · P.O. Box 910 · Gulfport, MS 39502 · 601-863-8827

Leigh B. Allen III · Brunini, Grantham, Grower & Hewes · 1400 Trustmark Building · P.O. Drawer 119 · Jackson, MS 39205 · 601-948-3101

D. Carl Black, Jr. · Butler, Snow, O'Mara, Stevens & Cannada · Deposit Guaranty Plaza, 17th Floor · P.O. Box 22567 · Jackson, MS 39225-2567 · 601-948-5711

William O. Carter, Jr. · Wise Carter Child & Caraway · 600 Heritage Building · Congress at Capitol · P.O. Box 651 · Jackson, MS 39205 · 601-354-2385

Lauch M. Magruder, Jr. · (Estate Planning, Estate Administration) · Butler, Snow, O'Mara, Stevens & Cannada · P.O. Box 22567 · Jackson, MS 39225-2567 601-948-5711

Jay A. Travis III · Butler, Snow, O'Mara, Stevens & Cannada · Deposit Guaranty Plaza, 17th Floor · P.O. Box 22567 · Jackson, MS 39225-2567 · 601-948-5711

F. M. Bush III · Phelps Dunbar · One Mississippi Plaza, Suite 700 · P.O. Box 1220 Tupelo, MS 38802-1220 · 601-842-7907

MISSOURI

BANKRUPTCY LAW

James C. Mordy · Morrison, Hecker, Curtis, Kuder & Parrish · 1700 Bryant Building · 1102 Grand Avenue · Kansas City, MO 64106-2370 · 816-842-5910

Michael R. Roser* · (Business Reorganization, Creditors' Rights, Bankruptcy Litigation) · Lathrop, Norquist & Miller · 2600 Mutual Benefit Life Building · 2345 Grand Avenue · Kansas City, MO 64108 · 816-842-0820

Mendel Small · (Business Reorganization, Creditors' Rights, Debtors' Rights, Bankruptcy Litigation) · Spencer Fane Britt & Browne · 1400 Commerce Bank Building · 1000 Walnut Street · Kansas City, MO 64106-2140 · 816-474-8100

R. Pete Smith* · (Business Reorganization, Creditors' Rights, Debtors' Rights, Bankruptcy Litigation) · McDowell, Rice & Smith · 12 Wyandotte Plaza, Suite 1300 · 120 West 12th Street · Kansas City, MO 64105-1932 · 816-221-5400

Donald B. Stelle · Morrison, Hecker, Curtis, Kuder & Parrish · 1700 Bryant Building · 1102 Grand Avenue · Kansas City, MO 64106-2370 · 816-842-5910

Robert H. Brownlee · Thompson & Mitchell · One Mercantile Center, Suite 3300 · St. Louis, MO 63101 · 314-231-7676

Steven Goldstein · Husch, Eppenberger, Donohue, Cornfeld & Jenkins · The Boatmen's Tower, 13th Floor · 100 North Broadway · St. Louis, MO 63102 · 314-421-4800

David A. Lander · (Business Reorganization, Creditors' Rights, Debtors' Rights, Bankruptcy Litigation) · Thompson & Mitchell · One Mercantile Center, Suite 3400 · St. Louis, MO 63101 · 314-342-1618

Lloyd A. Palans · Bryan, Cave, McPheeters & McRoberts · 500 North Broadway St. Louis, MO 63102-2186 · 314-231-8600

Gregory D. Willard · (Business Reorganization, Creditors' Rights, Debtors' Rights, Bankruptcy Litigation) · Bryan, Cave, McPheeters & McRoberts · 500 North Broadway · St. Louis, MO 63102-2186 · 314-231-8600

BUSINESS LITIGATION

James E. Reeves · Ward & Reeves · 711 Ward Avenue · P.O. Box 169 · Caruthersville, MO 63830 · 314-333-2396

Spencer Brown* · Deacy and Deacy · 1000 Bryant Building · 1102 Grant Avenue Kansas City, MO 64106 · 816-421-4000

Thomas E. Deacy, Jr. · Deacy & Dearcy · 1000 Bryant Building · 1102 Grand Street · Kansas City, MO 64106 · 816-421-4000

Robert L. Driscoll* · (Commercial, Energy) · Stinson, Mag & Fizzell · 1201 Walnut, Suite 2800 · P.O. Box 419251 · Kansas City, MO 64141-6251 · 816-842-8600

Reed O. Gentry* · Field, Gentry, Benjamin & Robertson · 600 East 11th Street Kansas City, MO 64106 · 816-842-6031

John M. Kilroy · Shughart, Thomson & Kilroy · 12 Wyandotte Plaza, Suite 1800 · 120 West 12th Street · Kansas City, MO 64105 · 816-421-3355

William H. Sanders, Sr.* · Blackwell Sanders Matheny Weary & Lombardi · Two Pershing Square, Suite 1100 · 2300 Main Street · P.O. Box 419777 · Kansas City, MO 64141-6777 · 816-274-6800

R. Lawrence Ward* · (Antitrust, Commercial, Securities) · Shughart, Thomson & Kilroy · 12 Wyandotte Plaza, Suite 1800 · 120 West 12th Street · Kansas City, MO 64105 · 816-421-3355

Roger D. Stanton* · (Banking, Commercial, Energy, Finance, Securities) · Stinson, Mag & Fizzell · 7500 West 110th Street · Overland Park, MO 66210-2329 · 913-451-8600

Jerry L. Redfern · Neil, Newman, Bradshaw & Freeman · One Corporate Center, Suite 1-130 · 1949 East Sunshine · P.O. Box 10327 · Springfield, MO 65808 · 417-882-9090

Robert Smith Allen* · Lewis, Rice & Fingersh · 611 Olive Street, 14th Floor · St. Louis, MO 63101 · 314-444-7600

Alan C. Kohn · Kohn, Shands, Elbert, Gianoulakis & Giljum · One Mercantile Center, 24th Floor · St. Louis, MO 63101 · 314-241-3963

Henry D. Menghini · Evans & Dixon · Marquette Building, 16th Floor · 314 North Broadway · St. Louis, MO 63102-2093 · 314-621-7755

Alan E. Popkin · Popkin & Stern · 8182 Maryland Avenue, 15th Floor · St. Louis, MO 63105 · 314-862-0900

William A. Richter · Peper, Martin, Jensen, Maichel and Hetlage · 720 Olive Street, 24th Floor · St. Louis, MO 63101 · 314-421-3850

Veryl L. Riddle* · Bryan, Cave, McPheeters & McRoberts · 500 North Broadway · St. Louis, MO 63102-2186 · 314-231-8600

John C. Shepherd · Armstrong, Teasdale, Schlafly, Davis & Dicus · One Metropolitan Square · St. Louis, MO 63102-2740 · 314-621-5070

Thomas E. Wack* · (Antitrust, Appellate, Finance, Securities) · Bryan, Cave, McPheeters & McRoberts · 500 North Broadway · St. Louis, MO 63102-2186 · 314-231-8600

W. Stanley Walch* · (Banking, Commercial, RICO, Securities) · Thompson & Mitchell · One Mercantile Center, Suite 3400 · St. Louis, MO 63101 · 314-231-7676

Thomas C. Walsh* · (Appellate, Commercial, Securities, Trademarks) · Bryan, Cave, McPheeters & McRoberts · 500 North Broadway · St. Louis, MO 63102-2186 · 314-231-8600

CORPORATE LAW

John R. Bancroft · (Corporate Finance, Insurance, Mergers & Acquisitions, Securities) · Morrison, Hecker, Curtis, Kuder & Parrish · 1700 Bryant Building · 1102 Grand Avenue · Kansas City, MO 64106-2370 · 816-691-2600

Thomas I. Gill · Smith, Gill, Fisher & Butts · One Kansas City Place, 35th Floor 1200 Main Street · Kansas City, MO 64105 · 816-474-7400

William A. Hirsch · Morrison, Hecker, Curtis, Kuder & Parrish · 1700 Bryant Building · 1102 Grand Avenue · Kansas City, MO 64106-2370 · 816-842-5910

Basil W. Kelsey · (Utilities) · Spencer Fane Britt & Browne · 1400 Commerce Bank Building · 1000 Walnut Street · Kansas City, MO 64106-2140 · 816-474-8100

C. Maxwell Logan · Shook, Hardy & Bacon · One Kansas City Place · 1200 Main Street · Kansas City, MO 64105 · 816-474-6550

Robert P. Lyons · Spencer Fane Britt & Browne · 1400 Commerce Bank Building 1000 Walnut Street · Kansas City, MO 64106-2140 · 816-474-8100

John F. Marvin · Watson, Ess, Marshall & Enggas · 1010 Grand Avenue · Kansas City, MO 64106-2271 · 816-842-3132

Howard H. Mick · (Banking, Corporate Finance, Financial Institutions, Mergers & Acquisitions) · Stinson, Mag & Fizzell · 1201 Walnut, Suite 2800 · P.O. Box 419251 · Kansas City, MO 64141-6251 · 816-842-8600

Jennings J. Newcom · Shook, Hardy & Bacon · One Kansas City Place · 1200 Main Street · Kansas City, MO 64105 · 816-474-6550

Richard N. Nixon · (Banking, Corporate Finance, Financial Institutions, Mergers & Acquisitions) · Stinson, Mag & Fizzell · 1201 Walnut, Suite 2800 · P.O. Box 419251 · Kansas City, MO 64141-6251 · 816-842-8600

William M. Stapleton · Lathrop, Norquist & Miller · 2600 Mutual Benefit Life Building · 2345 Grand Avenue · Kansas City, MO 64108 · 816-842-0820

Daniel C. Weary · Blackwell Sanders Matheny Weary & Lombardi · Two Pershing Square, Suite 1100 · 2300 Main Street · P.O. Box 419777 · Kansas City, MO 64141-6777 · 816-274-6800

Ralph G. Wrobley · Bryan, Cave, McPheeters & McRoberts · 2500 City Center Square · 1100 Main Street · Kansas City, MO 64105 · 816-842-7444

Jerry L. Redfern · Neil, Newman, Bradshaw & Freeman · One Corporate Center, Suite 1-130 · 1949 East Sunshine · P.O. Box 10327 · Springfield, MO 65808 · 417-882-9090

Charles C. Allen, Jr. · Lewis, Rice & Fingersh · 611 Olive Street, 14th Floor · St. Louis, MO 63101 · 314-444-7600

Thomas V. Connelly · Bryan, Cave, McPheeters & McRoberts · 500 North Broadway · St. Louis, MO 63102-2186 · 314-231-8600

John J. Goebel · Bryan, Cave, McPheeters & McRoberts · 500 North Broadway St. Louis, MO 63102-2186 · 314-231-8600

Edward B. Greensfelder · Greensfelder, Hemker & Gale · 1800 Equitable Building · Ten South Broadway · St. Louis, MO 63102 · 314-241-9090

William G. Guerri · Thompson & Mitchell · One Mercantile Center, Suite 3400 St. Louis, MO 63101 · 314-231-7676

Michael F. Lause · Thompson & Mitchell · One Mercantile Center, Suite 3400 St. Louis, MO 63101 · 314-231-7676

Don G. Lents · (Corporate Finance, International, Leveraged Buyouts, Mergers & Acquisitions) · Bryan, Cave, McPheeters & McRoberts · 500 North Broadway St. Louis, MO 63102-2186 · 314-231-8600

John V. Lonsberg · Bryan, Cave, McPheeters & McRoberts · 500 North Broadway · St. Louis, MO 63102-2186 · 314-231-8600

Walter L. Metcalfe, Jr. · Bryan, Cave, McPheeters & McRoberts · 500 North Broadway · St. Louis, MO 63102-2186 · 314-231-8600

Paul F. Pautler · (Corporate Finance, Financial Institutions, Mergers & Acquisitions, Securities) · Thompson & Mitchell · One Mercantile Center, Suite 3400 · St. Louis, MO 63101 · 314-231-7676

Robert L. Sweney · Bryan, Cave, McPheeters & McRoberts · 500 North Broadway · St. Louis, MO 63102-2186 · 314-231-8600

David F. Ulmer · (Banking, Financial Institutions, Mergers & Acquisitions) · Thompson & Mitchell · One Mercantile Center, Suite 3400 · St. Louis, MO 63101 314-231-7676

William M. Van Cleve · Bryan, Cave, McPheeters & McRoberts · 500 North Broadway · St. Louis, MO 63102-2186 · 314-231-8600

W. Stanley Walch* · (Antitrust, Corporate Finance, Leveraged Buyouts, Mergers & Acquisitions) · Thompson & Mitchell · One Mercantile Center, Suite 3400 · St. Louis, MO 63101 · 314-231-7676

Bruce E. Woodruff · Armstrong, Teasdale, Schlafly, Davis & Dicus · One Metropolitan Square · St. Louis, MO 63102-2740 · 314-621-5070

CRIMINAL DEFENSE

Charles M. Shaw · 168 North Meramec, Suite 150 · Clayton, MO 63105 · 314-725-9700

Robert C. Welch · Paden, Welch, Martin & Albano · Law Building · 311 West Kansas Avenue · Independence, MO 64050 · 816-836-8000

Charles E. Atwell · Koenigsdorf & Wyrsch · 1006 Grand Avenue, 10th Floor · Kansas City, MO 64106 · 816-221-0080

Robert Beaird · Law Offices of Robert Beaird · 1125 Grand Avenue, Suite 1717 · Kansas City, MO 64106 · 816-471-7535

Robert G. Duncan* · Duncan, Coulson, Schloss, Chancellor & Norris · 2800-B Kendallwood Parkway · Kansas City, MO 64119-2196 · 816-455-0555

Gerald M. Handley · Speck and Handley · Palace Building, Suite 810 · 1150 Grand Avenue · Kansas City, MO 64106 · 816-471-7145

James R. Wyrsch* · (Federal Court, State Court) · Koenigsdorf & Wyrsch · 1006 Grand Avenue, 10th Floor · Kansas City, MO 64106 · 816-221-0080

William H. Wendt · Building H, Suite 400 · 1200 East Woodhurst Drive · Springfield, MO 65804 · 417-883-5277

Irl B. Baris · Law Offices of Irl B. Baris · 1600 Boatmen's Tower · 100 North Broadway · St. Louis, MO 63102 · 314-231-8700

Norman S. London* · 1600 Boatmen's Tower · 100 North Broadway · St. Louis, MO 63102 · 314-231-8700

Donald L. Wolff* · (Violent Crimes, Non-Violent Crimes, Federal Court, State Court) · 8019 Forsyth · St. Louis (Clayton), MO 63105 · 314-725-8019

FAMILY LAW

Jack Cochran* · (Child Custody, Divorce, Marital Settlement Agreements, Equitable Division) · Cochran, Oswald, Barton, McDonald & Graham · One Jefferson Place · P.O. Box 550 · Blue Springs, MO 64014 · 816-229-8121

Gina M. Graham · Cochran, Oswald, Barton, McDonald & Graham · One Jefferson Place · P.O. Box 550 · Blue Springs, MO 64014 · 816-229-8121

Douglas R. Beach · Beach, Burcke, Mooney & Lake · 222 South Central, Suite 900 · Clayton, MO 63105 · 314-863-8484

David B. Lacks · Love, Lacks & Paule · Pierre Laclede Building, Suite 680 · 11 South Meramec Avenue, Seventh Floor · Clayton, MO 63105 · 314-863-4100

Roger P. Krumm · Krumm & Shryock · 14 West Fifth Street · Fulton, MO 65251 314-642-9183

Michael S. J. Albano* · (Child Custody,Divorce, Marital Settlement Agreements, Equitable Division) · Paden, Welch, Martin & Albano · Law Building · 311 West Kansas Avenue · Independence, MO 64050 · 816-836-8000

John W. Dennis, Jr. · Paden, Welch, Martin & Albano · Law Building · 311 West Kansas Avenue · Independence, MO 64050 · 816-836-8000

Robert C. Paden · Paden, Welch, Martin & Albano · Law Building · 311 West Kansas Avenue · Independence, MO 64050 · 816-836-8000

Lori J. Levine* · Carson & Coil · 211 East Capitol Avenue · P.O. Box 235 · Jefferson City, MO 65102-0235 · 314-636-2177

Regina Keelan Bass* · (Child Custody, Divorce, Marital Settlement Agreements) Thayer, Bernstein, Bass & Monaco · 8900 Ward Parkway, Suite 210 · Kansas City, MO 64114 · 816-444-8030

Karen A. Plax · United Missouri Bank Building, Suite 303 · 1310 Carondelet Drive · Kansas City, MO 64114 · 816-942-1900

Charlotte P. Thayer* · Thayer, Bernstein, Bass & Monaco · 8900 Ward Parkway, Suite 210 · Kansas City, MO 64114 · 816-444-8030

Robert C. Fields* · (Child Custody, Divorce, Marital Settlement Agreements, Equitable Division) · 333 Park Central East, Suite 221 · Springfield, MO 65806 · 417-831-1505

Merle L. Silverstein* · (Divorce, Marital Settlement Agreements) · Rosenblum, Goldenhersh, Silverstein & Zafft · 7733 Forsythe · St. Louis, MO 63105 · 314-726-6868

Charles P. Todt* · (Child Custody, Divorce, Marital Settlement Agreements, Equitable Division) · Charles P. Todt and Associates · 212 South Meramec · St. Louis, MO 63105 · 314-862-5520

John A. Turcotte, Jr. · Diekemper, Hammond, Shinners, Turcotte and Larrew · 7730 Carondelet Avenue, Suite 222 · St. Louis, MO 63105 · 314-727-1015

Allan H. Zerman · 100 South Brentwood · St. Louis, MO 63105 · 314-862-4444

FIRST AMENDMENT LAW

Samuel L. Colville · Shook, Hardy & Bacon · One Kansas City Place · 1200 Main Street · Kansas City, MO 64105 · 816-474-6550

M. Errol Copilevitz · Copilevitz, Bryant, Gray & Jennings · 1500 One Kansas City Place · 1200 Main Street · Kansas City, MO 64105 · 816-471-3977

Robert B. Hoemeke · Lewis, Rice & Fingersh · 611 Olive Street, 14th Floor · St. Louis, MO 63101 · 314-444-7600

HEALTH CARE LAW

James M. Beck · Shook, Hardy & Bacon · One Kansas City Place · 1200 Main Street · Kansas City, MO 64105 · 816-474-6550

Paul P. Cacioppo · Stinson, Mag & Fizzell · 1201 Walnut, Suite 2800 · P.O. Box 419251 · Kansas City, MO 64141-6251 · 816-842-8600

E. J. Holland, Jr. · Spencer Fane Britt & Browne · 1400 Commerce Bank Building 1000 Walnut Street · Kansas City, MO 64106-2140 · 816-474-8100

Thomas G. Kokoruda · Shughart, Thomson & Kilroy · 12 Wyandotte Plaza, Suite 1800 · 120 West 12th Street · Kansas City, MO 64105 · 816-421-3335

Charles F. Myers · Spencer Fane Britt & Browne · 1400 Commerce Bank Building · 1000 Walnut Street · Kansas City, MO 64106-2140 · 816-474-8100

Tracy L. Mathis · Thompson & Mitchell · 200 North Third Street · St. Charles, MO 63301 · 314-946-7717

Diane E. Felix · Armstrong, Teasdale, Schlafly, Davis & Dicus · One Metropolitan Square · St. Louis, MO 63102-2740 · 314-621-5070

David M. Harris · Greensfelder, Hemker & Gale · 1800 Equitable Building · Ten South Broadway · St. Louis, MO 63102 · 314-241-9090

Daniel L. Human · Ziercher & Hocker · 130 South Bemiston Avenue, Fourth Floor · St. Louis, MO 63105 · 314-727-5822

Richard D. Watters · Lashly & Baer · 714 Locust Street · St. Louis, MO 63101 · 314-621-2939

IMMIGRATION LAW

George S. Newman · Blumenfeld, Kaplan & Sandweiss · 168 North Merramec, Suite 400 · Clayton, MO 63105 · 314-863-0800

Robert Frager · Winston & Frager · 1150 Grand Avenue, Suite 250 · Kansas City, MO 64106 · 816-842-0044

INTELLECTUAL PROPERTY LAW

John M. Collins · Hovey, Williams, Timmons & Collins · 1101 Walnut Street, Suite 400 · Kansas City, MO 64106 · 816-474-9050

Clayton E. Dickey · Watson, Ess, Marshall & Enggas · 1010 Grand Avenue · Kansas City, MO 64106-2271 · 816-842-3132

Robert D. Hovey · Hovey, Williams, Timmons & Collins · 1101 Walnut Street, Suite 400 · Kansas City, MO 64106 · 816-474-9050

William B. Kircher · Kokjer, Kircher, Bradley · 2414 Commerce Tower · 911 Main · Kansas City, MO 64105 · 816-474-5300

Carter H. Kokjer · Kokjer, Kircher, Bradley · 2414 Commerce Tower · 911 Main Kansas City, MO 64105 · 816-474-5300

I. E. Marquette · Spencer Fane Britt & Browne · 1400 Commerce Bank Building 1000 Walnut Street · Kansas City, MO 64106-2140 · 816-474-8100

John M. Howell · Rogers, Howell & Haferkamp · 7777 Bonhomme Avenue, Suite 1700 · St. Louis, MO 63105 · 314-727-5188

Roy A. Lieder · (Trademark) · Gravely, Lieder & Woodruff · 705 Olive Street · St. Louis, MO 63101 · 314-621-1457

Lionel L. Lucchesi · Polster, Polster & Lucchesi · 763 South New Ballas Street, Suite 160 · St. Louis, MO 63141 · 314-872-8118

Philip B. Polster · Polster, Polster & Lucchesi · 763 South New Ballas Street, Suite 160 · St. Louis, MO 63141 · 314-872-8118

Stuart N. Senninger · Senninger, Powers, Leavitt & Roedel · 611 Olive Street, Suite 2050 · St. Louis, MO 63101 · 314-231-0109

LABOR AND EMPLOYMENT LAW

Arthur A. Benson II · (Individuals) · Benson & McKay · 1000 Walnut Street, Suite 1125 · Kansas City, MO 64106 · 816-842-7603

Allan L. Bioff* · (Management) · Bioff, Singer and Finucane · The Stilwell Building, Suite 400 · 104 West Ninth Street · Kansas City, MO 64105 · 816-842-8770

Clifton L. Elliott · (Management) · Watson, Ess, Marshall & Enggas · 1010 Grand Avenue · Kansas City, MO 64106-2271 · 816-842-3132

William A. Jolley* · (Labor) · Jolley, Walsh & Hager · 204 West Linwood Boulevard · Kansas City, MO 64111 · 816-561-3755

Jack L. Whitacre · (Management) · Spencer Fane Britt & Browne · 1400 Commerce Bank Building · 1000 Walnut Street · Kansas City, MO 64106-2140 · 816-474-8100

James R. Willard · (Management) · Spencer Fane Britt & Browne · 1400 Commerce Bank Building · 1000 Walnut Street · Kansas City, MO 64106-2140 · 816-474-8100

Alan I. Berger · (Management) · McMahon, Berger, Hanna, Linihan, Cody & McCarthy · 2730 North Ballas Road, Suite 200 · St. Louis, MO 63131 · 314-567-7350

James K. Cook · (Labor) · Schuchat, Cook & Werner · The Shell Building, Suite 250 · 1221 Locust Street · St. Louis, MO 63103-2364 · 314-621-2626

Jerome A. Diekemper* · (Labor, Individuals) · Diekemper, Hammond, Shinners, Turcotte and Larrew · 7730 Carondelet Avenue, Suite 222 · St. Louis, MO 63105 · 314-727-1015

Dennis C. Donnelly · (Management) · Bryan, Cave, McPheeters & McRoberts · 500 North Broadway · St. Louis, MO 63012-2186 · 314-231-8600

Bruce S. Feldacker · (Labor) · Feldacker & Cohen · 720 Olive Street, Suite 2222 St. Louis, MO 63101 · 314-231-2970

Ronald K. Fisher · (Management) · Harris, Dowell & Fisher · 15400 South Outer Highway 40, Suite 202 · St. Louis, MO 63017 · 314-532-0300

Louis Gilden* · (Individuals) · Louderman Building, Suite 1220 · 317 North 11th Street · St. Louis, MO 63101 · 314-241-6607

Michael J. Hoare* · (Individuals) · 314 North Broadway · St. Louis, MO 63102 314-241-7961

Fred Leicht · (Management) · Armstrong, Teasdale, Schlafly, Davis & Dicus · One Metropolitan Square · St. Louis, MO 63102-2740 · 314-621-5070

Ned O. Lemkemeier · (Management) · Bryan, Cave, McPheeters & McRoberts · 500 North Broadway · St. Louis, MO 63012-2186 · 314-231-8600

Morris J. Levin · (Labor) · Levin and Weinhaus · 906 Olive Street, Suite 900 · St. Louis, MO 63101 · 314-621-8363

Daniel J. Sullivan · (Management) · Lewis, Rice & Fingersh · 611 Olive Street, 14th Floor · St. Louis, MO 63101 · 314-444-7600

Charles A. Werner* · (Labor) · Schuchat, Cook & Werner · The Shell Building, Suite 250 · 1221 Locust Street · St. Louis, MO 63103-2364 · 314-621-2626

MARITIME LAW

Michael D. O'Keefe · Thompson & Mitchell · One Mercantile Center, Suite 3400 St. Louis, MO 63101 · 314-231-7676

Elmer Price* · Goldstein & Price · 1300 Paul Brown Building · 818 Olive Street St. Louis, MO 63101 · 314-421-0710

Gary T. Sacks · Goldstein & Price · 1300 Paul Brown Building · 818 Olive Street St. Louis, MO 63101 · 314-421-0710

NATURAL RESOURCES AND ENVIRONMENTAL LAW

Robert L. Driscoll* · (Air, Hazardous Waste) · Stinson, Mag & Fizzell · 1201 Walnut, Suite 2800 · P.O. Box 419251 · Kansas City, MO 64141-6251 · 816-842-8600

Stephen J. Owens* · Stinson, Mag & Fizzell · 1201 Walnut, Suite 2800 · P.O. Box 419251 · Kansas City, MO 64141-6251 · 816-842-8600

James T. Price · (Water, Air, Solid Waste, Hazardous Waste) · Spencer Fane Britt & Browne · 1400 Commerce Bank Building · 1000 Walnut Street · Kansas City, MO 64106-2140 · 816-474-8100

David R. Tripp · Stinson, Mag & Fizzell · 1201 Walnut, Suite 2800 · P.O. Box 419251 · Kansas City, MO 64141-6251 · 816-842-8600

Nicholas C. Gladding · (Water, Air, Solid Waste, Hazardous Waste) · Bryan, Cave, McPheeters & McRoberts · 500 North Broadway · St. Louis, MO 63102-2186 · 314-231-8600

Lewis C. Green* · (Plaintiffs) · Green, Hennings & Henry · Marquette Building, Suite 1830 · 314 North Broadway · St. Louis, MO 63102 · 314-231-4181

Maxine I. Lipeles · Husch, Eppenberger, Donohue, Cornfeld & Jenkins · The Boatmen's Tower, 13th Floor · 100 North Broadway · St. Louis, MO 63102 · 314-421-4800

Edwin L. Noel · Armstrong, Teasdale, Schlafly, Davis & Dicus · One Metropolitan Square · St. Louis, MO 63102-2740 · 314-621-5070

George M. Von Stamwitz · Armstrong, Teasdale, Schlafly, Davis & Dicus · One Metropolitan Square, Suite 2600 · St. Louis, MO 63102-2740 · 314-621-5070

PERSONAL INJURY LITIGATION

Raymond C. Lewis, Jr.* · (Defendants) · Smith, Lewis, Beckett & Powell · Haden Building · 901 East Broadway · Columbia, MO 65201-4894 · 314-443-3141

Michael Manners · Paden, Welch, Martin & Albano · Law Building · 311 West Kansas Avenue · Independence, MO 64050 · 816-836-8000

Spencer Brown · Deacy and Deacy · 1000 Bryant Building · 1102 Grant Avenue Kansas City, MO 64106 · 816-421-4000

Lyman Field* · (Medical Malpractice, Products Liability, Automobile Collision, Airplane Collision) · Field, Gentry, Benjamin & Robertson · 600 East 11th Street Kansas City, MO 64106-2680 · 816-842-6031

Max W. Foust* · (Plaintiffs, Medical Malpractice, Products Liability, Professional Malpractice, Automobile Collision) · Foust, Strother & Frickleton · 2390 City Center Square · 1100 Main Street · P.O. Box 26490 · Kansas City, MO 64196 · 816-474-6050

Reed O. Gentry* · (Defendants) · Field, Gentry, Benjamin & Robertson · 600 East 11th Street · Kansas City, MO 64106 · 816-842-6031

John M. Kilroy · (Defendants, Medical Malpractice, Products Liability, Professional Malpractice, Airplane Collision) · Shughart, Thomson & Kilroy · 12 Wyandotte Plaza, Suite 1800 · 120 West 12th Street · Kansas City, MO 64105 · 816-421-3355

Patrick McLarney* · (Defendants) · Shook, Hardy & Bacon · One Kansas City Place, 29th Floor · 1200 Main Street · Kansas City, MO 64105 · 816-474-6550

Larry L. McMullen · (Defendants) · Blackwell Sanders Matheny Weary & Lombardi · Two Pershing Square, Suite 1100 · 2300 Main Street · P.O. Box 419777 · Kansas City, MO 64141-6777 · 816-274-6800

William H. Sanders, Sr.* · (Defendants) · Blackwell Sanders Matheny Weary & Lombardi · Two Pershing Square, Suite 1100 · 2300 Main Street · P.O. Box 419777 · Kansas City, MO 64141-6777 · 816-274-6800

R. Lawrence Ward · Shughart, Thomson & Kilroy · 12 Wyandotte Plaza, Suite 1800 · 120 West 12th Street · Kansas City, MO 64105 · 816-421-3355

Lantz Welch* · (Plaintiffs, Medical Malpractice, Products Liability, Automobile Collision) · 2930 City Center Square · 1100 Main · P.O. Box 26250 · Kansas City, MO 64196 · 816-421-1600

Roger D. Stanton* · (Products Liability) · Stinson, Mag & Fizzell · 7500 West 110th Street · Overland Park, MO 66210-2329 · 913-451-8600

Thomas Strong · (Plaintiffs) · Strong & Associates · 901 East Battlefield · Springfield, MO 65807 · 417-887-4300

Paul S. Brown · (Defendants, Products Liability, Professional Malpractice) · Brown & James · 705 Olive Street, Suite 1100 · St. Louis, MO 63101-2270 · 314-421-3400

Eugene K. Buckley* · (Defendants) · Evans & Dixon · Marquette Building, 16th Floor · 314 North Broadway · St. Louis, MO 63102-2093 · 314-621-7755

Ben Ely, Jr.* · (Defendants) · Kortenhof & Ely · 1015 Locust Street, Suite 300 · St. Louis, MO 63101 · 314-621-5757

Robert C. Ely · (Defendants) · Law Offices of Robert C. Ely · 1015 Locust Street, Suite 600 · St. Louis, MO 63101 · 314-231-9191

William W. Evans* · (Defendants, Products Liability, Automobile Collision, Appellate) · Evans & Dixon · Marquette Building, 16th Floor · 314 North Broadway St. Louis, MO 63102-2093 · 314-621-7755

Theodore Hoffman · (Plaintiffs) · Hoffman & Wallach · 1015 Locust Street, Suite 700 · St. Louis, MO 63101 · 314-241-1020

James E. Hullverson · (Plaintiffs) · The Hullverson Law Firm · 1010 Market Street, Suite 1550 · St. Louis, MO 63101-2091 · 314-421-2313

Thomas C. Hullverson* · (Plaintiffs, Medical Malpractice, Products Liability, Professional Malpractice, Automobile Collision) · The Hullverson Law Firm · 1010 Market Street, Suite 1550 · St. Louis, MO 63101-2091 · 314-421-2313

Joseph M. Kortenhof* · (Defendants) · Kortenhof & Ely · 1015 Locust Street, Suite 300 · St. Louis, MO 63101 · 314-621-5757

Daniel T. Rabbitt* · (Defendants) · Rabbitt, Pitzer & Snodgrass · One Boatmen's Plaza · 800 Market Street · St. Louis, MO 63101 · 314-421-5545

Robert F. Ritter · Gray & Ritter · 701 Market Street, Suite 800 · St. Louis, MO 63101 · 314-241-5620

Donald L. Schlapprizzi · 1015 Locust, Suite 914 · St. Louis, MO 63101 · 314-241-0763

John C. Shepherd · Armstrong, Teasdale, Schlafly, Davis & Dicus · One Metropolitan Square · St. Louis, MO 63102-2740 · 314-621-5070

Don B. Sommers* · (Plaintiffs, Defendants, Products Liability, F.E.L.A.) · Paul Brown Building, Suite 1630 · 818 Olive Street · St. Louis, MO 63101 · 314-436-2088

PUBLIC UTILITY LAW

Gary W. Duffy · (Electric, Gas) · Brydon, Swearengen & England · 312 East Capitol Street · Jefferson City, MO 65101 · 314-635-7166

W. R. England III · (Telecommunications) · Brydon, Swearengen & England · 312 East Capitol Street · Jefferson City, MO 65101 · 314-635-7166

James C. Swearengen · (Electric, Gas) · Brydon, Swearengen & England · 312 East Capitol Street · Jefferson City, MO 65101 · 314-635-7166

Basil W. Kelsey · Spencer Fane Britt & Browne · 1400 Commerce Bank Building 1000 Walnut Street · Kansas City, MO 64106-2140 · 816-474-8100

Leland B. Curtis · (Telecommunications) · Curtis, Etting, Heinz, Garrett & Soule · 130 South Bemiston Street, Suite 200 · St. Louis, MO 63105 · 314-725-8788

REAL ESTATE LAW

Sherwin L. Epstein · (Zoning, Eminent Domain, Commercial Transactions, Real Estate Taxation) · Sherwin L. Epstein & Associates · Home Savings Bank Building, Suite 1700 · 1006 Grand Avenue · Kansas City, MO 64106-2276 · 816-421-6200

Larrie C. Hindman · (Commercial Transactions, Real Estate Finance) · Morrison, Hecker, Curtis, Kuder & Parrish · 1700 Bryant Building · 1102 Grand Avenue · Kansas City, MO 64106-2370 · 816-842-5910

James M. Jenkins · Husch, Eppenberger, Donohue, Cornfeld & Jenkins · 1200 Main, Suite 1700 · Kansas City, MO 64105 · 816-421-4800

Michael G. O'Flaherty · Stinson, Mag & Fizzell · 1201 Walnut, Suite 2800 · P.O. Box 419251 · Kansas City, MO 64141-6251 · 816-842-8600

Richard W. Scarritt · (Zoning, Commercial Transactions, Industrial Transactions) · Spencer Fane Britt & Browne · 1400 Commerce Bank Building · 1000 Walnut Street · Kansas City, MO 64106-2140 · 816-474-8100

Stephen K. Taylor · Watson, Ess, Marshall & Enggas · 1010 Grand Avenue · Kansas City, MO 64106-2271 · 816-842-3132

Fred E. Arnold · Thompson & Mitchell · One Mercantile Center, Suite 3400 · St. Louis, MO 63101 · 314-231-7676

Donald U. Beimdiek* · (Land Use, Eminent Domain, Commercial Transactions, Industrial Transactions) · Armstrong, Teasdale, Schlafly, Davis & Dicus · One Metropolitan Square · St. Louis, MO 63102-2740 · 314-621-5070

John A. Blumenfeld · Blumenfeld, Kaplan, Sandweiss, Marx, Ponfil & Kaskowitz 168 North Meramec Avenue, Fourth Floor · St. Louis, MO 63105 · 314-863-0800

Robert S. Goldenhersh · (Eminent Domain, Commercial Transactions, Industrial Transactions, Real Estate Taxation) · Rosenblum, Goldenhersh, Silverstein & Zafft · Pierre Laclede Center · 7733 Forsyth Boulevard, Fourth Floor · St. Louis, MO 63105 · 314-726-6868

Harvey A. Harris · (Workouts, Troubled Projects) · The Stolar Partnership · The Lammert Building, Seventh Floor · 911 Washington Avenue · St. Louis, MO 63101 · 314-231-2800

James L. Hawkins · (Construction) · Greensfelder, Hemker & Gale · 1800 Equitable Building · Ten South Broadway · St. Louis, MO 63102 · 314-241-9090

Richard A. Hetlage · Peper, Martin, Jensen, Maichel and Hetlage · 720 Olive Street, 24th Floor · St. Louis, MO 63101 · 314-421-3850

Robert O. Hetlage · Peper, Martin, Jensen, Maichel and Hetlage · 720 Olive Street, 24th Floor · St. Louis, MO 63101 · 314-421-3850

Andrew S. Love, Jr. · Bryan, Cave, McPheeters & McRoberts · 500 North Broadway · St. Louis, MO 63102-2186 · 314-231-8600

George V. Meisel · Bryan, Cave, McPheeters & McRoberts · 500 North Broadway St. Louis, MO 63102-2186 · 314-231-8600

Jerome M. Rubenstein · Bryan, Cave, McPheeters & McRoberts · 500 North Broadway · St. Louis, MO 63102-2186 · 314-231-8600

Shulamith Simon · Husch, Eppenberger, Donohue, Cornfeld & Jenins · The Boatmen's Tower, 13th Floor · 100 North Broadway · St. Louis, MO 63102 · 314-421-4800

Walter J. Taylor · Lewis, Rice & Fingersh · 611 Olive Street, 14th Floor · St. Louis, MO 63101 · 314-444-7600

TAX AND EMPLOYEE BENEFITS LAW

James R. Hudek · (Employee Benefits) · Spencer Fane Britt & Browne · 1400 Commerce Bank Building · 1000 Walnut Street · Kansas City, MO 64106-2140 · 816-474-8100

Thomas R. Brous · (Employee Benefits) · Watson, Ess, Marshall & Enggas · 1010 Grand Avenue · Kansas City, MO 64106-2271 · 816-842-3132

Thomas C. Graves · (Employee Benefits) · Morrison, Hecker, Curtis, Kuder & Parrish · 1700 Bryant Building · 1102 Grand Avenue · Kansas City, MO 64106-2370 · 816-842-5910

Ronald L. Langstaff · Spencer Fane Britt & Browne · 1400 Commerce Bank Building · 1000 Walnut Street · Kansas City, MO 64106-2140 · 816-474-8100

Ross W. Lillard · (Employee Benefits) · Stinson, Mag & Fizzell · 1201 Walnut, Suite 2800 · P.O. Box 419251 · Kansas City, MO 64141-6251 · 816-842-8600

C. Maxwell Logan · Shook, Hardy & Bacon · One Kansas City Place · 1200 Main Street · Kansas City, MO 64105 · 816-474-6550

Robert P. Lyons · Spencer Fane Britt & Browne · 1400 Commerce Bank Building 1000 Walnut Street · Kansas City, MO 64106-2140 · 816-474-8100

Morton Y. Rosenberg · Stinson, Mag & Fizzell · 1201 Walnut, Suite 2800 · P.O. Box 419251 · Kansas City, MO 64141-6251 · 816-842-8600

Sylvan Siegler · Shook, Hardy & Bacon · One Kansas City Place, 29th Floor · 1200 Main Street · Kansas City, MO 64105 · 816-474-6550

Myron E. Sildon · (Tax, Employee Benefits) · Sildon Law Group · 2800 City Center Square · 1100 Main Street · Kansas City, MO 64105 · 816-474-7777

Perry M. Toll · (Employee Benefits) · Shughart, Thomson & Kilroy · 12 Wyandotte Plaza, Suite 1800 · 120 West 12th Street · Kansas City, MO 64105 · 816-421-3355

Daniel C. Weary · Blackwell Sanders Matheny Weary & Lombardi · Two Pershing Square, Suite 1100 · 2300 Main Street · P.O. Box 419777 · Kansas City, MO 64141-6777 · 816-274-6800

Stanley P. Weiner · (Corporate & Partnership Transactions, Tax Disputes) · Shook, Hardy & Bacon · One Kansas City Place, 31st Floor · 1200 Main Street · Kansas City, MO 64105 · 816-474-6550

John P. Williams · (Employee Benefits) · Blackwell Sanders Matheny Weary & Lombardi · Two Pershing Square, Suite 1100 · 2300 Main Street · P.O. Box 419777 · Kansas City, MO 64141-6777 · 816-274-6800

Charles M. Babington III · (Employee Benefits) · Thompson & Mitchell · One Mercantile Center, Suite 3400 · St. Louis, MO 63101 · 314-231-7676

John P. Barrie · (Employee Benefits) · Gallop, Johnson & Neuman · Interco Corporate Tower · 101 South Hanley Road, Suite 1600 · St. Louis, MO 63105 · 314-862-1200

Brian Berglund · (Employee Benefits) · Bryan, Cave, McPheeters & McRoberts 500 North Broadway · St. Louis, MO 63102-2186 · 314-231-8600

Harold G. Blatt · (Employee Benefits) · Bryan, Cave, McPheeters & McRoberts 500 North Broadway · St. Louis, MO 63102-2186 · 314-231-8600

Lawrence Brody* · Bryan, Cave, McPheeters & McRoberts · 500 North Broadway · St. Louis, MO 63102-2186 · 314-231-8600

Dave L. Cornfeld · Husch, Eppenberger, Donohue, Cornfeld & Jenkins · The Boatmen's Tower, 13th Floor · 100 North Broadway · St. Louis, MO 63102 · 314-421-4800

William D. Crampton · Bryan, Cave, McPheeters & McRoberts · 500 North Broadway · St. Louis, MO 63102-2186 · 314-231-8600

Joseph P. Giljum · Kohn, Shands, Elbert, Gianoulakis & Giljum · One Mercantile Center, 24th Floor · St. Louis, MO 63101 · 314-241-3963

Paul G. Griesemer · (Employee Benefits) · Peper, Martin, Jensen, Maichel and Hetlage · 720 Olive Street, 24th Floor · St. Louis, MO 63101 · 314-421-3850

Juan D. Keller · Bryan, Cave, McPheeters & McRoberts · 500 North Broadway St. Louis, MO 63102-2186 · 314-231-8600

Warren L. Maichel · Peper, Martin, Jensen, Maichel and Hetlage · 720 Olive Street, 24th Floor · St. Louis, MO 63101 · 314-421-3850

Joan M. Newman · (Employee Benefits) · Thompson & Mitchell · One Mercantile Center, Suite 3400 · St. Louis, MO 63101 · 314-231-7676

Michael N. Newmark · (Corporate & Partnership Transactions, Tax Disputes) · Gallop, Johnson & Neuman · Interco Corporate Tower · 101 South Hanley Road, Suite 1600 · St. Louis, MO 63105 · 314-862-1200

Edward W. Rataj · (Employee Benefits) · Bryan, Cave, McPheeters & McRoberts 500 North Broadway · St. Louis, MO 63102-2186 · 314-231-8600

Douglas D. Ritterskamp · (Employee Benefits) · Bryan, Cave, McPheeters & McRoberts · 500 North Broadway · St. Louis, MO 63102-2186 · 314-231-8600

Llewellyn Sale III · (Employee Benefits) · Bryan, Cave, McPheeters & McRoberts · 500 North Broadway · St. Louis, MO 63102-2186 · 314-231-8600

TRUSTS AND ESTATES

Byron A. Stewart, Jr. · Constance, Stewart & Cook · 501 West Lexington Avenue Independence, MO 64050 · 816-833-1800

Peter W. Brown · Husch, Eppenberger, Donohue, Cornfeld & Jenkins · 1200 Main, Suite 1700 · Kansas City, MO 64105 · 816-421-4800

Donald H. Chisholm · Stinson, Mag & Fizzell · 1201 Walnut, Suite 2800 · P.O. Box 419251 · Kansas City, MO 64141-6251 · 816-842-8600

John C. Davis · Stinson, Mag & Fizzell · 1201 Walnut, Suite 2800 · P.O. Box 419251 · Kansas City, MO 64141-6251 · 816-842-8600

George R. Haydon, Jr. · Watson, Ess, Marshall & Enggas · 1010 Grand Avenue Kansas City, MO 64106-2271 · 816-842-3132

Roger T. Hurwitz · Morrison, Hecker, Curtis, Kuder & Parrish · 1700 Bryant Building · 1102 Grand Avenue · Kansas City, MO 64106-2370 · 816-842-5910

Guy A. Magruder, Jr.* · Van Osdol, Magruder, Erickson and Redmond · 515 Commerce Trust Building · Kansas City, MO 64106 · 816-421-0644

Maurice J. O'Sullivan, Jr. · Lathrop Norquist & Miller · 2600 Mutual Benefit Life Building · 2345 Grand Avenue · Kansas City, MO 64108 · 816-842-0820

Edward A. Setzler · (Estate Planning, Estate Administration, Charitable Trusts, Fiduciary Tax) · Spencer Fane Britt & Browne · 1400 Commerce Bank Building 1000 Walnut Street · Kansas City, MO 64106-2140 · 816-474-8100

Sylvan Siegler · Shook, Hardy & Bacon · One Kansas City Place, 31st Floor · 1200 Main Street · Kansas City, MO 64105 · 816-474-6550

Myron E. Sildon · Sildon Law Group · 2800 City Center Square · 1100 Main Street · Kansas City, MO 64105 · 816-474-7777

David L. West · Blackwell Sanders Matheny Weary & Lombardi · Two Pershing Square, Suite 1100 · 2300 Main Street · P.O. Box 419777 · Kansas City, MO 64141-6777 · 816-274-6800

Richard D. Woods · Shook, Hardy & Bacon · One Kansas City Place, 31st Floor 1200 Main Street · Kansas City, MO 64105 · 816-474-6550

Lawrence Brody* · Bryan, Cave, McPheeters & McRoberts · 500 North Broadway · St. Louis, MO 63102-2186 · 314-231-8600

Dave L. Cornfeld · Husch, Eppenberger, Donohue, Cornfeld & Jenkins · The Boatmen's Tower, 13th Floor · 100 North Broadway · St. Louis, MO 63102 · 314-421-4800

John E. Dooling, Jr. · Greensfelder, Hemker & Gale · 1800 Equitable Building Ten South Broadway · St. Louis, MO 63102 · 314-241-9090

Milton Greenfield, Jr. · (Estate Planning, Estate Administration) · 7751 Carondelet, Suite 500 · St. Louis, MO 63105 · 314-725-2627

Lawrence P. Katzenstein · The Stolar Partnership · 911 Washington Avenue, Seventh Floor · St. Louis, MO 63101 · 314-231-2800

Michael D. Mulligan · Lewis, Rice & Fingersh · 611 Olive Street, 14th Floor · St. Louis, MO 63101 · 314-444-7600

Charles A. Redd · Armstrong, Teasdale, Schlafly, Davis & Dicus · One Metropolitan Square, Suite 2600 · St. Louis MO 63102-2740 · 314-621-5070

Kathleen R. Sherby · Bryan, Cave, McPheeters & McRoberts · 500 North Broadway · St. Louis, MO 63102-2186 · 314-231-8600

Franklin F. Wallis · Bryan, Cave, McPheeters & McRoberts · 500 North Broadway · St. Louis, MO 63102-2186 · 314-231-8600

MONTANA

BANKRUPTCY LAW

Joel E. Guthals* · (Business Reorganization, Creditors' Rights, Debtors' Rights, Bankruptcy Litigation) · Wright, Tolliver & Guthals · Windsor Court · 10 North 27th Street · P.O. Box 1977 · Billings, MT 59103 · 406-245-3071

Charles W. Hingle* · (Creditors' Rights, Bankruptcy Litigation) · Dorsey & Whitney · 1200 First Interstate Center · 401 North 31st Street · P.O. Box 7188 · Billings, MT 59103 · 406-252-3800

Sherry Scheel Matteucci · Crowley, Haughey, Hanson, Toole & Dietrich · 500 Transwestern Plaza II · 490 North 31st Street · P.O. Box 2529 · Billings, MT 59103 · 406-252-3441

Sidney R. Thomas · Moulton, Bellingham, Longo & Mather · Sheridan Building, Suite 1900 · P.O. Box 2559 · Billings, MT 59103-2559 · 406-248-7731

Arthur G. Matteucci · Matteucci, Falcon & Squires · Norwest Bank Building, Suite 200 · 21 Third Street North · P.O. Box 149 · Great Falls, MT 59403 · 406-727-5740

Harold V. Dye · Milodragovich, Dale & Dye · Sunstone Building · 620 High Park Way · P.O. Box 4947 · Missoula, MT 59806-4947 · 406-728-1455

BUSINESS LITIGATION

George Dalthorp · Crowley, Haughey, Hanson, Toole & Dietrich · 500 Transwestern Plaza II · 490 North 31st Street · P.O. Box 2529 · Billings, MT 59103 · 406-252-3441

A. Clifford Edwards* · (Banking, Finance) · Edwards & Paoli · 1601 Lewis Avenue, Suite 206 · P.O. Box 20039 · Billings, MT 59104 · 406-256-8155

Stephen H. Foster* · (Commercial) · Holland & Hart · 175 North 27th Street, Suite 1400 · Billings, MT 59101 · 406-252-2166

Ronald R. Lodders · Crowley, Haughey, Hanson, Toole & Dietrich · 500 Transwestern Plaza II · 490 North 31st Street · P.O. Box 2529 · Billings, MT 59103-2529 406-252-3441

James H. Goetz · (Appellate) · Goetz, Madden & Dunn · 35 North Grand Avenue Bozeman, MT 59715 · 406-587-0618

Donald C. Robinson* · (Commercial) · Poore, Roth & Robinson · 1341 Harrison Avenue · P.O. Box 3328 · Butte, MT 59701-4898 · 406-782-1223

Urban L. Roth* · Poore, Roth & Robinson · 1341 Harrison Avenue · P.O. Box 3328 · Butte, MT 59701-4898 · 406-782-1223

John D. Stephenson, Jr.* · Jardine, Stephenson, Blewett & Weaver · First National Bank Building, Seventh Floor · P.O. Box 2269 · Great Falls, MT 59403-2269 · 406-727-5000

W. William Leaphart · (Appellate) · Leaphart Law Firm · One North Last Chance Gulch, Suite 6 · Helena, MT 59601 · 406-442-4930

Ronald F. Waterman · Gough, Shanahan, Johnson & Waterman · 301 First National Bank Building · P.O. Box 1715 · Helena, MT 59624 · 406-442-8560

Sam E. Haddon* · Boone, Karlberg and Haddon · Central Square, Suite 301 · 201 West Main Street · P.O. Box 9199 · Missoula, MT 59807-9199 · 406-543-6646

William Evan Jones* · (Commercial) · Garlington, Lohn & Robinson · 199 West Pine · P.O. Box 7909 · Missoula, MT 59807-7909 · 406-728-1200

Sherman V. Lohn · Garlington, Lohn & Robinson · 199 West Pine · P.O. Box 7909 · Missoula, MT 59807-7909 · 406-728-1200

CORPORATE LAW

John M. Dietrich · Crowley, Haughey, Hanson, Toole & Dietrich · 500 Transwestern Plaza II · 490 North 31st Street · P.O. Box 2529 · Billings, MT 59103 · 406-252-3441

Gareld F. Krieg · Crowley, Haughey, Hanson, Toole & Dietrich · 500 Transwestern Plaza II · 490 North 31st Street · P.O. Box 2529 · Billings, MT 59103 · 406-252-3441

L. W. Petersen · Dorsey & Whitney · 1200 First Interstate Center · 401 North 31st Street · P.O. Box 7188 · Billings, MT 59103 · 406-252-3800

Mark D. Safty · Holland & Hart · 175 North 27th Street, Suite 1400 · Billings, MT 59101 · 406-252-2166

Ward A. Shanahan* · Gough, Shanahan, Johnson & Waterman · 301 First National Bank Building · P.O. Box 1715 · Helena, MT 59624 · 406-442-8560

Thomas H. Boone · Boone, Karlberg & Haddon · Central Square, Suite 301 · 201 West Main Street · P.O. Box 9199 · Missoula, MT 59807-9199 · 406-543-6646

Harry A. Haines · Worden, Thane & Haines · P.O. Box 4747 · Missoula, MT 59806 · 406-721-3400

Sherman V. Lohn · Garlington, Lohn & Robinson · 199 West Pine · P.O. Box 7909 · Missoula, MT 59807-7909 · 406-728-1200

CRIMINAL DEFENSE

Charles F. Moses* · Moses Law Firm · The Terrace—Penthouse · 300 North 25th Street · P.O. Box 2533 · Billings, MT 59103 · 406-248-7702

Gregory A. Jackson · Jackson & Rice · 833 North Last Chance Gulch · Helena, MT 59601 · 406-443-2140

W. William Leaphart · Leaphart Law Firm · One North Last Chance Gulch, Suite Six · Helena, MT 59601 · 406-442-4930

FIRST AMENDMENT LAW

Sidney R. Thomas · Moulton, Bellingham, Longo & Mather · Sheridan Building, Suite 1900 · P.O. Box 2559 · Billings, MT 59103-2559 · 406-248-7731

HEALTH CARE LAW

Gareld F. Krieg · Crowley, Haughey, Hanson, Toole & Dietrich · 500 Transwestern Plaza II · 490 North 31st Street · P.O. Box 2529 · Billings, MT 59103-2529 406-252-3441

Jeremy G. Thane* · Worden, Thane & Haines · 11 North Higgins · P.O. Box 4747 · Missoula, MT 59806 · 406-721-3400

LABOR AND EMPLOYMENT LAW

Donald C. Robinson* · (Management) · Poore, Roth & Robinson · 1341 Harrison Avenue · P.O. Box 3328 · Butte, MT 59701-4898 · 406-782-1223

Tom L. Lewis* · (Labor) · Regnier, Lewis & Boland · 725 Third Avenue North P.O. Box 2325 · Great Falls, MT 59403 · 406-761-5595

D. Patrick McKittrick* · (Labor) · 410 Central Avenue, Suite 622 · P.O. Box 1184 Great Falls, MT 59403 · 406-727-4041

James M. Regnier* · (Individuals) · Regnier, Lewis & Boland · 725 Third Avenue North · P.O. Box 2325 · Great Falls, MT 59403 · 406-761-5595

Jeremy G. Thane* · (Management) · Worden, Thane & Haines · 11 North Higgins · P.O. Box 4747 · Missoula, MT 59806 · 406-721-3400

NATURAL RESOURCES AND ENVIRONMENTAL LAW

William H. Bellingham · Moulton, Bellingham, Longo & Mather · Sheridan Building, Suite 1900 · P.O. Box 2559 · Billings, MT 59103-2559 · 406-248-7731

Louis R. Moore · (Oil & Gas, Coal, Mining) · Crowley, Haughey, Hanson, Toole & Dietrich · 500 Transwestern Plaza II · 490 North 31st Street · P.O. Box 2529 · Billings, MT 59103 · 406-252-3441

James H. Goetz · (Plaintiffs) · Goetz, Madden & Dunn · 35 North Grand Avenue Bozeman, MT 59715 · 406-587-0618

Ted J. Doney · (Water) · Doney, Crowley & Shontz · 314 North Last Chance Gulch · P.O. Box 1185 · Helena, MT 59624 · 406-443-7018

PERSONAL INJURY LITIGATION

Wade J. Dahood* · (Plaintiffs, Medical Malpractice, Products Liability, Automobile Collision) · Knight, Dahood, McLean & Everett · P.O. Box 727 · Anaconda, MT 59711 · 406-563-3424

Bernard J. Everett · (Plaintiffs) · Knight, Dahood, McLean & Everett · P.O. Box 727 · Anaconda, MT 59711 · 406-563-3424

Gene Huntley · (Plaintiffs) · 204 South First Street, West · P.O. Box 760 · Baker, MT 59313 · 406-778-2831

William H. Bellingham · (Defendants) · Moulton, Bellingham, Longo & Mather Sheridan Building, Suite 1900 · P.O. Box 2559 · Billings, MT 59103-2559 · 406-248-7731

Richard F. Cebull* · (Defendants, Medical Malpractice) · Anderson, Brown, Gerbase, Cebull, Fulton, Harman & Ross · 315 North 24th Street · P.O. Drawer 849 · Billings, MT 59103-0849 · 406-248-2611

George C. Dalthorp · Crowley, Haughey, Hanson, Toole & Dietrich · 500 Transwestern Plaza II · 490 North 31st Street · P.O. Box 2529 · Billings, MT 59103-2529 406-252-3441

A. Clifford Edwards* · (Plaintiffs, Automobile Collision) · Edwards & Paoli · 1601 Lewis Avenue, Suite 206 · P.O. Box 20039 · Billings, MT 59103 · 406-256-8155

Steven J. Harman · (Defendants) · Anderson, Brown, Gerbase, Cebull, Fulton, Harman & Ross · 315 North 24th Street · P.O. Drawer 849 · Billings, MT 59103-0849 · 406-248-2611

Bruce R. Toole* · (Defendants) · Crowley, Haughey, Hanson, Toole & Dietrich 500 Transwestern Plaza II · 490 North 31st Street · P.O. Box 2529 · Billings, MT 59103-2529 · 406-252-3441

Donald C. Robinson* · (Plaintiffs) · Poore, Roth & Robinson · 1341 Harrison Avenue · P.O. Box 3328 · Butte, MT 59701-4898 · 406-782-1223

Urban L. Roth · (Products Liability, Professional Malpractice) · Poore, Roth & Robinson · 1341 Harrison Avenue · P.O. Box 3328 · Butte, MT 59701-4898 · 406-782-1223

Alexander Blewett III · Hoyt & Blewett · 501 Second Avenue North · P.O. Box 2807 · Great Falls, MT 59403-2807 · 406-761-1960

John C. Hoyt* · (Plaintiffs, Products Liability, Automobile Collision, Airplane Collision) · Hoyt & Blewett · 501 Second Avenue North · P.O. Box 2807 · Great Falls, MT 59403-2807 · 406-761-1960

Tom L. Lewis* · (Plaintiffs) · Regnier, Lewis & Boland · 725 Third Avenue North P.O. Box 2325 · Great Falls, MT 59403 · 406-761-5595

James M. Regnier* · (Plaintiffs) · Regnier, Lewis & Boland · 725 Third Avenue North · P.O. Box 2325 · Great Falls, MT 59403 · 406-761-5595

P. Keith Keller* · (Defendants) · Keller, Reynolds, Drake, Sternhagen and Johnson · 38 South Last Chance Gulch · Helena, MT 59601 · 406-442-0230

Stuart L. Kellner · (Defendants) · Hughes, Kellner, Sullivan & Alke · 406 Fuller Avenue · P.O. Box 1166 · Helena, MT 59624 · 406-442-3690

Sam E. Haddon* · (Defendants) · Boone, Karlberg & Haddon · Central Square, Suite 301 · 201 West Main Street · P.O. Box 9199 · Missoula, MT 59807-9199 · 406-543-6646

William Evan Jones* · (Defendants, Products Liability, Automobile Collision) · Garlington, Lohn & Robinson · 199 West Pine · P.O. Box 7909 · Missoula, MT 59807-7909 · 406-728-1200

Sherman V. Lohn · (Defendants) · Garlington, Lohn & Robinson · 199 West Pine P.O. Box 7909 · Missoula, MT 59807-7909 · 406-728-1200

Larry E. Riley · (Defendants) · Garlington, Lohn & Robinson · 199 West Pine · P.O. Box 7909 · Missoula, MT 59807-7909 · 406-728-1200

REAL ESTATE LAW

Richard W. Josephson · Josephson and Fredricks · 115 West Second Avenue · Big Timber, MT 59011 · 406-932-5440

John M. Dietrich · Crowley, Haughey, Hanson, Toole & Dietrich · 500 Transwestern Plaza II · 490 North 31st Street · P.O. Box 2529 · Billings, MT 59103 · 406-252-3441

Gareld F. Krieg · Crowley, Haughey, Hanson, Toole & Dietrich · 500 Transwestern Plaza II · 490 North 31st Street · P.O. Box 2529 · Billings, MT 59103 · 406-252-3441

Leonard A. Schulz · Schulz, Davis & Warren · 122 East Glendale Street · P.O. Box 28 · Dillon, MT 59725 · 406-683-2363

Harry A. Haines · Worden, Thane & Haines · P.O. Box 4747 · Missoula, MT 59806 · 406-721-3400

Robert M. Knight · Knight, Maclay & Maser · 300 Glacier Building · 111 North Higgins Avenue · P.O. Box 8957 · Missoula, MT 59807-8957 · 406-721-5440

TAX AND EMPLOYEE BENEFITS LAW

David L. Johnson · Crowley, Haughey, Hanson, Toole & Dietrich · 500 Transwestern Plaza II · 490 North 31st Street · P.O. Box 2529 · Billings, MT 59103 · 406-252-3441

L. W. Petersen · Dorsey & Whitney · 1200 First Interstate Center · 401 North 31st Street · P.O. Box 7188 · Billings, MT 59103 · 406-252-3800

Myles J. Thomas · (Corporate & Partnership Transactions) · Crowley, Haughey, Hanson, Toole & Dietrich · 500 Transwestern Plaza II · 490 North 31st Street · P.O. Box 2529 · Billings, MT 59103-2529 · 406-252-3441

Thomas F. Topel · Dorsey & Whitney · 1200 First Interstate Center · P.O. Box 7188 · Billings, MT 59103 · 406-252-3800

Dale Forbes · Church, Harris, Johnson & Williams · Norwest Bank Building, Third Floor · P.O. Box 1645 · Great Falls, MT 59403 · 406-761-3000

John R. Kline* · (Corporate & Partnership Transactions, State Tax, Tax Disputes) · Arcade Building, Suite 3J · 111 North Last Chance Gulch · P.O. Box 1705 Helena, MT 59624 · 406-442-8950

Harry A. Haines · Worden, Thane & Haines · P.O. Box 4747 · Missoula, MT 59806 · 406-721-3400

TRUSTS AND ESTATES

John M. Dietrich · Crowley, Haughey, Hanson, Toole & Dietrich · 500 Transwestern Plaza II · 490 North 31st Street · P.O. Box 2529 · Billings, MT 59103 · 406-252-3441

Myles J. Thomas · (Estate Planning, Estate Administration) · Crowley, Haughey, Hanson, Toole & Dietrich · 500 Transwestern Plaza II · 490 North 31st Street · P.O. Box 2529 · Billings, MT 59103 · 406-252-3441

Thomas F. Topel · Dorsey & Whitney · 1200 First Interstate Center · P.O. Box 7188 · Billings, MT 59103 · 406-252-3800

Dale Forbes · Church, Harris, Johnson & Williams · Norwest Bank Building, Third Floor · P.O. Box 1645 · Great Falls, MT 59403 · 406-761-3000

Cordell Johnson · Gough, Shanahan, Johnson & Waterman · 301 First National Bank Building · P.O. Box 1715 · Helena, MT 59624 · 406-442-8560

John R. Kline* · (Estate Planning, Estate Administration, Charitable Trusts) · Arcade Building, Suite 3J · 111 North Last Chance Gulch · P.O. Box 1705 · Helena, MT 59624 · 406-442-8950

George D. Goodrich · Garlington, Lohn & Robinson · 199 West Pine · P.O. Box 7909 · Missoula, MT 59807-7909 · 406-728-1200

NEBRASKA

BANKRUPTCY LAW

Joseph H. Badami · Woods & Atken · 206 South 13th Street, Suite 1500 · Lincoln, NE 68508 · 402-473-6464

Harry D. Dixon, Jr. · (Business Reorganization, Creditors' Rights) · Dixon & Dixon · One First National Center, Suite 1800 · 16th & Dodge Streets · Omaha, NE 68102 · 402-345-3900

Paul F. Festersen · Law Offices of Paul F. Festersen · 510 Service Life Building 19th & Farnam Streets · Omaha, NE 68102 · 402-344-3400

Jerrold L. Strasheim* · Baird, Holm, McEachen, Pedersen, Hamann & Strasheim · 1500 Woodmen Tower · Omaha, NE 68102-2069 · 402-344-0500

Steven C. Turner · Baird, Holm, McEachen, Pedersen, Hamann & Strasheim · 1500 Woodmen Tower · Omaha, NE 68102 · 402-344-0500

BUSINESS LITIGATION

M. J. "Jim" Bruckner · Bruckner, O'Gara, Keating, Sievers & Hendry · 530 South 13th Street, Suite A · Lincoln, NE 68508 · 402-475-8230

Fredric H. Kauffman · Cline, Williams, Wright, Johnson & Oldfather · 1900 FirsTier Bank Building · Lincoln, NE 68508 · 402-474-6900

Charles F. Gotch* · Cassem, Tierney, Adams, Gotch & Douglas · 8805 Indian Hills Drive, Suite 300 · Omaha, NE 68114 · 402-390-0300

Joseph K. Meusey* · Fraser, Stryker, Vaughn, Meusey, Olson, Boyer & Bloch · 500 Energy Plaza · 409 South 17th Street · Omaha, NE 68102-2663 · 402-341-6000

Warren S. Zweiback* · Zweiback, Holtz & Lamberty · Bozell & Jacobs Plaza, Suite 100 · 10250 Regency Circle · Omaha, NE 68114 · 402-397-1140

CORPORATE LAW

Warren C. Johnson · Cline, Williams, Wright, Johnson & Oldfather · 1900 FirsTier Bank Building · Lincoln, NE 68508 · 402-474-6900

Theodore L. Kessner · Crosby, Guenzel, Davis, Kessner & Kuester · 400 Lincoln Benefit Life Building · 134 South 13th Street · Lincoln, NE 68508 · 402-475-5131

Robert J. Routh · (Banking, Mergers & Acquisitions, Securities) · Knudsen, Berkheimer, Richardson & Endacott · 1000 NBC Center · Lincoln, NE 68508 · 402-475-7011

James W. R. Brown · Brown & Brown · 501 Scoular Building · 2027 Dodge Street Omaha, NE 68102 · 402-346-5010

Thomas R. Burke · Kennedy, Holland, DeLacy & Svoboda · Kennedy Holland Building · 10306 Regency Parkway Drive · Omaha, NE 68114 · 402-397-0203

Deryl F. Hamann · Baird, Holm, McEachen, Pedersen, Hamann & Strasheim · 1500 Woodmen Tower · Omaha, NE 68102 · 402-344-0500

Howard J. Kaslow · Abrahams, Kaslow & Cassman · 8712 West Dodge Road, Suite 300 · Omaha, NE 68114 · 402-392-1250

Edmund D. McEachen · Baird, Holm, McEachen, Pedersen, Hamann & Strasheim · 1500 Woodmen Tower · Omaha, NE 68102 · 402-344-0500

Stephen T. McGill · McGill, Gotsdiner, Workman & Lepp · 10010 Regency Circle, Suite 300 · Omaha, NE 68114 · 402-397-9988

Harold L. Rock · Kutak Rock & Campbell · The Omaha Building · 1650 Farnam Street · Omaha, NE 68102 · 402-346-6000

Bruce C. Rohde · McGrath, North, Mullin & Kratz · One Central Park Plaza, Suite 1100 · 222 South 15th Street · Omaha, NE 68102 · 402-341-3070

John S. Zeilinger · Baird, Holm, McEachen, Pedersen, Hamann & Strasheim · 1500 Woodmen Tower · Omaha, NE 68102 · 402-344-0500

CRIMINAL DEFENSE

Kirk E. Naylor, Jr. · Naylor & Blakeslee · 1111 Lincoln Mall, Suite 300 · Lincoln, NE 68508 · 402-474-5529

J. William Gallup* · Gallup & Schaefer · 1001 Farnam on The Mall · Omaha, NE 68102 · 402-341-0700

J. Joseph McQuillan · Walentine, O'Toole, McQuillan & Gordon · 11301 Davenport Street · Omaha, NE 68154 · 402-330-6300

FAMILY LAW

Paul E. Galter* · Bauer, Galter & O'Brien · 811 South 13th Street · Lincoln, NE 68508 · 402-475-0811

Con M. Keating · Bruckner, O'Gara, Keating, Sievers & Hendry · 530 South 13th Street, Suite A · Lincoln, NE 68508 · 402-475-8230

Albert L. Feldman · Harris, Feldman, Stumpf Law Offices · Regency One, Suite 101 · 10050 Regency Circle · Omaha, NE 68114 · 402-397-1200

Steven J. Lustgarten · Lustgarten and Roberts · 477 Continental Building · 209 South 19th Street · Omaha, NE 68102 · 402-346-1920

Warren S. Zweiback* · Zweiback, Holtz & Lamberty · Bozell & Jacobs Plaza, Suite 100 · 10250 Regency Circle · Omaha, NE 68114 · 402-397-1140

FIRST AMENDMENT LAW

Alan E. Peterson · Cline, Williams, Wright, Johnson & Oldfather · 1900 FirsTier Bank Building · Lincoln, NE 68508 · 402-474-6900

James L. Koley · Koley, Jessem, Daubman & Rupiper · One Pacific Place, Suite 800 · 1125 South 103rd Street · Omaha, NE 68124 · 402-390-9500

HEALTH CARE LAW

Douglas L. Curry · Erickson & Sederstrom · 301 South 13th Street, Suite 400 · Lincoln, NE 68508 · 402-476-1000

Charles M. Pallesen · Cline, Williams, Wright, Johnson & Oldfather · 1900 FirsTier Bank Building · Lincoln, NE 68508 · 402-474-6900

Alex (Kelly) Clarke · Baird, Holm, McEachen, Pedersen, Hamann & Strasheim 1500 Woodmen Tower · Omaha, NE 68102 · 402-344-0500

John R. Holdenried · Baird, Holm, McEachen, Pedersen, Hamann & Strasheim 1500 Woodmen Tower · Omaha, NE 68102 · 402-344-0500

Patricia A. Zieg · Kennedy, Holland, DeLacy & Svoboda · Kennedy Holland Building · 10306 Regency Parkway Drive · Omaha, NE 68114 · 402-397-0203

IMMIGRATION LAW

Stanley A. Krieger · 9290 West Dodge Road, Suite 302 · Omaha, NE 68114 · 402-392-1280

LABOR AND EMPLOYMENT LAW

Steven D. Burns* · (Labor, Individuals) · Burns & Associates · 3400 O Street · P.O. Box 30333 · Lincoln, NE 68503-0333 · 402-474-1513

Thom K. Cope* · (Individuals) · Bailey, Polsky, Cope & Wood · Cooper Plaza Building, Suite 400 · 211 North 12th Street · Lincoln, NE 68508 · 402-476-8877

William A. Harding* · (Management) · Harding & Ogborn · 500 The Atrium · 1200 N Street · P.O. Box 82028 · Lincoln, NE 68501-2028 · 402-475-6761

Theodore L. Kessner · (Labor) · Crosby, Guenzel, Davis, Kessner & Kuester · 400 Lincoln Benefit Life Building · 134 South 13th Street · Lincoln, NE 68508 · 402-475-5131

Mark D. McGuire* · (Labor, Individuals) · Crosby, Guenzel, Davis, Kessner & Kuester · 400 Lincoln Benefit Life Building · 134 South 13th Street · Lincoln, NE 68508 · 402-475-5131

A. Stevenson Bogue · McGrath, North, Mullin & Kratz · One Central Park Plaza, Suite 1100 · 222 South 15th Street · Omaha, NE 68102 · 402-341-3070

Thomas F. Dowd · (Labor) · Thomas F. Dowd & Associates · 1905 Harney Street, Suite 710 · Omaha, NE 68102 · 402-341-1020

Dean G. Kratz · (Management) · McGrath, North, Mullin & Kratz · One Central Park Plaza, Suite 1100 · 222 South 15th Street · Omaha, NE 68102 · 402-341-3070

Roger J. Miller · (Management) · McGrath, North, Mullin & Kratz · One Central Park Plaza, Suite 1100 · 222 South 15th Street · Omaha, NE 68102 · 402-341-3070

George C. Rozmarin · (Management) · Fraser, Stryker, Vaughn, Meusey, Olson, Boyer & Bloch · 500 Energy Plaza · 409 South 17th Street · Omaha, NE 68102-2663 · 402-341-6000

PERSONAL INJURY LITIGATION

M. J. "Jim" Bruckner · (Plaintiffs) · Bruckner, O'Gara, Keating, Sievers & Hendry · 530 South 13th Street, Suite A · Lincoln, NE 68508 · 402-475-8230

Fredric H. Kauffman · (Defendants) · Cline, Williams, Wright, Johnson & Oldfather · 1900 FirsTier Bank Building · Lincoln, NE 68508 · 402-474-6900

Daniel D. Jewell · (Defendants) · Jewell, Gatz, Collins, Dreier & Fitzgerald · 105 South Second Street · P.O. Box 1367 · Norfolk, NE 68702-1367 · 402-371-4844

John T. Carpenter · (Plaintiffs) · Carpenter, Rowen, & Fitzgerald · The Law Building, Suite 200 · 500 South 18th Street · Omaha, NE 68102 · 402-341-0994

Charles F. Gotch* · (Defendants, Medical Malpractice, Products Liability, Automobile Collision) · Cassem, Tierney, Adams, Gotch & Douglas · 8805 Indian Hills Drive, Suite 300 · Omaha, NE 68114 · 402-390-0300

William M. Lamson, Jr. · (Defendants) · Kennedy, Holland, DeLacy & Svoboda Kennedy Holland Building · 10306 Regency Parkway Drive · Omaha, NE 68114 402-397-0203

Joseph K. Meusey* · (Defendants) · Fraser, Stryker, Vaughn, Meusey, Olson, Boyer & Bloch · 500 Energy Plaza · 409 South 17th Street · Omaha, NE 68102-2663 · 402-341-6000

Robert Paul Chaloupka* · (Plaintiffs, Medical Malpractice, Products Liability, Automobile Collision) · Van Steenberg, Brower, Chaloupka, Mullin, Holyoke, Pahlke, Smith, Snyder & Hofmeister · 1904 First Avenue · P.O. Box 1204 · Scottsbluff, NE 69363-1204 · 308-635-3161

Francis L. Winner* · (Defendants) · 19 East Nineteenth Street · P.O. Box 99 · Scottsbluff, NE 69361-0099 · 308-635-3161

REAL ESTATE LAW

Thomas J. Fitchett · Pierson, Fitchett, Hunzeker, Blake & Loftis · 530 South 13th Street, Suite B · Lincoln, NE 68508 · 402-476-7621

William H. Coates · Abrahams, Kaslow & Cassman · 8712 West Dodge Road, Suite 300 · Omaha, NE 68114 · 402-392-1250

Richard E. Croker · Croker, Huck, Kasher, Lanphier, Dewitt & Anderson · Commercial Federal Tower, Suite 1250 · 2120 South 72nd Street · Omaha, NE 68124 · 402-391-6777

William A. Day, Jr. · Gross & Welch · 800 Commercial Federal Tower · 2120 South 72nd Street · Omaha, NE 68124 · 402-392-1500

John H. Fullenkamp · Walsh, Fullencamp & Doyle · 11440 West Center Road · Omaha, NE 68144 · 402-334-0700

Robert J. Huck · Croker, Huck, Kasher, Lanphier, Dewitt & Anderson · Commercial Federal Tower, Suite 1250 · 2120 South 72nd Street · Omaha, NE 68124 402-391-6777

TAX AND EMPLOYEE BENEFITS LAW

M. Douglas Deitchler · Baylor, Evnen, Curtiss, Grimit & Witt · 1200 American Charter Center · 206 South 13th Street · Lincoln, NE 68508 · 402-475-1075

David A. Ludtke · Rembolt Ludtke Parker & Berger · Century House, Suite 102 1201 Lincoln Mall · Lincoln, NE 68508 · 402-475-5100

Charles E. Wright · Cline, Williams, Wright, Johnson & Oldfather · 1900 FirsTier Bank Building · Lincoln, NE 68508 · 402-474-6900

L. Bruce Wright · (Employee Benefits) · Cline, Williams, Wright, Johnson & Oldfather · 1900 FirsTier Bank Building · Lincoln, NE 68508 · 402-474-6900

William A. Day, Jr. · Gross & Welch · 800 Commercial Federal Tower · 2120 South 72nd Street · Omaha, NE 68124 · 402-392-1500

Howard Fredrick Hahn · Gross & Welch · 800 Commercial Federal Tower · 2120 South 72nd Street · Omaha, NE 68124-2342 · 402-392-1500

Deryl F. Hamann · Baird, Holm, McEachen, Pedersen, Hamann & Strasheim · 1500 Woodmen Tower · Omaha, NE 68102 · 402-344-0500

David L. Hefflinger · McGrath, North, Mullin & Kratz · One Central Park Plaza, Suite 1100 · 222 South 15th Street · Omaha, NE 68102 · 402-341-3070

T. Geoffrey Lieben* · (State Tax, Employee Benefits, Tax Disputes) · Lieben, Dahlk, Whitted, Houghton & Jahn · 100 Scoular Building · 2027 Dodge Street · Omaha, NE 68102 · 402-344-4000

Kent O. Littlejohn · Baird, Holm, McEachen, Pedersen, Hamann & Strasheim · 1500 Woodmen Tower · Omaha, NE 68102 · 402-344-0500

William E. Mooney, Jr. · Schmid, Mooney & Frederick · 11404 West Dodge Road, Suite 700 · Omaha, NE 68154 · 402-493-7700

John E. North · McGrath, North, Mullin & Kratz · One Central Park Plaza, Suite 1100 · 222 South 15th Street · Omaha, NE 68102 · 402-341-3070

Gary W. Radil · (Employee Benefits) · Baird, Holm, McEachen, Pedersen, Hamann & Strasheim · 1500 Woodmen Tower · Omaha, NE 68102 · 402-344-0500

Arden J. Rupiper · (Employee Benefits) · Koley, Jessen, Daubman & Rupiper · 1125 South 103rd Street, Suite 800 · Omaha, NE 68124 · 402-390-9500

TRUSTS AND ESTATES

M. Douglas Deitchler · Baylor, Evnen, Curtiss, Grimit & Witt · 1200 American Charter Center · 206 South 13th Street · Lincoln, NE 68508 · 402-475-1075

Thomas J. Fitchett · Pierson, Fitchett, Hunzeker, Blake & Loftis · 530 South 13th Street, Suite B · Lincoln, NE 68508 · 402-476-7621

David A. Ludtke · Rembolt Ludtke Parker & Berger · Century House, Suite 102 1201 Lincoln Mall · Lincoln, NE 68508 · 402-475-5100

James E. Rembolt · Rembolt Ludtke Parker & Berger · Century House, Suite 102 · 1201 Lincoln Mall · Lincoln, NE 68508 · 402-475-5100

Charles E. Wright · (Estate Planning, Estate Administration, Charitable Trusts) Cline, Williams, Wright, Johnson & Oldfather · 1900 FirsTier Bank Building · Lincoln, NE 68508 · 402-474-6900

Dennis W. Collins · Jewell, Gatz, Collins, Dreier & Fitzgerald · 105 South Second Street · P.O. Box 1367 · Norfolk, NE 68702-1367 · 402-371-4844

Thomas R. Burke · Kennedy, Holland, DeLacy & Svoboda · Kennedy Holland Building · 10306 Regency Parkway Drive · Omaha, NE 68114 · 402-397-0203

William A. Day, Jr. · Gross & Welch · 800 Commercial Federal Tower · 2120 South 72nd Street · Omaha, NE 68124 · 402-392-1500

Deryl F. Hamann · Baird, Holm, McEachen, Pedersen, Hamann & Strasheim · 1500 Woodmen Tower · Omaha, NE 68102 · 402-344-0500

David L. Hefflinger · McGrath, North, Mullin & Kratz · One Central Park Plaza, Suite 1100 · 222 South 15th Street · Omaha, NE 68102 · 402-341-3070

Michael D. Jones · Ellick Jones Law Offices · 8805 Indian Hills Drive, Suite 280 Omaha, NE 68114 · 402-390-0390

T. Geoffrey Lieben* · (Estate Planning) · Lieben, Dahlk, Whitted, Houghton & Jahn · 100 Scoular Building · 2027 Dodge Street · Omaha, NE 68102 · 402-344-4000

William E. Mooney, Jr. · Schmid, Mooney & Frederick · 11404 West Dodge Road, Suite 700 · Omaha, NE 68154 · 402-493-7700

John E. North · McGrath, North, Mullin & Kratz · One Central Park Plaza, Suite 1100 · 222 South Fifteenth Street · Omaha, NE 68102 · 402-341-3070

NEVADA

BANKRUPTCY LAW

Gerald M. Gordon · Wiener, Waldman, Gordon & Silver · Chicago Title Building, Suite 801 · 701 East Bridger Avenue · Las Vegas, NV 89101 · 702-382-9666

William L. McGimsey · Law Offices of William L. McGimsey · 601 East Charleston Boulevard · Las Vegas, NV 89104 · 702-382-9948

Sallie Bernard Armstrong · Hartman & Armstrong · 417 West Plumb Lane · Reno, NV 89509 · 702-786-7600

Janet L. Chubb · Jones, Jones, Close & Brown · One East Liberty Street, Suite 614 · Reno, NV 89501 · 702-322-3811

Richard W. Horton* · Lionel Sawyer & Collins · 50 West Liberty Street, Suite 1100 · Reno, NV 89501 · 702-788-8666

BUSINESS LITIGATION

Morton R. Galane · First Interstate Bank Building, Suite 1100 · 302 East Carson Avenue · Las Vegas, NV 89101 · 702-382-3290

Paul Hejmanowski* · Lionel Sawyer & Collins · 1700 Valley Bank Plaza Building 300 South Fourth Street · Las Vegas, NV 89101 · 702-383-8888

Samuel S. Lionel · Lionel Sawyer & Collins · 1700 Valley Bank Plaza Building · 300 South Fourth Street · Las Vegas, NV 89101 · 702-383-8888

Steve Morris · Lionel Sawyer & Collins · 1700 Valley Bank Plaza Building · 300 South Fourth Street · Las Vegas, NV 89101 · 702-383-8888

Paul A. Bible · Bible, Hoy, Miller, Trachok & Wadhams · 232 Court Street · Reno, NV 89501-1808 · 702-786-8000

C. Robert Cox · Walther, Key, Maupin, Oats, Cox, Lee & Klaich · Lakeside Professional Plaza, Suite 200 · 3500 Lakeside Court · P.O. Box 30000 · Reno, NV 89520 · 702-827-2000

David W. Hagen* · (Appellate, Banking, Commercial, Energy) · Guild, Hagen & Clark · 102 Rolf Way · P.O. Box 2838 · Reno, NV 89505 · 702-786-2366

Richard W. Horton* · Lionel Sawyer & Collins · 50 West Liberty Street, Suite 1100 · Reno, NV 89501 · 702-788-8666

J. Stephen Peek · Hale, Lane, Peek, Dennison and Howard · Valley Bank Plaza, Suite 650 · 50 West Liberty Street · P.O. Box 3237 · Reno, NV 89505 · 702-786-7900

John C. Renshaw* · Vargas & Bartlett · 201 West Liberty Street, Third Floor · P.O. Box 281 · Reno, NV 89504 · 702-786-5000

CORPORATE LAW

Charles W. Deaner · Deaner, Deaner & Scann · 720 South Fourth Street, Suite 300 · Las Vegas, NV 89101 · 702-382-6911

Samuel S. Lionel · Lionel Sawyer & Collins · 1700 Valley Bank Plaza Building · 300 South Fourth Street · Las Vegas, NV 89101 · 702-383-8888

John D. O'Brien* · Valley Bank Plaza, Suite 1009 · 300 South Fourth Street · Las Vegas, NV 89101 · 702-382-5222

Robert C. Anderson · (Banking, Corporate Finance, Leveraged Buyouts, Mergers & Acquisitions) · Anderson, Pearl, Beecroft, Murphy & Stone · 245 East Liberty Street, Third Floor · P.O. Box 21150 · Reno, NV 89515 · 702-348-5000

Edward Everett Hale · Hale, Lane, Peek, Dennison and Howard · Valley Bank Plaza, Suite 650 · 50 West Liberty Street · P.O. Box 3237 · Reno, NV 89505 · 702-786-7900

F. DeArmond Sharp · Robison, Belaustegui, Robb & Sharp · 71 Washington Street · Reno, NV 89503 · 702-329-3151

CRIMINAL DEFENSE

Donald J. Campbell · Law Office of Donald J. Campbell · Valley Bank Plaza, Suite 1009 · 300 South Fourth Street · Las Vegas, NV 89101 · 702-382-5222

Dominic P. Gentile · Gentile, Porter & Kelesis · First Interstate Bank Building, Fourth Floor · 302 East Carson Avenue · Las Vegas, NV 89101 · 702-386-0066

Oscar B. Goodman · Goodman, Stein & Chesnoff · 520 South Fourth Street · Las Vegas, NV 89101-6593 · 702-384-5563

Richard A. Wright* · (Federal Court, State Court) · Wright & Stewart · First Interstate Bank Building, Third Floor · 302 East Carson Avenue · Las Vegas, NV 89101 · 702-382-4004

John Ohlson · Law Office of John Ohlson · 522 Lander Street · Reno, NV 89509 702-323-0300

C. Frederick Pinkerton · 543 Plumas Street · Reno, NV 89509 · 702-322-7553

Jerome M. Polaha · 450 Marsh Avenue · Reno, NV 89509 · 702-786-5344

FAMILY LAW

George M. Dickerson · Dickerson, Dickerson, Lieberman & Consul · 330 South Third Street, Suite 1130 · Las Vegas, NV 89101 · 702-388-8600

Ronald J. Logar* · Law Offices of Ronald J. Logar · 243 South Sierra Street · Reno, NV 89501 · 702-786-5040

Gary L. Manson · Law Offices of Ronald J. Logar · 243 South Sierra Street · Reno, NV 89501 · 702-786-5040

HEALTH CARE LAW

Dennis L. Kennedy · Lionel Sawyer & Collins · 1700 Valley Bank Plaza Building 300 South Fourth Street · Las Vegas, NV 89101 · 702-383-8888

Sherman B. Mayor · Hafen & Mayor · 525 South Ninth Street · Las Vegas, NV 89101 · 702-384-5800

Keith L. Lee · Walther, Key, Maupin, Oats, Cox, Lee & Klaich · Lakeside Professional Plaza, Suite 200 · 3500 Lakeside Court · P.O. Box 30000 · Reno, NV 89520 · 702-827-2000

Kim G. Rowe · Walther, Key, Maupin, Oats, Cox, Lee & Klaich · Lakeside Professional Plaza, Suite 200 · 3500 Lakeside Court · P.O. Box 30000 · Reno, NV 89520 · 702-827-2000

LABOR AND EMPLOYMENT LAW

Frederic I. Berkley* · (Labor) · Gang & Berkley · 415 South Sixth Street, Suite 101 · Las Vegas, NV 89101 · 702-385-3761

Kevin C. Efroymson · (Management) · 2915 West Charleston Boulevard, Suite Nine · Las Vegas, NV 89102 · 702-870-9601

Gregory J. Kamer · (Management) · Kamer & Ricciardi · Building D, Suite 208 2300 Paseo del Prado · Las Vegas, NV 89102 · 702-364-1014

Daniel Marks · (Individuals) · John Peter Lee · 830 South Las Vegas Boulevard Las Vegas, NV 89101 · 702-382-4044

Richard S. Segerblom · (Individuals) · Law Office of Richard S. Segerblom · 704 South Ninth Street · Las Vegas, NV 89101 · 702-388-9600

NATURAL RESOURCES AND ENVIRONMENTAL LAW

Jack E. Hull · Vaughan, Hull & Copenhaver · 530 Idaho Street · P.O. Box 1420 Elko, NV 89801 · 702-738-4031

John C. Miller · (Mining, Water) · Bible, Hoy, Miller, Trachok & Wadhams · Blohm Building, Suite 201 · Elko, NV 89801 · 702-738-8064

Earl M. Hill* · (Mining, Water, Public Land Law) · Hill Cassas de Lipkau and Erwin · Holcomb Professional Building, Suite 300 · 333 Holcomb Avenue · P.O. Box 2790 · Reno, NV 89505 · 702-323-1601

Roger W. Jeppson · (Mining, Water) · Woodburn Wedge & Jeppson · One East First Street · Reno, NV 89501 · 702-329-6131

PERSONAL INJURY LITIGATION

William S. Barker · (Defendants) · Barker, Gillock, Koning, Brown & Early · 430 South Third Street · Las Vegas, NV 89101 · 702-386-1086

Drake DeLanoy · (Defendants) · Beckley, Singleton, DeLanoy, Jemison & List · 530 Las Vegas Boulevard South · Las Vegas, NV 89101 · 702-385-3373

Allan R. Earl · (Plaintiffs) · Galatz, Earl, Catalano & Smith · 710 South Fourth Street · Las Vegas, NV 89101 · 702-386-0000

Morton R. Galane · (Plaintiffs) · First Interstate Bank Building, Suite 1100 · 302 East Carson Avenue · Las Vegas, NV 89101 · 702-382-3290

Neil G. Galatz* · (Plaintiffs, Medical Malpractice, Products Liability, Automobile Collision) · Galatz, Earl, Catalano & Smith · 710 South Fourth Street · Las Vegas, NV 89101 · 702-386-0000

Gerald I. Gillock · (Defendants) · Barker, Gillock, Koning, Brown & Early · 430 South Third Street · Las Vegas, NV 89101 · 702-386-1086

David Goldwater · 302 East Carson Avenue, Suite 1000 · Las Vegas, NV 89101 · 702-385-5266

Rex A. Jemison · (Defendants) · Beckley, Singleton, DeLanoy, Jemison & List · 530 Las Vegas Boulevard South · Las Vegas, NV 89101 · 702-385-3373

James F. Pico* · (Defendants) · Miles, Pico & Mitchell · 2000 South Eastern Avenue · Las Vegas, NV 89104 · 702-457-9099

William O. Bradley · (Plaintiffs) · Bradley & Drendel · 401 Flint Street · Reno, NV 89501 · 702-329-2273

C. James Georgeson* · (Defendants) · Shamberger, Georgeson, McQuaid & Thompson · 100 West Grove Street, Suite 500 · P.O. Box 3257 · Reno, NV 89509 · 702-827-6440

Peter Chase Neumann* · (Plaintiffs) · 136 Ridge Street · P.O. Box 1170 · Reno, NV 89504-1170 · 702-786-3750

Kent R. Robison · (Plaintiffs) · Robison, Belaustegui, Robb & Sharp · 71 Washington Street · Reno, NV 89503 · 702-329-3151

Eugene J. Wait, Jr. · (Defendants) · 305 West Moana Lane, Suite D · P.O. Box 719 · Reno, NV 89504-0719 · 702-827-5500

PUBLIC UTILITY LAW

Robert L. Crowell · Crowell, Susich, Owen & Tackes · 510 West Fourth Street Carson City, NV 89701 · 702-882-1311

Richard G. Campbell, Sr. · Lionel Sawyer & Collins · 50 West Liberty Street, Suite 1100 · P.O. Box 2610 · Reno, NV 89505 · 702-788-8666

REAL ESTATE LAW

Michael E. Buckley · Jones, Jones, Close & Brown · Valley Bank Plaza, Suite 700 300 South Fourth Street · Las Vegas, NV 89101-6026 · 702-385-4202

Charles W. Deaner · Deaner, Deaner & Scann · 720 South Fourth Street, Suite 300 · Las Vegas, NV 89101 · 702-382-6911

Jodi Raizin Goodheart · Sherman & Howard · 2300 West Saraha, Suite 500 · Las Vegas, NV 89102 · 702-368-6200

Barry Stephen Goold · Goold & Patterson · 905 Valley Bank Plaza · 300 South Fourth Street · Las Vegas, NV 89101 · 702-386-0038

Jeffrey P. Zucker · Lionel Sawyer & Collins · 1700 Valley Bank Plaza Building · 300 South Fourth Street · Las Vegas, NV 89101 · 702-383-8888

Edward Everett Hale · Hale, Lane, Peek, Dennison and Howard · Valley Bank Plaza, Suite 650 · 50 West Liberty Street · P.O. Box 3237 · Reno, NV 89505 · 702-786-7900

David R. Hoy* · (Commercial Transactions, Industrial Transactions, Litigation) · Bible, Hoy, Miller, Trachok & Wadhams · 232 Court Street · Reno, NV 89501-1808 · 702-786-8000

F. DeArmond Sharp · Robison, Belaustegui, Robb & Sharp · 71 Washington Street · Reno, NV 89503 · 702-329-3151

TAX AND EMPLOYEE BENEFITS LAW

Patricia L. Brown · (Tax, Employee Benefits) · Beckley, Singleton, Delanoy, Jemison & List · 530 Las Vegas Boulevard South · Las Vegas, NV 89101 · 702-385-3373

Jeffrey L. Burr · (Tax) · 1900 East Flamingo Road, Suite 252 · Las Vegas, NV 89119 · 702-369-9919

Douglas M. Edwards · (Tax) · Edwards & Kolesar · Nevada Savings Financial Center, Suite 380 · 3320 West Sahara Avenue · Las Vegas, NV 89102 · 702-362-7800

A. Kent Greene · (Employee Benefits) · Clark, Greene & Associates · 5606 South Eastern Avenue · Las Vegas, NV 89119 · 702-736-1844

Robert C. Anderson · (Corporate & Partnership Transactions, Tax Disputes, Mergers & Reorganizations) · Anderson, Pearl, Beecroft, Murphy & Stone · 245 East Liberty Street, Third Floor · P.O. Box 21150 · Reno, NV 89515 · 702-348-5000

L. Robert LeGoy, Jr. · (Employee Benefits) · Walther, Key, Maupin, Oats, Cox, Lee & Klaich · Lakeside Professional Plaza, Suite 200 · 3500 Lakeside Court · P.O. Box 30000 · Reno, NV 89520 · 702-827-2000

Ernest J. Maupin III* · (Corporate & Partnership Transactions, Tax Disputes, Individual Tax Planning, Real Property Transactions) · Walther, Key, Maupin, Oats, Cox, Lee & Klaich · Lakeside Professional Plaza, Suite 200 · 3500 Lakeside Court · P.O. Box 30000 · Reno, NV 89520 · 702-827-2000

G. Barton Mowry* · (Corporate & Partnership Transactions, Tax Disputes, Individual Tax Planning, Real Property Transactions) · Walther, Key, Maupin, Oats, Cox, Lee & Klaich · Lakeside Professional Plaza, Suite 200 · 3500 Lakeside Court · P.O. Box 30000 · Reno, NV 89520 · 702-827-2000

Andrew Pearl · Anderson & Pearl · 241 Ridge Street, Suite 300 · P.O. Box 21150 Reno, NV 89515 · 702-348-5000

TRUSTS AND ESTATES

Patricia L. Brown · Beckley, Singleton, Delanoy, Jemison & List · 530 Las Vegas Boulevard South · Las Vegas, NV 89101 · 702-385-3373

Jeffrey L. Burr · (Estate Planning, Estate Administration) · 1900 East Flamingo Road, Suite 252 · Las Vegas, NV 89119 · 702-369-9919

Charles William Johnson · 530 South Fourth Street · Las Vegas, NV 89101 · 702-384-2830

Richard A. Oshins · Oshins & Gibbons · 501 South Rancho Drive, Suite G-46 · Las Vegas, NV 89106 · 702-386-1935

Layne T. Rushforth · (Estate Planning, Estate Administration, Charitable Trusts) Beckley, Singleton, De Lanoy, Jemison & List · 530 Las Vegas Boulevard South Las Vegas, NV 89101 · 702-385-3373

Robert E. Armstrong · McDonald, Carano, Wilson, McCune, Bergin, Frankovick & Hicks · 241 Ridge Street · P.O. Box 2670 · Reno, NV 89505 · 702-322-0635

Ernest J. Maupin III* · (Estate Planning, Estate Administration, Charitable Trusts) · Walther, Key, Maupin, Oats, Cox, Lee & Klaich · Lakeside Professional Plaza, Suite 200 · 3500 Lakeside Court · P.O. Box 30000 · Reno, NV 89520 · 702-827-2000

G. Barton Mowry* · (Estate Planning, Estate Administration, Charitable Trusts) Walther, Key, Maupin, Oats, Cox, Lee & Klaich · Lakeside Professional Plaza, Suite 200 · 3500 Lakeside Court · P.O. Box 30000 · Reno, NV 89520 · 702-827-2000

Fred L. Oats · Walther, Key, Maupin, Oats, Cox, Lee & Klaich · Lakeside Professional Plaza, Suite 200 · 3500 Lakeside Court · P.O. Box 30000 · Reno, NV 89520 · 702-827-2000

Andrew Pearl · Anderson & Pearl · 241 Ridge Street, Suite 300 · P.O. Box 21150 Reno, NV 89515 · 702-348-5000

NEW HAMPSHIRE

BANKRUPTCY LAW

Daniel J. Callaghan · Devine, Millimet & Branch · 111 Amherst Street · P.O. Box 719 · Manchester, NH 03105 · 603-669-1000

Daniel W. Sklar · (Business Reorganization, Creditors' Rights, Bankruptcy Litigation) · Hampshire Plaza · 889 Elm Street · Manchester, NH 03101 · 603-669-3662

Mark W. Vaughn · (Business Reorganization, Creditors' Rights, Debtors' Rights, Bankruptcy Litigation) · Devine, Millimet & Branch · 111 Amherst Street · P.O. Box 719 · Manchester, NH 03105 · 603-669-1000

J. Michael Deasy · Deasy & Dwyer · 60 Main Street · Nashua, NH 03060 · 603-595-9700

BUSINESS LITIGATION

Richard B. Couser · Orr and Reno · One Eagle Square · P.O. Box 709 · Concord, NH 03302-0709 · 603-224-2381

Charles G. Douglas III* · (Appellate) · 197 Loudon Road · Concord, NH 03301 603-226-1988

Martin L. Gross · (Appellate) · Sulloway Hollis & Soden · Nine Capitol Street · P.O. Box 1256 · Concord, NH 03301 · 603-224-2341

Ronald L. Snow* · Orr and Reno · One Eagle Square · P.O. Box 709 · Concord, NH 03302-0709 · 603-224-2381

Frederic K. Upton · (Appellate) · Upton, Sanders and Smith · Ten Centre Street P.O. Box 1109 · Concord, NH 03302-1109 · 603-224-7791

W. Wright Danenbarger* · Wiggin & Nourie · The Parish House · Franklin & Market Streets · P.O. Box 808 · Manchester, NH 03105-0808 · 603-669-2211

E. Donald Dufresne* · (Banking, Securities) · Devine, Millimet & Branch · Victory Park · 111 Amherst Street · P.O. Box 719 · Manchester, NH 03105 · 603-669-1000

Jack B. Middleton* · McLane, Graf, Raulerson & Middleton · 40 Stark Street · P.O. Box 326 · Manchester, NH 03105-0326 · 603-625-6464

James R. Muirhead · McLane, Graf, Raulerson & Middleton · 40 Stark Street · P.O. Box 326 · Manchester, NH 03105-0326 · 603-625-6464

Thomas H. Richards · Sheehan, Phinney, Bass & Green · Hampshire Plaza · 1000 Elm Street · P.O. Box 3701 · Manchester, NH 03105-3701 · 603-668-0300

Eugene M. Van Loan III · Wadleigh, Starr, Peters, Dunn & Chiesa · 95 Market Street · Manchester, NH 03101 · 603-669-4140

CORPORATE LAW

Charles F. Leahy · Orr and Reno · One Eagle Square · P.O. Box 709 · Concord, NH 03302-0709 · 603-224-2381

Charles F. Sheridan, Jr. · Sulloway Hollis & Soden · Nine Capitol Street · P.O. Box 1256 · Concord, NH 03301 · 603-224-2341

T. William Bigelow · Wiggin & Nourie · The Parish House · Franklin & Market Streets · P.O. Box 808 · Manchester, NH 03105-0808 · 603-669-2211

Robert E. Dastin · Sheehan, Phinney, Bass & Green · Hampshire Plaza · 1000 Elm Street · P.O. Box 3701 · Manchester, NH 03105-3701 · 603-668-0300

Charles A. DeGrandpre · McLane, Graf, Raulerson & Middleton · 40 Stark Street · P.O. Box 326 · Manchester, NH 03105-0326 · 603-625-6464

John S. Holland · Devine, Millimet & Branch · 111 Amherst Street · P.O. Box 719 · Manchester, NH 03105 · 603-669-1000

Joseph A. Millimet · Devine, Millimet & Branch · 111 Amherst Street · P.O. Box 719 · Manchester, NH 03105 · 603-669-1000

John R. Monson · Wiggin & Nourie · The Parish House · Franklin & Market Streets · P.O. Box 808 · Manchester, NH 03105-0808 · 603-669-2211

Robert A. Raulerson · McLane, Graf, Raulerson & Middleton · 40 Stark Street P.O. Box 326 · Manchester, NH 03105-0326 · 603-625-6464

Alan L. Reische · Sheehan, Phinney, Bass & Green · Hampshire Plaza · 1000 Elm Street · P.O. Box 3701 · Manchester, NH 03105-3701 · 603-668-0300

William C. Tucker · Wadleigh, Starr, Peters, Dunn & Chiesa · 95 Market Street Manchester, NH 03101 · 603-669-4140

Chester H. Lopez, Jr. · Hamblett & Kerrigan · One Indian Head Plaza · P.O. Box 868X · Nashua, NH 03061 · 603-883-5501

CRIMINAL DEFENSE

Steven M. Gordon* · Shaheen, Cappiello, Stein & Gordon · One Barberry Lane P.O. Box 2159 · Concord, NH 03302-2159 · 603-228-1109

Robert A. Stein · Shaheen, Cappiello, Stein & Gordon · One Barberry Lane · P.O. Box 2159 · Concord, NH 03302-2159 · 603-228-1109

William E. Brennan · Brennan, Caron & Lenehan · 85 Brook Street · Manchester, NH 03104 · 603-668-8300

Cathy J. Green · (also Appellate) · Law Offices of Cathy J. Green · 108 Bay Street Manchester, NH 03104 · 603-669-7603

Richard B. McNamara · Wiggin & Nourie · The Parish House · Franklin & Market Streets · P.O. Box 808 · Manchester, NH 03105-0808 · 603-669-2211

FAMILY LAW

Charles G. Douglas III* · (Divorce) · 197 Loudon Road · Concord, NH 03301 · 603-226-1988

Michael R. Chamberlain · Chamberlain & Connor · 155 Myrtle Street · Manchester, NH 03104 · 603-622-3784

L. Jonathan Ross · (Divorce, Marital Settlement Agreements, Equitable Division) · Wiggin & Nourie · The Parish House · Franklin & Market Streets · P.O. Box 808 · Manchester, NH 03105-0808 · 603-669-2211

FIRST AMENDMENT LAW

William L. Chapman · Orr and Reno · One Eagle Square · P.O. Box 709 · Concord, NH 03302-0709 · 603-224-2381

Steven M. Gordon · Shaheen, Cappiello, Stein & Gordon · One Barberry Lane P.O. Box 2159 · Concord, NH 03302-2159 · 603-228-1109

Arnold R. Falk · Bell, Falk & Norton · Eight Middle Street · P.O. Box F · Keene, NH 03431 · 603-352-5950

Jon Meyer · Backus, Meyer & Solomon · 116 Lowell Street · P.O. Box 516 · Manchester, NH 03105 · 603-668-7272

HEALTH CARE LAW

Neil F. Castaldo · Castaldo, Hanna & Malmberg · 14 South Street · Concord, NH 03302-1477 · 603-224-9033

Eleanor Holmes MacLellan · Sulloway Hollis & Soden · Nine Capitol Street · P.O. Box 1256 · Concord, NH 03301 · 603-224-2341

David H. Barnes · Devine, Millimet & Branch · 111 Amherst Street · P.O. Box 719 · Manchester, NH 03105 · 603-669-1000

Jon S. Richardson · Sheehan, Phinney, Bass & Green · Hampshire Plaza · 1000 Elm Street · P.O. Box 3701 · Manchester, NH 03105-3701 · 603-668-0300

Eugene Van Loan III · Wadleigh, Starr, Peters, Dunn & Chiesa · 95 Market Street · Manchester, NH 03101 · 603-669-4140

LABOR AND EMPLOYMENT LAW

Alan Hall · (Management, Public & Private Sectors) · 15 North Main Street, Suite 202 · Concord, NH 03301 · 603-226-4855

Edward M. Kaplan · (Management, Individuals) · Sulloway Hollis & Soden · Nine Capitol Street · P.O. Box 1256 · Concord, NH 03301 · 603-224-2341

Edward E. Shumaker III* · (Management) · Gallagher, Callahan & Gartrell · 214 North Main Street · P.O. Box 1415 · Concord, NH 03302 · 603-228-1181

Richard E. Galway, Jr. · (Management) · Devine, Millimet & Branch · 111 Amherst Street · P.O. Box 719 · Manchester, NH 03105 · 603-669-1000

PERSONAL INJURY LITIGATION

Edward M. Kaplan · (Plaintiffs) · Sulloway Hollis & Soden · Nine Capitol Street P.O. Box 1256 · Concord, NH 03301 · 603-224-2341

Ernest T. Smith III · (Plaintiffs) · Upton, Sanders and Smith · Ten Centre Street P.O. Box 1109 · Concord, NH 03302-1109 · 603-224-7791

Ronald L. Snow* · (Defendants, Medical Malpractice, Airplane Collision) · Orr and Reno · One Eagle Square · P.O. Box 709 · Concord, NH 03302-0709 · 603-224-2381

Dort S. Bigg* · (Plaintiffs, Medical Malpractice, Products Liability, Professional Malpractice, Automobile Collision, Airplane Collision) · Wiggin & Nourie · The Parish House · Franklin & Market Streets · P.O. Box 808 · Manchester, NH 03105-0808 · 603-669-2211

John T. Broderick, Jr.* · (Defendants, Plaintiffs, Medical Malpractice) · Merrill & Broderick · 707 Chestnut Street · P.O. Box 1420 · Manchester, NH 03105 · 603-626-1000

E. Donald Dufresne* · (Medical Malpractice, Products Liability) · Devine, Millimet & Branch · 111 Amherst Street · P.O. Box 719 · Manchester, NH 03105 · 603-669-1000

John E. Friberg · (Defendants) · Wadleigh, Starr, Peters, Dunn & Chiesa · 95 Market Street · Manchester, NH 03101 · 603-669-4140

Joseph F. McDowell II · (Plaintiffs) · 282 North River Road · P.O. Box 3280 · Manchester, NH 03105 · 603-668-3353

Jack B. Middleton* · (Plaintiffs) · McLane, Graf, Raulerson & Middleton · 40 Stark Street · P.O. Box 326 · Manchester, NH 03105-0326 · 603-625-6464

David L. Nixon · (Plaintiffs) · Nixon, Hall & Hess · 80 Merrimack Street · Manchester, NH 03101 · 603-669-8080

William S. Orcutt* · (Defendants, Products Liability, Automobile Collision) · Wiggin & Nourie · The Parish House · Franklin & Market Streets · P.O. Box 808 Manchester, NH 03105-0808 · 603-669-2211

Jeffrey B. Osburn · (Defendants) · Wiggin & Nourie · The Parish House · Franklin & Market Streets · P.O. Box 808 · Manchester, NH 03105-0808 · 603-669-2211

Philip G. Peters · (Defendants) · Wadleigh, Starr, Peters, Dunn & Chiesa · 95 Market Street · Manchester, NH 03101 · 603-669-4140

Joseph M. Kerrigan* · (Defendants) · Hamblett & Kerrigan · One Indian Head Plaza · P.O. Box 868X · Nashua, NH 03061 · 603-883-5501

James John Kalled · (Plaintiffs) · Route 171 · Courthouse Square · Ossipee, NH 03864 · 603-539-2218

PUBLIC UTILITY LAW

Martin L. Gross · Sulloway Hollis & Soden · Nine Capitol Street · P.O. Box 1256 Concord, NH 03301 · 603-224-2341

Margaret H. Nelson · Sulloway Hollis & Soden · Nine Capitol Street · P.O. Box 1256 · Concord, NH 03301 · 603-224-2341

John B. Pendleton · Gallagher, Callahan and Gartrell · 214 North Main Street · P.O. Box 1415 · Concord, NH 03302 · 603-228-1181

Frederick J. Coolbroth · Devine, Millimet & Branch · 111 Amherst Street · P.O. Box 719 · Manchester, NH 03105 · 603-669-1000

Richard A. Samuels · McLane, Graf, Raulerson & Middleton · 40 Stark Street · P.O. Box 326 · Manchester, NH 03105-0326 · 603-625-6464

REAL ESTATE LAW

Donald E. Gartrell · Gallagher, Callahan & Gartrell · 214 North Main Street · P.O. Box 1415 · Concord, NH 03302 · 603-228-1181

John B. Pendleton · Gallagher, Callahan and Gartrell · 214 North Main Street · P.O. Box 1415 · Concord, NH 03302 · 603-228-1181

Eaton W. Tarbell, Jr. · Sulloway Hollis & Soden · Nine Capitol Street · P.O. Box 1256 · Concord, NH 03301 · 603-224-2341

John J. Ryan · Casassa and Ryan · 459 Lafayette Road · Hampton, NH 03842 · 603-926-6336

William C. Tucker · Wadleigh, Starr, Peters, Dunn & Chiesa · 95 Market Street Manchester, NH 03101 · 603-669-4140

TAX AND EMPLOYEE BENEFITS LAW

David F. Conley · Sulloway Hollis & Soden · Nine Capitol Street · P.O. Box 1256 Concord, NH 03301 · 603-224-2341

Douglas R. Chamberlain · (Employee Benefits) · Wiggin & Nourie · The Parish House · Franklin & Market Streets · P.O. Box 808 · Manchester, NH 03105-0808 603-669-2211

Alan P. Cleveland · (Employee Benefits) · Sheehan, Phinney, Bass & Green · Hampshire Plaza · 1000 Elm Street · P.O. Box 3701 · Manchester, NH 03105-3701 603-668-0300

John S. Holland · Devine, Millimet & Branch · 111 Amherst Street · P.O. Box 719 · Manchester, NH 03105 · 603-669-1000

William V. A. Zorn · McLane, Graf, Raulerson & Middleton · 40 Stark Street · P.O. Box 326 · Manchester, NH 03105-0326 · 603-625-6464

TRUSTS AND ESTATES

David F. Conley · Sulloway Hollis & Soden · Nine Capitol Street · P.O. Box 1256 Concord, NH 03301 · 603-224-2341

Malcolm McLane · Orr and Reno · One Eagle Square · P.O. Box 709 · Concord, NH 03302-0709 · 603-224-2381

Joseph S. Ransmeier · Ransmeier & Spellman · One Capitol Street · P.O. Box 1378 · Concord, NH 03301 · 603-228-0477

George R. Hanna · Faulkner, Plaut, Hanna, Zimmerman & Freund · 91 Court Street · P.O. Box 527 · Keene, NH 03431-0527 · 603-352-3630

Charles A. DeGrandpre · McLane, Graf, Raulerson & Middleton · 40 Stark Street · P.O. Box 326 · Manchester, NH 03105-0326 · 603-625-6464

John S. Holland · Devine, Millimet & Branch · 111 Amherst Street · P.O. Box 719 · Manchester, NH 03105 · 603-669-1000

Richard A. Morse · Sheehan, Phinney, Bass & Green · Hampshire Plaza · 1000 Elm Street · P.O. Box 3701 · Manchester, NH 03105-3701 · 603-668-0300

Robert A. Wells · (Estate Planning, Estate Administration, Charitable Trusts, Probate Litigation) · McLane, Graf, Raulerson & Middleton · 40 Stark Street · P.O. Box 326 · Manchester, NH 03105-0326 · 603-625-6464

William V. A. Zorn · McLane, Graf, Raulerson & Middleton · 40 Stark Street · P.O. Box 326 · Manchester, NH 03105-0326 · 603-625-6464

NEW JERSEY

BANKRUPTCY LAW

Arthur J. Abramowitz* · (Business Reorganization, Creditors' Rights, Debtors' Rights, Bankruptcy Litigation) · Davis, Reberkenny & Abramowitz · 499 Cooper Landing Road · P.O. Box 5459 · Cherry Hill, NJ 08002 · 609-667-6000

Myron S. Lehman · (Debtors' Rights) · Lehman, Wasserman, Jurista & Stolz · The Common · 225 Millburn Avenue · P.O. Box 1029 · Millburn, NJ 07041 · 201-467-2700

Nathan Ravin · Ravin, Greenberg & Marks · 101 Eisenhower Parkway · Roseland, NJ 07068 · 201-226-1500

Arthur Teich · (Business Reorganization, Creditors' Rights, Debtors' Rights, Bankruptcy Litigation) · Teich, Groh and Frost · 691 State Highway 33 · Trenton, NJ 08619-4492 · 609-394-3161

BUSINESS LITIGATION

Morrill J. Cole · Cole, Schotz, Bernstein, Meisel & Forman · Court Plaza North, Fourth Floor · 25 Main Street · Hackensack, NJ 07602-0800 · 201-489-3000

Paul A. Rowe · Greenbaum, Rowe, Smith, Ravin, Davis & Bergstein · 99 Wood Avenue South · P.O. Box 5600 · Iselin, NJ 08830 · 908-549-5600

David A. Parker* · (Commercial) · Parker, McCay & Criscuolo · Three Greentree Centre, Suite 401 · Route 73 & Greentree Road · Marlton, NJ 08053 · 609-267-2850

Thomas F. Campion* · Shanley & Fisher · 131 Madison Avenue · P.O. Box 1979 Morristown, NJ 07962-1979 · 201-285-1000

Clyde A. Szuch · Pitney, Hardin, Kipp & Szuch · Park Avenue at Morris County P.O. Box 1945 · Morristown, NJ 07962-1945 · 201-966-8041

Clive S. Cummis · Sills Cummis Zuckerman Radin Tischman Epstein & Gross · One Riverfront Plaza · Newark, NJ 07102-3179 · 201-643-3232

Michael R. Griffinger* · (Antitrust, Commercial, Securities) · Crummy, Del Deo, Dolan, Griffinger & Vecchione · One Riverfront Plaza · Newark, NJ 07102-5497 201-622-2235

Eugene M. Haring* · McCarter & English · Four Gateway Center · 100 Mulberry Street · P.O. Box 652 · Newark, NJ 07101-0652 · 201-622-4444

Joseph E. Irenas · McCarter & English · Four Gateway Center · 100 Mulberry Street · P.O. Box 652 · Newark, NJ 07101-0652 · 201-622-4444

Frederick B. Lacey · LeBoeuf, Lamb, Leiby & MacRae · One Gateway Center, Suite 603 · Newark, NJ 07102 · 201-643-8000

John L. McGoldrick · McCarter & English · Four Gateway Center · 100 Mulberry Street · P.O. Box 652 · Newark, NJ 07101-0652 · 201-622-4444

William B. McGuire* · Tompkins, McGuire & Wachenfeld · Four Gateway Center · 100 Mulberry Street · Newark, NJ 07102-4070 · 201-622-3000

H. Curtis Meanor* · Podvey, Sachs, Meanor, Catenacci, Hildner & Cocoziello · The Legal Center · One Riverfront Plaza · Newark, NJ 07102-5497 · 201-623-1000

Donald A. Robinson · Robinson, Wayne & LaSala · One Gateway Center · Newark, NJ 07102-5311 · 201-621-7900

William J. Brennan III · Smith, Stratton, Wise, Heher & Brennan · 600 College Road East · Princeton, NJ 08540 · 609-924-6000

Albert G. Besser · Hannoch Weisman · Four Becker Farm Road · Roseland, NJ 07068-3788 · 201-535-5300

Adrian M. Foley, Jr. · Connell, Foley & Geiser · 85 Livingston Avenue · Roseland, NJ 07068 · 201-535-0500

Laurence B. Orloff · Orloff, Lowenbach, Stifelman & Siegel · 101 Eisenhower Parkway · Roseland, NJ 07068 · 201-622-6200

Ronald M. Sturtz* · (Banking, Finance) · Hannoch Weisman · Four Becker Farm Road · Roseland, NJ 07068-3788 · 201-535-5300

Frederic K. Becker · Wilentz, Goldman & Spitzer · 90 Woodbridge Center Drive P.O. Box 10 · Woodbridge, NJ 07095 · 201-636-8000

CORPORATE LAW

Peter D. Hutcheon · Norris, McLaughlin & Marcus · 721 Route 202-206 · Bridgewater, NJ 08807 · 201-722-0700

Philip L. Chapman · Klein & Chapman · 935 Allwood Road · P.O. Box 2048 · Clifton, NJ 07015 · 201-777-8900

Alan E. Davis · Greenbaum, Rowe, Smith, Ravin, Davis & Bergstein · 99 Wood Avenue South · Iselin, NJ 08830 · 908-549-5600

Allen Ravin · Greenbaum, Rowe, Smith, Ravin, Davis & Bergstein · 99 Wood Avenue South · P.O. Box 5600 · Iselin, NJ 08830 · 908-549-5600

John A. Aiello · (Corporate Finance, Leveraged Buyouts, Mergers & Acquisitions, Securities) · Giordano, Halleran & Ciesla · 270 State Highway · 35 · P.O. Box 190 · Middletown, NJ 07748 · 201-741-3900

Thomas J. Bitar · Dillon, Bitar & Luther · 53 Maple Avenue · P.O. Box 398 · Morristown, NJ 07960-0398 · 201-539-3100

Thomas E. Colleton, Jr. · Riker, Danzig, Scherer, Hyland & Perretti · Headquarters Plaza · One Speedwell Avenue · P.O. Box 1981 · Morristown, NJ 07962-1981 · 201-538-0800

Robert Fischer III · Riker, Danzig, Scherer, Hyland & Perretti · Headquarters Plaza · One Speedwell Avenue · P.O. Box 1981 · Morristown, NJ 07962-1981 · 201-538-0800

William D. Hardin · Pitney, Hardin, Kipp & Szuch · Park Avenue at Morris County · P.O. Box 1945 · Morristown, NJ 07962-1945 · 201-966-8041

Joseph H. Kott · (Financial Institutions, Mergers & Acquisitions, Securities, General Business) · Pitney, Hardin, Kipp & Szuch · Park Avenue at Morris County · P.O. Box 1945 · Morristown, NJ 07962-1945 · 201-966-8041

Joseph Lunin · Pitney, Hardin, Kipp & Szuch · Park Avenue at Morris County · P.O. Box 1945 · Morristown, NJ 07962-1945 · 201-966-8041

Bart J. Colli · (Corporate Finance, Mergers & Acquisitions, Securities) · McCarter & English · Four Gateway Center · 100 Mulberry Street · P.O. Box 652 · Newark, NJ 07101-0652 · 201-622-4444

Steven E. Gross · Sills Cummis Zuckerman Radin Tischman Epstein & Gross · One Riverfront Plaza · Newark, NJ 07102-3179 · 201-643-3232

Joseph E. Irenas · McCarter & English · Four Gateway Center · 100 Mulberry Street · P.O. Box 652 · Newark, NJ 07101-0652 · 201-622-4444

Stephen H. Knee · Stryker, Tams & Dill · 33 Washington Street · Newark, NJ 07102 · 201-624-9300

Peter H. Ehrenberg · Lowenstein, Sandler, Kohl, Fisher & Boylan · 65 Livingston Avenue · Roseland, NJ 07068-1791 · 201-992-8700

Ellen B. Kulka · Hannoch Weisman · Four Becker Farm Road · Roseland, NJ 07068-3788 · 201-535-5300

Ralph M. Lowenbach · Orloff, Lowenbach, Stifelman & Siegel · 101 Eisenhower Parkway · Roseland, NJ 07068 · 201-622-6200

Alan V. Lowenstein · Lowenstein, Sandler, Kohl, Fisher & Boylan · 65 Livingston Avenue · Roseland, NJ 07068-1791 · 201-992-8700

John R. MacKay 2nd · Lowenstein, Sandler, Kohl, Fisher & Boylan · 65 Livingston Avenue · Roseland, NJ 07068-1791 · 201-992-8700

Richard M. Sandler · Lowenstein, Sandler, Kohl, Fisher & Boylan · 65 Livingston Avenue · Roseland, NJ 07068-1791 · 201-992-8700

John D. Schupper · Lowenstein, Sandler, Kohl, Fisher & Boylan · 65 Livingston Avenue · Roseland, NJ 07068-1791 · 201-992-8700

Bruce D. Shoulson · (Mergers & Acquisitions) · Lowenstein, Sandler, Kohl, Fisher & Boylan · 65 Livingston Avenue · Roseland, NJ 07068-1791 · 201-992-8700

Frederic K. Becker · Wilentz, Goldman & Spitzer · 90 Woodbridge Center Drive P.O. Box 10 · Woodbridge, NJ 07095 · 201-636-8000

Stuart A. Hoberman · Wilentz, Goldman & Spitzer · 90 Woodbridge Center Drive · P.O. Box 10 · Woodbridge, NJ 07095 · 201-636-8060

CRIMINAL DEFENSE

Edwin J. Jacobs, Jr.* · Jacobs, Bruso & Barbone · 1125 Pacific Avenue · Atlantic City, NJ 08401 · 609-348-1125

Carl D. Poplar · (Federal Court, State Court, Environmental Crimes, White Collar Business Crimes) · Building One, Suite C · 1010 Kings Highway South · Cherry Hill, NJ 08034 · 609-795-5560

Brian J. Neary · Law Offices of Brian J. Neary · 190 Moore Street · Hackensack, NJ 07601 · 201-488-0544

Miles Feinstein · Law Office of Miles Feinstein · 192 Boulevard · Hasbrouch Heights, NJ 07604 · 201-393-1661

Leonard Meyerson · Miller, Hochman, Meyerson & Schwartz · 955 West Side Avenue · Jersey City, NJ 07306 · 201-333-9000

Dino D. Bliablias* · (Environmental Crimes) · Stein, Bliablias, McGuire, Pantages & Gigl · Eisenhower Plaza II, Second Floor · 354 Eisenhower Parkway · P.O. Box 460 · Livingston, NJ 07039 · 201-992-1100

Francis J. Hartman · Law Offices of Francis J. Hartman · 300 Chester Avenue · Moorestown, NJ 08057 · 609-235-0220

Thomas R. Ashley · Ashley & Charles · 24 Commerce Street · Newark, NJ 07102 201-623-0501

Raymond A. Brown · Brown, Brown & Kologi · Gateway One, Suite 900 · Newark, NJ 07102 · 201-622-1846

Raymond M. Brown · Brown, Brown & Kologi · Gateway One, Suite 900 · Newark, NJ 07102 · 201-622-1846

Michael A. Querques · Law Offices of Michael A. Querques · 433 Central Avenue · Orange, NJ 07050 · 201-673-1400

Matthew P. Boylan · Lowenstein, Sandler, Kohl, Fisher & Boylan · 65 Livingston Avenue · Roseland, NJ 07068-1791 · 201-992-8700

Michael D'Alessio, Jr. · DeCotis, Philips & Lundsten · 103 Eisenhower Parkway Roseland, NJ 07068 · 201-736-1500

Justin P. Walder · Walder, Sondak, Berkeley & Brogan · Five Becker Farm Road Roseland, NJ 07068 · 201-992-5300

Theodore V. Wells, Jr. · Lowenstein, Sandler, Kohl, Fisher & Boylan · 65 Livingston Avenue · Roseland, NJ 07068-1791 · 201-992-8700

Robert F. Novins · Novins, York, DeVincens & Pentony · 202 Main Street, CN 2032 · Toms River, NJ 08754 · 201-349-7100

Joseph A. Hayden, Jr. · Hayden, Perle & Silber · 1500 Harbor Boulevard · Weehawken, NJ 07087 · 201-795-9681

Michael Critchley · Michael Critchley & Associates · 354 Main Street · West Orange, NJ 07052 · 201-731-9831

David A. Ruhnke · Ruhnke and Barrett · 20 Northfield Avenue · West Orange, NJ 07052 · 201-325-7970

Harvey Weissbard* · Weissbard & Wiewiorka · 20 Northfield Avenue · West Orange, NJ 07052 · 201-731-9770

FAMILY LAW

Richard J. Feinberg* · Feinberg, Dee & Feinberg · 554 Broadway · Bayonne, NJ 07002 · 201-339-5500

Harold M. Savage, Sr.* · Savage & Savage · 102-103 B Troy Towers · P.O. Box 487 · Bloomfield, NJ 07003 · 201-743-0900

Gardner B. Miller* · (Child Custody, Divorce, Marital Settlement Agreements, Equitable Division) · Miller & Lawless · The Canfield Office Park · 882 Pompton Avenue · P.O. Box 490 · Cedar Grove, NJ 07009 · 201-239-1040

Thomas S. Forkin* · (Divorce, Marital Settlement Agreements, Equitable Division, Divorce Tax Issue Resolution) · Forkin, McShane & Rotz · 750 North Kings Highway · Cherry Hill, NJ 08034 · 609-779-8500

Saverio R. Principato · Forkin, McShane & Rotz · 750 North Kings Highway · Cherry Hill, NJ 08034 · 609-779-8500

Arthur Rose* · Rose & De Fuccio · 35 Essex Street · Hackensack, NJ 07601 · 201-488-7800

Lee M. Hymerling · (Child Custody, Divorce, Marital Settlement Agreements, Equitable Division).. · ..Archer & Greiner · One Centennial Square · Haddonfield, NJ 08033 · 609-795-2121

Gary N. Skoloff · Skoloff & Wolfe · 293 Eisenhower Parkway · Livingston, NJ 07039 · 201-992-0900

Anne W. Elwell · Elwell and Crane · 38 Park Street · Montclair, NJ 07042 · 201-783-3390

Sheldon M. Simon* · 555 Speedwell Avenue · Morris Plains, NJ 07950 · 201-538-2266

Barry I. Croland · Stern, Steiger, Croland, Tanenbaum & Schielke · One Mack Centre Drive · Paramus, NJ 07652 · 201-262-9400

Bernard H. Hoffman* · (Child Custody, Divorce, Marital Settlement Agreements, Equitable Division) · Hoffman, Schreiber & Gladstone · 199 Broad Street P.O. Drawer 789 · Red Bank, NJ 07701 · 201-842-7272

Edward S. Snyder* · (Child Custody, Divorce, Marital Settlement Agreements, Equitable Division) · Law Offices of Edward S. Snyder · Five Becker Farm Road Roseland, NJ 07068 · 201-994-4442

Frank A. Louis · Pogarsky, Louis & Santangelo · 213 Washington Street · P.O. Box 461 · Tom's River, NJ 08753-0461 · 201-349-0600

David M. Wildstein · Wilentz, Goldman & Spitzer · 90 Woodbridge Center Drive P.O. Box 10 · Woodbridge, NJ 07095 · 201-636-8000

FIRST AMENDMENT LAW

Robert T. Lehman · Archer & Greiner · One Centennial Square · Haddonfield, NJ 08033 · 609-795-2121

John J. Gibbons · Crummy, Del Deo, Dolan, Griffinger & Vecchione · One Riverfront Plaza · Newark, NJ 07102-5497 · 201-622-2235

Edward F. Lamb · Robinson, St. John & Wayne · Gateway I · Newark, NJ 07102 201-622-3700

Donald A. Robinson · Robinson, St. John & Wayne · Gateway I · Newark, NJ 07102 · 201-622-3700

Richard A. Ragsdale · Strauss & Hall · 32 Nassau Street · Princeton, NJ 08542 · 609-924-2100

Thomas J. Cafferty · McGimpsey & Cafferty · 285 Davidson Avenue · Somerset, NJ 08873 · 908-560-1900

Warren W. Faulk · Brown & Connery · 360 Haddon Avenue · Westmont, NJ 08108 · 609-854-8900

HEALTH CARE LAW

Michael J. Kallison · Norris, McLaughlin & Marcus · 721 Route 202-206 · Bridgewater, NJ 08807 · 908-722-0700

Gary J. Lesneski · Archer & Greiner · One Centennial Square · Haddonfield, NJ 08033 · 609-795-2121

Leonard M. Fishman · (Nursing Homes) · Cohen, Shapiro, Polisher, Shiekman and Cohen · Princeton Pike Corporate Center · 1009 Lenox Drive, Building 4 · Lawrenceville, NJ 08648 · 609-895-1600

Murray J. Klein · Cohen, Shapiro, Polisher, Shiekman and Cohen · Princeton Pike Corporate Center · 1009 Lenox Drive, Building 4 · Lawrenceville, NJ 08648 609-895-1600

Jonathan D. Weiner · (Nursing Homes) · Fox, Rothschild, O'Brien & Frankel · 104 Carnegie Center, Suite 201 · Princeton, NJ 08543 · 609-520-2110

Burton L. Eichler · Brach, Eichler, Rosenberg, Silver, Bernstein, Hammer & Gladstone · 101 Eisenhower Parkway · Roseland, NJ 07068 · 201-228-5700

Joseph Gorrell · Brach, Eichler, Rosenberg, Silver, Bernstein, Hammer & Gladstone · 101 Eisenhower Parkway · Roseland, NJ 07068 · 201-228-5700

Barry H. Ostrowsky · Brach, Eichler, Rosenberg, Silver, Bernstein, Hammer & Gladstone · 101 Eisenhower Parkway · Roseland, NJ 07068 · 201-228-5700

Bruce D. Shoulson · Lowenstein, Sandler, Kohl, Fisher & Boylan · 65 Livingston Avenue · Roseland, NJ 07068-1791 · 201-992-8700

John R. Heher · Smith, Stratton, Wise, Heher & Brennan · One State Street Square · 50 West State Street · Trenton, NJ 08608 · 609-924-6000

IMMIGRATION LAW

William E. McAlvanah · Law Office of William R. Hilberth · 790 Bloomfield Avenue · Clifton, NJ 07012 · 201-773-4748

Melvin R. Solomon · Parsekian & Solomon · 140 Main Street · Hackensack, NJ 07601 · 201-487-2080

Vincent J. Agresti · 56-58 Ferry Street · Newark, NJ 07105 · 201-589-4707

Milton S. Kramer · Kramer & Kramer · 11 Commerce Street · Newark, NJ 07102 201-642-5035

Thomas E. Moseley · De Maria, Ellis, Hunt &Salsberg · 744 Broad Street, Suite 1400 · Newark, NJ 07102 · 201-623-1699

Edwin R. Rubin · Steel, Rubin & Rudnick · 744 Broad Street, Suite 1300 · Newark, NJ 07102 · 201-623-4444

INTELLECTUAL PROPERTY LAW

Sidney David · Lerner, David, Littenberg, Krumholz & Mentlik · 600 South Avenue West · Westfield, NJ 07090 · 908-654-5000

Joseph S. Littenberg · Lerner, David, Littenberg, Krumholz & Mentlik · 600 South Avenue West · Westfield, NJ 07090 · 908-654-5000

William L. Mentlick · Lerner, David, Littenberg, Krumholz & Mentlik · 600 South Avenue West · Westfield, NJ 07090 · 908-654-5000

LABOR AND EMPLOYMENT LAW

David Seliger · (Labor) · Law Offices of David Seliger · Commerce Bank Building, Suite 301 · 1701 Route 70 East · Cherry Hill, NJ 08003 · 609-751-6201

Edward A. Cohen · (Labor) · Schneider, Cohen, Solomon, Leder & Montalbano 1150 Raritan Road · Cranford, NJ 07016 · 201-272-1010

Bruce D. Leder · (Labor) · Schneider, Cohen, Solomon, Leder & Montalbano · 1150 Raritan Road · Cranford, NJ 07016 · 201-272-1010

Paul A. Montalbano · (Labor) · Schneider, Cohen, Solomon, Leder & Montalbano · 1150 Raritan Road · Cranford, NJ 07016 · 201-272-1010

Zachary Schneider · (Labor) · Schneider, Cohen, Solomon, Leder & Montalbano 1150 Raritan Road · Cranford, NJ 07016 · 201-272-1010

David S. Solomon · (Labor) · Schneider, Cohen, Solomon, Leder & Montalbano 1150 Raritan Road · Cranford, NJ 07016 · 201-272-1010

James Katz · Tomar, Simonoff, Adourian & O'Brien · 41 South Haddon Avenue Haddonfield, NJ 08033 · 609-429-1100

Robert F. O'Brien* · (Labor) · Tomar, Simonoff, Adourian & O'Brien · 41 South Haddon Avenue · Haddonfield, NJ 08033 · 609-429-1100

Howard S. Simonoff* · (Labor, Individuals) · Tomar, Simonoff, Adourian & O'Brien · 41 South Haddon Avenue · Haddonfield, NJ 08033 · 609-429-1100

Steven W. Suflas · (Management) · Archer & Greiner · One Centennial Square · Haddonfield, NJ 08033 · 609-795-2121

Vincent J. Apruzzese · (Management) · Apruzzese, McDermott, Mastro & Murphy · Somerset Hills Corporate Center · 25 Independence Boulevard · P.O. Box 112 · Liberty Corner, NJ 07938 · 901-580-1776

Francis A. Mastro* · (Management) · Apruzzese, McDermott, Mastro & Murphy Somerset Hills Corporate Center · 25 Independence Boulevard · P.O. Box 112 · Liberty Corner, NJ 07938 · 901-580-1776

Angelo J. Genova · (Management) · Genova, Burns & Schott · Eisenhower Plaza II 354 Eisenhower Parkway · Livingston, NJ 07039 · 201-533-0777

Patrick M. Stanton, · Shanley & Fisher · 131 Madison Avenue · P.O. Box 1979 Morristown, NJ 07962-1979 · 201-285-1000

Ronald H. De Maria · (Management) · De Maria, Ellis, Hunt &Salsberg · 744 Broad Street, Suite 1400 · Newark, NJ 07102 · 201-623-1699

Francis X. Dee* · (Management) · Carpenter, Bennett & Morrissey · Three Gateway Center · 100 Mulberry Street · Newark, NJ 07102-4082 · 201-622-7711

H. Reed Ellis · (Management) · De Maria, Ellis, Hunt & Salsberg · 744 Broad Street, Suite 1400 · Newark, NJ 07102 · 201-623-1699

Craig H. Livingston · (Labor, Individuals) · Ball, Livingston & Tykulsker · 108 Washington Street · Newark, NJ 07102 · 201-622-4545

Thomas L. Morrissey · (Management) · Carpenter, Bennett & Morrissey · Three Gateway Center · 100 Mulberry Street · Newark, NJ 07102-4082 · 201-622-7711

Denise Reinhardt · (Individuals) · Reinhardt & Schachter · 744 Broad Street, · 3101 · Newark, NJ 07102 · 201-623-1600

Donald A. Romano · (Management) · Carpenter, Bennett & Morrissey · Three Gateway Center · 100 Mulberry Street · Newark, NJ 07102-4082 · 201-622-7711

Edward F. Ryan · (Management) · Carpenter, Bennett & Morrissey · Three Gateway Center · 100 Mulberry Street · Newark, NJ 07102-4082 · 201-622-7711

Paul Schachter · (Individuals) · Reinhardt & Schachter · 744 Broad Street, · 3101 Newark, NJ 07102 · 201-623-1600

James R. Zazzali · (Labor) · Zazzali, Zazzali, Fagella & Nowak · One Riverfront Plaza · Newark, NJ 07102-5410 · 201-623-1822

Theodore M. Eisenberg · Grotta, Glassman & Hoffman · 75 Livingston Avenue Roseland, NJ 07068 · 201-992-4800

Jerold E. Glassman · (Management) · Grotta, Glassman & Hoffman · 75 Livingston Avenue · Roseland, NJ 07068 · 201-992-4800

Marvin M. Goldstein · (Management) · Grotta, Glassman & Hoffman · 75 Livingston Avenue · Roseland, NJ 07068 · 201-992-4800

Harold L. Hoffman* · (Management) · Grotta, Glassman & Hoffman · 75 Livingston Avenue · Roseland, NJ 07068 · 201-992-4800

Desmond Massey · (Management) · Grotta, Glassman & Hoffman · 75 Livingston Avenue · Roseland, NJ 07068 · 201-992-4800

Stephen A. Ploscowe · (Management) · Grotta, Glassman & Hoffman · 75 Livingston Avenue · Roseland, NJ 07068 · 201-992-4800

Steven B. Hunter · (Labor) · Klausner & Hunter · 63 East High Street · P.O. Box 1012 · Summerville, NJ 08876 · 201-685-1552

Albert G. Kroll · (Labor) · Law Offices of Albert G. Kroll · 25 Pompton Avenue, Suite 309 · Verona, NJ 07044 · 201-857-2100

Howard A. Goldberger* · (Labor) · Goldberger & Finn · 81 Northfield Avenue West Orange, NJ 07052 · 201-731-0500

Nancy Erika Smith · (Individuals) · Smith, Mullen & Kiernan · 200 Executive Drive, Suite 155 · West Orange, NJ 07052 · 201-736-7033

NATURAL RESOURCES AND ENVIRONMENTAL LAW

Lewis Goldshore · Goldshore, Wolf & Lewis · 2683 Main Street · Lawrenceville, NJ 08648 · 609-896-1660

Theodore A. Schwartz* · Schwartz Tobia & Stanziale · 22 Crestmont Road · Montclair, NJ 07042 · 201-746-6000

William H. Hyatt, Jr. · Pitney, Hardin, Kipp & Szuch · Park Avenue at Morris County · P.O. Box 1945 · Morristown, NJ 07962-1945 · 201-966-8041

John A. McKinney, Jr. · McCarter & English · Four Gateway Center · 100 Mulberry Street · P.O. Box 652 · Newark, NJ 07101-0652 · 201-622-4444

A. Patrick Nucciarone* · (Water, Hazardous Waste, Environmental Litigation) · Dechert Price & Rhoads · 214 Carnegie Center, Suite 202 · Princeton, NJ 08540-6237 · 609-520-3200

Michael L. Rodburg · Lowenstein, Sandler, Kohl, Fisher & Boylan · 65 Livingston Avenue · Roseland, NJ 07068-1791 · 201-992-8700

Steven J. Picco · Picco Mack Herbert Kennedy Jaffe Perrella & Yoskin · 50 West State Street, Suite 1000 · P.O. Box 1388 · Trenton, NJ 08607-1388 · 609-393-2400

David B. Farer · Farer, Siegal & Fersko · 600 South Avenue West · P.O. Box 580 Westfield, NJ 07091 · 201-789-8550

PERSONAL INJURY LITIGATION

Gerald B. O'Connor* · (Plaintiffs) · O'Connor & Rhatican · 383 Main Street · Chatham, NJ 07928-2105 · 201-635-2210

Joseph H. Kenney* · (Commercial) · Kenney & Kearney · Woodland Falls Corporate Park · 220 Lake Drive East, Suite 210 · P.O. Box 5034 · Cherry Hill, NJ 08034-0421 · 609-779-7000

David A. Parker* · (Defendants) · Parker, McCay & Criscuolo · Three Greentree Centre, Suite 401 · Route 73 & Greentree Road · Marlton, NJ 08053 · 609-267-2850

Myron J. Bromberg · Porzio, Bromberg & Newman · 163 Madison Avenue · Morristown, NJ 07960-1997 · 201-538-4006

Thomas F. Campion* · (Defendants) · Shanley & Fisher · 131 Madison Avenue P.O. Box 1979 · Morristown, NJ 07962-1979 · 201-285-1000

Raymond M. Tierney, Jr. · (Defendants) · Shanley & Fisher · 131 Madison Avenue · P.O. Box 1979 · Morristown, NJ 07962-1979 · 201-285-1000

Stephen S. Weinstein · 20 Park Place · Morristown, NJ 07960 · 201-267-5200

John M. Blume* · (Plaintiffs, Medical Malpractice, Products Liability, Professional Malpractice) · Blume, Vasquez, Goldfaden, Berkowitz, Oliveras & Donnelly · Five Commerce Street, Fourth Floor · Newark, NJ 07102-3989 · 201-622-1881

John E. Keale · (Defendants) · Carpenter, Bennett & Morrissey · Three Gateway Center · 100 Mulberry Street · Newark, NJ 07102-4082 · 201-622-7711

John L. McGoldrick · (Defendants) · McCarter & English · Four Gateway Center 100 Mulberry Street · P.O. Box 652 · Newark, NJ 07101-0652 · 201-622-4444

William B. McGuire* · (Defendants) · Tompkins, McGuire & Wachenfeld · Four Gateway Center · 400 Mulberry Street · Newark, NJ 07102-4070 · 201-622-3000

H. Curtis Meanor* · (Defendants) · Podvey, Sachs, Meanor, Catenacci, Hildner & Cocoziello · The Legal Center · One Riverfront Plaza · Newark, NJ 07102-5497 201-623-1000

Carl Greenberg* · Budd Larner Gross Rosenbaum Greenberg & Sade · 150 John F. Kennedy Parkway, CN 1000 · Short Hills, NJ 07078-0999 · 201-379-4800

David R. Gross · Budd Larner Gross Rosenbaum Greenberg & Sade · 150 John F. Kennedy Parkway, CN 1000 · Short Hills, NJ 07078-0999 · 201-379-4800

Burchard V. Martin · (Defendants) · Martin, Gunn & Martin · Sentry Office Plaza · 216 Haddon Avenue, Suite 420 · P.O. Box 358 · Westmont, NJ 08108 · 609-858-0900

Morris Brown · (Plaintiffs) · Wilentz, Goldman & Spitzer · 90 Woodbridge Center Drive · P.O. Box 10 · Woodbridge, NJ 07095 · 201-636-8000

PUBLIC UTILITY LAW

James H. Laskey · Norris, McLaughlin & Marcus · 721 Route 202-206 · Bridgewater, NJ 08807 · 908-722-0700

Vincent J. Sharkey, Jr. · (Cogeneration, Telecommunications, Water) · Riker, Danzig, Scherer, Hyland & Perretti · Headquarters Plaza · One Speedwell Avenue · P.O. Box 1981 · Morristown, NJ 07962-1981 · 201-538-0800

Stephen B. Genzer · Stryker, Tams & Dill · 33 Washington Street · Newark, NJ 07102 · 201-624-9300

William F. Hyland · Riker, Danzig, Scherer, Hyland & Perretti · Headquarters Plaza · One Speedwell Avenue · P.O. Box 1981 · Newark, NJ 07962-1981 · 201-538-0800

Richard B. McGlynn · Stryker, Tams & Dill · 33 Washington Street · Newark, NJ 07102 · 201-624-9300

Sidney M. Schreiber · Riker, Danzig, Scherer, Hyland & Perretti · Headquarters Plaza · One Speedwell Avenue · P.O. Box 1981 · Newark, NJ 07962-1981 · 201-538-0800

REAL ESTATE LAW

Edward M. Schotz · Cole, Schotz, Bernstein, Meisel & Forman · Court Plaza North, Fourth Floor · 25 Main Street · Hackensack, NJ 07601-7015 · 201-489-3000

Robert S. Greenbaum · Greenbaum, Rowe, Smith, Ravin, Davis & Bergstein · 99 Wood Avenue South · P.O. Box 5600 · Iselin, NJ 08830 · 908-549-5600

Wendell A. Smith · (Zoning, Land Use, Condominium & Planned Real Estate, Community Association) · Greenbaum, Rowe, Smith, Ravin, Davis & Bergstein · 99 Wood Avenue South · P.O. Box 5600 · Iselin, NJ 08830 · 908-549-5600

Peter L. Berkley · Riker, Danzig, Scherer, Hyland & Perretti · Headquarters Plaza · One Speedwell Avenue · P.O. Box 1981 · Morristown, NJ 07962-1981 · 201-538-0800

Gerald W. Hull, Jr. · Shanley & Fisher · 131 Madison Avenue · P.O. Box 1979 Morristown, NJ 07962-1979 · 201-285-1000

Lawrence B. Mink · Clapp & Eisenberg · 80 Park Plaza · Newark, NJ 07102 · 201-642-3900

George C. Witte, Jr. · McCarter & English · Four Gateway Center · 100 Mulberry Street · P.O. Box 652 · Newark, NJ 07101-0652 · 201-622-4444

Martin E. Dollinger · Dollinger & Dollinger · Mack Centre One · 365 West Passaic Street · Rochelle Park, NJ 07662 · 201-368-0640

Edward S. Radzely · Kimmelman, Wolff & Samson · 280 Corporate Center · Five Becker Farm Road · Roseland, NJ 07068 · 201-740-0500

Joseph LeVow Steinberg · Lowenstein, Sandler, Kohl, Fisher & Boylan · 65 Livingston Avenue · Roseland, NJ 07068-1791 · 201-992-8700

H. Harding Brown · Epstein, Epstein, Brown & Bosek · 505 Morris Avenue · P.O. Box 705 · Springfield, NJ 07081 · 201-467-4444

TAX AND EMPLOYEE BENEFITS LAW

Emmanuel Liebman · (Corporate & Partnership Transactions, Tax Disputes) · 409 East Marlton Pike · Cherry Hill, NJ 08034-2472 · 609-795-8600

Steven G. Siegel · Siegel, Witman & Stadtmauer · 26 Columbia Turnpike · Florham Park, NJ 07932 · 201-822-0220

Leonard J. Witman · (Employee Benefits) · Siegel, Witman & Stadtmauer · 26 Columbia Turnpike · Florham Park, NJ 07068 · 201-822-0220

Peter C. Aslanides · McCarter & English · Four Gateway Center · 100 Mulberry Street · P.O. Box 652 · Newark, NJ 07101-0652 · 201-622-4444

Laurence Reich · Carpenter, Bennett, & Morrissey · Three Gateway Center · 100 Mulberry Street · Newark, NJ 07102-4082 · 201-622-7711

Paul I. Rosenberg · (Corporate & Partnership Transactions) · Fox and Fox · 570 Broad Street · Newark, NJ 07102 · 201-622-3624

Arnold Fisher · Lowenstein, Sandler, Kohl, Fisher & Boylan · 65 Livingston Avenue · Roseland, NJ 07068-1791 · 201-992-8700

Benedict M. Kohl · Lowenstein, Sandler, Kohl, Fisher & Boylan · 65 Livingston Avenue · Roseland, NJ 07068-1791 · 201-992-8700

Stephen P. Lichtstein · (Employee Benefits) · Hannoch Weisman · Four Becker Farm Road · Roseland, NJ 07068-3788 · 201-535-5300

Milton H. Stern · Hannoch Weisman · Four Becker Farm Road · Roseland, NJ 07068-3788 · 201-535-5300

Joel A. Wolff · Wolff & Samson · 280 Corporate Center · Five Becker Farm Road Roseland, NJ 07068 · 201-740-0500

Robert B. Haines · Herold and Haines · 25 Independence Boulevard · Warren, NJ 07059-6747 · 201-647-1022

William T. Knox IV · (Employee Benefits) · Herold and Haines · 25 Independence Boulevard · Warren, NJ 07059-6747 · 201-647-1022

TRUSTS AND ESTATES

Stephen G. Siegel · Siegel, Witman & Stadtmauer · 26 Columbia Turnpike · Florham, NJ 07932 · 201-822-0220

Peter E. Driscoll · Archer & Greiner · One Centennial Square · Haddonfield, NJ 08033 · 609-795-2121

Sidney G. Dillon · Dillon, Bitar & Luther · 53 Maple Avenue · P.O. Box 398 · Morristown, NJ 07960-0398 · 201-539-3100

Richard Kahn · Dillon, Bitar & Luther · 53 Maple Avenue · P.O. Box 398 · Morristown, NJ 07960-0398 · 201-539-3100

George A. Aguilar · Stryker, Tams & Dill · 33 Washington Street · Newark, NJ 07102 · 201-624-9300

Rodney N. Houghton · McCarter & English · Four Gateway Center · 100 Mulberry Street · P.O. Box 652 · Newark, NJ 07101-0652 · 201-622-4444

Howard G. Wachenfeld · Tompkins, McGuire & Wachenfeld · Four Gateway Center · 100 Mulberry Street · Newark, NJ 07102-4070 · 201-622-3000

Bernard S. Berkowitz · Hannoch Weisman · Four Becker Farm Road · Roseland, NJ 07068-3788 · 201-535-5300

Arnold Fisher · Lowenstein, Sandler, Kohl, Fisher & Boylan · 65 Livingston Avenue · Roseland, NJ 07068-1791 · 201-992-8700

Joseph E. Imbriaco · Young, Rose, Millspaugh, Imbriaco & Burke · 20 Waterview Street · Roseland, NJ 07054 · 201-263-7777

Benedict M. Kohl · Lowenstein, Sandler, Kohl, Fisher & Boylan · 65 Livingston Avenue · Roseland, NJ 07068-1791 · 201-992-8700

Gordon A. Millspaugh, Jr. · Young, Rose, Millspaugh, Imbriaco & Burke · 20 Waterview Street · Roseland, NJ 07054 · 201-263-7777

Ashley Steinhart · (Estate Planning, Estate Administration, Federal & State Tax Implications, Fiduciary Counselling & Litigation) · Hannoch Weisman · Four Becker Farm Road · Roseland, NJ 07068-3788 · 201-535-5300

Richard H. Herold · Herold and Haines · 25 Independence Boulevard · Warren, NJ 07059-6747 · 201-647-1022

Richard F. Lert · Wilentz, Goldman & Spitzer · 90 Woodbridge Center Drive · P.O. Box 10 · Woodbridge, NJ 07095 · 201-636-8000

NEW MEXICO

BANKRUPTCY LAW

Paul M. Fish · (Business Reorganization, Creditors' Rights, Bankruptcy Litigation) · Modrall, Sperling, Roehl, Harris & Sisk · Sunwest Bank Building, Suite 1000 · 500 Fourth Street, NW · P.O. Box 2168 · Albuquerque, NM 87103 · 505-848-1800

Robert A. Johnson* · (Bankruptcy Litigation) · Kemp, Smith, Duncan & Hammond · 500 Marquette, NW, Suite 1200 · P.O. Box 1276 · Albuquerque, NM 87103-1276 · 505-247-2315

James S. Starzynski · Francis & Starzynski · 320 Gold Avenue, SW, Suite 800 · Albuquerque, NM 87102 · 505-242-2880

BUSINESS LITIGATION

Peter J. Adang* · (Antitrust, Commercial) · Modrall, Sperling, Roehl, Harris & Sisk · Sunwest Building, Suite 1000 · 500 Fourth Street, NW · P.O. Box 2168 · Albuquerque, NM 87103 · 505-848-1800

John R. Cooney* · Modrall, Sperling, Roehl, Harris & Sisk · Sunwest Bank Building · 500 Fourth Street, NW · P.O. Box 2168 · Albuquerque, NM 87103 · 505-848-1800

William S. Dixon · Rodey, Dickason, Sloan, Akin & Robb · Albuquerque Plaza, Suite 2200 · 201 Third Street, NW · P.O. Box 1888 · Albuquerque, NM 87103 · 505-765-5900

Bruce Hall* · (Appellate, Commercial) · Rodey, Dickason, Sloan, Akin & Robb Albuquerque Plaza, Suite 2200 · 201 Third Street, NW · P.O. Box 1888 · Albuquerque, NM 87103 · 505-765-5900

C. LeRoy Hansen · Civerolo, Hansen and Wolf · 500 Marquette, NW, Suite 1400 P.O. Drawer 887 · Albuquerque, NM 87103-0887 · 505-842-8255

Robert A. Johnson* · (Banking, Commercial, Finance) · Kemp, Smith, Duncan & Hammond · 500 Marquette, NW, Suite 1200 · P.O. Box 1276 · Albuquerque, NM 87103-1276 · 505-247-2315

Marshall G. Martin* · Hinkle, Cox, Eaton, Coffield,& Hensley · 500 Marquette Avenue, Suite 800 · Albuquerque, NM 87102 · 505-768-1500

Russell Moore · Keleher & McLeod · Public Service Building · 414 Silver Avenue, SW · P.O. Drawer AA · Albuquerque, NM 87103 · 505-842-6262

Norman S. Thayer, Jr.* · (Antitrust, Banking, Commercial) · Sutin, Thayer & Browne · 6565 Americas Parkway, NE, 10th Floor · P.O. Box 32500 · Albuquerque, NM 87190 · 505-883-2500

Rex D. Throckmorton* · (Antitrust, Banking, Commercial, Energy) · Rodey, Dickason, Sloan, Akin & Robb · Albuquerque Plaza, Suite 2200 · 201 Third Street, NW · P.O. Box 1888 · Albuquerque, NM 87103 · 505-765-5900

Harold L. Hensley, Jr. · Hinkle, Cox, Eaton, Coffield & Hensley · United Bank Plaza, Suite 700 · P.O. Box 10 · Roswell, NM 88201-0010 · 505-622-6510

Stuart D. Shanor · Hinkle, Cox, Eaton, Coffield & Hensley · United Bank Plaza, Suite 700 · P.O. Box 10 · Roswell, NM 88201-0010 · 505-622-6510

J. E. Gallegos · The Gallegos Law Firm · 141 East Palace · Santa Fe, NM 87501 505-983-6686

CORPORATE LAW

Mark K. Adams · Rodey, Dickason, Sloan, Akin & Robb · Albuquerque Plaza, Suite 2200 · 201 Third Street, NW · P.O. Box 1888 · Albuquerque, NM 87103 · 505-765-5900

Richard K. Barlow · (Corporate Finance, Leveraged Buyouts, Mergers & Acquisitions, Securities) · Chappell & Barlow · 2155 Louisiana Boulevard, NE, Suite 3500 · Albuquerque, NM 87110 · 505-889-3636

Graham Browne · Sutin, Thayer & Browne · 6565 Americas Parkway, NE, 10th Floor · P.O. Box 32500 · Albuquerque, NM 87190 · 505-883-2500

Dale Wallace Ek · (Banking) · Modrall, Sperling, Roehl, Harris & Sisk · Sunwest Bank Building, Suite 1000 · 500 Fourth Street, NW · P.O. Box 2168 · Albuquerque, NM 87103 · 505-848-1800

Dennis J. Falk · Modrall, Sperling, Roehl, Harris & Sisk · Sunwest Bank Building 500 Fourth Street, NW · P.O. Box 2168 · Albuquerque, NM 87103 · 505-848-1800

Robert G. Heyman · (Corporate Finance, Financial Institutions, Securities) · Sutin, Thayer & Browne · 6565 Americas Parkway, NE, 10th Floor · P.O. Box 32500 · Albuquerque, NM 87190 · 505-883-2500

William B. Keleher · Keleher & McLeod · Public Service Building · 414 Silver Avenue, SW · P.O. Drawer AA · Albuquerque, NM 87103 · 505-842-6262

Henry A. Kelly · The Poole Law Firm · 201 Third Street, NW, Suite 1600 · P.O. Box 1769 · Albuquerque, NM 87103-1769 · 505-842-8155

Dennis M. McCary · (Corporate Finance, Financial Institutions) · Dines, McCary & Wilson · City Centre Building, Suite 233W · 6400 Uptown Boulevard, NE · Albuquerque, NM 87110 · 505-889-4050

Charles L. Moore · Keleher & McLeod · Public Service Building · 414 Silver Avenue, SW · P.O. Drawer AA · Albuquerque, NM 87103 · 505-842-6262

Roberta C. Ramo · The Poole Law Firm · 201 Third Street, NW, Suite 1600 · P.O. Box 1769 · Albuquerque, NM 87103-1769 · 505-842-8155

William C. Schaab* · Rodey, Dickason, Sloan, Akin & Robb · Albuquerque Plaza, Suite 2200 · 201 Third Street, NW · P.O. Box 1888 · Albuquerque, NM 87103 · 505-765-5900

Daniel A. Sisk · (Banking) · Modrall, Sperling, Roehl, Harris & Sisk · Sunwest Bank Building · 500 Fourth Street, NW · P.O. Box 2168 · Albuquerque, NM 87103 · 505-848-1800

Robert M. St. John · Rodey, Dickason, Sloan, Akin & Robb · Albuquerque Plaza, Suite 2200 · 201 Third Street, NW · P.O. Box 1888 · Albuquerque, NM 87103 · 505-765-5900

Charles I. Wellborn · Modrall, Sperling, Roehl, Harris & Sisk · Sunwest Bank Building, Suite 1000 · 500 Fourth Street, NW · P.O. Box 2168 · Albuquerque, NM 87103 · 505-848-1800

CRIMINAL DEFENSE

James L. Brandenburg* · (Federal Court, State Court, Bank Fraud & White Collar Crime) · Brandenburg & Brandenburg · 715 Tijeras, NW . · Albuquerque, NM 87102 · 505-842-5924

Charles W. Daniels* · (Violent Crimes, Non-Violent Crimes, Federal Court, State Court) · Freedman, Boyd, Daniels, Peifer, Hollander & Guttmann · 20 First Plaza, Suite 212 · Albuquerque, NM 87102 · 505-842-9960

Nancy Hollander* · Freedman, Boyd, Daniels, Peifer, Hollander & Guttmann · 20 First Plaza, Suite 212 · Albuquerque, NM 87102 · 505-842-9960

Ronald Edwin Koch · 503 Slate Avenue, NW · Albuquerque, NM 87102 · 505-247-2972

Randi McGinn* · 420 Central, SW, Suite 200 · Albuquerque, NM 87102 · 505-843-6161

Ray Twohig* · (White Collar Crime) · 420 Central, SW · Albuquerque, NM 87102 505-843-6223

Michael W. Lilley · Lilley & Macias · 118 South Downtown Mall, Suite A · Las Cruces, NM 88001 · 505-524-7809

Michael L. Stout · Michael L. Stout & Associates · 215 West Sixth Street · Roswell, NM 88201 · 505-624-1471

Mark H. Donatelli* · Rothstein, Bennett, Daly, Donatelli & Hughes · 500 Montezuma, Suite 101 · P.O. Box 8180 · Santa Fe, NM 87504-8180 · 505-988-8004

Robert R. Rothstein* · (Violent Crimes, Non-Violent Crimes, White Collar Crimes, Drug Offenses) · Rothstein, Bennett, Daly, Donatelli & Hughes · 500 Montezuma, Suite 101 · P.O. Box 8180 · Santa Fe, NM 87504-8180 · 505-988-8004

FAMILY LAW

Jan B. Gilman · Atkinson & Kelsey · 6501 Americas Parkway, Suite 901 · P.O. Box 3070 · Albuquerque, NM 87190 · 505-883-3070

David H. Kelsey · Atkinson & Kelsey · 6501 Americas Parkway, Suite 901 · P.O. Box 3070 · Albuquerque, NM 87190 · 505-883-3070

Sandra Morgan Little · Atkinson & Kelsey · 6501 Americas Parkway, Suite 901 P.O. Box 3070 · Albuquerque, NM 87190 · 505-883-3070

Joseph J. Mullins · Rodey, Dickason, Sloan, Akin & Robb · Albuquerque Plaza, Suite 2200 · 201 Third Street, NW · P.O. Box 1888 · Albuquerque, NM 87103 · 505-765-5900

Betty Read · 801 Tijeras Avenue, NW · P.O. Box 27575 · Albuquerque, NM 87102 · 505-247-9933

Barbara L. Shapiro* · (Child Custody, Divorce, Marital Settlement Agreements, Prenuptial Agreements) · The Poole Law Firm · 201 Third Street, NW, Suite 1600 · P.O. Box 1769 · Albuquerque, NM 87103-1769 · 505-842-8155

Michael T. Murphy · Wein, Drenner, Richards, Paulowsky, Sandenaw & Ramirez P.O. Drawer O · Las Cruces, NM 88004-1719 · 505-524-8624

David L. Walther* · David L. Walther Associates · 119 East Marcy Street, Suite 207 · Santa Fe, NM 87501 · 505-984-0097

FIRST AMENDMENT LAW

John W. Boyd* · Freedman, Boyd, Daniels, Peifer, Hollander & Guttmann · 20 First Plaza, Suite 212 · Albuquerque, NM 87102 · 505-842-9960

William S. Dixon · Rodey, Dickason, Sloan, Akin & Robb · Albuquerque Plaza, Suite 2200 · 201 Third Street, NW · P.O. Box 1888 · Albuquerque, NM 87103 · 505-765-5900

Erik D. Lanphere · Hinckle Law Firn · 500 Marquette, NW, Suite 800 · Albuquerque, NM 87102 · 505-768-1500

Victor R. Marshall · Victor R. Marshall & Associates · 20 First Plaza, Suite 405 · Albuquerque, NM 87102 · 505-764-8180

HEALTH CARE LAW

George F. Koinis · Modrall, Sperling, Roehl, Harris & Sisk · Sunwest Bank Building, Suite 1000 · 5000 Fourth Street, NW · P.O.Box 2168 · Albuquerque, NM 87103 · 505-848-1800

James M. Parker · Modrall, Sperling, Roehl, Harris & Sisk · Sunwest Bank Building, Suite 1000 · 500 Fourth Street, NW · P.O. Box 2168 · Albuquerque, NM 87103 · 505-848-1800

Edward Ricco · Rodey, Dickason, Sloan, Akin & Robb · Albuquerque Plaza, Suite 2200 · 201 Third Street, NW · P.O. Box 1888 · Albuquerque, NM 87103 · 505-765-5900

Gene C. Walton · Rodey, Dickason, Sloan, Akin & Robb · Albuquerque Plaza, Suite 2200 · 201 Third Street, NW · P.O. Box 1888 · Albuquerque, NM 87103 · 505-765-5900

Robert J. Werner · Sutin, Thayer & Browne · 300 First Interstate Plaza · Santa Fe, NM 87504 · 505-883-2500

IMMIGRATION LAW

John W. Lawit · 900 Gold Avenue, SW · Albuquerque, NM 87102 · 505-243-0733

Sarah Reinhardt · Law Office of Sarah Reinhardt · 110 Quincy, NE · Albuquerque, NM 87108 · 505-266-8739

INTELLECTUAL PROPERTY LAW

Robert W. Harris · The Poole Law Firm · 201 Third Street, NW, Suite 1600 · P.O. Box 1769 · Albuquerque, NM 87103-1769 · 505-842-8155

DeWitt M. Morgan · Rodey, Dickason, Sloan, Akin & Robb · Albuquerque Plaza, Suite 2200 · 201 Third Street, NW · P.O. Box 1888 · Albuquerque, NM 87103 · 505-765-5900

Deborah A. Peacock · Chappell & Barlow · 2155 Louisiana Boulevard, NE, Suite 3500 · Albuquerque, NM 87110 · 505-889-3636

Saul Cohen · Sutin, Thayer & Browne · 300 First Interstate Plaza · P.O. Box 2187
Santa Fe, NM 87504 · 505-988-5521

LABOR AND EMPLOYMENT LAW

John W. Boyd* · (Individuals) · Freedman, Boyd, Daniels, Peifer, Hollander &
Guttmann · 20 First Plaza, Suite 212 · Albuquerque, NM 87102 · 505-842-9960

Duane C. Gilkey · (Management) · Rodey, Dickason, Sloan, Akin & Robb ·
Albuquerque Plaza, Suite 2200 · 201 Third Street, NW · P.O. Box 1888 · Albuquerque, NM 87103 · 505-765-5900

Roland B. Kool* · (Labor) · Kool, Kool, Bloomfield & Hollis · 1516 San Pedro
Boulevard, NE · Albuquerque, NM 87110 · 505-266-7841

Nicholas J. Noeding · (Management) · Sherman & Howard · 500 Marquette
Building · 500 Marquette, NW · P.O. Box 2043 · Albuquerque, NM 87103-2043
505-764-8100

K. Lee Peifer · (Labor, Individuals) · Freedman, Boyd, Daniels, Peifer, Hollander
& Guttmann · 20 First Plaza, Suite 212 · Albuquerque, NM 87102 · 505-842-9960

Eric Sirotkin · (Individuals) · Advocate for Equal Rights Law Office · 824 Gold
Avenue, SW · P.O. Box 450 · Albuquerque, NM 87103-0450 · 505-843-6581

Robert P. Tinnin, Jr.* · (Management) · Sherman & Howard · 500 Marquette
Building · 500 Marquette, NW · P.O. Box 2043 · Albuquerque, NM 87103-2043
505-764-8100

NATURAL RESOURCES AND ENVIRONMENTAL LAW

Mark K. Adams · (Oil & Gas, Coal, Mining, Water) · Rodey, Dickason, Sloan,
Akin & Robb · Albuquerque Plaza, Suite 2200 · 201 Third Street, NW · P.O. Box
1888 · Albuquerque, NM 87103 · 505-765-5900

Clifford K. Atkinson · (Water) · Modrall, Sperling, Roehl, Harris & Sisk · Sunwest Bank Building, Suite 1000 · 500 Fourth Street, NW · P.O. Box 2168 ·
Albuquerque, NM 87103 · 505-848-1800

Larry P. Ausherman · (Mining) · Modrall, Sperling, Roehl, Harris & Sisk ·
Sunwest Bank Building, Suite 1000 · 500 Fourth Street, NW · P.O. Box 2168 ·
Albuquerque, NM 87103 · 505-848-1800

Lynn H. Slade · (Indian Affairs, Oil & Gas) · Modrall, Sperling, Roehl, Harris &
Sisk · Sunwest Bank Building, Suite 1000 · 500 Fourth Street, NW · P.O. Box
2168 · Albuquerque, NM 87103 · 505-848-1800

Lester K. Taylor · (Oil & Gas,Water) · Nordhaus, Haltom, Taylor, Taradish & Frye · 500 Marquette Avenue, NW, Suite 1050 · Albuquerque, NM 87102 · 505-243-4275

A. J. Losee · (Oil & Gas) · Losee & Carson · 300 Yates Petroleum Building · P.O. Drawer 239 · Artesia, NM 88211-0239 · 505-746-3508

Grove T. Burnett · (Plaintiffs) · Route 1 · P.O. Box 9A · Glorieta, NM 87535 · 505-757-8408

Sim B. Christy IV* · (Oil & Gas) · 920 United Bank Plaza · 400 North Pennsylvania Avenue · P.O. Box 569 · Roswell, NM 88202-0569 · 505-625-2021

Louis C. Cox · (Oil & Gas) · Hinkle, Cox, Eaton, Coffield & Hensley · United Bank Plaza, Suite 700 · P.O. Box 10 · Roswell, NM 88201-0010 · 505-622-6510

Don M. Fedric · (Oil & Gas) · Hunker Fedric · Hinkle Building, Suite 210 · P.O. Box 1837 · Roswell, NM 88201 · 505-622-2700

Richard N. Carpenter · (Mining) · Carpenter, Crout & Olmstead · 141 East Palace Avenue · P.O. Box 669 · Santa Fe, NM 87504-0669 · 505-982-4611

William F. Carr* · (Oil & Gas) · Campbell & Black · 110 North Guadalupe · P.O. Box 2208 · Santa Fe, NM 87504-2208 · 505-988-4421

John B. Draper · (Water) · Montgomery & Andrews · 325 Paseo de Peralta · P.O. Box 2307 · Santa Fe, NM 87504-2307 · 505-982-3873

Richard A. Simms · (Water) · Simms & Stein · 121 Sandoval Street, Third Floor P.O. Box 280 · Santa Fe, NM 87504 · 505-983-3880

PERSONAL INJURY LITIGATION

Peter J. Adang · (Defendants) · Modrall, Sperling, Roehl, Harris & Sisk · Sunwest Building, Suite 1000 · 500 Fourth Street, NW · P.O. Box 2168 · Albuquerque, NM 87103 · 505-848-1800

William H. Carpenter · (Plaintiffs) · Carpenter & Goldberg · 1600 University Boulevard, Suite B · Albuquerque, NM 87102 · 505-243-1336

Stephen Durkovich · (Plaintiffs) · 412 Eleventh Street, NW · Albuquerque, NM 87102 · 505-247-2367

Bruce Hall* · (Defendants, Medical Malpractice, Products Liability, Appellate) · Rodey, Dickason, Sloan, Akin & Robb · Albuquerque Plaza, Suite 2200 · 201 Third Street, NW · P.O. Box 1888 · Albuquerque, NM 87103 · 505-765-5900

Kenneth L. Harrigan · (Defendants) · Modrall, Sperling, Roehl, Harris & Sisk · Sunwest Bank Building · 500 Fourth Street, NW · P.O. Box 2168 · Albuquerque, NM 87103 · 505-848-1800

W. Robert Lasater, Jr.* · (Defendants) · Rodey, Dickason, Sloan, Akin & Robb · Albuquerque Plaza, Suite 2200 · 201 Third Street, NW · P.O. Box 1888 · Albuquerque, NM 87103 · 505-765-5900

Robert G. McCorkle* · (Defendants, Products Liability, Airplane Collision) · Rodey, Dickason, Sloan, Akin & Robb · Albuquerque Plaza, Suite 2200 · 201 Third Street, NW · P.O. Box 1888 · Albuquerque, NM 87103 · 505-765-5900

Ranne B. Miller · (Defendants) · Miller, Stratvert, Torgerson & Schlenker · Cavan Building, Suite 1100 · 500 Marquette, NW · P.O. Box 25687 · Albuquerque, NM 87125 · 505-842-1950

Peter G. Prina · Rodey, Dickason, Sloan, Akin & Robb · Albuquerque Plaza, Suite 2200 · 201 Third Street, NW · P.O. Box 1888 · Albuquerque, NM 87103 · 505-765-5900

James C. Ritchie* · (Defendants, Products Liability) · Rodey, Dickason, Sloan, Akin & Robb · Albuquerque Plaza, Suite 2200 · 201 Third Street, NW · P.O. Box 1888 · Albuquerque, NM 87103 · 505-765-5900

William E. Snead · (Plaintiffs) · Law Offices of William E. Snead · 201 Twelfth Street, NW · P.O. Box 2226 · Albuquerque, NM 87102 · 505-842-8177

William K. Stratvert · Miller, Stratvert, Torgerson & Schlenker · Cavan Building, Suite 1100 · 500 Marquette, NW · P.O. Box 25687 · Albuquerque, NM 87125 · 505-842-1950

Alan C. Torgerson · Miller, Stratvert, Torgerson & Schlenker · Cavan Building, Suite 1100 · 500 Marquette, NW · P.O. Box 25687 · Albuquerque, NM 87125 · 505-842-1950

Wayne C. Wolf* · (Defendants) · Civerolo, Hansen and Wolf · 500 Marquette, NW, Suite 1400 · P.O. Drawer 887 · Albuquerque, NM 87103-0887 · 505-842-8255

Richard L. Gerding · Pansey, Roseborough, Gerding & Strother · 621 West Arrington Street · P.O. Box 1020 · Farmington, NM 87499 · 505-325-1801

Lowell Stout · (Plaintiffs) · Stout & Stout · 218 West Lea · P.O. Box 716 · Hobbs, NM 88240 · 505-393-1555

Harold L. Hensley, Jr. · Hinkle, Cox, Eaton, Coffield & Hensley · United Bank Plaza, Suite 700 · P.O. Box 10 · Roswell, NM 88201-0010 · 505-622-6510

Russell D. Mann* · (Defendants, Products Liability, Professional Malpractice, Airplane Collision) · Atwood, Malone, Mann & Turner · Sunwest Centre · P.O. Drawer 700 · Roswell, NM 88201-0700 · 505-622-6221

Bob F. Turner* · (Defendants) · Atwood, Malone, Mann & Turner · Sunwest Centre · P.O. Drawer 700 · Roswell, NM 88202-0700 · 505-622-6221

Matias A. Zamora · (Plaintiffs) · 444 Galisteo Street, Suite E · P.O. Box 1117 · Santa Fe, NM 87504-1117 · 505-982-4449

PUBLIC UTILITY LAW

Richard B. Cole · Keleher & McLeod · Public Service Building · 414 Silver Avenue, SW · P.O. Drawer AA · Albuquerque, NM 87103 · 505-842-6262

William B. Keleher · Keleher & McLeod · Public Service Building · 414 Silver Avenue, SW · P.O. Drawer AA · Albuquerque, NM 87103 · 505-842-6262

Richard N. Carpenter · Carpenter, Crout & Olmstead · 141 East Palace Avenue P.O. Box 669 · Santa Fe, NM 87504 · 505-982-4611

David S. Cohen · Cohen & Throne · 1660 Old Pecos Trail, Suite H · Santa Fe, NM 87501 · 505-983-9277

Paul J. Kelly, Jr. · Hinkle, Cox, Eaton, Coffield & Hensley · 218 Montezuma · P.O. Box 2068 · Santa Fe, NM 87504-2068 · 505-982-4554

REAL ESTATE LAW

Bill Chappell, Jr. · Chappell & Barlow · 2155 Louisiana Boulevard, NE, Suite 3500 · Albuquerque, NM 87110 · 505-889-3636

Dale Wallace Ek · Modrall, Sperling, Roehl, Harris & Sisk · Sunwest Bank Building, Suite 1000 · 500 Fourth Street, NW · P.O. Box 2168 · Albuquerque, NM 87103 · 505-848-1800

Patrick W. Hurley · Keleher & McLeod · Public Service Building · 414 Silver Avenue, SW · P.O. Drawer AA · Albuquerque, NM 87103 · 505-842-6262

Donald L. Jones · Rodey, Dickason, Sloan, Akin & Robb · Albuquerque Plaza, Suite 2200 · 201 Third Street, NW · P.O. Box 1888 · Albuquerque, NM 87103 · 505-765-5900

William B. Keleher · Keleher & McLeod · Public Service Building · 414 Silver Avenue, SW · P.O. Drawer AA · Albuquerque, NM 87103 · 505-842-6262

Dennis M. McCary · (Commercial Transactions) · Dines, McCary & Wilson · City Center Building, Suite 233W · 6400 Uptown Boulevard, NE · Albuquerque, NM 87110 · 505-889-4050

John A. Myers · (Zoning, Land Use, Eminent Domain, Commercial Transactions) · Myers & Oliver · 6400 Uptown Boulevard, NE, Suite 300 West · Albuquerque, NM 87110 · 505-889-4040

Charles P. Price III · Sutin, Thayer & Browne · 6565 Americas Parkway, NE, 10th Floor · P.O. Box 32500 · Albuquerque, NM 87190 · 505-883-2500

John P. Salazar* · (Zoning, Land Use, Eminent Domain, Commercial Transactions) · Rodey, Dickason, Sloan, Akin & Robb · Albuquerque Plaza, Suite 2200 · 201 Third Street, NW · P.O. Box 1888 · Albuquerque, NM 87103 · 505-765-5900

Robert M. St. John · Rodey, Dickason, Sloan, Akin & Robb · Albuquerque Plaza, Suite 2200 · 201 Third Street, NW · P.O. Box 1888 · Albuquerque, NM 87103 · 505-765-5900

Gene C. Walton · (Land Use, Commercial Transactions) · Rodey, Dickason, Sloan, Akin & Robb · Albuquerque Plaza, Suite 2200 · 201 Third Street, NW · P.O. Box 1888 · Albuquerque, NM 87103 · 505-765-5900

John P. Burton* · (Commercial Transactions, Industrial Transactions, Lending) Rodey, Dickason, Sloan, Akin & Robb · Marcy Plaza, Suite 101 · 123 East Marcy Street · P.O. Box 1357 · Santa Fe, NM 87504 · 505-984-0100

TAX AND EMPLOYEE BENEFITS LAW

Richard K. Barlow · (Corporate & Partnership Transactions, State Tax, Employee Benefits, Tax Disputes) · Chappell & Barlow · 2155 Louisiana Boulevard, NE, Suite 3500 · Albuquerque, NM 87110 · 505-889-3636

John E. Heer III · (Employee Benefits) · Modrall, Sperling, Roehl, Harris & Sisk Sunwest Bank Building · 500 Fourth Street, NW · P.O. Box 2168 · Albuquerque, NM 87103 · 505-848-1800

John D. Laflin · Laflin, Lieuwen, Tucker & Swaim · Building 5, Suite 600 · 2400 Louisiana Boulevard, NE · Albuquerque, NM 87110 · 505-883-0679

John Lieuwen · Corporate & Partnership Transactions, Employee Benefits) · Laflin, Lieuwen, Tucker & Swaim · Building 5, Suite 600 · 2400 Louisiana Boulevard, NE · Albuquerque, NM 87110 · 505-883-0679

James M. Parker · (Corporate & Partnership Transactions, Employee Benefits) · Modrall, Sperling, Roehl, Harris & Sisk · Sunwest Bank Building, Suite 1000 · 500 Fourth Street, NW · P.O. Box 2168 · Albuquerque, NM 87103 · 505-848-1800

Charles L. Saunders, Jr. · Kemp, Smith, Duncan & Hammond · 500 Marquette, NW, Suite 1200 · P.O. Box 1276 · Albuquerque, NM 87103-1276 · 505-247-2315

Thomas Smidt II · (Corporate & Partnership Transactions, State Tax, Tax Disputes) · Kemp, Smith, Duncan & Hammond · 500 Marquette, NW, Suite 1200 · P.O. Box 1276 · Albuquerque, NM 87103-1276 · 505-247-2315

Patricia Tucker* · (Tax Disputes) · Laflin, Lieuwen, Tucker & Swaim · Building 5, Suite 600 · 2400 Louisiana Boulevard, NE · Albuquerque, NM 87110 · 505-883-0679

Curtis W. Schwartz · (Corporate & Partnership Transactions, State Tax, Tax Disputes) · Modrall, Sperling, Roehl, Harris & Sisk · 119 East Marcy, Suite 200 Santa Fe, NM 87504 · 505-988-8039

TRUSTS AND ESTATES

Suzanne M. Barker · The Poole Law Firm · 201 Third Street, NW, Suite 1600 P.O. Box 1769 · Albuquerque, NM 87103-1769 · 505-842-8155

Richard K. Barlow · (Estate Planning, Estate Administration, Charitable Trusts) Chappell & Barlow · 2155 Louisiana Boulevard, NE, Suite 3500 · Albuquerque, NM 87110 · 505-889-3636

John D. Laflin · Laflin, Lieuwen, Tucker & Swaim · Building 5, Suite 600 · 2400 Louisiana Boulevard, NE · Albuquerque, NM 87110 · 505-883-0679

John Lieuwen · (Estate Planning) · Laflin, Lieuwen, Tucker & Swaim · Building 5, Suite 600 · 2400 Louisiana Boulevard, NE · Albuquerque, NM 87110 · 505-883-0679

Kendall O. Schlenker* · Miller, Stratvert, Torgerson & Schlenker · 500 Marquette, NW, Suite 1100 · P.O. Box 25687 · Albuquerque, NM 87125 · 505-842-1950

Thomas Smidt II · (Estate Planning, Estate Administration) · Kemp, Smith, Duncan & Hammond · 500 Marquette, NW, Suite 1200 · P.O. Box 1276 · Albuquerque, NM 87103-1276 · 505-247-2315

Beth R. Davenport · Modrall, Sperling, Roehl, Harris & Sisk · 119 East Marcy, Suite 200 · P.O. Box 9318 · Santa Fe, NM 87504-9318 · 505-983-2020

Robert P. Worcester · (Estate Planning, Estate Administration) · Montgomery & Andrews · 325 Paseo de Peralta · P.O. Box 2307 · Santa Fe, NM 87504-2307 · 505-982-3873

NEW YORK

BANKRUPTCY LAW

Donald G. Hatt · (Business Reorganization, Creditors' Rights, Debtors' Rights, Bankruptcy Litigation) · 11 North Pearl Street · Albany, NY 12207 · 518-463-1189

William M. McCarthy · (Business Reorganization, Creditors' Rights, Debtors' Rights, Bankruptcy Litigation) · McCarthy and Evanick · 60 South Swan Street · Albany, NY 12210 · 518-434-6141

Carl L. Bucki · Cohen, Swados, Wright, Hanifin, Bradford & Brett · 70 Niagra Street · Buffalo, NY 14202 · 716-856-4600

Harold P. Bulan · Goldstein, Navagh, Bulan & Chiari · Rand Building, Suite 1440 Buffalo, NY 14203 · 716-854-1332

William H. Gardner · Hodgson, Russ, Andrews, Woods & Goodyear · 1800 One M&T Plaza · Buffalo, NY 14203-2391 · 716-856-4000

Garry M. Graber · Hodgson, Russ, Andrews, Woods & Goodyear · 1800 One M&T Plaza · Buffalo, NY 14203-2391 · 716-856-4000

William E. Lawson · Aaron, Dautch, Sternberg & Lawson · 500 Convention Tower · Buffalo, NY 14202 · 716-854-3015

Donald P. Sheldon · 300 Pearl Street, Suite 200 · Buffalo, NY 14202 · 716-842-6009

Robert M. Spaulding · Phillips, Lytle, Hitchcock, Blaine & Huber · 3400 Marine Midland Center · Buffalo, NY 14203 · 716-847-8400

Donald S. Bernstein · Davis Polk & Wardwell · One Chase Manhattan Plaza · New York, NY 10005 · 212-530-4000

Richard F. Broude · Mayer, Brown & Platt · 787 Seventh Avenue · New York, NY 10019 · 212-554-3000

Michael L. Cook* · (Business Reorganization, Creditors' Rights, Debtors' Rights, Bankruptcy Litigation) · Skadden, Arps, Slate, Meagher & Flom · 919 Third Avenue · New York, NY 10022-3897 · 212-735-3000

Michael J. Crames · Kaye, Scholer, Firan, Hays & Handler · 425 Park Avenue · New York, NY 10022 · 212-836-8415

Denis F. Cronin · Wachtell, Lipton, Rosen & Katz · 299 Park Avenue · New York, NY 10171-0149 · 212-371-9200

Ronald DeKoven · Shearman & Sterling · 599 Lexington Avenue · New York, NY 10022 · 212-848-4000

Chaim J. Fortgang · Wachtell, Lipton, Rosen & Katz · 299 Park Avenue · New York, NY 10171-0149 · 212-371-9200

Marcia Landweber Goldstein · Weil, Gotshal & Manges · 767 Fifth Avenue · New York, NY 10153 · 212-310-8000

Henry L. Goodman · Zalkin, Rodin & Goodman · 750 Third Avenue · New York, NY 10017 · 212-682-6900

George A. Hahn · Hahn & Hessen · Empire State Building, Suite 3700 · 350 Fifth Avenue · New York, NY 10118 · 212-736-1000

Marvin E. Jacob · Weil, Gotshal & Manges · 767 Fifth Avenue · New York, NY 10153 · 212-310-8000

John J. Jerome · Milbank, Tweed, Hadley & McCloy · One Chase Manhattan Plaza · New York, NY 10005-1413 · 212-530-5000

Alan W. Kornberg · Paul, Weiss, Rifkind, Wharton & Garrison · 1285 Avenue of the Americas · New York, NY 10019-6064 · 212-373-3000

Lillian E. Kraemer · (Business Reorganization, Creditors' Rights) · Simpson Thacher & Bartlett · 425 Lexington Avenue · New York, NY 10017-3909 · 212-455-2000

Robert H. MacKinnon · Shearman & Sterling · 599 Lexington Avenue · New York, NY 10022 · 212-848-4000

Alan B. Miller · (Business Reorganization, Creditors' Rights, Debtors' Rights, Bankruptcy Litigation) · Weil, Gotshal & Manges · 767 Fifth Avenue · New York, NY 10153 · 212-310-8000

Harvey R. Miller · Weil, Gotshal & Manges · 767 Fifth Avenue · New York, NY 10153 · 212-310-8000

Herbert P. Minkel, Jr. · (Business Reorganization) · Fried, Frank, Harris, Shriver & Jacobson · One New York Plaza · New York, NY 10004-1980 · 212-820-8000

Harold S. Novikoff · Wachtell, Lipton, Rosen & Katz · 299 Park Avenue · New York, NY 10171-0149 · 212-371-9200

Barry G. Radick · Milbank, Tweed, Hadley & McCloy · One Chase Manhattan Plaza · New York, NY 10005-1413 · 212-530-5000

Leonard M. Rosen · Wachtell, Lipton, Rosen & Katz · 299 Park Avenue · New York, NY 10171-0149 · 212-371-9200

Robert J. Rosenberg · (Business Reorganization, Creditors' Rights) · Latham & Watkins · 885 Third Avenue, Suite 1000 · New York, NY 10022 · 212-906-1200

Brad E. Scheler · Fried, Frank, Harris, Shriver & Jacobson · One New York Plaza New York, NY 10004-1980 · 212-820-8000

Myron Trepper · Willkie Farr & Gallagher · One Citicorp Center · 153 East 53rd Street · New York, NY 10022-4669 · 212-935-8000

Joel B. Zweibel · O'Melveny & Myers · 153 East 53rd Street, 53rd Floor · New York, NY 10022-4611 · 212-326-2000

Warren H. Heilbronner · (Business Reorganization, Creditors' Rights, Debtors' Rights) · Mousaw, Vigdor, Reeves, Heilbronner & Kroll · 600 First Federal Plaza Rochester, NY 14614 · 716-325-2500

C. Bruce Lawrence · (Business Reorganization, Creditors' Rights, Debtors' Rights) · Suter Doyle Kesselring Lawrence & Werner · 700 First Federal Plaza · Rochester, NY 14614 · 716-325-6446

John C. Ninfo II · Underberg and Kessler · 1800 Lincoln First Tower · Rochester, NY 14604 · 716-258-2800

Louis A. Ryen · (Business Reorganization, Creditors' Rights, Debtors' Rights, Bankruptcy Litigation) · Lacy, Katzen, Ryen & Mittleman · The Granite Building 130 East Main Street · Rochester, NY 14604-1686 · 716-454-5650

Larry D. Scheafer · Harter, Secrest & Emery · 700 Midtown Tower · Rochester, NY 14604-2070 · 716-232-6500

William S. Thomas, Sr. · Nixon, Hargrave, Devans & Doyle · Clinton Square · P.O. Box 1051 · Rochester, NY 14603 · 716-546-8000

Richard P. Vullo · Weinstein, Vullo & Miller · Two State Street, Suite 950 · Rochester, NY 14614 · 716-325-3175

John R. Weider · Harter, Secrest & Emery · 700 Midtown Tower · Rochester, NY 14604-2070 · 716-232-6500

Michael J. Balanoff · Grass, Balanoff & Whitelaw · 247-259 West Fayette Street Syracuse, NY 13202 · 315-472-7832

Harold P. Goldberg* · (Business Reorganization, Creditors' Rights, Debtors' Rights, Bankruptcy Litigation) · 1408 West Genesee Street · Syracuse, NY 13204 315-422-6191

Peter L. Hubbard · Menter, Rudin & Trivelpiece · 500 South Salina Street, Suite 500 · Syracuse, NY 13202-3300 · 315-474-7541

Edward M. Zachary · Menter, Rudin & Trivelpiece · 500 South Salina Street, Suite 500 · Syracuse, NY 13202-3300 · 315-474-7541

BUSINESS LITIGATION

John T. DeGraff, Jr.* · DeGraff, Foy, Conway, Holt-Harris & Mealey · 90 State Street · Albany, NY 12207 · 518-462-5301

Carroll J. Mealey · DeGraff, Foy, Conway, Holt-Harris & Mealey · 90 State Street · Albany, NY 12207 · 518-462-5301

N. Theodore Sommer · Hinman, Howard & Kattell · 700 Security Mutual Building · 80 Exchange Street · Binghamton, NY 13901 · 607-723-5341

Robert B. Conklin · Hodgson, Russ, Andrews, Woods & Goodyear · 1800 One M&T Plaza · Buffalo, NY 14203-2391 · 716-856-4000

Alexander C. Cordes* · Phillips, Lytle, Hitchcock, Blaine & Huber · 3400 Marine Midland Center · Buffalo, NY 14203 · 716-847-8400

David K. Floyd · Phillips, Lytle, Hitchcock, Blaine & Huber · 3400 Marine Midland Center · Buffalo, NY 14203 · 716-847-8400

Victor T. Fuzak* · (Antitrust, Appellate, Banking, Public Utility) · Hodgson, Russ, Andrews, Woods & Goodyear · 1800 One M&T Plaza · Buffalo, NY 14203-2391 · 716-856-4000

Richard F. Griffin* · (Commercial, Securities) · Phillips, Lytle, Hitchcock, Blaine & Huber · 3400 Marine Midland Center · Buffalo, NY 14202 · 716-847-7082

Richard E. Moot · Damon & Morey · 1000 Cathedral Place · 298 Main Street · Buffalo, NY 14202 · 716-858-3875

H. Kenneth Schroeder, Jr. · Hodgson, Russ, Andrews, Woods & Goodyear · 1800 One M&T Plaza · Buffalo, NY 14203-2391 · 716-856-4000

John H. Stenger · Jaeckle, Fleischman & Mugel · 800 Norstar Building · 12 Fountain Plaza · Buffalo, NY 14202 · 716-856-0600

Floyd Abrams · Cahill Gordon & Reindel · 80 Pine Street · New York, NY 10005 212-701-3000

Kenneth C. Anderson · (Antitrust, Trade Regulation) · Lord Day & Lord, Barrett Smith · 1675 Broadway · New York, NY 10019 · 212-969-6000

Michael F. Armstrong · Lord Day & Lord, Barrett Smith · 1675 Broadway · New York, NY 10019 · 212-969-6000

Jack C. Auspitz · Morrison & Foerster · 1290 Avenue of the Americas · New York, NY 10019 · 212-468-8000

Stephen M. Axinn · Skadden, Arps, Slate, Meagher & Flom · 919 Third Avenue New York, NY 10022-3897 · 212-735-3000

Thomas D. Barr · Cravath, Swaine & Moore · Worldwide Plaza · 825 Eighth Avenue, 38th Floor · New York, NY 10019 · 212-474-1000

Dennis J. Block · Weil, Gotshal & Manges · 767 Fifth Avenue · New York, NY 10153 · 212-310-8000

David Boies · Cravath, Swaine & Moore · Worldwide Plaza · 825 Eighth Avenue, 38th Floor · New York, NY 10019 · 212-474-1000

Michael E. Bradley · Brown & Wood · One World Trade Center · New York, NY 10048-0557 · 212-839-5300

Edward Brodsky · Spengler Carlson Gubar Brodsky & Frischling · 520 Madison Avenue · New York, NY 10022 · 212-935-5000

Melvyn L. Cantor* · Simpson Thacher & Bartlett · 425 Lexington Avenue · New York, NY 10017-3909 · 212-455-2000

Michael A. Cardozo · Proskauer Rose Goetz & Mendelsohn · 1585 Broadway · New York, NY 10036 · 212-969-3000

Marc P. Cherno · Fried, Frank, Harris, Shriver & Jacobson · One New York Plaza New York, NY 10004-1980 · 212-820-8000

Arthur H. Christy* · Christy & Viener · 620 Fifth Avenue · New York, NY 10020 212-632-5507

Merrell E. Clark, Jr. · Winthrop, Stimson, Putnam & Roberts · One Battery Park Plaza · New York, NY 10004-1490 · 212-858-1719

Robert Stephan Cohen* · Morrison Cohen Singer & Weinstein · 750 Lexington Avenue, Eighth Floor · New York, NY 10022 · 212-735-8600

Donald J. Cohn · 425 Park Avenue · New York, NY 10022 · 212-355-1444

Michael A. Cooper · Sullivan & Cromwell · 125 Broad Street, 28th Floor · New York, NY 10004 · 212-558-4000

Edward N. Costikyan · Paul, Weiss, Rifkind, Wharton & Garrison · 1285 Avenue of the Americas · New York, NY 10019-6064 · 212-373-3000

Louis A. Craco · Willkie Farr & Gallagher · One Citicorp Center · 153 East 53rd Street · New York, NY 10022-4669 · 212-935-8000

Thomas F. Curnin · Cahill Gordon & Reindel · 80 Pine Street · New York, NY 10005 · 212-701-3000

Paul J. Curran · Kaye, Scholer, Fierman, Hays & Handler · 425 Park Avenue · New York, NY 10022 · 212-836-8000

Jeremy G. Epstein · Shearman & Sterling · 599 Lexington Avenue · New York, NY 10022 · 212-848-4000

Raymond L. Falls, Jr. · Cahill Gordon & Reindel · 80 Pine Street · New York, NY 10005 · 212-701-3000

Peter M. Fishbein · Kaye, Scholer, Fierman, Hays & Handler · 425 Park Avenue New York, NY 10022 · 212-836-8000

Robert B. Fiske, Jr. · Davis Polk & Wardwell · One Chase Manhattan Plaza · New York, NY 10005 · 212-530-4000

Joseph M. Fitzpatrick · Fitzpatrick, Cella, Harper & Scinto · 277 Park Avenue · New York, NY 10172 · 212-758-2400

Peter E. Fleming, Jr. · Curtis, Mallet-Prevost, Colt & Mosle · 101 Park Avenue New York, NY 10178 · 212-696-6000

David L. Foster* · (Antitrust, Insurance) · Willkie Farr & Gallagher · One Citicorp Center · 153 East 53rd Street · New York, NY 10022-4669 · 212-935-8000

William P. Frank · Skadden, Arps, Slate, Meagher & Flom · 919 Third Avenue New York, NY 10022-3897 · 212-735-2500

Marvin E. Frankel · Kramer, Levin, Nessen, Kamin & Frankel · 919 Third Avenue · New York, NY 10022 · 212-715-9100

Victor S. Friedman · Fried, Frank, Harris, Shriver & Jacobson · One New York Plaza · New York, NY 10004-1980 · 212-820-8000

Barry H. Garfinkel · Skadden, Arps, Slate, Meagher & Flom · 919 Third Avenue New York, NY 10022-3897 · 212-735-2500

Milton S. Gould · Shea & Gould · 1251 Avenue of the Americas · New York, NY 10020-1193 · 212-827-3000

Jay Greenfield · Paul, Weiss, Rifkind, Wharton & Garrison · 1285 Avenue of the Americas · New York, NY 10019-6064 · 212-373-3223

Michael D. Hess · White & Case · 1155 Avenue of the Americas · New York, NY 10036 · 212-819-8200

Alan J. Hruska · Cravath, Swaine & Moore · Worldwide Plaza · 825 Eighth Avenue, 38th Floor · New York, NY 10019 · 212-474-1000

John Roscoe Hupper · Cravath, Swaine & Moore · Worldwide Plaza · 825 Eighth Avenue, 38th Floor · New York, NY 10019 · 212-474-1000

Jacob Imberman · Proskauer Rose Goetz & Mendelsohn · 1585 Broadway · New York, NY 10036 · 212-969-3000

William E. Jackson · Milbank, Tweed, Hadley & McCloy · One Chase Manhattan Plaza · New York, NY 10005-1413 · 212-530-5538

Gregory P. Joseph · Fried, Frank, Harris, Shriver & Jacobson · One New York Plaza · New York, NY 10004-1980 · 212-820-8000

Lewis A. Kaplan · Paul, Weiss, Rifkind, Wharton & Garrison · 1285 Avenue of the Americas · New York, NY 10019-6064 · 212-373-3000

Lewis A. Kaplan · (Antitrust, Appellate, International, Securities) · Paul, Weiss, Rifkind, Wharton & Garrison · 1285 Avenue of the Americas · New York, NY 10019-6064 · 212-373-3000

Edmund H. Kerr · (Commercial, Securities) · Cleary, Gottlieb, Steen & Hamilton One Liberty Plaza · New York, NY 10006 · 212-225-2000

Allen Kezsbom · Fried, Frank, Harris, Shriver & Jacobson · One New York Plaza New York, NY 10004-1980 · 212-820-8000

Henry L. King · Davis Polk & Wardwell · One Chase Manhattan Plaza · New York, NY 10005 · 212-530-4000

T. Barry Kingham · Curtis, Mallet-Prevost, Colt & Mosle · 101 Park Avenue · New York, NY 10178 · 212-696-6000

David Klingsberg* · (Antitrust, Commercial, Securities) · Kaye, Scholer, Fierman, Hays & Handler · 425 Park Avenue · New York, NY 10022 · 212-836-8000

John G. Koeltl · Debevoise & Plimpton · 875 Third Avenue · New York, NY 10022 · 212-909-6000

Daniel F. Kolb · (Accounting, Antitrust, Securities) · Davis Polk & Wardwell · One Chase Manhattan Plaza · New York, NY 10005 · 212-530-4000

Daniel J. Kornstein · Kornstein Veisz & Wexler · 757 Third Avenue · New York, NY 10017 · 212-418-8600

Frederick B. Lacey · LeBoeuf, Lamb, Leiby & MacRae · 520 Madison Avenue New York, NY 10022 · 212-715-8000

Martin N. Leaf* · (International) · Morrison Cohen Singer & Weinstein · 750 Lexington Avenue, Eighth Floor · New York, NY 10022 · 212-735-8729

Daniel P. Levitt · Reid & Priest · 40 West 57th Street · New York, NY 10019 · 212-603-2000

Arthur L. Liman · Paul, Weiss, Rifkind, Wharton & Garrison · 1285 Avenue of the Americas · New York, NY 10019-6064 · 212-373-3000

Sanford M. Litvack* · Dewey Ballantine · 1301 Avenue of the Americas · New York, NY 10019-6092 · 212-259-8000

Martin London* · Paul, Weiss, Rifkind, Wharton & Garrison · 1285 Avenue of the Americas · New York, NY 10019-6064 · 212-373-3000

Robert MacCrate · Sullivan & Cromwell · 125 Broad Street, 29th Floor · New York, NY 10004 · 212-558-4000

William J. Manning · Simpson Thacher & Bartlett · 425 Lexington Avenue · New York, NY 10017-3909 · 212-455-2000

Denis McInerney* · (Antitrust, Appellate, International, Securities) · Cahill Gordon & Reindel · 80 Pine Street · New York, NY 10005 · 212-701-3000

Ira M. Millstein · Weil, Gotshal & Manges · 767 Fifth Avenue · New York, NY 10153 · 212-310-8000

Edwin B. Mishkin · Cleary, Gottlieb, Steen & Hamilton · One Liberty Plaza · New York, NY 10006 · 212-225-2120

Michael W. Mitchell · (Commercial, Securities) · Skadden, Arps, Slate, Meagher & Flom · 919 Third Avenue · New York, NY 10022-3897 · 212-735-3000

Maurice N. Nessen · Kramer, Levin, Nessen, Kamin & Frankel · 919 Third Avenue · New York, NY 10022 · 212-715-9100

Bernard W. Nussbaum · Wachtell, Lipton, Rosen & Katz · 299 Park Avenue · New York, NY 10171-0149 · 212-371-9200

Sheldon Oliensis* · Kaye, Scholer, Fierman, Hays & Handler · 425 Park Avenue New York, NY 10022 · 212-836-8000

Barrington D. Parker, Jr. · Morrison & Foerster · 1290 Avenue of the Americas New York, NY 10019 · 212-468-8000

Daniel A. Pollack · Pollack & Kaminsky · 114 West 42nd Street, 19th Floor · New York, NY 10036 · 212-575-4700

Philip C. Potter, Jr. · Davis Polk & Wardwell · One Chase Manhattan Plaza · New York, NY 10005 · 212-530-4000

Sheldon Raab · Fried, Frank, Harris, Shriver & Jacobson · One New York Plaza New York, NY 10004-1980 · 212-820-8000

Jed S. Rakoff · (RICO, Securities) · Fried, Frank, Harris, Shriver & Jacobson · One New York Plaza · New York, NY 10004-1980 · 212-820-8000

James W. Rayhill · Carter, Ledyard & Milburn · Two Wall Street, 15th Floor · New York, NY 10005 · 212-732-3200

Roy L. Reardon · Simpson Thacher & Bartlett · 425 Lexington Avenue · New York, NY 10017-3909 · 212-455-2000

Edward J. Reilly · Milbank, Tweed, Hadley & McCloy · One Chase Manhattan Plaza · New York, NY 10005-1413 · 212-530-5000

George D. Reycraft* · Cadwalader, Wickersham & Taft · 100 Maiden Lane · New York, NY 10038 · 212-504-6000

Robert S. Rifkind* · Cravath, Swaine & Moore · Worldwide Plaza · 825 Eighth Avenue, 38th Floor · New York, NY 10019 · 212-474-1450

Stanley D. Robinson · Kaye, Scholer, Fierman, Hays & Handler · 425 Park Avenue · New York, NY 10022 · 212-836-8000

Asa Rountree · Debevoise & Plimpton · 875 Third Avenue · New York, NY 10022 · 212-909-6000

Allen G. Schwartz* · (Commercial, Securities) · Proskauer Rose Goetz & Mendelsohn · 1585 Broadway · New York, NY 10036 · 212-969-3000

Marvin Schwartz* · Sullivan & Cromwell · 125 Broad Street, 28th Floor · New York, NY 10004 · 212-558-4000

Jerome G. Shapiro · Hughes Hubbard & Reed · One Battery Park Plaza · New York, NY 10004 · 212-837-6020

Leon Silverman · Fried, Frank, Harris, Shriver & Jacobson · One New York Plaza New York, NY 10004-1980 · 212-820-8000

Robert J. Sisk · Hughes Hubbard & Reed · One Battery Park Plaza · New York, NY 10004 · 212-837-6020

Eugene P. Souther · Seward & Kissel · One Battery Park Plaza · New York, NY 10004 · 212-574-1200

Gordon B. Spivack* · (Antitrust) · Coudert Brothers · 200 Park Avenue · New York, NY 10166 · 212-880-4400

Alvin M. Stein · Parker Chapin Flattau & Klimpl · 1211 Avenue of the Americas New York, NY 10036 · 212-704-6000

Stephen R. Steinberg* · (Class Actions, Security Actions, Antitrust Actions, Commercial Litigation) · Milberg Weiss Bershad Specthrie & Lerach · One Pennsylvania Plaza, 49th Floor · New York, NY 10119 · 212-594-5300

Jay Topkis · Paul, Weiss, Rifkind, Wharton & Garrison · 1285 Avenue of the Americas · New York, NY 10019-6064 · 212-373-3000

Harold R. Tyler, Jr. · Patterson, Belknap, Webb & Tyler · 30 Rockefeller Center New York, NY 10112 · 212-698-2500

Herbert M. Wachtell · Wachtell, Lipton, Rosen & Katz · 299 Park Avenue · New York, NY 10171-0149 · 212-371-9200

Gerald Walpin · (Appellate, Commercial, Securities) · Rosenman & Colin · 575 Madison Avenue · New York, NY 10022-2585 · 212-940-8600

Stephen A. Weiner* · (Banking, Commercial, Securities) · Winthrop, Stimson, Putnam & Roberts · One Battery Park Plaza · New York, NY 10004-1490 · 212-858-1000

Melvyn I. Weiss · Milberg Weiss Bershad Specthrie & Lerach · One Pennsylvania Plaza · New York, NY 10119 · 212-594-5300

George Weisz · Cleary, Gottlieb, Steen & Hamilton · One Liberty Plaza · New York, NY 10006 · 212-225-2000

George Weisz · Cleary, Gottlieb, Steen & Hamilton · One Liberty Plaza · New York, NY 10006 · 212-225-2060

William E. Willis · Sullivan & Cromwell · 125 Broad Street, 28th Floor · New York, NY 10004 · 212-558-4000

William Lent Dorr* · Harris, Beach & Wilcox · The Granite Building · 130 East Main Street · Rochester, NY 14604 · 716-232-4440

Edward H. Fox* · Harris, Beach & Wilcox · The Granite Building · 130 East Main Street · Rochester, NY 14604 · 716-232-4440

David M. Lascell* · (Appellate, Commercial) · Nixon, Hargrave, Devans & Doyle Clinton Square · P.O. Box 1051 · Rochester, NY 14603 · 716-546-8000

Anthony R. Palermo · (Commercial) · Harter, Secrest & Emery · 700 Midtown Tower · Rochester, NY 14604-2070 · 716-232-6500

Kenneth A. Payment* · (Antitrust, Commercial, Securities, Intellectual Property Rights) · Harter, Secrest & Emery · 700 Midtown Tower · Rochester, NY 14604-2070 · 716-232-6500

John J. Dee · Bond, Schoeneck & King · One Lincoln Center, 15th Floor · Syracuse, NY 13202-1355 · 315-422-0121

Paul M. Hanrahan* · (Commercial) · Hancock & Estabrook · One Mony Plaza, 14th Floor · 100 Madison Street · P.O. Box 4976 · Syracuse, NY 13221-4976 · 315-471-3151

George H. Lowe · Bond, Schoeneck & King · One Lincoln Center, 16th Floor · Syracuse, NY 13202-1355 · 315-422-0121

Kevin M. Reilly* · Mackenzie Smith Lewis Michell & Hughes · 600 Onondaga Savings Bank Building · P.O. Box 4967 · Syracuse, NY 13221-4967 · 315-474-7571

Carter H. Strickland · Mackenzie Smith Lewis Michell & Hughes · 600 Onondaga Savings Bank Building · P.O. Box 4967 · Syracuse, NY 13221-4967 · 315-474-7571

E. Stewart Jones, Jr.* · Jones Building · 28 Second Street · Troy, NY 12181 · 518-274-5820

Henry G. Miller · Clark, Gagliardi & Miller · Inns of Court Building · 99 Court Street · White Plains, NY 10601 · 914-946-8900

CORPORATE LAW

John A. Beach · Bond, Schoeneck & King · 111 Washington Avenue · Albany, NY 12210-2280 · 518-462-7421

John E. Holt-Harris, Jr. · DeGraff, Foy, Conway, Holt-Harris & Mealey · 90 State Street · Albany, NY 12207 · 518-462-5301

Michael Whiteman · Whiteman Osterman & Hanna · One Commerce Plaza · Albany, NY 12260 · 518-487-7600

Frederick G. Attea · Phillips, Lytle, Hitchcock, Blaine & Huber · 3400 Marine Midland Center · Buffalo, NY 14203 · 716-847-8400

John C. Barber, Jr. · (International) · Hodgson, Russ, Andrews, Woods & Goodyear · 1800 One M&T Plaza · Buffalo, NY 14203-2391 · 716-856-4000

Donald S. Day · Saperston & Day · Goldome Center, One Fountain Plaza · Buffalo, NY 14203-1486 · 716-856-5400

Arnold B. Gardner · (Corporate Finance, Investment, Mergers & Acquisitions) · Kavinoky & Cook · 120 Delaware Avenue · Buffalo, NY 14202 · 716-856-9234

Alvin M. Glick · Falk & Siemer · 2600 Main Place Tower · Buffalo, NY 14202 · 716-852-6670

Waldron S. Hayes, Jr. · Phillips, Lytle, Hitchcock, Blaine & Huber · 3400 Marine Midland Center · Buffalo, NY 14203 · 716-847-8400

Richard E. Heath · Hodgson, Russ, Andrews, Woods & Goodyear · 1800 One M&T Plaza · Buffalo, NY 14203-2391 · 716-856-4000

William I. Schapiro · Jaeckle, Fleischmann & Mugel · 800 Norstar Building · 12 Fountain Plaza · Buffalo, NY 14202-2222 · 716-856-0600

Robert O. Swados · Cohen Swados Wright Hanifin Bradford & Brett · 70 Niagara Street · Buffalo, NY 14202 · 716-856-4600

George M. Zimmermann · Albrecht, Maguire, Heffern & Gregg · 2100 Empire Tower · Buffalo, NY 14202 · 716-853-1521

J. Robert LaPann · LaPann, Jensen & LaPann · 107 Bay Street · Glens Falls, NY 12801 · 518-792-5634

Roger S. Aaron · (Mergers & Acquisitions) · Skadden, Arps, Slate, Meagher & Flom · 919 Third Avenue · New York, NY 10022-3897 · 212-735-3000

George B. Adams, Jr. · (Corporate Finance, International, International Finance, Securities) · Debevoise & Plimpton · 875 Third Avenue · New York, NY 10022 · 212-909-6000

Richard Marlow Allen · (Bankruptcy, Project Finance) · Cravath, Swaine & Moore · Worldwide Plaza · 825 Eighth Avenue, 38th Floor · New York, NY 10019 · 212-474-1000

Neil T. Anderson · Sullivan & Cromwell · 125 Broad Street, 28th Floor · New York, NY 10004 · 212-558-4000

Alan Appelbaum · Cleary, Gottlieb, Steen & Hamilton · One Liberty Plaza · New York, NY 10006 · 212-225-2000

James M. Asher · (Finance, Mergers & Acquisitions, Securities) · Rogers & Wells Pan Am Building · 200 Park Avenue · New York, NY 10166 · 212-878-8000

Peter A. Atkins · (Mergers & Acquisitions, Securities) · Skadden, Arps, Slate, Meagher & Flom · 919 Third Avenue · New York, NY 10022-3897 · 212-735-3000

Gerald S. Backman · Weil, Gotshal & Manges · 767 Fifth Avenue · New York, NY 10153 · 212-310-8000

Martin Balsam · (Securities) · Kramer, Levin, Nessen, Kamin & Frankel · 919 Third Avenue · New York, NY 10022 · 212-715-9100

Stephen E. Banner · (Mergers & Acquisitions, Securities) · Simpson Thacher & Bartlett · 425 Lexington Avenue · New York, NY 10017-3909 · 212-455-2000

David E. Baudler · (Banking, Finance, Mergers & Acquisitions) · Morrison & Foerster · 1290 Avenue of the Americas · New York, NY 10019 · 212-468-8000

Richard I. Beattie · (Corporate Finance, Leveraged Buyouts, Mergers & Acquisitions) · Simpson Thacher & Bartlett · 425 Lexington Avenue · New York, NY 10017-3909 · 212-455-2000

Melvin Leonard Bedrick · Cravath, Swaine & Moore · Worldwide Plaza · 825 Eighth Avenue, 38th Floor · New York, NY 10019 · 212-474-1000

Louis Begley · (International, International Finance, Investment, Mergers & Acquisitions) · Debevoise & Plimpton · 875 Third Avenue · New York, NY 10022 212-909-6000

John W. Belash · (Mutual Funds, Securities) · Gordon, Hurwitz, Butowsky, Weitzen, Shalov & Wein · 101 Park Avenue · New York, NY 10178 · 212-557-8000

Joshua M. Berman · Kramer, Levin, Nessen, Kamin & Frankel · 919 Third Avenue · New York, NY 10022 · 212-715-9100

David W. Bernstein · (Finance, Mergers & Acquisitions, Securities) · Rogers & Wells · Pan Am Building · 200 Park Avenue · New York, NY 10166 · 212-878-8000

Kenneth J. Bialkin · (Corporate Finance, International Finance, Mergers & Acquisitions, Securities Regulations) · Skadden, Arps, Slate, Meagher & Flom · 919 Third Avenue · New York, NY 10022-3897 · 212-735-3000

Eugene L. Bondy, Jr. · Rogers & Wells · Pan Am Building · 200 Park Avenue · New York, NY 10166 · 212-878-8000

Ronald E. Brackett · (Finance, Mergers & Acquisitions, Securities) · Rogers & Wells · Pan Am Building · 200 Park Avenue · New York, NY 10166 · 212-878-8000

Floyd E. Brandow, Jr. · (Securities Regulation) · Milbank, Tweed, Hadley & McCloy · One Chase Manhattan Plaza · New York, NY 10005-1413 · 212-530-5000

Meredith M. Brown · (Leveraged Buyouts, Mergers & Acquisitions, Securities Regulation) · Debevoise & Plimpton · 875 Third Avenue · New York, NY 10022 212-909-6000

F. Sedgwick Browne · (Insurance, Reinsurance) · Lord Day & Lord, Barrett Smith · 1675 Broadway · New York, NY 10019 · 212-969-6000

David Owen Brownwood · (Banking, Securities) · Cravath, Swaine & Moore · Worldwide Plaza · 825 Eighth Avenue, 38th Floor · New York, NY 10019 · 212-474-1218

Barry R. Bryan · (Finance, International) · Debevoise & Plimpton · 875 Third Avenue · New York, NY 10022 · 212-909-6000

Samuel Coles Butler · (International, Mergers & Acquisitions, Securities) · Cravath, Swaine & Moore · Worldwide Plaza · 825 Eighth Avenue, 38th Floor · New York, NY 10019 · 212-474-1000

Robert Carswell · (Banking) · Shearman & Sterling · 599 Lexington Avenue · New York, NY 10022 · 212-848-4000

Seymour H. Chalif · Kaye, Scholer, Fierman, Hays & Handler · 425 Park Avenue New York, NY 10022 · 212-836-8000

David B. Chapnick · (Mergers & Acquisitions, Securities) · Simpson Thacher & Bartlett · 425 Lexington Avenue · New York, NY 10017-3909 · 212-455-2000

Michael A. Chapnick · (Bank Finance for Lenders, Government Securities) · Lord Day & Lord, Barrett Smith · 1675 Broadway · New York, NY 10019 · 212-969-6000

Jonathan M. Clark · (Securities) · Davis Polk & Wardwell · One Chase Manhattan Plaza · New York, NY 10005 · 212-530-4000

George M. Cohen · (International Banking & Finance) · Cleary, Gottlieb, Steen & Hamilton · One Liberty Plaza · New York, NY 10006 · 212-225-2000

H. Rodgin Cohen · (Banking) · Sullivan & Cromwell · 125 Broad Street, 28th Floor · New York, NY 10004 · 212-558-4000

Jerome Alan Cohen · (Chinese) · Paul, Weiss, Rifkind, Wharton & Garrison · 1285 Avenue of the Americas · New York, NY 10019-6064 · 212-373-3000

C. Payson Coleman, Jr. · (Aviation Finance, International, Securities) · Winthrop, Stimson, Putnam & Roberts · One Battery Park Plaza · New York, NY 10004-1490 · 212-858-1426

Martin A. Coleman · Rubin Baum Levin Constant & Friedman · 30 Rockefeller Plaza, 29th Floor · New York, NY 10112 · 212-698-7700

Sydney M. Cone III · (Finance, International) · Cleary, Gottlieb, Steen & Hamilton · One Liberty Plaza · New York, NY 10006 · 212-225-2000

Thomas E. Constance · (Securities) · Shea & Gould · 1251 Avenue of the Americas · New York, NY 10020-1193 · 212-827-3000

Stephen H. Cooper · Weil, Gotshal & Manges · 767 Fifth Avenue · New York, NY 10153 · 212-310-8000

Laurence E. Cranch · (Finance, Mergers & Acquisitions, Securities) · Rogers & Wells · Pan Am Building · 200 Park Avenue · New York, NY 10166 · 212-878-8000

Benjamin Field Crane · (Finance, Mergers & Acquisitions) · Cravath, Swaine & Moore · Worldwide Plaza · 825 Eighth Avenue, 38th Floor · New York, NY 10019 212-474-1000

John S. D'Alimonte · Willkie Farr & Gallagher · One Citicorp Center · 153 East 53rd Street · New York, NY 10022-4669 · 212-935-8000

Ronald F. Daitz · (Finance, Mergers & Acquisitions, Securities) · Weil, Gotshal & Manges · 767 Fifth Avenue · New York, NY 10153 · 212-310-8000

Stephen J. Dannhauser · (Finance, Mergers & Acquisitions, Restructurings, Securities) · Weil, Gotshal & Manges · 767 Fifth Avenue · New York, NY 10153 212-310-8000

Peter H. Darrow · (Finance, Securities) · Cleary, Gottlieb, Steen & Hamilton · One Liberty Plaza · New York, NY 10006 · 212-225-2000

Edward S. Davis · (International, Securities) · Hughes Hubbard & Reed · One Battery Park Plaza · New York, NY 10004 · 212-837-6020

Joseph Diamond · (Banking, Financial Services) · Skadden, Arps, Slate, Meagher & Flom · 919 Third Avenue · New York, NY 10022-3897 · 212-735-3000

Robert E. Dineen, Jr. · (Banking, Securities) · Shearman & Sterling · 599 Lexington Avenue · New York, NY 10022 · 212-848-4000

Peter R. Douglas · (Financial Institutions, Leveraged Buyouts, Mergers & Acquisitions) · Davis Polk & Wardwell · One Chase Manhattan Plaza · New York, NY 10005 · 212-530-4000

W. Leslie Duffy · Cahill Gordon & Reindel · 80 Pine Street · New York, NY 10005 212-701-3000

John T. Dunne · Kaye, Scholer, Fierman, Hays & Handler · 425 Park Avenue · New York, NY 10022 · 212-836-8000

Cornelius J. Dwyer, Jr. · (Finance, International) · Shearman & Sterling · 599 Lexington Avenue · New York, NY 10022 · 212-848-4000

Klaus Eppler · (Mergers & Acquisitions, Securities) · Proskauer Rose Goetz & Mendelsohn · 1585 Broadway · New York, NY 10036 · 212-969-3000

Jeffrey M. Epstein · (Banking, Finance) · Kaye, Scholer, Fierman, Hays & Handler · 425 Park Avenue · New York, NY 10022 · 212-836-8000

William M. Evarts, Jr. · (Mergers & Acquisitions, Securities) · Winthrop, Stimson, Putnam & Roberts · One Battery Park Plaza · New York, NY 10004-1490 · 212-858-1000

Robert H. Falk · (Leveraged Buyouts, Securities) · Skadden, Arps, Slate, Meagher & Flom · 919 Third Avenue · New York, NY 10022-3897 · 212-735-3000

Gerald Feller · Kaye, Scholer, Fierman, Hays & Handler · 425 Park Avenue · New York, NY 10022 · 212-836-8000

Allen Finkelson · Cravath, Swaine & Moore · Worldwide Plaza · 825 Eighth Avenue, 38th Floor · New York, NY 10019 · 212-474-1000

Fred N. Fishman · Kaye, Scholer, Fierman, Hays & Handler · 425 Park Avenue New York, NY 10022 · 212-836-8000

Arthur Fleischer, Jr. · (Mergers & Acquisitions) · Fried, Frank, Harris, Shriver & Jacobson · One New York Plaza · New York, NY 10004-1980 · 212-820-8000

Joseph H. Flom · (Mergers & Acquisitions) · Skadden, Arps, Slate, Meagher & Flom · 919 Third Avenue · New York, NY 10022-3897 · 212-735-3000

James H. Fogelson · (Mergers & Acquisitions) · Wachtell, Lipton, Rosen & Katz 299 Park Avenue · New York, NY 10171-0149 · 212-371-9200

Blaine V. Fogg · (Mergers & Acquisitions) · Skadden, Arps, Slate, Meagher & Flom · 919 Third Avenue · New York, NY 10022-3897 · 212-735-3000

John C. Fontaine · (International, Securities) · Hughes Hubbard & Reed · One Battery Park Plaza · New York, NY 10004 · 212-837-6020

George J. Forsyth · Milbank, Tweed, Hadley & McCloy · One Chase Manhattan Plaza · New York, NY 10005-1413 · 212-530-5000

Stephen Fraidin · (Leveraged Buyouts, Mergers & Acquisitions, Securities, Securities Regulation) · Fried, Frank, Harris, Shriver & Jacobson · One New York Plaza · New York, NY 10004-1980 · 212-820-8000

Arthur H. Fredston · (Finance, International, Mergers & Acquisitions) · Winthrop, Stimson, Putnam & Roberts · One Battery Park Plaza · New York, NY 10004-1490 · 212-858-1000

James C. Freund · (Mergers & Acquisitions) · Skadden, Arps, Slate, Meagher & Flom · 919 Third Avenue · New York, NY 10022-3897 · 212-735-3000

Robert L. Friedman · (Corporate Finance, Financial Institutions, Leveraged Buyouts, Mergers & Acquisitions, Securities, Securities Regulation) · Simpson Thacher & Bartlett · 425 Lexington Avenue · New York, NY 10017-3909 · 212-455-2000

Stanley J. Friedman · (Securities) · Shereff, Friedman, Hoffman & Goodman · 919 Third Avenue · New York, NY 10022 · 212-758-9500

James J. Fuld · (Finance, Securities) · Proskauer Rose Goetz & Mendelsohn · 1585 Broadway · New York, NY 10036 · 212-969-3000

Herbert L. Galant · (Finance, Mergers & Acquisitions, Securities) · Fried, Frank, Harris, Shriver & Jacobson · One New York Plaza · New York, NY 10004-1980 · 212-820-8000

Sean J. Geary · (Capital Markets) · White & Case · 1155 Avenue of the Americas New York, NY 10036 · 212-819-8200

Thomas Gilroy · (International, Mergers & Acquisitions, Securities) · Hughes Hubbard & Reed · One Battery Park Plaza · New York, NY 10004 · 212-837-6020

Lawrence G. Graev · O'Sullivan, Graev & Karabel · 30 Rockefeller Plaza, 41st Floor · New York, NY 10112 · 212-408-2400

Stephen Allen Grant · (International, Mergers & Acquisitions, Securities) · Sullivan & Cromwell · 125 Broad Street, 28th Floor · New York, NY 10004 · 212-558-4000

David G. Gray · (Bank Regulations) · Simpson Thacher & Bartlett · 425 Lexington Avenue · New York, NY 10017-3909 · 212-455-2000

Gilson B. Gray III · (Banking, International) · Hughes Hubbard & Reed · One Battery Park Plaza · New York, NY 10004 · 212-837-6020

Robert W. Gray · Winthrop, Stimson, Putnam & Roberts · One Battery Park Plaza · New York, NY 10004-1490 · 212-858-1000

Edward F. Greene · Cleary, Gottlieb, Steen & Hamilton · One Liberty Plaza · New York, NY 10006 · 212-225-2000

Michael Gruson · (Banking, International) · Shearman & Sterling · 599 Lexington Avenue · New York, NY 10022 · 212-848-4000

William A. Hagan, Jr. · (Banking) · Shea & Gould · 1251 Avenue of the Americas New York, NY 10020-1193 · 212-827-3000

Joseph W. Halliday · (Banking) · Skadden, Arps, Slate, Meagher & Flom · 919 Third Avenue · New York, NY 10022-3897 · 212-735-3000

Joseph Daniel Hansen · (Finance, Mergers & Acquisitions, Securities) · Kaye, Scholer, Fierman, Hays & Handler · 425 Park Avenue · New York, NY 10022 · 212-836-8000

David W. Heleniak · (Mergers & Acquisitions) · Shearman & Sterling · 599 Lexington Avenue · New York, NY 10022 · 212-848-4000

Edwin Heller · (Securities) · Fried, Frank, Harris, Shriver & Jacobson · One New York Plaza · New York, NY 10004-1980 · 212-820-8000

Dennis S. Hersch · (Mergers & Acquisitions) · Davis Polk & Wardwell · One Chase Manhattan Plaza · New York, NY 10005 · 212-530-4000

Seymour Hertz · (Mergers & Acquisitions, Public & Private Finance, Securities) Paul, Weiss, Rifkind, Wharton & Garrison · 1285 Avenue of the Americas · New York, NY 10019-6064 · 212-373-3000

Robert B. Hiden, Jr. · (Corporate Finance, Mergers & Acquisitions, Securities Regulation, Futures, Options & Derivative Products) · Sullivan & Cromwell · 250 Park Avenue · New York, NY 10177 · 212-558-3812

William E. Hirschberg · (Banking, Finance) · Shearman & Sterling · 599 Lexington Avenue · New York, NY 10022 · 212-848-4000

Robert B. Hodes · Willkie Farr & Gallagher · One Citicorp Center · 153 East 53rd Street · New York, NY 10022-4669 · 212-935-8000

Joel S. Hoffman · Simpson Thacher & Bartlett · 425 Lexington Avenue · New York, NY 10017-3909 · 212-455-2000

Lawrence J. Hohlt · (International Banking) · Hughes Hubbard & Reed · One Battery Park Plaza · New York, NY 10004 · 212-837-6000

G. Malcolm Holderness · (Corporate Finance, Insurance Industry, Mergers & Acquisitions) · Milbank, Tweed, Hadley & McCloy · One Chase Manhattan Plaza New York, NY 10005-1413 · 212-530-5000

Arne Hovdesven · (Corporate Finance, Securities, Securities Regulation) · Shearman & Sterling · 599 Lexington Avenue · New York, NY 10022 · 212-848-4000

David M. Huggin · (Banking) · Sullivan & Cromwell · 125 Broad Street, 28th Floor · New York, NY 10004 · 212-558-4000

John Francis Hunt · (Finance) · Cravath, Swaine & Moore · Worldwide Plaza · 825 Eighth Avenue, 38th Floor · New York, NY 10019 · 212-474-1000

James B. Hurlock · (International Financial Transactions) · White & Case · 1155 Avenue of the Americas · New York, NY 10036 · 212-819-8200

Jerome E. Hyman · (Aviation, Securities) · Cleary, Gottlieb, Steen & Hamilton One Liberty Plaza · New York, NY 10006 · 212-225-2000

Michael Iovenko · (Banking, Insurance) · Breed, Abbott & Morgan · 153 East 53rd Street · New York, NY 10022 · 212-888-0800

Allen I. Isaacson · (International Financial Institutions, Mergers & Acquisitions) Fried, Frank, Harris, Shriver & Jacobson · One New York Plaza · New York, NY 10004-1980 · 212-820-8000

Arnold S. Jacobs · (Corporate, Finance, Securities) · Shea & Gould · 1251 Avenue of the Americas · New York, NY 10020 · 212-827-3000

Arthur P. Jacobs · (Mergers & Acquisitions) · Weil, Gotshal & Manges · 767 Fifth Avenue · New York, NY 10153 · 212-310-8000

Stephen E. Jacobs · Weil, Gotshal & Manges · 767 Fifth Avenue · New York, NY 10153 · 212-310-8000

Douglas W. Jones · Milbank, Tweed, Hadley & McCloy · One Chase Manhattan Plaza · New York, NY 10005-1413 · 212-530-5000

Lewis A. Kaplan · (Antitrust, International, Securities, Mergers & Acquisitions) · Paul, Weiss, Rifkind, Wharton & Garrison · 1285 Avenue of the Americas · New York, NY 10019-6064 · 212-373-3000

Peter Karasz · (International, Oil & Gas, Mergers & Acquisitions) · Cleary, Gottlieb, Steen & Hamilton · One Liberty Plaza · New York, NY 10006 · 212-225-2000

Roberta S. Karmel · (Securities, Securities & Banking Regulation) · Kelley Drye & Warren · 101 Park Avenue · New York, NY 10178 · 202-808-7800

Richard D. Katcher · (Mergers & Acquisitions, Securities) · Wachtell, Lipton, Rosen & Katz · 299 Park Avenue · New York, NY 10171-0149 · 212-371-9200

Stuart Z. Katz · (Mergers & Acquisitions) · Fried, Frank, Harris, Shriver & Jacobson · One New York Plaza · New York, NY 10004-1980 · 212-820-8000

Ed Kaufmann · (International, Securities) · Hughes Hubbard & Reed · One Battery Park Plaza · New York, NY 10004 · 212-837-6020

Peter L. Keane · Lord Day & Lord, Barrett Smith · 1675 Broadway · New York, NY 10019 · 212-969-6000

Howard S. Kelberg · (Finance, Securities) · Winthrop, Stimson, Putnam & Roberts · One Battery Park Plaza · New York, NY 10004-1490 · 212-858-1000

George C. Kern, Jr. · Sullivan & Cromwell · 250 Park Avenue · New York, NY 10177 · 212-558-4000

Jerome H. Kern · Shea & Gould · 1251 Avenue of the Americas · New York, NY 10020-1193 · 212-827-3000

B. Robbins Kiessling · Cravath, Swaine & Moore · Worldwide Plaza · 825 Eighth Avenue, 38th Floor · New York, NY 10019 · 212-474-1000

Fredric J. Klink · (Finance, Mergers & Acquisitions, Securities) · Dechert Price & Rhoads · 477 Madison Avenue, 12th Floor · New York, NY 10022 · 212-326-3500

Immanuel Kohn · (Corporate Reorganizations & Financing Transactions, Mergers & Acquisitions) · Cahill Gordon & Reindel · 80 Pine Street · New York, NY 10005 · 212-701-3000

Roy M. Korins · (General Commercial, International) · Esanu Katsky Korins & Siger · 605 Third Avenue, 16th Floor · New York, NY 10158 · 212-953-6000

Morris J. Kramer · (Mergers & Acquisitions) · Skadden, Arps, Slate, Meagher & Flom · 919 Third Avenue · New York, NY 10022-3897 · 212-735-3000

Sanford Krieger · (Mergers & Acquisitions) · Fried, Frank, Harris, Shriver & Jacobson · One New York Plaza · New York, NY 10004-1980 · 212-820-8000

William C. F. Kurz · Winthrop, Stimson, Putnam & Roberts · One Battery Park Plaza · New York, NY 10004-1490 · 212-858-1000

Dennis W. LaBarre · (Financial Institutions, Project Finance) · Jones, Day, Reavis & Pogue · 599 Lexington Avenue · New York, NY 10022 · 212-326-3939

W. Loeber Landau · (Finance, Mergers & Acquisitions, Securities) · Sullivan & Cromwell · 250 Park Avenue · New York, NY 10177 · 212-558-4000

Robert Todd Lang · (Mergers & Acquisitions, Securities) · Weil, Gotshal & Manges · 767 Fifth Avenue · New York, NY 10153 · 212-310-8000

Martin N. Leaf* · (Corporate Finance, International, Mergers & Acquisitions) · Morrison Cohen Singer & Weinstein · 750 Lexington Avenue, Eighth Floor · New York, NY 10022 · 212-735-8729

Lawrence Lederman · (Finance, Mergers & Acquisitions, Securities) · Wachtell, Lipton, Rosen & Katz · 299 Park Avenue · New York, NY 10171-0149 · 212-371-9200

Edwin Deane Leonard · (Mergers & Acquisitions) · Davis Polk & Wardwell · One Chase Manhattan Plaza · New York, NY 10005 · 212-530-4000

Joseph H. Levie · (Banking, International Banking, International Trade) · Rogers & Wells · Pan Am Building · 200 Park Avenue · New York, NY 10166 · 212-878-8000

Ezra G. Levin · (Banking, Mergers & Acquisitions, Securities) · Kramer, Levin, Nessen, Kamin & Frankel · 919 Third Avenue · New York, NY 10022 · 212-715-9100

Victor I. Lewkow · (Mergers & Acquisitions) · Cleary, Gottlieb, Steen & Hamilton · One Liberty Plaza · New York, NY 10006 · 212-225-2000

Albert F. Lilley · (Corporate Governance, Public Utility Finance, Securities Regulation) · Milbank, Tweed, Hadley & McCloy · One Chase Manhattan Plaza · New York, NY 10005-1413 · 212-530-5000

S. Troland Link · (International Banking) · Davis Polk & Wardwell · One Chase Manhattan Plaza · New York, NY 10005 · 212-530-4000

Martin Lipton · Wachtell, Lipton, Rosen & Katz · 299 Park Avenue · New York, NY 10171-0149 · 212-371-9200

Bevis Longstreth · (Finance, Securities) · Debevoise & Plimpton · 875 Third Avenue · New York, NY 10022 · 212-909-6000

George Theodore Lowy · (International, Mergers & Acquisitions, Securities) · Cravath, Swaine & Moore · Worldwide Plaza · 825 Eighth Avenue, 38th Floor · New York, NY 10019 · 212-474-1000

John J. Madden · (Mergers & Acquisitions) · Shearman & Sterling · 599 Lexington Avenue · New York, NY 10022 · 212-848-4000

Matthew J. Mallow · (Corporate Finance) · Skadden, Arps, Slate, Meagher & Flom · 919 Third Avenue · New York, NY 10022-3897 · 212-735-3000

Edgar M. Masinter · (Banking, Securities) · Simpson Thacher & Bartlett · 425 Lexington Avenue · New York, NY 10017-3909 · 212-455-2000

William B. Matteson · (International, Mergers & Acquisitions) · Debevoise & Plimpton · 875 Third Avenue · New York, NY 10022 · 212-909-6000

David A. McCabe · (Corporate Finance, International, Mergers & Acquisitions, Securities Regulation) · Shearman & Sterling · 599 Lexington Avenue · New York, NY 10022 · 212-848-4000

Willis McDonald IV · (Mergers & Acquisitions, Securities) · White & Case · 1155 Avenue of the Americas · New York, NY 10036 · 212-819-8200

John J. McNally · (Mergers & Acquisitions, Securities) · White & Case · 1155 Avenue of the Americas · New York, NY 10036 · 212-819-8200

Walter G. McNeill · (Structured Finance) · Skadden, Arps, Slate, Meagher & Flom · 919 Third Avenue · New York, NY 10022-3897 · 212-735-3000

John E. Merow · Sullivan & Cromwell · 125 Broad Street, 28th Floor · New York, NY 10004 · 212-558-4000

Ricardo A. Mestres, Jr. · (Mergers & Acquisitions, Securities) · Sullivan & Cromwell · 125 Broad Street, 28th Floor · New York, NY 10004 · 212-558-4000

Roger M. Milgrim · (Intellectual Property, Licensing) · Milgrim Thomajan Jacobs & Lee · 53 Wall Street · New York, NY 10005-2718 · 212-858-5300

Clyde Mitchell · White & Case · 1155 Avenue of the Americas · New York, NY 10036 · 212-819-8200

Franklin H. Moore, Jr. · (Securities) · Shearman & Sterling · 599 Lexington Avenue · New York, NY 10022 · 212-848-4000

Francis J. Morison · (International, Securities) · Davis Polk & Wardwell · One Chase Manhattan Plaza · New York, NY 10005 · 212-530-4000

Morton Moskin · White & Case · 1155 Avenue of the Americas · New York, NY 10036 · 212-819-8200

James F. Munsell · Cleary, Gottlieb, Steen & Hamilton · One Liberty Plaza · New York, NY 10006 · 212-225-2000

Jiro Murase · (Banking, International, Mergers & Acquisitions) · Marks Murase & White · 400 Park Avenue · New York, NY 10022 · 212-832-3333

William O. Murphy · (Banking) · Simpson Thacher & Bartlett · 425 Lexington Avenue · New York, NY 10017-3909 · 212-455-2000

Toby S. Myerson · (Banking, Finance, Mergers & Acquisitions) · Paul, Weiss, Rifkind, Wharton & Garrison · 1285 Avenue of the Americas · New York, NY 10019-6064 · 212-373-3000

Andre W. G. Newburg · (International, Securities) · Cleary, Gottlieb, Steen & Hamilton · One Liberty Plaza · New York, NY 10006 · 212-225-2000

Matthew Nimetz · (International Transactions, Mergers & Acquisitions) · Paul, Weiss, Rifkind, Wharton & Garrison · 1285 Avenue of the Americas · New York, NY 10019-6064 · 212-373-3000

Bernard William Nimkin · (Corporate Finance, Mergers & Acquisitions, Securities) · Kaye, Scholer, Fierman, Hays & Handler · 425 Park Avenue · New York, NY 10022 · 212-836-8000

Jack H. Nusbaum · (Mergers & Acquisitions) · Willkie Farr & Gallagher · One Citicorp Center · 153 East 53rd Street · New York, NY 10022-4669 · 212-935-8000

Robert S. O'Hara, Jr. · (Banking, Finance, Mergers & Acquisitions) · Milbank, Tweed, Hadley & McCloy · One Chase Manhattan Plaza · New York, NY 10005-1413 · 212-530-5000

Stuart I. Oran · Paul, Weiss, Rifkind, Wharton & Garrison · 1285 Avenue of the Americas · New York, NY 10019-6064 · 212-373-3000

David G. Ormsby · Cravath, Swaine & Moore · Worldwide Plaza · 825 Eighth Avenue, 38th Floor · New York, NY 10019 · 212-474-1000

Alan H. Paley · (Mergers & Acquisitions, Venture Capital)) · Debevoise & Plimpton · 875 Third Avenue · New York, NY 10022 · 212-909-6000

Joel I. Papernik · (Corporate Finance, International, Mergers & Acquisitions, Securities Regulation) · Shea & Gould · 1251 Avenue of the Americas · New York, NY 10020-1193 · 212-827-3000

Guy Paschal · (Corporate Finance, Investment) · Debevoise & Plimpton · 875 Third Avenue · New York, NY 10022 · 212-909-6000

Roswell B. Perkins · (Mergers & Acquisitions, Securities) · Debevoise & Plimpton · 875 Third Avenue · New York, NY 10022 · 212-909-6000

Donaldson C. Pillsbury · (Banking, International) · Davis Polk & Wardwell · One Chase Manhattan Plaza · New York, NY 10005 · 212-530-4000

Frank C. Puleo · (Banking, Federal Securities Laws) · Milbank, Tweed, Hadley & McCloy · One Chase Manhattan Plaza · New York, NY 10005-1413 · 212-530-5000

Leonard V. Quigley · (International, Mergers & Acquisitions, Securities Financings) · Paul, Weiss, Rifkind, Wharton & Garrison · 1285 Avenue of the Americas · New York, NY 10019-6064 · 212-373-3000

Edward S. Reid · (Mergers & Acquisitions, Securities) · Davis Polk & Wardwell · One Chase Manhattan Plaza · New York, NY 10005 · 212-530-4000

William P. Rogers · (International) · Rogers & Wells · Pan Am Building · 200 Park Avenue · New York, NY 10166 · 212-878-8000

Robert Rosenman · Cravath, Swaine & Moore · Worldwide Plaza · 825 Eighth Avenue, 38th Floor · New York, NY 10019 · 212-474-1000

Michael A. Ross · (Banking) · Shearman & Sterling · 599 Lexington Avenue · New York, NY 10022 · 212-848-4000

Peter D. Rowntree · (International Banking) · Milbank, Tweed, Hadley & McCloy · One Chase Manhattan Plaza · New York, NY 10005-1413 · 212-530-5000

Ernest Rubenstein · (Mergers & Acquisitions) · Paul, Weiss, Rifkind, Wharton & Garrison · 1285 Avenue of the Americas · New York, NY 10019-6064 · 212-373-3000

Frederic A. Rubinstein · (Corporate Finance, Investment, Mergers & Acquisitions, Venture Capital) · Kelley Drye & Warren · 101 Park Avenue · New York, NY 10178 · 202-808-7800

John S. Russell, Jr. · Winthrop, Stimson, Putnam & Roberts · One Battery Park Plaza · New York, NY 10004-1490 · 212-858-1000

Thomas A. Russo · Cadwalader, Wickersham & Taft · 100 Maiden Lane · New York, NY 10038 · 212-504-6000

Howard Schneider · (Corporate Finance, Mergers & Acquisitions, Securities Regulation, Futures Regulation) · Rosenman & Colin · 575 Madison Avenue · New York, NY 10022-2585 · 212-940-8600

Paul S. Schreiber · (International, Mutual Funds, Securities & Securities Regulation) · Kramer, Levin, Nessen, Kamin & Frankel · 919 Third Avenue · New York, NY 10022 · 212-715-9100

Stephen J. Schulte · (Mergers & Acquisitions) · Schulte Roth & Zabel · 900 Third Avenue · New York, NY 10022 · 212-758-0404

Michael P. Schumaecker · (Banking, Finance) · Winthrop, Stimson, Putnam & Roberts · One Battery Park Plaza · New York, NY 10004-1490 · 212-858-1433

Terrance W. Schwab · (Banking) · Kelley Drye & Warren · 101 Park Avenue · New York, NY 10178 · 202-808-7800

George M. Shapiro · (Banking, Private International Trade) · Proskauer Rose Goetz & Mendelsohn · 1585 Broadway · New York, NY 10036 · 212-969-3000

Isaac Shapiro · (International Commercial Transactions) · Skadden, Arps, Slate, Meagher & Flom · 919 Third Avenue, 46th Floor · New York, NY 10022-3897 · 212-735-3000

Sidney J. Silberman · Kaye, Scholer, Fierman, Hays & Handler · 425 Park Avenue · New York, NY 10022 · 212-836-8000

Joseph R. Siphron · Milbank, Tweed, Hadley & McCloy · One Chase Manhattan Plaza · New York, NY 10005-1413 · 212-530-5000

David V. Smalley · (Finance, Securities) · Debevoise & Plimpton · 875 Third Avenue · New York, NY 10022 · 212-909-6000

Bradley Y. Smith · (Banking) · Davis Polk & Wardwell · One Chase Manhattan Plaza · New York, NY 10005 · 212-530-4000

Theodore C. Sorensen · (International Business Transactions) · Paul, Weiss, Rifkind, Wharton & Garrison · 1285 Avenue of the Americas · New York, NY 10019-6064 · 212-373-3000

Lee B. Spencer, Jr. · (Securities) · Gibson, Dunn & Crutcher · 200 Park Avenue, 47th Floor · New York, NY 10166 · 212-351-4000

Allan G. Sperling · Cleary, Gottlieb, Steen & Hamilton · One Liberty Plaza · New York, NY 10006 · 212-225-2000

Richard D. Spizzirri · (Limited Partnerships, Mergers & Acquisitions, Research & Development Finance) · Davis Polk & Wardwell · One Chase Manhattan Plaza New York, NY 10005 · 212-530-4000

Benjamin F. Stapleton · (Mergers & Acquisitions) · Sullivan & Cromwell · 125 Broad Street, 28th Floor · New York, NY 10004 · 212-558-4000

Richard A. Stark · (Mergers & Acquisitions, Securities Offerings) · Milbank, Tweed, Hadley & McCloy · One Chase Manhattan Plaza · New York, NY 10005-1413 · 212-530-5000

Ned B. Stiles · (Finance, Mergers & Acquisitions, Securities) · Cleary, Gottlieb, Steen & Hamilton · One Liberty Plaza · New York, NY 10006 · 212-225-2000

David P. Stone · Weil, Gotshal & Manges · 767 Fifth Avenue · New York, NY 10153 · 212-310-8000

Milton G. Strom · (Mergers & Acquisitions, Securities) · Skadden, Arps, Slate, Meagher & Flom · 919 Third Avenue · New York, NY 10022-3897 · 212-735-3000

David W. Swanson · White & Case · 1155 Avenue of the Americas · New York, NY 10036 · 212-819-8200

John C. Taylor III · (Leveraged Buyouts, Mergers & Acquisitions) · Paul, Weiss, Rifkind, Wharton & Garrison · 1285 Avenue of the Americas · New York, NY 10019-6064 · 212-373-3000

Arbie R. Thalacker · (International Joint Ventures, Mergers & Acquisitions, Securities) · Shearman & Sterling · 599 Lexington Avenue · New York, NY 10022 · 212-848-4000

Allen L. Thomas · Paul, Weiss, Rifkind, Wharton & Garrison · 1285 Avenue of the Americas · New York, NY 10019-6064 · 212-373-3000

Robert M. Thomas, Jr. · (Corporate Finance, International Finance, Mergers & Acquisitions, Securities) · Sullivan & Cromwell · 125 Broad Street, 28th Floor · New York, NY 10004 · 212-558-4000

Judith R. Thoyer · Paul, Weiss, Rifkind, Wharton & Garrison · 1285 Avenue of the Americas · New York, NY 10019-6064 · 212-373-3000

Robert L. Tortoriello · (Banking) · Cleary, Gottlieb, Steen & Hamilton · One Liberty Plaza · New York, NY 10006 · 212-225-2000

Cyrus R. Vance · (Antitrust) · Simpson Thacher & Bartlett · 425 Lexington Avenue · New York, NY 10017-3909 · 212-455-2000

Charles H. Vejvoda · (Banking, Creditors' Rights) · Winthrop, Stimson, Putnam & Roberts · One Battery Park Plaza · New York, NY 10004-1490 · 212-858-1000

Stephen R. Volk · (Mergers & Acquisitions) · Shearman & Sterling · 599 Lexington Avenue · New York, NY 10022 · 212-848-4000

Mark A. Walker · (International Business Transactions, International Finance, Sovereign Debt Restructuring) · Cleary, Gottlieb, Steen & Hamilton · One Liberty Plaza · New York, NY 10006 · 212-225-2000

Duane D. Wall · (Banking, International Finance) · White & Case · 1155 Avenue of the Americas · New York, NY 10036 · 212-819-8200

Robert D. Webster · (Banking, International) · Winthrop, Stimson, Putnam & Roberts · One Battery Park Plaza · New York, NY 10004-1490 · 212-858-1000

Rohan S. Weerasinghe · Shearman & Sterling · 599 Lexington Avenue · New York, NY 10022 · 212-848-4000

Peter H. Weil · (Asset-Based Lending, Corporate Finance, Reorganizations) · Kaye, Scholer, Fierman, Hays & Handler · 425 Park Avenue · New York, NY 10022 · 212-836-8000

Stephen K. West · Sullivan & Cromwell · 125 Broad Street, 28th Floor · New York, NY 10004 · 212-558-4000

John W. White · (Corporate Finance, Securities, Securities Regulation) · Cravath, Swaine & Moore · Worldwide Plaza · 825 Eighth Avenue, 38th Floor · New York, NY 10019 · 212-474-1000

Charles S. Whitman III · (Corporate Finance, International, Securities, Securities Regulation) · Davis Polk & Wardwell · One Chase Manhattan Plaza · New York, NY 10005 · 212-530-4888

Peter Whitridge Williams · (Banking, Finance) · Rogers & Wells · Pan Am Building · 200 Park Avenue · New York, NY 10166 · 212-878-8000

Thomas A. Williams · (Banking, Financial Institutions, Mergers & Acquisitions, Securities Regulation) · Milbank, Tweed, Hadley & McCloy · One Chase Manhattan Plaza · New York, NY 10005-1413 · 212-530-5000

William J. Williams, Jr. · (Finance) · Sullivan & Cromwell · 125 Broad Street, 28th Floor · New York, NY 10004 · 212-558-4000

Paul H. Wilson, Jr. · (Business, Securities) · Debevoise & Plimpton · 875 Third Avenue · New York, NY 10022 · 212-909-6000

James Ronald Wolfe · (Lease Finance, Project Finance) · Simpson Thacher & Bartlett · 425 Lexington Avenue · New York, NY 10017-3909 · 212-455-2000

Jacob J. Worenklein · (Project Finance & Development) · Milbank, Tweed, Hadley & McCloy · One Chase Manhattan Plaza · New York, NY 10005-1413 · 212-530-5000

Cecil Wray, Jr. · (Finance, Securities) · Debevoise & Plimpton · 875 Third Avenue · New York, NY 10022 · 212-909-6000

William F. Wynne, Jr. · (Mergers & Acquisitions) · White & Case · 1155 Avenue of the Americas · New York, NY 10036 · 212-819-8200

John Edward Young · Cravath, Swaine & Moore · Worldwide Plaza · 825 Eighth Avenue, 38th Floor · New York, NY 10019 · 212-474-1000

Julian W. Atwater · Nixon, Hargrave, Devans & Doyle · Clinton Square · P.O. Box 1051 · Rochester, NY 14603 · 716-546-8000

Thomas E. Clement · Nixon, Hargrave, Devans & Doyle · Clinton Square · P.O. Box 1051 · Rochester, NY 14603 · 716-546-8000

Alfred J. Giuffrida · Nixon, Hargrave, Devans & Doyle · Clinton Square · P.O. Box 1051 · Rochester, NY 14603 · 716-546-8000

B. G. Staffan Lundback · Nixon, Hargrave, Devans & Doyle · Clinton Square · P.O. Box 1051 · Rochester, NY 14603 · 716-546-8000

Thomas A. Solberg · (Closely Held Businesses) · Harter, Secrest & Emery · 700 Midtown Tower · Rochester, NY 14604-2070 · 716-232-6500

Alan J. Underberg · (Corporate Finance, Mergers & Acquisitions) · Underberg & Kessler · 1800 Lincoln First Tower · Rochester, NY 14604 · 716-258-2800

Justin L. Vigdor · Mousaw, Vigdor, Reeves, Heilbronner & Kroll · 600 First Federal Plaza · Rochester, NY 14614 · 716-325-2500

John A. Beach · Bond, Schoeneck & King · One Lincoln Center, 18th Floor · Syracuse, NY 13202-1355 · 315-422-0121

Charles T. Beeching, Jr. · (Banking, Insurance, Mergers & Acquisitions, Securities Regulation) · Bond, Schoeneck & King · One Lincoln Center, 18th Floor · Syracuse, NY 13202-1355 · 315-422-0121

Donald A. Denton · Hancock & Estabrook · One Mony Plaza, 14th Floor · 100 Madison Street · P.O. Box 4976 · Syracuse, NY 13221-4976 · 315-471-3151

George S. Deptula · Hiscock & Barclay · Financial Plaza, Suite 500 · P.O. Box 4878 · Syracuse, NY 13221 · 315-422-2131

James R. McVety · Hancock & Estabrook · One Mony Plaza, 14th Floor · 100 Madison Street · P.O. Box 4976 · Syracuse, NY 13221-4976 · 315-471-3151

Richard S. Scolaro · Scolaro, Shulman, Cohen, Lawler & Burstein · 90 Presidential Plaza, Fifth Floor · Syracuse, NY 13202 · 315-471-8111

Edward M. Zachary · Menter, Rudin & Trivelpiece · 500 South Salina Street, Suite 500 · Syracuse, NY 13202 · 315-474-7541

Ivan Serchuk · (Banking, Financial Institutions) · Serchuk & Zelermyer · 81 Main Street · White Plains, NY 10601 · 914-761-2100

CRIMINAL DEFENSE

Stephen R. Coffey · O'Connell and Aronowitz · 100 State Street, Eighth Floor · Albany, NY 12207 · 518-462-5601

William J. Dreyer · Dreyer, Kinsella, Boyajian & Tuttle · 75 Columbia Street · Albany, NY 12210 · 518-463-7784

Harold J. Boreanaz* · (Federal & White Collar Crimes) · Boreanaz, Carra & Boreanaz · 736 Brisbane Building · 403 Main Street · Buffalo, NY 14203 · 716-854-5800

Paul J. Cambria, Jr. · Lipsitz, Green, Fahringer, Roll, Salisbury & Cambria · 42 Delaware Avenue, Suite 300 · Buffalo, NY 14202-3901 · 716-849-1333

John W. Condon, Jr.* · (Federal Court, State Court, Environmental Crimes, Federal & State Tax Fraud) · Condon, Pieri & Taheri · 300 Statler Towers · Buffalo, NY 14202-2868 · 716-856-2183

Terrence M. Connors · Connors & Vilardo · Old City Court Building · 42 Delaware Avenue, Suite 710 · Buffalo, NY 14202 · 716-852-5533

Joel L. Daniels · 444 Statler Towers · Buffalo, NY 14202 · 716-856-5140

Herbert L. Greenman* · Lipsitz, Green, Fahringer, Roll, Salisbury & Cambria · 42 Delaware Avenue, Suite 300 · Buffalo, NY 14202-3901 · 716-849-1333

Joseph M. LaTona · Lipsitz, Green, Fahringer, Roll, Salisbury & Cambria · 42 Delaware Avenue, Suite 300 · Buffalo, NY 14202-3901 · 716-849-1333

Mark J. Mahoney* · Bermingham, Cook & Mahoney · 1620 Statler Towers · Buffalo, NY 14202-3066 · 716-854-6800

Joseph V. Sedita* · (Federal Court, Environmental Crimes, Government Procurement Investigations) · Moot & Sprague · 2300 Empire Tower · Buffalo, NY 14202 · 716-845-5200

Felix V. Lapine · (Violent Crimes, Non-Violent Crimes, Federal Court, State Court) · Nine West State Street · Dolgeville, NY 13329 · 315-429-9873

Elkan Abramowitz · Morvillo, Abramowitz & Grand · 530 Fifth Avenue, 16th Floor · New York, NY 10036 · 212-221-1414

Stanley S. Arkin · Chadbourne & Parke · 30 Rockefeller Plaza · New York, NY 10112 · 212-408-5100

Michael F. Armstrong · Lord Day & Lord, Barrett Smith · 1675 Broadway · New York, NY 10019 · 212-969-6000

Herald Price Fahringer · Lipsitz, Green, Fahringer, Roll, Salisbury & Cambria 540 Madison Avenue · New York, NY 10022 · 212-751-1330

Robert B. Fiske, Jr. · Davis Polk & Wardwell · One Chase Manhattan Plaza · New York, NY 10005 · 212-530-4000

Peter E. Fleming, Jr. · Curtis, Mallet-Prevost, Colt & Mosle · 101 Park Avenue New York, NY 10178 · 212-696-6000

Jay Goldberg · 250 Park Avenue, 14th Floor · New York, NY 10177-0077 · 212-983-6000

Paul R. Grand* · (Non-Violent Crimes, Federal Court, State Court) · Morvillo, Abramowitz & Grand · 530 Fifth Avenue, 16th Floor · New York, NY 10036 · 212-221-1414

Frederick P. Hafetz · Goldman & Hafetz · 60 East 42nd Street, Suite 950 · New York, NY 10165 · 212-682-7000

Jack S. Hoffinger · Hoffinger Friedland Dobrish Bernfeld & Hasen · 110 East 59th Street · New York, NY 10022-1392 · 212-421-4000

Robert Kasanof* · (Non-Violent Crimes, Federal Court, State Court, Environmental Crimes) · 767 Third Avenue · New York, NY 10017 · 212-355-6505

Stephen E. Kaufman* · 277 Park Avenue · New York, NY 10017 · 212-826-0820

Michael Kennedy · Law Offices of Michael Kennedy · 425 Park Avenue, 26th Floor · New York, NY 10022 · 212-935-4500

James M. LaRossa · LaRossa, Mitchell & Ross · 41 Madison Avenue · New York, NY 10010 · 212-696-9700

Andrew M. Lawler · 220 East 42nd Street · New York, NY 10017 · 212-687-8850

Gerald B. Lefcourt* · 148 East 78th Street · New York, NY 10021 · 212-737-0400

Jack T. Litman · Litman, Asche, Lupkin & Gioiella · 45 Broadway Atrium, 30th Floor · New York, NY 10006 · 212-809-4500

Robert G. Morvillo · Morvillo, Abramowitz & Grand · 530 Fifth Avenue, 16th Floor · New York, NY 10036 · 212-221-1414

Gary P. Naftalis · Kramer, Levin, Nessen, Kamin & Frankel · 919 Third Avenue New York, NY 10022 · 212-715-9100

Gustave H. Newman · Newman & Schwartz · 641 Lexington Avenue · New York, NY 10022 · 212-308-7900

Jed S. Rakoff · (Non-Violent Crimes, Federal Court, RICO) · Fried, Frank, Harris, Shriver & Jacobson · One New York Plaza · New York, NY 10004-1980 · 212-820-8000

Jules Ritholz* · (Tax Fraud, Federal Court) · Kostelanetz Ritholz Tigue & Fink 80 Pine Street · New York, NY 10005 · 212-422-4030

Paul K. Rooney* · 26 Broadway · New York, NY 10004 · 212-269-4420

Edward M. Shaw · Stillman, Friedman & Shaw · 425 Park Avenue · New York, NY 10022 · 212-223-0200

Charles A. Stillman · Stillman, Friedman & Shaw · 425 Park Avenue · New York, NY 10022 · 212-223-0200

Patrick M. Wall · 36 West 44th Street, Suite 905 · New York, NY 10036 · 212-840-7188

John R. Wing* · Weil, Gotshal & Manges · 767 Fifth Avenue · New York, NY 10153 · 212-310-8364

Lawrence J. Andolina · Harris Beach & Wilcox · The Granite Building · 130 East Main Street · Rochester, NY 14604 · 716-232-4440

Michael T. DiPrima · Law Offices of Michael T. DiPrima · 2024 West Henrietta Road · Rochester, NY 14623 · 716-292-0170

Felix V. Lapine · (Violent Crimes, Non-Violent Crimes, Federal Court, State Court) · 17 East Main Street, Suite 500 · Rochester, NY 14614 · 716-454-6690

David A. Murante* · (Violent Crimes, Non-Violent Crimes, Federal Court, State Court) · 700 Wilder Building · Eight Exchange Street · Rochester, NY 14614 · 716-232-6830

Norman A. Palmiere, Sr. · Palmiere & Pellegrino · Chapin Building, Third Floor 205 St. Paul Street · Rochester, NY 14604 · 716-232-6144

John R. Parrinello · Redmond & Parrinello · 400 Executive Office Building · Rochester, NY 14614 · 716-454-2321

David Rothenberg · Geiger and Rothenberg · 800 Times Square Building · 45 Exchange Street · Rochester, NY 14614 · 716-232-1946

Karl F. Salzer · (Violent Crimes, Non-Violent Crimes, Federal Court, State Court) · Gough, Skipworth, Summers, Eves & Trevett · 700 Reynolds Arcade · 16 East Main Street · Rochester, NY 14614-1803 · 716-454-2181

John F. Speranza · 13 South Fitzhugh Street · Rochester, NY 14614 · 716-454-1500

Joseph E. Fahey* · Wiles & Fahey · 1010 State Tower Building · Syracuse, NY 13202 · 315-474-4648

Edward F. Gerber · (Non-Violent Crimes, Federal Court, State Court, Environmental Crimes) · 214 South Warren Street, Ninth Floor · Syracuse, NY 13202-4171 315-472-4484

Emil M. Rossi · Rouizzigno, Rossi & Vavonse · The Lowe Building · 108 West Jefferson Street, Suite 500 · Syracuse, NY 13202 · 315-471-0126

E. Stewart Jones, Jr.* · Jones Building · 28 Second Street · Troy, NY 12181 · 518-274-5820

ENTERTAINMENT LAW

Richard L. Barovick · Loeb and Loeb · 230 Park Avenue · New York, NY 10169
212-692-4800

John F. Breglio · Paul, Weiss, Rifkind, Wharton & Garrison · 1285 Avenue of the
Americas · New York, NY 10019-6064 · 212-373-3000

Alvin Deutsch · Deutsch, Klagsbrun & Blasband · 800 Third Avenue, Third Floor
New York, NY 10022 · 212-758-1100

Michael P. Frankfurt · Frankfurt, Garbus, Klein & Selz · 488 Madison Avenue,
Ninth Floor · New York, NY 10022 · 212-980-0120

Leonard Franklin · Franklin, Weinrib, Rudell & Vassallo · 488 Madison Avenue,
Eighth Floor · New York, NY 10022 · 212-935-5500

Martin Garbus · Frankfurt, Garbus, Klein & Selz · 488 Madison Avenue, Ninth
Floor · New York, NY 10022 · 212-980-0120

Allen J. Grubman · Grubman, Indursky, Schindler, Goldstein & Flax · 152 West
57th Street · New York, NY 10019 · 212-554-0400

Arthur J. Klein · Frankfurt, Garbus, Klein & Selz · 488 Madison Avenue, Ninth
Floor · New York, NY 10022 · 212-980-0120

Thomas M. Lewyn · Simpson Thacher & Bartlett · 425 Lexington Avenue · New
York, NY 10017-3909 · 212-455-2000

Paul G. Marshall · Marshall Morris Wattenberg & Platt · 130 West 57th Street ·
New York, NY 10019 · 212-582-1122

Robert H. Montgomery, Jr. · (Film, Theatrical, Musical, Literary) · Paul, Weiss,
Rifkind, Wharton & Garrison · 1285 Avenue of the Americas · New York, NY
10019-6064 · 212-373-3000

E. Gabriel Perle · Proskauer Rose Goetz & Mendelsohn · 1585 Broadway · New
York, NY 10036 · 212-969-3000

Harriet F. Pilpel · Weil, Gotshal & Manges · 767 Fifth Avenue · New York, NY
10153 · 212-310-8000

Michael I. Rudell · Franklin, Weinrib, Rudell & Vassallo · 488 Madison Avenue,
Eighth Floor · New York, NY 10022 · 212-935-5500

Paul Sawyer · Phillips, Nizer, Benjamin, Krim & Ballon · 40 West 57th Street ·
New York, NY 10019 · 212-977-9700

Paul J. Sherman · Pryor, Cashman, Sherman & Flynn · 410 Park Avenue · New York, NY 10022 · 212-421-4100

Lee N. Steiner · Loeb and Loeb · 230 Park Avenue · New York, NY 10169 · 212-692-4800

Nancy F. Wechsler · Deutsch, Klagsbrun & Blasband · 800 Third Avenue, Third Floor · New York, NY 10022 · 212-758-1100

FAMILY LAW

Stanley A. Rosen* · McNamee, Lochner, Titus & Williams · 75 State Street · P.O. Box 459 · Albany, NY 12201-0459 · 518-434-3136

Bruno Colapietro* · Chernin & Gold · Bache Building · 71 State Street · P.O. Box 1563 · Binghamton, NY 13902 · 607-723-9581

Donald M. Sukloff* · Bernstein, Gitlitz & Sukloff · Key Bank Building · 59-61 Court Street, Sixth Floor · State Street Entrance · Binghamton, NY 13901 · 607-723-7913

Saul Edelstein · Edelstein & Brown · 26 Court Street · Brooklyn, NY 11242 · 718-875-3550

Grace Marie Ange · Ange & Gordon · 560 Statler Towers · Buffalo, NY 14202 · 716-854-8888

Paul Ivan Birzon · Birzon & Zakia · 360 Statler Towers · Buffalo, NY 14202 · 716-847-6060

William J. Cunningham, Jr.* · 900 Cathedral Park Tower · 37 Franklin Street · Buffalo, NY 14202 · 716-856-7177

Peter J. Fiorella, Jr. · Fiorella, Palmer & Leiter · 877 Delaware Avenue · Buffalo, NY 14209 · 716-882-3333

Mark G. Hirschorn* · (Divorce, Marital Settlement Agreements, Equitable Division, Enforcement & Modification) · Siegel, Kelleher & Kahn · 426 Franklin Street · Buffalo, NY 14202 · 716-881-5800

Thomas Allan Palmer · Fiorella, Palmer & Leiter · 877 Delaware Avenue · Buffalo NY 14209 · 716-882-3333

Herbert M. Siegel · Siegel, Kelleher & Kahn · 426 Franklin Street · Buffalo, NY 14202 · 716-881-5800

David G. Stiller · Heimerl, Stiller, Keenan & Longo · 1566 Statler Towers · Buffalo, NY 14202 · 716-854-5063

Leonard Swagler* · (Child Custody, Divorce, Marital Settlement Agreements, Equitable Division) · 704 Statler Towers · Buffalo, NY 14202 · 716-856-3315

Michael B. Atkins* · (Child Custody, Divorce, Marital Settlement Agreements, Appeals) · Taylor, Atkins & Ostrow · 200 Garden City Plaza · Garden City, NY 11530 · 516-877-1800

Joel R. Brandes* · (Child Custody, Divorce, Equitable Division, Trial & Appellate) · Brandes, Weidman & Spatz · 200 Garden City Plaza · Garden City, NY 11530 · 516-746-6995

Willard H. DaSilva · 585 Stewart Avenue · Garden City, NY 11530 · 516-222-0700

Stephen Gassman* · (Child Custody, Divorce, Marital Settlement Agreements, Equitable Division) · Gassman Gouz & Fisher · 666 Old Country Road · Garden City, NY 11530 · 516-228-9181

Michael J. Ostrow · (Child Custody, Divorce, Marital Settlement Agreements, Equitable Division) · Taylor, Atkins & Ostrow · 200 Garden City Plaza · Garden City, NY 11530 · 516-877-1800

Michael Dikman* · (Child Custody, Divorce, Marital Settlement Agreements, Equitable Division) · Dikman, Dikman and Botter · 161-10 Jamaica Avenue · Jamaica, NY 11432 · 718-739-4830

Kenneth Koopersmith* · Koopersmith, Feigenbaum & Potruch · 3000 Marcus Avenue, Suite 3W7 · Lake Success, NY 11042 · 516-354-0800

Stephen W. Schlissel · (Child Custody, Divorce, Marital Settlement Agreements, Equitable Division) · Ruskin, Schlissel, Moscou, Evans & Faltischek · 170 Old Country Road · Mineola, NY 11501-4366 · 516-248-9500

Eleanor Breitel Alter · Rosenman & Colin · 575 Madison Avenue · New York, NY 10022 · 212-940-8600

Robert Stephan Cohen* · Morrison Cohen Singer & Weinstein · 750 Lexington Avenue · New York, NY 10022 · 212-735-8600

Robert Z. Dobrish* · Hoffinger Friedland Dobrish Bernfeld & Hasen · 110 East 59th Street · New York, NY 10022-1392 · 212-421-4000

Joan L. Ellenbogen · Ellenbogen & Goldstein · 142 West 57th Street · New York, NY 10019 · 212-245-3260

Myrna Felder · The Firm of Raoul Lionel Felder · 437 Madison Avenue · New York, NY 10022 · 212-832-3939

Raoul Lionel Felder · The Firm of Raoul Lionel Felder · 437 Madison Avenue New York, NY 10022 · 212-832-3939

William C. Herman · Rosenthal, Herman & Mantel · 310 Madison Avenue, Suite 2024 · New York, NY 10017 · 212-972-8911

Stanford G. Lotwin* · Tenzer, Greenblatt, Fallon & Kaplan · The Chrysler Building · 405 Lexington Avenue · New York, NY 10174 · 212-573-4300

Julia Perles* · Phillips, Nizer, Benjamin, Krim & Ballon · 40 West 57th Street · New York, NY 10019 · 212-977-9700

Stanley Plesent · Squadron, Ellenoff, Plesent & Lehrer · 551 Fifth Avenue · New York, NY 10017 · 212-661-6500

Miriam M. Robinson · Leddle, O'Connor, Finkelstein & Robinson · 685 Third Avenue · New York, NY 10117 · 212-687-8500

Rona J. Shays · Rosenthal & Shays · 276 Fifth Avenue · New York, NY 10001 · 212-684-1700

Norman M. Sheresky* · (Child Custody, Divorce, Marital Settlement Agreements, Equitable Division) · Colton, Hartnick, Yamin & Sheresky · 79 Madsion Avenue · New York, NY 10016 · 212-532-5100

Sanford S. Dranoff* · Dranoff & Johnson · One Blue Hill Plaza, Suite 900 · P.O. Box 1629 · Pearl River, NY 10965-8629 · 914-735-7100

Perry Satz* · Satz and Kirshon · 309 Mill Street · Poughkeepsie, NY 12601 · 914-454-4040

Brian J. Barney · Pauley & Barney · 130 Linden Oaks, Suite 130D · Rochester, NY 14625 · 716-248-0140

S. Gerald Davidson* · Davidson, Fink, Cook and Gates · 900 First Federal Plaza Rochester, NY 14614 · 716-546-6448

Joel J. Goldman* · (Divorce, Marital Settlement Agreements, Equitable Division) · Kaman, Berlove, Marafioti, Jacobstein & Goldman · The Academy, Suite 400 · 13 South Fitzhugh Street · Rochester, NY 14614 · 716-325-7440

Lewis J. Gould* · (Child Custody, Divorce, Marital Settlement Agreements, Equitable Division) · Gould & Peck · 45 Exchange Street · Rochester, NY 14614 716-546-3065

Gregory J. Mott* · Davidson, Fink, Cook and Gates · 900 First Federal Plaza · Rochester, NY 14614 · 716-546-6448

Joan de R. O'Byrne · 19 West Main Street · Rochester, NY 14614 · 716-546-3340

Raymond J. Pauley · Pauley & Barney · 130 Linden Oaks, Suite 130D · Rochester, NY 14625 · 716-248-0140

Bruce G. Behrins · Bruce G. Behrins & Associates · 1492 Victory Boulevard · Staten Island, NY 10301 · 718-447-5540

Edward B. Alderman* · (Child Custody, Divorce, Marital Settlement Agreements, Equitable Division) · Alderman and Alderman · Empire Building, Suite 555 · 472 South Salina Street · Syracuse, NY 13202 · 315-422-8131

Anthony J. Di Caprio, Jr.* · Di Caprio and Di Caprio · 503 Myrtle Street · Syracuse, NY 13204-1823 · 315-468-1109

Richard E. Gordon · Nottingham, Engel, Gordon & Kerr · One Lincoln Center, Suite 880 · Syracuse, NY 13201 · 315-474-6046

Gary L. Orenstein · Orenstein Law Office · 818 State Tower Building · 109 South Warren Street · Syracuse, NY 13202 · 315-422-8185

Timothy M. Tippins · Tippins Law Firm · 102 Third Street · Troy, NY 12180 · 518-271-0707

Henry S. Berman · Fink, Weinberger, Fredman, Berman, Lowell & Fensterheim 11 Martine Avenue · White Plains, NY 10606 · 914-682-7700

Ronnie Parker Gouz · Fink, Weinberger, Fredman, Berman, Lowell & Fensterheim · 11 Martine Avenue · White Plains, NY 10606 · 914-682-7700

FIRST AMENDMENT LAW

Peter Danzinger · O'Connell & Aronowitz · 100 State Street · Albany, NY 12207 518-462-5601

Michael T. Wallender · DeGraff, Foy, Conway, Holt-Harris & Mealey · 90 State Street · Albany, NY 12207 · 518-462-5301

John H. Stenger · Jaeckle, Fleischman & Mugel · 800 Norstar Building · 12 Fountain Plaza · Buffalo, NY 14202 · 716-856-0600

Floyd Abrams · Cahill Gordon & Reindel · 80 Pine Street · New York, NY 10005 212-701-3000

Michael A. Bamberger · Sonnenschein Nath & Rosenthal · 900 Third Avenue, Suite 1600 · New York, NY 10022 · 212-891-2000

Jerry S. Birenz · Sabin, Bermant & Gould · 350 Madison Avenue · New York, NY 10017 · 212-692-4411

Robert M. Callagy · Shatterlee, Stephens, Burke & Burke · 230 Park Avenue · New York, NY 10169 · 212-818-9200

Leon Friedman · 148 East 78th Street · New York, NY 10021 · 212-737-0400

Alexander Gigante · Mailman & Gigante · 780 Third Avenue, 32nd Floor · New York, NY 10017 · 212-832-7400

James C. Goodale · Debevoise & Plimpton · 875 Third Avenue · New York, NY 10022 · 212-909-6000

Peter C. Gould · Sabin, Bermant & Gould · 350 Madison Avenue · New York, NY 10017 · 212-692-4411

Jonathan W. Lubell · Morrison Cohen Singer & Weinstein · 750 Lexington Avenue, Eighth Floor · New York, NY 10022 · 212-735-8600

Robert D. Sack · Gibson, Dunn & Crutcher · 200 Park Avenue · New York, NY 01066 · 212-351-4000

Robert G. Sugarman · Weil, Gotshal & Manges · 767 Fifth Avenue · New York, NY 10153 · 212-310-8000

John J. Walsh · Cadwalader, Wickersham & Taft · 100 Maiden Lane · New York, NY 10038 · 212-504-6000

Richard N. Winfield · Rogers & Wells · Pan Am Building · 200 Park Avenue · New York, NY 10166 · 212-878-8000

Melvin L. Wulf · Beldock Levine & Hoffman · 99 Park Avenue, 16th Floor · New York, NY 10016 · 212-490-0400

William S. Brandt · Nixon, Hargrave, Devans & Doyle · Clinton Square · P.O. Box 1051 · Rochester, NY 14603 · 716-546-8000

S. Paul Battaglia* · (Media) · Bond, Schoeneck & King · One Lincoln Center, 17th Floor · Syracuse, NY 13202-1355 · 315-422-0121

HEALTH CARE LAW

Robert H. Iseman · DeGraff, Foy, Conway, Holt-Harris & Mealey · 90 State Street · Albany, NY 12207 · 518-462-5301

Cornelius D. Murray · O'Connell & Aronowitz · 100 State Street · Albany, NY 12207 · 518-462-5601

Jeffrey J. Sherrin · Sherrin & Glasel · 74 North Pearl Street · Albany, NY 12207-2710 · 518-465-1275

Ellen V. Weissman · Hodgson, Russ, Andrews, Woods & Goodyear · 1800 One M&T Plaza · Buffalo, NY 14203-2391 · 716-856-4000

Norton L. Travis · Garfunkel, Wild & Travis · 175 Great Neck Road · Great Neck, NY 11021 · 516-466-3090

Robert A. Wild · Garfunkel, Wild & Travis · 175 Great Neck Road · Great Neck, NY 11021 · 516-466-3090

Jeffrey H. Becker · Epstein, Becker & Green · 250 Park Avenue · New York, NY 10177 · 212-351-4500

Peter G. Bergmann · (Nursing Homes) · Cadwalader, Wickersham & Taft · 100 Maiden Lane · New York, NY 10038 · 212-504-6000

William S. Bernstein · Kalkines, Arky, Zall & Bernstein · 1675 Broadway · New York, NY 10019 · 212-541-9090

Irwin M. Birnbaum · Proskauer Rose Goetz & Mendelsohn · 1585 Broadway · New York, NY 10036 · 212-969-3000

Robert P. Borsody · Epstein, Becker & Green · 250 Park Avenue · New York, NY 10177 · 212-351-4500

George Kalkines · Kalkines, Arky, Zall & Bernstein · 1675 Broadway · New York, NY 10019 · 212-541-9090

Robert M. Kaufman · Proskauer Rose Goetz & Mendelsohn · 1585 Broadway · New York, NY 10036 · 212-969-3000

Edward S. Kornreich · Proskauer Rose Goetz & Mendelsohn · 1585 Broadway · New York, NY 10036 · 212-969-3000

Bruce S. Wolff · (Nursing Homes) · McDermott, Will & Emery · 1211 Sixth Avenue, 43rd Floor · New York, NY 10036 · 212-768-5400

Rick J. Zall · Kalkines, Arky, Zall & Bernstein · 1675 Broadway · New York, NY 10019 · 212-541-9090

C. Richard Cole · Harter, Secrest & Emery · 700 Midtown Tower · Rochester, NY 14604-2070 · 716-232-6500

Judith M. Norman · Nixon, Hargrave, Devans & Doyle · Clinton Square · P.O. Box 1051 · Rochester, NY 14603 · 716-546-8000

Susan S. Robfogel · Nixon, Hargrave, Devans & Doyle · Clinton Square · P.O. Box 1051 · Rochester, NY 14603 · 716-546-8000

Sue S. Stewart · Nixon, Hargrave, Devans & Doyle · Clinton Square · P.O. Box 1051 · Rochester, NY 14603 · 716-546-8000

Eric Stonehill · Harris, Beach & Wilcox · The Granite Building · 130 East Main Street · Rochester, NY 14604 · 716-232-4440

William P. Burrows · Bond, Schoeneck & King · One Lincoln Center, 18th Floor Syracuse, NY 13202-1355 · 315-422-0121

IMMIGRATION LAW

Jules E. Coven · Lebenkoff & Coven · 505 Fifth Avenue · New York, NY 10017 212-687-3541

Austin T. Fragomen, Jr. · Fragomen, Del Ray & Bernsen · 515 Madison Avenue, 15th Floor · New York, NY 10022 · 212-688-8555

Benjamin Gim · Gim & Wong · 217 Park Row · New York, NY 10038 · 212-233-1088

Robert E. Juceam · Fried, Frank, Harris, Shriver & Jacobson · One New York Plaza · New York, NY 10004-1980 · 212-820-8000

Esther M. Kaufman · Law Offices of Esther M. Kaufman · 350 Broadway, Suite 210 · New York, NY 10013 · 212-431-8030

Stanley Mailman · Shatterlee, Stephens, Burke & Burke · 230 Park Avenue · New York, NY 10169 · 212-818-9200

Theodore Ruthizer · Winston & Strawn, Cole & Dietz · 175 Water Street · New York, NY 10038-4981 · 212-269-2500

Alan H. Wernick · Wernick & Berger · 335 Broadway, Suite 1103 · New York, NY 10013 · 212-925-6688

Leon Wildes · Wildes & Weinberg · 515 Madison Avenue · New York, NY 10017 212-753-3468

Margaret A. Catillaz · Harter, Secrest & Emery · 700 Midtown Tower · Rochester, NY 14604-2070 · 716-232-6500

INTELLECTUAL PROPERTY LAW

Edwin T. Bean · Hodgson, Russ, Andrews, Woods & Goodyear · 1800 One M&T Plaza · Buffalo, NY 14203-2391 · 716-856-4000

Daniel C. Oliverio · Sommer, Oliverio & Sommer · 920 Liberty Building · Buffalo, NY 14202 · 716-853-7761

Peter K. Sommer · Sommer, Oliverio & Sommer · 920 Liberty Building · Buffalo, NY 14202 · 716-853-7761

Robert J. Bernstein · (Copyright) · Cowan Liebowitz & Latman · 605 Third Avenue · New York, NY 10158 · 212-503-6200

Francis T. Carr · (Patent) · Kenyon & Kenyon · One Broadway · New York, NY 10004 · 212-425-7200

Richard Dannay · (Copyright) · Schwab, Goldberg, Price & Dannay · 1185 Avenue of the Americas · New York, NY 10036 · 212-575-8150

Marie V. Driscoll · (Trademark) · Robin, Blecker, Daley & Driscoll · 330 Madison Avenue · New York, NY 10017 · 212-682-9640

Albert E. Fey · (Patent) · Fish & Neave · 875 Third Avenue · New York, NY 10022 · 212-715-0600

Joseph M. Fitzpatrick · (Patent) · Fitzpatrick, Chella, Harper & Scinto · 277 Park Avenue · New York, NY 10172 · 212-758-2400

John D. Foley · (Patent) · Morgan & Finnegan · 345 Park Avenue · New York, NY 10154 · 212-758-4800

William J. Gilbreth · (Patent) · Fish & Neave · 875 Third Avenue · New York, NY 10022 · 212-715-0600

David Goldberg · (Trademark, Copyright) · Cowan, Liebowitz & Latman · 605 Third Avenue · New York, NY 10158 · 212-503-6250

Morton D. Goldberg · (Trademark, Copyright) · Schwab Goldberg Price & Dannay · 1185 Broadway · New York, NY 10036 · 212-575-8150

Arthur J. Greenbaum · (Trademark, Copyright) · Cowan Liebowitz & Latman · 605 Third Avenue · New York, NY 10158 · 212-503-6200

James F. Haley, Jr. · Fish & Neave · 875 Third Avenue · New York, NY 10022 212-715-0600

Jerome G. Lee · (Patent) · Morgan & Finnegan · 345 Park Avenue · New York, NY 10154 · 212-758-4800

Kenneth E. Madsen · (Patent) · Kenyon & Kenyon · One Broadway · New York, NY 10004 · 212-425-7200

Leslie S. Misrock · (Patent) · Pennies & Edmonds · 1155 Avenue of the Americas New York, NY 10036 · 212-790-9090

Robert C. Osterberg · (Copyright) · Abeles, Clark & Osterberg · 224 East 50th Street · New York, NY 10022 · 212-755-0812

Albert Robin · (Trademark) · Robin, Blecker, Daley & Driscoll · 330 Madison Avenue · New York, NY 10017 · 212-682-9640

Frank F. Scheck · (Patent) · Pennies & Edmonds · 1155 Avenue of the Americas New York, NY 10036 · 212-790-9090

Herbert F. Schwartz · (Patent) · Fish & Neave · 875 Third Avenue · New York, NY 10022 · 212-715-0600

Lawrence F. Scinto · (Patent) · Fitzpatrick, Chella, Harper & Scinto · 277 Park Avenue · New York, NY 10172 · 212-758-2400

John O. Tramontine · (Patent) · Fish & Neave · 875 Third Avenue · New York, NY 10022 · 212-715-0600

Alan Zelnick · (Trademark) · Weiss, Dawid, Fross, Zelnick & Lehrman · 633 Third Avenue · New York, NY 10017 · 212-953-9090

Roger Zissu · (Copyright, Trademark) · Weiss, Dawid, Fross, Zelnick & Lehrman · 633 Third Avenue · New York, NY 10017 · 212-953-9090

LABOR AND EMPLOYMENT LAW

Edward L. Bookstein · (Management) · Kohn, Bookstein & Karp · 90 State Street, Suite 929 · Albany, NY 12207 · 518-449-8810

Bruce C. Bramley* · (Labor) · Pozefsky, Bramley & Murphy · 90 State Street · Albany, NY 12207 · 518-434-2622

Richard C. Heffern · (Management) · Bond, Schoeneck & King · 111 Washington Avenue · Albany, NY 12210 · 518-462-7421

Melvin H. Osterman, Jr. · (Management) · Whiteman Osterman & Hanna · One Commerce Plaza · Albany, NY 12260 · 518-487-7600

William Pozefsky · (Labor) · Pozefsky, Bramley & Murphy · 90 State Street · Albany, NY 12207 · 518-434-2622

Richard R. Rowley · (Labor, Individuals) · Rowley, Forrest, O'Donnell & Hite 90 State Street · Albany, NY 12207 · 518-434-6187

Frank A. Nemia · (Management) · Twining, Nemia, Hill & Steflik · 53 Front Street · Binghamton, NY 13905 · 607-772-1700

Jeremy V. Cohen · (Management) · Flaherty, Cohen, Grande, Randazzo & Doren Firstmark Building · 135 Delaware Avenue, Suite 210 · Buffalo, NY 14202 · 716-853-7262

John F. Donovan · (Management) · Phillips, Lytle, Hitchcock, Blaine & Huber 3400 Marine Midland Center · Buffalo, NY 14203 · 716-847-8400

Robert A. Doren · (Management) · Flaherty, Cohen, Grande, Randazzo & Doren Firstmark Building · 135 Delaware Avenue, Suite 210 · Buffalo, NY 14202 · 716-853-7262

E. Joseph Giroux, Jr. · (Labor) · Law Offices of E. Joseph Giroux, Jr. · 181 Franklin Street · Buffalo, NY 14202 · 716-853-6300

Genuino J. Grande · (Management) · Flaherty, Cohen, Grande, Randazzo & Doren · Firstmark Building · 135 Delaware Avenue, Suite 210 · Buffalo, NY 14202 716-853-7262

David E. Hall · (Management) · Hodgson, Russ, Andrews, Woods & Goodyear · 1800 One M&T Plaza · Buffalo, NY 14203-2391 · 716-856-4000

Ronald L. Jaros · (Labor) · Lipsitz, Green, Fahringer, Roll, Salisbury & Cambria 42 Delaware Avenue, Suite 300 · Buffalo, NY 14202-3901 · 716-849-1333

Richard Lipsitz · (Labor) · Lipsitz, Green, Fahringer, Roll, Salisbury & Cambria 42 Delaware Avenue, Suite 300 · Buffalo, NY 14202-3901 · 716-849-1333

Randall M. Odza · (Management) · Jaeckle, Fleischmann & Mugel · 800 Norstar Building · 12 Fountain Plaza · Buffalo, NY 14202 · 716-856-0600

Edward G. Piwowarczyk · (Management) · Jaeckle, Fleischmann & Mugel · 800 Norstar Building · 12 Fountain Plaza · Buffalo, NY 14202 · 716-856-0600

Joseph L. Randazzo · (Management) · Flaherty Cohen Grande Randazzo Doren Firstmark Building · 135 Delaware Avenue, Suite 210 · Buffalo, NY 14202 · 716-853-7262

Eugene W. Salisbury* · (Labor, Individuals) · Lipsitz, Green, Fahringer, Roll, Salisbury & Cambria · 42 Delaware Avenue, Suite 300 · Buffalo, NY 14202-3901 716-849-1333

James N. Schmit · (Management) · Damon & Morey · 1000 Cathedral Place · 298 Main Street · Buffalo, NY 14202-4096 · 716-856-5500

W. James Schwan · (Labor, Individuals) · Wyssling, Schwan & Montgomery · 1230 Delaware Avenue · Buffalo, NY 14209-1430 · 716-882-2243

Brian J. Troy · (Management) · Jaeckle, Fleischmann & Mugel · 800 Norstar Building · 12 Fountain Plaza · Buffalo, NY 14202 · 716-865-0600

Robert M. Walker · (Management) · Hodgson, Russ, Andrews, Woods & Goodyear · 1800 One M&T Plaza · Buffalo, NY 14203-2391 · 716-856-4000

Martin F. Idzik · (Management) · Phillips, Lytle, Hitchcock, Blaine & Huber · 307 Chase Lincoln First Bank Building · P.O. Box 1279 · Jamestown, NY 14702-1279 · 716-664-3906

Albert X. Bader, Jr. · (Management) · Simpson Thacher & Bartlett · 425 Lexington Avenue · New York, NY 10017-3909 · 212-455-2000

Charles G. Bakaly, Jr. · (Management) · O'Melveny & Myers · 153 East 53rd Street, 53rd Floor · New York, NY 10022-4611 · 212-326-2000

L. Robert Batterman · (Management) · Proskauer Rose Goetz & Mendelsohn · 1585 Broadway · New York, NY 10036 · 212-969-3000

Warren J. Bennia · (Individuals) · 507 East 80th Street · New York, NY 10021 · 212-744-2020

Michael I. Bernstein · (Management) · Benetar Bernstein Schair & Stein · 330 Madison Avenue · New York, NY 10017 · 212-697-4433

Stuart H. Bompey · (Management) · Baer Marks & Upham · 805 Third Avenue New York, NY 10022-7513 · 212-702-5853

John D. Canoni* · (Management) · Townley & Updike · Chrysler Building · 405 Lexington Avenue · New York, NY 10174 · 212-682-4567

Marvin Dicker · (Management) · Proskauer Rose Goetz & Mendelsohn · 1585 Broadway · New York, NY 10036 · 212-969-3000

Eugene G. Eisner · (Labor) · Eisner, Levy, Pollack & Ratner · 113 University Place, Eighth Floor · New York, NY 10003-4588 · 212-473-1122

Sheldon Engelhard · (Labor) · Vladeck, Waldman, Elias & Engelhard · 1501 Broadway · New York, NY 10036 · 212-354-8330

Allen I. Fagin · (Management) · Proskauer Rose Goetz & Mendelsohn · 1585 Broadway · New York, NY 10036 · 212-969-3000

Leonard N. Flamm* · (Individuals) · 880 Third Avenue · New York, NY 10022 212-752-3380

Eugene S. Friedman* · (Labor) · Friedman & Levy-Warren · 1500 Broadway, Suite 2303 · New York, NY 10036-4015 · 212-354-4500

Howard L. Ganz · (Management) · Proskauer Rose Goetz & Mendelsohn · 1585 Broadway · New York, NY 10036 · 212-969-3000

Amy Gladstein · (Labor, Individuals) · Gladstein, Reis & Meginniss · 361 Broadway, Suite 610 · New York, NY 10013 · 212-941-6161

Janice Goodman* · (Individuals) · 500 Fifth Avenue, Suite 5530 · New York, NY 10110 · 212-869-1940

Kenneth E. Gordon* · (Labor, Individuals, Civil Rights) · Gordon & Gordon · Three Park Avenue, 28th Floor · New York, NY 10016 · 212-725-3700

Ronald M. Green · (Management) · Epstein, Becker & Green · 250 Park Avenue, 14th Floor · New York, NY 10177 · 212-370-9800

Jerold D. Jacobson · (Management) · Patterson, Belknap, Webb & Tyler · 30 Rockefeller Plaza · New York, NY 10112 · 212-698-2500

Mark A. Jacoby · (Management) · Weil, Gotschal & Manges · 767 Fifth Avenue New York, NY 10153 · 212-310-8000

Alan S. Jaffe · (Management) · Proskauer Rose Goetz & Mendelsohn · 1585 Broadway · New York, NY 10036 · 212-969-3000

Jerome B. Kauff · (Management) · Dretzin, Kauff, McClain & McGuire · 950 Third Avenue, 15th Floor · New York, NY 10022 · 212-644-1010

Saul G. Kramer · (Management) · Proskauer Rose Goetz & Mendelsohn · 1585 Broadway · New York, NY 10036 · 212-969-3000

William A. Krupman · (Management) · Jackson, Lewis, Schnitzler & Krupman · 261 Madison Avenue · New York, NY 10016 · 212-697-8200

Leonard Leibowitz · (Labor) · 400 Madison Avenue · New York, NY 10017 · 212-593-3310

Richard A. Levy* · (Labor) · Eisner, Levy, Pollack & Ratner · 113 University Place, Eighth Floor · New York, NY 10003-4588 · 212-473-1122

Everett E. Lewis · (Labor) · Lewis, Greenwald, Kennedy & Lewis · 232 West 40th Street · New York, NY 10018 · 212-382-0029

Walter M. Meginniss · (Labor, Individuals) · Gladstein, Reis & Meginniss · 361 Broadway, Suite 610 · New York, NY 10013 · 212-941-6161

Martin J. Oppenheimer · (Management) · Proskauer Rose Goetz & Mendelsohn 1585 Broadway · New York, NY 10036 · 212-969-3000

Wayne N. Outten · (Individuals) · Lankenau & Bickford · 1740 Broadway, 25th Floor · New York, NY 10019 · 212-489-8230

Peter M. Panken · (Management) · Parker Chapin Flattau & Klimpl · 1211 Avenue of the Americas · New York, NY 10036 · 212-704-6000

Bertrand B. Pogrebin · (Management) · Rains & Pogrebin · 425 Park Avenue · New York, NY 10022 · 212-980-3560

Gregory I. Rasin · (Management) · Jackson, Lewis, Schnitzler & Krupman · 261 Madison Avenue · New York, NY 10016 · 212-697-8200

Eric Rosenfeld* · (Management) · Seyfarth, Shaw, Fairweather & Geraldson · 767 Third Avenue · New York, NY 10017-2013 · 212-715-9000

Stanley Schair · (Management) · Benetar Bernstein Schair & Stein · 330 Madison Avenue · New York, NY 10017 · 212-697-4433

Martin C. Seham · (Management) · Seham, Klein & Zelman · 485 Madison Avenue, 15th Floor · New York, NY 10022 · 212-935-6020

Martin N. Silberman · (Individuals) · Silberman & Rhine · 35 Worth Street, Fourth Floor · New York, NY 10013 · 212-219-2100

Edward Silver · (Management) · Proskauer Rose Goetz & Mendelsohn · 1585 Broadway · New York, NY 10036 · 212-969-3000

Bruce H. Simon · (Labor) · Cohen, Weiss and Simon · 330 West 42nd Street · New York, NY 10036 · 212-563-4100

I. Philip Sipser · (Labor) · Sipser, Weinstock, Harper & Dorn · 380 Madison Avenue · New York, NY 10017 · 212-867-2100

Lewis M. Steel* · (Employment Discrimination) · Steel, Bellman & Ritz · 351 Broadway · New York, NY 10013 · 212-925-7400

Jerome Y. Sturm · (Labor) · Sturm and Perl · 21 East 40th Street · New York, NY 10016 · 212-685-8487

Judith P. Vladeck · (Labor, Individuals) · Vladeck, Waldman, Elias & Engelhard 1501 Broadway · New York, NY 10036 · 212-354-8330

Jay W. Waks* · (Management) · Kaye, Scholer, Fierman, Hays & Handler · 425 Park Avenue · New York, NY 10023 · 212-836-8000

Seymour M. Waldman · (Labor) · Vladeck, Waldman, Elias & Engelhard · 1501 Broadway · New York, NY 10036 · 212-354-8330

Henry Weiss · (Labor) · Cohen, Weiss and Simon · 330 West 42nd Street · New York, NY 10036 · 212-563-4100

Richard N. Chapman · (Management) · Harris Beach & Wilcox · The Granite Building · 130 East Main Street · Rochester, NY 14604 · 716-232-4440

Thomas G. Dignan · (Management) · Nixon, Hargrave, Devans & Doyle · Clinton Square · P.O. Box 1051 · Rochester, NY 14603 · 716-546-8000

Michael T. Harren · (Labor, Individuals) · Chamberlain, D'Amanda, Oppenheimer and Greenfield · 1600 Crossroads Building · Two State Street · Rochester, NY 14614 · 716-232-3730

Carl R. Krause · (Management) · Harris, Beach & Wilcox · The Granite Building 130 East Main Street · Rochester, NY 14604 · 716-232-4440

Emmelyn S. Logan-Baldwin · (Individuals, Employment) · Century Row, Suite 400 · 171 State Street · Rochester, NY 14614 · 716-232-2292

Gerald L. Paley · (Management) · Phillips, Lytle, Hitchcock, Blaine & Huber · 1400 First Federal Plaza · Rochester, NY 14614 · 716-238-2000

Susan Robfogel · (Management) · Nixon, Hargrave, Devans & Doyle · Clinton Square · P.O. Box 1051 · Rochester, NY 14603 · 716-546-8000

Jules L. Smith* · Blitman and King · The Fitch Building, Suite 200 · 315 Alexander Street · Rochester, NY 14604 · 716-232-5600

Peter G. Smith · Harter, Secrest & Emery · 700 Midtown Tower · Rochester, NY 14604-2070 · 716-232-6500

Eugene D. Ulterino* · (Management) · Nixon, Hargrave, Devans & Doyle · Clinton Square · P.O. Box 1051 · Rochester, NY 14603 · 716-546-8000

Franklin H. Goldberger · (Management) · Ogletree, Deakins, Nash, Smoak & Stewart · 215 State Street · Schenectady, NY 12305 · 518-374-4029

William L. Bergan · (Management) · Bond, Schoeneck & King · One Lincoln Center, 16th Floor · Syracuse, NY 13202-1355 · 315-422-0121

Earl P. Boyle · (Labor) · Boyle & Cantone · University Building, Suite 731 · 120 East Washington Street · Syracuse, NY 13202 · 315-422-2208

W. Carroll Coyne · (Management) · Hancock & Estabrook · One Mony Plaza, 14th Floor · 100 Madison Street · P.O. Box 4976 · Syracuse, NY 13221-4976 · 315-471-3151

Bernard T. King · (Labor) · Blitman and King · The 500 Building, Suite 1100 · 500 South Salina Street · Syracuse, NY 13202 · 315-422-7111

Robert W. Kopp · (Management) · Bond, Schoeneck & King · One Lincoln Center, 16th Floor · Syracuse, NY 13202-1355 · 315-422-0121

James R. LaVaute · (Labor, Individuals) · Blitman and King · The 500 Building, Suite 1100 · 500 South Salina Street · Syracuse, NY 13202 · 315-422-7111

Raymond W. Murray, Jr. · (Management) · Bond, Schoeneck & King · One Lincoln Center, 16th Floor · Syracuse, NY 13202-1355 · 315-422-0121

Patrick L. Vaccaro · (Management) · Jackson, Lewis, Schnitzler & Krupman · One North Broadway, Suite 1502 · White Plains, NY 10601 · 914-328-0404

MARITIME LAW

Richard G. Ashworth · Haight, Gardner, Poor & Havens · 195 Broadway, 24th Floor · New York, NY 10007 · 212-341-7000

Richard B. Barnett · Haight, Gardner, Poor & Havens · 195 Broadway, 24th Floor New York, NY 10007 · 212-341-7000

R. Glenn Bauer* · (Charter Parties) · Haight, Gardner, Poor & Havens · 195 Broadway, 24th Floor · New York, NY 10007 · 212-341-7000

Arthur J. Blank, Jr. · Hill, Betts & Nash · One World Trade Center, Suite 5215 New York, NY 10048 · 212-839-7000

Lawrence Bowles · Nourse & Bowles · One Exchange Plaza at 55 Broadway · New York, NY 10006 · 212-952-6200

Richard H. Brown, Jr.* · (Ship Collision) · Kirlin, Campbell & Keating · 14 Wall Street, 23rd Floor · New York, NY 10005 · 212-732-5520

Raymond J. Burke, Jr. · (Charter Parties Marine Insurance) · Burke & Parsons · 1114 Avenue of the Americas, 34th Floor · New York, NY 10036 · 212-354-3800

Francis X. Byrn* · Haight, Gardner, Poor & Havens · 195 Broadway, 24th Floor New York, NY 10007 · 212-341-7000

Stephen K. Carr · Haight, Gardner, Poor & Havens · 195 Broadway, 24th Floor New York, NY 10007 · 212-341-7000

Michael Marks Cohen* · (Charter Parties) · Burlingham Underwood & Lord · One Battery Park Plaza, 25th Floor · New York, NY 10004-1484 · 212-422-7585

Leroy S. Corsa · Walker & Corsa · One Wall Street Court · New York, NY 10005 212-344-4700

M. E. DeOrchis · DeOrchis & Partners · 71 Broadway, Suite 2200 · New York, NY 10006 · 212-425-9797

Vincent M. DeOrchis* · (Charter Parties, Cargo, Hull) · DeOrchis & Partners · 71 Broadway, Suite 2200 · New York, NY 10006 · 212-425-9797

Steve C. Dune · Cadwalader, Wickersham & Taft · 100 Maiden Lane · New York, NY 10038 · 212-504-6000

Emery W. Harper · (Ship Financing) · Lord Day & Lord, Barrett Smith · 1675 Broadway · New York, NY 10019 · 212-969-6000

Nicholas J. Healy · Healy & Baillie · 29 Broadway, 25th Floor · New York, NY 10006 · 212-943-3980

Chester D. Hooper · Haight, Gardner, Poor & Havens · 195 Broadway, 24th Floor New York, NY 10007 · 212-341-7000

Franklin G. Hunt · Lord Day & Lord, Barrett Smith · 1675 Broadway · New York, NY 10019 · 212-969-6000

John G. Ingram · Burlingham Underwood & Lord · One Battery Park Plaza, 25th Floor · New York, NY 10004-1484 · 212-422-7585

Douglas A. Jacobsen* · (Charter Parties, Casualty & Collision) · Bigham Englar Jones & Houston · 14 Wall Street · New York, NY 10005-2140 · 212-732-4646

Marshall P. Keating · Kirlin, Campbell & Keating · 14 Wall Street, 23rd Floor · New York, NY 10005 · 212-732-5520

John D. Kimball · Healy & Baillie · 29 Broadway · New York, NY 10006 · 212-943-3980

Alan S. Loesberg · Hill Rivkins Loesberg O'Brien Mulroy & Hayden · 21 West Street · New York, NY 10006 · 212-825-1000

Herbert M. Lord · Burlingham Underwood & Lord · One Battery Park Plaza, 25th Floor · New York, NY 10004-1484 · 212-422-7585

David L. Maloof · Badiak, Will & Maloof · 90 John Street, Suite 1703 · New York, NY 10038 · 212-791-9696

David A. Nourse · Nourse & Bowles · One Exchange Plaza at 55 Broadway · New York, NY 10006 · 212-952-6200

Francis J. O'Brien · Hill Rivkins Loesberg O'Brien Mulroy & Hayden · 21 West Street · New York, NY 10006 · 212-825-1000

Gordon W. Paulsen · Healy & Baillie · 29 Broadway, 25th Floor · New York, NY 10006 · 212-943-3980

John G. Poles · Poles, Tublin, Patestides & Stratakis · 46 Trinity Place, Fifth Floor · New York, NY 10006 · 212-943-0110

Richard E. Repetto* · Donovan Parry Walsh & Repetto · 161 William Street · New York, NY 10038-2681 · 212-964-3553

Richard H. Sommer* · (Charter Parties, Ship Financing, Arbitration, Bills of Landing) · Kirlin, Campbell & Keating · 14 Wall Street, 23rd Floor · New York, NY 10005 · 212-732-5520

Brian D. Starer · Haight, Gardner, Poor & Havens · 195 Broadway, 24th Floor · New York, NY 10007 · 212-341-7000

Bernard J. Tansey · Mendes & Mount · Three Park Avenue · New York, NY 10016 · 212-951-2200

Charles L. Trowbridge · Walker & Corsa · One Wall Street Court · New York, NY 10005 · 212-344-4700

Melvin J. Tublin · Poles, Tublin, Patestides & Stratakis · 46 Trinity Place, Fifth Floor · New York, NY 10006 · 212-943-0110

Kenneth H. Volk* · Burlingham Underwood & Lord · One Battery Park Plaza, 25th Floor · New York, NY 10004-1484 · 212-422-7585

Donald M. Waesche, Jr. · Waesche, Sheinbaum & O'Regan · 111 Broadway, Fourth Floor · New York, NY 10006 · 212-227-3550

Richard H. Webber · Hill Rivkins Loesberg O'Brien Mulroy & Hayden · 21 West Street · New York, NY 10006 · 212-825-1000

NATURAL RESOURCES AND ENVIRONMENTAL LAW

Richard F. Griffin · (Oil & Gas) · Phillips, Lytle, Hitchcock, Blaine & Huber · 3400 Marine Midland Center · Buffalo, NY 14202 · 716-847-7082

Donald W. Stever · Sidley & Austin · 875 Third Avenue · New York, NY 10022 · 212-906-2000

Steven A. Tasher* · (Water, Solid Waste, Hazardous Waste, Impact of Environmental Law on Real Estate & Business Transactions) · Willkie Farr & Gallagher · One Citicorp Center · 153 Fifty-Third Street · New York, NY 10022-4669 · 212-935-8000

Neal D. Madden · Harter, Secrest & Emery · 700 Midtown Tower · Rochester, NY 14604-2070 · 716-232-6500

PERSONAL INJURY LITIGATION

Stephen R. Coffey · (Plaintiffs) · O'Connell and Aronowitz · 100 State Street, Eighth Floor · Albany, NY 12207 · 518-462-5601

Mae A. D'Agostino · (Defendants) · Maynard, O'Connor & Smith · 80 State Street · Albany, NY 12207 · 518-465-3553

John T. DeGraff, Jr.* · (Plaintiffs) · DeGraff, Foy, Conway, Holt-Harris & Mealey · 90 State Street · Albany, NY 12207 · 518-462-5301

Richard M. Gershon* · (Defendants, Medical Malpractice, Products Liability, Professional Malpractice) · Thorn & Gershon · 19 Aviation Road · Albany, NY 12205 · 518-459-8971

John K. Powers* · (Plaintiffs, Medical Malpractice, Products Liability, Automobile Collision) · Powers & Santola · 600 Broadway · Albany, NY 12207 · 518-465-5995

Daniel R. Santola · (Plaintiffs) · Powers & Santola · 600 Broadway · Albany, NY 12207 · 518-465-5995

Lee S. Michaels* · (Plaintiffs) · 71 South Street · P.O. Box 308 · Auburn, NY 13021 · 315-253-3293

Sanford P. Tanenhaus · (Plaintiffs, Defendants) · Chernin & Gold · Bache Building · 71 State Street · P.O. Box 1563 · Binghamton, NY 13902 · 607-723-9581

Carlton F. Thompson · (Defendants) · Levene, Gouldin & Thompson · 902 Press Building · P.O. Box F-1706 · Binghamton, NY 13902 · 607-772-9200

Joseph M. Irom · (Plaintiffs) · Irom & Wittels · 349 East 149th Street · Bronx, NY 10451 · 212-665-0220

Paul W. Beltz · (Plaintiffs) · 36 Church Street · Buffalo, NY 14202 · 716-852-0111

John F. Canale · (Defendants) · Canale, Madden and Burke · 43 Court Street, Suite 530 · Buffalo, NY 14202 · 716-853-7100

David K. Floyd · (Defendants) · Phillips, Lytle, Hitchcock, Blaine & Huber · 3400 Marine Midland Center · Buffalo, NY 14203 · 716-847-8400

George M. Gibson* · (Defendants) · Gibson, McAskill & Crobsy · Chemical Bank Building, Suite 900 · 69 Delaware Avenue · Buffalo, NY 14202 · 716-856-4200

Carl A. Green · (Plaintiffs) · Lipsitz, Green, Fahringer, Roll, Salisbury & Cambria 42 Delaware Avenue, Suite 300 · Buffalo, NY 14202-3901 · 716-849-1333

Richard F. Griffin* · (Defendants, Plaintiffs, Product Liability, Railroad) · Phillips, Lytle, Hitchcock, Blaine & Huber · 3400 Marine Midland Center · Buffalo, NY 14202 · 716-847-7082

Sheldon Hurwitz · (Defendants) · Hurwitz & Fine · 1400 Liberty Building · Buffalo, NY 14202 · 716-853-6100

Philip H. Magner, Jr.* · (Plaintiffs, Medical Malpractice, Professional Malpractice, Automobile Collision) · Magner, Love & Morris · 1725 Statler Towers · Buffalo, NY 14202 · 716-856-8480

James S. McAskill · (Defendants) · Gibson, McAskill & Crosby · 900 Chemical Bank Building · 69 Delaware Avenue · Buffalo, NY 14202 · 716-856-4200

Samuel R. Miserendino · (Plaintiffs) · Miserendino, Krull & Foley · 964 Ellicott Square Building · Buffalo, NY 14203 · 716-854-1002

William S. Reynolds · (Defendants) · O'Shea, Reynolds, Napier, Cummings & Kirby · 181 Franklin Street · Buffalo, NY 14202 · 716-853-6341

Daniel T. Roach* · (Defendants) · Maloney, Gallup, Roach, Brown & McCarthy 1620 Liberty Building · 420 Main Street · Buffalo, NY 14202 · 716-852-0400

Terry D. Smith* · (Plaintiffs, Medical Malpractice, Products Liability, Automobile Collision) · Smith, Keller, Hayes & Miner · 1212 Chemical Bank Building · 69 Delaware Avenue · Buffalo, NY 14202 · 716-855-3611

Terry D. Smith · (Plaintiffs) · Smith, Keller, Hayes & Miner · 69 Delaware Avenue, Suite 1212 · Buffalo, NY 14202 · 716-855-3611

Emmet J. Agoglia · Agoglia, Fassberg, Magee & Crowe · 80 East Old Country Road · Mineola, NY 11501 · 516-741-2422

James P. Barrett · (Defendants) · Simpson Thacher & Bartlett · 425 Lexington Avenue · New York, NY 10017-3909 · 212-455-2000

Francis P. Bensel · (Defendants) · Martin, Clearwater & Bell · 220 East 42nd Street · New York, NY 10017 · 212-697-3122

Sheila L. Birnbaum · (Defendants) · Skadden, Arps, Slate, Meagher & Flom · 919 Third Avenue · New York, NY 10022-3897 · 212-735-3000

John J. Bower* · (Defendants) · Bower & Gardner · 110 East 59th Street · New York, NY 10022 · 212-751-2900

Robert L. Conason · (Plaintiffs) · Gair, Gair & Conason · 80 Pine Street · New York, NY 10005 · 212-943-1090

Joseph M. Costello · (Defendants) · Costello & Shea · One Battery Park Plaza · New York, NY 10004 · 212-483-9600

Peter E. De Blasio* · (Plaintiffs, Medical Malpractice, Professional Malpractice, Airplane Collision) · De Blasio & Alton · 233 Broadway, 43rd Floor · New York, NY 10279 · 212-732-2620

Stanley D. Friedman* · (Defendants) · McAloon, Friedman & Mandell · 116 John Street, 29th Floor · New York, NY 10038 · 212-732-8700

John Gardner · (Defendants) · Bower & Gardner · 110 East 59th Street · New York, NY 10022 · 212-751-2900

Richard Godosky · Damashek, Godosky & Gentile · 35 Worth Street · New York, NY 10013 · 212-431-9100

Peter James Johnson · Leahey & Johnson · 120 Wall Street, Suite 2220 · New York, NY 10005 · 212-269-7308

Gunther H. Kilsch · (Defendants) · McAloon, Friedman & Mandell · 116 John Street, 29th Floor · New York, NY 10038 · 212-732-8700

Norman J. Landau · (Plaintiffs) · Landau & Miller · 233 Broadway · New York, NY 10279-0048 · 212-962-7545

Roger P. McTiernan · (Defendants) · Barry, McTiernan & Moore · 22 Cortlandt Street, Ninth Floor · New York, NY 10007 · 212-964-4270

David G. Miller* · (Plaintiffs) · Gair, Gair, Conason, Steigman & Mackauf · 80 Pine Street · New York, NY 10005 · 212-943-1090

Donald Miller* · (Plaintiffs, Medical Malpractice, Products Liability, Automobile Collision) · Landau & Miller · 233 Broadway · New York, NY 10279-0048 · 212-962-7545

Thomas A. Moore · (Plaintiffs) · Kramer, Dillof, Tessel, Duffy & Moore · 233 Broadway, 45th Floor · New York, NY 10279 · 212-267-4177

Luke M. Pittoni · (Defendants) · Heidell, Pittoni, Murphy & Bach · 99 Park Avenue, Seventh Floor · New York, NY 10016 · 212-286-8585

Fred Queller* · (Plaintiffs, Medical Malpractice, Products Liability, Automobile Collision) · Queller, Fisher & Wisotsky · 110 Wall Street · New York, NY 10005 212-422-3600

Roy L. Reardon · (Defendants) · Simpson Thacher & Bartlett · 425 Lexington Avenue · New York, NY 10017-3909 · 212-455-2000

Ivan S. Schneider · (Plaintiffs) · Schneider, Kleinick & Weitz · 11 Park Place, 10th Floor · New York, NY 10007 · 212-962-1780

Harold L. Schwab* · (Defendants, Products Liability) · Lester Schwab Katz & Dwyer · 120 Broadway · New York, NY 10271 · 212-964-6611

Robert G. Sullivan · (Plaintiffs) · Sullivan & Liapakis · 100 Church Street · New York, NY 10007 · 212-732-9000

George G. Van Setter · (Defendants) · Martin, Clearwater & Bell · 220 East 42nd Street · New York, NY 10017 · 212-697-3122

Edwin N. Weidman · (Plaintiffs) · 150 Broadway · New York, NY 10038 · 212-349-4123

Harvey Weitz · (Plaintiffs) · Schneider, Kleinick & Weitz · 11 Park Place, 10th Floor · New York, NY 10007 · 212-962-1780

Angelo G. Faraci · (Plaintiffs) · Faraci, Guadagnino, Lange & Johns · 45 Exchange Street · Rochester, NY 14614 · 716-325-5150

Alexander Geiger · (Plaintiffs) · Geiger and Rothenberg · 800 Times Square Building · 45 Exchange Street · Rochester, NY 14614 · 716-232-1946

David M. Lascell* · (Defendants, Products Liability, Appellate) · Nixon, Hargrave, Devans & Doyle · Clinton Square · P.O. Box 1051 · Rochester, NY 14603 716-546-8000

James C. Moore* · (Defendants, Products Liability, Professional Malpractice) · Harter, Secrest & Emery · 700 Midtown Tower · Rochester, NY 14604-2070 · 716-232-6500

Anthony R. Palermo · (Products Liability) · Harter, Secrest & Emery · 700 Midtown Tower · Rochester, NY 14604-2070 · 716-232-6500

Norman A. Palmiere · (Plaintiffs) · Palmiere & Pellegrino · Chapin Building, Third Floor · 205 St. Paul Street · Rochester, NY 14604 · 716-232-6144

David Rothenberg · (Plaintiffs) · Geiger and Rothenberg · 800 Times Square Building · 45 Exchange Street · Rochester, NY 14614 · 716-232-1946

Jeffrey M. Wilkens* · (Defendants, Medical Malpractice, Products Liability, Professional Malpractice) · Osborn, Reed, Van de Vate & Burke · Watts Building, Fourth Floor · 47 South Fitzhugh Street · Rochester, NY 14614 · 716-454-6480

S. Paul Battaglia* · (Defendants) · Bond, Schoeneck & King · One Lincoln Center, 17th Floor · Syracuse, NY 13202-1355 · 315-422-0121

Irwin Birnbaum* · (Plaintiffs, Medical Malpractice, Products Liability, Automobile Collision, Airplane Collision) · Birnbaum McDermott & Friedman · 300 Lowe's Landmark · 108 West Jefferson Street, Suite 300 · Syracuse, NY 13202-2507 · 315-422-0246

John C. Cherundolo · (Plaintiffs) · Cherundolo, Bottar & Del Duchetto · One Lincoln Center, Suite 1180 · Syracuse, NY 13202 · 315-422-3466

John J. Dee* · (Plaintiffs) · Bond, Schoeneck & King · One Lincoln Center, 15th Floor · Syracuse, NY 13202-1355 · 315-422-0121

Hilbert I. Greene · Greene, Hershdorfer & Sharpe · The 500 Building, Suite 830 500 South Salina Street · Syracuse, NY 13202 · 315-422-6154

Paul M. Hanrahan* · (Plaintiffs, Defendants, Medical Malpractice, Products Liability) · Hancock & Estabrook · One Mony Plaza, 14th Floor · 100 Madison Street P.O. Box 4976 · Syracuse, NY 13221-4976 · 315-471-3151

William F. Lynn · (Plaintiffs) · Lynn Law Office · 802 Onondaga Bank Building Syracuse, NY 13202-4983 · 315-474-1267

Kevin M. Reilly* · (Defendants, Products Liability, Automobile Collision) · Mackenzie Smith Lewis Michell & Hughes · 600 Onondaga Savings Bank Building · P.O. Box 4967 · Syracuse, NY 13221-4967 · 315-474-7571

Edward C. Schepp · (Plaintiffs) · 500 State Tower Building · Syracuse, NY 13202 315-428-1111

Laurence F. Sovik* · (Defendants, Medical Malpractice, Products Liability, Professional Malpractice) · Smith, Sovik, Kendrick, Schwarzer & Sugnet · 300 Empire Building · 472 South Salina Street · Syracuse, NY 13202-2473 · 315-474-2911

E. Stewart Jones, Jr.* · Jones Building · 28 Second Street · Troy, NY 12181 · 518-274-5820

Henry G. Miller · (Plaintiffs) · Clark, Gagliardi & Miller · Inns of Court Building 99 Court Street · White Plains, NY 10601 · 914-946-8900

PUBLIC UTILITY LAW

David E. Blabey · Hiscock & Barclay · One Keycorp Plaza, Suite 1100 · 30 South Pearl Street · Albany, NY 12207-3411 · 518-434-2163

William T. Baker, Jr. · Reid & Priest · 40 West 57th Street · New York, NY 10019 212-603-2000

M. Douglas Dunn · Milbank, Tweed, Hadley & McCloy · One Chase Manhattan Plaza · New York, NY 10005-1413 · 212-530-5000

David P. Falck · Winthrop, Stimson, Putnam & Roberts · One Battery Park Plaza New York, NY 10004-1490 · 212-858-1000

Ronald D. Jones · LeBoeuf, Lamb, Leiby & MacRae · 520 Madison Avenue · New York, NY 10022 · 212-715-8000

K. William Kolbe · (Public Utility Tax Matters) · Reid & Priest · 40 West 57th Street · New York, NY 10019 · 212-603-2000

Robert G. Schuur · Reid & Priest · 40 West 57th Street · New York, NY 10019 212-603-2000

Samuel M. Sugden · (Electric) · LeBoeuf, Lamb, Leiby & MacRae · 520 Madison Avenue · New York, NY 10022 · 212-715-8000

Steven K. Waite · Winthrop, Stimson, Putnam & Roberts · One Battery Park Plaza · New York, NY 10004-1490 · 212-858-1000

Michael T. Tomaino · Nixon, Hargrave, Devans & Doyle · Clinton Square · P.O. Box 1051 · Rochester, NY 14603 · 716-546-8000

REAL ESTATE LAW

Lawrence F. Anito, Jr. · Helm, Shapiro, Anito & Aldrich · 111 Washington Avenue · Albany, NY 12210 · 518-465-7563

Harold C. Hanson · Hinman, Straub, Pigors & Manning · 121 State Street · Albany, NY 12207-1622 · 518-436-0751

John W. Tabner* · (Zoning, Assessment Litigation) · Tabner and Laudato · 26 Computer Drive West · P.O. Box 12605 · Albany, NY 12212-2605 · 518-459-9000

Edward J. Trombly · Hiscock & Barclay · One Keycorp Plaza, Suite 1100 · 30 South Pearl Street · Albany, NY 12207-3411 · 518-434-2163

Peter J. Battaglia · Williams, Stevens, McCarville & Frizzell · 1920 Liberty Building · Buffalo, NY 14202 · 716-856-2112

Marvin R. Baum · 1400 Statler Towers · Buffalo, NY 14202 · 716-847-8800

George R. Grasser · Phillips, Lytle, Hitchcock, Blaine & Huber · 3400 Marine Midland Center · Buffalo, NY 14203 · 716-847-8400

F. William Gray III · Hodgson, Russ, Andrews, Woods & Goodyear · 1800 One M&T Plaza · Buffalo, NY 14203-2391 · 716-856-4000

Franklin Pack · (Commercial Transactions, Industrial Transactions, Real Estate Taxation, Developing & Subdividing Land for Building) · Pack, Hartman, Ball & Huckabone · 230 Brisbane Building · Buffalo, NY 14203 · 716-856-9533

Michael M. Blinkoff · Blinkoff, Viksjo, Robinson & Saeli · 2746 Delaware Avenue Kenmore, NY 14217 · 716-875-8916

Jack Adelman · Cadwalader, Wickersham & Taft · 100 Maiden Lane · New York, NY 10038 · 212-504-6000

Steven M. Alden · Debevoise & Plimpton · 875 Third Avenue · New York, NY 10022 · 212-909-6000

Alan J. B. Aronsohn · Robinson, Silverman, Pearce, Aronsohn & Berman · 1290 Avenue of the Americas · New York, NY 10104 · 212-541-2000

Franklin L. Bass · Fried, Frank, Harris, Shriver & Jacobson · One New York Plaza · New York, NY 10004-1980 · 212-820-8000

Donald A. Bettex · Wien, Malkin & Bettex · Lincoln Building · 60 East 42nd Street, 48th Floor · New York, NY 10165-0015 · 212-687-8700

Leonard Boxer · (Real Property Tax Certiorari) · Stroock & Stroock & Lavan · Seven Hanover Square · New York, NY 10004-2594 · 212-806-5400

John D. Cohen · Tenzer, Greenblatt, Fallon & Kaplan · The Chrysler Building 405 Lexington Avenue · New York, NY 10174 · 212-573-4300

Robert M. Feely · Shearman & Sterling · Citicorp Center · 153 East 53rd Street New York, NY 10022 · 212-848-4000

Charles A. Goldstein · (Commercial Transactions, Industrial Transactions, Real Estate Financing, International Transactions) · Shea & Gould · 1251 Avenue of the Americas · New York, NY 10020-1193 · 212-827-3000

Philip H. Hedges · White & Case · 1155 Avenue of the Americas · New York, NY 10036 · 212-819-8200

Samuel W. Ingram, Jr. · Hutton, Ingram, Yuzek, Gainen, Carroll & Bertolotti · 530 Fifth Avenue · New York, NY 10036 · 212-642-0800

William M. Kufeld · Carb, Luria, Glassner, Cook & Kufeld · 529 Fifth Avenue · New York, NY 10017 · 212-986-3131

Anthony B. Kuklin · Paul, Weiss, Rifkind, Wharton & Garrison · 1285 Avenue of the Americas · New York, NY 10019-6064 · 212-373-3000

Walter F. Leinhardt · Paul, Weiss, Rifkind, Wharton & Garrison · 1285 Avenue of the Americas · New York, NY 10019-6064 · 212-373-3000

Samuel H. Lindenbaum · Rosenman & Colin · 575 Madison Avenue · New York, NY 10022 · 212-940-8600

Lawrence J. Lipson · Shea & Gould · 1251 Avenue of the Americas · New York, NY 10020-1193 · 212-827-3000

Sydney A. Luria · Carb, Luria, Glassner, Cook & Kufeld · 529 Fifth Avenue · New York, NY 10017 · 212-986-3131

Peter L. Malkin · Wien, Malkin & Bettex · Lincoln Building · 60 East 42nd Street, 48th Floor · New York, NY 10165-0015 · 212-687-8700

Melvin Michaelson · Kaye, Scholer, Fierman, Hays & Handler · 425 Park Avenue New York, NY 10022 · 212-836-8000

Benjamin F. Needell · Skadden, Arps, Slate, Meagher & Flom · 919 Third Avenue · New York, NY 10022-3897 · 212-735-3000

John C. Nelson · Milbank, Tweed, Hadley & McCloy · One Chase Manhattan Plaza · New York, NY 10005-1413 · 212-530-5000

Benet Polikoff, Jr. · Rosenman & Colin · 575 Madison Avenue · New York, NY 10022 · 212-940-8600

David Alan Richards · Sidley & Austin · 875 Third Avenue · New York, NY 10022 · 212-418-2100

Paul E. Roberts · Morgan, Lewis & Bockius · 101 Park Avenue · New York, NY 10178 · 212-309-6000

Martin S. Saiman · Kaye, Scholer, Fierman, Hays & Handler · 425 Park Avenue New York, NY 10022 · 212-836-8427

Flora Schnall · Milbank, Tweed, Hadley & McCloy · One Chase Manhattan Plaza · New York, NY 10005-1413 · 212-530-5000

Gerald N. Schrager · Dreyer and Traub · 101 Park Avenue · New York, NY 10178 212-661-8800

Alvin Silverman · Wien, Malkin & Bettex · Lincoln Building · 60 East 42nd Street, 48th Floor · New York, NY 10165-0015 · 212-687-8700

Donald H. Siskind · Rosenman & Colin · 575 Madison Avenue · New York, NY 10022 · 212-940-8600

Neil Underberg · Whitman & Ransom · 200 Park Avenue, 27th Floor · New York, NY 10166 · 212-351-3000

John E. Zuccotti · Brown & Wood · One World Trade Center · New York, NY 10048 · 212-839-5300 850-9610

John E. Blyth · Harter, Secrest & Emery · 700 Midtown Tower · Rochester, NY 14604-2070 · 716-232-6500

Richard A. Calabrese · Elliott, Stern & Calabrese · One East Main Street, 10th Floor · Rochester, NY 14614 · 716-232-4724

John B. Hood · Nixon, Hargrave, Devans & Doyle · Clinton Square · P.O. Box 1051 · Rochester, NY 14603 · 716-546-8000

Frank B. Iacovangelo · Gallo & Iacovangelo · 80 West Main Street, Suite 200 · Rochester, NY 14614 · 716-454-7145

Charles E. Littlefield · Harris, Beach & Wilcox · The Granite Building · 130 East Main Street · Rochester, NY 14604 · 716-232-4440

Thomas P. Moonan · Harris, Beach & Wilcox · The Granite Building · 130 East Main Street · Rochester, NY 14604 · 716-232-4440

William D. Smith · Harter, Secrest & Emery · 700 Midtown Tower · Rochester, NY 14604-2070 · 716-232-6500

Stephen L. Johnson · Bond, Schoeneck & King · One Lincoln Center, 18th Floor Syracuse, NY 13202-1355 · 315-422-0121

C. Daniel Shulman · Shulman Law Offices · 250 Clinton Street · Syracuse, NY 13202 · 315-424-8944

Gregory R. Thornton · Hancock & Estabrook · One Mony Plaza, 14th Floor · 100 Madison Street · P.O. Box 4976 · Syracuse, NY 13221-4976 · 315-471-3151

Charles H. Umbrecht, Jr. · Hancock & Estabrook · One Mony Plaza, 14th Floor 100 Madison Street · P.O. Box 4976 · Syracuse, NY 13221-4976 · 315-471-3151

TAX AND EMPLOYEE BENEFITS LAW

Richard V. D'Alessandro · 69 Columbia Street · Albany, NY 12210 · 518-449-1421

Robert E. Helm · (Corporate & Partnership Transactions, State Tax, Employee Benefits) · Helm, Shapiro, Anito & Aldrich · 111 Washington Avenue · Albany, NY 12210 · 518-465-7563

Dianne Bennett · (Tax, Employee Benefits) · Hodgson, Russ, Andrews, Woods & Goodyear · 1800 One M&T Plaza · Buffalo, NY 14203-2391 · 716-856-4000

Irving D. Brott, Jr. · (Employee Benefits) · Phillips, Lytle, Hitchcock, Blaine & Huber · 3400 Marine Midland Center · Buffalo, NY 14203 · 716-847-8400

Richard F. Campbell · Hodgson, Russ, Andrews, Woods & Goodyear · 1800 One M&T Plaza · Buffalo, NY 14203-2391 · 716-856-4000

Paul R. Comeau · Hodgson, Russ, Andrews, Woods & Goodyear · 1800 One M&T Plaza · Buffalo, NY 14203-2391 · 716-856-4000

Richard E. Heath · Hodgson, Russ, Andrews, Woods & Goodyear · 1800 One M&T Plaza · Buffalo, NY 14203-2391 · 716-856-4000

Donald C. Lubick · Hodgson, Russ, Andrews, Woods & Goodyear · 1800 One M&T Plaza · Buffalo, NY 14203-2391 · 716-856-4000

Albert R. Mugel · Jaeckle, Fleischmann & Mugel · 800 Norstar Building · 12 Fountain Plaza · Buffalo, NY 14202 · 716-856-0600

Daniel R. Sharpe · (Employee Benefits) · Hodgson, Russ, Andrews, Woods & Goodyear · 1800 One M&T Plaza · Buffalo, NY 14203-2391 · 716-856-4000

M. Bernard Aidinoff · Sullivan & Cromwell · 125 Broad Street, 28th Floor · New York, NY 10004 · 212-558-4000

Martin B. Amdur · Weil, Gotshal & Manges · 767 Fifth Avenue · New York, NY 10153 · 212-310-8000

Richard C. Blake · Simpson Thacher & Bartlett · 425 Lexington Avenue · New York, NY 10017-3909 · 212-455-2000

David H. Brockway · Dewey Ballantine · 1301 Avenue of the Americas · New York, NY 10019-6092 · 212-259-8000

Herbert L. Camp · Cravath, Swaine & Moore · Worldwide Plaza · 825 Eighth Avenue, 38th Floor · New York, NY 10019 · 212-474-1000

Peter C. Canellos · Wachtell, Lipton, Rosen & Katz · 299 Park Avenue · New York, NY 10171-0149 · 212-371-9200

Walter C. Cliff · Cahill Gordon & Reindel · 80 Pine Street · New York, NY 10005 212-701-3000

Richard G. Cohen · Winthrop, Stimson, Putnam & Roberts · One Battery Park Plaza · New York, NY 10004-1490 · 212-858-1000

Dale S. Collinson · (Corporate & Partnership Transactions, Tax-Exempt Bonds, Regulated Investment Companies) · Willkie Farr & Gallagher · One Citicorp Center · 153 East 53rd Street · New York, NY 10022-4669 · 212-935-8000

Kenneth C. Edgar, Jr. · (Employee Benefits) · Simpson Thacher & Bartlett · 425 Lexington Avenue · New York, NY 10017-3909 · 212-455-2000

James S. Eustice · Kronish, Lieb, Weiner & Hellman · 1345 Avenue of the Americas · New York, NY 10105 · 212-841-6000

Peter L. Faber · Kaye, Scholer, Fierman, Hays & Handler · 425 Park Avenue · New York, NY 10022 · 212-836-8000

Arthur A. Feder · Fried, Frank, Harris, Shriver & Jacobson · One New York Plaza New York, NY 10004-1980 · 212-820-8000

M. Carr Ferguson* · Davis Polk & Wardwell · One Chase Manhattan Plaza · New York, NY 10005 · 212-530-4000

Robert C. Fleder · (Employee Benefits) · Paul, Weiss, Rifkind, Wharton & Garrison · 1285 Avenue of the Americas · New York, NY 10019-6064 · 212-373-3000

Frederick Gelberg · Moses & Singer · 1271 Avenue of the Americas, 45th Floor New York, NY 10020 · 212-246-3700

Sanford H. Goldberg · Roberts & Holland · 30 Rockefeller Plaza, 20th Floor · New York, NY 10112 · 212-903-8700

Harold R. Handler · Simpson Thacher & Bartlett · 425 Lexington Avenue · New York, NY 10017-3909 · 212-455-2000

Kenneth H. Heitner · Weil, Gotshal & Manges · 767 Fifth Avenue · New York, NY 10153 · 212-310-8000

Gordon D. Henderson · (Corporate & Partnership Transactions) · Weil, Gotshal & Manges · 767 Fifth Avenue · New York, NY 10153 · 212-310-8000

Richard Joseph Hiegel · Cravath, Swaine & Moore · Worldwide Plaza · 825 Eighth Avenue, 38th Floor · New York, NY 10019 · 212-474-1000

Robert A. Jacobs · Milbank, Tweed, Hadley & McCloy · One Chase Manhattan Plaza · New York, NY 10005-1413 · 212-530-5000

Everett L. Jassy · Dewey Ballantine · 1301 Avenue of the Americas · New York, NY 10019-6092 · 212-259-8000

Arthur Kalish · Paul, Weiss, Rifkind, Wharton & Garrison · 1285 Avenue of the Americas · New York, NY 10019-6064 · 212-373-3000

Sherwin Kamin · Kramer, Levin, Nessen, Kamin & Frankel · 919 Third Avenue New York, NY 10022 · 212-715-9100

Lydia E. Kess · (Corporate & Partnership Transactions) · Davis Polk & Wardwell One Chase Manhattan Plaza · New York, NY 10005 · 212-530-4606

Charles I. Kingson · Willkie Farr & Gallagher · One Citicorp Center · 153 East 53rd Street · New York, NY 10022-4669 · 212-935-8000

Edward D. Kleinbard · Cleary, Gottlieb, Steen & Hamilton · One Liberty Plaza New York, NY 10006 · 212-225-2000

Frederick C. Kneip · (Employee Benefits) · Milbank, Tweed, Hadley & McCloy One Chase Manhattan Plaza · New York, NY 10005-1413 · 212-530-5000

Boris Kostelanetz · Kostelanetz & Ritholz · 80 Pine Street · New York, NY 10005 212-422-4030

William N. Kravitz · (Employee Benefits) · Skadden, Arps, Slate, Meagher & Flom · 919 Third Avenue · New York, NY 10022-3897 · 212-735-3000

James P. Lawton · Davis Polk & Wardwell · One Chase Manhattan Plaza · New York, NY 10005 · 212-530-4626

James Patrick Lawton · (Employee Benefits) · Davis Polk & Wardwell · One Chase Manhattan Plaza · New York, NY 10005 · 212-530-4000

Richard M. Leder · Chadbourne & Parke · 30 Rockefeller Plaza · New York, NY 10112 · 212-408-5100

Richard O. Loengard, Jr. · Fried, Frank, Harris, Shriver & Jacobson · One New York Plaza · New York, NY 10004-1980 · 212-820-8000

Thomas S. Monfried · (Employee Benefits) · Willkie Farr & Gallagher · One Citicorp Center · 153 East 53rd Street · New York, NY 10022-4669 · 212-935-8000

Michael J. Nassau · (Employee Benefits) · Kramer, Levin, Nessen, Kamin & Frankel · 919 Third Avenue · New York, NY 10022 · 212-715-9100

Stuart I. Odell · (Corporate & Partnership Transactions) · Dewey Ballantine · 1301 Avenue of the Americas · New York, NY 10019-6092 · 212-259-8000

James M. Peaslee · Cleary, Gottlieb, Steen & Hamilton · One Liberty Plaza · New York, NY 10006 · 212-225-2000

Howard Pianko · (Employee Benefits) · Hughes Hubbard & Reed · One Battery Park Plaza · New York, NY 10004 · 212-837-6000

Robert H. Preiskel · Fried, Frank, Harris, Shriver & Jacobson · One New York Plaza · New York, NY 10004-1980 · 212-820-8000

John C. Richardson · LeBoeuf, Lamb, Leiby & MacRae · 520 Madison Avenue New York, NY 10022 · 212-715-8000

Jules Ritholz* · (Tax Disputes) · Kostelanetz Ritholz Tigue & Fink · 80 Pine Street · New York, NY 10005 · 212-422-4030

James R. Rowen · Shearman & Sterling · 599 Lexington Avenue · New York, NY 10022 · 212-848-4000

Hugh Rowland, Jr. · Debevoise & Plimpton · 875 Third Avenue · New York, NY 10022 · 212-909-6000

Stanley I. Rubenfeld · (Corporate & Partnership Transactions, Tax Disputes) · Shearman & Sterling · Citicorp Center · 153 East 53rd Street · New York, NY 10022 · 212-848-4000

David Sachs · White & Case · 1155 Avenue of the Americas · New York, NY 10036 · 212-819-8200

Irving Salem · Latham & Watkins · 885 Third Avenue, Suite 1000 · New York, NY 10022-4802 · 212-906-1200

Leslie B. Samuels · Cleary, Gottlieb, Steen & Hamilton · One Liberty Plaza · New York, NY 10006 · 212-225-2000

Donald Schapiro · Chadbourne & Parke · 30 Rockefeller Plaza · New York, NY 10112 · 212-408-5100

Ruth G. Schapiro · Proskauer Rose Goetz & Mendelsohn · 1585 Broadway · New York, NY 10036 · 212-969-3000

Michael L. Schler · (Corporate & Partnership Transactions) · Cravath, Swaine & Moore · Worldwide Plaza · 825 Eighth Avenue, 38th Floor · New York, NY 10019 212-474-1588

Stuart E. Seigel · Arnold & Porter · Park Avenue Tower · 65 East 55th Street · New York, NY 10022 · 212-750-5372

Susan P. Serota · (Employee Benefits) · Winthrop, Stimson, Putnam & Roberts One Battery Park Plaza · New York, NY 10004-1490 · 212-858-1125

Mayer Siegel · (Employee Benefits) · Fried, Frank, Harris, Shriver & Jacobson · One New York Plaza · New York, NY 10004-1980 · 212-820-8000

Jesse G. Silverman, Jr. · Roberts & Holland · 30 Rockefeller Plaza, 20th Floor · New York, NY 10112 · 212-903-8700

Robert J. Stokes · (Employee Benefits) · Cravath, Swaine & Moore · Worldwide Plaza · 825 Eighth Avenue, 38th Floor · New York, NY 10019 · 212-474-1594

A. Richard Susko · (Employee Benefits) · Cleary, Gottlieb, Steen & Hamilton · One Liberty Plaza · New York, NY 10006 · 212-225-2410

Willard B. Taylor · Sullivan & Cromwell · 125 Broad Street, 28th Floor · New York, NY 10004 · 212-558-4000

David R. Tillinghast · Chadbourne & Park · 30 Rockefeller Plaza · New York, NY 10112 · 212-408-5100

B. Cary Tolley · Hunton & Williams · 200 Park Avenue · New York, NY 10166 · 212-309-1000

David E. Watts · Dewey Ballantine · 1301 Avenue of the Americas · New York, NY 10019-6092 · 212-259-6060

Philip S. Winterer · Debevoise & Plimpton · 875 Third Avenue · New York, NY 10022 · 212-909-6000

Alfred D. Youngwood · Paul, Weiss, Rifkind, Wharton & Garrison · 1285 Avenue of the Americas · New York, NY 10019-6064 · 212-373-3000

Victor Zonana · Arnold & Porter · 65 East 55th Street, 31st Floor · 425 Park Avenue · New York, NY 10022 · 212-750-5050

Richard S. Fischer · (Employee Benefits) · Nixon, Hargrave, Devans & Doyle · Clinton Square · P.O. Box 1051 · Rochester, NY 14603 · 716-546-8000

Sherman F. Levey · Harris, Beach & Wilcox · The Granite Building · 130 East Main Street · Rochester, NY 14604 · 716-232-4440

E. Parker Brown II · Hiscock & Barclay · Financial Plaza · P.O. Box 4878 · Syracuse, NY 13221 · 315-422-2131

Stephen H. Cohen · (Employee Benefits) · Scolaro, Shulman, Cohen, Lawler & Burstein · 90 Presidential Plaza, Fifth Floor · Syracuse, NY 13202 · 315-471-8111

Gary R. Germain · (Corporate & Partnership Transactions, State Tax, Tax Disputes) · Bond, Schoeneck & King · One Lincoln Center, 17th Floor · Syracuse, NY 13202-1355 · 315-422-0121

Clayton H. Hale, Jr. · Mackenzie Smith Lewis Michell & Hughes · 600 Onondaga Savings Bank Building · P.O. Box 4967 · Syracuse, NY 13221-4967 · 315-474-7571

Richard D. Hole · (Employee Benefits) · Bond, Schoeneck & King · One Lincoln Center, 18th Floor · Syracuse, NY 13202-1355 · 315-422-0121

Robert V. Hunter · Hunter & Hartnett · The Clinton Exchange, Suite 106 · Four Clinton Square · Syracuse, NY 13202-1075 · 315-476-0532

Richard S. Scolaro · Scolaro, Shulman, Cohen, Lawler & Burstein · 90 Presidential Plaza, Fifth Floor · Syracuse, NY 13202 · 315-471-8111

George C. Shattuck · (Corporate & Partnership Transactions, State Tax, Tax Disputes) · Bond, Schoeneck & King · One Lincoln Center, 17th Floor · Syracuse, NY 13202-1355 · 315-422-0121

TRUSTS AND ESTATES

James B. Ayers · DeGraff, Foy, Conway, Holt-Harris & Mealey · 90 State Street Albany, NY 12207 · 518-462-5301

Thomas E. Dolin · Hiscock & Barclay · One Keycorp Plaza, Suite 1100 · 30 South Pearl Street · Albany, NY 12207-3411 · 518-434-2163

William S. Haase · McNamee, Lochner, Titus & Williams · 75 State Street, Room 1200 · P.O. Box 459 · Albany, NY 12201-0459 · 518-434-3136

Albert A. Manning · Hinman, Straub, Pigors & Manning · 121 State Street · Albany, NY 12207-1622 · 518-436-0751

Timothy B. Thornton · McNamee, Lochner, Titus & Williams · 75 State Street P.O. Box 459 · Albany, NY 12201-0459 · 518-434-3136

John P. McLane · (Estate Planning, Estate Administration, Charitable Trusts) · Boyle & Anderson · 120 Genesee Street, Suite 4 · Auburn, NY 13021 · 315-253-0326

Thomas M. Barney · Phillips, Lytle, Hitchcock, Blaine & Huber · 3400 Marine Midland Center · Buffalo, NY 14203 · 716-847-8400

Gordon A. MacLeod · Hodgson, Russ, Andrews, Woods & Goodyear · 1800 One M&T Plaza · Buffalo, NY 14203-2391 · 716-856-4000

Albert R. Mugel · Jaeckle, Fleischmann & Mugel · 800 Norstar Building · 12 Fountain Plaza · Buffalo, NY 14202-2222 · 716-856-0600

Stephen M. Newman · Hodgson, Russ, Andrews, Woods & Goodyear · 1800 One M&T Plaza · Buffalo, NY 14203-2391 · 716-856-4000

Robert J. Plache · Damon & Morey · 1000 Cathedral Place · Buffalo, NY 14202 716-858-3875

Arthur M. Sherwood · Phillips, Lytle, Hitchcock, Blaine & Huber · 3400 Marine Midland Center · Buffalo, NY 14203 · 716-847-8400

Mal L. Barasch · Rosenman & Colin · 575 Madison Avenue · New York, NY 10022 · 212-940-8600

Christine Beshar · Cravath, Swaine & Moore · Worldwide Plaza · 825 Eighth Avenue, 38th Floor · New York, NY 10019 · 212-474-1000

Jonathan Blattmachr · Milbank, Tweed, Hadley & McCloy · One Chase Manhattan Plaza · New York, NY 10005-1413 · 212-530-5000

Herbert H. Chaice · Patterson, Belknap, Webb & Tyler · 30 Rockefeller Plaza · New York, NY 10112 · 212-698-2500

Donald C. Christ · Sullivan & Cromwell · 250 Park Avenue · New York, NY 10177 · 212-558-4000

Henry Christensen III · Sullivan & Cromwell · 250 Park Avenue, 15th Floor · New York, NY 10177 · 212-558-4000

Carolyn C. Clark* · (Estate Planning, Estate Administration, Charitable Trusts, Non-Profit Organizations & Charitable Giving) · Milbank, Tweed, Hadley & McCloy · One Chase Manhattan Plaza · New York, NY 10005-1413 · 212-530-5000

Richard B. Covey · Carter, Ledyard & Milburn · Two Wall Street, 15th Floor · New York, NY 10005 · 212-732-3200

James F. Dolan · Davis Polk & Wardwell · 499 Park Avenue, 24th Floor · New York, NY 10022 · 212-446-3000

Bernard Finkelstein · Paul, Weiss, Rifkind, Wharton & Garrison · 1285 Avenue of the Americas · New York, NY 10019-6064 · 212-373-3000

Alexander D. Forger · Milbank, Tweed, Hadley & McCloy · One Chase Manhattan Plaza · New York, NY 10005-1413 · 212-530-5000

Michael I. Frankel · Carter, Ledyard & Milburn · Two Wall Street, 15th Floor · New York, NY 10005 · 212-732-3200

Charles F. Gibbs · Breed, Abbott & Morgan · Citicorp Center, 56th Floor · 153 East 53rd Street · New York, NY 10022 · 212-888-0800

George J. Gillespie · Cravath, Swaine & Moore · Worldwide Plaza · 825 Eighth Avenue, 38th Floor · New York, NY 10019 · 212-474-1000

Bernard H. Greene · Paul, Weiss, Rifkind, Wharton & Garrison · 1285 Avenue of the Americas · New York, NY 10019-6064 · 212-373-3000

Dan T. Hastings · (Estate Planning, Estate Administration, Charitable Trusts) · Milbank, Tweed, Hadley & McCloy · One Chase Manhattan Plaza · New York, NY 10005-1413 · 212-530-5000

Philip J. Hirsch · Proskauer Rose Goetz & Mendelsohn · 1585 Broadway · New York, NY 10036 · 212-969-3000

Linda B. Hirschson · Gilbert, Segall and Young · 430 Park Avenue, 11th Floor · New York, NY 10022 · 212-644-4000

Philip G. Hull · Winthrop, Stimson, Putnam & Roberts · One Battery Park Plaza New York, NY 10004-1490 · 212-858-1000

Jane B. Jacobs · (Estate Planning, Estate Administration, Charitable Trusts) · Patterson, Belknap, Webb & Tyler · 30 Rockefeller Plaza · New York, NY 10112 212-698-2500

Mildred E. Kalik · Simpson Thacher & Bartlett · 425 Lexington Avenue · New York, NY 10017-3909 · 212-455-2000

Joseph Kartiganer · Simpson Thacher & Bartlett · 425 Lexington Avenue · New York, NY 10017-3909 · 212-455-2000

Theodore A. Kurz · Debevoise & Plimpton · 875 Third Avenue · New York, NY 10022 · 212-909-6000

James Woodman Lloyd · Davis Polk & Wardwell · One Chase Manhattan Plaza New York, NY 10005 · 212-530-4000

Ira H. Lustgarten · (Estate Planning, Estate Administration, Charitable Trusts, Estate Litigation) · Willkie Farr & Gallagher · One Citicorp Center · 153 East 53rd Street · New York, NY 10022-4669 · 212-935-8000

Jerome A. Manning · Stroock & Stroock & Lavan · Seven Hanover Square · New York, NY 10004-2594 · 212-806-5400

Carlyn S. McCaffrey · Weil, Gotshal & Manges · 767 Fifth Avenue · New York, NY 10153 · 212-310-8000

Lawrence Newman · Kaye, Scholer, Fierman, Hays & Handler · 425 Park Avenue New York, NY 10022 · 212-836-8000

David C. Oxman · (Estate Planning, Estate Administration, Charitable Trusts) · Davis Polk & Wardwell · 499 Park Avenue, 24th Floor · New York, NY 10022 · 212-446-3000

William Parsons, Jr. · Davis Polk & Wardwell · One Chase Manhattan Plaza · New York, NY 10005 · 212-530-4000

Richard Henry Pershan · LeBoeuf, Lamb, Leiby & MacRae · 520 Madison Avenue · New York, NY 10022 · 212-715-8000

Samuel S. Polk · Milbank, Tweed, Hadley & McCloy · One Chase Manhattan Plaza · New York, NY 10005-1413 · 212-530-5000

Barbara Paul Robinson · Debevoise & Plimpton · 875 Third Avenue · New York, NY 10022 · 212-909-6000

Edward S. Schlesinger · Law Offices of Edward S. Schlesinger · 600 Third Avenue, 25th Floor · New York, NY 10016 · 212-682-3540

Sanford J. Schlesinger · (Estate Planning, Estate Administration, Charitable Trusts, Elder Law) · Shea & Gould · 1251 Avenue of the Americas · New York, NY 10020-1193 · 212-827-3000

Arthur D. Sederbaum · (Estate Planning, Estate Administration, Charitable Trusts) · Olshan Grundman Frome Rosenzweig & Orens · 505 Park Avenue · New York, NY 10022 · 212-753-7200

Michael V. Sterlacci · Winthrop, Stimson, Putnam & Roberts · One Battery Park Plaza · New York, NY 10004-1490 · 212-858-1000

Lawrence B. Thompson · Emmet, Marvin & Martin · 48 Wall Street · New York, NY 10005 · 212-422-2974

Charles W. Ufford, Jr. · Skadden, Arps, Slate, Meagher & Flom · 919 Third Avenue · New York, NY 10022-3897 · 212-735-3000

Theodore R. Wagner · Carter, Ledyard & Milburn · Two Wall Street, 15th Floor New York, NY 10005 · 212-732-3200

William B. Warren · Dewey Ballantine · 1301 Avenue of the Americas · New York, NY 10019-6092 · 212-259-8000

Douglas F. Williamson, Jr. · Winthrop, Stimson, Putnam & Roberts · One Battery Park Plaza · New York, NY 10004-1490 · 212-858-1000

E. Lisk Wyckoff, Jr. · Kelley Drye & Warren · 101 Park Avenue · New York, NY 10178 · 212-808-7800

William D. Zabel · Schulte, Roth & Zabel · 900 Third Avenue · New York, NY 10022 · 212-758-0404

Henry S. Ziegler · Shearman & Sterling · Citicorp Center · 153 East 53rd Street New York, NY 10022 · 212-848-8000

Harvey F. Zimand · Kelley Drye & Warren · 101 Park Avenue · New York, NY 10178 · 212-808-7800

Crandall Melvin, Jr. · (Estate Planning, Estate Administration) · Melvin Law Firm · 6834 Buckley Road · North Syracuse, NY 13212-4264 · 315-451-7955

Edward D. Bloom · Harris, Beach & Wilcox · The Granite Building · 130 East Main Street · Rochester, NY 14604 · 716-232-4440

Michael Buckley · Harter, Secrest & Emery · 700 Midtown Tower · Rochester, NY 14604-2070 · 716-232-6500

John T. Fitzgerald, Jr. · Nixon, Hargrave, Devans & Doyle · Clinton Square · P.O. Box 1051 · Rochester, NY 14603 · 716-546-8000

John L. Goldman · Underberg and Kessler · 1800 Lincoln First Tower · Rochester, NY 14604 · 716-258-2800

Alan Illig · (Estate Planning, Estate Administration) · Harter, Secrest & Emery · 700 Midtown Tower · Rochester, NY 14604-2070 · 716-232-6500

George R. Parsons, Jr. · Nixon, Hargrave, Devans & Doyle · Clinton Square · P.O. Box 1051 · Rochester, NY 14603 · 716-546-8000

Jon L. Schumacher · Nixon, Hargrave, Devans & Doyle · Clinton Square · P.O. Box 1051 · Rochester, NY 14603 · 716-263-1263

John E. Swett · Harter, Secrest & Emery · 700 Midtown Tower · Rochester, NY 14604-2070 · 716-232-6500

John W. Tarbox · (Estate Planning, Estate Administration, Charitable Trusts) · Harris, Beach & Wilcox · The Granite Building · 130 East Main Street · Rochester, NY 14604 · 716-232-4440

Michael R. Suprunowicz · Higgins, Roberts, Beyerl & Coan · 502 State Street · Schenectady, NY 12305 · 518-374-3399

Robert F. Baldwin, Jr. · Green & Seifter · One Lincoln Center, Ninth Floor · Syracuse, NY 13202 · 315-422-1391

Arthur E. Bongiovanni · Bond, Schoeneck & King · One Lincoln Center, 17th Floor · Syracuse, NY 13202-1355 · 315-422-0121

Roger J. Edinger · Hiscock & Barclay · Financial Plaza · P.O. Box 4878 · Syracuse, NY 13221 · 315-422-2131

Robert J. Hughes, Jr. · Harter, Secrest & Emery · 431 East Fayette Street · Syracuse, NY 13202 · 315-474-4000

Michael E. O'Connor · Hancock & Estabrook · One Mony Plaza, 15th Floor · 100 Madison Street · P.O. Box 4976 · Syracuse, NY 13221-4976 · 315-471-3151

Richard P. Wallace · Martin, Shudt, Wallace, DiLorenzo, Copps & Johnson · 279 River Street · P.O. Box 1530 · Troy, NY 12181 · 518-272-6565

Harris Markhoff · Danziger & Markhoff · Centroplex, Suite 900 · 123 Main Street White Plains, NY 10601 · 914-948-1556

John G. McQuaid · McCarthy, Fingar, Donovan, Drazen & Smith · 11 Martine Avenue · White Plains, NY 10606 · 914-946-3700

Conrad Teitell · Prerau & Teitell · 50 Main Street, Ninth Floor · White Plains, NY 10606 · 914-682-9300

NORTH CAROLINA

BANKRUPTCY LAW

Albert L. Sneed, Jr. · Van Winkle, Buck, Wall, Starnes and Davis · 11 North Market Street · P.O. Box 7376 · Asheville, NC 28802 · 704-258-2991

J. Michael Booe · Petree Stockton & Robinson · 3500 One First Union Center · 301 South College Street · P.O. Box 32397 · Charlotte, NC 28232-2397 · 704-372-9110

W. B. Hawfield, Jr. · Moore & Van Allen · 3000 NCNB Plaza · Charlotte, NC 28280 · 704-331-1000

Thomas B. Henson · Robinson, Bradshaw & Hinson · 1900 Independence Center 101 North Tryon Street · Charlotte, NC 28246 · 704-377-2536

Richard M. Hutson II · Maxwell & Hutson · 300 West Morgan Street · P.O. Drawer 2252A · Durham, NC 27702 · 919-683-1561

Richard A. Leippe · Smith Helms Mulliss & Moore · 300 North Greene, Suite 1400 · P.O. Box 21927 · Greensboro, NC 27420 · 919-378-5200

David F. Meschan · Tuggle Duggins & Meschan · 228 West Market Street · P.O. Drawer X · Greensboro, NC 27402 · 919-378-1431

William L. Stocks · (Defendants) · Nichols, Caffrey, Hill, Evans & Murelle · 1400 Renaissance Plaza · P.O. Box 989 · Greensboro, NC 27402 · 919-379-1390

Trawick H. Stubbs, Jr.* · Stubbs, Perdue, Chesnutt, Wheeler & Clemmons · 215 Broad Street · P.O. Drawer 1654 · New Bern, NC 28560 · 919-633-2700

Gregory B. Crampton · Merriman, Nicholls & Crampton · 100 St. Albans Drive P.O. Box 18237 · Raleigh, NC 27619 · 919-781-1311

J. Larkin Pahl · Smith, Debnam, Hibbert & Pahl · 4700 New Bern Avenue · P.O. Drawer 26268 · Raleigh, NC 27611 · 919-250-2000

Stephen L. Beaman · Beaman and King · 304 West Nash Street · P.O. Box 1907 Wilson, NC 27894-1907 · 919-237-9020

R. Bradford Leggett · Allman Spry Humphreys Leggett & Howington · 380 Knollwood Street, Suite 700 · P.O. Drawer 5129 · Winston-Salem, NC 27113-5129 919-722-2300

BUSINESS LITIGATION

E. Osborne Ayscue, Jr. · Smith Helms Mulliss & Moore · 227 North Tryon Street P.O. Box 31247 · Charlotte, NC 28231 · 704-343-2000

Harry C. Hewson* · Jones, Hewson & Woolard · 1000 Law Building · 730 East Trade Street, Suite 1000 · Charlotte, NC 28202 · 704-372-6541

A. Ward McKeithen* · (Appellate, Banking, Commercial, Securities) · Robinson, Bradshaw & Hinson · 1900 Independence Center · 101 North Tryon Street · Charlotte, NC 28246 · 704-377-2536

William C. Raper* · (Commercial, Finance, RICO, Securities) · Womble Carlyle Sandridge & Rice · 3300 One First Union Center · 301 South College Street · Charlotte, NC 28202-6025 · 704-331-4900

Robert B. Glenn, Jr. · Glenn, Mills & Fisher · 709 First Federal Building · P.O. Box 3865 · Durham, NC 27702-3865 · 919-683-2135

Jack W. Floyd* · Floyd, Greeson, Allen and Jacobs · 400 West Market Street, Suite 400 · P.O. Box 2460 · Greensboro, NC 27402 · 919-273-1797

Charles T. Hagan, Jr. · Adams, Kleemeier, Hagan, Hannah & Fouts · One Southern Life Center · P.O. Box 3463 · Greensboro, NC 27402 · 919-373-1600

Hubert Humphrey · Brooks, Pierce, McLendon, Humphrey & Leonard · 2000 Renaissance Place · 230 North Elm Street · P.O. Drawer U · Greensboro, NC 27402 · 919-373-8850

Charles E. Nichols* · Nichols, Caffrey, Hill, Evans & Murrelle · 1400 Renaissance Plaza · P.O. Box 989 · Greensboro, NC 27402 · 919-379-1390

McNeill Smith* · (Antitrust, Commercial, Securities) · Smith Helms Mulliss & Moore · 300 North Greene, Suite 1400 · P.O. Box 21927 · Greensboro, NC 27420 919-378-5200

James T. Williams · Brooks, Pierce, McLendon, Humphrey & Leonard · 2000 Renaissance Place · 230 North Elm Street · P.O. Drawer U · Greensboro, NC 27402 · 919-373-8850

Walter F. Brinkley, Jr. · Brinkley, Walser, McGirt, Miller, Smith & Coles · 10 LSB Plaza · P.O. Box 1657 · Lexington, NC 27293-1657 · 704-249-2101

James D. Blount, Jr.* · (Commercial, Securities) · Smith, Anderson, Blount, Dorsett, Mitchell & Jernigan · 1300 St. Mary's Street · P.O. Box 12807 · Raleigh, NC 27605 · 919-821-1220

C. Eugene Boyce · Womble Carlyle Sandridge & Rice · 901 Wachovia Building · P.O. Box 831 · Raleigh, NC 27602 · 919-828-7214

David W. Long · Poyner & Spruill · 3600 Glenwood Avenue · P.O. Box 10096 · Raleigh, NC 27605-0096 · 919-783-6400

Howard E. Manning · Manning, Fulton & Skinner · 500 UCB Plaza · 3605 Glenwood Avenue · P.O. Box 20389 · Raleigh, NC 27619-0389 · 919-787-8880

H. Grady Barnhill, Jr.* · Womble Carlyle Sandridge & Rice · 1600 One Triad Park · 200 West Second Street · P.O. Drawer 84 · Winston-Salem, NC 27102-0084 919-721-3600

Jimmy H. Barnhill* · (Commercial) · Womble Carlyle Sandridge & Rice · 1600 One Triad Park · 200 West Second Street · P.O. Drawer 84 · Winston-Salem, NC 27102-0084 · 919-721-3628

J. Robert Elster* · Petree Stockton & Robinson · 1001 West Fourth Street · P.O. Box 2860 · Winston-Salem, NC 27102-2400 · 919-725-2351

William F. Maready* · (Complex Litigation) · Petree Stockton & Robinson · 1001 West Fourth Street · P.O. Box 2860 · Winston-Salem, NC 27102-2400 · 919-725-2351

Norwood Robinson · Petree Stockton & Robinson · 1001 West Fourth Street · P.O. Box 2860 · Winston-Salem, NC 27102-2400 · 919-725-2351

Ralph M. Stockton, Jr. · Petree Stockton & Robinson · 1001 West Fourth Street P.O. Box 2860 · Winston-Salem, NC 27102-2400 · 919-725-2351

CORPORATE LAW

Larry J. Dagenhart · (Corporate Finance, Financial Institutions, Mergers & Acquisitions, Securities Regulation) · Smith Helms Mulliss & Moore · 227 North Tryon Street · P.O. Box 31247 · Charlotte, NC 28231 · 704-343-2010

J. Carlton Fleming · Womble Carlyle Sandridge & Rice · 3300 One First Union Center · 301 South College Street · Charlotte, NC 28202-6025 · 704-331-4900

Russell M. Robinson II · Robinson, Bradshaw & Hinson · 1900 Independence Center · 101 North Tryon Street · Charlotte, NC 28246 · 704-377-2536

Clarence W. Walker · Kennedy Covington Lobdell & Hickman · 3300 NCNB Plaza · Charlotte, NC 28280 · 704-377-6000

Michael R. Abel · Schell, Bray, Aycock, Abel & Livingston · 230 North Elm Street, Suite 1500 · P.O. Box 21847 · Greensboro, NC 27420 · 919-370-8800

Doris R. Bray · Schell, Bray, Aycock, Abel & Livingston · 230 North Elm Street, Suite 1500 · P.O. Box 21847 · Greensboro, NC 27420 · 919-370-8800

Braxton Schell · (Corporate Finance, Mergers & Acquisitions) · Schell, Bray, Aycock, Abel & Livingston · 230 North Elm Street, Suite 1500 · P.O. Box 21847 Greensboro, NC 27420 · 919-370-8800

J. Troy Smith, Jr. · Ward and Smith · 1001 College Court · P.O. Box 867 · New Bern, NC 28563-0867 · 919-633-1000

David L. Ward, Jr. · Ward and Smith · 1001 College Court · P.O. Box 867 · New Bern, NC 28563-0867 · 919-633-1000

E. Lawrence Davis III · (Corporate Finance, International Trade, Mergers & Acquisitions, Securities) · Womble Carlyle Sandridge & Rice · 901 Wachovia Building · P.O. Box 831 · Raleigh, NC 27602 · 919-828-7214

James K. Dorsett, Jr. · Smith, Anderson, Blount, Dorsett, Mitchell & Jernigan · 1300 St. Mary's Street · P.O. Box 12807 · Raleigh, NC 27605 · 919-821-1220

Henry A. Mitchell, Jr. · Smith, Anderson, Blount, Dorsett, Mitchell & Jernigan 1300 St. Mary's Street · P.O. Box 12807 · Raleigh, NC 27605 · 919-821-1220

Linwood L. Davis · Womble Carlyle Sandridge & Rice · 1600 One Triad Park · 200 West Second Street · P.O. Drawer 84 · Winston-Salem, NC 27102-0084 · 919-721-3621

James S. Dockery, Jr. · Petree Stockton & Robinson · 1001 West Fourth Street P.O. Box 2860 · Winston-Salem, NC 27102-2400 · 919-725-2351

John L. W. Garrou · Womble Carlyle Sandridge & Rice · 1600 One Triad Park 200 West Second Street · P.O. Drawer 84 · Winston-Salem, NC 27102-0084 · 919-721-3600

CRIMINAL DEFENSE

Charles T. Browne* · Bell and Browne · 151 North Fayetteville Street · Asheboro, NC 27203 · 919-625-2111

Allen A. Bailey* · Bailey, Patterson, Caddell & Bailey · Equity Building, Suite One · 701 East Trade Street · Charlotte, NC 28202 · 704-333-8612

Martin L. Brackett, Jr. · Robinson, Bradshaw & Hinson · 1900 Independence Center · 101 North Tryon Street · Charlotte, NC 28246 · 704-377-2536

James E. Ferguson II* · Ferguson, Stein, Watt, Wallas, Adkins & Gresham · East Independence Plaza, Suite 730 · 700 East Stonewall Street · Charlotte, NC 28202 704-375-8461

James E. Walker* · (Federal Court) · Kennedy Covington Lobdell & Hickman · 3300 NCNB Plaza · Charlotte, NC 28280-8082 · 704-377-6000

Robert S. Cahoon* · Cahoon & Swisher · 232 West Market Street · Greensboro, NC 27401 · 919-275-9867

Locke T. Clifford · McNairy, Clifford, Clendenin & Parks · 300 Southern National Bank Building · 127 North Greene Street · Greensboro, NC 27401 · 919-378-1212

William L. Osteen · Osteen & Adams · Gate City Savings & Loan Building, Suite 305 · 201 West Market Street · P.O. Box 2489 · Greensboro, NC 27402 · 919-274-2947

Percy L. Wall* · 301 South Greene Street, Suite One · P.O. Box 3483 · Greensboro, NC 27402 · 919-275-7915

W. B. Jack Byerly, Jr. · Byerly & Byerly · 505 East Commerce Street · P.O. Box 2221 · High Point, NC 27261 · 919-883-9181

C. Richard Tate, Jr.* · 115 West High Street · P.O. Box 2726 · High Point, NC 27261 · 919-885-0176

Norman B. Kellum, Jr. · Beaman, Kellum & Hollows · 219 Broad Street · P.O. Box 866 · New Bern, NC 28560 · 919-633-2550

James R. Van Camp* · Van Camp, West, Webb & Hayes · The Theater Building, Third Floor · Village Green West · P.O. Box 1389 · Pinehurst, NC 28374-1389 · 919-295-2525

Joseph B. Cheshire V · Cheshire, Parker, Hughes & Manning · 133 Fayetteville Street Mall · P.O. Box 1029 · Raleigh, NC 27602 · 919-833-3114

Russell W. DeMent, Jr. · DeMent, Askew, Gammon & Salisbury · Branch Bank Building, Suite 1513 · P.O. Box 711 · Raleigh, NC 27602 · 919-833-5555

Thomas C. Manning · Cheshire, Parker, Hughes & Manning · 133 Fayetteville Street Mall · P.O. Box 1029 · Raleigh, NC 27602 · 919-833-3114

Robert L. McMillan, Jr. · McMillan, Kimzey & Smith · 205 West Martin Street P.O. Box 150 · Raleigh, NC 27602 · 919-821-5124

Roger W. Smith* · Tharrington, Smith & Hargrove · 209 Fayetteville Street Mall P.O. Box 1151 · Raleigh, NC 27602 · 919-821-4711

Wade M. Smith · Tharrington, Smith & Hargrove · 209 Fayetteville Street Mall P.O. Box 1151 · Raleigh, NC 27602 · 919-821-4711

James L. Nelson* · 124 Market Street · P.O. Box 1767 · Wilmington, NC 28402 919-763-7760

Fred G. Crumpler, Jr. · White and Crumpler · 11 West Fourth Street · Winston-Salem, NC 27101 · 919-725-1304

FAMILY LAW

Robert E. Riddle · Riddle, Kelly & Cagle · 35 North Market Street · P.O. Box 7206 · Asheville, NC 28802 · 704-258-2394

Thomas R. Cannon · Hamel, Helms, Cannon & Hamel · Two First Union Center, Suite 2300 · Charlotte, NC 28282 · 704-372-4884

William K. Diehl, Jr. · James, McElroy & Diehl · 600 South College Street, Suite 3000 · Charlotte, NC 28202 · 704-372-9870

Fred A. Hicks · Hicks, Hodge & Cranford · 1308 East Fourth Street · Charlotte, NC 28204 · 704-377-9714

Richard D. Stephens* · Kennedy Covington Lobdell & Hickman · 3300 NCNB Plaza · Charlotte, NC 28280-8082 · 704-377-6000

James B. Maxwell* · (Equitable Division) · Maxwell & Hutson · 300 West Morgan Street, Suite 1500 · P.O. Drawer 2252A · Durham, NC 27702 · 919-683-1561

Ronnie M. Mitchell · Harris, Mitchell, Hancox & Van Story · 308 Person Street P.O. Box 2917 · Fayetteville, NC 28302 · 919-323-2666

C. Richard Tate, Jr.* · 115 West High Street · P.O. Box 2726 · High Point, NC 27261 · 919-885-0176

Lana S. Warlick* · 410 New Bridge Street, Suite 1A · P.O. Box 1393 · Jacksonville, NC 28541-1393 · 919-347-4400

Robert L. Huffman* · (Child Custody, Divorce, Equitable Division, Alimony Claims) · 340 West Morgan Street · P.O. Box 1008 · Monroe, NC 28110 · 704-283-1529

John Maclachlan Boxley* · (Equitable Division) · Boxley, Bolton & Garber · The Nash Square Building · 227 West Martin Street · P.O. Drawer 1429 · Raleigh, NC 27602 · 919-832-3915

John H. Parker* · Cheshire, Parker, Hughes & Manning · 133 Fayetteville Street Mall · P.O. Box 1029 · Raleigh, NC 27602 · 919-833-3114

Carlyn G. Poole · Tharrington, Smith & Hargrove · 209 Fayetteville Street Mall P.O. Box 1151 · Raleigh, NC 27602 · 919-821-4711

J. Harold Tharrington* · (Child Custody, Marital Settlement Agreements, Equitable Division, Alimony) · Tharrington, Smith & Hargrove · 209 Fayetteville Street Mall · P.O. Box 1151 · Raleigh, NC 27602 · 919-821-4711

J. Edgar Moore* · (Child Custody, Marital Settlement Agreements, Equitable Division) · Moore, Diedrick, Carlisle & Hester · Two Federal Square · 512 West Thomas Street · P.O. Box 2626 · Rocky Mount, NC 27802-2626 · 919-977-1911

James L. Nelson* · 124 Market Street · P.O. Box 1767 · Wilmington, NC 28402 919-763-7760

Fred G. Crumpler, Jr. · White and Crumpler · 11 West Fourth Street · Winston-Salem, NC 27101 · 919-725-1304

FIRST AMENDMENT LAW

E. Osborne Ayscue, Jr. · Smith Helms Mulliss & Moore · 227 North Tryon Street P.O. Box 31247 · Charlotte, NC 28231 · 704-343-2000

Jonathan E. Buchan · Smith Helms Mulliss & Moore · 227 North Tryon Street P.O. Box 31247 · Charlotte, NC 28231 · 704-343-2000

George Daly* · One North McDowell, Suite 226 · 101 North McDowell Street · Charlotte, NC 28204 · 704-333-5196

John H. Hasty · Waggoner, Hamrick, Hasty, Monteith, Kratt & McDonnell · Two First Union Center, Suite 2500 · Charlotte, NC 28282 · 704-332-6141

Hugh H. Stevens · Everett, Gaskins, Hancock & Stevens · 127 West Hargett Street · P.O. Box 919 · Raleigh, NC 27602 · 919-755-0025

Michael K. Curtis · Smith, Patterson, Follin, Curtis, James, Harkavy & Lawrence 101 South Elm Street · P.O. Box 990 · Greensboro, NC 27402 · 919-274-2992

McNeill Smith* · Smith Helms Mulliss & Moore · 300 North Greene, Suite 1400 P.O. Box 21927 · Greensboro, NC 27420 · 919-378-5200

Norman B. Smith · Smith, Patterson, Follin, Curtis, James, Harkavy & Lawrence 101 South Elm Street · P.O. Box 21927 · Greensboro, NC 27402 · 919-274-2992

Richard W. Ellis · Smith Helms Mulliss & Moore · 316 West Edenton Street · Raleigh, NC 27603 · 919-828-8207

Wade H. Hargrove · Tharrington, Smith & Hargrove · 209 Fayetteville Street Mall · P.O. Box 1151 · Raleigh, NC 27602 · 919-821-4711

Mark J. Prak · Tharrington, Smith & Hargrove · 209 Fayetteville Street Mall · P.O. Box 1151 · Raleigh, NC 27602 · 919-821-4711

HEALTH CARE LAW

Maureen Demarest Murray · Smith Helms Mulliss & Moore · 300 North Greene, Suite 1400 · P.O. Box 21927 · Greensboro, NC 27420 · 919-378-5200

Wendell H. Ott · Turner, Enochs & Lloyd · 100 South Elm Street, Suite 400 · P.O. Box 160 · Greensboro, NC 27402-0160 · 919-373-1300

Noah H. HuffstetlerIII · Petree Stockton & Robinson · 4101 Lake Boone Trail, Suite 400 · Raleigh, NC 27607-6519 · 919-782-5092

John R. McArthur · Hunton & Williams · One Hannover Square, Suite 1400 · Fayetteville Street Mall · P.O. Box 109 · Raleigh, NC 27602 · 919-899-3000

Robert L. Wilson, Jr. · Maupin Taylor Ellis & Adams · Merrill Lynch Building 3201 Glenwood Avenue · P.O. Drawer 19764 · Raleigh, NC 27619-9764 · 919-781-6800

Anthony H. Brett · Womble Carlyle Sandridge & Rice · 1600 One Triad Park · 200 West Second Street · P.O. Drawer 84 · Winston-Salem, NC 27102-0084 · 919-721-3600

Roddey M. Ligon, Jr. · Womble Carlyle Sandridge & Rice · 1600 One Triad Park 200 West Second Street · P.O. Drawer 84 · Winston-Salem, NC 27102-0084 · 919-721-3620

IMMIGRATION LAW

Alan S. Gordon · Law Offices of Alan S. Gordon · 1018 East Boulevard, Suite 7 Charlotte, NC 28203 · 704-332-2555

A. Frank Johns · Booth, Harrington, Johns & Campbell · 239 North Edgeworth Street · P.O. Box 3585 · Greensboro, NC 27402 · 919-275-1567

C. Lynn Calder · Allen & Pinnix · 20 Market Plaza, Suite 200 · P.O. Drawer 1270 Raleigh, NC 27602 · 919-755-0505

John L. Pinnix · Allen & Pinnix · 20 Market Plaza, Suite 200 · P.O. Drawer 1270 Raleigh, NC 27602 · 919-755-0505

Jessica Bagg Radermacher · Maupin Taylor Ellis & Adams · Merrill Lynch Building · 3201 Glenwood Avenue · P.O. Drawer 19764 · Raleigh, NC 27619-9764 919-781-6800

Mary C. Tolton · Parker, Poe, Adams & Bernstein · Research Triangle Park · P.O. Box 13039 · Raleigh, NC 27709 · 919-832-3639

LABOR AND EMPLOYMENT LAW

George Daly* · (Labor, Individuals) · One North McDowell, Suite 226 · 101 North McDowell Street · Charlotte, NC 28204 · 704-333-5196

John J. Doyle, Jr. · (Management) · Weinstein & Sturges · 1100 South Tryon Street · Charlotte, NC 28203-4244 · 704-372-4800

John O. Pollard* · (Management) · Blakeney, Alexander & Machen · 3700 NCNB Plaza · Charlotte, NC 28280 · 704-372-3680

Jonathan Wallas* · (Individuals) · Ferguson, Stein, Watt, Wallas & Adkins · East Independence Plaza, Suite 730 · 700 East Stonewall Street · Charlotte, NC 28202 704-375-8461

R. D. Douglas, Jr. · (Management) · Douglas, Ravenel, Hardy, Crihfield & Moseley · 110 Commerce Place · P.O. Box 419 · Greensboro, NC 27401 · 919-378-0580

Martin N. Erwin* · (Management) · Smith Helms Mulliss & Moore · 300 North Greene, Suite 1400 · P.O. Box 21927 · Greensboro, NC 27420 · 919-378-5200

Jonathan Ross Harkavy* · (Labor, Individuals) · Smith, Patterson, Follin, Curtis, James, Harkavy & Lawrence · 101 South Elm Street · P.O. Box 990 · Greensboro, NC 27402 · 919-274-2992

Norman B. Smith* · (Individuals) · Smith, Patterson, Follin, Curtis, James, Harkavy & Lawrence · 101 South Elm Street · P.O. Box 990 · Greensboro, NC 27402 · 919-274-2992

Michael G. Okun · Smith, Patterson, Follin, Curtis, James, Harkavy & Lawrence 206 New Bern Place · Raleigh, NC 27601 · 919-755-1812

Henry N. Patterson, Jr. · (Labor, Individuals) · Smith, Patterson, Follin, Curtis, James, Harkavy & Lawrence · 206 New Bern Place · Raleigh, NC 27601 · 919-755-1812

Robert A. Valois · (Management) · Maupin Taylor Ellis & Adams · Merrill Lynch Building · 3201 Glenwood Avenue · P.O. Drawer 19764 · Raleigh, NC 27619-9764 919-781-6800

Frank P. Ward, Jr. · (Management) · Maupin Taylor Ellis & Adams · Merrill Lynch Building · 3201 Glenwood Avenue · P.O. Drawer 19764 · Raleigh, NC 27619-9764 · 919-781-6800

Guy F. Driver, Jr. · (Management) · Womble Carlyle Sandridge & Rice · 1600 One Triad Park · 200 West Second Street · P.O. Drawer 84 · Winston-Salem, NC 27102-0084 · 919-721-3600

David A. Irvin · (Management) · Womble Carlyle Sandridge & Rice · 1600 One Triad Park · 200 West Second Street · P.O. Drawer 84 · Winston-Salem, NC 27102-0084 · 919-721-3600

W. Randolph Loftis, Jr. · Constangy, Brooks & Smith · First Stratford Building 101 South Stratford Road · Winston-Salem, NC 27104-4213 · 919-721-1001

Charles F. Vance, Jr. · (Management) · Womble Carlyle Sandridge & Rice · 1600 One Triad Park · 200 West Second Street · P.O. Drawer 84 · Winston-Salem, NC 27102-0084 · 919-721-3600

NATURAL RESOURCES AND ENVIRONMENTAL LAW

Harold N. Bynum · Smith Helms Mulliss & Moore · 300 North Greene, Suite 1400 · P.O. Box 21927 · Greensboro, NC 27420 · 919-378-5200

Stephen W. Earp · Smith Helms Mulliss & Moore · 300 North Greene, Suite 1400 P.O. Box 21927 · Greensboro, NC 27420 · 919-378-5200

George W. House* · (Mining, Water, Air, Hazardous Waste) · Brooks, Pierce, McLendon, Humphrey & Leonard · 2000 Renaissance Place · 230 North Elm Street · P.O. Drawer U · Greensboro, NC 27402 · 919-373-8850

William G. Ross, Jr. · Brooks, Pierce, McLendon, Humphrey & Leonard · 2000 Renaissance Place · 230 North Elm Street · P.O. Drawer U · Greensboro, NC 27402 · 919-373-8850

Charles D. Case · Moore & Van Allen · One Hanover Square, Suite 1700 · P.O. Box 26507 · Raleigh, NC 27611 · 919-828-4481

Amos C. Dawson III* · Maupin Taylor Ellis & Adams · Merrill Lynch Building 3201 Glenwood Avenue · P.O. Drawer 19764 · Raleigh, NC 27619-9764 · 919-781-6800

H. Glenn T. Dunn · (Water, Air, Solid Waste, Hazardous Waste) · Poyner & Spruill · 3600 Glenwood Avenue · P.O. Box 10096 · Raleigh, NC 27605-0096 · 919-783-6400

PERSONAL INJURY LITIGATION

Allen A. Bailey* · (Plaintiffs, Automobile Collision) · Bailey, Patterson, Caddell & Bailey · Equity Building, Suite One · 701 East Trade Street · Charlotte, NC 28202 · 704-333-8612

James E. Ferguson II* · (Plaintiffs) · Ferguson, Stein, Watt, Wallas, Adkins & Gresham · East Independence Plaza, Suite 730 · 700 East Stonewall Street · Charlotte, NC 28202 · 704-375-8461

John G. Golding · (Defendants, Medical Malpractice, Professional Malpractice) Golding, Meekins, Holden, Cosper & Stiles · Attorneys Building, Suite 400 · 806 East Trade Street · Charlotte, NC 28202 · 704-374-1600

Harry C. Hewson* · (Defendants) · Jones, Hewson & Woolard · 1000 Law Building · 730 East Trade Street, Suite 1000 · Charlotte, NC 28202 · 704-372-6541

Charles V. Tomkins · (Defendants, Medical Malpractice) · Kennedy Covington Lobdell & Hickman · 3300 NCNB Plaza · Charlotte, NC 28280-8082 · 704-377-6000

James B. Maxwell* · (Plaintiffs, Medical Malpractice, Professional Malpractice) · Maxwell & Hutson · 300 West Morgan Street, Suite 1500 · P.O. Drawer 2252A · Durham, NC 27702 · 919-683-1561

W. Paul Pulley, Jr. · (Plaintiffs) · Pulley, Watson, King & Hofler · Brightleaf Square · P.O. Box 3600 · Durham, NC 27702 · 919-682-9691

Joe McLeod* · (Plaintiffs, Medical Malpractice, Automobile Collision, Airplane Collision) · McLeod, Senter & Hockman · 705 First Citizens Bank Building · P.O. Box 1539 · Fayetteville, NC 28302 · 919-323-1425

Tim L. Harris · (Plaintiffs) · 223 West Main Avenue · P.O. Box 249 · Gastonia, NC 28053 · 704-864-3409

J. Donald Cowan, Jr. · (Defendants) · Smith Helms Mulliss & Moore · 300 North Greene, Suite 1400 · P.O. Box 21927 · Greensboro, NC 27420 · 919-378-5200

Joseph E. Elrod III · (Defendants) · Elrod & Lawing · 826 North Elm Street · P.O. Box 22106 · Greensboro, NC 27402 · 919-333-6400

Perry C. Henson · (Defendants) · Henson Henson Bayliss & Teague · 601 Wachovia Building · P.O. Box 3525 · Greensboro, NC 27402 · 919-275-0587

Charles E. Nichols* · (Defendants) · Nichols, Caffrey, Hill, Evans & Murelle · 1400 Renaissance Plaza · P.O. Box 989 · Greensboro, NC 27402 · 919-379-1390

McNeill Smith* · (Defendants, Products Liability) · Smith Helms Mulliss & Moore · 300 North Greene, Suite 1400 · P.O. Box 21927 · Greensboro, NC 27420 919-378-5200

Marvin K. Blount, Jr. · (Plaintiffs) · 400 West First Street · P.O. Drawer 58 · Greenville, NC 27835-0058 · 919-752-6000

Arch K. Schoch, Jr.* · (Plaintiffs) · Schoch, Schoch and Schoch · 310 South Main Street · P.O. Box 1893 · High Point, NC 27261 · 919-884-4151

John D. Warlick, Jr.* · (Plaintiffs, Medical Malpractice, Automobile Collision) · Ellis, Hooper, Warlick, Waters & Morgan · 313 New Bridge Street · P.O. Drawer 1006 · Jacksonville, NC 28541-1006 · 919-455-3637

Thomas E. Harris* · (Defendants, Medical Malpractice, Products Liability, Professional Malpractice, Automobile Collision) · Harris and Associates · 229 Pollock Street · P.O. Box 1184 · New Bern, NC 28563-1184 · 919-638-6666

James G. Billings · (Defendants) · Smith, Anderson, Blount, Dorsett, Mitchell & Jernigan · 1300 St. Mary's Street · P.O. Box 12807 · Raleigh, NC 27605 · 919-821-1220

Charles F. Blanchard* · (Plaintiffs) · Blanchard, Twiggs, Abrams & Strickland · 200 West Morgan Street, Suite 300 · P.O. Drawer 30 · Raleigh, NC 27602 · 919-828-4357

James D. Blount, Jr.* · (Defendants, Medical Malpractice) · Smith, Anderson, Blount, Dorsett, Mitchell & Jernigan · 1300 St. Mary's Street · P.O. Box 12807 · Raleigh, NC 27605 · 919-821-1220

Robert M. Clay* · (Defendants, Medical Malpractice) · Patterson, Dilthey, Clay, Cranfill, Sumner & Hartzog · 225 Hillsborough Street, Suite 300 · P.O. Box 310 Raleigh, NC 27602-0310 · 919-821-7052

Ronald C. Dilthey* · (Defendants, Products Liability, Professional Malpractice) Patterson, Dilthey, Clay, Cranfill, Sumner & Hartzog · 225 Hillsboro Street, Suite 300 · P.O. Box 310 · Raleigh, NC 27602-0310 · 919-821-7052

John R. Edwards · (Plaintiffs) · Tharrington, Smith & Hargrove · 209 Fayetteville Street Mall · P.O. Box 1151 · Raleigh, NC 27602 · 919-821-4711

James C. Fuller, Jr. · (Plaintiffs) · Becton, Slifkin & Fuller · 908 West Morgan Street · Raleigh, NC 27603 · 919-755-1068

Anne R. Slifkin · (Plaintiffs) · Becton, Slifkin & Fuller · 908 West Morgan Street Raleigh, NC 27603 · 919-755-1068

William L. Thorp* · (Plaintiffs) · William L. Thorp & Associates · 225 Hillsborough Street, Suite 325 · Raleigh, NC 27603 · 919-755-1367

Howard F. Twiggs · (Plaintiffs) · Blanchard, Twiggs, Abrams & Strickland · 200 West Morgan Street, Suite 300 · P.O. Drawer 30 · Raleigh, NC 27602 · 919-828-4357

Joseph W. Yates III* · (Defendants, Medical Malpractice, Products Liability) · Yates, McLamb & Weyher · Carolina Place, Suite 350 · 2626 Glenwood Avenue P.O. Box 18037 · Raleigh, NC 27619 · 919-783-5300

Daniel L. Brawley · Roundtree, Seagle & Brawley · 2419 Market Street · P.O. Box 1409 · Wilmington, NC 28402 · 919-763-3404

Lonnie B. Williams · (Defendants) · Marshall, Williams & Gorham · 14 South Fifth Street · P.O. Drawer 2088 · Wilmington, NC 28402-2088 · 919-763-9891

H. Grady Barnhill, Jr.* · (Defendants) · Womble Carlyle Sandridge & Rice · 1600 One Triad Park · 200 West Second Street · P.O. Drawer 84 · Winston-Salem, NC 27102-0084 · 919-721-3600

Jimmy H. Barnhill* · (Products Liability) · Womble Carlyle Sandridge & Rice · 1600 One Triad Park · 200 West Second Street · P.O. Drawer 84 · Winston-Salem, NC 27102-0084 · 919-721-3628

William Kearns Davis · (Defendants) · Bell, Davis & Pitt · 635 West Fourth Street, Suite 200 · P.O. Box 49 · Winston-Salem, NC 27102 · 919-722-3700

Allan R. Gitter* · (Defendants, Medical Malpractice, Professional Malpractice, Automobile Collision) · Womble Carlyle Sandridge & Rice · 1600 One Triad Park 200 West Second Street · P.O. Drawer 84 · Winston-Salem, NC 27102-0084 · 919-721-3615

Ralph M. Stockton, Jr.* · (Defendants) · Petree Stockton & Robinson · 1001 West Fourth Street · P.O. Box 2860 · Winston-Salem, NC 27102-2400 · 919-725-2351

PUBLIC UTILITY LAW

Clarence W. Walker · Kennedy Covington Lobdell & Hickman · 3300 NCNB Plaza · Charlotte, NC 28280 · 704-377-6000

Jerry W. Amos · Brooks, Pierce, McLendon, Humphrey & Leonard · 2000 Renaissance Place · 230 North Elm Street · P.O. Drawer U · Greensboro, NC 27402 919-373-8850

Edgar M. Roach, Jr. · Hunton & Williams · One Hannover Square, Suite 1400 · Fayetteville Street Mall · P.O. Box 109 · Raleigh, NC 27602 · 919-899-3000

REAL ESTATE LAW

Alfred G. Adams · (Commercial Transactions, Industrial Transactions) · Van Winkle, Buck, Wall, Starnes and Davis · 11 North Market Street · P.O. Box 7376 Asheville, NC 28802 · 704-258-2991

Ashley L. Hogewood, Jr. · Parker, Poe, Adams & Bernstein · 2600 Charlotte Plaza · Charlotte, NC 28244 · 704-372-9000

Henry C. Lomax · Kennedy Covington Lobdell & Hickman · 3300 NCNB Plaza Charlotte, NC 28280-8082 · 704-377-6000

Bailey Patrick, Jr. · Perry, Patrick, Farmer & Michaux · 900 Baxter Street, Suite 300 · P.O. Box 35566 · Charlotte, NC 28235 · 704-372-1120

Robert E. Perry, Jr. · Perry, Patrick, Farmer & Michaux · 900 Baxter Street, Suite 300 · P.O. Box 35566 · Charlotte, NC 28235 · 704-372-1120

Robert C. Sink · Robinson, Bradshaw & Hinson · 1900 Independence Center · 101 North Tryon Street · Charlotte, NC 28246 · 704-377-2536

Gibson L. Smith, Jr. · Robinson, Bradshaw & Hinson · 1900 Independence Center · 101 North Tryon Street · Charlotte, NC 28246 · 704-377-2536

William P. Aycock II · (Corporate Finance, Leveraged Buyouts, Mergers & Acquisitions, Securities Regulation) · Schell, Bray, Aycock, Abel & Livingston · 230 North Elm Street, Suite 1500 · P.O. Box 21847 · Greensboro, NC 27420 · 919-370-8800

Charles E. Melvin, Jr. · Smith Helms Mulliss & Moore · 300 North Greene, Suite 1400 · P.O. Box 21927 · Greensboro, NC 27420 · 919-378-5200

Thomas F. Adams, Jr. · Maupin Taylor Ellis & Adams · Merrill Lynch Building 3201 Glenwood Avenue · P.O. Drawer 19764 · Raleigh, NC 27619-9764 · 919-781-6800

Charles L. Fulton · Manning, Fulton & Skinner · 500 UCB Plaza · 3605 Glenwood Avenue · P.O. Box 20389 · Raleigh, NC 27619-0389 · 919-787-8880

Marshall B. Hartsfield · Poyner & Spruill · 3600 Glenwood Avenue · P.O. Box 10096 · Raleigh, NC 27605-0096 · 919-783-6400

James Lee Seay · Seay, Titchener & Horne · 4934 Windy Hill Drive · P.O. Box 18807 · Raleigh, NC 27619-8807 · 919-876-4100

Frank M. Bell, Jr. · Bell, Davis & Pitt · 635 West Fourth Street, Suite 200 · P.O. Box 49 · Winston-Salem, NC 27102 · 919-722-3700

Leslie E. Browder · Womble Carlyle Sandridge & Rice · 1600 One Triad Park · 200 West Second Street · P.O. Drawer 84 · Winston-Salem, NC 27102-0084 · 919-721-3600

Richard E. Glaze, Sr. · Petree Stockton & Robinson · 1001 West Fourth Street · P.O. Box 2860 · Winston-Salem, NC 27102-2400 · 919-725-2351

TAX AND EMPLOYEE BENEFITS LAW

Brian F. D. Lavelle · Van Winkle, Buck, Wall, Starnes and Davis · 11 North Market Street · P.O. Box 7376 · Asheville, NC 28802 · 704-258-2991

Michael L. Miller · BB&T Building, Suite 508 · Asheville, NC 28801 · 704-251-1200

Steve C. Horowitz · (Corporate & Partnership Transactions, IRS Practice & Procedures) · Weinstein & Sturges · 1100 South Tryon Street · Charlotte, NC 28203-4244 · 704-372-4800

James E. Johnson, Jr. · 2400 NCNB Plaza · Charlotte, NC 28280 · 704-333-7177

Raleigh A. Shoemaker · (Employee Benefits) · Kennedy Covington Lobdell & Hickman · 3300 NCNB Plaza · Charlotte, NC 28280 · 704-377-6000

Richard E. Thigpen, Jr. · (Corporate & Partnership Transactions, State Tax, Tax Disputes) · Poyner & Spruill · 128 South Tryon Street, Suite 1600 · Charlotte, NC 28202 · 704-342-5250

Joseph B. Alala, Jr.* · (Corporate & Partnership Transactions, Tax Disputes) · Alala, Drum, Kersh, Solomon & Sigmon · 301 South York Street · P.O. Box 859 Gastonia, NC 28053 · 704-864-2634

Michael R. Abel · Schell, Bray, Aycock, Abel & Livingston · 230 North Elm Street, Suite 1500 · P.O. Box 21847 · Greensboro, NC 27420 · 919-370-8800

James N. Duggins, Jr. · Tuggle Duggins & Meschan · 228 West Market Street · P.O. Drawer X · Greensboro, NC 27402 · 919-378-1431

Richard J. Tuggle · Tuggle Duggins & Meschan · 228 West Market Street · P.O. Drawer X · Greensboro, NC 27402 · 919-378-1431

Jasper L. Cummings, Jr. · (Corporate & Partnership Transactions, State Tax) · Womble Carlyle Sandridge & Rice · 800 Wachovia Building · P.O. Box 831 · Raleigh, NC 27602 · 919-755-2108

Thomas L. Norris, Jr. · (Employee Benefits) · Poyner & Spruill · 3600 Glenwood Avenue · P.O. Box 10096 · Raleigh, NC 27605-0096 · 919-783-6400

W. Gerald Thornton · Manning, Fulton & Skinner · 500 UCB Plaza · 3605 Glenwood Avenue · P.O. Box 20389 · Raleigh, NC 27619-0389 · 919-787-8880

William Allison Davis II · (Employee Benefits) · Womble Carlyle Sandridge & Rice · 1600 One Triad Park · 200 West Second Street · P.O. Drawer 84 · Winston-Salem, NC 27102-0084 · 919-721-3600

Murray C. Greason, Jr. · Womble Carlyle Sandridge & Rice · 1600 One Triad Park · 200 West Second Street · P.O. Drawer 84 · Winston-Salem, NC 27102-0084 919-721-3600

Michael D. Gunter · (Employee Benefits) · Womble Carlyle Sandridge & Rice · 1600 One Triad Park · 200 West Second Street · P.O. Drawer 84 · Winston-Salem, NC 27102-0084 · 919-721-3607

R. Frank Murphy II · (Employee Benefits) · Petree Stockton & Robinson · 1001 West Fourth Street · P.O. Box 2860 · Winston-Salem, NC 27102-2400 · 919-725-2351

Robert C. Vaughn, Jr. · Petree Stockton & Robinson · 1001 West Fourth Street P.O. Box 2860 · Winston-Salem, NC 27102-2400 · 919-725-2351

TRUSTS AND ESTATES

Barry B. Kempson · Van Winkle, Buck, Wall, Starnes and Davis · 11 North Market Street · P.O. Box 7376 · Asheville, NC 28802 · 704-258-2991

Brian F. D. Lavelle · Van Winkle, Buck, Wall, Starnes and Davis · 11 North Market Street · P.O. Box 7376 · Asheville, NC 28802 · 704-258-2991

Herbert H. Browne, Jr. · Smith Helms Mulliss & Moore · 227 North Tryon Street P.O. Box 31247 · Charlotte, NC 28231 · 704-343-2000

William F. Drew, Jr. · Kennedy Covington Lobdell & Hickman · 3300 NCNB Plaza · Charlotte, NC 28280 · 704-377-6000

Mark B. Edwards · Poyner & Spruill · 128 South Tryon Street, Suite 1600 · Charlotte, NC 28202 · 704-342-5250

Neill G. McBryde · Moore & Van Allen · 3000 NCNB Plaza · Charlotte, NC 28280 704-331-1000

Robert B. Lloyd, Jr. · (Estate Planning, Estate Administration, Charitable Trusts) Turner, Enochs & Lloyd · 100 South Elm Street, Suite 401 · P.O. Box 160 · Greensboro, NC 27402 · 919-373-1300

David S. Evans · (Estate Planning, Estate Administration, Charitable Trusts, Premarital Agreements) · Ward and Smith · 1001 College Court · P.O. Box 867 · New Bern, NC 28563-0867 · 919-633-1000

Maria M. Lynch · Hunter, Wharton & Lynch · 2626 Glenwood Avenue, Suite 430 P.O. Drawer 10037 · Raleigh, NC 27605 · 919-881-9110

Curtis A. Twiddy · Poyner & Spruill · 3600 Glenwood Avenue · P.O. Box 10096
Raleigh, NC 27605-0096 · 919-783-6400

Jeff. D. Batts · 505 Sunset Avenue · P.O. Drawer 4847 · Rocky Mount, NC 27803
919-977-6450

Elizabeth L. Quick · Womble Carlyle Sandridge & Rice · 1600 One Triad Park
200 West Second Street · P.O. Drawer 84 · Winston-Salem, NC 27102-0084 ·
919-721-3600

Robert C. Vaughn, Jr. · Petree Stockton & Robinson · 1001 West Fourth Street
P.O. Box 2860 · Winston-Salem, NC 27102-2400 · 919-725-2351

NORTH DAKOTA

BANKRUPTCY LAW

Max D. Rosenberg · 105 East Broadway · P.O. Box 1278 · Bismarck, ND 58502 701-222-3968

David T. DeMars · DeMars & Turman · 600 First Interstate Center · Fargo, ND 58124 · 701-293-5592

John S. Foster* · (Creditors' Rights, Bankruptcy Litigation) · Vaaler, Warcup, Woutat, Zimney & Foster · Metropolitan Building, Fifth Floor · 600 De Mers Avenue · P.O. Box 1617 · Grand Forks, ND 58206-1617 · 701-772-8111

Richard P. Olson* · (Creditors' Rights, Bankruptcy Litigation) · Olson, Sturdevant & Burns · 17 First Avenue, SE · P.O. Box 1180 · Minot, ND 58702-1180 · 701-839-1740

BUSINESS LITIGATION

Lyle W. Kirmis* · (Commercial) · Zuger, Kirmis, Bolinske & Smith · Provident Life Building · 316 North Fifth Street · P.O. Box 1695 · Bismarck, ND 58501-1695 · 701-223-2711

David L. Peterson* · (Banking) · Wheeler Wolf · 116 North Fourth Street · P.O. Box 773 · Bismarck, ND 58502-0773 · 701-223-5300

John R. Brakke · Vogel, Brantner, Kelly, Knutson, Weir & Bye · 502 First Avenue North · P.O. Box 1389 · Fargo, ND 58107 · 701-237-6983

Kermit Edward Bye · Vogel, Brantner, Kelly, Knutson, Weir & Bye · 502 First Avenue North · P.O. Box 1389 · Fargo, ND 58107 · 701-237-6983

Timothy Q. Davies · (Commercial) · Nilles, Hansen & Davies · 1800 Radisson Tower · P.O. Box 2626 · Fargo, ND 58108 · 701-237-5544

Charles A. Feste · Conmy, Feste, Bossart, Hubbard & Corwin · 400 Norwest Center · Fourth Street and Main Avenue · Fargo, ND 58126 · 701-293-9911

John S. Foster* · (Banking, Commercial, Finance) · Vaaler, Warcup, Woutat, Zimney & Foster · Metropolitan Building, Fifth Floor · 600 De Mers Avenue · P.O. Box 1617 · Grand Forks, ND 58206-1617 · 701-772-8111

Garry A. Pearson · Pearson, Christensen & Fischer · 24 North Fourth Street · P.O. Box 1075 · Grand Forks, ND 58206-1075 · 701-775-0521

Robert Vaaler* · (Commercial) · Vaaler, Warcup, Woutat, Zimney & Foster · Metropolitan Building, Fifth Floor · 600 De Mers Avenue · P.O. Box 1617 · Grand Forks, ND 58206-1617 · 701-772-8111

Malcolm H. Brown* · (Commercial) · Bair, Brown and Kautzmann · 210 First Avenue, NW · P.O. Box 100 · Mandan, ND 58554-0100 · 701-663-6568

Richard P. Olson* · (Banking, Commercial, Finance) · Olson, Sturdevant & Burns · 17 First Avenue, SE · P.O. Box 1180 · Minot, ND 58702-1180 · 701-839-1740

CORPORATE LAW

Ernest R. Fleck · Fleck, Mather & Strutz · Norwest Bank Building, Sixth Floor 400 East Broadway · P.O. Box 2798 · Bismarck, ND 58502 · 701-223-6585

Lyle W. Kirmis* · Zuger, Kirmis, Bolinske & Smith · Provident Life Building · 316 North Fifth Street · P.O. Box 1695 · Bismarck, ND 58501-1695 · 701-223-2711

William P. Pearce · Pearce and Durick · 314 East Thayer Avenue, Third Floor · P.O. Box 400 · Bismarck, ND 58502 · 701-223-2890

R. W. Wheeler · Wheeler Wolf · 220 North Fourth Street · P.O. Box 2056 · Bismarck, ND 58502-2056 · 701-223-5300

Kermit Edward Bye · Vogel, Brantner, Kelly, Knutson, Weir & Bye · 502 First Avenue North · P.O. Box 1389 · Fargo, ND 58107 · 701-237-6983

Timothy Q. Davies · (Banking, Financial Institutions) · Nilles, Hansen & Davies 1800 Radisson Tower · P.O. Box 2626 · Fargo, ND 58108 · 701-237-5544

Charles A. Feste · Conmy, Feste, Bossart, Hubbard & Corwin · 400 Norwest Center · Fourth Street & Main Avenue · Fargo, ND 58126 · 701-293-9911

Russell F. Freeman · Nilles, Hansen & Davies · 1800 Radisson Tower · P.O. Box 2626 · Fargo, ND 58108 · 701-237-5544

Garry A. Pearson · Pearson, Christensen & Fischer · 24 North Fourth Street · P.O. Box 1075 · Grand Forks, ND 58206-1075 · 701-775-0521

Malcolm H. Brown* · Bair, Brown and Kautzmann · 210 First Avenue, NW · P.O. Box 100 · Mandan, ND 58554-0100 · 701-663-6568

Richard P. Olson* · (Banking, Corporate Finance, Financial Institutions) · Olson, Sturdevant & Burns · 17 First Avenue, SE · P.O. Box 1180 · Minot, ND 58702-1180 · 701-839-1740

CRIMINAL DEFENSE

Irvin B. Nodland · Nodland, Tharaldson & Dickson · 109 North Fourth Street, Suite 300 · P.O. Box 640 · Bismarck, ND 58502 · 701-222-2222

Ralph A. Vinje · 523 North Fourth Street · Bismarck, ND 58501 · 701-258-9475

Ronald A. Reichert · Freed, Dynes, Reichert & Buresh · 34 East First Street · P.O. Drawer K · Dickinson, ND 58601 · 701-225-6711

Kenneth A. Olson · Lanier, Knox, Olson & Racek · 115 University Drive · P.O. Box 1007 · Fargo, ND 58107-1932 · 701-232-4437

William D. Yuill · Yuill, Wold, Johnson & Feder · Gate City Building, Suite 414 P.O. Box 1680 · Fargo, ND 58107 · 701-235-5515

Alan J. Larivee · 215 North Third Street, Suite 208B · Grand Forks, ND 58201 701-775-3921

Thomas M. Tuntland · 104 Third Avenue, NW · P.O. Box 1315 · Mandan, ND 58554 · 701-667-1888

FAMILY LAW

Carma Christensen · Christensen & Thompson · 1720 Burnt Boat Drive · Bismarck, ND 58502 · 701-223-9787

James R. Brothers · Schuster, Brothers & Beauchene · 124 North Eighth Street P.O. Box 2842 · Fargo, ND 58108-2842 · 701-293-7935

Robert A. Feder* · Yuill, Wold, Johnson & Feder · Gate City Building, Suite 414 P.O. Box 1680 · Fargo, ND 58107 · 701-235-5515

Kenneth A. Olson · Lanier, Knox, Olson & Racek · 115 University Drive · P.O. Box 1007 · Fargo, ND 58107-1932 · 701-232-4437

William D. Yuill · Yuill, Wold, Johnson & Feder · Gate City Building, Suite 414 P.O. Box 1680 · Fargo, ND 58107 · 701-235-5515

Dwight C. H. Kautzmann* · Bair, Brown & Kautzmann · 210 First Avenue, NW P.O. Box 100 · Mandan, ND 58554-0100 · 701-663-6568

FIRST AMENDMENT LAW

Jack McDonald · Wheeler Wolf · 220 North Fourth Street · P.O. Box 2056 · Bismarck, ND 58502-2056 · 701-223-5300

Robert A. Feder* · Yuill, Wold, Johnson & Feder · Gate City Building, Suite 414 P.O. Box 1680 · Fargo, ND 58107 · 701-235-5515

LABOR AND EMPLOYMENT LAW

Patrick J. Ward* · (Management) · Zuger, Kirmis, Bolinske & Smith · 316 North Fifth Street · P.O. Box 1695 · Bismarck, ND 58502 · 701-223-2711

Robert A. Feder* · (Management) · Yuill, Wold, Johnson & Feder · Gate City Building, Suite 414 · P.O. Box 1680 · Fargo, ND 58107 · 701-235-5515

Douglas R. Herman · Vogel, Brantner, Kelly, Knutson, Weir & Bye · 502 First Avenue North · P.O. Box 1389 · Fargo, ND 58107 · 701-237-6983

NATURAL RESOURCES AND ENVIRONMENTAL LAW

Ernest R. Fleck · Fleck, Mather & Strutz · Norwest Bank Building, Sixth Floor 400 East Broadway · P.O. Box 2798 · Bismarck, ND 58502 · 701-223-6585

William P. Pearce · Pearce and Durick · 314 East Thayer Avenue, Third Floor · P.O. Box 400 · Bismarck, ND 58502 · 701-223-2890

John L. Sherman* · Mackoff, Kellogg, Kirby & Kloster · 46 West Second Street P.O. Box 1097 · Dickinson, ND 58601 · 701-227-1841

Robert A. Wheeler · McGee, Hankla, Backes & Wheeler · P.O. Box 998 · Minot, ND 58702 · 701-852-2544

Fred C. Rathert · (Oil & Gas) · Bjella Neff Rathert Wahl & Eiken · 111 East Broadway · P.O. Drawer 1526 · Williston, ND 58802-1526 · 701-572-3794

PERSONAL INJURY LITIGATION

Leonard H. Bucklin* · (Products Liability, Automobile Collision, Fires & Explosions) · Bucklin Trial Lawyers · Norwest Bank Building, Suite 500 · P.O. Box 955 · Bismarck, ND 58502 · 701-258-8988

B. Timothy Durick · (Defendants) · Pearce and Durick · 314 East Thayer Avenue, Third Floor · P.O. Box 400 · Bismarck, ND 58502 · 701-223-2890

Irvin B. Nodland · (Plaintiffs) · Nodland, Tharaldson & Dickson · 109 North Fourth Street, Suite 300 · P.O. Box 640 · Bismarck, ND 58502 · 701-222-2222

David L. Peterson* · (Products Liability, Automobile Collision) · Wheeler Wolf 116 North Fourth Street · P.O. Box 773 · Bismarck, ND 58502-0773 · 701-223-5300

Orell D. Schmitz · (Plaintiffs) · Wheeler Wolf · 220 North Fourth Street · P.O. Box 2056 · Bismarck, ND 58502-2056 · 701-223-5300

William A. Strutz · (Defendants) · Fleck, Mather & Strutz · Norwest Bank Building, Sixth Floor · 400 East Broadway · P.O. Box 2798 · Bismarck, ND 58502 701-223-6585

Paul G. Kloster · (Defendants) · Mackoff, Kellogg, Kirby & Kloster · 46 West Second Street · P.O. Box 1097 · Dickinson, ND 58601 · 701-227-1841

Ronald A. Reichert · (Plaintiffs) · Freed, Dynes, Reichert & Buresh · 34 East First Street · Drawer K · Dickinson, ND 58601 · 701-225-6711

David R. Bossart · (Plaintiffs) · Conmy, Feste, Bossart, Hubbard & Corwin · 400 Norwest Center · Fourth Street & Main Avenue · Fargo, ND 58126 · 701-293-9911

Lee Hagen · (Plaintiffs) · Pioneer Plaza, Suite 302 · 101 North 10th Street · P.O. Box 2982 · Fargo, ND 58108-2982 · 701-293-8425

Donald R. Hansen · (Defendants) · Nilles, Hansen & Davies · 1800 Radisson Tower · P.O. Box 2626 · Fargo, ND 58108 · 701-237-5544

Carlton J. Hunke · (Defendants) · Vogel, Brantner, Kelly, Knutson, Weir & Bye 502 First Avenue North · P.O. Box 1389 · Fargo, ND 58107 · 701-237-6983

Duane H. Ilvedson · (Defendants) · Nilles, Hansen & Davies · 1800 Radisson Tower · P.O. Box 2626 · Fargo, ND 58108 · 701-237-5544

John D. Kelly · (Defendants) · Vogel, Brantner, Kelly, Knutson, Weir & Bye · 502 First Avenue North · P.O. Box 1389 · Fargo, ND 58107 · 701-237-6983

Frank T. Knox · (Plaintiffs) · Lanier, Knox, Olson & Racek · 115 University Drive P.O. Box 1007 · Fargo, ND 58107-1932 · 701-232-4437

Jack G. Marcil* · (Plaintiffs, Defendants, Products Liability, Automobile Collision) · Serkland, Lundberg, Erickson, Marcil & McLean · 10 Roberts Street · P.O. Box 6017 · Fargo, ND 58108-6017 · 701-232-8957

Mart R. Vogel · (Defendants) · Vogel, Brantner, Kelly, Knutson, Weir & Bye · 502 First Avenue North · P.O. Box 1389 · Fargo, ND 58107 · 701-237-6983

H. Patrick Weir · Vogel, Brantner, Kelly, Knutson, Weir & Bye · 502 First Avenue North · P.O. Box 1389 · Fargo, ND 58107 · 701-237-6983

Robert Vaaler* · (Defendants, Medical Malpractice, Products Liability) · Vaaler, Warcup, Woutat, Zimney & Foster · Metropolitan Building, Fifth Floor · 600 De Mers Avenue · P.O. Box 1617 · Grand Forks, ND 58206-1617 · 701-772-8111

Robert Vogel* · (Medical Malpractice, Professional Malpractice) · The Robert Vogel Law Office · 106 North Third Street, Suite M102 · P.O. Box 1376 · Grand Forks, ND 58206-1376 · 701-775-3117

Bruce B. Bair* · Bair, Brown & Kautzmann · 210 First Avenue, NW · P.O. Box 100 · Mandan, ND 58554-0100 · 701-663-6568

PUBLIC UTILITY LAW

William P. Pearce · Pearce and Durick · 314 East Thayer Avenue, Third Floor · P.O. Box 400 · Bismarck, ND 58502 · 701-223-2890

R. W. Wheeler · Wheeler Wolf · 220 North Fourth Street · P.O. Box 2056 · Bismarck, ND 58502-2056 · 701-223-5300

REAL ESTATE LAW

John L. Sherman* · (Land Use, Commercial Transactions, Industrial Transactions, Foreclosure of Mortgages) · Mackoff, Kellogg, Kirby & Kloster · 46 West Second Street · P.O. Box 1097 · Dickinson, ND 58601 · 701-227-1841

Paul M. Hubbard · Conmy, Feste, Bossart, Hubbard & Corwin · 400 Norwest Center · Fourth Street & Main Avenue · Fargo, ND 58126 · 701-293-9911

J. Philip Johnson · Yuill, Wold, Johnson & Feder · Gate City Building, Suite 414 P.O. Box 1680 · Fargo, ND 58107 · 701-235-5515

David F. Knutson · Vogel, Brantner, Kelly, Knutson, Weir & Bye · 502 First Avenue North · P.O. Box 1389 · Fargo, ND 58107 · 701-237-6983

Robert L. Stroup II · Nilles, Hansen & Davies · 1800 Radisson Tower · P.O. Box 2626 · Fargo, ND 58108 · 701-237-5544

Theodore M. Camrud · Degnan, McElroy, Lamb, Camrud, Maddock & Olson · First National Bank Building, Fifth Floor · P.O. Box 818 · Grand Forks, ND 58201-0818 · 701-775-5595

TAX AND EMPLOYEE BENEFITS LAW

C. Nicholas Vogel · Vogel, Brantner, Kelly, Knutson, Weir & Bye · 502 First Avenue North · P.O. Box 1389 · Fargo, ND 58107 · 701-237-6983

Garry A. Pearson · Pearson, Christensen & Fischer · 24 North Fourth Street · P.O. Box 1075 · Grand Forks, ND 58206-1075 · 701-775-0521

Robert J. Lamont · Lamont Law Office · 111 Eleventh Avenue, SW · P.O. Box 2226 · Minot, ND 58702 · 701-852-7002

TRUSTS AND ESTATES

Sean O. Smith · Tschider & Smith · 418 East Rosser Avenue · Bismarck, ND 58501 · 701-258-4000

Charles A. Feste · Conmy, Feste, Bossart, Hubbard & Corwin · 400 Norwest Center · Fourth Street & Main Avenue · Fargo, ND 58126 · 701-293-9911

C. Nicholas Vogel · Vogel, Brantner, Kelly, Knutson, Weir & Bye · 502 First Avenue North · P.O. Box 1389 · Fargo, ND 58107 · 701-237-6983

Garry A. Pearson · Pearson, Christensen & Fischer · 24 North Fourth Street · P.O. Box 1075 · Grand Forks, ND 58206-1075 · 701-775-0521

Walfrid B. Hankla · McGee, Hankla, Backes & Wheeler · Norwest Bank Building, Suite 305 · P.O. Box 998 · Minot, ND 58702-0998 · 701-852-2544

Robert J. Lamont · Lamont Law Office · 111 Eleventh Avenue, SW · P.O. Box 2226 · Minot, ND 58702 · 701-852-7002

Robert E. Rosenvold · Ohnstad & Twitchell · 901 Thirteenth Avenue East · P.O. Box 458 · West Fargo, ND 58078-0455 · 701-282-3249

OHIO

BANKRUPTCY LAW

John J. Guy · Guy, Lammert & Towne · 2210 First National Tower · Akron, OH 44308-1449 · 216-535-2151

David M. Hunter · (Business Reorganization) · Brouse & McDowell · 500 First National Tower · Akron, OH 44308-1471 · 216-535-5711

John A. Schwemler* · Brouse & McDowell · 500 First National Tower · Akron, OH 44308-1471 · 216-535-5711

Ronald N. Towne · Guy, Lammert & Towne · 2210 First National Tower · Akron, OH 44308-1449 · 216-535-2151

Wallace W. Walker · Roetzel & Andress · 75 East Market Street · Akron, OH 44308-2098 · 216-376-2700

Stephen L. Black · Graydon, Head & Ritchey · 1900 Fifth Third Center · 511 Walnut Street · P.O. Box 6464 · Cincinnati, OH 45202-6464 · 513-621-6464

Timothy J. Hurley · Taft, Stettinius & Hollister · 1800 Star Bank Center · Cincinnati, OH 45202 · 513-381-2838

Frederick R. Reed · Vorys, Sater, Seymour and Pease · 52 East Gay Street · P.O. Box 1008 · Cincinnati, OH 43216-1008 · 513-723-4000

Jay A. Rosenberg · (Business Reorganization, Creditors' Rights) · Dinsmore & Shohl · 255 East Fifth Street · Cincinnati, OH 45202-3172 · 513-977-8200

Peter J. Strauss · Graydon, Head & Ritchey · 1900 Fifth Third Center · 511 Walnut Street · P.O. Box 6464 · Cincinnati, OH 45202-6464 · 513-621-6464

Robert S. Balantzow · Benesch, Friedlander, Coplan & Aronoff · 1100 Citizens Building · 850 Euclid Avenue · Cleveland, OH 44114-3399 · 216-363-4638

Richard A. Baumgart* · Dettelbach, Sicherman & Baumgart · 1100 Ohio Savings Plaza · 1801 East Ninth Street · Cleveland, OH 44114-3169 · 216-696-6000

David G. Heiman · Jones, Day, Reavis & Pogue · North Point · 901 Lakeside Avenue · Cleveland, OH 44114 · 216-586-3939

G. Christopher Meyer · (Business Reorganization, Creditors' Rights, Debtors' Rights, Workouts & Restructurings) · Squire, Sanders & Dempsey · 1800 Huntington Building · Cleveland, OH 44115 · 216-687-8500

Joseph Patchan · Baker & Hostetler · 3200 National City Center · Cleveland, OH 44114 · 216-621-0200

Lee D. Powar · (Business Reorganization, Creditors' Rights, Bankruptcy Litigation, Environmental) · Hahn Loeser & Parks · 800 National City East Sixth Building · 1965 East Sixth Street · Cleveland, OH 44114-2262 · 216-621-0150

Marvin A. Sicherman* · Dettelbach, Sicherman & Baumgart · 1100 Ohio Savings Plaza · 1801 East Ninth Street · Cleveland, OH 44114-3169 · 216-696-6000

Howard L. Sokolsky · Benesch, Friedlander, Coplan & Aronoff · 1100 Citizens Building · 850 Euclid Avenue · Cleveland, OH 44114-3399 · 216-363-4500

Nick V. Cavalieri · Arter & Hadden · One Columbus, 21st Floor · 10 West Broad Street · Columbus, OH 43215 · 614-221-3155

R. P. Cunningham · Arter & Hadden · One Columbus, 21st Floor · 10 West Broad Street · Columbus, OH 43215 · 614-221-3155

John J. Dilenschneider · Squire, Sanders & Dempsey · 41 South High Street · Columbus, OH 43215 · 614-365-2789

E. James Hopple · (Business Reorganization, Creditors' Rights) · Schottenstein, Zox & Dunn · The Huntington Center, 26th Floor · 41 South High Street · Columbus, OH 43215 · 614-221-3211

William B. Logan, Jr.* · (Business Reorganization, Creditors' Rights, Bankruptcy Litigation) · Luper, Wolinetz, Sheriff & Neidenthal · 1200 LeVeque Tower · 50 West Broad Street · Columbus, OH 43215-3374 · 614-221-7663

Frederick M. Luper · Luper, Wolinetz, Sheriff & Neidenthal · 1200 LeVeque Tower · 50 West Broad Street · Columbus, OH 43215-3374 · 614-221-7663

Grady L. Pettigrew, Jr. · Arter & Hadden · One Columbus, 21st Floor · 10 West Broad Street · Columbus, OH 43215 · 614-221-3155

Jack R. Pigman · (Business Reorganization, Creditors' Rights, Bankruptcy Litigation) · Porter, Wright, Morris & Arthur · 41 South High Street · Columbus, OH 43215-3406 · 614-227-2000

Thomas C. Scott* · Thompson, Hine and Flory · The Bank One Building, 18th Floor · 100 East Broad Street · Columbus, OH 43215 · 614-469-7200

Robert J. Sidman · Vorys, Sater, Seymour and Pease · 52 East Gay Street · P.O. Box 1008 · Columbus, OH 43216-1008 · 614-464-6400

Philip E. Langer · Chernesky, Heyman & Kress · 10 Courthouse Plaza Southwest, Suite 1100 · P.O. Box 3808 · Dayton, OH 45401-3808 · 513-449-2828

Dennis L. Patterson* · (Creditors' Rights, Bankruptcy Litigation, Creditors' Committees) · Bogin & Patterson · 1200 Talbott Tower · 131 North Ludlow Street Dayton, OH 45402-1737 · 513-226-1200

Ira Rubin · Goldman, Rubin & Shapiro · 2050 Miami Valley Tower · Dayton, OH 45402 · 513-222-2376

H. Buswell Roberts, Jr. · Nathan & Roberts · 644 Spitzer Building · 520 Madison Avenue · Toledo, OH 43604-1302 · 419-255-3036

Michael A. Gallo · Nadler, Nadler & Bergman · 20 Federal Plaza West, Suite 600
Youngstown, OH 44503 · 216-744-0247

BUSINESS LITIGATION

Norman S. Carr* · Roetzel & Andress · 75 East Market Street · Akron, OH
44308-2098 · 216-376-2700

John W. Beatty · Dinsmore & Shohl · 255 East Fifth Street · Cincinnati, OH
45202-3172 · 513-977-8200

Thomas S. Calder · Dinsmore & Shohl · 255 East Fifth Street · Cincinnati, OH
45202-3172 · 513-977-8200

Murray S. Monroe* · (Antitrust, Appellate, RICO) · Taft, Stettinius & Hollister
1800 Star Bank Center · Cincinnati, OH 45202 · 513-381-2838

Robert A. Pitcairn, Jr. · Katz, Teller, Brant & Hild · 1400 Tri-State Building ·
432 Walnut Street · Cincinnati, OH 45202-3961 · 513-721-4532

Robert G. Stachler* · (Appellate, Commercial, RICO, Securities) · Taft, Stettinius & Hollister · 1800 Star Bank Center · Cincinnati, OH 45202 · 513-381-2838

Jacob K. Stein* · Thompson, Hine and Flory · 1700 Central Trust Tower · One
West Fourth Street · Cincinnati, OH 45202-3675 · 513-352-6700

Glenn V. Whitaker* · (Commercial) · Graydon, Head & Ritchey · 1900 Fifth
Third Center · 511 Walnut Street · P.O. Box 6464 · Cincinnati, OH 45202-6464
513-629-2733

Richard Cusick* · (Antitrust, Commercial, Securities) · Calfee, Halter & Griswold · 1800 Society Building · East Ninth and Superior · Cleveland, OH 44114-
2688 · 216-622-8200

Daniel W. Hammer* · Thompson, Hine and Flory · 1100 National City Bank
Building · 629 Euclid Avenue · Cleveland, OH 44114-3070 · 216-566-5500

Marvin L. Karp · Ulmer & Berne · 900 Bond Court Building · 1300 East Ninth
Street · Cleveland, OH 44114-1583 · 216-621-8400

Thomas S. Kilbane · Squire, Sanders & Dempsey · 1800 Huntington Building ·
Cleveland, OH 44115 · 216-687-8500

H. Stephen Madsen* · Baker & Hostetler · 3200 National City Center · Cleveland, OH 44114 · 216-621-0200

Patrick F. McCartan · Jones, Day, Reavis & Pogue · North Point · 901 Lakeside Avenue · Cleveland, OH 44114 · 216-586-3939

Gerald A. Messerman · Messerman & Messerman · 1525 Ohio Savings Plaza · 1801 East Ninth Street · Cleveland, OH 44114 · 216-574-9990

Mark O'Neill* · Weston, Hurd, Fallon, Paisley & Howley · 2500 Terminal Tower Cleveland, OH 44113-2241 · 216-241-6602

James M. Porter · (Antitrust, Commercial) · Squire, Sanders & Dempsey · 1800 Huntington Building · Cleveland, OH 44115 · 216-687-8500

James A. Smith · Squire, Sanders & Dempsey · 1800 Huntington Building · Cleveland, OH 44115 · 216-687-8500

John L. Strauch · Jones, Day, Reavis & Pogue · North Point · 901 Lakeside Avenue · Cleveland, OH 44114 · 216-586-3939

Alan L. Briggs · Squire, Sanders & Dempsey · 1300 Huntington Center · 41 South High Street · Columbus, OH 43215 · 614-365-2800

John J. Chester* · Chester, Hoffman, Willcox and Saxbe · 17 South High Street, Suite 900 · Columbus, OH 43215-3413 · 614-221-4000

David S. Cupps · Vorys, Sater, Seymour and Pease · 52 East Gay Street · P.O. Box 1008 · Columbus, OH 43216-1008 · 614-464-6400

Gerald L. Draper* · (Commercial) · Thompson, Hine and Flory · The Bank One Building, 18th Floor · 100 East Broad Street · Columbus, OH 43215 · 614-469-7200

Robert M. Duncan* · Jones, Day, Reavis & Pogue · 1900 Huntington Center · 41 South High Street · Columbus, OH 43215 · 614-469-3939

John C. Elam · Vorys, Sater, Seymour and Pease · 52 East Gay Street · P.O. Box 1008 · Columbus, OH 43216-1008 · 614-464-6400

Denis J. Murphy · Carlile Patchen Murphy & Allison · 366 East Broad Street · Columbus, OH 43215 · 614-228-6135

Thomas E. Palmer · Squire, Sanders & Dempsey · 1300 Huntington Center · 41 South High Street · Columbus, OH 43215 · 614-365-2800

James E. Pohlman · Porter, Wright, Morris & Arthur · 41 South High Street · Columbus, OH 43215-3406 · 614-227-2000

Thomas B. Ridgley · (Commercial, Toxic Tort) · Vorys, Sater, Seymour and Pease · 52 East Gay Street · P.O. Box 1008 · Columbus, OH 43216-1008 · 614-464-6400

Edgar A. Strause* · Vorys, Sater, Seymour and Pease · 52 East Gay Street · P.O. Box 1008 · Columbus, OH 43216-1008 · 614-464-6257

Duke W. Thomas* · Vorys, Sater, Seymour and Pease · 52 East Gay Street · P.O. Box 1008 · Columbus, OH 43216-1008 · 614-464-6400

David J. Young · Squire, Sanders & Dempsey · 1300 Huntington Center · 41 South High Street · Columbus, OH 43215 · 614-365-2800

John W. Zeiger* · Jones, Day, Reavis & Pogue · 1900 Huntington Center · 41 South High Street · Columbus, OH 43215 · 614-469-3939

Charles J. Faruki* · Faruki Gilliam & Ireland · 600 Courthouse Plaza, SW · 10 North Ludlow Street · Dayton, OH 45402 · 513-227-3700

Armistead W. Gilliam, Jr.* · (Antitrust, Commercial, Energy, Securities) · Faruki Gilliam & Ireland · 600 Courthouse Plaza, SW · 10 North Ludlow Street · Dayton, OH 45402 · 513-227-3700

David C. Greer* · Bieser, Greer & Landis · 400 Gem Plaza · Third and Main Streets · Dayton, OH 45402 · 513-223-3277

Roger J. Makley* · (Banking, Commercial, Securities) · Coolidge, Wall, Womsley & Lombard · 600 IBM Building · 33 West First Street · Dayton, OH 45402 · 513-223-8177

Irving I. Saul* · (Plaintiffs, Antitrust, Banking, Commercial, RICO, Securities) · 113 Bethpolamy Court · Dayton, OH 45415 · 513-278-4858

Robert G. Clayton, Jr.* · Shumaker, Loop & Kendrick · North Courthouse Square · 1000 Jackson · Toledo, OH 43624-1573 · 419-241-9000

Cary Rodman Cooper* · (Antitrust, Commercial) · Cooper, Straub, Walinski & Cramer · 900 Adams Street, Third Floor · P.O. Box 1568 · Toledo, OH 43603-1568 · 419-241-1200

John M. Curphey · Robison, Curphey & O'Connell · Four Seagate, Ninth Floor · Toledo, OH 43604 · 419-249-7900

Jamille G. Jamra · Eastman & Smith · 800 United Savings Building · 240 Huron Street · Toledo, OH 43604-1141 · 419-241-6000

James R. Jeffrey · Spengler, Nathanson, Heyman, McCarthy & Durfee · 1000 National Bank Building · Toledo, OH 43604-1169 · 419-241-2201

Richard M. Kerger* · Marshall & Melhorn · Four Seagate, Eighth Floor · Toledo, OH 43604 · 419-249-7100

John G. Mattimoe · Marshall & Melhorn · Four Seagate, Eighth Floor · Toledo, OH 43604 · 419-249-7100

CORPORATE LAW

Richard A. Chenoweth · Buckingham, Doolittle & Burroughs · Akron Centre Plaza · 50 South Main Street · P.O. Box 1500 · Akron, OH 44309-1500 · 216-376-5300

Duane L. Isham · Roetzel & Andress · 75 East Market Street · Akron, OH 44308-2098 · 216-376-2700

Robert P. Reffner · Brouse & McDowell · 500 First National Tower · Akron, OH 44308-1471 · 216-535-5711

Edmund J. Adams · (Banking, Mergers & Acquisitions) · Frost & Jacobs · 2500 Central Trust Center · 201 East Fourth Street · P.O. Box 5715 · Cincinnati, OH 45201-5715 · 513-651-6800

James M. Anderson · Taft, Stettinius & Hollister · 1800 Star Bank Center · Cincinnati, OH 45202 · 513-381-2838

Dennis J. Barron · Frost & Jacobs · 2500 Central Trust Center · 201 East Fourth Street · P.O. Box 5715 · Cincinnati, OH 45201-5715 · 513-651-6800

J. Leland Brewster · Frost & Jacobs · 2500 Central Trust Center · 201 East Fourth Street · P.O. Box 5715 · Cincinnati, OH 45201-5715 · 513-651-6800

James R. Bridgeland, Jr. · Taft, Stettinius & Hollister · 1800 Star Bank Center Cincinnati, OH 45202 · 513-381-2838

Nolan W. Carson · Dinsmore & Shohl · 255 East Fifth Street · Cincinnati, OH 45202-3172 · 513-977-8200

Timothy E. Hoberg · (Corporate Finance, Mergers & Acquisitions, Securities, Securities Regulation) · Taft, Stettinius & Hollister · 1800 Star Bank Center · Cincinnati, OH 45202 · 513-381-2838

Reuven J. Katz · Katz, Teller, Brant & Hild · 1400 Tri-State Building · 432 Walnut Street · Cincinnati, OH 45202-3961 · 513-721-4532

Gary P. Kreider · Keating, Muething & Klekamp · Provident Tower, 18th Floor One East Fourth Street · Cincinnati, OH 45202 · 513-579-6400

Charles D. Lindberg · Taft, Stettinius & Hollister · 1800 Star Bank Center · Cincinnati, OH 45202 · 513-381-2838

Leonard S. Meranus · (Corporate Finance, Mergers & Acquisitions) · Thompson, Hine and Flory · 312 Walnut Street, Suite 1400 · Cincinnati, OH 45202-3675 · 513-352-6700

Murray S. Monroe* · (Antitrust) · Taft, Stettinius & Hollister · 1800 Star Bank Center · Cincinnati, OH 45202 · 513-381-2838

Clifford A. Roe, Jr. · (Corporate Finance, Financial Institutions, Mergers & Acquisitions, Securities) · Dinsmore & Shohl · 255 East Fifth Street · Cincinnati, OH 45202-3172 · 513-977-8200

John S. Stith · Frost & Jacobs · 2500 Central Trust Center · 201 East Fourth Street · P.O. Box 5715 · Cincinnati, OH 45201-5715 · 513-651-6800

George N. Aronoff · (Corporate Finance, Mergers & Acquisitions, Securities) · Benesch, Friedlander, Coplan & Aronoff · 1100 Citizens Building · 850 Euclid Avenue · Cleveland, OH 44114-3399 · 216-363-4500

Lawrence M. Bell · Benesch, Friedlander, Coplan & Aronoff · 1100 Citizens Building · 850 Euclid Avenue · Cleveland, OH 44114-3399 · 216-363-4500

James H. Berick · Berick, Pearlman & Mills · 1350 Eaton Center · 1111 Superior Avenue · Cleveland, OH 44114-2569 · 216-861-4900

Albert I. Borowitz · Jones, Day, Reavis & Pogue · North Point · 901 Lakeside Avenue · Cleveland, OH 44114 · 216-586-3939

John H. Burlingame · Baker & Hostetler · 3200 National City Center · Cleveland, OH 44114 · 216-621-0200

Paul B. Campbell · Squire, Sanders & Dempsey · 1800 Huntington Building · Cleveland, OH 44115 · 216-687-8500

Joseph R. Cortese · (International Finance, Investment Banking) · Squire, Sanders & Dempsey · 1800 Huntington Building · Cleveland, OH 44115 · 216-687-8500

John L. Dampeer · Thompson, Hine and Flory · 1100 National City Bank Building · 629 Euclid Avenue · Cleveland, OH 44114-3070 · 216-566-5500

Daniel L. Ekelman · Calfee, Halter & Griswold · 1800 Society Building · East Ninth and Superior · Cleveland, OH 44114-2688 · 216-622-8200

John H. Gherlein · Thompson, Hine and Flory · 1100 National City Bank Building · 629 Euclid Avenue · Cleveland, OH 44114-3070 · 216-566-5500

Donald W. Gruettner · Baker & Hostetler · 3200 National City Center · Cleveland, OH 44114 · 216-621-0200

David H. Gunning · Jones, Day, Reavis & Pogue · North Point · 901 Lakeside Avenue · Cleveland, OH 44114 · 216-586-3939

Alan L. Hyde · Thompson, Hine and Flory · 1100 National City Bank Building · 629 Euclid Avenue · Cleveland, OH 44114-3070 · 216-566-5500

Mary Ann Jorgenson · Squire, Sanders & Dempsey · 1800 Huntington Building Cleveland, OH 44115 · 216-687-8654

Robert G. Markey · (Corporate Finance, Mergers & Acquisitions, Securities) · Baker & Hostetler · 3200 National City Center · Cleveland, OH 44114 · 216-621-0200

William A. Papenbrock · Calfee, Halter & Griswold · 1800 Society Building · East Ninth and Superior · Cleveland, OH 44114-2688 · 216-622-8200

Richard W. Pogue · Jones, Day, Reavis & Pogue · North Point · 901 Lakeside Avenue · Cleveland, OH 44114 · 216-586-3939

Frank M. Rasmussen · Squire, Sanders & Dempsey · 1800 Huntington Building Cleveland, OH 44115 · 216-687-8654

Carlton B. Schnell · Arter & Hadden · 1100 Huntington Building · Cleveland, OH 44115 · 216-696-1100

Wilton S. Sogg · Hahn Loeser & Parks · 800 National City East Sixth Building · 1965 East Sixth Street · Cleveland, OH 44114-2262 · 216-621-0150

William H. Steinbrink · Jones, Day, Reavis & Pogue · North Point · 901 Lakeside Avenue · Cleveland, OH 44114 · 216-586-3939

Richard E. Streeter · Thompson, Hine and Flory · 1100 National City Bank Building · 629 Euclid Avenue · Cleveland, OH 44114-3070 · 216-566-5500

Leigh B. Trevor · Jones, Day, Reavis & Pogue · North Point · 901 Lakeside Avenue · Cleveland, OH 44114 · 216-586-3939

Richard T. Watson · Spieth, Bell, McCurdy & Newell · 2000 Huntington Building · Cleveland, OH 44115-1496 · 216-696-4700

William E. Arthur · Porter, Wright, Morris & Arthur · 41 South High Street · Columbus, OH 43215-3406 · 614-227-2000

John P. Beavers · (Corporate Finance, Mergers & Acquisitions, Securities, Securities Regulation) · Bricker & Eckler · 100 South Third Street · Columbus, OH 43215-4291 · 614-227-2300

Susan E. Brown · Vorys, Sater, Seymour and Pease · 52 East Gay Street · P.O. Box 1008 · Columbus, OH 43216-1008 · 614-464-6400

J. Richard Emens · Emens, Hurd, Kegler & Ritter · Capitol Square · 65 East State Street · Columbus, OH 43215 · 614-462-5400

Philip C. Johnston · Vorys, Sater, Seymour and Pease · 52 East Gay Street · P.O. Box 1008 · Columbus, OH 43216-1008 · 614-464-6400

G. Robert Lucas II · (Corporate Finance, Mergers & Acquisitions, Securities, Securities Regulation) · Vorys, Sater, Seymour and Pease · 52 East Gay Street · P.O. Box 1008 · Columbus, OH 43216-1008 · 614-464-6400

Robert W. Minor · Vorys, Sater, Seymour and Pease · 52 East Gay Street · P.O. Box 1008 · Columbus, OH 43216-1008 · 614-464-6400

Michael E. Moritz · Baker & Hostetler · 65 East State Street, Suite 2100 · Columbus, OH 43215 · 614-228-1541

Frank R. Morris, Jr. · Porter, Wright, Morris & Arthur · 41 South High Street · Columbus, OH 43215-3406 · 614-227-2000

Richard R. Murphey, Jr. · Squire, Sanders & Dempsey · 1300 Huntington Center 41 South High Street · Columbus, OH 43215 · 614-365-2700

Edward A. Schrag, Jr. · Vorys, Sater, Seymour and Pease · 52 East Gay Street · P.O. Box 1008 · Columbus, OH 43216-1008 · 614-464-6400

Stanley Schwartz, Jr. · Schwartz, Kelm, Warren & Rubenstein · Huntington Center, 23rd Floor · 41 South High Street · Columbus, OH 43215-6188 · 614-224-3168

Roger R. Stinehart · Jones, Day, Reavis & Pogue · 1900 Huntington Center · 41 South High Street · Columbus, OH 43215 · 614-469-3939

Michael F. Sullivan · Bricker & Eckler · 100 South Third Street · Columbus, OH 43215-4291 · 614-227-2300

John R. Thomas · Emens, Hurd, Kegler & Ritter · Capitol Square · 65 East State Street · Columbus, OH 43215 · 614-462-5400

James M. Tobin · Squire, Sanders & Dempsey · 1300 Huntington Center · 41 South High Street · Columbus, OH 43215 · 614-365-2700

Arthur I. Vorys · Vorys, Sater, Seymour and Pease · 52 East Gay Street · P.O. Box 1008 · Columbus, OH 43216-1008 · 614-464-6400

Richard A. Broock · Chernesky, Heyman & Kress · 10 Courthouse Plaza Southwest, Suite 1100 · P.O. Box 3808 · Dayton, OH 45401-3808 · 513-449-2840

Richard J. Chernesky · (Corporate Finance, Mergers & Acquisitions) · Chernesky, Heyman & Kress · 10 Courthouse Plaza Southwest, Suite 1100 · P.O. Box 3808 · Dayton, OH 45401-3808 · 513-449-2828

Andrew K. Cherney · (Banking, Corporate Finance, Mergers & Acquisitions) · Chernesky, Heyman & Kress · 10 Courthouse Plaza Southwest, Suite 1100 · P.O. Box 3808 · Dayton, OH 45401-3808 · 513-449-2800

Stanley A. Freedman · Thompson, Hine and Flory · 2000 Courthouse Plaza, NE P.O. Box 8801 · Dayton, OH 45401-8801 · 513-443-6500

J. Michael Herr · Thompson, Hine and Flory · 2000 Courthouse Plaza, NE · P.O. Box 8801 · Dayton, OH 45401-8801 · 513-443-6500

Edward M. Kress · Chernesky, Heyman & Kress · 10 Courthouse Plaza Southwest, Suite 1100 · P.O. Box 3808 · Dayton, OH 45401-3808 · 513-449-2828

James J. Mulligan · Thompson, Hine and Flory · 2000 Courthouse Plaza, NE · P.O. Box 8801 · Dayton, OH 45401-8801 · 513-443-6500

Joseph M. Rigot · Thompson, Hine and Flory · 2000 Courthouse Plaza, NE · P.O. Box 8801 · Dayton, OH 45401-8801 · 513-443-6500

James W. Baehren · (Corporate Finance, Mergers & Acquisitions) · Fuller & Henry · One SeaGate, 17th Floor · P.O. Box 2088 · Toledo, OH 43603-2088 · 419-247-2500

George L. Chapman · Shumaker, Loop & Kendrick · North Courthouse Square 1000 Jackson · Toledo, OH 43624-1573 · 419-241-9000

David A. Katz · Spengler, Nathanson, Heyman, McCarthy & Durfee · 1000 National Bank Building · Toledo, OH 43604-1169 · 419-241-2201

David F. Waterman · Shumaker, Loop & Kendrick · North Courthouse Square · 1000 Jackson · Toledo, OH 43624-1573 · 419-241-9000

James F. White, Jr. · (Banking, Corporate Finance, Mergers & Acquisitions, Securities) · Shumaker, Loop & Kendrick · North Courthouse Square · 1000 Jackson · Toledo, OH 43624-1573 · 419-241-9000

CRIMINAL DEFENSE

James L. Burdon* · Burdon and Merlitti · 73 East Mill Street · Akron, OH 44308 216-253-7171

Arnold Morelli · Bauer, Morelli & Heyd · 1029 Main Street · Cincinnati, OH 45202 · 513-241-3676

James N. Perry · 601 Main Street, Third Floor · Cincinnati, OH 45202 · 513-621-0442

Martin S. Pinales · Sirkin, Pinales, Mezibov & Schwartz · 105 West Fourth Street, Suite 920 · Cincinnati, OH 45202 · 513-721-4876

Jack C. Rubenstein · Rubenstein and Thurman · 36 East Fourth Street, Suite 1206 · Cincinnati, OH 45202 · 513-241-7460

Glenn V. Whitaker · Graydon, Head & Ritchey · 1900 Fifth Third Center · 511 Walnut Street · P.O. Box 6464 · Cincinnati, OH 45202-6464 · 513-629-2733

Elmer A. Giuliani · Law Offices of Elmer A. Giuliani · The Leader Building, Suite 410 · 526 Superior Avenue, NE · Cleveland, OH 44114 · 216-241-0520

Gerald S. Gold* · Gold, Rotatori, Schwartz & Gibbons · 1500 Leader Building · 526 Superior Avenue, NE · Cleveland, OH 44114-1498 · 216-696-6122

Gerald A. Messerman · Messerman & Messerman · 1525 Ohio Savings Plaza · 1801 East Ninth Street · Cleveland, OH 44114 · 216-574-9990

Jerome P. Milano* · Milano, Attorneys at Law · 600 Standard Building · Cleveland, OH 44113 · 216-241-5050

George J. Moscarino · Jones, Day, Reavis & Pogue · North Point · 901 Lakeside Avenue · Cleveland, OH 44114 · 216-586-3939

Robert J. Rotatori · Gold, Rotatori, Schwartz & Gibbons · 1500 Leader Building 526 Superior Avenue, NE · Cleveland, OH 44114-1498 · 216-696-6122

James R. Willis · Willis & Blackwell · Bond Court Building, Suite 610 · 1300 East Ninth Street · Cleveland, OH 44114 · 216-523-1100

Paul D. Cassidy · Cassidy & Meeks · 511 South High Street · Columbus, OH 43215 · 614-228-3569

R. William Meeks* · Cassidy & Meeks · 511 South High Street · Columbus, OH 43215 · 614-228-3569

Thomas M. Tyack · Thomas M. Tyack & Associates · 536 South High Street · Columbus, OH 43215 · 614-221-1341

Samuel B. Weiner* · (Forfeiture) · Law Offices of Samuel B. Weiner · 743 South Front Street · Columbus, OH 43206 · 614-443-6581

Harold E. Wonnell · Law Offices of Harold E. Wonnell · 326 South High Street ,Suite 400 · Columbus, OH 43215 · 614-224-7291

Dennis A. Lieberman · Flanagan, Lieberman, Hoffman & Swaim · 318 West Fourth Street · Dayton, OH 45402 · 513-223-5200

Daniel J. O'Brien* · (Violent Crimes, Non-Violent Crimes, Federal Court, State Court) · Talbott Tower, Suite 1410 · 131 North Ludlow Street · Dayton, OH 45402 · 513-228-6001

John H. Rion* · John H. Rion & Associates · One First National Plaza · P.O. Box 1262 · Dayton, OH 45402 · 513-223-9133

Roger L. Clark · Kimble, Stevens, Young, Clark & Rodeheffer · 622 Sixth Street Portsmouth, OH 45662 · 614-354-3214

Jack D. Young · Kimble, Stevens, Young, Clark & Rodeheffer · 622 Sixth Street Portsmouth, OH 45662 · 614-354-3214

John J. Callahan · Secor, Ide & Callahan · 1400 National Bank Building · 608 Madison Avenue · Toledo, OH 43604 · 419-243-2101

William M. Connelly* · Connelly, Soutar & Jackson · 2100 Ohio Citizens Bank Building · Toledo, OH 43604-1207 · 419-243-2100

Alan S. Konop · Konop & Cameron · 413 North Michigan Street · Toledo, OH 43624-1606 · 419-255-0571

Jon D. Richardson · Kaplan, Richardson and Rost · 524 Spitzer Building · Toledo, OH 43604 · 419-241-6168

J. Gerald Ingram · 7330 Market Street · Youngstown, OH 44512 · 216-758-2308

Carmen A. Policy · Flask Policy Weimer & White · 20 Federal Plaza West, Suite 610 · P.O. Box 959 · Youngstown, OH 44501 · 216-746-3217

FAMILY LAW

David A. Lieberth · 1221 West Market Street · Akron, OH 44313 · 216-836-1505

Michael R. Barrett · Graydon, Head & Ritchey · 1900 Fifth Third Center · 511 Walnut Street · P.O. Box 6464 · Cincinnati, OH 45202-6464 · 513-621-6464

Don C. Bolsinger* · (Child Custody, Divorce, Marital Settlement Agreements, Equitable Division) · Bolsinger & Brinkman · 105 East Fourth Street, Suite 1520 Cincinnati, OH 45202 · 513-621-7878

Guy M. Hild* · (Divorce, Marital Settlement Agreements, Equitable Division) · Katz, Teller, Brant & Hild · 1400 Tri-State Building · 432 Walnut Street · Cincinnati, OH 45202-3961 · 513-721-4532

Bea V. Larsen · 30 Garfield Place, Suite 920 · Cincinnati, OH 45202 · 513-241-9844

Jerome S. Teller · Katz, Teller, Brant & Hild · 1400 Tri-State Building · 432 Walnut Street · Cincinnati, OH 45202-3961 · 513-721-4532

Deborah Rowley Akers* · Wolf & Akers · 1515 The East Ohio Building · 1717 East Ninth Street · Cleveland, OH 44114 · 216-623-9999

Joyce E. Barrett* · (Child Custody, Divorce, Marital Settlement Agreements, Equitable Division) · 800 Standard Building · 1370 Ontario Street · Cleveland, OH 44113 · 216-696-1545

Herbert Palkovitz · Law Office of Herbert Palkovitz · 1300 Standard Building · 1370 Ontario Street · Cleveland, OH 44113-1701 · 216-771-3777

James M. Wilsman* · Kelley, McCann & Livingstone · BP America Building, 35th Floor · 200 Public Square · Cleveland, OH 44114-2302 · 216-241-3141

Marshall J. Wolf · (Child Custody, Divorce, Marital Settlement Agreements, Equitable Division) · Wolf & Akers · 1515 The East Ohio Building · 1717 East Ninth Street · Cleveland, OH 44114 · 216-623-9999

Robert I. Zashin* · (Child Custody, Marital Settlement Agreements, Equitable Division) · Zashin, Rich, Sutula & Monastra · 250 Standard Building · Ontario at St. Clair Avenue · Cleveland, OH 44113-1701 · 216-696-4441

John A. Carnahan · Arter & Hadden · One Columbus, 21st Floor · 10 West Broad Street · Columbus, OH 43215 · 614-221-3155

William S. Friedman · Friedman & Babbitt · 500 South Front Street · Columbus, OH 43215 · 614-221-0090

Jeffrey A. Grossman · 32 West Hoster Street · Columbus, OH 43215 · 614-221-7711

Harry Lewis* · (Child Custody, Divorce, Marital Settlement Agreements, Equitable Division) · 625 City Park Avenue · Columbus, OH 43206-1003 · 614-221-3938

Stanley Z. Greenberg · Rogers & Greenberg · 2160 Kettering Tower · Dayton, OH 45423 · 513-223-8171

Charles D. Lowe* · Cowden, Pfarrer, Crew & Becker · 2580 Kettering Tower · Dayton, OH 45423-2580 · 513-223-6211

Jude T. Aubry · (Divorce, Marital Settlement Agreements, Equitable Division) · Aubry, Meyer, Yosses & Rudge · Lawyers Building on Library Square · 329 Tenth Street · P.O. Box 2068 · Toledo, OH 43603-2068 · 419-241-4288

Peter L. Moran* · Peppers & Moran · Louisville Building, Suite 300 · 626 Madison Avenue · Toledo, OH 43604 · 419-241-8171

Melvin G. Nusbaum · Lackey, Nusbaum, Harris, Reny & Torzewski · Two Maritime Plaza, Third Floor · Toledo, OH 43604-1803 · 419-243-1105

Ron L. Rimelspach · Rimelspach, Gibson & Turner · 414 North Erie Street, Suite 200 · Toledo, OH 43624 · 419-241-2153

Eugene B. Fox · Law Offices of Eugene B. Fox · 20 West Boardman Street · Youngstown, OH 44503 · 216-747-4481

FIRST AMENDMENT LAW

Marc D. Mezibov · Sirkin, Pinales, Mezibov & Schwartz · 105 West Fourth Street, Suite 920 · Cincinnati, OH 45202 · 513-721-4876

Robert B. Newman · Kircher and Phalen · 125 East Court Street, Suite 1000 · Cincinnati, OH 45202-1299 · 513-381-3525

H. Louis Sirkin · Sirkin, Pinales, Mezibov & Schwartz · 105 West Fourth Street, Suite 920 · Cincinnati, OH 45202 · 513-721-4876

Frederick M. Gittes* · Spater, Gittes, Schulte & Kolman · 723 Oak Street · Columbus, OH 43205 · 614-221-1160

Benson A. Wolman · Moots, Cope, Stanton & Kizer · 3600 Olentangy River Road · Columbus, OH 43214-3913 · 614-459-4140

John W. Zeiger · Jones, Day, Reavis & Pogue · 1900 Huntington Center · 41 South High Street · Columbus, OH 43215 · 614-469-3939

John Czarnecki · Cooper, Straub, Walinski & Cramer · 900 Adams Street, Third Floor · P.O. Box 1568 · Toledo, OH 43603-1568 · 419-241-1200

HEALTH CARE LAW

Harry M. Brown · Benesch, Friedlander, Coplan & Aronoff · 1100 Citizens Building · 850 Euclid Avenue · Cleveland, OH 44114-3399 · 216-363-4500

Ruth Anna Carlson · Ulmer & Berne · 900 Bond Court Building · 1300 East Ninth Street · Cleveland, OH 44114-1583 · 216-621-8400

Arthur L. Cobb · Hahn Loeser & Parks · 800 National City East Sixth Building 1965 East Sixth Street · Cleveland, OH 44114-2262 · 216-621-0150

John D. Leech · Calfee, Halter & Griswold · 1800 Society Building · East Ninth and Superior · Cleveland, OH 44114-2688 · 216-622-8200

Thomas J. Onusko · Arter & Hadden · 1100 Huntington Building · Cleveland, OH 44115 · 216-696-1100

Susan Scheutzow · Ulmer & Berne · 900 Bond Court Building · 1300 East Ninth Street · Cleveland, OH 44114-1583 · 216-621-8400

Don Antram · Emens, Hurd, Kegler & Ritter · Capitol Square · 65 East State Street · Columbus, OH 43215 · 614-462-5400

Donald A. Davies · Arter & Hadden · One Columbus, 21st Floor · 10 West Broad Street · Columbus, OH 43215 · 614-221-3155

Michael K. Gire · Jones, Day, Reavis & Pogue · 1900 Huntington Center · 41 South High Street · Columbus, OH 43215 · 614-469-3939

James J. Hughes, Jr. · Bricker & Eckler · 100 South Third Street · Columbus, OH 43215-4291 · 614-227-2300

G. Roger King · Jones, Day, Reavis & Pogue · 1900 Huntington Center · 41 South High Street · Columbus, OH 43215 · 614-469-3939

Gretchen McBeath · Bricker & Eckler · 100 South Third Street · Columbus, OH 43215-4291 · 614-227-2300

Peter A. Pavarini · Schottenstein, Zox & Dunn · The Huntington Center, 26th Floor · 41 South High Street · Columbus, OH 43215 · 614-221-3211

David J. Young · Squire, Sanders & Dempsey · 41 South High Street · Columbus, OH 43215 · 614-365-2789

Dennis P. Witherell · Shumaker, Loop & Kendrick · North Courthouse Square · 1000 Jackson · Toledo, OH 43624-1573 · 419-241-9000

IMMIGRATION LAW

Gregory P. Adams · Frost & Jacobs · 2500 Central Trust Center · 201 East Fourth Street · P.O. Box 5715 · Cincinnati, OH 45201-5715 · 513-651-6800

Douglas S. Weigle · Bartlett, Junewick & Weigle · 432 Walnut Street, Suite 1100 Cincinnati, OH 45202 · 513-241-3992

Margaret W. Wong · Margaret W. Wong & Associates · 1128 Standard Building Cleveland, OH 44113 · 216-566-9908

William G. Meyer · Lawyers Building on Library Square · 329 Tenth Street · P.O. Box 2068 · Toledo, OH 43603-2068 · 419-241-4288

INTELLECTUAL PROPERTY LAW

Jack L. Renner · Renner, Kenner, Greiva, Bobak, Taylor & Weber · First National Tower, 16th Floor · Akron, OH 44308 · 216-376-1242

Ray L. Weber · Renner, Kenner, Greive, Bobak, Taylor & Weber · First National Tower, 16th Floor · Akron, OH 44308-1456 · 216-376-1242

Herbert C. Brinkman · Wood, Herron & Evans · 2700 Carew Tower · Cincinnati, OH 45202 · 513-241-2324

Donald F. Frei · Wood, Herron & Evans · 2700 Carew Tower · Cincinnati, OH 45202 · 513-241-2324

Kenneth B. Germain · Frost & Jacobs · 2500 Central Trust Center · 201 East Fourth Street · P.O. Box 5715 · Cincinnati, OH 45201-5715 · 513-651-6800

David J. Josephic · Wood, Herron & Evans · 2700 Carew Tower · Cincinnati, OH 45202 · 513-241-2324

David S. Stallard · Wood, Herron & Evans · 2700 Carew Tower · Cincinnati, OH 45202 · 513-241-2324

Bruce Tittel · Wood, Herron & Evans · 2700 Carew Tower · Cincinnati, OH 45202 · 513-241-2324

Kenneth R. Adamo · Jones, Day, Reavis & Pogue · North Point · 901 Lakeside Avenue · Cleveland, OH 44114 · 216-586-3939

Christopher B. Fagan · Fay, Sharpe, Beall, Fagan, Minnich & McKee · 1100 Superior Avenue · Cleveland, OH 44114 · 216-861-5582

Daniel J. Sammon · Watts Hoffman Fisher & Heinke · 100 Erieview Plaza, Suite 2850 · Cleveland, OH 44114 · 216-623-0775

Thomas W. Flynn · Biebel, French & Nauman · 2500 Kettering Tower · Dayton, OH 45423 · 513-461-4543

Timothy W. Hagan · Killworth, Gottman, Hagan & Schaeff · 1400 First National Plaza · Dayton, OH 45402-1502 · 513-223-2050

Richard A. Killworth · Killworth, Gottman, Hagan & Schaeff · 1400 First National Bank Building · Dayton, OH 45402 · 513-223-2050

Mark P. Levy · Thompson, Hine and Flory · 2000 Courthouse Plaza, NE · P.O. Box 8801 · Dayton, OH 45401-8801 · 513-443-6800

LABOR AND EMPLOYMENT LAW

William B. Gore · (Labor) · Laybourne, Smith, Gore & Goldsmith · Society Building, Suite 503 · 159 South Main Street · Akron, OH 44308 · 216-434-7167

Edward C. Kaminski · (Management) · Buckingham, Doolittle & Burroughs · Akron Centre Plaza · 50 South Main Street · P.O. Box 1500 · Akron, OH 44309-1500 · 216-376-5300

Dean E. Denlinger · (Management) · Denlinger, Rosenthal & Greenberg · 2310 First National Bank Center · 425 Walnut Street · Cincinnati, OH 45202 · 513-621-3440

Michael W. Hawkins · (Management, Employment Litigation) · Dinsmore & Shohl · 255 East Fifth Street · Cincinnati, OH 45202-3172 · 513-977-8200

James B. Helmer, Jr.* · (Individuals) · Helmer, Lugbill & Whitman · 1900 Clopay Building · 105 East Fourth Street · Cincinnati, OH 45202 · 513-421-2400

Thomas J. Kircher · (Labor) · 125 East Court Street, Suite 1000 · Cincinnati, OH 45202-1299 · 513-381-3525

James K. L. Lawrence · (Management) · Frost & Jacobs · 2500 Central Trust Center · 201 East Fifth Street · P.O. Box 5715 · Cincinnati, OH 45201-5715 · 513-651-6800

J. Alan Lips* · (Management, Employment) · Taft, Stettinius & Hollister · 1800 Star Bank Center · Cincinnati, OH 45202 · 513-381-2838

Marc D. Mezibov · (Individuals) · Sirkin, Pinales, Mezibov & Schwartz · 105 West Fourth Street, Suite 920 · Cincinnati, OH 45202 · 513-721-4876

Thomas F. Phalen, Jr. · (Labor) · 700 Gwynne Building · 602 Main Street · Cincinnati, OH 45202 · 513-651-0559

James B. Robinson* · (Labor, Individuals) · Kircher and Robinson · 125 East Court Street, Suite 1000 · Cincinnati, OH 45202-1299 · 513-381-3525

Frank H. Stewart · (Management) · Taft, Stettinius & Hollister · 1800 Star Bank Center · Cincinnati, OH 45202 · 513-381-2838

Paul H. Tobias* · (Individuals) · Tobias & Kraus · 911 Mercantile Library Building · 414 Walnut Street · Cincinnati, OH 45202 · 513-241-8137

Roger A. Weber · (Management) · Taft, Stettinius & Hollister · 1800 Star Bank Center · Cincinnati, OH 45202 · 513-381-2838

Thomas H. Barnard · (Management) · Duvin, Cahn & Barnard · Erieview Tower, 20th Floor · 1301 East Ninth Street · Cleveland, OH 44114 · 216-696-7600

Jeffrey A. Belkin · (Management) · Hahn, Loeser & Parks · 800 National City East Sixth Building · 1965 East Sixth Street · Cleveland, OH 44114-2262 · 216-621-0150

Gerald B. Chattman · Chattman, Garfield, Friedlander & Paul · 400 Engineers Building · Cleveland, OH 44114 · 216-328-8000

Ronald L. Coleman · (Management) · Squire, Sanders & Dempsey · 1800 Huntington Building · Cleveland, OH 44115 · 216-687-8500

Robert P. Duvin · (Management) · Duvin, Cahn & Barnard · Erieview Tower, 20th Floor · Cleveland, OH 44114 · 216-696-7600

Arthur A. Kola · (Management) · Squire, Sanders & Dempsey · 1800 Huntington Building · Cleveland, OH 44115 · 216-687-8500

Andrew M. Kramer · (Management) · Jones, Day, Reavis & Pogue · North Point 901 Lakeside Avenue · Cleveland, OH 44114 · 216-586-1019

Robert L. Larson · (Management) · Thompson, Hine and Flory · 1100 National City Bank Building · 629 Euclid Avenue · Cleveland, OH 44114-3070 · 216-566-5500

Paul S. Lefkowitz · (Labor) · Climaco & Seminatore · 1228 Euclid Avenue, Suite 900 · Cleveland, OH 44115 · 216-621-8484

Kenneth R. Millisor · (Management) · Millisor & Nobil · 9150 South Hills Boulevard · Cleveland, OH 44147-3599 · 216-838-8800

Joseph A. Rotolo · (Management) · Arter & Hadden · 1100 Huntington Building Cleveland, OH 44115 · 216-696-1100

Joseph S. Ruggie, Jr. · (Management) · Thompson, Hine and Flory · 1100 National City Bank Building · 629 Euclid Avenue · Cleveland, OH 44114-3070 · 216-566-5500

Melvin S. Schwarzwald · (Labor, Individuals) · Schwarzwald & Rock · 616 Bond Court Building · 1300 East Ninth Street · Cleveland, OH 44114 · 216-566-1600

Victor Strimbu, Jr. · (Management) · Baker & Hostetler · 3200 National City Center · Cleveland, OH 44114 · 216-621-0200

Richard V. Whelan, Jr. · (Management) · Thompson, Hine and Flory · 1100 National City Bank Building · 629 Euclid Avenue · Cleveland, OH 44114-3070 · 216-566-5500

Frederick M. Gittes* · (Individuals) · Spater, Gittes, Schulte & Kolman · 723 Oak Street · Columbus, OH 43205 · 614-221-1160

N. Victor Goodman · (Labor) · Benesch, Friedlander, Coplan & Aronoff · 88 East Broad Street · Columbus, OH 44114-3399 · 614-223-9300

Stuart M. Gordon · (Management) · Porter, Wright, Morris & Arthur · 41 South High Street · Columbus, OH 43215-3406 · 614-227-2000

Dennis D. Grant · (Management) · Arter & Hadden · One Columbus, 21st Floor 10 West Broad Street · Columbus, OH 43215 · 614-221-3155

Louis A. Jacobs · (Individuals) · 3040 Riverside Drive · Columbus, OH 43221 · 614-486-0407

Stewart R. Jaffy · (Labor) · Stewart Jaffy & Associates · 306 East Gay Street · Columbus, OH 43215-3212 · 614-228-6148

G. Roger King · (Management) · Jones, Day, Reavis & Pogue · 1900 Huntington Center · 41 South High Street · Columbus, OH 43215 · 614-469-3939

Alvin J. McKenna · (Management) · Porter, Wright, Morris & Arthur · 41 South High Street · Columbus, OH 43215-3406 · 614-227-2000

Charles D. Minor · (Management) · Vorys, Sater, Seymour and Pease · 52 East Gay Street · P.O. Box 1008 · Columbus, OH 43216-1008 · 614-464-6400

Andrew J. Ruzicho* · (Management, Individuals) · Law Offices of Andrew J. Ruzicho · 3040 Riverside Drive, Suite 201 · Columbus, OH 43221-2551 · 614-486-0407

David M. Selcer · (Management) · Baker & Hostetler · 65 East State Street, Suite 2100 · Columbus, OH 43215 · 614-228-1541

Bradd N. Siegel · (Management) · Porter, Wright, Morris & Arthur · 41 South High Street · Columbus, OH 43215-3406 · 614-227-2000

Alexander M. Spater · (Individuals) · Spater, Gittes, Schulte & Kolman · 723 Oak Street · Columbus, OH 43205 · 614-221-1160

Robert J. Brown · (Management) · Thompson, Hine and Flory · 2000 Courthouse Plaza, NE · P.O. Box 8801 · Dayton, OH 45401-8801 · 513-443-6500

Sorrell Logothetis · (Labor, Individuals) · Logothetis and Pence · 111 West First Street, Suite 1100 · Dayton, OH 45402 · 513-461-5310

Leonard S. Sigall · (Labor) · Law Offices of Leonard S. Sigall · 6470 East Main Street · Reynoldsburg, OH 43068 · 614-866-3731

Harland M. Britz* · (Individuals) · Britz and Zemmelman · 414 North Erie Street, Suite 100 · Toledo, OH 43624-2399 · 419-242-7415

Donald W. Fisher* · (Labor) · 1320 National Bank Building · Toledo, OH 43604-1108 · 419-255-7368

Jack E. Gallon* · (Labor) · Gallon, Kalniz & Iorio · 3161 North Republic Boulevard · P.O. Box 7417 · Toledo, OH 43615 · 419-535-1976

Theodore M. Iorio* · (Labor) · Gallon, Kalniz & Iorio · 3161 North Republic Boulevard · P.O. Box 7417 · Toledo, OH 43615 · 419-535-1976

Justice G. Johnson, Jr. · (Management) · Marshall & Melhorn · Four Seagate, Eighth Floor · Toledo, OH 43604 · 419-249-7100

Patrick J. Johnson · (Management) · Eastman & Smith · 800 United Savings Building · 240 Huron Street · Toledo, OH 43604-1141 · 419-241-6000

Jeffrey Julius · (Labor) · Gallon, Kalniz & Iorio · 3161 North Republic Boulevard P.O. Box 7417 · Toledo, OH 43615 · 419-535-1976

Gerald B. Lackey · (Labor) · Lackey, Nusbaum, Harris, Reny & Torzewski · Two Maritime Plaza, Third Floor · Toledo, OH 43604-1803 · 419-243-1105

John T. Landwehr · Eastman & Smith · 800 United Savings Building · 240 Huron Street · Toledo, OH 43604-1141 · 419-241-6000

John G. Mattimoe · (Management) · Marshall & Melhorn · Four Seagate, Eighth Floor · Toledo, OH 43604 · 419-249-7100

Donald M. Mewhort, Jr. · (Management) · Shumaker, Loop & Kendrick · North Courthouse Square · 1000 Jackson · Toledo, OH 43624-1573 · 419-241-9000

Rolf H. Scheidel* · (Management) · Shumaker, Loop & Kendrick · North Courthouse Square · 1000 Jackson · Toledo, OH 43624-1573 · 419-241-9000

Anthony P. Sgambati II · (Labor) · Green, Haines, Sgambati, Murphy & Macala Dollar Bank Building, Fourth Floor · P.O. Box 849 · Youngstown, OH 44501 · 216-743-5101

MARITIME LAW

David G. Davies* · Ray, Robinson, Hanninen & Carle · 1650 East Ohio Building 1717 East Ninth Street · Cleveland, OH 44114-2898 · 216-861-4533

Robert G. McCreary · Arter & Hadden · 1100 Huntington Building · Cleveland, OH 44115 · 216-696-1100

Thomas O. Murphy · Thompson, Hine and Flory · 1100 National City Bank Building · 629 Euclid Avenue · Cleveland, OH 44114-3070 · 216-566-5500

NATURAL RESOURCES AND ENVIRONMENTAL LAW

William L. Caplan · (Hazardous Waste) · Buckingham, Doolittle & Burroughs · Akron Centre Plaza · 50 South Main Street · P.O. Box 1500 · Akron, OH 44309-1500 · 216-376-5300

Kim K. Burke · Taft, Stettinius & Hollister · 1800 Star Bank Center · Cincinnati, OH 45202 · 513-381-2838

Thomas T. Terp* · Taft, Stettinius & Hollister · 1800 Star Bank Center · Cincinnati, OH 45202 · 513-381-2838

G. David Van Epps · Vorys, Sater, Seymour and Pease · 221 East Fourth Street, Suite 2100 · Cincinnati, OH 45202 · 513-723-4058

Van Carson · Squire, Sanders & Dempsey · 1800 Huntington Building · Cleveland, OH 44115 · 216-687-8500

Michael A. Cyphert · Thompson, Hine and Flory · 1100 National City Bank Building · 629 Euclid Avenue · Cleveland, OH 44114-3070 · 216-566-5500

William W. Falsgraf · Baker & Hostetler · 3200 National City Center · Cleveland, OH 44114 · 216-621-0200

James M. Friedman · Benesch, Friedlander, Coplan & Aronoff · 1100 Citizens Building · 850 Euclid Avenue · Cleveland, OH 44114-3399 · 216-363-4500

Michael L. Hardy* · (Solid Waste, Hazardous Waste) · Thompson, Hine and Flory · 1100 National City Bank Building · 629 Euclid Avenue · Cleveland, OH 44114-3070 · 216-566-5500

Kenneth C. Moore · Squire, Sanders & Dempsey · 1800 Huntington Building · Cleveland, OH 44115 · 216-687-8500

John W. Edwards · (Coal) · Jones, Day, Reavis & Pogue · 1900 Huntington Center · 41 South High Street · Columbus, OH 43215 · 614-469-3939

J. Richard Emens · (Oil & Gas) · Emens, Hurd, Kegler & Ritter · Capitol Square 65 East State Street · Columbus, OH 43215 · 614-462-5400

John W. Hoberg · Vorys, Sater, Seymour and Pease · 52 East Gay Street · P.O. Box 1008 · Columbus, OH 43216-1008 · 614-464-6400

Joseph D. Lonardo · Vorys, Sater, Seymour and Pease · 52 East Gay Street · P.O. Box 1008 · Columbus, OH 43216-1008 · 614-464-6400

Robert H. Maynard · Vorys, Sater, Seymour and Pease · 52 East Gay Street · P.O. Box 1008 · Columbus, OH 43216-1008 · 614-464-6400

J. Jeffrey McNealey · Porter, Wright, Morris & Arthur · 41 South High Street · Columbus, OH 43215-3406 · 614-227-2000

Christopher R. Schraff · Porter, Wright, Morris & Arthur · 41 South High Street Columbus, OH 43215-3406 · 614-227-2000

Elizabeth Tullman · Vorys, Sater, Seymour and Pease · 52 East Gay Street · P.O. Box 1008 · Columbus, OH 43216-1008 · 614-464-6400

Richard T. Sargeant* · (Water, Air, Solid Waste, Hazardous Waste) · Eastman & Smith · 800 United Savings Building · 240 Huron Street · Toledo, OH 43604-1141 419-241-6000

Louis E. Tosi* · Fuller & Henry · One SeaGate, 17th Floor · P.O. Box 2088 · Toledo, OH 43603-2088 · 419-247-2500

PERSONAL INJURY LITIGATION

K. Richard Aughenbaugh* · (Defendants, Medical Malpractice, Railroad) · Roetzel & Andress · 75 East Market Street · Akron, OH 44308-2098 · 216-376-2700

Norman S. Carr* · (Products Liability) · Roetzel & Andress · 75 East Market Street · Akron, OH 44308-2098 · 216-376-2700

Orville L. Reed III* · (Defendants, Plaintiffs) · Buckingham, Doolittle & Burroughs · Akron Centre Plaza · 50 South Main Street · P.O. Box 1500 · Akron, OH 44309-1500 · 216-376-5300

Timothy F. Scanlon · (Plaintiffs) · Scanlon & Gearinger · 1100 First National Tower · 106 South Main Street · Akron, OH 44308-1463 · 216-376-4558

Stanley M. Chesley* · (Plaintiffs) · Waite, Schneider, Bayless & Chesley · 1513 Central Trust Tower · Fourth & Vine Streets · Cincinnati, OH 45202 · 513-621-0267

Clement J. DeMichelis · (Defendants) · McCaslin, Imbus & McCaslin · 1200 Gwynne Building · 602 Main Street · Cincinnati, OH 45202 · 513-421-4646

Louis F. Gilligan · (Medical Malpractice, Products Liability, Automobile Collision) · Keating, Muething & Klekamp · Provident Tower, 18th Floor · One East Fourth Street · P.O. Box 1800 · Cincinnati, OH 45202 · 513-579-6400

Jacob K. Stein* · (Defendants) · Thompson, Hine and Flory · 1700 Central Trust Tower · One West Fourth Street · Cincinnati, OH 45202-3675 · 513-352-6700

Glenn V. Whitaker* · (Plaintiffs) · Graydon, Head & Ritchey · 1900 Fifth Third Center · 511 Walnut Street · P.O. Box 6464 · Cincinnati, OH 45202-6464 · 513-629-2733

Frank C. Woodside III* · (Defendants, Medical Malpractice, Products Liability) Dinsmore & Shohl · 255 East Fifth Street · Cincinnati, OH 45202-3172 · 513-977-8200

Charles F. Clarke · (Defendants) · Squire, Sanders & Dempsey · 1800 Huntington Building · Cleveland, OH 44115 · 216-687-8500

Burt J. Fulton · (Defendants) · Gallagher, Sharp, Fulton & Norman · Bulkley Building, Seventh Floor · 1501 Euclid Avenue · Cleveland, OH 44115 · 216-241-5310

Michael R. Gallagher* · (Defendants, Products Liability, Airplane Collision) · Gallagher, Sharp, Fulton & Norman · Bulkley Building, Seventh Floor · 1501 Euclid Avenue · Cleveland, OH 44115 · 216-241-5310

Jerome S. Kalur · (Medical Malpractice) · Jacobson, Maynard, Tuschman & Kalur · 1001 Lakeside Avenue, Suite 1600 · Cleveland, OH 44114-1192 · 216-736-8600

Charles Kampinski* · (Plaintiffs) · 1530 Standard Building · 1370 Ontario Street Cleveland, OH 44113 · 216-781-4110

Robert Eric Kennedy · (Plaintiffs) · Weisman, Goldberg, Weisman & Kaufman · 1600 Midland Building · 101 Prospect Avenue · Cleveland, OH 44115 · 216-781-1111

Charles W. Kitchen* · (Defendants, Medical Malpractice, Products Liability, Professional Malpractice) · Kitchen, Messner & Deery · Illuminating Building, Suite 1100 · 55 Public Square · Cleveland, OH 44113 · 216-241-5614

John D. Liber* · (Plaintiffs, Products Liability, Automobile Collision) · Spangenberg, Shibley, Traci & Lancione · 1500 National City Bank Building · Cleveland, OH 44114-3062 · 216-696-3232

Robert C. Maynard · (Defendants) · Jacobson, Maynard, Tuschman & Kalur · 100 Lakeside Avenue, Suite 1600 · Cleveland, OH 44114-1192 · 216-736-8600

Patrick F. McCartan · (Defendants) · Jones, Day, Reavis & Pogue · North Point 901 Lakeside Avenue · Cleveland, OH 44114 · 216-586-3939

Forrest A. Norman* · (Defendants) · Gallagher, Sharp, Fulton & Norman · Bulkley Building, Seventh Floor · 1501 Euclid Avenue · Cleveland, OH 44115 · 216-241-5310

Marshall I. Nurenberg · (Plaintiffs) · Nurenberg, Plevin, Heller & McCarthy · Stander Building, First Floor · 1370 Ontario Street · Cleveland, OH 44113 · 216-621-2300

Mark O'Neill* · (Defendants) · Weston, Hurd, Fallon, Paisley & Howley · 2500 Terminal Tower · Cleveland, OH 44113-2241 · 216-241-6602

Louis Paisley · (Defendants) · Weston, Hurd, Fallon, Paisley & Howley · 2500 Terminal Tower · Cleveland, OH 44113-2241 · 216-241-6602

Keith E. Spero* · (Plaintiffs, Medical Malpractice, Products Liability, Automobile Collision) · Spero & Rosenfield · 113 St. Clair Avenue, Suite 500 · Cleveland, OH 44114-1211 · 216-771-1255

Lawrence E. Stewart · (Plaintiffs) · Stewart and DeChant · The Atrium Office Plaza, Suite 850 · 668 Euclid Avenue · Cleveland, OH 44114-3060 · 216-781-2258

Donald P. Traci* · (Plaintiffs, Medical Malpractice, Products Liability, Automobile Collision, Airplane Collision) · Spangenberg, Shibley, Traci & Lancione · 1500 National City Bank Building · 629 Euclid Avenue · Cleveland, OH 44114-3062 · 216-696-3232

Fred Weisman · (Plaintiffs) · Weisman, Goldberg, Weisman & Kaufman · 1600 Midland Building · 101 Prospect Avenue · Cleveland, OH 44115 · 216-781-1111

Louis E. Gerber* · (Defendants) · Arter & Hadden · One Columbus, 21st Floor 10 West Broad Street · Columbus, OH 43215 · 614-221-3155

C. Richard Grieser · (Plaintiffs) · Grieser, Schafer, Blumenstiel & Slane · 261 West Johnstown Road · Columbus, OH 43230 · 614-475-9511

Terrance M. Miller* · (Defendants, Products Liability, Professional Malpractice) Porter, Wright, Morris & Arthur · 41 South High Street · Columbus, OH 43215-3406 · 614-227-2142

James S. Monahan · (Defendants) · Bricker & Eckler · 100 South Third Street · Columbus, OH 43215-4291 · 614-227-2300

James S. Oliphant* · (Defendants, Medical Malpractice, Toxic Tort) · Porter, Wright, Morris & Arthur · 41 South High Street · Columbus, OH 43215-3406 · 614-227-2000

James E. Pohlman · (Defendants) · Porter, Wright, Morris & Arthur · 41 South High Street · Columbus, OH 43215-3406 · 614-227-2000

Alan T. Radnor* · (Plaintiffs, Defendants, Medical Malpractice, Airplane Collision) · Vorys, Sater, Seymour and Pease · 52 East Gay Street · P.O. Box 1008 · Columbus, OH 43216-1008 · 614-464-6400

Frank A. Ray* · (Plaintiffs) · 330 South High Street · Columbus, OH 43215 · 614-221-7791

Hans Scherner* · (Plaintiffs, Medical Malpractice, Products Liability, Professional Malpractice) · Scherner & Hanson · 130 Northwoods Boulevard · Columbus, OH 43235-4414 · 614-431-7200

Paul O. Scott · (Wrongful Death) · 35 East Livingston Avenue · Columbus, OH 43215-5770 · 614-461-6666

Edgar A. Strause* · (Defendants) · Vorys, Sater, Seymour and Pease · 52 East Gay Street · P.O. Box 1008 · Columbus, OH 43216-1008 · 614-464-6257

Gerald J. Todaro · (Plaintiffs, Medical Malpractice) · 330 South High Street · Columbus, OH 43215 · 614-221-4013

Thomas M. Tyack · (Plaintiffs) · Thomas M. Tyack & Associates · 536 South High Street · Columbus, OH 43215 · 614-221-1341

David C. Greer* · (Defendants) · Bieser, Greer & Landis · 400 Gem Plaza · Third and Main Streets · Dayton, OH 45402 · 513-223-3277

Thomas E. Jenks · (Defendants) · Jenks, Surdyk & Cowdrey · 205 East First Street · Dayton, OH 45402 · 513-222-2333

Charles D. Lowe* · (Plaintiffs) · Cowden, Pfarrer, Crew & Becker · 2580 Kettering Tower · Dayton, OH 45423-2580 · 513-223-6211

Irving I. Saul* · (Plaintiffs, Medical Malpractice, Products Liability, Automobile Collision, Appellate) · 113 Bethpolamy Court · Dayton, OH 45415 · 513-278-4858

William M. Connelly* · (Plaintiffs) · Connelly, Soutar & Jackson · 2100 Ohio Citizens Bank Building · Toledo, OH 43604 · 419-243-2100

John M. Curphey · (Defendants) · Robison, Curphey & O'Connell · Four Sea-Gate, Ninth Floor · Toledo, OH 43604 · 419-249-7900

John A. (Jay) Harris III* · (Plaintiffs, Medical Malpractice, Products Liability) · Lackey, Nusbaum, Harris, Reny & Torzewski · Two Maritime Plaza, Third Floor Toledo, OH 43604-1803 · 419-243-1105

James M. Tuschman* · (Medical Malpractice) · Jacobson, Maynard, Tuschman & Kalur · Four SeaGate, Ninth Floor · Toledo, OH 43604 · 419-249-7373

Martin W. Williams · (Plaintiffs) · Williams, Jilek, Lafferty & Gallagher · 500 Toledo Legal Building · 416 North Erie Street · Toledo, OH 43624-1696 · 419-241-2122

David C. Comstock* · (Defendants) · Comstock, Springer & Wilson · 926 City Centre One · P.O. Box 6306 · Youngstown, OH 44501-6306 · 216-746-5643

PUBLIC UTILITY LAW

Alan P. Buchmann · Squire, Sanders & Dempsey · 1800 Huntington Building · Cleveland, OH 44115 · 216-687-8705

Paul T. Ruxin · Jones, Day, Reavis & Pogue · North Point · 901 Lakeside Avenue Cleveland, OH 44114 · 216-586-3939

William S. Newcomb, Jr. · Vorys, Sater, Seymour and Pease · 52 East Gay Street P.O. Box 1008 · Columbus, OH 43216-1008 · 614-464-5681

Samuel H. Porter · Porter, Wright, Morris & Arthur · 41 South High Street · Columbus, OH 43215-3406 · 614-227-2000

REAL ESTATE LAW

John N. Teeple · Geiger, Teeple, Smith & Hahn · 404 Bank One Building · Alliance, OH 44601 · 216-821-1430

Edward D. Diller · Taft, Stettinius & Hollister · 1800 Star Bank Center · Cincinnati, OH 45202 · 513-381-2838

Richard S. Roberts · Taft, Stettinius & Hollister · 1800 Star Bank Center · Cincinnati, OH 45202 · 513-381-2838

Jay A. Rosenberg · (Commercial Transactions, Industrial Transactions, Title Insurance) · Dinsmore & Shohl · 255 East Fifth Street · Cincinnati, OH 45202-3172 · 513-977-8200

Herbert B. Weiss · Keating, Muething & Klekamp · 1800 Provident Tower · One East Fourth Street · P.O. Box 1800 · Cincinnati, OH 45202 · 513-579-6400

Jordan C. Band · (Commercial Transactions, Industrial Transations) · Ulmer & Berne · 900 Bond Court Building · 1300 East Ninth Street · Cleveland, OH 44114-1583 · 216-621-8400

George R. Barry · Squire, Sanders & Dempsey · 1800 Huntington Building · Cleveland, OH 44115 · 216-687-8500

Bernard D. Goodman · Benesch, Friedlander, Coplan & Aronoff · 1100 Citizens Building · 850 Euclid Avenue · Cleveland, OH 44114-3399 · 216-363-4500

Norman W. Gutmacher · Benesch, Friedlander, Coplan & Aronoff · 1100 Citizens Building · 850 Euclid Avenue · Cleveland, OH 44114-3399 · 216-363-4500

Sidney B. Hopps · (Zoning, Land Use, Commercial Transactions, Industrial Transactions) · Squire, Sanders & Dempsey · 1800 Huntington Building · Cleveland, OH 44115 · 216-687-8500

Thomas A. Mason · (Zoning, Land Use, Commercial Transactions, Industrial Transactions) · Thompson, Hine and Flory · 1100 National City Bank Building · 629 Euclid Avenue · Cleveland, OH 44114-3070 · 216-566-5500

James P. McAndrews · (Land Use, Eminent Domain, Commercial Transactions, Industrial Transactions) · Benesch, Friedlander, Coplan & Aronoff · 1100 Citizens Building · 850 Euclid Avenue · Cleveland, OH 44114-3399 · 216-363-4500

Albert P. Pickus · Squire, Sanders & Dempsey · 1800 Huntington Building · Cleveland, OH 44115 · 216-687-8500

Richard L. Reppert · Jones, Day, Reavis & Pogue · North Point · 901 Lakeside Avenue · Cleveland, OH 44114 · 216-586-3939

Richard A. Rosner · Kahn, Kleinman, Yanowitz & Arnson · 100 Erieview Plaza, Suite 2600 · Cleveland, OH 44114 · 216-696-3311

Lawrence C. Sherman · Kahn, Kleinman, Yanowitz & Arnson · 100 Erieview Plaza, Suite 2600 · Cleveland, OH 44114 · 216-696-3311

Howard A. Steindler · Benesch, Friedlander, Coplan & Aronoff · 1100 Citizens Building · 850 Euclid Avenue · Cleveland, OH 44114-3399 · 216-363-4500

Stanley A. Williams · Arter & Hadden · 1100 Huntington Building · Cleveland, OH 44115 · 216-696-1100

David G. Baker · (Commercial Transactions, Industrial Transactions, Mortgage Financing) · Bricker & Eckler · 100 South Third Street · Columbus, OH 43215-4291 · 614-227-2300

Stephen R. Buchenroth · Vorys, Sater, Seymour and Pease · 52 East Gay Street P.O. Box 1008 · Columbus, OH 43216-1008 · 614-464-6400

James B. Cushman · (Zoning, Land Use, Commercial Transactions, Development & Financing) · Vorys, Sater, Seymour and Pease · 52 East Gay Street · P.O. Box 1008 · Columbus, OH 43216-1008 · 614-464-6254

James J. Erb · Jones, Day, Reavis & Pogue · 1900 Huntington Center · 41 South High Street · Columbus, OH 43215 · 614-469-3939

Howard J. Haddow · Folkerth, O'Brien, Haddow & Davis · 580 South High Street · Columbus, OH 43215 · 614-228-2945

Richard G. Ison · Vorys, Sater, Seymour and Pease · 52 East Gay Street · P.O. Box 1008 · Columbus, OH 43216-1008 · 614-464-6400

Robert C. Kiger · Porter, Wright, Morris & Arthur · 41 South High Street · Columbus, OH 43215-3406 · 614-227-2000

Kenton L. Kuehnle · Thompson, Hine and Flory · The Bank One Building, 18th Floor · 100 East Broad Street · Columbus, OH 43215 · 614-469-7200

Richard L. Loveland · (Land Use, Commercial Transactions, Industrial Transactions, Condominiums & PUDs) · Loveland & Brosius · 50 West Broad Street, Suite 1016 · Columbus, OH 43215 · 614-464-3563

Steven J. McCoy · Vorys, Sater, Seymour and Pease · 52 East Gay Street · P.O. Box 1008 · Columbus, OH 43216-1008 · 614-464-6400

Robert H. Schottenstein · Schottenstein, Zox & Dunn · The Huntington Center, 26th Floor · 41 South High Street · Columbus, OH 43215 · 614-462-2249

David S. Sidor · Squire, Sanders & Dempsey · 1300 Huntington Center · 41 South High Street · Columbus, OH 43215 · 614-365-2700

Norman T. Smith · Porter, Wright, Morris & Arthur · 41 South High Street · Columbus, OH 43215-3406 · 614-227-2000

Robert M. Curry · Thompson, Hine and Flory · 2000 Courthouse Plaza, NE · P.O. Box 8801 · Dayton, OH 45401-8801 · 513-443-6500

J. Stephen Herbert · Coolidge, Wall, Womsley & Lombard · 600 IBM Building 33 West First Street · Dayton, OH 45402 · 513-223-8177

Richard H. Packard · Porter, Wright, Morris & Arthur · 2100 First National Bank Building · 130 West Second Street · P.O. Box 1805 · Dayton, OH 45402-1805 · 513-228-2411

Edward L. Shank · Bieser, Greer & Landis · 400 Gem Plaza · Third and Main Streets · Dayton, OH 45402 · 513-223-3277

Jerome R. Parker · Gressley, Kaplin, Parker & Frederickson · 1600 Toledo Trust Building · 245 North Summit Street · Toledo, OH 43604-1539 · 419-244-8336

Joseph A. Rideout · (Zoning, Land Use, Commercial Transactions, Financing Transactions) · Shumaker, Loop & Kendrick · North Courthouse Square · 1000 Jackson · Toledo, OH 43624-1573 · 419-241-9000

Barton L. Wagenman · Shumaker, Loop & Kendrick · North Courthouse Square 1000 Jackson · Toledo, OH 43624-1573 · 419-241-9000

TAX AND EMPLOYEE BENEFITS LAW

Frank A. Lettieri · Amer Cunningham Brennan · Society Building, Sixth Floor · Akron, OH 44308 · 216-762-2411

Robert W. Malone · (Corporate & Partnership Transactions, State Tax, Tax Disputes) · Buckingham, Doolittle & Burroughs · 50 South Main Street · Akron Centre Plaza · P.O Box 1500 · Akron, OH 44309-1500 · 216-376-5300

Mark H. Berliant · Strauss & Troy · 2100 Central Trust Center · 201 East Fifth Street · Cincinnati, OH 45202 · 513-621-2120

Bart A. Brown, Jr. · Keating, Muething & Klekamp · Provident Tower, 18th Floor · One East Fourth Street · Cincinnati, OH 45202 · 513-579-6400

Scott B. Crooks · (Employee Benefits) · Thompson, Hine and Flory · 312 Walnut Street, Suite 1400 · Cincinnati, OH 45202-4029 · 513-352-6700

Jerold A. Fink · (Employee Benefits) · Taft, Stettinius & Hollister · 1800 Star Bank Center · Cincinnati, OH 45202 · 513-381-2838

William M. Freedman · (Tax, Employee Benefits) · Dinsmore & Shohl · 255 East Fifth Street · Cincinnati, OH 45202-3172 · 513-977-8200

Ronald E. Heinlen · Frost & Jacobs · 2500 Central Trust Center · 201 East Fifth Street · P.O. Box 5715 · Cincinnati, OH 45201-5715 · 513-651-6800

Stephen M. Nechemias · Taft, Stettinius & Hollister · 1800 Star Bank Center · Cincinnati, OH 45202 · 513-381-2838

James J. Ryan · Taft, Stettinius & Hollister · 1800 Star Bank Center · Cincinnati, OH 45202 · 513-381-2838

Stephen J. Alfred · Squire, Sanders & Dempsey · 1800 Huntington Building · Cleveland, OH 44115 · 216-687-8500

Patrick J. Amer · Spieth, Bell, McCurdy & Newell · 2000 Huntington Building Cleveland, OH 44115-1496 · 216-696-4700

Malvin E. Bank · Thompson, Hine and Flory · 1100 National City Bank Building 629 Euclid Avenue · Cleveland, OH 44114-3070 · 216-566-5500

Lewis T. Barr · Weston, Hurd, Fallon, Paisley & Howley · 2500 Terminal Tower Cleveland, OH 44113-2241 · 216-241-6602

David Lyle Carpenter · Calfee, Halter & Griswold · 1800 Society Building · East Ninth and Superior · Cleveland, OH 44114-2688 · 216-622-8200

William H. Conner · Squire, Sanders & Dempsey · 1800 Huntington Building · Cleveland, OH 44115 · 216-687-8500

Alan Doris · (Corporate & Partnership Transactions, Tax Disputes, Leasing Transactions) · Benesch, Friedlander, Coplan & Aronoff · 1100 Citizens Building 850 Euclid Avenue · Cleveland, OH 44114-3399 · 216-363-4500

Robert E. Glaser · (Corporate & Partnership Transactions, State Tax, Tax Disputes) · Arter & Hadden · 1100 Huntington Building · Cleveland, OH 44115 · 216-696-1100

Thomas A. Jorgensen · (Employee Benefits) · Calfee, Halter & Griswold · 1800 Society Building · East Ninth and Superior · Cleveland, OH 44114-2688 · 216-622-8200

Stephen L. Kadish · Kadish & Bender · 2112 East Ohio Building · Cleveland, OH 44114 · 216-696-3030

Charles J. Kerester · Jones, Day, Reavis & Pogue · North Point · 901 Lakeside Avenue · Cleveland, OH 44114 · 216-586-3939

N. Herschel Koblenz · Hahn Loeser & Parks · 800 National City East Sixth Building · 1965 East Sixth Street · Cleveland, OH 44114-2262 · 216-621-0150

Donald L. Korb · Thompson, Hine and Flory · 1100 National City Bank Building 629 Euclid Avenue · Cleveland, OH 44114-3070 · 216-566-5500

Herbert B. Levine · Ulmer & Berne · 900 Bond Court Building · 1300 East Ninth Street · Cleveland, OH 44114-1583 · 216-621-8400

Michael G. Meissner · Squire, Sanders & Dempsey · 1800 Huntington Building · Cleveland, OH 44115 · 216-687-8593

W. James Ollinger · (Employee Benefits) · Baker & Hostetler · 3200 National City Center · Cleveland, OH 44114 · 216-621-0200

Terrence G. Perris · Squire, Sanders & Dempsey · 1800 Huntington Building · Cleveland, OH 44115 · 216-687-8500

Carlton B. Schnell · Arter & Hadden · 1100 Huntington Building · Cleveland, OH 44115 · 216-696-1100

John L. Sterling · Jones, Day, Reavis & Pogue · North Point · 901 Lakeside Avenue · Cleveland, OH 44114 · 216-586-3939

William R. Stewart · (Corporate & Partnership Transactions, State Tax, Tax Disputes, Tax Exempt Organizations) · Thompson, Hine and Flory · 1100 National City Bank Building · 629 Euclid Avenue · Cleveland, OH 44114-3070 · 216-566-5500

William M. Toomajian · Baker & Hostetler · 3200 National City Center · Cleveland, OH 44114 · 216-621-0200

Kenneth E. Updegraft, Jr. · (Corporate & Partnership Transactions) · Jones, Day, Reavis & Pogue · North Point · 901 Lakeside Avenue · Cleveland, OH 44114 · 216-586-3939

Jeffry L. Weiler · (State Tax, Tax Disputes) · Benesch, Friedlander, Coplan & Aronoff · 1100 Citizens Building · 850 Euclid Avenue · Cleveland, OH 44114-3399 216-363-4551

Jon M. Anderson · Porter, Wright, Morris & Arthur · 41 South High Street · Columbus, OH 43215-3406 · 614-227-2000

Kenneth D. Beck · Vorys, Sater, Seymour and Pease · 52 East Gay Street · P.O. Box 1008 · Columbus, OH 43216-1008 · 614-464-6400

Michael R. Becker · (Corporate & Partnership Transactions, Tax Disputes) · Isaac, Brant, Ledman & Becker · The Midland Building, Suite 800 · 250 East Broad Street · Columbus, OH 43215-3742 · 614-221-2121

William W. Ellis, Jr. · (Tax, Employee Benefits) · Vorys, Sater, Seymour and Pease · 52 East Gay Street · P.O. Box 1008 · Columbus, OH 43216-1008 · 614-464-6400

Daniel M. Maher · (Employee Benefits) · Squire, Sanders & Dempsey · 1300 Huntington Center · 41 South High Street · Columbus, OH 43215 · 614-365-2700

Michael A. Mess · Bricker & Eckler · 100 South Third Street · Columbus, OH 43215-4291 · 614-227-2300

Richard R. Murphey, Jr. · Squire, Sanders & Dempsey · 1300 Huntington Center 41 South High Street · Columbus, OH 43215 · 614-365-2700

Thomas J. Riley · Hahn Loeser & Parks · 431 East Broad Street, Suite 200 · Columbus, OH 43215 · 614-221-0240

Paul D. Ritter, Jr. · (Tax, Employee Benefits) · Emens, Hurd, Kegler & Ritter Capitol Square · 65 East State Street · Columbus, OH 43215 · 614-462-5400

Ronald L. Rowland · (Corporate & Partnership Transactions) · Vorys, Sater, Seymour and Pease · 52 East Gay Street · P.O. Box 1008 · Columbus, OH 43216-1008 · 614-464-6400

Fredric L. Smith · Squire, Sanders & Dempsey · 1300 Huntington Center · 41 South High Street · Columbus, OH 43215 · 614-365-2700

Richard R. Stedman · Vorys, Sater, Seymour and Pease · 52 East Gay Street · P.O. Box 1008 · Columbus, OH 43216-1008 · 614-464-6400

John Terakedis, Jr. · (Employee Benefits, Corporate & Partnership Transactions, Tax Disputes) · Schottenstein, Zox & Dunn · The Huntington Center, 26th Floor 41 South High Street · Columbus, OH 43215 · 614-221-3211

Richard F. Carlile · (Employee Benefits) · Thompson, Hine and Flory · 2000 Courthouse Plaza, NE · P.O. Box 8801 · Dayton, OH 45401-8801 · 513-443-6721

Frederick J. Caspar · Chernesky, Heyman & Kress · 10 Courthouse Plaza Southwest, Suite 1100 · P.O. Box 3808 · Dayton, OH 45401-3808 · 513-449-2818

Ralph E. Heyman · Chernesky, Heyman & Kress · 10 Courthouse Plaza Southwest, Suite 1100 · P.O. Box 3808 · Dayton, OH 45401-3808 · 513-449-2800

Bruce R. Lowry · (Corporate & Partnership Transactions, Tax Disputes, International Transactions) · Thompson, Hine and Flory · 2000 Courthouse Plaza, NE P.O. Box 8801 · Dayton, OH 45401-8801 · 513-443-6500

Marc Gertner · (Employee Benefits) · Shumaker, Loop & Kendrick · North Courthouse Square · 1000 Jackson · Toledo, OH 43624-1573 · 419-241-9000

Frank D. Jacobs · Eastman & Smith · 800 United Savings Building · 240 Huron Street · Toledo, OH 43604-1141 · 419-241-6000

David F. Waterman · Shumaker, Loop & Kendrick · North Courthouse Square · 1000 Jackson · Toledo, OH 43624-1573 · 419-241-9000

James F. White, Jr. · Shumaker, Loop & Kendrick · North Courthouse Square · 1000 Jackson · Toledo, OH 43624-1573 · 419-241-9000

TRUSTS AND ESTATES

Patricia A. Pacenta · Buckingham, Doolittle & Burroughs · Akron Centre Plaza · 50 South Main Street · P.O. Box 1500 · Akron, OH 44309-1500 · 216-376-5300

Michael L. Stark · Stark & Knoll · 1512 Ohio Edison Building · 76 South Main Street · Akron, OH 44308 · 216-376-3300

Joseph A. Brant · Katz, Teller, Brant & Hild · 1400 Tri-State Building · 432 Walnut Street · Cincinnati, OH 45202-3961 · 513-721-4532

J. Michael Cooney · Dinsmore & Shohl · 255 East Fifth Street · Cincinnati, OH 45202-3172 · 513-977-8200

Wiley Dinsmore* · Dinsmore & Shohl · 255 East Fifth Street · Cincinnati, OH 45202-3172 · 513-977-8200

John W. Eilers, Jr. · Clark & Eyrich · 525 Vine Street, Suite 2200 · Cincinnati, OH 45202 · 513-241-5540

Jon Hoffheimer · 808 Mercantile Library Building · 414 Walnut Street · Cincinnati, OH 45202 · 513-421-7666

Robert S. Marriott · (Estate Planning) · Graydon, Head & Ritchey · 1900 Fifth Third Center · 511 Walnut Street · P.O. Box 6464 · Cincinnati, OH 45202-6464 513-621-6464

T. Stephen Phillips · Frost & Jacobs · 2500 Central Trust Center · 201 East Fifth Street · P.O. Box 5715 · Cincinnati, OH 45201-5715 · 513-651-6800

James S. Wachs · (Estate Planning, Estate Administration, Charitable Trusts) · Frost & Jacobs · 2500 Central Trust Center · 201 East Fifth Street · P.O. Box 5715 Cincinnati, OH 45201-5715 · 513-651-6800

Oakley V. Andrews* · (Estate Planning, Estate Administration, Trusts & Estates Litigation) · Baker & Hostetler · 3200 National City Center · Cleveland, OH 44114 · 216-621-0200

Robert M. Brucken · Baker & Hostetler · 3200 National City Center · Cleveland, OH 44114 · 216-621-0200

J. Donald Cairns · Squire, Sanders & Dempsey · 1800 Huntington Building · Cleveland, OH 44115 · 216-687-8500

Charles M. Driggs · Squire, Sanders & Dempsey · 1800 Huntington Building · Cleveland, OH 44115 · 216-687-8500

Andrew L. Fabens III · Thompson, Hine and Flory · 1100 National City Bank Building · 629 Euclid Avenue · Cleveland, OH 44114-3070 · 216-566-5500

Kenneth G. Hochman · Jones, Day, Reavis & Pogue · North Point · 901 Lakeside Avenue · Cleveland, OH 44114 · 216-586-3939

Leslie L. Knowlton · Arter & Hadden · 1100 Huntington Building · Cleveland, OH 44115 · 216-696-1100

Charles W. Landefeld · Arter & Hadden · 1100 Huntington Building · Cleveland, OH 44115 · 216-696-1100

Paul L. Millet · Millet & Sprague · Four Commerce Park Square, Suite 805 · 23200 Chagrin Boulevard · Cleveland, OH 44122 · 216-765-1188

Jerome D. Neifach · Arter & Hadden · 1100 Huntington Building · Cleveland, OH 44115 · 216-696-1100

Robert B. Nelson · Jones, Day, Reavis & Pogue · North Point · 901 Lakeside Avenue · Cleveland, OH 44114 · 216-586-3939

Sidney Nudelman · Hahn Loeser & Parks · 800 National City East Sixth Building 1965 East Sixth Street · Cleveland, OH 44114-2262 · 216-621-0150

Lincoln Reavis · (Estate Planning, Estate Administration, Charitable Trusts) · Spieth, Bell, McCurdy & Newell · 2000 Huntington Building · Cleveland, OH 44115-1496 · 216-696-4700

Richard C. Renkert · Jones, Day, Reavis & Pogue · North Point · 901 Lakeside Avenue · Cleveland, OH 44114 · 216-586-3939

John E. Smeltz · Schneider, Smeltz, Ranney & La Fond · 1525 National City Bank Building · Cleveland, OH 44114 · 216-696-4200

Roger L. Shumaker · McDonald, Hopkins, Burke & Haber · 629 Euclid Avenue, Suite 300 · Cleveland, OH 44114 · 216-771-2700

Jeffry L. Weiler · (Estate Planning) · Benesch, Friedlander, Coplan & Aronoff · 1100 Citizens Building · 850 Euclid Avenue · Cleveland, OH 44114-3399 · 216-363-4551

Leon A. Weiss · Reminger & Reminger · 113 St. Clair Building · Cleveland, OH 44114-1273 · 216-687-1311

Nelson E. Weiss · McDonald, Hopkins, Burke & Haber · 300 National City Bank Building · 629 Euclid Avenue · Cleveland, OH 44114 · 216-771-2700

Lawrence L. Fisher · Vorys, Sater, Seymour and Pease · 52 East Gay Street · P.O. Box 1008 · Columbus, OH 43216-1008 · 614-464-6400

Lloyd E. Fisher, Jr. · Porter, Wright, Morris & Arthur · 41 South High Street · Columbus, OH 43215-3406 · 614-227-2000

Richard Heer Oman · Vorys, Sater, Seymour and Pease · 52 East Gay Street · P.O. Box 1008 · Columbus, OH 43216-1008 · 614-464-6453

Marvin R. Pliskin · Porter, Wright, Morris & Arthur · 41 South High Street · Columbus, OH 43215-3406 · 614-227-2000

R. Douglas Wrightsel · Arter & Hadden · One Columbus, 21st Floor · 10 West Broad Street · Columbus, OH 43215 · 614-221-3155

Kenneth L. Bailey · (Estate Planning) · 226 Talbott Tower · Dayton, OH 45402 513-228-8080

C. Terry Johnson · Thompson, Hine and Flory · 2000 Courthouse Plaza, NE · P.O. Box 8801 · Dayton, OH 45401-8801 · 513-443-6721

Crofford J. Macklin, Jr. · (Estate Planning, Estate Administration) · Thompson, Hine and Flory · 2000 Courthouse Plaza, NE · P.O. Box 8801 · Dayton, OH 45401-8801 · 513-443-6730

Donald G. Schweller · Pickrel, Schaeffer and Ebeling · 2700 Kettering Tower · Dayton, OH 45423 · 513-223-1130

Robert V. Sterling · Weber & Sterling · 1745 Indian Wood Circle · Maumee, OH 43537 · 419-893-7216

Edward F. Weber · (Estate Planning, Estate Administration, Charitable Trusts, Private Foundations) · Weber & Sterling · 1745 Indian Wood Circle · Maumee, OH 43537 · 419-893-7216

William F. Bates · Watkins & Bates · 1200 National Bank Building · Toledo, OH 43604 · 419-241-2100

Morton Bobowick · (Estate Planning, Estate Administration) · Eastman & Smith 800 United Savings Building · 240 Huron Street · Toledo, OH 43604-1141 · 419-241-6000

Frank D. Jacobs · Eastman & Smith · 800 United Savings Building · 240 Huron Street · Toledo, OH 43604-1141 · 419-241-6000

Donald J. Keune · Law Office of Donald J. Keune · 2727 North Holland-Sylvania Road, Suite E · Toledo, OH 43615 · 419-535-5728

OKLAHOMA

BANKRUPTCY LAW

W. Rogers Abbott II* · Abbott & Gordon · 500 Bank of Oklahoma Plaza · Oklahoma City, OK 73102 · 405-232-2166

Richard R. Bailey · McClelland, Collins, Bailey, Bailey & Bellingham · Colcord Building, 11th Floor · 15 North Robinson · Oklahoma City, OK 73102 · 405-235-9371

Robert C. Bailey · McClelland, Collins, Bailey, Bailey & Bellingham · Colcord Building, 11th Floor · 15 North Robinson · Oklahoma City, OK 73102 · 405-235-9371

Gary A. Bryant · Mock, Schwabe, Waldo, Elder, Reeves & Bryant · One Leadership Square, 15th Floor · 211 North Robinson Avenue · Oklahoma City, OK 73102 · 405-235-5500

V. Burns Hargis · (Business Reorganization) · Hartzog Conger Cason & Hargis · 1600 Bank of Oklahoma Plaza · 201 Robert S. Kerr · Oklahoma City, OK 73102 · 405-235-7000

Kenneth I. Jones, Jr. · Jones, Blaney & Williams · First City Place Building, 13th Floor · 204 North Robinson · P.O. Box 657 · Oklahoma City, OK 73101 · 405-235-8445

Michael Paul Kirschner* · (Business Reorganization, Bankruptcy Litigation) · Hastie and Kirschner · 3000 First Oklahoma Tower · 210 West Park Avenue · Oklahoma City, OK 73102 · 405-239-6404

David A. Kline · (Business Reorganization, Creditors' Rights, Debtors' Rights, Bankruptcy Litigation) · Kline & Kline · Kline Law Building · 720 Northeast 63rd Street · Oklahoma City, OK 73105 · 405-848-4448

Timothy D. Kline · Kline & Kline · Kline Law Building · 720 Northeast 63rd Street · Oklahoma City, OK 73105 · 405-848-4448

Bruce McClelland · McClelland, Collins, Bailey, Bailey & Bellingham · Colcord Building, 11th Floor · 15 North Robinson · Oklahoma City, OK 73102 · 405-235-9371

D. Kent Meyers* · (Business Reorganization, Bankruptcy Litigation) · Crowe & Dunlevy · 1800 Mid-America Tower · 20 North Broadway · Oklahoma City, OK 73102 · 405-235-7700

Ray G. Moss · (Business Reorganization, Bankruptcy Litigation) · Daugherty, Bradford, Fowler & Moss · 900 City Place · 204 North Robinson · Oklahoma City, OK 73102 · 405-232-0003

Don R. Nicholson II · Eagleton and Nicholson · Bank of Oklahoma Plaza, Suite 310 · 201 West Robert S. Kerr Avenue · Oklahoma City, OK 73120 · 405-236-0550

Louis J. Price · McAfee & Taft · Two Leadership Square, 10th Floor · Oklahoma City, OK 73102 · 405-235-9621

Lynn A. Pringle · Jones, Blaney & Williams · First City Place Building, 13th Floor 204 North Robinson · P.O. Box 657 · Oklahoma City, OK 73101 · 405-235-8445

Norman E. Reynolds · Reynolds & Ridings · 2808 First National Center · Oklahoma City, OK 73102 · 405-232-8131

G. Blaine Schwabe III · Mock, Schwabe, Waldo, Elder, Reeves & Bryant · One Leadership Square, 15th Floor · 211 North Robinson Avenue · Oklahoma City, OK 73102 · 405-235-5500

John W. Swinford, Jr. · Hastie and Kirschner · 3000 First Oklahoma Tower · 210 West Park Avenue · Oklahoma City, OK 73102 · 405-239-6404

Jerry Tubb · Fuller, Tubb & Pomeroy · 800 Bank of Oklahoma Plaza · 201 Robert S. Kerr Avenue · Oklahoma City, OK 73102-4292 · 405-235-2575

James W. Vogt · Reynolds & Ridings · 2808 First National Center · Oklahoma City, OK 73102 · 405-232-8131

Sam G. Bratton II · Doerner, Stuart, Saunders, Daniel & Anderson · 320 South Boston Avenue, Suite 500 · Tulsa, OK 74103-3725 · 918-582-1211

Gary C. Clark · Baker, Hoster, McSpadden, Clark, Rasure & Slicker · 800 Kennedy Building · Tulsa, OK 74103 · 918-592-5555

Thomas E. English · English, Jones & Faulkner · 1700 Fourth National Bank Building · Tulsa, OK 74119 · 918-582-1564

Gary M. McDonald · Doerner, Stuart, Saunders, Daniel & Anderson · 320 South Boston Avenue, Suite 500 · Tulsa, OK 74103-3725 · 918-582-1211

A. F. Ringold · Rosenstein, Fist & Ringold · 525 South Main, Suite 300 · Tulsa, OK 74103 · 918-585-9211

James R. Ryan · Conner & Winters · 2400 First National Tower · Tulsa, OK 74103 · 918-586-5711

BUSINESS LITIGATION

Burck Bailey* · Fellers, Snider, Blankenship, Bailey & Tippens · 2400 First National Center · Oklahoma City, OK 73102 · 405-232-0621

Peter B. Bradford* · (Antitrust, Securities) · Daugherty, Bradford, Fowler & Moss · 900 City Place · 204 North Robinson · Oklahoma City, OK 73102 · 405-232-0003

Andrew M. Coats · Crowe & Dunlevy · 1800 Mid-America Tower · 20 North Broadway · Oklahoma City, OK 73102 · 405-235-7700

George S. Corbyn · Ryan, Holloman, Corbyn & Geister · 900 Robinson Renaissance · 119 North Robinson · Oklahoma City, OK 73102-4608 · 405-239-6041

Roy J. Davis* · Murrah & Davis · One Leadership Square, 12th Floor · 211 North Robinson · Oklahoma City, OK 73102 · 405-235-1681

John T. Edwards* · (Appellate, Energy) · Monnet, Hayes, Bullis, Thompson & Edwards · First National Center West, Suite 1719 · Oklahoma City, OK 73102 · 405-232-5481

Stephen P. Friot* · Spradling, Alpern, Friot & Gum · 101 Park Avenue, Suite 700 · Oklahoma City, OK 73102-7283 · 405-272-0211

Robert H. Gilliland, Jr.* · (Commercial, Energy) · McAfee & Taft · Two Leadership Square, 10th Floor · Oklahoma City, OK 73102 · 405-235-9621

James A. Kirk · Kirk & Chaney · Midland Center, Suite 1300 · Oklahoma City, OK 73102-6695 · 405-235-1333

James P. Linn · Linn & Helms · 1200 Bank of Oklahoma Plaza · 201 Robert S. Kerr · Oklahoma City, OK 73102-4289 · 405-239-6781

Kenneth N. McKinney* · (Energy, Environmental) · McKinney, Stringer & Webster · BancFirst Building, Eighth Floor · 101 North Broadway · Oklahoma City, OK 73102 · 405-239-6444

Clyde A. Muchmore* · Crowe & Dunlevy · 1800 Mid-America Tower · 20 North Broadway · Oklahoma City, OK 73102 · 405-235-7734

Jack L. (Drew) Neville, Jr.* · (Antitrust, Commercial, RICO, Securities) · Linn & Helms · 1200 Bank of Oklahoma Plaza · 201 Robert S. Kerr · Oklahoma City, OK 73102-4289 · 405-239-6781

Reid E. Robison* · McAfee & Taft · Two Leadership Square, 10th Floor · Oklahoma City, OK 73102 · 405-235-9621

Patrick M. Ryan · Ryan, Holloman, Corbyn & Geister · 900 Robinson Renaissance · 119 North Robinson · Oklahoma City, OK 73102-4608 · 405-239-6041

Terry W. Tippens* · (Banking, Commercial, Finance, Securities) · Fellers, Snider, Blankenship, Bailey & Tippens · 2400 First National Center · Oklahoma City, OK 73102 · 405-232-0621

Harry A. Woods, Jr.* · Crowe & Dunlevy · 1800 Mid-America Tower · 20 North Broadway · Oklahoma City, OK 73102 · 405-235-7754

William C. Anderson · Doerner, Stuart, Saunders, Daniel & Anderson · 320 South Boston Avenue, Suite 500 · Tulsa, OK 74103-3725 · 918-582-1211

John S. Athens* · Conner & Winters · 2400 First National Tower · Tulsa, OK 74103 · 918-586-5711

B. Hayden Crawford* · (Antitrust, Appellate, Energy, Securities) · Crawford, Crowe & Bainbridge · 1714 First National Building · Tulsa, OK 74103 · 918-587-1128

Samuel P. Daniel, Jr.* · Doerner, Stuart, Saunders, Daniel & Anderson · 320 South Boston Avenue, Suite 500 · Tulsa, OK 74103-3725 · 918-582-1211

Sidney G. Dunagan* · Gable & Gotwals · 2000 Fourth National Bank Building · 15 West Sixth Street · Tulsa, OK 74119-5447 · 918-582-9201

Jack R. Givens · Jones, Givins, Gotcher, Bogan & Hillborne · 3800 First National Tower · Tulsa, OK 74103 · 918-581-8200

John M. Imel* · (Banking, Commercial, Securities) · Moyers, Martin, Santee, Imel & Tetrick · 320 South Boston Building, Suite 920 · Tulsa, OK 74103 · 918-582-5281

J. Warren Jackman* · Pray, Walker, Jackman, Williamson & Marlar · ONEOK Plaza, Ninth Floor · 100 West Fifth Street · Tulsa, OK 74103 · 918-584-4136

James L. Kincaid* · Crowe & Dunlevy · The Kennedy Building, Suite 500 · 321 South Boston · Tulsa, OK 74103-3313 · 918-59209800

L. K. Smith · Boone, Smith, Davis, Hurst & Dickman · 500 ONEOK Plaza · 100 West Fifth Street · Tulsa, OK 74103 · 918-587-0000

Lance Stockwell · Boesche, McDermott & Eskridge · ONEOK Plaza, Suite 800 100 West Fifth Street · Tulsa, OK 74103 · 918-583-1777

James M. Sturdivant* · (Commercial, Energy, Securities) · Gable & Gotwals · 2000 Fourth National Bank Building · 15 West Sixth Street · Tulsa, OK 74119-5447 · 918-582-9201

CORPORATE LAW

John C. Andrews · Andrews Davis Legg Bixler Milsten & Price · 500 West Main Oklahoma City, OK 73102 · 405-272-9241

J. Edward Barth · Andrews Davis Legg Bixler Milsten & Price · 500 West Main Oklahoma City, OK 73102 · 405-272-9241

James F. Davis · Andrews Davis Legg Bixler Milsten & Price · 500 West Main · Oklahoma City, OK 73102 · 405-272-9241

Theodore M. Elam · (Corporate Finance, Investment, Mergers & Acquisitions, Securities) · McAfee & Taft · Two Leadership Square, 10th Floor · Oklahoma City, OK 73102 · 405-235-9621

Irving L. Faught · (Corporate Finance, Mergers & Acquisitions, Securities, Securities Regulation) · Andrews Davis Legg Bixler Milsten & Price · 500 West Main Oklahoma City, OK 73102 · 405-272-9241

James D. Fellers · Fellers, Snider, Blankenship, Bailey & Tippens · 2400 First National Center · Oklahoma City, OK 73102 · 405-232-0621

Lon Foster III · (Corporate Finance, Mergers & Acquisitions, Securities) · Crowe & Dunlevy · 1800 Mid-America Tower · 20 North Broadway · Oklahoma City, OK 73102 · 405-235-7700

Daniel J. Fowler · (Corporate Finance, Aircraft Finance) · Daugherty, Bradford, Fowler & Moss · 900 City Place · 204 North Robinson · Oklahoma City, OK 73102 405-232-0003

Kent F. Frates* · (Insurance) · Frates & Farris · Colcord Building, Suite 610 · 15 North Robinson Avenue · Oklahoma City, OK 73102 · 405-272-0616

Gary F. Fuller · McAfee & Taft · Two Leadership Square, 10th Floor · Oklahoma City, OK 73102 · 405-235-9621

James C. Gibbens · Crowe & Dunlevy · 1800 Mid-America Tower · 20 North Broadway · Oklahoma City, OK 73102 · 405-235-7700

James L. Hall, Jr. · (Corporate Finance, Financial Institutions, Mergers & Acquisitions, Securities Regulation) · Crowe & Dunlevy · 1800 Mid-America Tower 20 North Broadway · Oklahoma City, OK 73102 · 405-235-7700

John M. Mee · McAfee & Taft · Two Leadership Square, 10th Floor · Oklahoma City, OK 73102 · 405-235-9621

D. Joe Rockett · Andrews Davis Legg Bixler Milsten & Price · 500 West Main · Oklahoma City, OK 73102 · 405-272-9241

Michael M. Stewart · Crowe & Dunlevy · 1800 Mid-America Tower · 20 North Broadway · Oklahoma City, OK 73102 · 405-235-7700

Jerry Tubb · Fuller, Tubb & Pomeroy · 800 Bank of Oklahoma Plaza · 201 Robert S. Kerr Avenue · Oklahoma City, OK 73102-4292 · 405-235-2575

John E. Barry · Conner & Winters · 2400 First National Tower · Tulsa, OK 74103 918-586-5711

Charles S. Chapel · Chapel, Riggs, Abney, Neal & Turpen · Frisco Building · 502 West Sixth Street · Tulsa, OK 74119 · 918-587-3161

Thomas D. Gable · Hall, Estill, Hardwick, Gable, Golden & Nelson · 4100 Bank of Oklahoma Tower · One Williams Center · Tulsa, OK 74172-0154 · 918-588-2700

Thomas F. Golden · Hall, Estill, Hardwick, Gable, Golden & Nelson · 4100 Bank of Oklahoma Tower · One Williams Center · Tulsa, OK 74172-0154 · 918-588-2700

John B. Johnson, Jr. · (Corporate Finance, Mergers & Acquisitions, Securities, General Corporate) · Gable & Gotwals · 2000 Fourth National Bank Building · 15 West Sixth Street · Tulsa, OK 74119-5447 · 918-582-9201

Donald E. Pray · Pray, Walker, Jackman, Williamson & Marlar · ONEOK Plaza, Ninth Floor · Tulsa, OK 74103 · 918-584-4136

Patrick O. Waddel · Gable & Gotwals · 2000 Fourth National Bank Building · 15 West Sixth Street · Tulsa, OK 74119-5447 · 918-582-9201

CRIMINAL DEFENSE

Warren Gotcher* · Gotcher, Brown & Bland · The Centre · 209 East Wyandotte Street · P.O. Box 160 · McAlester, OK 74502 · 918-423-0412

Gene Stipe* · (Violent Crimes, Non-Violent Crimes, Federal Court, Environmental Crimes) · Stipe, Gossett, Stipe, Harper, Estes, McCune and Parks · 323 East Carl Albert Parkway · P.O. Box 1368 · McAlester, OK 74501 · 918-423-0421

Burck Bailey* · Fellers, Snider, Blankenship, Bailey & Tippens · 2400 First National Center · Oklahoma City, OK 73102 · 405-232-0621

James W. Bill Berry · City Place, Suite 2500 · 204 North Robinson · Oklahoma City, OK 73102 · 405-236-3167

Frank R. Courbois III · Courbois Law Office · 2200 Classen Boulevard, Suite 2000 · Oklahoma City, OK 73106 · 405-235-7507

James P. Linn · Linn & Helms · 1200 Bank of Oklahoma Plaza · 201 Robert S. Kerr · Oklahoma City, OK 73102-4289 · 405-239-6781

D. C. Thomas · (Violent Crimes, Non-Violent Crimes, Federal Court, State Court) · Fidelity Plaza, Suite 504 · Oklahoma City, OK 73102 · 405-235-4300

Robert J. (Jim) Turner · Turner, Turner & Braun · 1319 Classen Drive · Oklahoma City, OK 73103 · 405-236-1646

Thomas D. Frasier · Frasier & Frasier · 1700 Southwest Boulevard, Suite 100 · Tulsa, OK 74107 · 918-584-4724

Ronald H. Mook · 16 East 16th Street, Suite 302 · Tulsa, OK 74119 · 918-583-7094

Larry L. Oliver* · (Violent Crimes, Non-Violent Crimes, Federal Court, State Court) · Larry L. Oliver & Associates · Oliver Building · 2211 East Skelly Drive Tulsa, OK 74105-5913 · 918-745-6084

Patrick A. Williams · 324 Main Mall, Suite 600 · Tulsa, OK 74103 · 918-583-1338

FAMILY LAW

James W. Bill Berry · City Place, Suite 2500 · 204 North Robinson · Oklahoma City, OK 73102 · 405-236-3167

Arnold D. Fagin · Fagin & Fagin · 210 West Park Avenue, Suite 2650 · Oklahoma City, OK 73102 · 405-239-6771

Jon L. Hester* · Hester and Schem · 5400 Northwest Grand Boulevard, Suite 500 Oklahoma City, OK 73112 · 405-947-8866

Philip F. Horning · Horning, Johnson, Grove, Moore, Hulett & Thompson · First City Place, Suite 1800 · 204 North Robinson Avenue · Oklahoma City, OK 73102 405-232-3407

James A. Kirk · Kirk & Chaney · Midland Center, Suite 1300 · Oklahoma City, OK 73102-6695 · 405-235-1333

Carolyn S. Thompson · Horning, Johnson, Grove, Moore, Hulett & Thompson First City Place, Suite 1800 · 204 North Robinson Avenue · Oklahoma City, OK 73102 · 405-232-3407

Robert J. (Jim) Turner · Turner, Turner & Braun · 1319 Classen Drive · Oklahoma City, OK 73103 · 405-236-1646

Samuel P. Daniel, Jr. · Doerner, Stuart, Saunders, Daniel & Anderson · 320 South Boston Avenue, Suite 500 · Tulsa, OK 74103-3725 · 918-582-1211

William W. Hood* · (Child Custody, Divorce, Equitable Division) · Hood, Thornbrugh & Raynolds · 1914 South Boston · Tulsa, OK 74119 · 918-583-5825

Arthur E. Rubin* · James R. Gotwals and Associates · 525 South Main Street, Suite 1130 · Tulsa, OK 74103 · 918-599-7088

Don E. Williams · Naylor & Williams · 1701 South Boston Avenue · Tulsa, OK 74119 · 918-582-8000

FIRST AMENDMENT LAW

Roy J. Davis* · Murrah & Davis · One Leadership Square, 12th Floor · 211 North Robinson · Oklahoma City, OK 73102 · 405-235-1681

Michael Minnis* · First Oklahoma Tower, Suite 1310 · 210 West Park Avenue · Oklahoma City, OK 73102 · 405-235-7686

Clyde A. Muchmore* · Crowe & Dunlevy · 1800 Mid-America Tower · 20 North Broadway · Oklahoma City, OK 73102 · 405-235-7734

Robert D. Nelon · Andrews Davis Legg Bixler Milsten & Price · 500 West Main Oklahoma City, OK 73102 · 405-272-9241

Louis W. Bullock · Bullock and Bullock · 320 South Boston, Suite 718 · Tulsa, OK 74103 · 918-584-2001

John Henry Rule* · Gable & Gotwals · 2000 Fourth National Bank Building · 15 West Sixth Street · Tulsa, OK 74119-5447 · 918-582-9201

HEALTH CARE LAW

James L. Hall, Jr. · Crowe & Dunlevy · 1800 Mid-America Tower · 20 North Broadway · Oklahoma City, OK 73102 · 405-235-7720

Michael E. Joseph · McAfee & Taft · Two Leadership Square, 10th Floor · Oklahoma City, OK 73102 · 405-235-9621

Mary Holloway Richard · Spradling, Alpern, Friot & Gum · 101 Park Avenue, Suite 700 · Oklahoma City, OK 73102-7283 · 405-272-0211

Karen S. Rieger · Crowe & Dunlevy · 1800 Mid-America Tower · 20 North Broadway · Oklahoma City, OK 73102 · 405-235-7788

Linda G. Scoggins · Spradling, Alpern, Friot & Gum · 101 Park Avenue, Suite 700 · Oklahoma City, OK 73102-7283 · 405-272-0211

Elise Dunitz Brennan · Doerner, Stuart, Saunders, Daniel & Anderson · 320 South Boston Avenue, Suite 500 · Tulsa, OK 74103-3725 · 918-582-1211

John A. Gaberino · Huffman Arrington · 1000 ONEOK Plaza · Tulsa, OK 74103 918-585-8141

Teresa A. Meinders · Boone, Smith, Davis, Hurst & Dickman · 500 ONEOK Plaza · 100 West Fifth Street · Tulsa, OK 74103 · 918-587-0000

IMMIGRATION LAW

E. Vance Winningham · Winningham & Associates · 911 Northwest 57th Street Oklahoma City, OK 73118 · 405-843-1037

INTELLECTUAL PROPERTY LAW

E. Harrison Gilbert · Laney, Dougherty, Hessin & Beavers · 211 North Robinson Oklahoma City, OK 73102-7114 · 405-232-5586

Robert M. Hessin · Laney, Dougherty, Hessin & Beavers · 211 North Robinson Oklahoma City, OK 73102-7114 · 405-232-5586

William R. Laney · Laney, Dougherty, Hessin & Beavers · 211 North Robinson Oklahoma City, OK 73102-7114 · 405-232-5586

LABOR AND EMPLOYMENT LAW

H. Leonard Court* · (Management) · Crowe & Dunlevy · 1800 Mid-American Tower · 20 North Broadway · Oklahoma City, OK 73102 · 405-235-7700

Charles W. Ellis · (Management) · Lawrence & Ellis · Union Plaza, Suite 600 · 3030 Northwest Expressway · Oklahoma City, OK 73112 · 405-948-6000

James L. Hall, Jr. · (Management) · Crowe & Dunlevy · 1800 Mid-American Tower · 20 North Broadway · Oklahoma City, OK 73102 · 405-235-7700

Mona S. Lambird · (Management) · Andrews Davis Legg Bixler Milsten & Price 500 West Main · Oklahoma City, OK 73102 · 405-272-9241

George J. McCaffrey · (Labor, Individuals) · Lampkin, McCaffrey & Tawwater 201 Robert S. Kerr, Suite 1100 · Oklahoma City, OK 73102 · 405-272-9611

James R. Moore · (Labor, Individuals) · Horning, Johnson, Grove, Moore, Hulett & Thompson · First City Place, Suite 1800 · 204 North Robinson Avenue · Oklahoma City, OK 73102 · 405-232-3407

Jerry D. Sokolosky · (Labor) · Abel, Musser, Sokolosky & Clark · One Leadership Square · 211 North Robinson, Suite 600 · Oklahoma City, OK 73102 · 405-239-7046

Peter T. Van Dyke · (Management) · Lytle Soule & Curlee · 1200 Robinson Renaissance · 119 North Robinson · Oklahoma City, OK 73102 · 405-235-7471

Thomas F. Birmingham · (Labor) · Ungerman & Iola · Riverbridge Office Park, Suite 300 · 1323 East 71st Street · P.O. Box 701917 · Tulsa, OK 74170-1917 · 918-495-0550

D. Gregory Bledsoe* · (Individuals) · 1515 South Denver · Tulsa, OK 74119-3828 918-599-8118

Louis W. Bullock · (Individuals) · Bullock and Bullock · 320 South Boston, Suite 718 · Tulsa, OK 74103 · 918-584-2001

J. Patrick Cremin* · (Management) · Hall, Estill, Hardwick, Gable, Golden & Nelson · 4100 Bank of Oklahoma Tower · One Williams Center · Tulsa, OK 74172-0154 · 918-588-2700

Lynn Paul Mattson · (Management) · Doerner, Stuart, Saunders, Daniel & Anderson · 320 South Boston Avenue, Suite 500 · Tulsa, OK 74103-3725 · 918-582-1211

J. Ronald Petrikin · (Management) · Gable & Gotwals · 2000 Fourth National Bank Building · 15 West Sixth Street · Tulsa, OK 74119-5447 · 918-582-9201

David E. Strecker · (Management) · Conner & Winters · 2400 First National Tower · Tulsa, OK 74103 · 918-586-5711

Maynard I. Ungerman · (Labor) · Ungerman & Iola · Riverbridge Office Park, Suite 300 · 1323 East 71st Street · P.O. Box 701917 · Tulsa, OK 74170-1917 · 918-495-0550

NATURAL RESOURCES AND ENVIRONMENTAL LAW

Stanley L. Cunningham · (Oil & Gas) · McAfee & Taft · Two Leadership Square, 10th Floor · Oklahoma City, OK 73102 · 405-235-9621

Philip D. Hart* · (Oil & Gas) · McAfee & Taft · Two Leadership Square, 10th Floor · Oklahoma City, OK 73102 · 405-235-9621

William J. Legg* · (Oil & Gas) · Andrews Davis Legg Bixler Milsten & Price · 500 West Main · Oklahoma City, OK 73102 · 405-272-9241

Kenneth N. McKinney* · (Environmental Litigation) · McKinney, Stringer & Webster · BancFirst Building, Eighth Floor · 101 North Broadway · Oklahoma City, OK 73102 · 405-239-6444

Barth P. Walker · (Oil & Gas) · Walker, Walker & Driskill · 950 Landmark Towers East · 3535 Northwest 58th Street · Oklahoma City, OK 73112 · 405-943-9693

H. B. Watson, Jr. · (Oil & Gas) · Watson & McKenzie · 2900 Liberty Tower · 100 North Broadway · Oklahoma City, OK 73102 · 405-232-2501

James C. T. Hardwick · (Oil & Gas) · Hall, Estill, Hardwick, Gable, Golden & Nelson · 4100 Bank of Oklahoma Tower · One Williams Center · Tulsa, OK 74172-0154 · 918-588-2700

Joseph W. Morris · (Oil & Gas, Coal) · Gable & Gotwals · 2000 Fourth National Bank Building · 15 West Sixth Street · Tulsa, OK 74119-5447 · 918-582-9201

W. Bland Williamson, Jr. · (Oil & Gas) · Pray, Walker, Jackman, Williamson & Marlar · ONEOK Plaza, Ninth Floor · Tulsa, OK 74103 · 918-584-4136

PERSONAL INJURY LITIGATION

Gene Stipe* · (Plaintiffs, Medical Malpractice, Products Liability, Automobile Collision, Workmen's Compensation) · Stipe, Gossett, Stipe, Harper, Estes, McCune and Parks · 323 East Carl Albert Parkway · P.O. Box 1368 · McAlester, OK 74502 · 918-423-0421

Ed Abel · (Plaintiffs) · Abel, Musser, Sokolosky & Clark · One Leadership Square 211 North Robinson, Suite 600 · Oklahoma City, OK 73102-7107 · 405-239-7046

Murray E. Abowitz · (Defendants) · Abowitz and Welch · 15 North Robinson, 10th Floor · P.O. Box 1937 · Oklahoma City, OK 73101 · 405-236-4645

Robert S. Baker · (Defendants) · Baker, Baker, Smith & Tait · 2140 Liberty Tower · Oklahoma City, OK 73102 · 405-232-3487

Howard K. Berry, Jr.* · (Plaintiffs) · Berry & Durland · 300 Equity Tower · 1601 Northwest Expressway · Oklahoma City, OK 73118 · 405-840-0060

James W. Bill Berry · (Plaintiffs) · City Place, Suite 2500 · 204 North Robinson Oklahoma City, OK 73102 · 405-236-3167

John R. Couch* · (Defendants, Products Liability, Professional Malpractice) · Pierce Couch Hendrickson Johnston & Baysinger · 1109 North Francis · P.O. Box 26350 · Oklahoma City, OK 73126 · 405-235-1611

James D. Foliart * · (Defendants) · Foliart, Huff, Ottaway & Caldwell · First National Center, 20th Floor · 120 North Robinson · Oklahoma City, OK 73102 · 405-232-4633

Calvin W. Hendrickson* · (Plaintiffs, Defendants, Medical Malpractice, Products Liability) · Pierce Couch Hendrickson Johnston & Baysinger · 1109 North Francis · P.O. Box 26350 · Oklahoma City, OK 73126 · 405-235-1611

Kenneth N. McKinney* · (Defendants) · McKinney, Stringer & Webster · BancFirst Building, Eighth Floor · 101 North Broadway · Oklahoma City, OK 73102 · 405-239-6444

Earl D. Mills · (Defendants) · Mills, Whitten, Mills, Mills & Hinkle · One Leadership Square, Suite 500 · 211 North Robinson · Oklahoma City, OK 73102 405-239-2500

John W. Norman* · (Plaintiffs) · Renaissance Centre East · 127 North 10th Street Oklahoma City, OK 73103-4903 · 405-272-0200

Patrick M. Ryan · Ryan, Holloman, Corbyn & Geister · 900 Robinson Renaissance · 119 North Robinson · Oklahoma City, OK 73102-4608 · 405-239-6041

George F. Short* · (Defendants, Medical Malpractice, Products Liability, Professional Malpractice) · Short Barnes Wiggins Margo & Adler · 1400 American First Tower · 101 North Robinson · Oklahoma City, OK 73102 · 405-232-1211

Kenneth R. Webster · McKinney, Stringer & Webster · BancFirst Building, Eighth Floor · Main & Broadway · Oklahoma City, OK 73102 · 405-239-6444

Michael P. Atkinson · Thomas, Glass, Atkinson, Haskins, Nellis & Boudreaux · 525 South Main, Suite 1500 · Tulsa, OK 74103 · 918-582-8877

Joseph M. Best · (Defendants) · Best, Sharp, Sheridan & Stritzke · Kennedy Building, Suite 700 · 100 West Fifth Street · Tulsa, OK 74104 · 918-582-1234

James E. Frasier* · (Plaintiffs) · Frasier & Frasier · 1700 Southwest Boulevard, Suite 100 · Tulsa, OK 74107 · 918-584-4724

Richard D. Gibbon · (Defendants) · Richard D. Gibbon & Associates · 1611 South Harvard · Tulsa, OK 74112 · 918-745-0687

John A. Gladd · Gladd & Darrah · 2642 East 21st Street, Suite 150 · Tulsa, OK 74114 · 918-744-5657

J. Warren Jackman · Pray, Walker, Jackman, Williamson & Marlar · ONEOK Plaza, Ninth Floor · 100 West Fifth Street · Tulsa, OK 74103 · 918-584-4136

Alfred B. Knight* · (Defendants, Products Liability, Professional Malpractice, Appellate) · Knight, Wilkerson & Parrish · 233 West 11th · P.O. Box 1560 · Tulsa, OK 74101-1560 · 918-584-6457

James E. Poe* · (Defendants) · Covington & Poe · Grantson Building, Suite 740
Fifth & Boulder · Tulsa, OK 74103 · 918-585-5537

PUBLIC UTILITY LAW

James W. George · Crowe & Dunlevy · 1800 Mid-America Tower · 20 North
Broadway · Oklahoma City, OK 73102 · 405-235-7700

H. B. Watson, Jr. · Watson & McKinzie · 2900 Liberty Tower · 100 Broadway ·
Oklahoma City, OK 73102 · 405-232-2501

John L. Arrington · (State Utilities) · Huffman Arrington · 1000 ONEOK Plaza
Tulsa, OK 74103 · 918-585-8141

Harry M. Crowe, Jr. · (Natural Gas, Municipal Utilities) · Crawford, Crowe &
Bainbridge · 1714 First National Building · Tulsa, OK 74103 · 918-587-1128

REAL ESTATE LAW

Monty L. Bratcher · 2000 Southeast 15th Street, Suite 150B · P.O. Box 1347 ·
Edmond, OK 73083-1347 · 405-340-6983

James C. Elder · (Commercial Transactions) · Mock, Schwabe, Waldo, Elder,
Reeves & Bryant · One Leadership Square, 15th Floor · 211 North Robinson
Avenue · Oklahoma City, OK 73102 · 405-235-5500

James F. Hartmann, Jr. · Crowe & Dunlevy · 1800 Mid-America Tower · 20
North Broadway · Oklahoma City, OK 73102 · 405-235-7700

John D. Hastie · Hastie and Kirschner · 3000 First Oklahoma Tower · 210 West
Park Avenue, Suite 3000 · Oklahoma City, OK 73102 · 405-239-6404

Frank D. Hill · (Real Estate Taxation) · McAfee & Taft · Two Leadership
Square, 10th Floor · Oklahoma City, OK 73102 · 405-235-9621

Robert M. Johnson · (Commercial Transactions, Industrial Transactions, Real
Estate Financing) · Crowe & Dunlevy · 1800 Mid-America Tower · 20 North
Broadway · Oklahoma City, OK 73102 · 405-235-7700

Warren E. Jones · Law Office of Warren E. Jones · 1900 North Robinson, Suite
900 · Oklahoma City, OK 73102 · 405-239-6041

Sally Mock · McAfee & Taft · Two Leadership Square, 10th Floor · Oklahoma
City, OK 73102 · 405-235-9621

Henry P. Rheinberger · Crowe & Dunlevy · 1800 Mid-America Tower · 20 North Broadway · Oklahoma City, OK 73102 · 405-235-7700

Richard A. Riggs · (Commercial Transactions) · McAfee & Taft · Two Leadership Square, 10th Floor · Oklahoma City, OK 73102 · 405-235-9621

Joe S. Rolston III · Woodard Rolston Kelley & Associates · Lake Park Tower, Suite 201 · 6525 North Meridian · Oklahoma City, OK 73116 · 405-728-2242

John E. Sargent · McAfee & Taft · Two Leadership Square, 10th Floor · Oklahoma City, OK 73102 · 405-235-9621

John T. Spradling · Spradling, Alpern, Friot & Gum · 101 Park Avenue, Suite 700 Oklahoma City, OK 73102-7283 · 405-272-0211

T. Scott Spradling · Spradling, Alpern, Friot & Gum · 101 Park Avenue, Suite 700 · Oklahoma City, OK 73102-7283 · 405-272-0211

Richard Cleverdon · 111 West Fifth Street, Suite 400 · Tulsa, OK 74103 · 918-583-9700

Charles P. Gotwals, Jr. · Gable & Gotwals · 2000 Fourth National Bank Building 15 West Sixth Street · Tulsa, OK 74119-5447 · 918-582-9201

Roy D. Johnsen · Epperson & Johnsen · 324 Main Mall, Suite 900 · Tulsa, OK 74103 · 918-585-5641

William B. Jones · Jones, Givens, Gotcher, Bogan & Hilborne · 3800 First National Tower · Tulsa, OK 74103 · 918-581-8200

TAX AND EMPLOYEE BENEFITS LAW

Thomas G. Potts · (Tax Disputes) · Houston and Klein · 320 South Boston, Suite 700 · Tulsa, OK 74103 · 918-583-2131

Len Cason · Hartzog Conger Cason & Hargis · 1600 Bank of Oklahoma Plaza · 201 Robert S. Kerr · Oklahoma City, OK 73102 · 405-235-7000

Gary F. Fuller · McAfee & Taft · Two Leadership Square, 10th Floor · Oklahoma City, OK 73102 · 405-235-9621

James H. Holloman, Jr. · (Corporate & Partnership Transactions, State Tax, Employee Benefits, Tax Disputes) · Crowe & Dunlevy · 1800 Mid-America Tower · 20 North Broadway · Oklahoma City, OK 73102-4608 · 405-235-7700

J. Dudley Hyde · (Employee Benefits) · McAfee & Taft · Two Leadership Square, 10th Floor · Oklahoma City, OK 73102 · 405-235-9621

Richard B. Kells, Jr. · (State Tax) · Andrews Davis Legg Bixler Milsten & Price 500 West Main · Oklahoma City, OK 73102 · 405-272-9241

Timothy M. Larason · (Corporate & Partnership Transactions, State Tax, Tax Disputes, Oil & Gas) · Andrews Davis Legg Bixler Milsten & Price · 500 West Main · Oklahoma City, OK 73102 · 405-272-9241

Jean A. McDonald · (Tax, Employee Benefits) · Crowe & Dunlevy · 1800 Mid-America Tower · 20 North Broadway · Oklahoma City, OK 73102 · 405-235-7700

Randall D. Mock · Mock, Schwabe, Waldo, Elder, Reeves & Bryant · One Leadership Square, 15th Floor · 211 North Robinson Avenue · Oklahoma City, OK 73102 · 405-235-5500

Dee A. Replogle · (Corporate & Partnership Transactions) · McAfee & Taft · Two Leadership Square, 10th Floor · Oklahoma City, OK 73102 · 405-235-9621

Jon H. Trudgeon · Speck, Philbin, Fleig, Trudgeon & Lutz · First City Place, Suite 800 · Oklahoma City, OK 73102 · 405-235-1603

E. John Eagleton* · (Corporate & Partnership Transactions, State Task, Employee Benefits, Tax Disputes) · Houston and Klein · 320 South Boston, Suite 700 Tulsa, OK 74103 · 918-583-2131

C. Robert Jones · (Corporate & Partnership Transactions, State Tax, Employee Benefits) · Gable & Gotwals · 2000 Fourth National Bank Building · 15 West Sixth Street · Tulsa, OK 74119-5447 · 918-582-9201

Gail R. Runnels · Holliman, Langholz, Runnels & Dorwart · Holarud Building, Suite 700 · 10 East Third Street · Tulsa, OK 74103-3695 · 918-584-1471

Varley H. Taylor, Jr. · (Tax, Employee Benefits) · Doerner, Stuart, Saunders, Daniel & Anderson · 320 South Boston Avenue, Suite 500 · Tulsa, OK 74103-3725 918-582-1211

John B. Turner · (State Tax, Tax Disputes) · Doerner, Stuart, Saunders, Daniel & Anderson · 320 South Boston Avenue, Suite 500 · Tulsa, OK 74103-3725 · 918-582-1211

Henry G. Will · (Tax, Employee Benefits) · Conner & Winters · 2400 First National Tower · Tulsa, OK 74103 · 918-586-5711

Andrew M. Wolov · (Corporate & Partnership Transactions) · Hall, Estill, Hardwick, Gable, Golden & Nelson · 4100 Bank of Oklahoma Tower · One Williams Center · Tulsa, OK 74172-0154 · 918-588-2700

TRUSTS AND ESTATES

James F. Davis · Andrews Davis Legg Bixler Milsten & Price · 500 West Main · Oklahoma City, OK 73102 · 405-272-9241

Allen D. Evans · Crowe & Dunlevy · 1800 Mid-America Tower · 20 North Broadway · Oklahoma City, OK 73102 · 405-235-7700

Gary F. Fuller · McAfee & Taft · Two Leadership Square, 10th Floor · Oklahoma City, OK 73102 · 405-235-9621

James H. Holloman, Jr. · (Estate Planning, Estate Administration, Charitable Trusts) · Crowe & Dunlevy · 1800 Mid-America Tower · 20 North Broadway · Oklahoma City, OK 73102-4608 · 405-235-7700

Richard B. Kells, Jr. · Andrews Davis Legg Bixler Milsten & Price · 500 West Main · Oklahoma City, OK 73102 · 405-272-9241

Randall D. Mock · Mock, Schwabe, Waldo, Elder, Reeves & Bryant · One Leadership Square, 15th Floor · 211 North Robinson Avenue · Oklahoma City, OK 73102 · 405-235-5500

Alan Newman · Hartzog Conger Cason & Hargis · 1600 Bank of Oklahoma Plaza 201 Robert S. Kerr · Oklahoma City, OK 73102 · 405-235-7000

Cynda C. Ottaway · Crowe & Dunlevy · 1800 Mid-America Tower · 20 North Broadway · Oklahoma City, OK 73102 · 405-235-7700

Michael W. Thom · Thom & Hendrick · Union Bank Building, Suite 326 · 3030 Northwest Expressway · Oklahoma City, OK 73112 · 405-947-5551

W. Thomas Coffman (Estate Planning, Estate Administration, Charitable Trusts, Estate Taxation) · Gable & Gotwals · 2000 Fourth National Bank Building · 15 West Sixth Street · Tulsa, OK 74119-5447 · 918-582-9201

David F. James · Houston and Klein · 320 South Boston, Suite 700 · Tulsa, OK 74103 · 918-583-2131

John B. Johnson, Jr. · (Estate Planning) · Gable & Gotwals · 2000 Fourth National Bank Building · 15 West Sixth Street · Tulsa, OK 74119-5447 · 918-582-9201

Henry G. Will · Conner & Winters · 2400 First National Tower · Tulsa, OK 74103 918-586-5711

OREGON

BANKRUPTCY LAW

Keith Y. Boyd · (Business Reorganization, Creditors' Rights, Debtors' Rights, Bankruptcy Litigation) · McGavic & Boyd · 700 Lawrence Street · Eugene, OR 97401 · 503-485-4555

Wilson C. Muhlheim · Harrang, Long, Watkinson, Arnold & Laird · 101 East Broadway, Suite 400 · P.O. Box 11620 · Eugene, OR 97440-3820 · 503-485-0220

Richard C. Josephson · Stoel Rives Boley Jones & Grey · Standard Insurance Center, Suite 2300 · 900 Southwest Fifth Avenue · Portland, OR 97204-1268 · 503-224-3380

Albert N. Kennedy · Tonkon, Torp, Galen, Marmaduke & Booth · 1600 Pioneer Tower · 888 Southwest Fifth Avenue · Portland, OR 97204-2099 · 503-221-1440

William M. McAllister · Stoel Rives Boley Jones & Grey · Standard Insurance Center, Suite 2300 · 900 Southwest Fifth Avenue · Portland, OR 97204-1268 · 503-224-3380

Kevin D. Padrick · (Business Reorganization, Creditors' Rights, Debtors' Rights, Bankruptcy Litigation) · Miller, Nash, Wiener, Hager & Carlsen · 3500 U.S. Bancorp Tower · 111 Southwest Fifth Avenue · Portland, OR 97204-3699 · 503-224-5858

Jerome B. Shank · Sussman, Shank, Wapnick, Caplan & Stiles · 1111 Security Pacific Plaza · 1001 Southwest Fifth Avenue · Portland, OR 97204 · 503-227-1111

Leon Simson · Ball, Janik & Novack · One Main Place, Suite 1100 · 101 Southwest Main Street · Portland, OR 97204 · 503-228-2525

Norman Wapnick · (Business Reorganization, Creditors' Rights, Debtors' Rights, Bankruptcy Litigation) · Sussman, Shank, Wapnick, Caplan & Stiles · 1111 Security Pacific Plaza · 1001 Southwest Fifth Avenue · Portland, OR 97204-1111 · 503-227-1111

BUSINESS LITIGATION

William F. Gary · Harrang, Long, Watkinson, Arnold & Laird · 101 East Broadway, Suite 400 · P.O. Box 11620 · Eugene, OR 97440-3820 · 503-485-0220

K. Patrick Neill · Hershner, Hunter, Moulton, Andrews & Neill · 180 East 11th Avenue · P.O. Box 1475 · Eugene, OR 97440 · 503-686-8511

Mark W. Perrin · Perrin, Gartland, Doyle & Nelson · 44 Club Road, Suite 200 · P.O. Box 11229 · Eugene, OR 97440 · 503-344-2174

William G. Wheatley* · Jaqua & Wheatley · 825 East Park Street · Eugene, OR 97401-2909 · 503-686-8485

James H. Clarke · (Appellate) · Lane Powell Spears Lubersky · 520 Southwest Yamhill Street, Suite 800 · Portland, OR 97204 · 503-226-6151

Barnes H. Ellis* · (Antitrust, Commercial, Securities) · Stoel Rives Boley Jones & Grey · Standard Insurance Center, Suite 2300 · 900 Southwest Fifth Avenue · Portland, OR 97204-1268 · 503-224-3380

John R. Faust, Jr.* · (Appellate) · Schwabe, Williamson & Wyatt · Pacwest Center, Suites 1600-1950 · 1211 Southwest Fifth Avenue · Portland, OR 97204-3795 · 503-222-9981

Wayne Hilliard* · (Antitrust, Commercial Securities) · Lane Powell Spears Lubersky · 520 Southwest Yamhill Street, Suite 800 · Portland, OR 97204 · 503-226-6151

Jack L. Kennedy* · Kennedy, King & Zimmer · 2600 Pacwest Center · 1211 Southwest Fifth Avenue · Portland, OR 97204-3726 · 503-228-6191

Garr M. King · Kennedy, King & Zimmer · 2600 Pacwest Center · 1211 Southwest Fifth Avenue · Portland, OR 97204-3726 · 503-228-6191

David B. Markowitz · Markowitz, Herbold, Glade & Mehlhaf · One Southwest Columbia Street, Suite 300 · Portland, OR 97258 · 503-295-3085

Wayne A. Williamson* · Schwabe, Williamson & Wyatt · Pacwest Center, Suites 1600-1950 · 1211 Southwest Fifth Avenue · Portland, OR 97204-3795 · 503-222-9981

CORPORATE LAW

Vernon D. Gleaves · Gleaves Swearingen Larson & Potter · 975 Oak Street, Eighth Floor · P.O. Box 1147 · Eugene, OR 97440-1147 · 503-686-8833

James L. Hershner · Hershner, Hunter, Moulton, Andrews & Neill · 180 East 11th Avenue · P.O. Box 1475 · Eugene, OR 97440 · 503-686-8511

Malcolm H. Scott · Cass, Scott, Woods & Smith · 101 East Broadway, Suite 200 · Eugene, OR 97401 · 503-687-1515

Arlen C. Swearingen · (Mergers & Acquisitions) · Gleaves Swearingen Larsen & Potter · 975 Oak Street, Eighth Floor · P.O. Box 1147 · Eugene, OR 97440-1147 · 503-686-8833

John P. Bledsoe · Lane Powell Spears Lubersky · 520 Southwest Yamhill Street, Suite 800 · Portland, OR 97204 · 503-226-6151

Brian G. Booth · Tonkon, Torp, Galen, Marmaduke & Booth · 1600 Pioneer Tower · 888 Southwest Fifth Avenue · Portland, OR 97204-2099 · 503-221-1440

Edward L. Epstein · (Mergers & Acquisitions) · Stoel Rives Boley Jones & Grey Standard Insurance Center, Suite 2300 · 900 Southwest Fifth Avenue · Portland, OR 97204-1268 · 503-224-3380

David G. Hayhurst · (Banking, Corporate Finance, Mergers & Acquisitions, Securities Regulation) · Stoel Rives Boley Jones & Grey · Standard Insurance Center, Suite 2300 · 900 Southwest Fifth Avenue · Portland, OR 97204-1268 · 503-224-3380

Kenneth W. Hergenhan · Miller, Nash, Wiener, Hager & Carlsen · 3500 U.S. Bancorp Tower · 111 Southwest Fifth Avenue · Portland, OR 97204-3699 · 503-224-5858

Henry H. Hewitt · Stoel Rives Boley Jones & Grey · Standard Insurance Center, Suite 2300 · 900 Southwest Fifth Avenue · Portland, OR 97204-1268 · 503-224-3380

James M. Kennedy · (Closely-Held Corporations) · Kennedy & Kennedy · 222 Southwest Columbia Street · Portland, OR 97201 · 503-226-6555

Dexter E. Martin · Stoel Rives Boley Jones & Grey · Standard Insurance Center, Suite 2300 · 900 Southwest Fifth Avenue · Portland, OR 97204-1268 · 503-224-3380

Richard E. Roy · (Corporate Finance, Leveraged Buyouts, Mergers & Acquisitions) · Stoel Rives Boley Jones & Grey · Standard Insurance Center, Suite 2300 900 Southwest Fifth Avenue · Portland, OR 97204-1268 · 503-224-3380

CRIMINAL DEFENSE

Donald D. Diment, Jr. · Diment, Billings & Walker · 767 Willamette, Suite 208 Eugene, OR 97401 · 503-484-2422

Robert J. McCrea* · (Federal Court, State Court) · 1147 High Street · Eugene, OR 97401-3270 · 503-485-1182

Kenneth A. Morrow · Morrow Monks & Sharp · 310 East 11th Avenue · Eugene, OR 97401 · 503-345-2002

Wendell R. Birkland* · (Violent Crimes, Non-Violent Crimes, State Court) · Security Pacific Plaza · 1001 Southwest Fifth Avenue, Suite 1215 · Portland, OR 97204-1199 · 503-241-8601

Marc D. Blackman · Ransom, Blackman & Weil · 900 American Bank Building · 621 Southwest Morrison Street · Portland, OR 97205 · 503-228-0487

Desmond D. Connall · (Violent Crimes, Non-Violent Crimes, Federal Court, State Court) · 1501 Southwest Harrison Street · Portland, OR 97201 · 503-227-2688

Ronald H. Hoevet · Hoevet, Snyder & Miller · 900 Southwest Fifth Avenue, Suite 2100 · Portland, OR 97204 · 503-228-0497

Stephen A. Houze* · (Violent Crimes, Non-Violent Crimes, Federal Court, State Court) · Security Pacific Plaza · 1001 Southwest Fifth Avenue, Suite 1215 · Portland, OR 97204-1199 · 503-241-8601

John S. Ransom* · Ransom, Blackman & Weil · 900 American Bank Building · 621 Southwest Morrison Street · Portland, OR 97205 · 503-228-0487

Norman Sepenuk* · 1800 Security Pacific Plaza · 1001 Southwest Fifth Avenue Portland, OR 97204-1134 · 503-221-1633

FAMILY LAW

Douglas L. McCool · 400 Country Club Road, Suite 210 · Eugene, OR 97401 · 503-485-8114

Ronald I. Gevurtz* · Gevurtz, Menashe, Hergert, Larson & Kurshner · The 1515 Building, Suite 808 · 1515 Southwest Fifth Avenue · Portland, OR 97201-5472 · 503-227-1515

Ira L. Gottlieb* · (Child Custody, Divorce, Marital Settlement Agreements, Equitable Division) · Keller, Gottlieb & Gorin · 350 American Bank Building · 621 Southwest Morrison Street · Portland, OR 97205-3812 · 503-224-7563

Jack L. Kennedy · Kennedy, King & Zimmer · 2600 Pacwest Center · 1211 Southwest Fifth Avenue · Portland, OR 97204-3726 · 503-228-6191

Albert A. Menashe* · Gevurtz, Menashe, Hergert, Larson & Kurshner · The 1515 Building, Suite 808 · 1515 Southwest Fifth Avenue · Portland, OR 97201-5472 · 503-227-1515

William F. Schulte, Jr. · Schulte, Anderson, DeFrancq, Downes & Carter · 811 Southwest Front Avenue, Suite 500 · Portland, OR 97204-3379 · 503-223-4131

Gary J. Zimmer* · Kennedy, King & Zimmer · 2600 Pacwest Center · 1211 Southwest Fifth Avenue · Portland, OR 97204-3726 · 503-228-6191

FIRST AMENDMENT LAW

Charles F. Hinkle · Stoel Rives Boley Jones & Grey · Standard Insurance Center, Suite 2300 · 900 Southwest Fifth Avenue · Portland, OR 97204-1268 · 503-224-3380

HEALTH CARE LAW

Craig A. Smith · Hershner, Hunter, Moulton, Andrews & Neill · 180 East 11th Avenue · P.O. Box 1475 · Eugene, OR 97440 · 503-686-8511

Thomas E. Cooney · Cooney, Moscato & Crew · 1515 Southwest Fifth Avenue, Suite 920 · Portland, OR 97201 · 503-224-7600

Edward L. Epstein · Stoel Rives Boley Jones & Grey · Standard Insurance Center, Suite 2300 · 900 Southwest Fifth Avenue · Portland, OR 97204-1268 · 503-224-3380

Theodore C. Falk · Lane Powell Spears Lubersky · 520 Southwest Yamhill Street, Suite 800 · Portland, OR 97204 · 503-226-6151

J. Barrett Marks · Miller, Nash, Wiener, Hager & Carlsen · 3500 U.S. Bancorp Tower · 111 Southwest Fifth Avenue · Portland, OR 97204-3699 · 503-224-5858

Peter F. Stoloff · One Financial Center, Suite 1000 · 121 Southwest Morrison · Portland, OR 97204 · 503-224-4664

IMMIGRATION LAW

Gerald H. Robinson · Black Helterline · 700 Southwest Washington Street, Suite 1200 · Portland, OR 97205 · 503-224-5560

INTELLECTUAL PROPERTY LAW

Paul S. Angello · Stoel Rives Boley Jones & Grey · Standard Insurance Center, Suite 2300 · 900 Southwest Fifth Avenue · Portland, OR 97204-1268 · 503-224-3380

Daniel P. Chernoff · (Patent, Computer) · Chernoff, Vilhauer, McClung & Stenzel · 600 Benjamin Franklin Plaza · One Southwest Columbia · Portland, OR 97258 · 503-227-5631

Kenneth S. Klarquist, Sr. · Klarquist, Sparkman, Cambell, Leigh & Winston · 121 Southwest Salmon Street, Suite 1600 · Portland, OR 97204 · 503-226-7391

J. Pierre Kolisch · Kolisch, Hartwell, Dickinson, McCormack & Heuser · 520 Southwest Yamhill, Suite 200 · Portland, OR 97204 · 503-224-6655

James S. Leigh · Klarquist, Sparkman, Cambell, Leigh & Winston · 121 Southwest Salmon Street, Suite 1600 · Portland, OR 97204 · 503-226-7391

LABOR AND EMPLOYMENT LAW

Harlan Bernstein* · (Labor, Individuals) · Jolles, Sokol & Bernstein · 721 Southwest Oak Street · Portland, OR 97205-3791 · 503-228-6474

Garry R. Bullard · (Management) · Bullard, Korshoj, Smith & Jernstedt · 1515 Southwest Fifth Avenue, Suite 1000 · Portland, OR 97201 · 503-248-1134

Richard C. Busse, Jr.* · (Individuals) · American Bank Building · 621 Southwest Morrison Street, Suite 521 · Portland, OR 97205 · 503-248-0504

Richard R. Carney* · (Labor) · Carney, Buckley, Kasameyer & Hays · 410 Riviera Plaza · 1618 Southwest First Avenue, Suite 410 · Portland, OR 97201 · 503-221-0611

Kenneth E. Jernstedt · (Management) · Bullard, Korshoj, Smith & Jernstedt · 1515 Southwest Fifth Avenue, Suite 1000 · Portland, OR 97201 · 503-248-1134

Bernard Jolles · (Labor, Individuals) · Jolles, Sokol & Bernstein · 721 Southwest Oak Street · Portland, OR 97205 · 503-228-6474

Louis B. Livingston · (Management) · Miller, Nash, Wiener, Hager & Carlsen · 3500 U.S. Bancorp Tower · 111 Southwest Fifth Avenue · Portland, OR 97204-3699 · 503-224-5858

William F. Lubersky · (Management) · Lane Powell Spears Lubersky · 520 Southwest Yamhill Street, Suite 800 · Portland, OR 97204 · 503-226-6151

Donald S. Richardson · (Labor) · Carney, Buckley, Kasameyer & Hays · 1618 Southwest First Avenue, Suite 410 · Portland, OR 97201 · 503-221-0611

Elden M. Rosenthal* · (Individuals) · Rosenthal & Greene · 1907 Orbanco Building · 1001 Southwest Fifth Avenue · Portland, OR 97204-1165 · 503-228-3015

Lewis K. Scott · (Management) · Lane Powell Spears Lubersky · 520 Southwest Yamhill Street, Suite 800 · Portland, OR 97204 · 503-226-6151

Lester V. Smith, Jr. · (Management) · Bullard, Korshoj, Smith & Jernstedt · 1515 Southwest Fifth Avenue, Suite 1000 · Portland, OR 97201 · 503-248-1134

MARITIME LAW

Dean D. DeChaine* · Miller, Nash, Wiener, Hager & Carlsen · 3500 U.S. Bancorp Tower · 111 Southwest Fifth Avenue · Portland, OR 97204-3699 · 503-224-5858

Carl R. Neil · Lindsay, Hart, Neil & Weigler · 222 Southwest Columbia Street, Suite 1600 · Portland, OR 97201 · 503-226-7677

Kenneth E. Roberts · Schwabe, Williamson & Wyatt · Pacwest Center, Suites 1600-1950 · 1211 Southwest Fifth Avenue · Portland, OR 97204-3795 · 503-222-9981

Robert I. Sanders · Wood Tatum Landis Wonacott & Landis · 1001 Southwest Fifth Avenue, Suite 1300 · Portland, OR 97204-1129 · 503-224-5430

Paul N. Wonacott* · Wood Tatum Mosser Brooke & Landis · 1001 Southwest Fifth Avenue, Suite 1300 · Portland, OR 97204-1129 · 503-224-5430

NATURAL RESOURCES AND ENVIRONMENTAL LAW

Richard D. Bach · (Environmental) · Stoel Rives Boley Jones & Grey · Standard Insurance Center, Suite 2300 · 900 Southwest Fifth Avenue · Portland, OR 97204-1268 · 503-224-3380

John P. Bledsoe · (Timber) · Lane Powell Spears Lubersky · 520 Southwest Yamhill Street, Suite 800 · Portland, OR 97204 · 503-226-6151

David L. Blount · Copeland Landye Bennett and Wolf · 3500 First Interstate Tower · One Southwest Columbia · Portland, OR 97201 · 503-224-4100

John B. Crowell, Jr.* · (Timber) · Lane Powell Spears Lubersky · 520 Southwest Yamhill Street, Suite 800 · Portland, OR 97204 · 503-226-6151

Jerry R. Fish · (Oil & Gas, Coal, Mining) · Stoel Rives Boley Jones & Grey · Standard Insurance Center, Suite 2300 · 900 Southwest Fifth Avenue · Portland, OR 97204-1268 · 503-224-3380

Kirk Johansen · (Timber) · Schwabe, Williamson & Wyatt · Pacwest Center, Suites 1600-1950 · 1211 Southwest Fifth Avenue · Portland, OR 97204-3795 · 503-222-9981

David P. Miller · (Timber) · Stoel Rives Boley Jones & Grey · Standard Insurance Center, Suite 2300 · 900 Southwest Fifth Avenue · Portland, OR 97204-1268 · 503-224-3380

Mark A. Norby · (Oil & Gas, Mining, Timber) · Stoel Rives Boley Jones & Grey Standard Insurance Center, Suite 2300 · 900 Southwest Fifth Avenue · Portland, OR 97204-1268 · 503-224-3380

James N. Westwood · (Timber) · Miller, Nash, Wiener, Hager & Carlsen · 3500 U.S. Bancorp Tower · 111 Southwest Fifth Avenue · Portland, OR 97204-3699 · 503-224-5858

PERSONAL INJURY LITIGATION

Arthur C. Johnson · (Plaintiffs) · Johnson, Clifton, Larson & Eolin · Citizens Building, 10th Floor · 975 Oak Street · Eugene, OR 97401-3176 · 503-484-2434

William G. Wheatley* · (Medical Malpractice, Products Liability, Professional Malpractice, Automobile Collision) · Jaqua & Wheatley · 825 East Park · Eugene, OR 97401-2909 · 503-686-8485

Richard P. Noble · (Plaintiffs) · One Centerpointe Drive, Suite 170 · Lake Oswego, OR 97035 · 503-620-3870

E. Richard Bodyfelt* · (Defendants, Products Liability, Airplane Collision) · Bodyfelt, Mount, Stroup & Chamberlain · 300 Powers Building · 65 Southwest Yamhill Street · Portland, OR 97204-3377 · 503-243-1022

John E. Hart* · (Defendants, Medical Malpractice) · Schwabe, Williamson & Wyatt · Pacwest Center, Suites 1600-1950 · 1211 Southwest Fifth Avenue · Portland, OR 97204-3795 · 503-222-9981

Wayne Hilliard* · (Defendants, Products Liability, Professional Malpractice) · Lane Powell Spears Lubersky · 520 Southwest Yamhill Street, Suite 800 · Portland, OR 97204 · 503-226-6151

Jack L. Kennedy · (Defendants) · Kennedy, King & Zimmer · 2600 Pacwest Center · 1211 Southwest Fifth Avenue · Portland, OR 97204-3726 · 503-228-6191

George L. Kirklin · Lane Powell Spears Lubersky · 520 Southwest Yamhill Street, Suite 800 · Portland, OR 97204 · 503-226-6151

Dan O'Leary* · (Plaintiffs) · Pozzi, Wilson, Atchison, O'Leary & Conboy · Standard Plaza,14th Floor · 1100 Southwest Sixth Avenue · Portland, OR 97204 · 503-226-3232

Charles Paulson · (Plaintiffs) · Paulson & Baisch · Security Pacific Plaza, Suite 1905 · 1001 Southwest Fifth Avenue · Portland, OR 97204-1166 · 503-226-6361

Wayne A. Williamson* · (Defendants) · Schwabe, Williamson & Wyatt · Pacwest Center, Suites 1600-1950 · 1211 Southwest Fifth Avenue · Portland, OR 97204-3795 · 503-222-9981

PUBLIC UTILITY LAW

James F. Fell · Stoel Rives Boley Jones & Grey · Standard Insurance Center, Suite 2300 · 900 Southwest Fifth Avenue · Portland, OR 97204-1268 · 503-224-3380

George M. Galloway · Stoel Rives Boley Jones & Grey · Standard Insurance Center, Suite 2300 · 900 Southwest Fifth Avenue · Portland, OR 97204-1268 · 503-224-3380

Michael M. Morgan · Tonkon, Torp, Galen, Marmaduke & Booth · 1600 Pioneer Tower · 888 Southwest Fifth Avenue · Portland, OR 97204-2099 · 503-221-1440

REAL ESTATE LAW

Vernon D. Gleaves · Gleaves Swearingen Larson & Potter · 975 Oak Street, Eighth Floor · P.O. Box 1147 · Eugene, OR 97440-1147 · 503-686-8833

James P. Harrang · Harrang, Long, Watkinson, Arnold & Laird · 101 East Broadway, Suite 400 · P.O. Box 11620 · Eugene, OR 97440-3820 · 503-485-0220

Arlen C. Swearingen · (Commercial Transactions, Industrial Transactions) · Gleaves Swearingen Larsen & Potter · 975 Oak Street, Eighth Floor · P.O. Box 1147 · Eugene, OR 97440-1147 · 503-686-8833

Robert S. Ball · Ball, Janik & Novack · One Main Place, Suite 1100 · 101 Southwest Main Street · Portland, OR 97204 · 503-228-2525

Richard A. Cantlin · Perkins Coie · U.S. Bancorp Tower, Suite 2500 · 111 Southwest Fifth Avenue · Portland, OR 97204 · 503-295-4400

Howard M. Feuerstein · (Commercial Transactions, Industrial Transactions) · Stoel Rives Boley Jones & Grey · Standard Insurance Center, Suite 2300 · 900 Southwest Fifth Avenue · Portland, OR 97204-1268 · 503-224-3380

Terry C. Hauck · Schwabe, Williamson & Wyatt · Pacwest Center, Suites 1600-1950 · 1211 Southwest Fifth Avenue · Portland, OR 97204-3795 · 503-222-9981

Stephen Thomas Janik · Ball, Janik & Novack · One Main Place, Suite 1100 · 101 Southwest Main Street · Portland, OR 97204 · 503-228-2525

David P. Miller · Stoel Rives Boley Jones & Grey · Standard Insurance Center, Suite 2300 · 900 Southwest Fifth Avenue · Portland, OR 97204-1268 · 503-224-3380

Stanley M. Samuels · Preston, Thorgrimson, Shidler, Gates & Ellis · 3200 U.S. Bancorp Tower · 111 Southwest Fifth Avenue · Portland, OR 97204-3635 · 503-228-3200

David P. Weiner · Samuels, Yoelin, Weiner, Kantor & Seymour · 200 Willamette Wharf · 4640 Southwest Macadam Avenue · Portland, OR 97201 · 503-226-2966

TAX AND EMPLOYEE BENEFITS LAW

Craig A. Smith · (Employee Benefits) · Hershner, Hunter, Moulton, Andrews & Neill · 180 East 11th Avenue · P.O. Box 1475 · Eugene, OR 97440 · 503-686-8511

Donald A. Burns · (Employee Benefits) · Miller, Nash, Wiener, Hager & Carlsen · 3500 U.S. Bancorp Tower · 111 Southwest Fifth Avenue · Portland, OR 97204-3699 · 503-224-5858

Joyle C. Dahl · (Corporate & Partnership Transactions, Employee Benefits, Tax Disputes) · Schwabe, Williamson & Wyatt · Pacwest Center, Suites 1600-1950 · 1211 Southwest Fifth Avenue · Portland, OR 97204-3795 · 503-222-9981

Thomas P. Deering · (Employee Benefits) · Stoel Rives Boley Jones & Grey · Standard Insurance Center, Suite 2300 · 900 Southwest Fifth Avenue · Portland, OR 97204-1268 · 503-224-3380

John H. Doran · (Corporate & Partnership Transactions, State Tax) · Lane Powell Spears Lubersky · 520 Southwest Yamhill Street, Suite 800 · Portland, OR 97204-1383 · 503-226-6151

Charles P. Duffy* · (Corporate & Partnership Transactions, Tax Disputes, Timber Valuations) · Duffy, Kekel, Jensen & Bernard · 1200 Standard Plaza · 1100 Southwest Sixth Avenue · Portland, OR 97204-1019 · 503-226-1371

Gerald A. Froebe · Miller, Nash, Wiener, Hager & Carlsen · 3500 U.S. Bancorp Tower · 111 Southwest Fifth Avenue · Portland, OR 97204-3699 · 503-224-5858

Gersham Goldstein · Stoel Rives Boley Jones & Grey · Standard Insurance Center, Suite 2300 · 900 Southwest Fifth Avenue · Portland, OR 97204-1268 · 503-224-3380

Joseph J. Hanna, Jr. · Hanna, Spencer, Kerns & Strader · 1300 Southwest Sixth Avenue, Suite 300 · Portland, OR 97201 · 503-273-2700

Joel D. Kuntz · Stoel Rives Boley Jones & Grey · Standard Insurance Center, Suite 2300 · 900 Southwest Fifth Avenue · Portland, OR 97204-1268 · 503-224-3380

Robert L. Weiss · Weiss, Jensen, Ellis & Botteri · 2300 U.S. Bancorp Tower · 111 Southwest Fifth Avenue · Portland, OR 97204 · 503-243-2300

Morton H. Zalutsky · (Employee Benefits) · Zalutsky, Klarquist & Johnson · The Waldo Building, Third Floor · 215 Southwest Washington Street · Portland, OR 97204 · 503-248-0300

TRUSTS AND ESTATES

David N. Andrews · (Estate Planning, Estate Administration, Charitable Trusts) Hershner, Hunter, Moulton, Andrews & Neill · 180 East 11th Avenue · P.O. Box 1475 · Eugene, OR 97440 · 503-686-8511

Nancy L. Cowgill · Stoel Rives Boley Jones & Grey · Standard Insurance Center, Suite 2300 · 900 Southwest Fifth Avenue · Portland, OR 97204-1268 · 503-224-3380

Robert D. Dayton · Schwabe, Williamson & Wyatt · Pacwest Center, Suites 1600-1950 · 1211 Southwest Fifth Avenue · Portland, OR 97204-3795 · 503-222-9981

Joseph J. Hanna, Jr. · Hanna, Spencer, Kerns & Strader · 1300 Southwest Sixth Avenue, Suite 300 · Portland, OR 97201 · 503-273-2700

David A. Kekel · Duffy, Kekel, Jensen & Bernard · 1200 Standard Plaza · 1100 Southwest Sixth Avenue · Portland, OR 97204-1019 · 503-226-1371

Kenneth S. Klarquist, Jr. · Zalutsky, Klarquist & Johnson · The Waldo Building, Third Floor · 215 Southwest Washington Street · Portland, OR 97204 · 503-248-0300

Charles J. McMurchie · (Estate Planning, Estate Administration, Charitable Trusts, Personal Income Tax) · Stoel Rives Boley Jones & Grey · Standard Insurance Center, Suite 2300 · 900 Southwest Fifth Avenue · Portland, OR 97204-1268 · 503-224-3380

Conrad L. Moore · (Estate Planning, Estate Administration, Estate & Fiduciary Income) · Miller, Nash, Wiener, Hager & Carlsen · 3500 U.S. Bancorp Tower · 111 Southwest Fifth Avenue · Portland, OR 97204-3699 · 503-224-5858

Campbell Richardson · (Estate Planning, Estate Administration, Charitable Trusts, Fiduciary Income Tax) · Stoel Rives Boley Jones & Grey · Standard Insurance Center, Suite 2300 · 900 Southwest Fifth Avenue · Portland, OR 97204-1268 · 503-224-3380

Daniel A. Ritter · Harland, Ritter, Saalfeld, Griggs & Gorsuch · 693 Chemeketa Street, NE · P.O. Box 470 · Salem, OR 97308 · 503-399-1070

PENNSYLVANIA

BANKRUPTCY LAW

Robert L. Knupp · (Business Reorganization, Bankruptcy Litigation) · Knupp & Kodak · Cameron Mansion · 407 North Front Street · P.O. Box 11848 · Harrisburg, PA 17108-1848 · 717-238-7151

Edward W. Rothman* · (Business Reorganization, Creditors' Rights, Debtors' Rights, Bankruptcy Litigation) · McNees, Wallace & Nurick · 100 Pine Street · P.O. Box 1166 · Harrisburg, PA 17108 · 717-232-8000

Thomas E. Biron · Blank, Rome, Comisky & McCauley · Four Penn Center Plaza, 10th-13th Floors · Philadelphia, PA 19103-2599 · 215-569-5500

Neal D. Colton · (Business Reorganization, Creditors' Rights, Debtors' Rights) · Dechert Price & Rhoads · 4000 Bell Atlantic Tower · 1717 Arch Street · Philadelphia, PA 19103-2793 · 215-994-4000

Leon S. Forman · Blank, Rome, Comisky & McCauley · Four Penn Center Plaza, 10th-13th Floors · Philadelphia, PA 19103-2599 · 215-569-5500

Howard T. Glassman · Blank, Rome, Comisky & McCauley · Four Penn Center Plaza, 10th-13th Floors · Philadelphia, PA 19103-2599 · 215-569-5568

Marvin Krasny · (Business Reorganization, Creditors' Rights, Debtors' Rights) · Wolf, Block, Schorr and Solis-Cohen · Packard Building, 12th Floor · 15th and Chestnut Streets · Philadelphia, PA 19102-2678 · 215-977-2000

Alexander N. Rubin, Jr. · Rubin, Quinn, Moss & Heaney · 1800 Penn Mutual Tower · 510 Walnut Street · Philadelphia, PA 19106 · 215-925-8300

Raymond L. Shapiro · (Business Reorganization, Creditors' Rights) · Blank, Rome, Comisky & McCauley · Four Penn Center Plaza, 10th-13th Floors · Philadelphia, PA 19103-2599 · 215-569-5500

David T. Sykes · Duane, Morris & Heckscher · One Liberty Place, Suite 4200 · Philadelphia, PA 19102 · 215-979-1500

Michael L. Temin · Wolf, Block, Schorr and Solis-Cohen · Packard Building, 12th Floor · 15th and Chestnut Streets · Philadelphia, PA 19102-2678 · 215-977-2000

Phillip E. Beard · Stonecipher, Cunningham, Beard & Schmitt · 125 First Avenue Building · Pittsburgh, PA 15222 · 412-391-8510

Douglas A. Campbell · (Business Reorganization, Creditors' Rights, Debtors' Rights, Bankruptcy Litigation) · Campbell & Levine · 3100 Grant Building · Pittsburgh, PA 15219-2399 · 412-261-0310

George L. Cass · Buchanan Ingersoll · USX Tower, 58th Floor · 600 Grant Street Pittsburgh, PA 15219-2887 · 412-562-8800

Stanley E. Levine · Campbell & Levine · 3100 Grant Building · Pittsburgh, PA 15219 · 412-261-0310

M. Bruce McCullough · Buchanan Ingersoll · USX Tower, 58th Floor · 600 Grant Street · Pittsburgh, PA 15219-2887 · 412-562-8800

David A. Murdoch · Kirkpatrick & Lockhart · 1500 Oliver Building · Pittsburgh, PA 15222-5379 · 412-355-6472

Robert G. Sable · Sable, Makoroff, Sherman & Gusky · The Frick Building, Seventh Floor · Pittsburgh, PA 15219-6002 · 412-471-4996

Bernhard Schaffler* · Schaffler & Bohm · 967 Liberty Avenue · Pittsburgh, PA 15222 · 412-765-3888

William H. Schorling · Klett Lieber Rooney & Schorling · One Oxford Centre, 40th Floor · Pittsburgh, PA 15219-6498 · 412-392-2060

Paul M. Singer · Reed Smith Shaw & McClay · James H. Reed Building, Mellon Square · 435 Sixth Avenue · P.O. Box 2009 · Pittsburgh, PA 15230-2009 · 412-288-3131

Joel M. Walker · Pollard, Walker & Vollmer · Grant Building, Suite 1320 · Pittsburgh, PA 15219 · 412-391-2121

BUSINESS LITIGATION

John M. McLaughlin · Knox McLaughlin Gornall and Sennett · 120 West 10th Street · Erie, PA 16501 · 814-459-2800

Thomas D. Caldwell, Jr.* · Caldwell & Kearns · 3631 North Front Street · Harrisburg, PA 17110 · 717-232-7661

Ronald M. Katzman* · Goldberg, Katzman & Shipman · Strawberry Square · 320E Market Street · P.O. Box 1268 · Harrisburg, PA 17108-1266 · 717-234-4161

David E. Lehman · (Defendants) · McNees, Wallace & Nurick · 100 Pine Street P.O. Box 1166 · Harrisburg, PA 17108-1166 · 717-232-8000

R. Stephen Shibla · Rhoads & Sinon · One South Market Square · P.O. Box 1146 Harrisburg, PA 17108-1146 · 717-233-5731

David Berger · Berger & Montague · 1622 Locust Street · Philadelphia, PA 19103 215-875-3000

James D. Crawford · Schnader, Harrison, Segal & Lewis · 1600 Market Street, Suite 3600 · Philadelphia, PA 19103 · 215-751-2000

Alan J. Davis · Ballard, Spahr, Andrews & Ingersoll · 1735 Market Street, 51st Floor · Philadelphia, PA 19103-7599 · 215-564-8500

John G. Harkins, Jr.* · Pepper, Hamilton & Scheetz · 3000 Two Logan Square 18th and Arch Streets · Philadelphia, PA 19103-2799 · 215-981-4355

Lawrence T. Hoyle, Jr. · Hoyle, Morris & Kerr · One Liberty Place, Suite 4900 1650 Market Street · Philadelphia, PA 19103 · 215-981-5700

Arthur H. Kahn · Schnader, Harrison, Segal & Lewis · 1600 Market Street, Suite 3600 · Philadelphia, PA 19103 · 215-751-2000

Harold E. Kohn* · Kohn, Savett, Klein & Graf · 2400 One Reading Center · 1101 Market Street · Philadelphia, PA 19107 · 215-238-1700

John H. Lewis, Jr. · Morgan, Lewis & Bockius · 2000 One Logan Square · Philadelphia, PA 19103-6993 · 215-963-5000

Henry T. Reath · Duane, Morris & Heckscher · One Liberty Place, Suite 4200 · Philadelphia, PA 19102 · 215-979-1000

Thomas B. Rutter* · Rutter, Turner, Solomon & DiPiero · The Curtis Center · Independence Square West, Suite 750 · One Walnut Street · Philadelphia, PA 19106 · 215-925-9200

Robert S. Ryan · Drinker Biddle & Reath · 1100 Philadelphia National Bank Building · Broad & Chestnut Streets · Philadelphia, PA 19107 · 215-988-2700

Henry W. Sawyer III · Drinker Biddle & Reath · 1100 Philadelphia National Bank Building · Broad & Chestnut Streets · Philadelphia, PA 19107 · 215-988-2700

David J. Armstrong* · Dickie, McCamey & Chilcote · Two PPG Place, Suite 400 Pittsburgh, PA 15222-5402 · 412-281-7272

David B. Fawcett* · Dickie, McCamey & Chilcote · Two PPG Place, Suite 400 Pittsburgh, PA 15222-5402 · 412-281-7272

J. Tomlinson Fort* · (Administrative, Antitrust, Securities) · Reed Smith Shaw & McClay · James H. Reed Building, Mellon Square · 435 Sixth Avenue · P.O. Box 2009 · Pittsburgh, PA 15230-2009 · 412-288-3131

Joseph A. Katarincic* · (RICO, Securities) · Katarincic & Salmon · CNG Tower, Suite 2600 · 625 Liberty Avenue · Pittsburgh, PA 15222 · 412-338-2900

Edwin L. Klett* · (Banking, Securities) · Klett Lieber Rooney & Schorling · One Oxford Centre, 40th Floor · Pittsburgh, PA 15219-6498 · 412-392-2000

Roslyn M. Litman · Litman Litman Harris Brown and Watzman · One Oxford Centre, Suite 3600 · Pittsburgh, PA 15219 · 412-456-2000

David L. McClenahan* · (Antitrust, Commercial, Securities) · Kirkpatrick & Lockhart · 1500 Oliver Building · Pittsburgh, PA 15222-5379 · 412-355-6484

James D. Morton* · (Commercial, RICO, Securities, Class Actions) · Buchanan Ingersoll · USX Tower, 58th Floor · 600 Grant Street · Pittsburgh, PA 15219-2887 412-562-8800

Charles Weiss* · Thorp, Reed & Armstrong · One Riverfront Center · Pittsburgh, PA 15222 · 412-394-7711

William M. Wycoff · Thorp, Reed & Armstrong · One Riverfront Center · Pittsburgh, PA 15222 · 412-394-7711

CORPORATE LAW

William D. Boswell · Boswell, Snyder, Tintner & Piccola · 315 North Front Street Harrisburg, PA 17108-0741 · 717-236-9377

Francis B. Haas, Jr. · McNees, Wallace & Nurick · 100 Pine Street · P.O. Box 1166 · Harrisburg, PA 17108 · 717-232-8000

John P. Manbeck · Rhoads & Sinon · One South Market Square · P.O. Box 1146 Harrisburg, PA 17108-1146 · 717-233-5731

Gerald K. Morrison · (Mergers & Acquisitions) · Rhoads & Sinon · One South Market Square · P.O. Box 1146 · Harrisburg, PA 17108-1146 · 717-233-5731

Rod J. Pera · McNees, Wallace & Nurick · 100 Pine Street · P.O. Box 1166 · Harrisburg, PA 17108 · 717-232-8000

Henry W. Rhoads · Rhoads & Sinon · One South Market Square · P.O. Box 1146 Harrisburg, PA 17108-1146 · 717-233-5731

Richard W. Stevenson · (Mergers & Acquisitions) · McNees, Wallace & Nurick 100 Pine Street · P.O. Box 1166 · Harrisburg, PA 17108 · 717-232-8000

John J. Brennan · Dechert Price & Rhoads · 4000 Bell Atlantic Tower · 1717 Arch Street · Philadelphia, PA 19103-2793 · 215-994-4000

J. Gordon Cooney · (Mergers & Acquisitions, Securities, Corporate Governance) Schnader, Harrison, Segal & Lewis · 1600 Market Street, Suite 3600 · Philadelphia, PA 19103 · 215-751-2000

Park B. Dilks, Jr. · (Banking, International) · Morgan, Lewis & Bockius · 2000 One Logan Square · Philadelphia, PA 19103-6993 · 215-963-5000

Vincent F. Garrity, Jr. · (Corporate Finance, Leveraged Buyouts, Mergers & Acquisitions) · Duane, Morris & Heckscher · One Liberty Place, Suite 4200 · Philadelphia, PA 19102 · 215-979-1242

Henry A. Gladstone · Wolf, Block, Schorr and Solis-Cohen · Packard Building, 12th Floor · 15th and Chestnut Streets · Philadelphia, PA 19102-2678 · 215-977-2102

F. John Hagele · Pepper, Hamilton & Scheetz · 3000 Two Logan Square · 18th and Arch Streets · Philadelphia, PA 19103-2799 · 215-981-4397

Stephen J. Harmelin · Dilworth, Paxson, Kalish & Kauffman · 2600 The Fidelity Building · 123 South Broad Street · Philadelphia, PA 19109-1094 · 215-875-7000

Thomas M. Hyndman, Jr. · Duane, Morris & Heckscher · One Liberty Place, Suite 4200 · Philadelphia, PA 19102 · 215-979-1284

William R. Klaus · (International, International Trade, Leveraged Buyouts, Mergers & Acquisitions) · Pepper, Hamilton & Scheetz · 3000 Two Logan Square 18th and Arch Streets · Philadelphia, PA 19103-2799 · 215-981-4000

Frederick D. Lipman · Blank, Rome, Comisky & McCauley · Four Penn Center Plaza, 10th-13th Floors · Philadelphia, PA 19103-2599 · 215-569-5500

Carl W. Schneider · Wolf, Block, Schorr and Solis-Cohen · Packard Building, 12th Floor · 15th and Chestnut Streets · Philadelphia, PA 19102-2678 · 215-977-2000

James W. Schwartz · Saul, Ewing, Remick & Saul · 3800 Center Square West · Philadelphia, PA 19102-2186 · 215-972-7735

Donald A. Scott · Morgan, Lewis & Bockius · 2000 One Logan Square · Philadelphia, PA 19103-6993 · 215-963-5000

Howard L. Shecter · Morgan, Lewis & Bockius · 2000 One Logan Square · Philadelphia, PA 19103-6993 · 215-963-5442

Robert E. Shields · Drinker Biddle & Reath · 1100 Philadelphia National Bank Building · Broad & Chestnut Streets · Philadelphia, PA 19107 · 215-988-2821

Robert Deland Williams · Dechert Price & Rhoads · 4000 Bell Atlantic Tower · 1717 Arch Street · Philadelphia, PA 19103-2793 · 215-994-4000

Barton J. Winokur · Dechert Price & Rhoads · 4000 Bell Atlantic Tower · 1717 Arch Street · Philadelphia, PA 19103-2793 · 215-994-4000

Minturn T. Wright · Dechert Price & Rhoads · 4000 Bell Atlantic Tower · 1717 Arch Street · Philadelphia, PA 19103-2793 · 215-994-4000

Robert H. Young · Morgan, Lewis & Bockius · 2000 One Logan Square · Philadelphia, PA 19103-6993 · 215-963-5297

William E. Zeiter · Morgan, Lewis & Bockius · 2000 One Logan Square · Philadelphia, PA 19103-6993 · 215-963-5367

Carl F. Barger · Eckert Seamans Cherin & Mellott · 600 Grant Street, 42nd Floor Pittsburgh, PA 15219 · 412-566-6000

Charles C. Cohen · Cohen & Grisby · 2900 CNG Tower · 625 Liberty Avenue · Pittsburgh, PA 15222 · 412-394-4900

Bruce D. Evans · Reed Smith Shaw & McClay · James H. Reed Building, Mellon Square · 435 Sixth Avenue · P.O. Box 2009 · Pittsburgh, PA 15230-2009 · 412-288-3131

William P. Hackney · Reed Smith Shaw & McClay · James H. Reed Building, Mellon Square · 435 Sixth Avenue · P.O. Box 2009 · Pittsburgh, PA 15230-2009 412-288-3131

James H. Hardie · (Corporate Finance, Mergers & Acquisitions, Securities Regulation) · Reed Smith Shaw & McClay · James H. Reed Building, Mellon Square 435 Sixth Avenue · P.O. Box 2009 · Pittsburgh, PA 15230-2009 · 412-288-3131

C. Kent May · (Corporate Finance, Leveraged Buyouts, Mergers & Acquisitions, Securities) · Eckert Seamans Cherin & Mellott · 600 Grant Street, 42nd Floor · Pittsburgh, PA 15219 · 412-566-6000

Michael C. McLean · Kirkpatrick & Lockhart · 1500 Oliver Building · Pittsburgh, PA 15222-5379 · 412-355-6500

William R. Newlin · (Corporate Finance, Mergers & Acquisitions, Securities) · Buchanan Ingersoll · USX Tower, 58th Floor · 600 Grant Street · Pittsburgh, PA 15219-2887 · 412-562-8800

John R. Previs · (Leveraged Buyouts, Cable Television) · Buchanan Ingersoll · USX Tower, 58th Floor · 600 Grant Street · Pittsburgh, PA 15219-2887 · 412-562-8800

William Dwight Sutton · (International, International Banking, International Finance) · Thorp, Reed & Armstrong · One Riverfront Center · Pittsburgh, PA 15222 · 412-394-7711

Thomas D. Wright · Eckert Seamans Cherin & Mellott · 600 Grant Street, 42nd Floor · Pittsburgh, PA 15219 · 412-566-6000

CRIMINAL DEFENSE

Thomas R. Ceraso · 126 North Maple Street · Greensburg, PA 15601 · 412-836-1720

Arthur K. Dils · Dils, Dixon & Zulli · 101 South Second Street · Harrisburg, PA 17101 · 717-233-8743

Joshua D. Lock · Law Offices of Joshua D. Lock · 106 Walnut Street · P.O. Box 949 · Harrisburg, PA 17108 · 717-234-7025

William C. Costopoulos · Kollas, Costopoulos, Foster & Fields · 831 Market Street · P.O. Box 222 · Lemoyne, PA 17043 · 717-761-2121

John R. Carroll · Carroll & Carroll · 400 Market Street, Suite 850 · Philadelphia, PA 19106 · 215-925-4100

Thomas Colas Carroll · (Appellate) · The Curtis Center, Suite 750 · Independence Square West · Philadelphia, PA 19106 · 215-925-2500

James D. Crawford · Schnader, Harrison, Segal & Lewis · 1600 Market Street, Suite 3600 · Philadelphia, PA 19103 · 215-751-2000

Donald J. Goldberg · 1310 One Meridian Plaza Center · Philadelphia, PA 19102 215-563-6345

Ronald F. Kidd · Duane, Morris & Heckscher · One Liberty Place, Suite 4200 · Philadelphia, PA 19102 · 215-979-1000

A. Charles Peruto, Sr.* · (Violent Crimes, Non-Violent Crimes, Federal Court, State Court) · Peruto, Ryan & Vitullo · Washington West Building · Northeast Corner Eighth & Locust Streets · Philadelphia, PA 19106-3598 · 215-925-5800

Thomas B. Rutter* · Rutter, Turner, Solomon & DiPiero · The Curtis Center · Independence Square West, Suite 750 · One Walnut Street · Philadelphia, PA 19106 · 215-925-9200

Stanford Shmukler* · (Violent Crimes, Non-Violent Crimes, Federal Court, State Court) · Packard Building, 24th Floor · 111 South 15th Street · Philadelphia, PA 19102 · 215-751-9500

Joel Harvey Slomsky · 1600 Market Street, Suite 1720 · Philadelphia, PA 19103 215-568-3700

Richard A. Sprague · Sprague, Higgins, Creamer & Sprague · The Wellington Building, Suite 400 · 135 South 19th Street · Philadelphia, PA 19103 · 215-561-7681

J. Clayton Undercofler III* · (Environmental Crimes) · Saul, Ewing, Remick & Saul · 3800 Centre Square West · Philadelphia, PA 19102-2186 · 215-972-7777

David J. Armstrong* · (Non-Violent Crimes) · Dickie, McCamey & Chilcote · Two PPG Place, Suite 400 · Pittsburgh, PA 15222-5402 · 412-281-7272

John L. Doherty* · Manifesto, Doherty & Donahoe · 1550 Koppers Building · 436 Seventh Avenue · Pittsburgh, PA 15219-1818 · 412-471-8893

Harold Gondelman · Pietragallo, Bosick & Gordon · One Oxford Centre, 13th Floor · Pittsburgh, PA 15219 · 412-263-2000

Stanley W. Greenfield · Greenfield & Associates · 1035 Fifth Avenue · Pittsburgh, PA 15219 · 412-261-4466

Thomas A. Livingston · Livingston & Clark · The Colonial Building · 205 Ross Street · Pittsburgh, PA 15219 · 412-391-7686

William F. Manifesto* · (Non-Violent Crimes, Federal Court, State Court, Environmental Crimes) · Manifesto, Doherty & Donahoe · 1550 Koppers Building · 436 Seventh Avenue · Pittsburgh, PA 15219-1818 · 412-471-8893

James K. O'Malley · The Colonial Building · 205 Ross Street · Pittsburgh, PA 15219 · 412-391-1148

Charles F. Scarlata · Scarlata & Plastino · 1550 Koppers Building · Pittsburgh, PA 15219 · 412-765-2855

Emmanuel H. Dimitriou · Law Office of Emmanuel H. Dimitriou · 522-24 Court Street · P.O. Box 677 · Reading, PA 19603 · 215-376-7466

FAMILY LAW

Sandra Schultz Newman · Astor, Weiss & Newman · Three Bala Plaza West, Suite 100 · P.O. Box 1665 · Bala Cynwyd, PA 19004 · 215-667-8660

Norman Perlberger · Perlberger Law Associates · 401 City Avenue, Suite 200 · Bala Cynwyd, PA 19004 · 215-668-5400

William L. Goldman* · 90 East State Street · P.O. Box 1989 · Doylestown, PA 18901 · 215-348-2605

Maria P. Cognetti* · (Child Custody, Divorce, Marital Settlement Agreements, Equitable Division) · Mette, Evans & Woodside · 1801 North Front Street · P.O. Box 729 · Harrisburg, PA 17108-0729 · 717-232-5000

Bruce D. Desfor · Meyers, Desfor & Shollenberger · 410 North Second Street · Harrisburg, PA 17101 · 717-236-9428

John C. Howett, Jr. · Law Offices of John C. Howett · 132 Walnut Street · P.O. Box 810 · Harrisburg, PA 17108 · 717-234-2616

Neil Hurowitz · Law Office of Neil Hurowitz · 900 East Eighth Avenue, Suite 300 · King of Prussia, PA 19406 · 215-265-7370

I. B. Sinclair* · Sinclair, McErlean, Rubin and Dinsmore · 30 West Third Street · Media, PA 19063 · 215-565-2500

Michael R. Sweeney · Sweeney & Mencini · The Madison Building · 108 Chesley Drive · Media, PA 19063 · 215-566-0900

Eric D. Turner · Eckell, Sparks, Levy, Auerbach, Monte & Moses · Legal Arts Building · 344 West Front Street · Media, PA 19063 · 215-565-3700

Mason Avrigian · Schnader, Harrison, Segal & Lewis · One Montgomery Plaza, Suite 700 · Norristown, PA 19401 · 215-277-7700

Emanuel A. Bertin · One Meetinghouse Place, Suite 102 · Norristown, PA 19401 · 215-277-1500

Frederick Cohen · Blank, Rome, Comisky & McCauley · Four Penn Center Plaza, 10th-13th Floors · Philadelphia, PA 19103 · 215-569-5669

Leonard Dubin* · (Child Custody, Divorce, Marital Settlement Agreements, Equitable Division) · Blank, Rome, Comisky & McCauley · Four Penn Center Plaza, 10th-13th Floors · Philadelphia, PA 19103-2599 · 215-569-5602

Michael E. Fingerman* · (Child Custody, Divorce, Marital Settlement Agreements, Equitable Division) · Shainberg & Fingerman · 1525 Locust Street, 15th Floor · Philadelphia, PA 19102 · 215-546-9300

Saul Levit · Schnader, Harrison, Segal & Lewis · 1600 Market Street, Suite 3600 · Philadelphia, PA 19103 · 215-751-2518

Alfred Mariletti · Alfred Mariletti & Associates · 1000 Two Mellon Bank Center · Philadelphia, PA 19102 · 215-563-0400

Albert Momjian* · Schnader, Harrison, Segal & Lewis · 1600 Market Street, Suite 3600 · Philadelphia, PA 19103 · 215-751-2516

Charles C. Shainberg* · (Adoption, Child Custody, Divorce, Equitable Division) · Shainberg & Fingerman · 1525 Locust Street, 15th Floor · Philadelphia, PA 19102 · 215-546-9300

Stewart B. Barmen* · Buchanan Ingersoll · USX Tower · 600 Grant Street, 57th Floor · Pittsburgh, PA 15219 · 412-562-1028

Robert C. Capristo · Gillotti, Goldberg & Capristo · Grant Building, Suite 215 · 310 Grant Street · Pittsburgh, PA 15219-2201 · 412-391-4242

Chris F. Gillotti* · (Child Custody, Divorce, Equitable Division, Prenuptial Agreements) · Gillotti, Goldberg & Capristo · Grant Building, Suite 215 · 310 Grant Street · Pittsburgh, PA 15219-2201 · 412-391-4242

Mark J. Goldberg* · (Child Custody, Divorce, Marital Settlement Agreements, Equitable Division) · Gillotti, Goldberg & Capristo · Grant Building, Suite 215 · 310 Grant Street · Pittsburgh, PA 15219-2201 · 412-391-4242

Harry J. Gruener* · (Child Custody, Divorce, Marital Settlement Agreements, Equitable Division) · Raphael, Gruener, Raphael & Horoho · Grant Building, 35th Floor · Pittsburgh, PA 15219 · 412-471-8822

Patricia G. Miller · Reed Smith Shaw & McClay · James H. Reed Building, Mellon Square · 435 Sixth Avenue · P.O. Box 2009 · Pittsburgh, PA 15230-2009 412-288-3131

Robert Raphael* · (Child Custody, Divorce, Marital Settlement Agreements, Equitable Division) · Raphael, Gruener, Raphael & Horoho · Grant Building, 35th Floor · Pittsburgh, PA 15219 · 412-471-8822

Joanne Ross Wilder* · Wilder & Mahood · 816 Frick Building · Pittsburgh, PA 15219-6192 · 412-261-4040

FIRST AMENDMENT LAW

James E. Beasley · (Plaintiffs) · Beasley, Casey, Colleran, Erbstein, Thistle & Kline · 21 South 12th Street · Philadelphia, PA 19107 · 215-665-1000

Samuel E. Klein · Kohn, Savett, Klein & Graf · 2400 One Reading Center · 1101 Market Street · Philadelphia, PA 19107 · 215-238-1700

Jerome J. Shestack · Schnader, Harrison, Segal & Lewis · 1600 Market Street, Suite 3600 · Philadelphia, PA 19103 · 215-751-2446

John H. Bingler, Jr. · Thorp, Reed & Armstrong · One Riverfront Center · Pittsburgh, PA 15222 · 412-394-7711

Roslyn M. Litman · Litman, Litman, Harris, Brown & Watszman · 3600 One Oxford Centre · Pittsburgh, PA 15219 · 412-456-2002

W. Thomas McGough, Jr. · Reed Smith Shaw & McClay · James H. Reed Building, Mellon Square · 435 Sixth Avenue · P.O. Box 2009 · Pittsburgh, PA 15230-2009 · 412-288-3131

Walter T. (Bud) McGough · Reed Smith Shaw & McClay · James H. Reed Building, Mellon Square · 435 Sixth Avenue · P.O. Box 2009 · Pittsburgh, PA 15230-2009 · 412-288-3131

HEALTH CARE LAW

Charles O. Barto, Jr. · Charles O. Barto & Associates · 608 North Third Street · Harrisburg, PA 17101-1102 · 717-236-6257

Alice G. Gosfield · Alice G. Gosfield & Associates · 2309 Delancey Place · Philadelphia, PA 19103 · 215-735-2384

Reed Hamilton · Blank, Rome, Comisky & McCauley · Four Penn Center Plaza, 10th-13th Floors · Philadelphia, PA 19103-2599 · 215-569-5538

William A. Humenuk · Dechert Price & Rhoads · 4000 Bell Atlantic Tower · 1717 Arch Street · Philadelphia, PA 19103-2793 · 215-994-4000

John C. S. Kepner · Saul, Ewing, Remick & Saul · 3800 Centre Square West · Philadelphia, PA 19102-2186 · 215-972-7704

Robert M. McNair · Drinker Biddle & Reath · 1100 Philadelphia National Bank Building · Broad & Chestnut Streets · Philadelphia, PA 19107 · 215-988-2700

Roland Morris · Duane, Morris & Heckscher · One Liberty Place, Suite 4200 · Philadelphia, PA 19102 · 215-979-1000

Jeffrey B. Schwartz · Wolf, Block, Schorr and Solis-Cohen · Packard Building, 12th Floor · 15th and Chestnut Streets · Philadelphia, PA 19102-2678 · 215-977-2533

Barbara Blackmond · Hortey, Springer & Mattern · 4614 Fifth Avenue · Pittsburgh, PA 15213 · 412-687-7677

Thomas E. Boyle · Buchanan Ingersoll · USX Tower, 58th Floor · 600 Grant Street · Pittsburgh, PA 15219-2887 · 412-562-8800

John Hortey · Hortey, Springer & Mattern · 4614 Fifth Avenue · Pittsburgh, PA 15213 · 412-687-7677

J. Jerome Mansmann · Mansmann, Cindrich & Titus · Four Gateway Center · Pittsburgh, PA 15222 · 412-642-2000

David L. McClenahan · Kirkpatrick & Lockhart · 1500 Oliver Building · Pittsburgh, PA 15222-5379 · 412-355-6484

Edward V. Weisgerber · Kirkpatrick & Lockhart · 1500 Oliver Building · Pittsburgh, PA 15222-5379 · 412-355-8980

IMMIGRATION LAW

H. Ronald Klasko · Dechert Price & Rhoads · 4000 Bell Atlantic Tower · 1717 Arch Street · Philadelphia, PA 19103-2793 · 215-994-4000

Lawrence H. Rudnick · Steel, Rubin & Rudnick · Public Ledger Building, Suite 936 · Sixth and Chestnut Streets · Philadelphia, PA 19106 · 215-922-1181

Richard D. Steel · Steel, Rubin & Rudnick · Public Ledger Building, Suite 936 Sixth and Chestnut Streets · Philadelphia, PA 19106 · 215-922-1181

John S. Brendel · Buchanan Ingersoll · USX Tower, 58th Floor · 600 Grant Street Pittsburgh, PA 15219-2887 · 412-562-8800

Robert P. Deasy · Healey Whitehill · Law and Finance Building, Fifth Floor · Pittsburgh, PA 15219 · 412-391-7707

Robert S. Whitehill · Healey Whitehill · Law and Finance Building, Fifth Floor Pittsburgh, PA 15219 · 412-391-7707

INTELLECTUAL PROPERTY LAW

James A. Drobile · Schnader, Harrison, Segal & Lewis · 1600 Market Street, Suite 3600 · Philadelphia, PA 19103 · 215-751-2242

William H. Elliott, Jr. · Synnestvedt & Lechner · 1600 ARA Tower · 1101 Market Street · Philadelphia, PA 19107 · 215-923-4466

Robert B. Washburn · Woodcock & Washburn · One Liberty Place, 46th Floor 1650 Market Street · Philadelphia, PA 19103 · 215-568-3100

William H. Webb · Webb, Burden, Ziesenheim & Webb · 515 Oliver Building · P.O. Box 2009 · Pittsburgh, PA 15222 · 412-471-8815

Robert D. Yeager · Kirkpatrick & Lockhart · 1500 Oliver Building · Pittsburgh, PA 15222-5379 · 412-355-8605

LABOR AND EMPLOYMENT LAW

John S. Hayes · (Management) · Duane, Morris & Heckscher · Commerce Plaza III · 5050 Tilghman Street, Suite 430 · Allentown, PA 18104 · 215-391-1225

Irwin W. Aronson · (Labor) · Handler, Gerber, Johnston & Aronson · 150 Corporate Center Drive, Suite 100 · Camphill, PA 17011 · 717-975-5500

Jerome H. Gerber · (Labor) · Handler, Gerber, Johnston & Aronson · 150 Corporate Center Drive, Suite 100 · Camphill, PA 17011 · 717-975-5500

Ira H. Weinstock* · (Labor) · 800 North Second Street, Suite 100 · Harrisburg, PA 17102 · 717-238-1657

Norman I. White · (Management) · McNees, Wallace & Nurick · 100 Pine Street P.O. Box 1166 · Harrisburg, PA 17108 · 717-232-8000

John J. McAleese, Jr. · (Management) · McAleese, McGoldrick & Susanin · Executive Terrace, Suite 240 · 455 South Gulph Road · King of Prussia, PA 19406 215-337-4510

Frank H. Abbott · (Management) · Schnader, Harrison, Segal & Lewis · 1600 Market Street, Suite 3600 · Philadelphia, PA 19103 · 215-751-2452

Alice W. Ballard* · (Individuals) · Samuel and Ballard · 225 South 15th Street, Suite 1700 · Philadelphia, PA 19102 · 215-893-9990

Warren J. Borish · (Labor) · Spear, Wilderman, Borish, Endy, Browning & Spear 260 South Broad Street, Suite 1500 · Philadelphia, PA 19102 · 215-732-0101

Carter R. Buller · (Management) · Montgomery, McCracken, Walker & Rhoads Three Parkway, 20th Floor · Philadelphia, PA 19102 · 215-563-0650

Alfred J. D'Angelo, Jr. · (Management) · Pepper, Hamilton & Scheetz · 3000 Two Logan Square · 18th and Arch Streets · Philadelphia, PA 19103-2799 · 215-981-4000

Mark S. Dichter · (Management) · Morgan, Lewis & Bockius · 2000 One Logan Square · Philadelphia, PA 19103-6993 · 215-963-5000

H. Thomas Felix II · (Management) · Montgomery, McCracken, Walker & Rhoads · Three Parkway, 20th Floor · Philadelphia, PA 19102 · 215-665-7200

Miriam L. Gafni · (Individuals) · Freedman and Lorry · Continental Building · Fourth and Market Street, Ninth Floor · Philadelphia, PA 19106-5096 · 215-925-8400

Howard I. Hatoff · (Management) · Blank, Rome, Comisky & McCauley · Four Penn Center Plaza, 10th-13th Floors · Philadelphia, PA 19103 · 215-569-5500

Thomas W. Jennings · (Labor) · Sagot, Jennings & Sigmond · Public Ledger Building, Suite 1172 · Independence Square · Philadelphia, PA 19106 · 215-922-6700

Jonathan A. Kane · (Management) · Drinker Biddle & Reath · 1100 Philadelphia National Bank Building · Broad and Chestnut Streets · Philadelphia, PA 19107 · 215-988-2924

Bernard N. Katz · (Labor) · Meranze and Katz · Lewis Tower Building, 12th Floor · Northeast Corner 15th & Locust Streets · Philadelphia, PA 19102 · 215-546-4183

Alan M. Lerner · (Management, Individuals) · Cohen, Shapiro, Polisher, Shiekman and Cohen · PSFS Building, 22nd Floor · 12 South 12th Street · Philadelphia, PA 19107-3981 · 215-922-1300

John Markle, Jr. · (Management) · Drinker Biddle & Reath · 1100 Philadelphia National Bank Building · Broad and Chestnut Streets · Philadelphia, PA 19107 · 215-988-2922

Richard H. Markowitz · (Labor) · Markowitz & Richman · 1100 North American Building · 121 South Broad Street, 11th Floor · Philadelphia, PA 19107 · 215-875-3100

J. Anthony Messina · (Management) · Pepper, Hamilton & Scheetz · 3000 Two Logan Square · 18th and Arch Streets · Philadelphia, PA 19103-2799 · 215-981-4000

Mark P. Muller · (Labor) · Freedman and Lorry · Lafayette Building, Eighth Floor · Chestnut Street at Fifth Street · Philadelphia, PA 19106-2493 · 215-925-8400

John B. Nason III · (Management) · Kleinbard, Bell & Brecker · 1900 Market Street, Suite 700 · Philadelphia, PA 19103 · 215-496-7241

Timothy P. O'Reilly · (Management) · Morgan, Lewis & Bockius · 2000 One Logan Square · Philadelphia, PA 19103-6993 · 215-963-5470

Harry Reagan · (Management) · Morgan, Lewis & Bockius · 2000 One Logan Square · Philadelphia, PA 19103-6993 · 215-963-5000

Stephen C. Richman* · (Labor) · Markowitz & Richman · 1100 North American Building · 121 South Broad Street, 11th Floor · Philadelphia, PA 19107 · 215-875-3100

Richard B. Sigmond · (Labor) · Sagot, Jennings & Sigmond · The Public Ledger Building, Suite 1172 · Independence Square · Philadelphia, PA 19106 · 215-922-6700

Robert E. Wachs · (Management) · Wolf, Block, Schorr and Solis-Cohen · Packard Building, 12th Floor · 15th and Chestnut Streets · Philadelphia, PA 19102-2678 · 215-977-2000

Martin Wald* · (Management) · Schnader, Harrison, Segal & Lewis · 1600 Market Street, Suite 3600 · Philadelphia, PA 19103 · 215-751-2000

Steven R. Waxman · (Individuals) · Fox, Rothschild, O'Brien & Frankel · 2000 Market Street, 10th Floor · Philadelphia, PA 19103 · 215-299-2718

William A. Whiteside, Jr. · (Management) · Fox, Rothschild, O'Brien & Frankel 2000 Market Street, Ninth Floor · Philadelphia, PA 19103 · 215-299-2000

Deborah R. Willig · (Labor) · Walters Willig Williams & Davidson · 1608 Walnut Street · Philadelphia, PA 19103 · 215-893-9000

William Bevan III · (Management) · Reed Smith Shaw & McClay · James H. Reed Building, Mellon Square · 435 Sixth Avenue · P.O. Box 2009 · Pittsburgh, PA 15230-2009 · 412-288-3131

Aims C. Coney, Jr. · (Management) · Kirkpatrick & Lockhart · 1500 Oliver Building · Pittsburgh, PA 15222-5379 · 412-355-6500

Walter P. DeForest III* · (Management) · Reed Smith Shaw & McClay · James H. Reed Building, Mellon Square · 435 Sixth Avenue · P.O. Box 2009 · Pittsburgh, PA 15230-2009 · 412-288-3131

John F. Dugan · (Management) · Kirkpatrick & Lockhart · 1500 Oliver Building Pittsburgh, PA 15222-5379 · 412-355-6500

Robert W. Hartland · (Management) · Reed Smith Shaw & McClay · James H. Reed Building, Mellon Square · 435 Sixth Avenue · P.O. Box 2009 · Pittsburgh, PA 15230-2009 · 412-288-3131

James Q. Harty · (Management) · Reed Smith Shaw & McClay · James H. Reed Building, Mellon Square · 435 Sixth Avenue · P.O. Box 2009 · Pittsburgh, PA 15230-2009 · 412-288-3131

Stephen H. Jordan · (Labor) · Rothman & Gordon · 300 Grant Building, Third Floor · Pittsburgh, PA 15219 · 412-281-0705

Louis B. Kushner · (Labor, Individuals) · Rothman & Gordon · 300 Grant Building, Third Floor · Pittsburgh, PA 15219 · 412-281-0705

William A. Meyer, Jr. · (Management) · Meyer, Unkovic & Scott · 1300 Oliver Building · Pittsburgh, PA 15222 · 412-456-2800

Joseph J. Pass, Jr.* · (Labor) · Jubelirer, Pass & Intrieri · 219 Fort Pitt Boulevard Pittsburgh, PA 15222-1505 · 412-281-3850

Patrick W. Ritchey · (Management) · Reed Smith Shaw & McClay · James H. Reed Building, Mellon Square · 435 Sixth Avenue · P.O. Box 2009 · Pittsburgh, PA 15230-2009 · 412-288-3131

Leonard L. Scheinholtz · (Management) · Reed Smith Shaw & McClay · James H. Reed Building, Mellon Square · 435 Sixth Avenue · P.O. Box 2009 · Pittsburgh, PA 15230-2009 · 412-288-3131

Stanford A. Segal · (Labor) · Gatz, Cohen, Segal & Koerner · 400 Law & Finance Building · 429 Fourth Avenue · Pittsburgh, PA 15219 · 412-261-1380

Hayes C. Stover* · (Management) · Kirkpatrick & Lockhart · 1500 Oliver Building · Pittsburgh, PA 15222-5379 · 412-355-6500

John C. Unkovic · (Management) · Reed Smith Shaw & McClay · James H. Reed Building, Mellon Square · 435 Sixth Avenue · P.O. Box 2009 · Pittsburgh, PA 15230-2009 · 412-288-3131

Charles R. Volk · (Management) · Volk, Frankovitch, Anetakis, Recht, Robertson & Hellerstedt · Three Gateway Center, 15th Floor East · Pittsburgh, PA 15222 · 412-392-2300

Scott F. Zimmerman · (Management) · Reed Smith Shaw & McClay · James H. Reed Building, Mellon Square · 435 Sixth Avenue · P.O. Box 2009 · Pittsburgh, PA 15230-2009 · 412-288-3131

MARITIME LAW

Henry C. Lucas III · Rawle & Henderson · 211 South Broad Street, 15th Floor · Philadelphia, PA 19107 · 215-875-4000

Richard W. Palmer* · (Charter Parties, Ship Financing, Collisions, Fires, Explosions, Groundlings) · Palmer Biezup & Henderson · Public Ledger Building, Suite 956 · Independence Square · Philadelphia, PA 19106 · 215-625-9900

Marc E. Gold · Manko, Gold & Katcher · 401 City Avenue, Suite 500 · Bala Cynwyd, PA 19004 · 215-660-5700

NATURAL RESOURCES AND ENVIRONMENTAL LAW

Joseph Manko · Manko, Gold & Katcher · 401 City Avenue, Suite 500 · Bala Cynwyd, PA 19004 · 215-660-5700

Terry R. Bossert · McNees, Wallace & Nurick · 100 Pine Street · P.O. Box 1166 Harrisburg, PA 17108 · 717-232-8000

Eugene E. Dice* · (Water, Air, Solid Waste, Hazardous Waste) · 1721 North Front Street, Suite 101 · Harrisburg, PA 17102 · 717-238-4256

John A. Bonya · (Coal) · Bonya & Douglass · 134 South Sixth Street · Indiana, PA 15701 · 412-465-9685

Robert L. Collings · Morgan, Lewis & Bockius · 2000 One Logan Square · Philadelphia, PA 19103-6993 · 215-963-5000

Donald K. Joseph* · (Superfund Litigation) · Wolf, Block, Schorr and Solis-Cohen · Packard Building, 12th Floor · 15th and Chestnut Streets · Philadelphia, PA 19102-2678 · 215-977-2000

Kenneth R. Myers · Morgan, Lewis & Bockius · 2000 One Logan Square · Philadelphia, PA 19103-6993 · 215-963-5000

Hershel J. Richman* · (Water, Air, Solid Waste, Wetlands) · Cohen, Shapiro, Polisher, Shiekman and Cohen · PSFS Building, 22nd Floor · 12 South 12th Street Philadelphia, PA 19107-3981 · 215-922-1300

Bradford F. Whitman · Reed Smith Shaw & McClay · 2500 One Liberty Place · Philadelphia, PA 19103 · 215-851-8100

Minturn T. Wright III · (Coal) · Dechert Price & Rhoads · 4000 Bell Atlantic Tower · 1717 Arch Street · Philadelphia, PA 19103-2793 · 215-994-4000

Blair S. McMillin* · Reed Smith Shaw & McClay · James H. Reed Building, Mellon Square · 435 Sixth Avenue · P.O. Box 2009 · Pittsburgh, PA 15230-2009 412-288-3228

Harley N. Trice II · Reed Smith Shaw & McClay · James H. Reed Building, Mellon Square · 435 Sixth Avenue · P.O. Box 2009 · Pittsburgh, PA 15230-2009 412-288-3131

Peter Greig Veeder · Thorp, Reed & Armstrong · One Riverfront Center · Pittsburgh, PA 15222 · 412-394-7711

PERSONAL INJURY LITIGATION

James Lewis Griffith* · (Products Liability, Professional Malpractice) · Griffith & Burr · 101 West City Avenue · Bala Cynwyd, PA 19104-3113 · 215-893-1234

Andrew J. Conner · Conner & Associates · 17 West 10th Street · Erie, PA 16501 814-453-3343

Richard C. Angino* · (Plaintiffs) · Angino & Rovner · 4503 North Front Street · Harrisburg, PA 17110-1799 · 717-238-6791

Thomas D. Caldwell, Jr.* · (Defendants) · Caldwell & Kearns · 3631 North Front Street · Harrisburg, PA 17110 · 717-232-7661

James W. Evans* · (Defendants) · Mette, Evans & Woodside · 1801 North Front Street · P.O. Box 729 · Harrisburg, PA 17108-0729 · 717-232-5000

Joseph P. Hafer* · (Defendants, Medical Malpractice, Professional Malpractice) Thomas, Thomas & Hafer · 305 North Front Street · P.O. Box 999 · Harrisburg, PA 17108 · 717-255-7613

David E. Lehman · (Defendants) · McNees, Wallace & Nurick · 100 Pine Street P.O. Box 1166 · Harrisburg, PA 17108-1166 · 717-232-8000

James E. Beasley* · (Plaintiffs) · Beasley, Casey, Colleran, Erbstein, Thistle & Kline · 21 South 12th Street, Fifth Floor · Philadelphia, PA 19107-3638 · 215-665-1000

Perry S. Bechtle* · (Defendants) · LaBrum and Doak · 1700 Market Street, Suite 700 · Philadelphia, PA 19103-3997 · 215-561-4400

Marshall A. Bernstein* · (Plaintiffs) · Bernstein, Bernstein & Harrison · 1600 Market Street, Suite 2500 · Philadelphia, PA 19103 · 215-864-0770

Stephen M. Feldman · (Plaintiffs) · 1715 Rittenhouse Square · Philadelphia, PA 19103 · 215-546-2604

Joseph H. Foster* · (Defendants) · White and Williams · One Liberty Place · 1650 Market Street, Suite 1800 · Philadelphia, PA 19103-7301 · 215-864-7043

Robert St. Leger Goggin · Marshall, Dennehey, Warner, Coleman & Goggin · 1515 Locust Street · Philadelphia, PA 19102 · 215-893-3800

Herbert F. Kolsby · (Plaintiffs) · Kolsby & Gordon · One Liberty Place · 1650 Market Street, 22nd Floor · Philadelphia, PA 19103 · 215-851-9000

George J. Lavin, Jr. · (Defendants) · Lavin, Coleman, Finarelli & Gray · Penn Mutual Tower, 12th Floor · 510 Walnut Street · Philadelphia, PA 19106 · 215-627-0303

S. Gerald Litvin* · (Plaintiffs, Medical Malpractice, Products Liability, Automobile Collision) · Litvin, Blumberg, Matusow & Young · 210 West Washington Square, Fifth Floor · Philadelphia, PA 19106 · 215-925-4500

James J. McCabe · Duane, Morris & Heckscher · One Liberty Place, Suite 4200 Philadelphia, PA 19103-7394 · 215-979-1107

William J. O'Brien · (Defendants) · Gellman DeStefno & Rohn · 1515 Market Street · Philadelphia, PA 19102 · 215-864-9600

Joseph V. Pinto* · (Defendants) · White and Williams · One Liberty Place · 1650 Market Street, Suite 1800 · Philadelphia, PA 19103-7301 · 215-864-7000

Thomas B. Rutter* · (Plaintiffs) · Rutter, Turner, Solomon & DiPiero · The Curtis Center · Independence Square West, Suite 750 · One Walnut Street · Philadelphia, PA 19106 · 215-925-9200

Daniel J. Ryan* · (Defendants) · LaBrum and Doak · 1700 Market Street, Seventh Floor · Philadelphia, PA 19103-3997 · 215-561-4400

David S. Shrager · (Plaintiffs) · Shrager, McDaid, Loftus, Flum & Spivey · Eight Penn Center Plaza, 17th Floor · 17th & John F. Kennedy Boulevard · Philadelphia, PA 19103 · 215-568-7771

David J. Armstrong* · Dickie, McCamey & Chilcote · Two PPG Place, Suite 400 Pittsburgh, PA 15222-5402 · 412-281-7272

Edward J. Balzarini, Sr. · (Plaintiffs) · Balzarini, Carey & Watson · 3303 Grant Building · Pittsburgh, PA 15219 · 412-471-1200

William R. Caroselli* · (Plaintiffs, Medical Malpractice, Products Liability, Automobile Collision) · Caroselli, Spagnolli & Beachler · 322 Boulevard of the Allies, Eighth Floor · Pittsburgh, PA 15222 · 412-391-9860

Thomas L. Cooper · (Plaintiffs) · Gilardi & Cooper · 808 Grant Building · Pittsburgh, PA 15219 · 412-391-9770

Carl A. Eck · (Defendants) · Meyer, Darragh, Buckler, Bebenek, Eck & Hall · 2000 The Frick Building · Pittsburgh, PA 15219 · 412-261-6600

David B. Fawcett* · (Plaintiffs, Defendants) · Dickie, McCamey & Chilcote · Two PPG Place, Suite 400 · Pittsburgh, PA 15222-5402 · 412-281-7272

Robert S. Grigsby · (Defendants) · Alder Cohen & Grigsby · 600 Grant Street, Fifth Floor · Pittsburgh, PA 15219 · 412-394-4900

Dennis C. Harrington · (Plaintiffs) · Harrington & Schweers · 100 Ross Street · Pittsburgh, PA 15219 · 412-391-3477

Thomas Hollander · (Plaintiffs) · Evans, Ivory, Moses, Hollander & MacVay · 1311 Frick Building · Pittsburgh, PA 15219 · 412-471-3740

Herman C. Kimpel · (Defendants) · Dickie, McCamey & Chilcote · Two PPG Place, Suite 400 · Pittsburgh, PA 15222-5402 · 412-281-7272

David H. Trushel · (Defendants) · Trushel, Klym & Olszewski · 1207 Fifth Avenue · Pittsburgh, PA 15219 · 412-232-3800

William M. Wycoff · Thorp, Reed & Armstrong · One Riverfront Center · Pittsburgh, PA 15222 · 412-394-7711

Ronald H. Sherr · (Defendants) · Sherr, Joffe & Zuckerman · 100 Four Falls Corporate Center, Suite 400 · P.O. Box 800 · West Conshohochen, PA 19428 · 215-941-5400

Joseph A. Quinn, Jr. · (Plaintiffs) · Hourigan, Kluger, Spohrer & Quinn · 700 United Penn Bank Building · Wilkes Barre, PA 18701 · 717-825-9401

PUBLIC UTILITY LAW

David M. Kleppinger · McNees, Wallace & Nurick · 100 Pine Street · P.O. Box 1166 · Harrisburg, PA 17108 · 717-232-8000

Charles E. Thomas, Jr. · Thomas, Thomas, Armstrong & Niesen · 212 Locust Street · P.O. Box 9500 · Harrisburg, PA 17108 · 717-255-7600

Thomas P. Gadsden · Morgan, Lewis & Bockius · 2000 One Logan Square · Philadelphia, PA 19103-6993 · 215-963-5000

Robert L. Kendall, Jr. · Schnader, Harrison, Segal & Lewis · 1600 Market Street, Suite 3600 · Philadelphia, PA 19103 · 215-751-2478

David B. MacGregor · Morgan, Lewis & Bockius · 2000 One Logan Square · Philadelphia, PA 19103-6993 · 215-963-5000

Alan L. Reed · Morgan, Lewis & Bockius · 2000 One Logan Square · Philadelphia, PA 19103-6993 · 215-963-5000

REAL ESTATE LAW

Robert M. Cherry · McNees, Wallace & Nurick · 100 Pine Street · P.O. Box 1166 Harrisburg, PA 17108-1166 · 717-237-5326

Kenelm L. Shirk, Jr. · Shirk, Reist, Wagen, Seller and Shirk · 132 East Chestnut Street · P.O. Box 1552 · Lancaster, PA 17603 · 717-394-7247

David C. Auten · Reed Smith Shaw & McClay · 2500 One Liberty Place · Philadelphia, PA 19103 · 215-851-8100

Edward F. Beatty, Jr. · Saul, Ewing, Remick & Saul · 3800 Center Square West Philadelphia, PA 19102-2186 · 215-972-7777

Michael M. Dean · Wolf, Block, Schorr and Solis-Cohen · Packard Building, 12th Floor · 15th and Chestnut Streets · Philadelphia, PA 19102-2678 · 215-977-2000

Morris J. Dean · Blank, Rome, Comisky & McCauley · Four Penn Center Plaza, 10th-13th Floors · Philadelphia, PA 19103-2599 · 215-569-5500

Alvin H. Dorsky · Wolf, Block, Schorr and Solis-Cohen · Packard Building, 12th Floor · 15th and Chestnut Streets · Philadelphia, PA 19102-2678 · 215-977-2000

Stuart F. Ebby · Toll, Ebby, Langer & Marvin · 1760 Market Street, Sixth Floor Philadelphia, PA 19103 · 215-567-5770

Herman C. Fala · Wolf, Block, Schorr and Solis-Cohen · Packard Building, 12th Floor · 15th and Chestnut Streets · Philadelphia, PA 19102-2678 · 215-977-2102

Frank J. Ferro · Dechert Price & Rhoads · 4000 Bell Atlantic Tower · 1717 Arch Street · Philadelphia, PA 19103-2793 · 215-994-4000

Marvin Garfinkel · (Commercial Transactions, Real Estate Finance, Condominiums & Plan Unit Development, Defaults & Workouts) · Mesirov, Gelman, Jaffe, Cramer & Jamieson · 1735 Market Street, 38th Floor · Philadelphia, PA 19103 · 215-994-1450

Ronald B. Glazer · (Commercial Transactions, Condominiums & PUDs) · Wolf, Block, Schorr and Solis-Cohen · Packard Building, 12th Floor · 15th and Chestnut Streets · Philadelphia, PA 19102-2678 · 215-977-2000

Morris C. Kellett · Dechert Price & Rhoads · 4000 Bell Atlantic Tower · 1717 Arch Street · Philadelphia, PA 19103-2793 · 215-994-4000

David W. Maxey · Drinker Biddle & Reath · 1100 Philadelphia National Bank Building · Broad & Chestnut Streets · Philadelphia, PA 19107 · 215-988-2700

Henry F. Miller · Wolf, Block, Schorr and Solis-Cohen · Packard Building, 12th Floor · 15th and Chestnut Streets · Philadelphia, PA 19102-2678 · 215-977-2000

Harris Ominsky · Blank, Rome, Comisky & McCauley · Four Penn Center Plaza, 10th-13th Floors · Philadelphia, PA 19103-2599 · 215-569-5500

Mitchell E. Panzer · Wolf, Block, Schorr and Solis-Cohen · Packard Building, 12th Floor · 15th and Chestnut Streets · Philadelphia, PA 19102-2678 · 215-977-2000

Julian P. Rackow · Blank, Rome, Comisky & McCauley · Four Penn Center Plaza, 10th-13th Floors · Philadelphia, PA 19103-2599 · 215-569-5500

Kenneth I. Rosenberg · Mesirov, Gelman, Jaffe, Cramer & Jamieson · 1735 Market Street, 38th Floor · Philadelphia, PA 19103 · 215-994-1058

Sanford M. Rosenbloom · (Zoning, Commercial Transactions, Industrial Transactions, Construction & Other Financing) · Schnader, Harrison, Segal & Lewis · 1600 Market Street, Suite 3600 · Philadelphia, PA 19103 · 215-751-2484

James A. Rosenstein · Wolf, Block, Schorr and Solis-Cohen · Packard Building, 12th Floor · 15th and Chestnut Streets · Philadelphia, PA 19102-2678 · 215-977-2000

Robert M. Schwartz · White and Williams · One Liberty Place · 1650 Market Street, Suite 1800 · Philadelphia, PA 19103-7301 · 215-864-7188

Robert M. Segal · Wolf, Block, Schorr and Solis-Cohen · Packard Building, 12th Floor · 15th and Chestnut Streets · Philadelphia, PA 19102-2678 · 215-977-2000

Russell W. Whitman · Dechert Price & Rhoads · 4000 Bell Atlantic Tower · 1717 Arch Street · Philadelphia, PA 19103-2793 · 215-994-4000

Alan L. Ackerman* · Citron Ackerman & Alex · 1700 Allegheny Building · 429 Forbes Avenue · Pittsburgh, PA 15219 · 412-765-2720

Alexander Black · Buchanan Ingersoll · USX Tower, 58th Floor · 600 Grant Street · Pittsburgh, PA 15219-2887 · 412-562-8800

Raymond W. Cromer* · (Eminent Domain, Commercial Transactions, Real Estate Taxation) · Cromer & Reinbold · 450 Porter Building · Pittsburgh, PA 15219 · 412-281-2738

Thomas J. Dempsey, Sr. · 820 Frick Building · Pittsburgh, PA 15219 · 412-281-2442

Daniel B. Dixon · Rose, Schmidt, Hasley & DiSalle · 900 Oliver Building · Pittsburgh, PA 15222-5369 · 412-434-8600

Samuel L. Douglass · Rose, Schmidt, Hasley & DiSalle · 900 Oliver Building · Pittsburgh, PA 15222-5369 · 412-434-8600

Vincent J. Grogan* · (Zoning, Land Use, Commercial Transactions, Industrial Transactions) · Grogan, Graffam, McGinley & Lucchino · Three Gateway Center, 22nd Floor · Pittsburgh, PA 15222 · 412-553-6327

Calvin R. Harvey · (Banking, Financial Institutions) · Buchanan Ingersoll · USX Tower, 58th Floor · 600 Grant Street · Pittsburgh, PA 15219-2887 · 412-562-8800

E. D. Hollinshead · Hollinshead, Mendelson & Nixon · 230 Grant Building · Pittsburgh, PA 15219 · 412-355-7070

Leonard M. Mendelson* · (Zoning, Eminent Domain, Real Estate Taxation) · Hollinshead, Mendelson & Nixon · 230 Grant Building · Pittsburgh, PA 15219 · 412-355-7070

Regis D. Murrin · Reed Smith Shaw & McClay · James H. Reed Building, Mellon Square · 435 Sixth Avenue · P.O. Box 2009 · Pittsburgh, PA 15230-2009 · 412-288-3131

Alan Papernick · Papernick & Gefsky · One Oxford Centre, 34th Floor · Pittsburgh, PA 15219 · 412-765-2212

Harvey E. Robins · Brennan, Robins & Daley · 445 Fort Pitt Boulevard, Suite 500 Pittsburgh, PA 15219 · 412-281-0776

Edward W. Seifert · Reed Smith Shaw & McClay · James H. Reed Building, Mellon Square · 435 Sixth Avenue · P.O. Box 2009 · Pittsburgh, PA 15230-2009 412-288-3131

Herbert G. Sheinberg · Sheinberg & Hoover · 617 Grant Building · Pittsburgh, PA 15219-2201 · 412-261-6300

William J. Staley · Tucker Arensberg · 1200 Pittsburgh National Building · Pittsburgh, PA 15222 · 412-566-1212

John H. White · Reed Smith Shaw & McClay · James H. Reed Building, Mellon Square · 435 Sixth Avenue · P.O. Box 2009 · Pittsburgh, PA 15230-2009 · 412-288-3131

Nelson P. Young · (Commercial Transactions) · Reed Smith Shaw & McClay · James H. Reed Building, Mellon Square · 435 Sixth Avenue · P.O. Box 2009 · Pittsburgh, PA 15230-2009 · 412-288-3131

TAX AND EMPLOYEE BENEFITS LAW

Howell C. Mette · Mette, Evans & Woodside · 1801 North Front Street · P.O. Box 729 · Harrisburg, PA 17108-0729 · 717-232-5000

Gerald K. Morrison · (Corporate & Partnership Transactions, Tax Disputes) · Rhoads & Sinon · One South Market Square · P.O. Box 1146 · Harrisburg, PA 17108-1146 · 717-233-5731

John S. Oyler · (Mergers & Acquisitions) · McNees, Wallace & Nurick · 100 Pine Street · P.O. Box 1166 · Harrisburg, PA 17108 · 717-232-8000

Richard W. Stevenson · McNees, Wallace & Nurick · 100 Pine Street · P.O. Box 1166 · Harrisburg, PA 17108 · 717-232-8000

Robert L. Abramowitz · (Employee Benefits) · Morgan, Lewis & Bockius · 2000 One Logan Square · Philadelphia, PA 19103-6993 · 215-963-5000

Anthony L. Bartolini · Dechert Price & Rhoads · 4000 Bell Atlantic Tower · 1717 Arch Street · Philadelphia, PA 19103-2793 · 215-994-4000

John Marley Bernard · (Employee Benefits) · Ballard, Spahr, Andrews & Ingersoll · 1735 Market Street, 51st Floor · Philadelphia, PA 19103-7599 · 215-665-8500

Robert A. Bildersee · (Employee Benefits) · Morgan, Lewis & Bockius · 2000 One Logan Square · Philadelphia, PA 19103-6993 · 215-963-5000

Sheldon M. Bonovitz · Duane, Morris & Heckscher · One Liberty Place, Suite 4200 · Philadelphia, PA 19102 · 215-979-1000

Christopher Branda, Jr. · Dechert Price & Rhoads · 4000 Bell Atlantic Tower · 1717 Arch Street · Philadelphia, PA 19103-2793 · 215-994-4000

Robert D. Comfort · Morgan, Lewis & Bockius · 2000 One Logan Square · Philadelphia, PA 19103-6993 · 215-963-5000

William M. Goldstein · Drinker Biddle & Reath · 1100 Philadelphia National Bank Building · Broad & Chestnut Streets · Philadelphia, PA 19107 · 215-988-2700

Harry L. Gutman · Drinker Biddle & Reath · 1100 Philadelphia National Bank Building · Broad & Chestnut Streets · Philadelphia, PA 19107 · 215-988-2984

Selwyn A. Horvitz · Horvitz, Fisher, Miller & Sedlack · 1515 Locust Street, Suite 400 · Philadelphia, PA 19102 · 215-732-3232

Paul S. Kimbol · (Employee Benefits) · Dechert Price & Rhoads · 4000 Bell Atlantic Tower · 1717 Arch Street · Philadelphia, PA 19103-2793 · 215-994-4000

Charles G. Kopp · Wolf, Block, Schorr and Solis-Cohen · Packard Building, 12th Floor · 15th and Chestnut Streets · Philadelphia, PA 19102-2678 · 215-977-2000

Joseph Lundy · Ballard Spahr, Andrews & Ingersoll · 1735 Market Street, 51st Floor · Philadelphia, PA 19103-7599 · 215-665-8500

William Scott Magargee III · (Employee Benefits) · Dechert Price & Rhoads · 4000 Bell Atlantic Tower · 1717 Arch Street · Philadelphia, PA 19103-2793 · 215-994-4000

Robert E. McQuiston · Ballard, Spahr, Andrews & Ingersoll · 1735 Market Street, 51st Floor · Philadelphia, PA 19103-7599 · 215-665-8500

William A. Rosoff · Wolf, Block, Schorr and Solis-Cohen · Packard Building, 12th Floor · 15th and Chestnut Streets · Philadelphia, PA 19102-2678 · 215-977-2000

Ronald M. Wiener · (Corporate & Partnership Transactions, Tax Disputes, Real Estate Transactions) · Wolf, Block, Schorr and Solis-Cohen · Packard Building, 12th Floor · 15th and Chestnut Streets · Philadelphia, PA 19102-2678 · 215-977-2266

Richard P. Wild · Dechert Price & Rhoads · 4000 Bell Atlantic Tower · 1717 Arch Street · Philadelphia, PA 19103-2793 · 215-994-4000

Thomas D. Arbogast · (Corporate & Partnership Transactions, Tax Disputes) · Reed Smith Shaw & McClay · James H. Reed Building, Mellon Square · 435 Sixth Avenue · P.O. Box 2009 · Pittsburgh, PA 15230-2009 · 412-288-3131

Edward A. Craig III · Kirkpatrick & Lockhart · 1500 Oliver Building · Pittsburgh, PA 15222-5379 · 412-355-6500

Alan H. Finegold · Kirkpatrick & Lockhart · 1500 Oliver Building · Pittsburgh, PA 15222-5379 · 412-355-6500

Robert A. Johnson · (Employee Benefits) · Buchanan Ingersoll · USX Tower, 58th Floor · 600 Grant Street · Pittsburgh, PA 15219-2887 · 412-562-8832

David L. Ketter · Kirkpatrick & Lockhart · 1500 Oliver Building · Pittsburgh, PA 15222-5379 · 412-355-6420

Marvin S. Lieber · (Corporate & Partnership Transactions, Tax Disputes) · Klett Lieber Rooney & Schorling · One Oxford Centre, 40th Floor · Pittsburgh, PA 15219-6498 · 412-392-2000

Larry E. Phillips · Buchanan Ingersoll · USX Tower, 58th Floor · 600 Grant Street Pittsburgh, PA 15219-2887 · 412-562-8800

William H. Powderly III · (Employee Benefits) · Jones, Day, Reavis & Pogue · One Mellon Bank Center · Pittsburgh, PA 15219 · 412-394-7921

Charles J. Queenan, Jr. · Kirkpatrick & Lockhart · 1500 Oliver Building · Pittsburgh, PA 15222-5379 · 412-355-6500

Charles R. Smith, Jr. · (Employee Benefits) · Kirkpatrick & Lockhart · 1500 Oliver Building · Pittsburgh, PA 15222-5379 · 412-355-6536

Robert B. Williams · Eckert Seamans Cherin & Mellott · 600 Grant Street, 42nd Floor · Pittsburgh, PA 15219 · 412-566-6000

Patrick J. Di Quinzio · Law Office of Patrick J. Di Quinzio · 310 North High Street · Westchester, PA 19308 · 215-436-6535

TRUSTS AND ESTATES

Heath L. Allen · Keefer, Wood, Allen & Rahal · Walnut-Court Building · 210 Walnut Street · P.O. Box 11963 · Harrisburg, PA 17108-1963 · 717-255-8000

William D. Boswell · Boswell, Snyder, Tintner & Piccola · 315 North Front Street P.O. Box 741 · Harrisburg, PA 17108-0741 · 717-236-9377

Richard R. Lefever · McNees, Wallace & Nurick · 100 Pine Street · P.O. Box 1166 · Harrisburg, PA 17108 · 717-232-8000

Howell C. Mette · Mette, Evans & Woodside · 1801 North Front Street · P.O. Box 729 · Harrisburg, PA 17108-0729 · 717-232-5000

Henry W. Rhoads · Rhoads & Sinon · One South Market Square · P.O. Box 1146 Harrisburg, PA 17108-1146 · 717-233-5731

Donald R. Waisel · McNees, Wallace & Nurick · 100 Pine Street · P.O. Box 1166 Harrisburg, PA 17108 · 717-232-8000

S. Jonathan Emerson · Montgomery, McCracken, Walker & Rhoads · 300 West State Street · Media, PA 19603 · 215-566-0249

J. Brooke Aker* · Smith, Aker, Grossman & Hollinger · 60 East Penn Street · P.O. Box 150 · Norristown, PA 19404 · 215-275-8200

Richard L. Grossman · Smith, Aker, Grossman & Hollinger · 60 East Penn Street P.O. Box 150 · Norristown, PA 19404 · 215-275-8200

James L. Hollinger · Smith, Aker, Grossman & Hollinger · 60 East Penn Street P.O. Box 150 · Norristown, PA 19404 · 215-275-8200

William C. Bullitt · Drinker Biddle & Reath · 1100 Philadelphia National Bank Building · Broad & Chestnut Streets · Philadelphia, PA 19107 · 215-988-2700

Bruce L. Castor · Ballard, Spahr, Andrews & Ingersoll · 1735 Market Street, 51st Floor · Philadelphia, PA 19103-7599 · 215-665-8500

Linda A. Fisher · Dechert Price & Rhoads · 4000 Bell Atlantic Tower · 1717 Arch Street · Philadelphia, PA 19103-2793 · 215-994-4000

George S. Forde, Jr. · Stradley, Ronon, Stevens & Young · 2600 One Commerce Square · Philadelphia, PA 19103 · 215-564-8000

Robert L. Freedman · Dechert Price & Rhoads · 4000 Bell Atlantic Tower · 1717 Arch Street · Philadelphia, PA 19103-2793 · 215-994-4000

Christopher H. Gadsden · Drinker Biddle & Reath · 1100 Philadelphia National Bank Building · Broad & Chestnut Streets · Philadelphia, PA 19107 · 215-988-2700

George J. Hauptfuhrer · Dechert Price & Rhoads · 4000 Bell Atlantic Tower · 1717 Arch Street · Philadelphia, PA 19103-2793 · 215-994-4000

Martin A. Heckscher · Duane, Morris & Heckscher · One Liberty Place, Suite 4200 · Philadelphia, PA 19102 · 215-979-1979

Paul C. Heintz · Obermayer, Rebmann, Maxwell & Hippel · Packard Building, 14th Floor · Philadelphia, PA 19102 · 215-665-3000

H. Ober Hess · Ballard, Spahr, Andrews & Ingersoll · 1735 Market Street, 51st Floor · Philadelphia, PA 19103-7599 · 215-665-8500

David J. Kaufman · (Estate Planning, Estate Administration, Charitable Trusts) Wolf, Block, Schorr and Solis-Cohen · Packard Building, 12th Floor · 15th and Chestnut Streets · Philadelphia, PA 19102-2678 · 215-977-2000

James R. Ledwith · Pepper, Hamilton & Scheetz · 3000 Two Logan Square · 18th and Arch Streets · Philadelphia, PA 19103-2799 · 215-981-4315

John J. Lombard, Jr. · Morgan, Lewis & Bockius · 2000 One Logan Square · Philadelphia, PA 19103-6993 · 215-963-5000

Francis J. Mirabello · Morgan, Lewis & Bockius · 2000 One Logan Square · Philadelphia, PA 19103-6993 · 215-963-5000

George H. Nofer · Schnader, Harrison, Segal & Lewis · 1600 Market Street, Suite 3600 · Philadelphia, PA 19103 · 215-751-2464

Samuel N. Rabinowitz · Blank, Rome, Comisky & McCauley · Four Penn Center Plaza, 10th-13th Floors · Philadelphia, PA 19103-2599 · 215-569-5572

J. Pennington Straus · Schnader, Harrison, Segal & Lewis · 1600 Market Street, Suite 3600 · Philadelphia, PA 19103 · 215-751-2000

Regina O'Brien Thomas · Ballard, Spahr, Andrews & Ingersoll · 1735 Market Street, 51st Floor · Philadelphia, PA 19103-7599 · 215-665-8500

Minturn T. Wright III · Dechert Price & Rhoads · 4000 Bell Atlantic Tower · 1717 Arch Street · Philadelphia, PA 19103-2793 · 215-994-4000

Jack G. Armstrong · Buchanan Ingersoll · USX Tower, 58th Floor · 600 Grant Street · Pittsburgh, PA 15219-2887 · 412-562-8800

G. Donald Gerlach · Reed, Smith, Shaw & McClay · James H. Reed Building, Mellon Square · 435 Sixth Avenue · P.O. Box 2009 · Pittsburgh, PA 15230-2009 412-288-3131

William McC. Houston* · (Estate Planning, Estate Administration) · Houston, Houston & Donnelly · 2510 Centre City Tower · 650 Smithfield Street · Pittsburgh, PA 15222 · 412-471-5828

Robert G. Lovett · Reed, Smith, Shaw & McClay · James H. Reed Building, Mellon Square · 435 Sixth Avenue · P.O. Box 2009 · Pittsburgh, PA 15230-2009 412-288-3131

W. Reid Lowe · Meyer, Unkovic & Scott · 1300 Oliver Building · Pittsburgh, PA 15222 · 412-456-2800

Stephen E. Nash · Meyer, Unkovic & Scott · 1300 Oliver Building · Pittsburgh, PA 15222 · 412-456-2800

K. Sidney Neuman · Buchanan Ingersoll · USX Tower, 58th Floor · 600 Grant Street · Pittsburgh, PA 15219-2887 · 412-562-8800

James W. Ummer · (Estate Planning, Estate Administration, Charitable Trusts) · Buchanan Ingersoll · USX Tower, 58th Floor · 600 Grant Street · Pittsburgh, PA 15219-2887 · 412-562-8800

Robert B. Williams · Eckert Seamans Cherin & Mellott · 600 Grant Street, 42nd Floor · Pittsburgh, PA 15219 · 412-566-6000

RHODE ISLAND

BANKRUPTCY LAW

John R. Allen · Hinckley, Allen, Snyder & Comen · 1500 Fleet Center · Providence, RI 02903 · 401-274-2000

Edward J. Bertozzi, Jr. · Edwards & Angell · 2700 Hospital Trust Tower · Providence, RI 02903 · 401-274-9200

Allan M. Shine · Winograd, Shine & Zacks · 123 Dyer Street · Providence, RI 02903 · 401-273-8300

Michael A. Silverstein · Hinckley, Allen, Snyder & Comen · 1500 Fleet Center Providence, RI 02903 · 401-274-2000

BUSINESS LITIGATION

John H. Blish* · Blish & Cavanagh · Commerce Center · 30 Exchange Terrace · Providence, RI 02903 · 401-831-8900

Joseph V. Cavanagh, Jr.* · (Antitrust, Banking, Commercial) · Blish & Cavanagh Commerce Center · 30 Exchange Terrace · Providence, RI 02903 · 401-831-8900

Michael P. DeFanti* · Hinckley, Allen, Snyder & Comen · 1500 Fleet Center · Providence, RI 02903 · 401-274-2000

Robert G. Flanders, Jr. · Flanders + Madeiros · One Turks Head Place, Suite 700 · Providence, RI 02903 · 401-831-0700

Peter Lawson Kennedy* · (Commercial, Securities, Construction) · Adler Pollock & Sheehan · 2300 Hospital Trust Tower · Providence, RI 02903 · 401-274-7200

Matthew F. Medeiros* · Flanders + Madeiros · One Turks Head Place, Suite 700 · Providence, RI 02903 · 401-831-0700

George Vetter · Vetter & White · 20 Washington Place · Providence, RI 02903 · 401-421-3060

CORPORATE LAW

John F. Corrigan · (Corporate Finance, International, Mergers & Acquisitions, Securities) · Adler Pollock & Sheehan · 2300 Hospital Trust Tower · Providence, RI 02903 · 401-274-7200

Robert Spink Davis · Edwards & Angell · 2700 Hospital Trust Tower · Providence, RI 02903 · 401-274-9200

David K. Duffell · Edwards & Angell · 2700 Hospital Trust Tower · Providence, RI 02903 · 401-274-9200

Malcolm Farmer III · Hinckley, Allen, Snyder & Comen · 1500 Fleet Center · Providence, RI 02903 · 401-274-2000

Jacques V. Hopkins · Hinckley, Allen, Snyder & Comen · 1500 Fleet Center · Providence, RI 02903 · 401-274-2000

James A. Jackson · Hinckley, Allen, Snyder & Comen · 1500 Fleet Center · Providence, RI 02903 · 401-274-2000

V. Duncan Johnson · Edwards & Angell · 2700 Hospital Trust Tower · Providence, RI 02903 · 401-274-9200

Eustace T. Pliakas · Tillinghast, Collins & Graham · One Old Stone Square · Providence, RI 02903 · 401-456-1200

James J. Skeffington · Edwards & Angell · 2700 Hospital Trust Tower · Providence, RI 02903 · 401-274-9200

Richard G. Small · Hinckley, Allen, Snyder & Comen · 1500 Fleet Center · Providence, RI 02903 · 401-274-2000

Bentley Tobin · Hinckley, Allen, Snyder & Comen · 1500 Fleet Center · Providence, RI 02903 · 401-274-2000

Edwin G. Torrance · Hinckley, Allen, Snyder & Comen · 1500 Fleet Center · Providence, RI 02903 · 401-274-2000

Joachim A. Weissfeld · Hinckley, Allen, Snyder & Comen · 1500 Fleet Center · Providence, RI 02903 · 401-274-2000

CRIMINAL DEFENSE

Harold C. Arcaro, Jr. · Arcaro & Reilly · 1500 Turks Head Building · Providence, RI 02903 · 401-751-1040

Peter A. Di Biase · Toro Law Associates · 91 Friendship Street · Providence, RI 02903 · 401-351-7752

William A. Dimitri, Jr. · Dimitri & Dimitri · 733 Douglas Avenue · Providence, RI 02908 · 401-273-9092

John A. MacFadyen III* · (Appellate) · The Remington Building · 91 Friendship Street · Providence, RI 02903-3819 · 401-521-4420

Eugene F. Toro · Toro Law Associates · 91 Friendship Street · Providence, RI 02903 · 401-351-7752

John Tramonti, Jr. · 808 Hospital Trust Building · Providence, RI 02903 · 401-751-5433

FAMILY LAW

Alfred Factor* · Kirshenbaum & Kirshenbaum · 888 Reservoir Avenue · Cranston, RI 02910 · 401-946-3200

Joseph T. Houlihan · Corcoran, Peckham & Hayes · 61 Long Wharf · P.O. Box 389 · Newport, RI 02840 · 401-847-0872

Jerry L. McIntyre* · Edwards & Angell · 130 Bellevue Avenue · Newport, RI 02840 · 401-849-7800

Howard I. Lipsey* · Lipsey & Skolnik · 369 South Main Street · Providence, RI 02903 · 401-351-7700

FIRST AMENDMENT LAW

Joseph V. Cavanagh, Jr.* · Blish & Cavanagh · Commerce Center · 30 Exchange Terrace · Providence, RI 02903 · 401-831-8900

HEALTH CARE LAW

Jeffery M. Alexander · Edwards & Angell · 2700 Hospital Trust Tower · Providence, RI 02903 · 401-274-9200

Thomas R. Courage · Hinckley, Allen, Snyder & Comen · 1500 Fleet Center · Providence, RI 02903 · 401-274-2000

Gerard R. Goulet · Hinckley, Allen, Snyder & Comen · 1500 Fleet Center · Providence, RI 02903 · 401-274-2000

LABOR AND EMPLOYMENT LAW

Patrick A. Liguori · (Management) · Adler Pollock & Sheehan · 2300 Hospital Trust Tower · Providence, RI 02903 · 401-274-7200

John J. Pendergast III · (Management) · Hinckley, Allen, Snyder & Comen · 1500 Fleet Center · Providence, RI 02903 · 401-274-2000

William R. Powers III · (Management) · Powers, Kinder, Keeney & Brody · 56 Exchange Terrace · Providence, RI 02903 · 401-454-2000

Richard A. Skolnik · (Labor) · Lipsey & Skolnik · 369 South Main Street · Providence, RI 02903 · 401-351-7700

NATURAL RESOURCES AND ENVIRONMENTAL LAW

Gregory L. Benik · Hinckley, Allen, Snyder & Comen · 1500 Fleet Center · Providence, RI 02903 · 401-274-2000

Deming E. Sherman · Edwards & Angell · 2700 Hospital Trust Tower · Providence, RI 02903 · 401-274-9200

PERSONAL INJURY LITIGATION

Leonard Decof* · (Plaintiffs, Medical Malpractice, Products Liability) · Decof & Grimm · One Smith Hill · Providence, RI 02903 · 401-272-1110

John F. Dolan* · (Defendants) · Rice, Dolan & Kershaw · 101 Dyer Street, Suite 3-A · Providence, RI 02903 · 401-272-8800

Joseph A. Kelly · (Defendants) · Carroll, Kelly & Murphy · The Packet Building, Suite 200 · 155 South Main Street · Providence, RI 02903 · 401-331-7272

A. Lauriston Parks* · (Defendants) · Hanson, Curran, Parks & Whitman · The Francis Building · 146 Westminster Street · Providence, RI 02903-2218 · 401-421-2154

George Vetter · (Defendants) · Vetter & White · 20 Washington Place · Providence, RI 02903 · 401-421-3060

Max Wistow* · (Plaintiffs) · Wistow & Barylick · Hanley Building · 56 Pine Street Providence, RI 02903 · 401-831-2700

REAL ESTATE LAW

E. Jerome Batty · Hinckley, Allen, Snyder & Comen · 1500 Fleet Center · Providence, RI 02903 · 401-274-2000

Michael R. Goldenberg · Goldenberg & Muri · 15 Westminster Street · Providence, RI 02903 · 401-421-7300

Timothy T. More · Edwards & Angell · 2700 Hospital Trust Tower · Providence, RI 02903 · 401-274-9200

Robert A. Pitassi · (Land Use, Eminent Domain, Commercial Transactions, Industrial Transactions) · Licht & Semonoff · One Park Row · Providence, RI 02903 · 401-421-8030

Charles F. Rogers · Edwards & Angell · 2700 Hospital Trust Tower · Providence, RI 02903 · 401-274-9200

David J. Tracy · (Zoning, Land Use, Commercial Transactions, Real Estate Financing & Development) · Hinckley, Allen, Snyder & Comen · 1500 Fleet Center · Providence, RI 02903 · 401-274-2000

TAX AND EMPLOYEE BENEFITS LAW

Harold C. Arcaro, Jr. · Arcaro & Reilly · 1500 Turks Head Building · Providence, RI 02903 · 401-751-1040

Edmund C. Bennett · Hinckley, Allen, Snyder & Comen · 1500 Fleet Center · Providence, RI 02903 · 401-274-2000

Alfred S. Lombardi · Edwards & Angell · 2700 Hospital Trust Tower · Providence, RI 02903 · 401-274-9200

Frederick P. McClure · (Employee Benefits) · Hinckley, Allen, Snyder & Comen 1500 Fleet Center · Providence, RI 02903 · 401-274-2000

H. Peter Olsen · Hinckley, Allen, Snyder & Comen · 1500 Fleet Center · Providence, RI 02903 · 401-274-2000

John H. Reid III · (Employee Benefits) · Edwards & Angell · 2700 Hospital Trust Tower · Providence, RI 02903 · 401-274-9200

TRUSTS AND ESTATES

James H. Barnett · Edwards & Angell · 2700 Hospital Trust Tower · Providence, RI 02903 · 401-274-9200

Noel M. Field, Jr. · Hinckley, Allen, Snyder & Comen · 1500 Fleet Center · Providence, RI 02903 · 401-274-2000

Mary Louise Kennedy · Edwards & Angell · 2700 Hospital Trust Tower · Providence, RI 02903 · 401-274-9200

Benjamin G. Paster · Adler Pollock & Sheehan · 2300 Hospital Trust Tower · Providence, RI 02903 · 401-274-7200

Richard H. Pierce · Hinckley, Allen, Snyder & Comen · 1500 Fleet Center · Providence, RI 02903 · 401-274-2000

David T. Riedel · Tillinghast, Collins & Graham · One Old Stone Square · Providence, RI 02903 · 401-456-1200

Joachim A. Weissfeld · Hinckley, Allen, Snyder & Comen · 1500 Fleet Center · Providence, RI 02903 · 401-274-2000

SOUTH CAROLINA

BANKRUPTCY LAW

Gerald M. Finkel* · (Business Reorganization, Creditors' Rights, Debtors' Rights, Bankruptcy Litigation) · Finkel, Goldberg, Sheftman & Altman · 1331 Elmwood Avenue · P.O. Box 1799 · Columbia, SC 29202 · 803-765-2935

Donald H. Stubbs · (Business Reorganization, Creditors' Rights) · Nelson, Mullins, Riley & Scarborough · Keenan Building, Third Floor · 1330 Lady Street · P.O. Box 11070 · Columbia, SC 29211 · 803-799-2000

BUSINESS LITIGATION

Robert H. Hood* · Hood Law Firm · 172 Meeting Street · P.O. Box 1508 · Charleston, SC 29402 · 803-577-4435

Joseph H. McGee · Buist, Moore, Smythe & McGee · Five Exchange Street · P.O. Box 999 · Charleston, SC 29402-0999 · 803-722-8375

Morris D. Rosen · Rosen, Rosen & Hagood · 45 Broad Street · P.O. Box 893 · Charleston, SC 29402 · 803-577-6726

Robert B. Wallace · Wallace and Tinkler · 129 Broad Street · P.O. Box 388 · Charleston, SC 29402 · 803-722-8313

Wilburn Brewer, Jr.* · Nexsen Pruet Jacobs & Pollard · 1441 Main Street, 15th Floor · P.O. Drawer 2426 · Columbia, SC 29202 · 803-771-8900

Harold Jacobs · Nexsen Pruet Jacobs & Pollard · 1441 Main Street, 15th Floor · P.O. Drawer 2426 · Columbia, SC 29202 · 803-771-8900

Thomas E. McCutchen · Whaley, McCutchen, Blanton & Rhodes · 1414 Lady Street · P.O. Drawer 11209 · Columbia, SC 29211-1209 · 803-799-9791

Stephen G. Morrison · Nelson, Mullins, Riley & Scarborough · Keenan Building, Third Floor · 1330 Lady Street · P.O. Box 11070 · Columbia, SC 29211 · 803-799-2000

Edward W. Mullins, Jr. · Nelson, Mullins, Riley & Scarborough · Keenan Building, Third Floor · 1330 Lady Street · P.O. Box 11070 · Columbia, SC 29211 · 803-799-2000

William L. Pope · Pope & Rodgers · 1330 Lady Street, Suite 615 · P.O. Box 5907 · Columbia, SC 29250 · 803-254-0700

Saunders M. Bridges* · Bridges and Orr · Bridges Building · 318 West Palmetto Street · P.O. Box 130 · Florence, SC 29503 · 803-662-1418

Mark W. Buyck, Jr.* · Willcox, McLeod, Buyck, Baker & Williams · Willcox Building · 248 West Evans Street · P.O. Box 1909 · Florence, SC 29503 · 803-662-3258

Frank H. Gibbes, Jr. · Gibbes & Clarkson · 330 East Coffee Street · P.O. Box 10589 · Greenville, SC 29603 · 803-271-9580

John E. Johnston · Leatherwood, Walker, Todd & Mann · 100 East Coffee Street · P.O. Box 87 · Greenville, SC 29602 · 803-242-6440

Fletcher C. Mann* · Leatherwood, Walker, Todd & Mann · 100 East C[ ] Street · P.O. Box 87 · Greenville, SC 29602 · 803-242-6440

William Francis Marion, Sr. · Haynsworth, Marion, McKay & Guerard · Tw[ ] Shelter Centre, 11th Floor · 75 Beattie Place · P.O. Box 2048 · Greenville, SC 29602 · 803-240-3200

G. Dewey Oxner, Jr. · Haynsworth, Marion, McKay & Guerard · Two Shelter Centre, 11th Floor · 75 Beattie Place · P.O. Box 2048 · Greenville, SC 29602 · 803-240-3200

James C. Parham, Jr. · Wyche, Burgess, Freeman & Parham · 44 East Camperdown Way · P.O. Box 728 · Greenville, SC 29602 · 803-242-3131

R. Frank Plaxco · Leatherwood, Walker, Todd & Mann · 100 East Coffee Street P.O. Box 87 · Greenville, SC 29602 · 803-242-6440

J. D. Todd, Jr.* · Leatherwood, Walker, Todd & Mann · 100 East Coffee Street P.O. Box 87 · Greenville, SC 29602 · 803-242-6440

Wesley M. Walker · Leatherwood, Walker, Todd & Mann · 100 East Coffee Street · P.O. Box 87 · Greenville, SC 29602 · 803-242-6440

James H. Watson · Leatherwood, Walker, Todd & Mann · 100 East Coffee Street P.O. Box 87 · Greenville, SC 29602 · 803-242-6440

Thomas H. Pope · Pope and Hudgens · 1508 College Street · P.O. Box 190 · Newberry, SC 29108 · 803-276-2532

CORPORATE LAW

Robert L. Clement, Jr. · Young, Clement, Rivers & Tisdale · 28 Broad Street · P.O. Box 993 · Charleston, SC 29402 · 803-577-4000

Theodore B. Guerard · Haynsworth, Marion, McKay & Guerard · Two Prioleau Street · P.O. Box 1119 · Charleston, SC 29402 · 803-722-7606

Augustine T. Smythe · Buist, Moore, Smythe & McGee · Five Exchange Street P.O. Box 999 · Charleston, SC 29402-0999 · 803-722-8375

Susan M. Smythe · (Corporate Finance, Mergers & Acquisitions, Financial Institutions) · Buist, Moore, Smythe & McGee · Five Exchange Street · P.O. Box 999 · Charleston, SC 29402-0999 · 803-722-8375

John W. Foster · McNair Law Firm · NCNB Tower, 18th Floor · 1301 Gervais Street · P.O. Box 11390 · Columbia, SC 29211 · 803-799-9800

George S. King, Jr. · Sinkler & Boyd · The Palmetto Center, Suite 1200 · 1426 Main Street · P.O. Box 11889 · Columbia, SC 29211 · 803-779-3080

Julian J. Nexsen · Nexsen Pruet Jacobs & Pollard · 1441 Main Street, 15th Floor · P.O. Drawer 2426 · Columbia, SC 29202 · 803-771-8900

David W. Robinson II · Robinson, McFadden & Moore · Jefferson Square, Suite 600 · 1801 Main Street · P.O. Box 944 · Columbia, SC 29202 · 803-779-8900

David L. Freeman · Wyche, Burgess, Freeman & Parham · 44 East Camperdown Way · P.O. Box 728 · Greenville, SC 29602 · 803-242-3131

David A. Quattlebaum III · Leatherwood, Walker, Todd & Mann · 100 East Coffee Street · P.O. Box 87 · Greenville, SC 29602 · 803-242-6440

CRIMINAL DEFENSE

B. Henderson Johnson, Jr. · Johnson Johnson Maxwell Whittle Snelgrove & Weeks · 117 Pendleton Street, NW · P.O. Box 2619 · Aiken, SC 29802-2619 · 803-649-5338

Coming B. Gibbs, Jr.* · Gibbs & Holmes · 171 Church Street, Suite 270 · P.O. Box 938 · Charleston, SC 29402-0938 · 803-722-0033

Arthur G. Howe · Uricchio, Howe & Krell · 171-2 Broad Street · P.O. Box 399 · Charleston, SC 29402 · 803-723-7491

Gedney M. Howe III · Law Office of Gedney M. Howe · Eight Chalmers Street · P.O. Box 1440 · Charleston, SC 29402 · 803-722-8048

Lionel S. Loftin · Law Offices of Lionel S. Loftin · 174 East Bay Street, Suite 302 · P.O. Box 449 · Charleston, SC 29402 · 803-722-6319

Andrew J. Savage · 174 East Bay Street, Suite 302 · Charleston, SC 29402 · 803-722-6319

Robert Wallace · Wallace and Tinkler · 129 Broad Street · P.O. Box 388 · Charleston, SC 29402 · 803-722-8313

Terrell L. Glenn · Glenn, Irvin, Murphy, Gray & Stepp · 1500 Calhoun Street · P.O. Box 1550 · Columbia, SC 29202 · 803-765-1100

O. W. Bannister, Jr. · Hill, Wyatt & Bannister · 100 Williams Street · P.O. Box 2585 · Greenville, SC 29602 · 803-242-5133

Belton O. Thomason · Love, Thornton, Arnold & Thomason · 410 East Washington Street · P.O. Box 10045 · Greenville, SC 29603 · 803-242-6360

FAMILY LAW

Robert N. Rosen · Rosen, Rosen & Hagood · 45 Broad Street · P.O. Box 893 · Charleston, SC 29402 · 803-577-6726

Robert B. Wallace* · Wallace and Tinkler · 129 Broad Street · P.O. Box 388 · Charleston, SC 29402-0388 · 803-722-8313

Harvey L. Golden* · (Child Custody, Divorce, Marital Settlement Agreements, Equitable Division) · 1712-1714 Main Street · Columbia, SC 29201 · 803-779-3700

Kermit S. King* · 1426 Richland Street · P.O. Box 7667 · Columbia, SC 29202 · 803-779-3090

David H. Wilkins* · Wilkins, Nelson, & Kittredge · 408 East North Street · Greenville, SC 29601-3098 · 803-232-5629

John O. McDougall · Weinberg, Brown & McDougall · 109 North Main Street · P.O. Drawer 1289 · Sumter, SC 29151 · 803-775-1274

FIRST AMENDMENT LAW

Thomas S. Tisdale, Jr. · Young, Clement, Rivers & Tisdale · 28 Broad Street · P.O. Box 993 · Charleston, SC 29402 · 803-577-4000

James M. Brailsford III · Robinson, McFadden & Moore · Jefferson Square, Suite 600 · 1801 Main Street · P.O. Box 944 · Columbia, SC 29202 · 803-779-8900

David L. Freeman · Wyche, Burgess, Freeman & Parham · 44 East Camperdown Way · P.O. Box 728 · Greenville, SC 29602 · 803-242-3131

INTELLECTUAL PROPERTY LAW

Ralph Bailey · Bailey & Hardaway · 125 Broadus Avenue · Greenville, SC 29601 803-233-1338

Julian W. Dority · Dority & Manning · 700 East North Street, Suite 15 · Greenville, SC 29601 · 803-271-1592

LABOR AND EMPLOYMENT LAW

Homer L. Deakins, Jr.* · (Management) · Ogletree, Deakins, Nash, Smoak & Stewart · 300 North Main Street · P.O. Box 2757 · Greenville, SC 29602 · 803-271-1300

Knox L. Haynsworth, Jr. · (Management) · Haynsworth, Baldwin, Johnson & Greaves · 918 South Pleasantburg Drive · P.O. Box 10888 · Greenville, SC 29603 · 803-271-7410

Melvin R. Hutson · (Management) · Thompson, Mann & Hutson · The Daniel Building, Suite 2200 · Greenville, SC 29602 · 803-242-3200

Lewis T. Smoak · Ogletree, Deakins, Nash, Smoak & Stewart · 300 North Main Street · P.O. Box 2757 · Greenville, SC 29602 · 803-271-1300

Robert T. Thompson, Sr. · (Management) · Thompson, Mann & Hutson · The Daniel Building, Suite 2200 · Greenville, SC 29602 · 803-242-3200

MARITIME LAW

Benj. Allston Moore, Jr. · Buist, Moore, Smythe & McGee · Five Exchange Street · P.O. Box 999 · Charleston, SC 29402-0999 · 803-722-8375

Gordon D. Schreck* · (Charter Parties, Ship Financing, Personal Injury, Collision & Salvage) · Buist, Moore, Smythe & McGee · Five Exchange Street · P.O. Box 999 · Charleston, SC 29402-0999 · 803-722-8375

NATURAL RESOURCES AND ENVIRONMENTAL LAW

William L. Want · 174 East Bay Street, Suite 202 · P.O. Box 1088 · Charleston, SC 29402 · 803-723-5148

Ralph M. Mellom · (Hazardous Waste) · Ogletree, Deakins, Nash, Smoak & Stewart · 300 North Main Street · P.O. Box 2757 · Greenville, SC 29602 · 803-271-1300

PERSONAL INJURY LITIGATION

Julian B. Salley, Jr. · Henderson & Salley · 111 Park Avenue, SW · Aiken, SC 29801 · 803-648-4213

Robert H. Hood* · (Defendants) · Hood Law Firm · 172 Meeting Street · P.O. Box 1508 · Charleston, SC 29402 · 803-577-4435

Arthur G. Howe · (Plaintiffs) · Uricchio, Howe & Krell · 171-2 Broad Street · P.O. Box 399 · Charleston, SC 29402 · 803-723-7491

Joseph H. McGee · (Defendants) · Buist, Moore, Smythe & McGee · Five Exchange Street · P.O. Box 999 · Charleston, SC 29402-0999 · 803-722-8375

Morris D. Rosen · Rosen, Rosen & Hagood · 45 Broad Street · P.O. Box 893 · Charleston, SC 29402 · 803-577-6726

Robert B. Wallace* · (Plaintiffs, Medical Malpractice, Products Liability, Automobile Collision) · Wallace and Tinkler · 129 Broad Street · P.O. Box 388 · Charleston, SC 29402 · 803-722-8313

Wilburn Brewer, Jr.* · (Defendants) · Nexsen Pruet Jacobs & Pollard · 1441 Main Street, 15th Floor · P.O. Drawer 2426 · Columbia, SC 29202 · 803-771-8900

Terrell L. Glenn · Glenn, Irvin, Murphy, Gray & Stepp · 1500 Calhoun Street · P.O. Box 1550 · Columbia, SC 29202 · 803-765-1100

Thomas E. McCutchen · Whaley, McCutchen, Blanton & Rhodes · 1414 Lady Street · P.O. Drawer 11209 · Columbia, SC 29211-1209 · 803-799-9791

Haywood E. McDonald · (Defendants) · McDonald, McKenzie, Fuller, Rubin & Miller · 1704 Main Street · P.O. Box 58 · Columbia, SC 29201 · 803-252-0500

Stephen G. Morrison · (Defendants) · Nelson, Mullins, Riley & Scarborough · Keenan Building, Third Floor · 1330 Lady Street · P.O.Box 11070 · Columbia, SC 29211 · 803-799-2000

Edward W. Mullins, Jr. · (Defendants) · Nelson, Mullins, Riley & Scarborough Keenan Building, Third Floor · 1330 Lady Street · P.O. Box 11070 · Columbia, SC 29211 · 803-799-2000

Kenneth M. Suggs · (Plaintiffs) · Suggs & Kelly · 1821 Hampton Street · P.O. Box 8113 · Columbia, SC 29202-8113 · 803-256-7550

Saunders M. Bridges* · Bridges and Orr · Bridges Building · 318 West Palmetto Street · P.O. Box 130 · Florence, SC 29503 · 803-662-1418

J. Kendall Few · (Plaintiffs) · Few & Few · 850 Wade Hampton Boulevard · P.O. Box 10085 Fed. Station · Greenville, SC 29603 · 803-232-6456

Richard J. Foster · (Plaintiffs) · Foster, Covington & Patrick · 117 Manly Street P.O. Box 2146 · Greenville, SC 29602 · 803-232-5662

Fletcher C. Mann* · (Defendants) · Leatherwood, Walker, Todd & Mann · 100 East Coffee Street · P.O. Box 87 · Greenville, SC 29602 · 803-242-6440

William Francis Marion, Sr. · (Defendants) · Haynsworth, Marion, McKay & Guerard · Two Shelter Centre, 11th Floor · 75 Beattie Place · P.O. Box 2048 · Greenville, SC 29602 · 803-240-3200

G. Dewey Oxner, Jr. · (Defendants) · Haynsworth, Marion, McKay & Guerard · Two Shelter Centre, 11th Floor · 75 Beattie Place · P.O. Box 2048 · Greenville, SC 29602 · 803-240-3200

R. Frank Plaxco · (Defendants) · Leatherwood, Walker, Todd & Mann · 100 East Coffee Street · P.O. Box 87 · Greenville, SC 29602 · 803-242-6440

J. D. Todd, Jr.* · Leatherwood, Walker, Todd & Mann · 100 East Coffee Street P.O. Box 87 · Greenville, SC 29602 · 803-242-6440

Wesley M. Walker · (Defendants) · Leatherwood, Walker, Todd & Mann · 100 East Coffee Street · P.O. Box 87 · Greenville, SC 29602 · 803-242-6440

James H. Watson · (Defendants) · Leatherwood, Walker, Todd & Mann · 100 East Coffee Street · P.O. Box 87 · Greenville, SC 29602 · 803-242-6440

Thomas H. Pope, Jr. · (Defendants) · Pope and Hudgens · 1508 College Street P.O. Box 190 · Newberry, SC 29108 · 803-276-2532

William U. Gunn* · (Defendants, Medical Malpractice, Products Liability, Automobile Collision) · Holcombe, Bomar, Wynn, Cothran and Gunn · Spartan Food Systems' Plaza · 203 East Main Street · P.O. Drawer 1897 · Spartanburg, SC 29304 803-585-4273

PUBLIC UTILITY LAW

Leo H. Hill · Hill, Wyatt & Bannister · 100 Williams Street · Greenville, SC 10601 803-242-5133

REAL ESTATE LAW

Susan M. Smythe · Buist, Moore, Smythe & McGee · Five Exchange Street · P.O. Box 999 · Charleston, SC 29402-0999 · 803-722-8375

John H. Warren · Hutchinson & Warren · 171 Church Street, Suite 30 · Charleston, SC 29401 · 803-577-0660

Rudolph C. Barnes, Sr. · Barnes, Alford, Stork & Johnson · 1613 Main Street · P.O. Box 8448 · Columbia, SC 29202 · 803-799-1111

Edward G. Menzie · Nexsen Pruet Jacobs & Pollard · 1441 Main Street, 15th Floor · P.O. Drawer 2426 · Columbia, SC 29202 · 803-771-8900

Ralston B. Vanzant II · Nelson, Mullins, Riley & Scarborough · Keenan Building, Third Floor · 1330 Lady Street · P.O. Box 11070 · Columbia, SC 29211 · 803-799-2000

Larry D. Estridge · Wyche, Burgess, Freeman & Parham · 44 East Camperdown Way · P.O. Box 728 · Greenville, SC 29602 · 803-242-3131

Patrick H. Grayson, Jr. · Bozeman, Grayson, Smith & Price · 300 College Street Greenville, SC 29601 · 803-242-1120

TAX AND EMPLOYEE BENEFITS LAW

Scott Y. Barnes · (Corporate & Partnership Transactions, State Tax, Tax Disputes) · Holmes & Thomson · 100 Broad Street · P.O. Box 858 · Charleston, SC 29402-0858 · 803-723-2000

John C. Von Lehe, Jr. · Young, Clement, Rivers & Tisdale · 28 Broad Street · P.O. Box 993 · Charleston, SC 29402 · 803-577-4000

J. Donald Dial, Jr. · Sinkler & Boyd · The Palmetto Center, Suite 1200 · 1426 Main Street · P.O. Box 11889 · Columbia, SC 29211 · 803-779-3080

Robert M. Nettles, Jr. · (Employee Benefits) · Ewing & Nettles · SCN Bank Building, Suite 601 · 1401 Main Street · Columbia, SC 29201 · 803-765-2424

Robert Young · 1330 Richland Street · P.O. Box 12525 · Columbia, SC 29211 · 803-254-2020

J. Munford Scott, Jr. · Scott & Associates · 1807 Cherokee Road · P.O. Box 6105 Florence, SC 29502 · 803-662-8204

David A. Merline · Merline & Thomas · 665 North Academy Street · P.O. Box 10796 · Greenville, SC 29603 · 803-242-4080

John R. Thomas · (Employee Benefits) · Merline & Thomas · 665 North Academy Street · P.O. Box 10796 · Greenville, SC 29603 · 803-242-4080

Johnnie M. Walters · (Tax Disputes) · Leatherwood Walker Todd & Mann · 100 East Coffee Street · P.O. Box 87 · Greenville, SC 29602 · 803-242-6440

TRUSTS AND ESTATES

Robert M. Kunes · Evans, Carter, Kunes and Grant · 151 Meeting Street, Suite 415 · P.O. Box 369 · Charleston, SC 29402-0369 · 803-577-2300

Robert M. Earle · Nexsen Pruet Jacobs & Pollard · 1441 Main Street, 15th Floor P.O. Drawer 2426 · Columbia, SC 29202 · 803-771-8900

Albert L. Moses · Sherrill & Rogers · 1337 Assembly Street · P.O. Drawer 447 · Columbia, SC 29202 · 803-771-8880

Albert C. Todd III · Todd, Johnson & Weatherly · Standard Federal Savings & Loan Building, Suite 600 · 1136 Washington Street · P.O. Box 11262 · Columbia, SC 29211 · 803-252-1500

David A. Merline · Merline & Thomas · 665 North Academy Street · P.O. Box 10796 · Greenville, SC 29603 · 803-242-4080

Charles M. Stuart, Jr. · 630 East Washington Street, Suite D2 · Greenville, SC 29601 · 803-232-5411

William A. Ruth · Ruth, Clabaugh & Hack · One Sea Pine Circle · P.O. Drawer 5706 · Hilton Head, SC 29938 · 803-785-4251

Robert P. Wilkins · Nelson, Mullins, Riley & Scarborough · 334 Old Chapin Road · P.O. Box 729 · Lexington, SC 29071 · 803-359-9940

James Carlisle Hardin III · (Estate Planning, Estate Administration) · Kennedy Covington Lobdell & Hickman · The Guardian Building, Suite 301 · P.O. Drawer 11429 · Rock Hill, SC 29731-1421 · 803-327-6171

James B. Drennan III* · (Estate Planning, Estate Administration, Charitable Trusts, Estate/Trust Litigation) · Drennan, Shelor, Cole & Evins · 126 Advent Street · P.O. Box 5446 · Spartanburg, SC 29304 · 803-585-5800

SOUTH DAKOTA

BANKRUPTCY LAW

Brent A. Wilbur* · (Creditors' Rights, Bankruptcy Litigation) · May, Adams, Gerdes & Thompson · 503 South Pierre Street · P.O. Box 160 · Pierre, SD 57501-0160 · 605-224-8803

James P. Hurley · (Debtors' Rights) · Bangs, McCullen, Butler, Foye & Simmons · 818 St. Joseph Street · P.O. Box 2760 · Rapid City, SD 57709 · 605-343-1040

J. Bruce Blake · Law Center, Suite 201 · 505 West Ninth Street · Sioux Falls, SD 57104-3698 · 605-336-0948

Roger W. Damgaard · Woods, Fuller, Shultz & Smith · 310 South First Avenue · Sioux Falls, SD 57102 · 605-336-3890

Vance R. C. Goldhammer · Boyce, Murphy, McDowell & Greenfield · 101 North Phillips Avenue, Suite 505 · P.O. Box 5015 · Sioux Falls, SD 57117-5015 · 605-336-2424

Robert E. Hayes · Davenport, Evans, Hurwitz & Smith · National Reserve Building · 513 South Main Avenue · P.O. Box 1030 · Sioux Falls, SD 57101-1030 · 605-336-2880

BUSINESS LITIGATION

Brent A. Wilbur* · (Banking) · May, Adams, Gerdes & Thompson · 503 South Pierre Street · P.O. Box 160 · Pierre, SD 57501-0160 · 605-224-8803

Ronald W. Banks · Banks & Johnson · 3202 West Main Street · Rapid City, SD 57702-2398 · 605-348-7300

Joseph M. Butler · Bangs, McCullen, Butler, Foye & Simmons · 818 St. Joseph Street · P.O. Box 2670 · Rapid City, SD 57709 · 605-343-1040

William G. Taylor, Jr.* · Woods, Fuller, Shultz & Smith · 310 South First Avenue Sioux Falls, SD 57102 · 605-336-3890

CORPORATE LAW

Thomas H. Foye · (Antitrust, Corporate Finance, Mergers & Acquisitions) · Bangs, McCullen, Butler, Foye & Simmons · 818 St. Joseph Street · P.O. Box 2670 · Rapid City, SD 57709 · 605-343-1040

Richard A. Cutler · Davenport, Evans, Hurwitz & Smith · National Reserve Building · 513 South Main Avenue · P.O. Box 1030 · Sioux Falls, SD 57101-1030 605-336-2880

Vance R. C. Goldhammer · Boyce, Murphy, McDowell & Greenfield · 101 North Phillips Avenue, Suite 505 · P.O. Box 5015 · Sioux Falls, SD 57117-5015 · 605-336-2424

David L. Knudson · (Banking, Mergers & Acquisitions) · Davenport, Evans, Hurwitz & Smith · National Reserve Building · 513 South Main Avenue · P.O. Box 1030 · Sioux Falls, SD 57101-1030 · 605-336-2880

Jeremiah D. Murphy · Boyce, Murphy, McDowell & Greenfield · 101 North Phillips Avenue, Suite 505 · P.O. Box 5015 · Sioux Falls, SD 57117-5015 · 605-336-2424

William G. Taylor, Jr.* · Woods, Fuller, Shultz & Smith · 310 South First Avenue Sioux Falls, SD 57102 · 605-336-3890

William G. Taylor, Jr.* · Woods, Fuller, Shultz & Smith · 310 South First Avenue Sioux Falls, SD 57102 · 605-336-3890

CRIMINAL DEFENSE

Charles Rick Johnson · Johnson, Eklund & Abourezk · 405 Main Street · P.O. Box 149 · Gregory, SD 57533 · 605-835-8391

David Gienapp · Arenson, Issenhuth and Gienapp · 205 North Egan Avenue · Madison, SD 57042 · 605-256-9161

Gary C. Colbath* · Banks, Johnson, Johnson, Colbath & Huffman · 3202 West Main Street · P.O. Box 6100 · Rapid City, SD 57709-6100 · 605-348-7300

John E. Fitzgerald, Jr. · Fitzgerald Law Office · 403 National Street · Rapid City, SD 57702 · 605-348-7250

Sidney B. Strange · Strange & Palmer · 226 North Phillips Avenue · Sioux Falls, SD 57102 · 605-339-0780

LABOR AND EMPLOYMENT LAW

Ronald W. Banks · Management · Banks & Johnson · 3202 West Main Street · Rapid City, SD 57702-2398 · 605-348-730

NATURAL RESOURCES AND ENVIRONMENTAL LAW

Donn Bennett · (Oil & Gas, Mining, Hazardous Waste) · Bennett & Main · 618 State Street · Belle Fourche, SD 57717 · 605-892-2011

Max Main · (Oil & Gas, Mining, Water) · Bennett & Main · 618 State Street · Belle Fourche, SD 57717 · 605-892-2011

Marvin D. Truhe · Truhe Law Offices · First Federal Plaza, Fifth Floor · Ninth and St. Joseph Streets · P.O. Box 8106 · Rapid City, SD 57709 · 605-342-2800

PERSONAL INJURY LITIGATION

Charles Rick Johnson · (Plaintiffs) · Johnson, Eklund & Abourezk · 405 Main Street · P.O. Box 149 · Gregory, SD 57533 · 605-835-8391

Ronald W. Banks · Banks & Johnson · 3202 West Main · Rapid City, SD 57702-2398 · 605-348-7300

Joseph M. Butler · Bangs, McCullen, Butler, Foye & Simmons · 818 St. Joseph Street · P.O. Box 2670 · Rapid City, SD 57709 · 605-343-1040

William G. Porter · (Defendants) · Costello, Porter, Hill, Heisterkamp & Bushnell · 200 Security Building · 704 St. Joseph Street · P.O. Box 290 · Rapid City, SD 57709 · 605-343-2410

William F. Day, Jr.* · (Defendants) · Lynn, Jackson, Shultz & Lebrun · 409 South Second Avenue · Sioux Falls, SD 57102 · 605-332-5999

Edwin E. Evans · Davenport, Evans, Hurwitz & Smith · 513 South Main Avenue P.O. Box 1030 · Sioux Falls, SD 57101-1030 · 605-336-2880

Carleton R. Hoy* · (Defendants) · Hoy & Hoy · 401 South Second Avenue · Sioux Falls, SD 57102 · 605-336-2600

Gary J. Pashby* · (Plaintiffs, Defendants, Products Liability, Automobile Collision) · Boyce, Murphy, McDowell & Greenfield · 101 North Phillips Avenue, Suite 505 · P.O. Box 5015 · Sioux Falls, SD 57117-5015 · 605-336-2424

John E. Simko · (Defendants) · Woods, Fuller, Shultz & Smith · 310 South First Avenue · Sioux Falls, SD 57102 · 605-336-3890

Deming Smith* · (Defendants, Medical Malpractice, Products Liability) · Davenport, Evans, Hurwitz & Smith · National Reserve Building · 513 South Main Avenue · P.O. Box 1030 · Sioux Falls, SD 57101-1030 · 605-336-2880

Arlo D. Sommervold · (Plaintiffs, Defendants, Products Liability, Toxic Torts) Woods, Fuller, Shultz & Smith · 310 South First Avenue · Sioux Falls, SD 57102 605-336-3890

Steven M. Johnson* · (Plaintiffs, Products Liability) · Brady, Reade and Johnson 200 West Third Street · P.O. Box 735 · Yankton, SD 57078-0735 · 605-665-7468

PUBLIC UTILITY LAW

Warren W. May · May, Adams, Gerdes & Thompson · 503 South Pierre Street · P.O. Box 160 · Pierre, SD 57501-0160 · 605-224-8803

Thomas Welk · Boyce, Murphy, McDowell & Greenfield · 101 North Phillips Avenue, Suite 505 · P.O. Box 5015 · Sioux Falls, SD 57117-5015 · 605-336-2424

REAL ESTATE LAW

Thomas C. Adam · May, Adams, Gerdes & Thompson · 503 South Pierre Street P.O. Box 160 · Pierre, SD 57501-0160 · 605-224-8803

Thomas H. Foye · (Land Use, Commercial Transactions, Industrial Transactions, Real Estate Taxation) · Bangs, McCullen, Butler, Foye & Simmons · 818 St. Joseph Street · P.O. Box 2670 · Rapid City, SD 57709 · 605-343-1040

Charles L. Riter · Bangs, McCullen, Butler, Foye & Simmons · 818 St. Joseph Street · P.O. Box 2670 · Rapid City, SD 57709 · 605-343-1040

Richard A. Cutler · Davenport, Evans, Hurwitz & Smith · National Reserve Building · 513 South Main Avenue · P.O. Box 1030 · Sioux Falls, SD 57101-1030 605-336-2880

Vance R. C. Goldammer · Boyce, Murphy, McDowell & Greenfield · 101 North Phillips Avenue, Suite 505 · P.O. Box 5015 · Sioux Falls, SD 57117-5015 · 605-336-2424

Russell R. Greenfield · Boyce, Murphy, McDowell & Greenfield · 101 North Phillips Avenue, Suite 505 · P.O. Box 5015 · Sioux Falls, SD 57117-5015 · 605-336-2424

William G. Taylor, Jr.* · Woods, Fuller, Shultz & Smith · 310 South First Avenue Sioux Falls, SD 57102 · 605-336-3890

TAX AND EMPLOYEE BENEFITS LAW

Thomas H. Foye · (Corporate & Partnership Transactions, Employee Benefits, Tax Disputes) · Bangs, McCullen, Butler, Foye & Simmons · 818 St. Joseph Street · P.O. Box 2670 · Rapid City, SD 57709 · 605-343-1040

Charles L. Riter · Bangs, McCullen, Butler, Foye & Simmons · 818 St. Joseph Street · P.O. Box 2670 · Rapid City, SD 57709 · 605-343-1040

Bradley C. Grossenburg · Woods, Fuller, Shultz & Smith · 310 South First Avenue · Sioux Falls, SD 57102 · 605-335-3890

David L. Knudson · Davenport, Evans, Hurwitz & Smith · National Reserve Building · 513 South Main Avenue · P.O. Box 1030 · Sioux Falls, SD 57101-1030 605-336-2880

TRUSTS AND ESTATES

Thomas H. Foye · (Estate Planning, Estate Administration, Charitable Trusts) · Bangs, McCullen, Butler, Foye & Simmons · 818 St. Joseph Street · P.O. Box 2670 · Rapid City, SD 57709 · 605-343-1040

Charles L. Riter · Bangs, McCullen, Butler, Foye & Simmons · 818 St. Joseph Street · P.O. Box 2670 · Rapid City, SD 57709 · 605-343-1040

Merle A. Johnson · Woods, Fuller, Shultz & Smith · 310 South First Avenue · Sioux Falls, SD 57102 · 605-335-3890

Richard Moe · May, Johnson, Dole & Becker · Western Surety Building, Suite 420 · 101 South Phillips Avenue · P.O. Box 1443 · Sioux Falls, SD 57101-1443 · 605-336-2565

Irving A. Hinderaker · Austin, Hinderaker, Hackett & Hopper · 25 First Avenue, SW · P.O. Box 966 · Watertown, SD 57201-0966 · 605-886-5823

TENNESSEE

BANKRUPTCY LAW

Richard C. Kennedy · Kennedy, Fulton & Koontz · 320 North Holtzclaw Avenue Chattanooga, TN 37404 · 615-622-4535

Thomas E. Ray · Patrick, Beard, Richardson & Ray · Market Court, Suite 202 · 537 Market Street · Chattanooga, TN 37402 · 615-756-7117

Glenn C. Stophel · (Business Reorganization) · Stophel & Stophel · Maclellan Building, Third Floor · Chattanooga, TN 37402-1789 · 615-756-2333

Kyle R. Weems · Weems & Beckham · 1810 McCallie Avenue · Chattanooga, TN 37404 · 615-624-1000

John A. Walker, Jr. · Walker & Walker · 715 First American Center · P.O. Box 2774 · Knoxville, TN 37901 · 615-523-0700

John David Blaylock · Udelsohn, Blaylock & Marlow · 44 North Second Street, Suite 700 · Memphis, TN 38103 · 901-527-7613

John R. Dunlap · Humphreys Dunlap & Wellford · First Tennessee Building, Suite 2200 · 165 Madison Avenue · Memphis, TN 38103 · 901-523-8088

Jack F. Marlow · Udelsohn, Blaylock & Marlow · 44 North Second Street, Suite 700 · Memphis, TN 38103 · 901-527-7613

John W. McQuiston* · (Business Reorganization, Bankrutpcy Litigation) · Goodman, Glazer, Greener, Schneider, McQuiston & Kremer · 1500 First Tennessee Bank Building · 165 Madison Avenue · Memphis, TN 38103-0001 · 901-525-4466

John L. Ryder · Apperson, Crump, Duzane & Maxwell · One Commerce Building, Suite 2100 · Memphis, TN 38103 · 901-525-1711

Robert A. Udelsohn · Udelsohn, Blaylock & Marlow · 44 North Second Street, Suite 700 · Memphis, TN 38103 · 901-527-7613

Lawrence R. Ahern III* · (Business Reorganization, Creditors' Rights, Bankruptcy Litigation) · Bass, Berry & Sims · 2700 First American Center · Nashville, TN 37238 · 615-742-6249

John H. Bailey III · Bass, Berry & Sims · 2700 First American Center · Nashville, TN 37238 · 615-742-6200

Rhea G. Bucy · Gullett, Sanford, Robinson & Martin · Metropolitan Federal Building, Third Floor · 230 Fourth Avenue North · P.O. Box 2757 · Nashville, TN 37219-0757 · 615-244-4994

C. Kinian Cosner, Jr. · (Business Reorganization, Bankruptcy Litigation) · Manier, Herod, Hollabaugh & Smith · 2200 One Nashville Place · 150 Fourth Avenue North · Nashville, TN 37219 · 615-244-0030

Craig V. Gabbert, Jr. · (Business Reorganization, Creditors' Rights, Bankruptcy Litigation) · Harwell Martin & Stegall · 172 Second Avenue North · P.O. Box 2960 Nashville, TN 37219-0960 · 615-256-0500

Russell H. Hippe, Jr. · Trabue, Sturdivant & DeWitt · Nashville City Center, 25th Floor · 511 Union Street · Nashville, TN 37219 · 615-244-9270

James R. Kelley · (Business Reorganization, Creditors' Rights, Debtors' Rights) Neal & Harwell · 2000 One Nashville Place · Nashville, TN 37219 · 615-244-1713

Bradley A. MacLean · Farris, Warfield & Kanaday · Third National Financial Center, Suite 1900 · 424 Church Street · Nashville, TN 37219 · 615-244-5200

Marc T. McNamee · Neal & Harwell · 2000 One Nashville Place · Nashville, TN 37219 · 615-244-1713

BUSINESS LITIGATION

Thomas Maxfield Bahner* · Chambliss & Bahner · Tallan Building, Suite 1000 Two Union Square · Chattanooga, TN 37402-2502 · 615-756-3000

George M. Derryberry · Derryberry & Associates · 1110 Market Street, Suite 502 Chattanooga, TN 37402 · 615-267-9777

Charles J. Gearhiser · Gearhiser, Peters & Horton · 320 McCallie Avenue · Chattanooga, TN 37402 · 615-756-5171

Thomas O. Helton · Caldwell, Heggie & Helton · 1800 Republic Centre · 630 Chestnut Street · Chattanooga, TN 37450 · 615-756-2010

Raymond R. Murphy, Jr.* · (Banking, Commercial, Securities) · Miller & Martin Volunteer Building, Suite 1000 · Chattanooga, TN 37402 · 615-756-6600

John R. Seymour · Speed & Taintor · One Republic Centre, Suite 1310 · 633 Chestnut Street · Chattanooga, TN 37450 · 615-266-4655

J. Houston Gordon* · (Banking, Commercial) · Gordon & Forrester · Hotel Lindo Building, Suite 200 · 114 West Liberty Avenue · P.O. Box 865 · Covington, TN 38019 · 901-476-5229

Bernard E. Bernstein* · (Commercial) · Bernstein, Stair & McAdams · First Tennessee Bank Building, Suite 600 · 530 South Gay Street · Knoxville, TN 37902 · 615-546-8030

Robert R. Campbell · Hodges, Doughty & Carson · 617 West Main Avenue · P.O. Box 869 · Knoxville, TN 37902 · 615-546-9611

Donald F. Paine · Paine, Swiney & Tarwater · 500 First Tennessee Bank Building, Suite 880 · 530 South Gay Street · P.O. Box 198 · Knoxville, TN 37901 · 615-525-0880

Don C. Stansberry, Jr.* · (Banking, Commercial, Transportation) · Baker, Worthington, Crossley, Stansberry & Woolf · Bank of East Tennessee Building, 22nd Floor · 900 Gay Street, SW · P.O. Box 1792 · Knoxville, TN 37901 · 615-549-7000

Leo Bearman, Jr. · Heiskell, Donelson, Bearman, Adams, Williams & Kirsch · 165 Madison Avenue, 20th Floor · Memphis, TN 38103 · 901-526-2000

Lucius E. Burch, Jr. · Burch, Porter & Johnson · 130 North Court Avenue · Memphis, TN 38103 · 901-523-2311

James D. Causey · 230 Adams Avenue · Memphis, TN 38103 · 901-526-0206

Ronald Lee Gilman* · Farris, Hancock, Gilman, Branan & Hellen · Morgan Keegan Tower, Suite 1400 · 50 North Front Street · Memphis, TN 38103 · 901-576-8200

Frank J. Glankler, Jr. · Glankler, Brown, Gilliland, Chase, Robinson & Raines One Commerce Square, Suite 1700 · Memphis, TN 38103 · 901-525-1322

Thomas F. Johnston* · Armstrong Allen Prewitt Gentry Johnston & Holmes · 1900 One Commerce Square · Memphis, TN 38103-2568 · 901-523-8211

James W. McDonnell, Jr. · McDonnell & Boyd · 67 Madison Avenue, 12th Floor Memphis, TN 38103 · 901-521-1111

Joel H. Porter* · Burch, Porter & Johnson · 130 North Court Avenue · Memphis, TN 38103 · 901-523-2311

Thomas R. Prewitt, Sr. · Armstrong Allen Prewitt Gentry Johnston & Holmes · 1900 One Commerce Square · Memphis, TN 38103-2568 · 901-523-8211

Ames Davis* · (Securities) · Waller Lansden Dortch & Davis · 2100 One Commerce Place · Nashville, TN 37239 · 615-244-6380

Ward DeWitt, Jr. · Trabue, Sturdivant & DeWitt · Nashville City Center, 25th Floor · 511 Union Street · Nashville, TN 37219 · 615-244-9270

Frank C. Gorrell · Bass, Berry & Sims · 2700 First American Center · Nashville, TN 37238 · 615-742-6200

Thomas P. Kanaday, Jr.* · (Banking, Commercial) · Farris, Warfield & Kanaday Third National Financial Center, Suite 1900 · 424 Church Street · Nashville, TN 37219 · 615-244-5200

Thomas H. Peebles III · Trabue, Sturdivant & DeWitt · Nashville City Center, 25th Floor · 511 Union Street · Nashville, TN 37219 · 615-244-9270

Wilson Sims* · Bass, Berry & Sims · 2700 First American Center · Nashville, TN 37238 · 615-742-6200

Robert J. Walker* · (Antitrust, Commercial, Securities) · Bass, Berry & Sims · 2700 First American Center · Nashville, TN 37238 · 615-742-6200

William R. Willis, Jr. · Willis & Knight · 215 Second Avenue North · Nashville, TN 37201 · 615-259-9600

CORPORATE LAW

J. Guy Beatty, Jr. · Miller & Martin · Volunteer Building, Suite 1000 · Chattanooga, TN 37402 · 615-756-6600

Thomas A. Caldwell · Caldwell, Heggie & Helton · 1800 Republic Centre · 630 Chestnut Street · Chattanooga, TN 37450 · 615-756-2010

Joel W. Richardson, Jr. · Miller & Martin · Volunteer Building, Suite 1000 · Chattanooga, TN 37402 · 615-756-6600

John C. Stophel · Stophel & Stophel · Maclellan Building, Third Floor · Chattanooga, TN 37402-1789 · 615-756-2333

Robert Kirk Walker · Strang, Fletcher, Carriger, Walker, Hodge & Smith · 400 Krystal Building · One Union Square · Chattanooga, TN 37402 · 615-265-2000

Robert L. Crossley* · Baker, Worthington, Crossley, Stansberry & Woolf · Bank of East Tennessee Building, 22nd Floor · 900 Gay Street, SW · P.O. Box 1792 · Knoxville, TN 37901 · 615-549-7000

E. Bruce Foster, Jr. · Bass, Berry & Sims · Riverview Tower, Suite 1700 · 900 South Gay Street · P.O. Box 1509 · Knoxville, TN 37901-1509 · 615-521-6200

Jackson C. Kramer · Kramer, Rayson, Leake, Rogers & Morgan · Plaza Tower, Suite 2500 · P.O. Box 629 · Knoxville, TN 37901-0629 · 615-525-5134

Herbert S. Sanger, Jr. · Wagner, Myers & Sanger · 1801 Plaza Tower · P.O. Box 1308 · Knoxville, TN 37901-1308 · 615-525-4600

Arthur G. Seymour · Frantz, McConnell & Seymour · 500 Sovran Center · 550 West Main Avenue · P.O. Box 39 · Knoxville, TN 37901 · 615-546-9321

Robert F. Worthington, Jr.* · Baker, Worthington, Crossley, Stansberry & Woolf · Bank of East Tennessee Building, 22nd Floor · 900 Gay Street, SW · P.O. Box 1792 · Knoxville, TN 37901 · 615-549-7000

Richard H. Allen · Armstrong Allen Prewitt Gentry Johnston & Holmes · 1900 One Commerce Square · Memphis, TN 38103-2568 · 901-523-8211

Robert Grattan Brown, Jr. · Glankler, Brown, Gilliland, Chase, Robinson & Raines · One Commerce Square, Suite 1700 · Memphis, TN 38103 · 901-525-1322

Samuel D. Chafetz · (Corporate Finance, Securities, Securities Regulation) · Waring Cox · Morgan Keegan Tower, Suite 1300 · 50 North Front Street · Memphis, TN 38103 · 901-543-8000

Robert L. Cox · Waring Cox · Morgan Keegan Tower, Suite 1300 · 50 North Front Street · Memphis, TN 38103 · 901-543-8000

Lewis R. Donelson III · Heiskell, Donelson, Bearman, Adams, Williams & Kirsch 165 Madison Avenue, 20th Floor · Memphis, TN 38103 · 901-526-2000

Ronald Lee Gilman* · Farris, Hancock, Gilman, Branan & Hellen · Morgan Keegan Tower, Suite 1400 · 50 North Front Street · Memphis, TN 38103 · 901-576-8200

Charles Forrest Newman* · Burch, Porter & Johnson · 130 North Court Avenue Memphis, TN 38103 · 901-523-2311

S. Shepherd Tate · Martin, Tate, Morrow & Marston · 6060 Poplar Avenue, Suite 295 · Memphis, TN 38119-3901 · 901-763-4800

Charles T. Tuggle, Jr. · Heiskell, Donelson, Bearman, Adams, Williams & Kirsch 165 Madison Avenue, 20th Floor · Memphis, TN 38103 · 901-526-2000

Alfred T. Adams, Jr. · (Administrative) · Adams, Taylor, Philbin, Pigue and Marchetti · One Union Street · P.O. Box 198169 · Nashville, TN 37219-8169 · 615-244-5361

J. O. Bass, Jr. · Bass, Berry & Sims · 2700 First American Center · Nashville, TN 37238 · 615-742-6200

James H. Cheek III · Bass, Berry & Sims · 2700 First American Center · Nashville, TN 37238 · 615-742-6200

Thomas P. Kanaday, Jr.* · (Banking, Financial Institutions) · Farris, Warfield & Kanaday · Third National Financial Center, Suite 1900 · 424 Church Street · Nashville, TN 37219 · 615-244-5200

James T. O'Hare · O'Hare, Sherrard & Roe · 424 Church Street, Suite 2000 · Nashville, TN 37219 · 615-742-4200

T. G. Pappas · Bass, Berry & Sims · 2700 First American Center · Nashville, TN 37238 · 615-742-6200

Thomas J. Sherrard III · O'Hare, Sherrard & Roe · 424 Church Street, Suite 2000 Nashville, TN 37219 · 615-742-4200

Wilson Sims* · Bass, Berry & Sims · 2700 First American Center · Nashville, TN 37238 · 615-742-6200

Robert D. Tuke · (Corporate Finance, International Trade, Mergers & Acquisitions) · Farris, Warfield & Kanaday · Third National Financial Center, Suite 1900 424 Church Street · Nashville, TN 37219 · 615-244-5200

CRIMINAL DEFENSE

Leroy Phillips, Jr. · Phillips & Caputo · 312 Vine Street · Chattanooga, TN 37402 615-266-1211

Jerry H. Summers* · Summers, McCrea & Wyatt · 500 Lindsay Street · Chattanooga, TN 37402-1490 · 615-265-2385

Jerry C. Colley · Colley and Colley · 710 North Main Street · P.O. Box 1476 · Columbia, TN 38402-1476 · 615-388-8564

Charles W. B. Fels* · Ritchie, Fels & Dillard · Main Place, Suite 300 · 606 West Main Avenue · P.O. Box 1126 · Knoxville, TN 37901-1126 · 615-637-0661

Robert W. Ritchie* · Ritchie, Fels & Dillard · Main Place, Suite 300 · 606 West Main Avenue · P.O. Box 1126 · Knoxville, TN 37901-1126 · 615-637-0661

James D. Causey · 230 Adams Avenue · Memphis, TN 38103 · 901-526-0206

Hal Gerber · Gerber Law Offices · 800 Monroe Avenue, Suite 410 · Memphis, TN 38103 · 901-523-0019

Frank J. Glankler, Jr. · Glankler, Brown, Gilliland, Chase, Robinson & Raines One Commerce Square, Suite 1700 · Memphis, TN 38103 · 901-525-1322

J. N. Raines · (Federal Court, Non-Violent Crime) · Glankler, Brown, Gilliland, Chase, Robinson & Raines · One Commerce Square, Suite 1700 · Memphis, TN 38103 · 901-525-1322

Lionel R. Barrett, Jr.* · Washington Square Two, Suite 417 · 222 Second Avenue North · Nashville, TN 37201 · 615-254-1471

Joe P. Binkley, Sr. · 174 Third Avenue North · Nashville, TN 37201 · 615-244-8630

Cecil D. Branstetter* · (Federal Court, State Court, Environmental Crimes) · Branstetter, Kilgore, Stranch & Jennings · 200 Church Street, Fourth Floor · Nashville, TN 37201 · 615-254-8801

E. E. Edwards III · Edwards & Simmons · 1707 Division Street, Suite 100 · Nashville, TN 37203 · 615-254-3334

Aubrey B. Harwell, Jr.* · (Non-Violent Crimes, Federal Court, Environmental Crimes, White Collar Crimes) · Neal & Harwell · 2000 One Nashville Place · 150 Fourth Avenue North · Nashville, TN 37219-2417 · 615-244-1713

John J. Hollins · Hollins, Wagster & Yarbrough · Third National Bank Building, Eighth Floor · Nashville, TN 37219 · 615-256-6666

Alfred H. Knight · Willis & Knight · 215 Second Avenue North · Nashville, TN 37201 · 615-259-9600

James F. Neal · Neal & Harwell · 2000 One Nashville Place · 150 Fourth Avenue North · Nashville, TN 37219-2417 · 615-244-1713

Charles R. Ray · Ray & Housch · 211 Third Avenue North · Nashville, TN 37201 615-256-2111

James F. Sanders · Neal & Harwell · 2000 One Nashville Place · 150 Fourth Avenue North · Nashville, TN 37219-2417 · 615-244-1713

Edward M. Yarbrough* · (Violent Crimes, Non-Violent Crimes, Federal Court, State Court) · Hollins, Wagster & Yarbrough · Third National Bank Building, Eighth Floor · Nashville, TN 37219 · 615-256-6666

W. Gordon Ball* · (Violent Crimes, Non-Violent Crimes, Federal Court, Environmental Crimes) · Ball & Dunn · Sovran Center, Suite 750 · 550 Main Avenue Newport, TN 37902 · 615-525-7028

FAMILY LAW

Michael Ross Campbell · Campbell & Campbell · 1200 James Building · 735 Broad Street · Chattanooga, TN 37402 · 615-266-1108

William H. Horton · Gearhiser, Peters & Horton · 320 McCallie Avenue · Chattanooga, TN 37402 · 615-756-5171

James C. Lee* · (Divorce, Marital Settlement Agreements, Equitable Division) · 1200 James Building · 735 Broad Street · Chattanooga, TN 37402-1835 · 615-266-1108

James D. Causey · 230 Adams Avenue · Memphis, TN 38103 · 901-526-0206

David E. Caywood · Picard & Caywood · 200 Jefferson, Suite 750 · Memphis, TN 38103 · 901-527-3561

James S. Cox · James S. Cox & Associates · 60 North Third Street · Memphis, TN 38103 · 901-575-2040

Joe M. Duncan · Burch, Porter & Johnson · 130 North Court Avenue · Memphis, TN 38103 · 901-523-2311

Hal Gerber · Gerber Law Offices · 800 Monroe Avenue, Suite 410 · Memphis, TN 38103 · 901-523-0019

Jack A. Butler* · (Divorce) · Butler & Phillips · First American Center, Suite 2395 315 Deaderick Street · Nashville, TN 37238-2395 · 615-244-3300

Lew Conner* · (Child Custody, Divorce, Child Abuse) · Boult, Cummings, Conner & Berry · 222 Third Avenue North · P.O. Box 188062 · Nashville, TN 37219 · 615-144-2582

Maclin P. Davis, Jr.* · (Divorce) · Heiskell, Donelson, Bearman, Adams, Williams & Kirsch · Nashville City Central, Suite 600 · 511 Union Street · Nashville, TN 37219 · 615-256-0815

John J. Hollins · Hollins, Wagster & Yarbrough · Third National Bank Building, Eighth Floor · Nashville, TN 37219 · 615-256-6666

Robert L. Jackson · Robert L. Jackson & Associates · One Washington Square, Suite 103 · 214 Second Avenue North · Nashville, TN 37201 · 615-256-2602

James G. Martin III · Farris, Warfield & Kanaday · Third National Financial Center, Suite 1900 · 424 Church Street · Nashville, TN 37219 · 615-244-5200

Jack Norman, Jr. · 213 Third Avenue North · Nashville, TN 37201 · 615-254-0656

Charles H. Warfield · Farris, Warfield & Kanaday · Third National Financial Center, Suite 1900 · 424 Church Street · Nashville, TN 37219 · 615-244-5200

FIRST AMENDMENT LAW

Richard L. Hollow · McCampbell & Young · 800 South Gay Street · P.O. Box 550 Knoxville, TN 37901-0550 · 615-637-1440

S. Russell Headrick · Armstrong Allen Prewitt Gentry Johnston & Holmes · 1900 One Commerce Square · Memphis, TN 38103-2568 · 901-523-8211

Charles Forrest Newman* · Burch, Porter & Johnson · 130 North Court Avenue Memphis, TN 38103 · 901-523-2311

Alfred H. Knight · Willis & Knight · 215 Second Avenue North · Nashville, TN 37201 · 615-259-9600

William R. Willis, Jr. · Willis & Knight · 215 Second Avenue North · Nashville, TN 37201 · 615-259-9600

HEALTH CARE LAW

William P. Aiken · Chambliss & Bahner · Tallan Building, Suite 1000 · Two Union Square · Chattanooga, TN 37402-2502 · 615-756-3000

Howard I. Levine · Miller & Martin · Volunteer Building, Suite 1000 · Chattanooga, TN 37402 · 615-756-6600

Fred H. Moore · Spears, Moore, Rebman & Williams · Blue Cross Building, Eighth Floor · 801 Pine Street · P.O. Box 1749 · Chattanooga, TN 37401-1749 · 615-756-5020

William T. Gamble · Wilson Worley Gamble & Ward · 110 East Center Street · P.O. Box 1007 · Kingsport, TN 37662 · 615-246-8181

Douglas S. Tweed · Hunter, Smith & Davis · Law Center · 1212 North Eastman Road · P.O. Box 3740 · Kingsport, TN 37664 · 615-378-8814

Foster D. Arnett · Arnett, Draper & Hagood · Plaza Tower, Suite 2300 · Knoxville, TN 37929-2300 · 615-546-7000

Lee J. Chase III · Glankler, Brown, Gilliland, Chase, Robinson & Raines · One Commerce Square, Suite 1700 · Memphis, TN 38103 · 901-525-1322

Gavin M. Gentry · Armstrong Allen Prewitt Gentry Johnston & Holmes · 1900 One Commerce Square · Memphis, TN 38103-2568 · 901-523-8211

Robert L. Green · Neely, Green, Fargarson & Brooke · 65 Union Avenue, Ninth Floor · Memphis, TN 38103 · 901-523-2500

Thomas R. Prewitt, Jr. · Armstrong Allen Prewitt Gentry Johnston & Holmes · 1900 One Commerce Square · Memphis, TN 38103-2568 · 901-523-8211

Max Shelton · Harris, Shelton, Dunlap & Cobb · 1900 One Commerce Square · One Commerce Square, Suite 2700 · Memphis, TN 38103 · 901-525-1455

H. Lee Barfield II · Bass, Berry & Sims · 2700 First American Center · Nashville, TN 37238 · 615-742-6200

George W. Bishop III · Waller Lansden Dortch & Davis · 2100 One Commerce Place · Nashville, TN 37239 · 615-244-6380

Frank Grace, Jr. · Willis & Knight · 215 Second Avenue North · Nashville, TN 37201 · 615-259-9600

William E. Martin · Harwell, Martin & Stegall · 172 Second Avenue North · P.O. Box 2960 · Nashville, TN 37219 · 615-256-0500

Mary M. Schaffner · Howell, Fisher & Branham · 300 James Robertson Parkway Nashville, TN 37201 · 615-244-3370

John R. Voigt · O'Hare, Sherrard & Roe · 424 Church Street, Suite 200 · Nashville, TN 37219 · 615-742-4200

Howard T. Wall III · Waller Lansden Dortch & Davis · 2100 One Commerce Place · Nashville, TN 37239 · 615-244-6380

William R. Willis, Jr. · Willis & Knight · 215 Second Avenue North · Nashville, TN 37201 · 615-259-9600

Charles K. Wray · Bass, Berry & Sims · 2700 First American Center · Nashville, TN 37238 · 615-742-6200

INTELLECTUAL PROPERTY LAW

John R. Walker III · Walker & McKenzie · 6363 Poplar Avenue, Suite 434 · Memphis, TN 38119 · 901-685-7428

LABOR AND EMPLOYMENT LAW

Harry F. Burnette · (Individuals) · Brown, Dobson, Burnette & Kesler · 713 Cherry Street · Chattanooga, TN 37402 · 615-266-2121

Hal F. S. Clements* · (Management, Employment) · Miller & Martin · Volunteer Building, Suite 1000 · Chattanooga, TN 37402 · 615-756-6600

Ronald G. Ingham · (Management) · Miller & Martin · Volunteer Building, Suite 1000 · Chattanooga, TN 37402 · 615-756-6000

Frank P. Pinchak · (Management) · Hutcheson, Moseley, Pinchak, Powers & Disheroon · One Central Plaza, Suite 600 · Chattanooga, TN 37402 · 615-756-5600

Edwin O. Norris* · (Management) · Hunter, Smith & Davis · Law Center · 1212 North Eastman Road · P.O. Box 3740 · Kingsport, TN 37664 · 615-378-8814

Lewis R. Hagood · Arnett, Draper and Hagood · Plaza Tower, Suite 2300 · Knoxville, TN 37929-2300 · 615-546-7000

E. H. Rayson · (Management) · Kramer, Rayson, Leake, Rogers & Morgan · Plaza Tower, Suite 2500 · P.O. Box 629 · Knoxville, TN 37901 · 615-525-5134

John B. Rayson · (Management) · Kramer, Rayson, Leake, Rogers & Morgan · Plaza Tower, Suite 2500 · P.O. Box 629 · Knoxville, TN 37901 · 615-525-5134

Lynn A. Agee · (Labor) · Agee, Allen, Godwin, Morris & Laurenzi · 263 Court Avenue, Second Floor · Memphis, TN 38103 · 901-528-1702

Allen S. Blair · (Labor) · Hanover, Walsh, Jalenak & Blair · Falls Building, Fifth Floor · 22 North Front Street · Memphis, TN 38103 · 901-526-0621

Donald A. Donati · (Individuals) · Donati & Associates · 629 Poplar Avenue · Memphis, TN 38105-4509 · 901-521-0570

Fletcher L. Hudson · (Management) · McKnight, Hudson, Lewis, Henderson & Clark · 1709 Kirby Parkway · P.O. Box 171375 · Memphis, TN 38187-1375 · 901-756-1550

Frederick J. Lewis* · (Management) · McKnight, Hudson, Lewis, Henderson & Clark · 1709 Kirby Parkway · P.O. Box 171375 · Memphis, TN 38187-1375 · 901-756-1550

Dan M. Norwood · (Labor, Individuals) · The Norwood Law Firm · 5400 Poplar Avenue, Suite 300 · Memphis, TN 38119 · 901-682-0066

Arnold E. Perl · (Management) · Young & Perl · One Commerce Square, Suite 2380 · Memphis, TN 38103 · 901-525-2761

Stephen L. Shields · (Management) · Jackson, Shields, Yeiser & Cantrell · 8001 Center View Parkway, Suite 100 · Memphis, TN 38018 · 901-754-8001

Samuel J. Weintraub · (Management) · Weintraub, Robinson, Weintraub & Stock · One Commerce Square, Suite 2560 · Memphis, TN 38103 · 901-526-0431

Robert L. Ballow · (Management) · King & Ballow · 1200 Noel Place · 200 Fourth Avenue North · Nashville, TN 37219 · 615-259-3456

George E. Barrett* · (Labor) · Barrett, Johnston & Parsley · 217 Second Avenue North · Nashville, TN 37201-1697 · 615-244-2202

Cecil D. Branstetter* · (Labor) · Branstetter, Kilgore, Stranch & Jennings · 200 Church Street, Fourth Floor · Nashville, TN 37201 · 615-254-8801

Joseph Martin, Jr. · (Management) · Gullett, Sanford, Robinson & Martin · Metropolitan Federal Building, Third Floor · 230 Fourth Avenue North · P.O. Box 2757 · Nashville, TN 37219-0757 · 615-244-4994

Russell F. Morris, Jr. · (Management) · Bass, Berry & Sims · 2700 First American Center · Nashville, TN 37238 · 615-742-6200

William N. Ozier* · (Management) · Bass, Berry & Sims · 2700 First American Center · Nashville, TN 37238 · 615-742-6200

James G. Stranch III* · (Labor, Individuals) · Branstetter, Kilgore, Stranch & Jennings · 200 Church Street, Fourth Floor · Nashville, TN 37201 · 615-254-8801

Charles Hampton White · (Management) · Cornelius & Collins · Third National Financial Center, 29th Floor · P.O. Box 2808 · Nashville, TN 37219 · 615-244-1440

NATURAL RESOURCES AND ENVIRONMENTAL LAW

James Gentry, Jr.* · (Water, Air, Hazardous Waste, Toxic Torts) · Spears, Moore, Rebman & Williams · Blue Cross Building, Eighth Floor · 801 Pine Street P.O. Box 1749 · Chattanooga, TN 37401-1749 · 615-756-5020

Oscar C. Carr III* · Glankler, Brown, Gilliland, Chase, Robinson & Raines · One Commerce Square, Suite 1700 · Memphis, TN 38103 · 901-525-1322

Charles Forrest Newman* · (Hazardous Waste, Environmental) · Burch, Porter & Johnson · 130 North Court Avenue · Memphis, TN 38103 · 901-523-2311

J. Andrew Goddard · Bass, Berry & Sims · 2700 First American Center · Nashville, TN 37238 · 615-742-6200

PERSONAL INJURY LITIGATION

Michael R. Campbell · (Defendants) · Campbell & Campbell · 1200 James Building · 735 Broad Street · Chattanooga, TN 37402-1835 · 615-266-1108

Charles J. Gearhiser · Gearhiser, Peters & Horton · 320 McCallie Avenue · Chattanooga, TN 37402 · 615-756-5171

Paul R. Leitner · (Defendants) · Leitner, Warner, Moffitt, Williams, Dooley, Carpenter & Napolitan · Pioneer Building, Third Floor · Chattanooga, TN 37402 615-265-0214

Ray H. Moseley · (Defendants) · Hutcheson, Moseley, Pinchak, Powers & Disheroon · One Central Plaza, Suite 600 · Chattanooga, TN 37402 · 615-756-5600

Thomas H. O'Neal · (Plaintiffs) · O'Neal & Walker · 808 Maclellan Building · 721 Broad Street · Chattanooga, TN 37402 · 615-756-5111

Jerry H. Summers* · (Plaintiffs) · Summers, McCrea & Wyatt · 500 Lindsay Street · Chattanooga, TN 37402-1490 · 615-265-2385

J. Houston Gordon* · (Plaintiffs, Medical Malpractice) · Gordon & Forrester · Hotel Lindo Building, Suite 200 · 114 West Liberty Avenue · P.O. Box 865 · Covington, TN 38019 · 901-476-5229

Robert R. Campbell* · (Defendants, Products Liability) · Hodges, Doughty & Carson · 617 West Main Avenue · P.O. Box 869 · Knoxville, TN 37902 · 615-546-9611

Sidney W. Gilreath* · (Plaintiffs, Medical Malpractice, Products Liability, Automobile Collision) · Gilreath & Associates · 550 Main Avenue, Suite 600 · P.O. Box 1270 · Knoxville, TN 37901-1270 · 615-637-2442

Donald F. Paine · Paine, Swiney & Tarwater · 500 First Tennessee Bank Building, Suite 880 · 530 South Gay Street · P.O. Box 198 · Knoxville, TN 37901 · 615-525-0880

Don C. Stansberry, Jr.* · (Defendants, Products Liability) · Baker, Worthington, Crossley, Stansberry & Woolf · Bank of East Tennessee Building, 22nd Floor · 900 Gay Street, SW · P.O. Box 1792 · Knoxville, TN 37901 · 615-549-7000

Louis C. Woolf · (Defendants) · Baker, Worthington, Crossley, Stansberry & Woolf · Bank of East Tennessee Building, 22nd Floor · 900 Gay Street, SW · P.O. Box 1792 · Knoxville, TN 37901 · 615-549-7000

Leo Bearman, Jr. · (Defendants) · Heiskell, Donelson, Bearman, Adams, Williams & Kirsch · 165 Madison Avenue, 20th Floor · Memphis, TN 38103 · 901-526-2000

Lucius E. Burch, Jr. · Burch, Porter & Johnson · 130 North Court Avenue · Memphis, TN 38103 · 901-523-2311

James D. Causey · (Defendants) · 230 Adams Avenue · Memphis, TN 38103 · 901-526-0206

James S. Cox · (Plaintiffs) · James S. Cox & Associates · 60 North Third Street Memphis, TN 38103 · 901-575-2040

Frank J. Glankler, Jr. · Glankler, Brown, Gilliland, Chase, Robinson & Raines One Commerce Square, Suite 1700 · Memphis, TN 38103 · 901-525-1322

Albert C. Harvey · Thomason, Hendrix, Harvey, Johnson, Mitchell, Blanchard & Adams · First American Bank Building, Ninth Floor · 44 North Second · Memphis, TN 38103 · 901-525-8721

Thomas R. Prewitt, Sr. · Armstrong Allen Prewitt Gentry Johnston & Holmes · 1900 One Commerce Square · Memphis, TN 38103-2568 · 901-523-8211

Joe D. Spicer* · (Defendants) · Spicer, Ridolphi, Flynn & Rudstrom · 200 Claridge House · 1109 North Mid-America Mall · Memphis, TN 38103-5072 · 901-523-1333

John J. Thomason* · (Defendants) · Thomason, Hendrix, Harvey, Johnson, Mitchell, Blanchard & Adams · First American Bank Building, Ninth Floor · 44 North Second · Memphis, TN 38103 · 901-525-8721

Cecil D. Branstetter* · (Plaintiffs, Medical Malpractice, Products Liability, Automobile Collision) · Branstetter, Kilgore, Stranch & Jennings · 200 Church Street, Fourth Floor · Nashville, TN 37201 · 615-254-8801

Jack A. Butler* · (Plaintiffs) · Butler & Phillips · First American Center, Suite 2395 · 315 Deaderick Street · Nashville, TN 37238-2395 · 615-244-3300

John T. Conners, Jr. · (Plaintiffs) · Boult, Cummings, Conners & Berry · 222 Third Avenue North · P.O. Box 198062 · Nashville, TN 37219 · 615-244-2582

Ward DeWitt, Jr. · (Defendants) · Trabue, Sturdivant & DeWitt · Nashville City Center, 25th Floor · 511 Union Street · Nashville, TN 37219 · 615-244-9270

Douglas M. Fisher* · (Defendants) · Howell, Fisher & Branham · Court Square Building · 300 James Robertson Parkway · Nashville, TN 37201-1107 · 615-244-3370

Clarence J. Gideon, Jr. · North & Gideon · One Commerce Place, Suite 1450 · Nashville, TN 37239 · 615-254-0400

James F. Neal · (Plaintiffs) · Neal & Harwell · 2000 One Nashville Place · 150 Fourth Avenue North · Nashville, TN 37219-2417 · 615-244-1713

Thomas H. Peebles III · Trabue, Sturdivant & DeWitt · Nashville City Center, 25th Floor · 511 Union Street · Nashville, TN 37219 · 615-244-9270

Robert J. Walker* · (Plaintiffs, Products Liability, Airplane Collision) · Bass, Berry & Sims · 2700 First American Center · Nashville, TN 37238 · 615-742-6200

William R. Willis, Jr. · Willis & Knight · 215 Second Avenue North · Nashville, TN 37201 · 615-259-9600

REAL ESTATE LAW

Richard D. Crotteau · Miller & Martin · Volunteer Building, Suite 1000 · Chattanooga, TN 37402 · 615-756-6600

James M. Haley IV · Miller & Martin · Volunteer Building, Suite 1000 · Chattanooga, TN 37402 · 615-756-6600

G. Richard Hostetter · Whitfield Mills Ragland & Hostetter · Warehouse Row · 1110 Market Street, Suite 505 · P.O. Box 150 · Chattanooga, TN 37401 · 615-265-7461

C. Thomas Cates · Burch, Porter & Johnson · 6060 Poplar Avenue, Suite 411 · Memphis, TN 38119 · 901-763-1221

W. Emmett Marston · Martin, Tate, Morrow & Marston · 6060 Poplar Avenue, Suite 295 · Memphis, TN 38119-3901 · 901-763-4800

Wm. Rowlett Scott · (Commercial Transactions) · Armstrong Allen Prewitt Gentry Johnston & Holmes · 1900 One Commerce Square · Memphis, TN 38103-2568 901-523-8211

David G. Williams · Heiskell, Donelson, Bearman, Adams, Williams & Kirsch · 165 Madison Avenue, 20th Floor · Memphis, TN 38103 · 901-526-2000

Alfred E. Abbey · Trabue, Sturdivant & DeWitt · Nashville City Center, 25th Floor · 511 Union Street · Nashville, TN 37219 · 615-244-9270

Joseph N. Barker · Dearborn & Ewing · One Commerce Place, Suite 1200 · Nashville, TN 37239 · 615-259-3560

E. Warner Bass · Bass, Berry & Sims · 2700 First American Center · Nashville, TN 37238 · 615-742-6200

James I. Vance Berry · Boult, Cummings, Conners & Berry · 222 Third Avenue North · P.O. Box 198062 · Nashville, TN 37219 · 615-244-2582

Robert P. Thomas · Boult, Cummings, Conners & Berry · 222 Third Avenue North · P.O. Box 198062 · Nashville, TN 37219 · 615-244-2582

Charles K. Wray · Bass, Berry & Sims · 2700 First American Center · Nashville, TN 37238 · 615-742-6200

TAX AND EMPLOYEE BENEFITS LAW

Thomas A Caldwell · Caldwell, Heggie & Helton · 1800 Republic Centre · 630 Chestnut Street · Chattanooga, TN 37450 · 615-756-2010

Wallace M. Davies · (Employee Benefits) · 811 Chestnut Street · Chattanooga, TN 37402 · 615-756-7533

Albert W. Secor · Hogshead Building, Suite Eight · 600 Georgia Avenue · Chattanooga, TN 37402 · 615-265-3433

Glenn C. Stophel · (Corporate & Partnership Transactions) · Stophel & Stophel Maclellan Building, Third Floor · Chattanooga, TN 37402-1789 · 615-756-2333

John C. Stophel · Stophel & Stophel · Maclellan Building, Third Floor · Chattanooga, TN 37402-1789 · 615-756-2333

William L. Taylor · (Corporate & Partnership Transactions, Employee Benefits) Spears, Moore, Rebman & Williams · Blue Cross Building, Eighth Floor · 801 Pine Street · P.O. Box 1749 · Chattanooga, TN 37402-1749 · 615-756-7000

Mack A. Gentry · Gentry, Tipton, Kaizer & Little · 2610 Plaza Tower · Knoxville, TN 37901 · 615-524-0313

Robert S. Marquis · (Tax, Employee Benefits) · McCampbell & Young · 2021 Plaza Tower · P.O. Box 550 · Knoxville, TN 37901-0550 · 615-637-1440

William C. Myers, Jr. · Wagner, Myers & Sanger · 1801 Plaza Tower · P.O. Box 1308 · Knoxville, TN 37901-1308 · 615-525-4600

William P. Kenworthy · (Employee Benefits) · Heiskell, Donelson, Bearman, Adams, Williams & Kirsch · 165 Madison Avenue, 20th Floor · Memphis, TN 38103 · 901-526-2000

William H. Lawson, Jr. · Bogatin, Lawson & Chiapella · 245 Wagner Place, Suite 280 · Memphis, TN 38103 · 901-522-1234

B. Percy Magness · (Employee Benefits) · Thomason, Hendrix, Harvey, Johnson, Mitchell, Blanchard & Adams · First American Bank Building, Ninth Floor · 44 North Second Street · Memphis, TN 38103 · 901-525-8721

Shellie G. McCain, Jr. · Waring Cox · Morgan Keegan Tower, Suite 1300 · 50 North Front Street · Memphis, TN 38103 · 901-543-8000

R. Michael Potter · Burch, Porter & Johnson · 130 North Court Avenue · Memphis, TN 38103 · 901-523-2311

Michael A. Robinson · (Corporate & Partnership Transactions, State Tax, Tax Disputes) · Glankler, Brown, Gilliland, Chase, Robinson & Raines · One Commerce Square, Suite 1700 · Memphis, TN 38103 · 901-525-1322

Clayton D. Smith · Waring Cox · Morgan Keegan Tower, Suite 1300 · 50 North Front Street · Memphis, TN 38103 · 901-543-8000

James W. Berry, Jr. · (Employee Benefits) · Bass, Berry & Sims · 2700 First American Center · Nashville, TN 37238 · 615-742-6200

W. W. Berry · (Tax Disputes) · Bass, Berry & Sims · 2700 First American Center Nashville, TN 37238 · 615-742-6200

James C. Gooch · Bass, Berry & Sims · 2700 First American Center · Nashville, TN 37238 · 615-742-6200

H. Wynne James III · (Corporate & Partnership Transactions, State Tax, Tax Disputes) · Heiskell, Donelson, Bearman, Adams, Williams & Kirsch · Nashville City Central, Suite 600 · 511 Union Street · Nashville, TN 37219 · 615-256-0815

Michel G. Kaplan · Boult, Cummings, Conners & Berry · 222 Third Avenue North · P.O. Box 198062 · Nashville, TN 37219 · 615-244-2582

James D. Leckrone · Manier, Herod, Hollabaugh & Smith · 2200 One Nashville Place · 150 Fourth Avenue North · Nashville, TN 37219 · 615-742-9311

H. Stennis Little, Jr. · Blackburn, Little, Smith & Slobey · 1275 First American Center · 315 Deaderick Street · Nashville, TN 37238 · 615-254-7770

James T. O'Hare · O'Hare, Sherrard & Roe · 424 Church Street, Suite 2000 · Nashville, TN 37219 · 615-742-4200

Larry T. Thrailkill · (Corporate & Partnership Transactions, Employee Benefits, Tax Disputes, Criminal Tax Cases) · Boult, Cummings, Conners & Berry · 222 Third Avenue North · P.O. Box 198062 · Nashville, TN 37219 · 615-244-2582

Charles A. Trost* · (State Tax, Tax Disputes) · Waller Lansden Dortch & Davis 2100 One Commerce Place · Nashville, TN 37239 · 615-244-6380

TRUSTS AND ESTATES

Thomas A. Caldwell · Caldwell, Heggie & Helton · 1800 Republic Centre · 630 Chestnut Street · Chattanooga, TN 37450 · 615-756-2010

Jon O. Fullerton · Caldwell, Heggie & Helton · 1800 Republic Centre · 630 Chestnut Street · Chattanooga, TN 37450 · 615-756-2010

Hunter D. Heggie · Caldwell, Heggie & Helton · 1800 Republic Centre · 630 Chestnut Street · Chattanooga, TN 37450 · 615-756-2010

Albert W. Secor · Hogshead Building, Suite Eight · 600 Georgia Avenue · Chattanooga, TN 37402 · 615-265-3433

Robert L. McMurray · Bell and Associates · Merchants Bank Building · P.O. Box 1169 · Cleveland, TN 37364-1169 · 615-476-8541

Mack A. Gentry · Gentry, Tipton, Kaizer & Little · 2610 Plaza Tower · P.O. Box 1275 · Knoxville, TN 37901 · 615-524-0313

Dan W. Holbrook · (Estate Planning, Estate Administration, Charitable Trusts) Egerton, McAfee, Armistead & Davis · 500 First American National Bank Center P.O. Box 2047 · Knoxville, TN 37901 · 615-546-0500

Robert S. Marquis · McCampbell & Young · 2021 Plaza Tower · P.O. Box 550 · Knoxville, TN 37901-0550 · 615-637-1440

James T. Bland · Armstrong Allen Prewitt Gentry Johnston & Holmes · 1900 One Commerce Square · Memphis, TN 38103-2568 · 901-523-8211

John A. Chiapella · Bogatin, Lawson & Chiapella · 5170 Sanderlin Avenue, Suite 101 · Memphis, TN 38117 · 901-767-1234

Kenneth F. Clark, Jr. · MacDonell Boyd · 6075 Poplar Avenue, Suite 623 · Memphis, TN 38119 · 901-685-2550

Joe M. Duncan · Burch, Porter & Johnson · 130 North Court Avenue · Memphis, TN 38103 · 901-523-2311

Ronald Lee Gilman* · Farris, Hancock, Gilman, Branan & Hellen · Morgan Keegan Tower, Suite 1400 · 50 North Front Street · Memphis, TN 38103 · 901-576-8200

W. Thomas Hutton · Martin, Tate, Morrow & Marston · 6060 Poplar Avenue, Suite 295 · Memphis, TN 38119-3901 · 901-763-4800

William H. Lawson, Jr. · Bogatin, Lawson & Chiapella · 245 Wagner Place, Suite 280 · Memphis, TN 38103 · 901-522-1234

Joseph Brent Walker · Armstrong Allen Prewitt Gentry Johnston & Holmes · 1900 One Commerce Square · Memphis, TN 38103-2568 · 901-523-8211

W. W. Berry · (Estate Planning, Estate Administration, Charitable Trusts) · Bass, Berry & Sims · 2700 First American Center · Nashville, TN 37238 · 615-742-6200

James C. Gooch · Bass, Berry & Sims · 2700 First American Center · Nashville, TN 37238 · 615-742-6200

Richard D. Holton · (Estate Planning, Estate Administration, Exempt Organizations, Charitable Trusts) · Holton & Walker · Financial Center, Suite 2700 · 424 Church Street · Nashville, TN 37219 · 615-256-3338

Michel G. Kaplan · Boult, Cummings, Conners & Berry · 222 Third Avenue North · P.O. Box 198062 · Nashville, TN 37219 · 615-244-2582

James T. O'Hare · O'Hare, Sherrard & Roe · 424 Church Street, Suite 2000 · Nashville, TN 37219 · 615-742-4200

Jack Wright Robinson, Sr. · Gullett, Sanford, Robinson & Martin · Metropolitan Federal Building, Third Floor · 230 Fourth Avenue, North · P.O. Box 2757 · Nashville, TN 37219-0757 · 615-244-4994

Charles A. Trost* · (Estate Planning, Estate Administration) · Waller Lansden Dortch & Davis · 2100 One Commerce Place · Nashville, TN 37239 · 615-244-6380

TEXAS

BANKRUPTCY LAW

Eric R. Borsheim · Eric Borsheim & Associates · 910 West Avenue · Austin, TX 78701 · 512-478-9089

Mina A. Clark · Jones, Day, Reavis & Pogue · 301 Congress Avenue, Suite 1200 Austin, TX 78701 · 512-499-3986

George E. Henderson · Fulbright & Jaworski · One American Center, Suite 2400 600 Congress Avenue · Austin, TX 78701 · 512-474-5201

Joseph D. Martinec · 701 Brazos, Suite 1010 · Austin, TX 78701 · 512-477-7599

Adrian Overstreet · (Bankruptcy Litigation) · Overstreet, Winn & Edwards · 1209 West Fifth Street · Austin, TX 78703 · 512-474-6436

Shelby A. Jordan* · (Business Reorganization, Bankruptcy Litigation) · Jordan & Shaw · CCNB Center North, Suite 900 · 500 North Water Street · Corpus Christi, TX 78471 · 512-884-5678

James A. Donohoe · Sullivan & Ave · 3535 Travis, Suite 130 · Dallas, TX 75204 214-528-9560

Dean M. Gandy* · (Business Reorganization, Creditors' Rights, Debtors' Rights, Bankruptcy Litigation) · Akin, Gump, Strauss, Hauer & Feld · 4100 First City Center · 1700 Pacific Avenue · Dallas, TX 75201-4618 · 214-969-2800

D. M. Lynn · Weil, Gotshal & Manges · 901 Main Street, Suite 4100 · Dallas, TX 75202 · 214-746-7700

Mark E. MacDonald · (Business Reorganization, Creditors' Rights, Debtors' Rights, Bankruptcy Litigation) · Johnson & Gibbs · Founders Square, Suite 100 900 Jackson Street · Dallas, TX 75202-4499 · 214-977-9000

Robin E. Phelan* · (Business Reorganization, Creditors' Rights, Debtors' Rights, Bankruptcy Litigation) · Haynes and Boone · 3100 NCNB Plaza · 901 Main Street Dallas, TX 75202-3714 · 214-651-5000

David R. Snodgrass · Gardere & Wynne · Thanksgiving Tower, Suite 3000 · 1601 Elm Street · Dallas, TX 75201 · 214-979-4500

Daniel Clark Stewart · Winstead,Sechrest & Minich · 5400 Renaissance Tower · 1201 Elm Street · Dallas, TX 75270 · 214-742-1700

Vernon O. Teofan · (Business Reorganization, Creditors' Rights, Debtors' Rights, Bankruptcy Litigation) · Jenkens & Gilchrist · 3200 First Interstate Tower · 1445 Ross Avenue · Dallas, TX 75202-2711 · 214-855-4500

Gerald P. Keith · Ginnings Birkelbach Keith and Delgado · SunWest Bank Building, Suite 700 · 416 North Stanton · P.O. Box 54 · El Paso, TX 79940 · 915-532-5929

Larry C. Wood · Kemp, Smith, Duncan & Hammond · 2000 MBank Plaza · P.O. Drawer 2800 · El Paso, TX 79999-2800 · 915-533-4424

John R. Blinn · Leonard Marsh Hurt Terry & Blinn · City Center Tower II · 301 Commerce Street, Suite 1100 · Fort Worth, TX 76102 · 817-332-6500

Theodore Mack · Wynn, Brown, Mack, Renfro & Thompson · 1800 First City Bank Tower · 201 Main Street · Fort Worth, TX 76102-3186 · 817-335-6261

Michael A. McConnell · Jackson & Walker · City Center Tower II, Suite 2700 · 301 Commerce Street · Fort Worth, TX 76102 · 817-334-7200

D. Jansing Baker · Weil, Gotshal & Manges · 1600 NCNB Center · 700 Louisiana Houston, TX 77002 · 713-546-5000

Thad Grundy · Hutcheson & Grundy · 3300 Citicorp Center · 1200 Smith Street Houston, TX 77002-4579 · 713-951-2800

Jarrel D. McDaniel · Vinson & Elkins · 3300 First City Tower · 1001 Fannin Street · Houston, TX 77002-6760 · 713-758-2222

Hugh M. Ray · (Business Reorganization, Bankruptcy Litigation) · Andrews & Kurth · 4200 Texas Commerce Tower · 600 Travis Street · Houston, TX 77002 · 713-220-4200

Myron M. Sheinfeld · Sheinfeld, Maley & Kay · 3700 First City Tower · Houston, TX 77002-6797 · 713-754-6261

Roderick G. Ayers, Jr. · Cox & Smith · 2000 NBC Bank Plaza · 112 East Pecan Street · San Antonio, TX 78205 · 512-554-5500

Evelyn H. Biery · (Business Reorganization, Creditors' Rights, Bankruptcy Litigation) · Fulbright & Jaworski · 2200 NCNB Plaza · 300 Convent Street · San Antonio, TX 78205 · 512-270-7130

Claiborne B. Gregory, Jr. · Gresham, Davis, Gregory, Worthy & Moore · 1800 Frost Bank Tower · San Antonio, TX 78205 · 512-226-4157

Ronald Hornberger · (Business Reorganization, Creditors' Rights, Debtors' Rights, Bankruptcy Litigation) · Plunkett, Gibson & Allen · Financial Center Northwest, Sixth Floor · 6243 Northwest Expressway · P.O. Box BH002 · San Antonio, TX 78201 · 512-734-7092

William A. Jeffers, Jr.* · Jeffers, Brook, Kreager & Gragg · 660 North Main Street, Suite 300 · San Antonio, TX 78205-1295 · 512-227-3400

William H. Lemons III · Cox & Smith · 2000 NBC Bank Plaza · 112 East Pecan Street · San Antonio, TX 78205 · 512-554-5500

Jack M. Partain, Jr. · Fulbright & Jaworski · 2200 NCNB Plaza · 300 Convent Street · San Antonio, TX 78205 · 512-270-7130

John H. Tate II · Oppenheimer, Rosenberg, Kelleher & Wheatley · 711 Navarro, Sixth Floor · San Antonio, TX 78205 · 512-224-2000

BUSINESS LITIGATION

R. James George, Jr.* · Graves, Dougherty, Hearon & Moody · 2300 NCNB Tower · P.O. Box 98 · Austin, TX 78767 · 512-480-5600

Douglass D. Hearne* · (Banking, Commercial) · Hearne, Knolle, Livingston & Holcomb · 1500 Texas Commerce Bank Building · 700 Lavaca · P.O. Drawer 1687 Austin, TX 78767 · 512-478-1500

Robert J. Hearon, Jr. · Graves, Dougherty, Hearon & Moody · 2300 NCNB Tower · P.O. Box 98 · Austin, TX 78767 · 512-480-5600

Patton G. Lochridge* · (Commercial, Energy) · McGinnis, Lockridge & Kilgore 1300 Capitol Center · 919 Congress Avenue · Austin, TX 78701 · 512-476-6982

Richard T. McCarroll · Brown Maroney & Oaks Hartline · 1400 Franklin Plaza · 111 Congress Avenue · Austin, TX 78701 · 512-472-5456

John J. McKetta III* · Graves, Dougherty, Hearon & Moody · 2300 NCNB Tower · P.O. Box 98 · Austin, TX 78767 · 512-480-5600

Shannon H. Ratliff · McGinnis, Lockridge & Kilgore · 1300 Capitol Center · 919 Congress Avenue · Austin, TX 78701 · 512-495-6007

Paul J. Van Osselaer* · Jenkens & Gilchrist · 2200 One American Center · 600 Congress Avenue · Austin, TX 78701 · 512-499-3800

Thomas H. Watkins · Hilgers & Watkins · 98 San Jacinto Boulevard, Suite 1300 P.O. Box 2063 · Austin, TX 78768 · 512-476-4716

G. Cleve Bachman · Orgain, Bell & Tucker · 470 Orleans Street · Beaumont, TX 77701 · 409-838-6412

Gilbert I. Low* · (General) · Orgain, Bell & Tucker · 470 Orleans Street · Beaumont, TX 77701 · 409-838-6412

Otto J. Weber, Jr. · Mehaffy & Weber · NCNB Building, Eighth Floor · P.O. Box 16 · Beaumont, TX 77704 · 409-835-5011

James R. Harris* · Harris & Thomas · 1700 First City Bank Tower · P.O. Drawer 1901 · Corpus Christi, TX 78403 · 512-883-1946

Glenn A. Sodd · (Eminent Domain) · Dawson, Sodd, Moe & Means · 121 North Main · P.O. Box 837 · Corsicana, TX 75151 · 903-872-8181

Louis P. Bickel · Akin, Gump, Strauss, Hauer & Feld · 4100 First City Center · 1700 Pacific Avenue · Dallas, TX 75201-4618 · 214-969-2800

George W. Bramblett, Jr. · Haynes and Boone · 3100 NCNB Plaza · 901 Main Street · Dallas, TX 75202-3714 · 214-651-5574

George C. Chapman · Thompson & Knight · 3300 First City Center · 1700 Pacific Avenue · Dallas, TX 75201 · 214-969-1700

James E. Coleman, Jr. · Carrington, Coleman, Sloman & Blumenthal · 200 Crescent Court, Suite 1500 · Dallas, TX 75201 · 214-855-3000

Mark T. Davenport · Figari & Davenport · 4800 NCNB Plaza, LB 125 · 901 Main Street · Dallas, TX 75202 · 214-939-2000

J. Carlisle DeHay, Jr.* · DeHay & Blanchard · 2500 South Tower, LB 201 · Plaza of the Americas · Dallas, TX 75201-2880 · 214-953-1313

Ernest E. Figari, Jr.* · (Commercial, Finance, RICO, Securities) · Figari & Davenport · 4800 NCNB Plaza, LB 125 · 901 Main Street · Dallas, TX 75202 · 214-939-2000

John A. Gilliam* · Jenkens & Gilchrist · 3200 First Interstate Tower · 1445 Ross Avenue · Dallas, TX 75202-2711 · 214-855-4500

John H. Hall · Strasburger & Price · 4300 NCNB Plaza · 901 Main Street · P.O. Box 50100 · Dallas, TX 75250 · 214-651-4300

Morris Harrell · Locke Purnell Rain Harrell · 2200 Ross Avenue, Suite 2200 · Dallas, TX 75201-6776 · 214-740-8000

John L. Hauer · Akin, Gump, Strauss, Hauer & Feld · 4100 First City Center · 1700 Pacific Avenue · Dallas, TX 75201-4618 · 214-969-2800

Jerry P. Jones · Thompson & Knight · 3300 First City Center · 1700 Pacific Avenue · Dallas, TX 75201 · 214-969-1700

David S. Kidder* · Thompson & Knight · 3300 First City Center · 1700 Pacific Avenue · Dallas, TX 75201 · 214-969-1700

Jack D. Maroney · (RICO) · Brown Maroney & Oaks Hartline · 3012 Fairmount Dallas, TX 75201 · 214-871-2121

Schuyler B. Marshall · Thompson & Knight · 3300 First City Center · 1700 Pacific Avenue · Dallas, TX 75201 · 214-969-1700

John H. McElhaney* · (Antitrust, Commercial, Finance) · Locke Purnell Rain Harrell · 2200 Ross Avenue, Suite 2200 · Dallas, TX 75201-6776 · 214-740-8000

Robert H. Mow, Jr.* · Hughes & Luce · Bank One Center, Suite 2800 · 1717 Main Street · Dallas, TX 75201 · 214-939-5500

David R. Noteware · Thompson & Knight · 3300 First City Center · 1700 Pacific Avenue · Dallas, TX 75201 · 214-969-1700

Ronald L. Palmer · (Banking, Commercial, Energy, Finance) · Baker & Botts · 800 Trammell Crow Center · 2001 Ross Avenue · Dallas, TX 75201-2916 · 214-953-6500

Marvin S. Sloman · (Appellate) · Carrington, Coleman, Sloman & Blumenthal · 200 Crescent Court, Suite 1500 · Dallas, TX 75201 · 214-855-3000

Fletcher L. Yarbrough · Carrington, Coleman, Sloman & Blumenthal · 200 Crescent Court, Suite 1500 · Dallas, TX 75201 · 214-855-3000

E. Link Beck · Beck & James · 218 West Franklin · El Paso, TX 79901 · 915-544-5545

W. Royal Furgeson, Jr.* · Kemp, Smith, Duncan & Hammond · 2000 MBank Plaza · P.O. Drawer 2800 · El Paso, TX 79999-2800 · 915-533-4424

Richard G. Munzinger · Scott, Hulse, Marshall, Feuille, Finger & Thurmond · Texas Commerce Bank Building, 11th Floor · El Paso, TX 79901 · 915-533-2493

Sam Sparks · Grambling & Mounce · Texas Commerce Bank Building, Seventh Floor · P.O. Drawer 1977 · El Paso, TX 79901-1977 · 915-532-3911

R. David Broiles* · Brown, Herman, Scott, Dean & Miles · Fort Worth Club Building, Suite 203 · 306 West Seventh Street · Fort Worth, TX 76102-4988 · 817-332-1391

Beale Dean* · Brown, Herman, Scott, Dean & Miles · Fort Worth Club Building, Suite 203 · 306 West Seventh Street · Fort Worth, TX 76102-4988 · 817-332-1391

Kleber C. Miller* · (Commercial, Securities) · Shannon, Gracey, Ratliff & Miller 2200 First City Bank Tower · 201 Main Street · Fort Worth, TX 76102-9990 · 817-336-9333

Cecil E. Munn · Cantey & Hanger · 2100 Burnett Plaza · 801 Cherry Street · Fort Worth, TX 76102 · 817-877-2800

E. William Barnett · Baker & Botts · One Shell Plaza · 910 Louisiana · Houston, TX 77002-4995 · 713-229-1234

David J. Beck · Fulbright & Jaworski · Chevron Tower, 51st Floor · 1301 McKinney Street, Suite 5100 · Houston, TX 77010-3095 · 713-651-5151

Richard H. Caldwell* · (Antitrust, Commercial, Securities) · Mayor, Day, Caldwell & Keeton · 1900 NCNB Center · 700 Louisiana · P.O. Box 61269 · Houston, TX 77002-2778 · 713-225-7000

Richard N. Carrell · Fulbright & Jaworski · Chevron Tower, 51st Floor · 1301 McKinney Street, Suite 5100 · Houston, TX 77010-3095 · 713-651-5151

Ralph S. Carrigan · Baker & Botts · One Shell Plaza · 910 Louisiana · Houston, TX 77002-4995 · 713-229-1234

Finis E. Cowan · Baker & Botts · One Shell Plaza · 910 Louisiana · Houston, TX 77002-4995 · 713-229-1234

Alfred H. Ebert, Jr.* · Andrews & Kurth · 4200 Texas Commerce Tower · 600 Travis Street · Houston, TX 77002 · 713-220-4200

Robin C. Gibbs* · (Antitrust, Commercial, Securities) · Gibbs & Ratliff · 3400 InterFirst Plaza · 1100 Louisiana · Houston, TX 77002 · 713-650-8805

H. Lee Godfrey · Susman Godfrey · 5100 First Interstate Bank Plaza · 1000 Louisiana · Houston, TX 77002-5096 · 713-651-9366

David T. Harvin* · (Antitrust, Energy, Securities, Corporate) · Vinson & Elkins 3300 First City Tower · 1001 Fannin Street · Houston, TX 77002-6760 · 713-758-2368

David T. Hedges, Jr. · Vinson & Elkins · 3300 First City Tower · 1001 Fannin Street · Houston, TX 77002-6760 · 713-758-2676

Joseph D. Jamail · Jamail & Kolius · 500 Dallas Street, Suite 3300 · Houston, TX 77002-4793 · 713-651-3000

Richard P. Keeton · Mayor, Day, Caldwell & Keeton · 1900 NCNB Center · 700 Louisiana · P.O. Box 61269 · Houston, TX 77002-2778 · 713-225-7000

Robert J. Malinak · Baker & Botts · One Shell Plaza · 910 Louisiana · Houston, TX 77002-4995 · 713-229-1234

John L. McConn, Jr. · McConn & Hardy · 6700 Texas Commerce Tower · 600 Travis Street · Houston, TX 77002 · 713-237-0222

Richard B. Miller · Miller, Bristow & Brown · 3900 Two Houston Center · Houston, TX 77010 · 713-759-1234

John L. Murchison, Jr. · Vinson & Elkins · 3300 First City Tower · 1001 Fannin Street · Houston, TX 77002-6760 · 713-758-2222

Harry M. Reasoner* · Vinson & Elkins · 3300 First City Tower · 1001 Fannin Street · Houston, TX 77002-6760 · 713-758-2258

Joe H. Reynolds* · (Antitrust, Commercial, Energy, Finance) · Reynolds, Cunningham, Peterson & Cordell · 3300 First Interstate Bank Plaza · 1000 Louisiana Houston, TX 77002-5087 · 713-951-9400

James B. Sales · Fulbright & Jaworski · Chevron Tower, 51st Floor · 1301 McKinney Street, Suite 5100 · Houston, TX 77010-3095 · 713-651-5151

Stephen D. Susman* · Susman Godfrey · 5100 First Interstate Bank Plaza · 1000 Louisiana · Houston, TX 77002-5096 · 713-651-9366

G. Irvin Terrell · Baker & Botts · One Shell Plaza · 910 Louisiana · Houston, TX 77002-4995 · 713-229-1234

Rufus Wallingford · Fulbright & Jaworski · Chevron Tower, 51st Floor · 1301 McKinney Street, Suite 5100 · Houston, TX 77010-3095 · 713-651-5151

Ewing Werlein, Jr. · Vinson & Elkins · 3300 First City Tower · 1001 Fannin Street · Houston, TX 77002-6760 · 713-758-2222

Walter E. Workman · Baker & Botts · One Shell Plaza · 910 Louisiana · Houston, TX 77002-4995 · 713-229-1234

W. O. Shafer · Shafer, Davis, McCollum, Ashley, O'Leary & Stoker · NCNB Texas Bank Building, Suite 201 · 700 North Grant Street · P.O. Drawer 1552 · Odessa, TX 79760-1552 · 915-332-0893

Reese L. Harrison, Jr.* · Oppenheimer, Rosenberg, Kelleher & Wheatley · 711 Navarro, Sixth Floor · San Antonio, TX 78205 · 512-224-2000

Ralph G. Langley · Foster, Lewis, Langley, Gardner & Banack · 1100 NBC Bank Plaza · 112 East Pecan Street · San Antonio, TX 78205-1533 · 512-226-3116

R. Laurence Macon* · (Appellate, Commercial, Securities) · Cox & Smith · 2000 NBC Bank Plaza · 112 East Pecan Street · San Antonio, TX 78205 · 512-554-5500

Thomas G. Sharpe · Oppenheimer, Rosenberg, Kelleher & Wheatley · 711 Navarro, Sixth Floor · San Antonio, TX 78205 · 512-224-2000

George H. Spencer, Sr.* · Clemens & Spencer · 1500 NBC Bank Plaza · 112 East Pecan Street · San Antonio, TX 78205 · 512-227-7121

Seagal V. Wheatley · Oppenheimer, Rosenberg, Kelleher & Wheatley · 711 Navarro, Sixth Floor · San Antonio, TX 78205 · 512-224-2000

CORPORATE LAW

Karen J. Bartoletti · Graves, Dougherty, Hearon & Moody · 2300 NCNB Tower P.O. Box 98 · Austin, TX 78767 · 512-480-5600

W. Amon Burton, Jr. · (Corporate Finance, Mergers & Acquisitions, Securities, Entertainment) · 1306 Guadalupe · Austin, TX 78701 · 512-473-8903

J. Rowland Cook · (Corporate Finance, Leveraged Buyouts, Mergers & Acquisitions, Securities) · Johnson & Gibbs · 100 Congress Avenue, Suite 1400 · Austin, TX 78701 · 512-322-8000

C. Morris Davis · McGinnis, Lochridge & Kilgore · 1300 Capitol Center · 919 Congress Avenue · Austin, TX 78701 · 512-476-6982

Rod Edens, Jr. · (Corporate Finance, Leveraged Buyouts, Mergers & Acquisitions, Securities) · Jenkens & Gilchrist · 2200 One American Center · 600 Congress Avenue · Austin, TX 78701 · 512-499-3800

John E. Gangstad · (Banking, Corporate Finance, Mergers & Acquisitions, Securities) · Brown Maroney & Oaks Hartline · 1400 Franklin Plaza · 111 Congress Avenue · Austin, TX 78701 · 512-472-5456

P. Michael Hebert · (Corporate Finance, Financial Institutions, Investment, Mergers & Acquisitions) · Capitol Center, Suite 601 · 919 Congress Avenue · Austin, TX 78701 · 512-476-2884

R. Clarke Heidrick, Jr. · (Banking, Corporate Finance, Mergers & Acquisitions) Graves, Dougherty, Hearon & Moody · 2300 NCNB Tower · P.O. Box 98 · Austin, TX 78767 · 512-480-5600

Lloyd Lochridge · McGinnis, Lochridge & Kilgore · 1300 Capitol Center · 919 Congress Avenue · Austin, TX 78701 · 512-476-6982

Frank Oliver · McGinnis, Lochridge & Kilgore · 1300 Capitol Center · 919 Congress Avenue · Austin, TX 78701 · 512-476-6982

William R. Volk · (Corporate Finance, Mergers & Acquisitions, Venture Capital) Jenkens & Gilchrist · 2200 One American Center · 600 Congress Avenue · Austin, TX 78701 · 512-499-3800

James A. Williams · Graves, Dougherty, Hearon & Moody · 2300 NCNB Tower P.O. Box 98 · Austin, TX 78767 · 512-480-5600

Charles W. Thomasson · Gary, Thomasson, Hall & Marks · 210 South Carancahua · P.O. Box 2888 · Corpus Christi, TX 78403 · 512-884-1961

Michael M. Boone · Haynes and Boone · 3100 NCNB Plaza · 901 Main Street · Dallas, TX 75202-3714 · 214-651-5000

Sam P. Burford, Jr. · Thompson & Knight · 3300 First City Center · 1700 Pacific Avenue · Dallas, TX 75201 · 214-969-1700

Dan Busbee · (Corporate Finance, International Finance, Mergers & Acquisitions, Securities) · Locke Purnell Rain Harrell · 2200 Ross Avenue, Suite 2200 · Dallas, TX 75201-6776 · 214-740-8000

Steven K. Cochran · Thompson & Knight · 3300 First City Center · 1700 Pacific Avenue · Dallas, TX 75201 · 214-969-1387

George W. Coleman · Jenkens & Gilchrist · 3200 First Interstate Tower · 1445 Ross Avenue · Dallas, TX 75202-2711 · 214-855-4500

John D. Curtis · Johnson & Gibbs · 100 Founders Square · 900 Jackson Street · Dallas, TX 75202-4499 · 214-977-9000

D. Gilbert Friedlander · Johnson & Gibbs · Founders Square, Suite 100 · 900 Jackson Street · Dallas, TX 75202-4499 · 214-977-9023

Henry Gilchrist · Jenkens & Gilchrist · 3200 First Interstate Tower · 1445 Ross Avenue · Dallas, TX 75202-2711 · 214-855-4500

Daniel K. Hennessy · (Banking, Financial Institutions, International) · Hughes & Luce · Bank One Center, Suite 2800 · 1717 Main Street · Dallas, TX 75201 · 214-939-5500

James L. Irish III · (Energy Finance) · Thompson & Knight · 3300 First City Center · 1700 Pacific Avenue · Dallas, TX 75201 · 214-969-1700

John T. Kipp · Gardere & Wynne · Thanksgiving Tower, Suite 3000 · 1601 Elm Street · Dallas, TX 75201 · 214-979-4500

Harold F. Kleinman · Thompson & Knight · 3300 First City Center · 1700 Pacific Avenue · Dallas, TX 75201 · 214-969-1700

Jack M. Little · Thompson & Knight · 3300 First City Center · 1700 Pacific Avenue · Dallas, TX 75201 · 214-969-1700

Larry L. Schoenbrun · Gardere & Wynne · Thanksgiving Tower, Suite 3000 · 1601 Elm Street · Dallas, TX 75201 · 214-979-4500

Laurence D. Stuart, Jr. · Weil, Gotshal & Manges · 901 Main Street, Suite 4100 Dallas, TX 75202 · 214-746-7700

Jim A. Watson · Johnson & Gibbs · Founders Square, Suite 100 · 900 Jackson Street · Dallas, TX 75202-4499 · 214-977-9000

Fletcher L. Yarbrough · Carrington, Coleman, Sloman, & Blumenthal · 200 Crescent Court, Suite 1500 · Dallas, TX 75201 · 214-855-3000

Barney T. Young · Locke Purnell Rain Harrell · 2200 Ross Avenue, Suite 2200 · Dallas, TX 75201-6776 · 214-740-8000

C. Michael Ginnings · Ginnings Birkelbach Keith and Delgado · SunWest Bank Building, Suite 700 · 416 North Stanton · P.O. Box 54 · El Paso, TX 79940 · 915-532-5929

Tad R. Smith · (Corporate Finance, Mergers & Acquisitions, Securities, Securities Regulation) · Kemp, Smith, Duncan & Hammond · 2000 MBank Plaza · P.O. Drawer 2800 · El Paso, TX 79999-2800 · 915-533-4424

Mark L. Hart, Jr. · Kelly, Hart & Hallman · 2500 First City Bank Tower · 201 Main Street · Fort Worth, TX 76102 · 817-332-2500

Dee J. Kelly · Kelly, Hart & Hallman · 2500 First City Bank Tower · 201 Main Street · Fort Worth, TX 76102 · 817-332-2500

Robert F. Watson · (Securities, Securities Regulation) · Law, Snakard & Gambill 3200 Team Bank Building · Fort Worth, TX 76102 · 817-335-7373

Milton H. Anders · (Financial Institutions) · Vinson & Elkins · 3300 First City Tower · 1001 Fannin Street · Houston, TX 77002-6760 · 713-758-2406

Eric S. Anderson · (Corporate Finance, Insurance, Securities) · Fulbright & Jaworski · Chevron Tower, 51st Floor · 1301 McKinney Street, Suite 5100 · Houston, TX 77010-3095 · 713-651-5151

R. Dennis Anderson · Fulbright & Jaworski · Chevron Tower, 51st Floor · 1301 McKinney Street, Suite 5100 · Houston, TX 77010-3095 · 713-651-5151

Robert J. Bachman · Vinson & Elkins · 3300 First City Tower · 1001 Fannin Street · Houston, TX 77002-6760 · 713-758-2222

Robert S. Baird · Vinson & Elkins · 3300 First City Tower · 1001 Fannin Street Houston, TX 77002-6760 · 713-758-2222

Robert F. Barrett · Vinson & Elkins · 3300 First City Tower · 1001 Fannin Street Houston, TX 77002-6760 · 713-758-2222

Douglas Y. Bech · Andrews & Kurth · 4200 Texas Commerce Tower · 600 Travis Street · Houston, TX 77002 · 713-220-4200

Bruce R. Bilger · Vinson & Elkins · 3300 First City Tower · 1001 Fannin Street Houston, TX 77002-6760 · 713-758-2222

John L. Bland · Bracewell & Patterson · 2900 South Tower, Pennzoil Place · Houston, TX 77002 · 713-223-2900

John H. Buck · Buck, Rouner, Keenan & Ballard · 700 Louisiana Street, Suite 5100 · Houston, TX 77002 · 713-225-4500

David Alan Burns · Baker & Botts · One Shell Plaza · 910 Louisiana · Houston, TX 77002-4995 · 713-229-1234

John T. Cabaniss · Andrews & Kurth · 4200 Texas Commerce Tower · 600 Travis Street · Houston, TX 77002 · 713-220-4200

Joseph A. Cialone II · Baker & Botts · One Shell Plaza · 910 Louisiana · Houston, TX 77002-4995 · 713-229-1234

Michael W. Conlon · Fulbright & Jaworski · Chevron Tower, 51st Floor · 1301 McKinney Street, Suite 5100 · Houston, TX 77010-3095 · 713-651-5151

Rufus Cormier, Jr. · Baker & Botts · One Shell Plaza · 910 Louisiana · Houston, TX 77002-4995 · 713-229-1234

Alton F. Curry · Fulbright & Jaworski · Chevron Tower, 51st Floor · 1301 McKinney Street, Suite 5100 · Houston, TX 77010-3095 · 713-651-5151

Christopher E. H. Dack · Fulbright & Jaworski · Chevron Tower, 51st Floor · 1301 McKinney Street, Suite 5100 · Houston, TX 77010-3095 · 713-651-5151

John C. Dawson, Jr. · Vinson & Elkins · 3300 First City Tower · 1001 Fannin Street · Houston, TX 77002-6760 · 713-758-2222

Richard B. Dewey · Baker & Botts · One Shell Plaza · 910 Louisiana · Houston, TX 77002-4995 · 713-229-1234

Joseph C. Dilg · Vinson & Elkins · 3300 First City Tower · 1001 Fannin Street Houston, TX 77002-6760 · 713-758-2222

Michael P. Finch · Vinson & Elkins · 3300 First City Tower · 1001 Fannin Street Houston, TX 77002-6760 · 713-758-2222

William T. Fleming, Jr. · Vinson & Elkins · 3300 First City Tower · 1001 Fannin Street · Houston, TX 77002-6760 · 713-758-2222

Frank T. Garcia · Fulbright & Jaworski · Chevron Tower, 51st Floor · 1301 McKinney Street, Suite 5100 · Houston, TX 77010-3095 · 713-651-5151

J. Patrick Garrett · Baker & Botts · One Shell Plaza · 910 Louisiana · Houston, TX 77002-4995 · 713-229-1234

Moulton Goodrum, Jr. · Baker & Botts · One Shell Plaza · 910 Louisiana · Houston, TX 77002-4995 · 713-229-1234

Charles R. Gregg · Hutcheson & Grundy · 3300 Citicorp Center · 1200 Smith Street · Houston, TX 77002-4579 · 713-951-2800

Campbell A. Griffin, Jr. · Vinson & Elkins · 3300 First City Tower · 1001 Fannin Street · Houston, TX 77002-6760 · 713-758-2222

S. Tevis Grinstead · Vinson & Elkins · 3300 First City Tower · 1001 Fannin Street Houston, TX 77002-6760 · 713-758-2222

Dewuse Guyton, Jr. · Butler & Binion · 1600 First Interstate Bank Plaza · 1000 Louisiana Street · Houston, TX 77002 · 713-237-3111

Ralph A. Harper · Vinson & Elkins · 3300 First City Tower · 1001 Fannin Street Houston, TX 77002-6760 · 713-758-2222

Thomas L. Healey · Andrews & Kurth · 4200 Texas Commerce Tower · 600 Travis Street · Houston, TX 77002 · 713-220-4200

Donald L. Howell · Vinson & Elkins · 3300 First City Tower · 1001 Fannin Street Houston, TX 77002-6760 · 713-758-2222

John M. Huggins · Baker & Botts · One Shell Plaza · 910 Louisiana · Houston, TX 77002-4995 · 713-229-1234

Thad T. Hutcheson, Jr. · Baker & Botts · One Shell Plaza · 910 Louisiana · Houston, TX 77002-4995 · 713-229-1234

J. Rolfe Johnson · One Riverway, Suite 1700 · Houston, TX 77056 · 713-225-7000

William E. Joor III · Vinson & Elkins · 3300 First City Tower · 1001 Fannin Street · Houston, TX 77002-6760 · 713-758-2222

Wm. Franklin Kelly, Jr. · (Corporate Finance, Mergers & Acquisitions, Securities) · Vinson & Elkins · 3300 First City Tower · 1001 Fannin Street · Houston, TX 77002-6760 · 713-758-2222

David R. Keyes · Vinson & Elkins · 3300 First City Tower · 1001 Fannin Street Houston, TX 77002-6760 · 713-758-2222

Jerry V. Kyle · Andrews & Kurth · 4200 Texas Commerce Tower · 600 Travis Street · Houston, TX 77002 · 713-220-4200

James L. Leader · Baker & Botts · One Shell Plaza · 910 Louisiana · Houston, TX 77002-4995 · 713-229-1234

Edgar J. Marston III · Bracewell & Patterson · 2900 South Tower, Pennzoil Place Houston, TX 77002 · 713-223-2900

Stephen A. Massad · Baker & Botts · One Shell Plaza · 910 Louisiana · Houston, TX 77002-4995 · 713-229-1234

Richard B. Mayor · Mayor, Day, Caldwell & Keeton · 1900 NCNB Center · 700 Louisiana · P.O. Box 61269 · Houston, TX 77002-2778 · 713-225-7000

Edward C. Norwood · Sewell & Riggs · 333 Clay Avenue, Suite 800 · Houston, TX 77002-4086 · 713-759-1937

Dallas Parker · Baker, Brown, Sharman & Parker · Citicorp Center, Suite 3600 · 1200 Smith Street · Houston, TX 77002 · 713-654-8111

P. Dexter Peacock · Andrews & Kurth · 4200 Texas Commerce Tower · 600 Travis Street · Houston, TX 77002 · 713-220-4200

T. William Porter · (Corporate Finance, International Finance, Mergers & Acquisitions, Securities) · Porter & Clements · NCNB Center · 700 Louisiana, Suite 3500 · P.O. Box 4744 · Houston, TX 77210-4744 · 713-226-0600

James D. Randall · Baker & Botts · One Shell Plaza · 910 Louisiana · Houston, TX 77002-4995 · 713-229-1234

Rush H. Record · (Corporate Finance, Mergers & Acquisitions) · Vinson & Elkins 3300 First City Tower · 1001 Fannin Street · Houston, TX 77002-6760 · 713-758-2222

Arthur H. Rogers III · Fulbright & Jaworski · Chevron Tower, 51st Floor · 1301 McKinney Street, Suite 5100 · Houston, TX 77010-3095 · 713-651-5151

Michael Q. Rosenwasser · Andrews & Kurth · 4200 Texas Commerce Tower · 600 Travis Street · Houston, TX 77002 · 713-220-4200

Richard A. Royds · Bracewell & Patterson · 2900 South Tower, Pennzoil Place · Houston, TX 77002 · 713-223-2900

John M. Sanders · Fulbright & Jaworski · Chevron Tower, 51st Floor · 1301 McKinney Street, Suite 5100 · Houston, TX 77010-3095 · 713-651-5151

George A. Shannon, Jr. · Johnson & Gibbs · 1200 First City Tower · 1001 Fannin Street · Houston, TX 77002 · 713-752-3300

Walter J. Smith · Baker & Botts · One Shell Plaza · 910 Louisiana · Houston, TX 77002-4995 · 713-229-1234

Charles H. Still · Fulbright & Jaworski · Chevron Tower, 51st Floor · 1301 McKinney Street, Suite 5100 · Houston, TX 77010-3095 · 713-651-5151

Robert L. Stillwell · Baker & Botts · One Shell Plaza · 910 Louisiana · Houston, TX 77002-4995 · 713-229-1234

Walter B. Stuart IV · Vinson & Elkins · 3300 First City Tower · 1001 Fannin Street · Houston, TX 77002-6760 · 713-758-1086

H. Don Teague · (Banking, Financial Institutions) · Vinson & Elkins · 3300 First City Tower · 1001 Fannin Street · Houston, TX 77002-6760 · 713-758-2222

Geoffrey K. Walker · Mayor, Day, Caldwell & Keeton · 1900 NCNB Center · 700 Louisiana · P.O. Box 61269 · Houston, TX 77002-2778 · 713-225-7000

John A. Watson · Fulbright & Jaworski · Chevron Tower, 51st Floor · 1301 McKinney Street, Suite 5100 · Houston, TX 77010-3095 · 713-651-5151

John S. Watson · Vinson & Elkins · 3300 First City Tower · 1001 Fannin Street · Houston, TX 77002-6760 · 713-758-2222

Robert H. Whilden, Jr. · Vinson & Elkins · 3300 First City Tower · 1001 Fannin Street · Houston, TX 77002-6760 · 713-758-2222

Jerry L. Wickliffe · Fulbright & Jaworski · Chevron Tower, 51st Floor · 1301 McKinney Street, Suite 5100 · Houston, TX 77010-3095 · 713-651-5151

R. Daniel Witschey, Jr. · Bracewell & Patterson · 2900 South Tower, Pennzoil Place · Houston, TX 77002 · 713-223-2900

Howard Wolf · Fulbright & Jaworski · Chevron Tower, 51st Floor · 1301 McKinney Street, Suite 5100 · Houston, TX 77010-3095 · 713-651-5151

Frank M. Wozencraft · Baker & Botts · One Shell Plaza · 910 Louisiana · Houston, TX 77002-4995 · 713-229-1234

Richard E. Goldsmith · Matthews & Branscomb · One Alamo Center, Suite 800 · San Antonio, TX 78205 · 512-226-4211

J. David Oppenheimer · Oppenheimer, Rosenberg, Kelleher & Wheatley · 711 Navarro, Sixth Floor · San Antonio, TX 78205 · 512-224-2000

J. Burleson Smith · Cox & Smith · 2000 NBC Bank Plaza · 112 East Pecan Street · San Antonio, TX 78205 · 512-554-5500

Dan G. Webster III · Cox & Smith · 2000 NBC Bank Plaza · 112 East Pecan Street
San Antonio, TX 78205 · 512-554-5500

CRIMINAL DEFENSE

Charles R. Burton · Minton, Burton, Foster & Collins · 1100 Guadalupe Street
Austin, TX 78701 · 512-476-4873

Bill Fitzgerald · Fitzgerald & Meissner · 1812 San Antonio, Suite 400 · Austin,
TX 78701 · 512-474-4700

Roy Q. Minton · Minton, Burton, Foster & Collins · 1100 Guadalupe Street ·
Austin, TX 78701 · 512-476-4873

Michael E. Tigar* · (Federal Court) · University of Texas · 727 East 26th Street
Austin, TX 78705 · 512-471-5151

Joseph C. Hawthorn* · Hawthorn & Black · 485 Milam · Beaumont, TX 77701-
3518 · 409-838-3969

J. A. Canales · Canales & Simonson · 2601 Morgan Avenue · P.O. Box 5624 ·
Corpus Christi, TX 78405 · 512-883-0601

J. Douglas Tinker* · Tinker & Muschenheim · 622 South Tancahua Street · P.O.
Box 276 · Corpus Christi, TX 78403 · 512-882-4378

Melvyn Carson Bruder · (Appellate) · Three Forest Plaza · 12221 Merit Drive,
Suite 150 · Dallas, TX 75251 · 214-991-6474

Emmett Colvin* · (Federal Court, State Court) · 4054 McKinney, Suite 200 ·
Dallas, TX 75204 · 214-522-1181

Michael S. Fawer · 2311 Cedar Springs Road, Suite 250 · Dallas, TX 75201 ·
214-953-1000

Michael P. Gibson · Burleson, Pate & Gibson · 2414 North Akard, Suite 700 ·
P.O. Box 190623 · Dallas, TX 75201 · 214-871-4900

Robert C. Hinton · Burleson, Pate & Gibson · 2414 North Akard, Suite 700 · P.O.
Box 190623 · Dallas, TX 75201 · 214-871-4900

George R. Milner, Jr. · Milner, Goranson, Sorrels, Udashen, Wells & Parker ·
Chateau Plaza, Suite 1500 · 2515 McKinney Avenue, Lock Box 21 · Dallas, TX
75201 · 214-651-1121

Charles W. Tessmer · One Elm Place · 1015 Elm Street, Suite 2300 · Dallas, TX
75202 · 214-748-3433

Joseph (Sib) Abraham, Jr. · Law Office of Joseph (Sib) Abraham · Caples Building, Suite 505 · P.O. Box D · El Paso, TX 79951-0004 · 915-532-1601

Bernard J. Panetta, Jr. · Caballero Panetta & Ortega · 521 Texas Avenue · El Paso, TX 79901 · 915-544-0042

Tim Evans* · 115 West Second Street, Suite 202 · Fort Worth, TX 76102 · 817-332-3822

Jeffery A. Kearney · Casey & Kearney · 1055 Burnett Plaza · 801 Cherry Street Fort Worth, TX 76102 · 817-336-5600

Jack V. Strickland · 500 Main Street · Fort Worth, TX 76102 · 817-338-1000

Mike DeGeurin · Forman, DeGeurin & Nugent · 909 Fannin Street, Suite 590 · Houston, TX 77010 · 713-655-9000

Dick DeGuerin · DeGuerin & Dickson · The Republic Building, Seventh Floor 1018 Preston Avenue · Houston, TX 77002 · 713-223-5959

Richard Haynes · 4300 Scotland Street · Houston, TX 77007 · 713-868-1111

Michael Ramsey* · (Violent Crimes, Non-Violent Crimes, Federal Court, State Court) · Ramsey & Tyson · River Oaks/Welch Building · 2120 Welch · Houston, TX 77019 · 713-224-2001

Randolph Lee Schaffer* · Schaffer, Lambright, Odom & Sparks · Chevron Tower, Suite 3100 · 1301 McKinney Street · Houston, TX 77010 · 713-951-9555

Travis D. Shelton · Shelton & Jones · 1801 Avenue Q · Lubbock, TX 79401 · 806-763-5201

Warren Burnett · 307 South East Loop 338 · Odessa, TX 79762 · 915-332-0106

Roy R. Barrera, Sr. · Nicholas & Barrera · 424 East Nueva · San Antonio, TX 78205 · 512-224-5811

Charles D. Butts · 120 Villita Street · San Antonio, TX 78205 · 512-223-2941

Gerald H. Goldstein · Goldstein, Goldstein & Hilley · Tower Life Building, 29th Floor · San Antonio, TX 78205 · 512-226-1463

Jack Paul Leon · Law Offices of Jack Paul Leon · 500 Lexington Avenue · San Antonio, TX 78215 · 512-223-4254

Anthony Nicholas · Nicholas & Barrera · 424 East Nueva · San Antonio, TX 78205 · 512-224-5811

Mark Stevens · 442 Dwyer Avenue · San Antonio, TX 78204 · 512-226-1433

F. R. "Buck" Files, Jr. · Bain Files Allen & Worthen · 109 West Ferguson Street · P.O. Box 2013 · Tyler, TX 75710 · 903-595-3573

FAMILY LAW

Thomas L. Ausley* · Ausley & Slaikeu · 3307 Northland Drive, Suite 420 · Mopac at Northland · Austin, TX 78731 · 512-454-8791

Jon N. Coffee · Jon N. Coffee & Associates · 327 Congress Avenue, Suite 600 · Austin, TX 78701 · 512-472-2272

Patricia A. English · Bankston, Wright & Greenhill · 1800 One Bank Tower · 221 West Sixth Street · P.O. Box 2166-78768 · Austin, TX 78701-3495 · 512-476-4600

Barbara Anne Kazen · 1717 West Sixth Street, Suite 350 · Austin, TX 78703 · 512-474-8200

Dan R. Price · 3001 Lake Austin Boulevard, Suite 205 · Austin, TX 78703 · 512-476-7086

Scott T. Cook* · Scott T. Cook & Associates · 2820 South Padre Island Drive, Suite 290 · Corpus Christi, TX 78415 · 512-855-6655

Kenneth D. Fuller · Koons, Fuller, McCurley & Vanden Eykel · 2311 Cedar Springs, Suite 300 · Dallas, TX 75201 · 214-871-2727

Thomas P. Goranson · Law Office of Thomas P. Goranson · 2750 One Dallas Centre · 350 North St. Paul Street · Dallas, TX 75201-4205 · 214-220-9033

William C. Koons · Koons, Fuller, McCurley & Vanden Eykel · 2311 Cedar Springs, Suite 300 · Dallas, TX 75201 · 214-871-2727

Mike McCurley* · (Adoption, Child Custody, Divorce, Marital Settlement Agreements) · Koons, Fuller, McCurley & Vanden Eykel · 2311 Cedar Springs, Suite 300 · Dallas, TX 75201 · 214-871-2727

Louise Raggio · Raggio & Raggio · 3316 Oak Grove Avenue, Suite 100 · Dallas, TX 75204 · 214-880-7500

Reba Graham Rasor · Passman & Jones · 2500 Renaissance Tower · 1201 Elm Street · Dallas, TX 75270 · 214-742-2121

Charles H. Robertson · Robertson & Merrill · 705 Ross Avenue · Dallas, TX 75202 · 214-748-9211

Donald R. Smith* · (Divorce, Equitable Division, Characterization of Marital Property) · Law Offices of Donald R. Smith · 5950 Berkshire Lane, Suite 1616 · Dallas, TX 75225 · 214-696-2100

Brian L. Webb · Webb, Kinser & Luce · 4620 Renaissance Tower · 1201 Elm Street · Dallas, TX 75270 · 214-744-4620

Curtis M. Loveless · Law Office of Curtis M. Loveless · 218 North Elm · P.O. Box 1566 · Denton, TX 76201 · 817-383-1618

Ann C. McClure · 6541 Vasco Way · El Paso, TX 79912 · 915-584-6033

David R. McClure* · (Child Custody, Divorce) · Schwartz, Earp, McClure, Cohen & Stewart · 609 Laurel Street · El Paso, TX 79903 · 915-542-1533

Larry H. Schwartz* · Schwartz, Earp, McClure, Cohen & Stewart · 609 Laurel Street · El Paso, TX 79903 · 915-542-1533

James M. Loveless · 5601 Airport Highway · Fort Worth, TX 76117 · 817-831-6800

Joe Shannon, Jr. · Bennett Shannon & Cruz · 2300 Team Bank Building · 500 Throckmorton Street · Fort Worth, TX 76102 · 817-332-6178

Donn C. Fullenweider* · (Divorce, Marital Settlement Agreements, Equitable Division, Complex Property Cases) · 4300 Scotland Street · Houston, TX 77007 713-880-4600

Roy W. Moore* · (Child Custody, Divorce, Marital Settlement Agreements) · Gray & Moore · 1301 McKinney Street, Suite 3550 · Houston, TX 77010-3091 · 713-651-9777

John F. Nichols · Piro * Nichols * Lilly · 1400 Post Oak Boulevard, Suite 600 · Houston, TX 77056 · 713-966-4444

Robert J. Piro · Piro * Nichols * Lilly · 1400 Post Oak Boulevard, Suite 600 · Houston, TX 77056 · 713-966-4444

Donald R. Royall* · (Adoption, Child Custody, Divorce, Equitable Division) · The Royalls · 13430 Northwest Freeway, Suite 650 · Houston, TX 77040 · 713-462-6500

J. Lindsey Short, Jr. · Lindsey Short & Associates · 3200 Southwest Freeway, Suite 3150 · Houston, TX 77027 · 713-626-0208

Harry L. Tindall · Tindall & Foster · 2800 Texas Commerce Tower · Houston, TX 77002-3094 · 713-229-8733

Thomas J. Purdom · Purdom Law Offices · 1801 Avenue Q · Lubbock, TX 79401
806-747-4653

William M. Boyd · Boyd, Veigel & Hance · 218 East Louisiana Street · McKinney, TX 75069 · 214-542-0191

Sam C. Bashara · Law Offices of Sam C. Bashara · Commerce Plaza Building, Suite 1800 · 111 Solodad Street · San Antonio, TX 78205 · 512-227-1496

John Compere* · (Child Custody, Divorce, Marital Settlement Agreements, Equitable Division) · Shaddox, Compere, Walraven & Good · The North Frost Center, Suite 725 · 1250 North East Loop 410 · San Antonio, TX 78209-1535 · 512-822-2018

Richard R. Orsinger · Law Office of Richard R. Orsinger · 1616 Tower Life Building · San Antonio, TX 78205 · 512-225-5567

James D. Stewart · (Child Custody, Divorce, Marital Settlement Agreements) · James D. Stewart and Associates · Milam Building, Suite 1900 · 115 East Travis Street · San Antonio, TX 78205 · 512-225-4321

Cheryl L. Wilson · Wilson & Bickley · 405 South Presa · San Antonio, TX 78205 512-227-4010

Jerry E. Bain · Bain Files Allen & Worthen · 109 West Ferguson Street · P.O. Box 2013 · Tyler, TX 75710 · 903-595-3573

Coye Conner, Jr. · Connor, Gillen & Yarbrough · 3301 Golden Road, Suite 211 Tyler, TX 75701 · 903-595-0755

FIRST AMENDMENT LAW

David H. Donaldson · Graves, Dougherty, Hearon & Moody · 2300 NCNB Tower · P.O. Box 98 · Austin, TX 78767 · 512-480-5600

R. James George, Jr. · Graves, Dougherty, Hearon & Moody · 2300 NCNB Tower · P.O. Box 98 · Austin, TX 78767 · 512-480-5600

Charles L. Babcock · Jackson & Walker · 6000 NCNB Plaza · 901 Main Street · Dallas, TX 75202 · 214-953-6000

Thomas S. Leatherbury · Locke Purnell Rain Harrell · 2200 Ross Avenue, Suite 2200 · Dallas, TX 75201-6776 · 214-740-8000

John H. McElhaney* · Locke Purnell Rain Harrell · 2200 Ross Avenue, Suite 2200 · Dallas, TX 75201-6776 · 214-740-8000

Richard G. Munzinger · Scott, Hulse, Marshall, Feuille, Finger & Thurmond · Texas Commerce Bank Building, 11th Floor · El Paso, TX 79901 · 915-533-2493

Thomas J. Williams · Bishop, Payne, Lamsens, Williams & Werley · 500 West Seventh Street, Suite 1800 · Fort Worth, TX 76102 · 817-335-4911

W. W. Ogden · Liddell, Sapp, Zivley, Hill & LaBoon · Texas Commerce Tower, 35th Floor · Houston, TX 77002 · 713-226-1200

Mark J. Cannan · Lang, Ladon, Green, Clochlan & Fisher · NCNB Plaza, Suite 1700 · 300 Convent · San Antonio, TX 78205 · 512-227-3106

HEALTH CARE LAW

Jerry A. Bell, Jr. · Fulbright & Jaworski · One American Center, Suite 2400 · 600 Congress Avenue · Austin, TX 78701 · 512-474-5201

Michael Sharp · 600 Congress Avenue, Suite 1820 · Austin, TX 78701 · 512-473-2265

Terry O. Tottenham · Fulbright & Jaworski · One American Center, Suite 2400 600 Congress Avenue · Austin, TX 78701 · 512-474-5201

Patricia D. Chamblin · Mehaffy & Weber · NCNB Center, Eighth Floor · 2615 Calder Avenue · P.O. Box 16 · Beaumont, TX 77704 · 409-835-5011

Edward Hopkins · Johnson & Gibbs · Founders Square, Suite 100 · 900 Jackson Street · Dallas, TX 75202-4499 · 214-977-9000

Ann N. James · Johnson & Gibbs · Founders Square, Suite 100 · 900 Jackson Street · Dallas, TX 75202-4499 · 214-977-9000

Richard G. Munzinger · Scott, Hulse, Marshall, Feuille, Finger & Thurmond · Texas Commerce Bank Building, 11th Floor · El Paso, TX 79901 · 915-533-2493

Yvonne K. Puig · Grambling & Mounce · Texas Commerce Bank Building, Seventh Floor · P.O. Drawer 1977 · El Paso, TX 79950-1977 · 915-532-3911

Richard L. Griffith* · Cantey & Hanger · 2100 Burnett Plaza · 801 Cherry Street Fort Worth, TX 76102 · 817-877-2800

Michael L. Malone · Law, Snakard & Gambill · 3200 Team Bank Building · Fort Worth, TX 76102 · 817-335-7373

Charles D. Boston · Fulbright & Jaworski · Chevron Tower, 51st Floor · 1301 McKinney Street, Suite 5100 · Houston, TX 77010-3095 · 713-651-5151

Burt L. Campbell · Vinson & Elkins · 3300 First City Tower · 1001 Fannin Street Houston, TX 77002-6760 · 713-758-2222

Gary W. Eiland · Vinson & Elkins · 3300 First City Tower · 1001 Fannin Street Houston, TX 77002-6760 · 713-758-2222

John D. Epstein · Vinson & Elkins · 3300 First City Tower · 1001 Fannin Street Houston, TX 77002-6760 · 713-758-2222

Hugh C. Wilfong II · Vinson & Elkins · 3300 First City Tower · 1001 Fannin Street · Houston, TX 77002-6760 · 713-758-2222

Jerry A. Gibson · Plunkett, Gibson & Allen · 6243 Northwest Expressway, Suite 600 · San Antonio, TX 78201 · 512-734-7092

Cynthia Day King · Groce, Locke & Hebdon · 2000 Frost Bank Tower · San Antonio, TX 78205-1497 · 512-225-3031

IMMIGRATION LAW

Paul D. Parsons · 704 Rio Grande · Austin, TX 78701 · 512-477-7887

Harry J. Joe · 1445 Ross Avenue · Dallas, TX 75202 · 214-855-4302

Laurier McDonald · 200 South Street, Highway 281 · Edinburgh, TX 78539 · 512-381-8181

David W. Chew · Chew & Douglas · 604 Myrtle Street · El Paso, TX 79901 · 915-533-2274

Kathleen C. Walker · Ginnings Birkelbach Keith and Delgado · SunWest Bank Building, Suite 700 · 416 North Stanton · P.O. Box 54 · El Paso, TX 79940 · 915-532-5929

Charles C. Foster · Tindall & Foster · 2800 Texas Commerce Tower · Houston, TX 77002-3094 · 713-229-8733

Harry Gee, Jr. · Law Office of Harry Gee, Jr. · 5847 San Felipe, Suite 2950 · Houston, TX 77057 · 713-781-0071

Nancy Taylor Shivers · Shivers & Shivers · 1146 South Alamo Street · San Antonio, TX 78210 · 512-226-9725

Robert A. Shivers · Shivers & Shivers · 1146 South Alamo Street · San Antonio, TX 78210 · 512-226-9725

INTELLECTUAL PROPERTY LAW

Floyd R. Nation · (Patent) · Arnold, White & Durkee · 2300 One American Center · 600 Congress Avenue · Austin, TX 78701 · 512-320-7200

Louis T. Pirkey · (Trademark) · Arnold, White & Durkee · 2300 One American Center · 600 Congress Avenue · Austin, TX 78701 · 512-320-7200

Garland P. Andrews · Richards, Medlock & Andrews · 4500 Renaissance Tower 1201 Elm Street · Dallas, TX 75270 · 214-939-4500

V. Bryan Medlock · Richards, Medlock & Andrews · 4500 Renaissance Tower · 1201 Elm Street · Dallas, TX 75270 · 214-939-4500

Jerry W. Mills · Baker & Botts · 800 Trammell Crow Center · 2001 Ross Avenue Dallas, TX 75201-2916 · 214-953-6500

Ronald V. Thurman · Hubbard, Thurman, Tucker & Harris · One Galleria Tower, Suite 2100 · 13355 Noel Road · Dallas, TX 75240-6604 · 214-23305712

Robert W. Turner · Jones, Day, Reavis & Pogue · 2300 Trammell Crow Center 2001 Ross Avenue · P.O. Box 660623 · Dallas, TX 75266 · 214-220-3939

M. R. Feldsman · Feldsman, Bradley & Gunter · 6805 Bennington Drive · Fort Worth, TX 76148 · 817-485-0030

Tom Arnold · Arnold, White & Durkee · 750 Bering Drive · Houston, TX 77210 713-787-1400

Ronald G. Bliss · Fulbright & Jaworski · Chevron Tower, 51st Floor · 1301 McKinney Street, Suite 5100 · Houston, TX 77010-3095 · 713-651-3446

James B. Gambrell · Pravel, Gambrell, Hewitt, Kimball & Krieger · 1177 West Loop South, 10th Floor · Houston, TX 77027 · 713-850-0909

Jack C. Goldstein · Arnold, White & Durkee · 750 Bering Drive · Houston, TX 77210 · 713-787-1400

Paul M. Janicke · Arnold, White & Durkee · 750 Bering Drive · Houston, TX 77210 · 713-787-1400

William L. LaFuze · Vinson & Elkins · 3300 First City Tower · 1001 Fannin Street · Houston, TX 77002-6760 · 713-758-2222

John F. Lynch · Arnold, White & Durkee · 750 Bering Drive · Houston, TX 77210 · 713-787-1400

J. Clark Martin · Vinson & Elkins · 3300 First City Tower · 1001 Fannin Street Houston, TX 77002-6760 · 713-758-2222

Bernarr Roe Pravel · Pravel, Gambrell, Hewitt, Kimball & Krieger · 1177 West Loop South, 10th Floor · Houston, TX 77027 · 713-850-0909

Alan D. Rosenthal · Baker & Botts · One Shell Plaza · 910 Louisiana · Houston, TX 77002-4995 · 713-229-1234

Gale R. Peterson · (Patent) · Cox & Smith · 2000 NBC Bank Plaza · 112 East Pecan Street · San Antonio, TX 78205 · 512-554-5500

LABOR AND EMPLOYMENT LAW

Brian S. Greig* · (Management) · Fulbright & Jaworski · One American Center, Suite 2400 · 600 Congress Avenue · Austin, TX 78701 · 512-474-5201

David R. Richards · (Labor, Individuals) · Richards, Wiseman & Durst · 600 West Seventh Street · Austin, TX 78701 · 512-479-5017

David Van Os · (Labor) · Van Os, Deats, Rubinett & Owen · 900 Congress Avenue, Suite 400 · Austin, TX 78701 · 512-479-6155

Robert J. Hambright · (Management) · Orgain, Bell & Tucker · 470 Orleans Street · Beaumont, TX 77701 · 409-838-6412

Hershell L. Barnes · (Management) · Haynes and Boone · 3100 NCNB Plaza · 901 Main Street · Dallas, TX 75202-3714 · 214-651-5000

Allen Butler · (Management) · Clark, West, Keller, Butler & Ellis · 4800 Renaissance Tower · 1201 Elm Street · Dallas, TX 75270-2146 · 214-741-1001

Bennett W. Cervin · (Management) · Thompson & Knight · 3300 First City Center · 1700 Pacific Avenue · Dallas, TX 75201 · 214-969-1700

Edward B. Cloutman III* · (Labor, Individuals) · Cloutman, Albright & Bower 3301 Elm Street · Dallas, TX 75226-1637 · 214-939-9222

George C. Dunlap · (Management) · Strasburger & Price · 4300 NCNB Plaza · 901 Main Street · P.O. Box 50100 · Dallas, TX 75250 · 214-651-4300

David M. Ellis · (Management) · Clark, West, Keller, Butler & Ellis · 4800 Renaissance Tower · 1201 Elm Street · Dallas, TX 75270-2146 · 214-741-1001

Stephen F. Fink · (Management) · Thompson & Knight · 3300 First City Center 1700 Pacific Avenue · Dallas, TX 75201 · 214-969-1700

James L. Hicks, Jr. · (Labor, Individuals) · Hicks, James & Preston · 1420 West Mockingbird Lane, Suite 760 · P.O. Box 560388 · Dallas, TX 75356-0388 · 214-630-8621

Phillip R. Jones · (Management) · Jenkens & Gilchrist · 3200 First Interstate Tower · 1445 Ross Avenue · Dallas, TX 75202-2711 · 214-855-4500

William L. Keller* · (Management) · Clark, West, Keller, Butler & Ellis · 4800 Renaissance Tower · 1201 Elm Street · Dallas, TX 75270-2146 · 214-741-1001

John F. McCarthy · (Management) · Johnson, Bromberg & Leeds · 2600 Lincoln Plaza · 500 North Akard · Dallas, TX 75201-3398 · 214-740-2622

Steven McCown · (Management) · Jenkens & Gilchrist · 3200 First Interstate Tower · 1445 Ross Avenue · Dallas, TX 75202-2711 · 214-855-4500

Robert G. Mebus · (Management) · Haynes and Boone · 3100 NCNB Plaza · 901 Main Street · Dallas, TX 75202-3714 · 214-651-5000

Marvin Menaker · (Labor) · Menaker & Huffman · 11311 North Central Expressway, Suite 208 · Dallas, TX 75243-6786 · 214-696-5441

Kenneth H. Molberg* · (Individuals) · Wilson, Williams & Molberg · 2214 Main Street · Dallas, TX 75201-4324 · 214-748-5276

William C. Strock* · (Management) · Haynes and Boone · 3100 NCNB Plaza · 901 Main Street · Dallas, TX 75202-3714 · 214-651-5623

Kenneth R. Carr* · (Management) · Grambling & Mounce · Texas Commerce Bank Building, Seventh Floor · P.O. Drawer 1977 · El Paso, TX 79901-1977 · 915-532-3911

Charles C. High, Jr. · (Management) · Kemp, Smith, Duncan & Hammond · 2000 MBank Plaza · P.O. Drawer 2800 · El Paso, TX 79999-2800 · 915-533-4424

Thomas A. Spieczny · (Labor) · Law Office of Thomas A. Spieczny · 521 Texas Avenue · El Paso, TX 79901 · 915-533-5581

Robert S. Bambace · (Management) · Fulbright & Jaworski · Chevron Tower, 51st Floor · 1301 McKinney Street, Suite 5100 · Houston, TX 77010-3095 · 713-651-5151

Richard R. Brann · (Management) · Baker & Botts · One Shell Plaza · 910 Louisiana · Houston, TX 77002-4995 · 713-229-1563

V. Reagan Burch* · (Management) · Baker & Botts · One Shell Plaza · 910 Louisiana · Houston, TX 77002-4995 · 713-229-1234

Bruce A. Fickman · (Labor) · 3303 Main Street, Suite 300 · Houston, TX 77002 713-223-4444

Patrick M. Flynn · (Labor) · Watson, Flynn & Bensik · 1225 North Loop West, Suite 800 · Houston, TX 77008 · 713-861-6163

A. J. Harper II* · (Management) · Fulbright & Jaworski · Chevron Tower, 51st Floor · 1301 McKinney Street, Suite 5100 · Houston, TX 77010-3095 · 713-651-5151

W. Carl Jordan* · (Management) · Vinson & Elkins · 3300 First City Tower · 1001 Fannin Street · Houston, TX 77002-6760 · 713-758-2222

V. Scott Kneese · (Management) · Bracewell & Patterson · 2900 South Tower, Pennzoil Place · Houston, TX 77002 · 713-223-2900

Thomas M. Melo · (Management) · Bracewell & Patterson · 2900 South Tower, Pennzoil Place · Houston, TX 77002 · 713-223-2900

Stuart M. Nelkin* · (Individuals) · Nelkin & Nelkin · 5417 Chaucer · P.O. Box 25303 · Houston, TX 77265 · 713-526-4500

Anthony P. Rosenstein · Baker & Botts · One Shell Plaza · 910 Louisiana · Houston, TX 77002-4995 · 713-229-1582

L. Chapman Smith · (Management) · Baker & Botts · One Shell Plaza · 910 Louisiana · Houston, TX 77002-4995 · 713-229-1234

John H. Smither · (Management) · Vinson & Elkins · 3300 First City Tower · 1001 Fannin Street · Houston, TX 77002-6760 · 713-758-2222

Eliot P. Tucker* · (Individuals) · Mandell & Wright · Texas Commerce Bank Building, Suite 1600 · 712 Main Street · Houston, TX 77002-3297 · 713-228-1521

James R. Watson, Jr. · (Labor) · Watson, Flynn & Bensik · 1225 North Loop West, Suite 800 · Houston, TX 77008 · 713-861-6163

G. William Baab · (Labor) · Cigna Tower, Suite 1202 · 600 Las Colinas Boulevard Irving, TX 75039-5606 · 214-556-2999

L.N.D. Wells, Jr. · (Labor, Individuals) · Cigna Tower, Suite 1202 · 600 Las Colinas Boulevard · Irving, TX 75039 · 214-556-2999

J. Joe Harris · (Management) · Matthews & Branscomb · One Alamo Center, Suite 800 · San Antonio, TX 78205 · 512-226-4211

Frank Herrera, Jr. · (Labor) · Herrera & Vega · 175 East Houston Street, Suite 250 · San Antonio, TX 78205 · 512-224-1054

Shelton E. Padgett · (Management) · Akin Gump Strauss Hauer & Feld · 1500 NCNB Plaza · 300 Convent Street · San Antonio, TX 78205 · 512-270-0800

Philip J. Pfeiffer · (Management) · Fulbright & Jaworski · 2200 NCNB Plaza · 300 Convent Street · San Antonio, TX 78205 · 512-270-7130

MARITIME LAW

Jack L. Allbritton · Fulbright & Jaworski · Chevron Tower, 51st Floor · 1301 McKinney Street, Suite 5100 · Houston, TX 77010-3095 · 713-651-5151

Ed Bluestein, Jr.* · Fulbright & Jaworski · Chevron Tower, 51st Floor · 1301 McKinney Street, Suite 5100 · Houston, TX 77010-3095 · 713-651-5151

Joseph D. Cheavens* · Baker & Botts · One Shell Plaza · 910 Louisiana · Houston, TX 77002-4995 · 713-229-1234

Theodore G. Dimitry* · Vinson & Elkins · 3300 First City Tower · 1001 Fannin Street · Houston, TX 77002-6760 · 713-758-2222

Eugene J. Silva · Vinson & Elkins · 3300 First City Tower · 1001 Fannin Street Houston, TX 77002-6760 · 713-758-2222

Edward D. Vickery · Royston, Rayzor, Vickery & Williams · 2200 Texas Commerce Tower · Houston, TX 77002 · 713-224-8380

NATURAL RESOURCES AND ENVIRONMENTAL LAW

Molly J. Cagle · Vinson & Elkins · First City Centre · 816 Congress Avenue · Austin, TX 78701-2496 · 512-495-8400

Jeff Civins · (Water, Air, Solid Waste, Hazardous Waste) · Kelly, Hart & Hallman 301 Congress Avenue, Suite 2000 · Austin, TX 78701 · 512-495-6410

Frank Douglass · (Oil & Gas) · Scott, Douglass & Luton · One American Center, Suite 1500 · 600 Congress Avenue · Austin, TX 78701 · 512-476-6337

Pamela M. Giblin · Jones, Day, Reavis & Pogue · 301 Congress Avenue, Suite 1200 · Austin, TX 78701 · 512-499-3986

R. Kinnan Golemon · (Water, Air, hazardous Waste, Governmental Relations—Lobbying) · Brown Maroney & Oaks Hartline · 1400 Franklin Plaza · 111 Congress Avenue · Austin, TX 78701 · 512-472-5456

Dan Moody, Jr.* · (Oil & Gas) · Graves, Dougherty, Hearon & Moody · 2300 NCNB Tower · P.O. Box 98 · Austin, TX 78767 · 512-480-5600

Roger P. Nevola · (Water) · Vinson & Elkins · First City Centre · 816 Congress Avenue · Austin, TX 78701-2496 · 512-495-8400

Shannon H. Ratliff · (Oil & Gas) · McGinnis, Lockridge & Kilgore · 1300 Capitol Center · 919 Congress Avenue · Austin, TX 78701 · 512-495-6007

Louis Seymour Zimmerman* · (Water, Solid Waste, Hazardous Waste, Litigation) · Fulbright & Jaworski · One American Center, Suite 2400 · 600 Congress Avenue · Austin, TX 78701 · 512-474-5201

Linton E. Barbee · (Oil & Gas) · Fulbright & Jaworski · 2200 Ross Avenue, Suite 2800 · Dallas, TX 75201 · 214-855-8119

Theodore R. Borrego · (Oil & Gas) · Johnson & Gibbs · Founders Square, Suite 100 · 900 Jackson Street · Dallas, TX 75202-4499 · 214-977-9000

James B. Harris · Thompson & Knight · 3300 First City Center · 1700 Pacific Avenue · Dallas, TX 75201 · 214-969-1700

James C. Morriss III · Thompson & Knight · 3300 First City Center · 1700 Pacific Avenue · Dallas, TX 75201 · 214-969-1700

Norman D. Radford, Jr. · (Water, Air, Solid Waste, Hazardous Waste) · Vinson & Elkins · 3700 Trammell Crow Center · 2001 Ross Avenue · Dallas, TX 75201-2916 · 214-220-7722

David J. Beck · Fulbright & Jaworski · Chevron Tower, 51st Floor · 1301 McKinney Street, Suite 5100 · Houston, TX 77010-3095 · 713-651-5151

Charles L. Berry · Vinson & Elkins · 3300 First City Tower · 1001 Fannin Street Houston, TX 77002-6760 · 713-758-2222

James B. Blackburn · (Environmental, Plaintiffs) · Blackburn & Carter · 3131 Eastside, Suite 450 · Houston, TX 77098 · 713-524-1012

Larry B. Briggs · (Oil & Gas) · Deaton & Briggs · San Felipe Plaza, 40th Floor · 5847 San Felipe · Houston, TX 77057-3063 · 713-780-1111

F. Walter Conrad, Jr. · Baker & Botts · One Shell Plaza · 910 Louisiana · Houston, TX 77002-4995 · 713-229-1234

Carol E. Dinkins · Vinson & Elkins · 3300 First City Tower · 1001 Fannin Street Houston, TX 77002-6760 · 713-758-2222

William H. Drushel, Jr. · (Oil & Gas) · Vinson & Elkins · 3300 First City Tower 1001 Fannin Street · Houston, TX 77002-6760 · 713-758-2222

Uriel E. Dutton · (Oil & Gas) · Fulbright & Jaworski · Chevron Tower, 51st Floor 1301 McKinney Street, Suite 5100 · Houston, TX 77010-3095 · 713-651-5151

Larry B. Feldcamp · Baker & Botts · One Shell Plaza · 910 Louisiana · Houston, TX 77002-4995 · 713-229-1234

John E. Kolb · (Oil & Gas) · Vinson & Elkins · 3300 First City Tower · 1001 Fannin Street · Houston, TX 77002-6760 · 713-758-2222

Rush H. Record · (Oil & Gas) · Vinson & Elkins · 3300 First City Tower · 1001 Fannin Street · Houston, TX 77002-6760 · 713-758-2222

George L. Robertson · (Oil & Gas) · Butler & Binion · 1600 First Interstate Bank Plaza · 1000 Louisiana Street · Houston, TX 77002 · 713-237-3111

John S. Sellingsloh · (Oil & Gas) · Baker & Botts · One Shell Plaza · 910 Louisiana · Houston, TX 77002-4995 · 713-229-1234

William Byron White · (Oil & Gas) · Fulbright & Jaworski · Chevron Tower, 51st Floor · 1301 McKinney Street, Suite 5100 · Houston, TX 77010-3095 · 713-651-3728

Richard T. Brady · (Oil & Gas) · Cox & Smith · 2000 NBC Bank Plaza · 112 East Pecan Street · San Antonio, TX 78205 · 512-554-5500

Paul H. Smith · (Oil & Gas) · Cox & Smith · 2000 NBC Bank Plaza · 112 East Pecan Street · San Antonio, TX 78205 · 512-554-5306

PERSONAL INJURY LITIGATION

L. Tonnett Byrd · (Plaintiffs) · Byrd, Davis and Eisenberg · 707 West 34th Street Austin, TX 78705 · 512-454-3751

John H. Coates* · (Defendants, Medical Malpractice, Products Liability) · Brown Maroney & Oaks Hartline · 1400 Franklin Plaza · 111 Congress Avenue · P.O. Box 1148 · Austin, TX 78701 · 512-479-9739

Tom H. Davis · (Plaintiffs) · Byrd, Davis and Eisenberg · 707 West 34th Street · Austin, TX 78705 · 512-454-3751

Robert Gibbins · (Plaintiffs) · Gibbins, Winckler & Bayer · 500 West 13th Street Austin, TX 78701 · 512-474-2441

Richard T. McCarroll · (Defendants) · Brown Maroney & Oaks Hartline · 1400 Franklin Plaza · 111 Congress Avenue · Austin, TX 78701 · 512-472-5456

Charles (Lefty) Morris* · (Plaintiffs, Medical Malpractice, Products Liability, Automobile Collision, Airplane Collision) · Morris, Craven & Sulak · 2350 One American Center · 600 Congress Avenue · Austin, TX 78701 · 512-478-9535

Broadus A. Spivey* · (Plaintiffs, Products Liability, Professional Malpractice, Airplane Collision) · Spivey, Grigg, Kelly & Knisely · 48 East Avenue, Suite 300 P.O. Box 2011 · Austin, TX 78768-2011 · 512-474-6061

T. B. Wright* · (Defendants, Products Liability, Professional Malpractice) · Bankston, Wright & Greenhill · 1800 Bank One Tower · 221 West Sixth Street · P.O. Box 2166-78768 · Austin, TX 78701 · 512-476-4600

G. Cleve Bachman · (Defendants) · Orgain, Bell & Tucker · 470 Orleans Street Beaumont, TX 77701 · 409-838-6412

Gilbert I. Low* · (Defendants) · Orgain, Bell & Tucker · 470 Orleans Street · Beaumont, TX 77701 · 409-838-6412

Walter Umphrey · Umphrey, Eddins & Carver · Stedman Building · 490 Park Street · Beaumont, TX 77701 · 409-835-6000

Otto J. Weber, Jr. · (Defendants) · Mehaffy & Weber · NCNB Building, Eighth Floor · P.O. Box 16 · Beaumont, TX 77704 · 409-835-5011

Guy H. Allison · 920 Leopard Street · Corpus Christi, TX 78401 · 512-884-1632

Darrell L. Barger · (Defendants) · Hermansen, McKibben & Barge · 1100 First City Tower · Corpus Christi, TX 78478 · 512-882-6611

Ronald B. Brin · (Defendants) · Brin & Brin · 1202 Third Street · Corpus Christi, TX 78404 · 512-881-9643

William R. Edwards* · (Plaintiffs) · Edwards & Terry · Texas Commerce Plaza, Suite 1400 · P.O. Drawer 480 · Corpus Christi, TX 78403 · 512-883-0971

David L. Perry · (Plaintiffs) · David L. Perry & Associates · 2300 Texas Commerce Plaza · 802 North Carancahua · P.O. Drawer 1500 · Corpus Christi, TX 78403-1500 · 512-887-7500

Frank L. Branson* · (Plaintiffs, Products Liability, Professional Negligence, Aviation Negligence, Negligence Actions) · Law Offices of Frank L. Branson · Highland Park Place, 18th Floor · 4514 Cole Avenue · Dallas, TX 75205-4185 · 214-522-0200

Arlen (Spider) Bynum · (Defendants) · Law Offices of Arlen D. (Spider) Bynum Hampton Court, Suite 444 · 4311 Oak Lawn Street · Dallas, TX 75219 · 214-559-0500

James E. Coleman, Jr. · (Defendants) · Carrington, Coleman, Solman & Blumenthal · 200 Crescent Court, Suite 1500 · Dallas, TX 75201 · 214-855-3000

Jim E. Cowles · (Defendants) · Cowles & Thompson · 4000 NCNB Plaza · 901 Main Street · Dallas, TX 75202 · 214-670-1100

W. Richard Davis · (Defendants) · Strasburger & Price · 4300 NCNB Plaza · 901 Main Street · P.O. Box 50100 · Dallas, TX 75250 · 214-651-4300

J. Carlisle DeHay, Jr.* · (Defendants) · DeHay & Blanchard · 2500 South Tower, LB 201 · Plaza of the Americas · Dallas, TX 75201-2880 · 214-953-1313

John H. Hall · (Defendants) · Strasburger & Price · 4300 NCNB Plaza · 901 Main Street · P.O. Box 50100 · Dallas, TX 75250 · 214-651-4300

John Howie · (Plaintiffs) · Misko, Howie & Sweeney · Turtle Creek Centre, Suite 1900 · 3811 Turtle Creek Boulevard · Dallas, TX 75219 · 214-443-8000

Joe Hill Jones · (Plaintiffs) · Carter, Jones, Magee, Rudberg & Mayes · One Main Place, Suite 2400 · 1201 Main Street · Dallas, TX 75202-3973 · 214-742-6261

David S. Kidder* · (Products Liability) · Thompson & Knight · 3300 First City Center · 1700 Pacific Avenue · Dallas, TX 75201 · 214-969-1700

John L. Lancaster III* · (Defendants) · Jackson & Walker · 6000 NCNB Plaza · 901 Main Street · Dallas, TX 75202 · 214-953-6000

Jack D. Maroney* · (Defendants, Medical Malpractice, Products Liability, Professional Malpractice, Airplane Collision) · Brown Maroney & Oaks Hartline · 3012 Fairmount · Dallas, TX 75201 · 214-871-2121

Fred Misko, Jr.* · (Plaintiffs, Medical Malpractice, Products Liability, Airplane Collision) · Misko, Howie & Sweeney · Turtle Creek Centre, Suite 1900 · 3811 Turtle Creek Boulevard · Dallas, TX 75219 · 214-443-8000

Robert H. Mow, Jr.* · (Products Liability) · Hughes & Luce · Bank One Center, Suite 2800 · 1717 Main Street · Dallas, TX 75201 · 214-939-5500

C. L. Mike Schmidt* · Stradley, Schmidt & Wright · One Campbell Centre · 8350 North Central Expressway · Dallas, TX 75206 · 214-696-4880

Fred S. Stradley* · (Defendants) · Stradley, Schmidt & Wright · One Campbell Centre · 8350 North Central Expressway · Dallas, TX 75206 · 214-696-4880

Windle Turley · (Plaintiffs) · Law Offices of Windle Turley · University Tower, Suite 1000 · 6440 North Central Expressway · Dallas, TX 75206 · 214-691-4025

Edwin E. Wright III · (Defendants) · Stradley, Schmidt & Wright · One Campbell Centre · 8350 North Central Expressway · Dallas, TX 75206 · 214-696-4880

James Curtis · (Defendants) · Kemp, Smith, Duncan & Hammond · 2000 MBank Plaza · P.O. Drawer 2800 · El Paso, TX 79999-2800 · 915-533-4424

John A. Grambling · (Defendants) · Grambling & Mounce · Texas Commerce Bank Building, Seventh Floor · P.O. Drawer 1977 · El Paso, TX 79901-1977 · 915-532-3911

Sam Sparks · (Defendants) · Grambling & Mounce · Texas Commerce Bank Building, Seventh Floor · P.O. Drawer 1977 · El Paso, TX 79901-1977 · 915-532-3911

John P. Camp · Camp, Hartley, O'Neill & Clark · 1300 South University Drive, Suite 308 · Fort Worth, TX 76107 · 817-335-4275

Beale Dean* · (Defendants) · Brown, Herman, Scott, Dean & Miles · Fort Worth Club Building, Suite 203 · 306 West Seventh Street · Fort Worth, TX 76102-4988 817-332-1391

Richard L. Griffith* · (Defendants, Medical Malpractice) · Cantey & Hanger · 2100 Burnett Plaza · 801 Cherry Street · Fort Worth, TX 76102 · 817-877-2800

Darrell L. Keith · (Medical Malpractice) · Keith, Link & Smith · 1400 First City 201 Main Street · Fort Worth, TX 76102 · 817-338-1400

Kleber C. Miller* · (Defendants, Professional Malpractice) · Shannon, Gracey, Ratliff & Miller · 2200 First City Bank Tower · 201 Main Street · Fort Worth, TX 76102-9990 · 817-336-9333

Richard U. Simon · McLean & Sanders · 100 Main Street · Fort Worth, TX 76102 817-338-1700

Estil A. Vance · (Defendants) · Cantey & Hanger · 2100 Burnett Plaza · 801 Cherry Street · Fort Worth, TX 76102 · 817-877-2800

J. Donald Bowen · (Plaintiffs) · Helm, Pletcher, Hogan, Bowen & Saunders · 2700 America Tower · 2929 Allen Parkway at Waugh · Houston, TX 77019-2120 713-522-4550

David H. Burrow* · (Plaintiffs) · Burrow & Williams · 1301 McKinney Street · Houston, TX 77010-3034 · 713-222-6333

Richard H. Caldwell* · (Defendants, Products Liability, Airplane Collision) · Mayor, Day, Caldwell & Keeton · 1900 NCNB Center · 700 Louisiana · P.O. Box 61269 · Houston, TX 77002-2778 · 713-225-7000

Lamberth S. Carsey · (Defendants) · Fulbright & Jaworski · Chevron Tower, 51st Floor · 1301 McKinney Street, Suite 5100 · Houston, TX 77010-3095 · 713-651-5151

Wayne Fisher · (Plaintiffs) · Fisher, Gallagher, Perrin & Lewis · First Interstate Bank Plaza, 70th Floor · 1000 Louisiana · Houston, TX 77002 · 713-654-4433

Michael T. Gallagher · (Plaintiffs) · Fisher, Gallagher, Perrin & Lewis · First Interstate Bank Plaza, 70th Floor · 1000 Louisiana · Houston, TX 77002 · 713-654-4433

Charles W. Hurd* · (Defendants) · Fulbright & Jaworski · Chevron Tower, 51st Floor · 1301 McKinney Street, Suite 5100 · Houston, TX 77010-3095 · 713-651-5151

Joseph D. Jamail · (Plaintiffs) · Jamail & Kolius · 500 Dallas Street, Suite 3300 · Houston, TX 77002-4793 · 713-651-3000

Ronald D. Krist* · (Plaintiffs) · Krist, Gunn, Weller, Neumann & Morrison · 17050 El Camino Real · Houston, TX 77058 · 713-488-2313

W. James Kronzer · Law Office of W. James Kronzer · 1900 Memorial Avenue · Houston, TX 77007 · 713-236-1722

John L. McConn, Jr. · (Defendants) · McConn & Hardy · 6700 Texas Commerce Tower · 600 Travis Street · Houston, TX 77002 · 713-237-0222

Richard B. Miller · (Defendants) · Miller, Bristow & Brown · 3900 Two Houston Center · Houston, TX 77010 · 713-759-1234

Richard Warren Mithoff · (Plaintiffs) · Mithoff & Jacks · 3450 One Allen Center, Penthouse · Houston, TX 77002 · 713-654-1122

Nick C. Nichols* · (Plaintiffs) · Abraham, Watkins, Nichols, Ballard, Onstad & Friend · 800 Commerce Street · Houston, TX 77002-1776 · 713-222-7211

Jim M. Perdue · (Plaintiffs) · Perdue & Todesco · Lyric Office Centre, Suite 1900 440 Louisiana · P.O. Box 1364 · Houston, TX 77215-1364 · 713-227-1403

George E. Pletcher · (Plaintiffs) · Helm, Pletcher, Hogan, Bowen & Saunders · 2700 America Tower · 2929 Allen Parkway at Waugh · Houston, TX 77019-2120 713-522-4550

James B. Sales · (Defendants) · Fulbright & Jaworski · Chevron Tower, 51st Floor · 1301 McKinney Street, Suite 5100 · Houston, TX 77010-3095 · 713-651-5151

Paul E. Stallings · (Defendants) · Vinson & Elkins · 3300 First City Tower · 1001 Fannin Street · Houston, TX 77002-6760 · 713-758-2222

Kenneth Tekell* · (Defendants) · Tekell, Book, Matthews & Limmer · 3600 Two Houston Center · 909 Fannin Street · Houston, TX 77010 · 713-222-9542

Joe H. Tonahill* · (Plaintiffs) · Tonahill, Hile, Leister & Jacobellis · Tonahill Building · 270 East Lamar · Jasper, TX 75951 · 409-384-2501

F. Scott Baldwin, Sr. · (Plaintiffs) · Baldwin & Baldwin · 115 North Wellington Street · P.O. Drawer 1349 · Marshall, TX 75671-1349 · 214-935-4131

Franklin Jones, Jr. · (Plaintiffs) · Jones, Jones, Curry & Roth · 201 West Houston Street · P.O. Drawer 1249 · Marshall, TX 75671-1249 · 214-938-4395

Warren Burnett · (Plaintiffs) · 307 South East Loop 338 · Odessa, TX 79762 · 915-332-0106

James L. Branton · (Plaintiffs) · Branton & Hall · 737 Travis Park Plaza Building San Antonio, TX 78205 · 512-224-4474

George B. Brin · (Defendants) · Brin & Brin · 10940 Laureate Drive, Suite 8480 San Antonio, TX 78429 · 512-697-3100

Paul M. Green · (Defendants, Medical Malpractice) · 1700 NCNB Plaza · San Antonio, TX 78205-3718 · 512-227-3106

Franklin D. Houser* · (Plaintiffs) · Tinsman & Houser · One Riverwalk Place, 14th Floor · 700 North St. Mary's Street · San Antonio, TX 78205 · 512-225-3121

Clarence Lyons · (Plaintiffs) · Southers & Lyons · 126 Villita Street · San Antonio, TX 78205 · 512-225-5251

George H. Spencer, Sr.* · (Defendants) · Clemens & Spencer · 1500 NBC Bank Plaza · 112 East Pecan Street · San Antonio, TX 78205 · 512-227-7121

Richard D. Cullen* · (Defendants, Medical Malpractice, Products Liability, Professional Malpractice) · Cullen, Carsner, Seerden & Cullen · 119 South Main Street · P.O. Box 2938 · Victoria, TX 77902 · 512-573-6318

Jack G. Banner · (Plaintiffs) · Banner & Briley · Hamilton Building, Suite 1200 900 Eighth Street · Wichita Falls, TX 76301 · 817-723-6644

PUBLIC UTILITY LAW

Walter Demond · (Natural Gas, Electricity) · Clark, Thomas, Winters & Newton · 1200 Texas Commerce Bank Building · P.O. Box 1148 · Austin, TX 78767 · 512-472-8800

Geoffrey Gay · (Municipal) · Butler Porter & Gay · 901 Mopac South · 525 Barton Oaks Plaza Two · Austin, TX 78746 · 512-327-2812

Robert J. Hearon, Jr. · (Electricity & Telecommunications) · Graves, Dougherty, Hearon & Moody · 2300 NCNB Tower · P.O. Box 98 · Austin, TX 78767 · 512-480-5600

J. Alan Holman · (Natural Gas, Electricity, Telecommunications) · Brown Maroney & Oaks Hartline · 1400 Franklin Plaza · 111 Congress Avenue · Austin, TX 78701 · 512-479-9732

Thomas B. Hudson, Jr. · Graves, Dougherty, Hearon & Moody · 2300 NCNB Tower · P.O. Box 98 · Austin, TX 78767 · 512-480-5600

Carolyn E. Shellmann · (Telecommunications) · Bickerstaff, Heath & Smiley · 98 San Jacinto Boulevard, Suite 1800 · Austin, TX 78701 · 512-472-8021

Robert A. Webb · (Natural Gas, Electricity, Telecommunications) · Jordan & Webb · 111 Congress Avenue · Austin, TX 78701 · 512-478-5336

William N. Woolsey · Redford, Wray & Woolsey · CCNB Center North · 500 North Water Street, Suite 1000 · Corpus Christi, TX 78471 · 512-886-3213

J. Dan Bohannan · Worsham, Forsythe, Samples & Wooldridge · 2001 Bryan Tower, Suite 3200 · Dallas, TX 75201 · 214-979-3000

Robert A. Wooldridge · Worsham, Forsythe, Samples & Wooldridge · 2001 Bryan Tower, Suite 3200 · Dallas, TX 75201 · 214-979-3000

Norman Gordon · (Municipal) · Diamond, Rash, Leslie, Smith & Samaniego · 300 East Main Street, Seventh Floor · El Paso, TX 79901 · 915-533-2277

Michael D. McQueen · Kemp, Smith, Duncan & Hammond · 2000 MBank Plaza · P.O. Drawer 2800 · El Paso, TX 79999-2800 · 915-533-4424

Jonathan Day · Mayor, Day, Caldwell & Keeton · 1900 NCNB Center · 700 Louisiana · P.O. Box 61269 · Houston, TX 77002-2778 · 713-225-7000

Scott E. Rozzelle · Baker & Botts · One Shell Plaza · 910 Louisiana · Houston, TX 77002-4995 · 713-229-1234

Jon C. Wood · Matthews & Branscomb · One Alamo Center, Suite 800 · San Antonio, TX 78205 · 512-226-4211

REAL ESTATE LAW

David B. Armbrust · (Zoning, Land Use) · Strasburger & Price, Armbrust & Brown · 2600 One American Center · 600 Congress Avenue · Austin, TX 78701 · 512-499-3600

Richard C. Baker · Brown Maroney & Oaks Hartline · 1400 Franklin Plaza · 111 Congress Avenue · Austin, TX 78701 · 512-472-5456

Wm. Terry Bray · Graves, Dougherty, Hearon & Moody · 2300 NCNB Tower · P.O. Box 98 · Austin, TX 78767 · 512-480-5600

Robert G. Converse · Fulbright & Jaworski · One American Center, Suite 2400 600 Congress Avenue · Austin, TX 78701 · 512-474-5201

Michael L. Cook · Jenkens & Gilchrist · 2200 One American Center · 600 Congress Avenue · Austin, TX 78701 · 512-499-3800

R. Alan Haywood · Graves, Dougherty, Hearon & Moody · 2300 NCNB Tower · P.O. Box 98 · Austin, TX 78767 · 512-480-5600

P. Michael Hebert · (Commercial Transactions, Industrial Transactions) · Capitol Center, Suite 601 · 919 Congress Avenue · Austin, TX 78701 · 512-476-2884

Brian C. Rider · Brown Maroney & Oaks Hartline · 1400 Franklin Plaza · 111 Congress Avenue · Austin, TX 78701 · 512-472-5456

Roy C. Snodgrass III · Jenkens & Gilchrist · 2200 One American Center · 600 Congress Avenue · Austin, TX 78701 · 512-499-3800

G. Bickford Shaw · Jordan & Shaw · 900 CCNB Center North · 500 North Water Street · Corpus Christi, TX 78471 · 512-884-5678

Robert M. Allen · Clements, Allen & Warren · 5429 LBJ Freeway, Suite 800 · Dallas, TX 75240 · 214-991-2600

Lawrence J. Brannian · Johnson & Gibbs · Founders Square, Suite 100 · 900 Jackson Street · Dallas, TX 75202-4499 · 214-977-9000

Daniel K. Hennessy · Hughes & Luce · Bank One Center, Suite 2800 · 1717 Main Street · Dallas, TX 75201 · 214-939-5500

Daniel K. Hennessy · (Commercial Transactions) · Hughes & Luce · Bank One Center, Suite 2800 · 1717 Main Street · Dallas, TX 75201 · 214-939-5500

Steven R. Jenkins · Johnson & Gibbs · Founders Square, Suite 100 · 900 Jackson Street · Dallas, TX 75202-4499 · 214-977-9000

John R. Johnson · Johnson & Gibbs · Founders Square, Suite 100 · 900 Jackson Street · Dallas, TX 75202-4499 · 214-977-9000

Dan B. Miller · Jones, Day, Reavis & Pogue · 2300 Trammell Crow Center · 2001 Ross Avenue · P.O. Box 660623 · Dallas, TX 75266-0623 · 214-220-3939

Mark V. Murray · Geary, Stahl & Spencer · 6400 NCNB Plaza · 901 Main Street Dallas, TX 75202 · 214-748-9901

Edward A. Peterson · Winstead, Sechrest & Minich · 5400 Renaissance Tower · 1201 Elm Street · Dallas, TX 75270 · 214-745-5642

William D. Powell · Johnson, Bromberg & Leeds · 2600 Lincoln Plaza · 500 North Akard · Dallas, TX 75201-3398 · 214-740-2600

Gary R. Rice · Payne & Vendig · 3700 Renaissance Tower · 1201 Elm Street · Dallas, TX 75270 · 214-742-3700

Harry M. Roberts, Jr. · Thompson & Knight · 3300 First City Center · 1700 Pacific Avenue · Dallas, TX 75201 · 214-969-1700

James W. Rose · Thompson & Knight · 3300 First City Center · 1700 Pacific Avenue · Dallas, TX 75201 · 214-969-1700

William B. Sechrest · Winstead, Sechrest & Minick · 5400 Renaissance Tower · 1201 Elm Street · Dallas, TX 75270 · 214-742-1700

Robert F. See, Jr. · Locke Purnell Rain Harrell · 2200 Ross Avenue, Suite 2200 Dallas, TX 75201-6776 · 214-740-8000

Philip B. Smith, Jr. · Locke Purnell Rain Harrell · 2200 Ross Avenue, Suite 2200 Dallas, TX 75201-6776 · 214-740-8000

Charles W. Spencer · Geary, Stahl & Spencer · 6400 NCNB Plaza · 901 Main Street · Dallas, TX 75202 · 214-748-9901

Lewis T. Sweet, Jr. · Hughes & Luce · Bank One Center, Suite 2800 · 1717 Main Street · Dallas, TX 75201 · 214-939-5500

William A. Thau · Jenkens & Gilchrist · 3200 First Interstate Tower · 1445 Ross Avenue · Dallas, TX 75202-2711 · 214-855-4500

James H. Wallenstein · Jenkens & Gilchrist · 3200 First Interstate Tower · 1445 Ross Avenue · Dallas, TX 75202-2711 · 214-855-4500

Philip D. Weller · Vinson & Elkins · 3700 Trammell Crow Center · 2001 Ross Avenue · Dallas, TX 75201-2916 · 214-220-7700

Ben B. West · (Eminent Domain, Commercial Transactions) · Jackson & Walker 6000 NCNB Plaza · 901 Main Street · Dallas, TX 75202 · 214-953-6000

Robert E. Wilson · Haynes and Boone · 3100 NCNB Plaza · 901 Main Street · Dallas, TX 75202-3714 · 214-651-5000

Eldon L. Youngblood · Baker, Glast & Middleton · 2001 Ross Avenue, Suite 500 Dallas, TX 75201 · 214-220-8533

Marc P. Bernat · Potash, Bernat, Sipes & Bernat · 300 East Main, Suite 1424 · El Paso, TX 79901-1380 · 915-532-1491

Raymond H. Marshall · Kemp, Smith, Duncan & Hammond · 2000 MBank Plaza P.O. Drawer 2800 · El Paso, TX 79999-2800 · 915-533-4424

William J. Mounce · Grambling & Mounce · Texas Commerce Bank Building, Seventh Floor · P.O. Drawer 1977 · El Paso, TX 79901-1977 · 915-532-3911

Billie J. Ellis, Jr. · (Commercial Transactions, Industrial Transactions) · Kelly, Hart & Hallman · 2500 First City Bank Tower · 201 Main Street · Fort Worth, TX 76102 · 817-332-2500

William Kendall Adam · Fulbright & Jaworski · Chevron Tower, 51st Floor · 1301 McKinney Street, Suite 5100 · Houston, TX 77010-3095 · 713-651-5151

Gus Block · Hirsch & Westheimer · NCNC Center, Suite 2500 · 700 Louisiana Street · Houston, TX 77002 · 713-223-5181

Bernard O. Dow · Dow, Cogburn & Friedman · Coastal Tower, Suite 2300 · Nine Greenway Plaza · Houston, TX 77046 · 713-626-5800

Melvin A. Dow · Dow, Cogburn & Friedman · Coastal Tower, Suite 2300 · Nine Greenway Plaza · Houston, TX 77046 · 713-626-5800

Fred H. Dunlop · Baker & Botts · One Shell Plaza · 910 Louisiana · Houston, TX 77002-4995 · 713-229-1234

Uriel E. Dutton · Fulbright & Jaworski · Chevron Tower, 51st Floor · 1301 McKinney Street, Suite 5100 · Houston, TX 77010-3095 · 713-651-5151

Jack E. Fields · Andrews & Kurth · 4200 Texas Commerce Tower · 600 Travis Street · Houston, TX 77002 · 713-220-4200

Abraham P. Friedman · Dow, Cogburn & Friedman · Coastal Tower, Suite 2300 Nine Greenway Plaza · Houston, TX 77046 · 713-626-5870

Jesse B. Heath, Jr. · (Commercial Transactions) · Mayor, Day, Caldwell & Keeton · 1900 NCNB Center · 700 Louisiana · P.O. Box 61269 · Houston, TX 77002-2778 · 713-225-7000

John S. Hollyfield · (Commercial Transactions, Industrial Transactions) · Fulbright & Jaworski · Chevron Tower, 51st Floor · 1301 McKinney Street, Suite 5100 · Houston, TX 77010-3095 · 713-651-5151

Randall K. Howard · Sheinfeld, Maley & Kay · 3700 First City Tower · Houston, TX 77002-6797 · 713-658-8881

Frank W. R. Hubert, Jr. · (Commercial, Industrial) · Baker & Botts · One Shell Plaza · 910 Louisiana · Houston, TX 77002-4995 · 713-229-1453

M. Marvin Katz · Mayer Brown & Platt · NCNB Center, Suite 3600 · 700 Louisiana · Houston, TX 77002-2730 · 713-221-1651

Darrell C. Morrow · Vinson & Elkins · 3300 First City Tower · 1001 Fannin Street · Houston, TX 77002-6760 · 713-758-2222

Carl G. Mueller, Jr. · 515 Post Oak Boulevard, Suite 715 · Houston, TX 77046 · 713-622-7992

Lee D. Schlanger · Schlanger, Cook, Cohn, Mills & Grossberg · 5847 San Felipe, Suite 1700 · Houston, TX 77057 · 713-785-1700

John S. Sellingsloh · Baker & Botts · One Shell Plaza · 910 Louisiana · Houston, TX 77002-4995 · 713-229-1234

Joel I. Shannon · Andrews & Kurth · 4200 Texas Commerce Tower · 600 Travis Street · Houston, TX 77002 · 713-220-4200

Frank F. Smith, Jr. · Vinson & Elkins · 3300 First City Tower · 1001 Fannin Street · Houston, TX 77002-6760 · 713-758-2222

Jack R. Sowell · Vinson & Elkins · 3300 First City Tower · 1001 Fannin Street Houston, TX 77002-6760 · 713-758-2142

Sanford A. Weiner · (Land Use, Commercial Transactions, Usury/Interest) · Vinson & Elkins · 3300 First City Tower · 1001 Fannin Street · Houston, TX 77002-6760 · 713-758-2558

William Byron White · (Commercial Transactions, Industrial Transactions) · Fulbright & Jaworski · Chevron Tower, 51st Floor · 1301 McKinney Street, Suite 5100 · Houston, TX 77010-3095 · 713-651-3728

Douglas W. Becker · Kaufman, Becker, Pullen & Reibach · 2300 NCNB Plaza · 300 Convent Street · San Antonio, TX 78205-3724 · 512-227-2000

Patricia G. Bridwell · Groce, Locke & Hebdon · 2000 Frost Bank Tower · San Antonio, TX 78205-1497 · 512-225-3031

Norman S. Davis · Davis, Adami & Cedillo · Concord Plaza, Suite 400 · 200 Concord Plaza Drive · San Antonio, TX 78216 · 512-822-6666

W. Bebb Francis III · Groce, Locke & Hebdon · 2000 Frost Bank Tower · San Antonio, TX 78205-1497 · 512-225-3031

Kenneth M. Gindy · Oppenheimer, Rosenberg, Kelleher & Wheatley · 711 Navarro, Sixth Floor · San Antonio, TX 78205 · 512-224-2000

David C. Spoor · (Construction) · Cox & Smith · 2000 NBC Bank Plaza · 112 East Pecan Street · San Antonio, TX 78205 · 512-554-5500

Lewis T. Tarver, Jr. · Matthews & Branscomb · One Alamo Center · San Antonio, TX 78205 · 512-226-4211

TAX AND EMPLOYEE BENEFITS LAW

Lydia Wommack Barton · (Employee Benefits) · Graves, Dougherty, Hearon & Moody · 2300 NCNB Tower · P.O. Box 98 · Austin, TX 78767 · 512-480-5600

Thomas J. Brorby · Johnson & Gibbs · 100 Congress Avenue, Suite 1400 · Austin, TX 78701 · 512-322-8000

Michael L. Cook · Jenkens & Gilchrist · 2200 One American Center · 600 Congress Avenue · Austin, TX 78701 · 512-499-3800

J. Chrys Dougherty · Graves, Dougherty, Hearon & Moody · 2300 NCNB Tower P.O. Box 98 · Austin, TX 78767 · 512-480-5600

David I. Kuperman · (Tax, Employee Benefits) · Johnson & Gibbs · 100 Congress Avenue, Suite 1400 · Austin, TX 78701 · 512-322-8000

Sander W. Shapiro · Jenkens & Gilchrist · 2200 One American Center · 600 Congress Avenue · Austin, TX 78701 · 512-499-3800

Peter Winstead · Winstead, Sechrest & Minick · 100 Congress Avenue, Suite 800 Austin, TX 78701 · 512-370-2801

Harvie Branscomb, Jr. · Matthews & Branscomb · 1800 First City Bank Tower Corpus Christi, TX 78477-0129 · 512-888-9261

Gerald W. Ostarch · Gary, Thomasson, Hall & Marks · 210 South Carancahua · P.O. Box 2888 · Corpus Christi, TX 78403 · 512-884-1961

Buford P. Berry · Thompson & Knight · 3300 First City Center · 1700 Pacific Avenue · Dallas, TX 75201 · 214-969-1700

Stuart M. Bumpas · (Employee Benefits) · Locke Purnell Rain Harrell · 2200 Ross Avenue, Suite 2200 · Dallas, TX 75201-6776 · 214-740-8000

Robert Edwin Davis · Johnson & Gibbs · Founders Square, Suite 100 · 900 Jackson Street · Dallas, TX 75202-4499 · 214-977-9000

Henry D. De Berry III · Johnson & Gibbs · Founders Square, Suite 100 · 900 Jackson Street · Dallas, TX 75202-4499 · 214-977-9000

Dennis B. Drapkin · Jones, Day, Reavis & Pogue · 2300 Trammell Crow Center 2001 Ross Avenue · P.O. Box 660623 · Dallas, TX 75266-0623 · 214-220-3939

H. Gene Emery · Locke Purnell Rain Harrell · 2200 Ross Avenue, Suite 2200 · Dallas, TX 75201-6776 · 214-740-8000

Richard A. Freling · Johnson & Gibbs · Founders Square, Suite 100 · 900 Jackson Street · Dallas, TX 75202-4499 · 214-977-9000

Joseph J. French, Jr. · (Corporate & Partnership Transactions) · Locke Purnell Rain Harrell · 2200 Ross Avenue, Suite 2200 · Dallas, TX 75201-6776 · 214-740-8000

W. John Glancy · (Corporate & Partnership Transactions, Tax Disputes) · 8117 Preston Road, Suite 210 · Dallas, TX 75225 · 214-369-5353

David G. Glickman · Johnson & Gibbs · Founders Square, Suite 100 · 900 Jackson Street · Dallas, TX 75202-4499 · 214-977-9000

John Michael Holt · (Employee Benefits) · Thompson & Knight · 3300 First City Center · 1700 Pacific Avenue · Dallas, TX 75201 · 214-969-1700

Vester T. Hughes, Jr. · Hughes & Luce · Bank One Center, Suite 2800 · 1717 Main Street · Dallas, TX 75201 · 214-939-5500

William D. Jordan · Jackson & Walker · 6000 NCNB Plaza · 901 Main Street · Dallas, TX 75202 · 214-953-6000

Cym H. Lowell · Johnson & Gibbs · Founders Square, Suite 100 · 900 Jackson Street · Dallas, TX 75202-4499 · 214-977-9000

Richard A. Massman · Johnson & Gibbs · Founders Square, Suite 100 · 900 Jackson Street · Dallas, TX 75202-4499 · 214-977-9000

William B. McClure, Jr. · (Employee Benefits) · Johnson & Gibbs · Founders Square, Suite 100 · 900 Jackson Street · Dallas, TX 75202-4499 · 214-977-9000

P. Mike McCullough · Thompson & Knight · 3300 First City Center · 1700 Pacific Avenue · Dallas, TX 75201 · 214-969-1476

Emily A. Parker · Thompson & Knight · 3300 First City Center · 1700 Pacific Avenue · Dallas, TX 75201 · 214-969-1700

Bruce D. Pingree · (Employee Benefits) · Johnson & Gibbs · Founders Square, Suite 100 · 900 Jackson Street · Dallas, TX 75202-4499 · 214-977-9000

Cecil A. Ray, Jr. · (Employee Benefits) · Haynes & Boone · 3100 NCNB Plaza · 901 Main Street · Dallas, TX 75202-3714 · 214-651-5599

David L. Sinak · Hughes & Luce · Bank One Center, Suite 2800 · 1717 Main Street · Dallas, TX 75201 · 214-939-5500

Donald J. Zahn · Akin, Gump, Strauss, Hauer & Feld · 4100 First City Center · 1700 Pacific Avenue · Dallas, TX 75201-4618 · 214-969-2800

Hector Delgado · Ginnings Birkelbach Keith and Delgado · SunWest Bank Building, Suite 700 · 416 North Stanton · P.O. Box 54 · El Paso, TX 79940 · 915-532-5929

R. Gordon Appleman · Thompson & Knight · 801 Cherry Street, Suite 1600 · Fort Worth, TX 76102 · 817-347-1700

Whitfield J. Collins · Cantey & Hanger · 2100 Burnett Plaza · 801 Cherry Street Fort Worth, TX 76102 · 817-877-2800

Gary P. Amoan · (Employee Benefits) · Vinson & Elkins · 3300 First City Tower 1001 Fannin Street · Houston, TX 77002-6760 · 713-758-2222

Paul H. Asofsky · Weil, Gotshal & Manges · 1600 NCNB Center · 700 Louisiana Houston, TX 77002 · 713-546-5000

Stanley C. Beyer · Baker & Botts · One Shell Plaza · 910 Louisiana · Houston, TX 77002-4995 · 713-229-1234

A. T. Blackshear, Jr. · Fulbright & Jaworski · Chevron Tower, 51st Floor · 1301 McKinney Street, Suite 5100 · Houston, TX 77010-3095 · 713-651-5151

Richard P. Bogatto · (Employee Benefits) · Fulbright & Jaworski · Chevron Tower, 51st Floor · 1301 McKinney Street, Suite 5100 · Houston, TX 77010-3095 713-651-5151

Gareth W. Cook · (Employee Benefits) · Vinson & Elkins · 3300 First City Tower 1001 Fannin Street · Houston, TX 77002-6760 · 713-758-2222

J. Cal Courtney, Jr. · (Employee Benefits) · Fulbright & Jaworski · Chevron Tower, 51st Floor · 1301 McKinney Street, Suite 5100 · Houston, TX 77010-3095 713-651-5151

Sam G. Croom, Jr. · (Employee Benefits) · Baker & Botts · One Shell Plaza · 910 Louisiana · Houston, TX 77002-4995 · 713-229-1234

William C. Griffith · Baker & Botts · One Shell Plaza · 910 Louisiana · Houston, TX 77002-4995 · 713-229-1234

Charles W. Hall · Fulbright & Jaworski · Chevron Tower, 51st Floor · 1301 McKinney Street, Suite 5100 · Houston, TX 77010-3095 · 713-651-5151

Donald O. Jansen · (Employee Benefits) · Fulbright & Jaworski · Chevron Tower, 51st Floor · 1301 McKinney Street, Suite 5100 · Houston, TX 77010-3095 713-651-5151

George H. Jewell · Baker & Botts · One Shell Plaza · 910 Louisiana · Houston, TX 77002-4995 · 713-229-1234

Carol H. Jewett · (Employee Benefits) · Vinson & Elkins · 3300 First City Tower 1001 Fannin Street · Houston, TX 77002-6760 · 713-758-2222

Lawrence Kalinec · Fulbright & Jaworski · Chevron Tower, 51st Floor · 1301 McKinney Street, Suite 5100 · Houston, TX 77010-3095 · 713-651-5151

William M. Linden · Vinson & Elkins · 3300 First City Tower · 1001 Fannin Street · Houston, TX 77002-6760 · 713-758-2222

Thomas P. Marinis, Jr. · Vinson & Elkins · 3300 First City Tower · 1001 Fannin Street · Houston, TX 77002-6760 · 713-758-2222

J. Holland McGuirt · (Employee Benefits) · Butler & Binion · 1600 First Interstate Bank Plaza · 1000 Louisiana Street · Houston, TX 77002 · 713-237-3111

John Edward Neslage · (Employee Benefits) · Baker & Botts · One Shell Plaza 910 Louisiana · Houston, TX 77002-4995 · 713-229-1234

Edward C. Osterberg, Jr. · (Corporate & Partnership Transactions, International) Vinson & Elkins · 3300 First City Tower · 1001 Fannin Street · Houston, TX 77002-6760 · 713-758-2222

James R. Raborn · (Employee Benefits) · Baker & Botts · One Shell Plaza · 910 Louisiana · Houston, TX 77002-4995 · 713-229-1234

Steven C. Salch · Fulbright & Jaworski · Chevron Tower, 51st Floor · 1301 McKinney Street, Suite 5100 · Houston, TX 77010-3095 · 713-651-5151

Laurence D. Sikes, Jr. · Andrews & Kurth · 4200 Texas Commerce Tower · 600 Travis Street · Houston, TX 77002 · 713-220-4200

Herbert D. Simons · Butler & Binion · 1600 First Interstate Bank Plaza · 1000 Louisiana Street · Houston, TX 77002 · 713-237-3111

Michael Dean Stewart · (Employee Benefits) · Andrews & Kurth · 4200 Texas Commerce Tower · 600 Travis Street · Houston, TX 77002 · 713-220-4200

C. W. Wellen · Fulbright & Jaworski · Chevron Tower, 51st Floor · 1301 McKinney Street, Suite 5100 · Houston, TX 77010-3095 · 713-651-5151

Donald F. Wood · Vinson & Elkins · 3300 First City Tower · 1001 Fannin Street Houston, TX 77002-6760 · 713-758-2222

Stanley L. Blend · Oppenheimer, Rosenberg, Kelleher & Wheatley · 711 Navarro, Sixth Floor · San Antonio, TX 78205 · 512-224-2000

R. James Curphy · Schoenbaum, Curphy & Scanlan · 300 Convent Street, Suite 1775 · San Antonio, TX 78205-3744 · 512-224-4491

Richard E. Goldsmith · Matthews & Branscomb · One Alamo Center, Suite 800 San Antonio, TX 78205 · 512-226-4211

Farley P. Katz · Matthews & Branscomb · One Alamo Center · San Antonio, TX 78205 · 512-226-4211

Mary M. Potter · (Employee Benefits) · Matthews & Branscomb · One Alamo Center, Suite 800 · San Antonio, TX 78205 · 512-226-4211

William Scanlan, Jr. · (Employee Benefits) · Schoenbaum, Curphy & Scanlan · 300 Convent Street, Suite 1775 · San Antonio, TX 78205-3744 · 512-224-4491

Stanley Schoenbaum · Schoenbaum, Curphy & Scanlan · 300 Convent Street, Suite 1775 · San Antonio, TX 78205-3744 · 512-224-4491

Richard N. Weinstein · (Employee Benefits, Tax Disputes, Business Tax) · Oppenheimer, Rosenberg, Kelleher & Wheatley · 711 Navarro, Sixth Floor · San Antonio, TX 78205 · 512-224-2000

W. Thomas Weir · Akin, Gump, Strauss, Hauer & Feld · 1500 NCNB Plaza · 300 Convent Street · San Antonio, TX 78205 · 512-270-0800

TRUSTS AND ESTATES

J. Chrys Dougherty · Graves, Dougherty, Hearon & Moody · 2300 NCNB Tower P.O. Box 98 · Austin, TX 78767 · 512-480-5600

Alvin J. Golden · Johnson & Gibbs · 100 Congress Avenue, Suite 1400 · Austin, TX 78701 · 512-322-8000

H. David Hughes · Brown Maroney & Oaks Hartline · 1400 Franklin Plaza · 111 Congress Avenue · Austin, TX 78701 · 512-472-5456

Duncan Elliott Osborne · Graves, Dougherty, Hearon & Moody · 2300 NCNB Tower · P.O. Box 98 · Austin, TX 78767 · 512-480-5627

John L. Bell, Jr. · Mehaffy & Weber · Interfirst Tower, Eighth Floor · P.O. Box 16 · Beaumont, TX 77704 · 409-835-5011

Stephen R. Akers · Jenkens & Gilchrist · 3200 First Interstate Tower · 1445 Ross Avenue · Dallas, TX 75202-2711 · 214-855-4500

Barbara McComas Anderson · Locke Purnell Rain Harrell · 2200 Ross Avenue, Suite 2200 · Dallas, TX 75201-6776 · 214-740-8000

R. W. Calloway · Turner, Rodgers, Calloway & Norris · 2700 First City Center · 1700 Pacific Avenue · Dallas, TX 75201 · 214-969-7422

Thomas H. Cantrill · Jenkens & Gilchrist · 3200 First Interstate Tower · 1445 Ross Avenue · Dallas, TX 75202-2711 · 214-855-4500

Ronald R. Cresswell* · (Estate Planning, Estate Administration, Charitable Trusts, Probate Litigation) · Locke Purnell Rain Harrell · 2200 Ross Avenue, Suite 2200 · Dallas, TX 75201-6776 · 214-740-8000

James J. Hartnett, Sr. · The Hartnett Law Firm · 2800 MBank Building · 1704 Main Street · Dallas, TX 75201 · 214-742-4655

Jack W. Hawkins · Gardere & Wynne · Thanksgiving Tower, Suite 3000 · 1601 Elm Street · Dallas, TX 75201 · 214-979-4500

Jack M. Kinnebrew · Strasburger & Price · 4300 NCNB Plaza · 901 Main Street P.O. Box 50100 · Dallas, TX 75250 · 214-651-4613

Robert Kroney · Kroney—Silverman—Mincey · 1210 Three Forrest Plaza · 12221 Merit Drive · Dallas, TX 75251 · 214-386-8500

Donald J. Malouf · Malouf Lynch Jackson Kessler & Collins · 8117 Preston Road, Suite 700 West · Dallas, TX 75225 · 214-750-0722

P. Mike McCullough · Thompson & Knight · 3300 First City Center · 1700 Pacific Avenue · Dallas, TX 75201 · 214-969-1476

Rust E. Reid · Thompson & Knight · 3300 First City Center · 1700 Pacific Avenue Dallas, TX 75201 · 214-969-1700

Edward V. Smith III* · Taylor & Mizell · 3000 Lincoln Plaza, L.B.5 · 500 North Akard · Dallas, TX 75201 · 214-954-3400

Donald A. Swanson, Jr. · Storey, Armstrong, Steger & Martin · 4600 First Interstate Bank Tower · 1445 Ross Avenue · Dallas, TX 75202 · 214-855-6800

Robert Hyer Thomas* · (Estate Administration) · Strasburger & Price · 4300 NCNB Plaza · 901 Main Street · P.O. Box 50100 · Dallas, TX 75250 · 214-651-4300

Ronald M. Weiss · Carrington, Coleman, Sloman & Blumenthal · 200 Crescent Court, Suite 1500 · Dallas, TX 75201 · 214-855-3000

Edward B. Winn · (Estate Planning, Estate Administration, Charitable Trusts, Trusts & Estates Litigation) · Winn, Beaudry & Virden · NCNB Center, 3330 Tower I · 300 North Ervay Street · Dallas, TX 75201 · 214-969-0001

Richard H. Feuille · Scott, Hulse, Marshall, Feuille, Finger & Thurmond · Texas Commerce Bank Building, 11th Floor · El Paso, TX 79901 · 915-533-2493

Joseph P. Hammond · Kemp, Smith, Duncan & Hammond · 2000 MBank Plaza P.O. Drawer 2800 · El Paso, TX 79999-2800 · 915-533-4424

J. Sam Moore, Jr. · Scott, Hulse, Marshall, Feuille, Finger & Thurmond · Texas Commerce Bank Building, 11th Floor · El Paso, TX 79901 · 915-533-2493

Brainerd S. Parrish · Studdard & Melby · Franklin Plaza, Third Floor · 415 North Mesa Street · El Paso, TX 79901 · 915-533-5938

R. Gordon Appleman · Thompson & Knight · 801 Cherry Street, Suite 1600 · Fort Worth, TX 76102 · 817-347-1700

Allan Howeth · Cantey & Hanger · 2100 Burnett Plaza · 801 Cherry Street · Fort Worth, TX 76102 · 817-877-2800

Rice M. Tilley, Jr. · (Estate Planning, Charitable Trusts) · Law, Snakard & Gambill · 3200 Team Bank Building · Fort Worth, TX 76102 · 817-878-6350

Thomas E. Berry · (Estate Planning, Estate Administration, Charitable Trusts) · Thomas E. Berry & Associates · 255 Houston Club Building · 811 Rusk Avenue Houston, TX 77002-2811 · 713-223-8061

W. Fred Cameron · Fulbright & Jaworski · Chevron Tower, 51st Floor · 1301 McKinney Street, Suite 5100 · Houston, TX 77010-3095 · 713-651-5151

Richard R. Cruse · Woodard, Hall & Primm · 7000 Texas Commerce Tower · Houston, TX 77002 · 713-221-3957

S. Stacy Eastland · Baker & Botts · One Shell Plaza · 910 Louisiana · Houston, TX 77002-4995 · 713-229-1234

J. Thomas Eubank · 1745 South Tower · 711 Louisiana · Houston, TX 77002 · 713-228-3555

Don E. Fizer · Fizer, Beck, Webster & Bentley · 1360 Post Oak Boulevard, Suite 1600 · Houston, TX 77056 · 713-840-7710

Charles W. Giraud · Butler & Binion · 1600 First Interstate Bank Plaza · 1000 Louisiana Street · Houston, TX 77002 · 713-237-3111

L. Henry Gissel, Jr. · Fulbright & Jaworski · Chevron Tower, 51st Floor · 1301 McKinney Street, Suite 5100 · Houston, TX 77010-3095 · 713-651-5151

John L. Hopwood · Liddell, Sapp, Zivley, Hill & LaBoon · Texas Commerce Tower, 35th Floor · Houston, TX 77002 · 713-226-1200

Rodney C. Koenig · Fulbright & Jaworski · Chevron Tower, 51st Floor · 1301 McKinney Street, Suite 5100 · Houston, TX 77010-3095 · 713-651-5151

Everett A. Marley, Jr. · Butler & Binion · 1600 First Interstate Bank Plaza · 1000 Louisiana Street · Houston, TX 77002 · 713-237-3281

Kent H. McMahan · Fulbright & Jaworski · Chevron Tower, 51st Floor · 1301 McKinney Street, Suite 5100 · Houston, TX 77010-3095 · 713-651-5151

Harold L. Metts · Baker & Botts · One Shell Plaza · 910 Louisiana · Houston, TX 77002-4995 · 713-229-1234

William T. Miller · Andrews & Kurth · 4200 Texas Commerce Tower · 600 Travis Street · Houston, TX 77002 · 713-220-4200

Lawrence J. Pirtle · Sewell & Riggs · 333 Clay Avenue, Suite 800 · Houston, TX 77002-4086 · 713-652-8700

Charles A. Saunders, Jr. · Fulbright & Jaworski · Chevron Tower, 51st Floor · 1301 McKinney Street, Suite 5100 · Houston, TX 77010-3095 · 713-651-5151

Walter P. Zivley · (Estate Planning, Estate Administration, Charitable Trusts) · Liddell, Sapp, Zivley, Hill & LaBoon · Texas Commerce Tower, 35th Floor · Houston, TX 77002 · 713-226-1200

Arthur H. Bayern · Bayern, Paterson, Aycock & Amen · 112 East Pecan Street, Suite 2300 · San Antonio, TX 78205 · 512-223-6306

Taylor S. Boone · Oppenheimer, Rosenberg, Kelleher & Wheatley · 711 Navarro, Sixth Floor · San Antonio, TX 78205 · 512-224-2000

Richard E. Goldsmith · Matthews & Branscomb · One Alamo Center, Suite 800 San Antonio, TX 78205 · 512-226-4211

Jesse H. Oppenheimer · Oppenheimer, Rosenberg, Kelleher & Wheatley · 711 Navarro, Sixth Floor · San Antonio, TX 78205 · 512-224-2000

Allan G. Paterson, Jr. · Bayern, Paterson, Aycock & Amen · 112 East Pecan Street, Suite 2300 · San Antonio, TX 78205 · 512-223-6306

William Scanlan, Jr. · Schoenbaum, Curphy & Scanlan · 300 Convent Street, Suite 1775 · San Antonio, TX 78205-3744 · 512-224-4491

Jim D. Bowmer · Bowmer, Courtney, Burleson, Normand & Moore · First National Bank Building, Sixth Floor · P.O. Box 844 · Temple, TX 76503 · 817-778-1354

UTAH

BANKRUPTCY LAW

Peter W. Billings, Jr.* · Fabian & Clendenin · 215 South State Street, 12th Floor
P.O. Box 510210 · Salt Lake City, UT 84151 · 801-531-8900

William G. Fowler* · (Business Reorganization, Creditors' Rights, Debtors'
Rights, Bankruptcy Litigation) · Van Cott, Bagley, Cornwall & McCarthy · 50
South Main Street, Suite 1600 · P.O. Box 45340 · Salt Lake City, UT 84145 ·
801-532-3333

Ralph R. Mabey · LeBoeuf, Lamb, Leiby & MacRae · 1000 Kearns Building · 136 South Main · Salt Lake City, UT 84101 · 801-355-6900

Robert D. Merrill · (Business Reorganization, Creditors' Rights) · Van Cott, Bagley, Cornwall & McCarthy · 50 South Main Street, Suite 1600 · P.O. Box 45340 · Salt Lake City, UT 84145 · 801-532-3333

Herschel J. Saperstein* · (Business Reorganization, Creditors' Rights, Debtors' Rights, Bankruptcy Litigation) · Watkiss & Saperstein · 310 South Main Street, 12th Floor · Salt Lake City, UT 84101-2171 · 801-363-3300

Alan L. Smith · 31 L Street, Suite 107 · Salt Lake City, UT 84103 · 801-521-3321

BUSINESS LITIGATION

Daniel L. Berman* · Berman & O'Rorke · 50 South Main Street, Suite 1250 · Salt Lake City, UT 84144 · 801-328-2200

Robert S. Campbell, Jr.* · Campbell Maack & Sessions · First Interstate Plaza, Suite 400 · 170 South Main Street · Salt Lake City, UT 84101-1605 · 801-537-5555

Harold G. Christensen · Snow, Christensen & Martineau · 10 Exchange Place, 11th Floor · P.O. Box 45000 · Salt Lake City, UT 84145-5000 · 801-521-9000

Stephen G. Crockett · Giauque, Crockett & Bendinger · 500 Kearns Building · 136 South Main Street · Salt Lake City, UT 84101 · 801-533-8383

Richard W. Giauque* · (Antitrust, Commercial, Securities) · Giauque, Crockett & Bendinger · 500 Kearns Building · 136 South Main · Salt Lake City, UT 84101 801-533-8383

Gordon L. Roberts · Parsons, Behle & Latimer · 185 South State Street, Suite 700 · P.O. Box 11898 · Salt Lake City, UT 84147-0898 · 801-532-1234

David K. Watkiss, Sr. · Watkiss & Saperstein · 310 South Main Street, 12th Floor Salt Lake City, UT 84101-2171 · 801-363-3300

CORPORATE LAW

Don B. Allen · (Banking, Corporate Finance, Financial Institutions) · Ray, Quinney & Nebeker · 400 Deseret Building · 79 South Main Street · P.O. Box 45385 Salt Lake City, UT 84145-0385 · 801-532-1500

Robert M. Anderson · Anderson & Watkins · 50 West Broadway, Suite 700 · Salt Lake City, UT 84101 · 801-534-1700

Peter W. Billings, Jr.* · Fabian & Clendenin · 215 South State Street, 12th Floor P.O. Box 510210 · Salt Lake City, UT 84151 · 801-531-8900

Edward W. Clyde* · (Antitrust, Banking) · Clyde, Pratt & Snow · American Savings Plaza, Suite 200 · 77 West Second South · Salt Lake City, UT 84101 · 801-322-2516

Donald B. Holbrook · Jones, Waldo, Holbrook & McDonough · 1500 First Interstate Plaza · 170 South Main Street · Salt Lake City, UT 84101 · 801-521-3200

Wilford W. Kirton, Jr. · Kirton, McConkie & Poelman · 60 East South Temple, Suite 1800 · Salt Lake City, UT 84111 · 801-521-3680

James B. Lee · Parsons, Behle & Latimer · 185 South State Street, Suite 700 · P.O. Box 11898 · Salt Lake City, UT 84147-0898 · 801-532-1234

David E. Salisbury · (Administrative, Banking, Corporate Finance, Financial Institutions) · Van Cott, Bagley, Cornwall & McCarthy · 50 South Main Street, Suite 1600 · P.O. Box 45340 · Salt Lake City, UT 84145-0898 · 801-532-3333

Alonzo W. Watson, Jr. · Ray, Quinney & Nebeker · 400 Deseret Building · 79 South Main Street · P.O. Box 45385 · Salt Lake City, UT 84145-0385 · 801-532-1500

M. Scott Woodland · Van Cott, Bagley, Cornwall & McCarthy · 50 South Main Street, Suite 1600 · P.O. Box 45340 · Salt Lake City, UT 84145-0898 · 801-532-3333

CRIMINAL DEFENSE

Brian R. Florence · Florence and Hutchison · 818 Twenty-Sixth Street · Ogden, UT 84401 · 801-399-9291

John Blair Hutchison* · Florence and Hutchison · 818 Twenty-Sixth Street · Ogden, UT 84401 · 801-399-9291

D. Gilbert Athay · Law Offices of D. Gilbert Athay · 72 East Fourth South, Suite 325 · Salt Lake City, UT 84111 · 801-363-7074

Stephen R. McCaughey* · (Violent Crimes, Non-Violent Crimes, Federal Court, State Court) · Hatch and McCaughey · 72 East 400 South Street, Suite 330 · Salt Lake City, UT 84111 · 801-364-6474

G. Fred Metos* · Yengich, Rich, Xaiz & Metos · 175 East 400 South, Suite 400 Salt Lake City, UT 84111 · 801-355-0320

Ronald J. Yengich* · (Violent Crimes, Non-Violent Crimes, Federal Court, State Court) · Yengich, Rich, Xaiz & Metos · 175 East 400 South, Suite 400 · Salt Lake City, UT 84111 · 801-355-0320

FAMILY LAW

Brian R. Florence · Florence and Hutchison · 818 Twenty-Sixth Street · Ogden, UT 84401 · 801-399-9291

James P. Cowley* · Van Cott, Bagley, Cornwall & McCarthy · 50 South Main Street, Suite 1600 · Salt Lake City, UT 84145 · 801-532-3333

B. L. Dart · Dart, Adamson & Kasting · 310 South Main Street, Suite 1330 · Salt Lake City, UT 84101 · 801-521-6383

David S. Dolowitz* · Cohne, Rappaport & Segal · 525 East First South, Suite 500 P.O. Box 11008 · Salt Lake City, UT 84147-0008 · 801-532-2666

Frank J. Gustin · Gustin, Green, Stegall & Liapis · New York Building, Third Floor · 48 Post Office Place · Salt Lake City, UT 84101 · 801-532-6996

Kent M. Kasting · Dart, Adamson & Kasting · 310 South Main Street, Suite 1330 Salt Lake City, UT 84101 · 801-521-6383

Clark W. Sessions* · Campbell Maack & Sessions · First Interstate Plaza, Suite 400 · 170 South Main Street · Salt Lake City, UT 84101-1605 · 801-537-5555

FIRST AMENDMENT LAW

Robert M. Anderson · Anderson & Watkins · 50 West Broadway, Suite 700 · Salt Lake City, UT 84101 · 801-534-1700

Randy Dryer · Parsons, Behle & Latimer · 185 South State Street, Suite 800 · P.O. Box 11898 · Salt Lake City, UT 84147-0898 · 801-532-1234

D. Miles Holman · Jones, Waldo, Holbrook & McDonough · 1500 First Interstate Plaza · 170 South Main Street · Salt Lake City, UT 84101 · 801-521-3200

Thomas R. Karrenberg · Anderson & Watkins · 50 West Broadway, Suite 700 · Salt Lake City, UT 84101 · 801-534-1700

David B. Watkiss · Watkiss & Saperstein · 310 South Main Street, 12th Floor · Salt Lake City, UT 84101 · 801-363-3300

IMMIGRATION LAW

Arnold G. Gardner, Jr. · Littlefield & Peterson · 426 South 500 East · Salt Lake City, UT 84102 · 801-531-0435

David E. Littlefield · Littlefield & Peterson · 426 South 500 East · Salt Lake City, UT 84102 · 801-531-0435

Oscar W. McConkie III · Kirton, McConkie & Bushnell · 330 South Third East Salt Lake City, UT 84111 · 801-521-3680

INTELLECTUAL PROPERTY LAW

William S. Britt · Trask, Britt & Rossa · 525 South 300 East · P.O. Box 2550 · Salt Lake City, UT 84110 · 801-532-1922

Allen R. Jensen · Workman, Nydeger & Jensen · 1000 Eagle Gate Tower · 60 East South Temple · Salt Lake City, UT 84111 · 801-533-9800

Rick D. Nydeger · Workman, Nydeger & Jensen · 1000 Eagle Gate Tower · 60 East South Temple · Salt Lake City, UT 84111 · 801-533-9800

David V. Trask · Trask, Britt & Rossa · 525 South 300 East · P.O. Box 2550 · Salt Lake City, UT 84110 · 801-532-1922

H. Ross Workman · Workman, Nydeger & Jensen · 1000 Eagle Gate Tower · 60 East South Temple · Salt Lake City, UT 84111 · 801-533-9800

Calvin E. Thorpe · Thorpe, North & Western · 9035 South 700 East, Suite 200 Sandy, UT 84070 · 801-566-6633

LABOR AND EMPLOYMENT LAW

Stephen W. Cook · (Labor) · Cook & Wilde · Union Park Center, Suite 490 · 6925 Union Park Avenue · Midvale, UT 84047 · 801-255-6000

David A. Anderson* · (Management, ERISA Litigation) · Parsons, Behle & Latimer · 185 South State Street, Suite 700 · P.O. Box 11898 · Salt Lake City, UT 84147-0898 · 801-532-1234

Elizabeth Dunning* · (Individuals) · Watkiss & Saperstein · 310 South Main Street, 12th Floor · Salt Lake City, UT 84101-2171 · 801-363-3300

Nathan J. Fullmer · (Management) · McIntyre Building, Suite 800 · 68 South Main Street · Salt Lake City, UT 84101 · 801-531-8300

Gordon L. Roberts · (Management) · Parsons, Behle & Latimer · 185 South State Street, Suite 700 · P.O. Box 11898 · Salt Lake City, UT 84147-0898 · 801-532-1234

A. Wally Sandack · (Labor) · 370 East Fifth South Street · Salt Lake City, UT 84111 · 801-531-0555

Janet Hugie Smith · (Management) · Ray, Quinney & Nebeker · 400 Deseret Building · 79 South Main Street · P.O. Box 45385 · Salt Lake City, UT 84145-0385 · 801-532-1500

Ronald F. Sysak* · (Management) · Prince, Yeates & Geldzahler · City Centre I, Suite 900 · 175 East Fourth South · Salt Lake City, UT 84111 · 801-524-1000

Keith E. Taylor · (Management) · Parsons, Behle & Latimer · 185 South State Street, Suite 700 · P.O. Box 11898 · Salt Lake City, UT 84147-0898 · 801-532-1234

Charles H. Thronson* · (Management) · Parsons, Behle & Latimer · 185 South State Street, Suite 700 · P.O. Box 11898 · Salt Lake City, UT 84147-0898 · 801-532-1234

Robert M. Yeates · (Management) · Prince, Yeates & Geldzahler · City Centre I, Suite 900 · 175 East Fourth South · Salt Lake City, UT 84111 · 801-524-1000

NATURAL RESOURCES AND ENVIRONMENTAL LAW

Stephen G. Boyden · (Indian Affairs) · 1100 South 1500 East · Salt Lake City, UT 84105 · 801-581-9305

Edward W. Clyde* · (Oil & Gas, Mining, Water, Hazardous Waste) · Clyde, Pratt & Snow · American Savings Plaza, Suite 200 · 77 West Second South · Salt Lake City, UT 84101 · 801-322-2516

Patrick J. Garver · Parsons, Behle & Latimer · 185 South State Street, Suite 700 P.O. Box 11898 · Salt Lake City, UT 84147-0898 · 801-532-1234

Oliver W. Gushee, Jr. · (Oil & Gas) · Pruitt, Gushee & Bachtell · Beneficial Life Tower, Suite 1850 · 36 South State Street · Salt Lake City, UT 84111 · 801-531-8446

James A. Holtkamp · Davis, Graham & Stubbs · Eagle Gate Tower, Suite 1600 60 East South Temple · Salt Lake City, UT 84111 · 801-328-6000

Dallin W. Jensen · (Water, State Lands) · Parsons, Behle & Latimer · 185 South State Street, Suite 700 · P.O. Box 11898 · Salt Lake City, UT 84147-0898 · 801-532-1234

Lee Kapaloski · Parsons, Behle & Latimer · 185 South State Street, Suite 700 · P.O. Box 11898 · Salt Lake City, UT 84147-0898 · 801-532-1234

James B. Lee · (Mining, Water) · Parsons, Behle & Latimer · 185 South State Street, Suite 700 · P.O. Box 11898 · Salt Lake City, UT 84147-0898 · 801-532-1234

Joseph Novak · (Water) · Snow, Christensen & Martineau · 10 Exchange Place, 11th Floor · P.O. Box 45000 · Salt Lake City, UT 84145-5000 · 801-521-9000

Clayton J. Parr · Kimball, Parr, Waddoups, Brown & Gee · 185 South State Street, Suite 1300 · P.O. Box 11019 · Salt Lake City, UT 84147 · 801-532-7840

Robert G. Pruitt, Jr. · (Oil & Gas) · Pruitt, Gushee & Bachtell · Beneficial Life Tower, Suite 1850 · 36 South State Street · Salt Lake City, UT 84111 · 801-531-8446

Richard K. Sager · (Mining, Water, Public Lands) · Van Cott, Bagley, Cornwall & McCarthy · 50 South Main Street, Suite 1600 · P.O. Box 45340 · Salt Lake City, UT 84145 · 801-532-3333

Gregory P. Williams · Van Cott, Bagley, Cornwall & McCarthy · 50 South Main Street, Suite 1600 · P.O. Box 45340 · Salt Lake City, UT 84145 · 801-532-3333

PERSONAL INJURY LITIGATION

Richard W. Campbell* · (Defendants) · Campbell & Neeley · 2485 Grant Avenue, Suite 200 · Ogden, UT 84401 · 801-621-3646

David S. Kunz · (Plaintiffs) · Kunz, Kunz & Hadley · Bank of Utah Building, Suite 300 · 2605 Washington Boulevard · Ogden, UT 84401 · 801-394-4573

Jackson B. Howard* · Howard, Lewis & Petersen · Delphi Building · 120 East 300 North Street · P.O. Box 778 · Provo, UT 84603 · 801-373-6345

Harold G. Christensen · (Defendants) · Snow, Christensen & Martineau · 10 Exchange Place, 11th Floor · P.O. Box 45000 · Salt Lake City, UT 84145-5000 · 801-521-9000

Ray R. Christensen* · (Defendants, Products Liability, Professional Malpractice, Airplane Collision) · Christensen, Jensen & Powell · 510 Clark Leaming Building 175 South West Temple · Salt Lake City, UT 84101 · 801-355-3431

Glenn C. Hanni · Strong & Hanni · Boston Building, Suite 600 · Nine Exchange Place · Salt Lake City, UT 84111 · 801-532-7080

Carman E. Kipp · (Defendants) · Kipp and Christian · City Centre I, Suite 330 175 East 400 South · Salt Lake City, UT 84111-2314 · 801-521-3773

Stephen B. Nebeker · (Defendants) · Ray, Quinney & Nebeker · 400 Deseret Building · 79 South Main Street · P.O. Box 45385 · Salt Lake City, UT 84145-0385 · 801-532-1500

Gordon L. Roberts · (Plaintiffs) · Parsons, Behle & Latimer · 185 South State Street, Suite 700 · P.O. Box 11898 · Salt Lake City, UT 84147-0898 · 801-532-1234

David K. Watkiss, Sr. · Watkiss & Saperstein · 310 South Main Street, 12th Floor Salt Lake City, UT 84101-2171 · 801-363-3300

W. Brent Wilcox* · (Plaintiffs, Products Liability, Automobile Collision, Mining & Oil Fields) · Wilcox, Dewsnup & King · 20020 Beneficial Life Tower · 36 South State Street · Salt Lake City, UT 84111 · 801-533-0400

PUBLIC UTILITY LAW

Gregory B. Monson · Watkiss & Saperstein · 310 South Main Street, 12th Floor Salt Lake City, UT 84101 · 801-363-3300

F. Robert Reeder · Parsons, Behle & Latimer · 185 South State Street, Suite 700 P.O. Box 11898 · Salt Lake City, UT 84147-0898 · 801-532-1234

REAL ESTATE LAW

Charles L. Maak · Maak & Maak · l85 South State Street, Suite 1300 · Salt Lake City, UT 84111 · 801-532-7840

Reed L. Martineau* · (Zoning, Land Use, Eminent Domain, Commercial Transactions) · Snow, Christensen & Martineau · 10 Exchange Place, 11th Floor · P.O. Box 45000 · Salt Lake City, UT 84145-5000 · 801-521-9000

Denis Roy Morrill · Prince, Yeates & Geldzahler · City Centre I, Suite 900 · 175 East Fourth South · Salt Lake City, UT 84111 · 801-524-1000

TAX AND EMPLOYEE BENEFITS LAW

K. Jay Holdsworth · Holdsworth, Vogel & Swenson · CSB Tower, Suite 1200 · 50 South Main · Salt Lake City, UT 84144 · 801-322-1100

David E. Salisbury · (Corporate & Partnership Transactions) · Van Cott, Bagley, Cornwall & McCarthy · 50 South Main Street, Suite 1600 · P.O. Box 45340 · Salt Lake City, UT 84145 · 801-532-3333

William Vogel · Holdsworth, Vogel & Swenson · Key Tower, Suite 1200 · 50 South Main Street · Salt Lake City, UT 84144 · 801-322-1100

TRUSTS AND ESTATES

Clark P. Giles · Ray, Quinney & Nebeker · 400 Deseret Building · 79 South Main Street · P.O. Box 45385 · Salt Lake City, UT 84145-0385 · 801-532-1500

K. Jay Holdsworth · Holdsworth, Vogel & Swenson · CSB Tower, Suite 1200 · 50 South Main · Salt Lake City, UT 84144 · 801-322-1100

David E. Salisbury · (Estate Planning, Estate Administration) · Van Cott, Bagley, Cornwall & McCarthy · 50 South Main Street, Suite 1600 · P.O. Box 45340 · Salt Lake City, UT 84145 · 801-532-3333

William Vogel · Holdsworth, Vogel & Swenson · Key Tower, Suite 1200 · 50 South Main Street · Salt Lake City, UT 84144 · 801-322-1100

VERMONT

BANKRUPTCY LAW

Douglas J. Wolinsky · Saxer, Anderson, Wolinsky & Sunshine · One Lawson Lane · P.O. Box 1505 · Burlington, VT 05402-1505 · 802-658-2826

Jerome I. Meyers · Pine and Maple Streets · P.O. Box 919 · White River Junction, VT 05001 · 802-296-2100

BUSINESS LITIGATION

Richard E. Davis* · Richard E. Davis & Associates · 30 Washington Street · Box 666 · Barre, VT 05641 · 802-476-3123

John G. Kristensen · Kristensen, Cummings, Murtha & Stewart · Five Grove Street · P.O. Box 677 · Battleboro, VT 05302 · 802-254-8733

William B. Gray · Sheehey, Brue, Gray & Furlong · 119 South Winooski Avenue P.O. Box 66 · Burlington, VT 05402 · 802-864-9891

Robert B. Hemley · Gravel and Shea · Corporate Plaza · 76 St. Paul Street · P.O. Box 369 · Burlington, VT 05402-0369 · 802-658-0220

Robert D. Rachlin* · (Commercial) · Downs Rachlin & Martin · 199 Main Street P.O. Box 190 · Burlington, VT 05402-0190 · 802-863-2375

John T. Sartore* · (Commercial, RICO, Securities) · Paul, Frank & Collins · One Church Street · P.O. Box 1307 · Burlington, VT 05402-1307 · 802-658-2311

Peter B. Joslin · (Defendants) · Theriault & Joslin · 141 Main Street · P.O. Box 552 · Montpelier, VT 05601 · 802-223-2381

David L. Cleary · Miller, Cleary & Faignant · 36-38 Merchants Row · P.O. Box 6567 · Rutland, VT 05701-6567 · 802-775-2521

CORPORATE LAW

John G. Kristensen · Kristensen, Cummings, Murtha & Stewart · Five Grove Street · P.O. Box 677 · Battleboro, VT 05302 · 802-254-8733

Allen Martin · Downs Rachlin & Martin · 199 Main Street · P.O. Box 190 · Burlington, VT 05402-0190 · 802-863-2375

Stewart H. McConaughy · Gravel and Shea · Corporate Plaza · 76 St. Paul Street P.O. Box 369 · Burlington, VT 05402-0369 · 802-658-0220

J. Paul Giuliani · McKee, Giuliani & Cleveland · 94 Main Street · P.O. Box F · Montpelier, VT 05602 · 802-223-3479

Thomas M. Dowling · Ryan Smith & Carbine · Mead Building · P.O. Box 310 · Rutland, VT 05702-0310 · 802-773-3344

John L. Primmer · Primmer & Wilson · 12 Prospect Street · P.O. Box 159 · St. Johnsbury, VT 05819 · 802-748-5061

CRIMINAL DEFENSE

Richard E. Davis* · (Violent Crimes, Non-Violent Crimes, Federal Court, State Court) · Richard E. Davis & Associates · 30 Washington Street · Box 666 · Barre, VT 05641 · 802-476-3123

Richard I. Rubin · Rubin Rona Kidney & Myer · 237 North Main Street · Barre, VT 05641 · 802-479-2514

Oreste V. Valsangiacomo, Jr.* · Valsangiacomo, Detora, McQuesten, Rose & Grearson · 162 North Main Street · P.O. Box 625 · Barre, VT 05641 · 802-476-4181

Robert B. Hemley · Gravel and Shea · Corporate Plaza · 76 St. Paul Street · P.O. Box 369 · Burlington, VT 05402-0369 · 802-658-0220

Jerome F. O'Neill · O'Neill and Crawford · One Lawson Lane · P.O. Box 5359 Burlington, VT 05402-5359 · 802-865-4700

Charles R. Tetzlaff* · Latham, Eastman, Schweyer & Tetzlaff · 308 Main Street P.O. Box 568 · Burlington, VT 05402-0568 · 802-863-2826

Peter F. Langrock* · Langrock Sperry & Wool · 15 South Pleasant Street · P.O. Drawer 351 · Middlebury, VT 05753-0351 · 802-864-0217

William K. Sessions III* · (Violent Crimes, Non-Violent Crimes, Federal Court, State Court) · Sessions, Keiner, Dumont, Barnes & Everitt · 72 Court Street · Middlebury, VT 05753 · 802-388-4906

Donald A. Graham · Welch, Graham & Manby · Gilman Office Center, Building 4 Holiday Inn Drive · P.O. Box 858 · White River Junction, VT 05001-0858 · 802-295-9347

FAMILY LAW

Richard E. Davis* · (Child Custody, Divorce, Marital Settlement Agreements) · Richard E. Davis & Associates · 30 Washington Street · Box 666 · Barre, VT 05641 802-476-3123

E. Bruce Weber · Weber, Perra & Wilson · 16 Linden Street · P.O. Box 558 · Brattleboro, VT 05302 · 802-257-7161

Charles R. Tetzlaff* · Latham, Eastman, Schweyer & Tetzlaff · 308 Main Street P.O. Box 568 · Burlington, VT 05402-0568 · 802-863-2826

Stephen A. Dardeck · Tepper & Dardeck · 73 Center Street · Rutland, VT 05701 802-775-7525

FIRST AMENDMENT LAW

Robert B. Hemley · Gravel and Shea · Corporate Plaza · 76 St. Paul Street · P.O. Box 369 · Burlington, VT 05402-0369 · 802-658-0220

Peter F. Langrock* · (Plaintiffs) · Langrock Sperry & Wool · 15 South Pleasant Street · P.O. Drawer 351 · Middlebury, VT 05753-0351 · 802-388-6356

HEALTH CARE LAW

Anne Kramer Hong · Miller, Eggleston & Rosenberg · 150 South Champlain Street · P.O. Box 1489 · Burlington, VT 05402-1489 · 802-864-0880

Spencer R. Knapp · Dinse, Erdmann & Clapp · 209 Battery Street · P.O. Box 988 Burlington, VT 05402-0988 · 802-864-5751

Martin K. Miller · Miller, Eggleston & Rosenberg · 150 South Champlain Street P.O. Box 1489 · Burlington, VT 05402-1489 · 802-864-0880

David M. Wilson · Primmer & Wilson · City Center · 89 Main Street · P.O. Box 159 · Montpelier, VT 05601-1059 · 802-229-4914

IMMIGRATION LAW

Oswald I. Kramer · Carroll, Obuchowski & Scribner · 74 Main Street · P.O. Box 932 · Burlington, VT 05402 · 802-862-2855

NATURAL RESOURCES AND ENVIRONMENTAL LAW

Raymond P. Perra · Weber, Perra & Wilson · 16 Linden Street · P.O. Box 558 · Brattleboro, VT 05302 · 802-257-7161

Stephen R. Crampton · Gravel and Shea · Corporate Plaza · 76 St. Paul Street · P.O. Box 369 · Burlington, VT 05402-0369 · 802-658-0220

John R. Ponsetto · Gravel and Shea · Corporate Plaza · 76 St. Paul Street · P.O. Box 369 · Burlington, VT 05402-0369 · 802-658-0220

Jonathan N. Brownell · Brownell & Moeser · RFD 1524 · Corinth, VT 05039 · 802-439-5312

A. Jay Kenlan · Abell, Kenlan, Schwiebert & Hall · 71 Allen Street · P.O. Box 578 Rutland, VT 05702-0578 · 802-773-2754

John H. Marshall · Downs Rachlin & Martin · Nine Prospect Street · St. Johnsbury, VT 05819 · 802-748-8324

PERSONAL INJURY LITIGATION

Richard E. Davis* · (Plaintiffs, Medical Malpractice, Products Liability, Professional Malpractice, Automobile Collision, Airplane Collision) · Richard E. Davis & Associates · 30 Washington Street · Box 666 · Barre, VT 05641 · 802-476-3123

Robert B. Hemley · Gravel and Shea · Corporate Plaza · 76 St. Paul Street · P.O. Box 369 · Burlington, VT 05402-0369 · 802-658-0220

Robert E. Manchester · (Plaintiffs) · Manchester Law Offices · One Lawson Lane, 3rd Floor · P.O. Box 1459 · Burlington, VT 05402-1459 · 802-658-7444

Robert D. Rachlin* · (Medical Malpractice, Products Liability) · Downs Rachlin & Martin · 199 Main Street · P.O. Box 190 · Burlington, VT 05402-0190 · 802-863-2375

John T. Sartore* · (Plaintiffs, Defendants, Products Liability, Professional Malpractice) · Paul, Frank & Collins · One Church Street · P.O. Box 1307 · Burlington, VT 05402-1307 · 802-658-2311

Alan F. Sylvester · (Plaintiffs) · Sylvester & Maley · 78 Pine Street · P.O. Box 1053 · Burlington, VT 05401 · 802-864-5722

Peter F. Langrock* · (Plaintiffs) · Langrock Sperry & Wool · 15 South Pleasant Street · P.O. Drawer 351 · Middlebury, VT 05753-0351 · 802-388-6356

David L. Cleary · (Plaintiffs, Defendants, Medical Malpractice, Airplane Collision) · Miller, Cleary & Faignant · 36-38 Merchants Row · P.O. Box 6567 · Rutland, VT 05701-6567 · 802-775-2521

PUBLIC UTILITY LAW

Allen Martin · Downs Rachlin & Martin · 199 Main Street · P.O. Box 190 · Burlington, VT 05402-0190 · 802-863-2375

Martin K. Miller · Miller, Eggleston & Rosenberg · 150 South Champlain Street P.O. Box 1489 · Burlington, VT 05402-1489 · 802-864-0880

John H. Marshall · Downs Rachlin & Martin · Nine Prospect Street · St. Johnsbury, VT 05819 · 802-748-8324

William B. Piper · Primmer & Wilson · 12 Prospect Street · P.O. Box 159 · St. Johnsbury, VT 05819 · 802-748-5061

REAL ESTATE LAW

Jonathan Bump · Eight Park Place · P.O. Box 658 · Brattleboro, VT 05302 · 802-257-0687

Peter M. Collins · Paul, Frank & Collins · One Church Street · P.O. Box 1307 · Burlington, VT 05402-1307 · 802-658-2311

Stephen R. Crampton · (Zoning, Land Use, Commercial Transactions) · Gravel and Shea · Corporate Plaza · 76 St. Paul Street · P.O. Box 369 · Burlington, VT 05402-0369 · 802-658-0220

Carl H. Lisman* · Lisman & Lisman · 84 Pine Street · P.O. Box 728 · Burlington, VT 05402 · 802-864-5756

Mark L. Sperry III · Langrock Sperry & Wool · 275 College Street · P.O. Box 721 Burlington, VT 05402-0721 · 802-864-0217

Jonathan N. Brownell · Brownell & Moeser · RFD 1524 · Corinth, VT 05039 · 802-439-5312

A. Jay Kenlan · Abell, Kenlan, Schwiebert & Hall · 71 Allen Street · P.O. Box 578 Rutland, VT 05702-0578 · 802-773-2754

James G. Wheeler, Jr. · Downs Rachlin & Martin · Nine Prospect Street · St. Johnsbury, VT 05819 · 802-748-8324

TAX AND EMPLOYEE BENEFITS LAW

Jon R. Eggleston · Miller, Eggleston & Rosenberg · 150 South Champlain Street P.O. Box 1489 · Burlington, VT 05402-1489 · 802-864-0880

Charles T. Shea · Gravel and Shea · Corporate Plaza · 76 St. Paul Street · P.O. Box 369 · Burlington, VT 05402-0369 · 802-658-0220

Thomas M. Dowling · (Corporate & Partnership Transactions) · Ryan Smith & Carbine · Mead Building · P.O. Box 310 · Rutland, VT 05702-0310 · 802-773-3344

TRUSTS AND ESTATES

Harvey B. Otterman, Jr. · Otterman and Allen · 162 North Main Street · P.O. Box 273 · Barre, VT 05641 · 802-479-2552

Paul N. Olson · Fitts, Olson, Carnahan, Anderson and Giddings · 16 High Street P.O. Box 801 · Brattleboro, VT 05301 · 802-254-2345

Clarke A. Gravel · Gravel and Shea · Corporate Plaza · 76 St. Paul Street · P.O. Box 369 · Burlington, VT 05402-0369 · 802-658-0220

William G. Post, Jr. · Gravel and Shea · Corporate Plaza · 76 St. Paul Street · P.O. Box 369 · Burlington, VT 05402-0369 · 802-658-0220

Christopher G. Stoneman · Downs Rachlin & Martin · 199 Main Street · P.O. Box 190 · Burlington, VT 05402-0190 · 802-863-2375

Thomas M. Dowling · (Estate Planning) · Ryan Smith & Carbine · Mead Building P.O. Box 310 · Rutland, VT 05702-0310 · 802-773-3344

Christopher A. Webber, Jr. · Webber, Costello & Chapman · 110 Merchants Row · P.O. Box 807 · Rutland, VT 05702-0807 · 802-773-9109

VIRGINIA

BANKRUPTCY LAW

Richard A. Bartl · Tyler, Bartl, Burke & Albert · 300 North Washington Street, Suite 500 · Alexandria, VA 22314 · 703-549-5000

H. Bradley Evans, Jr.* · (Bankruptcy Litigation) · Hazel & Thomas · 510 King Street, Suite 200 · P.O. Box 820 · Alexandria, VA 22313-0820 · 703-836-8400

Robert O. Tyler · Tyler, Bartl, Burke & Albert · 300 North Washington Street, Suite 500 · Alexandria, VA 22314 · 703-549-5000

Ross C. Reeves · Willcox & Savage · 1800 Sovran Center · One Commercial Place Norfolk, VA 23510-2197 · 804-628-5545

Jerrold G. Weinberg* · (Business Reorganization, Creditors' Rights, Debtors' Rights) · Weinberg & Stein · 1825 Dominion Tower · 999 Waterside Drive · P.O. Box 3789 · Norfolk, VA 23514 · 804-627-1066

Frank J. Santoro · Marcus, Santoro & Kozak · 341 High Street · P.O. Box 69 · Portsmouth, VA 23705 · 804-393-2555

Benjamin C. Ackerly* · Hunton & Williams · Riverfront Plaza, East Tower · 951 East Byrd Street · P.O. Box 1535 · Richmond, VA 23212 · 804-788-8479

H. Slayton Dabney, Jr. · McGuire, Woods, Battle & Boothe · One James Center 901 East Cary Street · Richmond, VA 23219 · 804-775-1000

Harry Shaia, Jr. · Spinella, Owings & Shaia · 8550 Mayland Drive · Richmond, VA 23294-4704 · 804-747-0920

M. Caldwell Butler · Woods, Rogers & Hazlegrove · 105 Franklin Road, SW · P.O. Box 720 · Roanoke, VA 24004-0720 · 703-982-4200

David H. Adams* · (Business Reorganization, Creditors' Rights, Bankruptcy Litigation, Trustee Representation) · Clark & Stant · 900 Sovran Bank Building · One Columbus Center · Virginia Beach, VA 23462 · 804-499-8800

BUSINESS LITIGATION

Edward B. Lowry · Michie, Hamlett, Lowry, Rasmussen & Tweel · 500 Court Square, Suite 300 · P.O. Box 298 · Charlottesville, VA 22902-0298 · 804-977-3390

Dexter S. Odin · Odin, Feldman & Pittleman · 9302 Lee Highway, Suite 1100 · Fairfax, VA 22031 · 703-218-2100

Robert C. Wood III · Edmunds & Williams · 800 Main Street · P.O. Box 958 · Lynchburg, VA 24505 · 804-846-9000

David McC. Estabrook* · Gordon Estabrook & Yeonas · 7926 Jones Branch Drive, Suite 570 · P.O. Box 459 · McLean, VA 22102 · 703-506-9441

R. Terrence Ney* · (Appellate) · McGuire, Woods, Battle & Boothe · Tysons Corner · 8280 Greensboro Drive, Suite 900 · P.O. Box 9346 · McLean, VA 22102 703-712-5000

Lee A. Rau · Reed Smith Shaw & McClay · 8201 Greensboro Drive, Suite 820 · McLean, VA 22102-3604 · 703-556-8440

John S. Stump · McGuire, Woods, Battle & Boothe · Tysons Corner · 8280 Greensboro Drive, Suite 900 · P.O. Box 9346 · McLean, VA 22102 · 703-712-5457

Jack E. Greer* · (Commercial) · Williams, Kelly, & Greer · 600 Crestar Bank Building · P.O. Box 3416 · Norfolk, VA 23514 · 804-624-2600

John Y. Pearson, Jr. · Willcox & Savage · 1800 Sovran Center · One Commercial Place · Norfolk, VA 23510-2197 · 804-628-5503

John M. Ryan* · Vandeventer, Black, Meredith & Martin · 500 World Trade Center · Norfolk, VA 23510 · 804-446-8600

Conrad M. Shumadine* · (Antitrust, Appellate, Banking, Commercial) · Willcox & Savage · 1800 Sovran Center · One Commercial Place · Norfolk, VA 23510-2197 804-628-5500

Gregory N. Stillman* · (Antitrust) · Hunton & Williams · First Virginia Bank Tower, Suite 1300 · P.O. Box 3889 · Norfolk, VA 23514 · 804-625-5501

Jerrold G. Weinberg* · (Appellate, Banking, Commercial, Finance) · Weinberg & Stein · 1825 Dominion Tower · 999 Waterside Drive · P.O. Box 3789 · Norfolk, VA 23514 · 804-627-1066

Everette G. Allen, Jr. · Hirschler, Fleischer, Weinberg, Cox & Allen · Main Street Centre · 629 East Main Street · P.O. Box 1Q · Richmond, VA 23202 · 804-771-9500

Lewis Thomas Booker · Hunton & Williams · Riverfront Plaza, East Tower · 951 East Byrd Street · P.O. Box 1535 · Richmond, VA 23212 · 804-788-8200

J. Robert Brame III* · (Administrative, Antitrust) · McGuire, Woods, Battle & Boothe · One James Center · 901 East Cary Street · Richmond, VA 23219 · 804-775-1000

Robert F. Brooks* · Hunton & Williams · Riverfront Plaza, East Tower · 951 East Byrd Street · P.O. Box 1535 · Richmond, VA 23212 · 804-788-8200

R. Harvey Chappell, Jr. · Christian, Barton, Epps, Brent & Chappell · 1200 Mutual Building · 909 East Main Street · Richmond, VA 23219-3095 · 804-644-7851

William R. Cogar* · Mays & Valentine · Sovran Center · 1111 East Main Street P.O. Box 1122 · Richmond, VA 23208-1122 · 804-697-1200

James E. Farnham* · (Securities) · Hunton & Williams · Riverfront Plaza, East Tower · 951 East Byrd Street · P.O. Box 1535 · Richmond, VA 23212 · 804-788-8200

J. Waller Harrison* · McGuire, Woods, Battle & Boothe · One James Center · 901 East Cary Street · Richmond, VA 23219 · 804-775-1000

John F. Kay, Jr. · Mays & Valentine · Sovran Center · 1111 East Main Street · P.O. Box 1122 · Richmond, VA 23208-1122 · 804-697-1200

William H. King, Jr. · McGuire, Woods, Battle & Boothe · One James Center · 901 East Cary Street · Richmond, VA 23219 · 804-775-1000

Jack E. McClard* · (Commercial, Securities, Construction) · Hunton & Williams Riverfront Plaza, East Tower · 951 East Byrd Street · P.O. Box 1535 · Richmond, VA 23212 · 804-788-8200

John H. OBrion, Jr. · (Commercial) · Cowan & Owen · 1930 Huguenot Road · P.O. Box 35655 · Richmond, VA 23235-0655 · 804-320-8918

Rosewell Page III · McGuire, Woods, Battle & Boothe · One James Center · 901 East Cary Street · Richmond, VA 23219 · 804-775-1000

Robert H. Patterson, Jr. · McGuire, Woods, Battle & Boothe · One James Center 901 East Cary Street · Richmond, VA 23219 · 804-775-1000

Robert E. Payne* · (Banking, Commercial, International Securities) · McGuire, Woods, Battle & Boothe · One James Center · 901 East Cary Street · Richmond, VA 23219 · 804-775-1000

Virginia W. Powell* · Hunton & Williams · Riverfront Plaza, East Tower · 951 East Byrd Street · P.O. Box 1535 · Richmond, VA 23212 · 804-788-8200

James C. Roberts* · Mays & Valentine · Sovran Center · 1111 East Main Street P.O. Box 1122 · Richmond, VA 23208-1122 · 804-697-1200

James L. Sanderlin · McGuire, Woods, Battle & Boothe · One James Center · 901 East Cary Street · Richmond, VA 23219 · 804-775-1000

Thomas G. Slater, Jr. · Hunton & Williams · Riverfront Plaza, East Tower · 951 East Byrd Street · P.O. Box 1535 · Richmond, VA 23212 · 804-788-8200

Alexander H. Slaughter · McGuire, Woods, Battle & Boothe · One James Center 901 East Cary Street · Richmond, VA 23219 · 804-775-1000

Michael W. Smith · Christian, Barton, Epps, Brent & Chappell · 1200 Mutual Building · 909 East Main Street · Richmond, VA 23219-3095 · 804-644-7851

Joseph M. Spivey III* · (Commercial) · Hunton & Williams · Riverfront Plaza, East Tower · 951 East Byrd Street · P.O. Box 1535 · Richmond, VA 23212 · 804-788-8200

Anthony F. Troy* · (Administrative, Antitrust) · Mays & Valentine · Sovran Center · 1111 East Main Street · P.O. Box 1122 · Richmond, VA 23208-1122 · 804-697-1200

Anne Marie Whittemore · McGuire, Woods, Battle & Boothe · One James Center · 901 East Cary Street · Richmond, VA 23219 · 804-775-1000

Murray H. Wright* · Wright, Robinson, McCammon, Osthimer & Tatum · 411 East Franklin Street · Richmond, VA 23219-2205 · 804-783-1100

William B. Poff* · Woods, Rogers & Hazlegrove · 105 Franklin Road, SW · P.O. Box 720 · Roanoke, VA 24004-0720 · 703-982-4200

William R. Rakes* · (Antitrust, Banking, Securities, Health Care) · Gentry, Locke, Rakes & Moore · 800 Crestar Plaza · P.O. Box 1018 · Roanoke, VA 24005 703-982-8000

Donald H. Clark · Clark & Stant · 900 Sovran Bank Building · One Columbus Center · Virginia Beach, VA 23462 · 804-499-8800

Vernon M. Geddy, Jr.* · Geddy, Harris & Geddy · 137 York Street · P.O. Box 379 · Williamsburg, VA 23187 · 804-229-2393

CORPORATE LAW

Neal D. Peterson · (Banking, Financial Institutions) · 9401 Lee Highway, Suite 101 · Fairfax, VA 22031 · 703-934-0008

James B. Pittleman · Odin, Feldman & Pittleman · 9302 Lee Highway, Suite 1100 · Fairfax, VA 22031 · 703-218-2100

Jesse B. Wilson III · Miles & Stockbridge · 11350 Random Hills Road, Suite 500 Fairfax, VA 22030 · 703-273-2440

Duane W. Beckhorn · Hazel & Thomas · 3110 Fairview Park Drive, Suite 1400 P.O. Box 12001 · Falls Church, VA 22042 · 703-641-4200

Thomas C. Brown, Jr. · McGuire, Woods, Battle & Boothe · Tysons Corner · 8280 Greensboro Drive, Suite 900 · P.O. Box 9346 · McLean, VA 22102 · 703-712-5393

C. Thomas Hicks III · Shaw, Pittman, Potts & Trowbridge · 1501 Farm Credit Drive, Suite 4400 · McLean, VA 22102 · 703-790-7900

Arthur P. Scibelli · (Financial Institutions, Mergers & Acquisitions, Securities, Securities Regulation) · McGuire, Woods, Battle & Boothe · Tysons Corner · 8280 Greensboro Drive, Suite 900 · P.O. Box 9346 · McLean, VA 22102 · 703-712-5445

Charles W. Best, Jr. · Wilks & Best · 700 Town Pont Center · 150 Boush Street Norfolk, VA 23510-1626 · 804-623-6500

Leroy T. Canoles, Jr. · Kaufman & Canoles · Sovran Center, Suite 2000 · One Commercial Place · P.O. Box 3037 · Norfolk, VA 23514-3037 · 804-624-3000

Robert C. Goodman, Jr. · Kaufman & Canoles · Sovran Center, Suite 2000 · One Commercial Place · P.O. Box 3037 · Norfolk, VA 23514-3037 · 804-624-3000

Thomas G. Johnson, Jr. · Willcox & Savage · 1800 Sovran Center · One Commercial Place · Norfolk, VA 23510-2197 · 804-628-5500

Vincent J. Mastracco, Jr. · Kaufman & Canoles · Sovran Center, Suite 2000 · One Commercial Place · P.O. Box 3037 · Norfolk, VA 23514-3037 · 804-624-3000

Robert C. Nusbaum* · Hofheimer, Nusbaum, McPhaul & Samuels · 1700 Dominion Tower · P.O. Box 3460 · Norfolk, VA 23514-3460 · 804-622-3366

Toy D. Savage, Jr. · Willcox & Savage · 1800 Sovran Center · One Commercial Place · Norfolk, VA 23510-2197 · 804-628-5500

Guy K. Tower · Kaufman & Canoles · Sovran Center, Suite 2000 · One Commercial Place · P.O. Box 3037 · Norfolk, VA 23514-3037 · 804-624-3000

Albert J. Taylor, Jr. · Cooper, Spong & Davis · Central Fidelity Bank Building High & Crawford Streets · P.O. Box 1475 · Portsmouth, VA 23705-1475 · 804-397-3481

Evans B. Brasfield · Hunton & Williams · Riverfront Plaza, East Tower · 951 East Byrd Street · P.O. Box 1535 · Richmond, VA 23212 · 804-788-8200

Robert L. Burrus, Jr. · McGuire, Woods, Battle & Boothe · One James Center 901 East Cary Street · Richmond, VA 23219 · 804-775-1000

Joseph C. Carter, Jr. · Hunton & Williams · Riverfront Plaza, East Tower · 951 East Byrd Street · P.O. Box 1535 · Richmond, VA 23212 · 804-788-8200

Richard H. Catlett, Jr. · McGuire, Woods, Battle & Boothe · One James Center 901 East Cary Street · Richmond, VA 23219 · 804-775-1000

Marshall H. Earl, Jr. · McGuire, Woods, Battle & Boothe · One James Center · 901 East Cary Street · Richmond, VA 23219 · 804-775-1000

John W. Edmonds III · Mays & Valentine · Sovran Center · 1111 East Main Street · P.O. Box 1122 · Richmond, VA 23208-1122 · 804-697-1200

George C. Freeman, Jr. · Hunton & Williams · Riverfront Plaza, East Tower · 951 East Byrd Street · P.O. Box 1535 · Richmond, VA 23212 · 804-788-8200

Allen C. Goolsby III · Hunton & Williams · Riverfront Plaza, East Tower · 951 East Byrd Street · P.O. Box 1535 · Richmond, VA 23212 · 804-788-8200

Leslie A. Grandis · McGuire, Woods, Battle & Boothe · One James Center · 901 East Cary Street · Richmond, VA 23219 · 804-775-1000

F. Claiborne Johnston, Jr. · (Banking, Corporate Finance, Financial Institutions, Securities Regulation) · Mays & Valentine · Sovran Center · 1111 East Main Street P.O. Box 1122 · Richmond, VA 23208-1122 · 804-697-1200

Stephen R. Larson · Christian, Barton, Epps, Brent & Chappell · 1200 Mutual Building · 909 East Main Street · Richmond, VA 23219-3095 · 804-644-7851

Michael W. Maupin · Hunton & Williams · Riverfront Plaza, East Tower · 951 East Byrd Street · P.O. Box 1535 · Richmond, VA 23212 · 804-788-8200

C. Cotesworth Pinckney · Mays & Valentine · Sovran Center · 1111 East Main Street · P.O. Box 1122 · Richmond, VA 23208-1122 · 804-697-1200

Gordon F. Rainey, Jr. · (Banking) · Hunton & Williams · Riverfront Plaza, East Tower · 951 East Byrd Street · P.O. Box 1535 · Richmond, VA 23212 · 804-788-8200

R. Gordon Smith · McGuire, Woods, Battle & Boothe · One James Center · 901 East Cary Street · Richmond, VA 23219 · 804-775-1000

Randolph F. Totten · Hunton & Williams · Riverfront Plaza, East Tower · 951 East Byrd Street · P.O. Box 1535 · Richmond, VA 23212 · 804-788-8200

C. Porter Vaughan III · (Corporate Finance, Leveraged Buyouts, Mergers & Acquisitions, Securities) · Hunton & Williams · Riverfront Plaza, East Tower · 951 East Byrd Street · P.O. Box 1535 · Richmond, VA 23212 · 804-788-8200

William R. Waddell · McGuire, Woods, Battle & Boothe · One James Center · 901 East Cary Street · Richmond, VA 23219 · 804-775-1000

Hugh V. White, Jr. · Hunton & Williams · Riverfront Plaza, East Tower · 951 East Byrd Street · P.O. Box 1535 · Richmond, VA 23212 · 804-788-8200

Douglas W. Densmore · (Banking) · Woods, Rogers & Hazlegrove · 105 Franklin Road, SW · P.O. Box 720 · Roanoke, VA 24004-0720 · 703-982-4200

G. Franklin Flippin* · (Banking, Corporate Finance, Mergers & Acquisitions) · Glenn, Flippin, Feldman & Darby · 200 First Campbell Square · P.O. Box 2887 Roanoke, VA 24001 · 703-344-3000

Talfourd H. Kemper · Woods, Rogers & Hazlegrove · 105 Franklin Road, SW · P.O. Box 720 · Roanoke, VA 24004-0720 · 703-982-4200

Joel M. Birken · (Administrative) · Rees, Broome & Diaz · 8133 Leesburg Pike, Ninth Floor · Vienna, VA 22182 · 703-442-8183

Vernon M. Geddy, Jr.* · Geddy, Harris & Geddy · 137 York Street · P.O. Box 379 · Williamsburg, VA 23187 · 804-229-2393

CRIMINAL DEFENSE

James C. Clark · Land, Clark, Carroll & Mendelson · 600 Cameron Street · Alexandria, VA 22320-0888 · 703-549-3335

Blair D. Howard · Howard, Leino & Howard · 128 North Pitt Street · Alexandria, VA 22314 · 703-549-1188

William B. Moffitt · William B. Moffitt & Associates · 317 South Patrick Street · Alexandria, VA 22314 · 703-548-0572

J. Frederick Sinclair · Cohen, Dunn & Sinclair · 221 South Alfred Street · P.O. Box 117 · Alexandria, VA 22313-0117 · 703-836-9000

Frank W. Dunham, Jr. · Cohen, Gettings, Alper & Dunham · 2200 Wilson Boulevard, Suite 800 · Arlington, VA 22201 · 703-525-2260

Brian P. Gettings · Cohen, Gettings, Alper & Dunham · 2200 Wilson Boulevard, Suite 800 · Arlington, VA 22201 · 703-525-2260

Louis Koutoulakos · Varoutsos & Koutoulakos · 2009 North 14th Street, Suite 708 · Arlington, VA 22201 · 703-527-0124

John C. Lowe · Lowe and Jacobs · 300 Court Square · Charlottesville, VA 22901-5163 · 804-296-8188

Wayne Lustig* · (Non-Violent Crimes, Federal Court, State Court) · Mays & Valentine · Town Point Center, Eighth Floor · 150 Boush Street · Norfolk, VA 23510 · 804-627-5500

Stanley E. Sacks* · Sacks & Sacks · Town Point Center, Suite 501 · 150 Boush Street · P.O. Box 3874 · Norfolk, VA 23514-3874 · 804-623-2753

Franklin A. Swartz · Rabinowitz, Rafal, Swartz, Taliaferro & Gilbert · Wainwright Building, Seventh Floor · 229 West Bute Street · P.O. Box 3332 · Norfolk, VA 23514-3332 · 804-622-3931

Dennis W. Dohnal · Bremner, Baber & Janus · Jefferson Bank Building, Suite 1500 · 701 East Franklin Street · P.O. Box 826 · Richmond, VA 23207 · 804-644-0721

Murray J. Janus* · Bremner, Baber & Janus · Jefferson Bank Building, Suite 1500 701 East Franklin Street · P.O. Box 826 · Richmond, VA 23207 · 804-644-0721

Michael Morchower · Morchower, Luxton and Whaley · Nine East Franklin Street · Richmond, VA 23219 · 804-643-0147

James C. Roberts* · Mays & Valentine · Sovran Center · 1111 East Main Street P.O. Box 1122 · Richmond, VA 23208-1122 · 804-697-1200

Robert F. Rider* · Rider, Thomas, Cleaveland, Ferris & Eakin · Southwest Virginia Savings and Loan Building · Campbell Avenue and Second Street, SW · P.O. Box 1791 · Roanoke, VA 24008-1791 · 703-344-3233

Richard G. Brydges · Brydges, Brydges and Mahan · Professional Building · 1369 Laskin Road · P.O. Box 625 · Virginia Beach, VA 23451 · 804-428-6021

FAMILY LAW

James Ray Cottrell* · (Child Custody, Divorce, Marital Settlement Agreements, Equitable Division) · Gannon, Cottrell & Ward · 411 North Washington Street · P.O. Box 1286 · Alexandria, VA 22313 · 703-836-2770

Ilona Ely Freedman (Grenadier)* · Grenadier, Davis & Simpson · 649 South Washington Street · Alexandria, VA 22314 · 703-683-9000

Martin A. Gannon · Gannon, Cottrell & Ward · 411 North Washington Street · P.O. Box 1286 · Alexandria, VA 22313-1286 · 703-836-2770

Joanne Fogel Alper · Cohen, Gettings, Alper & Dunham · 2200 Wilson Boulevard, Suite 800 · Arlington, VA 22201 · 703-525-2260

Betty A. Thompson · Law Office of Betty A. Thompson · 1800 North Kent Street, Suite 1001 · Arlington, VA 22209 · 703-522-8100

Annie Lee Jacobs · Parker, McElwain & Jacobs · 1425 Seminole Trail, Fourth Floor · P.O. Box 6186 · Charlottesville, VA 22906 · 804-973-3331

Ronald R. Tweel · Michie, Hamlett, Lowry, Rasmussen & Tweel · 500 Court Square, Suite 300 · P.O. Box 298 · Charlottesville, VA 22902-0298 · 804-977-3390

Richard J. Colten* · Surovell, Jackson, Colten & Dugan · 4010 University Drive, Suite 300 · Fairfax, VA 22030 · 703-591-1300

Robert E. Shoun · Shoun, Smith & Bach · 12700 Fairlakes Circle · Fairfax, VA 22033 · 703-222-3330

Robert J. Surovell · Surovell, Jackson, Colten & Dugan · 4010 University Drive, Suite 300 · Fairfax, VA 22030 · 703-591-1300

Lawrence D. Diehl · Marks & Harrison · 320 East Broadway · P.O. Box 170 · Hopewell, VA 23860 · 804-748-0999

Burke F. McCahill · Hanes, Sevila, Saunders & McCahill · 30 North King Street P.O. Box 678 · Leesburg, VA 22075 · 703-777-5700

William Rosenberger, Jr.* · Central Fidelity Bank Building, Suite 1904 · P.O. Box 1328 · Lynchburg, VA 24505 · 804-845-2393

Henry M. Schwan · 806 Crestar Bank Building · Norfolk, VA 23510 · 804-625-4221

Jerrold G. Weinberg* · (Child Custody, Divorce, Marital Settlement Agreements, Equitable Division) · Weinberg & Stein · 1825 Dominion Tower · 999 Waterside Drive · P.O. Box 3789 · Norfolk, VA 23514 · 804-627-1066

Morton B. Spero · 135 South Adams Street · Petersburg, VA 23803 · 804-733-0151

Donald K. Butler · (Child Custody, Divorce, Marital Settlement Agreements, Equitable Division) · Morano, Colan and Butler · 526 North Boulevard · Richmond, VA 23220 · 804-353-4931

Murray J. Janus* · Bremner, Baber & Janus · Jefferson Bank Building, Suite 1500 701 East Franklin Street · P.O. Box 826 · Richmond, VA 23207 · 804-644-0721

Matthew N. Ott · 2222 Monument Avenue · Richmond, VA 23220 · 804-358-5044

Harwell M. Darby, Jr. · Glenn, Flippin, Feldmann & Darby · 200 First Campbell Square · P.O. Box 2887 · Roanoke, VA 24001 · 703-344-3000

G. Marshall Mundy · Mundy Rogers & Frith · Third Street & Woods Avenue, SW · P.O. Box 2240 · Roanoke, VA 24009 · 703-982-1351

Arthur E. Smith* · 404 Shenandoah Building · 301 First Street, SW · Roanoke, VA 24011 · 703-344-2121

Joseph A. Condo* · Rees, Broome & Diaz · 8133 Leesburg Pike, Ninth Floor · Vienna, VA 22182 · 703-442-8183

Barry Kantor · (Child Custody, Divorce, Marital Settlement Agreements, Equitable Division) · Christie, Held & Kantor · 209 Business Park Drive · P.O. Box 62525 · Virginia Beach, VA 23462 · 804-499-9222

Grover C. Wright, Jr. · Beach Tower Building, Suite 303 · 3330 Pacific Avenue Virginia Beach, VA 23451 · 804-428-2741

FIRST AMENDMENT LAW

Conrad M. Shumadine · Willcox & Savage · 1800 Sovran Center · One Commercial Place · Norfolk, VA 23510-2197 · 804-628-5500

Alexander Wellford · Christian, Barton, Epps, Brent & Chappell · 1200 Mutual Building · 909 East Main Street · Richmond, VA 23219-3095 · 804-644-7851

HEALTH CARE LAW

Leigh B. Middleditch, Jr. · McGuire, Woods, Battle & Boothe · Court Square Building · 418 East Jefferson Street · P.O. Box 1288 · Charlottesville, VA 22902 804-977-2500

Barent L. Fake · Miles & Stockbridge · 11350 Random Hills Road, Suite 500 · Fairfax, VA 22030 · 703-273-2440

Thomas C. Brown, Jr. · McGuire, Woods, Battle & Boothe · Tysons Corner · 8280 Greensboro Drive, Suite 900 · P.O. Box 9346 · McLean, VA 22102 · 703-712-5393

J. Robert McAllister III · Adams, Porter & Radigan · 1650 Tysons Boulevard, Suite 700 · McLean, VA 22102 · 703-448-6600

Hugh L. Patterson · Willcox & Savage · 1800 Sovran Center · One Commercial Place · Norfolk, VA 23510-2197 · 804-628-5500

Anita O. Poston · Vandeventer, Black, Meredith & Martin · 500 World Trade Center · Norfolk, VA 23510 · 804-446-8600

Robert T. Adams · McGuire, Woods, Battle & Boothe · One James Center · 901 East Cary Street · Richmond, VA 23219 · 804-775-4365

John William Crews · Crews & Hancock · 700 Building · 700 East Main Street Richmond, VA 23219 · 804-649-9333

Virginia H. Hackney · Hunton & Williams · Riverfront Plaza, East Tower · 951 East Byrd Street · P.O. Box 1535 · Richmond, VA 23212 · 804-788-8200

Thomas Francis Hancock · Crews & Hancock · 700 Building · 700 East Main Street · Richmond, VA 23219 · 804-649-9333

Thomas W. McCandlish · Mezzullo & McCandlish · 700 East Main Street, Suite 804 · P.O. Box 796 · Richmond, VA 23206 · 804-782-9250

Nicholas A. Spinella · Spinella, Owings & Shaia · 8550 Mayland Drive · Richmond, VA 23294-4704 · 804-747-0920

Heman A. Marshall · Woods, Rogers & Hazlegrove · 105 Franklin Road, SW · P.O. Box 720 · Roanoke, VA 24004-0720 · 703-982-4200

IMMIGRATION LAW

Robert W. Goodlatte · Bird, Kinder & Huffman · 126 Church Avenue, SW, Suite 200 · P.O. Box 2795 · Roanoke, VA 24001-2795 · 703-982-1755

LABOR AND EMPLOYMENT LAW

Thomas J. Cawley · (Management) · Hunton & Williams · 3050 Chain Bridge Road · P.O. Box 1147 · Fairfax, VA 22030 · 703-352-2200

Christine H. Perdue · (Management) · Hunton & Williams · 3050 Chain Bridge Road · Fairfax, VA 22030 · 703-352-2200

Michael F. Marino* · (Management) · Reed Smith Shaw & McClay · 8201 Greensboro Drive, Suite 820 · McLean, VA 22102-3604 · 703-556-8440

Stanley G. Barr, Jr.* · (Management) · Kaufman & Canoles · Sovran Center, Suite 2000 · One Commercial Place · P.O. Box 3037 · Norfolk, VA 23514-3037 · 804-624-3000

Henry E. Howell, Jr. · (Labor) · Howell, Daugherty, Brown & Lawrence · One East Plume Street · P.O. Box 3929 · Norfolk, VA 23514 · 804-623-7334

William E. Rachels, Jr.* · (Management) · Willcox & Savage · 1800 Sovran Center · One Commercial Place · Norfolk, VA 23510-2197 · 804-628-5500

John M. Ryan* · (Management) · Vandeventer, Black, Meredith & Martin · 500 World Trade Center · Norfolk, VA 23510 · 804-446-8600

Abram W. VanderMeer, Jr. · (Management) · Hunton & Williams · First Virginia Bank Tower, Suite 1300 · P.O. Box 3889 · Norfolk, VA 23514 · 804-625-5501

Burt H. Whitt · (Management) · Kaufman & Canoles · Sovran Center, Suite 2000 One Commercial Place · P.O. Box 3037 · Norfolk, VA 23514-3037 · 804-624-3000

John S. Barr* · (Individuals) · Maloney, Yeatts & Barr · 600 Ross Building · 801 East Main Street · Richmond, VA 23219-2906 · 804-644-0313

J. Robert Brame III* · (Management) · McGuire, Woods, Battle & Boothe · One James Center · 901 East Cary Street · Richmond, VA 23219 · 804-775-1000

Jack W. Burtch, Jr. · (Management, Individuals) · McSweeney, Burtch & Crump 11 South 12th Street · P.O. Box 1463 · Richmond, VA 23212 · 804-783-6800

Jay J. Levit* · (Management, Labor, Individuals) · Levit & Mann · 419 North Boulevard · Richmond, VA 23220 · 804-355-7766

James V. Meath · (Management) · Williams, Mullen, Christian & Dobbins · Two James Center · 1021 East Cary Street · P.O. Box 1320 · Richmond, VA 23210-1320 804-783-6412

Paul M. Thompson · (Management) · Hunton & Williams · Riverfront Plaza, East Tower · 951 East Byrd Street · P.O. Box 1535 · Richmond, VA 23212 · 804-788-8200

William E. Twomey, Jr. · (Management) · McGuire, Woods, Battle & Boothe · One James Center · 901 East Cary Street · Richmond, VA 23219 · 804-775-1000

D. Eugene Webb, Jr. · (Management) · Mays & Valentine · Sovran Center · 111 East Main Street · P.O. Box 1122 · Richmond, VA 23208-1122 · 804-697-1200

Hill B. Wellford, Jr. · (Management) · Hunton & Williams · Riverfront Plaza, East Tower · 951 East Byrd Street · P.O. Box 1535 · Richmond, VA 23212 · 804-788-8200

W. Carter Younger · (Management) · McGuire, Woods, Battle & Boothe · One James Center · 901 East Cary Street · Richmond, VA 23219 · 804-775-1000

Bayard E. Harris* · (Management) · The Center for Employment Law · 2965 Colonnade Drive, SW · P.O. Box 21669 · Roanoke, VA 24018-0580 · 703-989-1021

Donald Wise Huffman · (Individuals) · Bird, Kinder & Huffman · 126 Church Avenue, SW, Suite 200 · P.O. Box 2795 · Roanoke, VA 24001-2795 · 703-982-1755

Clinton S. Morse · (Management) · Woods, Rogers & Hazlegrove · 105 Franklin Road, SW · P.O. Box 720 · Roanoke, VA 24004-0720 · 703-982-4200

MARITIME LAW

Morton H. Clark · Vandeventer, Black, Meredith & Martin · 500 World Trade Center · Norfolk, VA 23510 · 804-446-8600

Walter B. Martin, Jr. · (Charter Parties, Personal Injury, Collision) · Vandeventer, Black, Meredith & Martin · 500 World Trade Center · Norfolk, VA 23510 · 804-446-8600

A. Jackson Timms* · Hunton & Williams · First Virginia Bank Tower, Suite 1300 P.O. Box 3889 · Norfolk, VA 23510 · 804-625-5501

Charles F. Tucker* · (Personal Injury) · Vandeventer, Black, Meredith & Martin 500 World Trade Center · Norfolk, VA 23510 · 804-446-8600

Braden Vandeventer, Jr. · Vandeventer, Black, Meredith & Martin · 500 World Trade Center · Norfolk, VA 23510 · 804-446-8600

NATURAL RESOURCES AND ENVIRONMENTAL LAW

David E. Evans · McGuire, Woods, Battle & Boothe · One James Center · 901 East Cary Street · Richmond, VA 23219 · 804-775-1000

Manning Gasch, Jr. · (Hazardous Waste) · Hunton & Williams · Riverfront Plaza, East Tower · 951 East Byrd Street · P.O. Box 1535 · Richmond, VA 23212 · 804-788-8200

Jeremiah J. Jewett III · (Water, Air, Solid Waste, Hazardous Waste) · McGuire, Woods, Battle & Boothe · One James Center · 901 East Cary Street · Richmond, VA 23219 · 804-775-1005

William L. Rosbe · Hunton & Williams · Riverfront Plaza, East Tower · 951 East Byrd Street · P.O. Box 1535 · Richmond, VA 23212 · 804-788-8200

PERSONAL INJURY LITIGATION

Fred C. Alexander, Jr. · (Defendants, Medical Malpractice) · McGuire, Woods, Battle & Boothe · TransPotomac Plaza · 1199 North Fairfax Street · P.O. Box 25047 · Alexandria, VA 22313-5047 · 703-739-6200

Thomas P. Mains, Jr. · (Plaintiffs) · Mains & Maines · 1199 North Fairfax Street, Suite 800 · P.O. Box 428 · Alexandria, Va 22313 · 703-548-1112

Robert J. Arthur* · (Plaintiffs, Products Liability, Automobile Collision) · Arthur and Speed · 5549 Lee Highway · Arlington, VA 22207-1687 · 703-241-7171

Brian C. Shevlin · (Plaintiffs) · Shevlin & Glass · 1655 North Fort Myer Drive, Suite 610 · Arlington, VA 22209 · 703-522-2202

Christopher K. Speed* · (Plaintiffs) · Arthur and Speed · 5549 Lee Highway · Arlington, VA 22207-1687 · 703-241-7171

Thomas E. Albro* · (Plaintiffs) · Tremblay & Smith · 105-109 East High Street P.O. Box 1585 · Charlottesville, VA 22902 · 804-977-4455

L. B. Chandler, Jr.* · (Plaintiffs, Products Liability, Automobile Collision) · Chandler, Franklin & O'Bryan · Ednam Professional Center · 2564 Ivy Road · P.O. Box 6747 · Charlottesville, VA 22906 · 804-971-7273

John C. Lowe · (Plaintiffs) · Lowe and Jacobs · 300 Court Square · Charlottesville, VA 22901 · 804-296-8188

Bruce D. Rasmussen* · (Plaintiffs, Medical Malpractice, Products Liability, Automobile Collision) · Michie, Hamlett, Lowry, Rasmussen & Tweel · 500 Court Square, Suite 300 · P.O. Box 298 · Charlottesville, VA 22902-0298 · 804-977-3390

John W. Zunka* · (Defendants) · Taylor & Zunka · 414 Park Street · P.O. Box 1567 · Charlottesville, VA 22902 · 804-977-0191

Charles E. Carter · (Plaintiffs) · Carter, Craig, Bass, Blair & Kushner · 126 South Union Street · P.O. Box 601 · Danville, VA 24543 · 804-792-9311

James A. L. Daniel · (Defendants) · Daniel, Vaughan, Medley & Smitherman · 116 South Ridge Street · P.O. Box 720 · Danville, VA 24543 · 804-792-3911

Frank O. Meade · (Defendants) · Woods, Rogers & Hazlegrove · 530 Main Street P.O. Box 560 · Danville, VA 24543-0560 · 804-791-1321

John J. Brandt · (Defendants) · Slenker, Brandt, Jennings & Johnston · 3026 Javier Road · P.O. Box 2908 · Fairfax, VA 22116-2908 · 703-849-8600

Joseph P. Dyer · (Defendants) · Siciliano, Ellis, Dyer & Boccarosse · 10521 Judicial Drive, Suite 300 · Fairfax, VA 22030 · 703-385-6692

Robert T. Hall · (Plaintiffs) · Hall, Markle, Sickels & Fudala · 4010 University Drive · Fairfax, VA 22030 · 703-591-8600

Richard H. Lewis · (Defendants) · Lewis, Trichilo & Bancroft · 4117 Chain Bridge Road, Suite 400 · Fairfax, VA 22030 · 703-385-1000

Norman F. Slenker* · (Defendants, Medical Malpractice, Professional Malpractice) · Slenker, Brandt, Jennings & Johnston · 3026 Javier Road · P.O. Box 2908 Fairfax, VA 22116-2908 · 703-849-8600

William O. P. Snead III · (Plaintiffs) · Law Offices of William O. P. Snead · 3923 Old Lee Highway, Suite 62B · Fairfax, VA 22030 · 703-359-8111

Ronald D. Hodges* · (Defendants) · Wharton, Aldhizer & Weaver · 100 South Mason Street · P.O. Box 809 · Harrisonburg, VA 22801 · 703-434-0316

Phillip C. Stone · (Defendants) · Wharton, Aldhizer & Weaver · 100 South Mason Street · P.O. Box 809 · Harrisonburg, VA 22801 · 703-434-0316

John R. Alford · (Defendants) · Caskie & Frost · 2306 Atherholt Road · P.O. Box 6360 · Lynchburg, VA 24505 · 804-846-2731

Henry M. Sackett III* · (Defendants, Medical Malpractice, Products Liability) · Edmunds & Williams · 800 Main Street · P.O. Box 958 · Lynchburg, VA 24505 · 804-846-9000

S. James Thompson, Jr. · (Defendants) · Caskie & Frost · 2306 Atherholt Road P.O. Box 6360 · Lynchburg, VA 24505 · 804-846-2731

Thomas C. Palmer, Jr.* · (Defendants, Products Liability, Professional Malpractice) · Brault, Palmer, Grove and Zimmerman · 8567-D Sudley Road · P.O. Box 534 · Manassas, VA 22110-0534 · 703-631-9727

J. Jay Corson IV · (Defendants) · McGuire, Woods, Battle & Boothe · Tysons Corner · 8280 Greensboro Drive, Suite 900 · P.O. Box 9346 · McLean, VA 22102 703-712-5000

Haynie Seay Trotter · McGuire, Woods, Battle & Boothe · Tysons Corner · 8280 Greensboro Drive, Suite 900 · P.O. Box 9346 · McLean, VA 22102 · 703-712-5413

Stanley G. Barr, Jr.* · (Medical Malpractice) · Kaufman & Canoles · Sovran Center, Suite 2000 · One Commercial Place · P.O. Box 3037 · Norfolk, VA 23514-3037 · 804-624-3000

Bruce T. Bishop · Willcox & Savage · 1800 Sovran Center · One Commercial Place · Norfolk, VA 23510-2197 · 804-628-5573

Guy E. Daugherty · (Plaintiffs) · Howell, Daugherty, Brown & Lawrence · One East Plume Street · P.O. 3929 · Norfolk, VA 23514 · 804-623-7334

Richard S. Glasser · (Plaintiffs) · Glasser and Glasser · 125 St. Paul's Boulevard, Suite 400 · Norfolk, VA 23510 · 804-625-6787

Jack E. Greer* · (Defendants, Products Liability, Professional Malpractice, Appellate) · Williams, Kelly, & Greer · 600 Crestar Bank Building · P.O. Box 3416 Norfolk, VA 23514-3416 · 804-624-2600

John A. Heilig* · (Defendants) · Heilig, McKenry, Fraim & Lollar · Stoney Point Center · 700 Newtown Road · Norfolk, VA 23502 · 804-461-2500

Wayne Lustig* · (Plaintiffs, Defendants, Products Liability, Professional Malpractice) · Mays & Valentine · Town Point Center, Eighth Floor · 150 Boush Street · Norfolk, VA 23510 · 804-627-5500

Stanley E. Sacks* · (Plaintiffs) · Sacks & Sacks · Town Point Center, Suite 501 150 Bush Street · P.O. Box 3874 · Norfolk, VA 23514-3874 · 804-623-2753

Gregory N. Stillman* · (Defendants, Products Liability, Appellate) · Hunton & Williams · First Virginia Bank Tower, Suite 1300 · P.O. Box 3889 · Norfolk, VA 23514 · 804-625-5501

Charles F. Tucker* · (Defendants) · Vandeventer, Black, Meredith & Martin · 500 World Trade Center · Norfolk, VA 23510 · 804-446-8600

J. Darrell Foster* · (Plaintiffs) · Bangel, Bangel & Bangel · 505 Court Street · P.O. Box 760 · Portsmouth, VA 23705-0760 · 804-397-3471

Robert J. Ingram, Sr.* · (Plaintiffs) · Gilmer, Sadler, Ingram, Sutherland & Hutton · Midtown Professional Office Building · 65 East Main Street · P.O. Box 878 · Pulaski, VA 24301 · 703-980-1360

George E. Allen III · (Plaintiffs) · Allen, Allen, Allen & Allen · 1809 Staples Mill Road · P.O. Box 6855 · Richmond, VA 23230 · 804-359-9151

Lewis Thomas Booker · (Defendants) · Hunton & Williams · Riverfront Plaza, East Tower · 951 East Byrd Street · P.O. Box 1535 · Richmond, VA 23212 · 804-788-8200

Robert F. Brooks* · (Products Liability) · Hunton & Williams · Riverfront Plaza, East Tower · 951 East Byrd Street · P.O. Box 1535 · Richmond, VA 23212 · 804-788-8200

William R. Cogar · Mays & Valentine · Sovran Center · 1111 East Main Street · P.O. Box 1122 · Richmond, VA 23208-1122 · 804-697-1200

Frank N. Cowan · Cowan & Owen · 1930 Huguenot Road · P.O. Box 35655 · Richmond, VA 23235-0655 · 804-320-8918

Emanuel Emroch · (Plaintiffs) · Emroch & Williamson · 6800 Paragon Place, Suite 233 · P.O. Box 8692 · Richmond, VA 23226 · 804-288-1661

James E. Farnham* · (Products Liability) · Hunton & Williams · Riverfront Plaza, East Tower · 951 East Byrd Street · P.O. Box 1535 · Richmond, VA 23212 804-788-8200

John F. Kay, Jr. · (Defendants) · Mays & Valentine · Sovran Center · 1111 East Main Street · P.O. Box 1122 · Richmond, VA 23208-1122 · 804-697-1200

William H. King, Jr.* · (Defendants) · McGuire, Woods, Battle & Boothe · One James Center · 901 East Cary Street · Richmond, VA 23219 · 804-775-1000

David Craig Landin · (Defendants) · McGuire, Woods, Battle & Boothe · One James Center · 901 East Cary Street · Richmond, VA 23219 · 804-775-1000

Henry H. McVey III* · (Defendants) · McGuire, Woods, Battle & Boothe · One James Center · 901 East Cary Street · Richmond, VA 23219 · 804-775-1000

Frank B. Miller III* · (Defendants, Medical Malpractice, Products Liability, Professional Malpractice) · Sands, Anderson, Marks & Miller · 1400 Ross Building 801 East Main Street · P.O. Box 1998 · Richmond, VA 23216-1998 · 804-648-1636

James W. Morris III* · (Defendants) · Morris & Morris · 1200 Ross Building · 801 East Main Street · Richmond, VA 23219 · 804-344-8300

Philip B. Morris · (Defendants) · Morris & Morris · 1200 Ross Building · 801 East Main Street · Richmond, VA 23219 · 804-344-8300

John H. O'Brion, Jr. · (Plaintiffs, Defendants, Products Liability) · Cowan & Owen · 1930 Huguenot Road · P.O. Box 35655 · Richmond, VA 23235-0655 · 804-320-8918

John M. Oakey, Jr.* · (Defendants) · McGuire, Woods, Battle & Boothe · One James Center · 901 East Cary Street · Richmond, VA 23219 · 804-775-1000

Albert M. Orgain IV · (Defendants) · Sands, Anderson, Marks & Miller · 1400 Ross Building · 801 East Main Street · P.O. Box 1998 · Richmond, VA 23216-1998 804-648-1636

Rosewell Page III · (Defendants) · McGuire, Woods, Battle & Boothe · One James Center · 901 East Cary Street · Richmond, VA 23219 · 804-775-1000

James C. Roberts* · (Defendants) · Mays & Valentine · Sovran Center · 1111 East Main Street · P.O. Box 1122 · Richmond, VA 23208-1122 · 804-697-1200

John B. Russell · (Defendants) · Browder, Russell, Morris and Butcher · One James Center, Suite 1100 · 901 East Cary Street · Richmond, VA 23219 · 804-771-9300

Joseph M. Spivey III* · (Defendants) · Hunton & Williams · Riverfront Plaza, East Tower · 951 East Byrd Street · P.O. Box 1535 · Richmond, VA 23212 · 804-788-8200

Thomas W. Williamson, Jr. · (Plaintiffs) · Emroch & Williamson · 6800 Paragon Place, Suite 233 · P.O. Box 8692 · Richmond, VA 23226 · 804-288-1661

James R. Austin · Gentry, Locke, Rakes & Moore · 800 Crestar Plaza · P.O. Box 1018 · Roanoke, VA 24005 · 703-982-8000

David B. Hart* · (Defendants, Products Liability, Professional Malpractice) · Wooten & Hart · 707 Building, Suite 310 · P.O. Box 12247 · Roanoke, VA 24024-2247 · 703-343-2451

James F. Johnson* · (Defendants) · Johnson, Ayers & Matthews · Southwest Virginia Bank Building, Second Floor · 302 Second Street, SW · P.O. Box 2200 · Roanoke, VA 24009 · 703-982-3666

S. D. Roberts Moore · Gentry, Locke, Rakes & Moore · 800 Crestar Plaza · P.O. Box 1018 · Roanoke, VA 24005 · 703-982-8000

G. Marshall Mundy · (Plaintiffs) · Mundy Rogers & Frith · Third Street & Woods Avenue, SW · P.O. Box 2240 · Roanoke, VA 24009 · 703-982-1351

William B. Poff* · (Defendants) · Woods, Rogers & Hazlegrove · 105 Franklin Road, SW · P.O. Box 720 · Roanoke, VA 24004-0720 · 703-982-4200

George W. Wooten · (Defendants) · Wooten & Hart · 707 Building, Suite 310 · Roanoke, VA 24024 · 703-343-2451

Thomas L. Phillips · (Plaintiffs) · Phillips, Phillips & Phillips · Route Three · P.O. Box 179-P · Rustburg, VA 24588 · 804-821-5022

Frank D. Harris · (Defendants) · Harris, Matthews & Warren · 115 West Danville Street · P.O. Box 369 · South Hill, VA 23970 · 804-447-3128

Colin J. S. Thomas, Jr.* · (Plaintiffs, Defendants, Products Liability, Automobile Collision) · Timberlake, Smith, Thomas & Moses · The Virginia Building · 25 North Central Avenue · P.O. Box 108 · Staunton, VA 24401 · 703-885-1517

John F. Gionfriddo · (Defendants) · Law Office of John F. Gionfriddo · 311 Edwin Lane · Vienna, VA 22180 · 703-938-0328

Thomas B. Shuttleworth · (Plaintiffs) · Shuttleworth, Ruloff, Giordano & Kahle 4425 Corporation Lane, Suite 300 · Virginia Beach, VA 23462 · 804-671-6000

Thomas V. Monahan · Hall, Monahan, Engle, Mahan & Mitchell · Nine East Boscawen Street · P.O. Box 848 · Winchester, VA 22601 · 703-662-3200

PUBLIC UTILITY LAW

Evans B. Brasfield · Hunton & Williams · Riverfront Plaza, East Tower · 951 East Byrd Street · P.O. Box 1535 · Richmond, VA 23212 · 804-788-8200

Edward L. Flippen · Mays & Valentine · Sovran Center · 1111 East Main Street P.O. Box 1122 · Richmond, VA 23208-1122 · 804-697-1200

Richard D. Gary · Hunton & Williams · Riverfront Plaza, East Tower · 951 East Byrd Street · P.O. Box 1535 · Richmond, VA 23212 · 804-788-8200

Hullihen W. Moore · Christian, Barton, Epps, Brent & Chappell · 1200 Mutual Building · 909 East Main Street · Richmond, VA 23219-3095 · 804-644-7851

Guy T. Tripp III · Hunton & Williams · Riverfront Plaza, East Tower · 951 East Byrd Street · P.O. Box 1535 · Richmond, VA 23212 · 804-788-8200

John L. Walker, Jr. · Woods, Rogers & Hazlegrove · 105 Franklin Road, SW · P.O. Box 720 · Roanoke, VA 24004-0720 · 703-982-4200

REAL ESTATE LAW

Fred S. Landess · (Zoning, Land Use, Commercial Transactions) · McGuire, Woods, Battle & Boothe · Court Square Building · 418 East Jefferson Street · P.O. Box 1288 · Charlottesville, VA 22902 · 804-977-2500

Gary C. McGee · (Zoning, Land Use, Commercial Transactions) · McGuire, Woods, Battle & Boothe · Court Square Building · 418 East Jefferson Street · P.O. Box 1288 · Charlottesville, VA 22902 · 804-977-2500

A. Hugo Blankingship, Jr.* · (Eminent Domain, Real Estate Taxation) · Blankingship & Keith · 4020 University Drive · Fairfax, VA 22030 · 703-691-1235

C. Christopher Giragosian · Hunton & Williams · 3050 Chain Bridge Road · P.O. Box 1147 · Fairfax, VA 22030 · 703-352-2200

Henry C. Mackall · Mackall, Mackall, Walker & Gibb · 4031 Chain Bridge Road Fairfax, VA 22030 · 703-273-0320

Edgar Allen Prichard · McGuire, Woods, Battle & Boothe · 3950 Chain Bridge Road · P.O. Box 338 · Fairfax, VA 22030 · 703-359-1000

Grayson P. Hanes · Hazel & Thomas · 3110 Fairview Park Drive, Suite 1400 · P.O. Box 547 · Falls Church, VA 22042 · 703-641-4200

Minerva Wilson Andrews · McGuire, Woods, Battle & Boothe · Tysons Corner 8280 Greensboro Drive, Suite 900 · P.O. Box 9346 · McLean, VA 22102 · 703-712-5439

M. Langhorne Keith · (Land Use, Municipal Corporations) · Hogan & Hartson · 8300 Greensboro Drive, Suite 1100 · McLean, VA 22102 · 703-847-6010

R. Dennis McArver · McGuire, Woods, Battle & Boothe · Tysons Corner · 8280 Greensboro Drive, Suite 900 · P.O. Box 9346 · McLean, VA 22102 · 703-712-5429

Courtland L. Traver · McGuire, Woods, Battle & Boothe · Tysons Corner · 8280 Greensboro Drive, Suite 900 · P.O. Box 9346 · McLean, VA 22102 · 703-712-5461

Robert E. Farmer · Kaufman & Canoles · Sovran Center, Suite 2000 · One Commercial Place · P.O. Box 3037 · Norfolk, VA 23514-3037 · 804-624-3000

Thomas G. Johnson, Jr. · Willcox & Savage · 1800 Sovran Center · One Commercial Place · Norfolk, VA 23510-2197 · 804-628-5500

Jay F. Wilks · (Zoning, Land Use, Commercial Transactions) · Wilks & Best · 700 Town Pont Center · 150 Boush Street · Norfolk, VA 23510-1626 · 804-623-6500

Philip J. Bagley III · Mays & Valentine · Sovran Center · 1111 East Main Street P.O. Box 1122 · Richmond, VA 23208-1122 · 804-697-1444

John W. Bates III · McGuire, Woods, Battle & Boothe · One James Center · 901 East Cary Street · Richmond, VA 23219 · 804-775-1000

David S. Cohn · Mays & Valentine · Sovran Center · 1111 East Main Street · P.O. Box 1122 · Richmond, VA 23208-1122 · 804-697-1470

William F. Gieg · (Commercial Transactions, Industrial Transactions, Real Estate Taxation) · McGuire, Woods, Battle & Boothe · One James Center · 901 East Cary Street · Richmond, VA 23219 · 804-775-1000

L. Charles Long, Jr. · Hirschler, Fleischer, Weinberg, Cox & Allen · Main Street Centre · 629 East Main Street · P.O. Box 1Q · Richmond, VA 23202 · 804-771-9524

Patrick J. Milmoe · Hunton & Williams · Riverfront Plaza, East Tower · 951 East Byrd Street · P.O. Box 1535 · Richmond, VA 23212 · 804-788-8200

Thomas L. Newton, Jr. · McGuire, Woods, Battle & Boothe · One James Center 901 East Cary Street · Richmond, VA 23219 · 804-775-1000

Willam A. Walsh, Jr. · Hunton & Williams · Riverfront Plaza, East Tower · 951 East Byrd Street · P.O. Box 1535 · Richmond, VA 23212 · 804-788-8200

Jay M. Weinberg · Hirschler, Fleischer, Weinberg, Cox & Allen · Main Street Centre · 629 East Main Street · P.O. Box 1Q · Richmond, VA 23202 · 804-771-9500

W. Heywood Fralin · Jolly, Place, Fralin & Prillaman · 3912 Electric Road · P.O. Box 2865 · Roanoke, VA 24001 · 703-989-0000

Talfourd H. Kemper · Woods, Rogers & Hazlegrove · 105 Franklin Road, SW · P.O. Box 720 · Roanoke, VA 24004-0720 · 703-982-4200

Michael K. Smeltzer · Woods, Rogers & Hazlegrove · 105 Franklin Road, SW · P.O. Box 720 · Roanoke, VA 24004-0720 · 703-982-4200

TAX AND EMPLOYEE BENEFITS LAW

Philip Tierney · McGuire, Woods, Battle & Boothe · Trans Potomac Plaza · 1199 North Fairfax Street · P.O. Box 25047 · Alexandria, VA 22313-5047 · 703-739-6200

David W. Kudravetz · McCallum Kudravetz · 250 East High Street · P.O. Box 224 · Charlottesville, VA 22902 · 804-293-8191

Leigh B. Middleditch, Jr. · McGuire, Woods, Battle & Boothe · Court Square Building · 418 East Jefferson Street · P.O. Box 1288 · Charlottesville, VA 22902 804-977-2500

Robert E. Stroud · McGuire, Woods, Battle & Boothe · Court Square Building · 418 East Jefferson Street · P.O. Box 1288 · Charlottesville, VA 22902 · 804-977-2500

James B. Pittleman · Odin, Feldman & Pittleman · 9302 Lee Highway, Suite 1100 · Fairfax, VA 22031 · 703-218-2100

Duane W. Beckhorn · Hazel & Thomas · 3110 Fairview Park Drive, Suite 1400 P.O. Box 12001 · Falls Church, VA 22042 · 703-641-4200

Carrington Williams · McGuire, Woods, Battle & Boothe · Tysons Corner · 8280 Greensboro Drive, Suite 900 · P.O. Box 9346 · McLean, VA 22102 · 703-712-5451

Leroy T. Canoles, Jr. · Kaufman & Canoles · Sovran Center, Suite 2000 · One Commercial Place · P.O. Box 3037 · Norfolk, VA 23514-3037 · 804-624-3000

Allan G. Donn · Willcox & Savage · 1800 Sovran Center · One Commercial Place Norfolk, VA 23510-2197 · 804-628-5500

Robert C. Nusbaum* · Hofheimer, Nusbaum, McPhaul & Samuels · 1700 Dominion Tower · P.O. Box 3460 · Norfolk, VA 23514-3460 · 804-622-3366

William A. Old, Jr. · Hofheimer, Nusbaum, McPhaul & Samuels · 1700 Dominion Tower · P.O. Box 3460 · Norfolk, VA 23514-3460 · 804-622-3366

Toy D. Savage, Jr. · Willcox & Savage · 1800 Sovran Center · One Commercial Place · Norfolk, VA 23510-2197 · 804-628-5500

Albert J. Taylor, Jr. · Cooper, Spong & Davis · Central Fidelity Bank Building High & Crawford Streets · P.O. Box 1475 · Portsmouth, VA 23705-1475 · 804-397-3481

Carle E. Davis · McGuire, Woods, Battle & Boothe · One James Center · 901 East Cary Street · Richmond, VA 23219 · 804-775-1000

Thomas F. Dean · (Employee Benefits) · McGuire, Woods, Battle & Boothe · One James Center · 901 East Cary Street · Richmond, VA 23219 · 804-775-4314

W. Birch Douglass III · (Corporate & Partnership Transactions, State Tax) · McGuire, Woods, Battle & Boothe · One James Center · 901 East Cary Street · Richmond, VA 23219 · 804-775-4315

Mark S. Dray · (Employee Benefits) · Hunton & Williams · Riverfront Plaza, East Tower · 951 East Byrd Street · P.O. Box 1535 · Richmond, VA 23212 · 804-788-8200

Louis A. Mezzullo · (Corporate & Partnership Transactions, Employee Benefits) Mezzullo & McCandlish · 700 East Main Street, Suite 804 · P.O. Box 796 · Richmond, VA 23206 · 804-782-9250

Mims Maynard Powell · (Employee Benefits) · McGuire, Woods, Battle & Boothe · One James Center · 901 East Cary Street · Richmond, VA 23219 · 804-775-1000

William M. Richardson · (Corporate & Partnership Transactions) · Hunton & Williams · Riverfront Plaza, East Tower · 951 East Byrd Street · P.O. Box 1535 · Richmond, VA 23212 · 804-788-8200

J. G. Ritter · (Employee Benefits) · Hunton & Williams · Riverfront Plaza, East Tower · 951 East Byrd Street · P.O. Box 1535 · Richmond, VA 23212 · 804-788-8200

William L. S. Rowe · (State Tax) · Hunton & Williams · Riverfront Plaza, East Tower · 951 East Byrd Street · P.O. Box 1535 · Richmond, VA 23212 · 804-788-8200

Wallace M. Starke · (Employee Benefits) · Mays & Valentine · Sovran Center · 1111 East Main Street · P.O. Box 1122 · Richmond, VA 23208-1122 · 804-697-1369

Frank W. Rogers, Jr. · Woods, Rogers & Hazlegrove · 105 Franklin Road, SW · P.O. Box 720 · Roanoke, VA 24004-0720 · 703-982-4200

Bruce C. Stockburger · Gentry, Locke, Rakes & Moore · 800 Crestar Plaza · P.O. Box 1018 · Roanoke, VA 24005 · 703-982-8000

Thomas R. Frantz · Clark & Stant · 900 Sovran Bank Building · One Columbus Center · Virginia Beach, VA 23462 · 804-499-8800

R. Braxton Hill III · Kaufman & Canoles · 1104 Laskin Road · P.O. Box 626 · Virginia Beach, VA 23451 · 804-491-4000

Lewis M. Costello* · Hazel & Thomas · 107 North Kent Street, Fourth Floor · P.O. Box 2740 · Winchester, VA 22601 · 703-665-0050

TRUSTS AND ESTATES

James G. Arthur · Mays & Valentine · 2300 South Ninth Street · Alexandria, VA 22204 · 703-521-5252

Philip Tierney · McGuire, Woods, Battle & Boothe · TransPotomac Plaza · 1199 North Fairfax Street · P.O. Box 25047 · Alexandria, VA 22313-5047 · 703-739-6200

Donald O. Manning · Manning & Murray · Plaza Suite 3 · 4141 North Henderson Road · Arlington, VA 22203 · 703-243-5000

William G. Murray · Manning & Murray · Plaza Suite 3 · 4141 North Henderson Road · Arlington, VA 22203 · 703-243-5000

Lucius H. Bracey, Jr. · McGuire, Woods, Battle & Boothe · Court Square Building · 418 East Jefferson Street · P.O. Box 1288 · Charlottesville, VA 22902 · 804-977-2500

Dennis W. Good, Jr. · (Estate Planning, Estate Administration) · McGuire, Woods, Battle & Boothe · Court Square Building · 418 East Jefferson Street · P.O. Box 1288 · Charlottesville, VA 22902 · 804-977-2500

Howard M. Zaritsky · Zaritsky & Zaritsky · 3040 Williams Drive, Suite 402 · Fairfax, VA 22031 · 703-698-7540

George F. Albright, Jr. · Hazel & Thomas · 3110 Fairview Park Drive, Suite 1400 · P.O. Box 12001 · Falls Church, VA 22042 · 703-641-4200

Constantine L. Dimos · McGuire, Woods, Battle & Boothe · Tysons Corner · 8280 Greensboro Drive, Suite 900 · P.O. Box 9346 · McLean, VA 22102 · 703-712-5449

Patrick J. Vaughan · Adams, Porter & Radigan · 1650 Tysons Boulevard, Suite 700 · McLean, VA 22102 · 703-448-6600

Leroy T. Canoles, Jr. · Kaufman & Canoles · Sovran Center, Suite 2000 · One Commercial Place · P.O. Box 3037 · Norfolk, VA 23514-3037 · 804-624-3000

Allan G. Donn · Willcox & Savage · 1800 Sovran Center · One Commercial Place Norfolk, VA 23510-2197 · 804-628-5500

Robert C. Nusbaum* · Hofheimer, Nusbaum, McPhaul & Samuels · 1700 Dominion Tower · P.O. Box 3460 · Norfolk, VA 23514-3460 · 804-622-3366

Toy D. Savage, Jr. · Willcox & Savage · 1800 Sovran Center · One Commercial Place · Norfolk, VA 23510-2197 · 804-628-5500

J. Hume Taylor, Jr. · Taylor & Walker · 223 East City Hall Avenue, Suite 400 · Norfolk, VA 23514-3490 · 804-625-7300

E. Diane Thompson · Hofheimer, Nusbaum, McPhaul & Samuels · 1700 Dominion Tower · P.O. Box 3460 · Norfolk, VA 23514-3460 · 804-622-3366

Michael Armstrong · Mays & Valentine · Sovran Center · 1111 East Main Street P.O. Box 1122 · Richmond, VA 23208-1122 · 804-697-1200

Dennis I. Belcher · (Estate Planning, Estate Administration, Charitable Trusts, Fiduciary Litigation) · McGuire, Woods, Battle & Boothe · One James Center · 901 East Cary Street · Richmond, VA 23219 · 804-775-1000

Waller H. Horsley · (Estate Planning, Estate Administration, Charitable Trusts) Hunton & Williams · Riverfront Plaza, East Tower · 951 East Byrd Street · P.O. Box 1535 · Richmond, VA 23212 · 804-788-8200

Louis A. Mezzullo · Mezzullo & McCandlish · 700 East Main Street, Suite 804 P.O. Box 796 · Richmond, VA 23206 · 804-782-9250

Julious P. Smith, Jr. · Williams, Mullen, Christian & Dobbins · Two James Center · P.O. Box 1320 · Richmond, VA 23210-1320 · 804-643-1991

C. Daniel Stevens · Christian, Barton, Epps, Brent & Chappell · 1200 Mutual Building · 909 East Main Street · Richmond, VA 23219-3095 · 804-644-7851

Harry J. Warthen III · Hunton & Williams · Riverfront Plaza, East Tower · 951 East Byrd Street · P.O. Box 1535 · Richmond, VA 23212 · 804-788-8200

Thomas S. Word, Jr. · McGuire, Woods, Battle & Boothe · One James Center · 901 East Cary Street · Richmond, VA 23219 · 804-775-1000

Frank W. Rogers, Jr. · Woods, Rogers & Hazlegrove · 105 Franklin Road, SW · P.O. Box 720 · Roanoke, VA 24004-0720 · 703-982-4200

Thomas R. Frantz · Clark & Stant · 900 Sovran Bank Building · One Columbus Center · Virginia Beach, VA 23462 · 804-499-8800

R. Braxton Hill III · Kaufman & Canoles · 1104 Laskin Road · P.O. Box 626 · Virginia Beach, VA 23451 · 804-491-4000

Lewis M. Costello* · Hazel & Thomas · 107 North Kent Street, Fourth Floor · P.O. Box 2740 · Winchester, VA 22601 · 703-665-0050

WASHINGTON

BANKRUPTCY LAW

Sheena Ramona Aebig · Shulkin, Hutton & Bucknell · 1201 Third Avenue, Suite 1900 · Seattle, WA 98101-3066 · 206-623-3515

C. Keith Allred · Davis Wright Tremaine · 2600 Century Square · 1501 Fourth Avenue · Seattle, WA 98101-1688 · 206-622-3150

Thomas N. Bucknell · Shulkin, Hutton & Bucknell · 1201 Third Avenue, Suite 1900 · Seattle, WA 98101-3066 · 206-623-3515

Gayle E. Bush · (Business Reorganization, Creditors' Rights, Debtors' Rights, Bankruptcy Litigation) · Culp, Guterson & Grader · One Union Square, 27th Floor · 600 University Street · Seattle, WA 98101-3143 · 206-624-7141

Daniel M. Caine* · Fountain Rhoades · 1350 Key Tower · 1000 Second Avenue Seattle, WA 98104 · 206-682-4405

Jack J. Cullen* · (Business Reorganization, Creditors' Rights, Debtors' Rights, Bankruptcy Litigation) · Hatch & Leslie · 2700 Columbia Seafirst Center · 701 Fifth Avenue · Seattle, WA 98104 · 206-622-0090

Charles R. Ekberg · Lane Powell Spears Lubersky · Pacific First Center, Suite 4100 · 1420 Fifth Avenue · Seattle, WA 98101-2338 · 206-223-7000

Willard Hatch · Hatch & Leslie · 2700 Columbia Seafirst Center · 701 Fifth Avenue · Seattle, WA 98104 · 206-622-0090

Arthur J. Hutton, Jr. · Shulkin, Hutton & Bucknell · 1201 Third Avenue, Suite 1900 · Seattle, WA 98101-3066 · 206-623-3515

Dillon E. Jackson · Hatch & Leslie · 2700 Columbia Seafirst Center · 701 Fifth Avenue · Seattle, WA 98104 · 206-622-0090

Jerome Shulkin · Shulkin, Hutton & Bucknell · 1201 Third Avenue, Suite 1900 Seattle, WA 98101-3066 · 206-623-3515

Thomas G. Thorbeck · Davis Wright Tremaine · 2600 Century Square · 1501 Fourth Avenue · Seattle, WA 98101-1688 · 206-622-3150

Thomas T. Bassett · (Creditors' Rights, Bankruptcy Litigation) · Lukins & Annis 1600 Washington Trust Financial Center · West 717 Sprague Avenue · Spokane, WA 99204-0466 · 509-455-9555

John F. Bury · Murphy, Bantz & Bury · West 818 Riverside Avenue, Suite 631 Spokane, WA 99201 · 509-838-4458

Barry W. Davidson · Barry W. Davidson & Associates · 1280 SeaFirst Building · Spokane, WA 99201 · 509-624-4600

Joseph A. Esposito* · (Business Reorganization, Creditors' Rights, Bankruptcy Litigation, Trustee) · Esposito, Tombari & George · 960 Paulsen Building · Spokane, WA 99201 · 509-624-9219

Daniel O'Rourke* · (Business Reorganization, Creditors' Rights, Debtors' Rights, Bankruptcy Litigation) · Southwell, O'Rourke, Jalbert & Kappelman · Paulsen Center, Suite 820 · West 421 Riverside Avenue · Spokane, WA 99201 · 509-624-0159

Charles F. Van Marter · Lukins & Annis · 1600 Washington Trust Financial Center · West 717 Sprague Avenue · Spokane, WA 99204-0466 · 509-455-9555

Frank L. Kurtz · Kurtz, Hurley & Lara · 411 North Second Street · Yakima, WA 98901 · 509-248-4282

BUSINESS LITIGATION

John O. Burgess* · (Commercial, Construction) · Short, Cressman & Burgess · First Interstate Center, 30th Floor · 999 Third Avenue · Seattle, WA 98104-4008 206-682-3333

Peter D. Byrnes · Byrnes & Keller · Key Tower, 38th Floor · 1000 Second Avenue Seattle, WA 98104 · 206-622-2000

Thomas J. Greenan · Ferguson & Burdell · Security Pacific Plaza, Suite 3400 · 1420 Fifth Avenue · Seattle, WA 98101-2339 · 206-622-1711

William A. Helsell · Helsell, Fetterman, Martin, Todd & Hokanson · 1500 Puget Sound Building · P.O. Box 21846 · Seattle, WA 98111 · 206-292-1144

Ronald E. McKinstry · Bogle & Gates · Two Union Square, Suite 4700 · 601 Union Street · Seattle, WA 98101-2322 · 206-682-5151

Michael Mines* · Betts, Patterson & Mines · The Financial Center, Suite 800 · 1215 Fourth Avenue · Seattle, WA 98161-1090 · 206-292-9988

Evan L. Schwab · Bogle & Gates · Two Union Square, Suite 4700 · 601 Union Street · Seattle, WA 98101-2322 · 206-682-5151

Payton Smith* · (Antitrust, International) · Davis Wright Tremaine · 2600 Century Square · 1501 Fourth Avenue · Seattle, WA 98101-1688 · 206-628-7767

Fredric C. Tausend · Preston, Thorgrimson, Shidler, Gates & Ellis · 5400 Columbia Center · 701 Fifth Avenue · Seattle, WA 98104-7078 · 206-623-7580

Paul J. Allison · Randall & Danskin · 1500 Seafirst Financial Center · West 601 Riverside · Spokane, WA 99201 · 509-747-2052

Eugene I. Annis · Lukins & Annis · 1600 Washington Trust Financial Center · West 717 Sprague Avenue · Spokane, WA 99204-0466 · 509-455-9555

Joseph P. Delay* · Delay, Curran, Thompson & Pontarolo · 1212 Washington Mutual Financial Center · West 601 Main · Spokane, WA 99201-0684 · 509-455-9500

John G. Layman · Layman, Loft, Arpin & White · 820 Lincoln Building · Spokane, WA 99210 · 509-455-8883

William D. Symmes* · (Antitrust, Commercial, Securities) · Witherspoon, Kelley, Davenport & Toole · Old National Bank Building, 11th Floor · West 428 Riverside Avenue · Spokane, WA 99201-0390 · 509-624-5265

Robert H. Whaley* · Winston & Cashatt · Seafirst Financial Center, Suite 1900 West 601 Riverside Avenue · Spokane, WA 99201-0695 · 509-838-6131

Albert R. Malanca* · (Antitrust, Energy, Securities) · Gordon, Thomas, Honeywell, Malanca, Peterson & Daheim · 2200 First Interstate Plaza · P.O. Box 1157 Tacoma, WA 98401-1157 · 206-572-5050

William J. Rush · Rush, Hannula & Harkins · 715 Tacoma Avenue South · Tacoma, WA 98402 · 206-383-5388

James A. Perkins* · Bogle & Gates · 105 North Third Street · P.O. Box 550 · Yakima, WA 98907 · 509-457-1515

CORPORATE LAW

Richard S. Sprague · Bogle & Gates · 10500 Northeast Eighth Street, Suite 1500 Bellevue, WA 98004-4398 · 206-455-3940

C. Kent Carlson · Preston, Thorgrimson, Shidler, Gates & Ellis · 5400 Columbia Center · 701 Fifth Avenue · Seattle, WA 98104-7078 · 206-623-7580

Richard A. Clark · Stoel Rives Boley Jones & Grey · One Union Square, 36th Floor · 600 University Street · Seattle, WA 98101-3197 · 206-624-0900

John M. Davis · Davis Wright Tremaine · 2600 Century Square · 1501 Fourth Avenue · Seattle, WA 98101-1688 · 206-622-3150

P. Cameron DeVore · Davis Wright Tremaine · 2600 Century Square · 1501 Fourth Avenue · Seattle, WA 98101-1688 · 206-622-3150

Robert J. Diercks · Foster, Pepper & Shefelman · 1111 Third Avenue, 34th Floor Seattle, WA 98101 · 206-447-4400

Richard B. Dodd · (Corporate Finance, Mergers & Acquisitions, Securities) · Preston Thorgrimson Shidler Gates & Ellis · 5400 Columbia Center · 701 Fifth Avenue · Seattle, WA 98104-7078 · 206-623-7580

Karl J. Ege · Bogle & Gates · Two Union Square, Suite 4700 · 601 Union Street Seattle, WA 98101-2322 · 206-682-5151

James R. Ellis · (Corporate Finance, Public Corporations) · Preston, Thorgrimson, Shidler, Gates & Ellis · 5400 Columbia Center · 701 Fifth Avenue · Seattle, WA 98104-7078 · 206-623-7580

William H. Gates · Preston Thorgrimson Shidler Gates & Ellis · 5400 Columbia Center · 701 Fifth Avenue · Seattle, WA 98104-7078 · 206-623-7580

Robert Edward Giles · Perkins Coie · 1201 Third Avenue, 40th Floor · Seattle, WA 98101-3099 · 206-583-8888

D. Wayne Gittinger · Lane Powell Spears Lubersky · Pacific First Center, Suite 4100 · 1420 Fifth Avenue · Seattle, WA 98101-2338 · 206-223-7000

Raymond W. Haman · Lane Powell Spears Lubersky · Pacific First Center, Suite 4100 · 1420 Fifth Avenue · Seattle, WA 98101-2338 · 206-223-7000

James M. Hilton · (Corporate Finance) · Perkins Coie · 1201 Third Avenue, 40th Floor · Seattle, WA 98101-3099 · 206-583-8888

Dan P. Hungate · Bogle & Gates · Two Union Square, Suite 4700 · 601 Union Street · Seattle, WA 98101-2322 · 206-682-5151

Harold D. Johnson · Williams, Kastner & Gibbs · Two Union Square · 601 Union Street · P.O. Box 21926 · Seattle, WA 98111-3926 · 206-628-6600

Robert D. Kaplan · Bogle & Gates · Two Union Square, Suite 4700 · 601 Union Street · Seattle, WA 98101-2322 · 206-682-5151

Francis A. Kareken · Davis Wright Tremaine · 2600 Century Square · 1501 Fourth Avenue · Seattle, WA 98101-1688 · 206-622-3150

Charles J. Katz, Jr. · Perkins Coie · 1201 Third Avenue, 40th Floor · Seattle, WA 98101-3099 · 206-583-8888

Earl P. Lasher III* · Lasher Holzapfel Sperry & Ebberson · 6000 Westland Building · 100 South King Street · Seattle, WA 98104-2869 · 206-624-1230

Michael E. Morgan · Lane Powell Spears Lubersky · Pacific First Center, Suite 4100 · 1420 Fifth Avenue · Seattle, WA 98101-2338 · 206-223-7000

J. Shan Mullin · (International Trade) · Perkins Coie · 1201 Third Avenue, 40th Floor · Seattle, WA 98101-3099 · 206-583-8888

Harold F. Olsen · Perkins Coie · 1201 Third Avenue, 40th Floor · Seattle, WA 98101-3099 · 206-583-8888

Charles F. Osborn · Bogle & Gates · Two Union Square, Suite 4700 · 601 Union Street · Seattle, WA 98101-2322 · 206-682-5151

William G. Pusch · Davis Wright Tremaine · 2600 Century Square · 1501 Fourth Avenue · Seattle, WA 98101-1688 · 206-622-3150

Bruce M. Pym · Graham & Dunn · Security Pacific Plaza, 33rd Floor · 1420 Fifth Avenue · Seattle, WA 98101-2390 · 206-624-8300

Daniel B. Ritter · (Banking, Corporate Finance) · Davis Wright Tremaine · 2600 Century Square · 1501 Fourth Avenue · Seattle, WA 98101-1688 · 206-622-3150

Evelyn Sroufe · Perkins Coie · 1201 Third Avenue, 40th Floor · Seattle, WA 98101-3099 · 206-583-8888

Michael E. Stansbury · Perkins Coie · 1201 Third Avenue, 40th Floor · Seattle, WA 98101-3099 · 206-583-8888

John M. Steel · Riddell, Williams, Bullitt & Walkinshaw · 1001 Fourth Avenue Plaza, Suite 4400 · Seattle, WA 98154 · 206-624-3600

Irwin L. Treiger · Bogle & Gates · Two Union Square, Suite 4700 · 601 Union Street · Seattle, WA 98101-2322 · 206-682-5151

Jerome D. Whalen · Foster, Pepper & Shefelman · 1111 Third Avenue, 34th Floor · Seattle, WA 98101 · 206-447-4400

Paul J. Allison · Randall & Danskin · 1500 Seafirst Financial Center · West 601 Riverside · Spokane, WA 99201 · 509-747-2052

Ned M. Barnes · Witherspoon, Kelley, Davenport & Toole · Old National Bank Building, 11th Floor · West 428 Riverside Avenue · Spokane, WA 99201-0390 · 509-624-5265

R. Calvin Cathcart · Lukins & Annis · 1600 Washington Trust Financial Center West 717 Sprague Avenue · Spokane, WA 99204-0466 · 509-455-9555

Patrick B. Cerutti · Underwood, Campbell, Brock & Cerutti · 1100 Seafirst Financial Center · West 601 Riverside Avenue · Spokane, WA 99201 · 509-455-8500

Lawrence R. Small · Paine, Hamblen, Coffin, Brooke & Miller · 1200 Washington Trust Financial Center · Spokane, WA 99204 · 509-455-6000

Charles F. Van Marter · Lukins & Annis · 1600 Washington Trust Financial Center · West 717 Sprague Avenue · Spokane, WA 99204-0466 · 509-455-9555

James J. Gallagher · Graham & Dunn · 1300 Tacoma Financial Center · 1145 Broadway Plaza · Tacoma, WA 98401 · 206-572-9294

Paul M. Larson · Bogle & Gates · 105 North Third Street · P.O. Box 550 · Yakima, WA 98907 · 509-457-1515

Morris G. Shore · Velikanje, Moore & Shore · 405 East Lincoln Avenue · Yakima, WA 98901 · 509-248-6030

William L. Weigand, Jr. · Lyon, Beaulaurier, Weigand, Suko & Gustafson · 222 North Third Street · P.O. Box 1689 · Yakima, WA 98907 · 509-248-7220

CRIMINAL DEFENSE

David B. Bukey · (Federal Court) · Bukey & Bentley · 111 Third Avenue, 10th Floor · Seattle, WA 98101 · 206-343-9391

Dan R. Dubitzky* · (Federal Court, Environmental Crimes, White Collar Crimes) 803 Waterfront Place One · 1011 Western Avenue · Seattle, WA 98104 · 206-467-6709

Laurence B. Finegold · Finegold & Zulauf · Tower Building, 13th Floor · Seattle, WA 98101 · 206-682-9274

Murray B. Guterson* · Culp, Guterson & Grader · One Union Square, 27th Floor 600 University Street · Seattle, WA 98101-3143 · 206-624-7141

Darrell D. Hallett · Chicoine & Hallett · Waterfront Place One, Suite 803 · 1011 Western Avenue · Seattle, WA 98104 · 206-223-0800

Richard A. Hansen · Allen & Hansen · 600 Pioneer Building · 600 First Avenue Seattle, WA 98104 · 206-447-9681

Peter K. Mair* · (Federal Court, State Court, Environmental Crimes, Regulatory Fraud) · Mair, Abercrombie, Camiel & Rummonds · 710 Cherry Street · Seattle, WA 98104 · 206-624-1551

Katrina C. Pflaumer* · 2300 Smith Tower · Seattle, WA 98104 · 206-622-5943

Anthony Savage · 615 Lyon Building · 607 Third Avenue · Seattle, WA 98104 · 206-682-1882

Irwin H. Schwartz · 710 Cherry Street · Seattle, WA 98104 · 206-623-5084

L. Carl Maxey · Maxey Law Offices · Maxey Building · West 1835 Broadway · Spokane, WA 99201 · 509-326-0338

Mark E. Vovos* · (Federal Court, State Court) · Delphi Building · West 1309 Dean Avenue · Spokane, WA 99201 · 509-326-5220

Robert H. Whaley* · (Federal Court, Environmental Crimes) · Winston & Cashatt · Seafirst Financial Center, Suite 1900 · West 601 Riverside Avenue · Spokane, WA 99201-0695 · 509-838-6131

Monte E. Hester · Law Offices of Monte E. Hester · 1008 South Yakima Avenue Tacoma, WA 98405 · 206-272-2157

FAMILY LAW

William L. Kinzel* · Kinzel, Allen & Skone · The Redwood Building, Suite 206 845 One-Hundred-Sixth Avenue Northeast · Bellevue, WA 98004 · 206-455-3333

Lowell K. Halverson · Law Offices of Lowell K. Halverson · 3035 Island Crest Way · Mercer Island, WA 98040-2919 · 206-236-9000

John O. Burgess* · Short, Cressman & Burgess · First Interstate Center, 30th Floor · 999 Third Avenue · Seattle, WA 98104-4008 · 206-682-3333

Janet A. George* · 5700 Columbia Center · 701 Fifth Avenue · Seattle, WA 98104 206-447-0717

Martin A. Godsil · Casey & Pruzan · Pacific Building, 18th Floor · Third & Columbia · Seattle, WA 98104 · 206-623-3577

James M. Hilton · (Divorce, Marital Settlement Agreements) · Perkins Coie · 1201 Third Avenue, 40th Floor · Seattle, WA 98101-3099 · 206-583-8888

Bernice Jonson* · (Divorce) · Jonson, Hurley, Olson & Olson · 1734 Northwest Market Street · Seattle, WA 98107 · 206-789-4700

Carl Pruzan · Casey & Pruzan · Pacific Building, 18th Floor · Third & Columbia Seattle, WA 98104 · 206-623-3577

Richard H. Riddell · Riddell, Williams, Bullitt & Walkinshaw · 1001 Fourth Avenue Plaza, Suite 4400 · Seattle, WA 98154 · 206-624-3600

Gordon W. Wilcox · Riddell, Williams, Bullitt & Walkinshaw · 1001 Fourth Avenue Plaza, Suite 4400 · Seattle, WA 98154 · 206-624-3600

FIRST AMENDMENT LAW

David J. Burman · Perkins Coie · 1201 Third Avenue, 40th Floor · Seattle, WA 98101-3099 · 206-583-8426

P. Cameron DeVore · Davis Wright Tremaine · 2600 Century Square · 1501 Fourth Avenue · Seattle, WA 98101-1688 · 206-622-3150

Marshall J. Nelson · Davis Wright Tremaine · 2600 Century Square · 1501 Fourth Avenue · Seattle, WA 98101-1688 · 206-622-3150

David Utevsky · Foster, Pepper & Shefelman · 1111 Third Avenue, 34th Floor · Seattle, WA 98101 · 206-447-4400

Daniel M. Waggoner · Davis Wright Tremaine · 2600 Century Square · 1501 Fourth Avenue · Seattle, WA 98101-1688 · 206-622-3150

Duane M. Swinton · Witherspoon, Kelley, Davenport & Toole · Old National Bank Building, 11th Floor · West 428 Riverside Avenue · Spokane, WA 99201-0390 · 509-624-5265

HEALTH CARE LAW

Andrew K. Dolan · Bogle & Gates · Two Union Square, Suite 4700 · 601 Union Street · Seattle, WA 98101-2322 · 206-682-5151

R. Bruce Johnston · Lane Powell Spears Lubersky · Pacific First Center, Suite 4100 · 1420 Fifth Avenue · Seattle, WA 98101-2338 · 206-223-7000

Terry L. Kukuk · Garvey, Schubert & Barer · Waterfront Place Building, 10th Floor · 1011 Western Avenue · Seattle, WA 98104 · 206-464-3939

Mitchell J. Olejko · Davis Wright Tremaine · 2600 Century Square · 1501 Fourth Avenue · Seattle, WA 98101-1688 · 206-622-3150

Lee R. Voorhees · Foster, Pepper & Shefelman · 1111 Third Avenue, 34th Floor Seattle, WA 98101 · 206-447-4400

Robert J. Walerius · Reed McClure · 3600 Columbia Center · 701 Fifth Avenue Seattle, WA 98104 · 206-292-4900

Roger F. Chase · Chase, Haskell, Hayes & Kalamon · 1000 Seafirst Financial Center · Spokane, WA 99201 · 509-456-0333

K. Thomas Connolly · Witherspoon, Kelley, Davenport & Toole · Old National Bank Building, 11th Floor · West 428 Riverside Avenue · Spokane, WA 99201-0390 · 509-624-5265

IMMIGRATION LAW

Robert A. Free · MacDonald, Hoague & Bayless · 705 Second Avenue, Suite 1500 Seattle, WA 98104 · 206-622-1604

Joel H. Paget · Ryan, Swanson & Cleveland · 1201 Third Avenue, Suite 3400 · Seattle, WA 98101 · 206-464-4224

Daniel Hoyt Smith · MacDonald, Hoague & Bayless · 705 Second Avenue, Suite 1500 · Seattle, WA 98104 · 206-622-1604

Jimmy Wu · 2525 First Interstate Center · 999 Third Avenue · Seattle, WA 98104 206-464-1520

INTELLECTUAL PROPERTY LAW

Edward W. Bulchis · Seed & Berry · 6300 Columbia Center · 701 Fifth Avenue Seattle, WA 98104-7092 · 206-622-4900

William O. Ferron, Jr. · Seed & Berry · 6300 Columbia Center · 701 Fifth Avenue Seattle, WA 98104-7092 · 206-622-4900

Lee E. Johnson · Christensen, O'Connor, Johnson & Kindness · 2800 Pacific First Centre · 1420 Fifth Avenue · Seattle, WA 98101 · 206-682-8100

David J. Maki · (Bio-Technology Patent) · Seed & Berry · 6300 Columbia Center 701 Fifth Avenue · Seattle, WA 98104-7092 · 206-622-4900

Jerald E. Nagae · (Patent, Trademark) · Christensen, O'Connor, Johnson & Kindness · 2800 Pacific First Centre · 1420 Fifth Avenue · Seattle, WA 98101 · 206-682-8100

Richard W. Seed · Seed & Berry · 6300 Columbia Center · 701 Fifth Avenue · Seattle, WA 98104-7092 · 206-622-4900

Michael G. Toner · (Electronics, Software, Patent) · Christensen, O'Connor, Johnson & Kindness · 2800 Pacific First Centre · 1420 Fifth Avenue · Seattle, WA 98101 · 206-682-8100

James R. Uhlir · Christensen, O'Connor, Johnson & Kindness · 2800 Pacific First Centre · 1420 Fifth Avenue · Seattle, WA 98101 · 206-682-8100

LABOR AND EMPLOYMENT LAW

Peter M. Anderson · (Management) · Bogle & Gates · Two Union Square, Suite 4700 · 601 Union Street · Seattle, WA 98101-2322 · 206-682-5151

John F. Aslin* · (Management) · Perkins Coie · 1201 Third Avenue, 40th Floor Seattle, WA 98101-3099 · 206-583-8888

Clemens H. Barnes · (Management) · Graham & Dunn · Security Pacific Plaza, 33rd Floor · 1420 Fifth Avenue · Seattle, WA 98101-2390 · 206-624-8300

John Burns · (Labor) · Hafer, Price, Rinehart & Schwerin · 2505 Third Avenue, Suite 309 · Seattle, WA 98121 · 206-728-7280

Carolyn Cairns · (Individuals) · Monroe, Stokes, Eitelbach & Lawrence · 800 Fifth Avenue, Suite 4000 · Seattle, WA 98104 · 206-626-6000

Michael E. Cavanaugh · Boyle & Gates · Two Union Square, Suite 4700 · Seattle, WA 98101-2346 · 206-682-5151

Bruce Michael Cross* · (Management) · Perkins Coie · 1201 Third Avenue, 40th Floor · Seattle, WA 98101-3099 · 206-583-8888

Patrick J. Donnelly · (Management) · Bullivant, Houser, Bailey, Pendergrass & Hoffman · 4100 Columbia Center · 701 Fifth Avenue · Seattle, WA 98104 · 206-292-8930

Kelby D. Fletcher* · (Individuals) · Peterson, Bracelin, Young, Putra, Fletcher & Zeder · 2500 Smith Tower · 506 Second Avenue · Seattle, WA 98104-2399 · 206-624-6800

Steven B. Frank · (Individuals) · Frank & Rosen · Hoge Building, 12th Floor · 705 Second Avenue · Seattle, WA 98104 · 206-682-6711

Hugh Hafer* · (Labor) · Hafer, Price, Rinehart & Schwerin · 2505 Third Avenue, Suite 309 · Seattle, WA 98121 · 206-728-7280

Wayne W. Hansen · (Management) · Lane Powell Spears Lubersky · Pacific First Center, Suite 4100 · 1420 Fifth Avenue · Seattle, WA 98101-2338 · 206-223-7000

Mark A. Hutcheson · (Management) · Davis Wright Tremaine · 2600 Century Square · 1501 Fourth Avenue · Seattle, WA 98101-1688 · 206-622-3150

Thomas A. Lemly* · (Management, Employment Litigation) · Davis Wright Tremaine · 2600 Century Square · 1501 Fourth Avenue · Seattle, WA 98101-1688 206-622-3150

Judith A. Lonnquist · (Individuals) · Law Offices of Judith A. Lonnquist · 1500 Seattle Tower · 1218 Third Avenue · Seattle, WA 98104 · 206-622-2086

James Markham Marshall* · (Management) · Preston, Thorgrimson, Shidler, Gates & Ellis · 5400 Columbia Center · 701 Fifth Avenue · Seattle, WA 98104-7078 · 206-623-7580

Douglas G. Mooney · (Management) · Bogle & Gates · Two Union Square, Suite 4700 · 601 Union Street · Seattle, WA 98101-2322 · 206-682-5151

Frederick T. Rasmussen · (Management) · Riddell, Williams, Bullitt & Walkinshaw · 1001 Fourth Avenue Plaza, Suite 4400 · Seattle, WA 98154 · 206-624-3600

John E. Rinehart, Jr. · (Labor) · Hafer, Price, Rinehart & Schwerin · 2505 Third Avenue, Suite 309 · Seattle, WA 98121 · 206-728-7280

William A. Roberts · (Labor) · Davies, Roberts & Reid · 101 Elliott Avenue West, Suite 550 · Seattle, WA 98119 · 206-285-3610

Jon Howard Rosen · (Labor, Individuals) · Frank & Rosen · Hoge Building, 12th Floor · 705 Second Avenue · Seattle, WA 98104 · 206-682-6711

Jerome L. Rubin · (Management) · Stoel Rives Boley Jones & Grey · One Union Square, 36th Floor · 600 University Street · Seattle, WA 98101-3197 · 206-624-0900

Lawrence Schwerin · (Labor) · Hafer, Price, Rinehart & Schwerin · 2505 Third Avenue, Suite 309 · Seattle, WA 98121 · 206-728-7280

Sidney J. Strong · (Individuals) · Strong & Kydd · 1616 The Bank of California Center · 900 Fourth Avenue · Seattle, WA 98104 · 206-623-5221

Herman L. Wacker · (Management) · Riddell, Williams, Bullitt & Walkinshaw · 1001 Fourth Avenue Plaza, Suite 4400 · Seattle, WA 98154 · 206-624-3600

Jerome F. McCarthy* · (Management) · Vandeberg & Johnson · 1900 First Interstate Plaza · Tacoma, WA 98402 · 206-383-3791

MARITIME LAW

David Danielson · Danielson Harrigan & Tollefson · First Interstate Center, 44th Floor · 999 Third Avenue · Seattle, WA 98104 · 206-623-1700

Vincent R. Larson · Riddell, Williams, Bullitt & Walkinshaw · 1001 Fourth Avenue Plaza, Suite 4400 · Seattle, WA 98154 · 206-624-3600

Thomas J. McKey* · Bogle & Gates · Two Union Square, Suite 4700 · 601 Union Street · Seattle, WA 98101-2322 · 206-682-5151

Harold F. Vhugen · (Personal Injury) · Levinson, Friedman, Vhugen, Duggan, Bland & Horowitz · One Union Square, Suite 2900 · 600 University Street · Seattle, WA 98101 · 206-624-8844

NATURAL RESOURCES AND ENVIRONMENTAL LAW

J. Richard Aramburu · (Plaintiffs) · Law Offices of J. Richard Aramburu · 505 Madison Street, Suite 209 · Seattle, WA 98104 · 206-625-9515

Peter L. Buck · Buck & Gordon · Waterfront Place, Suite 902 · 1011 Western Avenue · Seattle, WA 98104 · 206-382-9540

Peter J. Eglick · (Plaintiffs) · Peter J. Eglick & Associates · Bank of California Building, Suite 1212 · 900 Fourth Avenue · Seattle, WA 98164 · 206-464-1435

Richard L. Hames · Davis Wright Tremaine · 2600 Century Square · 1501 Fourth Avenue · Seattle, WA 98101-1688 · 206-622-3150

Jerome L. Hillis* · Hillis, Clark, Martin & Peterson · 500 Galland Building · 1221 Second Avenue · Seattle, WA 98101-2925 · 206-623-1745

James R. Moore* · (Water, Solid Waste, Hazardous Waste, Environmental Crimes) · Perkins Coie · 1201 Third Avenue, 40th Floor · Seattle, WA 98101-3099 206-583-8888

Ralph H. Palumbo · Heller, Ehrman, White & McAuliffe · Columbia SeaFirst Center, 61st Floor · 701 Fifth Avenue · Seattle, WA 98104 · 206-447-0900

Judith M. Runstad · Foster, Pepper & Shefelman · 1111 Third Avenue, 34th Floor · Seattle, WA 98101 · 206-447-4400

Daniel D. Syrdal · Heller, Ehrman, White & McAuliffe · Columbia SeaFirst Center, 61st Floor · 701 Fifth Avenue · Seattle, WA 98104 · 206-447-0900

Kenneth S. Weiner · Preston, Thorgrimson, Shidler, Gates & Ellis · 5400 Columbia Center · 701 Fifth Avenue · Seattle, WA 98104-7078 · 206-623-7580

John L. Neff · (Mining) · Neff Law Firm · SeaFirst Financial Center, Suite 1370 West 601 Riverside Avenue · Spokane, WA 99201 · 509-838-6033

PERSONAL INJURY LITIGATION

Paul L. Stritmatter · (Plaintiffs) · Stritmatter, Kessler & McCauley · 407 Eighth Street · Hoquiam, WA 98550-3692 · 206-533-2710

Paul N. Luvera, Jr.* · (Plaintiffs) · Law Offices of Paul N. Luvera · 917 South Third Avenue · P.O. Box 427 · Mount Vernon, WA 98273-0427 · 206-336-6561

Arthur D. Swanson · (Plaintiffs) · 4512 Talbot Road South · Renton, WA 98055 206-226-7920

Craig P. Campbell · (Defendants) · Karr Tuttle Campbell · 1201 Third Avenue, Suite 2900 · Seattle, WA 98101-3028 · 206-223-1313

Thomas Chambers · (Plaintiffs) · Law Offices of Thomas Chambers · 1400 Broadway · Seattle, WA 98122 · 206-328-5561

John Patrick Cook* · (Defendants) · Lee, Smart, Cook, Martin & Patterson · 800 Puget Sound Plaza · 1325 Fourth Avenue · Seattle, WA 98101 · 206-624-7990

Joel D. Cunningham* · (Defendants, Medical Malpractice, Products Liability, Professional Malpractice) · Williams, Kastner & Gibbs · Two Union Square · 601 Union Street · P.O. Box 21926 · Seattle, WA 98111-3926 · 206-628-6600

William A. Helsell · (Defendants) · Helsell, Fetterman, Martin, Todd & Hokanson · Puget Sound Plaza, Suite 1500 · 1325 Fourth Avenue · P.O. Box 21846 · Seattle, WA 98111 · 206-292-1144

Lembhard G. Howell* · (Plaintiffs, Medical Malpractice, Products Liability, Automobile Collision, Airplane Collision) · Law Offices of Lembhard G. Howell · Arctic Building, Penthouse · 700 Third Avenue · Seattle, WA 98104 · 206-623-5296

J. Murray Kleist · (Plaintiffs) · Schroeter, Goldmark & Bender · 810 Third Avenue, Suite 500 · Seattle, WA 98104 · 206-622-8000

David L. Martin* · (Defendants) · Lee, Smart, Cook, Martin & Patterson · 800 Puget Sound Plaza · 1325 Fourth Avenue · Seattle, WA 98101-22585 · 206-624-7990

Jan Eric Peterson · (Plaintiffs) · Peterson, Bracelin, Young, Putra, Fletcher & Zeder · 2500 Smith Tower · 506 Second Avenue · Seattle, WA 98104-2399 · 206-624-6800

Leonard W. Schroeter · (Plaintiffs) · Schroeter, Goldmark & Bender · 810 Third Avenue, Suite 500 · Seattle, WA 98104 · 206-622-8506

Daniel F. Sullivan · (Plaintiffs) · Sullivan & Golden · Hoge Building, 10th Floor 705 Second Avenue · Seattle, WA 98104 · 206-682-8813

Robert W. Thomas · (Defendants) · Lane Powell Spears Lubersky · Pacific First Center, Suite 4100 · 1420 Fifth Avenue · Seattle, WA 98101-2338 · 206-223-7000

Eugene I. Annis · (Defendants) · Lukins & Annis · 1600 Washington Trust Financial Center · West 717 Sprague Avenue · Spokane, WA 99204-0466 · 509-455-9555

Dan W. Keefe* · (Defendants, Medical Malpractice) · Keefe, King & Boman · Washington Mutual Financial Center · West 601 Main Street, Suite 1102 · Spokane, WA 99201 · 509-624-8988

Daniel E. McKelvey, Jr. · (Plaintiffs) · McKelvey & Associates · North 222 Wall Street, Suite 402 · Spokane, WA 99201 · 509-624-0888

F. Ross Burgess* · (Defendants) · Burgess, Fitzer, Leighton & Phillips · 1551 Broadway, Suite 400 · Tacoma, WA 98402-3300 · 206-572-5324

John L. Messina* · (Plaintiffs, Products Liability, Airplane Collision) · Messina & Duffy · Benjamin Franklin Building · 4002 Tacoma Mall Boulevard, Suite 200 · Tacoma, WA 98409 · 206-472-6000

Jack G. Rosenow · (Defendants) · Rosenow, Hale & Johnson · 2115 North 30th, Suite 101 · Tacoma, WA 98403 · 206-572-5323

William J. Rush · Rush, Hannula & Harkins · 715 Tacoma Avenue South · Tacoma, WA 98402 · 206-383-5388

H. Frank Stubbs · 955 Tacoma Avenue South, Suite 309 · P.O. Box 1738 · Tacoma, WA 98401 · 206-383-5891

Dennis L. Fluegge* · (Defendants, Medical Malpractice) · Meyer, Fluegge & Tenney · 230 South Second Street · P.O. Box 22680 · Yakima, WA 98907 · 509-575-8500

PUBLIC UTILITY LAW

Richard R. Rohde · Perkins Coie · One Bellevue Center, Suite 1800 · 411 One-Hundred-Eighth Avenue, NE · Bellevue, WA 98004 · 206-453-7304

William S. Weaver · Perkins Coie · One Bellevue Center, Suite 1800 · 411 One-Hundred-Eighth Avenue, NE · Bellevue, WA 98004 · 206-453-7308

Terence L. Mundorf · Marsh, Mundorf & Pratt · 16000 Bothell Everett Highway, Suite 160 · Mill Creek, WA 98012 · 206-742-4545

Douglas H. Rosenberg · Preston Thorgrimson Shidler Gates & Ellis · 5400 Columbia Center · 701 Fifth Avenue · Seattle, WA 98104-7078 · 206-623-7580

Gary A. Dahlke · Paine, Hamblen, Coffin, Brooke & Miller · Washington Trust Financial Center Building, Suite 1200 · West 717 Sprague Avenue · Spokane, WA 99204 · 509-455-6540

REAL ESTATE LAW

Richard U. Chapin · Inslee, Best, Doezie & Ryder · Building D · 2340 One-Hundred-Thirtieth Avenue, NE · P.O. Box C-90016 · Bellevue, WA 98009-9016 206-455-1234

Omar S. Parker, Jr. · Perkins Coie · One Bellevue Center, Suite 1800 · 411 One-Hundred-Eighth Avenue, NE · Bellevue, WA 98004 · 206-453-6980

Richard S. Sprague · Bogle & Gates · 10500 Northeast Eighth Street, Suite 1500 Bellevue, WA 98004-4398 · 206-455-3940

Thaddas L. Alston · Alston, Courtnage, MacAulay & Proctor · 1000 Second Avenue, Suite 3900 · Seattle, WA 98104 · 206-623-7600

Timothy R. Clifford · Foster, Pepper & Shefelman · 1111 Third Avenue, 34th Floor · Seattle, WA 98101 · 206-447-4400

John A. Gose · Preston, Thorgrimson, Shidler, Gates & Ellis · 5400 Columbia Center · 701 Fifth Avenue · Seattle, WA 98104-7078 · 206-623-7580

Joel E. Haggard* · (Zoning, Land Use) · Haggard Law Office · IBM Building, Suite 1515 · 1200 Fifth Avenue · Seattle, WA 98101 · 206-682-5635

Jerome L. Hillis* · (Zoning, Land Use, Commercial Transactions, Industrial Transactions) · Hillis, Clark, Martin & Peterson · 500 Galland Building · 1221 Second Avenue · Seattle, WA 98101-2925 · 206-623-1745

Richard E. Keefe · Foster, Pepper & Shefelman · 1111 Third Avenue, 34th Floor Seattle, WA 98101 · 206-447-4400

Edward W. Kuhrau · Perkins Coie · 1201 Third Avenue, 40th Floor · Seattle, WA 98101-3099 · 206-583-8888

Richard E. McCann · (Zoning, Land Use) · Perkins Coie · 1201 Third Avenue, 40th Floor · Seattle, WA 98101-3099 · 206-583-8888

Dennis E. McLean · (Commercial Transactions) · Davis Wright Tremaine · 2600 Century Square · 1501 Fourth Avenue · Seattle, WA 98101-1688 · 206-622-3150

Scott B. Osborne · Graham & Dunn · Security Pacific Plaza, 33rd Floor · 1420 Fifth Avenue · Seattle, WA 98101-2390 · 206-624-8300

John E. Phillips · Phillips & Wilson · Marketplace One, Suite 500 · 2001 Western Avenue · Seattle, WA 98102 · 206-448-1818

David H. Rockwell · Stoel Rives Boley Jones & Grey · One Union Square, 36th Floor · 600 University Street · Seattle, WA 98101-3197 · 206-624-0900

Judith M. Runstad · Foster, Pepper & Shefelman · 1111 Third Avenue, 34th Floor · Seattle, WA 98101 · 206-447-4400

David W. Thorne · Davis Wright Tremaine · 2600 Century Square · 1501 Fourth Avenue · Seattle, WA 98101-1688 · 206-622-3150

Russell F. Tousley · Tousley Brain · AT&T Gateway Tower, 56th Floor · 700 Fifth Avenue · Seattle, WA 98104 · 206-682-5600

Jerome D. Whalen · Foster, Pepper & Shefelman · 1111 Third Avenue, 34th Floor · Seattle, WA 98101 · 206-447-4400

Paul J. Allison · Randall & Danskin · 1500 Seafirst Financial Center · West 601 Riverside · Spokane, WA 99201 · 509-747-2052

Ned M. Barnes · Witherspoon, Kelley, Davenport & Toole · Old National Bank Building, 11th Floor · West 428 Riverside Avenue · Spokane, WA 99201-0390 · 509-624-5265

Joseph P. Delay · Delay, Curran, Thompson & Pontarolo · 1212 Washington Mutual Financial Center · West 601 Main · Spokane, WA 99201-0684 · 509-455-9500

Stanley R. Schultz · Winston & Cashatt · Seafirst Financial Center, Suite 1900 · West 601 Riverside Avenue · Spokane, WA 99201-0695 · 509-838-6131

William A. Tombari, Jr. · Esposito, Tombari & George · 960 Paulsen Building · Spokane, WA 99201 · 509-624-9219

Dale L. Carlisle · Gordon, Thomas, Honeywell, Malanca, Peterson & Daheim · 2200 First Interstate Plaza · Tacoma, WA 98402 · 206-572-5050

Warren J. Daheim · Gordon, Thomas, Honeywell, Malanca, Peterson & Daheim · 2200 First Interstate Plaza · Tacoma, WA 98402 · 206-572-5050

William F. Almon · Almon, Berg & Adams · 811 Summitview Avenue, Suite 2 · P.O. Box 588 · Yakima, WA 98907-0588 · 509-575-6500

Thomas B. Grahn · Halverson & Applegate · 311 North Fourth Street · P.O. Box 526 · Yakima, WA 98907 · 509-575-6611

TAX AND EMPLOYEE BENEFITS LAW

Dwight J. Drake · Foster, Pepper & Shefelman · Security Pacific Plaza, 15th Floor · 7770 One-Hundred-Eighth Avenue, NE · Bellevue, WA 98004 · 206-451-0500

William H. Burkhart · Preston, Thorgrimson, Shidler, Gates & Ellis · 5400 Columbia Center · 701 Fifth Avenue · Seattle, WA 98104-7078 · 206-623-7580

C. Kent Carlson · Preston, Thorgrimson, Shidler, Gates & Ellis · 5400 Columbia Center · 701 Fifth Avenue · Seattle, WA 98104-7078 · 206-623-7580

Donald C. Dahlgren · (Employee Benefits) · Dahlgren & Dauenhauer · 1702 Norton Building · 801 Second Avenue · Seattle, WA 98104 · 206-624-0450

Meade Emory* · Lane Powell Spears Lubersky · Pacific First Center, Suite 4100 1420 Fifth Avenue · Seattle, WA 98101-2338 · 206-223-7000

Graham H. Fernald · Perkins Coie · 1201 Third Avenue, 40th Floor · Seattle, WA 98101-3099 · 206-583-8888

G. Keith Grim · Lane Powell Spears Lubersky · Pacific First Center, Suite 4100 1420 Fifth Avenue · Seattle, WA 98101-2338 · 206-223-7000

W. Michael Hafferty · (Corporate & Partnership Transactions, State Tax, Real Estate Taxation) · Riddell, Williams, Bullitt & Walkinshaw · 1001 Fourth Avenue Plaza, Suite 4400 · Seattle, WA 98154 · 206-624-3600

Darrell D. Hallett · Chicoine & Hallett · Waterfront Place One, Suite 803 · 1011 Western Avenue · Seattle, WA 98104 · 206-223-0800

James M. Hilton · (Corporate & Partnership Transactions) · Perkins Coie · 1201 Third Avenue, 40th Floor · Seattle, WA 98101-3099 · 206-583-8888

Roland L. Hjorth · Perkins Coie · 1201 Third Avenue, 40th Floor · Seattle, WA 98101-3099 · 206-583-8888

Richard A. Hopp · (Employee Benefits) · Stoel Rives Boley Jones & Grey · One Union Square, 36th Floor · 600 University Street · Seattle, WA 98101-3197 · 206-624-0900

C. James Judson · (Corporate & Partnership Transactions, State Tax) · Davis Wright Tremaine · 2600 Century Square · 1501 Fourth Avenue · Seattle, WA 98101-1688 · 206-628-7686

Robert D. Kaplan · Bogle & Gates · Two Union Square, Suite 4700 · 601 Union Street · Seattle, WA 98101-2322 · 206-682-5151

Patrick F. Kennedy · Foster, Pepper & Shefelman · 1111 Third Avenue, 34th Floor · Seattle, WA 98101 · 206-447-4400

Francis A. LeSourd · LeSourd & Patten · 2400 Columbia Center · 701 Fifth Avenue · Seattle, WA 98104-7095 · 206-624-1040

Judd R. Marten · (Employee Benefits) · LeSourd & Patten · 2400 Columbia Center · 701 Fifth Avenue · Seattle, WA 98104-7095 · 206-624-1040

Gerhardt Morrison · Bogle & Gates · Two Union Square, Suite 4700 · 601 Union Street · Seattle, WA 98101-2322 · 206-682-5151

Richard L. Mull · Perkins Coie · 1201 Third Avenue, 40th Floor · Seattle, WA 98101-3099 · 206-583-8629

Anne L. Northrop · (Employee Benefits) · Davis Wright Tremaine · 2600 Century Square · 1501 Fourth Avenue · Seattle, WA 98101-1688 · 206-622-3150

David F. P. O'Connor · Bogle & Gates · Two Union Square, Suite 4700 · 601 Union Street · Seattle, WA 98101-2322 · 206-682-5151

Charles F. Osborn · Bogle & Gates · Two Union Square, Suite 4700 · 601 Union Street · Seattle, WA 98101-2322 · 206-682-5151

John T. Piper · Bogle & Gates · Two Union Square, Suite 4700 · 601 Union Street Seattle, WA 98101-2322 · 206-682-5151

Samuel F. Saracino · Davis Wright Tremaine · 2600 Century Square · 1501 Fourth Avenue · Seattle, WA 98101-1688 · 206-622-3150

Jon M. Schorr · Heller, Ehrman, White & McAuliffe · Columbia SeaFirst Center, 61st Floor · 701 Fifth Avenue · Seattle, WA 98104 · 206-447-0900

Lee Thorson · (Employee Benefits) · Lane Powell Spears Lubersky · Pacific First Center, Suite 4100 · 1420 Fifth Avenue · Seattle, WA 98101-2338 · 206-223-7000

Irwin L. Treiger · Bogle & Gates · Two Union Square, Suite 4700 · 601 Union Street · Seattle, WA 98101-2322 · 206-682-5151

Rodney J. Waldbaum* · (Corporate & Partnership Transactions, State Tax, Tax Disputes, Criminal Tax) · LeSourd & Patten · 2400 Columbia Center · 701 Fifth Avenue · Seattle, WA 98104-7095 · 206-624-1040

Andrew H. Zuccotti · Stoel Rives Boley Jones & Grey · One Union Square, 36th Floor · 600 University Street · Seattle, WA 98101-3197 · 206-624-0900

James S. Black, Jr. · Lukins & Annis · 1600 Washington Trust Financial Center West 717 Sprague Avenue · Spokane, WA 99204-0466 · 509-455-9555

K. Thomas Connolly · (Corporate & Partnership Transactions, Employee Benefits) · Witherspoon, Kelley, Davenport & Toole · Old National Bank Building, 11th Floor · West 428 Riverside Avenue · Spokane, WA 99201-0390 · 509-624-5265

Scott B. Lukins · Lukins & Annis · 1600 Washington Trust Financial Center · West 717 Sprague Avenue · Spokane, WA 99204-0466 · 509-455-9555

Gary C. Randall · (Tax Disputes) · Gonzaga Law School · 502 Boone Avenue East Box 3528 · Spokane, WA 99220-3528 · 509-484-6481

James A. Furber · Gordon, Thomas, Honeywell, Malanca, Peterson & Daheim 2200 First Interstate Plaza · Tacoma, WA 98402 · 206-572-5050

TRUSTS AND ESTATES

Albert J. Schauble · Aitken, Schauble, Patrick, Neill & Ruff · 210 US Bank Building · P.O. Box 307 · Pullman, WA 99163 · 509-334-3505

Steven W. Andreasen · Davis Wright Tremaine · 2600 Century Square · 1501 Fourth Avenue · Seattle, WA 98101-1688 · 206-628-7613

Janis A. Cunningham · Perkins Coie · 1201 Third Avenue, Suite 400 · Seattle, WA 98101-3099 · 206-583-8888

Bruce P. Flynn · Perkins Coie · 1201 Third Avenue, 40th Floor · Seattle, WA 98101-3099 · 206-583-8888

Thomas C. Gores · Bogle & Gates · Two Union Square, Suite 4700 · 601 Union Street · Seattle, WA 98101-2322 · 206-682-5151

Alan H. Kane · Preston, Thorgrimson, Shidler, Gates & Ellis · 5400 Columbia Center · 701 Fifth Avenue · Seattle, WA 98104-7078 · 206-623-7580

Richard A. Klobucher · Davis Wright Tremaine · 2600 Century Square · 1501 Fourth Avenue · Seattle, WA 98101-1688 · 206-622-3150

Reginald S. Koehler III · Perkins Coie · 1201 Third Avenue, 40th Floor · Seattle, WA 98101-3099 · 206-583-8888

Malcolm A. Moore · Davis Wright Tremaine · 2600 Century Square · 1501 Fourth Avenue · Seattle, WA 98101-1688 · 206-622-3150

Robert S. Mucklestone · Perkins Coie · 1201 Third Avenue, 40th Floor · Seattle, WA 98101-3099 · 206-583-8464

John R. Price · Perkins Coie · 1201 Third Avenue, 40th Floor · Seattle, WA 98101-3099 · 206-583-8888

Kenneth L. Schubert, Jr. · Garvey, Schubert & Barer · Waterfront Place Building, 10th Floor · 1011 Western Avenue · Seattle, WA 98104 · 206-464-3939

John F. Sherwood · 510 Rainier Avenue South · Seattle, WA 98144 · 206-323-8031

Kimbrough Street · Davis Wright Tremaine · 2600 Century Square · 1501 Fourth Avenue · Seattle, WA 98101-1688 · 206-622-3150

Scott B. Lukins · Lukins & Annis · 1600 Washington Trust Financial Center · West 717 Sprague Avenue · Spokane, WA 99204-0466 · 509-455-9555

Donald K. Querna · Randall & Danskin · 1500 Seafirst Financial Center · West 601 Riverside Avenue · Spokane, WA 99201 · 509-747-2052

Allan H. Toole · Witherspoon, Kelley, Davenport & Toole · Old National Bank Building, 11th Floor · West 428 Riverside Avenue · Spokane, WA 99201-0390 · 509-624-5265

Roger H. Underwood · Underwood, Campbell, Brock & Cerutti · 1100 Seafirst Financial Center · West 601 Riverside Avenue · Spokane, WA 99201 · 509-455-8500

S. Alan Weaver · Eisenhower, Carlson, Newlands, Reha, Henriot & Quinn · First Interstate Plaza, Suite 1200 · Tacoma, WA 98402 · 206-572-4500

Herman H. Hayner · Minnick-Hayner · 249 West Alder Street · P.O. Box 1757 · Walla Walla, WA 99362-0348 · 509-527-3500

James K. Hayner* · Minnick-Hayner · 249 West Alder Street · P.O. Box 1757 · Walla Walla, WA 99362-0348 · 509-527-3500

John M. Reese · Reese, Baffney, Schrag, Siegel & Hedine · Baker Building, Seventh Floor · Walla Walla, WA 99362 · 509-525-8130

George F. Velikanje · Velikanje, Moore & Shore · 405 East Lincoln Avenue · Yakima, WA 98901 · 509-248-6030

WEST VIRGINIA

BANKRUPTCY LAW

Thomas B. Bennett* · (Business Reorganization, Creditors' Rights, Bankruptcy Litigation) · Bowles Rice McDavid Graff & Love · Commerce Square, 16th Floor P.O. Box 1386 · Charleston, WV 25325-1386 · 304-347-1100

William W. Booker · Kay, Casto, Chaney, Love & Wise · 1600 Charleston National Plaza · P.O. Box 2031 · Charleston, WV 25327 · 304-343-4841

Ellen S. Cappellanti · Jackson & Kelly · 1600 Laidley Tower · P.O. Box 553 · Charleston, WV 25322 · 304-340-1000

William F. Dobbs, Jr.* · (Business Reorganization, Creditors' Rights, Bankruptcy Litigation) · Jackson & Kelly · 1600 Laidley Tower · P.O. Box 553 · Charleston, WV 25322 · 304-340-1000

Thomas R. Goodwin · Goodwin & Goodwin · 1500 One Valley Square · P.O. Box 2107 · Charleston, WV 25301 · 304-346-0321

Michael L. Bray · Steptoe & Johnson · Union National Center East, Sixth Floor
P.O. Box 2190 · Clarksburg, WV 26302-2190 · 304-624-8000

BUSINESS LITIGATION

James K. Brown* · Jackson & Kelly · 1600 Laidley Tower · P.O. Box 553 ·
Charleston, WV 25322 · 304-340-1000

John S. Haight · Kay, Casto, Chaney, Love & Wise · 1600 Charleston National
Plaza · P.O. Box 2031 · Charleston, WV 25327 · 304-345-8900

Charles M. Love III · Bowles Rice McDavid Graff & Love · Commerce Square,
16th Floor · P.O. Box 1386 · Charleston, WV 25325-1386 · 304-347-1100

Herbert G. Underwood · Steptoe & Johnson · Union National Center East, Sixth
Floor · P.O. Box 2190 · Clarksburg, WV 26302-2190 · 304-624-8000

John E. Jenkins, Jr. · Jenkins, Fenstermaker, Krieger, Kayes & Farrell · Coal
Exchange Building, llth Floor · 401 Eleventh Street · P.O. Drawer 2688 · Huntington, WV 25726 · 304-523-2100

CORPORATE LAW

Michael A. Albert · Jackson & Kelly · 1600 Laidley Tower · P.O. Box 553 ·
Charleston, WV 25322 · 304-340-1000

James K. Brown* · Jackson & Kelly · 1600 Laidley Tower · P.O. Box 553 ·
Charleston, WV 25322 · 304-340-1000

Thomas R. Goodwin · Goodwin & Goodwin · 1500 One Valley Square · P.O. Box
2107 · Charleston, WV 25301 · 304-346-0321

F. Thomas Graff, Jr. · (Administrative, Banking) · Bowles Rice McDavid Graff &
Love · Commerce Square, 16th Floor · P.O. Box 1386 · Charleston, WV 25325-
1386 · 304-347-1100

John R. Lukens · Jackson & Kelly · 1600 Laidley Tower · P.O. Box 553 ·
Charleston, WV 25322 · 304-340-1000

Charles R. McElwee · Robinson & McElwee · 600 United Center · 500 Virginia
Street East · P.O. Box 1791 · Charleston, WV 25326 · 304-344-5800

John E. Jenkins, Jr. · Jenkins, Fenstermaker, Krieger, Kayes & Farrell · Coal
Exchange Building, 11th Floor · 401 Eleventh Street · P.O. Drawer 2688 · Huntington, WV 25726 · 304-523-2100

CRIMINAL DEFENSE

Arthur T. Ciccarello* · (Violent Crimes, Non-Violent Crimes, Federal Court, State Court) · Lewis, Ciccarello & Friedberg · One Valley Square, Suite 700 · P.O. Box 1746 · Charleston, WV 25326 · 304-345-2000

Rudolph L. DiTrapano · DiTrapano & Jackson · 604-Virginia Street East · Charleston, WV 25301 · 304-342-0133

Robert B. King · King, Betts & Allen · 1320 Charleston National Plaza · P.O. Box 3394 · Charleston, WV 25333 · 304-345-7250

James B. McIntyre · McIntyre, Haviland & Jordan · 124 Capitol Street · Charleston, WV 25301 · 304-344-3652

LABOR AND EMPLOYMENT LAW

Grant Crandall* · (Labor, Individuals) · Crandall & Pyles · Medical Arts Building 1021 Quarrier Street, Suite 414 · P.O. Box 3465 · Charleston, WV 25334 · 304-345-3080

James M. Haviland · (Labor) · McIntyre, Haviland & Jordan · 124 Capitol Street Charleston, WV 25301 · 304-344-3652

Forrest H. Roles · (Management) · Smith, Heenan & Althen · One Valley Square, Suite 1380 · Charleston, WV 25301 · 304-342-8960

Robert M. Steptoe, Jr.* · (Management) · Steptoe & Johnson · Union National Center East, Sixth Floor · P.O. Box 2190 · Clarksburg, WV 26302-2190 · 304-624-8000

NATURAL RESOURCES AND ENVIRONMENTAL LAW

M. Ann Bradley · Robinson & McElwee · 600 United Center · 500 Virginia Street East · P.O. Box 1791 · Charleston, WV 25326 · 304-344-5800

David M. Flannery · (Water, Air, Solid Waste, Hazardous Waste) · Robinson & McElwee · 600 United Center · 500 Virginia Street East · P.O. Box 1791 · Charleston, WV 25326 · 304-344-5800

F. Thomas Graff, Jr. · (Oil & Gas, Coal) · Bowles Rice McDavid Graff & Love Commerce Square, 16th Floor · P.O. Box 1386 · Charleston, WV 25325-1386 · 304-347-1100

J. Thomas Lane* · (Oil & Gas, Coal) · Bowles Rice McDavid Graff & Love · Commerce Square, 16th Floor · P.O. Box 1386 · Charleston, WV 25325-1386 · 304-347-1100

Kim Brown Poland · (Environmental) · Robinson & McElwee · 600 United Center · 500 Virginia Street East · P.O. Box 1791 · Charleston, WV 25326 · 304-344-5800

Patrick D. Deem · (Oil & Gas, Coal) · Steptoe & Johnson · Union National Center East, Sixth Floor · P.O. Box 2190 · Clarksburg, WV 26302-2190 · 304-624-8000

Charles Q. Gage · (Coal) · Jackson & Kelly · 1600 Laidley Tower · P.O. Box 553 Charleston, WV 25322 · 304-340-1112

PERSONAL INJURY LITIGATION

Rudolph L. DiTrapano · (Plaintiffs) · DiTrapano & Jackson · 604 Virginia Street East · Charleston, WV 25301 · 304-342-0133

John S. Haight · (Defendants) · Kay, Casto, Chaney, Love & Wise · 1600 Charleston National Plaza · P.O. Box 2031 · Charleston, WV 25327 · 304-345-8900

Phillip Rodney Jackson* · (Plaintiffs, Medical Malpractice, Automobile Collision) · DiTrapano & Jackson · 604 Virginia Street East · Charleston, WV 25301 · 304-342-0133

Menis E. Ketchum* · (Plaintiffs, Medical Malpractice, Products Liability, Automobile Collision) · Greene, Ketchum, Bailey & Tweel · 419 Eleventh Street · P.O. Box 2389 · Huntington, WV 25724 · 304-525-9115

PUBLIC UTILITY LAW

Michael A. Albert · Jackson & Kelly · 1600 Laidley Tower · P.O. Box 553 · Charleston, WV 25322 · 304-340-1000

E. Dandridge McDonald · McDonald & Rodecker · 920 Charleston National Plaza · P.O. Box 2151 · Charleston, WV 25328 · 304-344-5046

Charles R. McElwee · Robinson & McElwee · 600 United Center · 500 Virginia Street East · P.O. Box 1791 · Charleston, WV 25326 · 304-344-5800

REAL ESTATE LAW

Charles E. Barnett · Kay, Casto, Chaney, Love & Wise · 1600 Charleston National Plaza · P.O. Box 2031 · Charleston, WV 25327 · 304-343-4841

George C. Leslie · (Commercial Transactions) · Kay, Casto, Chaney, Love & Wise · 1600 Charleston National Plaza · P.O. Box 2031 · Charleston, WV 25327 · 304-345-8900

Harvey Alan Siler · Jackson & Kelly · 1600 Laidley Tower · P.O. Box 553 · Charleston, WV 25322 · 304-340-1000

TAX AND EMPLOYEE BENEFITS LAW

Michael D. Foster · (Employee Benefits) · Jackson & Kelly · 1600 Laidley Tower P.O. Box 553 · Charleston, WV 25322 · 304-340-1000

John T. Kay, Jr. · (Corporate & Partnership Transactions) · Kay, Casto, Chaney, Love & Wise · 1600 Charleston National Plaza · P.O. Box 2031 · Charleston, WV 25327 · 304-345-8900

Gordon C. Lane · Bowles Rice McDavid Graff & Love · Commerce Square, 16th Floor · P.O. Box 1386 · Charleston, WV 25325-1386 · 304-347-1100

Charles W. Loeb · Payne, Loeb & Ray · 1210 One Valley Square · Charleston, WV 25301 · 304-342-1141

Louis S. Southworth II · (Corporate & Partnership Transactions, State Tax) · Jackson & Kelly · 1600 Laidley Tower · P.O. Box 553 · Charleston, WV 25322 · 304-340-1000

Charles B. Stacy · Spilman, Thomas, Battle & Klostermeyer · 1200 United Center · 500 Virginia Street East · P.O. Box 273 · Charleston, WV 25321 · 304-340-3855

TRUSTS AND ESTATES

Thomas G. Freeman II · Jackson & Kelly · 1600 Laidley Tower · P.O. Box 553 Charleston, WV 25322 · 304-340-1000

Harry P. Henshaw III · Shuman, Annand & Poe · 405 Capitol Street · P.O. Box 3953 · Charleston, WV 25339 · 304-345-1400

Milton T. Herndon · Campbell, Woods, Bagley, Emerson, McNeer & Herndon Charleston National Plaza, Suite 1400 · P.O. Box 2393 · Charleston, WV 25328-2393 · 304-346-2391

George C. Leslie · (Estate Planning) · Kay, Casto, Chaney, Love & Wise · 1600 Charleston National Plaza · P.O. Box 2031 · Charleston, WV 25327 · 304-345-8900

Charles W. Loeb · Payne, Loeb & Ray · 1210 One Valley Square · Charleston, WV 25301 · 304-342-1141

Charles B. Stacy · Spilman, Thomas, Battle & Klostermeyer · 1200 United Center · 500 Virginia Street East · P.O. Box 273 · Charleston, WV 25321 · 304-340-3855

WISCONSIN

BANKRUPTCY LAW

Mark Bromley · 151 West Maple Street, · P.O. Box 528 · Lancaster, WI 53813 · 608-723-7661

Denis P. Bartell · (Business Reorganization, Creditors' Rights, Bankruptcy Litigation) · Ross & Stevens · Capitol Square Office · First Wisconsin Plaza · P.O. Box 2599 · Madison, WI 53701-2599 · 608-257-5353

Patricia M. Gibeault · Axley Brynelson · Two East Mifflin · P.O. Box 1767 · Madison, WI 53701-1767 · 608-257-5661

Michael E. Kepler · Kepler & Peyton · 353 West Mifflin Street · Madison, WI 53703 · 608-257-5424

Roy L. Prange, Jr.* · (Creditors' Rights, Bankruptcy Litigation) · Quarles & Brady · First Wisconsin Plaza · One South Pinckney Street · P.O. Box 2113 · Madison, WI 53701-2113 · 608-251-5000

William J. Rameker · Murphy & Desmond · Manchester Place · Two East Mifflin Street, Suite 800 · P.O. Box 2038 · Madison, WI 53701-2038 · 608-257-7181

James D. Sweet · Murphy & Desmond · Manchester Place · Two East Mifflin Street, Suite 800 · P.O. Box 2038 · Madison, WI 53701-2038 · 608-257-7181

David G. Walsh · Foley & Lardner · First Wisconsin Plaza, Seventh Floor · One South Pinckney Street · P.O. Box 1497 · Madison, WI 53701-1497 · 608-257-5035

Andrew M. Barnes · Quarles & Brady · 411 East Wisconsin Avenue · Milwaukee, WI 53202-4497 · 414-277-5000

Peter C. Blain · Reinhart, Boerner, Van Deuren, Norris & Rieselbach · Bank One Plaza, Suite 1800 · 111 East Wisconsin Avenue · Milwaukee, WI 53202-4884 · 414-271-1190

Richard H. Casper · (Business Reorganization, Creditors' Rights) · Foley & Lardner · First Wisconsin Center · 777 East Wisconsin Avenue · Milwaukee, WI 53202-5367 · 414-289-3560

Randall D. Crocker · von Briesen & Purtell · 411 East Wisconsin Avenue, Suite 700 · Milwaukee, WI 53202 · 414-276-1122

Robert A. DuPuy · Foley & Lardner · First Wisconsin Center · 777 East Wisconsin Avenue · Milwaukee, WI 53202-5367 · 414-271-2400

David A. Erne · Reinhart, Boerner, Van Deuren, Norris & Rieselbach · Bank One Plaza, Suite 1800 · 111 East Wisconsin Avenue · Milwaukee, WI 53202-4884 · 414-271-1190

Floyd A. Harris · Polacheck and Harris · 710 North Plankinton Avenue · Milwaukee, WI 53203 · 414-276-1941

R. Arthur Ludwig · Ludwig & Shlimovitz · 1568 North Farwell Avenue · Milwaukee, WI 53202 · 414-271-4550

K. Thor Lundgren · Michael, Best & Friedrich · 100 East Wisconsin Avenue, Suite 3300 · Milwaukee, WI 53202-4108 · 414-271-6560

Paul S. Medved* · Michael, Best & Friedrich · 100 East Wisconsin Avenue, Suite 3300 · Milwaukee, WI 53202-4108 · 414-271-6560

Jack U. Shlimovitz · Ludwig & Shlimovitz · 1568 North Farwell Avenue · Milwaukee, WI 53202 · 414-271-4550

Albert Solochek · Howard, Solochek & Weber · 324 East Wisconsin Avenue · Milwaukee, WI 53202 · 414-272-0760

BUSINESS LITIGATION

Brian E. Butler · (Antitrust, RICO, Dealership/Franchise) · Stafford, Rosenbaum, Rieser & Hansen · Tenney Plaza, Suite 1000 · Three South Pinckney Street · P.O. Box 1784 · Madison, WI 53701-1784 · 608-256-0226

Daniel W. Hildebrand* · Ross & Stevens · Capitol Square Office · First Wisconsin Plaza · P.O. Box 2599 · Madison, WI 53701-2599 · 608-257-5353

John C. Mitby* · (Banking) · Axley Brynelson · Manchester Place · Two East Mifflin Street · P.O. Box 1767 · Madison, WI 53701-1767 · 800-369-5661

John S. Skilton · Foley & Lardner · First Wisconsin Plaza, Seventh Floor · One South Pinckney Street · P.O. Box 1497 · Madison, WI 53701-1497 · 608-257-5035

Robert V. Abendroth · Whyte & Hirschboeck · 111 East Wisconsin Avenue, Suite 2100 · Milwaukee, WI 53202-4894 · 414-271-8210

David E. Beckwith · Foley & Lardner · First Wisconsin Center · 777 East Wisconsin Avenue · Milwaukee, WI 53202-5367 · 414-271-2400

James R. Clark · Foley & Lardner · First Wisconsin Center · 777 East Wisconsin Avenue · Milwaukee, WI 53202-5367 · 414-271-2400

Frank J. Daily · Quarles & Brady · 411 East Wisconsin Avenue · Milwaukee, WI 53202-4497 · 414-277-5381

Robert A. DuPuy · Foley & Lardner · First Wisconsin Center · 777 East Wisconsin Avenue · Milwaukee, WI 53202-5367 · 414-271-2400

Laurence C. Hammond, Jr.* · Quarles & Brady · 411 East Wisconsin Avenue · Milwaukee, WI 53202-4497 · 414-277-5000

Maurice J. McSweeney* · (Antitrust, Commercial, Securities) · Foley & Lardner First Wisconsin Center · 777 East Wisconsin Avenue · Milwaukee, WI 53202-5367 414-271-2400

Richard C. Ninneman* · Quarles & Brady · 411 East Wisconsin Avenue · Milwaukee, WI 53202-4497 · 414-277-5000

W. Stuart Parsons* · Quarles & Brady · 411 East Wisconsin Avenue · Milwaukee, WI 53202-4497 · 414-277-5000

Thomas L. Shriner, Jr. · Foley & Lardner · First Wisconsin Center · 777 East Wisconsin Avenue · Milwaukee, WI 53202-5367 · 414-271-2400

Clay R. Williams* · Gibbs, Roper, Loots & Williams · 735 North Water Street · Milwaukee, WI 53202 · 414-273-7010

CORPORATE LAW

Robert H. Consigny · Consigny, Andrews, Hemming & Grant · 303 East Court Street · P.O. Box 1449 · Janesville, WI 53547 · 608-755-5050

Jeffrey B. Bartell · Quarles & Brady · First Wisconsin Plaza · One South Pinckney Street · P.O. Box 2113 · Madison, WI 53701-2113 · 608-251-5000

Lawrence J. Bugge · (Banking, Corporate Finance, Financial Institutions) · Foley & Lardner · First Wisconsin Plaza, Seventh Floor · One South Pinckney Street · P.O. Box 1497 · Madison, WI 53701-1497 · 608-257-5035

Joseph P. Hildebrandt · Foley & Lardner · First Wisconsin Plaza, Seventh Floor One South Pinckney Street · P.O. Box 1497 · Madison, WI 53701-1497 · 608-257-5035

John E. Knight · Boardman, Suhr, Curry & Field · One South Pinckney Street, Suite 410 · P.O. Box 927 · Madison, WI 53701-0927 · 608-257-9521

Tod B. Linstroth · (Corporate Finance, Leveraged Buyouts, Mergers & Acquisitions) · Michael, Best & Friedrich · First Wisconsin Plaza · One South Pinckney Street · P.O. Box 1806 · Madison, WI 53701-1806 · 608-257-3501

Thomas G. Ragatz* · (Administrative, Investment, Leveraged Buyouts, Mergers & Acquisitions) · Foley & Lardner · First Wisconsin Plaza, Seventh Floor · One South Pinckney Street · P.O. Box 1497 · Madison, WI 53701-1497 · 608-257-5035

Jeremy C. Shea · (Banking, Corporate Finance, Financial Institutions, Mergers & Acquisitions) · Ross & Stevens · Capitol Square Office · First Wisconsin Plaza · P.O. Box 2599 · Madison, WI 53701-2599 · 608-257-5353

Seward Ritchey Stroud · Stroud, Stroud, Willink, Thompson & Howard · 25 West Main Street, Suite 300 · P.O. Box 2236 · Madison, WI 53701 · 608-257-2281

David G. Walsh · (Mergers & Acquisitions, Communications) · Foley & Lardner First Wisconsin Plaza, Seventh Floor · One South Pinckney Street · P.O. Box 1497 Madison, WI 53701-1497 · 608-257-5035

Thomas D. Zilavy · Ross & Stevens · Capitol Square Office · First Wisconsin Plaza · P.O. Box 2599 · Madison, WI 53701-2599 · 608-257-5353

William J. Abraham, Jr. · (Corporate Finance, Leveraged Buyouts, Mergers & Acquisitions, Securities) · Foley & Lardner · First Wisconsin Center · 777 East Wisconsin Avenue · Milwaukee, WI 53202-5367 · 414-271-2400

A. William Asmuth, Jr. · Whyte & Hirschboeck · 111 East Wisconsin Avenue, Suite 2100 · Milwaukee, WI 53202-4894 · 414-271-8210

Roger L. Boerner · (Corporate Finance, Leveraged Buyouts) · Reinhart, Boerner, Van Deuren, Norris & Rieselbach · Bank One Plaza, Suite 1800 · 111 East Wisconsin Avenue · Milwaukee, WI 53202-4884 · 414-271-1190

Walter S. Davis · Davis & Kuelthau · 111 East Kilbourne, Suite 1400 · Milwaukee, WI 53202-6613 · 414-276-0200

Benjamin F. Garmer, III · (Leveraged Buyouts, Mergers & Acquisitions, Securities, Securities Regulation) · Foley & Lardner · First Wisconsin Center · 777 East Wisconsin Avenue · Milwaukee, WI 53202-5367 · 414-271-2400

Dudley J. Godfrey, Jr. · Godfrey & Kahn · 780 North Water Street · Milwaukee, WI 53202-3590 · 414-273-3500

Conrad G. Goodkind · (Corporate Finance, Mergers & Acquisitions, Mutual Funds, Securities) · Quarles & Brady · 411 East Wisconsin Avenue · Milwaukee, WI 53202-4497 · 414-277-5000

Michael W. Grebe · Foley & Lardner · First Wisconsin Center · 777 East Wisconsin Avenue · Milwaukee, WI 53202-5367 · 414-271-2400

Robert J. Kalupa · Quarles & Brady · 411 East Wisconsin Avenue · Milwaukee, WI 53202-4497 · 414-277-5000

Bernard S. Kubale · Foley & Lardner · First Wisconsin Center · 777 East Wisconsin Avenue · Milwaukee, WI 53202-5367 · 414-271-2400

Roy C. LaBudde · (Leveraged Buyouts, Mergers & Acquisitions) · Michael, Best & Friedrich · 100 East Wisconsin Avenue, Suite 3300 · Milwaukee, WI 53202-4108 · 414-271-6560

Arthur H. Laun · Quarles & Brady · 411 East Wisconsin Avenue · Milwaukee, WI 53202-4497 · 414-277-5000

Robert J. Loots · (Mergers & Acquisitions, Securities) · Gibbs, Roper, Loots & Williams · 735 North Water Street · Milwaukee, WI 53202 · 414-273-7000

John K. MacIver · Michael, Best & Friedrich · 100 East Wisconsin Avenue, Suite 3300 · Milwaukee, WI 53202-4108 · 414-271-6560

Larry J. Martin · Quarles & Brady · 411 East Wisconsin Avenue · Milwaukee, WI 53202-4497 · 414-277-5000

Jere D. McGaffey · Foley & Lardner · First Wisconsin Center · 777 East Wisconsin Avenue · Milwaukee, WI 53202-5367 · 414-271-2400

Maurice J. McSweeney* · (Antitrust) · Foley & Lardner · First Wisconsin Center 777 East Wisconsin Avenue · Milwaukee, WI 53202-5367 · 414-271-2400

Charles C. Mulcahy · Frisch Dudek · 825 North Jefferson Street, Suite 500 · Milwaukee, WI 53202 · 414-273-4000

Richard H. Norris III · Reinhart, Boerner, Van Deuren, Norris & Rieselbach · Bank One Plaza, Suite 1800 · 111 East Wisconsin Avenue · Milwaukee, WI 53202-4884 · 414-271-1190

Frank J. Pelisek · (Banking, Corporate Finance, Mergers & Acquisitions, Securities) · Michael, Best & Friedrich · 100 East Wisconsin Avenue, Suite 3300 · Milwaukee, WI 53202-4108 · 414-271-6560

Wayne J. Roper · Gibbs, Roper, Loots & Williams · 735 North Water Street · Milwaukee, WI 53202 · 414-273-7010

Patrick M. Ryan · Quarles & Brady · 411 East Wisconsin Avenue · Milwaukee, WI 53202-4497 · 414-277-5000

James Urdan · (Banking, Financial Institutions) · Quarles & Brady · 411 East Wisconsin Avenue · Milwaukee, WI 53202-4497 · 414-277-5000

Richard A. Van Deuren · Reinhart, Boerner, Van Deuren, Norris & Rieselbach Bank One Plaza, Suite 1800 · 111 East Wisconsin Avenue · Milwaukee, WI 53202-4884 · 414-271-1190

Edwin P. Wiley · (Antitrust, Corporate Finance, International) · Foley & Lardner First Wisconsin Center · 777 East Wisconsin Avenue · Milwaukee, WI 53202-5367 414-271-2400

Elwin J. Zarwell · Quarles & Brady · 411 East Wisconsin Avenue · Milwaukee, WI 53202-4497 · 414-277-5000

Rodney O. Kittelsen · (Banking) · Kittelsen, Barry, Ross, Wellington and Thompson · 916 Seventeenth Avenue · P.O. Box 710 · Monroe, WI 53566 · 608-325-2191

G. Lane Ware · Ruder Ware & Michler · 500 Third Street · Wausau, WI 54402-8050 · 715-845-4336

CRIMINAL DEFENSE

Sarah Furey Crandall* · Crandall Law Office · 330 East Wilson Street · Madison, WI 53703 · 608-255-6400

Charles W. Giesen · Giesen & Berman · 306 East Wilson Street · Madison, WI 53703 · 608-255-8200

Bruce J. Rosen* · (Violent Crimes, Non-Violent Crimes, Federal Court, State Court) · Pellino, Rosen, Mowris & Kirkhuff · James Wilson Plaza · 131 West Wilson Street, Suite 1201 · Madison, WI 53703 · 608-255-4501

Thomas E. Brown · Gimbel, Reilly, Guerin & Brown · 111 East Kilbourne Avenue, Suite 2400 · Milwaukee, WI 53202 · 414-271-1440

David J. Cannon* · Michael, Best & Friedrich · 100 East Wisconsin Avenue, Suite 3300 · Milwaukee, WI 53202-4108 · 414-271-6560

Dennis P. Coffey* · (Violent Crimes, Non-Violent Crimes, Federal Court) · Coffey, Coffey & Geraghty · 3127 West Wisconsin Avenue · Milwaukee, WI 53208 · 414-344-5700

Francis R. Croak* · (Federal Court, State Court, Environmental Crimes) · Cook & Franke · 660 Building, Suite 401 · 660 East Mason Street · Milwaukee, WI 53202 · 414-271-5900

Franklyn M. Gimbel · Gimbel, Reilly, Guerin & Brown · 111 East Kilbourne Avenue, Suite 2400 · Milwaukee, WI 53202 · 414-271-1440

Stephen M. Glynn* · Shellow, Shellow & Glynn · 222 East Mason Street · Milwaukee, WI 53202 · 414-271-8535

Stephen Kravit · Kravit, Lammiman & DeBruin · 757 North Broadway, Suite 600 · Milwaukee, WI 53202 · 414-271-7444

Robert J. Lerner · Perry, Lerner & Quindel · 823 North Cass Street · Milwaukee, WI 53202 · 414-272-7400

James M. Shellow* · Shellow, Shellow & Glynn · 222 East Mason Street · Milwaukee, WI 53202 · 414-271-8535

Martin I. Hanson* · Hanson, Gasiorkiewicz & Weber · 514 Wisconsin Avenue · P.O. Box 1875 · Racine, WI 53401 · 414-632-5550

Kenneth H. Conway, Jr.* · (Child Custody, Divorce, Marital Settlement Agreements, Equitable Division) · Conway, Gerhardt & Seefeld · 121 Fifth Street · Baraboo, WI 53913 · 608-356-9441

Donald A. Levy · Levy & Levy · N61 W6058 Columbia Road · P.O. Box 127 · Cedarburg, WI 53012 · 414-377-5555

J. Michael Jerry · Liebmann, Conway, Olejniczak & Jerry · 231 South Adams Street · P.O. Box 1241 · Green Bay, WI 54305 · 414-437-0476

Thomas W. Anderson · Anderson, Sumpter & Anderson · 5401 Sixtieth Street · Kenosha, WI 53144 · 414-654-0999

Steven A. Bach · Cullen, Weston, Pines & Bach · 20 North Carroll Street · Madison, WI 53703 · 608-251-0101

Allan R. Koritzinsky · Stolper, Koritzinsky, Brewster & Neider · 7617 Mineral Point Road · P.O. Box 5510 · Madison, WI 53705-0510 · 608-833-7617

Robert E. Cook · Cook & Franke · 660 Building, Suite 401 · 660 East Mason Street · Milwaukee, WI 53202 · 414-271-5900

C. Michael Hausman · Slattery & Hausman · 111 East Kilbourn Avenue, Suite 1800 · Milwaukee, WI 53202 · 414-271-4555

Leonard L. Loeb* · Bank One Plaza, Suite 1125 · 111 East Wisconsin Avenue · Milwaukee, WI 53202 · 414-272-5632

Marvin A. Margolis · Margolis & Cassidy · 324 East Wisconsin Avenue, Suite 700 · Milwaukee, WI 53202 · 414-272-5333

Clifford K. Meldman* · (Child Custody, Divorce, Marital Settlement Agreements, Equitable Division) · Meldman & Meldman · 5150 North Port Washington Road · P.O. Box 17397 · Milwaukee, WI 53217 · 414-962-6299

Bruce M. Peckerman* · Meldman & Meldman · M. G. Atrium, Suite 133 · 5150 North Port Washington Road · P.O. Box 17397 · Milwaukee, WI 53217 · 414-962-6299

James J. Podell · Podell & Podell · Security Savings Building, Suite 207 · 5555 North Port Washington Road · Milwaukee, WI 53217 · 414-961-0323

Gary L. Bakke* · (Child Custody, Divorce, Marital Settlement Agreements, Equitable Division) · Bakke, Norman, Schumacher, Skinner & Walter · 1200 Heritage Drive · P.O. Box 50 · New Richmond, WI 54017 · 715-246-3800

Gerald M. Crawford · Stewart, Peyton, Crawford, Crawford & Stutt · Lake Forum Building · 840 Lake Avenue · Racine, WI 53403 · 414-634-6659

Herbert C. Humke · Hayes, Neumann, Humke, Moir & Bolgert · North Eighth Street, Suite 350 · Sheboygan, WI 53081 · 414-458-4654

Charles I. Phillips* · Law Offices of Charles I. Phillips · 358 West Main Street · Waukesha, WI 53186-4611 · 414-544-9998

William F. Alderson, Jr. · Schloemer, Alderson, Seefeldt & Spella · Sixth & Hickory Streets · P.O. Box 176 · West Bend, WI 53095 · 414-334-3471

Thomas A. Bailey · Law Office of Thomas A. Bailey · 705 East Silver Spring Drive · Whitefish Bay, WI 53217 · 414-962-8200

FIRST AMENDMENT LAW

Brady C. Williamson · LaFollette & Sinykin · One East Main Street, Suite 500 P.O. Box 2719 · Madison, WI 53701 · 608-257-3911

Robert A. Christensen · Foley & Lardner · First Wisconsin Center · 777 East Wisconsin Avenue · Milwaukee, WI 53202-5367 · 414-271-2400

John R. Dawson · Foley & Lardner · First Wisconsin Center · 777 East Wisconsin Avenue · Milwaukee, WI 53202-5367 · 414-289-3507

Thomas L. Shriner, Jr. · Foley & Lardner · First Wisconsin Center, Suite 3800 777 East Wisconsin Avenue · Milwaukee, WI 53202-5367 · 414-271-2400

HEALTH CARE LAW

Michael S. Weiden · Quarles & Brady · First Wisconsin Plaza · One South Pinckney Street · P.O. Box 2113 · Madison, WI 53701-2113 · 608-251-5000

Richard J. Canter · Michael, Best & Friedrich · 100 East Wisconsin Avenue, Suite 3300 · Milwaukee, WI 53202-4108 · 414-271-6560

James P. Connelly · Foley & Lardner · First Wisconsin Center · 777 East Wisconsin Avenue · Milwaukee, WI 53202-5367 · 414-271-2400

Alyce C. Katayama · Quarles & Brady · 411 East Wisconsin Avenue · Milwaukee, WI 53202-4497 · 414-277-5000

IMMIGRATION LAW

Thomas Hochstatter · Hochstatter, McCarthy & Rivas · Security Savings Building, Suite 302 · 5555 North Port Washington Road · Milwaukee, WI 53217 · 414-962-7440

Alyce C. Katayama · Quarles & Brady · 411 East Wisconsin Avenue · Milwaukee, WI 53202-4497 · 414-277-5000

Mary Corbett Stevenson · Sullivan & Stevenson · 611 North Broadway · Milwaukee, WI 53202 · 414-271-5272

Deborah McKeithan Sullivan · Sullivan & Stevenson · 611 North Broadway · Milwaukee, WI 53202 · 414-271-5272

Dennis M. Sullivan · Sullivan & Stevenson · 611 North Broadway · Milwaukee, WI 53202 · 414-271-5272

INTELLECTUAL PROPERTY LAW

Robert E. Clemency · Michael, Best & Friedrich · 100 East Wisconsin Avenue, Suite 3300 · Milwaukee, WI 53202-4108 · 414-271-6560

John C. CooperIII · Foley & Lardner · First Wisconsin Center · 777 East Wisconsin Avenue · Milwaukee, WI 53202-5367 · 414-271-2400

Thomas W. Ehrmann · Quarles & Brady · 411 East Wisconsin Avenue · Milwaukee, WI 53202-4497 · 414-277-5729

Daniel D. Fetterley · Andrus, Sceales, Starke & Sawall · 100 East Wisconsin Avenue, Suite 1100 · Milwaukee, WI 53202 · 414-271-7590

Joseph A. Gemignani · Michael, Best & Friedrich · 100 East Wisconsin Avenue, Suite 3300 · Milwaukee, WI 53202-4108 · 414-271-6560

Thad F. Kryshak · Quarles & Brady · 411 East Wisconsin Avenue · Milwaukee, WI 53202-4497 · 414-277-5781

Allan W. Leiser · Quarles & Brady · 411 East Wisconsin Avenue · Milwaukee, WI 53202-4497 · 414-277-5613

Paul R. Puerner · Paul R. Puerner Law Offices · 633 West Wisconsin Avenue, Suite 1305 · Milwaukee, WI 53203 · 414-223-4281

Daniel D. Ryan · Fuller, Ryan & Hohenfeldt · 633 West Wisconsin Avenue · Milwaukee, WI 53203 · 414-271-6555

Barry E. Sammons · Quarles & Brady · 411 East Wisconsin Avenue · Milwaukee, WI 53202-4497 · 414-277-5000

Eugene R. Sawall · Andrus, Sceales, Starke & Sawall · 100 East Wisconsin Avenue, Suite 1100 · Milwaukee, WI 53202 · 414-271-7590

Carl R. Schwartz · (Trademark) · Quarles & Brady · 411 East Wisconsin Avenue Milwaukee, WI 53202-4497 · 414-277-5000

David B. Smith · Michael, Best & Friedrich · 100 East Wisconsin Avenue, Suite 3300 · Milwaukee, WI 53202-4108 · 414-271-6560

Glenn O. Starke · Andrus, Sceales, Starke & Sawall · 100 East Wisconsin Avenue, Suite 1100 · Milwaukee, WI 53202 · 414-271-7590

LABOR AND EMPLOYMENT LAW

Dennis W. Rader · (Management) · Godfrey & Kahn · 333 Main Street, Suite 600 P.O. Box 13067 · Green Bay, WI 54307-3067 · 414-435-4471

Michael H. Auen* · (Management) · Foley & Lardner · First Wisconsin Plaza, Seventh Floor · One South Pinckney Street · P.O. Box 1497 · Madison, WI 53701-1497 · 608-257-5035

Charles Barnhill, Jr. · (Individuals) · Davis, Minar, Barnhill & Galland · 44 East Mifflin, Suite 803 · Madison, WI 53703 · 608-255-5200

Lee Cullen · (Labor) · Cullen Weston Pines & Bach · 20 North Carroll Street · Madison, WI 53703 · 608-251-0101

Bruce M. Davey · (Labor) · Lawton & Cates · 214 West Mifflin Street · Madison, WI 53703-2594 · 608-256-9031

Michael R. Fox · (Individuals) · Fox & Fox · 44 East Mifflin Street, Suite 403 · Madison, WI 53703 · 608-258-9588

Robert J. Gingras · (Individuals) · Fox, Fox, Schaefer & Gingras · 131 West Wilson, Suite 610 · Madison, WI 53703 · 608-255-0061

Robert C. Kelly · (Labor) · Kelly & Haus · 121 East Wilson Street · Madison, WI 53703 · 608-257-0420

Joseph A. Melli* · (Management) · Melli, Walker, Pease & Ruhly · Insurance Building, Suite 600 · 119 Martin Luther King, Jr. Boulevard · P.O. Box 1664 · Madison, WI 53701-1664 · 608-257-4812

Jeff Scott Olson* · (Plaintiffs) · Julian, Olson & Lasker · 330 East Wilson Street · P.O. Box 2206 · Madison, WI 53701-2206 · 608-255-6400

James K. Pease, Jr. · (Management) · Melli, Walker, Pease & Ruhly · Insurance Building, Suite 600 · 119 Martin Luther King, Jr. Boulevard · P.O. Box 1664 · Madison, WI 53701-1664 · 608-257-4812

James K. Ruhly · (Management) · Melli, Walker, Pease & Ruhly · Insurance Building, Suite 600 · 119 Martin Luther King, Jr. Boulevard · P.O. Box 1664 · Madison, WI 53701-1664 · 608-257-4812

Jack D. Walker · (Management) · Melli, Walker, Pease & Ruhly · Insurance Building, Suite 600 · 119 Martin Luther King, Jr. Boulevard · P.O. Box 1664 · Madison, WI 53701-1664 · 608-257-4812

Marshall R. Berkoff · (Management) · Michael, Best & Friedrich · 100 East Wisconsin Avenue, Suite 3300 · Milwaukee, WI 53202-4108 · 414-271-6560

Jacob L. Bernheim · (Management) · Michael, Best & Friedrich · 100 East Wisconsin Avenue, Suite 3300 · Milwaukee, WI 53202-4108 · 414-271-6560

John W. Brahm · (Management) · Foley & Lardner · First Wisconsin Center · 777 East Wisconsin Avenue · Milwaukee, WI 53202-5367 · 414-271-2400

Walter S. Davis · (Management) · Davis & Kuelthau · 111 East Kilbourne, Suite 1400 · Milwaukee, WI 53202-6613 · 414-276-0200

Laurence E. Gooding, Jr. · (Management) · Quarles & Brady · 411 East Wisconsin Avenue · Milwaukee, WI 53202-4497 · 414-277-5000

George F. Graf · (Labor) · Gillick, Murphy, Wicht & Prachthauser · Brookfield Lakes Corporate Center · 300 Corporate Drive · Milwaukee, WI 53205 · 414-792-0888

Timothy E. Hawks · (Labor) · Shneidman, Myers, Dowling & Blumenfield · 700 West Michigan Street, Suite 500 · Milwaukee, WI 53233 · 414-271-8650

Walter F. Kelly* · (Labor, Individuals) · Sutton & Kelly · 1409 East Capitol Drive · Milwaukee, WI 53211 · 414-961-0802

Kenneth R. Loebel · (Labor) · Previant, Goldberg, Uelmen, Gratz, Miller & Brueggeman · Office on the Square, Sixth Floor · 788 North Jefferson Street · P.O. Box 92099 · Milwaukee, WI 53202 · 414-271-4500

James C. Mallatt · (Management) · Michael, Best & Friedrich · 100 East Wisconsin Avenue, Suite 3300 · Milwaukee, WI 53202-4108 · 414-271-6560

Gerry M. Miller · (Labor) · Previant, Goldberg, Uelmen, Gratz, Miller & Brueggeman · Office on the Square, Sixth Floor · 788 North Jefferson Street · P.O. Box 92099 · Milwaukee, WI 53202 · 414-271-4500

Robert W. Mulcahy · (Management) · Michael Best & Friedrich · 100 East Wisconsin Avenue, Suite 3300 · Milwaukee, WI 53202-4108 · 414-271-6560

Howard N. Myers · (Labor) · Shneidman, Myers, Dowling & Blumenfield · 700 West Michigan Street, Suite 500 · Milwaukee, WI 53233 · 414-271-8650

Thomas E. Obenberger · (Management) · Michael, Best & Friedrich · 100 East Wisconsin Avenue, Suite 3300 · Milwaukee, WI 53202-4108 · 414-271-6560

David Previant · (Labor) · Previant, Goldberg, Uelmen, Gratz, Miller & Brueggeman · Office on the Square, Sixth Floor · 788 North Jefferson Street · P.O. Box 92099 · Milwaukee, WI 53202 · 414-271-4500

Barbara Zack Quindel · (Labor, Individuals) · Perry, Lerner & Quindel · 823 North Cass Street · Milwaukee, WI 53202 · 414-272-7400

John R. Sapp · (Management) · Michael, Best & Friedrich · 100 East Wisconsin Avenue, Suite 3300 · Milwaukee, WI 53202-4108 · 414-271-6560

Thomas W. Scrivner · (Management) · Michael, Best & Friedrich · 100 East Wisconsin Avenue, Suite 3300 · Milwaukee, WI 53202-4108 · 414-271-6560

Daniel L. Shneidman · (Labor) · Shneidman, Myers, Dowling & Blumenfield · 700 West Michigan Street, Suite 500 · Milwaukee, WI 53233 · 414-271-8650

David L. Uelmen · (Labor) · Previant, Goldberg, Uelmen, Gratz, Miller & Brueggeman · Office on the Square, Sixth Floor · 788 North Jefferson Street · P.O. Box 92099 · Milwaukee, WI 53202 · 414-271-4500

Roger E. Walsh · (Management) · Davis & Kuelthau · 111 East Kilbourne, Suite 1400 · Milwaukee, WI 53202-6613 · 414-276-0200

George K. Whyte, Jr. · (Management) · Quarles & Brady · 411 East Wisconsin Avenue · Milwaukee, WI 53202-4497 · 414-277-5000

Herbert P. Wiedemann · (Management) · Foley & Lardner · First Wisconsin Center · 777 East Wisconsin Avenue · Milwaukee, WI 53202-5367 · 414-271-2400

NATURAL RESOURCES AND ENVIRONMENTAL LAW

Henry J. Handzel, Jr. · Dewitt, Porter, Huggett, Schumacher & Morgan · Two East Mifflin Street, Suite 600 · Madison, WI 53703 · 608-255-8891

Richard S. Heymann · Foley & Lardner · First Wisconsin Plaza, Seventh Floor One South Pinckney Street · P.O. Box 1497 · Madison, WI 53701-1497 · 608-257-5035

Richard J. Lewandowski · Dewitt, Porter, Huggett, Schumacher & Morgan · Two East Mifflin Street, Suite 600 · Madison, WI 53703 · 608-255-8891

Arthur J. Harrington* · Godfrey & Kahn · 780 North Water Street · Milwaukee, WI 53202-3590 · 414-273-3500

Charles Q. Kamps · (Water, AIr, Solid Waste) · Quarles & Brady · 411 East Wisconsin Avenue · Milwaukee, WI 53202-4497 · 414-277-5000

Raymond R. Krueger · Charne, Clancy & Taitelman · 100 East Wisconsin Avenue, Suite 2400 · Milwaukee, WI 53202-4113 · 414-273-2000

Kevin J. Lyons · Cook & Franke · 660 Building, Suite 401 · 660 East Mason Street Milwaukee, WI 53202 · 414-271-5900

Michael S. McCauley · (Environmental) · Quarles & Brady · 411 East Wisconsin Avenue · Milwaukee, WI 53202-4497 · 414-277-5000

Mark A. Thimke · Foley & Lardner · First Wisconsin Center · 777 East Wisconsin Avenue · Milwaukee, WI 53202-5367 · 414-271-2400

Allen W. Williams, Jr. · Foley & Lardner · First Wisconsin Center · 777 East Wisconsin Avenue · Milwaukee, WI 53202-5367 · 414-289-3537

PERSONAL INJURY LITIGATION

Ardell W. Skow · (Plaintiffs) · Doar, Drill & Skow · Office Park · Baldwin, WI 54002 · 715-684-3227

James E. Garvey · (Defendants) · Garvey, Anderson, Johnson, Gabler & Geraci 402 Graham Avenue · P.O. Box 187 · Eau Claire, WI 54702-0187 · 715-834-3425

Roy S. Wilcox · (Defendants) · Wilcox, Wilcox, Duplessie, Westerlund & Enright 1030 Regis Court · P.O. Box 128 · Eau Claire, WI 54702-0128 · 715-832-6645

Richard L. Cates · (Plaintiffs) · Lawton & Cates · 214 West Mifflin Street · Madison, WI 53703-2594 · 608-256-9031

Steven J. Caulum* · (Defendants, Medical Malpractice, Products Liability, Professional Malpractice) · Bell, Metzner, Gierhart & Moore · 44 East Mifflin Street P.O. Box 1807 · Madison, WI 53701-1807 · 608-257-3764

Henry A. Field, Jr. · (Defendants) · Boardman, Suhr, Curry & Field · One South Pinckney Street, Suite 410 · P.O. Box 927 · Madison, WI 53701-0927 · 608-257-9521

Richard A. Hollern* · (Defendants) · Stafford, Rosenbaum, Rieser & Hansen · Tenney Plaza, Suite 1000 · Three South Pinckney Street · P.O. Box 1784 · Madison, WI 53701-1784 · 608-256-0226

Curtis M. Kirkhuff · (Plaintiffs) · Pellino, Rosen, Mowris & Kirkhuff · 131 West Wilson Street, Suite 1201 · Madison, WI 53703 · 608-255-4501

William L. McCusker* · (Plaintiffs, Medical Malpractice, Products Liability, Automobile Collision, Airplane Collision) · McCusker and Robertson · Anchor Building, Suite 731 · 25 West Main Street · P.O. Box 1483 · Madison, WI 53703-3395 · 608-256-1841

Carroll E. Metzner · (Defendants) · Bell, Metzner, Gierhart & Moore · 44 East Mifflin Street · P.O. Box 1807 · Madison, WI 53701-1807 · 608-257-3764

John M. Moore · (Defendants) · Bell, Metzner, Gierhart & Moore · 44 East Mifflin Street · P.O. Box 1807 · Madison, WI 53701-1807 · 608-257-3764

Ward I. Richter · Bell, Metzner, Gierhart & Moore · 44 East Mifflin Street · P.O. Box 1807 · Madison, WI 53701-1807 · 608-257-3764

John D. Winner · Winner, Wixson & Pernitz · 121 East Wilson Street · P.O. Box 2626 · Madison, WI 53701 · 608-257-0257

Gerald J. Bloch · (Plaintiffs) · Warshafsky, Rotter, Tarnoff, Gesler, Reinhardt & Bloch · 839 North Jefferson Street · Milwaukee, WI 53202 · 414-276-4970

William M. Cannon · Cannon & Dunphy · 1110 North Old World Third Street, Suite 600 · Milwaukee, WI 53203 · 414-276-0111

Robert E. Cook · (Defendants) · Cook & Franke · 660 Building, Suite 401 · 660 East Mason Street · Milwaukee, WI 53202 · 414-271-5900

Kurt H. Frauen* · (Defendants, Products Liability) · Borgelt, Powell, Peterson & Frauen · 735 North Water Street, 15th Floor · Milwaukee, WI 53202-4188 · 414-276-3600

Alan E. Gesler* · (Plaintiffs, Products Liability, Automobile Collision, Railroad Crossings) · Warshafsky, Rotter, Tarnoff, Gesler, Reinhardt & Bloch · 839 North Jefferson Street · Milwaukee, WI 53202 · 414-276-4970

Robert L. Habush · (Plaintiffs) · Habush, Habush & Davis · First Wisconsin Center, Suite 2200 · 777 East Wisconsin Avenue · Milwaukee, WI 53202 · 414-271-0900

James J. Murphy · (Plaintiffs) · Gillick, Murphy, Gillick & Wicht · 330 East Kilbourne Avenue, Suite 1200 · Milwaukee, WI 53202 · 414-271-1011

James Peter O'Neill · (Defendants) · O'Neill, Schimmel, Quirk & Carroll · 312 East Wisconsin Avenue · Milwaukee, WI 53202 · 414-271-3282

Donald R. Peterson* · (Defendants, Medical Malpractice, Products Liability, Professional Malpractice) · Peterson, Johnson & Murray · 733 North Van Buren Street · Milwaukee, WI 53202 · 414-278-8800

John M. Swietlik · (Defendants) · Kasdorf, Lewis & Swietlik · 1551 South 108th Street · Milwaukee, WI 53214 · 414-257-1055

Ted M. Warshafsky* · (Plaintiffs, Medical Malpractice, Products Liability, Automobile Collision) · Warshafsky, Rotter, Tarnoff, Gesler, Reinhardt & Bloch · 839 North Jefferson Street · Milwaukee, WI 53202-3796 · 414-276-4970

Einer Christensen* · (Defendants) · Constantine, Christensen, Krohn & Kerscher · 723 Main Street · P.O. Box 1823 · Racine, WI 53401 · 414-631-6140

Adrian P. Schoone* · (Plaintiffs, Defendants, Products Liability) · Schoone, Ware, Fortune & Leuck · Racine Professional Center · 1300 South Green Bay Road · P.O. Box 97 · Racine, WI 53406-0097 · 414-637-6791

PUBLIC UTILITY LAW

John A. Hansen · Stafford, Rosenbaum, Rieser & Hansen · Tenney Plaza, Suite 1000 · Three South Pinckney Street · P.O. Box 1784 · Madison, WI 53701-1784 608-256-0226

Michael G. Stuart · (Municipal) · Boardman, Suhr, Curry & Field · One South Pinckney Street, Suite 410 · P.O. Box 927 · Madison, WI 53701-0927 · 608-257-9521

J. LeRoy Thilly · (Municipal) · Boardman, Suhr, Curry & Field · One South Pinckney Street, Suite 410 · P.O. Box 927 · Madison, WI 53701-0927 · 608-257-9521

Larry J. Martin · Quarles & Brady · 411 East Wisconsin Avenue · Milwaukee, WI 53202-4497 · 414-277-5000

Allen W. Williams, Jr. · Foley & Lardner · First Wisconsin Center · 777 East Wisconsin Avenue · Milwaukee, WI 53202-5367 · 414-289-3537

REAL ESTATE LAW

David G. Anderson · Garvey, Anderson, Johnson, Gabler & Geraci · 402 Graham Avenue · P.O. Box 187 · Eau Claire, WI 54702-0187 · 715-834-3425

John F. Wilcox · Wilcox, Wilcox, Duplessie, Westerlund & Enright · 1030 Regis Court · P.O. Box 128 · Eau Claire, WI 54702-0128 · 715-832-6645

Lowell E. Sweet · (Zoning, Land Use, Eminent Domain, Development) · Sweet, Leece & Phillips · Inns of Court Building · 114 North Church Street · P.O. Box 318 · Elkhorn, WI 53121 · 414-723-5480

James J. Vance · Vance, Wilcox, Short & Ristow · 79 North Main Street · Fort Atkinson, WI 53538-1897 · 414-563-9523

Pharis Horton · Tenney Building, Suite Three · Three South Pinckney Street · Madison, WI 53703 · 608-257-0404

Tod B. Linstroth · Michael, Best & Friedrich · First Wisconsin Plaza · One South Pinckney Street · P.O. Box 1806 · Madison, WI 53701-1806 · 608-257-3501

Jeremy C. Shea · Ross & Stevens · Capitol Square Office · First Wisconsin Plaza P.O. Box 2599 · Madison, WI 53701-2599 · 608-257-5353

Seward Ritchey Stroud · Stroud, Stroud, Willink, Thompson & Howard · 25 West Main Street, Suite 300 · P.O. Box 2236 · Madison, WI 53701 · 608-257-2281

Benjamin J. Abrohams · Foley & Lardner · First Wisconsin Center · 777 East Wisconsin Avenue · Milwaukee, WI 53202-5367 · 414-271-2400

Robert B. Bradley · Foley & Lardner · First Wisconsin Center · 777 East Wisconsin Avenue · Milwaukee, WI 53202-5367 · 414-271-2400

Gerald E. Connolly · Minahan & Peterson · 411 East Wisconsin Avenue, Suite 2200 · Milwaukee, WI 53202-4499 · 414-276-1400

Michael W. Hatch · Foley & Lardner · First Wisconsin Center · 777 East Wisconsin Avenue · Milwaukee, WI 53202-5367 · 414-271-2400

Lawrence J. Jost · Quarles & Brady · 411 East Wisconsin Avenue · Milwaukee, WI 53202-4497 · 414-277-5000

David L. Petersen · Quarles & Brady · 411 East Wisconsin Avenue · Milwaukee, WI 53202-4497 · 414-277-5000

Lyman A. Precourt · Foley & Lardner · First Wisconsin Center · 777 East Wisconsin Avenue · Milwaukee, WI 53202-5367 · 414-271-2400

Allen N. Rieselbach · Reinhart, Boerner, Van Deuren, Norris & Rieselbach · Bank One Plaza, Suite 1800 · 111 East Wisconsin Avenue · Milwaukee, WI 53202-4884 · 414-271-1190

TAX AND EMPLOYEE BENEFITS LAW

Sebastian J. Geraci · Garvey, Anderson, Johnson, Gabler & Geraci · 402 Graham Avenue · P.O. Box 187 · Eau Claire, WI 54702-0187 · 715-834-3425

Thomas A. Hoffner · (Employee Benefits) · LaFollette & Sinykin · One East Main Street, Suite 500 · P.O. Box 2719 · Madison, WI 53701 · 608-257-3911

George R. Kamperschroer · (Employee Benefits) · Boardman, Suhr, Curry & Field · One South Pinckney Street, Suite 410 · P.O. Box 927 · Madison, WI 53701-0927 · 608-257-9521

Richard W. Pitzner · Murphy & Desmond · Manchester Place · Two East Mifflin Street, Suite 800 · P.O. Box 2038 · Madison, WI 53701-2038 · 608-257-7181

Thomas G. Ragatz* · (Corporate & Partnership Transactions, State Tax, Tax Disputes) · Foley & Lardner · First Wisconsin Plaza, Seventh Floor · One South Pinckney Street · P.O. Box 1497 · Madison, WI 53701-1497 · 608-257-5035

John Rashke · (Employee Benefits) · Ross & Stevens · 8000 Excelsior Drive, Suite 401 · Madison, WI 53701-2599 · 608-831-2100

Leonard S. Sosnowski · Foley & Lardner · First Wisconsin Plaza · One South Pinckney Street · P.O. Box 1497 · Madison, WI 53701-1497 · 608-257-5035

Warren H. Stolper · Stolper, Koritzinsky, Brewster & Neider · 7617 Mineral Point Road · P.O. Box 5510 · Madison, WI 53705-0510 · 608-833-7617

Seward Ritchey Stroud · Stroud, Stroud, Willink, Thompson & Howard · 25 West Main Street, Suite 300 · P.O. Box 2236 · Madison, WI 53701 · 608-257-2281

Lloyd J. Dickinson · (Employee Benefits) · Foley & Lardner · 777 East Wisconsin Avenue · Milwaukee, WI 53202-5367 · 414-289-7036

Thomas J. Donnelly · Quarles & Brady · 411 East Wisconsin Avenue · Milwaukee, WI 53202-4497 · 414-277-5000

Timothy C. Frautschi* · (State Tax, Tax Disputes) · Foley & Lardner · First Wisconsin Center · 777 East Wisconsin Avenue · Milwaukee, WI 53202-5367 · 414-271-2400

Richard S. Gallagher · Foley & Lardner · First Wisconsin Center · 777 East Wisconsin Avenue · Milwaukee, WI 53202-5367 · 414-271-2400

Dudley J. Godfrey, Jr. · Godfrey & Kahn · 780 North Water Street · Milwaukee, WI 53202-3590 · 414-273-3500

John A. Hazelwood · (Corporate & Partnership Transactions, State Tax, Tax Disputes) · Quarles & Brady · 411 East Wisconsin Avenue · Milwaukee, WI 53202-4497 · 414-277-5000

Kenneth C. Hunt · Godfrey & Kahn · 780 North Water Street · Milwaukee, WI 53202-3590 · 414-273-3500

Gerald J. Kahn · Godfrey & Kahn · 780 North Water Street · Milwaukee, WI 53202-3590 · 414-273-3500

Jere D. McGaffey · (Corporate & Partnership Transactions) · Foley & Lardner · First Wisconsin Center · 777 East Wisconsin Avenue · Milwaukee, WI 53202-5367 414-271-2400

Robert E. Meldman · Reinhart, Boerner, Van Deuren, Norris & Rieselbach · Bank One Plaza, Suite 1800 · 111 East Wisconsin Avenue · Milwaukee, WI 53202-4884 · 414-271-1190

Greg W. Renz · (Employee Benefits) · Foley & Lardner · First Wisconsin Center 777 East Wisconsin Avenue · Milwaukee, WI 53202-5367 · 414-271-2400

Robert A. Schnur · (Corporate & Partnership Transactions, State Tax, Tax Disputes) · Michael, Best & Friedrich · 100 East Wisconsin Avenue, Suite 3300 · Milwaukee, WI 53202-4108 · 414-271-6560

Robert M. Weiss · Weiss, Berzowski, Brady & Donahue · 700 North Water Street Milwaukee, WI 53202 · 414-276-5800

Richard C. Brodek · (Employee Benefits) · DeMark, Kolbe & Brodek · 6216 Washington Avenue · P.O. Box 085009 · Racine, WI 53408 · 414-886-9720

William F. Kolbe · DeMark, Kolbe & Brodek · 6216 Washington Avenue · Racine, WI 53406 · 414-886-9720

TRUSTS AND ESTATES

Sebastian J. Geraci · Garvey, Anderson, Johnson, Gabler & Geraci · 402 Graham Avenue · P.O. Box 187 · Eau Claire, WI 54702-0187 · 715-834-3425

Stephen R. Schrage · (Estate Planning, Estate Administration) · Schrage Marjala Kaiser & Welter · 204 East Grand Avenue · P.O. Box 358 · Eau Claire, WI 54702-0358 · 715-832-3494

John F. Wilcox · Wilcox, Wilcox, Duplessie, Westerlund & Enright · 1030 Regis Court · P.O. Box 128 · Eau Claire, WI 54702-0128 · 715-832-6645

Robert H. Consigny · Consigny, Andrews, Hemming & Grant · 303 East Court Street · P.O. Box 1449 · Janesville, WI 53547 · 608-755-5050

James R. Cripe · Nowlan & Mouat · 100 South Main Street · P.O. Box 546 · Janesville, WI 53547 · 608-755-4747

C. Vernon Howard · Stroud, Stroud, Willink, Thompson & Howard · 25 West Main Street, Suite 300 · P.O. Box 2236 · Madison, WI 53701 · 608-257-2281

Richard Z. Kabaker* · Lee, Kilkelly, Paulson & Kabaker · One West Main Street P.O. Box 2189 · Madison, WI 53701-2189 · 608-256-9046

Warren H. Stolper · Stolper, Koritzinsky, Brewster & Neider · 7617 Mineral Point Road · P.O. Box 5510 · Madison, WI 53705-0510 · 608-833-7617

Seward Ritchey Stroud · Stroud, Stroud, Willink, Thompson & Howard · 25 West Main Street, Suite 300 · P.O. Box 2236 · Madison, WI 53701 · 608-257-2281

Michael W. Wilcox · Stolper, Koritzinsky, Brewster & Neider · 7617 Mineral Point Road · P.O. Box 5510 · Madison, WI 53705-0510 · 608-833-7617

Robert J. Bonner · Foley & Lardner · First Wisconsin Center · 777 East Wisconsin Avenue · Milwaukee, WI 53202-5367 · 414-271-2400

Jackson M. Bruce, Jr. · (Estate Planning, Estate Administration, Estate Litigation) · Quarles & Brady · 411 East Wisconsin Avenue · Milwaukee, WI 53202-4497 414-277-5000

Keith A. Christiansen* · Foley & Lardner · First Wisconsin Center · 777 East Wisconsin Avenue · Milwaukee, WI 53202-5367 · 414-271-2400

Thomas J. Drought · (Estate Planning, Estate Administration, Marital Agreements) · Cook & Franke · 660 Building, Suite 401 · 660 East Mason Street · Milwaukee, WI 53202 · 414-271-5900

Henry E. Fuldner · Godfrey & Kahn · 780 North Water Street · Milwaukee, WI 53202-3590 · 414-273-3500

Richard S. Gallagher · (Charitable Trusts) · Foley & Lardner · First Wisconsin Center · 777 East Wisconsin Avenue · Milwaukee, WI 53202-5367 · 414-271-2400

F. William Haberman · Michael, Best & Friedrich · 100 East Wisconsin Avenue, Suite 3300 · Milwaukee, WI 53202-4108 · 414-271-6560

John B. Haydon · (Estate Planning, Estate Administration) · Whyte & Hirschboeck · 111 East Wisconsin Avenue, Suite 2100 · Milwaukee, WI 53202-4894 · 414-271-8210

David L. Kinnamon · Quarles & Brady · 411 East Wisconsin Avenue · Milwaukee, WI 53202-4497 · 414-277-5000

Roy C. LaBudde · (Estate Planning, Estate Administration) · Michael, Best & Friedrich · 100 East Wisconsin Avenue, Suite 3300 · Milwaukee, WI 53202-4108 414-271-6560

Henry J. Loos · Quarles & Brady · 411 East Wisconsin Avenue · Milwaukee, WI 53202-4497 · 414-277-5735

Robert J. Loots · (Estate Planning) · Gibbs, Roper, Loots & Williams · 735 North Water Street · Milwaukee, WI 53202 · 414-273-7000

Arthur F. Lubke, Jr. · Reinhart, Boerner, Van Deuren, Norris & Rieselbach · Bank One Plaza, Suite 1800 · 111 East Wisconsin Avenue · Milwaukee, WI 53202-4884 · 414-271-1190

Wayne R. Lueders · Foley & Lardner · First Wisconsin Center · 777 East Wisconsin Avenue · Milwaukee, WI 53202-5367 · 414-271-2400

David L. MacGregor · (Estate Planning, Estate Administration, Planning for Closely Held Businesses) · Quarles & Brady · 411 East Wisconsin Avenue · Milwaukee, WI 53202-4497 · 414-277-5000

Harrold J. McComas · Foley & Lardner · First Wisconsin Center · 777 East Wisconsin Avenue · Milwaukee, WI 53202-5367 · 414-289-3528

Jere D. McGaffey · (Estate Planning, Charitable Trusts) · Foley & Lardner · First Wisconsin Center · 777 East Wisconsin Avenue · Milwaukee, WI 53202-5367 · 414-271-2400

Paul F. Meissner · Meissner & Tierney · 735 North Water Street, Suite 1328 · Milwaukee, WI 53202 · 414-273-4390

Timothy M. Dempsey · Dempsey, Magnusen, Williamson & Lampe · First Wisconsin National Bank Building · P.O. Box 886 · Oshkosh, WI 54902 · 414-235-7300

Mark J. Bradley · Ruder, Ware & Michler · 500 Third Street · Wausau, WI 54402-8050 · 715-845-4336

C. Duane Patterson · Patterson, Richards & Hessert · 630 Fourth Street · P.O. Box 1144 · Wausau, WI 54402-1144 · 715-845-1151

WYOMING

BANKRUPTCY LAW

Donn J. McCall · Brown & Drew · Casper Business Center · 123 West First Street, Suite 800 · Casper, WY 82601 · 307-234-1000

Barry G. Williams · Williams, Porter, Day & Neville · Durbin Center, Suite 300 145 South Durbin Street · Casper, WY 82601 · 307-265-0700

Georg Jensen · Law Offices of Georg Jensen · 1613 Evans Avenue · Cheyenne, WY 82001 · 307-634-0991

BUSINESS LITIGATION

William S. Bon · Schwartz, Bon, McCrary & Walker · Consolidated Royalty Building, Suite 505 · 141 South Center Street · Casper, WY 82601 · 307-235-6681

Richard E. Day · Williams, Porter, Day & Neville · Durbin Center, Suite 300 · 145 South Durbin Street · Casper, WY 82601 · 307-265-0700

William T. Schwartz · Schwartz, Bon, McCrary & Walker · Consolidated Royalty Building, Suite 505 · 141 South Center Street · Casper, WY 82601 · 307-235-6681

James L. Applegate · Hirst & Applegate · 200 Boyd Building · P.O. Box 1083 · Cheyenne, WY 82003-1083 · 307-632-0541

Richard P. Boley · Boley & McKellar · 2424 Pioneer Avenue, Suite 100 · P.O. Box 748 · Cheyenne, WY 82003-0748 · 307-637-5575

James E. Fitzgerald · Fitzgerald Law Firm · 2108 Warren Avenue · Cheyenne, WY 82001 · 307-635-1108

Paul B. Godfrey* · Godfrey & Sundahl · 403 Rocky Mountain Plaza, Suite 403 · P.O. Box 328 · Cheyenne, WY 82001 · 307-632-6421

Carl L. Lathrop* · Lathrop, Rutledge & Michael · City Center Building, Suite 500 · 1920 Thomes Avenue · P.O. Box 4068 · Cheyenne, WY 82003-4068 · 307-632-0554

Edward P. Moriarity · Spence, Moriarity & Schuster · 15 South Jefferson Street P.O. Box 548 · Jackson, WY 83001 · 307-733-7290

Gerald L. Spence · Spence, Moriarity & Schuster · 15 South Jefferson Street · P.O. Box 548 · Jackson, WY 83001 · 307-733-7290

CORPORATE LAW

William J. Kirven · Kirven & Kirven · 104 Fort Street · P.O. Box 640 · Buffalo, WY 82834 · 307-684-2248

Morris R. Massey · Brown & Drew · Casper Business Center · 123 West First Street, Suite 800 · Casper, WY 82601 · 307-234-1000

William T. Schwartz · Schwartz, Bon, McCrary & Walker · Consolidated Royalty Building, Suite 505 · 141 South Center Street · Casper, WY 82601 · 307-235-6681

Houston G. Williams · Williams, Porter, Day & Neville · Durbin Center, Suite 300 · 145 South Durbin Street · Casper, WY 82601 · 307-265-0700

Paul B. Godfrey* · Godfrey, Sundahl & Jorgenson · 403 Rocky Mountain Plaza, Suite 403 · P.O. Box 328 · Cheyenne, WY 82001 · 307-632-6421

Carl L. Lathrop* · Lathrop, Rutledge & Michael · City Center Building, Suite 500 · 1920 Thomes Avenue · P.O. Box 4068 · Cheyenne, WY 82003-4068 · 307-632-0554

James L. Hettinger · Hettinger & Leedy · Masonic Temple Building, Suite 214
107 South Broadway · Riverton, WY 82501-4380 · 307-856-2239

Richard I. Leedy · Hettinger & Leedy · Masonic Temple Building, Suite 214 ·
107 South Broadway · Riverton, WY 82501-4380 · 307-856-2239

Richard M. Davis, Jr.* · Burgess, Davis, Carmichael & Cannon · 40 South Main
P.O. Box 728 · Sheridan, WY 82801 · 307-672-7491

CRIMINAL DEFENSE

Terry W. Mackey* · (Federal Court, State Court) · American National Bank
Building · 1912 Capitol Avenue, Suite 400 · Cheyenne, WY 82001 · 307-637-7841

Richard C. Wolf* · (Federal Court, State Court) · Equality State Bank Building,
Suite 300 · 19th & Pioneer · P.O. Box 491 · Cheyenne, WY 82003 · 307-635-2876

Edward P. Moriarity · Spence, Moriarity & Schuster · 15 South Jefferson Street
P.O. Box 548 · Jackson, WY 83001 · 307-733-7290

Gerald L. Spence · Spence, Moriarity & Schuster · 15 South Jefferson Street ·
P.O. Box 548 · Jackson, WY 83001 · 307-733-7290

FAMILY LAW

Robert L. Nelson · Nelson & Associates · 1717 Carey Avenue · Cheyenne, WY
82001 · 307-632-2870

HEALTH CARE LAW

James L. Applegate · Hirst & Applegate · 200 Boyd Building · P.O. Box 1083 ·
Cheyenne, WY 82003-1083 · 307-632-0541

LABOR AND EMPLOYMENT LAW

George M. Apostolos · Brown & Drew · Casper Business Center · 123 West First
Street, Suite 800 · Casper, WY 82601 · 307-234-1000

NATURAL RESOURCES AND ENVIRONMENTAL LAW

Morris R. Massey · Brown & Drew · Casper Business Center · 123 West First
Street, Suite 800 · Casper, WY 82601 · 307-234-1000

Craig Newman · Brown & Drew · Casper Business Center · 123 West First Street, Suite 800 · Casper, WY 82601 · 307-234-1000

William T. Schwartz · Schwartz, Bon, McCrary & Walker · Consolidated Royalty Building, Suite 505 · 141 South Center Street · Casper, WY 82601 · 307-235-6681

Houston G. Williams · Williams, Porter, Day & Neville · Durbin Center, Suite 300 · 145 South Durbin Street · Casper, WY 82601 · 307-265-0700

Paul B. Godfrey* · Godfrey, Sundahl & Jorgenson · 403 Rocky Mountain Plaza, Suite 403 · P.O. Box 328 · Cheyenne, WY 82001 · 307-632-6421

Charles G. Kepler · Simpson, Kepler & Edwards · 1239 Rumsey Avenue, Suite 100 · P.O. Box 490 · Cody, WY 82414-0490 · 307-527-7891

Harry L. Harris · Harris, Morton & Cowan · 927 Main Street · P.O. Box 130 · Evanston, WY 82931-0130 · 307-789-3210

Richard M. Davis, Jr.* · Burgess, Davis, Carmichael & Cannon · 40 South Main P.O. Box 728 · Sheridan, WY 82801 · 307-672-7491

PERSONAL INJURY LITIGATION

William S. Bon · (Defendants) · Schwartz, Bon, McCrary & Walker · Consolidated Royalty Building, Suite 505 · 141 South Center Street · Casper, WY 82601 307-235-6681

Richard R. Bostwick · (Defendants) · Murane & Bostwick · 201 North Wolcott Street · Casper, WY 82601 · 307-234-9345

Richard E. Day · (Defendants) · Williams, Porter, Day & Neville · Durbin Center, Suite 300 · 145 South Durbin Street · Casper, WY 82601 · 307-265-0700

William F. Downes · (Defendants, Medical Malpractice) · Brown & Drew · Casper Business Center · 123 West First Street, Suite 800 · Casper, WY 82601 · 307-234-1000

Frank D. Neville · (Defendants) · Williams, Porter, Day & Neville · 145 South Durbin, Suite 300 · Casper, WY 82601 · 307-265-0700

J. E. Vlastos · (Defendants) · Vlastos, Brooks & Henley · Key Bank Building, Suite 320 · 300 South Wolcott Street · P.O. Box 10 · Casper, WY 82602 · 307-235-6613

James L. Applegate · (Defendants) · Hirst & Applegate · 200 Boyd Building · P.O. Box 1083 · Cheyenne, WY 82003-1083 · 307-632-0541

Richard P. Boley · Boley & McKellar · 2424 Pioneer Avenue, Suite 100 · P.O. Box 748 · Cheyenne, WY 82003-0748 · 307-637-5575

James E. Fitzgerald · (Plaintiffs) · Fitzgerald Law Firm · 2108 Warren Avenue · Cheyenne, WY 82001 · 307-635-1108

Paul B. Godfrey* · (Defendants) · Godfrey, Sundahl & Jorgenson · Rocky Mountain Plaza, Suite 403 · 2020 Carey Avenue · P.O. Box 328 · Cheyenne, WY 82001 307-632-6421

Carl L. Lathrop* · (Defendants) · Lathrop, Rutledge & Michael · City Center Building, Suite 500 · 1920 Thomes Avenue · P.O. Box 4068 · Cheyenne, WY 82003-4068 · 307-632-0554

Terry W. Mackey · (Plaintiffs) · American National Bank Building · 1912 Capitol Avenue, Suite 400 · Cheyenne, WY 82001 · 307-637-7841

Richard C. Wolf* · (Plaintiffs, Automobile Collision) · Equality State Bank Building, Suite 300 · 19th & Pioneer · P.O. Box 491 · Cheyenne, WY 82003 · 307-635-2876

Edward P. Moriarity · (Plaintiffs) · Spence, Moriarity & Schuster · 15 South Jefferson Street · P.O. Box 548 · Jackson, WY 83001 · 307-733-7290

Gerald L. Spence · (Plaintiffs) · Spence, Moriarity & Schuster · 15 South Jefferson Street · P.O. Box 548 · Jackson, WY 83001 · 307-733-7290

John E. Stanfield · (Plaintiffs) · Smith, Stanfield & Scott · 515 Ivinson Avenue · P.O. Box 971 · Laramie, WY 82070 · 307-745-7358

John R. Hursh* · (Plaintiffs, Medical Malpractice, Products Liability, Airplane Collision) · Hursh & Donohoue · 105-107 South Sixth Street East · P.O. Box 1783 Riverton, WY 82501 · 307-856-4157

John R. Vincent · Vincent & Vincent · 606 East Washington Street · Riverton, WY 82501 · 307-856-1902

Kim O. Cannon · Burgess, Davis, Carmichael & Cannon · 40 South Main · P.O. Box 728 · Sheridan, WY 82801 · 307-672-7491

REAL ESTATE LAW

Dennis M. Kirven · Kirven & Kirven · 104 Fort Street · P.O. Box 640 · Buffalo, WY 82834 · 307-684-2248

William J. Kirven · Kirven & Kirven · 104 Fort Street · P.O. Box 640 · Buffalo, WY 82834 · 307-684-2248

Morris R. Massey · Brown & Drew · Casper Business Center · 123 West First Street, Suite 800 · Casper, WY 82601 · 307-234-1000

William T. Schwartz · Schwartz, Bon, McCrary & Walker · Consolidated Royalty Building, Suite 505 · 141 South Center Street · Casper, WY 82601 · 307-235-6681

Houston G. Williams · Williams, Porter, Day & Neville · Durbin Center, Suite 300 · 145 South Durbin Street · Casper, WY 82601 · 307-265-0700

Carl L. Lathrop* · Lathrop, Rutledge & Michael · City Center Building, Suite 500 · 1920 Thomes Avenue · P.O. Box 4068 · Cheyenne, WY 82003-4068 · 307-632-0554

Larry L. Jorgenson* · One Broadway Centre · 235 East Broadway · P.O. Box 3103 · Jackson Hole, WY 83001 · 307-733-6021

Richard M. Davis, Jr.* · Burgess, Davis, Carmichael & Cannon · 40 South Main P.O. Box 728 · Sheridan, WY 82801 · 307-672-7491

TAX AND EMPLOYEE BENEFITS LAW

Thomas N. Long* · Hirst & Applegate · 200 Boyd Building · P.O. Box 1083 · Cheyenne, WY 82003-1083 · 307-632-0541

TRUSTS AND ESTATES

William J. Kirven · Kirven & Kirven · 104 Fort Street · P.O. Box 640 · Buffalo, WY 82834 · 307-684-2248

William T. Schwartz · Schwartz, Bon, McCrary & Walker · Consolidated Royalty Building, Suite 505 · 141 South Center Street · Casper, WY 82601 · 307-235-6681

Houston G. Williams · Williams, Porter, Day & Neville · Durbin Center, Suite 300 · 145 South Durbin Street · Casper, WY 82601 · 307-265-0700

Carl L. Lathrop* · Lathrop, Rutledge & Michael · City Center Building, Suite 500 · 1920 Thomes Avenue · P.O. Box 4068 · Cheyenne, WY 82003-4068 · 307-632-0554

Robert J. Wyatt · Burgess, Davis, Carmichael & Cannon · 40 South Main · P.O. Box 728 · Sheridan, WY 82801 · 307-672-7491